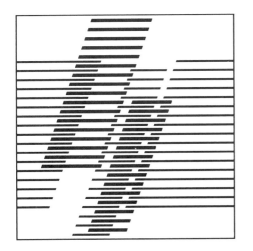

THIRD EDITION

STRATEGIC MANAGEMENT AND BUSINESS POLICY

Thomas L. Wheelen
University of South Florida

J. David Hunger
Iowa State University

▲
▼▼
ADDISON-WESLEY PUBLISHING COMPANY

Reading, Massachusetts · Menlo Park, California
New York · Don Mills, Ontario · Wokingham, England
Amsterdam · Bonn · Sydney · Singapore · Tokyo
Madrid · San Juan

Sponsoring Editor: Susan K. Badger
Senior Production Supervisor: Kazia Navas
Production Coordinator: Sarah Hallet
Text Designer: Deborah Schneck
Cover Designer: Marshall Henrichs
Technical Art Consultant: Dick Morton
Copyeditor: Fannie Toldi
Permissions Editor: Mary Dyer
Manufacturing Media Supervisor: Lu Anne Piskadlo
Software Production: Glenn Hoffman

Library of Congress Cataloging-in-Publication Data

Wheelen, Thomas L.
  Strategic management and business policy.
  Includes bibliographies and indexes.
  1. Strategic planning. I. Hunger, J. David,
1941–   . II. Title.
HD30.28.W43 1988   658.4'012   88–1263
ISBN 0-201-60000-5

Many of the designations used by manufacturers and sellers to distinguish their products are claimed as trademarks. Where those designations appear in this book, and Addison-Wesley was aware of a trademark claim, the designations have been printed in initial caps or all caps.

Lotus and 1-2-3 are registered trademarks of Lotus Development Corporation. IBM and IBM-PC are registered trademarks of International Business Machines Corporation.

The programs and applications presented in this book have been included for their instructional value. They have been tested with care but are not guaranteed for any particular purpose. The publisher does not offer warranties or representations, nor does it accept any liabilities with respect to the programs or applications.

Addison-Wesley Publishing Company, Inc., makes no representations or warranties, express or implied, with respect to this software and its documentation, including without limitations, any implied warranties of merchantability or fitness for a particular purpose, all of which are expressly disclaimed. The exclusion of implied warranties is not permitted by some states. The above exclusion may not apply to you. This warranty provides you with specific legal rights. There may be other rights that you have which may vary from state to state.

It is a violation of copyright law to make a copy of the accompanying software except for backup purposes to guard against accidental loss or damage. Addison-Wesley assumes no responsibility for errors arising from duplication of the original programs.

5678910-DO-9594939291

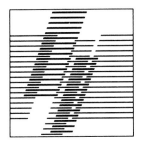

Preface

The corporate world is becoming a very different place. Mergers and acquisitions have transformed the landscape. International boundaries have faded as businesses take on a more global perspective, and the technology of the "Information Age" has telescoped the time it takes to communicate and make decisions. Strategic management takes a panoramic view of this changing corporate terrain and dares to ask *why*.

As a capstone course, strategic management, or business policy, unites the various departments, majors, and subdisciplines usually found in a school of business. Other courses deal in depth with procedures and activities designed to answer *how* corporations exist. Because strategic management itself is in a constant state of flux, and because the course takes a holistic approach, business policy is often a difficult course to teach and to take. Consequently, this book is organized around a strategic management model, which prefaces each chapter and provides a structure for content and for complex case analyses by students.

Both the text and the cases have been class-tested in policy courses and revised based on feedback from those classes. In response to students and professors, we have emphasized in the text primarily those concepts that have proved to be most useful in case analysis. Our goal was to make the text as comprehensive and useful as possible while addressing the following AACSB concerns described in the 1988 report of the "Futures Project" by Porter and McKibbin (published by McGraw-Hill as *Management Education and Development: Drift or Thrust into the 21st Century):* balanced coverage of internal and external environments; a global perspective; cross-functional integration; and attention to the information/service society. As in previous editions, all of the cases are about actual corporations. The firms range in size and maturity from large, established multinationals to small entrepreneurial ventures, and cover a broad range of issues and questions.

NEW TO THIS EDITION

This edition includes many of the same features and content that helped make previous editions successful. In addition to updating and fine-tuning these tested features, there are a number of additions to make the book more useful to students and professors, and more representative of the rapidly growing field of strategic management and business policy:

- A *new chapter*—"Strategic Issues in Entrepreneurial Ventures and Small Businesses"—has been included to reflect the increasing interest in innovation and entrepreneurship in today's world. In addition, nine cases are included to complement this chapter.

- Recent developments in the management of *technology* and *organizational innovation,* as well as research and development, receive expanded coverage in Chapters 5 and 8.

- An *integrative case* dealing with a successful company (CSX Corporation) operating in a rapidly changing, deregulated industry (transportation) follows Chapters 1 through 10 in a series of ten discrete segments. Each segment of the integrative case relates to the content discussed in the preceding chapter. The case thus gives the reader an opportunity to apply the concepts and techniques discussed in each chapter to CSX Corporation's particular situation.

- Increased emphasis is placed on *industry analysis* by including, as an appendix to Chapter 4, Michael Porter's now-classic *Harvard Business Review* article "How Competitive Forces Shape Strategy." In addition, *strategic groups* and *mobility barriers* are discussed in Chapter 6.

- A totally revised section on *corporate strategies* is added to Chapter 7 in order to more clearly explain the many corporate-level strategies and how they differ from business and functional strategies.

- A strengthened and expanded section on *scenario construction* in Chapter 7 now enables the reader to actually develop optimistic, pessimistic, and most likely scenarios for each strategic alternative under consideration. This ties in directly with the new software, Financial ANalyzer (FAN) available with this book.

- The concepts of *strategic control* and the *hierarchy of control* are discussed in Chapter 9 as a natural extension of the well-accepted hierarchy of strategy.

- Work by Kenichi Ohmae, the "Peter Drucker of Japan," on the importance of the *triad countries,* and by Michael Porter, on the significance of *multidomestic* versus *global industries,* expands the discussion of multinational corporations in Chapter 10.

- A special section of *entrepreneurial and small business cases* reflects an increasing interest in the strategic management of these types of companies.

- *29 cases* new to this edition on organizations ranging from product-oriented Harley-Davidson, Volvo, and Springfield Remanufacturing to service-oriented Kmart, Home Shopping Network, and Springfield Ballet. Cases also range from the fairly glamorous Apple Computer and Federal Express to the more mundane Inner-City Paint Corporation and Patton Septic Tank.

- An enhanced supplements package is available with the new edition. A detailed description of this expanded package is provided on page viii of this Preface.

OBJECTIVES

This book focuses on the following objectives, typically found in most business policy and strategic management courses:

- To develop *conceptual skills* so that a student is able to integrate previously learned aspects of corporations.
- To develop a *framework of analysis* to enable a student to identify central issues and problems in complex, comprehensive cases; to suggest alternative courses of action; and to present well-supported recommendations for future action.
- To develop an understanding of strategic management *concepts, research,* and *theories.*
- To develop an understanding of the *roles* and *responsibilities* of the Board of Directors, Chief Executive Officer, and other key managers in strategic management positions.
- To develop the ability to analyze and evaluate the *performance* of the people responsible for strategic management.
- To bridge the gap between theory and practice by developing an understanding of when and how to apply *concepts* and *techniques* learned in earlier courses on marketing, accounting, finance, management, and production.
- To improve the *research capabilities* necessary to gather and interpret key environmental data.
- To develop a better understanding of the *present and future environments* within which corporations must function.
- To develop and refine *analytical and decision-making skills* for dealing with complex conceptual problems.

This book achieves these objectives by presenting and explaining concepts and theories useful in understanding the strategic management process. It provides studies in the field of strategy and policy in order to acquaint the student with the literature of this area and to help develop the student's research capabilities. It also describes the people who manage strategically and suggests a model of strategic management. It recommends a strategic audit as one approach to the systematic analysis of complex organization-wide issues. Through a series of comprehensive cases, it provides the student with an opportunity to apply concepts, skills, and techniques to real-world corporate problems. The book focuses on the business corporation because of its crucial position in the economic system of the free world.

STRUCTURE

Part I is an overview of the subject, surveying the basic skills and competencies needed to deal with strategic issues in modern corporations. Chapter 1 presents a descriptive model as well as key terms and concepts that will be used throughout the book. Chapter 2 focuses on the development of the skills necessary for understanding and applying strategic concepts to actual situations.

Part II discusses important concepts that arise from both the external and internal environments of a corporation. It also describes key people in the corporation who are responsible for strategic management. Chapter 3 discusses the role and importance of a corporation's board of directors and top management in the strategic management process. Chapter 4 discusses both the task and societal environments of a corporation and suggests environmental scanning and forecasting as key corporate tasks. Michael Porter's article on competitive forces is included as an appendix to Chapter 4 to emphasize the importance of industry analysis. Chapter 5 examines the importance of a corporation's structure, culture, and resources to its strategic management.

Part III deals with strategy formulation. It emphasizes long-range planning and the development of alternative courses of action at both the corporate and business levels. Chapter 6 discusses situational analysis. Chapter 7 examines the many possible corporate, business, and functional strategies.

Part IV considers the implementation of strategies and policies, as well as the process of evaluation and control, with continued emphasis on corporate and division-level strategic management. Chapter 8 explains strategy implementation in terms of programs, budgets, and procedures. It describes the people in charge of implementation, what they need to do, and how they should do it. Chapter 9 focuses on evaluation and control. It considers the monitoring of corporate processes and the accomplishment of goals, as well as various methods and criteria used in evaluating performance.

Part V summarizes and examines strategic concerns in particular types of organizations. Chapter 10 looks at strategic issues in multinational corporations and deals with the implications of operating within an international environment. Chapter 11 examines the not-for-profit organization and explains how it differs from the typical business firm. Chapter 12, *a new addition to the text,* discusses strategic issues in entrepreneurial ventures and small businesses.

Part VI is composed of 38 case studies of strategic situations in actual organizations. These cases were written by experienced case writers from a number of countries, whose contributions greatly enhance the quality of the book. The cases cover a wide range of situations illustrating the material in Parts I through V. There are three cases on strategic managers, three cases dealing with environmental issues, twenty-seven comprehensive strategy cases (eighteen focusing on large corporations and nine focusing on entrepreneurial and small businesses), three cases on multinational corporations, and two cases dealing with not-for-profit organizations. In addition, a number of the cases can be grouped by type of industry, such as the following:

- *Personal Transportation.* Harley-Davidson, Volvo, and Piper Aircraft.
- *Entertainment.* Walt Disney, Springfield Ballet Company, and National Jazz Hall of Fame.

- *Information Technology.* Apple Computer, Tandy, VLSI Technology, Comdial, Multicon, Xerox, and Byte, Inc.
- *Petroleum.* Standard Oil and Global Marine.
- *Consumer Products.* Anheuser-Busch, American Greetings, Johnson Products, Hershey Foods, and Allen Corporation *(Crisis in Geneva).*
- *Manufacturing.* Springfield Remanufacturing, UMC, Dakotah, International Mining and Carbon *(Problem of Silicosis),* Urshel Laboratories, Wallace Group, Quasar, Byte, Inc., VLSI, Comdial, and Patton Septic Tank.
- *Construction.* Inner City Paint, Patton Septic Tank, and Southern Cabinet.
- *Agricultural Products.* Pioneer Hi-Bred and Cotton Belt Exporters.
- *Services.* Federal Express, Christian's, Brookstreet Hospice, Home Shopping Network, National Jazz Hall of Fame, and Multicon.
- *Retailing.* Austad's, Kmart, Home Shopping Network, Tandy, and Christians.

New, updated versions of favorite cases—Anheuser-Busch, Apple Computers, Johnson Products, Standard Oil, and Hershey Foods—are included. Dealing with the real problems of a real organization, each case helps the student bridge the gap between theories and the practices of the business world. The high quality of these cases is attested to by the fact that 30 of them have been professionally refereed and critiqued at workshops conducted by the North American Case Research Association and the Midwest Society for Case Research and/or accepted for publication in leading case journals, such as the *Case Research Journal,* the *Journal of Management Case Studies,* and *Annual Advances in Business Cases.*

FINANCIAL ANALYZER (FAN) DECISION-SUPPORT DISKETTES

Financial ANalyzer (FAN)™ was specially developed for students of strategic management and business policy. This software allows the instructor to introduce students to meaningful *computer-assisted strategic and financial analysis.* Financial ANalyzer (FAN) consists of two disks that contain the software plus balance sheets and income statements from over 20 cases in the book. The disks are to be used with the Lotus 1-2-3® spreadsheet program on IBM-compatible (MS-DOS) personal computers with two drives. FAN is "user friendly" and requires minimal knowledge of Lotus 1-2-3, programming, or microcomputers beyond the basic knowledge of "booting up." The student can learn to use FAN in less than one hour. Step-by-step instructions are provided for the student so that the instructor need not be involved.

Students are not required to purchase a supplemental book to obtain FAN. Instead, the text is available with the disks and instructions packaged in the back of the book. The order code for this package is #17895. Please contact the Marketing Manager for Business and Economics at Addison-Wesley or your bookstore for further details.

FAN is the most comprehensive software package available for students of strategic management and will enhance the student's knowledge of financial and strategic management analytical techniques. It links the classroom with the methods that strategic managers use in their companies.

Financial ANalyzer (FAN) helps students to more quickly and easily complete *on their own* the financial analysis of complex strategy/policy cases. It uses historical financial information in the form of balance sheets and income statements from the cases to generate:

- Balance sheets in 1967 constant dollars (see pages 37–39).
- Income statements in 1967 constant dollars (see pages 37–39).
- 27 financial ratios plus Altman's Z-value (see Table 2.1 and pages 33–37).
- Common-size balance sheets (see page 36).
- Common-size income statements (see page 36).
- Scenario construction box which enables the students to develop *pro forma* projected financial statements to accompany their recommendations (see pages 227–229). *A special feature of this box is that it interacts directly with Lotus 1-2-3 for ease of operation.*

In addition, as a special feature, FAN automatically calculates financial ratios and develops common-size balance sheets and income statements for the *pro forma* projections generated by the students in their scenario construction. This enables the student to check to see if the recommendation is feasible and in general agreement with the historical ratios and relationships.

SUPPLEMENTS   ## Instructor's Manual

A comprehensive Instructor's Manual has been carefully constructed to accompany this book. It is composed of the following five parts.

Part A–*Ideas for Instructors and Chapter Notes*. Suggested course outlines, case sequences, and teaching aids. A standardized format is provided for each chapter: (1) chapter abstract, (2) list of key concepts/terms, (3) suggested answers to discussion questions, and (4) multiple choice questions.

Part B–*Case Notes*. A standardized format is provided for each case: (1) case abstract, (2) case issues and subjects, (3) steps covered in the strategic decision-making process (see Fig. 6.1, p. 169), (4) case objectives, (5) suggested classroom approaches, (6) discussion questions, (7) student paper, (8) case author's teaching note, (9) student strategic audit, and (10) a complete list of 28 calculated financial ratios.

Part C–*Transparency Masters*. Selected figures and tables from the text chapters plus other masters highlighting key strategic management concepts and techniques.

Computerized Testing

Multiple choice questions from the Instructor's Manual are available free to adopters in a computerized test bank.

Transparency Acetates

Acetates of the transparency masters from the Instructor's Manual are available free to adopters of the text.

FAN Decision-Support Disks

As described earlier, FAN is specially prepared software for use with IBM-compatible (MS-DOS) personal computers. The disks include balance sheet and income statements from selected cases in the book plus a program that uses Lotus 1-2-3 to *calculate financial ratios*. This feature should allow students to reduce time spent on calculations and increase time spent on case analysis. The FAN disks are available packaged with the text.

Student Edition of Lotus 1-2-3

Available separately from Addison-Wesley, the Student Edition is a full-function version of Lotus 1-2-3 with a 64 column × 256 row spreadsheet. The Student Edition is compatible with the decision-support disks available with the text.

ACKNOWLEDGMENTS

We are grateful to the many people who reviewed drafts of the various editions of this book for their constructive comments and suggestions. Their thought and effort has resulted in a book far superior to our original manuscript.

Ivan Abel, *Baruch College, CUNY*
Sol Ahiarah, *University of Pittsburgh at Johnstown*
Sumer Aggarwal, *University of Massachusetts, Boston*
William Boulton, *University of Georgia*

Barry Baysinger, *Texas A&M University*
Richard Castaldi, *San Diego State University*
William Crittenden, *Northeastern University*
T. K. Das, *Baruch College, CUNY*
Keith Davis, *Arizona State University*
Richard Deane, *Georgia State University*
Donald Del Mar, *University of Idaho*
Cathy Enz, *Indiana University*
Roger Evered, *Naval Postgraduate School*
Jerry Geisler, *Sangamon State University*
Fred Haas, *Virginia Commonwealth University*
Kathryn Harrigan, *Columbia University*
R. Duane Ireland, *Baylor University*
Rose Knotts, *North Texas State University*
Bruce Lamont, *Texas A&M University*
William Litzinger, *University of Texas at San Antonio*
John Logan, *University of South Carolina*
John Mahon, *Boston University*
Martin Marsh, *California State University at Bakersfield*
Stan Mendenhall, *Eastern Montana College*
James Miller, *Georgia State University*
Thomas Navin, *University of Arizona*
Henry Odell, *University of Virginia*
Neil Snyder, *University of Virginia*
Jeffrey Susbauer, *Cleveland State University*
Natalie T. Taylor, *Babson College*
James Thurman, *George Washington University*
John P. van Gigch, *California State University*
Robert Viches, *Old Dominion University*
William Warren, *College of William and Mary*
Carl Zeithaml, *Texas A&M University*

Our special thanks go to Janis Jackson Hill, Connie Spatz, Cindy Johnson, Jim Heitker, and Susan Badger who served in turn as editors for the three editions of this text. We are extremely grateful to Mary Clare McEwing, Kazia Navas, and Fannie Toldi for their careful copyediting of text and cases. The valuable contributions of these people at Addison-Wesley Publishing Company are reflected in the overall quality of the book and in the fact that it was published on time—every time!

We thank Betty Hunger for her cheerful typing of the text revisions and Kari Hunger for her work in indexing. We are also grateful to Kari Hunger and Kathy Wheelen for their help in proofreading page proofs. Kim Hammonds and Karen Jackson were invaluable in helping us produce the Instructor's Manual accompanying this book. We are very thankful to the many students who tried out the cases we chose to include in this book and to the following graduate assistants who searched to uncover any flaws in the cases before the cases went to the printer: Jeffrey Allenby, Kyle Dryden, Phyllis Feddeler, Janiece Gallagher, Gilbert Gonzalez, Vicki Griftis, Lisa Hoard, Kathy Holmes, and Sharon James. A special note of thanks go to Glenn Wilt and Gilbert Gonzalez for their assistance in developing the software, Financial ANalyzer (FAN).

In addition, we express our appreciation to Dr. Charles B. Handy, Dean, and to Dr. Thomas Chacko, Management Department Chairman, of Iowa State's College of Business Administration for their provision of the resources so necessary to write a textbook. A note of thanks is also given to Dr. James L. Pappas, Dean, and to Dr. Alton Bartlett, Management Department Chairman, of the University of South Florida's College of Business Administration.

Both of us also acknowledge our debt to the University of Virginia and specifically to Dr. William Shenkir, Dean of the McIntire School of Commerce, for the provision of a work climate most supportive to the development of this textbook. A special note of thanks is offered to Dr. Frank S. Kaulback, Jr., former Dean of Virginia's McIntire School of Commerce, for encouraging the faculty to pursue individual research and consulting interests. His emphasis on quality teaching as a top priority and his willingness to let faculty experiment in teaching and in research enabled people to develop their talents in ways that helped both them and the school.

Lastly, to the many policy instructors and students who have moaned to us about their problems with the policy course: We have tried to respond to your problems as best we could by providing a comprehensive yet usable text coupled with recent and complex cases. To you, the people who work hard in the policy trenches, we acknowledge our debt. This book is yours.

Tampa, Florida   T. L. W.
Ames, Iowa   J. D. H.

To

**Kathy, Richard,
and Tom**

**Betty
Kari, Suzi, Lori, Merry**

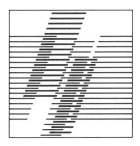

Contents*

*Chapter Summary and Discussion Questions follow each chapter.

PART THREE

Strategy Formulation   165

PART FOUR

Strategy Implementation and Control   241

About the Contributors

Moustafa H. Abdelsmad, D.B.A. (George Washington University), is Dean of the College of Business and Industry at Southeastern Massachusetts University. He previously served as Professor of Finance and Associate Dean for Graduate Studies in Business at Virginia Commonwealth University. He is Editor-in-Chief, *SAM Advanced Management Journal* and past International President of the Society for Advancement of Management. He is the author of *A Guide to Capital Expenditure Analysis,* and two chapters in the *Dow Jones-Irwin Capital Budgeting Handbook.* He is the author or coauthor of numerous articles in various publications.

Sexton Adams, Ph.D. is Professor of Management at North Texas State University. He is actively engaged as consultant to various organizations in strategic planning and management development. He is the author of the textbook *Personnel Management* and coauthor of *The Corporate Promotables* and *Modern Personnel Management.* He has published business policy cases in over 20 casebooks.

Hans J. Bocker, Ph.D. (University of South Africa), is Associate Professor of Production and Operations Management at Western Illinois University. He has taught in South Africa, West Germany, and Canada, and currently is a visiting professor in the European Business School, London. An internationally known expert on international finance, Dr. Bocker has written numerous articles for many international journals and is a senior contributor to *Finanz Und Wirtschaft* of Zurich, Switzerland.

Charles Boyd, Ph.D. (Kansas State University), is Associate Professor of Management at Southwest Missouri State University. His work in teaching, research, and consulting is primarily in the area of strategic management. He has authored or coauthored several articles and research papers. His cases appear in eight management textbooks and in the *Journal of Management Case Studies.*

Donna E. Bush is a Graduate/Teaching Assistant with the Management and Marketing Department at Middle Tennessee State University. She is concluding her studies for a Master of Business Administration. Ms. Bush plans to attend Vanderbilt University to work toward a doctorate in Management.

James W. Clinton, Ph.D. (St. Louis University), is Professor of Management, University of Northern Colorado. Previously he was a research analyst and project leader with the Department of Defense. He has authored six business policy cases, several of which appear in strategic management texts, as well as articles in *Computerworld* and *SAM Advanced Management Journal.*

Thomas Conquest, M.S. (Iowa State University), is an electrical engineer with Lear Siegler, Inc., Grand Rapids, Michigan. Previously he was with the Collins Group of Rockwell International.

Richard A. Cosier, Ph.D. (University of Iowa), is Chairman and Professor of Management at Indiana University. He was formerly a planning engineer with the Western Electric Company and Instructor of Management and Quantitative Methods at the University of Notre Dame. Dr. Cosier is interested in researching the managerial decision-making process, organizational responses to external forces, and participative management. He has published in *The Academy of Management Journal, The Academy of Management Review, Organizational Behavior and Human Performance, Management Science, Business Horizons, Decision Sciences, Personnel Psychology, Journal of Creative Behavior, International Journal of Management, The Business Quarterly,* and other journals. In addition, Professor Cosier has presented numerous papers at professional meetings, has coauthored a management textbook and has a chapter on conflict that is included in a popular management text. He has been active in many executive development programs and has acted as a management-education consultant for several organizations. Dr. Cosier was the recipient of a Teaching Excellence Award in the MBA program at Indiana and a Richard D. Irwin Fellowship. He belongs to Beta Gamma Sigma, the Academy of Management, Sigma Iota Epsilon, and the American Institute for Decision Sciences.

Mary K. Coulter, Ph.D. (University of Arkansas), is Assistant Professor of Management, Southwest Missouri State University. She has presented several papers at professional meetings and has authored a number of articles. Her current research interest is in the strategic management of nonprofit organizations, especially organizations devoted to the arts.

Ronald L. Coulter, Ph.D. (University of Arkansas), is Assistant Professor of Marketing at Southwest Missouri State University. He has published a variety of papers and articles in scholarly journals. His works have appeared in the *Journal of Retail Banking,* the *Journal of Bank Marketing,* the *Proceedings of the Southern Marketing Association* and the *American Marketing Association.* Dr. Coulter reviews for the *Journal of Business Research* and the *North American Case Research Journal.* He was the 1987 *Proceedings* Editor for the Atlantic Marketing Association. Dr. Coulter is presently a member of the American Marketing Association, the Academy of Marketing Science, the Atlantic Marketing Association, the Southern Marketing Association, and the North American Case Research Association. He was selected as runner-up for the Hugh G. Wales American Marketing Association Student Chapter Advisor of the Year in 1985–1986. His SMSU chapter won the AMA's 50th Anniversary Best "Marketing Week Award" for the 1986–1987 school year.

Dan R. Dalton, Ph.D. (University of California, Irvine), is Associate Professor of Management and Director of Doctoral Programs, Graduate School of Business, Indiana University. He was formerly with General Telephone & Electronics for thirteen years. Widely published in business and psychology, his articles have appeared in the *Academy of Management Journal, Journal of Applied Psychology, Personnel Psychology, Journal of Business Strategy, Academy of Management Review, Strategic Management Journal, Personnel Administrator,* and *Strategy and Executive Action* as well as many others. He is the coauthor of *Applied Readings in Personnel and Human Resource Management,* and *Case Problems in Management.*

William H. Davidson, D.B.A. (Harvard Business School), is Associate Professor of Management and Organization at the University of Southern California. He has written a series of books on international management issues, including *U.S. Industrial Competitiveness* (D.C. Heath, 1987), *Revitalizing American Industry* (Bollinger, 1985), *The Amazing Race* (Wiley, 1984) and *Global Strategic Management* (Wiley, 1982). He serves on the editorial boards of the *Journal of International Business Studies* and the *Journal of Management Case Studies.*

Cornelis A. de Kluyver, Ph.D., is Professor of Management at the Colgate Darden Graduate School of Business Administration at the University of Virginia. Prior to joining the Darden School, Dr. de Kluyver held positions as Associate Professor of Management at the Krannert Graduate School of Management at Purdue University and as Senior Lecturer of Operations Research at the University of Canterbury in Christchurch, New Zealand. He has served as Editor-at-Large for *Interfaces* and was Associate Editor of *New Zealand Operational Research* for five years. His publications have appeared in a wide variety of professional and scholarly journals including *Management Science,* the *Journal of Marketing Research, Industrial Marketing Management,* the *Sloan Management Review,* and *Business Horizons.* His cases have appeared in a number of texts on strategic and industrial marketing.

D. Keith Denton, Ph.D. (Southern Illinois University), is Associate Professor of Management, Southwest Missouri State University. He has published over 45 articles in management journals and magazines such as *Personnel Administration, Personnel Journal, Business, Management Review, SAM Advanced Management Journal, Industrial Engineering,* and *P&IM Review.* He has also authored or coauthored three books and is included in the 45th Edition of "Who's Who in America."

Cathy A. Enz, Ph.D. (The Ohio State University), is Assistant Professor of Management, Indiana University. She is the author of *Power and Shared Values in the Corporate Culture* and numerous articles and book chapters on value sharing, organizational culture, and influence. She has served as an ad hoc reviewer for *Administrative Science Quarterly* and *Academy of Management Review.* Dr. Enz is a member of the Academy of Management, the American Sociological Association, and the Institute for Decision Sciences.

Phyllis Feddeler, B.Sc. (Florida State University), is working towards an M.B.A. with a concentration in finance at the University of South Florida. She served as a teaching assistant for strategic management.

Sharon Ferguson, B.S., R.N., Greenwood, Mississippi, currently provides consulting services to hospitals, particularly in the area of cost control. She has ten years experience in nursing as floor nurse, nurse director, and nurse for the terminally ill.

Phil Fisher, Ph.D. (Stanford University), is Professor of Management, University of South Dakota. He has been President of the Midwest Society for Case Research (1988–1989) and is coauthor of several published cases.

Janiece L. Gallagher, M.B.A. (University of South Florida), is a consultant in strategic planning/strategic management and Instructor in Strategic Management and Business Policy at the University of South Florida. Previously she was a private consultant working with major multinational corporations and foreign governments, and a technical editor for a major publishing company.

Norman J. Gierlasinski, D.B.A., C.P.A., is Associate Professor of Accounting at Central Washington University. Formerly he was with the University of Montana. He served as Chairman of the Small Business Division of the Midwest Business Administration Association for 1986–1987. He has authored and coauthored cases for professional associations and the Harvard Case Study Series. He has authored various articles in professional journals as well as serving as a contributing author for textbooks and as a consultant to many organizations. He has also served as a reviewer for various publications.

Adelaide Griffin, Ph.D., is Associate Professor of Management at Texas Woman's University, and has served as Visiting Professor to the University of Texas at Arlington. She has published articles in the field of strategic planning with special emphasis on health care industry, a monograph on the special problems and successful strategies used by executive women, as well as numerous cases and papers. She is coauthor of the textbook, *Modern Personnel Management,* and the monograph, *Executive Women in the Dallas/Ft. Worth Metroplex: Significant Problems and Successful Strategies.*

Rolf Hackman, Dr. rer. pol. (Graz University, Austria), is Assistant Professor in the Marketing, Finance, and Transportation Department of Western Illinois University in Macomb, Illinois. His special field of interest is International Business and Marketing, Sales Management, and General Management. He worked for 20 years in the pharmaceutical and consumer goods industry in Europe and the United States. His business experience includes the Western European free market system and that of the socialistic societies of Eastern Europe. His special field of research interest centers on the effect of private direct foreign investment made by U.S. and other national companies and industries.

Stuart C. Hinrichs, formerly a naval officer assigned to the Navy ROTC unit at Iowa State University, is currently a pilot for Pan American Airlines.

Diane B. Hoadley, M.B.A., J.D. (University of Illinois), is Instructor of Management, University of South Dakota. She is a member of the Midwest Society for Case Research and is active in the Critical Thinking Skills Network.

Alan N. Hoffman, D.B.A. (Indiana University), is Associate Professor of Management, Bentley College, Waltham, Massachusetts. He has published articles in *The Academy of Management Journal, Journal of Business Strategy, Business Forum,* and *Human Relations.*

J. David Hunger, Ph.D. (Ohio State University), is Professor of Management at Iowa State University. Previously he was with George Mason University and the University of Virginia. His research interests lie in strategic management, conflict management, and leadership. He has worked in management positions for Procter & Gamble, Lazarus Department Store, and the U.S. Army. He has been active as consultant and trainer to business corporations, as well as to state and federal government agencies. He has written numerous articles and cases appearing in the *Academy of Management Journal, Journal of Management, Case Research Journal, Journal of Management Case Studies, Human Resource Management,* and *SAM Advanced Management Journal,* among others. Dr. Hunger is a member of the Academy of Management, Midwest Society for Case Research, North American Case Research Association, and Strategic Management Society. He presently serves as Vice President of the Midwest Society for Case Research and on the Board of Directors of the Midwest Management Society and on the editorial review boards of the *SAM Advanced Management Journal* and the *Journal of Management Case Studies.* He is coauthor of *Cases in Strategic Management and Business Policy* and *Strategic Management.*

Per V. Jenster, Ph.D. (University of Pittsburgh), is Assistant Professor at the McIntire School of Commerce at the Uni-

versity of Virginia, where he teaches and conducts research in the area of strategic management. His research has been published in *Long Range Planning, Journal of Information Systems, Organization Behavior Teaching Review, Case Research Journal* and *Computer Personnel,* as well as in numerous books. He is also a well-known consultant on strategic planning and organizational issues.

Paul N. Keaton, Ph.D. (University of Minnesota), is Associate Professor of Management at the University of Wisconsin-La Crosse. He previously taught at the University of Maryland at College Park and the University of Tennessee-Chattanooga. He is a member of the Midwest Society for Case Research, American Society for Personnel Administration, and the Midwest Business Administration Association. He serves as a manuscript reviewer for *Personnel Administrator* and is a contributor to *Non-Profit World Report.*

Daniel G. Kopp, Ph.D. (Virginia Tech), is Associate Professor of Management, Southwest Missouri State University. He has written articles and cases which have appeared in the *Academy of Management Journal,* the *Academy of Management Review,* and the *Journal of Management Case Studies.* His current focus is on case writing and research in the health care field.

Donald F. Kuratko, D.B.A., is Associate Professor of Management Science and Coordinator of the Small Business Management/Entrepreneurship Program, College of Business, Ball State University. He has published numerous articles on aspects of small business/entrepreneurship and has made a variety of presentations throughout the United States on management topics. Dr. Kuratko has written *Management,* and *Effective Small Business Management,* with a third book, *Entrepreneurship* currently in progress. He is a member of the Academy of Management, the International Council for Small Business, the Midwest Society for Case Research, and the Board of Directors of the Indiana Statewide Certified Development Corporation, among other organizations. He served as Program Chair for the 1986 Small Business/Entrepreneurship Division of the Midwest Business Administration Association and is currently on the editorial board of the Mid-American Journal of Business.

Melton L. Martin, Jr., M.B.A. (University of South Florida), is a civil engineer with the school board of Hillsborough County, Tampa, Florida. He received his undergraduate degree in Building Construction from the University of Florida.

Larry Maxwell is a financial analyst with the 3M Company, St. Paul, Minnesota.

Robert McGlashan, Ph.D. (University of Texas at Austin), is Professor of Management at the University of Houston-Clear Lake. He is the author of numerous articles, cases, and papers. He is past President of both the Southwest Division of the Academy of Management and the Southwestern Federation of Administrative Disciplines. He is coauthor of *Strategic Management.*

Robert E. Meadows, D.B.A. (Kent State University), is Professor of Management at Morehead State University (Kentucky) and formerly taught at Westminster College (Pennsylvania). He worked for more than thirteen years in middle management positions in the rubber industry. He is active in the Midwest Decision Sciences Institute and the Midwest Society for Case Research.

Charles E. Michaels, Ph.D. (University of South Florida), is Assistant Professor of Management at the University of South Florida. He has served on the Editorial Review Board for *SAM Advanced Management Journal* and has authored articles and papers in the fields of business management and industrial psychology.

William Miller, M.S. (Iowa State University), is an Industrial Engineer Specialist in the Process Development Department of the Collins Transmission Systems Division of Rockwell International, Dallas, Texas.

Robert L. Nixon, Ph.D. (Cornell University), is Associate Professor of Management and Organizational Behavior and Theory at the University of South Florida. His publications focus on the effects of information systems in the organization. He is the author of numerous papers and articles.

Shirley F. Olson, D.B.A., is Associate Professor with the Else School of Management, Millsaps College, Jackson, Mississippi. She teaches strategy and various behavioral courses at both the graduate and undergraduate level. She owns her own consulting firm, the Olson Consulting Group, providing management consulting to business and government and is a widely sought public speaker.

Jyoti N. Prasad, Ph.D. (University of Arkansas), is Assistant Professor of Strategic Management at Western Illinois University. He has written numerous articles and cases and has presented papers at national and international conferences.

Deborah Reading, M.S. (Iowa State University), is a program coordinator with the Office of International Educational Services, Iowa State University.

Foster C. Rinefort, Ph.D. (Texas A&M University), is Coordinator of Graduate Business Studies and Associate Professor at the College of Business, Eastern Illinois University. He previously served as an instructor at Texas A&M University. He has fifteen years of business experience with Procter & Gamble and a large chemical firm. As a consultant he has provided services to a variety of clients on a worldwide basis as well as to state and federal agencies. He is the author of numerous articles, papers, and cases. Memberships include the Academy of Management, Midwest Business Administration Association, and Midwest Society for Case Research.

David W. Rosenthal, D.B.A. (University of Virginia), is Associate Professor of Marketing, Miami University, Oxford, Ohio. He is coauthor of *Careers in Marketing,* and has written numerous articles, papers, and cases on the subject of marketing employment and positions. His case writing covers a broad variety of topics, including marketing strategy, marketing of high technology, and sales force management. He is active in consulting through Burke Marketing Services, and Miami Valley Marketing Group, Ltd.

David Saveraid, M.S. (Iowa State University), is a project specialist with the Farm Information Management Services Division of Pioneer Hi-Bred International, Johnston, Iowa.

William E. Schlender, Ph.D. (Ohio State University), is the Richard E. Meier Professor Emeritus of Management, Valparaiso University. He has also held faculty and administrative positions at Ohio State, Cleveland State, University of Texas at Austin, and Bowling Green State University. He has been a visiting faculty member at Columbia University, University of Texas at Arlington, and Denver University. He has served on the editorial board of the *Academy of Management Journal,* coauthored *Elements of Managerial Action,* edited *Executive Leadership in a Dynamic Society,* coedited *Management in Perspective,* and authored journal articles, cases, and papers. He is a Fellow of the Academy of Management, and has served as Vice President of its Southwest Division. He is a founding member and first president of the Northeast Ohio Chapter of the Industrial Relations Research Association. He has also served on the board of directors of five corporations.

Fazal J. Seyyed, Ph.D. candidate (University of Arkansas), is Assistant Professor in the Department of Marketing and Finance, Western Illinois University. He has written and published several articles and cases in the areas of international marketing and finance.

Charles B. Shrader, Ph.D. (Indiana University), is Assistant Professor of Management, Iowa State University. He is the author or coauthor of several articles and professional papers on strategic planning, organization structure, and organization performance.

Lois M. Shufeldt, Ph.D. (New Mexico State University), is Associate Professor of Computer Information Systems, Southwest Missouri State University. Prior to her teaching career, she worked for Allyn Bacon, Inc. and with a center for business research. She has authored several published articles in professional and academic journals and proceedings of various professional conferences.

Timothy M. Singleton, Ph.D. (Georgia State University), is Associate Professor of Management at the University of Houston-Clear Lake. He is coauthor of *The Practice of Management: Text, Readings, and Cases,* and *Strategic Management.* He is the author of many cases, articles, and papers and is an active member of the North American Case Research Association.

Laurence J. Stybel, D.B.A. (Harvard University), is General Partner of Stybel, Peabody & Associates of Boston. Previously he was a management consultant with Hay Associates in the area of executive compensation and Assistant Professor of Management at Babson College. Areas of expertise include outplacement, evaluation of management potential, and management succession planning.

Megan E. Sutton, M.B.A. (Western Illinois University), is a research associate for an international advertising and marketing firm in London, England.

James Taylor, Ph.D. (University of Iowa), is Professor of Marketing, University of South Dakota. He has authored and coauthored several cases that have appeared in marketing and policy case books over the past 19 years.

Joe G. Thomas, Ph.D. (Texas A&M University), is Associate Professor of Management, University of Central Arkansas, Conway, Arkansas. Dr. Thomas is the author of articles appearing in *Long Range Planning, Academy of Management Review, Human Relations, Business Horizons,* and numerous other journals. His cases appear in more than a dozen texts. He is also a member of the Academy of Management, Association of Human Resource Management and Organizational Behavior, and Midwest Case Research Association. He is editor of the *Newsletter* for the Association of Human Resources Management and is a member of the Editorial Review Board for the *Journal of the Association of Human Resource Management and Organizational Behavior.* He is author of the book, *Strategic Management.*

Robert L. Trewatha, Ph.D. (University of Arkansas), is Professor and head of the Management Department, Southwest Missouri State University. He has served on the Board of Directors of the Southern Management Association and is active in the presentation of papers in the areas of leadership, strategic management, and international business. He is coauthor of *Management Functions and Behavior* and *Management* and the author of articles and cases.

Albert O. Trostel, Ph.D. (University of Minnesota), is Visiting Professor at Instituto Centroamericano de Administración de Empresas (INCAE) in Costa Rica and Professor of Strategic Management at College of St. Thomas, St. Paul, Minnesota. He formerly worked in manufacturing. At the College of St. Thomas he also served as Chairman of the Business Administration Department. At INCAE he is teaching, offering seminars, and writing cases in production and operations management throughout Central America.

Joyce P. Vincelette, D.B.A. (Indiana University), is Associate Professor of Management at the University of South Florida. Her primary areas of teaching and research are in human resource management and organizational behavior. She has served on the Board of Directors of the Southern Management Association and is a member of the *SAM Advanced Management Journal* editorial review board.

Thomas L. Wheelen, D.B.A. (George Washington University), is a Professor of Strategic Management, University of South Florida, and was formerly the Ralph A. Beeton Professor of Free Enterprise at the McIntire School of Commerce, University of Virginia. He was Visiting Professor at both the University of Arizona and Northeastern University. He has worked in management positions for General Electric and the U.S. Navy. He has been active as a consultant and trainer to business corporations, as well as to federal and state government agencies. He served on the editorial boards of the *Journal of Management* and the *Journal of Retail Banking.* He is currently serving on the boards of the *Journal of Management Case Studies, SAM Advancement Management Journal,* and *Case Research Journal.* He is Associate Editor of *SAM Advanced Management Journal,* coauthor of *Cases in Strategic Management and Business Policy,* and *Strategic Management,* as well as coeditor of *Developments in Management Information Systems* and *Collective Bargaining in the Public Sector.* He has authored 35 articles appearing in such journals as *Journal of Management, Business Quarterly, Personnel Journal, SAM Advanced Management Journal, Journal of Retailing,* and *International Journal of Management.* His cases appear in 25 management textbooks, plus the *Journal of Management Case Studies* and *Case Research Journal.* He has served on the Board of Directors of the Southern Management Association, as Vice President at Large for the Society for the Advancement of Management, and as President of the North American Case Research Association. He is a member of the Academy of Management, Southern Management Association, North American Case Research Association, Society for Advancement of Management, Institute for Decision Sciences, Midwest Society for Case Research, Strategic Management Association and Strategic Planning Society. He is serving as Vice President for Strategic Management for the Society for the Advancement of Management.

L. K. Williams, D.B.A. (University of Kentucky), is Assistant Professor of Accounting, Tennessee Technological University. He is a C.P.A. in Kentucky and has public accounting experience working for the accounting firm of Coopers & Lybrand. He is a member of the American Institute of CPAs and the American Accounting Association.

Other Contributing Authors

Jeff Curry

Mike Harris

Dean Salpini

Stephen J. Schewe

Art Scibelli

Gordon Shanks

Marrett Varghese

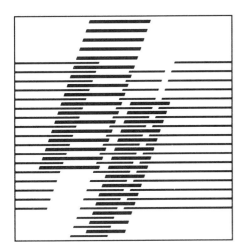

PART ONE

INTRODUCTION TO STRATEGIC MANAGEMENT AND BUSINESS POLICY

CHAPTER 1

INTRODUCTION

CHAPTER 2

DEVELOPING CONCEPTUAL SKILLS: THE CASE METHOD AND THE STRATEGIC AUDIT

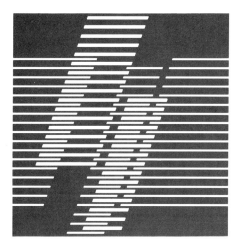

CHAPTER 1

INTRODUCTION

STRATEGIC MANAGEMENT MODEL

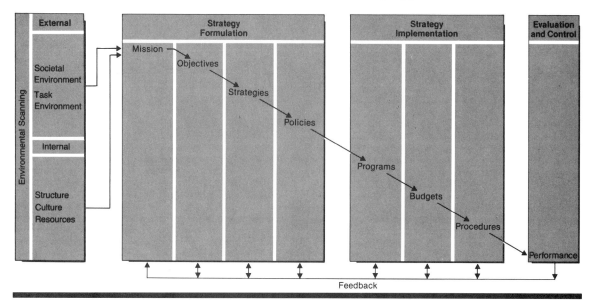

Who remembers Beaunit Mills, Hercules Powder, or Liebmann Breweries? These companies, along with 250 others that appeared in the first Fortune 500 list of top business corporations in 1955, have vanished from the major ranks of American industry. Why did so many fail to thrive? Although some of the changes are due to mergers and acquisitions, most of the turnover can be attributed to the company's inability to adapt to changing conditions.[1] One example of such a failure to adapt is the vacuum tube industry. During the first half of the twentieth century, the vacuum tube was a key electronic part of radios and televisions. Most televisions in the 1950s contained around ten to twenty vacuum tubes. They worked well, but took up a lot of space and gave off a large amount of heat—significant drawbacks for their use in early computers. One would assume that once the transistor was invented, most vacuum tube manufacturers would convert to the new technology. Surprisingly, that did not occur. Instead manufacturers spent more money in attempts to improve their current vacuum tube technology. As a result, the top ten manufacturers of vacuum tubes in 1955 gave way to other firms exploiting semiconductor technology and are no longer market leaders in this industry.[2]

With an 80% share of the market, National Cash Register (NCR) of Dayton, Ohio dominated the U.S. mechanical cash register business in 1971. NCR's management had invested millions of dollars in a highly sophisticated manufacturing facility. Also in 1971, Data Terminal Systems introduced the first electronic cash register in the U.S.A. This was the product of the future.

NCR, however, continued to emphasize its tried and true mechanical products until its profits turned to losses. In a frantic effort to recover its lost sales, the company fired 80% of its top managers and destroyed its expensive manufacturing facility to make room for a new plant. Despite the introduction of NCR's own electronic cash register, NCR's market share dropped from 80% in 1971 to 25% in 1978. It never regained industry dominance.[3]

These examples show how a leading company can quickly become an also-ran because of its failure to adapt to change or, even worse, its failure to create change. Current predictions are that the environment will become even more complex and turbulent as the world enters the twenty-first century. A recent report prepared by the American Assembly of Collegiate Schools of Business and the European Foundation for Management Development states, "Living with uncertainty is likely to be management's biggest challenge."[4]

Strategic management is a quickly developing field of study that has emerged in response to this environment of increasing turbulence. This field of study looks at the corporation as a whole and attempts to explain why some firms develop and thrive while others stagnate and go bankrupt. Strategic management typically focuses on analyzing the problems and opportunities faced by people in top management. Unlike many decisions made at lower levels in a corporation, **strategic decisions** deal with the long-run future of the entire organization and have three characteristics:

1. *Rare:* strategic decisions are unusual and typically have no precedent to follow.
2. *Consequential:* strategic decisions commit substantial resources and demand a great deal of commitment.
3. *Percursive:* strategic decisions set precedents for lesser decisions and future actions throughout the organization.[5]

Because strategic decisions have these characteristics, the stakes can be very high. For instance, the strategic decision made after World War II by Sears, Roebuck and Company to expand from catalog sales into retail stores and insurance gave Sears many years of successful profits. A similar decision made independently during the 1960s by the top managements of General Motors, Ford, and Chrysler to emphasize the production of large, powerful automobiles over small, fuel-efficient ones resulted in their low profits and even the threat of bankruptcy in the early 1980s.

Another example of a strategic decision was that made by the top management of International Rectifier Corporation (IR) in the mid-1980s. Founded in 1947 by Lithuanian immigrant Eric Ludlow and subsequently managed by Ludlow and his two sons, Alex and Derek, the company attempted to transform itself from a small firm in the U.S. microchip industry to an industry leader. From 1985 to 1987, top management poured $82 million into a state-of-the-art chipmaking plant designed to cut production costs in half, slash production time from eight weeks to one, and boost the yield of quality semiconductor silicon wafers. If the plant proved to be successful, the resulting output per worker would be $350,000 annually—more than double the industry's average.

Industry analysts criticized management's decision to build a plant at a cost that was more than half of International Rectifier's annual revenues and greater than the company's current book value of $55 million—especially when the semiconductor industry was in a prolonged slump. "There's no way a niche player like IR can use up new capacity," commented Adam Cuhney, vice-president for research at Kidder, Peabody and Company. Paul White, a vice-president of marketing at Motorola warned: "If they don't pull it off, they're going to sink." Nevertheless, the Ludlows remained confident in their decision. They pointed to experts' prediction that the world consumption of microchips would soar from $160 million in 1986 to $450 million by 1990. Accepting the fact that the company was deeply in debt after struggling with losses for three of the past five years, Alex Ludlow admitted that this was a strategic gamble: "We're putting everything on the line. We're betting we can produce a high-volume item in the U.S. better than anywhere else in the world."[6]

Alex Ludlow's comment suggests why the managers of today's business corporations must manage firms strategically. They cannot make decisions based on long-standing rules, policies, or standard operating procedures. Instead, they must look to the future as they plan organization-wide objectives, initiate strategy, and set policies. They must rise above their training and experience in such functional/operational areas as accounting, marketing, production, or finance, and grasp the overall picture. They must be willing to ask these key strategic questions:

1. Where is the corporation now?

2. If no changes are made, where will the corporation be in one year, two years, five years, ten years? Are the answers acceptable?

3. If the answers are not acceptable, what specific actions should the corporation undertake? What are the risks and payoffs involved?

1.1

STUDY OF STRATEGIC MANAGEMENT AND BUSINESS POLICY

Most business schools offer a strategic management or business policy course. Although this course typically serves as a capstone or final integrative class in a business administration program, it—also typically—takes on some of the characteristics of a separate discipline.

In the 1950s the Ford Foundation and the Carnegie Corporation sponsored investigations into the business school curriculum.[7] The resulting Gordon and Howell report, sponsored by the Ford Foundation, recommended a broad business education and a course in business policy to "give students an opportunity to pull together what they have learned in the separate business fields and utilize this knowledge in the analysis of complex business problems."[8] The report also suggested the content that should be part of such a course:

> The business policy course can offer the student something he [or she] will find nowhere else in the curriculum: consideration of business problems which are not prejudged as being marketing problems, finance problems, etc.; emphasis on the development of skills in identifying, analyzing, and solving problems in a situation which is as close as the classroom can ever be to the real business world; opportunity to consider problems which draw on a wide range of substantive areas in business; opportunity to consider the external, nonmarket implications of problems at the same time that internal decisions must be made; situations which enable the student to exercise qualities of judgment and of mind which were not explicitly called for in any prior course. Questions of social responsibility and of personal attitudes can be brought in as a regular aspect of this kind of problem-solving practice. Without the responsibility of having to transmit some specific body of knowledge, the business policy course can concentrate on integrating what already has been acquired and on developing further the student's skill in using that knowledge.[9]

By the late 1960s most business schools included such a business policy course in their curriculum. But since that time the typical policy course has evolved to one that emphasizes the total organization and strategic management, with an increased interest in business social responsibilities and ethics. This evolution is in line with a recent survey of business school deans that reported that a primary objective of undergraduate business education is to develop an understanding of the political, social, and economic environment of business.[10] This increasing concern with the effect of environmental issues on the management of the total organization has led leaders in the field to replace the term *business policy* with the more comprehensive *strategic management.*[11] **Strategic management** is that set of managerial decisions and actions that determines the long-run performance of a corporation. It includes strategy formulation, strategy implementation, and evaluation and control. The study of strategic management therefore emphasizes the monitoring and evaluating of environmental opportunities and constraints in light of a corporation's strengths and weaknesses. In contrast, the study of **business policy,** with its integrative orientation, tends to look inward. By focusing on the efficient utilization of a corporation's assets, it thus emphasizes the formulation of general guidelines that will better accomplish a firm's mission and objectives. We see, then, that strategic management incorporates the concerns of business policy with a heavier environmental and strategic emphasis.

1.2

RESEARCH ON THE EFFECTIVENESS OF STRATEGIC MANAGEMENT

Many of the concepts and techniques dealing with long-range planning and strategic management have been developed and used successfully by business corporations such as General Electric and the Boston Consulting Group, among others. Nevertheless, not all organizations use these tools or even attempt to manage strategically. Many are able to succeed for a while with unstated objectives and intuitive strategies. American Hospital Supply Corporation (AHS) was one such organization until Karl Bays became chief executive in 1971 and introduced strategic planning to a sales-dominated management. Previously, the company's idea of long-range planning was "Maybe in December we should look at next year's budget," recalled a former AHS executive.[12]

From his extensive work in the area, Bruce Henderson of the Boston Consulting Group concluded that intuitive strategies cannot be continued successfully if (1) the corporation becomes large, (2) the layers of management increase, or (3) the environment changes substantially.[13] Research suggests that the increasing risks of error, costly mistakes, and even economic ruin are causing today's professional managers to take strategic management seriously in order to keep their company competitive in an increasingly volatile environment.[14] Research by Gluck, Kaufman, and Walleck proposes that, as top managers attempt to better deal with their changing world, strategic planning evolves through *four sequential phases:*

Phase 1. *Basic financial planning:* seeking better operational control through the meeting of budgets.

Phase 2. *Forecast-based planning:* seeking more effective planning for growth by trying to predict the future beyond the next year.

Phase 3. *Externally oriented planning:* seeking increased responsiveness to markets and competition by trying to think strategically.

Phase 4. *Strategic management:* seeking to manage all resources to develop competitive advantage and to help create the future.[15]

Concern about external as well as internal factors seems to be increasing in today's large corporations. Research conducted by Henry indicates that the planning systems of fifty large companies are becoming increasingly sophisticated. For example, there is more effort to formulate, implement, and evaluate strategic plans. There is also a greater emphasis on strategic factors in the evaluation of a manager's performance.[16] Gordon Brunton, president of Britain's International Thomson Organisation, Ltd. emphasized this point when he made the following statement:

All International Thomson senior managers now understand that unless they demonstrate their ability to think strategically, their future career potential will be limited accordingly.[17]

William Rothschild, staff executive for business development and strategy at General Electric (GE), notes the current trend to push strategic management duties down the organizational hierarchy to operating line managers. He observes that at GE, "over half of our managers are strategic thinkers. Another 20 percent to 25 percent lean that way. The rest don't understand it, and if they're fortunate enough to be in the right business where there is a stable environment, it doesn't matter too much."[18]

Many researchers have conducted studies of corporations to reveal whether organizations that engage in strategic planning outperform those that do not. One analysis of five companies with sales ranging from $1 billion to $17 billion reports that the impact of strategic planning has been to

- help the companies sort their businesses into "winners and losers,"
- focus attention on critical issues and choices, and
- develop a strategic frame of mind among top and upper-level managers.

The study concludes that management should expect strategic planning to improve a company's competitive position and long-term profits, plus yield growth in earnings per share.[19]

Research studies attempting to measure objectively this anticipated connection between a corporation's use of formal strategic planning and its performance have found mixed results.[20] Rhyne, however, explains these contradictory findings as resulting from the use of varying measures for planning and performance plus a typical failure to consider industry effects. When he controlled for industry variation, focused only on the total return to stockholders, and considered strategic planning as being different from less-evolved stages of planning (such as budgeting or annual planning), Rhyne found a positive relationship between strategic planning and performance. He concluded that "these results provide assurance that the prescriptions of strategic management theory are indeed valid."[21] Research by Smith and Grimm on the impact of deregulation upon the U.S. railroad industry adds further support to Rhyne's conclusion. The study reveals that those railroads that changed their strategy as their environment changed out-performed those railroads that did not change.[22]

From this evidence we can conclude that a knowledge of strategic management is very important for business performance to be effective in a changing environment. The use of strategic planning and the selection of alternative courses of action based on an assessment of important external and internal factors are becoming key parts of a general manager's job.

1.3
HIERARCHY OF STRATEGY

The typical large, multidivisional business firm has three levels of strategy: (1) corporate, (2) business, and (3) functional.[23]

Corporate strategy explores the ways in which a firm can develop a favorable "portfolio strategy" for its many activities. It is the pattern of decisions regarding the types of businesses in which a firm should be involved, the flow of financial and other resources to and from its divisions, the relationship of the corporation to key groups in its environment, and the ways in which a corporation can increase its return on investment (ROI). Corporate strategy may be one of stability, growth, or retrenchment.

Business strategy, in contrast, usually occurs at the divisional level, and emphasizes improvement of the competitive position of a corporation's products or services in the specific industry or market segment served by the division. A division may be organized as a **Strategic Business Unit** (SBU) around a group of similar products, such as housewares or electric turbines. Top management usually treats an SBU as a semi-autonomous unit with, generally, the authority to develop its own strategy within corporate objectives and strategy. A division's business strategy probably would stress the increasing of its profit margin in the production and sales of its products and services. Business strategies also should integrate various functional activities so that divisional objectives are achieved. Sometimes called **competitive strategy,** business strategy may be one of overall cost leadership, differentiation, or focus.

The principal focus of **functional strategy**, is the maximizing of resource productivity.[24] Within the constraints of the corporate and business strategies around them, functional departments develop strategies in which their various activities and competencies are pulled together for the improvement of performance. For example, a typical strategy of a marketing department might center on developing the means to increase the current year's sales over those of the previous year. With a *market development* functional strategy, the department would attempt to sell current products to different customers in the current market or to new customers in a new geographical area. Examples of R&D functional strategies are *technological followership* (imitate the products of other companies) and *technological leadership* (pioneer an innovation).

The three levels of strategy—corporate, business, and functional—form a **hierarchy of strategy** within a large corporation. They interact closely with each other and must be well integrated if the total corporation is to be successful. As depicted in Fig. 1.1, each level of strategy forms the strategic environment of the next level in the corporation. (The interaction among the three levels is depicted later in the chapter in Fig. 1.5.)

1.4

DESCRIPTIVE MODEL OF STRATEGIC MANAGEMENT

The process of strategic management involves four basic elements: (1) **environmental scanning,** (2) **strategy formulation,** (3) **strategy implementation,** and (4) **evaluation and control.** Figure 1.2 shows how these four elements interact. We will discuss these interactions later in this section.

At the corporate level, the strategic management process includes activ-

FIGURE 1.1
Hierarchy of Strategy.

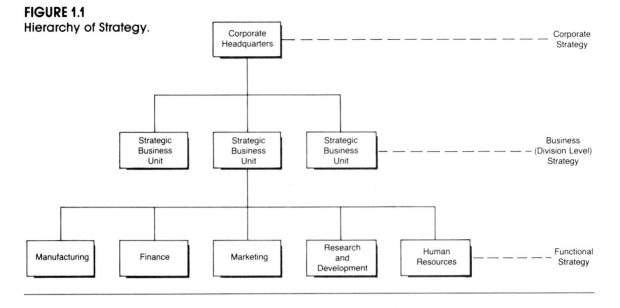

ities that range from environmental scanning to the evaluation of performance. Top management scans both the external environment for opportunities and threats, and the internal environment for strengths and weaknesses. The factors that are most important to the corporation's future are referred to as strategic factors and are summarized with the acronym **S.W.O.T.,** standing for **S**trengths, **W**eaknesses, **O**pportunities, and **T**hreats. Once these are identified, top management then evaluates the strategic factors and determines corporate mission. The first step in the formulation of strategy, a statement of mission leads to a determination of corporate objectives, strategies, and policies. These strategies and policies are implemented through programs, budgets, and procedures. Finally performance is evaluated, and information is fed back into the system so that adequate control of organizational activities is ensured. Figure 1.3 depicts this process as a continuous one. It is an expansion of the basic model presented in Fig. 1.2.

The model in Fig. 1.3, with minor changes, also reflects the strategic management process at both divisional and functional levels of the corporation. A division's external environment, for example, includes not only task and societal variables, but also the mission, objectives, strategy, and policies of corporate headquarters. Similarly, both corporate and divisional constraints form the external environment of a functional department. The model depicted in Fig. 1.3 therefore is appropriate to any strategic level of a corporation.

FIGURE 1.2
Basic Elements of the Strategic Management Process.

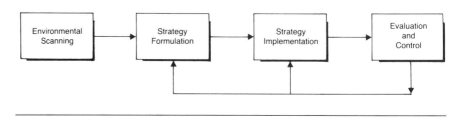

Environmental Scanning: External

The *external environment* consists of variables (**O**pportunities and **T**hreats) that are outside the organization and not typically within the short-run control of top management. These variables form the context within which the corporation exists. The external environment has two parts: task environment and societal environment. The **task environment** includes those elements or groups that directly affect and are affected by an organization's major operations. Some of these are stockholders, governments, suppliers, local communities, competitors, customers, creditors, labor unions, special

FIGURE 1.3
Strategic Management Model.

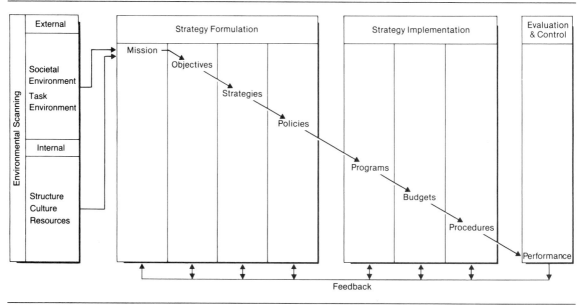

interest groups, and trade associations. The task environment of a corporation is often referred to as its *industry*. The **societal environment** includes more general forces—ones that do not directly touch the short-run activities of the organization but that can, and often do, influence its long-run decisions. Such economic, sociocultural, technological, and political-legal forces are depicted in Fig. 1.4 in relation to a firm's total environment. (These external variables are discussed in more detail in Chapter 4.)

Environmental Scanning: Internal

The *internal environment* of a corporation consists of variables (**S**trengths and **W**eaknesses) that are within the organization itself and are not usually within the short-run control of top management. These variables form the context in which work is done. They include the corporation's structure, culture, and resources. The **corporate structure** is the way a corporation is organized in terms of communication, authority, and workflow. It is often referred to as the "chain of command" and is graphically described in an

FIGURE 1.4
Environmental Variables.

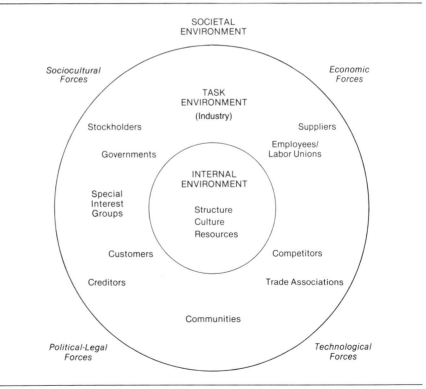

organization chart. The **corporation's culture** is that pattern of beliefs, expectations, and values shared by the corporation's members. In a firm norms typically emerge that define the acceptable behavior of people from top management down to the operative employees. **Corporate resources** are those assets that form the raw material for the production of an organization's products or services. These assets include people and managerial talent as well as financial assets, plant facilities, and the skills and abilities within functional areas. (These internal variables in a firm's environment are discussed in more detail in Chapter 5.)

Strategy Formulation

Strategy formulation is the development of long-range plans for the effective management of environmental opportunities and threats, in light of corporate strengths and weaknesses. It includes defining the corporate mission, specifying achievable objectives, developing strategies, and setting policy guidelines.[25]

Mission

The corporate mission is the purpose or reason for the corporation's existence. For example, the mission of a savings and loan association might be to provide mortgage money to people of the community. By fulfilling this mission, the S&L would hope to provide a reasonable rate of return to its depositors. A mission may be narrow or broad in scope. A **narrow mission** clearly limits the scope of the corporation's activities in terms of product or service offered, the technology used, and the market served. The above-mentioned S&L has the narrow mission of providing mortgage money to the people of the community. The problem with such a narrow statement of mission is that it might restrict the use of future opportunities for growth. A **broad mission** widens the scope of the corporation's activities to include many types of products or services, markets, and technologies. A broad mission of the same S&L might be to offer financial services to anyone, regardless of location. The problem with such a broad statement of mission is that it does not clearly identify which area the corporation wishes to emphasize and might confuse employees and customers. Other examples of narrow and broad missions are shown here.

NARROW SCOPE	BROAD SCOPE
Railroads	Transportation
Insurance	Financial services
Typewriters	Office equipment
Television	Telecommunications

Objectives

The corporate mission, as depicted in Fig. 1.3, determines the parameters of the specific objectives to be defined by top management. These objectives are listed as the end results of planned activity. They state *what* is to be accomplished by *when* and should be quantified if possible. (The term *goal* is often confused with *objective*. In contrast to an objective, a *goal* is an *open-ended* statement of what one wishes to accomplish with *no* quantification of what is to be achieved and *no* time criteria for completion.[26] For example, a goal of an S&L might be to increase its rate of return—a rather vague statement.) The achievement of corporate objectives, however, should result in a corporation's fulfilling its mission. An S&L, for example, might set an objective for the year of earning a 10% rate of return on its investment portfolio.

Strategies

A strategy of a corporation forms a comprehensive master plan stating *how* the corporation will achieve its mission and objectives. It maximizes competitive advantage and minimizes competitive disadvantage. For example, to achieve its objective of a 10% rate of return, an S&L could increase demand for its mortgages by offering special terms to a particular market segment, such as young professional people who can't meet the normal down-payment requirements. In order to increase the amount of money deposited in savings accounts that fund the mortgages, the S&L might offer large depositors special privileges and interest rates not available from other financial institutions. A different strategy would be to offer financial services so that the S&L's income becomes less dependent on mortgages.

Policies

Flowing from the strategy, policies provide broad guidance for decision making throughout the organization. Policies are thus broad guidelines which serve to link the formulation of strategy with its implementation. In attempting to increase the amount of mortgage loans as well as the amount of deposits available for mortgages, an S&L might set policies of always evaluating a mortgage candidate on the basis of *potential* rather than on current or historical income and of developing *creative* incentives for savings depositors. (Strategy formulation is discussed in detail in Chapters 6 and 7).

Strategy Implementation

Strategy implementation is the process by which strategies and policies are put into action through the development of programs, budgets, and procedures. This process might involve changes within the overall culture, structure, and/or management system of the entire organization. Except when such drastic corporate-wide changes are needed, however, the implementation of strategy is typically conducted by middle- and lower-level managers with review by top management. Sometimes referred to as operational planning, strategy implementation often involves day-to-day decisions in resource allocation.

Thus working under the guidance of top management, division and/or functional managers will fully develop the programs, budgets, and procedures that will be used to achieve the objectives of the corporate strategy. At the same time, these managers are involved in strategy formulation at the divisional or functional level. If, for example, the corporate strategy for an automobile manufacturer is to grow through international expansion through joint ventures, the business-level strategy of a particular division of the corporation might be to form a joint venture with a Brazilian auto firm in order to build the lowest-priced auto for sale in South America. Although this strategy formulation is at the business level of the corporation, it can also be viewed by top management as a program that implements its corporate strategy of international expansion through joint ventures.

Programs

A program is a statement of the activities or steps needed to accomplish a single-use plan. It makes the strategy action-oriented. For instance, to implement its strategy and policies, an S&L might initiate an advertising program in the local area, develop close ties with the local realtors' association, and offer free silverware with every $1,000 savings deposit.

Budgets

A budget is a statement of a corporation's programs in dollar terms. Used in planning and control, it lists the detailed cost of each program. The S&L might thus draw up separate budgets for each of its three programs: the advertising budget, the public relations budget, and the premium budget.

Procedures

Sometimes termed Standard Operating Procedures (SOP), procedures are a system of sequential steps or techniques that describe in detail how a particular task or job is to be done. They typically detail the various activities that must be carried out for completion of the corporation's program. The S&L, for example, might develop procedures for the placement of ads in newspapers and on radio. They might list persons to contact, techniques for the writing of acceptable copy (with samples), and details about payment. They might establish detailed procedures concerning eligibility requirements for silverware premiums. (Strategy implementation is discussed in more detail in Chapter 8.)

Evaluation and Control

Evaluation and control is the process in which corporate activities and performance results are monitored so that actual performance can be compared with desired performance. Managers at all levels use the resulting information to take corrective action and resolve problems. Although evaluation and control is the final major element of strategic management, it also can pinpoint weaknesses in previously implemented strategic plans and thus stimulate the entire process to begin again.

For evaluation and control to be effective, managers must obtain clear, prompt, and unbiased feedback from the people below them in the corporation's hierarchy. The model in Fig. 1.3 indicates how feedback in the forms of performance data and activity reports runs through the entire management process. Using this feedback, managers compare what is actually happening with what was originally planned in the formulation stage.

For example, the S&L management would probably ask its internal information systems people to keep track of both the number of mortgages being made and the level of deposits at the end of each week for each S&L branch office. It might also wish to develop special rewards for loan officers who increase their mortgage lending.

To monitor and evaluate broad-scale results, top management of large corporations typically uses periodic reports dealing with key performance indicators, such as return on investment, net profits, earnings per share, and net sales. From what these reports indicate, top management takes further action. For example, it might see a need to emphasize rewards for long-term performance improvement and thereby alter the corporation's current incentive system. To help managers pinpoint those areas with performance problems, corporations are sometimes structured with profit centers, investment centers, expense centers, cost centers, and revenue centers. (These are discussed in detail in Chapter 9.)

Activities are much harder to monitor and evaluate than are performance results. Because of the many difficulties in deciding which activities to monitor and because of the bias inherent in evaluating job performance, some firms now manage by objectives. Management By Objectives (MBO) has been criticized, however, for ignoring many of the intermediate activities that can lead to the desired results. To counter this criticism, consulting firms have developed management "audits," which assess key organizational activities and provide in-depth feedback to consultants and managers. Management audits complement standard measures of performance and help complete the picture of the corporation's activities. (We discuss an example of a comprehensive audit in Chapter 2.)

1.5

STRATEGIC MANAGEMENT MODEL IN ACTION

Most major corporations are structured on both a divisional and a functional basis. As depicted in Fig. 1.5, the corporate level goes through all three stages of the strategic management process. Top management *with input from the divisions* formulates strategies and makes plans for implementation. These implementation plans stimulate the strategy formulation process at the divisional level. To accomplish the corporate programs, each division formulates its own objectives, strategies, and policies. For example, a corporate-level program of CSX Corporation (a multidivisional major transportation company) in 1986 was to dispose of unproductive and marginal assets. To implement this program, the railroad business segment (or division) formulates an objective specifying how many miles of track would be abandoned or/and sold during the coming year and develops a strategy for accomplishing that objective. Then, as the division acts on its strategy, it feeds its evaluation and control information upward to the corporate level for its use in evaluation and control.

Responding to each division's programs for implementation, separate functional departments within each division begin to formulate their own objectives and strategies. For example, American Commercial Lines (ACL), CSX's barge subsidiary, might set an objective of increasing its barge tonnage by 10% over the previous year and propose this business strategy: to differentiate its service from that of the competition, it will guarantee fewer losses in transit. In response to this strategy, each functional department—such as operations and marketing—develops its own objectives and strategies. ACL's operations department would set an objective for loss reduction

FIGURE 1.5
Strategic Management Process at Three Corporate Levels.

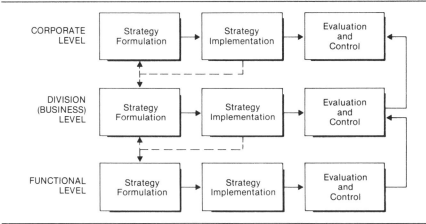

and begin formulating a strategy for the reduction of damage to goods being transported. ACL's marketing department would also set objectives specifying how many new customers will have to be attracted and how much tonnage from its current customers will have to be increased, to fulfill ACL's overall objective. Marketing would then formulate the appropriate advertising and promotion strategies. In this way each level of the corporation develops its own objectives, strategies, policies, programs, budgets, and procedures to complement those of the level above.

The specific operation of the hierarchy of strategy may vary from one corporation to another. The one described here of CSX Corporation is an example of **top-down strategic planning,** in which corporate-level top management initiates the strategy formulation process and calls upon divisions and functional units to formulate their own strategies as ways of implementing corporate-level strategies. Another approach is *bottom-up* strategic planning, in which the strategy formulation process is initiated by strategic proposals from divisional or functional units. This approach is shown by the arrows pointing upward in Fig. 1.5; strategy formulation leads from the functional level to the divisional level and from the divisional to the corporate level. Bechtel Group, the largest construction and engineering company in the U.S., uses bottom-up strategic planning because it uses autonomous divisions as independent profit centers.[27] Although an *interactive approach* is sometimes proposed as a third approach to strategic planning,[28] it is clear that in most companies the origin of the formulation process is not as important as the resultant interaction between levels. The process involves a lot of negotiation between levels in the hierarchy so that the various objectives, strategies, policies, programs, budgets, and procedures fit together and reinforce each other. It is a continuous process of adjustment between the formulation and implementation of each level of strategy.[29]

1.6

ILLUSTRATION OF THE CHAPTER: INTRODUCTION TO THE INTEGRATIVE CASE

To illustrate the strategic management model presented in this chapter, we will discuss CSX Corporation, a large multidivisional business corporation based in the United States. This example will also serve as an integrative case for the rest of the textbook. Each of the remaining chapters—except Chapters Eleven and Twelve, which cover special issues in strategic management—will include a part of the CSX Corporation case as an illustration of that chapter's content. By showing each part of the strategic management process as it operates within the same company, we can thus offer a consistent, integrated view of strategy formulation, strategy implementation, and evaluation and control.

The part of the integrative case at the end of this chapter presents a brief introduction to the CSX Corporation. It illustrates the strategic management model by providing the company's mission, objectives, strategies, policies, programs, budgets, procedures, and evaluation and control reports. Each of the following chapters will present an additional piece of the CSX case. Use the case to apply some of the concepts discussed in each chapter. Since the concepts are not applied for you (except for that part following Chapter One), the integrative case can be used for in-class discussions following each chapter. In this manner, the integrative case of CSX Corporation illustrates some of the many factors that need to be considered when a corporation is being managed strategically.

SUMMARY AND CONCLUSION

This chapter sets the stage for the study of strategic management and business policy. It explains the rationale for including the subject in a business school curriculum. In addition to serving as a capstone to integrate the various functional areas, the course provides a framework for the analysis of top management's decision process and the effects of environmental issues on the corporation. Research generally supports the conclusion that corporations that manage strategically perform at higher levels than do those firms that do not. Strategic management is thus an important area of study for anyone interested in organizational productivity.

Our model of strategic management includes environmental scanning, strategy formulation and implementation, plus evaluation and control. The mission of a corporation derives from the interaction of internal and external environmental factors, as modified by the needs and values of top management. A precise statement of mission guides the setting of objectives and the formulation of strategies and policies. Strategies are implemented through specific programs, budgets, and procedures. Management continuously monitors and evaluates performance and activities on the basis of measurable results and audits of key areas. These data feed back into the corporation at all phases of the strategic management process. If results and activities fail to measure up to the plans, managers may then take the appropriate actions.

Although top management and the board of directors have primary responsibility for the strategic management process, many levels of the corporation conduct strategy formulation, implementation, and evaluation and control. Large multidivisional corporations utilize divisional and functional levels that integrate the entire corporation by focusing their activities on the accomplishment of the corporate mission.

DISCUSSION QUESTIONS

1. What differentiates strategic decisions from other types of decisions?

2. How does strategic management typically evolve in a corporation? Why?

3. What is meant by the hierarchy of strategy?

4. Does every business firm have business strategies? Explain.

5. What information is needed for the proper formulation of strategy? Why?

6. What are the pros and cons of *bottom-up* as contrasted with *top-down* strategic planning?

NOTES

1. W. Shanklin, "Fortune 500 Dropouts," *Planning Review* (May 1986), pp. 12–17.

2. S. R. Craig, "Seeking Strategic Advantage with Technology? Focus on Customer Value!" *Long Range Planning* (April 1986), pp. 50–51.

3. Craig, p. 53.

4. J. Robertson, "The Changing Expectations of Society in the Next Thirty Years," in *Management for the XXI Century*, edited by the AACSB and EFMD (Boston/TheHague/London: Kluwer-Nijhoff Publishing, 1982), p. 5.

5. D. J. Hickson, R. J. Butler, D. Cray, G. R. Mallory, and D. C. Wilson, *Top Decisions: Strategic Decision-Making in Organizations* (San Francisco: Jossey-Bass, 1986), pp. 26–42.

6. R. Neff, "The Riverboat Gamblers of the Chip Business," *Business Week* (December 15, 1986), pp. 96–98.

7. R. A. Gordon and J. E. Howell, *Higher Education for Business* (New York: Columbia University Press, 1959).

F. C. Pierson et al., *The Education of American Businessmen* (New York: McGraw-Hill, 1959).

8. Gordon and Howell, p. 206.

9. Gordon and Howell, pp. 206–207.

10. J. D. Hunger and T. L. Wheelen, *An Assessment of Undergraduate Business Education in the United States* (Charlottesville, Va.: McIntire School of Commerce Foundation, 1980). Also summarized in "A Performance Appraisal of Undergraduate Business Education," *Human Resource Management* (Spring 1980), pp. 24–31.

11. M. Leontiades, "The Confusing Words of Business Policy," *Academy of Management Review* (January 1982), p. 46.

12. B. Lancaster, "American Hospital's Marketing Program Places Company Atop a Troubled Industry," *Wall Street Journal* (August 24, 1984), p. 19.

13. B. D. Henderson, *Henderson on Corporate Strategy* (Cambridge, Mass.: Abt Books, 1979), p. 33.

14. R. Lamb, *Advances in Strategic Management*, Vol. 2 (Greenwich, Conn.: Jai Press, Inc., 1983), p. x.

15. F. W. Gluck, S. P. Kaufman, and A. S. Walleck, "The Four Phases of Strategic Management," *The Journal of Business Strategy* (Winter 1982), pp. 9–21.

16. H. W. Henry, "Evolution of Strategic Planning in Major Corporations," *Proceedings, American Institute of Decision Sciences* (November 1980), pp. 454–456.

H. W. Henry, "Then and Now: A Look at Strategic Planning Systems," *Journal of Business Strategy* (Winter 1981), pp. 64–69.

17. G. C. Brunton, "Implementing Corporate Strategy: The Story of International Thomson," *Journal of Business Strategy* (Fall 1984), p. 14.

18. P. Pascarella, "Strategy Comes Down to Earth," *Industry Week* (January 9, 1984), p. 51.

19. W. B. Schaffir and T. J. Lobe, "Strategic Planning: The Impact at Five Companies," *Planning Review* (March 1984), pp. 40–41.

20. C. B. Shrader, L. Taylor, and D. R. Dalton, "Strategic Planning and Organizational Performance: A Critical Appraisal," *Journal of Management* (Summer 1984), pp. 149–179.

G. E. Greenley, "Does Strategic Planning Improve Company Performance?" *Long Range Planning* (April 1986), pp. 101–109.

J. A. Pearce II, E. A. Freeman, and R. B. Robinson, Jr., "The Tenuous Link Between Formal Strategic Planning and Financial Performance," *Academy of Management Review* (October 1987), pp. 658–675.

21. L. C. Rhyne, "The Relationship of Strategic Planning to Financial Performance," *Strategic Management Journal* (September-October 1986), p. 435.

22. K. G. Smith and C. M. Grimm, "Environmental Variation, Strategic Change and Firm Performance: A Study of Railroad Deregulation," *Strategic Management Journal* (July-August 1987), pp. 363–376.

23. Some theorists propose a fourth level of strategy called "enterprise," which seeks to position an organization within its broader environment. See R. E. Freeman and P. Lorange, "Theory Building in Strategic Management," in *Advances in Strategic Management, Volume 3*, edited by R. Lamb and P. Shrivastava (Greenwich, Conn.: Jai Press, 1985), p. 20. We chose, however, to include these broad environmental concerns with other factors considered in the development of corporate level strategy. See K. R. Andrews, *The Concept of Corporate Strategy*, Third Edition (Homewood, Illinois: Irwin, 1987), p. 13.

24. C. W. Hofer and D. Schendel, *Strategy Formulation: Analytical Concepts* (St. Paul, Minn.: West Publishing Co., 1978), p. 29.

25. Although some theorists propose that *both* objective setting and the consideration of competitive methods are a part of strategy, we agree with those who contend that objectives and strategy are separate means and ends considerations. See G. G. Dess, "Consensus on Strategy Formulation and Organizational Performance: Competitors in a Fragmented Industry," *Strategic Management Journal* (May-June 1987), pp. 259–260.

26. M. D. Richards, *Setting Strategic Goals and Objectives*, 2nd edition (St. Paul, Minn.: West Publishing Co., 1987), p. 12.

27. D. M. Slavick, "Planning at Bechtel: End of the Megaproject Era," *Planning Review* (September 1986), p. 20.

28. B. Ho Rho, "A Comparison of Long-Range Planning in South Korea, Japan, and the U.S.," *Planning Review* (March-April 1987), pp. 32–36.

29. M. E. Naylor, "Regaining Your Competitive Edge," *Long Range Planning* (February 1985), pp. 33–34.

R. G. Hamermesh, *Making Strategy Work* (New York: Wiley and Sons, 1986), p. 47.

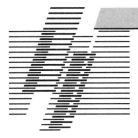

CSX CORPORATION

CSX Corporation is a major transportation company formed as a result of a merger in 1980 between two major railroad systems in the eastern United States and part of Canada. Through a series of acquisitions, CSX was by 1986 heavily involved in railroads, trucking, barge operations, and pipelines, and had real estate and managerial interests in coal mines and resort hotels. At that time, in order to integrate their five-year financial projection into the company's operating strategic plans, top management initiated formal strategic management. Statements from top management, published in media accounts and in CSX annual reports, infer that the following process occurred.

To begin the strategic management process described in Fig. 1.3, CSX top management first scanned the external environment for relevant information about opportunities and threats. As 1986 began, the U.S. government's deregulation of the transportation industries continued to be a strategic factor—deregulation opened the opportunity for mergers across traditional lines, such as railroads, trucking, and barge operations. Another external factor was the nation's economic health. The only depressed parts of the country were those dependent on agriculture and petroleum; otherwise, the economy was healthy and growing.

Top management also scanned its internal environment and assessed the strengths and weaknesses of its business units and functional areas. Corporate structure and culture continued to be a strategic factor as CSX attempted to integrate its many activities and manage its diverse assets in an effective and efficient manner. This environmental scanning provided the data for the formulation, implementation, and evaluation and control stages of strategic management. As depicted in Integrative Case Example 1.1, CSX top management begins with defining its mission and ends with developing a feedback system for evaluation and control.

INTEGRATIVE
CASE EXAMPLE
1.1

Strategic Management at CSX Corporation (Corporate Level—Early 1986)

STRATEGY FORMULATION

Mission

> **Broad:** become a national multimodal transportation system.
>
> **Narrow:** become an intermodal, one-stop freight transportation provider in the eastern United States.

Objectives

1. To reach and exceed a 15% return on invested capital by 1990.

2. Continue in the coming years to outperform the peer group and Standard and Poor's 500 in terms of stock price and earnings per share.

Strategies

1. Grow by *merging* with and *acquiring* other transportation companies whose transportation systems complement that of CSX.

2. Improve corporate productivity by *streamlining* the CSX transportation system and *divesting* those assets unrelated to the corporation's strategic mission.

Policies

1. Integrate the activities of the various transportation systems so that reliable, one-stop service is achieved and transportation efficiency is improved.

2. Expand only into those areas having long-term growth opportunity and promising a rate of return substantially exceeding the cost of capital.

3. Respect the history and traditions of the companies that comprise CSX so as to be a "partnership of equals."

4. Delegate responsibility for day-to-day operations to the divisions. The corporate office should be small and should focus on the three Ps—Policy, Planning, and Policing—while emphasizing finance.

STRATEGY IMPLEMENTATION

Programs

1. Initiate an acquisition program of finding a company that will complement current transportation businesses.

2. Restructure the corporation into four major business units—transportation, energy, technology, and properties.

3. Dispose of unproductive and marginal assets in all business units, especially railroads.

4. Reduce the number of rail employees through a buy-out program for contract and noncontract workers.

5. Institute a long-term incentive program to link management compensation to corporate financial performance.

6. Integrate the marketing and sales departments of the transportation business units so as to present the customer with a single representative of the corporation's many transportation modes.

Budgets

Prepare budgets showing a cost–benefit analysis of each planned program and a statement of how much the corporation can afford to spend for each program.

Procedures

1. Develop procedures for the sale of bonds or stock in quantities sufficient to finance the acquisition of a new transportation business.

2. Develop procedures for the reorganization in terms of accounting practices and personnel relocation.

3. Develop criteria to be used to determine asset productivity.

4. Develop the specifics of the early retirement program.

5. Develop the details of the long-term incentive program.

(Continued)

(Continued)

6. Develop procedures for combining the various transportation marketing and sales departments and handling human resources issues.

EVALUATION AND CONTROL

Require business units to provide monthly status reports on the following items:

1. Tonnage of originated coal by category (steam and metallurgical) and export coal dumpings.

2. Principal rail commodities (coal, automotive, chemicals, etc.) by carload and by revenues.

3. Miles of rail installed, ties laid, and track surfaced as well as track abandoned or sold.

4. Amount of principal barge commodities (coal, grain, liquids, etc.) by tons and by revenues.

5. Barge ton-miles traveled.

6. Average cost and average sales price of natural gas transmitted.

7. Sources of gas supply and volume transmitted.

8. Average revenue and volume of natural gas and oil condensate produced and sold.

Require business units to provide additional annual reports on the following items:

1. Operating revenues.

2. Operating costs and expenses for labor and fringe benefits, materials and supplies, fuel, equipment rental, and depreciation.

3. Identifiable assets in dollars plus property additions and deletions.

4. Number of rail employees.

SOURCE: Developed from "CSX Corporation" by J. D. Hunger, B. Ferrin, H. Felix-Gamez, and T. Goetzman in *Cases in Strategic Management and Business Policy* by T. L. Wheelen and J. D. Hunger (Reading, Mass.: Addison-Wesley Publishing Co., 1987), pp. 91–123 and from the 1985 Annual Report of CSX Corporation, published in early 1986. The above statements were developed by the authors strictly as pedagogical examples and were inferred from CSX publications and statements by CSX management.

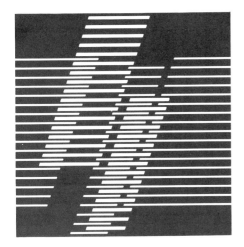

CHAPTER 2

DEVELOPING CONCEPTUAL SKILLS: THE CASE METHOD AND THE STRATEGIC AUDIT

STRATEGIC MANAGEMENT MODEL

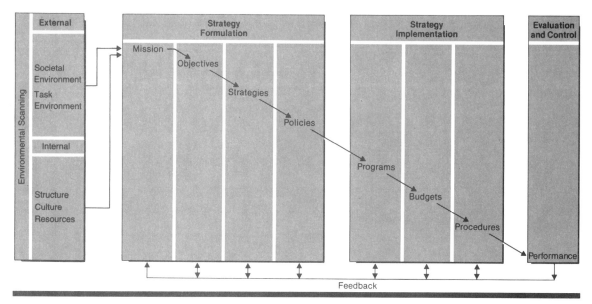

An analysis of a corporation's strategic management calls for a top-down view of the organization. In our analysis we view the corporation as an entity composed of interrelated units and systems, such as accounting, marketing, and finance. We examine the interrelationships of these units in light of the opportunities and threats in the corporation's environment. We carry out our analysis through the use of complex cases or management simulations. These techniques will give you the opportunity to move from a narrow, specialized view to a broader, less precise analysis of the overall corporate picture. Consequently, the emphasis in case analysis is on developing and refining conceptual skills, which are different from the skills you developed in your technical and function-oriented courses. As you will see, conceptual skills are vital to successful performance in the business world.

2.1

IMPORTANCE OF CONCEPTUAL SKILLS IN BUSINESS

Many have attempted to specify the characteristics necessary for a person to successfully advance from an entry-level position to one in top management. Few of these studies have been successful.[1] But Robert L. Katz has suggested one interesting approach. He focused on the skills successful managers exhibit in performing their jobs; this approach negates the need to identify specific personality traits.[2] These skills imply abilities that can be developed and are manifested in performance.

Katz suggests that effective administration rests on three basic skills: technical, human, and conceptual. He defines them as follows:[3]

- **Technical skills** pertain to *what* is done and to working with *things*. They comprise one's ability to use technology to perform an organizational task.
- **Human skills** pertain to *how* something is done and to working with *people*. They comprise one's ability to work with people in the achievement of goals.
- **Conceptual skills** pertain to *why* something is done and to one's view of the corporation as a *whole*. They comprise one's ability to understand the complexities of the corporation as it affects and is affected by its environment.

Katz further suggests that the optimal mix of these three skills varies at the different corporate levels:

> At lower levels, the major need is for technical and human skills. At higher levels, the administrator's effectiveness depends largely on human and conceptual skills. At the top, conceptual skill becomes the most important of all for successful administration.[4]

Results of a survey of 300 presidents of *Fortune*'s list of the top fifty banking, industrial, insurance, public utility, retailing, and transportation firms support Katz's conclusion regarding the different skill mixes needed at the different organizational levels.[5] As shown in Fig. 2.1, the need for technical skills decreases and the need for conceptual skills increases as a person moves from first-line supervision to top management.

In addition, when executives were asked, "Are there certain skills necessary to move from one organizational level to another?", 55% reported conceptual skills to be the most crucial in movement from middle to top management.[6] Similar results concerning accountants in CPA firms have been reported.[7] Most theorists therefore agree that conceptual work carried out by an organization's leaders is the heart of strategy-making.[8]

The strategic management and business policy course attempts to develop conceptual skills through the use of comprehensive cases or complex simulations. Of course, you also need technical skills in order to analyze various aspects of each case. And you will use human skills in team presentations, study groups, or team projects. But in this course, by focusing on strategic

FIGURE 2.1
Optimal Skill Mix of a Manager by Hierarchical Level.

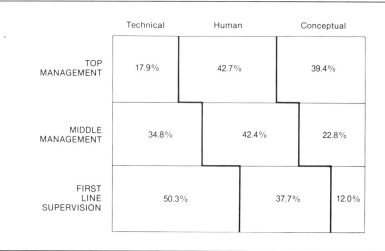

Source: T. L. Wheelen, G. K. Rakes, and J. D. Hunger, "Skills of an Executive," a paper presented to the Academy of Management, Kansas City, Mo., August 1976.

issues, you will primarily develop and refine your conceptual skills. Concentrating on strategic management processes forces you to develop a better understanding of the political, social, and economic environment of business, and to appreciate the interactions of the functional specialties required for corporate success.

2.2

AUDITS

Consulting firms, management scholars, boards of directors, and practicing managers suggest the use of audits of corporate activities.[9] An audit provides a checklist of questions, by area or issue, that enables a systematic analysis of various corporate activities to be made. It is extremely useful as a diagnostic tool to pinpoint problem areas and to highlight strengths and weaknesses.

Management Audit

The National Association of Regulatory Utility Commissioners analyzed thirty-one management audits that had been completed or were in progress. The report concluded that the regulatory agencies using management audits were pleased with the results and intended to continue using them. In general, these audits recommended changes in the operating practices of management and suggested areas where substantial reductions in operating costs could be made. The audits gave the boards of directors and management the opportunity to establish new priorities in their objectives and planning, and provided specific recommendations that had impact on the "bottom line."[10]

Typically, the term **management audit** is used to describe a list of questions that forms the basis for an in-depth analysis of a particular area of importance to the corporation. Examples are the sales-force management audit, the social audit, the stakeholder audit, the forecasting audit, the technology audit, the strategic-marketing audit, the culture audit, and the human-resource-management audit.[11] Rarely, however, does it include consideration of more than one issue or functional area. The **strategic audit** is, in comparison, a *type of management audit* that takes a corporate-wide perspective and provides a comprehensive assessment of a corporation's strategic situation. Most business analysts predict that the use of management audits of all kinds will increase. As corporate boards of directors become more aware of their expanding duties and responsibilities, they should call for more corporate-wide management audits to be conducted.

Strategic Audit

As contrasted with the typically more specialized management audit, the strategic audit considers external as well as internal factors and includes alternative selection, implementation, and evaluation and control. It therefore covers the key aspects of the strategic management process and places them within a decision-making framework. This framework is composed of the following eight interrelated steps:

1. **Evaluation of a corporation's current performance results**, in terms of (a) return on investment, profitability, etc., and (b) the current mission, objectives, strategies, and policies.

2. **Examination and evaluation of a corporation's strategic managers**—its board of directors and top management.

3. **A scan of the external environment**, to locate strategic factors that pose opportunities and threats.

4. **A scan of the internal corporate environment**, to determine strategic factors that are strengths and weaknesses.

5. **Analysis of the strategic factors**, to (a) pinpoint problem areas, and (b) review and revise the corporate mission and objectives as necessary.

6. **Generation, evaluation, and selection of the best alternative strategy** in light of the analysis conducted in step 5.

7. **Implementation** of selected strategies, via programs, budgets, and procedures.

8. **Evaluation** of the implemented strategies via feedback systems, and the **control** of activities to ensure their minimum deviation from plans.

This strategic decision-making process, depicted in Fig. 2.2, basically reflects the approach to strategic management being used successfully by corporations such as Warner-Lambert, Dayton Hudson, Avon Products, and Bechtel Group, Inc.[12] Although some research suggests that this type of "normative" approach might not work so well for firms in very unstable environments,[13] a recent survey of 956 corporate long-range planners reveals that actual business practice agrees generally with the model presented in Fig. 2.2.[14] This strategic decision-making process is made operational through the strategic audit.

The audit presents an integrated view of strategic management in action. It describes not only how objectives, strategies, and policies are formulated as long-range decisions, but also how they are implemented, evaluated, and controlled by programs, budgets, and procedures. The strategic audit, therefore, enables a person to better understand the *ways* in which various functional areas are interrelated and interdependent, as well as the *manner* in which they contribute to the achievement of the corporate mission.

FIGURE 2.2
Strategic Decision-making Process.

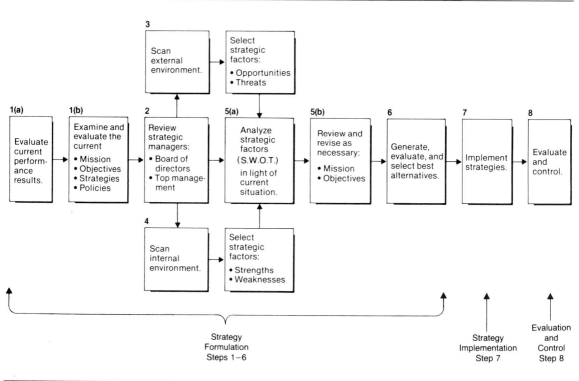

Consequently, the strategic audit is very useful to those people, such as boards of directors, whose jobs are to evaluate the overall performance of a corporation and its management.

Appendix 2.A (at the end of this chapter) is an example of a strategic audit proposed for use in the analysis of complex business policy cases and for strategic decision-making. The questions in the audit parallel the eight steps depicted in Fig. 2.2, the strategic decision-making process. It is *not* an all-inclusive list, but it presents many of the critical questions needed for the strategic analysis of any business corporation. You should consider the audit as a guide for analysis. Some questions or even some areas might be inappropriate for a particular case; in other cases, the questions may be insufficient for a complete analysis. However, each question in a particular area of the strategic audit can be broken down into an additional series of subquestions. It is up to you to develop these subquestions when they are needed.

A strategic audit fulfills three major *functions* in a case-oriented strategy and policy course:

1. It serves to highlight and review important concepts from previously studied subject areas.

2. It provides a systematic framework for the analysis of complex cases. (It is especially useful if you are unfamiliar with the case method.)

3. It generally improves the quality of case analysis and reduces the amount of time you might spend in learning how to analyze a case.

Students also find the audit helpful in their organizing a case for written or oral presentation and in seeing that all areas have been considered. The strategic audit thus enables both students and teachers to maximize their efficiency, both in analyzing why a certain area is creating problems for a corporation, and in considering solutions to the problems.

2.3

CASE METHOD

The analysis and discussion of case problems has been the most popular method of teaching strategy and policy for many years.[15] Cases present actual business situations and enable you to examine both successful and unsuccessful corporations. For example, you might be asked to critically analyze a situation in which a manager had to make a decision of long-run corporate importance. This approach gives you a feel for what it is like to work in a large corporation and to be faced with making a business decision.

Case Analysis and Presentation

There is no one best way to analyze or present a case report. Each instructor has personal preferences for format and approach. Nevertheless, we present one suggested approach for both written and oral reports in Appendix 2.B, at the end of the chapter. This approach provides a systematic method for successfully attacking a case.

The presentation of case analysis can be organized on the basis of a number of frameworks. One obvious framework to follow is the strategic audit as detailed in Appendix 2.A. Another is the McKinsey 7-S Framework, composed of the seven organizational variables of *structure, strategy, staff, management style, systems and procedures, skills,* and *shared values.*[16] Regardless of the framework chosen, be especially careful to include a complete analysis of key environmental variables—especially of trends in the industry and of the competition.

The focus in case discussion is on critical analysis and logical development of thought. A solution is satisfactory if it resolves important problems and is likely to be implemented successfully. How the corporation actually dealt with the case problems has no real bearing on the analysis, because its management might have analyzed its problems incorrectly and implemented a series of flawed solutions.

Researching the Case

You should undertake outside research into the environmental setting of the case. Check each case to find out when the case situation occurred and then screen the business periodicals for that time. This background will give you an appreciation for the situation as it was experienced by the people in the case. A company's annual report from that year can be very helpful.[17] An understanding of the economy during that period will help you avoid making a serious error in your analysis—for example, suggesting a sale of stock when the stock market is at an all-time low or taking on more debt when the prime interest rate is over 15%. Information on the industry will provide insights on its competitive activities. Some resources available for research into the economy and a corporation's industry are suggested in Appendix 2.C at the end of the chapter.

If you are unfamiliar with these business resources we urge you to read *How to Use the Business Library: With Sources of Business Information,* 5th ed., by H. W. Johnson, A. J. Faria, and E. L. Maier (Cincinnati: South-Western Publishing Co., 1984).

Financial Analysis: A Place To Begin

A review of key financial ratios can help you assess the company's overall situation and pinpoint some problem areas. Table 2.1 lists some of the most important financial ratios. Included are (1) **liquidity ratios,** which measure the corporation's ability to meet its financial obligations, (2) **profitability ratios,** which measure the degree of the corporation's success in achieving desired profit levels, (3) **activity ratios,** which measure the effectiveness of

TABLE 2.1
Financial Ratios

	FORMULA	HOW EXPRESSED	MEANING
1. Liquidity Ratios			
Current ratio	$\dfrac{\text{Current assets}}{\text{Current liabilities}}$	Decimal	A short-term indicator of the company's ability to pay its short-term liabilities from short-term assets; how much of current assets are available to cover each dollar of current liabilities.
Quick (acid test) ratio	$\dfrac{\text{Current assets} - \text{Inventory}}{\text{Current liabilities}}$	Decimal	Measures the company's ability to pay off its short-term obligations from current assets, excluding inventories.
Inventory to net working capital	$\dfrac{\text{Inventory}}{\text{Current assets} - \text{Current liabilities}}$	Decimal	A measure of inventory balance; measures the extent to which the cushion of excess current assets over current liabilities may be threatened by unfavorable changes in inventory.
Cash ratio	$\dfrac{\text{Cash} + \text{cash equivalents}}{\text{Current liabilities}}$	Decimal	Measures the extent to which the company's capital is in cash or cash equivalents; shows how much of the current obligations can be paid from cash or near-cash assets.
2. Profitability Ratios			
Net profit margin	$\dfrac{\text{Net profit after taxes}}{\text{Net sales}}$	Percentage	Shows how much after-tax profits are generated by each dollar of sales.
Gross profit margin	$\dfrac{\text{Sales} - \text{Cost of goods sold}}{\text{Net sales}}$	Percentage	Indicates the total margin available to cover other expenses beyond cost of goods sold, and still yield a profit.
Return on investment (ROI)	$\dfrac{\text{Net profit after taxes}}{\text{Total assets}}$	Percentage	Measures the rate of return on the total assets utilized in the company; a measure of management's efficiency, it shows the return on all the assets under its control regardless of source of financing.
Return on equity (ROE)	$\dfrac{\text{Net profit after taxes}}{\text{Stockholders equity}}$	Percentage	Measures the rate of return on the book value of stockholder's total investment in the company.

NOTE: In using ratios for analysis, calculate ratios for the corporation and compare them to the average ratios for the particular industry. Refer to Standard and Poor's and Robert Morris Associates for average industry data. For an in-depth discussion of ratios and their use, refer to J. F. Weston and E. F. Brigham, *Essentials of Managerial Finance*, 8th ed. (Chicago, Ill.: Dryden Press, 1987), pp. 240–259. Special thanks to Dr. Moustafa H. Abdelsamad, Dean of Southeastern Massachusetts University, for his writing of the meanings of these ratios.

(Continued)

TABLE 2.1 (Continued)

	FORMULA	HOW EXPRESSED	MEANING
Earnings Per Share (EPS)	$\dfrac{\text{Net profit after taxes} - \text{Preferred stock dividends}}{\text{Average number of common shares}}$	Dollar per share	Shows the after-tax earnings generated for each share of common stock.
3. Activity Ratios			
Inventory turnover	$\dfrac{\text{Net sales}}{\text{Inventory}}$	Decimal	Measures the number of times that average inventory of finished goods was turned over or sold during a period of time, usually a year.
Days of inventory	$\dfrac{\text{Inventory}}{\text{Cost of goods sold} \div 365}$	Days	Measures the number of one day's worth of inventory that a company has on-hand at any given time.
Net working capital turnover	$\dfrac{\text{Net sales}}{\text{Net working capital}}$	Decimal	Measures how effectively the net working capital is used to generate sales.
Asset turnover	$\dfrac{\text{Sales}}{\text{Total assets}}$	Decimal	Measures the utilization of all the company's assets; measures how many sales are generated by each dollar of assets.
Fixed asset turnover	$\dfrac{\text{Sales}}{\text{Fixed assets}}$	Decimal	Measures the utilization of the company's fixed assets (i.e., plant and equipment); measures how many sales are generated by each dollar of fixed assets.
Average collection period	$\dfrac{\text{Accounts receivable}}{\text{Sales for year} \div 365}$	Days	Indicates the average length of time in days that a company must wait to collect a sale after making it; may be compared to the credit terms offered by the company to its customers.
Accounts receivable turnover	$\dfrac{\text{Annual credit sales}}{\text{Accounts receivable}}$	Decimal	Indicates the number of times that accounts receivable are cycled during the period (usually a year).
Accounts payable period	$\dfrac{\text{Accounts Payable}}{\text{Purchases for year} \div 365}$	Days	Indicates the average length of time in days that the company takes to pay its credit purchases.
Days of cash	$\dfrac{\text{Cash}}{\text{Net sales for year} \div 365}$	Days	Indicates the number of days of cash on hand, at present sales levels.
4. Leverage Ratios			
Debt to asset ratio	$\dfrac{\text{Total debt}}{\text{Total assets}}$	Percentage	Measures the extent to which borrowed funds have been used to finance the company's assets.
Debt to equity ratio	$\dfrac{\text{Total debt}}{\text{Stockholders' equity}}$	Percentage	Measures the funds provided by creditors versus the funds provided by owners.

34

Ratio	Formula	Type	Description
Long-term debt to capital structure	$\dfrac{\text{Long-term debt}}{\text{Stockholders' equity}}$	Percentage	Measures the long-term component of capital structure.
Times interest earned	$\dfrac{\text{Profit before taxes} + \text{Interest charges}}{\text{Interest charges}}$	Decimal	Indicates the ability of the company to meet its annual interest costs.
Coverage of fixed charges	$\dfrac{\text{Profit before taxes} + \text{Interest charges} + \text{Lease charges}}{\text{Interest charges} + \text{Lease obligations}}$	Decimal	A measure of the company's ability to meet all of its fixed-charge obligations.
Current liabilities to equity	$\dfrac{\text{Current liabilities}}{\text{Stockholders' equity}}$	Percentage	Measures the short-term financing portion versus that provided by owners.

5. Other Ratios

Ratio	Formula	Type	Description
Price/Earning ratio	$\dfrac{\text{Market price per share}}{\text{Earnings per share}}$	Decimal	Shows the current market's evaluation of a stock, based on its earnings; shows how much the investor is willing to pay for each dollar of earnings.
Dividend payout ratio	$\dfrac{\text{Annual dividends per share}}{\text{Annual earnings per share}}$	Percentage	Indicates the percentage of profit that is paid out as dividends.
Dividend yield on common stock	$\dfrac{\text{Annual dividends per share}}{\text{Current market price per share}}$	Percentage	Indicates the dividend rate of return to common stockholders at the current market price.

NOTE: In using ratios for analysis, calculate ratios for the corporation and compare them to the average ratios for the particular industry. Refer to Standard and Poor's and Robert Morris Associates for average industry data. For an in-depth discussion of ratios and their use, refer to J. F. Weston and E. F. Brigham, *Essentials of Managerial Finance*, 8th ed. (Chicago, Ill.: Dryden Press, 1987). pp. 240–259. Special thanks to Dr. Moustafa H. Abdelsamad, Dean of Southeastern Massachusetts University, for his writing of the meanings of these ratios.

the corporation's use of resources, and (4) **leverage ratios,** which measure the contributions of owners' financing compared with creditors' financing.

In your analysis do *not* simply make an exhibit including all the ratios, but select and discuss only those ratios that have an impact on the company's problems. For instance, external resources, accounts receivable, and inventory may provide a source of funds. If receivables and inventories are double the industry average, reducing them may provide needed cash. In this situation, the case report should include not only sources of funds, but also the number of dollars freed for use.

A typical financial analysis of a firm would include a study of the operating statements for five or ten years, including a trend analysis of sales, profits, earnings per share, debt/equity ratio, return on investment, etc., plus a ratio study comparing the firm under study with industry standards. To begin, scrutinize historical income statements and balance sheets. These two basic statements provide most of the data needed for analysis. Compare the statements over time if a series of statements is available. Calculate changes that occur in individual categories from year to year, as well as the total change over the years. Determine the change as a percentage as well as an absolute amount, and determine the amount *adjusted for inflation* (constant dollars). Examination of this information may reveal developing trends. Compare trends in one category with trends in related categories. For example, an increase in sales of 15% over three years may appear to be satisfactory until you note an increase of 20% in the cost of goods sold during the same period. The outcome of this comparison might suggest that further investigation into the manufacturing process is necessary.

Another approach to the analysis of financial statements is to convert them into **common-size statements.** Convert every category from dollar terms to percentages. For the balance sheet, give the total assets or liabilities a value of 100%, and calculate all other categories as percentages of the total assets or liabilities. For the income statement, net sales represent 100%: calculate the percentage of each category so that the categories sum to the net sales percentage (100%). When you convert statements to this form, it is relatively easy to note the percentage that each category represents of the total. Comparisons of these percentages over the years can point out areas for additional analysis. To get a proper picture, however, make comparisons with industry data, if available, to see if fluctuations are merely reflecting industry-wide trends. If a firm's trends are generally in line with those of the rest of the industry, there is a lower likelihood of problems than if the firm's trends are worse than industry averages. These statements are especially helpful *in developing scenarios and pro forma statements,* since they provide a series of historical relationships (for example, cost of goods sold to sales, interest to sales, and inventories as a percent of assets).

If the corporation being studied appears to be in poor financial condition, calculate its "Z-value." Developed by Edward Altman, the formula com-

ILLUSTRATIVE EXAMPLE 2.1

The Altman Bankruptcy Formula

Edward I. Altman developed a formula to predict a company's likelihood of going bankrupt. His system of multiple discriminate analysis is used by stockholders to determine if the corporation is a good investment. The formula was developed from a study of thirty-three manufacturing companies with assets averaging $6.4 million that had filed Chapter X bankruptcies. These were paired with thirty-three similar but profitable firms with assets between $1 million and $25 million. The formula is:

$$Z = 1.2x_1 + 1.4x_2 + 3.3x_3 + 0.6x_4 + 1.0x_5$$

where

x_1 = Working capital divided by total assets.

x_2 = Retained earnings divided by total assets.

x_3 = Earnings before interest and taxes divided by total assets.

x_4 = Market value of equity divided by book value of total debt.

x_5 = Sales divided by total assets.

Z = Overall index of corporate fiscal health.

The range of the Z-value for most corporations is -4 to $+8$. According to Altman:

• Financially strong corporations have Z values above 2.99.

• Corporations in serious trouble have Z values below 1.81.

• Corporations between 1.81 and 2.99 are question marks that could go either way.

The closer a firm gets to bankruptcy, the more accurate is the Z value as a predictor.

SOURCE: M. Ball, "Z Factor: Rescue by the Numbers," *INC.* (December 1980), p. 48. Reprinted with permission, *INC.* magazine, (December, 1980). Copyright © 1980 by INC. Publishing Company, 38 Commercial Wharf, Boston, MA 02110.

bines five ratios by weighting them according to their importance to a corporation's financial strength (see Illustrative Example 2.1). The formula predicts the likelihood of the company going bankrupt. Firms in serious trouble have Z values below 1.81.

Adjusting for Inflation

Many of the cases in business policy/strategy textbooks take place during a period of inflation. When analyzing these cases, you should calculate sales and profits in constant dollars in order to perceive the "true" performance of the corporation in comparison with that of the industry, or of the economy in general. Remember that chief executive officers wish to keep their jobs and that some will tend to bias the figures in their favor. Sales stated in current dollars may seem to show substantial growth, but when they're converted to constant dollars, they may show a steady decline.

The return-on-investment ratio is doubly susceptible to distortion. Because net income is generally measured in current dollars, it rises with inflation. Meanwhile, investment (generally valued in historical dollars) effectively falls. Thus ROI may appear to be rising when it is actually stable, or appear to be stable when it is actually falling.[18]

To adjust for general inflation, most firms use the Consumer Price Index (CPI), as given in Table 2.2. The simplest way to adjust financial statements for inflation is to divide each item by the CPI for that year. This changes each figure to 1967 constant dollars. The CPI uses 1967 as the base year (with a CPI of 100.0) against which all other year's prices are compared. Remember that the CPI for each year is a percentage. For example, to convert 1985 reported sales of $950,000 to constant (1967) dollars, divide 950,000 by the CPI for 1985 (3.222); 1985 sales are thus converted to constant (1967) dollars of $294,848. This conversion displays the fact that, in terms of general purchasing power, a U.S. dollar in 1985 was worth only 32 cents in 1967 dollars.

For a comparison of recent financial statements, it might help to use a more recent base year than 1967 in the adjustment for inflation. For example, in Table 2.3 selected figures are taken from CSX Corporation's annual reports for 1982 through 1984. Instead of using 1967 as the base year for these comparisons, one may use 1982. To do so, divide the CPIs for 1983 and 1984 (as provided in Table 2.2) by the CPI for 1982; the appropriate adjustment factors are found to be 1.032 for 1983 and 1.076 for 1984. Table 2.3 shows operating revenue and net earnings figures first as reported (in 1983 and 1984 dollars) and second, divided by each year's adjustment factor, to result in 1982 constant dollars. Once this conversion is done, the impact of inflation on a firm's revenues and earnings can be clearly seen. Note, for example, that reported operating revenue increased by 62% from 1982 to 1984. In constant 1982 dollars, however, they increased only 50%. Although net earnings as reported in 1984 increased 12% from 1982, they increased only 4% when they are considered in constant dollar terms.

Another helpful aid in the analysis of cases in business policy is the chart

TABLE 2.2
Consumer Price Index for All Items (1967 = 100.0)

YEAR	CPI	YEAR	CPI
1974	147.7	1981	272.4
1975	161.2	1982	289.1
1976	170.5	1983	298.4
1977	181.5	1984	311.1
1978	195.4	1985	322.2
1979	217.4	1986	328.4
1980	246.8	1987	340.4

SOURCE: U.S. Department of Commerce, *1987 Statistical Abstract of the United States,* 107th edition, Chart no. 774, p. 463. *Monthly Labor Review* (March, 1988), p. 83.

TABLE 2.3

General Price Level Adjustment for Inflation Using Consumer Price Index

(In Millions of Dollars)

	1984	1983	1982
Operating Revenue, as reported	$7,934	$5,891	$4,909
% increase (decrease) over 1982	62%	20%	—
Operating Revenue			
Constant (1982) dollars	7,374	5,708	4,909
% increase over 1982	50%	16%	—
Net Earnings, as reported	465	272	414
% increase (decrease) over 1982	12%	(66%)	—
Net Earnings			
Constant (1982) dollars	432	263	414
% increase (decrease) over 1982	4%	(63%)	—
CPI Adjustment Factor (1982 = 100%)	1.076	1.032	1.000
$\dfrac{198x\ \text{CPI}}{1982\ \text{CPI}}$	$\left(\dfrac{311.1}{289.1}\right)$	$\left(\dfrac{298.4}{289.1}\right)$	$\left(\dfrac{289.1}{289.1}\right)$

SOURCE: Selected reported figures taken from CSX Corporation, *1984 Annual Report*, p. 20.

on prime interest rates given in Table 2.4. For better assessments of strategic decisions, it can be useful to note the level of the prime interest rate at the time of the case. A decision to borrow money to build a new plant would have been a good one in 1977, but somewhat foolhardy in 1981.

TABLE 2.4

Changes in Prime Interest Rates*

YEAR	LOW	HIGH	YEAR	LOW	HIGH
1974	8¾	12	1981	15¾	20½
1975	7	10½	1982	11½	17
1976	6¼	7¼	1983	10½	11½
1977	6½	7¾	1984	10¾	12¾
1978	6	11¾	1985	9½	10¾
1979	11½	15¾	1986	8	9½
1980	11	21½	1987	8	9¾

SOURCE: D. S. Benton, "Banking and Financial Information," Table 1.1, p. 2 in *Thorndike Encyclopedia of Banking and Financial Tables*, Revised Edition, *1987 Yearbook* (Boston, Mass.: Warren, Gorham & Lamont, 1987).

*The rate of interest that banks charge on the lowest-risk loans they make.

SUMMARY AND CONCLUSION

The strategic management/business policy course is concerned with developing the conceptual skills that successful top management needs. The emphasis is therefore on improving your analytical and problem-solving abilities. The case method develops those skills and gives you an appreciation of environmental issues and the interdependencies among the functional units of a large corporation. The strategic audit is one recommended technique for the systematization of the analysis of fairly long and complex policy cases. It also provides a basic checklist for the investigation of any large corporation. Nevertheless, the strategic audit is only one of many techniques with which you can analyze and diagnose case problems. We expect consultants, managers, and boards of directors to increasingly employ the audit as an analytical technique.

DISCUSSION QUESTIONS

1. Should people be selected for top management positions primarily on the basis of their having a particular combination of skills? Explain.

2. What are the strengths and weaknesses of the strategic audit as a technique for assessing corporate performance?

3. What value does the case method hold for the study of strategic management/business policy?

4. Why should one begin a case analysis with a financial analysis? When are other approaches appropriate?

5. Reconcile the strategic decision-making process depicted in Fig. 2.2 with the strategic management model depicted in Fig. 1.3.

6. Analyze the financial statements of CSX Corporation as provided in Tables 2.5 and 2.6 in the Integrative Case at the end of this chapter. What can you conclude?

NOTES

1. B. M. Bass, *Stogdill's Handbook of Leadership* (New York: Free Press, 1981), p. 73.

2. R. L. Katz, "Skills of an Effective Administrator," *Harvard Business Review* (January–February 1955), p. 33.

3. Katz, pp. 33–42. These definitions were adapted from the material in this article.

4. Katz, p. 42.

5. T. L. Wheelen, G. K. Rakes, and J. D. Hunger, "Skills of an Executive" (Paper presented at the Thirty-Sixth Annual Meeting of the Academy of Management, Kansas City, Mo., August 1976).

6. Wheelen, Rakes, and Hunger, p. 7.

7. W. G. Shenkir, T. L. Wheelen, and R. H. Strawser, "The Making of an Accountant," *CPA Journal* (March 1973), p. 219.

8. E. E. Chaffee, "Three Models of Strategy," *Academy of Management Review* (January 1985), pp. 89–90.

D. Norburn, "GOGOs, YOYOs and DODOs: Company Directors and Industry Performance," *Strategic Management Journal* (March–April 1986), p. 112.

B. C. Reimann, "Doers as Planners," *Planning Review* (September 1986), p. 45.

9. T. L. Wheelen and J. D. Hunger, "Using the Strategic Audit," *SAM Advanced Management Journal* (Winter 1987), pp. 4–12.

R. B. Buchele, "How to Evaluate a Firm," *California Management Review* (Fall 1962), pp. 5–16.

J. Martindell, *The Appraisal of Management* (New York: Harper & Row, 1962).

R. Bauer, L. T. Cauthorn, and R. P. Warner, "Management Audit Process Guide," (Boston: Intercollegiate Case Clearing House, no. 9-375-336, 1975).

J. D. Hunger and T. L. Wheelen, "The Strategic Audit: An Integrative Approach To Teaching Business Policy" (Paper presented at the Forty-Third Annual Meeting of the Academy of Management, Dallas, Texas, August 1983).

M. Lauenstein, "The Strategy Audit," *Journal of Business Strategy* (Winter 1984), pp. 87–91.

10. T. Barry, "What a Management Audit Can Do for

You," *Management Review* (June 1977), p. 43.

11. A. J. Dubinsky and R. W. Hansen, "The Sales Force Management Audit," *California Management Review* (Winter 1981), pp. 86–95.

A. B. Carroll and G. W. Beiler, "Landmarks in the Evolution of the Social Audit," *Academy of Management Journal* (September 1975), pp. 589–599.

R. E. Freeman, *Strategic Management: A Stakeholder Approach* (Boston: Pitman Publishing, 1984), p. 111.

J. S. Armstrong, "The Forecasting Audit," in S. Makridakis and S. C. Wheelwright (eds.), *The Handbook of Forecasting* (New York: Wiley and Sons, 1982), pp. 535–552.

D. Ford, "The Management and Marketing of Technology," in *Advances in Strategic Management, Vol. 3*, edited by R. Lamb and P. Shrivastava (Greenwich, Conn.: Jai Press, 1985), pp. 107–109.

M. P. Mokwa, "The Strategic Marketing Audit: An Adoption/Utilization Perspective," *Journal of Business Strategy* (Spring 1986), pp. 88–95.

J. W. Lorsch, "Strategic Myopia: Culture as an Invisible Barrier to Change," in *Gaining Control of the Corporate Culture*, edited by R. H. Kilmann, M. J. Saxton, and R. Serpa (San Francisco: Jossey Bass, 1985), pp. 97–98.

C. J. Fombrun, M. A. Devanna, and N. M. Tichy, in *Strategic Human Resources Management*, edited by C. J. Fombrun, N. M. Tichy, and M. A. Devanna (New York: John Wiley and Sons, 1984), pp. 235–248.

12. E. E. Tallett, "Repositioning Warner-Lambert as a High-Tech Health Care Company," *Planning Review* (May 1984), pp. 12–16, 41.

K. A. Macke, "Managing Change: How Dayton Hudson Meets the Challenge," *Journal of Business Strategy* (Summer 1983), pp. 78–81.

D. M. Slavick, "Planning at Bechtel: End of the Megaproject Era," *Planning Review* (September 1986), pp. 16–22.

H. Waldron, "Putting a New Face On Avon," *Planning Review* (July 1985), pp. 18–23.

13. J. W. Fredrickson, "The Comprehensiveness of Strategic Decision Processes: Extension, Observation, Future Directions," *Academy of Management Journal* (September 1984), pp. 445–466.

14. P. M. Ginter and A. C. Rucks, "Relative Emphasis Placed on the Steps of the Normative Model of Strategic Planning by Practitioners," *Proceedings, Southern Management Association* (November 1983), pp. 19–21.

15. C. Boyd, D. Kopp, and L. Shufelt, "Evaluative Criteria in Business Policy Case Analysis: An Exploratory Study," *Proceedings, Midwest Academy of Management* (April 1984), pp. 287–292.

16. T. J. Peters and R. W. Waterman, Jr., *In Search of Excellence* (New York: Harper & Row, 1982), pp. 9–12.

17. A survey of 6,000 investors and analysts in the United States, United Kingdom, and New Zealand, revealed a strong belief in the importance of annual reports, especially the financial statement sections, for investment decisions. See L. S. Chang and K. S. Most, "An International Study of the Importance of Financial Statements," *International Journal of Management* (December 1985), pp. 76–85.

18. M. J. Chussil, "Inflation and ROI," *The Pimsletter on Business Strategy, Number 22* (Cambridge, Mass.: The Strategic Planning Institute, 1980), p. 1.

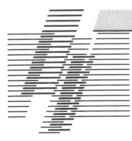

INTEGRATIVE CASE

CSX CORPORATION'S FINANCIAL STATEMENTS

Tables 2.5 and 2.6 are the consolidated financial statements of CSX Corporation for the years 1982 through 1984. As explained earlier, a detailed analysis of these statements first includes an adjustment for inflation. A *second* step is to convert the income statement (Table 2.5) and the balance sheet (Table 2.6) into common-size statements. To do this, convert operating revenue, total assets, and total liabilities into 100%, and list the other entries as percentages of each total. This will show, for example, if accounts receivable as a percentage of total assets had increased or decreased from 1982 to 1984. Dividing the accounts receivable for 1982 through 1984, as shown in Table 2.7, by the total assets for each of the three years, indicates that accounts receivable increased from 7.9% of total assets in 1982 to 10.7% in 1983 to 10.1% in 1984. Further analysis would be needed to ascertain if accounts receivable were mismanaged in 1983 or if the increase in accounts receivable in 1983 reflected a downturn in the economy.

The *third* step in initial case analysis is to calculate the financial ratios listed earlier in Table 2.1. Keep in mind that sometimes one has to make some decisions about which categories to lump together, so that one can ascertain the data needed in the calculation of a particular ratio. These decisions can explain why two people can calculate different ratios from the same financial statements—and yet both be correct, on the basis of different underlying assumptions. Also remember that not every ratio can be calculated for every case. In Tables 2.5 and 2.6, some of the needed data has been left out. That is why N.A. for Not Available is listed for certain ratios in Table 2.7.

TABLE 2.5
Consolidated Statement of Earnings and Retained Earnings: CSX Corporation
(In Millions of Dollars, Except Per-Share Amounts)

| | YEARS ENDED DECEMBER 31 | | |
	1984	1983	1982
Operating revenue	$7,934	$5,891	$4,909
Operating expense	6,916	5,255	4,432
Income from operations	1,018	636	447
Other income (mostly interest)	64	45	273[1]
Interest expense	242	215	171
Earnings before taxes and minority interest	840	466	579
Income taxes	344	165	138
Minority interest (in subsidiaries)	31	29	27
Net earnings	$ 465	$ 272	$ 414
Retained earnings—January 1	2,809	2,670	2,376
Dividends	154	133	120
Retained earnings—December 31	$3,120	$2,809	$2,670
Average common shares outstanding (thousands)	147,608	131,078	125,368
Common shares outstanding at year-end (thousands)	149,556	146,023	126,648
Per-share amounts			
Net earnings	$ 3.15	$ 2.07	$ 3.30
Dividends—common	$ 1.04	$ .99	$ .95

SOURCE: *1984 Annual Report,* CSX Corporation, p. 20.

NOTE: [1]Includes $171 million for sales of publishing and cable television subsidiaries plus $32 million from MCI for communications line right of way.

TABLE 2.6
Consolidated Statement of Financial Position: CSX Corporation
(In Millions of Dollars)

	DECEMBER 31		
	1984	1983	1982
Assets			
Current assets			
Cash and short-term investments	$ 377	$ 314	$ 528
Accounts receivable	1,178	1,175	728
Inventories	458	424	251
Other current assets	142	153	111
Total current assets	2,155	2,066	1,618
Investments			
Properties	9,143	8,589	7,257
Affiliates and other companies	137	115	96
Other assets	201	234	228
Total investments	9,481	8,938	7,581
Total assets	$11,636	$11,004	$9,199
Liabilities			
Current liabilities			
Accounts payable and other current liabilities	$ 1,663	$ 1,542	$1,229
Current maturities of long-term debt	261	282	167
Total current liabilities	1,924	1,824	1,396
Claims and other long-term liabilities	343	343	355
Deferred income taxes (due to investment tax credits)	1,828	1,511	1,321
Long-term debt	2,302	2,466	1,866
Redeemable preferred stock and minority interest	330	334	316
Common shareholders' equity			
Common stock	150	146	42
Other capital	1,639	1,571	1,233
Retained earnings	3,120	2,809	2,670
Total common shareholders' equity	4,909	4,526	3,945
Total liabilities and shareholders' equity	$11,636	$11,004	$9,199

SOURCE: CSX Corporation, *1984 Annual Report*, p. 24.

TABLE 2.7
Financial Ratio Analysis: CSX Corporation

	1984	1983	1982
Liquidity ratios			
Current	1.12	1.13	1.16
Quick	.88	0.90	0.98
Inventory to net working capital	1.98	1.75	1.13
Cash ratio	0.20	0.17	0.38
Profitability ratios			
Net profit margin	5.9	4.6	8.4
Gross profit margin	N.A.	N.A.	N.A.
ROI	4.0	2.5	4.5
ROE	9.5	6.0	10.5
EPS	3.15	2.07	3.30
Activity ratios			
Inventory turnover	17.3	13.9	19.6
Days of inventory	N.A.	N.A.	N.A.
Net working capital turnover	34.35	24.3	22.1
Asset turnover	0.7	0.5	0.5
Fixed asset turnover	0.9	0.7	0.7
Average collection period	54.2	72.8	54.1
A/R turnover	N.A.	N.A.	N.A.
Accounts payable period	N.A.	N.A.	N.A.
Days of cash	17.3	19.5	39.3
Leverage ratios			
Debt to asset	57.8	58.9	57.1
Debt to equity	137.0	143.1	133.2
L.-t. debt to capital structure	46.9	54.5	47.3
Times interest earned	N.A.	N.A.	N.A.
Coverage of fixed charges	N.A.	N.A.	N.A.
Current liabilities to equity	39.1	40.3	35.4
Other ratios			
Price/earnings	N.A.	N.A.	N.A.
Dividend payout	33.0	47.8	28.8
Dividend yield	N.A.	N.A.	N.A.
Net working capital (in $ millions)	231	242	222

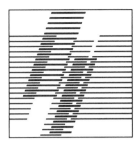

APPENDIX 2

AIDS FOR CASE ANALYSIS AND PRESENTATION

APPENDIX 2.A
STRATEGIC AUDIT OF A CORPORATION

I. Current Situation

A. How is the corporation performing in terms of return on investment, overall market share, profitability trends, earnings per share, etc.?

B. What are the corporation's current mission, objectives, strategies, and policies?

1. Are they clearly stated or are they merely implied from performance?

2. *Mission:* What business(es) is the corporation in? Why?

3. *Objectives:* What are the corporate, business, and functional objectives? Are they consistent with each other, with the mission, and with the internal and external environments?

4. *Strategies:* What strategy or mix of strategies is the corporation following? Are they consistent with each other, with the mission and objectives, and with the internal and external environments?

5. *Policies:* What are they? Are they consistent with each other, with the mission, objectives, and strategies, and with the internal and external environments?

II. Strategic Managers

A. Board of Directors

1. Who are they? Are they internal or external?

2. Do they own significant shares of stock?

3. Is the stock privately held or publicly traded?

4. What do they contribute to the corporation in terms of knowledge, skills, background, and connections?

5. How long have they served on the board?

6. What is their level of involvement in strategic management? Do they merely rubber-stamp top management's proposals or do they actively participate and suggest future directions?

B. Top Management

1. What person or group constitutes top management?

2. What are top management's chief characteristics in terms of knowledge, skills, background, and style?

3. Has top management been responsible for the corporation's performance over the past few years?

4. Has it established a systematic approach to the formulation, implementation, and evaluation and control of strategic management?

5. What is its level of involvement in the strategic management process?

6. How well does top management interact with lower-level management?

7. How well does top management interact with the board of directors?

8. Is top management sufficiently skilled to cope with likely future challenges?

III. External Environment: Opportunities and Threats (S.W.O.T.)

A. Societal Environment

1. What general environmental factors among the sociocultural, economic, political-legal, and technological forces are currently affecting both the corporation and the industries in which it competes? Which present current or future threats? Opportunities?

SOURCE: T. L. Wheelen and J. D. Hunger, "Strategic Audit of a Corporation." Copyright © 1982 by Wheelen and Hunger Associates. Reprinted by permission. Revised 1988.

2. Which of these are currently the most important (that is, are **strategic factors**) to the corporation and to the industries in which it competes? Which will be important in the future?

B. Task Environment

1. What forces in the immediate environment (that is, threat of new entrants, bargaining power of buyers, threat of substitute products or services, bargaining power of suppliers, rivalry among competing firms, and the relative power of unions, governments, etc.) are currently affecting the level of competitive intensity within the industries in which the corporation offers products or services?

2. What key factors in the immediate environment (that is, customers, competitors, suppliers, creditors, labor unions, governments, trade associations, interest groups, local communities, and stockholders) are currently affecting the corporation? Which present current or future threats? Opportunities?

3. Which of these forces and factors are the most important (that is, are strategic factors) at the present time? Which will be important in the future?

IV.   Internal Environment: Strengths and Weaknesses (S.W.O.T.)

A. Corporate Structure

1. How is the corporation presently structured?

   a) Is decision-making authority centralized around one group or decentralized to many groups or units?

   b) Is it organized on the basis of functions, projects, geography, or some combination of these?

2. Is the structure clearly understood by everyone in the corporation?

3. Is the present structure consistent with current corporate objectives, strategies, policies, and programs?

4. In what ways does this structure compare with those of similar corporations?

B. Corporate Culture

1. Is there a well-defined or emerging culture composed of shared beliefs, expectations, and values?

2. Is the culture consistent with the current objectives, strategies, policies, and programs?

3. What is the culture's position on important issues facing the corporation (that is, on productivity, quality of performance, adaptability to changing conditions)?

C. Corporate Resources

1. Marketing

   a) What are the corporation's current marketing objectives, strategies, policies, and programs?

      i) Are they clearly stated, or merely implied from performance and/or budgets?

      ii) Are they consistent with the corporation's mission, objectives, strategies, policies, and with internal and external environments?

   b) How well is the corporation performing in terms of analysis of market position and marketing mix (that is, of product, price, place, and promotion)?

      i) What trends emerge from this analysis?

      ii) What impact have these trends had on past performance and how will they probably affect future performance?

      iii) Does this analysis support the corporation's past and pending strategic decisions?

   c) How well does this corporation's marketing performance compare with those of similar corporations?

   d) Are marketing managers using accepted marketing concepts and techniques to evaluate and improve product performance? (Consider product life cycle, market segmentation, market research, and product portfolios.)

   e) What is the role of the marketing manager in the strategic management process?

2. Finance

   a) What are the corporation's current financial objectives, strategies, policies, and programs?

      i) Are they clearly stated or merely implied from performance and/or budgets?

ii) Are they consistent with the corporation's mission, objectives, strategies, policies, and with internal and external environments?

b) How well is the corporation performing in terms of financial analysis? (Consider liquidity ratios, profitability ratios, activity ratios, leverage ratios, capitalization structure, and constant dollars.)

  i) What trends emerge from this analysis?

  ii) Are there any significant differences when statements are calculated in constant versus reported dollars?

  iii) What impact have these trends had on past performance and how will they probably affect future performance?

  iv) Does this analysis support the corporation's past and pending strategic decisions?

c) How well does this corporation's financial performance compare with that of similar corporations?

d) Are financial managers using accepted financial concepts and techniques to evaluate and improve current corporate and divisional performance? (Consider financial leverage, capital budgeting, and ratio analysis.)

e) What is the role of the financial manager in the strategic management process?

3. Research and Development (R&D)

a) What are the corporation's current R&D objectives, strategies, policies, and programs?

  i) Are they clearly stated, or implied from performance and/or budgets?

  ii) Are they consistent with the corporation's mission, objectives, strategies, policies, and with internal and external environments?

  iii) What is the role of technology in corporate performance?

  iv) Is the mix of basic, applied, and engineering research appropriate given the corporate mission and strategies?

b) What return is the corporation receiving from its investment in R&D?

c) Is the corporation technologically competent?

d) How well does the corporation's investment in R&D compare with the investments of similar corporations?

e) What is the role of the R&D manager in the strategic management process?

4. Operations (Manufacturing/Service)*

a) What are the corporation's current manufacturing/service objectives, strategies, policies, and programs?

  i) Are they clearly stated, or merely implied from performance and/or budgets?

  ii) Are they consistent with the corporation's mission, objectives, strategies, policies, and with internal and external environments?

b) What is the type and extent of operations capabilities of the corporation?

  i) If product-oriented, consider plant facilities, type of manufacturing system (continuous mass production or intermittent job shop), age and type of equipment, degree and role of automation and/or robots, plant capacities and utilization, productivity ratings, availability and type of transportation.

  ii) If service-oriented, consider service facilities (e.g., hospital, theater, or school buildings), type of operations systems (continuous service over time to same clientele or intermittent service over time to varied clientele), age and type of supporting equipment, degree and role of automation and/or use of mass communication devices (e.g., diagnostic machinery, videotape machines), facility capacities and utilization rates, efficiency ratings of professional/service personnel, availability and type of transportation to bring service staff and clientele together.

c) Are manufacturing or service facilities vulnerable to natural disasters, local or national

---

*Research suggests that the strategic approach developed for manufacturing companies is very useful for service firms. See H. M. O'Neill, "Do Strategic Paradigms Work in Service Industries?" in *Handbook of Business Strategy, 1986/87 Yearbook*, edited by W. D. Guth (Boston: Warren, Gorham, and Lamont, 1986), pp. 19.1–19.14.

strikes, reduction or limitation of resources from suppliers, substantial cost increases of materials, or nationalization by governments?

d) Is operating leverage being used successfully with an appropriate mix of people and machines, in manufacturing firms, or of support staff to professionals, in service firms?

e) How well does the corporation perform relative to the competition? Consider costs per unit of labor, material, and overhead; downtime; inventory control management and/or scheduling of service staff; production ratings; facility utilization percentages; and number of clients successfully treated by category (if service firm), or percentage of orders shipped on time (if product firm).

i) What trends emerge from this analysis?

ii) What impact have these trends had on past performance and how will they probably affect future performance?

iii) Does this analysis support the corporation's past and pending strategic decisions?

f) Are operations managers using appropriate concepts and techniques to evaluate and improve current performance? Consider cost systems, quality control and reliability systems, inventory control management, personnel scheduling, learning curves, safety programs, engineering programs, that can improve efficiency of manufacturing or of service.

g) What is the role of the operations manager in the strategic management process?

5. Human Resources Management (HRM)

a) What are the corporation's current HRM objectives, strategies, policies, and programs?

i) Are they clearly stated, or merely implied from performance and/or budgets?

ii) Are they consistent with the corporation's mission, objectives, strategies, policies, and with internal and external environments?

b) How well is the corporation's HRM performing in terms of improving the fit between the individual employee and the job? Consider turnover, grievances, strikes, layoffs, employee training, quality of work life.

i) What trends emerge from this analysis?

ii) What impact have these trends had on past performance and how will they probably affect future performance?

iii) Does this analysis support the corporation's past and pending strategic decisions?

c) How does this corporation's HRM performance compare with that of similar corporations?

d) Are HRM managers using appropriate concepts and techniques to evaluate and improve corporate performance? Consider the job analysis program, performance appraisal system, up-to-date job descriptions, training and development programs, attitude surveys, job design programs, quality of relationship with unions.

e) What is the role of the HRM manager in the strategic management process?

6. Information Systems (IS)

a) What are the corporation's current IS objectives, strategies, policies, and programs?

i) Are they clearly stated, or merely implied from performance and/or budgets?

ii) Are they consistent with the corporation's mission, objectives, strategies, policies, and with internal and external environments?

b) How well is the corporation's IS performing in terms of providing a useful database, automating routine clerical operations, assisting managers in making routine decisions, and providing information necessary for strategic decisions?

i) What trends emerge from this analysis?

ii) What impact have these trends had on past performance and how will they probably affect future performance?

iii) Does this analysis support the corporation's past and pending strategic decisions?

c) How does this corporation's IS performance and stage of development compare with that of similar corporations?

d) Are IS managers using appropriate concepts and techniques to evaluate and improve corporate performance? Do they know how to build and manage a complex data-base, conduct system analyses, and implement interactive decision-support systems?

e) What is the role of the IS manager in the strategic management process?

V.   Analysis of Strategic Factors

A. What are the key internal and external factors (**S.W.O.T.**) that strongly affect the corporation's present and future performance?

1. What have been the key historical strategic factors for this corporation?

2. What are the key short-term (0–1 year) strategic factors for this corporation?

3. What are the key intermediate-term (1–3 year) strategic factors for this corporation?

4. What are the key long-term (3–10 year) strategic factors for this corporation?

B. Are the current mission and objectives appropriate in light of the key strategic factors and problems?

1. Should the mission and objectives be changed? If so, how?

2. If changed, what will the effects on the firm be?

VI.   Strategic Alternatives

A. Can the current or revised objectives be met by the simple, more careful implementing of those strategies presently in use (for example, fine tuning the strategies)?

B. What are the major feasible alternative strategies available to this corporation? What are the pros and cons of each? Can *scenarios* be developed and agreed upon?

1. Consider stability, growth, and retrenchment as corporate strategies.

2. Consider cost leadership, differentiation, and focus as business strategies.

3. Consider any functional strategic alternatives that might be needed for reinforcement of an important corporate or business strategic alternative.

VII.   Recommendation

A. Specify which of the strategic alternatives you are recommending for the corporate, business, and functional levels of the corporation. Do you recommend different business or functional strategies for different units of the corporation?

B. Justify your recommendation in terms of its ability to resolve both long- and short-term problems and effectively deal with the key strategic factors.

C. What policies should be developed or revised to guide effective implementation?

VIII.   Implementation

A. What kinds of programs (for example, restructuring the corporation) should be developed to implement the recommended strategy?

1. Who should develop these programs?

2. Who should be in charge of these programs?

B. Are the programs financially feasible? Can *pro forma* budgets be developed and agreed upon? Are priorities and timetables appropriate to individual programs?

C. Will new standard operating procedures need to be developed?

IX.   Evaluation and Control

A. Is the current information system capable of providing sufficient feedback on implementation activities and performance?

1. Can performance results be pinpointed by area, unit, project, or function?

2. Is the information timely?

B. Are adequate control measures, to ensure conformance with the recommended strategic plan, in place?

1. Are appropriate standards and measures being used?

2. Are reward systems capable of recognizing and rewarding good performance?

APPENDIX 2.B
SUGGESTED TECHNIQUES FOR CASE ANALYSIS AND PRESENTATION

A. Case Analysis

1. Read the case rapidly, to get an overview of the nature of the corporation and its environment. Note the date on which the case was written so that you can put it into proper context.

2. Read the case a second time, and give it a detailed analysis according to the strategic audit (see Appendix 2.A) when appropriate. The audit will provide a conceptual framework for the examination of the corporation's objectives, mission, policies, strategies, problems, symptoms of problems, and issues. You should end up with a list of the salient issues and problems in the case. Perform a financial analysis.

3. Undertake outside research, when appropriate, to uncover economic and industrial information. Appendix 2.C suggests possible sources for outside research. These data should provide the environmental setting for the corporation. Conduct an in-depth analysis of the industry. Analyze the important competitors. Consider the bargaining power of suppliers, as well as buyers that might affect the firm's situation. Consider also the possible threats of future competitors in the industry, as well as the likelihood of new or different products or services that might substitute for the company's present ones.

4. Marshal facts and evidence to support selected issues and problems. Develop a framework or outline to organize the analysis. Your method of organization could be one of the following:

   a) The case as organized around the strategic audit.

   b) The case as organized around the key individual(s) in the case.

   c) The case as organized around the corporation's functional areas: production, management, finance, marketing, and R&D.

   d) The case as organized around the decision-making process.

   e) The case as organized around the seven variables (McKinsey 7-S Framework) of structure, strategy, staff, management style, systems and procedures, skills, and shared values.

5. Clearly identify and state the central problem(s) as supported by the information in the case. Use the S.W.O.T. format to sum up the key **strategic factors** facing the corporation: Strengths and Weaknesses of the company; Opportunities and Threats in the environment.

6. Develop a logical series of alternatives that evolve from the analysis to resolve the problem(s) or issue(s) in the case.

7. Evaluate each of the alternatives in light of the company's environment (both external and internal), mission, objectives, strategies, and policies. For each alternative, consider both the possible obstacles to its implementation and its financial implications.

8. Make recommendations on the basis of the fact that action must be taken. (Don't say, "I don't have enough information." The individuals in the case may have had the same or even less information than is given by the case.)

   a) Base your recommendations on a total analysis of the case.

   b) Provide the evidence gathered in step A4 to justify suggested changes.

   c) List the recommendations in order of priority—those to be done immediately and those to be done in the future.

   d) Show clearly how your recommendations deal with each of the *strategic factors* that were mentioned earlier in step A5. How do they build upon corporate *Strengths* to take advantage of environmental *Opportunities*? How do they deal with environmental *Threats* and corporate *Weaknesses*?

   e) Explain how each recommendation will be implemented. How will the plan(s) deal with anticipated resistance?

   f) Suggest feedback and control systems, to ensure that the recommendations are carried out as planned and to give advance warning of needed adjustments.

B. Written Presentation

1. Use the outline from step A4 to write the first draft of the case analysis. Follow steps A5 through A8.

   a) Don't rehash the case material; rather, supply the salient evidence and data to support your recommendations.

b) Develop exhibits on financial ratios and other data for inclusion in your report. The exhibits should provide meaningful information. Mention key elements of an exhibit in the text of the written analysis. If you include a ratio analysis as an exhibit, explain the meaning of the ratios in the text and cite only the critical ones in your analysis.

2. After it is written, review your case analysis for content and grammar. Remember to compare the outline (step A4) with the final product. Make sure you've presented sufficient data or evidence to support your problem analysis and recommendations. If the final product requires rewriting, do so. Keep in mind that the written report is going to be judged not only on *what* is said but also on the *manner* in which it is said.

3. If your written or oral presentation requires *pro forma* statements, you may wish to develop a scenario for each quarter and/or year in your forecast. A well-constructed scenario will help improve the accuracy of your forecast. Chapters 4 and 7 suggest methods for the development of scenarios.

C. Oral Presentation by Teams

1. The team should first decide upon a framework or outline for analysis, as mentioned in step A4. Although teams often divide the analysis work among team members, it is helpful if each team member also follows steps A5 through A8 in developing a preliminary analysis of the entire case to share and compare with team members.

2. The team should combine member input into one consolidated team audit, including S.W.O.T. analysis, alternatives, and recommendation(s). Gain agreement on the strategic factors and the best alternative(s) to support.

3. Divide, among the team's members the further development and presentation of the case analysis and recommendation(s). Agree upon responsibilities for the preparation of visual aids and handouts.

4. Modify the team outline, if necessary, and have one or two rehearsals of the presentation. If there is a time constraint for the final presentation, apply it to the practice presentation. If exhibits are used, make sure to allow sufficient time for their explanation. Critique one another's presentations and make the necessary modifications to the analysis.

5. During the class presentation, if a presenter misses a key fact, either slip a note to him or her, or deal with it in the summary speech.

6. Answer the specific questions raised by the instructor or classmates. If one person acts as a moderator for the questions and refers the questions to the appropriate team member, the presentation runs more smoothly than it will if everyone (or no one!) tries to deal with each question.

APPENDIX 2.C
RESOURCES FOR CASE RESEARCH

A. Company Information

1. Annual Reports

2. *Moody's Manuals on Investment* (a listing of companies within certain industries, that contains a brief history and a five-year financial statement of each company)

3. Securities and Exchange Commission Annual Report Form 10-K

4. *Standard and Poor's Register of Corporations, Directors, and Executives*

5. *Value Line Investment Survey*

B. Economic Information

1. Regional statistics and local forecasts from large banks

2. *Business Cycle Development* (Department of Commerce)

3. Chase Econometric Associates' publications

4. Census Bureau publications on population, transportation, and housing

5. *Current Business Reports* (Department of Commerce)

6. *Economic Indicators* (Joint Economic Committee)

7. *Economic Report of the President to Congress*

8. *Long-Term Economic Growth* (Department of Commerce)

9. *Monthly Labor Review* (Department of Labor)

10. *Monthly Bulletin of Statistics* (United Nations)

11. "Survey of Buying Power," *Sales Management*

12. Standard and Poor's Statistical Service
13. *Statistical Abstract of the United States* (Department of Commerce)
14. *Statistical Yearbook* (United Nations)
15. *Survey of Current Business* (Department of Commerce)
16. *U.S. Industrial Outlook* (Department of Defense)
17. *World Trade Annual* (United Nations)
18. *Overseas Business Reports* (published by country, by U.S. Department of Commerce)

C. Industry Information
1. Analyses of companies and industries by investment brokerage firms
2. *Annual Report of American Industry* (a compilation of statistics by industry and company, published by *Fortune*)
3. *Business Week* (provides weekly economic and business information, and quarterly profit and sales rankings of corporations)
4. *Fortune Magazine* (publishes listings of financial information on corporations within certain industries)
5. *Industry Survey* (published quarterly by Standard and Poor Corporation)

D. Directory and Index Information
1. *Business Information: How to Find and Use It*
2. *Business Periodical Index*
3. *Directory of National Trade Associations*
4. *Encyclopedia of Associations*
5. *Funk and Scott Index of Corporations and Industries*
6. *Thomas's Register of American Manufacturers*
7. *Wall Street Journal Index*
8. *Where to Find Business Information*

E. Ratio Analysis Information
1. *Almanac of Business and Industrial Ratios* (Prentice-Hall)
2. *Annual Statement Studies* (Robert Morris Associates)
3. *Dun's Review* (Dun and Bradstreet: published annually in September-December issues)
4. *Industry Norms and Key Business Ratios* (Dun and Bradstreet)
5. *How to Read a Financial Report* (Merrill Lynch, Pierce, Fenner and Smith, Inc.)
6. *Quality of Earnings: The Investor's Guide to How Much Money a Company Is Really Making* (T. L. O'Glove, Free Press, 1987)

F. General Sources
1. *Commodity Yearbook*
2. *U.S. Census of Business*
3. *U.S. Census of Manufacturers*
4. *World Almanac and Book of Facts*

G. Business Periodicals
1. *Business Week*
2. *Forbes*
3. *Wall Street Journal*
4. *Fortune*
5. Industry-specific periodicals (e.g., *Oil and Gas Journal*)

H. Academic/Practitioner Journals
1. *Harvard Business Review*
2. *Journal of Business Strategy*
3. *Long-Range Planning*
4. *Strategic Management Journal*
5. *Planning Review*
6. *Academy of Management Review*
7. *SAM Advanced Management Journal*

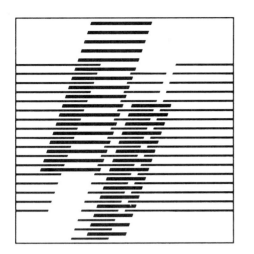

PART TWO

SCANNING THE ENVIRONMENT

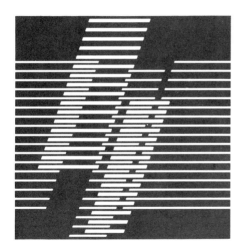

CHAPTER 3

STRATEGIC MANAGERS

STRATEGIC MANAGEMENT MODEL

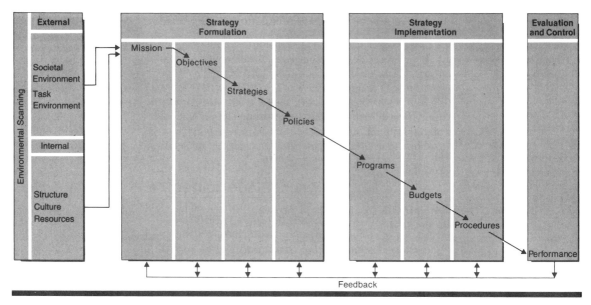

Strategic managers are the people in a corporation who are involved in the strategic management process. They are the people who scan the internal and external environments, formulate and implement objectives, strategies, and policies, and evaluate and control the results. The people with direct responsibility for this process are the board of directors and top management. The chief executive officer (CEO), the chief operations officer (COO) or president, the executive vice-president, and the vice-presidents in charge of operating divisions and functional areas typically form the top management group. Traditionally, boards of directors have engaged in strategic management only to the extent that they passively approved proposals from top management and hired and fired their CEOs. Their role, however, is changing dramatically. The strategic management process, therefore, is also changing.

3.1

CORPORATE BOARD OF DIRECTORS

Directors conduct a far different meeting from those in the past. Pressures—from regulatory agencies, shareholders, lenders, and the public—have practically forced greater awareness of directors' responsibilities. The board as a rubber stamp or a bastion of the "old-boy" selection system has largely been replaced by more active, more professional boards.[1]

Even in the recent past, boards of directors functioned rather passively. Members were selected because of their prestige in the community, regardless of their knowledge of the specific functioning of the corporation they were to oversee. Traditionally, members of the board were requested to simply approve proposals by top management or the firm's legal counsel, and the more important board activities generally were conducted by an executive committee composed of insiders.[2] Even now, the boards in some family-owned corporations are more figureheads than overseers; they exist on paper because the laws of incorporation require their presence, but rarely, if ever, do they question management's plans.

Lee Iacocca describes how such a situation existed at the Ford Motor Company under Henry Ford II.

> The Ford Motor Company had gone public in 1956, but Henry never really accepted the change. As he saw it, he was like his grandfather, the rightful owner—Henry Ford, Prop. (Proprietor)—and the company was his to do [with] as he pleased. When it came to the board, he, more than most CEO's, believed in the mushroom treatment—throw manure on them and keep them in the dark. That attitude, of course, was fostered by the fact that Henry and his family, with only 12% of the stock, held on to 40% of the voting rights.[3]

Over the past decade, stockholders and various interest groups have seriously questioned the role of the board of directors. A recent survey by the National Association of Corporate Directors, for example, revealed that almost half of stockholders believe that directors ignore stockholder interests when considering a merger.[4] As a result of these and other doubts, the general public has become more aware and more critical of many boards' apparent lack of responsibility for corporate activities. Who is responsible for radioactive leaks in nuclear power plants? For the manufacture and sale of unsafe toys? For not properly safeguarding employees from hazards in the workplace? For bribery attempts by corporate officers? Can boards, especially those of multinational corporations, realistically monitor the decisions and actions of corporate employees in countries halfway around the world? What are the legal liabilities of a board for the actions taken by the corporation?

Responsibilities of the Board

At this time, there are no national standards defining the accountability or responsibility of a board of directors. The law offers little guidance on this question. Specific requirements of directors vary, depending on the state in which the corporate charter is issued. According to Conference Board reports authored by Bacon and Brown, "State corporation laws give boards of directors rather sweeping powers couched in general language that does not specify to whom they are accountable nor clarify what it is they are accountable for."[5] There is, nevertheless, a developing consensus concerning the major responsibilities of a board.

The board of directors of a corporation is appointed or elected by the stockholders for the following purposes:

- To oversee the management of the corporation's assets;
- To establish or approve the corporation's mission, objectives, strategy, and policies;
- To review management's actions in light of the financial performance of the corporation; and
- To hire and fire the principal operating officers of the corporation.

In a legal sense, the board is required to direct the affairs of the corporation but not to manage them. It is charged by law to act with "due care." As Bacon and Brown put it, "Directors must act with that degree of diligence, care and skill which ordinarily prudent men would exercise under similar circumstances in like positions."[6] If a director or the board as a whole fails to act with due care and, as a result, the corporation is in some way harmed, the careless director or directors can be held personally liable for the harm done.

For example, after the Federal Deposit Insurance Corporation (FDIC) put together a $4.5 billion package to rescue the failing Continental Illinois Bank of Chicago in 1984, it dismissed nine of the bank's sixteen directors. Two other directors resigned. Even though each director had sworn the Joint Oath of the National Bank Directors to "diligently and honestly administer the affairs" of the bank, the FDIC contended that the directors should have monitored more carefully what was happening at Continental Illinois.[7] Another example was provided in 1986: A federal court in Delaware fined directors of Trans Union Corporation, a railcar-leasing company, for negligence in connection with the sale of the company.[8]

The increasing popularity of personal liability insurance for board members suggests that a number of people on boards of directors are becoming very concerned that they might be held personally responsible not only for their own actions but also for the actions of the corporation as a whole. This concern is reinforced by the requirement of the Securities and Exchange Commission (SEC) that a majority of directors must sign the Annual Report Form 10-K. A recent survey found that of 606 major U.S. corporations, 51% go beyond the SEC requirement by requiring that *all* directors sign the 10-K.[9]

Directors must make certain, in addition to these duties, that the corporation is managed in accordance with the laws of the state in which it is incorporated. They must also ensure management's adherence to laws and regulations, such as those dealing with the issuance of securities, insider trading, and other conflict-of-interest situations. They must also be aware of the needs and demands of constituent groups, so that they can achieve a judicious balance among the interests of these diverse groups while ensuring the continued functioning of the corporation. For example, the Delaware Supreme Court in 1986 concluded that when Revlon's directors authorized management to negotiate the sale of the company, the legal duties of the directors changed. In the court's words, the directors' role became that of "*auctioneers* charged with getting the best price for the stockholders in the sale of the company!"[10]

Role of the Board in Strategic Management

In terms of strategic management, a board of directors has three basic tasks.[11]

- **To initiate and determine.** A board can delineate a corporation's mission and specify strategic options to its management. Most boards still leave this task to top management.
- **To evaluate and influence.** A board can examine management's proposals, decisions, and actions; agree or disagree with them; give advice and offer suggestions; outline alternatives.
- **To monitor.** By acting through its committees, a board can keep abreast of developments both inside and outside the corporation. It can thus bring to management's attention developments it might have overlooked.

Even though every board will be composed of people with varying degrees of commitment to the corporation, we can make some generalizations about a board of directors as a whole, in its attempt to fulfill these three basic tasks. We can characterize a board as being at a specific point on a continuum, on the basis of its degree of involvement in corporate strategic affairs. As types, boards can range from phantom boards with no real involvement to catalyst boards with a very high degree of involvement. Highly involved boards tend to be very active. They take their tasks of initiating, evaluating and influencing, and monitoring very seriously; they provide advice when necessary and keep management alert. As depicted in Fig. 3.1, they can be deeply involved in the strategic management process. At Texas Instruments, for example, the board attends a four-day strategic planning conference each year, in which they discuss business opportunities of the next decade. Several members of the board also attend, during the following two days, management meetings attended by 500 managers from throughout the company.[12] Other corporations with active participation boards are Mead Corporation, Rohm and Haas, and Dayton-Hudson.[13]

As a board becomes less involved in the affairs of the corporation, it moves farther to the left on the continuum. On the far left are passive

FIGURE 3.1
Board of Directors Continuum.

←		DEGREE OF INVOLVEMENT IN STRATEGIC MANAGEMENT			→
LOW (Passive)					HIGH (Active)
Phantom	**Rubber Stamp**	**Minimal Review**	**Nominal Participation**	**Active Participation**	**Catalyst**
Never knows what to do, if anything; no degree of involvement.	Permits officers to make all decisions. It votes as the officers recommend on action issues.	Formally reviews selected issues that officers bring to its attention.	Involved to a limited degree in the performance or review of selected key decisions, indicators, or programs of management.	Approves, questions, and makes final decisions on mission, strategy, policies, and objectives. Has active board committees. Performs fiscal and management audits.	Takes the leading role in establishing and modifying the mission, objectives, strategy, and policies. It has a very active strategy committee.

boards that typically *never* initiate or determine strategy unless a crisis occurs. For example, when Mellon Bank Corporation suffered its first loss in its 118-year history in 1987, stockholders claimed that the directors had failed in their responsibilities. "The officers (management) were determining policy and the directors were just sitting around uninformed," reported a former director who had resigned from Mellon's board in 1984.[14]

Generally, the smaller the corporation, the less active is its board of directors. The board tends to be dominated by directors who are also owner-managers of the company. Other directors are usually friends or family members. As the corporation grows and goes public, however, the boards become more active in terms of roles and responsibilities.[15]

Most large, publicly owned corporations probably have boards that operate at some point between nominal and active participation. Few have catalyst boards, except for those with major problems (that is, pending bankruptcies, mergers, or acquisitions).

A survey of the nation's 2,235 largest commercial banks by Egon Zehnder International, a management consulting firm, supports this characterization of boards of directors.[16] The chief executive officers were asked:

"What phrase best characterizes the role of your Board of Directors in the *strategic* success of your bank?" They responded as follows:

- Critical contributor to our strategic success (catalyst)   5%
- Very active contributor (active participation)   22%
- Somewhat active contributor (nominal participation)   45%

- Passive (minimal review)   21%
- Largely ceremonial (phantom/rubber stamp)   8%

Many CEOs and board members do not want the board to be involved in strategy matters at more than a superficial level. Kenneth Andrews, an authority on strategic managers, suggests why:

> Many chief executive officers, rejecting the practicality of conscious strategy, preside over unstated, incremental, or intuitive strategies that have never been articulated or analyzed—and therefore could not be deliberated by the board. Others do not believe their outside directors know enough or have time enough to do more than assent to strategic recommendations. Still others may keep discussions of strategy within management to prevent board transgression onto management turf and consequent reduction of executives' power to shape by themselves the future of their companies.[17]

Nevertheless, recent surveys of directors reveal that one of the most pressing concerns of directors is strategic planning.[18] "In the past," said one director, "strategic planning has been exclusively a management function. But now it has been intertwined with the role and functions of the board."[19] Therefore, board members are now coming to think of themselves as participants in the corporation's strategic management.[20]

Board Membership: Inside versus Outside Directors

The boards of most publicly owned corporations are comprised of both inside and outside directors. Inside directors are typically officers or executives employed by the corporation. The outside director may be an executive of another firm but is not an employee of the board's corporation. A recent survey of large corporations in manufacturing and service industries found outsiders to account for almost 70% of board membership. The majority of these outside directors owned fewer than 500 shares—a rather minuscule amount—of the corporations for which they served.[21] A survey of small companies found that outsiders comprise only 40% of the average board.[22]

A recent Hay Survey of Directors reported outside directors to be compensated for their work at an average rate of $26,095 by industrial companies and $22,468 by financial companies. However, some such as Allied Signal pay as much as $45,000 annually. Generally, the compensation is composed of an annual retainer fee plus board- and committee-meeting fees.[23] Almost 60% of smaller companies compensated their directors. The average retainer fee was $4,300 and the average meeting fee, $510.[24] Few, if any, insider (management) directors are paid for assuming this extra duty.

The American Law Institute, an association of 1,800 leading lawyers, judges, and law professors, proposes in its "Principles of Corporate Governance and Structure: Restatement and Recommendations" that all corporations be required to have outside directors form a majority of the membership of their boards of directors.[25] The Securities and Exchange Commission (SEC) now requires corporations whose stock is listed on the New York Exchange to have at least two outside directors. The ALI and the SEC apparently take the view that outside directors are less biased and more likely to evaluate objectively management's performance than are inside directors. This view is in agreement with **agency theory**—a theory which states that problems arise in corporations because the agents (top management) no longer bear the full results of their decisions unless they own a substantial amount of stock in the corporation. The theory thus suggests that a majority of a board needs to be from outside the firm, so that top management is prevented from acting selfishly to the detriment of the stockholders.[26] Vance, an authority on boards of directors, contends, however, that outside directors are less effective than are insiders because the outsiders have "questionable interest, availability, or competency."[27] Although research by Kesner supports Vance's argument, there is some evidence that the amount of stock owned by directors can also have some impact on a corporation's stock price and profits.[28] Research by Pearce found that the directors' orientation toward the external environment was more associated with corporate performance than was the ratio of outsiders to insiders.[29] Nevertheless, the general trend seems to be one of an increasing percentage of outsiders on the boards of U.S. corporations.

Surveys of manufacturing companies disclose that a majority of the outside directors are presidents, managing partners, or chairmen of the boards of other corporations. Outside directors come from a variety of organizations, some even from the ministry, but a majority of them come from the manufacturing, banking, law, and investment industries. With the current concern for productivity, there appears to be a movement toward having more executives on boards with strong operating experience and fewer investment bankers and attorneys.

In 1986, 44% of corporations surveyed had women on their boards; 30% had members from minority groups. White males held 92.1% of directors' positions in 1987 compared to 95.4% in 1982.[30]

A majority of the inside directors include the president, chairman of the board, and vice-presidents; the rest are key officers or former employees. Lower-level operating employees, including managers, form only 1% of the total employee board membership of the companies surveyed.[31]

Codetermination

The dearth of nonmanagement-employee directors on the boards of U.S. corporations may be changing. Codetermination, the inclusion of a corporation's workers on its board, began only recently in the United States. Critics raise the issue of conflict of interest. Can a member of the board, who is privy to confidential managerial information, function for example as a union leader whose primary duty is to fight for the best benefits for his members?

The addition of Douglas Fraser, President of the United Auto Workers, to the board of Chrysler Corporation in 1980 was a controversial move designed to placate the union while Chrysler was attempting to avoid bankruptcy. With the replacement of Fraser in 1984 by Owen Bieber, the newly elected president of the UAW, a seat for labor in the Chrysler boardroom appeared to become permanent. Eastern Airlines, Western Air Lines, and Wheeling-Pittsburgh Steel Corporation have also added representatives from employee associations to their boards. As did Chrysler, these corporations have appointed employee directors in concordance with an agreement with their unions, that the unions accept major pay concessions.

Research in fourteen other U.S. firms with workers on the board found that "worker board representation is no guarantee that workers will have an effective role in the governance of the organization."[32] The need to work for the corporation as a whole as well as to represent the workers creates role conflict and stress among the worker directors—thus cutting into their effectiveness.

While the movement to place employees on the boards of directors of U.S. companies is only just beginning, the European experience reveals an increasing acceptance of worker participation on corporate boards. The Federal Republic of Germany pioneered the practice with its Co-Determination Acts of 1951 and 1976, and Works Constitution Act of 1952. Worker representatives in the coal, iron, and steel industries were given equal status with management on policy-making boards. Management in other industries, however, retained a two-thirds majority on policy-making boards.

Other countries, such as Sweden, Denmark, Norway, and Austria have passed similar codetermination legislation. Belgium, Luxembourg, France, Italy, Ireland, and the Netherlands use worker councils to work closely with management, but are seriously considering moving closer toward the German model.

However, the British government in the 1960s established the codetermination concept in nationalized industries but found it to be a failure. It did not cause better labor-management relations.[33] And recent research on German codetermination found that legislation requiring firms to put employee representatives on their boards "lowered dividend payments, led to a more conservative investment policy, and reduced firm values."[34]

Interlocking Directorates

Boards that are primarily composed of outside directors will not necessarily be more objective than those primarily composed of insiders. CEOs may nominate for board membership chief executives from other firms, for the exchange of important information and a guarantee of the stability of key marketplace relationships. One or more individuals serving on the boards of directors of two or more corporations create an *interlocking directorate*. Although the Clayton Act and the Banking Act of 1933 prohibit interlocking directorates by U.S. companies competing in the same industry, interlocking continues to occur in almost all corporations, especially large ones.[35] Research has shown that the larger the firm, the greater the number of different corporations represented on its board of directors. Interlocking occurs because large firms have a large impact on other corporations; and these other corporations, in turn, have some control over the firm's inputs and marketplace. Interlocking directorates are also a useful method for gaining both inside information about an uncertain environment and objective expertise about a firm's strategy.[36] Family-owned corporations, however, are less likely to have interlocking directorates than are corporations with highly dispersed stock ownership, probably because family-owned corporations do not like to dilute their corporate control by adding outsiders to boardroom discussions.[37]

Corporations also have members of their management teams on the boards of other corporations. In 1985, 74% of inside board members of large companies sat on one or more boards besides their own.[38] General Motors, for example, has 284 connections (11 through ownership, 67 through direct interlocking, and 206 through indirect interlocking).[39]

Nomination and Election of Board Members

Traditionally, the CEO of the corporation decided whom to invite to board membership and merely asked the stockholders for approval. The chief criteria used by most CEOs in nominating board members were that the persons be compatible with the CEO and that they bring some prestige to the board.

There are some dangers, however, in allowing the CEO free reign in nominating directors. The CEO might select only board members who, in the CEO's opinion, will not disturb the company's policies and functioning. More importantly, directors selected by the CEO often feel that they should go along with any proposals made by the CEO. Thus, board members find themselves accountable to the very management they are charged to oversee. Because of the likelihood of these occurrences, there is an increasing tendency for a special board committee to nominate new outside board members. A survey by Heidrick and Struggles revealed that the percentage of Fortune 1000 corporations using nominating committees to select new directors rose from 9% in 1976 to 90% in 1986.[40]

Term of Office

A recent study by the Hay Group reports that 46% of U.S. corporations surveyed elect all directors annually for a one-year term of office. In contrast, 35% elect directors for a three-year term.[41]

Virtually every corporation whose directors serve terms of more than one year divide the board into classes and stagger elections so that only a portion of the board stands for election each year. Arguments in favor of this practice are that it provides continuity by reducing the chance of an abrupt turnover in its membership and that it reduces the likelihood of people unfriendly to management being elected through cumulative voting. Among the many companies recently attempting to switch from one-year terms to longer-term staggered elections to reduce the likelihood of a takeover are Beatrice Foods, Union Oil, Sterling Drug, and Quaker Oats.

Cumulative Voting

The practice of cumulative voting allows a stockholder to concentrate his or her votes in an election of directors. Cumulative voting is required by law in eighteen states and is mandatory on request or permitted as a corporate option in thirty-two other states or territories. Under cumulative voting, the number of votes allowed is determined by multiplying the number of voting shares held by the number of directors to be elected. Thus, a person owning 1,000 shares in an election of 12 directors would have 12,000 votes. These votes may then be distributed in any manner—for instance, divided evenly (or unevenly) between two directors or concentrated on one. This method is contrasted with straight voting in which the stockholder votes simply yes or no for each director to be elected.[42] Although few stockholders use the privilege of cumulative voting, it is a powerful way for them to influence a board of directors. For example, a minority of stockholders could concentrate their voting power and elect one or more directors of their choice. In contrast, straight voting allows the holders of the majority of outstanding shares to prevent the election of any director not to their liking.

Those in favor of cumulative voting argue that it is the only system under which a candidate not on the management slate can hope to be elected to the board. Otherwise, under straight voting, an entrenched management could insulate itself from criticism and use the board as a rubber stamp. Critics of cumulative voting argue that it allows the board to deteriorate into interest groups more concerned with protecting their own special concerns than in working for the good of the corporation. This could become a serious problem if the corporation is in danger of being bought or controlled by another firm. For instance, by purchasing some shares, another firm (such as a potential acquirer) could, through cumulative voting, elect enough board members that it could directly influence or even incapacitate the board. It is for this reason that a number of U.S. corporations have recently re-incorporated in the state of Delaware where cumulative voting is not mandatory.[43] Nevertheless, the practice of cumulative voting has been recommended as a way to achieve minority representation on the boards of directors of major corporations.

Organization of the Board

The size of the board is determined by the corporation's charter and its bylaws in compliance with state laws. Although some states require a minimum number of board members, most corporations have quite a bit of discretion in determination of board size. Surveys of U.S. business corporations reveal that the average *privately* held company has eight board members who meet four times a year, as compared to the average *publicly* held corporation with thirteen directors who meet seven times a year. In addition, there appears to be a direct relationship between company size as measured by sales volume and the number of people on the board.[44]

Chairman

A fairly common practice in U.S. corporations is to have the chairman of the board also serve as the chief executive officer. The CEO concentrates on strategy, planning, external relations, and responsibility to the board. The chairman's responsibility is to ensure that the board and its committees perform their functions as stated in their charter. Further, the chairman schedules board meetings and presides over the annual stockholders' meeting. In over 75% of the Fortune 500 corporations, the CEO also serves as chairman of the board.[45]

Committees

The most effective boards of large corporations accomplish much of their work through committees.[46] Although the committees do not have legal duties, unless detailed in the bylaws, most committees are granted full power to act with the authority of the board between board meetings. Typical standing committees are the executive committee, audit committee, compensation committee, finance committee, and nominating committee. The executive committee is formed from local directors who can meet between board meetings to attend to matters that must be settled quickly. This committee acts as an extension of the board and, consequently, may have almost unrestricted authority in certain areas. A recent survey reports that in 68% of industrial and 72% of financial corporations, the executive committee includes at least a majority of outside directors.[47] Other less common committees are the strategic planning, social responsibility, investments (pension funds), stock options, conflict-of-interest, and research/technology committees.[48]

Trends for the Future

The role of the board of directors in the strategic management of the corporation is likely to be a more active one in the future. Change is more likely to be evolutionary than radical or revolutionary. Different boards are at different levels of maturity and will not be changing in the same direction or at the same speed.[49] There are, nevertheless, some current overall trends that should continue into the near-term future. Some of these are the following:[50]

- Boards will be held to increasingly high standards of conduct. Society will pay more attention to the board as the corporation's overseer of ethical, legal, and social standards.
- Directors will increasingly recognize that they are responsible for the long-run best interests of the corporation as a whole, not merely the interests of the stockholders. Although a key concern of strategic managers today is "shareholder value," corporations will need to pay more attention to other concerned groups in their task environments.
- There will be fewer successful law suits against boards as the legal system makes liability laws more rational. Already many U.S. state legislatures, beginning with Delaware, have passed laws limiting a director's personal liability as long as he/she acts in good faith, follows laws, and avoids conflicts of interest.[51]
- The board will be increasingly active in the evaluation and development of strategies. Expect more boards in corporations of all sizes to create and use a strategic planning committee.
- Directors will fulfill their larger responsibilities without a corresponding increase in the time they spend on board business. Although the average outside director of a typical large corporation spends 145 hours annually on board business, this amount should stabilize and could even drop as information provided to board members is made more appropriate and timely.[52]
- Corporations will work harder to select and keep active, qualified board members. John Nash, President of the National Association of Corporate Directors, has proposed a certification program that ensures the selection of competent directors. Although it is currently a pilot program, Nash predicts broad acceptance of the concept by the mid-1990s.[53]
- Boards will become more assertive in their selections of directors. More boards will use nominating committees to select an increasingly diverse pool of qualified candidates. Expect an increasing use of "professional" directors who will take the time to get involved in corporate affairs, to keep the board current on company activities, and to probe into areas in which most outside directors would not normally be knowledgeable.
- Directors will become more independent of the CEO. Although there will continue to be a commonality of purpose, the board will become more sensitive to its responsibility of being objective and independent of top management.

The importance of the board of directors and its likely future is aptly summarized by James Worthy and Robert Neuschel in their study on corporate governance:

> Boards of directors will be importantly concerned with helping to achieve the balance (between the degree of freedom necessary for business to function profitably and the need for society to preserve other freedoms and institutions) in the years ahead. More and more, society will expect the board to provide the fine line between achieving the economic objectives of the corporation and meeting the broader needs of society.[54]

3.2

TOP MANAGEMENT

The top management function is usually conducted by the CEO of the corporation in coordination with the COO or president, executive vice-president, and vice-presidents of divisions and functional areas. As we mentioned earlier in this chapter, some corporations combine the office of CEO with that of chairman of the board of directors. Although this plan has the advantage of freeing the president or COO of the firm from many strategic responsibilities so that he or she can focus primarily on operational matters, it has been criticized because it gives the combined CEO/chairman too much power and serves to undercut the independence of the board.[55]

Responsibilities of Top Management

Top management, and especially the CEO, is responsible to the board of directors for the overall management of the corporation. It is tasked with getting things accomplished through and with others, in order to meet the corporate objectives. Top management's job is thus multidimensional and is oriented toward the welfare of the total organization. Specific top management tasks vary from firm to firm and are developed from an analysis of the mission, objectives, strategies, and key activities of the corporation. But all top managers are people who see the business as a whole, who can balance the present needs of the business against the needs of the future, and who can make final and effective decisions.[56] The chief executive officer, in particular, must successfully handle three responsibilities crucial to the effective strategic management of the corporation: (1) fulfill key roles; (2) provide corporate leadership; and (3) manage the strategic planning process.

Fulfill Key Roles

From five weeks of in-depth observation of five chief executives, Henry Mintzberg concluded that the job of a top manager contains ten interrelated *roles*. The importance of each role and the amount of time demanded by each probably varies from one job to another. These roles are as follows:

- **Figurehead:** Acts as legal and symbolic head; performs obligatory social, ceremonial, or legal duties (hosts retirement dinners, luncheons for employees, and plant dedications; attends civic affairs; signs contracts on behalf of firm).
- **Leader:** Motivates, develops, and guides subordinates; oversees staffing, training, and associated activities (introduces Management By Objectives [MBO], develops a challenging work climate, provides a sense of direction, acts as a role model).
- **Liaison:** Maintains a network of contacts and information sources outside top management, in order to obtain information and assistance (meets with key people from the task environment, meets formally and informally with corporate division managers and with CEOs of other firms).

- **Monitor:** Seeks and obtains information needed for understanding the corporation and its environments; acts as nerve center for the corporation (reviews status reports from vice-presidents, reviews key indicators of corporate performance, scans *Wall Street Journal* and key trade journals, joins select clubs and societies).

- **Disseminator:** Transmits information to the rest of the top management team and other key people in the corporation (chairs staff meetings, transmits policy letters, communicates five-year plans).

- **Spokesman:** Transmits information to key groups and people in the task environment (prepares annual report to stockholders, talks to the Chamber of Commerce, states corporate policy to the media, participates in advertising campaigns, speaks before congressional committees).

- **Entrepreneur:** Searches the corporation and its environment for projects to improve products, processes, procedures, and structures: then supervises the design and implementation of these projects (introduces cost reduction programs, makes plant trips to divisions, changes forecasting system, brings in subcontract work to level the work load, reorganizes the corporation).

- **Disturbance Handler:** Takes corrective action in times of disturbance or crisis (personally talks with key creditors, interest groups, congressional committees, union leaders; establishes investigative committees; revises objectives, strategies, and policies).

- **Resource Allocator:** Allocates corporate resources by making and/or approving decisions (reviews budgets, revises program scheduling, initiates strategic planning, plans personnel load, sets objectives).

- **Negotiator:** Represents the corporation in negotiating important agreements; may speak directly with key representatives of groups in the task environment or work through a negotiator; negotiates disagreements within the corporation by working with conflicting division heads (works with labor negotiator; resolves jurisdictional disputes between divisions; negotiates with key creditors, suppliers, and customers).[57]

Provide Corporate Leadership

People who work in corporations look to top management for leadership. Their doing so, says Drucker, reflects a need for standard setting and example setting.[58] According to Mintzberg, this is a key role of any manager.

Corporate leadership is important because it sets the tone for the entire corporation. In a survey of top investment analysts and money managers, almost half responded that their personal evaluation of top management is worth 60% of their total evaluation of the company.[59] This is in agreement with research reporting that individual CEOs have a strong impact on the strategic direction of their firms.[60]

Most middle managers look to their boss for guidance and direction and so tend to emulate the characteristics and style of successful top managers. People in an organization want to have a vision of what they are working toward—a sense of mission. Only top management is in the position to specify and communicate this sense of mission to the general work force. Top management's enthusiasm (or lack of it) about the corporation tends to be contagious.

For instance, a positive attitude characterizing many well-known industrial leaders—such as Alfred Sloan at General Motors, Ed Watson at IBM, Robert Wood at Sears, Ray Kroc at McDonald's, and Lee Iacocca at Chrysler—have energized their respective corporations. In their book *In Search of Excellence*, Peters and Waterman report that "associated with almost every excellent company was a strong leader (or two) who seemed to have a lot to do with making his company excellent in the first place."[61] A two-year study by McKinsey & Co. found the CEOs of midsized, high-growth companies to be "almost inevitably consummate salesmen who radiate enormous contagious self-confidence" and "take pains to communicate their strong sense of mission to all who come in contact with them."[62]

Chief executive officers with a clear sense of mission are often perceived as dynamic and charismatic leaders. They are able to command respect and to influence strategy formulation and implementation because they tend to have three key characteristics.

1. The CEO *presents a role* for others to identify with and to follow. The leader sets an example in terms of behavior and dress. The CEO's attitudes and values concerning the corporation's purpose and activities are clear-cut and constantly communicated in words and deeds.

2. The CEO *articulates a transcendent goal* for the corporation. The CEO's vision of the corporation goes beyond the petty complaints and grievances of the average work day. Because this vision puts activities and conflicts in a new perspective, it gives renewed meaning to everyone's work activities and enables them to see beyond the details of their own jobs to the functioning of the total corporation. As John W. Teets, CEO and Chairman of The Greyhound Corporation, states, "Management's job is to see the company not as it is . . . but as it can become."[63]

3. The CEO *communicates high performance standards* but also *shows confidence* in the followers' abilities to meet these standards. No leader ever improved performance by setting easily attainable goals that provide no challenge. The CEO must be willing to follow through by coaching people.[64]

Manage Strategic Planning

Top management must initiate and manage the strategic planning process. To specify the corporate mission, delineate corporate objectives, and formulate appropriate strategies and policies, it must take a very long-range view. As depicted in Fig. 3.2, the ideal time horizon for management's planning varies according to level in the corporate hierarchy. The president of a corporation, for example, should allocate the largest proportion of planning time to looking two to four years ahead. One reason given for the

FIGURE 3.2
"Ideal" Allocations of Time for Planning in the "Average" Company.

	Today	1 Week Ahead	1 Month Ahead	3-6 Months Ahead	1 Year Ahead	2 Years Ahead	3-4 Years Ahead	5-10 Years Ahead
President	1%	2%	5%	10%	15%	27%	30%	10%
Executive Vice-President	2%	4%	10%	29%	20%	18%	13%	4%
Vice-President of Functional Area	4%	8%	15%	35%	20%	10%	5%	3%
General Manager of a Major Division	2%	5%	15%	30%	20%	12%	12%	4%
Department Manager	10%	10%	24%	39%	10%	5%	1%	1%
Section Supervisor	15%	20%	25%	37%	3%			
Group Supervisor	38%	40%	15%	5%	2%			

Source: Reprinted with permission of The Free Press, a division of Macmillan, Inc. from *Top Management Planning* by G. A. Steiner. Copyright © 1969 by the Trustees of Columbia University in the City of New York.

worldwide economic success of many Japanese corporations is the reputed ability of their top managers to conceptualize corporate mission and strategy far into the future. Mr. Ishihara, President of Nissan, has been quoted as saying "In what I do now, I am thinking twenty or thirty years ahead."[65] A department manager, however, should put the heaviest proportion of planning time on looking only three to six *months* ahead.

To accomplish its tasks, top management must use information provided by three key corporate groups: a long-range planning staff, divisional or SBU managers, and managers of functional departments.

A **long-range planning staff** typically consists of six people, headed by a senior vice-president or director of corporate planning.[66] In order to generate data for strategic decisions by top management, it continuously monitors both internal and external environments. It also suggests to top management possible changes in the corporate mission, objectives, strategies, and policies. Although only one in five companies with sales under $100 million have a separate, formal planning department, nearly all corporations with sales of at least $2 billion have such departments.[67] The size of corporate planning staffs in large corporations is currently decreasing, however, as strategic planning responsibilities are being shifted to line managers.[68]

Divisional or SBU managers, with the assistance of the long-range planning staff and with input from their product managers, perform the strategic planning function for each division. These SBU managers typically initiate proposals for top management's consideration and/or respond to requests for such proposals by corporate headquarters. They may also be tasked to carry out strategies and policies decided upon at the corporate level for organization-wide implementation. These division managers typically work with the heads of various functional units within the division to develop the appropriate functional strategies for the implementation of planned business-level strategies.

Managers of functional departments (marketing, engineering, R&D managers, etc.) report directly either to divisional managers in a multidivision corporation or to top management if the corporation has no divisions. Although they may develop specific functional strategies, they generally do so within the framework of divisional or corporate strategies. They also respond to initiatives from above that ask them for input or require them to develop strategies for the implementation of divisional plans.

Characteristics of Top Management Tasks

Top management tasks have two characteristics that differentiate them from other managerial tasks.[69] First, *very few of them are continuous*. Rarely does a manager work on these tasks all day. The responsibilities, however, are always present, even though the tasks themselves are sporadic. And when the tasks do arise, they are of crucial significance, such as the selection of a person to head a new division.

Mintzberg reports that the activities of most executives are characterized by brevity, variety, and fragmentation: "Half of the observed activities were completed in less than nine minutes and only one-tenth took more than an hour. In effect, the managers were seldom able or willing to spend much time on any one issue in any one session."[70]

It is likely that serious objective-setting and strategy formulation will not occur in corporations if most top managers are as activity-oriented as those in the Mintzberg study. John De Lorean suggests as much in his comments about "The Fourteenth Floor" (the executive offices) of General Motors.

> I was trying to bring a set of new eyes to the job of group executive, as one only can do in the first few months in a new position. But I had no time to perform the real function of my position. Instead, I was being tied down and totally consumed by this constant parade of paperwork and meetings.[71]

The second characteristic of top management tasks is that *they require a wide range of capabilities and temperaments*. Some tasks require the capacity to analyze and carefully weigh alternative courses of action. Some require an awareness of and an interest in people, whereas others call for the ability to pursue abstract ideas, concepts, and calculations.

One effect of tasks having these two characteristics is that top managers are often drawn back into the functional work of the corporation. Because their activities are not continuous, people in top management often have unplanned free time. They tend therefore to get caught up in the day-to-day work in manufacturing, marketing, accounting, engineering, or in other operations of the corporation. They may find themselves constantly solving crises that could probably have been better handled by lower-level managers. These managers are also usually fond of protesting, "How can I be expected to drain the swamp when I'm up to my eyeballs in alligators!?"

A second effect of the tasks' characteristics is that top managers tend to perceive only those aspects and responsibilities of the top management function that are compatible with their abilities, experience, and temperaments. And, if the board of directors fails to state explicitly what it considers to be the key responsibilities and activities of top management, the top managers are free to define the job themselves. Therefore, important tasks can be overlooked until a crisis occurs.

Top Management Team

The typical chief executive officer of the largest publicly held U.S. business corporations is around fifty-six years old, draws an average annual salary of $651,000, and has been with the company twenty-three years. Nearly half of these CEOs have graduate degrees. A high proportion are firstborn children who learned early to be family caretakers and mediators.[72] Nevertheless, these top managers are finding the job of the CEO to be increasingly difficult and unpredictable. Therefore, many scholars and executives propose that strategic planning and top management is a job for a team rather than for one person.[73]

The top management team could be organized as a chief executive "office" in which a number of people serve as equals, each with an assigned area of responsibility. Corporations such as DuPont, Schering A. G., Standard Oil of New Jersey, Royal Dutch Shell, Eastman Kodak, and Unilever have taken this approach.

Or the team may consist of one person who carries the title of CEO and several colleagues, each of whom has clearly assigned authority and responsibility for a segment of the top management task. General Motors and Xerox Corporation use this structure. GM's team includes a chairman, a vice-chairman, a chairman of the executive committee, and a president. General Electric has taken a similar approach, although it refers to its four-man top management group as the Corporate Executive Office.

The use of top management teams has increased dramatically from only 8% of large U.S. corporations in the 1960s to 25% in the 1980s.[74] An advantage of the team approach to top management is the sharing of roles, responsibilities, and tasks, a sharing that depends on the strengths and weaknesses of the people involved. It makes more sense for large corporations to put together a top management team to achieve synergy, than to try to find the perfect person to be CEO. Certainly succession problems are minimized by the team approach; decisions can be made even though the CEO has resigned, is incapacitated, or is otherwise absent.

3.3

STRATEGIC MANAGEMENT STYLES

Just as boards of directors vary widely on a continuum of involvement in the strategic management process, so do top management teams. For example, a top management team with low involvement in strategic management will tend to be functionally oriented and will focus its energies on day-to-day operational problems; this type of team is likely either to be disorganized or to have a dominant CEO who continues to identify with his or her old division. In contrast, a top management team with high involvement will be active in long-range planning. It will try to get divisional managers involved in planning so that top management will have more time to scan the environment for challenges and opportunities.

Both the board of directors and top management can be placed on a matrix that reflects four basic styles of corporate strategic management. These styles are depicted in Fig. 3.3.

Chaos Management

When both the board of directors and top management have little involvement in the strategic management process, their style is referred to as chaos

FIGURE 3.3
Strategic Management Styles.

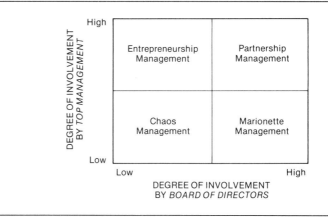

management. The board waits for top management to bring it proposals. Top management is operationally oriented and continues to carry out strategies, policies, and programs specified by the founding entrepreneur who died years ago. The basic strategic philosophy seems to be, "If it was good enough for old J. B., it's good enough for us." There is no strategic management being done here.

Entrepreneurship Management

A corporation with an uninvolved board of directors but a highly involved top management has entrepreneurship management. The board is willing to be used as a rubber stamp for top management's decisions. The CEO, operating alone or with a team, dominates the corporation and its strategic decisions. An example is Control Data Corporation under the leadership of its founder William C. Norris. For twenty-nine years, Norris dominated both the company's top management and its board of directors. Insisting that the company could profit by addressing "society's unmet needs," Norris directed corporate investments into the rejuvenation of ghettos and support of wind-powered generators and tundra farming, among other projects. Although these investments tended to result in losses, few people were willing to challenge his strategic decisions. Some employees even referred to him as "the Pope." A former Control Data executive noted, "More often than not, he's proven his critics wrong, so now his visions aren't challenged."[75]

Marionette Management

Probably the rarest form of strategic management styles, marionette management occurs when the board of directors is deeply involved in strategic decision making, but top management is primarily concerned with operations. Such a style evolves when a board is composed of key stockholders who refuse to delegate strategic decision making to the president. The president is forced into a COO role and can do only what the board allows him to do. This style also occurs when a board fires a CEO but is slow to find a replacement. The COO or executive vice-president stays on as "acting" president or CEO until the selection process is complete. In the meantime, strategic management is firmly in the hands of the board of directors.

This sequence occurred at Winnebago Industries in 1986 when the company's Board of Directors, chaired by its founder, 72-year-old John K. Hanson, took away Ronald Haugen's title as chief executive officer, but left him as company president. No new CEO was named. Hanson, whose family owned 46% of Winnebago's stock, had given up the CEO title in 1983 to President Haugen, a long-time employee. Outside observers noted that although Chairman Hanson did not also hold the title of CEO, he appeared to have taken on the CEO's responsibilities once again.[76]

Partnership Management

Probably the most effective style of strategic management, partnership management is epitomized by a highly involved board and top management. The board and the top management team work closely to establish the corporate mission, objectives, strategies, and policies. Board members are active in committee work and utilize strategic audits to provide feedback to top management on its implementations of agreed-upon strategies and policies. This appears to be the style emerging in a number of successful corporations such as Texas Instruments, Dayton Hudson Corporation, and General Electric Company.

SUMMARY AND CONCLUSION

The strategy-makers of a modern corporation are the board of directors and top management. Both must be actively involved in the strategic management process if the corporation is to have long-term success in accomplishing its mission.

An effective board is the keystone of the modern corporation. Without it, management would tend to focus on short-run problems and solutions or go off on tangents at odds with the basic mission. The personal needs and goals of executives would tend to overrule the interests of the corporation. Even the strongest critics of boards of directors are more interested in improving and upgrading boards than in eliminating them. An active board is critical in determining an organization's mission, objectives, strategy, and policies.

Top management, in contrast, is responsible for the overall functioning of the corporation. People in top management must view the corporation as a whole rather than as a series of functional departments or decentralized divisions. They must constantly visualize and plan for the future, and set objectives, strategies, and policies that will allow the corporation to successfully realize that future. They must set standards and provide a vision not only of what the corporation is but also of what it is trying to become. They must develop working relationships with the board of directors, key staff personnel, and managers from divisions and functional areas.

The interaction between the board of directors and the top management of a corporation usually results in an overall strategic management style. The long-run success of a corporation is best ensured through a partnership style in which both the board and top management are genuinely involved in strategic issues.

DISCUSSION QUESTIONS

1. Does a corporation really need a board of directors? Why or why not?

2. What aspects of a corporation's environment should be represented on a board of directors?

3. Should cumulative voting for the election of board members be *required* by law in all political jurisdictions?

4. Do you agree that a chief executive officer (CEO), in order to be effective, should fulfill Mintzberg's ten roles?

5. Is partnership management always the best style of strategic management?

6. What is your impression of the approach to strategic management being taken by the strategic managers of CSX Corporation in the Integrative Case following this chapter?

NOTES

1. W. L. Shanklin and J. K. Ryans, Jr., "Should the Board Consider This Agenda Item?" *MSU Business Topics* (Winter 1981), p. 35.

2. W. R. Boulton, "The Evolving Board: A Look at the Board's Changing Roles and Information Needs," *Academy of Management Review* (October 1978), p. 828.

3. L. Iacocca, *Iacocca: An Autobiography* (Toronto: Bantam Books, 1984), p. 104.

4. M. L. Weidenbaum, "The Best Defense Against the Raiders," *Business Week* (September 23, 1985), p. 21. This belief is supported by research reporting that the stockholders of an acquiring firm tend to lose in the transaction. See M. Weidenbaum and S. Vogt, "Takeovers and Stockholders: Winners and Losers," *California Management Review* (Summer 1987), pp. 157–168.

5. J. Bacon and J. K. Brown, *Corporate Directorship Practices: Role, Selection and Legal Status of the Board* (New York: The Conference Board, Report no. 646, 1975), p. 7.

6. Bacon and Brown, p. 75.

7. G. Smith, "Who Was Watching the Store?" *Forbes* (July 30, 1984), pp. 37–38.
"Rolling Heads," *Time* (December 17, 1984), p. 69.

8. "What's a Board For, Anyway?" *Business Week* (August 11, 1986), p. 84.

9. L. B. Korn and R. M. Ferry, *Board of Directors Ninth Annual Study* (New York: Korn/Ferry International, February 1982), p. 8.

10. L. A. Hamermesh, "The Director As Auctioneer," *Directors and Boards* (Winter 1987), p. 26.

11. Bacon and Brown, p. 15.

12. K. R. Andrews, "Corporate Strategy as a Vital Function of the Board," *Harvard Business Review* (November-December 1981), p. 175.

13. J. Rosenstein, "Why Don't U.S. Boards Get More Involved in Strategy?" *Long Range Planning* (June 1987), pp. 32–33.

14. C. Mitchell, "Mellon's Chairman Pearson Says Extent of Bad Loans Shocked Outside Directors," *Wall Street Journal* (April 21, 1987), p. 2.

15. C. N. Waldo, *Boards of Directors* (Westport, Conn.: Quorum Books, 1985), p. 2.
A. V. Bruno and J. K. Leidecker, "When to Convert From a Perfunctory Board or 'Staff Meeting' to an Operating Board of Directors," in *Handbook of Business Strategy, 1985/1986 Yearbook,* edited by W. D. Guth (Boston: Warren, Gorham, and Lamont, 1985), pp. 29.1–29.9.

16. *Third Annual Banking Survey of Chief Executive Officers* (Atlanta, Chicago, New York: Egon Zehnder International, Inc., 1984), p. 9.

17. K. R. Andrews, "Directors' Responsibility for Corporate Strategy," *Harvard Business Review* (November-December 1980), p. 30.

18. Annual survey of Korn/Ferry International as reported by A. Bennett, "Losing Ground? Surveyed Firms Report Fewer Women Directors," *Wall Street Journal* (July 17, 1987), p. 17.

19. T. R. Horton, "The Case for Planning Committees," *Directors & Boards* (Summer 1984), p. 26.

20. A. Tashakori and W. Boulton, "A Look to the Board's Role in Planning," *Journal of Business Strategy* (Winter 1983), pp. 64–70.

21. E. Mruk and J. Giardina, *Organization and Compensation of Boards of Directors* (New York: Financial Executives Institute, Arthur Young & Co., 1981), pp. 11 and 39.
A. Patton and J. C. Baker, "Why Won't Directors Rock the Boat?" *Harvard Business Review* (November-December 1987), p. 11.

22. R. J. Bronstein, "Good Pay on Small Boards," *Directors and Boards* (Spring 1987), pp. 36–37.

23. D. R. Simpson, "Board Fees and Benefits 1987," *Directors and Boards* (Spring 1987), pp. 33–37.

24. R. J. Bronstein, p. 36.

25. K. R. Andrews, "The American Law Institute's Proposals for Regulating Corporate Governance," *Harvard Business Review* (November-December 1982), p. 34.

26. R. D. Kosnik, "Greenmail: A Study of Board Performance in Corporate Governance," *Administrative Science Quarterly* (June 1987), pp. 163–185.
B. D. Baysinger and C. P. Zeithaml, "A Contingency Approach to Corporate Strategy and Board Composition: Theory and Empirical Research," Paper presented at the Annual Meetings of the Academy of Management, San Diego, August, 1985.

27. S. C. Vance, *Corporate Leadership: Boards, Directors, and Strategy* (New York: McGraw-Hill Book Company, 1983), p. 274.

28. I. F. Kesner, "Directors Stock Ownership and Organizational Performance: An Investigation of Fortune 500 Companies," *Journal of Management* (Fall 1987), pp. 499–507.
"A Little Ownership By Directors Is Good For Business," *Business Week* (December 8, 1986), p. 24.

29. J. A. Pearce, "The Relationship of Internal versus External Orientations to Financial Measures of Strategic Performance," *Strategic Management Journal* (December 1983), pp. 297–306.

30. P. Harrison, "On the Other Side of the Roadblock," *Directors and Boards* (Fall 1986), pp. 40–41; and *Wall Street Journal* (January 1, 1988), p. 1.

31. E. S. Buffa, "Making American Manufacturing Competitive," *California Management Review* (Spring 1984), p. 39.
J. Bacon, *Corporate Directorship Practices: Membership and Committees of the Board* (New York: The Conference Board, Report no. 588, 1973), pp. 28–29.

32. T. H. Hammer and R. N. Stern, "Worker Representation on Company Boards of Directors," *Proceedings, Academy of Management,* 1983, p. 368.

33. R. J. Kuhne, *Co-Determination in Business* (New York: Praeger Publishers, 1980), pp. 41–71.

34. L. H. Clark, Jr., "What Economists Say about Business—and Baboons," *Wall Street Journal* (June 7, 1983), p. 33. Article summarizes a research paper by G. Benelli, C. Loderer, and T. Lys presented to the Interlaken Seminar on Analysis and Ideology, Interlaken, Switzerland, 1983.

For further information on the German experience see articles by Thimm and by Thelen in the *California Management Review* (Spring 1987), pp. 115–148. The more radical Swedish approach is discussed by H. G. Jones in "Scenarios for Industrial Relations: Sweden Evolves a New Consensus," *Long Range Planning* (June 1987), pp. 65–76.

35. M. H. Bazerman and F. D. Schoorman, "A Limited Rationality Model of Interlocking Directorates," *Academy of Management Review* (April 1983), pp. 206–217.

M. Ornstein, "Interlocking Directorates in Canada: Intercorporate or Class Alliance?" *Administrative Science Quarterly* (June 1984), pp. 210–231.

36. R. S. Burt, "Cooptive Corporate Actor Networks: A Reconsideration of Interlocking Directorates Involving American Manufacturing," *Administrative Science Quarterly* (December 1980), p. 559.

L. B. Stearns and M. S. Mizruchi, "Broken-Tie Reconstitution and the Functions of Interorganizational Interlocks: A Reexamination," *Administrative Science Quarterly* (December 1986), pp. 522–538.

37. For a more in-depth discussion of this topic, refer to J. M. Pennings, *Interlocking Directorates* (San Francisco: Jossey-Bass, 1980), and M. S. Mizruchi, *The American Corporate Network 1904–1974* (Beverly Hills, Calif.: Sage Publications, 1982).

38. Patton and Baker.

39. Burt, p. 566.

40. G. R. Roche, "Committees Come to the Fore," *Directors and Boards* (Fall 1986), pp. 22–23.

41. R. C. Ochsner, "Directors Pay Develops Into a Dynamic Package," *Directors and Boards* (February 1986), p. 46.

42. Bacon, pp. 7–8.

43. A. C. Regan and A. Reichel, " 'Shark Repellents': How to Avoid Hostile Takeovers," *Long Range Planning* (December 1985), p. 62.

44. Korn and Ferry, p. 3; and Mruk and Giardina, p. 39.

45. I. F. Kesner, B. Victor, and B. T. Lamont, "Board Composition and the Commission of Illegal Acts: An Investigation of Fortune 500 Companies," *Academy of Management Journal* (December 1986), pp. 789–799.

46. J. C. Worthy and R. P. Neuschel, *Emerging Issues in Corporate Governance* (Evanston, Illinois: Northwestern University Press, 1983), pp. 15–18.

47. L. Barker, "Director Compensation 1984," *Directors & Boards* (Spring 1984), p. 39.

48. For further information on board committees, refer to Waldo, pp. 65–85; Roche, pp. 23–23; and J. R. Harrison, "The Strategic Use of Corporate Board Committees," *California Management Review* (Fall 1987), pp. 109–125.

49. Waldo, p. 173.

50. Taken from C. A. Anderson and R. N. Anthony, *The New Corporate Directors* (New York: John Wiley and Sons, 1986), pp. 221–241.

51. C. D. McCreesh, "Benchmark Changes in D & O Liability Statutes," *Directors and Boards* (Spring 1987), pp. 16–18.

52. W. E. Simon, "The Board Is at a Crossroad," *Directors and Boards* (Fall 1986), p. 4.

53. "Director Certification: Should You Prove Competence to Sit on a Board?" *Wall Street Journal* (February 17, 1987), p. 1.

54. Worthy and Neuschel, p. 100.

55. Bacon and Brown, p. 25.

Andrews, 1980, p. 36.

W. R. Boulton, "Effective Board Development: Five Areas of Concern," *Journal of Business Strategy* (Spring 1983), pp. 94–100.

H. S. Geneen, "Why Directors Can't Protect the Stockholders," *Fortune* (September 17, 1984), p. 29.

56. P. F. Drucker, *Management: Tasks, Responsibilities, Practices* (New York: Harper & Row, 1974), p. 613.

57. Adapted from H. Mintzberg, *The Nature of Managerial Work* (New York: Harper & Row, 1973), pp. 54–94.

58. Drucker, pp. 611–612.

59. T. H. Pincus, "A Crisis Parachute: Helping Stock Prices Have a Soft Landing," *Journal of Business Strategy* (Spring 1986), pp. 35–36.

60. R. P. Beatly and E. J. Zajac, "CEO Change and Firm Performance in Large Corporations: Succession Effects and Manager Effects," *Strategic Management Journal* (July-August 1987), p. 315.

61. T. J. Peters and R. H. Waterman, *In Search of Excellence* (New York: Harper & Row, 1982), p. 26.

62. A. Levitt, Jr., and J. Albertine, "The Successful Entrepreneur: A Personality Profile," *Wall Street Journal* (August 29, 1983), p. 12.

63. Advertisement in *Business Week* (October 23, 1987), pp. 118–119.

64. Adapted from R. J. House, "A 1976 Theory of Charismatic Leadership," *Leadership: The Cutting Edge*, eds. J. G. Hunt and L. L. Larson (Carbondale, Ill.: SIU Press, 1977), pp. 189–207.

This view of executive leadership is also referred to as *transformational leadership*. See *Emerging Leadership Vistas*, edited by J. G. Hunt, B. R. Baliga, H. P. Dachler, and C. A. Schriesheim (Lexington, Mass.: Lexington Books, 1988), pp. 5–84.

65. M. Trevor, "Japanese Decision-making and Global Strategy," in *Strategic Management Research: A European Perspective*, edited by J. McGee and H. Thomas (Chichester, U.K.: John Wiley and Sons, 1986), pp. 301.

66. S. Matlins and G. Knisely, "Update: Profile of the Corporate Planners," *Journal of Business Strategy* (Spring 1981), pp. 75 and 77.

67. C. D. Burnett, D. P. Yeskey, and D. Richardson, "New Roles for Corporate Planners in the 1980's," *Journal of Business Strategy* (Spring 1984), p. 67.

68. B. T. Houlden, "Developing a Company's Strategic Management Capability," *Long Range Planning* (October 1986), p. 92.

J. F. Orsini, "Artificial Intelligence: A Way Through the Strategic Planning Crisis?" *Long Range Planning* (August 1986), p. 71.

69. Drucker, pp. 615–617.

70. Mintzberg, p. 33.

71. J. P. Wright, *On a Clear Day You Can See General Motors* (Grosse Pointe, Mich.: Wright Enterprises, 1979), p. 28.

72. E. Ehrlich, "What the Boss Is Really Like," *Business Week* (October 23, 1987), pp. 37–44.

73. N. Gross, "Corporate Revitalization—Via Team Planning," in *Handbook of Business Strategy, 1985/1986 Year-*

book, edited by W. D. Guth (Boston: Warren, Gorham and Lamont, 1985), pp. 24.1–24.15.

E. Ginzberg and G. Vojta, *Beyond Human Scale: The Large Corporation At Risk* (New York: Basic Books, 1985).

J. R. Galbraith and R. K. Kazanjian, *Strategy Implementation* (St. Paul: West Publishing Company, 1986), pp. 147–149.

74. R. F. Vancil, "How Companies Pick New CEOs," *Fortune* (January 18, 1988), p. 75.

75. R. Gibson, "Control Data's Comeback Faces Rough Road," *Wall Street Journal* (June 17, 1985), p. 6.

76. J. R. Healey, "Hanson Cracks the Whip at Winnebago," *Des Moines Register* (January 19, 1986), pp. 1F and 4F.

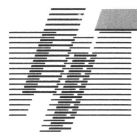

INTEGRATIVE CASE

CSX CORPORATION'S STRATEGIC MANAGERS

The first chairman of CSX was Prime F. Osborn, III, Chairman and CEO of Seaboard Coast Line Industries, Inc. Mr. Osborn acted as co-chief executive with Hays T. Watkins, who had served as Chairman and CEO of the Chessie System before the merger. From the very beginning of CSX, it was stressed that the corporation was to be a real partnership of equals. Even one year after the merger, *Business Week* reported that Osborn and Watkins "Practically make a fetish out of the partnership relationship of the two component railroads. Although one man is chairman and the other president, they insist they are truly co-chief executive officers."

This spirit of teamwork was embodied in the very name of the corporation. At the time of the merger, published reports quoted Hays T. Watkins as saying that the name CSX, originally chosen as a temporary working label, might become a permanent name. "Prime (Osborn) and I thought it up and like it because it's so anonymous and nondistinctive—the way we want the parent to be in relation to its operating railroads. . . . C is for Chessie, S is for Seaboard and X is for unknown, implying more," Watkins explained. One year after the merger, an article on CSX in *Business Week* carried the following statement, "Both Watkins and Prime F. Osborn, III, CSX's chairman, are fond of telling anyone who will listen that the 'X' in the name is the multiplication symbol, indicating that the company is much bigger than one plus one."

BOARDS OF DIRECTORS

To further reinforce this notion of a partnership, Osborn and Watkins adopted an interesting tactic: Chessie and Seaboard retained boards of directors that were distinct

---

SOURCE: Taken from "CSX Corporation" by J. D. Hunger, B. Ferrin, H. Felix-Gamez, and T. Goetzman in *Cases in Strategic Management and Business Policy* by T. L. Wheelen and J. D. Hunger (Reading, Mass.: Addison-Wesley, 1987), pp. 91–123.

from each other's and from the board of CSX. Watkins, who had been Chief Executive at Chessie, became Chairman of the Seaboard System board, while Osborn, who came from the Seaboard System, became Chairman of the Chessie board. "Flipping chairmanships is just one more device for cross-fertilization, for showing that this is a true partnership," said Watkins. Since the retirement of Osborn in 1982, Watkins assumed both roles of Chairman and CEO of CSX. The position of CSX President was assumed by Paul Funkhouser, who had been President and Chief Executive of the Seaboard System from the time of the merger until the retirement of Mr. Osborn.

The CSX Board was composed of twenty-seven members in 1985. (See Table 3.1.) Only five members of the Board were technically insiders, although a sixth (Mr. Osborn, the retired Chairman of the corporation) could have been considered an inside director. At the time of the merger creating the company, it was decided that Chessie and Seaboard would each have twelve seats on a twenty-four-person Board of Directors, even though the Seaboard shareholders wound up in control of slightly more stock in CSX than did the Chessie holders.

TABLE 3.1
CSX Board of Directors

Edward J. Boling*
President and Chief Executive Officer—The University of Tennessee, Knoxville, TN

Charles K. Cross, Sr.
Chairman of the Board and CEO—Barnett Bank of Central Florida, Orlando, FL

Frederick Deane, Jr.*
Chairman of the Board and CEO—Bank of Virginia Co., Richmond, VA

A. Paul Funkhouser*
President—CSX Corp., Richmond, VA

Richard A. Jay
Retired Vice-Chairman of the Board—Goodyear Tire and Rubber Co., Akron, OH

Clifford M. Kirtland, Jr.
Retired Chairman of the Board—Cox Communications, Inc., Atlanta, GA

John H. Lumpkin, Sr.
Honorary Chairman of the Board—South Carolina National Corp., Columbia, SC

William E. McGuirk, Jr.
Chairman of the Board—Mercantile Bankshares Corp., Baltimore, MD

Frank M. Northfleet
Chairman of the Board—Parts Industries Corp., Memphis, TN

Prime F. Osborn III
Retired Chairman of the Board—CSX Corp., Richmond, VA

Nicholas T. Camicia
Retired Chairman of the Board—The Pittston Co., Greenwich, CT

John T. Collinson
President and CEO—Chessie System Railroads, Cleveland, OH

John N. Dalton*
Senior Partner—McGuire, Woods & Battle, Richmond, VA

Alonzo G. Decker, Jr.
Honorary Chairman of the Board and Chairman of Executive Committee—The Black and Decker Mfr. Co., Baltimore, MD

Floyd D. Gottwald, Jr.
Chairman of the Board and CEO—Ethyl Corp., Richmond, VA

TOP MANAGEMENT

The role of the CSX parent was, according to Chairman and CEO Hayes Watkins, to coordinate operations, not to manage them. Major concerns of corporate management were to be finance, policy and shareholder relations, net income, and the company's progress against its major competitor, Norfolk Southern. According to Hays Watkins,

> Our management strategy . . . is to leave day-to-day operations largely with our subsidiaries. We at CSX . . . concentrate on what we call the three P's— Policy, Planning and Policing. We provide the broad policy and program guidance, and then we make sure that guidance is carried out. We at the CSX level also ensure that proper coordination is achieved among our various subsidiaries.
>
> We don't want to be an added bureaucracy that would run the organizations. We merely handle policy matters here. We're all overhead. We don't generate any mileage or freight. And we've been careful to keep our group small.

CSX and its subsidiaries were coordinated by a policy board composed of the top executives from each of the divisions plus the corporate office. Mr. Watkins reported,

---

Mary T. Kimpton
Economic Consultant to Business
and Government, Chicago, IL

Richard L. Leatherwood
President and CEO—Texas Gas
Resources Corp., Richmond, VA

Charles P. Lykes
Chairman of the Board and CEO—
Lykes Bros., Inc., Tampa, FL

Steven Muller
President—The Johns Hopkins
University, Baltimore, MD

James L. O'Keefe
Senior Partner—O'Keefe,
Ashendon, Lyons & Ward,
Chicago, IL

W. James Price
Managing Director—Alex, Brown
& Sons, Inc., Baltimore, MD

Robert H. Radcliff
Chairman of the Board and CEO—
Radcliff Marine Services, Inc.,
Mobile, AL

John K. Stevenson
Retired President—R.M. Stevenson
Co., Bloomfield Hills, MI

Alvin W. Vogtle, Jr.
Retired Chairman of the Board—
The Southern Co., Atlanta, GA

Richard D. Sandborn
President and CEO—Seaboard
System Railroad, Inc., Jacksonville,
FL

William B. Sturgill*
President—East Kentucky
Investment Co., Lexington, KY

Hays T. Watkins*
Chairman of the Board and CEO—
CSX Corp., Richmond, VA

SOURCE: *1984 Annual Report,* CSX Corporation, p. 44.
*Indicates Member of the Executive Committee.

TABLE 3.2
CSX Executive Officers

Hays T. Watkins Chairman of the Board and Chief Executive Officer	**Carl C. Hawk** Vice-President and Corporate Secretary
A. Paul Funkhouser President	**Kemper K. Hyers** Vice-President—Government Relations (State)
Robert L. Hintz Executive Vice-President	**Edward H. Latchford** Vice-President—Accounting and Financial Planning
John W. Snow Executive Vice-President	**James T. Lyon** Vice-President—Taxes
Gerald L. Nichols Senior Vice-President— Administration	**Woodruff M. Price** Vice-President—Government Relations
Josiah A. Stanley, Jr. Senior Vice-President—Audit	**Garth E. Griffith** General Counsel
Edwin E. Edel Vice-President—Corporate Communications	**Mark G. Aron** General Counsel—Special Projects
James Ermer Vice-President—Treasurer	
John H. Gobel Vice-President—Government Relations (State)	

SOURCE: *1984 Annual Report,* CSX Corporation, p. 15.

We meet at least once every other week and talk about policy matters. We also have three CSX staff people meeting with us regularly as members of the policy board; the senior vice-president of finance, the senior vice-president of corporate services (supervising the corporate secretary, public relations, the general counsel, and government affairs activities), and a recorder who is our office administrator.

Mr. Watkins emphasized the importance of finance at the corporate level. The financial person, according to Watkins, was "the key staff associate of CSX. He's the one that the president and I work with the most. . . . I guess we've had a culture around here for many years that the finance man is probably the single most important staff member of the company." This attitude was not surprising in view of Mr. Watkins's background, which included an M.B.A. from Northwestern University and a thirty-year career with the Chessie system in a variety of accounting and financial positions.

CSX corporate officers are listed in Table 3.2.

CHAPTER 4

THE EXTERNAL ENVIRONMENT

STRATEGIC MANAGEMENT MODEL

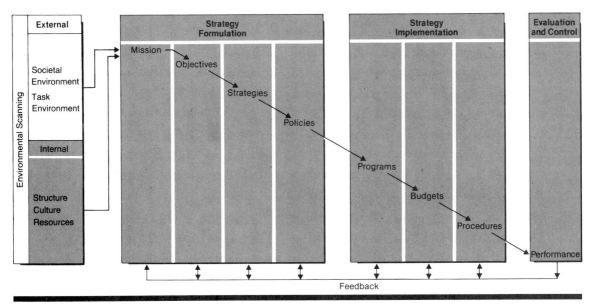

Business corporations do not exist in a vacuum. They arise out of society's need for a particular product or service and can continue to exist in freedom only so long as they acknowledge their role in the larger society. Therefore, corporations must constantly be aware of the key variables in their environment. These variables may be within a firm's task environment or in its larger societal environment (see Fig. 4.1). The **task environment** includes those elements or groups that directly affect the corporation and, in turn, are affected by it. These are governments, local communities, suppliers, competitors, customers, creditors, employees/labor unions, special interest groups, and trade associations. A corporation's task environment is the specific **industry** within which that corporation operates. The **societal environment** includes the more general forces that do not directly touch on the short-run activities of the organization but that can, and often do, influence its long-run decisions. These, also shown in Fig. 4.1, are as follows:

- **Economic forces** that regulate the exchange of materials, money, energy, and information.
- **Sociocultural forces** that regulate the values, mores, and customs of society.
- **Technological forces** that generate problem-solving inventions.
- **Political-legal forces** that allocate power and provide constraining and protecting laws and regulations.

All of these variables and forces constantly interact with each other. In the short run, societal forces affect the decisions and actions of a corporation

FIGURE 4.1
Key Environmental Variables.

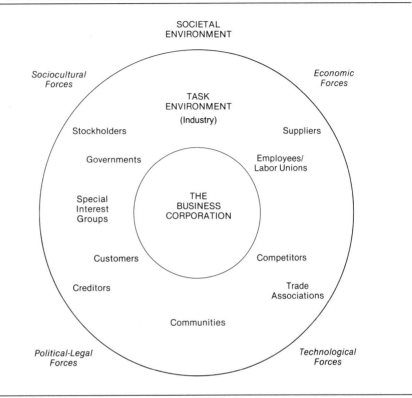

through the groups in its task environment. In the long run, however, the corporation also affects these groups through its activities. For example, the decision by a number of U.S. business corporations to relocate their manufacturing facilities to Asia and Latin America in order to reduce labor costs has increased the unemployment of U.S. blue-collar workers—and thus reduced union membership, adversely affected the country's balance of trade with other nations, and created economic depressions in those communities dependent for employment and tax revenue on the now-closed plants.

4.1

BUSINESS AND SOCIETY: A DELICATE RELATIONSHIP

For centuries, business corporations have lived in an uneasy truce with society. Exchange and commercial activities, along with laws governing them, are as old as recorded history. The Code of Hammurabi, established about 2000 B.C., provided guidelines for merchants and peddlers.[1] The Old Testament is filled with examples of commercial activity and the laws and regulations governing them. Greek philosophers, in general, regarded commercial activities as necessary but distasteful. The Romans, like the Greeks, were necessarily tolerant of commercial activity, but gave those so engaged a low status.[2] During the early years of the Middle Ages, the Roman Catholic Church held business and commercial activity in disdain and governed it through strict rules and limitations. Usury, the lending of money at interest, for instance, was decreed a mortal sin for Christians, who were forbidden the practice, although Jews were permitted to engage in it. Trade itself was of dubious purity, and the gathering of wealth was considered an action directly opposed to the charitable teachings of Jesus Christ. This view of trade and commerce and the associated accumulation of capital as necessary evils was commonly accepted in the Western world until the Protestant Reformation. The Eastern world, in contrast, was much more tolerant and accepting of business activities.

Development of the Capitalistic Ethic

With the end of the Middle Ages, values began to change in the West, and business activities were viewed more positively. Max Weber, noted economist and sociologist, postulated that changes in the religious ethic resulting from the Reformation and the Protestant movement provided an economic climate highly favorable for the development of capitalism.[3] A new spirit of individualism developed out of the Renaissance and was encouraged by humanism and Protestantism. Society placed a high value on frugality, thrift, and hard word—key elements of what is commonly referred to as the **Protestant ethic.**

Free trade was not, however, commonly accepted until much later. After the Reformation, kings and queens replaced the Church as earthly rulers. They established their right to regulate business activity through the concept of **mercantilism.** According to this concept, the individual was subordinate to the state, and all economic and business activity was dedicated to supporting the power of the state. Under mercantilism, Europeans set up organizations, such as the East India Company, to trade with the natives of distant lands and to return with goods valuable to crown and country.

In 1776, however, economist Adam Smith advanced a theory justifying capitalism in his book *An Inquiry into the Nature and Causes of the Wealth of Nations.* Smith argued that economic freedom would enable individuals through self-interest to fulfill themselves and would thereby benefit the total society. He used the term **laissez-faire** to suggest that government should leave business alone. The "invisible hand" of the marketplace would, through pure competition, ensure maximum benefit to society.

The doctrine of *laissez-faire,* as postulated by Smith and refined by others, called for society to give business corporations increasing autonomy so that they could accomplish their work—the production and sale of goods and services. In the rapidly changing world of the eighteenth and nineteenth centuries such work was considered worthwhile and valuable to society. For example, James Watt's development of a usable steam engine permitted muscle power to be replaced by an external power source and resulted in enormous increases in the production and distribution of scarce goods. Because of these benefits, governments relaxed many of their restrictions on commerce and trade, and allowed capital to accumulate and business to flourish.

Society Supports Free Enterprise

As changes in sociocultural values were fed by the benefits of new technology and *laissez-faire* economics, governments in the West began to support independent businesses. During much of the early part of the nineteenth century in the United States, government favored the development of commerce and industry. The Supreme Court, for example, ruled that the private corporation was a legal entity, and Congress passed tariff laws protecting business interests. In addition, the government provided vast sums of money and land for the rapidly expanding railroads.[4] As pointed out by McGuire,

> . . . the Federal government attempted to encourage business activities with a minimum of regulation and intervention. . . . Government's task in these years, it was thought by many politicians and businessmen, was to aid business enterprise in accord with the best principles of mercantilism and still leave business free to grow and develop without restraint, as set forth in the doctrine of *laissez-faire.* The tradition thus grew that businessmen in the United States could do what so few people were able to do—have their cake and eat it too.[5]

Beginnings of Regulation

In the late 1800s and early 1900s, the public began to find some business practices antisocial. This dissatisfaction was expressed increasingly. Karl Marx, who wrote *The Communist Manifesto* with Friedrich Engels in 1848 and *Das Kapital* in 1867, put into words much of this dissatisfaction. He, as well as many others, rejected the capitalistic ethic because of its many unsavory side-effects, such as child labor, unsafe working conditions, and subsistence wages. The development of monopolistic corporations and cartels caused various groups within the United States to demand some form of regulation. Although most U.S. citizens rejected the Marxist view, they challenged the *laissez-faire* concept and suggested that Adam Smith's economic system was based on a pure, competitive model that was ineffective in a system of entrenched monopolies and oligopolies. As a result, the U.S. federal government, to reclaim some of the freedom and autonomy it had granted business, enacted such legislation as the Interstate Commerce Act (1887), the Sherman Antitrust Act (1890), the Pure Food and Drug Act (1906), the Clayton Act (1914), and the Federal Trade Commission Act (1914). More restrictive laws were to follow.

A Question of Autonomy

The Great Depression of the 1930s, Keynesian economics, and the increasing popularity of socialism as a political force resulted in business losing even more of its autonomy to government. Governments all over the world assumed responsibility for their economies. In 1946, the U.S. Congress passed the Fair Employment Act, which states that the federal government has prime responsibility for the maintenance of full employment and full utilization of economic resources.[6] Through the decades of the 50s, 60s, and 70s, *laissez-faire,* if not dead, was certainly forgotten as people put their faith in a democratically elected central government rather than the self-interest of capitalists.

Consecutive years of profits earned by American big business during these prosperous decades suggested to a number of people that business was not truly paying its way in society. Increasingly, problems with product safety and environmental pollution were seen as the negative consequences of business peoples' selfish concern only with profits. Some of these feelings were expressed in 1962 by President Kennedy after the U.S. steel industry ignored his request to refrain from raising prices during a time of inflation.

> Some time ago I asked each American to consider what he would do for his country, and I asked steel companies. In the last 24 hours we had their answer. . . . My father always told me that all businessmen were sons of bitches, but I never believed it until now.[7]

Business people were increasingly constrained in their decision making by laws regarding air and water pollution, product safety, and employment practices, among others. In the United States, the number of federal agencies involved in regulating business activity increased from forty-nine in 1960 to eighty-three in 1970. Firms in the steel industry alone faced 5,600 regulations from twenty-seven federal agencies. The total cost of regulation to American business corporations in 1976 alone has been estimated at approximately $30 billion.[8] All around the world businesses were threatened by governments with more regulation or even by outright nationalization. Business autonomy was seriously threatened.

National Policy—Modern Mercantilism?

With the coming of the 1980s, the relationship between business and government changed. The labor productivity growth rate that had steadily increased in the United States for nearly two hundred years slowed and became negative during the period from 1978 to 1980.[9] Focusing upon high-volume standardized production, major Western firms found to their chagrin that companies in the developing nations had copied their technology. With lower production costs due to lower wages, among other factors, these companies in the third world were able to seriously erode the market share and profits of the business corporations in the industrialized countries of the West. Faced with serious problems of unemployment and balance of trade problems, governments of the United States, Great Britain, and other Western nations acted to reduce some of the constraints they had previously placed on business activity.

A number of people argued that not only should business be given more autonomy, but also that the national government should be an active supporter of business development. Stating that other nations with supportive industrial policies—such as Japan, Korea, and Singapore—had more competitive business corporations than did many Western nations, proposals for a sort of modern mercantilism were developed. Reich, in his influential book *The Next American Frontier,* contended that the federal government should develop a better system to help move U.S. industry more quickly out of high-volume standardized production into more flexible, quality-oriented systems of production using skilled labor.[10] National governments throughout the world were coming to think of business activity as the key to economic well-being. Questions of social responsibility were temporarily forgotten as people worried more about unemployment than pollution.

Unfortunately, by the latter half of the 1980s, problems of toxic waste, hazardous manufacturing plants, and unsafe products again became important topics for discussion as people once more became concerned about the disturbing side-effects of economic activity. Allegations of insider trading and other questionable activities in financial organizations around the world revealed some business people to have very low standards of ethics. Revelations in 1987 of automobile odometer tampering and the overexposure of workers to lead and arsenic in the workplace by Chrysler Corporation raised once again the issue of the extent to which business management is responsible to the society of which the organization is a part.[11]

4.2

SOCIAL RESPONSIBILITY

The concept that business must be socially responsible sounds appealing until one asks, "Responsible to whom?" As was shown in Fig. 4.1, the task environment includes a large number of groups with interest in a corporation's activities. These groups are referred to as **stakeholders** because they affect or are affected by the achievement of the firm's objectives.[12] Should a corporation be responsible only to some of these groups, or does business have a responsibility to all of them?

The corporation must pay close attention to its task environment, because its stakeholders are very responsive to the general trends in the societal environment and will typically translate these trends into direct pressure that affects corporate activities. Even if top management assumes the traditional *laissez-faire* stance that the major concern of its corporation is to make profits, it will find (often to its chagrin) that it must also be concerned with the effects of its profit-making on stakeholders within its task environment. Each stakeholder uses its own criteria to determine how well a corporation is performing, and each is constantly judging top management's actions in terms of their effect on itself. Therefore, top management must be aware not only of the key stakeholders in the corporation's task environment, but also of the criteria each group uses to judge the corporation's performance. The following is a list of some of these stakeholders and their probable criteria.

Stockholders	Price appreciation of securities. Dividends (How much and how often?).
Unions	Comparable wages. Stability of employment. Opportunity for advancement. Working conditions.
Governments	Support of government programs. Adherence to laws and regulations.
Suppliers	Rapidity of payment. Consistency of purchases.
Creditors	Adherence to contract terms. Dependability.
Customers/Distributors	Value given for the price paid. Availability of product or service.
Trade associations	Participation in association programs (time). Participation in association programs (money).
Competitors	Rate of growth (encroachment on their markets). Product or service innovation (source of new ideas to use).
Communities	Contribution to community development through taxes, participation in charitable activities, etc. Employment of local people. Minimum of negative side-effects (e.g., pollution).

Special interest groups Employment of minority groups.
Contributions to urban improvement programs.
Provision of free services to the disadvantaged.

Priority of Concerns

In any one decision regarding corporate strategy, the interests of one stakeholder can conflict with another. For example, a business firm's decision to build a plant in an inner-city location may have a positive effect on community relations but a negative effect on stockholder dividends. Which group's interests have priority?

In a survey sponsored by the American Management Association, 6,000 managers and executives were asked to rate on a seven-point scale the importance of a number of corporate stakeholders.[13] As shown in Table 4.1, executives felt customers to be the most important concern. Employees were also rated highly. Interestingly, the general public was felt to be of similar importance as stockholders. Owners (presumably those who own large blocks of stock), however, were rated as more important than either the public or more typical stockholders. Government representatives were rated as least important of all the groups considered.

Pressures on the Business Corporation

Because of the wide range of interests and concerns present in any corporation's task environment, one or more groups, at any one time, probably will be dissatisfied with a corporation's activities. For example, consider General Motors' decision in 1987 to close eleven of its manufacturing and assembly plants located throughout Michigan, Illinois, and Ohio. The com-

TABLE 4.1
Importance to Executives of Various Stakeholders

STAKEHOLDER	RANK
Customers	6.40
Employees	6.01
Owners	5.30
General public	4.52
Stockholders	4.51
Elected public officials	3.79
Government bureaucrats	2.90

SOURCE: Adapted from B. Z. Posner and W. H. Schmidt, "Values and the American Manager: An Update." Copyright © 1984 by the Regents of the University of California. Reprinted from the *California Management Review*, Vol. 26, No. 3, p. 206. By permission of The Regents.

NOTE: The ranking is calculated on a scale of 7 (most important) to 1 (least important).

pany's profits and market share had seriously dropped and it could no longer pay the costs of excess capacity. One of the plants to be closed was in Norwood, Ohio, where GM employed 4,200 workers and paid nearly 40% of the city's taxes. Faced with the imminent loss of its primary employer, the city of Norwood needed financial aid to provide essential services to its citizens.

City officials asked the GM management for extra money to help cover the tax shortage, but were refused. Consequently, Norwood filed a lawsuit against GM asking for $318.3 million as "alimony" for "breach of contract." The city contended that it had gone out of its way to build schools, add police and fire protection, plus widen streets and build an underpass in response to GM's requests and promises of expansion. Norwood argued that the company had implied responsibilities to the city beyond its service simply as an employer and tax payer. GM's top management was in a situation of being damned by its stockholders if it failed to close the plants and damned by the cities if it did![14]

Another controversial issue was the presence of more than 300 United States business corporations in South Africa. Because of the apartheid policy of strict racial segregation and discrimination against non-whites of the South African government, many critics of apartheid have been urging U.S. firms to withdraw their business. American corporations controlled nearly 70% of South Africa's computer industry and half of its petroleum business in the early 1980s. Anti-apartheid spokespeople argued that the presence of such important firms as IBM, Exxon, G.E., GM, Kodak, Johnson and Johnson, Hewlett-Packard, and Ford, among others, gave tacit approval and financial support to a "racist" government. Calls for the *disinvestment* of American business in South Africa were criticized, however, by some black South Africans with a different point of view. Mangosutu Gatsha Buthelezi, hereditary Prime Minister of the Zulu nation, commented, "No one has proved to us that the suffering which will ensue within the black community as a result of disinvestment will actually force the regime to effect the fundamental changes all of us are clamoring for."[15] Torn between two conflicting demands, around 150 U.S. business corporations chose a compromise position in 1985. They remained in South Africa, but signed and followed the *Sullivan Code,* a set of equal-opportunity and fair-treatment principles drawn up by Leon H. Sullivan, minister of Philadelphia's Zion Baptist Church and a director of General Motors. A number of Canadian companies followed a voluntary Canadian government code for conducting business in South Africa. Nevertheless, in 1987 Sullivan repudiated his code because of its failure to end apartheid. He urged the total withdrawal of all business firms. Increasing numbers of U.S. and Canadian business organizations chose to close or sell their holdings in South Africa. Even then, many of them were criticized because they continued to supply parts to the then-South African-owned businesses.[16]

The previous examples indicate how easily a business corporation can run into problems—even when top management is trying to achieve the best outcome for all involved. There are other examples, however, of business firms engaging in very questionable, unethical, or even illegal actions. These examples reveal the dark side of corporate decision making and support those arguments in favor of increased governmental regulation and decreased business autonomy. There is no doubt that the top managements of some business firms have sometimes made decisions emphasizing short-term profitability or personal gain over long-term relations with governments, local communities, suppliers, and even customers and employees. For example, here are some of the questionable practices that have been exposed in recent years:

- Possible negligent construction and management practices at nuclear power and chemical plants (for example, nuclear plants at Three Mile Island and Diablo Canyon, and Union Carbide's chemical plant in Bhopal, India).[17]
- Improper disposal of toxic wastes (for instance, at Love Canal).[18]
- Production and sale of defective products (for example, A. H. Robbins' Dalkon Shield birth-control device).[19]
- Declaring bankruptcy to cancel a labor contract and cut wages (for instance, Wilson Foods and Continental Airlines).[20]
- Insufficient safeguarding of employees from exposure to dangerous chemicals and materials in the workplace (for instance, the asbestos problem at Manville Corporation and cyanide poisoning at Film Recovery Systems).[21]
- Continuous instances of fraud, bribery, and price fixing at corporations of all sizes and locations (for example, National Semiconductor's defrauding the Defense Department by failure to test electronic components properly, General Electric's illegal claims for more than $800,000 in cost overruns on Minuteman missile contracts, and E. F. Hutton's overdraft scheme that cost banks an estimated $8 million over a two-year period).[22]

Ethics: A Question of Values

Such questionable practices by business corporations run counter to the values of society as a whole and are justly criticized and prosecuted. Why are actions taken that so obviously harm important stakeholders in the corporation's task environment? Are business corporations and the people who run them amoral, or are they simply ignorant of the many consequences of their actions?

Cultural Differences

One reason for such behavior is that there is no worldwide standard of conduct for businesspeople. Cultural norms and values vary between countries and even between different geographic regions and ethnic groups within a country. One example is the use of payoffs and bribes to influence a potential customer's decision to buy from a particular supplier. Although this practice is considered illegal in the United States, it is deeply entrenched in many countries. In Mexico, for instance, the payoff, referred to as *la mordida* (the bite), is considered a fringe benefit or *propina* (a tip).[23]

Personal Differences

Another possible reason for a corporation's questionable practices lies in differences in values between top management and key stakeholders in the task environment. Some businesspeople might believe that profit maximization is the key goal of their firm, whereas concerned interest groups might have other goals, such as the hiring of minorities and women or the safety of their neighborhoods.

Economist Milton Friedman, in urging a return to a *laissez-faire* style of worldwide economy, argues against the concept of social responsibility. If a businessperson acts "responsibly" by cutting the price of the firm's product to prevent inflation, or by making expenditures to reduce pollution, or by hiring the hard-core unemployed, that person, according to Friedman, is spending the stockholder's money for a general social interest. Even if the businessperson has stockholders' permission or encouragement to do so, he or she is still acting from motives other than economic and can, in the long run, cause harm to the very society the firm is trying to help. By taking on the burden of these social costs, the business becomes less efficient; and either prices go up to pay for the increased costs, or investment in new activities and research is postponed. These results negatively affect—perhaps fatally—the long-term efficiency of a business. Friedman thus referred to the social responsibility of business as a "fundamentally subversive doctrine" and stated that "there is one and only one social responsibility of business— to use its resources and engage in activities designed to increase its profits so long as it stays within the rules of the game, which is to say, engages in open and free competition without deception or fraud."[24]

Friedman's stand on free enterprise has been both criticized and praised. Business people tend to agree with Friedman because his views are compatible not only with their own self-interests but also with their hierarchy of values. When tested on the six values measured by the Allport-Vernon-Lindzey "Study of Values" test (aesthetic, economic, political, religious, social, and theoretical), both U.S. and British executives scored high on economic and political values, and low on social and religious ones. Protestant ministers, in contrast, scored high on religious and social values, and very low on economic values.[25]

Imagine the controversy that would result if a group composed of ministers and executives had to decide the following strategy issues: Should business firms close on Sunday? Should the corporation hire handicapped workers and accept the increased training costs associated with their employment? In discussing these issues, the executive would probably be very concerned with the effects on the "bottom line" (profits), whereas the minister would probably be concerned with the effects on society and salvation (a very different bottom line).

This conclusion is supported by a study of 6,000 executives and managers who were asked to rate a representative sample of typical organizational goals, as depicted in Table 4.2. The results clearly show community service and public service ranked at the bottom of the list under organizational effectiveness and profit maximization.[26] This study generally agrees with previous studies that revealed a desire by businesspeople to limit their social responsibilities to those areas in which they can clearly see benefits to the corporation, in terms of reduced costs and less governmental regulation.[27] This very narrow view of businesses' responsibilities to society typically will cause conflicts between the business corporation and certain members of its task environment.

Types of Responsibilities

Carroll, in his research on social responsibility, suggests that in addition to the obvious economic and legal responsibilities, businesses have ethical and discretionary ones.[28]

The **economic responsibilities** of a business organization's management are to produce goods and services of value to society, so that the firm can repay its creditors and stockholders. **Legal responsibilities** are defined by governments in laws that management is expected to obey. The **ethical responsibilities** of an organization's management are to follow the generally held beliefs about how one should act in the surrounding society. For example,

TABLE 4.2
Importance to Executives of Various Organizational Goals

ORGANIZATIONAL GOAL	DEGREE OF IMPORTANCE
Organizational effectiveness	6.26
High productivity	6.16
High morale	6.01
Organizational efficiency	5.93
Profit maximization	5.44
Organizational growth	5.20
Organizational value to community	4.82
Service to the public	4.68

SOURCE: Adapted from B. Z. Posner and W. H. Schmidt, "Values and the American Manager: An Update." Copyright © 1984 by the Regents of the University of California. Reprinted from the *California Management Review,* Vol. 26, No. 3, p. 205. By permission of The Regents.

NOTE: The ranking is calculated on a scale of 7 ("very important to me") to 1 ("of little or no importance to me").

although there may be no law requiring an organization to discuss the closing of a plant with representatives of the local community, society generally expects the firm to work with the community in planning for a plant closing. As in the Norwood, Ohio example mentioned earlier, the affected people can get very upset if an organization's management fails to act according to generally prevailing ethical values. **Discretionary responsibilities,** in contrast, are the purely voluntary obligations that a corporation assumes. Examples are philanthropic contributions, training the hard-core unemployed, and providing day-care centers. The difference between ethical and discretionary responsibilities is that no one expects an organization to fulfill discretionary responsibilities, whereas many expect an organization to fulfill ethical ones.

The term "social responsibility" can thus be viewed as the combination of an organization's ethical and discretionary responsibilities. The discretionary responsibilities of today may become the ethical responsibilities of tomorrow. Carroll suggests that to the extent that business organizations fail to acknowledge discretionary or ethical responsibilities, society, through government, will act, and make them legal responsibilities. This action can be taken by government, moreover, without regard to an organization's economic responsibilities. Because of such an act, the organization may have greater difficulty in earning a profit than it would have had if it had initially assumed voluntarily some ethical and discretionary responsibilities. For example, it has been suggested by some people in the American automobile industry that the large number of safety and pollution regulations passed in the 1960s and 1970s were partially responsible for the poor health of the U.S. industry in the early 1980s.[29]

Nevertheless, studies in the area have *failed* to find any significant relation between a business corporation's social responsibility and its financial performance. Examples can be cited of both highly profitable and marginally profitable companies with both poor and excellent social records.[30] One interesting example is Control Data Corporation. Under the leadership of socially concerned William C. Norris as founder, Chairman, and CEO, Control Data had organized assembly plants in ghettos and prisons and spent millions of dollars on computer systems for use in education and training in schools and industry. Unfortunately, corporate earnings have fallen and Norris has been criticized for allowing his "pet businesses" to drain investment away from the company's profitable ventures. He was subsequently forced to resign from the company.[31]

Even with the finding that social responsibility has no relationship to profits, one conclusion seems clear. The **iron law of responsibility** applies: If business corporations are unable or unwilling to police themselves by considering their responsibilities to all stakeholders in their task environment, then society—usually in the form of government—will police their doing so, and once again governments will reduce business's autonomy via increased rules and regulations.[32] During the late 1980s, there was already some pressure building in the United States for government regulations to take away some of business' decision-making freedom in some industries. Table 4.3 indicates that although general attitudes toward U.S. business in 1987 were still favorable, people questioned managers' ethics and appeared to be more disposed toward a return to government regulation. For example, bills were being proposed in the U.S. Congress to subject airlines to new restrictions (primarily because of an increasing number of complaints by customers and local communities) and to require pre-notification of major plant closings.[33] In addition, sixteen states were considering rules on mandatory pregnancy leave for employees. Fifteen states had already passed such laws.[34]

TABLE 4.3
Recent U.S. Attitudes Toward Business*

1. Overall attitude toward business:

Favorable	*Unsure*	*Unfavorable*
72%	4%	24%

2. Has the federal regulation of business changed from being too strict to being too lax?

Yes	*Unsure*	*No*
50%	5%	45%

3. Has the deregulation of various industries brought positive results?

Yes	*Unsure*	*No*
46%	5%	49%

4. Overall ethical standards of business executives:

Excellent/Good	*Unsure*	*Fair/Poor*
40%	2%	58%

5. Should there be new laws restricting hostile takeovers of one business firm by another?

Yes	*Unsure*	*No*
64%	6%	30%

6. Should companies be required by law to notify their workers and the local community in advance that they are planning to shut down an operation?

Yes	*Unsure*	*No*
86%	1%	13%

SOURCE: Based on data reported by S. Jackson and H. Collingwood, "Business Week/Harris Poll: Is An Antibusiness Backlash Growing?" *Business Week* (July 20, 1987), p. 71.

*Nationwide survey of 1,250 adults in the U.S. conducted May 8–12, 1987, by Louis Harris & Associates for *Business Week*.

4.3

ENVIRONMENTAL SCANNING AND INDUSTRY ANALYSIS

Because they are a part of a larger society that constantly affects them in many ways, corporations must be aware of changes and potential changes within the key variables in their task and societal environments. In 1973, for example, the Arab oil embargo caught many firms completely by surprise, with the result that goods dependent on oil as a raw material or energy source could not be produced. The resulting shortages and price adjustments caused chaos throughout the world's economy. The top managements of many business corporations then realized just how dependent they were on seemingly unpredictable external events. It was at this time, in the early 1970s, that many corporations established for the first time formal strategic planning systems. By 1984, between 92% and 95% of the world's largest corporations were using planning departments to monitor the environment and to prepare forecasts.[35]

Before strategy makers can begin formulating specific strategies, they must scan the external environment to identify possible *opportunities* and *threats*. Environmental scanning is the monitoring, evaluating, and disseminating of information from the external environment to key people within the corporation.[36] It is a tool that a corporation uses to avoid strategic surprise and to ensure its long-run health. Waterman argues that one reason excellent companies are able to constantly "renew" themselves is because they "know more" and "treat information as their main competitive advantage."[37] Both the societal and task environments must be monitored so that strategic factors that are likely to have a strong impact on corporate success or failure can be detected.

Monitoring Strategic Factors

Strategic managers should engage in environmental scanning through use of a *Strategic Issues Management System*.[38] By monitoring for weak as well as strong environmental signals, such a system continuously scans for possible trends and future developments. As mentioned in Chapter 1, NCR paid little attention to the appearance of the first electronic cash register in 1971—an example of a weak signal. By 1978, however, NCR's market share had dropped from 80% to 25%—a rather strong signal!

When analyzed, environmental data form a series of **strategic issues**—those trends and developments that are very likely to determine the future environment. Insofar as a corporation's strategic managers are concerned, however, these strategic environmental issues must be further analyzed so that those of most importance to the corporation's own future are identified. A corporation's **strategic factors** are those environmental strategic issues that are judged to have a high probability of occurrence and a high probability of impact on the corporation. As shown in Fig. 4.2, an **issues priority matrix** can be used to help managers decide which strategic issues should be merely

FIGURE 4.2
Issues Priority Matrix.

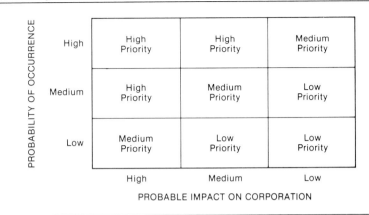

PROBABILITY OF OCCURRENCE

	High	Medium	Low
High	High Priority	High Priority	Medium Priority
Medium	High Priority	Medium Priority	Low Priority
Low	Medium Priority	Low Priority	Low Priority

PROBABLE IMPACT ON CORPORATION

Source: Adapted from L. L. Lederman, "Foresight Activities in the U.S.A.: Time for a Re-Assessment?" *Long-Range Planning* (June 1984), p. 46. Copyright © 1984 by Pergamon Press, Ltd. Reprinted by permission.

scanned (low priority) and which should be monitored as strategic factors (high priority). Those environmental issues judged to be a corporation's strategic factors are then categorized as *opportunities* and *threats,* and are included in strategy formulation.

Few firms, unfortunately, successfully monitor strategic issues.[39] The personal values of a corporation's top managers are likely to bias both their perception of what is important to monitor in the external environment and their interpretations of what they perceive. Therefore, different companies often respond differently to the same environmental changes because of differences in the ability of their strategic managers to recognize and understand strategic issues and factors.[40] For example, a study of presidents of savings and loan associations revealed that a president's perception of the environment strongly affected strategic planning. Those presidents who believed the present uncertain environment to be only temporary used no long-term planning staff or planning committees. They simply chose to wait for the "good old days" to return. In contrast, those presidents who believed the days of the stable, regulated environment to be long gone spent 30%–50% of their time considering long-range strategic issues and using planning staffs extensively.[41]

Societal Environment

The number of possible strategic factors in the societal environment is enormous. As noted in Table 4.4 large corporations categorize the societal

TABLE 4.4
Some Important Variables in the Societal Environment

SOCIOCULTURAL	ECONOMIC	TECHNOLOGICAL	POLITICAL-LEGAL
Lifestyle changes	GNP trends	Total federal spending for R&D	Antitrust regulations
Career expectations	Interest rates		Environmental protection laws
Consumer activism	Money supply	Total industry spending for R&D	
Rate of family formation	Inflation rates	Focus of technological efforts	Tax laws
Growth rate of population	Unemployment levels	Patent protection	Special incentives
Age distribution of population	Wage/Price controls	New products	Foreign trade regulations
Regional shifts in population	Devaluation/revaluation	New developments in technology transfer from lab to marketplace	Attitudes toward foreign companies
Life expectancies	Energy availability and cost		Laws on hiring and promotion
Birth rates	Disposable and discretionary income	Productivity improvements through automation	Stability of government

environment into four areas and focus their scanning in each area on trends with corporate-wide relevance. The economic area is usually the most significant, followed by the technological, political-legal, and sociocultural in decreasing order of importance.[42] Obviously, trends in any one area may be very important to the firms in one industry but of lesser importance to firms in other industries. For example, the demographic bulge in the U.S. population caused by the "baby boom" in the 1950s strongly affected the brewing industry, among others. As this demographic group became older during the 1980s, the percentage of the population that fell within the 18–25 years of age category—prime beer-drinking age—decreased. Thus sales and profits of breweries decreased and corporations like Anheuser-Busch found that they had to diversify if they were to stay profitable. In contrast, as the number of dual-career married couples in the 25–34 years of age category became larger, demand increased for day-care facilities like Kinder-Care Learning Centers.

Corporations throughout the developed nations of the world face some demographic societal pressures regardless of industry. The falling birth rates plus changing economic factors, for example, are leading to an aging of the workforce and to pressure for both men and women to have fulltime jobs. Because more than 60% of U.S. mothers with children under the age of 14 were actively employed in 1987 and there were predictions that the percentage would continue to rise, pressures were building on organizations to deal with the increasingly severe child-care dilemma facing their employees.[43] As the percentage of people in the U.S. workforce over 40 years of age increases from 37.8% in 1987 to nearly 50% in 2010, personnel practices and competitive strategies will be forced to change.[44] McDonald's fast-food chain has already begun to replace some of its teen aged employees with retired people. In attempts to change their offerings to match the changing lifestyles of their aging clientele, ski resorts are deemphasizing steep downhill slopes in favor of family-oriented lodges and scenic views.

John Naisbitt, in his influential book, *Megatrends,* states that America's present societal environment is turbulent because we are moving from one era to another. Having performed a content analysis of newspapers, he proposes that American society is being restructured by *ten broad influences* or "megatrends" that are defining the new society.

1. We are moving from an industrial to an information society.
2. We are moving from forced technology to a matching of each new technology with a compensatory human response ("Hi tech-hi touch").
3. We are moving from a national to a world economy.
4. We are moving from short-term to long-term considerations, with an emphasis on strategic planning.
5. We are moving from a period of centralization to decentralization of power.
6. We are shifting from reliance on institutional help to more self-reliance.
7. We are moving from representative democracy to more participative democracy, in politics as well as in the workplace.
8. We are giving up our dependence on traditional hierarchical structures in favor of informal networks of contacts.
9. We are moving geographically from the North to the South and West.
10. We are moving from a society with a limited number of personal choices to a multiple-option society.[45]

If Naisbitt is correct, these changes will have enormous impact not only upon American but also upon global society. To the extent that these trends are likely to have a strong impact on a particular corporation, they must be considered as strategic factors and be monitored closely by that firm's planners.

Task Environment/Industry Analysis

As was noted earlier, changes in the societal environment tend to be reflected in pressures on the corporation from task environment groups. As shown in Fig. 4.3, a corporation's scanning of the environment will include analyses of all the relevant elements in the task environment—interest groups, resources, the marketplace, competitors, suppliers, and governments. These analyses take the form of written reports, which, when boiled down to their essentials, act as a detailed list of strategic factors—those opportunities and

FIGURE 4.3
Scanning the External Environment.

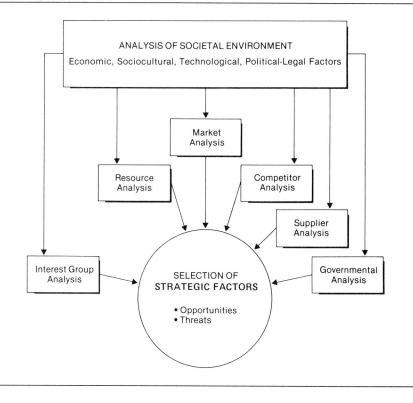

threats facing the corporation from its task environment. The task environment of a particular company is often referred to as its industry. Therefore, an examination of the task environment may also be called **industry analysis.** An *industry* is a group of firms producing a similar product or service, such as the automobile or soft drink industries.

Porter, an authority on competitive strategy, contends that a corporation is most concerned with the intensity of competition within its industry. The level of this intensity is determined by basic competitive forces, which are depicted in Fig. 4.4. "The collective strength of these forces," he contends, "determines the ultimate profit potential in the industry, where profit potential is measured in terms of long-run return on invested capital."[46] Although Porter mentions only five forces, a sixth—other stakeholders—is added to reflect the power of unions, governments, and other groups from the task environment on industry activities.

In carefully scanning the task environment, the corporation must assess the importance to its success of each of the following six forces.[47]

FIGURE 4.4
Forces Driving Industry Competition.

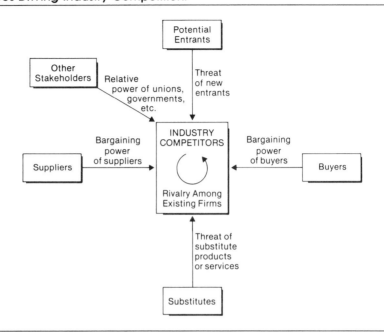

Source: Adapted/Reprinted with permission of The Free Press, a Division of Macmillan, Inc. from *Competitive Strategy: Techniques for Analyzing Industries and Competitors* by Michael E. Porter. Copyright © 1980 by The Free Press.

1. **Threat of New Entrants:** New entrants to an industry typically bring to it new capacity, a desire to gain market share, and substantial resources, and are, therefore, threats to an established corporation. The threat of entry depends on the presence of entry barriers and the reaction that can be expected from existing competitors. For example, there have been very few new automobile companies successfully established since the 1930s because of the high capital requirements to build production facilities and to develop a dealer distribution network.

2. **Rivalry among Existing Firms:** In most industries, corporations are mutually dependent. A competitive move by one firm can be expected to have a noticeable effect on its competitors and thus may cause retaliation or counter-efforts. For example, the entry of Philip Morris into the beer industry through the acquisition of Miller Brewing increased the level of competitive activity to such an extent that any introduction of a new product or promotion is now quickly followed by similar moves from other brewers.

3. **Threat of Substitute Products or Services:** In effect, all corporations within one industry are competing with other industries that produce substitute

products. According to Porter, "Substitutes limit the potential returns of an industry by placing a ceiling on the prices firms in the industry can profitably charge."[48] In the 1970s, for example, the high price of cane sugar caused soft drink manufacturers to turn to high-fructose corn syrup as a sugar substitute. Sometimes a difficult task, the identification of possible substitute products or services means searching for products or services that can perform the same *function*, even though they may not appear to be easily substitutable. Videotape recorders, for example, are becoming substitutes for home motion-picture projectors. The television screen thus substitutes for the portable projection screen.

4. **Bargaining Power of Buyers:** Buyers affect an industry through their ability to force down prices, bargain for higher quality or more services, and play competitors against each other. A buyer or a group of buyers is powerful if some of the following hold true:

   - It purchases a large proportion of the seller's product or service.

   - It has the potential to integrate backward by producing the product itself.

   - Alternative suppliers are plentiful.

   - Changing suppliers costs very little.

   For example, to the extent that General Motors purchases a large percentage of Firestone's total tire production, GM's purchasing department can easily make all sorts of demands on Firestone's marketing people. This would be the case especially if GM could easily get its tires from Goodyear or General Tire at no extra trouble or cost. Increasing demands by large manufacturing companies for "just-in-time delivery" means that, in order to get the orders, a small supplier dependent on the large firm's business must take over the warehousing functions previously handled by the large firm.

5. **Bargaining Power of Suppliers:** Suppliers can affect an industry through their ability to raise prices or reduce the quality of purchased goods and services. A supplier group is powerful if some of the following apply:

   - The supplier industry is dominated by a few companies, but sells to many.

   - Substitutes are not readily available.

   - Suppliers are able to integrate forward and compete directly with their present customers. An example was IBM's willingness in 1980 to open its own personal-computer stores instead of selling only through other established retailers.

   - A purchasing industry buys only a small portion of the supplier group's goods and services.

   For example, major oil companies in the 1970s were able to raise prices and reduce services because so many companies that purchased oil products had heavy energy needs and, in the short run, were unable to switch to substitute fuels, such as coal or nuclear power. Wishing to be less dependent on suppliers for the raw material so necessary to produce its synthetic materials, Dupont chose to buy Conoco, a major oil company.

6. **Relative Power of Other Stakeholders:** Freeman recommends adding this sixth force to Porter's list to include a variety of stakeholder groups from the task environment.[49] Some of these groups are governments, unions, local communities, creditors (if not included with suppliers), trade associations, special interest groups, and stockholders. The importance of these stakeholders will vary by industry. For example, environmental groups in Maine, Michigan, Oregon, and Iowa successfully fought to pass bills outlawing disposable bottles and cans, and thus deposits for most drink containers are now required. Although Porter contends that the government influences the level of competitive activity through the previously mentioned five forces, it is suggested here that governments deserve a special mention because of their strong relative power in all industries.

For additional information on industry analysis, refer to **"How Competitive Forces Shape Strategy"** by Michael E. Porter in Appendix 4.A at the end of this chapter.

Characterizing the Competition

In analyzing the level of competitive intensity within an industry, it is useful to characterize the competition for predictive purposes. According to Miles and Snow, competing firms within a single industry can be categorized on the basis of their general strategic orientation into one of four basic types: the Defender, the Prospector, the Analyzer, and the Reactor.[50] Each of these types has its own favorite strategy for responding to the environment, and has its own combination of structure, culture, and processes consistent with that strategy. This distinction helps explain why companies facing similar situations behave differently and why they continue to do so over a long period of time. These general types have the following characteristics:

- **Defenders** are corporations having a limited product line and focusing on improving the efficiency of their existing operations. This focus makes them unlikely to innovate in new areas. An example corporation is the Adolph Coors Company, which for so many years emphasized production efficiency in its one Colorado brewery and virtually ignored marketing.

- **Prospectors** are corporations having fairly broad product lines and focusing on product innovation and market opportunities. They tend to emphasize creativity over efficiency. An example would be the Miller Brewing Company, which successfully promoted light beer and generated aggressive, innovative advertising campaigns.

- **Analyzers** are corporations that operate in two different product-market areas, one stable and one changing. In the stable area, efficiency is emphasized. In the changing area, innovation is emphasized. An example would be Anheuser-Busch, which can take a defender orientation to protect its massive market share in beer and a prospector orientation to generate sales in its snack foods.

- **Reactors** are corporations that lack a consistent strategy-structure-culture relationship. Their (often ineffective) responses to environmental pressures tend to be piecemeal strategic changes. An example would be the Pabst Brewing Company, which, because of numerous takeover attempts, has been unable to generate a consistent strategy to keep its sales from dropping.

Dividing the competition into these four categories enables the strategic manager to not only monitor the effectiveness of certain strategic orientations, but also to develop scenarios of future industry developments (to be discussed later in this chapter).

Sources of Information

Studies have shown that much environmental scanning is done on an informal and individual basis. Information is obtained from a variety of sources, such as customers, suppliers, bankers, consultants, publications, personal observations, subordinates, superiors, and peers. For example, scientists and engineers working in a firm's R&D lab can learn about new products and competitors' ideas at professional meetings; someone from the purchasing department, speaking with supplier-representatives' personnel, may also uncover valuable bits of information about a competitor. A study of product innovation in the scientific instruments and machine tool industries found that 80% of all product innovations were initiated by the *customer* in the form of inquiries and complaints.[51] In these industries, the sales force and service departments must be especially vigilant.

Some of the main sources of information about an industry's environment are shown in Fig. 4.5. Because people throughout a corporation can obtain an extraordinary amount of data in any given month, top management must develop a system to get these data from those who obtained it to the people who can integrate it with other information to form a comprehensive environmental assessment.

As one would suspect, research suggests that corporations develop and implement more scanning procedures for following, anticipating, and responding to changes in the activities of *competitors* than of any other stakeholder in the environment.[52] At General Mills, for example, all members of the company have been trained to recognize and tap sources of competitive information. Janitors no longer simply place orders with suppliers of cleaning materials, they also ask about relevant practices at competing firms![53]

There is danger in focusing one's scanning efforts too closely on one's own industry, though. According to research by Snyder, "History teaches that most new developments which threaten existing business practices and technologies do not come from traditional industries."[54] For instance, **tech-**

FIGURE 4.5
Sources of Data for Industry Analysis.

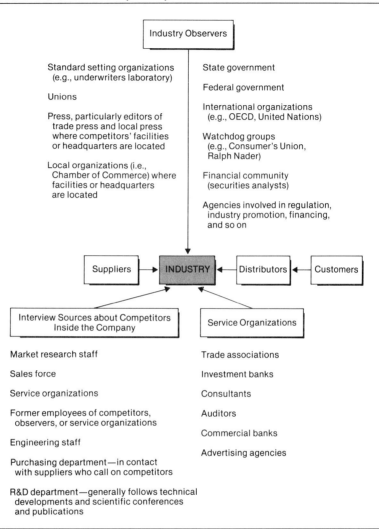

Source: Adapted/Reprinted with permission of The Free Press, a Division of Macmillan, Inc. from *Competitive Strategy: Techniques for Analyzing Industries and Competitors* by Michael E. Porter. Copyright © 1980 by The Free Press.

nology transfer, the process of taking new technology from the laboratory to the marketplace, has become an important issue in recent decades. Consider just one example. With the development of the integrated circuit, electronics firms, such as Texas Instruments, were able to introduce high-volume, low-cost electronic digital watches. These firms' entry into the watch-making industry took well-established mechanical watchmakers by surprise. Timex, Seiko, and especially the Swiss firms found that their market had changed overnight. Their production facilities, however, had not; and they spent a lot of money buying the new technology.

Most corporations rely on outside organizations to provide them with environmental data. Firms such as A. C. Nielsen Co. provide subscribers with bimonthly data on brand share, retail prices, percentages of stores stocking an item, and percentages of stock-out stores. These data can be used by management to spot regional and national trends as well as to assess market share. Information on market conditions, government regulations, competitors, and new products can be bought from "information brokers." Such firms as FIND/SVP, a New York company, and Finsbury Data Services, owned by Reuters in London, get their data from periodicals, reference books, computer data banks, directors, and experts in the area. Other firms, like Chase Econometrics, offer various data bases plus a software package that enables corporate planners to gain computer access to a large number of key indicators. Typically, the largest corporations spend from $25,000 to $30,000 per year for information services.[55] Close to 6,000 firms in the United States and Canada have established their own in-house libraries to deal with the growing mass of available information.[56]

Some companies, however, choose to use industrial espionage or other intelligence gathering techniques, to get their information straight from their competitors. For example, Hitachi Ltd., the large Japanese electronics firm, pleaded guilty in 1983 to conspiring to transport stolen IBM material to Japan.[57] In 1986, Kellogg Company closed its Battle Creek, Michigan, plant to public tours when it learned that industrial spies from two foreign competitors had gathered valuable information during visits. Experts report that modern "pirates" of information are inflicting billions of dollars worth of damage annually in missed sales and wasted R&D costs. Valuable information can slip out through managers, salespeople, and suppliers. Even cleaning workers have been caught selling trash to rival competitors![58]

4.4

FORECASTING

Once a business corporation has collected data about its current environmental situation, it must analyze present trends to learn if they will continue into the future. The strategic planning horizon for many large corporations is from five to ten years in the future. A long-term planning horizon is especially necessary for large, capital-intensive corporations, such as automobile or heavy-machinery manufacturers. In these corporations, moving from an accepted proposal to a finished product requires many years. Therefore, most corporations must base their future plans on a forecast, a set of assumptions about what that future will look like. These assumptions can be derived from an entrepreneur's vision, from a head-in-the-sand hope that the future will be similar to the present, or from the opinions of experts. Figure 4.6 depicts the role of forecasting in the strategy formulation process.

FIGURE 4.6
The Role of Forecasting.

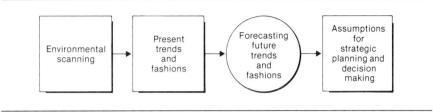

The Danger of Assumptions

A forecast is nothing more than a leap of faith into the future. Environmental scanning provides reasonably hard data on the present situation, but intuition and luck are needed to accurately predict the future. Faulty underlying assumptions appear to be the most frequent cause of forecasting errors.[59] Nevertheless, many managers who formulate and implement strategic plans have little or no realization that their success is based on a series of assumptions. Many long-range plans are simply based on projections of the current situation. One example of what can happen when a corporate strategy rests on the very questionable assumption that the future will simply be an extension of the present, is that of the Miller Brewing Company, a subsidiary of Philip Morris.

In 1980, Miller Brewing decided to construct a $412 million brewery in Trenton, Ohio. The decision was made after a decade of growth that saw Miller's beer volume increase 640% while that of the industry as a whole grew by only 40%. Miller's strategic managers assumed that with Philip Morris' marketing genius supporting the company, the sky was the limit for Miller beer. Unfortunately, that trend was not to continue. Of the total U.S. population, that percentage aged 18–25 years began to drop, and so did the overall demand for beer. The competition also increased its challenge: having been stung by Miller's marketing successes during the 1970s, Anheuser-Busch tripled its advertising budget and launched a $2 billion capital-expansion program. It became an aggressive competitor. Miller's Trenton brewery, completed in 1982, never opened. In 1986, the sales volume of Miller High Life (once the number two beer in America) had declined by 50% since the decade's beginning. Unable to reverse the trend, Miller took a $280 million writeoff on the Trenton brewery.[60]

Techniques

As depicted in Table 4.5, various techniques are used to forecast future situations. Each has its proponents and critics. A study of nearly 500 of the world's largest corporations revealed **trend extrapolation** to be the most

TABLE 4.5
Degree of Usage of Forecasting Techniques*

TECHNIQUE	TOP 1,000 U.S. INDUSTRIALS (n = 215)	TOP 100 U.S. INDUSTRIALS (n = 40)	TOP 300 U.S. NON-INDUSTRIALS (n = 85)	TOP 500 FOREIGN INDUSTRIALS (n = 105)
Trend extrapolation	73%	70%	74%	72%
Statistical modeling (i.e., regression analysis)	48	61	51	45
Scenarios	57	67	67	61
Relevance trees	5	3	7	4
Simulation	34	45	38	27
Brainstorming	65	61	69	52
Trend impact analysis	34	33	31	29
Expert opinion/Delphi	33	42	24	35
Morphological analysis	2	0	0	5
Signal monitoring	15	19	14	18
Cross-impact analysis	12	22	11	5

*Figures reflect the percentage of respondents indicating either "frequent" or "occasional" use. Respondents had been asked to classify their frequency of technique use as "not used," "rarely used," "used occasionally," or "used frequently."

SOURCE: H. E. Klein and R. E. Linneman, "Environmental Assessment: An International Study of Corporate Practices," *Journal of Business Strategy* (Summer 1984), p. 72. Copyright © 1984 by Warren, Gorham & Lamont, Inc. Reprinted by permission. All rights reserved.

widely practiced form of forecasting—over 70% use this technique either occasionally or frequently.[61] Simply stated, extrapolation is the extension of present trends into the future. As shown in the Miller Brewing example, it rests on the assumption that the world is reasonably consistent and changes slowly in the short run. Time-series methods are approaches of this type; these attempt to carry a series of historical events forward into the future. The basic problem with extrapolation is that a historical trend is based upon a series of patterns or relationships among so many different variables that a change in any one can drastically alter the future direction of the trend. As a rule of thumb, the further back into the past one can find relevant data supporting the trend, the more confidence one can have in the prediction. Nevertheless, even experts in forecasting admit: "Forecasts that cover a period of two years or more are typically very inaccurate."[62]

As shown in Table 4.5, brainstorming and statistical modeling are also very popular forecasting techniques. **Brainstorming** is a nonquantitative approach requiring simply the presence of people with some knowledge of the situation to be predicted. The basic ground rule is to propose ideas without first mentally screening them. No criticism is allowed. Ideas tend to build upon previous ideas until a consensus is reached. This is a good technique to use with operating managers who have more faith in "gut feel" than in more quantitative "number crunching" techniques.

Statistical modeling is a quantitative technique that attempts to discover causal or at least explanatory factors that link two or more time series together. Examples of statistical modeling are regression analysis and other econometric methods. Although very useful in the grasping of historic trends, statistical modeling, like trend extrapolation, is based on historical data. As the patterns of relationships change, the accuracy of the forecast deteriorates.[63]

Other forecasting techniques, such as *cross-impact analysis, trend impact analysis,* and *relevance trees* have not established themselves successfully as regularly employed tools. Research by Klein and Linneman reports that corporate planners found these techniques to be complicated, time-consuming, expensive, and academic. Usage was therefore concentrated among the very largest companies and there it was generally used to provide input for scenario-writing.[64]

Research further reports that **scenario-writing** appears to be the most widely used forecasting technique after trend extrapolation. Among corporations in the top Fortune 1,000 Industrials, the usage of scenarios increased from 22% in 1977 to 57% in 1981. Klein and Linneman predict that usage of this popular forecasting technique will increase, but point out that "most companies follow a very informal scenario-writing approach with little reliance on rigorous methodologies."[65] The scenario thus may be merely a written description of some future state, in terms of key variables and issues, or it may be generated in combination with other forecasting techniques.

A more complex version used by General Electric (depicted in Fig. 4.7) is based upon a Delphi panel of experts, a trend impact analysis, and a cross-impact analysis. The **Delphi technique** involves an anonymous panel of experts who are asked individually to estimate the probability of certain events' occurrence in the future. After seeing the anonymous responses from the other experts on the panel, each member of the panel is given several opportunities to revise his/her estimate. **Cross-impact analysis** (CIA), which is typically done on a computer, produces a matrix showing the interaction of the various likely developments that had been generated earlier by the Delphi panel. For example, in the lower right corner of Fig. 4.7, the CIA matrix indicates a prediction that the development of usable nuclear energy by the fusion (instead of the current fission) process will probably result in oil price-cuts by the members of OPEC and an increase in safety and environmental laws regarding the mining and burning of coal. **Trend-impact analysis** (TIA), in contrast, begins with an outside expert's or a Delphi panel's forecast of a trend or phenomenon. For example, if someone were interested in the future of cigarette smoking, one might use extrapolation to forecast a continuing downward trend in the number of smokers. Various possible influencing factors are then added to the forecast, and predictions

FIGURE 4.7
Scenario Construction at General Electric.

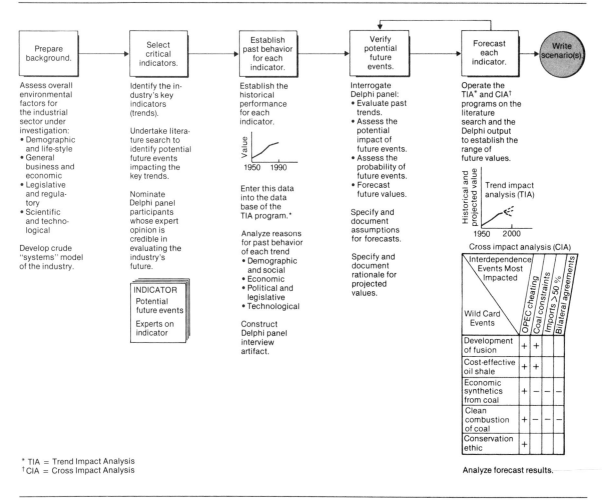

* TIA = Trend Impact Analysis
† CIA = Cross Impact Analysis

Source: General Electric Company. Used by permission.

of three or more alternative future trends result. For example, the likelihood that campaigns against public smoking will increase, might cause the trend in number of smokers to decline faster. The invention of smokeless tobacco might cause the trend to reverse its decline. The output from the Delphi panel, the cross-impact analysis, and the trend-impact analysis are then used in the development of a series of probable future scenarios.

In his book *Competitive Advantage,* Michael Porter strongly recommends the use of scenarios because they (1) allow a firm to move away from use of dangerous, single-point forecasts of the future in instances when the future cannot be predicted, and (2) encourage managers to make their assumptions explicit.[66] He recommends the use of **industry scenarios,** which utilize variables from the societal environment in terms of their effect on the key stakeholders in a corporation's task environment (industry). The process may operate as follows.[67]

1. **Examine possible shifts in the societal variables** (e.g., economic, socio-cultural, technological, and political-legal). Begin with the obvious variables listed in Table 4.4 and decide which of them might be changing so as to create a strategic issue. In order to identify those issues of most importance to the corporation and/or the industry, plot these variables on the issues-priority matrix depicted in Fig. 4.2.

2. **Identify uncertainties in each of the six forces from the task environment** (e.g., competitors, buyers, suppliers, likely substitutes, potential entrants, and other key stakeholders) as depicted in Fig. 4.4. Make sure that all the high-priority strategic issues identified in the first step are specified in terms of the appropriate forces in the task environment.

3. **Identify the causal factors behind the uncertainties.** These sources of uncertainty can be inside the industry (e.g., competitor behavior) or outside the industry (e.g., new regulations). It is likely that many of these causal factors were identified earlier when the societal environment was analyzed. It is also likely that new ones surfaced when the task environment was analyzed.

4. **Make a range of plausible assumptions about each important causal factor.** For example, if the price of oil is a causal factor, make reasonable assumptions about its future level in terms of high, low, and most probable price. A trend-impact analysis may be of some value here.

5. **Combine assumptions about individual causal factors into internally consistent scenarios.** Put various combinations of the assumptions together into sets of scenarios. Because one assumption may affect another, ensure that the scenarios are internally consistent. A simplified cross-impact analysis may be of some value in one's determining the interaction of likely trends. For example, if a scenario includes the assumptions of high oil prices and a low level of economic inflation, that scenario is not internally consistent and should be rejected. (It is an unlikely event because high oil prices tend to drive inflation upward.)

6. **Analyze the industry situation that would prevail under each scenario.** For example, if one scenario assumes that generic (no-name) drugs will be more in demand than brand-name drugs, the situation in the drug industry under that assumption will be very different than under the assumption that the demand for generic drugs will be negligible. For example, an industry dominated by generic drugs would have low profit margins for all firms and a very heavy degree of competition. It is likely that in that industry situation a few firms would leave the drug industry.

7. **Determine the sources of competitive advantage under each scenario.** For example, in an industry dominated by generic drugs, the combination

of low price backed up by low operating costs would provide competitive advantage to a firm. If brand-name drugs dominated, the combination of strong advertising, high-quality production, and heavy promotion would provide competitive advantage to the firm using them.

8. **Predict competitors' behavior under each scenario.** As the industry moves toward a particular scenario each competitor will make some adjustment. Some might leave the industry. New competitors might enter. Using each competitor's history and what is known about its management, estimate what each competitor is likely to do. Once this is done, management should be able to specify the *strategic factors* that are necessary for success (opportunities) as well as those that could cause failure (threats), in a variety of future scenarios. In order to choose the ones most likely to occur, one can also attach probabilities to each of the developed scenarios.[68]

Once management has scanned the external environment to identify strategic factors and forecasted their probable impact on future corporate activities, they must do the same for the corporation's internal environment, as will be shown next in Chapter 5.

SUMMARY AND CONCLUSION

Anyone concerned with how strategic decisions are made in large corporations should be aware of the impact of the external environment on top management and the board of directors. Long-run developments in the economic, technological, political-legal, and sociocultural aspects of the societal environment strongly affect the corporation's activities through the more immediate pressures in its task environment.

Business and commerce have lived an uneasy truce with society for centuries. Within societies that vacillate between heavy regulation and *laissez-faire* economics, business corporations are learning that they must be socially responsible if they are to operate with some autonomy. Top management and the board of directors must constantly balance the needs of one stakeholder in the corporation's task environment against the needs of another. They must ensure that the priorities of their corporation do not get too far away from those valued by society.

Before strategy can be formulated, strategy makers must scan the external environment for possible opportunities and threats. They must identify strategic issues to be monitored, as well as assess which are likely to affect the corporation in the future. Then they must analyze the resulting information and disseminate it to the people involved in strategic planning and decision making.

Just as environmental scanning provides an understanding of present trends in the environment, forecasting provides assumptions about the future that are crucial for strategic management. Most modern corporations use the techniques of trend extrapolation, scenario-writing, brainstorming, and statistical modeling to predict their future environment. Even if the predictions prove to be wrong, the very act of scanning and forecasting the environment helps managers take a broader perspective. These techniques also help prevent the development of reactive managers, who dare not take the time to plan for the future because they are caught up in the crises and problems of the present. Ward Hagan, Chief Executive Officer of Warner-Lambert, makes a strong argument in favor of environmental scanning and forecasting:

Nobody can plan accurately, strategically, five years ahead. But the intellectual discipline that

it imposes on operating people once a year is the best possible medicine I know for clear, sequential thinking.[69]

DISCUSSION QUESTIONS

1. When business corporations close a facility, should they be required to pay some sort of compensation to the communities they are leaving?

2. How appropriate is the theory of *laissez-faire* in today's world?

3. Why should a business corporation be socially responsible?

4. What can a corporation do to ensure that information about strategic environmental factors gets to the attention of strategy makers?

5. To what extent do you agree with the conclusion that the ultimate profit potential of an industry depends on the collective strength of six key forces: the threat of new entrants, the rivalry among existing firms, the threat of substitutable products or services, the bargaining power of buyers, the bargaining power of

suppliers, and the relative power of other stakeholders? Defend your view.

6. If most long-term forecasts are usually incorrect, why bother doing them?

7. Compare and contrast trend extrapolation with the writing of scenarios, as forecasting techniques.

8. List and discuss the major stakeholders in CSX Corporation's task environment as discussed in the Integrative Case at the end of this chapter. What do each of them want from the company?

9. What are some of the most important opportunities and threats present in the external environment of CSX Corporation as mentioned in the following Integrative Case? Which of these should have a major impact in strategy formulation at the time of the case and in the future?

NOTES

1. E. C. Bursk, D. T. Clark, and R. W. Hidy, "The Oldest Business Code: Nearly 4000 Years Ago," *The World of Business,* vol. 1 (New York: Simon and Schuster, 1962), pp. 9–10.

2. F. E. Kast and J. E. Rosenzweig, *Organization and Management,* 2nd ed. (New York: McGraw-Hill, 1974), p. 28.

3. M. Weber, *The Protestant Ethic and the Spirit of Capitalism,* trans. Talcott Parsons (New York: Charles Scribner's Sons, 1958).

4. Kast and Rosenzweig, p. 35.

5. J. W. McGuire, *Business and Society* (New York: McGraw-Hill, 1963), p. 78.

6. Kast and Rosenzweig, pp. 37–39.

7. *New York Times* (April 23, 1962) as quoted by H. L. Gabel, G. A. Becker, and B. S. Seng, "Armco—The 1978 Wage and Price Guidelines," in T. L. Wheelen and J. D. Hunger, *Strategic Management and Business Policy,* 1st ed. (Reading, Mass.: Addison-Wesley, 1983), p. 397.

8. G. A. Steiner, *The New CEO* (New York: Macmillan Publishing, 1983), p. 6.

W. E. Deming, *Out of the Crisis* (Cambridge, Mass.: M.I.T. Center for Advanced Study, 1986), p. 153.

9. K. Hughes, *Corporate Response to Declining Rates of Growth* (Lexington, Mass.: Lexington Books, 1982), p. 14.

10. R. B. Reich, *The Next American Frontier* (New York: Times Books, 1983).

11. A. R. Karr, "Chrysler Agrees to Pay $1.6 Million Fine to Settle OSHA Health, Safety Charges," *Wall Street Journal* (July 7, 1987), pp. 3 and 8.

12. R. E. Freeman, *Strategic Management: A Stakeholder Approach* (Boston: Pitman Publishing Co., 1984), p. 25.

13. B. Z. Posner and W. H. Schmidt, "Values and the American Manager: An Update," *California Management Review* (Spring 1984), pp. 202–216.

14. J. M. Schlesinger, "GM Sued by Town for $318.3 Million Over Breakup of 64-Year 'Marriage,' " *Wall Street Journal* (August 21, 1987), p. 4.

15. "Kennedy, Zulu Leader Discuss Investments," *Ames Tribune* (United Press International) (Ames, Iowa, January 10, 1985), p. 20.

16. D. Kneale, "Sullivan Urges Firms to Quit South Africa," *Wall Street Journal* (June 4, 1987), p. 6.

"Half of Canadian Concerns in South Africa Pulled Out," *Wall Street Journal* (June 26, 1987), p. 6.

For an excellent review of the arguments for and against business involvement in South Africa, see "Divestment and Disinvestment from South Africa: A Reappraisal," by D. Beaty and O. Harari, *California Management Review* (Summer, 1987), pp. 31–50.

17. "Three Mile Island's Lingering Ills," *Business Week* (October 22, 1979), p. 75.

T. Redburn, "Stalled Nuclear Power Plant: PG&E Feels Powerless," *Los Angeles Times* (February 24, 1980), part 4, p. 1.

J. H. Dobrzynski, W. B. Glaberson, R. W. King, W. J. Powell, Jr., and L. Helm, "Union Carbide Fights for Its Life," *Business Week* (December 24, 1984), pp. 52–56.

18. "Who Will Be Liable for Toxic Dumping?" *Business Week* (August 28, 1978), p. 32.

19. C. P. Alexander, B. R. Leavitt, and R. Samghabadi, "Robbins Runs for Shelter," *Business Week* (September 2, 1985), pp. 32–33.

20. L. Sorenson, "Chapter 11 Filing by Wilson Foods Roils Workers' Lives, Tests Law," *Wall Street Journal* (May 23, 1983), p. 25.

J. Fierman, "Safe in Chapter 11," *Fortune* (March 5, 1984), p. 143.

21. S. Soloman, "The Asbestos Fallout at Johns-Manville," *Fortune* (May 7, 1979), pp. 197–206.

B. Richards and A. Kotlowitz, "Judge Finds 3 Corporate Officials Guilty of Murder in Cyanide Death of Worker," *Wall Street Journal* (June 17, 1985), p. 2.

22. "Test Case: A Defense Contractor Is Fined," *Time* (March 19, 1984), p. 47.

F. Schwadel, "General Electric Pleads Guilty in Fraud Case," *Wall Street Journal* (May 14, 1985), p. 119.

C. P. Alexander, A. Constable, and J. M. Nash, "Crime in the Suites," *Time* (June 10, 1985), pp. 56–57.

S. W. Gellerman, "Why 'Good' Managers Make Bad Ethical Choices," *Harvard Business Review* (July-August 1986), pp. 85–90.

23. W. M. Pride and O. C. Ferrell, *Marketing*, 2nd ed. (Boston: Houghton Mifflin, 1980), p. 720.

24. M. Friedman, "The Social Responsibility of Business Is to Increase Its Profits," *New York Times Magazine* (September 13, 1970), pp. 30, 126–127; and *Capitalism and Freedom* (Chicago: University of Chicago Press, 1963), p. 133.

25. M. Gable and P. Arlow, "A Comparative Examination of the Value Orientations of British and American Executives," *International Journal of Management* (September 1986), pp. 97–106.

W. D. Guth and R. Tagiuri, "Personal Values and Corporate Strategy," *Harvard Business Review* (September-October 1965), pp. 126–127.

26. Posner and Schmidt, pp. 203–205.

27. S. N. Brenner and E. A. Molander, "Is the Ethics of Business Changing?" *Harvard Business Review* (January-February 1977), p. 70.

28. A. B. Carroll, "A Three-Dimensional Conceptual Model of Corporate Performance," *Academy of Management Review* (October 1979), pp. 497–505.

29. L. Iacocca, *Iacocca: An Autobiography* (Toronto: Bantam Books, 1984), pp. 196–197.

30. K. E. Aupperle, A. B. Carroll, and J. D. Hatfield, "An Empirical Examination of the Relationship between Corporate Social Responsibility and Profitability," *Academy of Management Journal* (June 1985), p. 459.

A. A. Ullmann, "Data in Search of a Theory: A Critical Examination of the Relationship Among Social Performance, Social Disclosure, and Economic Performance of U.S. Firms," *Academy of Management Review* (July 1985), pp. 540–557.

31. "A Visionary Exits," *Time* (January 20, 1986), p. 44.

32. K. Davis, "The Meaning and Scope of Social Responsibility," in J. W. McGuire (ed.), *Contemporary Management: Issues and Viewpoints* (Englewood Cliffs, N.J.: Prentice-Hall, 1974), p. 631.

33. S. Kilman, "An Unexpected Result of Airline Decontrol Is Return to Monopolies," *Wall Street Journal* (July 20, 1987), p. 1.

R. W. Crandall, "Don't Cartelize the Steel Industry," *Wall Street Journal* (July 20, 1987), p. 16.

34. *Wall Street Journal* (July 21, 1987), p. 1.

35. H. E. Klein and R. E. Linneman, "Environmental Assessment: An International Study of Corporate Practices," *Journal of Business Strategy* (Summer 1984), p. 67.

36. N. H. Snyder, "Environmental Volatility, Scanning Intensity and Organization Performance," *Journal of Contemporary Business* (September 1981), p. 7.

37. R. H. Waterman, Jr., "The Renewal Factor," *Business Week* (September 14, 1987), p. 101.

38. J. E. Dutton and E. Ottensmeyer, "Strategic Issue Management Systems: Forms, Functions, and Contexts," *Academy of Management Review* (April 1987), pp. 355–365.

P. Lorange, M. F. S. Morton, and S. Ghoshal, *Strategic Control* (St. Paul: West Publishing Co., 1986), pp. 101–104.

39. P. V. Jenster, "Using Critical Success Factors in Planning," *Long Range Planning* (August 1987), p. 108.

40. J. E. Dutton and R. B. Duncan, "The Creation of Momentum for Change Through the Process of Strategic Issue Diagnosis," *Strategic Management Journal* (May-June 1987), pp. 279–295.

41. M. Javidan. "The Impact of Environmental Uncertainty on Long-Range Planning and Practices of the U.S. Savings and Loan Industry," *Strategic Management Journal* (October-December 1984), pp. 381–392.

42. S. C. Jain, "Environmental Scanning in U.S. Corporations," *Long Range Planning* (April 1984), p. 119.

43. C. Wallis, "The Child-Care Dilemma," *Time* (June 22, 1987), pp. 54–60.

44. M. Levin-Epstein, ed., *Older Americans in the Workforce: Challenges and Solutions* (Rockville, Md.: Bureau of National Affairs, 1987) as reported by M. Memmott, "Companies Face Aging Work Force," *USA Today* (July 9, 1987), p. 5B.

Work Force 2000 (Indianapolis: The Hudson Institute, 1987) as reported by A. R. Karr, "Efficiency of Economy's Service Sector Must Be Buttressed, Study for U.S. Says," *Wall Street Journal* (July 3, 1987), p. 13.

45. J. Naisbitt, *Megatrends* (New York: Warner Books, 1982).

46. M. E. Porter, *Competitive Strategy* (New York: Free Press, 1980), p. 3.

47. This summary of the forces driving competitive strategy is taken from M. E. Porter, *Competitive Strategy* (New York: Free Press, 1980), pp. 7–29.

48. Porter, p. 23.

49. R. E. Freeman, *Strategic Management: A Stakeholder Approach* (Boston: Pitman Publishing, 1984), pp. 140–142.

50. R. E. Miles and C. C. Snow, *Organizational Strategy, Structure, and Process* (New York: McGraw-Hill Book Co., 1978).

51. R. T. Pascale, "Perspective on Strategy: The Real Story Behind Honda's Success," *California Management Review* (Spring 1981), p. 70.

52. B. Rosenbloom and R. V. Tripuraneni, "Strategic Planning Catches On In U.S. Retailers," *Long Range Planning* (August 1985), p. 59.

53. D. C. Smith and J. E. Prescott, "Demystifying Competitive Analysis," *Planning Review* (September/October 1987), p. 13. For more in-depth information on the gathering of competitor intelligence, refer to the entire September/October 1987 issue of *Planning Review*.

54. Snyder, p. 16.

55. C. Cox, "Planning in a Changing Environment: The Search for External Data," in *Handbook of Business Strategy, 1985/86 Yearbook,* edited by W. D. Guth (Boston: Warren, Gorham, and Lamont, 1985), p. 5.2.

56. J. L. Roberts, "As Information Swells, Firms Open Libraries," *Wall Street Journal* (September 25, 1983), p. 25.

57. J. Drinkhall, "Hitachi Ltd. Pleads Guilty in IBM Case," *Wall Street Journal* (February 9, 1983), p. 4.

58. G. L. Miles, "Information Thieves Are Now Corporate Enemy No. 1," *Business Week* (May 5, 1986), pp. 120–125.

59. S. P. Schnaars, "How to Develop and Use Scenarios," *Long Range Planning* (February 1987), p. 106.

60. J. Merwin, "A Billion in Blunders," *Forbes* (December 1, 1986), p. 104.

61. H. E. Klein and R. E. Linneman, "Environmental Assessment: An International Study of Corporate Practices," *Journal of Business Strategy* (Summer 1984), p. 72.

62. S. Makridakis and S. C. Wheelwright, "Introduction to Management Forecasting," *The Handbook of Forecasting* (New York: Wiley and Sons, 1982), p. 8.

63. Makridakis and Wheelwright, p. 6.

64. Klein and Linneman, p. 72.

65. Klein and Linneman, p. 73.

66. M. E. Porter, *Competitive Advantage* (New York: The Free Press, 1985), p. 447.

67. This process of scenario development is adapted from M. E. Porter, *Competitive Advantage* (New York: The Free Press, 1985), pp. 448–470.

68. For further information on scenario writing, cross-impact analysis, and the Delphi Technique, refer to *Microenvironmental Analysis for Strategic Management* by L. Fahey and V. K. Narayanan (St. Paul: West Publishing Co., 1986), pp. 213–219.

For information on trend-impact analysis, see W. R. Huss and E. J. Honton, "Scenario Planning—What Style Should You Use?" *Long Range Planning* (August 1987), pp. 23–24.

69. M. Magnet, "How Top Managers Make a Company's Toughest Decisions," *Fortune* (March 18, 1985), p. 55.

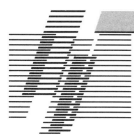

INTEGRATIVE CASE

CSX CORPORATION'S EXTERNAL ENVIRONMENT

During the 1970s, U.S. railroads had faced a bleak future. Starved for capital, the industry deferred maintenance and other badly needed capital improvements so it could meet the financial requirements of its day-to-day operations. The decrease in

SOURCE: J. D. Hunger, B. Ferrin, H. Felix-Gamez, and T. Goetzman, "CSX Corporation," *Cases in Strategic Management and Business Policy* by T. L. Wheelen and J. D. Hunger (Reading, Mass.: Addison-Wesley, 1987), pp. 91–123.

traffic levels and revenue over a three-decade period reflected a shifting industrial base, a changing marketplace, a maturing of competing transportation modes, and a regulatory system that made it almost impossible for the industry to adjust to changing market demands. Between 1947 and 1979, intercity freight tonnage doubled, but railroad tonnage increased only 1%. Barge tonnage in contrast increased 250%, while truck tonnage was up 300%. By the mid-1970s, about one fifth of the industry was facing annual losses and even bankruptcy. Nationalization of the railroads took its first step with the formation of the government-owned Consolidated Rail Corporation (Conrail) in 1976. Formed from the bankrupt Penn Central and five other ailing Northeastern railroads, Conrail was an attempt to keep rail service operating for businesses that were dependent on rail transportation in New York, New Jersey, and New England.

GOVERNMENT DEREGULATION CHANGES INDUSTRY

On October 14, 1980, President Carter signed into law the Staggers Rail Act, allowing the railroad industry to enjoy the first period of real regulatory freedom for many years. This act was the most significant change in federal policy toward this industry since the Interstate Commerce Act of 1887. The Staggers Act overturned many principles derived from the 1887 act and the long subsequent period of regulation.

The goals of the Staggers Act were (1) to assist the industry in its rehabilitation under private ownership, (2) to reform federal regulatory policy so that an efficient, economical, and stable system could be achieved, and (3) to provide the necessary regulation to balance the needs of carriers, shippers, and the public. Under Staggers, rail carriers no longer were obliged to provide unprofitable services. They were then allowed to set rates and services that could generate a profit. However, the Interstate Commerce Commission (ICC) still preserved the power to prevent monopolistic practices. Another important result of the Staggers Act had been the facilitation of rail mergers by speeding the decision process used by the ICC to review applications.

After the merger that formed CSX, the Norfolk and Western Railroad merged with the Southern Railway Company, to form Norfolk Southern Corporation. This combination was almost inevitable, because the Chessie System had been the traditional competitor of the N&W in the North, while Seaboard and Southern had been long-standing rivals in the South. In 1985 three rail systems dominated the eastern United States: *CSX, Norfolk Southern,* and *Conrail.* See Table 4.6 for a comparison of the three systems.

COMPETITIVE RIVALRY INCREASES

Since deregulation occurred, railroad rivalry was like "chess-type playing where you make a move and somebody else makes a countermove and you have to figure out what your next move is," said James A. Hagen, Conrail's Senior Vice-President for Marketing and Sales. This was definitely a new era for railroads. Learning to live in the deregulated environment became a must for everyone in the industry. Competition demanded that mentalities that had been constrained by excessive regulation and were more accustomed to cooperating with competitors than competing with them, be reshaped into outlooks that could generate the fresh ideas required by the newly invigorated market competition, resulting from deregulation.

TABLE 4.6

A Comparison of the Three Major Eastern Railroads

	12/31/84			12/31/83			12/31/82		
	Norfolk Southern	CSX	Conrail	Norfolk Southern	CSX	Conrail	Norfolk Southern	CSX	Conrail
Rail Operating Revenues[1]	3,524.6	5,058.0	3,379.4	3,148.1	4,554.0	3,076.4	3,359.0	4,554.0	3,616.6
Rail Operating Income[1]	734.0	657.0	466.0	543.7	446.0	288.2	659.3	365.0	48.6
Total Net Income[1]	482.2	465.0	500.2	356.5	272.0	313.0	461.8	414.0	174.2

		AS OF 12/31/84		
		Norfolk Southern	CSX	Conrail
	Route Miles	18,252	26,000	15,400
	Rail Employees	37,998	53,031	39,044

SOURCES: *Moody's Transportation Manual 1985;* CSX Corporation, *1984 Annual Report;* and *Standard Corporate Descriptions* (Standard & Poor's Corporation), October 1985.

NOTE: [1]In millions of dollars.

PRESSURES FOR RE-REGULATION

In March 1983, the National Industrial Traffic League (NITL), a shipper's trade and lobbying group, complained that what it called a growing "balkanization" of the nation's rail network could lead to regional monopolies. On October 22, 1984, both houses of Congress promised to look into shipper's complaints about alleged rate abuses resulting from rail deregulation. The specific issue was the criteria used by the ICC in its deciding whether a rate was excessively high and therefore subject to administrative action. Also at issue were the rate-making guidelines that the ICC recommended for the determining of maximum rates. A good deal of controversy had been generated by the application of these guidelines to coal shipments. "During the early part of 1985, we anticipate that Congress will closely examine the implementation of the Staggers Act, and take any legislative action that must be taken to assure the careful balance (between the interest of shippers and rail carriers) struck in the act," said a letter circulated in Congress and signed by sixteen senators.

Further, there appeared to be some resistance, by shippers, to the idea of a multimodal transportation conglomerate. Commonly held notions about the best relationship between supplier and customer dictated that a firm not let itself get too dependent on any one supplier. (This attitude was one of the major reasons that many coal-fired utility plants had been located along rivers as well as beside railway tracks. With this location the utility had the leverage of threatening to take its traffic elsewhere if rate negotiations with a railroad did not progress satisfactorily.) Many shippers thus were reluctant to become too dependent on railroads, even with promises of lower costs.

IMPACT OF THE PROPOSED SALE OF CONRAIL

Even though the corporation closed 1984 in a strong financial and physical position, a few strategic issues existed in early 1985 that could strongly affect the future of CSX. One of these was the future of Conrail, the largest customer of CSX. Although the U.S. Department of Transportation had decided to sell its 85% stake in Conrail to Norfolk Southern for $1.2 billion, the deal might not be approved by Congress. Both Watkins (Chairman of CSX) and Paul Funkhouser (President) agreed that a merger between Norfolk Southern and the big Northeastern railroad company Consolidated Rail Corporation (Conrail), could have serious consequences for CSX:

> A Norfolk Southern/Conrail combination would raise serious questions as to the ability of other carriers, including major portions of Chessie, to continue serving areas where so much market control is lodged in one rail system. Abandonment of large parts of Chessie's plant, therefore, would have to be seriously considered. The result could be withdrawal from several thousand miles of service, which would worsen, rather than improve, the competitive service picture.

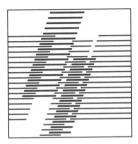

HOW COMPETITIVE FORCES SHAPE STRATEGY*

MICHAEL E. PORTER

The nature and degree of competition in an industry hinge on five forces: the threat of new entrants, the bargaining power of customers, the bargaining power of suppliers, the threat of substitute products or services (where applicable), and the jockeying among current contestants. To establish a strategic agenda for dealing with these contending currents and to grow despite them, a company must understand how they work in its industry and how they affect the company in its particular situation. The author details how these forces operate and suggests ways of adjusting to them and, where possible, of taking advantage of them.

The essence of strategy formulation is coping with competition. Yet it is easy to view competition too narrowly and too pessimistically. While one sometimes hears executives complaining to the contrary, intense competition in an industry is neither coincidence nor bad luck.

Moreover, in the fight for market share, competition is not manifested only in the other players. Rather, competition in an industry is rooted in its underlying economics, and competitive forces exist that go well beyond the established combatants in a particular industry. Customers, suppliers, potential entrants, and substitute products are all competitors that may be more or less prominent or active depending on the industry.

The state of competition in an industry depends on five basic forces, which are diagrammed in Figure 4.A.1. The collective strength of these forces determines the ultimate profit potential of an industry. It ranges from *intense* in industries like tires, metal cans, and steel,

where no company earns spectacular returns on investment, to *mild* in industries like oil field services and equipment, soft drinks, and toiletries, where there is room for quite high returns.

In the economists' "perfectly competitive" industry, jockeying for position is unbridled and entry to the industry very easy. This kind of industry structure, of course, offers the worst prospect for long-run profitability. The weaker the forces collectively, however, the greater the opportunity for superior performance.

Whatever their collective strength, the corporate strategist's goal is to find a position in the industry where his or her company can best defend itself against these forces or can influence them in its favor. The collective strength of the forces may be painfully apparent to all the antagonists; but to cope with them, the strategist must delve below the surface and analyze the sources of each. For example, what makes the industry vulnerable to entry? What determines the bargaining power of suppliers?

Knowledge of these underlying sources of competitive pressure provides the groundwork for a strategic agenda of action. They highlight the critical strengths and weaknesses of the company, animate the positioning of the company in its industry, clarify the areas where strategic changes may yield the greatest payoff, and highlight the places where industry trends promise to hold the greatest significance as either opportunities or threats. Understanding these sources also proves to be of help in considering areas for diversification.

CONTENDING FORCES

The strongest competitive force or forces determine the profitability of an industry and so are of greatest importance in strategy formulation. For example, even a company with a strong position in an industry unthreatened by potential entrants will earn low returns

FIGURE 4.A.1
Forces Governing Competition in an Industry.

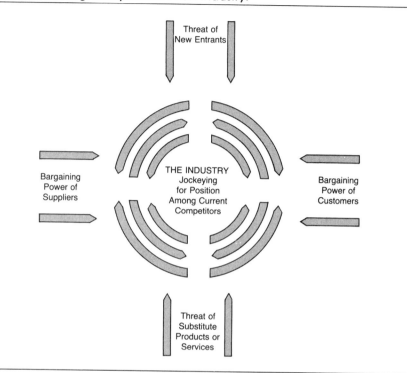

---

if it faces a superior or a lower-cost substitute prod-uct—as the leading manufacturers of vacuum tubes and coffee percolators have learned to their sorrow. In such a situation, coping with the substitute product becomes the number one strategic priority.

Different forces take on prominence, of course, in shaping competition in each industry. In the ocean-going tanker industry the key force is probably the buyers (the major oil companies), while in tires it is powerful OEM buyers coupled with tough competi-tors. In the steel industry the key forces are foreign competitors and substitute materials.

Every industry has an underlying structure, or a set of fundamental economic and technical characteristics, that gives rise to these competitive forces. The strat-egist, wanting to position his company to cope best with its industry environment or to influence that en-vironment in the company's favor, must learn what makes the environment tick.

This view of competition pertains equally to indus-tries dealing in services and to those selling products. To avoid monotony in this article, I refer to both products and services as "products." The same general principles apply to all types of business.

A few characteristics are critical to the strength of each competitive force. I shall discuss them in this section.

Threat of Entry

New entrants to an industry bring new capacity, the desire to gain market share, and often substantial re-sources. Companies diversifying through acquisition into the industry from other markets often leverage their resources to cause a shake-up, as Philip Morris did with Miller beer.

The seriousness of the threat of entry depends on the barriers present and on the reaction from existing competitors that the entrant can expect. If barriers to entry are high and a newcomer can expect sharp retaliation from the entrenched competitors, obviously he will not pose a serious threat of entering.

There are six major sources of barriers to entry:

1. **Economics of scale**—These economies deter entry by forcing the aspirant either to come in on large scale or to accept a cost disadvantage. Scale economies in production, research, marketing, and service are probably the key barriers to entry in the mainframe computer industry, as Xerox and GE sadly discovered. Economies of scale can also act as hurdles in distribution, utilization of the sales force, financing, and nearly any other part of a business.

2. **Product differentiation**—Brand identification creates a barrier by forcing entrants to spend heavily to overcome customer loyalty. Advertising, customer service, being first in the industry, and product differences are among the factors fostering brand identification. It is perhaps the most important entry barrier in soft drinks, over-the-counter drugs, cosmetics, investment banking, and public accounting. To create high fences around their businesses, brewers couple brand identification with economies of scale in production, distribution, and marketing.

3. **Capital requirements**—The need to invest large financial resources in order to compete creates a barrier to entry, particularly if the capital is required for unrecoverable expenditures in up-front advertising or R&D. Capital is necessary not only for fixed facilities but also for customer credit, inventories, and absorbing start-up losses. While major corporations have the financial resources to invade almost any industry, the high capital requirements in certain fields, such as computer manufacturing and mineral extraction, limit the pool of likely entrants.

4. **Cost disadvantages independent of size**—Entrenched companies may have cost advantages not available to potential rivals, no matter what their size and attainable economies of scale. These advantages can stem from the effects of the learning curve (and of its first cousin, the experience curve), proprietary technology, access to the best raw materials sources, assets purchased at preinflation prices, government subsidies, or favorable locations. Sometimes cost advantages are legally enforceable, as they are through patents. (For an analysis of the much-discussed experience curve as a barrier to entry, see the boxed insert.)

5. **Access to distribution channels**—The new boy on the block must, of course, secure distribution of his product or service. A new food product, for example, must displace others from the supermarket shelf via price breaks, promotions, intense selling efforts, or some other means. The more limited the wholesale or retail channels are and the more that existing competitors have these tied up, obviously the tougher that entry into the industry will be. Sometimes this barrier is so high that, to surmount it, a new contestant must create its own distribution channels, as Timex did in the watch industry in the 1950s.

6. **Government policy**—The government can limit or even foreclose entry to industries with such controls as license requirements and limits on access to raw materials. Regulated industries like trucking, liquor retailing, and freight forwarding are noticeable examples; more subtle government restrictions operate in fields like ski-area development and coal mining. The government also can play a major indirect role by affecting entry barriers through controls such as air and water pollution standards and safety regulations.

The potential rival's expectations about the reaction of existing competitors also will influence its decision on whether to enter. The company is likely to have second thoughts if incumbents have previously lashed out at new entrants or if:

- The incumbents possess substantial resources to fight back, including excess cash and unused borrowing power, productive capacity, or clout with distribution channels and customers.

- The incumbents seem likely to cut prices because of a desire to keep market shares or because of industrywide excess capacity.

- Industry growth is slow, affecting its ability to absorb the new arrival and probably causing the financial performance of all the parties involved to decline.

Changing Conditions. From a strategic standpoint there are two important additional points to note about the threat of entry.

First, it changes, of course, as these conditions change. The expiration of Polaroid's basic patents on instant photography, for instance, greatly reduced its absolute cost entry barrier built by proprietary technology. It is not surprising that Kodak plunged into the market. Product differentiation in printing has all but disappeared. Conversely, in the auto industry economies of scale increased enormously with post-World War II automation and vertical integration—virtually stopping successful new entry.

Second, strategic decisions involving a large segment of an industry can have a major impact on the conditions determining the threat of entry. For example, the actions of many U.S. wine producers in the 1960s to step up product introductions, raise advertising levels, and expand distribution nationally surely strengthened the entry roadblocks by raising economies of scale and making access to distribution channels more difficult. Similarly, decisions by members of the recreational vehicle industry to vertically integrate in order to lower costs have greatly increased the economies of scale and raised the capital cost barriers.

Powerful Suppliers and Buyers

Suppliers can exert bargaining power on participants in an industry by raising prices or reducing the quality of purchased goods and services. Powerful suppliers can thereby squeeze profitability out of an industry unable to recover cost increases in its own prices. By raising their prices, soft drink concentrate producers have contributed to the erosion of profitability of bottling companies because the bottlers, facing intense competition from powdered mixes, fruit drinks, and other beverages, have limited freedom to raise *their* prices accordingly. Customers likewise can force down prices, demand higher quality or more service, and play competitors off against each other—all at the expense of industry profits.

The power of each important supplier or buyer group depends on a number of characteristics of its market situation and on the relative importance of its sales or purchases to the industry compared with its overall business.

A *supplier* group is powerful if:

- It is dominated by a few companies and is more concentrated than the industry it sells to.
- Its product is unique or at least differentiated, or if it has built up switching costs. Switching costs are

---

THE EXPERIENCE CURVE AS AN ENTRY BARRIER

In recent years, the experience curve has become widely discussed as a key element of industry structure. According to this concept, unit costs in many manufacturing industries (some dogmatic adherents say in *all* manufacturing industries) as well as in some service industries decline with "experience," or a particular company's cumulative volume of production. (The experience curve, which encompasses many factors, is a broader concept than the better-known learning curve, which refers to the efficiency achieved over a period of time by workers through much repetition.)

The causes of the decline in unit costs are a combination of elements, including economies of scale, the learning curve for labor, and capital-labor substitution. The cost decline creates a barrier to entry because new competitors with no "experience" face higher costs than established ones, particularly the producer with the largest market share, and have difficulty catching up with the entrenched competitors.

Adherents of the experience curve concept stress the importance of achieving market leadership to maximize this barrier to entry, and they recommend aggressive action to achieve it, such as price cutting in anticipation of falling costs in order to build volume. For the combatant that cannot achieve a healthy market share, the prescription is usually, "Get out."

Is the experience curve an entry barrier on which strategies should be built? The answer is: not in every industry. In fact, in some industries, building a strategy on the experience curve can be potentially disastrous. That costs decline with experience in some industries is not news to corporate executives. The significance of the experience curve for strategy depends on what factors are causing the decline.

If costs are falling because a growing company can reap economies of scale through more efficient, automated facilities and vertical integration, then the cumulative volume of production is unimportant to its relative cost position. Here the lowest-cost producer is the one with the largest, most efficient facilities.

A new entrant may well be more efficient than the more experienced competitors; if it has built the newest plant, it will face no disadvantage in having to catch up. The strategic prescription, "You must have the fixed costs buyers face in changing suppliers. They arise because, among other things, a buyer's product specifications tie it to particular suppliers, it has invested heavily in specialized ancillary equipment or in learning how to operate a supplier's equipment (as in computer software), or its production lines are connected to the supplier's manufacturing facilities (as in some manufacture of beverage containers).

- It is not obliged to contend with other products for sale to the industry. For instance, the competition between the steel companies and the aluminum companies to sell to the can industry checks the power of each supplier.

- It poses a credible threat of integrating forward into the industry's business. This provides a check against the industry's ability to improve the terms on which it purchases.

- The industry is not an important customer of the supplier group. If the industry *is* an important customer, suppliers' fortunes will be closely tied to the industry, and they will want to protect the industry through reasonable pricing and assistance in activities like R&D and lobbying.

A *buyer* group is powerful if:

- It is concentrated or purchases in large volumes. Large-volume buyers are particularly potent forces if heavy fixed costs characterize the industry—as they do in metal containers, corn refining, and bulk chemicals, for example—which raise the stakes to keep capacity filled.

- The products it purchases from the industry are standard or undifferentiated. The buyers, sure that they can always find alternative suppliers, may play one company against another, as they do in aluminum extrusion.

- The products it purchases from the industry form a component of its product and represent a significant fraction of its cost. The buyers are likely to shop for a favorable price and purchase selectively. Where the product sold by the industry in question is a small fraction of buyers' costs, buyers are usually much less price sensitive.

- It earns low profits, which create great incentive to lower its purchasing costs. Highly profitable buyers, however, are generally less price sensitive (that is,

---

largest, most efficient plant," is a lot different from "You must produce the greatest cumulative output of the item to get your costs down."

Whether a drop in costs with cumulative (not absolute) volume erects an entry barrier also depends on the sources of the decline. If costs go down because of technical advances known generally in the industry or because of the development of improved equipment that can be copied or purchased from equipment suppliers, the experience curve is no entry barrier at all—in fact, new or less experienced competitors may actually enjoy a cost *advantage* over the leaders. Free of the legacy of heavy past investments, the newcomer or less experienced competitor can purchase or copy the newest and lowest-cost equipment and technology.

If, however, experience can be kept proprietary, the leaders will maintain a cost advantage. But new entrants may require less experience to reduce their costs than the leaders needed. All this suggests that the experience curve can be a shaky entry barrier on which to build a strategy.

While space does not permit a complete treatment here, I want to mention a few other crucial elements

in determining the appropriateness of a strategy built on the entry barrier provided by the experience curve:

- The height of the barrier depends on how important costs are to competition compared with other areas like marketing, selling, and innovation.

- The barrier can be nullified by product or process innovations leading to a substantially new technology and thereby creating an entirely new experience curve.* New entrants can leapfrog the industry leaders and alight on the new experience curve, to which those leaders may be poorly positioned to jump.

- If more than one strong company is building its strategy on the experience curve, the consequences can be nearly fatal. By the time only one rival is left pursuing such a strategy, industry growth may have stopped and the prospects of reaping the spoils of victory long since evaporated.

*For an example drawn from the history of the automobile industry, see William J. Abernathy and Kenneth Wayne, "The Limits of the Learning Curve," *Harvard Business Review,* September-October 1974, p. 109.

of course, if the item does not represent a large fraction of their costs).

- The industry's product is unimportant to the quality of the buyers' products or services. Where the quality of the buyers' products is very much affected by the industry's product, buyers are generally less price sensitive. Industries in which this situation [occurs] include oil field equipment, where a malfunction can lead to large losses, and enclosures for electronic medical and test instruments, where the quality of the enclosure can influence the user's impression about the quality of the equipment inside.

- The industry's product does not save the buyer money. Where the industry's product or service can pay for itself many times over, the buyer is rarely price sensitive; rather, he is interested in quality. This is true in services like investment banking and public accounting, where errors in judgment can be costly and embarrassing, and in business like the logging of oil wells, where an accurate survey can save thousands of dollars in drilling costs.

- The buyers pose a credible threat of integrating backward to make the industry's product. The Big Three auto producers and major buyers of cars have often used the threat of self-manufacture as a bargaining lever. But sometimes an industry engenders a threat to buyers that its members may integrate forward.

Most of these sources of buyer power can be attributed to consumers as a group as well as to industrial and commercial buyers; only a modification of the frame of reference is necessary. Consumers tend to be more price sensitive if they are purchasing products that are undifferentiated, expensive relative to their incomes, and of a sort where quality is not particularly important.

The buying power of retailers is determined by the same rules, with one important addition. Retailers can gain significant bargaining power over manufacturers when they can influence consumers' purchasing decisions, as they do in audio components, jewelry, appliances, sporting goods, and other goods.

Strategic Action. A company's choice of suppliers to buy from or buyer groups to sell to should be viewed as a crucial strategic decision. A company can improve its strategic posture by finding suppliers or buyers who possess the least power to influence it adversely.

Most common is the situation of a company being able to choose whom it will sell to—in other words,

buyer selection. Rarely do all the buyer groups a company sells to enjoy equal power. Even if a company sells to a single industry, segments usually exist within that industry that exercise less power (and that are therefore less price sensitive) than others. For example, the replacement market for most products is less price sensitive than the overall market.

As a rule, a company can sell to powerful buyers and still come away with above-average profitability only if it is a low-cost producer in its industry or if its product enjoys some unusual, if not unique, features. In supplying large customers with electric motors, Emerson Electric earns high returns because its low cost position permits the company to meet or undercut competitors' prices.

If the company lacks a low cost position or a unique product, selling to everyone is self-defeating because the more sales it achieves, the more vulnerable it becomes. The company may have to muster the courage to turn away business and sell only to less potent customers.

Buyer selection has been a key to the success of National Can and Crown Cork & Seal. They focus on the segments of the can industry where they can create product differentiation, minimize the threat of backward integration, and otherwise mitigate the awesome power of their customers. Of course, some industries do not enjoy the luxury of selecting "good" buyers.

As the factors creating supplier and buyer power change with time or as a result of a company's strategic decisions, naturally the power of these groups rises or declines. In the ready-to-wear clothing industry, as the buyers (department stores and clothing stores) have become more concentrated and control has passed to large chains, the industry has come under increasing pressure and suffered falling margins. The industry has been unable to differentiate its product or engender switching costs that lock in its buyers to neutralize these trends.

Substitute Products

By placing a ceiling on prices it can charge, substitute products, or services limit the potential of an industry. Unless it can upgrade the quality of the product or differentiate it somehow (as via marketing), the industry will suffer in earnings and possibly in growth.

Manifestly, the more attractive the price-performance tradeoff offered by substitute products, the firmer the lid placed on the industry's profit potential. Sugar producers confronted with the large-scale commercialization of high-fructose corn syrup, a sugar substitute, are learning this lesson today.

Substitutes not only limit profits in normal times; they also reduce the bonanza an industry can reap in boom times. In 1978 the producers of fiberglass insulation enjoyed unprecedented demand as a result of high energy costs and severe winter weather. But the industry's ability to raise prices was tempered by the plethora of insulation substitutes, including cellulose, rock wool, and styrofoam. These substitutes are bound to become an even stronger force once the current round of plant additions by fiberglass insulation producers has boosted capacity enough to meet demand (and then some).

Substitute products that deserve the most attention strategically are those that (a) are subject to trends improving their price-performance tradeoff with the industry's product, or (b) are produced by industries earning high profits. Substitutes often come rapidly into play if some development increases competition in their industries and causes price reduction or performance improvement.

Jockeying for Position

Rivalry among existing competitors takes the familiar form of jockeying for position—using tactics like price competition, product introduction, and advertising slugfests. Intense rivalry is related to the presence of a number of factors:

- Competitors are numerous or are roughly equal in size and power. In many U.S. industries in recent years foreign contenders, of course, have become part of the competitive picture.
- Industry growth is slow, precipitating fights for market share that involve expansion-minded members.
- The product or service lacks differentiation or switching costs, which lock in buyers and protect one combatant from raids on its customers by another.
- Fixed costs are high or the product is perishable, creating strong temptation to cut prices. Many basic materials businesses, like paper and aluminum, suffer from this problem when demand slackens.
- Capacity is normally augmented in large increments. Such additions, as in the chlorine and vinyl chloride businesses, disrupt the industry's supply-demand balance and often lead to periods of overcapacity and price cutting.

- Exit barriers are high. Exit barriers, like very specialized assets or management's loyalty to a particular business, keep companies competing even though they may be earning low or even negative returns on investment. Excess capacity remains functioning, and the profitability of the healthy competitors suffers as the sick ones hang on [1]. If the entire industry suffers from overcapacity, it may seek government help—particularly if foreign competition is present.
- The rivals are diverse in strategies, origins, and "personalities." They have different ideas about how to compete and continually run head-on into each other in the process.

As an industry matures, its growth rate changes, resulting in declining profits and (often) a shakeout. In the booming recreational vehicle industry of the early 1970s, nearly every producer did well; but slow growth since then has eliminated high returns, except for the strongest members, not to mention many of the weaker companies. The same profit story has been played out in industry after industry—snowmobiles, aerosal packaging, and sports equipment are just a few examples.

An acquisition can introduce a very different personality to an industry, as has been the case with Black & Decker's takeover of McCullough, the producer of chain saws. Technological innovation can boost the level of fixed costs in the production process, as it did in the shift from batch to continuous-line photo finishing in the 1960s.

While a company must live with many of these factors—because they are built into industry economics—it may have some latitude for improving matters through strategic shifts. For example, it may try to raise buyers' switching costs or increase product differentiation. A focus on selling efforts in the fastest-growing segments of the industry or on market areas with the lowest fixed costs can reduce the impact of industry rivalry. If it is feasible, a company can try to avoid confrontation with competitors having high exit barriers and can thus sidestep involvement in bitter price cutting.

FORMULATION OF STRATEGY

Once the corporate strategist has assessed the forces affecting competition in his industry and their underlying causes, he can identify his company's strengths and weaknesses. The crucial strengths and weaknesses from a strategic standpoint are the company's posture vis-à-vis the underlying causes of each force. Where does it stand against substitutes? Against the sources of entry barriers?

Then the strategist can devise a plan of action that may include (1) positioning the company so that its capabilities provide the best defense against the competitive force; and/or (2) influencing the balance of the forces through strategic moves, thereby improving the company's position; and/or (3) anticipating shifts in the factors underlying the forces and responding to them, with the hope of exploiting change by choosing a strategy appropriate for the new competitive balance before opponents recognize it. I shall consider each strategic approach in turn.

Positioning the Company

The first approach takes the structure of the industry as given and matches the company's strengths and weaknesses to it. Strategy can be viewed as building defenses against the competitive forces or as finding positions in the industry where the forces are weakest.

Knowledge of the company's capabilities and of the causes of the competitive forces will highlight the areas where the company should confront competition and where avoid it. If the company is a low-cost producer, it may choose to confront powerful buyers while it takes care to sell them only products not vulnerable to competition from substitutes.

The success of Dr Pepper in the soft drink industry illustrates the coupling of realistic knowledge of corporate strengths with sound industry analysis to yield a superior strategy. Coca-Cola and Pepsi-Cola dominate Dr Pepper's industry, where many small concentrate producers compete for a piece of the action. Dr Pepper chose a strategy of avoiding the largest-selling drink segment, maintaining a narrow flavor line, forgoing the development of a captive bottler network, and marketing heavily. The company positioned itself so as to be least vulnerable to its competitive forces while it exploited its small size.

In the $11.5 billion soft drink industry, barriers to entry in the form of brand identification, large-scale marketing, and access to a bottler network are enormous. Rather than accept the formidable costs and scale economies in having its own bottler network— that is, following the lead of the Big Two and of Seven-Up—Dr Pepper took advantage of the different flavor of its drink to "piggyback" on Coke and Pepsi bottlers who wanted a full line to sell to customers. Dr Pepper

coped with the power of these buyers through extraordinary service and other efforts to distinguish its treatment of them from that of Coke and Pepsi.

Many small companies in the soft drink business offer cola drinks that thrust them into head-to-head competition against the majors. Dr Pepper, however, maximized product differentiation by maintaining a narrow line of beverages built around an unusual flavor.

Finally, Dr Pepper met Coke and Pepsi with an advertising onslaught emphasizing the alleged uniqueness of its single flavor. This campaign built strong brand identification and great customer loyalty. Helping its efforts was the fact that Dr Pepper's formula involved lower raw materials cost, which gave the company an absolute cost advantage over its major competitors.

There are no economies of scale in soft drink concentrate production, so Dr Pepper could prosper despite its small share of the business (6%). Thus Dr Pepper confronted competition in marketing but avoided it in product line and in distribution. This artful positioning combined with good implementation has led to an enviable record in earnings and in the stock market.

Influencing the Balance

When dealing with the forces that drive industry competition, a company can devise a strategy that takes the offensive. This posture is designed to do more than merely cope with the forces themselves; it is meant to alter their causes.

Innovations in marketing can raise brand identification or otherwise differentiate the product. Capital investments in large-scale facilities or vertical integration affect entry barriers. The balance of forces is partly a result of external factors and partly in the company's control.

Exploiting Industry Change

Industry evolution is important strategically because evolution, of course, brings with it changes in the sources of competition I have identified. In the familiar product life-cycle pattern, for example, growth rates change, product differentiation is said to decline as the business becomes more mature, and the companies tend to integrate vertically.

These trends are not so important in themselves;

what is critical is whether they affect the sources of competition. Consider vertical integration. In the maturing minicomputer industry, extensive vertical integration, both in manufacturing and in software development, is taking place. This very significant trend is greatly raising economies of scale as well as the amount of capital necessary to compete in the industry. This in turn is raising barriers to entry and may drive some smaller competitors out of the industry once growth levels off.

Obviously, the trends carrying the highest priority from a strategic standpoint are those that affect the most important sources of competition in the industry and those that elevate new causes to the forefront. In contract aerosol packaging, for example, the trend toward less product differentiation is now dominant. It has increased buyers' power, lowered the barriers to entry, and intensified competition.

The framework for analyzing competition that I have described can also be used to predict the eventual profitability of an industry. In long-range planning the task is to examine each competitive force, forecast the magnitude of each underlying cause, and then construct a composite picture of the likely profit potential of the industry.

The outcome of such an exercise may differ a great deal from the existing industry structure. Today, for example, the solar heating business is populated by dozens and perhaps hundreds of companies, none with a major market position. Entry is easy, and competitors are battling to establish solar heating as a superior substitute for conventional methods.

The potential of this industry will depend largely on the shape of future barriers to entry, the improvement of the industry's position relative to substitutes, the ultimate intensity of competition, and the power captured by buyers and suppliers. These characteristics will in turn be influenced by such factors as the establishment of brand identities, significant economies of scale or experience curves in equipment manufacture wrought by technological change, the ultimate capital costs to compete, and the extent of overhead in production facilities.

The framework for analyzing industry competition has direct benefits in setting diversification strategy. It provides a road map for answering the extremely difficult question inherent in diversification decisions: "What is the potential of this business?" Combining the framework with judgment in its application, a company may be able to spot an industry with a good future before this good future is reflected in the prices of acquisition candidates.

MULTIFACETED RIVALRY

Corporate managers have directed a great deal of attention to defining their businesses as a crucial step in strategy formulation. Theodore Levitt, in his classic 1960 article in HBR, argued strongly for avoiding the myopia of narrow, product-oriented industry definition [2]. Numerous other authorities have also stressed the need to look beyond product function in defining a business, beyond national boundaries to potential international competition, and beyond the ranks of one's competitors today to those that may become competitors tomorrow. As a result of these urgings, the proper definition of a company's industry or industries has become an endlessly debated subject.

One motive behind this debate is the desire to exploit new markets. Another, perhaps more important motive is the fear of overlooking latent sources of competition that someday may threaten the industry. Many managers concentrate so single-mindedly on their direct antagonists in the fight for market share that they fail to realize that they are also competing with other customers and their suppliers for bargaining power. Meanwhile, they also neglect to keep a wary eye out for new entrants to the contest or fail to recognize the subtle threat of substitute products.

The key to growth—even survival—is to stake out a position that is less vulnerable to attack from head-to-head opponents, whether established or new, and less vulnerable to erosion from the direction of buyers, suppliers, and substitute goods. Establishing such a position can take many forms—solidifying relationships with favorable customers, differentiating the product either substantively or psychologically through marketing, integrating forward or backward, establishing technological leadership.

REFERENCES

1. For a complete discussion of exit barriers and their implications for strategy, see my article, "Please Note Location of Nearest Exit." *California Management Review,* Winter 1976, p. 21.

2. Theodore Levitt: "Marketing Myopia," reprinted as a *Harvard Business Review Classic,* September-October 1975, p. 26.

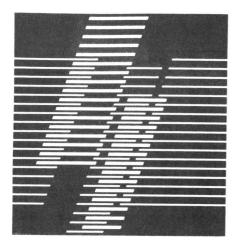

CHAPTER 5

THE INTERNAL ENVIRONMENT

STRATEGIC MANAGEMENT MODEL

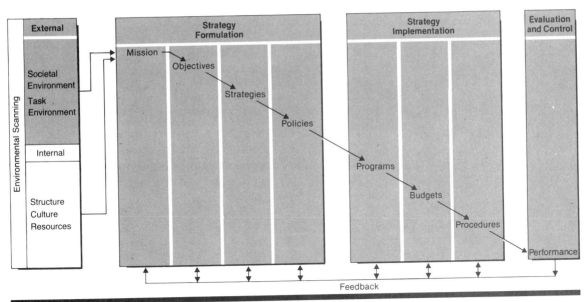

Managers cannot succeed in strategic planning and decision-making at the corporate level without an in-depth understanding of the strategic factors within the corporation. These factors are the internal *strengths* and *weaknesses* that act to either constrain or support a strategy. Part of a firm's internal environment, these factors are not within the short-run control of strategic managers. Instead they form the context within which work is accomplished. Strategic factors in a corporation's internal environment are (1) **structure,** (2) **culture,** and (3) **resources**.

131

5.1

STRUCTURE

The structure of a corporation is often defined in terms of communication, authority, and work flow. It is the corporation's pattern of relationships, its "anatomy." It is a formal arrangement of roles and relationships of people, so that the work is directed toward meeting the goals and accomplishing the mission of the corporation. Sometimes it is referred to as the chain of command and is often graphically described in an organization chart.[1]

Although there is an almost infinite variety of structural forms, certain types are predominant in modern complex organizations. These are simple, functional, divisional, matrix, and conglomerate structures.[2] Figure 5.1 illustrates some of these structures.

Simple Structure

Firms having a simple structure are usually small in size and undifferentiated laterally—that is, there are no functional or product categories. A firm with a simple structure is likely to be managed by an owner-manager who either does all the work or oversees a group of unspecialized people who do whatever needs to be done to provide a single product or service. A simple structure is appropriate when an organization is new and small and the owner-manager can personally grasp all the intricacies of the business. It becomes increasingly inappropriate as the organization grows, unless the owner-manager is able to find other competent people to whom he/she can delegate some responsibilities.

Functional Structure

In a functional structure, work is divided into subunits on the basis of such functions as manufacturing, finance, and sales. Functional structure enables a firm to take advantage of specialists and to deal with complex production or service-delivery problems more efficiently than it could if everyone performed an undifferentiated task. The functional structure is appropriate as long as top management is willing to invest a lot of energy in coordinating the many activities and as long as the company operates mostly in one industry. The long, specialized, vertical channels of communication and authority typical in large functionally structured companies tend to make the firm slow to respond to environmental changes that require coordination across departments, but are very successful when adaptability is not required and predictability is important.

Divisional Structure

When a corporation is organized on the basis of divisions, an extra management layer—division chiefs—is added between top management and

FIGURE 5.1
Basic Structures.

I. SIMPLE STRUCTURE

II. FUNCTIONAL STRUCTURE

III. DIVISIONAL STRUCTURE*

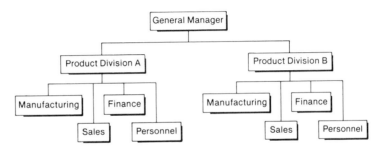

*Conglomerate structure is a variant of the division structure.

IV. MATRIX STRUCTURE

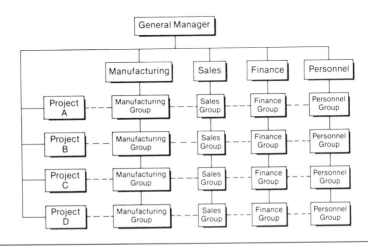

functional managers. The standard functions are then designed around products, clients, or territories. A recent innovation in this area is the use of **strategic business units** (SBUs), in which organizational groups composed of discrete, independent *product-market* segments are identified and given primary responsibility and authority for management of their functional areas. For example, instead of food preparation appliances being housed in three different divisions—such as large appliances, small appliances, and cookware—those divisions can be merged into a single SBU serving the housewares market.

An SBU may be of any size or level, but it must have (1) a unique mission, (2) identifiable competitors, (3) an external market focus, and (4) control of its business functions.[3] Once a large corporation is organized on a divisional basis around strategic business units, there still may be too many SBUs for top management to effectively manage. In this case, an additional management layer—*group executives*—is added between top management and the division or SBU chiefs. The group executive is thus responsible for the management of a number of similar SBUs, such as housewares, building materials, and auto accessories. Approximately 70% of the Fortune 500 corporations are combining divisions or SBUs around group executives.[4] (For more information on SBUs, refer to Chapter 8.)

The divisional structure is appropriate for a firm with many products serving many different markets. Organized so that they operate fairly independently of one another, the divisions can deal with different industries having varying degrees of change and complexity. This structure thus provides the company the flexibility it needs to operate in many industries. It can be inefficient, however, if there is much duplication of equipment and support staff. Furthermore, one division can be operating at overcapacity while another division underutilizes much of its facilities and staff.

Matrix Structure

In matrix structures, functional and divisional areas are combined *simultaneously* at the same level of the corporation. Employees have two superiors, a project manager and a functional manager. The "home" department—that is, engineering, manufacturing, or sales—is usually functional and is reasonably permanent. People from these functional units are assigned on a temporary basis to one or more project units. The project units act like divisions in that they are differentiated on a product-market basis. Pioneered in the aerospace industry, the matrix structure was developed to combine the stability of the functional structure with the flexibility of a project organization. The matrix structure is very useful when the external environment (especially the technological and market aspects) is very complex and changeable. It does, however, produce conflicts revolving around duties, authority, and resource allocation.

Conglomerate Structure

A variant of a divisional structure organized by product, the conglomerate structure is typically an assemblage of separate firms, having different products in different markets but operating together under one corporate umbrella. The divisions (subsidiaries) are independent of each other but share a dependence on central headquarters for financial resources and corporate planning. Its chief advantages to the corporation lie in the limitation of liability, a possible reduction in taxes, and, for the various divisions, the appearance of autonomy. For example, in response to a 1987 rule from the Financial Accounting Standards Board (FASB) requiring greater consolidation of financial statements, Tenneco created a holding company that would permit it to keep separate the heavy debt of its pipeline business from that of its other businesses.[5]

In addition, risks are spread over many different segments of the marketplace. The disadvantages of conglomerate structure derive from its heavy legalistic and financial orientation. In order to keep the legal advantages, the corporation cannot easily combine subsidiaries in attempts to generate operating or marketing synergy. And, the investment orientation at the corporate level can easily prevent top management from understanding divisional (subsidiary) problems in any sense other than financial. There is also a strong temptation for top management to choose a growth by acquisition strategy.[6] Furthermore, the ability to sell off a troubled division can lead to a short-run strategic orientation concerned only with the year-end bottom line.

An understanding of how a particular corporation is structured is very useful in the formulation of a strategy. If the structure is compatible with a proposed change in strategy, it is a corporate strength. If, however, the structure is not compatible with either the present or proposed strategy, it is a definite weakness, and will act to keep the strategy from being implemented properly. Intel Corporation, for example, has had some problems because its successful growth strategy had become incompatible with its centralized decision-making structure. The company had grown too big and its markets too turbulent for the CEO, Andy Grove, to control it so closely. Opportunities were in danger of being missed because of managers' dependence upon Grove for guidance.[7] For this reason, among others, the corporation's particular structure can predispose its strategic managers toward the selection of one strategy over another.[8] For example, research has revealed that diversified corporations using a divisional structure were more likely to move into international activities than were centralized companies using a functional structure.[9]

5.2

CULTURE

A corporation's culture is the collection of beliefs, expectations, and values shared by the corporation's members and transmitted from one generation of employees to another. These create norms (rules of conduct) that define acceptable behavior of people from top management to the operative employee. Myths and rituals, often unrecorded, that emerge over time will emphasize certain norms or values and explain why a certain aspect of the culture is important. Like the retelling of the vision and perseverance of the founder(s) of the corporation, the myth is often tied closely to the corporate mission.

Corporate culture shapes the behavior of people in the corporation. Analysts Schwartz and Davis point this out: "Apparently, the well-run corporations of the world have distinctive cultures that are somehow responsible for their ability to create, implement, and maintain their world leadership positions."[10] Because these cultures have a powerful influence on the behavior of managers, they can strongly affect a corporation's ability to shift its strategic direction.

For example, Exxon Corporation decided in the early 1970s to diversify away from its dependence on the declining petroleum business into the "office of the future." By buying firms from creative entrepreneurs, Exxon acquired three new word processing and printing technologies (named QWIP, QYX, and Vydec) to form Exxon Office Systems. As part of the bargain, the entrepreneurs who had developed these new products were also hired. Unfortunately, the entrepreneurs, who thrived in a helter-skelter world of exciting ideas and quick, risky decisions, were placed under the authority of Exxon's senior executives, people who lived by corporate policy and procedures manuals and made decisions only after many group meetings. One by one, the creative but undisciplined "kids" left the company with its meetings and paperwork and started something new somewhere else. Exxon replaced them with professional managers hired from other office-equipment companies like IBM, Xerox, and Burroughs. Accustomed to large staffs and generous support, the new managers staffed these small business units as if they were the large firms they had just left. Instead of emphasizing research and innovation, they focused on advertising and promotion. The result was an estimated loss of around $2 billion and the eventual sale of Exxon Office Systems to Olivetti and Lanier in 1985. One analyst summarized the basic problem:

> Obviously, Exxon never thought to analyze the subtle nuances of what it takes to run a collection of small technology-driven businesses because it simply wasn't a part of their culture . . . . [Management] never seemed to learn that the lethargic machinery and process technique that works so well in the oil business, simply wouldn't work in the fast-paced office equipment industry.[11]

Peters and Waterman, in their best-selling book *In Search of Excellence*, argue persuasively that the dominance and coherence of culture is an essential ingredient of the excellent companies they studied.

> The top performers create a broad, shared culture, a coherent framework within which charged-up people search for appropriate adaptations. Their ability to extract extraordinary contributions from very large numbers of people turns on the ability to create a sense of highly valued purpose. Such purpose invariably emanates from love of product, providing top-quality services, and honoring innovation and contribution from all.[12]

Peters and Waterman also state that poorer performing companies tend to have cultures that focus on internal politics instead of the customer and on "the numbers" instead of the product or the people who make it.

A study of thirty-four corporations by Denison supports the conclusions of Peters and Waterman. Denison found that companies with participative cultures (i.e., strong employee involvement in corporate decision making) not only have better performance records than those without such a culture, but that the performance difference widens over time. Data collected by Hay Associates in hundreds of companies from 1970 to 1985 also revealed that culture bears a significant relationship to corporate performance. The evidence thus suggests a possible cause and effect relationship between culture and performance.[13]

Corporate culture fulfills several important functions in an organization:

- First, culture conveys a sense of identity for employees;
- Second, culture helps generate employees' commitment to something greater than themselves;
- Third, culture adds to the stability of the organization as a social system;
- Fourth, culture serves as a frame of reference for employees to use to make sense out of organizational activities and to use as a guide for appropriate behavior.[14]

Corporate culture generally reflects the mission of firms. It gives a corporation a sense of *identity:* "This is who we are. This is what we do. This is what we stand for." The culture includes the dominant orientation of the company.[15] Some companies are *market-oriented.* Like IBM and John Deere they define themselves in terms of their customers and their customers' needs. For example, one of the secrets given for the success of Deere and Company during a period of agricultural recession is its rural roots. Unlike International Harvester, which had its headquarters in downtown Chicago, Deere has its headquarters in East Moline, Illinois, in the heart of an agricultural region responsible for two of the nation's major crops, corn and soybeans. Deere has "geographical awareness, because most of its executives live on a farm or near one . . . ."[16]

Other companies may be *materials-* or *product-oriented.* They define themselves in terms of the material they work on, the product they make, or the service they provide. They are first and foremost oil companies, steel companies, railroads, banks, or hospitals. This means that the people working for the company tend to identify themselves in the same way. They don't just work for a company; they *are* truckers, railroaders, bankers. This heavy emphasis on materials or product can partially explain why some industries, such as automobiles and steel, have their own distinct culture that reflects and is reflected in the individual cultures of the member companies.[17] This sharing of a common set of beliefs, values, and assumptions makes it easier for people to move among companies within the same industry than to move to companies in other industries with a different culture. For example, when he left Ford Motor Company, Lee Iacocca stated that he had no interest in pursuing possible offers from International Paper, Lockheed, or Tandy Corporation. Said Iacocca, ". . . cars were in my blood."[18]

Other companies are *technology-oriented*. These companies define themselves in terms of the technology they are organized to exploit. Eastman Kodak, for example, ignored the development of xerography and almost missed out on the change to electronic photography because of its strong commitment to the chemical film technology pioneered by George Eastman.[19] Similarly, high-tech firms in Silicon Valley think of themselves primarily as technological entrepreneurs.

The managers' understanding of a corporation's (or division's) culture is thus imperative if the firm is to be managed strategically. As suggested in Chapter 4's discussion of environmental scanning, an organization's culture can produce a **strategic myopia,** in which strategic managers fail to perceive the significance of changing external conditions because they are partially blinded by strongly held common beliefs. In this instance, a strongly held corporate culture can become a major deterrent to success at a time when the corporation most needs to change its strategic direction.[20] An additional problem with a strong culture is that a change in mission, objectives, strategies, or policies is not likely to be successful if it is in opposition to the accepted culture of the corporation. As was true for structure at a time of change, if the culture is compatible with the change, that culture is an internal strength. But if the corporate culture is not compatible with the change, it is, under circumstances of a changing environment, a serious weakness. This does not mean that a manager should *never* consider a strategy that runs counter to the established culture. However, if such a strategy is to be seriously considered, top management must be prepared to attempt to change the culture as well, a task that will take much time, effort, and persistence.

5.3

RESOURCES

William Newman, an authority in strategic management, points out that a practical way to develop a master strategy of the corporation is to "pick particular roles or niches that are appropriate in view of competition and the company's resources."[21] The company's resources are typically considered in terms of financial, physical, and human resources, as well as organizational systems and technological capabilities. Because these resources have functional significance, we can discuss them under the commonly accepted functional headings of Marketing, Finance, Research and Development, Operations, Human Resources, and Information Systems. These resources, among others, should be audited so that internal strengths and weaknesses can be ascertained.

Corporate-level strategy formulators must be aware of the many contributions each functional area can make to divisional and corporate performance. Functional resources include not only the people in each area but also that area's ability to formulate and implement under corporate guidance the necessary functional objectives, strategies, and policies. Thus the resources include both the knowledge of analytical concepts and procedural techniques common to each area and the ability of the people in each area to utilize them effectively. These are some of the most valuable and well-known concepts and techniques: market segmentation, product life-cycle, capital budgeting, financial leverage, technological competence, operating leverage, experience-curve analysis, job analysis, job design, and decision-support systems. There are many others, of course, but these are the basic ones. If used properly, these resources can improve overall strategic management.

Marketing

The major tasks of the marketing manager from a corporation's point of view is to regulate the level, timing, and character of demand, in a way that will help the corporation achieve its objectives.[22] The marketing manager is the corporation's primary link to the customer and the competition. The manager must therefore be especially concerned with the market position and marketing mix of the firm.

Market position deals with the question, "Who are our customers?" It refers to the selection of specific areas for marketing concentration, and can be expressed in terms of market, product, and geographical locations. Through market research, corporations are able to practice **market segmentation** with various products or services so that management can discover what niches to seek, which new types of products to develop, and how to ensure that a company's many products do not directly compete with one another.[23] For example, Procter and Gamble Company, which markets several shampoos, positioned Prell Concentrate shampoo as a practical, convenience-oriented product, in contrast to Liquid Prell's orientation as the more luxury, beauty-oriented product and Head and Shoulders' orientation as the dandruff-protection shampoo.

The **marketing mix** refers to the particular combination of key variables under the corporation's control, that can be used to affect demand and to gain competitive advantage. These variables are *product, place, promotion,* and *price*. Within each of these four variables are several subvariables, listed in Table 5.1, which should be analyzed in terms of their effects upon divisional and corporate performance.

TABLE 5.1
Marketing Mix Variables

PRODUCT	PLACE	PROMOTION	PRICE
Quality	Channels	Advertising	List price
Features	Coverage	Personal selling	Discounts
Options	Locations	Sales promotion	Allowances
Style	Inventory	Publicity	Payment periods
Brand name	Transport		Credit terms
Packaging			
Sizes			
Services			
Warranties			
Returns			

SOURCE: Philip Kotler, *Marketing Management: Analysis, Planning, and Control,* 4th ed. (Englewood Cliffs, N.J.: Prentice-Hall, 1980), p. 89. Copyright © 1980. Reprinted by permission of Prentice-Hall, Inc.

One of the most useful concepts in marketing insofar as strategic management is concerned is that of the **product life cycle.** As depicted in Figure 5.2, the product life-cycle is a graph showing time plotted against the dollar sales of a product as it moves from introduction through growth and maturity to decline. This concept enables a marketing manager to examine the marketing mix of a particular product or group of products in terms of its position in its life cycle. Although marketing people agree that different products will have differently shaped life cycles, research concludes that a consideration of the product life cycle is an important factor in strategy formulation.[24]

Finance

The job of the financial manager is the management of funds. The manager must ascertain the best *sources* of funds, *uses* of funds, and *control* of funds. Cash must be raised from internal or external financial sources and allocated for different uses. The flow of funds in the operations of the corporation must be monitored. Benefits, in the form of returns, repayments, or products and services, must be given to the sources of outside financing. All these tasks must be handled in a way that complements and supports overall corporate strategy.

From a strategic point of view, the financial area should be analyzed to see how well it deals with funds. The mix of externally generated short-term and long-term funds in relation to the amount and timing of internally generated funds should be appropriate to the corporate objectives, strategies,

FIGURE 5.2
The Product Life-Cycle

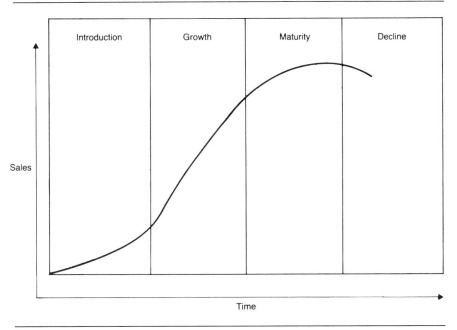

*The right end of the Growth stage is often called Competitive Turbulence because of price and distribution competition that shakes out the weaker competitors. For further information see C. R. Wasson, *Dynamic Competitive Strategy and Product Life Cycles*, 3rd ed., (Austin, Tex.: Austin Press, 1978).

and policies. The concept of **financial leverage** (the ratio of total debt to total assets) is very useful in descriptions of the use of debt to increase the earnings available to common stockholders.[25] When the corporation finances its activities by sales of bonds or notes instead of through stock, the earnings per share are boosted: the interest paid on the debt reduces taxable income, but there are fewer stockholders to share the profits. The debt, however, does raise the firm's break-even point above what it would have if the firm had financed from internally generated funds only. High leverage may therefore be perceived as a corporate strength in times of prosperity and ever-increasing sales, or as a weakness in times of a recession and dropping sales. This is because leverage acts to magnify the effect on earnings *per share* of an increase or decrease in dollar sales.

The knowledge and use of **capital budgeting** techniques is an important financial resource. A good finance department will be able to analyze and rank possible investments in such fixed assets as land, buildings, and equipment, in terms of the additional outlays and additional receipts that will result. Then it can rank investment proposals on the basis of some accepted criteria or "hurdle rate" (for example, years to pay back investment, rate of return, time to break-even point, etc.) and make its decisions. To select acquisition candidates and to analyze the amount of risk present in a corporation's portfolio of business units, financial analysts should also be able to utilize the Capital Asset Pricing Model (CAPM) and the Arbitrage Pricing Model (APM).[26]

Break-even analysis is an analytical technique used by approximately 80% of corporations in their study of the relations among fixed costs, variable costs, and profits.[27] It is a device used for determining the point at which sales will just cover total costs. When used in conjunction with some form of discounted cash flow analysis, like net present value or internal rate of return, it can provide useful information to strategic decision makers. Figure 5.3 shows a basic break-even chart for a hypothetical company. The chart is drawn on a unit basis; the volume produced is shown on the horizontal axis and costs and revenues are measured on the vertical axis. Fixed costs are $80,000, as represented by the horizontal line; variable costs are $2.40 per unit. Total costs rise by $2.40, the amount of the variable costs, for each additional unit produced past $80,000, and the product is sold at $4.00 per unit. The total-revenue line is a straight line increasing directly with production. As is usual, the slope of the total revenue line is steeper than that of the total cost line because, for every unit sold, the firm receives $4.00 of revenue for every $2.40 paid out for labor and material. Up to the break-even point (the intersection of the total revenue and total cost lines), the firm suffers losses. After that point, the firm earns profits at an increasing amount as volume increases. In this instance, the break-even point for the

FIGURE 5.3
Break-even Chart.

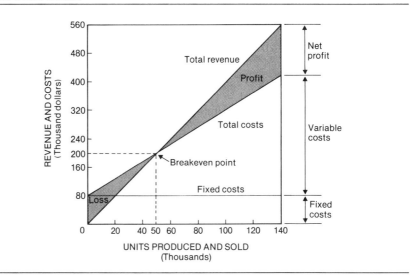

firm is at a sales and cost level of $200,000 and a production level of 50,000 units.

The financial manager must be very knowledgeable of these and other more sophisticated analytical techniques if management is to successfully implement functional strategies, such as internal financing or leveraged buyouts (discussed in Chapter 7).

Research and Development

The R&D manager is responsible for suggesting and implementing a corporation's technological strategy in light of its corporate objectives and policies. The manager's job therefore involves (1) choosing among alternative new technologies to use within the corporation, (2) developing methods of embodying the new technology in new products and processes, and (3) deploying resources so that the new technology can be successfully implemented.[28]

The term *research and development* is used to describe a wide range of activities. In some corporations R&D is conducted by scientists in well-equipped expensive laboratories where the focus is on theoretical problem areas. In other firms, R&D is heavily oriented toward marketing and is concerned with product or product-packaging improvements. In still other firms, R&D takes on an engineering orientation concentrating on quality control, the manufacturing of design specifications, and the development of improved production equipment. Most corporations will have a mix of basic, applied, and engineering R&D. The balance of these types of research is known as the **R&D mix** and should be appropriate to the corporate strategy.

A corporation's R&D unit should be evaluated for **technological competence** in both the development and use of innovative technology. Not only should the corporation make a consistent research effort (as measured by reasonably constant corporate expenditures that result in usable innovations), it should also be proficient in managing research personnel and integrating their innovations into its day-to-day operations. If a company is not proficient in **technology transfer**, the process of taking a new technology from the laboratory to the marketplace, it will not gain much advantage from new technological advances. Both American Telephone and Telegraph (AT&T) and Xerox Corporation have been criticized for their inability to take the research, ideas, and innovations bubbling up from their sophisticated R&D facilities (AT&T's Bell Labs and Xerox's Palo Alto Research Center) and packaging them in improved products and services.

Corporations operating in technology-based industries must be willing to make substantial investments in R&D. For example, the computer and pharmaceutical industries spend an average of 8.3% and 7.8% respectively of their sales dollars for R&D. As shown in Table 5.2 other industries, such as steel and tobacco, spend less than 1%. General Electric spends a large amount of money on R&D. Michael Carpenter, Vice-President of Corporate

TABLE 5.2
R&D Industry Expenditures—1986

INDUSTRY	SALES (Millions of Dollars)	PROFITS (Millions of Dollars)	R&D EXPENSES			
			(Millions of Dollars)	Percent of Sales	Percent of Pretax Profits	Dollars per Employee
Aerospace	79,124	1,680	3,584	4.5	116.7	4,616
Appliances	7,605	(5)	128	1.7	75.1	1,372
Automotive:						
Cars, trucks	201,809	7,577	7,402	3.7	74.0	5,076
Parts, equipment	14,459	334	341	2.4	52.8	2,119
Building materials	13,723	574	223	1.6	20.4	2,073
Chemicals	89,797	4,247	3,662	4.1	48.6	6,093
Conglomerates	52,114	(844)	1,354	2.6	140.9	2,187
Containers	1,192	65	19	1.6	15.7	1,879
Drugs	60,549	6,312	4,721	7.8	48.4	8,172
Electrical	57,211	3,759	1,864	3.3	33.4	2,984
Electronics	59,311	1,622	2,586	4.4	93.8	3,237
Food & beverage	71,748	3,311	611	0.9	10.5	780
Fuel	258,158	9,807	1,958	0.8	10.2	3,329
Informational processing:						
Computers	94,138	6,488	7,857	8.3	69.4	8,905
Office equipment	5,147	286	249	4.8	49.9	3,895
Peripherals	23,021	895	1,615	7.0	108.0	6,356
Software, services	6,086	482	468	7.7	55.8	6,528
Instruments	16,417	476	1,092	6.7	124.7	5,304
Leisure time	24,810	756	1,467	5.9	108.7	5,026
Machinery:						
Farm, construction	23,096	57	693	3.0	1,352	3,276
Machine tools, industrial, mining	14,983	213	487	3.3	121	2,788
Metals & mining	11,267	428	204	1.8	34.9	2,269

Miscellaneous manufacturing	61,055	3,115	1,693	2.8	30.5	2,305
Oil service & supply	21,257	(4,246)	699	3.3	NEG	2,939
Paper & paper products	29,517	1,440	349	1.2	14.7	1,561
Personal & home care products	30,664	1,431	794	2.6	32.6	3,793
Semiconductors	10,760	(327)	1,310	12.2	NEG	7,318
Steel	21,978	(2,069)	113	0.5	NEG	851
Telecommunications	54,502	1,664	2,762	5.1	103.4	5,300
Textiles, apparel	8,836	171	68	0.8	20.4	626
Tires, rubber	20,924	309	550	2.6	78.3	2,272
Tobacco	5,773	469	22	0.4	2.6	267
All-Industry Composite	1,451,300	50,500	50,900	3.5	55.5	4,201

SOURCE: Adapted from "R&D Scoreboard," *Business Week* (June 22, 1987), pp. 141–160.

Business Development and Planning at GE, points out that much of the company's growth has developed internally out of its R&D efforts. He states: "We spend half as much money each year on R&D as all the money going into the venture capital industry. . . . As a result GE has always been at the leading edge of technology."[29] A good rule of thumb for R&D spending is that a corporation should spend at a "normal" rate for that particular industry. According to PIMS data (to be discussed in Chapter 6), those companies that spend 1% of sales more or 1% of sales less than the average have lower ROIs.[30] Simply spending money on R&D or new projects does not mean, however, that the money will produce useful results. Between 1950 and 1979, the United States steel industry spent 20% more on plant maintenance and upgrading for each ton of production capacity added or replaced than did the Japanese steel industry. Nevertheless, U.S. steelmakers failed to recognize and adopt two "breakthroughs" in steel-making—the basic oxygen furnace and continuous casting. Their hesitancy to adopt new technology caused them to lose the world steel market.[31]

In addition to money, another important consideration in the effective management of research and development is the time factor. It is generally accepted that the time needed for meaningful profits to result from the inception of a specific R&D program is typically seven to eleven years.[32] If a corporation is unwilling to invest the large amounts of money and time for its own program of research and development, it might be able to purchase or lease the equipment, techniques, or patents necessary to stay abreast of the competition. To gain some manufacturing advantage over General Motors, Ford Motor Company, for instance, invested $20 million during 1985 in American Robot Corporation. Ford and American Robot planned to fully automate Ford's new electronic components plant near Toronto before GM would be able to complete a comparable facility. Ford's Chairman Donald E. Petersen reported that similar investments might follow: "If the best way to get technology is through acquisitions, we have an open-door policy."[33]

Those corporations that do purchase an innovative technology must, nevertheless, have the technological competence to make good use of it. Unfortunately, some managers who introduce the latest technology into their company's processes do not adequately assess the competence of their organization to handle it. For example, a survey conducted in Great Britain found that 44% of all companies that started to use robots met with initial failure, and that 22% of these firms abandoned the use of robots altogether, mainly because of inadequate technological knowledge and skills.[34] Similar problems with the introduction of robotization and computer-aided manufacturing have been noted at General Motors' new assembly plant in Hamtramck, Michigan, and at Ford's recently remodeled St. Louis assembly plant. "They're now discovering that if you don't have good management, you'll end up with a rotten automated plant," concluded David Cole, Director of the University of Michigan's Office for the Study of Automotive Transportation.[35]

The R&D manager must determine when to abandon present technology and when to develop or adopt new technology. After several years of studying progress and patterns in various technologies, Richard Foster of McKinsey and Company states that the displacement of one technology by another **(Technological Discontinuity)** is a frequent and strategically important phenomenon. For each technology within a given field or industry, the plotting of product performance against research effort/expenditures on a graph results in an S-shaped curve. Foster describes the process depicted in Figure 5.4.

> Early in the development of the technology a knowledge base is being built and progress requires a relatively large amount of effort. Later, progress comes more easily. And then, as the limits of that technology are approached, progress becomes slow and expensive. *That* is when R&D dollars should be allocated to technology with more potential. That is also—not so incidentally—when a competitor who has bet on a new technology can sweep away your business or topple an entire industry.[36]

The presence of such a *technological discontinuity* in the world's steel industry during the 1960s can explain why the large capital expenditures by U.S. steel companies failed to keep them competitive with the Japanese firms adopting the new technologies. As Foster points out: "History has

FIGURE 5.4
Technological Discontinuity.

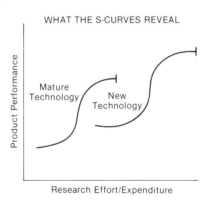

WHAT THE S-CURVES REVEAL

In the corporate planning process, it is generally assumed that incremental progress in technology will occur. But past developments in a given technology cannot be extrapolated into the future, because every technology has its limits. The key to competitiveness is to determine when to shift resources to a technology with more potential.

shown that as one technology nears the end of its S-curve, competitive leadership in a market generally changes hands."[37] This phenomenon continues to occur in the semiconductor industry with each new wave of microchip technology. Each time, the more established firms, which have much invested in the old technology, cannot risk cannibalizing themselves in a bet on future technology, and are subsequently left behind.[38] Even though numerous companies in various industries have invested substantially in the energy and resources needed for their conversion to leading-edge technologies, there have been relatively few successes.[39]

Ansoff recommends that strategic managers deal with technology substitution by (1) continually searching for sources from which new technologies are likely, (2) as the technology surfaces, making a timely commitment to either acquire the new technology or to prepare to leave the market, and (3) reallocating resources from improvements in the older process-oriented technology to investments in the newer, typically product-oriented, technology as the new technology approaches commercial realization. One way of assessing the need for technology conversion is by calculating a **Deterioration of Cost (DOC) Index,** which compares the average unit cost of the currently installed technology to that of the expected average unit cost of state-of-the-art (SOTA) technology. As proposed by Swamidass, the index is calculated as follows:

$$\text{DOC Index} = \frac{\text{Average unit cost for installed technology}}{\text{Average unit cost for SOTA technology}} \times 100\%$$

When the currently installed technology has a higher unit cost than does the state-of-the-art technology, the DOC Index would have a value greater than 100%. For example, when installed technology is inferior to SOTA technology, the DOC Index might be 135%, meaning that when the currently installed technology is used, the average unit cost is 35% more than the likely average unit cost attainable with the new technology. To reflect how quickly new technologies are gaining advantage over current ones, DOC Indexes could be calculated over time. Top management might agree on a specific DOC figure, such as 150%, to serve as the *modernization point* for conversion to the new technology. The index figure could be based on investment criteria, such as break even, pay back, or rate of return.[40]

Operations (Manufacturing/Service)

If the corporation is in business to transform tangible raw materials, like iron ore or petroleum, into usable products, like automobiles, machine parts, or plastic raincoats, the transformation process can be called *manufacturing*. If, however, the corporation is in the business of using people's skills and knowledge, such as those of doctors, lawyers, or loan officers, to provide services via hospitals, legal clinics, or banks, the work involved can be called *service*. These functions can be found in any corporation producing and providing either a tangible product or an intangible service. Many of the key concepts and techniques popularly used in manufacturing can therefore be applied to service businesses.[41]

The primary task of the manufacturing or service manager is to develop and operate a system that will produce the required number of products or services, with a certain quality, at a given cost, within an allotted time. However, manufacturing plants vary significantly depending on the type of product made. In very general terms, manufacturing can be intermittent or continuous. In **intermittent systems** (job shops), the item normally goes through a sequential process, but the work and sequence of the process vary. At each location, the tasks determine the details of processing and the time required for them. In contrast, **continuous systems** are those laid out as lines on which products can be continuously assembled or processed. An example is an automobile assembly line.

The type of manufacturing system used by a corporation determines divisional or corporate strategy. It makes no sense, for example, to plan to increase sales by saturating the market with low-priced products if the corporation's manufacturing process was designed as an intermittent "job shop" system that produces one-time-only products to a customer's specifications. Conversely, a plan to produce a number of specialty products might not be economically feasible if the manufacturing process was designed to be a mass-producing, continuous system using low-skilled labor or special purpose robots.

Continuous systems are popular because they allow a corporation to take advantage of manufacturing **operating leverage.** According to Weston and Copeland, operating leverage is the impact of a given change in sales volume on net operating income.[42] For example, a highly labor-intensive firm has little automated machinery and thus a small amount of fixed costs. It has a fairly low break-even point, but its variable cost line has a relatively steep slope. Because most of the costs associated with the product are variable (many employees earn piece rate wages), its variable costs are higher than those of automated firms. Its advantage over other firms is that it can operate at low levels and still be profitable. Once its sales reach break-even, however, the huge variable costs as a percentage of total costs keep the profit per unit at a relatively low level. Its low operating leverage thus prevents the firm from gathering the huge profits possible from a high volume of sales. In terms of strategy, this firm should look for a niche in the marketplace for which it can produce and sell a reasonably small quantity of goods.

In contrast, a capital-intensive firm has a lot of money in fixed investments, such as automated processes and highly sophisticated machinery. Its labor force, relatively small but highly skilled, earns salaries rather than piece-rate wages. Consequently, this firm has a high amount of fixed costs. It also has a relatively high break-even point, but its variable cost line rises slowly. Its advantage is that once it reaches break-even, its profits rise faster than do those of less automated firms. In terms of strategy, this firm needs to find a high-demand niche in the marketplace where it can produce and sell a large quantity of goods. Its high operating leverage makes it an extremely profitable and competitive firm once it reaches its high break-even point. Changes in the level of sales have a magnified (leveraged) impact on profits. In times of recession, however, this type of firm is likely to suffer huge losses. During an economic downturn, the firm with less automation and thus less leverage is more likely to survive comfortably, because a drop in sales affects primarily variable costs. It is often easier to lay off labor than to sell off specialized plants and machines.

The operations of a service business can also be continuous or intermittent. Continuous operations describe fairly similar services provided to the *same* clientele over a period of time (such as treatment of patients in a long-term-care hospital), whereas intermittent operations describe somewhat variable services provided to *different* clientele over a period of time (such as once-a-year auditing or income tax counseling by a CPA firm). To use operating leverage, service firms that use continuous operations might be able to substitute diagnostic machinery or videotape machines for highly paid professional personnel. Those using batch or intermittent operations might be able to substitute lower-paid support personnel for some of the more routine services performed by highly paid professionals.

A conceptual framework that many large corporations have used successfully is the **experience curve** (originally called learning curve). The concept as it applies to manufacturing is that unit production costs decline by some fixed percentage (commonly 20%–30%) each time the total accumulated volume of production in units doubles. The actual percentage varies by industry and is based upon many variables: the amount of time it takes a person to learn a new task; scale economies; product and process improvements; lower raw materials costs; and other variables. For example, in an industry where an 85% experience curve can be expected, a corporation might expect a 15% reduction in costs for every doubling of volume. The total costs per unit (adjusted for inflation) can be expected to drop from $100 when the total production is 10 units, to $85 ($100 × 85%) when production increases to 20 units, and to $72.25 ($85 × 85%) when it reaches 40 units.[43] Achieving these results often means making investments in R&D and fixed assets; higher operating leverage and less flexibility thus result. Nevertheless, the manufacturing strategy is one of building capacity ahead of demand, in order to achieve the lower unit costs that develop from the experience curve. On the basis of some future point on the experience curve, price the product or service very low, so as to preempt competition and increase market demand. The resulting high number of units sold and high market share should result in high profits, based on the low unit costs.[44] This idea of management's using the anticipated experience curve to price low, in order to gain high market share and thus high profits underlies the Boston Consulting Group's portfolio matrix (discussed in Chapter 6).

The experience curve is commonly used in management's estimating the production costs of (1) a product never before made with the present techniques and processes or (2) current products produced by newly introduced techniques or processes. The concept was first applied in the airframe industry and can be applied in the service industry as well. While many firms have used experience curves extensively, an unquestioning acceptance of the industry norm (such as 80% for the airframe industry or 70% for integrated circuits) is very risky. The experience curve of the industry as a whole might not hold true for a particular company for a variety of reasons.[45]

Recently, the use of large mass-production facilities to take advantage of experience-curve economies has been criticized. The use of CAD/CAM (computer-assisted design and computer-assisted manufacturing) and robot technology means that learning times are shorter and products can be economically manufactured in small, customized batches. Emphasizing *economies of scope* over *economies of scale,* a number of firms have introduced "flexible manufacturing." The new flexible factories permit a low-volume output of custom-tailored products to produce a profit.[46] It is thus possible to have the cost advantages of continuous systems with the customer-oriented advantages of intermittent systems. For example, Deere's new tractor assembly plant in Waterloo, Iowa, can produce more than 5,000 variations of its tractors to suit its customers' needs.[47]

In conclusion, the operations manager in charge of either manufacturing or services must be very knowledgeable of forecasting, scheduling, purchasing, quality assurance, process design, job design, work measurement, just-in-time production systems, and maintenance and reliability, among other things, in order to develop an appropriate operations functional strategy.[48]

Human Resources

The primary task of the manager of human resources is to improve the match between individuals and jobs. The quality of this match influences job performance, employee satisfaction, and employee turnover.[49] Consequently, human resource management (HRM) is concerned with the selection and training of new employees, appraisal of employee performance, the assessment of employees' promotion potential, and recruitment and personnel planning for the future. HRM is also highly involved in wage and salary administration, labor negotiations, job design, and employee morale.

A good HRM department should be competent in the use of attitude surveys and other feedback devices to assess employees' satisfaction with their jobs and with the corporation as a whole. HRM managers should also be knowledgeable in job analysis and competent in its use. **Job analysis** is a means of obtaining job-description information about what needs to be accomplished by each job in terms of quality and quantity. Up-to-date job descriptions are essential not only for proper employee selection, appraisal, training, and development; wage and salary administration; and labor negotiations, but also for summarizing the corporate-wide human resources in terms of employee-skill categories. Just as a corporation must know the number, type, and quality of its manufacturing facilities, it also must know the kinds of people it employs and the skills they possess. This knowledge is essential for the formulation and implementation of corporate strategy. The best strategies are meaningless if employees do not have the skills to carry them out or if jobs cannot be designed to accommodate the available workers. Honeywell, Inc., for example, uses *talent surveys* to ensure that it has the right mix of talents for implementation of its planned strategies.[50]

A good human resource manager should be able to work closely with the unions if the corporation is unionized. A recent development is the increasing desire by union leaders to work jointly with management in the formulation and implementation of strategic changes. For example, when General Electric announced its intention to close it Charleston, South Carolina, steam-turbine generator plant in 1985, the United Electrical Workers proposed to management eleven alternative products the plant could produce. To save jobs, other unions are making the same argument. The United Food and Commercial Workers Union and the Great Atlantic and Pacific Tea Company (A&P) management jointly developed a strategic plan in 1981 to reverse four years of financial losses. Employees in Philadelphia accepted a 25% pay cut in exchange for more input into store decision making and a cash bonus system equal to 1% of the store's sales—contingent upon their reducing labor costs from 15% to 10%. (The industry average was 12%). Stores were renamed Super Fresh to reflect the company's increased concern for both its customers and employees. By 1986, employees were much happier, costs had dropped to 11% of stores' sales, market shares had doubled, and management had expanded the program along the U.S. East Coast and into its stores in other states.[51] Jerome M. Rosow, President of the Work in America Institute, states that the involvement of union leaders in business decision making is a "major breakthrough which has great potential for improving the competitive edge of those companies."[52]

Human resource departments have found that, to reduce employee dissatisfaction and unionization efforts (or conversely, to improve employee satisfaction and existing union relations), they must consider the quality of work life (QWL) in the design of jobs. Partially a reaction to the traditionally heavy emphasis upon technical and economic factors in job design, QWL emphasizes the human dimension of work.

In general, **quality of work life** is "the degree to which members of a work organization are able to satisfy important personal needs through their experiences in the organization."[53] The knowledgeable human resource manager should therefore be able to improve the corporation's quality of work life by (1) introducing participative problem-solving, (2) restructuring work, (3) introducing innovative reward systems, and (4) improving the work environment.[54] These improvements will lead to hopefully a more participative corporate culture and thus higher performance.

Corporations such as General Motors, AT&T, Ford, Westinghouse, Xerox, Honeywell, Bethlehem Steel, and Procter and Gamble are just a few of the growing number of companies actively involved in improving QWL through job and plant redesigning. About 1,500 companies were using one version of the QWL programs, the quality circle, by the mid-1980s.[55]

The quality of work life becomes especially important in today's world of global communication and transportation systems. Advances in technology are copied almost immediately by competitors around the world. People, however, are not as willing to move to other companies in other countries. It is therefore argued that the only long-term resource advantage remaining to a corporation lies in the area of human resources. Paul Hagusa, President of the American subsidiary of Sharp Corporation of Japan, makes this point very clearly.

> Once there was a time when the Americans had very efficient machines and equipment, and Japan did not. At that time—regardless of the workers—those with the most modern machines had the competitive advantage. But now, one country soon has the same machinery as another. So, what makes the difference today is the quality of the people.[56]

Information Systems

The primary task of the manager of information systems (IS) is to design and manage the information flow of the corporation in ways that improve productivity and decision making. Information must be collected, stored, and synthesized in such a manner that it will answer important operating and strategic questions. This function is growing in importance for three reasons: (1) Corporations are growing in size and complexity. Managers must increasingly rely on second-hand, written information. (2) As corporations become more dispersed and decentralized, control techniques must become more sophisticated, so that managers are operating according to agreed plans. (3) The widespread application and falling costs of the computer make it an ideal aid to information processing.

Information systems can fulfill four major purposes.

- *Provide a basis for the analysis of early warning signals that can originate both externally and internally.* Any information system has a database. Like a library, the system collects, categorizes, and files the data so that the system can be used by other departments in the corporation.

- *Automate routine clerical operations.* Payroll, inventory reports, and other records can be generated automatically from the database and thus the need for fileclerks is reduced.

- *Assist managers in making routine (programmed) decisions.* Scheduling orders, assigning orders to machines, and reordering supplies are routine tasks that can be automated through a detailed analysis of the company's work flow.

- *Provide the information necessary for management to make strategic (non-programmed) decisions.* Increasingly, personal computers coupled with sophisticated software are being used to analyze large amounts of information and to calculate likely payoffs from alternate strategies. In order to fulfill this purpose, decision-support systems are needed that allow easy interaction by the user with the computer.[57]

In assessing the corporation's strengths and weaknesses, one should note the level of development of the firm's information system. There are at least four distinct stages of development.[58] These are depicted in Table 5.3. Stage one, **initiation,** generally involves accounting applications. The information-systems personnel are computer technicians who work to reduce clerical costs. Stage two, **growth,** emerges as applications spread beyond accounting into production and marketing. People now use the system to process information like budgets and sales forecasts. Stage three, **moratorium,** is a consolidation phase and calls for a stop to new applications. The spread of information systems is matched by increasing frustration in attempting to use it and by concern over the large costs of operating the system. Unfortunately, many corporations appear to be caught in this stage, with information systems managers being concerned more with computer technology than with its application.[59] Stage four, **integration,** stresses the acceptance of information systems as a major activity that must be integrated into the total corporation. Decision-support systems to aid managers at all levels of the corporation are now developed. A stage-four system is a significant internal strength for a corporation.

The requirements of a well-designed information system include the following:[60]

1. The system must focus managers' attention on the critical success factors in their jobs.

2. The system must present information that is accurate and of high quality.

3. The system must provide the necessary information when it is needed to those who most need it.

4. The system must process raw data so that it can be presented in a manner useful to the manager.

A corporation's information system can be a strength in all three elements of strategic management: formulation, implementation, and evaluation and control. For example, it can not only aid in environmental scanning and in controlling a corporation's many activities, it can also be used as a strategic weapon in the gaining of competitive advantage.[61] For example, American Hospital Supply (AHS), a leading manufacturer and distributor of a broad line of products for doctors, laboratories, and hospitals, has developed an order entry-distribution system that directly links the majority of its customers to AHS computers. The system has been successful because it simplifies ordering processes for customers, reduces costs for both AHS and

TABLE 5.3
Stages of Development of Information Systems

	STAGE ONE INITIATION	STAGE TWO GROWTH	STAGE THREE MORATORIUM	STAGE FOUR INTEGRATION
Application Focus	Accounting and cost reduction	Expansion of applications in many functional areas	Halt on new applications; emphasis on control	Integrating existing systems into the organization; decision support systems
Example Applications	Accounts payable, accounts receivable, payroll, billing	*Stage one plus*: cash flow, budgeting, forecasting, personnel inventory, sales, inventory control	*Stage two plus*: purchasing control, production scheduling	*Stage three plus*: simulation models, financial planning models, on-line personnel query system
MIS Staffing	Primarily computer experts and other skilled professionals	User-oriented system analysts and programmers	Entry of functional managers into MIS unit	Balance of technical and management specialists
Location of MIS in Structure	Embedded in accounting department	Growth in size of staff, still in accounting area	Separate MIS unit reporting to head financial officer	Same as stage three, or decentralization into divisions
What Top Management Wants from MIS	Speed computations with a reduction in clerical staff	Broader applications into operational areas	Concern over MIS costs and usefulness	Acceptance as a major organizational function, involved in planning and control
User Attitudes	Uncertainty; hands-off approach; anxiety over applications	Somewhat enthusiastic; minimum involvement in system design	Frustration and dissatisfaction over developed systems; concern over costs of developing and operating systems	Acceptance of MIS in their work; involvement in system design, implementation, and operation

SOURCE: Reprinted by permission of the *Harvard Business Review*. An exhibit from "Controlling the Costs of Data Services" by Richard L. Nolan (July/August 1977). Copyright © 1977 by the President and Fellows of Harvard College; all rights reserved.

the customer, and allows AHS to provide pricing incentives to the customer. As a result, customer loyalty is high and AHS's share of the market has become large. Other examples are the automated reservations systems American Airlines and United Airlines made available to travel agents. Because the reservations systems featured either American or United most prominently in the listings, other airlines complained that American and United had an unfair advantage in attracting customers.

Information Systems is quickly becoming a corporation's strategic resource. It can be used to monitor environmental changes, counter competitive threats, and assist in the implementation of strategy.[62]

SUMMARY AND CONCLUSION

Before strategies can be developed, top management needs to assess its internal corporate environment for strengths and weaknesses. Management must have an in-depth understanding of the internal strategic factors, such as the corporation's structure, culture, and resources.

A corporation's *structure* is its anatomy. It is often described graphically with an organizational chart. Corporate structures range from the simple structure of an owner-manager-operated business, to the complex series of structures of a large conglomerate. If compatible with present and potential strategies, a corporation's structure is a great internal strength. Otherwise, it can be a serious weakness that will either prevent a good strategy from being implemented properly or reduce the number of strategic alternatives available to a firm.

A corporation's *culture* is the collection of beliefs, expectations, and values shared by its members. A culture produces norms that shape the behavior of employees. Top management must

be aware of this culture and include it in its assessment of strategic factors. Those strategies that run counter to an established corporate culture are likely to be doomed by the poor motivation of the workforce. If a culture is thus antagonistic to a strategy change, the implementation plan will also have to include plans to change the culture.

A corporation's *resources* include not only such generally recognized assets as people, money, and facilities, but also those analytical concepts and procedural techniques known and in use within the functional areas. Because most top managers view their corporations in terms of functional activities, it is simplest to assess resource strengths and weaknesses by functional area. Each area should be audited in terms of financial, physical, and human resources, as well as its organization and technological competencies and capabilities. Just as the knowledge of key functional concepts and techniques is a corporate strength, its absence is a weakness.

DISCUSSION QUESTIONS

1. In what ways can a corporation's structure act as an internal strength or weakness to those formulating corporate strategies?

2. Why should top management be aware of a corporation's culture?

3. What kind of internal factors help determine whether a firm should emphasize the production and sales of a large number of low-priced products, or a small number of high-priced products?

4. What is the difference between operating and financial leverage? What are their implications to strategic planning?

5. Why is technological competence important in strategy formulation?

6. How can management's knowledge of technological discontinuity help to improve a corporation's efficiency?

7. What are the pros and cons of management's using the experience curve to determine strategy?

8. Why should information systems be included in the analysis of a corporation's strengths and weaknesses?

9. What are some of the most important strengths and weaknesses in the internal environment of CSX Corporation as described in the Integrative Case at the end of this chapter. Which of these should have a major impact on strategy formulation at the time of the case and in the future?

NOTES

1. R. L. Daft, *Organization Theory and Design* (St. Paul: West Publishing Co., 1986), pp. 211–212.

2. R. H. Miles, *Macro Organizational Behavior* (Santa Monica, Calif.: Goodyear Publishing, 1980), pp. 28–34.

3. M. Leontiades, "A Diagnostic Framework for Planning," *Strategic Management Journal* (January-March 1983), p. 14.

4. J. M. Stengrevics, "Managing the Group Executive's Job," *Organization Dynamics* (Winter 1984), p. 21.

5. L. Berton, "FASB Issues Rule Making Firms Combine Data of All Their Majority-Owned Firms," *Wall Street Journal* (November 2, 1987), p. 10.

6. D. K. Hurst, "Why Strategic Management Is Bankrupt," *Organizational Dynamics* (Autumn 1986), p. 9.

7. J. W. Wilson, "Can Andy Grove Practice What He Preaches?" *Business Week* (March 16, 1987), pp. 68–69.

8. J. W. Fredrickson, "The Strategic Decision Process and Organizational Structure," *Academy of Management Review* (April 1986), pp. 280–297.
D. Miller, "Configurations of Strategy and Structure: Towards a Synthesis," *Strategic Management Journal* (May-June 1986), pp. 233–249.

9. L. E. Fouraker and J. M. Stopford, "Organization Structure and the Multinational Strategy," *Administrative Science Quarterly* (June 1968), pp. 47–64.

10. H. Schwartz and S. M. Davis, "Matching Corporate Culture and Business Strategy," *Organizational Dynamics* (Summer 1981), p. 30.

11. R. M. Donnelly, "Exxon's 'Office of the Future' Fiasco," *Planning Review* (July/August, 1987), pp. 13 and 14.

12. T. J. Peters and R. H. Waterman, Jr., *In Search of Excellence* (New York: Harper & Row, 1982), pp. 293–294.

13. D. R. Denison, "Bringing Corporate Culture to the Bottom Line," *Organizational Dynamics* (Autumn 1984), pp. 5–22.
G. G. Gordon, "The Relationship of Corporate Culture to Industry Sector and Corporate Performance," in *Gaining Control of the Corporate Culture*, edited by R. H. Kilmann, M. J. Saxton, R. Serpa, and Associates (San Francisco: Jossey-Bass, 1985), p. 103.

14. L. Smircich, "Concepts of Culture and Organizational Analysis," *Administrative Science Quarterly* (September 1983), pp. 345–346.

15. S. C. Wheelwright, "Manufacturing Strategy: Defining the Missing Link," *Strategic Management Journal* (January-March 1984), p. 79.

16. D. Muhm, "John Deere's Company: 145 Years of Farming History," *Des Moines Register* (November 11, 1984), p. 2F.

17. I. I. Mitroff and S. Mohrman, "Correcting Tunnel Vision," *Journal of Business Strategy* (Winter 1987), pp. 49–59.

18. L. Iacocca, *Iacocca: An Autobiography* (Toronto: Bantam Books, 1984), p. 141.

19. T. Moore, "Embattled Kodak Enters the Electronic Era," *Fortune* (August 22, 1983), pp. 120–130.

20. J. Lorsch, "Strategic Myopia: Culture as an Invisible Barrier to Change," in *Gaining Control of the Corporate Culture*, edited by R. H. Kilmann, M. J. Saxton, R. Serpa and Associates (San Francisco: Jossey-Bass, 1985), pp. 84–102.
H. I. Ansoff and T. E. Baker, "Is Corporate Culture the Ultimate Answer?" in *Advances in Strategic Management, Volume 4*, edited by R. Lamb and P. Shrivastava (Greenwich, Conn.: Jai Press, 1986), p. 84.

21. W. H. Newman, "Shaping the Master Strategy of Your Firm," *California Management Review*, vol. 9, no. 3 (1967), p. 77.

22. P. Kotler, *Marketing Management*, 4th ed. (Englewood Cliffs, N.J.: Prentice-Hall, 1980), p. 22.

23. K. J. Roberts, "How to Define Your Market Segment," *Long Range Planning* (August 1986), pp. 53–58.

24. C. A. Anderson and C. P. Zeithaml, "Stage of the Product Life Cycle, Business Strategy, and Business Performance," *Academy of Management Journal* (March 1984), p. 22.

25. C. M. Sandberg, W. G. Lewellen, and K. L. Stanley, "Financial Strategy: Planning and Managing the Corporate Leverage Position," *Strategic Management Journal* (January-February 1987), pp. 15–24.

26. For further information on capital budgeting, discounted cash flow, CAPM, and APM Techniques, see J. F. Weston and T. E. Copeland, *Managerial Finance, 8th Edition* (Chicago: Dryden Press, 1986), pp. 99–138 and 427–478.

27. T. E. Conine, Jr., "The Potential Overreliance On Break-Even Analysis," *Journal of Business Strategy* (Fall, 1986), pp. 84–86.

28. M. A. Maidique and P. Patch, "Corporate Strategy and Technological Policy" (Boston: Intercollegiate Case Clearing House, no. 9-769-033, 1978, rev. March 1980), p. 3.

29. R. J. Allio, "G.E. = Giant Entrepreneur?" *Planning Review* (January 1985), p. 21.

30. M. J. Chussil, "How Much to Spend on R&D?" *The PIMS Letter of Business Strategy, No. 13* (Cambridge, Mass.: The Strategic Planning Institute, 1978), p. 5.

31. T. F. O'Boyle, "Steel's Management Has Itself to Blame," *Wall Street Journal* (May 17, 1983), p. 32.

32. E. F. Finkin, "Developing and Managing New Products," *Journal of Business Strategy* (Spring 1983), p. 45.

33. R. Brandt, M. Rothman, and A. Gabor, "Will Ford Beat GM in the Robot Race?" *Business Week* (May 27, 1985), p. 44.

34. "The Impact of Industrial Robotics on the World of Work," *International Labour Review*, Vol. 125, No. 1, 1986. Summarized in "The Risks of Robotization," *The Futurist* (May-June 1987), p. 56.

35. R. Mitchell, "Detroit Stumbles On Its Way to the Future," *Business Week* (June 16, 1986), p. 103.

36. P. Pascarella, "Are You Investing in the Wrong Technology?" *Industry Week* (July 25, 1983), p. 37.

37. Pascarella, p. 38.

38. M. S. Malone, "America's New Wave Chip Firms," *Wall Street Journal* (May 27, 1987), p. 30.

39. W. P. Sommers, J. Nemec, Jr., and J. M. Harris, "Repositioning With Technology: Making It Work," *Journal of Business Strategy* (Winter 1987), p. 16.

40. H. I. Ansoff, "Strategic Management of Technology," *Journal of Business Strategy* (Winter 1987), p. 35.
P. M. Swamidass, "Planning for Manufacturing Technology," *Long Range Planning* (October 1987), pp. 125–133.
For further information on technological discontinuity, the technology life cycle, and product versus process technology, see M. Tushman and D. Nadler, "Organizing For Innovation," *California Management Review* (Spring 1987), pp. 74–92 and F. Betz, *Managing Technology* (Englewood Cliffs, N.J.: Prentice-Hall, 1987).

41. L. J. Krajewski and L. P. Ritzman, *Operations Management* (Reading, Mass.: Addison-Wesley, 1987), p. 10.

42. Weston and Copeland, p. 220.

43. A. C. Hax and N. S. Majuf, "Competitive Cost Dynamics: The Experience Curve," in A. C. Hax (ed.), *Readings on Strategic Management* (Cambridge, Mass.: Ballinger Publishing Co., 1984), pp. 49–60.

44. B. D. Henderson, *Henderson on Corporate Strategy* (Cambridge, Mass.: Abt Books, 1979), p. 11.

45. G. Hall and S. Howell, "The Experience Curve from the Economist's Perspective," *Strategic Management Journal* (July-September, 1985), pp. 197–212.
R. Luchs, "Successful Businesses Compete on Quality—Not Costs," *Long Range Planning* (February 1986), pp. 16–17.

46. J. Meredith, "The Strategic Advantages of New Manufacturing Technologies for Small Firms," *Strategic Management Journal* (May-June 1987), pp. 249–258.
J. D. Goldhar and M. Jelinek, "Plan for Economies of Scope," *Harvard Business Review* (November-December 1983), pp. 141–148.

47. J. Holusa, "Deere & Co. Leads the Way in 'Flexible' Manufacturing," *Des Moines Register* (January 29, 1984), p. 10F.

48. R. B. Chase and E. L. Prentis, "Operations Management: A Field Rediscovered," *Journal of Management* (Summer 1987), pp. 351–366.

49. H. G. Heneman, D. P. Schwab, J. A. Fossum, and L. D. Dyer, *Personnel/Human Resource Management* (Homewood, Ill.: Richard D. Irwin, Inc., 1986), p. 7.

50. N. Tichy, "Conversation with Edson W. Spencer and Foster A. Boyle," *Organization Dynamics* (Spring 1983), p. 30.

51. C. S. Eklund, "How A&P Fattens Profits By Sharing Them," *Business Week* (December 22, 1986), p. 44.

52. J. Hoerr, "Now Unions Are Helping to Run the Business," *Business Week* (December 24, 1984), p. 69.
"A Bold Tactic to Hold On to Jobs," *Business Week* (October 29, 1984), pp. 70–72.

53. J. L. Suttle, "Improving Life at Work—Problems and Perspectives," *Improving Life at Work: Behavioral Science Approaches to Organizational Change,* eds. J. R. Hackman and J. L. Suttle (Santa Monica, Calif.: Goodyear Publishing, 1976), p. 4.

54. D. A. Nadler and E. E. Lawler III, "Quality of Work Life: Perspectives and Directions," *Organization Dynamics* (Winter 1983), p. 27.

55. C. Camman and G. E. Ledford, Jr., "Productivity Management Through Quality of Work Life Programs," in *Strategic Human Resource Management,* edited by C. J. Fombrun, N. M. Tichy, and M. A. Devanna (New York: John Wiley & Sons, 1984), p. 361.

56. L. E. Calonius, "In a Plant in Memphis, Japanese Firm Shows How to Attain Quality," *Wall Street Journal* (April 29, 1983), p. 14.

57. R. G. Murdick, *MIS: Concepts and Designs* (Englewood Cliffs, N.J.: Prentice-Hall, 1980), p. 253.

58. R. L. Nolan, "Controlling the Costs of Data Services," *Harvard Business Review* (July-August 1977), p. 117.

59. J. E. Izzo, *The Embattled Fortress* (San Francisco: Jossey-Bass, 1987).

60. R. H. Gregory and R. L. Van Horn, "Value and Cost of Information," in J. D. Cougar and R. W. Knapp (eds.), *Systems Analysis Techniques* (New York: Wiley, 1974), pp. 473–489.

61. R. I. Benjamin, J. F. Rockart, M. S. S. Morton, and J. Wyman, "Information Technology: A Strategic Opportunity," *Sloan Management Review* (Spring 1984), p. 5.

62. J. M. Ward, "Integrating Information Systems Into Business Strategies," *Long Range Planning* (June 1987), pp. 19–29.

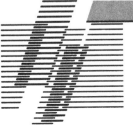

INTEGRATIVE CASE

CSX CORPORATION'S INTERNAL ENVIRONMENT

In early 1985, CSX was composed of two major business segments—*transportation* and *natural resources*. Each segment was composed of two or three business groups. Each business group was in turn made up of CSX subsidiaries, firms owned directly by CSX, or firms controlled by CSX through subsidiaries. Figure 5.5 shows the arrangement of CSX subsidiaries into business segments, business groups, and subsidiaries.

ORGANIZATIONAL STRUCTURE

In the transportation segment were three business groups. The first was the *Rail Transportation Group*, which was composed of the Chessie System Railroad, Seaboard System Railroad, and the Richmond, Fredericksburg and Potomac Railroad (R,F&P), which primarily moved general commodity merchandise and provided the most direct interchange between the Chessie and Seaboard. Chessie Motor Express, a trucking unit, was jointly owned by Chessie and Seaboard and provided coordinated pickup and delivery of intermodal shipments. Motor Express was one of CSX's fastest growing business units. The second business group in the transportation segment was *American Commercial Lines, Inc.*, the barge line acquired as a subsidiary of Texas Gas Resources. The third group was *Other Transportation*, which consisted of four units: CSX Beckett Aviation, a firm that provided aircraft maintenance services and managed the world's largest fleet of executive aircraft; CSX Communications, which represented CSX's participation in a joint venture with Southern New England Telephone; Cybernetics and Systems, a data-processing firm that was a subsidiary of Seaboard and provided MIS services to CSX and outside customers; and Fruit Growers Express, a manufacturer of specialized rail equipment that was owned jointly by Chessie, Seaboard, Conrail, Norfolk Southern, and Denver & Rio Grande Railway, although it was controlled by CSX. In January 1985, however, CSX entered into a letter of intent to sell its aviation subsidiary.

The natural resources segment contained two business groups. The *Energy Group* consisted of four units: Texas Gas Transmission, a natural gas pipeline acquired as part of the Texas Gas Resources (TXG) acquisition in 1983; Texas Gas Exploration, the oil and gas exploration firm also acquired as part of Texas Gas Resources; CSX

SOURCE: J. D. Hunger, B. Ferrin, H. Felix-Gamez, and T. Goetzman, "CSX Corporation," *Cases In Strategic Management and Business Policy* by T. L. Wheelen and J. D. Hunger (Reading, Mass.: Addison-Wesley, 1987), pp. 91–123.

FIGURE 5.5
Major Business Segments and Groups of CSX Corporation in
Early 1985

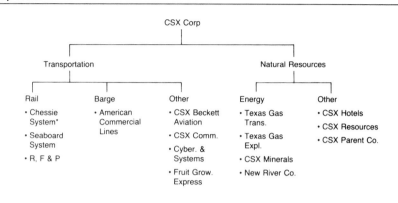

Chessie Motor Express: Trucking unit jointly owned by Chessie and Seaboard.

Minerals, which provided unified management of all CSX coal land development and thereby controlled the rights to 583,000 acres of coal land; and the New River Company, which operated four coal mines on CSX land near New River, West Virginia. The second business group in the natural resources segment was the *Other Natural Resources Group*. This business group consisted of three units: CSX Parent Company (CSX's Corporate Headquarters); CSX Hotels, which represented CSX's investment in the Greenbrier Resort Hotel and its interests in other hotel operations; and CSX Resources, which was established to provide centralized management of all real estate, oil, gas, and timber properties controlled by CSX. CSX Resources had an interest in 330 oil and gas wells and managed 350,000 acres of forest land.

UNIT PERFORMANCE

The transportation segment, with around 69% of CSX's total operating revenue and the same percentage of operating income, dominated the corporation. Rail operations alone accounted for 64% of CSX's operating revenue as well as its operating income. Seaboard was the largest of the three rail units and thus tended to contribute the largest toward the group's operating income. Although coal traffic typically accounted for around 35% of CSX rail units' total revenue, it accounted for around half of Chessie's revenue and around one quarter of Seaboard's revenue. Automobiles and chemicals were next in importance for the Chessie System, as contrasted with paper, phosphates, and fertilizers, for Seaboard. American Commercial Lines' actual annual operating revenue went from $295 million in 1982 to $237 million in 1983, and to $270 million in 1984. Its operating income followed a similar trend, going down from $41 million in 1982 to $22 million in 1983 and up to $32 million in 1984. CSX management indicated that the cause of the overall decline in revenue and income was a result of decreasing rates in the barge transportation industry, and that these decreases were due to equipment oversupply. A record high of 32.3 million tons were transported by American Commercial in 1984 (10% above 1983 and 4% above 1982).

Within the natural resources segment, the energy group accounted for 93% of the segment's operating revenue but only 67% of the segment's operating income. This situation seemed to be a result of low oil and gas prices, caused by depressed world energy demand and the abundance of crude oil and natural gas supplies during the mid-1980s. Insofar as CSX was concerned, the drop in oil and gas prices more than offset any gains in volume sold or transmitted during 1984. Refer to Tables 5.4 and 5.5 for detailed financial information on CSX's transportation and natural resources segments.

INTERNAL PROBLEMS

In early 1985, CSX top management was faced with a problem of strategic significance: *How should the corporation best manage its newly acquired businesses?* The stated mission of CSX was to become a multimodal, one-stop transportation conglomerate. This mission has been pursued throughout the development of the firm. In furthering its attempts to accomplish this mission, CSX continued to use a strategy that it had used successfully in the past. By trying to repeat the process by which Chessie and Seaboard were brought together, CSX management hoped to fully coordinate the operations of ACL with its rail network, without fully integrating the barge line.

However, CSX management faced some difficulties this time around. Barge lines have traditionally been fierce competitors of railroads. Extending CSX's philosophy of teamwork and cooperation was difficult because the railroad personnel and the barge operators were more used to fighting than functioning smoothly in a coordinated fashion. This situation was in direct contrast to the Chessie-Seaboard merger, in which the two partners had no history of competition and no overlap of lines. In addition, the barge industry was substantially different from the railroad industry. As a result, the process of communication that CSX relied so heavily on in its coordination efforts could be more difficult to establish in this acquisition than it had been in the Chessie-Seaboard merger, in which both parties were railroaders and could speak the same language.

The integration of the rest of Texas Gas Resources was also a problem for CSX's top management. Before the merger, more than 90% of CSX revenue had been derived from rail transportation. With the acquisition of TXG the corporation had become a major force in the gas pipeline business. (In 1982, $2.1 billion out of a total of $2.6 billion in TXG revenues came from its pipeline business.) Robert L. Hintz, Senior Vice-President of Finance for CSX, commented that the gas-transmission business had been considered a good fit because most of its revenue came in the winter months when railroads go through a seasonally lean period. Nevertheless, the addition of barge and pipeline businesses had created a serious organizational problem for a firm structured around the concept of separate but equal partnership of subsidiaries.

In their March 1985 letter to the stockholders, Watkins and Funkhouser acknowledged their concern about CSX's organization structure.

> Over the past four years, we have operated two corporately separate, but operationally coordinated, rail units. At the same time, we acquired Texas Gas, resulting in CSX having three essentially autonomous operating units.

TABLE 5.4
Financial Information, Transportation Segment of CSX
(In Millions of Dollars)

	1984				1983[1]				1982			
	Total	Rail	Barge	Other	Total	Rail	Barge	Other	Total	Rail	Barge	Other
Transportation operating revenue	$5,427	$5,058	$270	$99	$4,749	$4,554	$104	$91	$4,644	$4,554	$—	$90
Costs and other operating expenses												
Labor and fringe benefits	2,535	2,457	65	13	2,399	2,352	28	19	2,265	2,232	—	33
Materials, supplies, and other	889	728	112	49	715	633	42	40	839	813	—	26
Fuel	455	407	36	12	407	378	14	15	460	446	—	14
Equipment rent	550	538	10	2	500	493	4	3	417	415	—	2
Depreciation	297	271	15	11	269	252	6	11	294	283	—	11
Total	4,726	4,401	238	87	4,290	4,108	94	88	4,275	4,189	—	86
Transportation operating income	$ 701	$ 657	$ 32	$12	$ 459	$ 446	$ 10	$ 3	$ 369	$ 365	$—	$ 4

	IDENTIFIABLE ASSETS			CAPITAL EXPENDITURES			LONG-TERM DEBT AND MINORITY INTEREST		
	1984	1983	1982	1984	1983	1982	1984	1983	1982
Transportation									
Rail	$9,073	$8,624	$8,631	$748	$427	$511	$1,984	$2,064	$2,099
Barge	366	378	—	7	4	—	64	111	—
Other	213	174	197	8	11	12	47	52	54
Total	$9,652	$9,176	$8,828	$763	$442	$523	$2,095	$2,227	$2,153

SOURCE: CSX Corporation, *1984 Annual Report*, pp. 32–33.

[1]American Commercial Lines added August 1983.

TABLE 5.5
Financial Information, Natural Resources Segment of CSX
(In Millions of Dollars)

	1984			1983[1]			1982		
	Total	Energy	Other	Total	Energy	Other	Total	Energy	Other
Natural resource									
Operating revenue	$2,507	$2,329	$178	$1,142	$989	$153	$265	$55	$210
Costs and other operating expenses									
Gas purchased	1,589	1,589	—	689	689	—	—	—	—
Labor and fringe benefits	116	84	32	62	35	27	72	11	61
Materials, supplies, and other	267	232	35	119	79	40	68	20	48
NGL production payments	85	85	—	40	40	—	—	—	—
Depreciation	133	127	6	55	52	3	17	9	8
Total	2,190	2,117	73	965	895	70	157	40	117
Natural resource operating income	$ 317	$ 212	$105	$ 177	$ 94	$ 83	$108	$15	$ 93

	IDENTIFIABLE ASSETS		
	1984	1983	1982
Natural resource			
Energy	$1,764	$1,715	$151
Other	220	113	220
Total	$1,984	$1,828	$371

	CAPITAL EXPENDITURES		
	1984	1983	1982
Natural resource			
Energy	$235	$82	$28
Other	11	6	10
Total	$246	$88	$38

	LONG-TERM DEBT AND MINORITY INTEREST		
	1984	1983	1982
Natural resource			
Energy	$525	$561	$ 9
Other	12	12	20
Total	$537	$573	$29

SOURCE: CSX Corporation, *1984 Annual Report*, pp. 38–39.

[1]Texas Gas Resources Corporation added August 1983.

Early after the 1980 merger from which CSX was formed, and since mid-1983 in the case of Texas Gas, this organizational autonomy was critical to our success, as it assisted establishment of responsibility, promoted constructive competition between the units and dramatically eased the personnel distress usually associated with the mergers and major acquisitions.

In light of the accelerating dynamics of the transportation and energy marketplaces and the competitive demands of today's international economy, however, we are examining our overall corporate structure to determine the optimal organization for operating in this ever-changing environment.

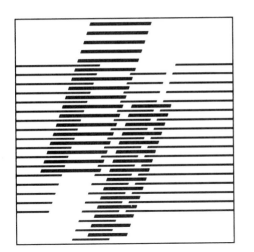

PART THREE

STRATEGY FORMULATION

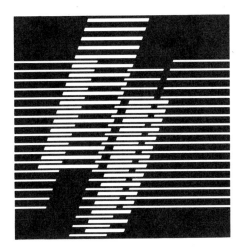

CHAPTER 6

STRATEGY FORMULATION: SITUATION ANALYSIS

STRATEGIC MANAGEMENT MODEL

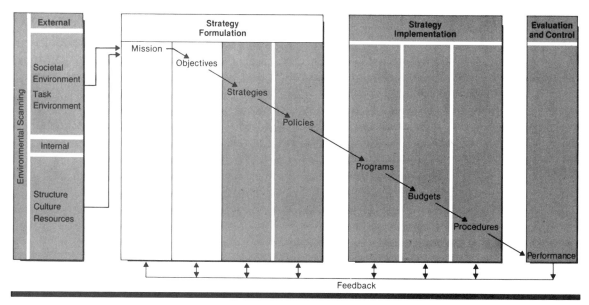

S trategy formulation is often referred to as strategic planning or long-range planning. Regardless of the term used, the process is primarily analytical, not action-oriented. The basic Strategic Management Model, shown first in Chapter 1, reflects the distinction between strategy formulation and strategy implementation. As shown in the model, the formulation process is concerned with developing a corporation's *mission, objectives, strategy,* and *policies.* In order to do this, corporate strategy makers must scan both the *external* and *internal environments* for needed information on strategic factors.

The Strategic Management Model does not show how the formulation process occurs. It merely describes the key *input variables* (internal and external environments) and the key *output factors* (mission, objectives, strategies, and policies). To supplement the Strategic Management Model, Chapters 6 and 7 therefore provide a more detailed discussion of the key activities in the process.

In Chapter 2, a strategic decision-making process was introduced as a graphic representation of the strategic audit. It is also included in this chapter as Fig. 6.1.

The first six steps commonly found in strategy formulation are a series of interrelated activities:

1. **Evaluation of a corporation's current performance results** in terms of (a) return on investment, profitability, etc., and (b) the current mission, objectives, strategies, and policies.

FIGURE 6.1
Strategic Decision-Making Process

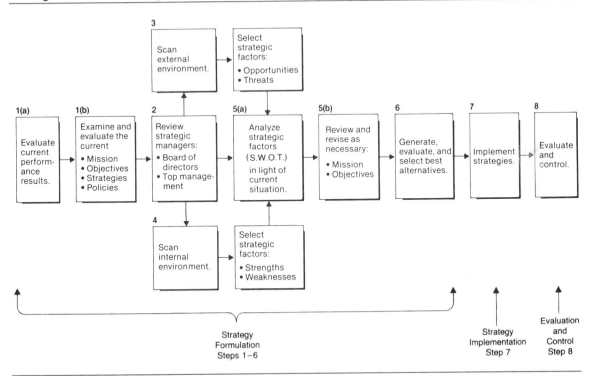

2. **Examination and evaluation of the corporation's strategic managers—** board of directors and top management.

3. **A scan of the external environment,** to locate strategic factors that pose opportunities and threats.

4. **A scan of the internal corporate environment,** to determine strategic factors that are strengths and weaknesses.

5. **Analysis of the strategic factors** from steps 3 and 4 to (a) pinpoint problem areas and (b) review and revise the corporate mission and objectives as necessary.

6. **Generation, evaluation, and selection of the best alternative strategy** in light of the analysis conducted in step 5.

Situation analysis is the first part of the strategy formulation process. Beginning with an evaluation of current performance and ending with the review and possible revision of mission and objectives, the process includes steps one through five. These steps are discussed in this chapter. Step six, the generation, evaluation, and selection of the best alternative strategy, is discussed in Chapter 7.

6.1

EVALUATION OF CURRENT RESULTS

After much research, Henry Mintzberg found that strategy formulation is typically not a regular, continuous process: "It is most often an irregular, discontinuous process, proceeding in fits and starts. There are periods of stability in strategy development, but also there are periods of flux, of groping, of piecemeal change, and of global change."[1] This view of strategy formulation as an irregular process can be explained by most people's tendency to continue on a particular course of action until something goes wrong. In a business corporation, the stimulus for a strategy review lies, in most instances, in current performance results.

Performance results are generally periodic measurements of the developments that have occurred during a given time period. At the corporate level, for example, the board and top management would be most concerned with overall measurements such as return on investment (ROI), profits after taxes, and earnings per share. To see whether a trend exists, management would compare the measurements for the current year to similar measurements from previous years. At the business or divisional level, the manager might be concerned with the return on the division's assets or its net contribution to corporate profits. At the functional level, various managers would be concerned with total sales and market share, plant efficiency, or number of new patents, depending upon their functional area.

Current performance results are compared with current objectives (desired results). If the results are equal to or greater than current objectives, most strategic managers are likely to assume that current strategies and policies are appropriate, as is. In this instance, only incremental changes to present objectives and strategy are likely to be recommended. The strategy formulation process might thus end rather abruptly with a summary statement suggesting that the corporation continue doing what it's already doing—only do it a little better next year. This is basically what occurred at Air Canada between 1955 and 1976. During this time the airline operated in a relatively stable and protected market. The very success of the company worked against any planning for change. The same mission and strategies went unchanged, for the most part, for twenty-one years. Mintzberg, Brunet, and Waters point out in their analysis of Air Canada: ". . . the system was clearly focused on operations, not strategy—the object was to program what was, not to create what hadn't been."[2]

Research does indicate that Air Canada is not an isolated example. Most organizations tend to follow a strategic orientation for around fifteen to twenty years before they make a significant change in direction.[3] After this rather long period of fine-tuning an existing strategy, some sort of **triggering event** is needed to motivate management to seriously reassess the corporation's situation. As shown in Illustrative Example 6.1, one act that is likely to serve as a triggering event is the emergence of a new chief executive officer. By asking a series of embarrassing questions, the new CEO cuts

ILLUSTRATIVE EXAMPLE 6.1

The New CEO: A Triggering Event at Alfred Dunhill PLC

When Anthony Greener became Managing Director of the family-owned British firm of Alfred Dunhill in 1975, he looked at the company's performance record and started to worry. Known widely for its pipes, lighters, and tobacco, nearly half of the company's revenues came from selling cigarette lighters to the Japanese. "We were very vulnerable," Greener stated. "What if the Japanese had suddenly stopped buying lighters?" After a complete reassessment of the firm, Greener used the tweedy, masculine image of Dunhill's English roots to build a world-wide men's fashion business. Following a strategy of growth by acquisition,

Greener plans to keep expanding until Dunhill becomes a premier marketer of luxury goods. By the mid-1980s, the company appeared to be well on its way to fulfilling its new mission. Annual revenues increased to 117 million pounds in 1984 from 20 million pounds in 1975. "This company is about marketing prestige, brand-name goods," stated Greener, emphasizing the change in mission.

SOURCE: "Breaking Dunhill's Dependence On Cigarette Lighters," *Business Week* (August 5, 1985), p. 68.

through the veil of complacency and forces people to question the very reason for the corporation's existence—a very frightening situation for most long-term employees.

Another triggering event is the **performance gap**—when the results of corporate performance do not meet expectations. A typical performance gap is when sales decline and profits fall off from previous years, or else sales and profits stagnate while those of competitors are rising. If top management chooses to confront the problem (and this is not always the case), the formulation process begins in earnest. People at all levels are urged by the board and top management to question present objectives, strategies, and policies. Even the mission may be questioned. Are we aiming too high? Do our strategies make sense? Environmental scanning of both internal and external variables begins. What went wrong? Why? Questions such as these prompt top management to review the corporation's mission, objectives, strategies and policies. As discussed in Illustrative Example 6.2, Eastman Kodak used a deteriorating situation to stimulate a strategy review.

Evaluation of Mission

A well-conceived mission statement defines the fundamental, unique purpose that sets a business apart from other firms of its type and identifies the scope of the business's operations in terms of products offered and markets served.[4] The breadth or narrowness of the corporate mission has an important effect upon corporate performance. The definition of the mission determines the broad limits of a company's growth. For example, amusement

ILLUSTRATIVE EXAMPLE 6.2

The Performance Gap: A Triggering Event at Eastman Kodak Company

Founded in 1880 by George Eastman, Kodak had been an American success story for many years. Unfortunately, its very success lulled management into complacency. Known as the staid, slumbering giant of Rochester, New York, the company had turned down early opportunities to move into xerography, instant photography, and electronic photography. As long as the amateur photography market remained strong, Kodak continued to earn annual profits in the billions of dollars. Unfortunately, the market changed in the early 1980s, but Kodak continued to emphasize its conservative tradition and slow, bureaucratic decision processes. In 1984, one year after earnings plunged by 51%, Chairman Colby H. Chandler commissioned a sweeping review of the company. He wanted to learn why Kodak had let competitors dominate markets like instant photography, 35-mm cameras, and video recorders—natural extensions of Kodak's photography business. The strategic assessment told Chandler that just as the silver-based film technology of George Eastman was being replaced by electronics, Kodak needed more than just a tune-up of its traditional business. "It's essential that we take more risks," contended Chandler. "We didn't need to take risks in the past."

To counter its chief competitor, the Japanese Fuji Photo Film Company, Kodak embarked on a series of acquisitions and restructured the company into seventeen small, autonomous business units. Top management realized that it could no longer afford to be just a photography company. They began investigating the drug industry among other things, as a possible outgrowth of Kodak's expertise in plastics and chemicals. Although the company had no drug products to sell as of mid–1987, management hoped to discover or acquire some soon. Said Leo J. Thomas, head of Kodak's effort in drugs and health care technology: "We need to broaden our base of business to where growth potential will carry us into the next century." Subsequently, Kodak acquired Sterling Drug, Inc. with its successful Lysol and Bayer Aspirin products.

SOURCES: B. Buell and R. Aikman, "Kodak Is Trying to Break Out of Its Shell," *Business Week* (June 10, 1985), pp. 92–95.

L. Helm, "Why Kodak Is Starting to Click Again," *Business Week* (February 23, 1987), pp. 134–138.

L. Helm and S. Benway, "Has Kodak Set Itself Up For a Fall?" *Business Week* (February 22, 1988), pp. 134–138.

parks traditionally defined themselves as in-place carnivals. After floundering in the 1950s, many such businesses went bankrupt. The success of Disneyland in the 1960s caused many parks such as Cedar Point, Inc. in Sandusky, Ohio to redefine themselves as "theme" parks with entertainment "packages" of shows, rides, and nationally known performers. With the aging of the American population, that mission is being further broadened to include a wider spectrum of entertainment, including golf courses and vacation resorts.

Surveys of large North American corporations reveal that approximately 60%–75% of them have formal, written statements of mission. A high percentage of the rest have an unwritten, informal mission.[5] The written mission statements of these corporations tend to contain the following eight components:

- Target customers/markets.
- Principal products/services.

- Geographic domain.
- Core technologies used.
- Commitment to survival, growth, and profitability.
- Key parts of the company's philosophy.
- Company's self-concept.
- Company's desired public image.[6]

The concept of a corporate mission implies that throughout a corporation's many activities there should be a **common thread** or unifying theme and that those corporations with such a common thread are better able to direct and administer their many activities.[7] In acquiring new firms or in developing new products, such a corporation looks for "strategic fit"; that is, the likelihood that new activities will mesh with present ones in such a way that the corporation's overall effectiveness and efficiency will be increased. A common thread may be common distribution channels or similar customers, warehousing economies or the mutual use of R&D, better use of managerial talent or any of a number of possible synergistic effects. For example, Ralston Purina recently acquired Union Carbide's battery business, including the Eveready and Energizer brands. Ralston's CEO, William Stiritz, argued that Ralston Purina would earn better profit margins on batteries than did Union Carbide because of Ralston's expertise in developing and marketing branded consumer products.[8]

Evaluation of Objectives

As pointed out in Chapter 4, each stakeholder in a corporation's task environment will have its own way of measuring the corporation's performance. Stockholders may want dividends and price appreciation, whereas unions want good wages, stability of employment, and opportunities for advancement. Customers, distributors, creditors, suppliers, local communities, and other governments, to name only a few, also have their own criteria by which they judge the corporation. By specifying and prioritizing objectives for the corporation to achieve, top management can recognize and deal with the needs of various corporate stakeholders. Some of the possible objectives a corporation might pursue are the following:

- Profitability (net profits)
- Efficiency (low costs, etc.)
- Growth (increase in total assets, sales, etc.)
- Shareholder wealth (dividends plus stock price appreciation)
- Utilization of resources (ROE or ROI)
- Contributions to customers (quality/price)
- Contributions to employees (employment security, wages)
- Contributions to society (taxes paid, participation in charities)

- Market leadership (market share, reputation)
- Technological leadership (innovations, creativity)
- Survival (avoiding bankruptcy)
- Personal needs of top management (using the firm for personal purposes, such as providing jobs for relatives)

The top management of most large, publicly-traded U.S. corporations like to announce their long-term objectives for the company—partially because that sets measurable goals to work toward and partially because they hope to impress stockholders and financial analysts. Under the direction of Chairman John F. Welch, Jr., for example, General Electric identified its primary objective of making GE worth more than any other U.S. company. In 1986, Chairman Lee Iacocca announced Chrysler's intention to boost its share of U.S. auto sales from its current 11% to 15% by the early 1990s. Admitting that market share drives profits in the auto industry, Iacocca stated, "It's a pretty big niche and we can make a lot of money doing that."[9]

It is likely, however, that many small, closely-held corporations have no formal objectives; rather they have vague, verbal ones that are typically not ranked by priority. It is even more likely that such a corporation's specified, written objectives are not the *real* (personal and probably unpublishable) objectives of top management.[10]

Evaluation of Strategies and Policies

Just as a number of firms have no formal objectives, many CEOs have unstated, incremental, or intuitive strategies that have never been articulated or analyzed. If pressured, these executives might state that they are following a certain strategy. This stated or "explicit" strategy is one with which few could quarrel, such as the development and acquisition of new product lines. Further investigation, however, might reveal the existence of a very different "implicit" strategy. For example, the prestige of a banker in one community is strictly a function of the bank's asset size. Top management, therefore, tends to choose strategies that will increase total bank assets rather than profits. An extremely profitable small bank in the eyes of the community is still just another unimportant small bank.

Often the only way to spot the implicit strategies of a corporation is to look not at what top management says, but at what it does. Implicit strategies can be derived from corporation policies, programs approved (and disapproved), and authorized budgets. Programs and divisions favored by budget increases and staffed by managers who are considered to be on the fast promotion track reveal where the corporation is putting its money and its energy.[11]

It is, nevertheless, not always necessary for strategic planning to be a formal process for it to be effective. Small corporations, for example, may plan informally and irregularly.[12] The president and a handful of top managers might get together casually, to resolve strategic issues and plan their next steps. As discussed in Chapter 12, they need no formal, elaborate planning system because the number of key executives is small enough that they can meet relatively often to discuss the company's future.

In large, multidivisional corporations, however, the planning of strategy can become quite complex. A study of strategic decisions made in thirty large organizations in England revealed that the average amount of time elapsed from the beginning of situation assessment to final decision agreement was a little over twelve months.[13] Because of the relatively large number of people affected by a strategic decision in such a firm, a formalized system is needed to ensure that a hierarchy of objectives and strategy exists. Otherwise, top management becomes isolated from developments in the divisions and lower-level managers lose sight of the corporate mission.

6.2
EVALUATION OF STRATEGIC MANAGERS

As discussed in Chapter 3, the interaction of a corporation's board with its top management is likely to reflect one of four basic styles of strategic management: chaos, entrepreneurial, marionette, and partnership. Firms like Adolph Coors Company, Winnebago, and Tandy Corporation have for years been so dominated by their founders that their boards probably operated passively as an instrument of the founder. Once the founder has died and an outsider is brought in to head the firm, however, the board may take an active role in representing the interests of the family. In such an instance, the new CEO might be quite constrained by the board in terms of strategic options.

The strategic management style of such a corporation can thus change abruptly from entrepreneurial (in which the founder dominates the board) to marionette management (in which the board, made up of the founder's family and friends, dominates top management and makes the significant decisions).

When the board is only moderately involved in strategic management, the CEO often has a free hand to set the direction of the corporation. Then the success or failure of a corporation's strategy must be evaluated in light of the CEO's managerial style.

For example, William Ylvisaker, former-Chairman and CEO of Gould Inc., had a reputation of being "mercurial" and "cavalier" with his people. Credited with reshaping the stodgy battery maker into a high-tech electronics concern, "the unpredictable Mr. Ylvisaker bought and sold properties like someone playing Monopoly."[14] In contrast, John Welch, Chairman of General Electric, carefully orchestrated the corporation's most wrenching change in its 109-year history. When Welch took charge of GE, he sketched three circles containing the fifteen businesses in which he thought GE should be involved. Apart from a few support operations, the rest were marked for sale. He proposed that for a business segment to be contributing to GE's primary objective, it must be either first or second in its market segment.[15] Welch's dynamic personality has radically altered GE's orientation toward strategic management.

Henry Mintzberg has pointed out that a corporation's objectives and strategies are strongly affected by top management's view of the world.[16] This view determines the approach or "mode" to be used in strategy formulation. He names three basic modes: entrepreneurial, adaptive, and planning. Characteristics of each mode are listed in Table 6.1.

- **Entrepreneurial mode.** Strategy is made by one powerful individual. The focus is on opportunities. Problems are secondary. Strategy is guided by the founder's own vision of direction and is exemplified by large, bold decisions. The dominant goal is growth of the corporation.

  As mentioned earlier, Gould Inc. under William Ylvisaker and General Electric under John Welch are examples of corporations being run in the entrepreneurial mode. Surprisingly, both are old, established firms with extremely dynamic and creative CEOs who have striven to change the character of their respective firms so that they will match their vision of the future.

- **Adaptive mode.** Sometimes referred to as "muddling through," this strategy-formulation mode is characterized by reactive solutions to existing problems, rather than a proactive search for new opportunities. Much bargaining goes on concerning priorities of objectives. Strategy is fragmented and is developed to move the corporation forward in incremental steps.

  This mode is typical of most universities, many large hospitals, a large number of governmental agencies, and a surprising number of large corporations. Western Union, for example, has for years successfully plodded along earning a small but predictable annual profit from businesses that largely were outgrowths of the telegraph. Only recently, when it tried to change modes and become more aggressive, did it fall on hard times.

- **Planning mode.** Analysts assume major responsibilities for strategy formulation. Strategic planning includes both the proactive search for new opportunities and the reactive solution of existing problems. Systematic comprehensive analysis is used for the development of strategies that integrate the corporation's decision-making processes.

  Sears, Roebuck and Company, in its strategic move into financial services, exemplified this mode. Rather than simply working to improve their then-stagnant merchandising group, top management chose to capitalize on the firm's successes in insurance and real estate, and to take advantage of unique opportunities emerging in the financial services industry.

In the *entrepreneurial* mode, top management believes that the environment is a force to be used and controlled. In the *adaptive* mode, it assumes the environment is too complex to be completely comprehended. In the

TABLE 6.1
Characteristics and Conditions of the Three Modes

CHARACTERISTIC	ENTREPRENEURIAL MODE	ADAPTIVE MODE	PLANNING MODE
Motive for decisions	Proactive	Reactive	Proactive and reactive
Goals of organization	Growth	Indeterminate	Efficiency and growth
Evaluation of proposals	Judgmental	Judgmental	Analytical
Choices made by	Entrepreneur	Bargaining	Management
Decision horizon	Long-term	Short-term	Long-term
Preferred environment	Uncertainty	Certainty	Risk
Decision linkages	Loosely coupled	Disjointed	Integrated
Flexibility of mode	Flexible	Adaptive	Constrained
Size of moves	Bold decisions	Incremental steps	Global strategies
Vision of direction	General	None	Specific
CONDITION FOR USE			
Source of power	Entrepreneur	Divided	Management
Objectives of organization	Operational	Nonoperational	Operational
Organizational environment	Yielding	Complex, dynamic	Predictable, stable
Status of organization	Young, small, or strong leadership	Established	Large

SOURCE: H. Mintzberg, "Strategy Making in Three Modes." Copyright © 1973 by the Regents of the University of California. Reprinted/Condensed from the *California Management Review*, Vol. No. 2, p. 49. By permission of The Regents.

planning mode, it works on the assumption that systematic scanning and analysis of the environment can provide the knowledge it needs to influence the environment to the corporation's advantage. The use of a specific planning mode reflects top management's perception of the corporation's environment. If we categorize a corporation's top management according to these three planning modes, we can better understand how and why key decisions are made. Then if we look at these decisions in light of the corporation's mission, objectives, strategies, and policies, we can then determine whether the dominant planning mode is appropriate.

In some instances, a corporation might follow an approach called **logical incrementalism,** which is a synthesis of the planning, adaptive, and to a lesser extent, the entrepreneurial modes of strategy formulation. As described by Quinn, top management might have a reasonably clear idea of the corporation's mission and objectives, but, in its development of strategies, chooses to use "an interactive process in which the organization probes the future, experiments and learns from a series of a partial (incremental) commitments rather than through global formulations of total strategies."[17] This approach appears to be useful when it is important to build consensus and develop needed resources before the entire corporation is committed to a new direction.

6.3

SCANNING THE EXTERNAL ENVIRONMENT

At the point in the strategy formulation process in which the external environment is scanned, strategic managers must examine both the societal and task environments for those strategic factors that are likely to strongly influence their corporation's success—factors that are, in other words, opportunities and threats. Long-run developments in the economic, technological, political-legal, and sociocultural aspects of the societal environment tend to affect strongly a corporation's activities: they assert immediate pressures on the corporation's task environment. Such societal issues as consumerism, governmental regulations, environmental pollution, energy cost and availability, inflation-fed wage demands, and heavy foreign competition tend to emerge from stakeholders in the firm's task environment. As indicated earlier in Chapter 4, the task environment of a particular company is often referred to as its industry. Therefore, an examination of the *task environment* may be called **industry analysis.**

As discussed in Chapter 4, strategic managers should evaluate environmental issues in terms of the probability of their occurrence and their probable impact on the corporation. In this manner, the possible societal issues listed in Table 4.4 can be placed on an issues priority matrix as shown in Fig. 4.2. Special emphasis can then be placed on the monitoring of these high-priority issues as strategic factors. Each of the six forces from the task environment depicted in Fig. 4.4, such as the threat of substitute products and services, also can be evaluated in this same manner and marked for special attention. Top management should then request its divisions and functional areas to report to it any significant developments in any of the high- or even medium-priority issues.

Strategic Groups

In the analysis of the various industries (task environments) in which a large multiproduct corporation competes, it can be very useful to categorize competitors within each industry into strategic groups. According to Hatten and Hatten, a **strategic group** is a set of business units or firms that "pursue similar strategies with similar resources."[18] Because a corporation's structure and culture tend to reflect the kinds of strategies it follows (to be discussed further in Chapter 8), companies or business units belonging to a particular strategic group within the same industry tend to be strong rivals and tend to be more similar to each other than to competitors in other strategic groups. For example, although Chevrolet and Rolls Royce are a part of the same automobile industry, they have different missions, objectives, and strategies, and thus belong to different strategic groups. They generally have very little in common and pay little attention to each other when planning competitive actions. Ford and Plymouth, however, have a great deal in common with Chevrolet, in terms of their similar strategy of producing a high volume of low-priced automobiles targeted for sale to the average person. Consequently, they are strong rivals and are organized and operated in a similar fashion.

Mobility Barriers

A corporation or business unit within a particular strategic group makes strategic decisions that competitors outside the group cannot easily imitate without substantial costs and a significant amount of time. These obstacles to casual imitation of a firm's strategy form what are called **mobility barriers** against entry into a particular strategic group.[19] These barriers are of great importance to a strategic manager because their presence in an industry can reduce the likelihood of potential competitors (See "Threat of New Entrants" in Fig. 4.4) in a particular market segment. Mobility barriers protect a particular strategic group from entry not only by competitors from other strategic groups within the industry, but also by companies currently outside the industry who wish to enter it.

The huge vertically integrated manufacturing and distribution facilities of General Motors, Chrysler, and Ford acted as a mobility barrier for many years in the United States. It prevented American Motors from successfully moving outside its niche in small cars and utility vehicles. The heavy costs involved in competing at even a small level in the U.S. acted as an entry (mobility) barrier to most foreign-based auto companies, until Volkswagen found a lucrative niche in the 1960s—that the Japanese soon followed and

TABLE 6.2

Examples of Mobility Barriers and Ways to Avoid or Overcome Them

EXAMPLES OF MOBILITY BARRIERS IN SOME INDUSTRIES

- High fixed asset requirement (steel industry)
- Heavy advertising expenses (beer industry)
- Scarce raw materials (petroleum industry)
- Difficult government requirements (electric utilities)
- Credit sales required (appliance industry)
- Ability to handle trade-ins (retail auto industry)
- Products protected by patents, trademarks, and trade secrets (drug industry)
- Control of key distribution channels (network television)
- Very low competitive prices (consumer electronics industry)

WAYS IN WHICH MOBILITY BARRIERS CAN BE AVOIDED OR OVERCOME

- Find an open niche (Neutrogena's mild soap)
- Find a substitute product (personal computers replace typewriters)
- Develop a technological improvement (P&G's low-fat cooking oil)
- Differentiate product through marketing mix (Zenith's sales of computers to colleges)
- Locate spot where competitors are weak (Toyota's emphasis on low-cost quality)
- Create process improvements (Deere's flexible manufacturing)

expanded. Some of the possible mobility barriers and ways in which they can be avoided or overcome are presented in Table 6.2.

6.4

SCANNING THE INTERNAL ENVIRONMENT

Before top management can properly address the issue of what possible strategies are appropriate for the corporation's future, it must assess its own internal situation—the environment within the firm itself. Strategic decisions should not be made until top management understands the strengths and weaknesses in divisional and functional areas.

In this instance management audits can be very useful as a diagnostic aid. As mentioned in Chapter 5, the key internal variables to be considered are the corporation's structure, culture, and resources. An example of a corporation (AT&T) in which a basic weakness in a functional area seriously hurt the implementation of a reasonable strategy is given in Illustrative Example 6.3.

PIMS Research

A current research effort to help pinpoint relevant strategic factors for business corporations is being made by the Strategic Planning Institute. Its

ILLUSTRATIVE EXAMPLE 6.3

Internal Weakness Negatively Affects Implementation of Strategic Decision at AT&T

In 1984, American Telephone and Telegraph (AT&T) bought 25% of Ing. C. Olivetti and Company, an Italian office-equipment company. AT&T wanted to become a full-blown information processing company and needed a strong presence in computers to complement its virtual domination of telephone networking. It agreed to sell Olivetti's M-24 personal computer in the United States as the AT&T 6300. The M-24 was basically another IBM "clone" with the then-standard MS-DOS operating system. Its price and features made it very competitive against the IBM personal computer in 1985, but it lost its temporary advantage in 1986 as other MS-DOS clones, such as Compaq, began offering more for the money. Sales of the AT&T 6300 dropped significantly from 1985 to 1986. Concerned with AT&T's apparent inability to market its computers, Olivetti arranged for Xerox Corporation to also sell the M-24 personal computer in North America, in competition with AT&T's 6300.

In 1986, AT&T posted an operating loss of $800 million on its computer business. An internal memo to Chairman James E. Olson of AT&T called for "priority" action to reverse the losses for "the successful execution of our strategy."

Former AT&T executives suggested that one reason the company was unable to make its computer business a success as of 1987 was its lack of a sales force dedicated solely to sales of computers. The current sales force did not report directly to the manager in charge of computers and was expected to sell communications equipment and long-distance telephone service, in addition to computers, to its business accounts. AT&T's lack of marketing expertise was also reflected in its one-year delay in meeting the industry-wide price cuts prevalent in 1986.

Even though the company in November 1986 hired Vittorio Cassoni from Olivetti to run its new Data Systems Division, computer sales continued to drop in 1987. Cassoni demanded a complete review of the computer-development projects. He argued that development money be concentrated on systems that would give AT&T computers distinct competitive advantages so that they would not be simply me-too products. In commenting on AT&T's apparent weaknesses in marketing, one analyst reported, "Corporate management by now realizes that they can't go out and sell computers by just saying 'We're AT&T.' "

SOURCES: J. J. Keller, G. Lewis, M. Maremont, and W. C. Symonds, "AT&T May Be Ready to Cut Its Losses In Computers," *Business Week* (July 6, 1987), p. 30; and J. Guyon, "AT&T to Unveil Desktop Computer and Minicomputer," *Wall Street Journal* (September 2, 1987), p. 6.

PIMS Program (Profit Impact of Market Strategy) is composed of various analyses of a data bank containing about 100 items of information on the strategic experiences of nearly 3,000 strategic business units throughout North America and Europe, for periods ranging from two to twelve years. The research conducted with the data has been aimed at discovering the empirical "principles" that determine which strategy, under which conditions, produces what results, in terms of return on investment and cash flows regardless of the specific product or services. To date, PIMS research has identified nine major strategic factors that account for around 80% of the variation in profitability across the businesses in the database.[20] In working with these factors, the Strategic Planning Institute has prepared profiles of high ROI companies as contrasted with low ROI companies. They found that the companies with high rates of return had the following characteristics:

- Low investment intensity (the amount of fixed capital and working capital required to produce a dollar of sales)
- High market share
- High relative product quality
- High capacity utilization
- High operating effectiveness (the ratio of actual to expected employee productivity)
- Low direct costs per unit, relative to competition[21]

These and other PIMS research findings are quite controversial. For example, PIMS research has reported consistently that a large market share should lead to greater profitability.[22] The reason appears to be that high market share results in low unit costs because of economies of scale. To gain share through low price, a company could therefore take advantage of the experience curve (discussed in Chapter 5). Unfortunately, a number of studies have found that high market share does not always lead to profitability. Firms selling products of high quality relative to the competition have been found to be very profitable even though they do not have large market share.[23] PIMS researchers respond, however, that the single most important factor affecting a business unit's performance relative to its competitors' is the quality of its products or services. They also state that market leaders tend to have products of higher quality relative to those of its competitors and market followers.[24]

From a practitioner's point of view, the most important criticism of PIMS research is that the "significant predictors of performance (investment intensity, market share, relative product quality, capacity utilization, etc.) generally have tended to be variables outside of management's control, at least in the short run."[25] As a result of these and other limitations, one can conclude that we are still quite a distance away from discovering "universal strategic laws." Nevertheless, the PIMS program is useful in helping strategic managers identify some key internal strategic factors, such as investment intensity, market share, product quality, capacity utilization, operating effectiveness, and direct costs per unit. In the assessment of a corporation's relative strengths and weaknesses, these factors can be measured and compared to those of other firms in the same industry.

Strategic Field Analysis

Strategic field analysis, as proposed by Lorange, Morton, and Ghoshal, is a way of examining the nature and extent of the synergies that do or do not exist between the internal components of a corporation.[26] First, one analyzes a company's **value-added chain** in terms of the various functional steps involved in the production of a product or service. Porter, who popularized the "value-chain" concept, identifies five **primary activities** that usually occur in any business corporation: (1) inbound logistics of raw materials, (2) operations, (3) outbound logistics of the finished goods, (4) marketing and sales, and (5) customer service—and four **support activities:** (1) the procurement process, (2) technology development, (3) human resource management, and (4) the infrastructure of planning, accounting, finance, legal, government affairs, and quality management.[27] Porter recommends that one should examine the "linkages" among the value activities. In seeking ways for a corporation to gain competitive advantage in the market place, the same function can be done in different ways with different results. For example, quality inspection of 100% of output instead of the usual 10% would increase production costs, but that increase might be more than offset by the savings obtained from the reduction in the number of repairmen needed to fix defective products and the increase in the amount of salespeople's time devoted to selling instead of exchanging already-sold, but defective, products.

The second step in strategic field analysis is to examine the potential synergies between the company's products, markets, or businesses. Not only does each value element, such as advertising or manufacturing, have an inherent **economy of scale** in which activities are conducted at their lowest possible cost per unit of output, but the value elements can also have **economies of scope** across elements. Such economies of scope come as the value chains of two separate products or services share activities. For example, the cost of joint production of two products can be less than the cost of separate production. This sharing of value-chain activities can take place across functions, products, or markets. In an example provided earlier in this chapter, Ralston Purina bought Union Carbide's battery business because it could apply its expertise in the marketing of its current products to the value chains of the Eveready and Energizer brands.

6.5

ANALYSIS OF STRATEGIC FACTORS

The analysis of the strategic factors in the strategic decision-making process calls for an integration and evaluation of data collected earlier from the scanning of the internal and external environments. External strategic factors are those opportunities and threats found in the present and future task and societal environments. Internal strategic factors are those important strengths and weaknesses within the corporation's divisional and functional areas. Step 5(a) in Fig. 6.1 requires that top management attempt to find a strategic fit between external opportunities and internal strengths. This can result in the identification of a corporation's **distinctive competence**—the company's unique position with regard to its competition and the company's use of its resources. For example, the emphasis by Urschel Laboratories in building high-quality, low-cost food processing machines has provided it a "distinctive competence" in manufacturing that enabled it to dominate the industry. This concept of distinctive competence is also exemplified by a statement from Sears, Roebuck and Company's 1986 annual report, concerning its diversification into financial services:

> Our diversification simply creates new channels and opens up new opportunities. . . . By design, Sears has carefully chosen those areas where our unique strengths give us an advantage over the competition.

S.W.O.T. Analysis

S.W.O.T. is a term used to stand for a summary listing of a corporation's key internal *Strengths* and *Weaknesses* and its external *Opportunities* and *Threats*. These are the strategic factors to be analyzed in step 5(a) of Fig. 6.1. They should include not only those external factors that are most likely to occur and to have a serious impact on the company, but also those internal factors that are most likely to affect the implementation of present and future strategic decisions. For the case of Illustrative Example 6.3, which discusses AT&T's entry into the computer business, a S.W.O.T. analysis should have reflected the great *opportunities* for profits emerging in the 1980s from personal-computers and for the integration of telecommunications with computer technology. It would also have shown the serious *threats* directed not only from IBM, but also from market-oriented, aggressive companies like Compaq. The S.W.O.T. analysis should also have listed AT&T's impressive strengths in research and development, human resources, and customer service. Nevertheless, an objective assessment of weaknesses should have highlighted AT&T's lack of experience in marketing products outside of telephone-related equipment and raised a "red flag" for management to seriously consider before it chose to sell Olivetti computers through its existing marketing channels. Because AT&T failed to note the seriousness of its marketing weaknesses, it was forced to hire an experienced computer executive from Olivetti to redirect AT&T's computer development and to possibly establish a separate sales force.

Finding a Niche

William Newman suggests that a corporation should seek to obtain a "propitious niche" in its strategy formulation process.[28] This niche is a corporation's specific competitive role. It should be so well-suited to the firm's internal and external environment that other corporations are not likely to challenge or dislodge it. The corporation thus has a *distinctive competence* that enables it to take advantage of specific environmental opportunities.

The finding of such a niche is not always easy. A firm's management must always be looking for **strategic windows,** that is, market opportunities.[29] As shown in the case of Electronic Technology Corporation, presented in Illustrative Example 6.4., the first one through the strategic window can occupy a propitious niche and discourage competition (if the firm has the

ILLUSTRATIVE EXAMPLE 6.4

High-Tech Electronic Technology Corporation and *Low-Tech* Zayre's Discount Stores Find Propitious Niches

SILICON VALLEY IN CEDAR RAPIDS?

Just one year after its founding, Electronic Technology Corporation (ETC), is succeeding beyond its founder's fondest dreams. The firm manufactures semi-custom integrated circuits and sells to customers throughout the Midwest. Founder Scott Clark brought the idea to Iowa from the famed "Silicon Valley" of northern California where such companies are more common than hamburger stands. "When we began, our plan was to have a typical production order of $35,000," says Clark. "Within six months, we revised it to $90,000. And by September, orders were averaging $240,000. In fiscal year 1985, orders will average $400,000. . . . We can't grow fast enough to keep up." A significant reason for its success is its location in Cedar Rapids. Because an estimated 90% of the industry is located in Silicon Valley, about 5% on the East Coast, and the remainder scattered throughout the United States, ETC leads the way in the upper Midwest. "We're between Chicago, Minneapolis, Milwaukee, St. Louis, and Kansas City. We're accessible and we're interested in our customers," states Clark. ETC offers its customers *service* and *security*. Clark says that it's not unusual for Silicon Valley engineers to stay with a company only a matter of months. When a company receives a big contract, it can hire the necessary design engineers from one of its competitors. "These guys jump from one job to another and think nothing of it. But what they do when they jump is take the secrets of the last company they did a contract for. They can offer it to a contractor's competitor. And that doesn't happen here. Our engineers come here planning to stay. They like the security of the job and they like being out of the rat race in California. We can guarantee our customers the security they must have," comments Clark. ETC's plans to expand over the next five years conjure up dreams of a Silicon Valley in the Midwest—located in Iowa. "I really believe it will

happen," predicts Clark. "The business is here and our only real competitors are in California."

ZAYRE'S FINDS SUCCESS IN INNER CITIES

In the late 1970s, Zayre Corporation was suffering from low earnings because of the "rummage sale" nature of its discount stores. Zayre responded by renovating its stores and improving its merchandise presentation and inventory. Unlike other discounters, who were leaving the inner city in droves, Zayre decided to stay. The chain made a "significant commitment to become very good at something that [other retailers] were running away from," says President Malcolm L. Sherman. Inner-city Chicago stores were the first to be upgraded. By 1984, approximately 20% of Zayre's 276 stores were in or near black and Hispanic neighborhoods in Chicago, Pittsburgh, Atlanta, Indianapolis, and other cities. They are generally the chain's profit leaders. Zayre has few competitors in the inner city. The inventory of the inner-city stores is tailored to the specific needs and tastes of area residents. The emphasis is on apparel. The inner-city stores stock more apparel than do suburban stores because inner-city residents "have fewer places to shop" and tend to have larger families, states Mr. Sherman. Its hiring and advertising practices also reflect the ethnic mix. Apparently, Zayre's concern for its inner-city customers is reciprocated by the people in the Zayre locations. When riots shook Miami's Liberty City in March, 1984, some residents of the area intervened to protect the store from troublemakers. "We had no damage," said Charles Howze, the inner-city store's manager.

SOURCES: J. Carlson, "Silicon Valley Comes to Iowa—and Sprouts," *Des Moines Register* (January 27, 1985), p. 6X. J. L. Roberts, "Zayre's Strategy of Ethnic Merchandising Proves To Be Successful in Inner-City Stores," *Wall Street Journal* (September 25, 1984), p. 37.

required internal strengths. Zayre's decision to improve and emphasize its inner-city discount stores at a time when competitors were leaving inner-city locations in droves enabled it to build a niche successfully where none had previously existed.

A recent study of high-performing, mid-sized growth companies found these successful corporations to have four characteristics in common:

- They innovate as a way of life.
- They compete on value, not price.
- They achieve leadership in *niche markets.*
- They build on their strengths by competing in *related niches.*[30]

In summary, research reveals that corporate performance is strongly influenced by how well a company positions itself within an industry.[31] The finding of a specific niche in which a corporation's strengths fit well with environmental opportunities is thus a desired outcome of situation analysis and a valuable means for a corporation to gain competitive advantage.

Portfolio Analysis

The business portfolio is the most recommended aid to the integration and evaluation of environmental data. Research suggests that roughly 75% of the U.S. Fortune 500 companies and many smaller companies with multiple product lines or services practice some form of portfolio analysis in their strategy formulations.[32] There is probably a similar rate of usage by companies located in other industrialized nations.

All corporations, except the simplest and smallest, are involved in more than one business. Even if a corporation sells only one product, it might benefit from handling separately a number of distinct product-market segments. Procter & Gamble, for example, managed Prell Liquid and Prell Concentrate as two separate brands of shampoo for a number of years because of their appeal to two separate and distinct market segments.

Portfolio analysis recommends that each product, strategic business unit (SBU), or division be considered separately for purposes of strategy formulation.

There are a number of matrixes available to reflect the variables under consideration in a portfolio. SBUs or products can be compared on the basis of their growth rate in sales, relative competitive position, stage of product/market evolution, market share, and industry attractiveness.

Four-Cell, BCG Growth-Share Matrix _____

The simplest matrix is the *growth-share matrix* developed by the Boston Consulting Group, as depicted in Fig. 6.2. Each of the corporation's SBUs or products is plotted on the matrix according to both the growth rate of the industry in which it competes and its relative market share. A product's or SBU's relative competitive position is defined as its market share in the industry divided by that of the largest other competitor. The business growth rate is the percentage of market growth—that is, the percentage by which sales of a particular product or SBU classification of products have increased.

The line separating areas of high and low relative competitive position is set at 1.5 times. A product or SBU must have relative strengths of this magnitude to ensure that it will have the dominant position needed to be a star or cash cow. On the other hand, a product or SBU having a relative competitive position of 1 times or less has dog status.[33] Each product or SBU is represented in Fig. 6.2 by a circle. The area of the circle represents the relative significance of each SBU or product to the corporation in terms of assets used or sales generated.

The growth-share matrix has a lot in common with the product life-cycle. New products are typically introduced in a fast growing industry. These initially are termed **question mark** products. If one of these products is to gain enough market share to become a market leader and thus a **star,** money must be taken from more mature **cash cow** products and spent on a *question mark. Stars* are typically at the peak of their product life-cycle and are usually able to generate cash enough for maintenance of their high share of the market. Once their market growth rate slows, *stars* become *cash cows.* These products typically bring in far more money than is needed for maintenance of their market share. As these products move along the decline stage of their life cycle, they are "milked" for cash to be invested in new *question mark* products. Those products unable to obtain a dominant market

FIGURE 6.2
The BCG Portfolio Matrix

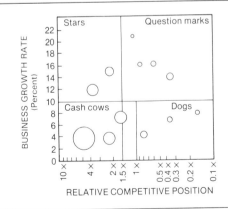

Source: B. Hedley, "Strategy and the Business Portfolio," *Long Range Planning* (February 1977), p. 12. Reprinted by permission.

share by the time the industry growth rate inevitably slows become **dogs,** which are either sold off or managed carefully for the small amount of cash they can generate.

Once the current positions of a corporation's products or SBUs have been plotted on a matrix, a projection can be made of its future position, if there are to be no changes in strategy. Present and projected matrixes can thus be used to assist in the identification of major strategic issues facing the corporation.

Research into the growth-share matrix generally supports its assumptions and recommendations except for the advice that dogs should be promptly harvested or liquidated.[34] A product with a low share in a declining industry can be very profitable if the product has a niche in which market demand remains stable and predictable.[35] If enough of the competition leaves the industry, a product's market share can increase by default until the dog becomes the market leader and thus a cash cow. All in all, the BCG growth-share matrix is a very popular technique. It is quantifiable and easy to use. The barnyard analogies of cash cows and dogs have become trendy buzz-words in management circles.

The growth-share matrix has been criticized for a number of reasons nevertheless:

- The use of highs and lows to make just four categories is too simplistic.
- The link between market share and profitability is not necessarily strong. Low-share businesses can be profitable, too (and vice versa).
- The highest-growth-rate markets are not always the best.
- It considers the product or SBU only in relation to one competitor— the market leader. It misses small competitors with fast-growing market shares.
- Growth rate is only one aspect of industry attractiveness.
- Market share is only one aspect of overall competitive position.[36]

Nine-Cell GE Business Screen

A more complicated matrix is that developed by General Electric with the assistance of the McKinsey and Company consulting firm. As depicted in Fig. 6.3, it includes nine cells based on long-term industry attractiveness and business strength/competitive position. Interestingly, this nine-cell matrix is almost identical to the *Directional Policy Matrix* developed by Shell Oil and used extensively by European firms. Both use the same factors and both use nine cells. The GE Business Screen, in contrast to the BCG growth-share matrix, includes much more data in its two key factors than just business growth rate and comparable market share. For example, at GE, industry attractiveness includes market growth rate, industry profitability, size, and pricing practices, among other possible opportunities and threats.

FIGURE 6.3
General Electric's Business Screen

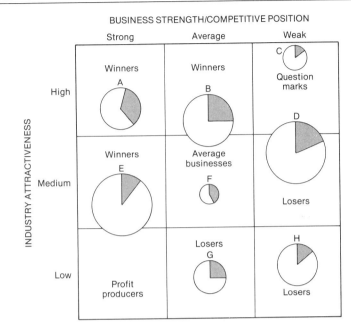

Source: Adapted from *Strategic Management in GE,* Corporate Planning and Development, General Electric Corporation. Used by permission of General Electric Company.

Business strength or competitive position includes market share as well as technological position, profitability, and size, among other possible strengths and weaknesses.[37]

The individual products or SBUs are identified by a letter and plotted as circles on the GE Screen. The area of each circle is in proportion to the size of the industry in terms of sales. The pie slices within the circles depict the market share of each product or SBU.

The following four steps are recommended for the plotting of products or SBUs on the GE Business Screen.[38]

1. **Assess industry attractiveness.**
   a) Select general criteria by which the industry will be rated. These criteria should be key aspects of the industry, such as its potential for sales growth and likely profitability. Table 6.3 lists fifteen criteria for one specific industry.
   b) Weight each criterion according to management's perception of the criterion's importance to the achievement of corporate objectives. For example, because the key criterion of the corporation in Table 6.3 is profitability, it receives the highest weight, 0.20.

TABLE 6.3

An Example of an Industry Attractiveness Assessment Matrix

ATTRACTIVENESS CRITERIA	WEIGHT*	RATING**	WEIGHTED SCORE
Size	0.15	4	0.60
Growth	0.12	3	0.36
Pricing	0.05	3	0.15
Market diversity	0.05	2	0.10
Competitive structure	0.05	3	0.15
Industry profitability	0.20	3	0.60
Technical role	0.05	4	0.20
Inflation vulnerability	0.05	2	0.10
Cyclicality	0.05	2	0.10
Customer financials	0.10	5	0.50
Energy impact	0.08	4	0.32
Social	GO	4	—
Environmental	GO	4	—
Legal	GO	4	—
Human	0.05	4	0.20
	1.00		3.38

SOURCE: Reprinted by permission from *Strategy Formulation: Analytical Concepts* by C. W. Hofer and D. Schendel. Copyright © 1978 by West Publishing Company. All rights reserved.

*Some criteria may be of a GO/NO GO type. For example, many *Fortune 500* firms probably would decide not to invest in industries that are viewed negatively by our society, such as gambling, even if it were both legal and very profitable to do so.

**1 *(very unattractive)* through 5 *(highly attractive)*.

    c) Rate the industry on each of these criteria from 1 (very unattractive) to 5 (very attractive). For example, if an industry is facing a long-term decline in profitability, this criterion should be rated 2 or less.

    d) To get a weighted score, multiply the weight for each criterion by its rating. When these scores are added, the weighted attractiveness score for the industry as a whole is provided for a particular SBU. (3.38 is the weighted industry attractiveness score for the SBU considered in Table 6.3.)

2. **Assess business strength/competitive position.**

    a) Identify the SBU's key factors for success in the industry. Table 6.4 lists seventeen such factors for a specific industry.

    b) Weight each success factor (market share, for instance) in terms of its relative importance to profitability or some other measure of success within the industry. For example, because market share was believed to have a relatively small impact on most firms in the

TABLE 6.4
An Example of a Business Strength/Competitive Position Assessment Matrix for an SBU

KEY SUCCESS FACTORS	WEIGHT	RATING**	WEIGHTED SCORE
Market share	0.10	5	.50
SBU growth rate	X*	3	—
Breadth of product line	.05	4	.20
Sales distribution effectiveness	.20	4	.80
Proprietary and key account advantages	X	3	—
Price competitiveness	X	4	—
Advertising and promotion effectiveness	.05	4	.20
Facilities location and newness	.05	5	.25
Capacity and productivity	X	3	—
Experience curve effects	.15	4	.60
Raw materials cost	.05	4	.20
Value added	X	4	—
Relative product quality	.15	4	.60
R&D advantages/position	.05	4	.20
Cash throw-off	.10	5	.50
Caliber of personnel	X	4	—
General image	.05	5	.25
	1.00		4.30

SOURCE: Reprinted by permission from *Strategy Formulation: Analytical Concepts* by C. W. Hofer and D. Schendel. Copyright © 1978 by West Publishing Company. All rights reserved.

*For any particular industry, there will be some factors that, while important in general, will have little or no effect on the relative competitive position of firms within that industry. It is usually better to drop such factors from the analysis than to assign them very low weights.

**1 *(very weak competitive position)* through 5 *(very strong competitive position)*.

industry of Table 6.4, this success factor was given a weight of only 0.10.

c) Rate the SBU on each of the factors from 1 (very weak competitive position) to 5 (very strong competitive position). For example, as the products of the SBU of Table 6.4 have a very high market share, market share received a rating of 5.

d) To get a weighted score, multiply the weight of each factor by its rating. When these scores are added, the sum provides a weighted business strength/competitive position score for the SBU as a whole.

(4.30 is the weighted business strength/competitive position score for the SBU considered in Table 6.4.)

3. **Plot each SBU's current position.**
Once industry attractiveness and business strength/competitive position are calculated for each SBU, the actual position of all the corporation's SBUs should be plotted on a matrix like the one illustrated in Fig. 6.3. The areas of the circles should be proportional to the sizes of the various industries involved (in terms of sales); the company's current market share in each industry should be depicted as a pie-shaped wedge; and the circles should be centered on the coordinates of the SBU's industry attractiveness and business strength/competitive position scores.

To develop a range of scores for the *industry attractiveness* axis of the matrix, look back at Table 6.3. A highly attractive industry should have mostly 5s in the rating column. An industry of medium attractiveness should have mostly 3s in the rating column. An industry of low attractiveness should have mostly 1s in the rating column. Because the weights of the criteria used for each industry must sum to 1.00 regardless of the number of criteria used, the attractiveness axis of the GE Business Screen matrix should range from 1.00 (low attractiveness) to 5.00 (high attractiveness), with 3.00 as the midpoint. The SBU evaluated in Table 6.3 with an industry attractiveness score of 3.38 is thus classified as "medium" on this factor.

Similarly, the range of scores for the *business strength/competitive position* axis of the GE Business Screen matrix should also range from 1.00 (weak) to 5.00 (strong), with 3.00 as the midpoint (average). This can be more clearly understood with another look at Table 6.4. Because the criteria weights must sum to 1.00 regardless of the number of criteria used for each SBU, an SBU with a very strong competitive position might have all 5s in the rating column and thus a total weighted score of 5.00. The SBU evaluated in Table 6.4 with a business strength/competitive position score of 4.30 is thus classified as "strong" on this factor.

The resulting matrix shows the corporation's current portfolio situation. This situation is then contrasted with an ideal portfolio. Figure 6.4 depicts what Hofer and Schendel consider to be such a portfolio. It is considered ideal because it includes primarily winners, and contains enough winners and profit producers to finance the growth of developing (or potential) winners. In reality, however, even a successful firm would probably have a few question marks and perhaps a small loser.

4. **Plot the firm's future portfolio.**
An assessment of the current situation is complete only when the present portfolio is projected into the future. Assuming that the present corporate and SBU strategies continue unchanged, top management should assess the probable impact that likely changes to the corporation's task and societal environments will have, on both future industry attractiveness and SBU competitive position. They should ask themselves whether future matrixes show an improving or deteriorating portfolio position. Is there a **performance gap** between projected and desired portfolios?

FIGURE 6.4
An Ideal Multi-Industry Corporate Portfolio

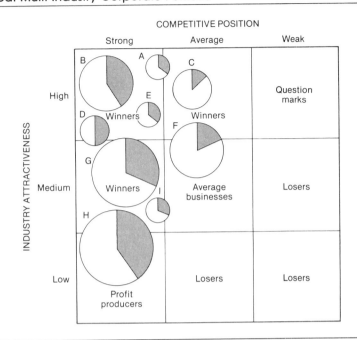

NOTE: It is impossible to identify the orientation (i.e. growth, profit, or balance) of an ideal portfolio based solely on the information contained in the GE Business Screen, because the screen does not reflect all the information needed to do so. For instance, SBUs B, C, F, G, and H could be developing winners in very large markets or established winners in smaller markets. Likewise, SBUs A, D, E, and I could represent either developing potential winners in large markets or established winners in small markets. In the majority of instances, however, the pattern of SBU sizes and positions depicted in this figure would correspond to a balanced ideal portfolio.

If the answer is yes, this gap should serve as a stimulus for them to seriously review the corporation's current mission, objectives, strategies, and policies.

Overall, the nine-cell GE Business Screen is an improvement over the Boston Consulting Group growth-share matrix. The GE Screen considers many more variables and does not lead to such simplistic conclusions. Nevertheless, it can get quite complicated and cumbersome. The calculations used in Tables 6.3 and 6.4 give the appearance of objectivity but are in reality subjective judgments that may vary from one person to another. Another shortcoming of this portfolio matrix is that it cannot effectively depict the positions of new products or SBUs in developing industries.

Fifteen-Cell Product/Market Evolution Matrix

Developed by Hofer and based on the product life-cycle, this matrix depicts the developing types of products or SBUs that cannot be easily shown on the GE Business Screen. Products or SBUs are plotted in terms of their competitive positions and their stages of product/market evolution.[39] As on the GE Business Screen, the circles represent the sizes of the industries involved and the pie wedges represent the market shares of the firm's SBUs or products. Present and future matrixes can be developed to identify strategic issues. In response to Fig. 6.5, for example, one could ask why product or SBU B does not have a greater share of the market, given its strong competitive position.

Advantages and Limitations of Portfolio Analysis

Portfolio analysis is commonly used in strategy formulation because it offers certain **advantages:**

- It encourages top management to evaluate each of the corporation's businesses individually and to set objectives and allocate resources for each.
- It stimulates the use of externally oriented data to supplement management's judgment.
- It raises the issue of cash flow availability for use in expansion and growth.
- Its graphic depiction facilitates communication.

Portfolio analysis does, however, have some very real **limitations** that have caused some companies to reduce their use of the matrixes:

- It is not easy to define product/market segments.
- It suggests the use of standard strategies that can miss opportunities or be impractical.
- It provides an illusion of scientific rigor when in reality positions are based on subjective judgments.
- Its value-laden terms like cash cow and dog can lead to self-fulfilling prophecies.[40]

6.6

REVIEW OF MISSION AND OBJECTIVES

A reexamination of a corporation's current mission and objectives must be done before alternative strategies can be generated and evaluated. The seriousness of this step is emphasized by Tregoe and Zimmerman.

> When making a decision, there is an almost universal tendency to concentrate on the alternatives—the action possibilities—rather than on the objectives we want to achieve. This tendency is widespread because it is much easier to deal

FIGURE 6.5
Product/Market Evolution Portfolio Matrix

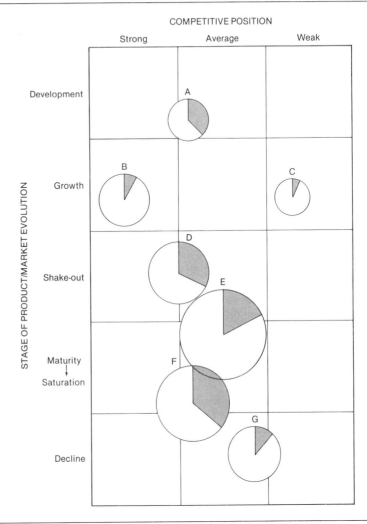

Source: C. W. Hofer and D. Schendel, *Strategy Formulation: Analytical Concepts* (St. Paul, Minn.: West Publishing Co., 1978), p. 34. From C. W. Hofer, "Conceptual Constructs for Formulating Corporate and Business Strategies" (Dover, Mass: Case Publishing), no. BP-0041, p. 3. Copyright © 1977 by Charles W. Hofer. Reprinted by permission.

with alternative courses of action that exist right here and now than to really think about what we want to accomplish in the future. Projecting a set of values forward is hard work. The end result is that we make choices that set our objectives for us, rather than having our choices incorporate clear objectives.[41]

Problems in corporate performance can derive from an inappropriate statement of mission, which may be too narrow or too broad. If the mission does not provide a common thread for a corporation's businesses, managers may be unclear about where the corporation is heading. Objectives and strategies might be in conflict with each other. Divisions might be competing against one another, rather than against outside competition—to the detriment of the corporation as a whole. According to Lorange, "Rapid changes in the environment suggest that the definition of businesses should be reviewed frequently, so that the relevance of the business definitions can be maintained.[42]

An example of a revision of a corporation's mission statement is that by American Telephone and Telegraph (AT&T). The revised mission was published in AT&T's 1980 annual report to the stockholders and had important implications for future corporate strategy:

> No longer do we perceive that our business will be limited to telephony or, for that matter, telecommunications. Ours is the business of information handling, the knowledge business. And the market that we seek is global.

A corporation's objectives can also be inappropriately stated. They can either focus too much on short-term operational goals or be so general that they provide little real guidance. Consequently, objectives should be constantly reviewed so that their usefulness is ensured.

SUMMARY AND CONCLUSION

This chapter describes the key activities involved in the process of strategy formulation. According to the strategic decision-making process introduced in Chapter 2, formulation is described as being composed of six distinct steps. Situation analysis incorporates five steps, beginning with the evaluation of current performance results and ending with the review and revision of mission and objectives. Step six—the generation, evaluation, and selection of the best alternative strategy—is discussed in the next chapter.

Step 1—the evaluation of current performance results and the review of the corporation's mission, objectives, strategies, and policies—deals with the initial stimulus that starts the formulation process. *Step 2*, the review of strategic managers, includes an evaluation of the competencies, level of involvement, and performance of the corporation's top management and board of directors. *Step 3*, scanning the external environment, focuses on the collection of information, the selection of strategic factors, and the forecasting of future events likely to affect the corporation's strategic decisions. An industry analysis includes a consideration of strategic groups and of mobility barriers. *Step 4*, scanning the internal environment, deals with the assessment of internal strengths and weaknesses in terms of structure, culture, and resources. PIMS research and strategic field analysis are valuable aids in the ascertaining of a company's strengths and weaknesses versus those of comparable firms in the company's industry. *Step 5(a)*, analysis of strategic factors in light of the current situation, proposes S.W.O.T. analysis and portfolio analysis as techniques to locate a business' propitious niche in light of its distinctive competence. Matrixes developed by the Boston Consulting Group,

General Electric, and Hofer are described as three ways by which business strengths and weaknesses can be compared to its environmental opportunities and threats. *Step 5(b)*, review and revision of the mission and objectives, completes the situation analysis: it forces a strategic manager to reexamine corporate purpose and objectives before initiating alternative strategies.

DISCUSSION QUESTIONS

1. Does strategy formulation need to be a regular, continuous process? Explain.

2. Is it necessary that a corporation have a "common thread" running through its many activities in order to be successful? Why or why not?

3. How can a knowledge of mobility barriers contribute to an understanding of competitive behavior within an industry?

4. What is likely to happen to an SBU that loses its propitious niche?

5. What value has portfolio analysis in the consideration of strategic factors?

6. Compare and contrast S.W.O.T. analysis with portfolio analysis.

7. Is the GE Business Screen just a more complicated version of the Boston Consulting Group growth/share matrix? Why or why not?

8. Is portfolio analysis used to formulate strategy at the corporate, divisional, or functional level of the corporation?

9. What are the key strategic factors facing CSX Corporation at the time of the case and in the future as described in the Integrative Case at the end of this chapter?

NOTES

1. H. Mintzberg, "Planning on the Left Side and Managing on the Right," *Harvard Business Review* (July-August 1976), p. 56.

2. H. Mintzberg, J. P. Brunet, and J. A. Waters, "Does Planning Impede Strategic Thinking? Tracking the Strategies of Air Canada from 1937 to 1976," in *Advances in Strategic Management, Vol. 4,* edited by R. Lamb and P. Shrivastava (Greenwich, Conn.: Jai Press, 1986), p. 29.

3. D. Miller and P. H. Friesen, "Momentum and Revolution in Organizational Adaptation," *Academy of Management Journal* (December 1980), pp. 600–601.
   H. Mintzberg and A. McHugh, "Strategy Formulation In An Adhocracy," *Administrative Science Quarterly* (June 1985), p. 190.

4. J. A. Pearce and F. David, "Corporate Mission Statements: The Bottom Line," *Academy of Management Executive* (May 1987), p. 109.

5. Pearce and David, p. 113.
   L. L. Byars and T. C. Neil, "Organizational Philosophy and Mission Statements," *Planning Review* (July-August 1987), p. 35.

6. Pearce and David, pp. 109–115.

7. H. I. Ansoff, *Corporate Strategy* (New York: McGraw-Hill, 1965), pp. 104–108.

8. K. Dreyfack, "What Purina Really Wanted From Carbide," *Business Week* (April 21, 1986), p. 33.

9. J. R. Norman, "General Electric Is Stalking Big Game Again," *Business Week* (March 16, 1987), p. 113.
   M. G. Guiles, "Chrysler Is Aiming to Boost Its Share of the U.S. Market," *Wall Street Journal* (September 25, 1986), p. 26.

10. M. D. Richards, *Setting Strategic Goals and Objectives,* 2nd ed. (St. Paul: West Publishing Co., 1986), pp. 30–32.

11. K. R. Andrews, *The Concept of Corporate Strategy,* 2nd ed. (Homewood, Ill.: Irwin, 1987), p. 18.

12. R. B. Robinson, Jr., and J. A. Pearce, III, "Research Thrusts in Small Firm Strategic Planning," *Academy of Management Review* (January 1984), pp. 128–137.

13. D. J. Hickson, R. J. Butler, D. Cray, G. R. Mallory, and D. C. Wilson, *Top Decisions: Strategic Decision-Making in Organizations* (San Francisco: Jossey-Bass, 1986), pp. 100–101.

14. J. Bussey, "Gould Reshapes Itself into High-Tech Outfit Amid Much Turmoil," *Wall Street Journal* (October 3, 1985), p. 1.

15. M. A. Harris, Z. Schiller, R. Mitchell, and C. Power, "Can Jack Welch Reinvent GE?" *Business Week* (June 30, 1986), pp. 62–67.

16. H. Mintzberg, "Strategy-Making in Three Modes," *California Management Review* (Winter 1973), pp. 44–53.

17. J. B. Quinn, *Strategies For Change: Logical Incrementalism* (Homewood, Ill.: Irwin, 1980), p. 58.

18. K. J. Hatten and M. L. Hatten, "Strategic Groups, Asymmetrical Mobility Barriers, and Contestability," *Strategic Management Journal* (July-August 1987), p. 329.

19. J. McGee and J. Thomas, "Strategic Groups: Theory, Research, and Taxonomy," *Strategic Management Journal* (March-April 1986), pp. 141–160. Mobility barrier is used here as a more general form of *entry barrier*—a term usually referring only to entry into an industry. See M. E. Porter, *Competitive Strategy* (New York: Free Press, 1980), pp. 132–135.

20. S. Schoeffler, "Nine Basic Findings On Business Strategy," *The PIMS Letter On Business Strategy*, No. 1 (Cambridge, Mass.: The Strategic Planning Institute, 1984), pp. 3–5.

21. G. Badler, "Strategizing for a Spectrum of Possibilities," *Planning Review* (July 1984), pp. 28–31.

22. R. D. Buzzell and B. T. Gale, *The PIMS Principles* (New York: The Free Press, 1987), pp. 8–10.

23. C. Y. Woo, "Market-Share Leadership—Not Always So Good," *Harvard Business Review* (January-February 1984), pp. 50–54.

J. K. Newton, "Market Share—Key to Higher Profitability?" *Long Range Planning* (February 1983), pp. 37–41.

D. Bourantas and Y. Mandes, "Does Market Share Lead to Profitability?" *Long Range Planning* (October 1987), pp. 102–108.

24. Buzzell and Gale, pp. 7 and 183.

25. V. Ramanujan and N. Venkatraman, "An Inventory and Critique of Strategy Research using the PIMS Database," *Academy of Management Review* (January 1984), p. 147.

26. P. Lorange, M. F. S. Morton, and S. Ghoshal, *Strategic Control* (St. Paul: West Publishing Co., 1986), pp. 104–107.

27. M. E. Porter, *Competitive Advantage* (New York: The Free Press, 1985), pp. 33–61.

28. W. H. Newman, "Shaping the Master Strategy of Your Firm," *California Management Review,* vol. 9, no. 3 (1967), pp. 77–88.

29. D. F. Abell, "Strategic Windows," *Journal of Marketing* (July 1978), pp. 21–26, as reported by K. R. Harrigan, "Entry Barriers in Mature Manufacturing Industries" in R. Lamb (ed.), *Advances in Strategic Management,* Vol. 2 (Greenwich, Conn.: Jai Press, 1983), pp. 67–97.

30. D. K. Clifford and R. E. Cavanagh, "The Winning Performance of Midsized Growth Companies," *Planning Review* (November 1984), pp. 18–23, 35.

31. L. Fahey and H. K. Christensen, "Evaluating the Research on Strategy Content," *Journal of Management* (Summer 1986), p. 180.

32. R. G. Hamermesh, "Making Planning Effective," *Harvard Business Review* (July-August 1986), p. 115.

33. B. Hedley, "Strategy and the Business Portfolio," *Long Range Planning* (February 1977), p. 9.

34. D. C. Hambrick, I. C. MacMillan, and D. L. Day, "Strategic Attributes and Performance in the BCG Matrix—A PIMS-Based Analysis of Industrial Product Businesses," *Academy of Management Journal* (September 1982), pp. 510–531.

35. C. Y. Woo and A. C. Cooper, "The Surprising Case for Low Market Share," *Harvard Business Review* (November-December 1982), pp. 106–113.

36. P. McNamee, "Competitive Analysis Using Matrix Displays," *Long Range Planning* (June 1984), pp. 98–114.

R. E. Walker, "Portfolio Analysis in Practice," *Long Range Planning* (June 1984), pp. 63–71.

D. A. Aaker and G. S. Day, "The Perils of High-growth Markets," *Strategic Management Journal* (September-October 1986), pp. 409–421.

37. R. G. Hamermesh, *Making Strategy Work* (New York: Wiley & Sons, 1986), p. 14.

For a more complete list of characteristics, see P. McNamee, pp. 102–103.

38. C. W. Hofer and D. Schendel, *Strategy Formulation: Analytical Concepts* (St. Paul: West Publishing Co., 1978), pp. 72–87.

39. Similar to the Hofer model, but using twenty instead of fifteen cells is the Arthur D. Little (ADL) strategic planning matrix. For details see M. B. Coate, "Pitfalls in Portfolio Planning," *Long Range Planning* (June 1983), pp. 47–56.

40. F. W. Gluck, "A Fresh Look at Strategic Management," *Journal of Business Strategy* (Fall 1985), pp. 4–19.

41. B. B. Tregoe and J. W. Zimmerman, "The New Strategic Manager," *Business* (May-June 1981), p. 19.

42. P. Lorange, *Implementation of Strategic Planning* (Englewood Cliffs, N.J.: Prentice-Hall, 1982, p. 211.

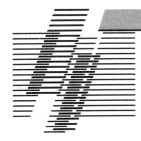

CSX CORPORATION'S STRATEGIC FACTORS

Three rail systems dominated the eastern United States in 1985: CSX, Norfolk Southern, and Conrail. West of the Mississippi also lay three major systems: Union Pacific, Santa Fe Southern Pacific Corporation (pending approval of the merger by the ICC), and the Burlington Northern Railroad. There appeared to be no one reason why railroads in the United States had developed into separate east-west domains generally separated by the Mississippi River. In some instances the personalities of the owner-managers kept railroads separate. According to Dr. Michael Crum at Iowa State University, an expert on rail transportation, rail traffic has traditionally been an interregional instead of transcontinental phenomenon. The emphasis has been on the gaining of access to individual markets, such as St. Louis or New York City, rather than the crossing of the country. Rail lines connected coastal population centers with the interior sources of commodities and products. What little traffic stretched from east to west coasts had typically been handled through standard interline agreements, allowing one railroad to transport for a fee the railcars of another railroad. Thus boxcars of the Seaboard Line (among many other railroads) could be seen traveling through California and Western Canada via agreements with Santa Fe, Canadian Pacific, and others. This phenomenon had made the management of such information a major task of any modern North American railroad. According to Dr. Crum, the interlining of rail traffic has created additional costs and some decrease in the quality of rail service in terms of time in transit. Negotiations for the division of revenues were often very complex. As a consequence, interlining, with its paperwork and delays, has been viewed by rail management as a necessary evil due to the historical fragmentation of rail system ownership.

KEY COMPETITORS

Although the Norfolk Southern and CSX rail systems had several characteristics in common, such as a high dependence upon coal as a revenue-producing commodity (coal composed around 32%–36% of CSX's total annual commodity revenues and approximately 36%–40% of Norfolk Southern's total annual commodity revenues), Norfolk Southern (NS) was a more efficient rail operation. NS has been characterized by analysts as a very lean operation in terms of costs and expenses, whereas both the Chessie and Seaboard systems have been criticized for having too many employees and higher salaries. CSX resulted from the merger of two railroads with high unit-labor costs, while NS represented a combination of two rail systems with historically low labor costs. Hays T. Watkins, Chairman of CSX, was well aware of the danger that NS, serving the same markets as CSX, could use its labor-cost advantage to undercut the rates of CSX. Mr. Watkins stated in 1981, "I don't think the CSX labor cost ratio will ever be as low as the Norfolk & Western and Southern despite

SOURCE: J. D. Hunger, B. Ferrin, H. Felix-Gamez, T. Goetzman, "CSX Corporation," in *Cases in Strategic Management and Business Policy* by T. L. Wheelen and J. D. Hunger (Reading, Mass.: Addison-Wesley, 1987), pp. 91–123.

anything we can do, due to geography, the locations of the mines, and the location of the facilities." He added,

> We have not found any practical way to run a good service railroad on the Chessie side and equal the N&W's figures. On the bottom line, I am not sure we can beat them. I'm not even sure we can match them, but we can't match AT&T or a lot of other companies. What we do is take what we have and do the best we can.

CSX management has worked hard, however, to reduce its rail employment from 75,336 employees in 1980 to 53,031 at year-end 1984.

Another significant difference between NS and CSX was that, after the respective mergers, NS had carried the consolidation of operations much farther than did CSX. While CSX operated its two rail systems as separate units, NS had combined most staff activities as well as the sales offices of its component railroads in every location. For example, all the functions commonly included in a traffic department—including sales, marketing, pricing, and industrial development—were directed by a chief marketing officer for the entire NS system.

Robert Claytor, NS Chairman, raised the possibility on October 23, 1984, that NS might also buy a barge line. NS already owned about 18% of Piedmont Aviation, a fast-growing regional airline. NS's acquisition plans did not stop there. The firm had expressed serious intentions of buying a major trucking operation and had entered an agreement for the purchase of North American Van Lines from Pepsico for over $300 million.

The third major railroad in the eastern United States was the government-owned Consolidated Rail Corporation (Conrail). Conrail operated a 15,400-mile track network that was basically oriented in a straight east-west line. Although analysts believed in 1976, when Conrail was formed, that it would take something of a minor miracle to make the system profitable, the miracle occurred thanks to significant government investment and easing of regulatory restrictions (e.g., branch line abandonments). Conrail's significant advantage over both CSX and Norfolk Southern was that it alone of the three major eastern systems had track north of Philadelphia and east of Rochester into the populous New York-New Jersey-New England area.

In early February 1985, Transportation Secretary Dole announced her decision to sell the government's 85% share of Conrail to Norfolk Southern. (The remaining 15% was owned by Conrail employees.) This decision took CSX top management by surprise. They had assumed that the bid by Norfolk Southern would never get past the Justice Department's anti-trust review.

RIVALRY INCREASES UNDER DEREGULATION

Deregulation had led to the industry-wide implementation of rate-cutting tactics designed to increase market share. The battle was taking place all over the country, but in the East the leading practitioner had been Conrail. On April 3, 1981, Conrail cut its rates 22% on import-export containers moving between Chicago and New York, Philadelphia, and Baltimore. "CSX Corporation, which controls 80% of the container traffic between Chicago and Baltimore, responded with a 25% reduction," reported Robert D. Long, analyst at First Boston Corporation.

In addition to the practice of cutting rates on desirable traffic, the railroads had employed several other tactics intended to increase market share and enhance profits.

Some companies had increased rates for services like short hauls in joint moves of cars; these companies argued that when the revenues were shared with the line offering the long-haul service, those carriers stuck with a very short-haul part of the movement were not justly compensated. Since the passage of the Staggers Act, railroads were allowed to charge joint rates that generated at least 110% of variable, or direct costs, or the cancel those routes.

Another tactic adopted by rail carriers was the canceling of joint routes with other railroads when they could provide service over the entire movement themselves. Railroads also substantially increased charges for switching services, in order to prevent competitors from entering certain of their markets. (The switching service was a mutual agreement that enabled one railroad to pick up or deliver a shipment for another carrier that did not have direct access to the shipper or receiver. The switching carrier received a per-car fee for its move, which was generally less than twenty miles.)

CONSIDERATION OF STRATEGIC FACTORS

Hays Watkins pondered the many variables still facing the industry and CSX in particular. CSX had come a long way in five short years. Leading the way in marketing innovations, the company's rail units had captured the rail industry's top marketing award twice in the last three years. At the same time, CSX had moved aggressively to broaden its transportation and natural resources horizons, improve rates of return, and accomplish its number one goal—increased shareholder wealth. The stated mission of CSX, to become a multimodal, one-stop transportation system, seemed to be within reach. The corporation's objectives for the near future would be directed toward increasing the returns on the assets, capital, and equity employed in its businesses. Given the company's internal strengths and weaknesses, and the various opportunities and threats within the transportation industry, how should CSX assess its position and plan for the future?

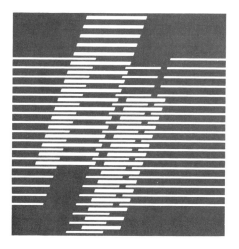

CHAPTER 7

STRATEGY FORMULATION: STRATEGIC ALTERNATIVES

STRATEGIC MANAGEMENT MODEL

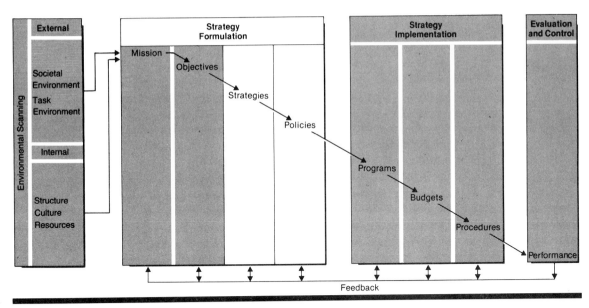

A key part of strategy formulation is the development of alternative courses of action that specify means by which the corporate mission and objectives are to be accomplished. As explained in Chapter 6 and depicted in Fig. 6.1, the generation, evaluation, and selection of the best strategic alternative is the sixth step of the strategic decision-making process. Once the best strategy is selected, appropriate policies must be established to define the ground rules for implementation. This chapter, therefore, will (a) explain the many alternative strategies available at the corporate, divisional, and functional levels of the corporation; (b) suggest criteria for use in the evaluation of these strategies; (c) explain how an optimal strategy is selected; and (d) suggest how strategy is translated into policies.

7.1

ALTERNATIVE STRATEGIES

As described in Chapter 1, the typical large, multidivisional business corporation operating in a number of different industries has three levels of strategy: corporate, business, and functional (see Fig. 1.1). **Corporate-level strategy** specifies the firm's portfolio of businesses, that is, the industries within which it will operate. **Business-level strategy** specifies how the company or its units will compete within each industry or industry segment. **Functional-level strategy** specifies how the company or its units will maximize resource productivity, so that it can develop the distinctive competence necessary for successful competition within each industry.[1] Even the smallest company operating in only one industry with one product line must, at one time or another, consider the questions embedded within each level of strategy:

> *Corporate:* Should we expand, cut back, or continue our operations with no change? If we want to grow and expand, should we do so through internal development or through external acquisitions, mergers, or joint ventures? Should we concentrate our activities within our current industry or should we diversify into other industries?

> *Business:* Should we compete on the basis of low cost or should we differentiate our products/services on some basis other than cost, such as quality or prestige? Should we compete head-to-head with our major competitors for the biggest but most sought-after share of the market, or should we focus on a niche in which we can satisfy a less sought-after but also profitable segment of the market?

> *Functional:* Depending on the corporate- and business-level strategies we're following, how should we carry out our functional activities so that we maximize productivity and develop a distinctive competence? For example, if we plan to concentrate our activities in one industry (concentration corporate-level growth strategy) and compete as the low cost producer (overall low cost business-level competitive strategy), should we, to keep costs down, use a follower rather than a leader R&D strategy? To finance our manufacturing facility, should we go into debt or sell stock? To generate market demand cheaply, should we emphasize promotion over advertising? Should we build a highly automated plant close to our markets, or a labor-intensive plant in a foreign country where labor is cheap?

Following is a discussion of the most popular strategies within each of the three levels. Regardless of which strategies are selected for a particular company or business unit, the corporate, business, and functional strategies must be internally consistent (that is, fit together in a mutually supportive manner that forms an integrated hierarchy of strategy).

Corporate Strategies

Corporate-level strategy looks at the entire firm and specifies the firm's overall approach to the achievement of its mission and objectives. It is composed of three grand strategies: **stability, growth,** and **retrenchment.** Each of these grand strategies is composed of appropriate sub-strategies.

Assume for the purposes of this section that the corporation either operates *only* in one industry, like Caterpillar in heavy construction equipment, or *primarily* in one industry, like Anheuser-Busch, which derives around 80% of its sales and over 90% of its profits from brewing beer and related products. For this type of company, strategic managers need to decide the overall direction of the firm through its corporate-level strategy. Management can do so by analyzing (1) the attractiveness of the industry in which the company primarily operates, and (2) the business strength/competitive position of the company within this primary industry. This analysis was discussed earlier in Chapter 6, under S.W.O.T. and portfolio analysis, and was depicted in Fig. 6.3. The nine-cell, GE business screen matrix, depicted in Figure 7.1, can plot the alternative corporate strategies that could fit the company's situation. This matrix suggests which corporate strategy from twelve possible strategies will be most appropriate for a firm's overall situation within its primary industry.

Stability Strategies

The *stability* family of strategies is appropriate for a successful corporation operating in an industry of medium attractiveness. The task environment

FIGURE 7.1
Corporate Strategies of a Company Operating Primarily in One Industry

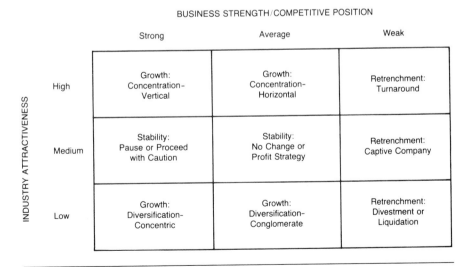

BUSINESS STRENGTH/COMPETITIVE POSITION

INDUSTRY ATTRACTIVENESS		Strong	Average	Weak
	High	Growth: Concentration–Vertical	Growth: Concentration–Horizontal	Retrenchment: Turnaround
	Medium	Stability: Pause or Proceed with Caution	Stability: No Change or Profit Strategy	Retrenchment: Captive Company
	Low	Growth: Diversification–Concentric	Growth: Diversification–Conglomerate	Retrenchment: Divestment or Liquidation

Source: Thomas L. Wheelen and J. David Hunger, "Corporate Strategies of a Company Operating Primarily in One Industry." Copyright © 1988 by Wheelen and Hunger Associates. Reprinted by permission.

may be reasonably predictable, with little change expected. The industry probably faces a moderate growth situation, so there is little current incentive for heavy investment in the business or diversification out of the industry. Epitomized by a steady-as-she-goes philosophy, these strategies involve no major changes. In order to build upon and improve its competitive advantage, a corporation concentrates its resources on its present businesses. It retains the same mission and similar objectives; it simply increases its level of achievement by approximately the same percentage each year. Its main strategic decisions concern improving the performance of functional areas, because its business-level competitive strategies continue to be successful. A stability strategy can also be used if the task environment is likely to change radically at any moment and top management wants to see what happens before they change the course of the company. Some stability strategies are as follows:

NO-CHANGE STRATEGY In this strategy, a corporation continues on its course and adjusts only for inflation in its objectives. Rarely articulated as a definite strategy, the success of a no-change strategy depends on a lack of change in a corporation's internal or external environments. This strategy might evolve from a lack of interest in or need to engage in hard strategic analysis. After all, if everything is going along fine, why change anything?

PROFIT STRATEGY The profit strategy involves the sacrifice of future growth for present profits. The result is often short-term success coupled to long-term stagnation. By reducing expenditures for R&D, maintenance, or advertising, short-term profits increase and are reflected in the stockholders' dividends. For example, many U.S. airlines were accused during the 1980s of reducing their maintenance budgets and of cutting back on their purchases of new planes so that they could stay profitable during a period of aggressive price competition. A corporation having a number of "cash cow" divisions or product lines can "milk" these of cash for dividends instead of investing the cash in new products or services. Obviously, the profit strategy is useful only to help a company get through a temporary difficulty. Unfortunately, the profit strategy is seductive and if continued long enough will lead to bankruptcy.

PAUSE STRATEGY After a period of prolonged fast growth, a corporation might become inefficient or unmanageable. The addition of new divisions through acquisition or internal development can stretch management and resources thin. A pause strategy involves reducing the levels of a corporation's objectives so that it is able to consolidate its resources. The strategy is generally considered temporary—a way to get a corporate house in order. For example, after making a series of acquisitions and internally developing new machines to put the company at the cutting edge of robotics and computer-controlled parts-making systems, Cincinnati Milicron decided in 1988 to emphasize reorganizing to improve its efficiency and to reduce its recent losses.[2]

PROCEED-WITH-CAUTION STRATEGY This strategy results from a specific decision to proceed slowly because of important factors developing in the external environment. Top management might believe that a growth strategy is no longer feasible, because of, for instance, a sudden scarcity of needed raw materials, new governmental regulations, or a poor economic climate. The top management of CSX, for example, was very hesitant in 1985 to take any major steps in the railroad industry until Conrail's future was definitely decided by the U.S. government.

Growth Strategies

Growth strategies are extremely popular because most executives tend to equate growth with success. Research by Glueck of 358 executives over a 45-year period revealed growth to be the most frequently used corporate strategy—it was used six times more often than stability and seven times more often than retrenchment.[3] Those corporations that are in dynamic environments *must* grow in order to survive. Continuing growth means increasing sales and a chance to take advantage of the experience curve to reduce the per unit cost of products sold and thereby increase profits. This cost reduction becomes extremely important if a corporation's industry is growing quickly and competitors are engaging in price wars in attempts to increase their shares of the market. Those firms that have not reached "critical mass" (that is, gained the necessary economy of large-scale production) will face large losses unless they can find and fill a small, but profitable, niche where higher prices can be offset by special product or service features.

Growth is a very seductive strategy for two key reasons:

- A growing firm can cover up mistakes and inefficiencies more easily than can a stable one. A growing flow of revenue into a highly leveraged corporation can create a large amount of "organization slack"[4] (unused resources) that can be used to quickly resolve problems and conflicts between departments and divisions. There is also a big cushion for a turnaround in case a strategic error is made. Larger firms also have more clout and are more likely to receive support in case of impending bankruptcy, as was the situation with Chrysler Corporation in 1979.

- There are more opportunities for advancement, promotion, and interesting jobs in a growing firm. Growth, per se, is exciting and ego-enhancing for CEOs. A growing corporation tends to be seen as a "winner" or "on the move" by the marketplace and by potential investors. Large firms are also more difficult to acquire than are smaller ones—thus an executive's job is more secure.[5]

There are two basic growth strategies at the corporate level: *concentration* in one industry and *diversification* into other industries. If, as depicted in Figure 7.1, the current industry is highly attractive in terms of growth rate and other criteria, concentration of resources on that one industry makes sense as a strategy for growth. If, however, the current industry has low attractiveness, it makes sense for a corporation to diversify out of that industry if management wishes to pursue growth. As shown in Table 7.1, each growth strategy has its own set of sub-strategies, such as horizontal and vertical growth under concentration, and concentric and conglomerate growth under diversification. Each of these corporate growth strategies can be conducted through *internal* development or through *external* acquisitions, mergers, or joint ventures. First, we examine some concentration and diversification strategies. Later, we consider internal versus external growth.

CONCENTRATION A corporation may choose to grow by the concentration of all or most of its resources in one industry; it emphasizes a single product or product line, single market, or single technology. Corporations such as McDonald's (fast food), Caterpillar (construction equipment), and Apple Computer (personal computers) that concentrate their efforts on a single product line are able to stay ahead of competitors who dilute their effort in many industries. Gerber, for example, failed miserably when it tried to diversify out of baby foods into adult foods, mail-order insurance, furniture, and day-care centers. A concentration strategy allows the corporation to put

TABLE 7.1
Major Corporate Growth Strategies

GROWTH STRATEGY	INTERNAL	EXTERNAL
I. Concentration (One-industry strategy)		
A. Horizontal	Coors move into Eastern U.S.	Chrysler's purchase of American Motors, Lamborghini, and part of Maserati
B. Vertical		
1. Backward	Ford's River Rouge steel mill	Turner Broadcasting's purchase of MGM/United Artists
2. Forward	Goodyear's & Firestone's retail tire stores	Boeing's purchase of part of Allegis (United Airlines)
II. Diversification (Multi-industry strategy)		
A. Concentric	Anheuser-Busch's Eagle Snacks	Reynold's purchase of Nabisco
B. Conglomerate	CSX's use of its land for resorts, hotels, office buildings	Xerox's purchase of Crum & Forster insurance

SOURCE: Thomas L. Wheelen and J. David Hunger, "Major Corporate Growth Strategies." Copyright © 1988 by Wheelen and Hunger Associates. Reprinted by permission.

more time, energy, and resources into the development of innovative product/service concepts so that it can better compete in an attractive industry. Two concentration strategies are horizontal and vertical growth. An example of an effective use of the concentration strategy is shown in Illustrative Example 7.1.

Horizontal Growth Strategy The horizontal growth strategy is an appropriate strategy for a company with an average competitive position wishing to increase its presence in an attractive industry. To enlarge its operations, the company spreads into other segments of its current market or into other geographic areas. The objectives are generally to increase the sales and profits of the firm's current business, through larger economies of scale in production and marketing, as well as to reduce current and/or potential competition for customers and supplies. As shown in Table 7.1, a company can grow horizontally through internal or external means. External horizontal growth, usually called **horizontal integration,** is defined as the acquisition by one corporation of another corporation or business unit in the same industry. Chrysler's purchase of American Motors, U.S. Air's merger with Piedmont Airlines, and Tonka's acquisition of Kenner Parker Toys are examples of external horizontal growth. In these instances, because the acquiring firm is buying a current competitor, the transaction can be liable to antitrust suits and/or government intervention to prevent the formation of a monopoly. The acquisition of a major competitor will also cost a lot of money and will probably force the acquiring firm into debt. A strong dislike of such debt is one reason why the Adolph Coors Company chose to expand into the eastern United States through internal means instead of through the acquisition of an eastern brewer.

Vertical Growth Strategy This strategy, often called **vertical integration,** is the strategy of a corporation that enters one or more businesses that provide goods or services necessary to the manufacture and distribution of its own products but that were previously purchased from other companies. These can range from the obtaining of raw materials to the merchandising of the product. **Backward vertical growth** (also called *backward integration*) is the corporation's entry into the business of supplying some of its present raw materials. Henry Ford I internally achieved this growth when he built his own steel mill at River Rouge to supply Ford's assembly lines. **Forward vertical growth** (also called *forward integration*) is the corporation's entry into the business of distributing its products: it enters marketing channels closer to the ultimate consumer. The internal form of this growth is common in the tire industry, where manufacturers, such as Firestone and Goodyear, build and manage their own retail outlets. Examples of vertical growth through external means are Turner Broadcasting's purchase of the MGM/United Artists film studios, by which TBC gained access to 2,200 films to be shown on its cable television channels (this is backward integration); and

ILLUSTRATIVE EXAMPLE 7.1

Concentration Strategy at Shell Oil

During the 1970s, oil companies throughout the world were awash in profits. Overwhelmed by cash inflows, they spent millions on acquisitions outside the oil industry and on expensive overhead. By the mid-1980s, these acquisitions, such as Exxon's purchase of Reliance Electric, Mobil's purchase of Montgomery Ward, and Standard Oil's purchase of Kennecott Copper, had turned to losses that measured in the hundreds of millions. By 1986, most of these acquisitions had been sold at a loss and the oil companies were laying off people and paring down their huge overhead costs.

Shell Oil Company was different. When John F. Bookout assumed the position of Chief Executive Officer in 1976 at Shell, the U.S. subsidiary of the Royal Dutch/Shell Group, the corporation ranked seventh in the industry in net profits. Nine years later Shell had moved to fourth place with net profits of $1.65 billion. "The first thing I was confronted with by our board was, 'Should Shell Oil diversify?'," recalled Bookout. After spending a year and a half weighing opportunities both inside and outside the oil business, Bookout decided against diversification. "It had to be almost egotistical to think that Shell could pay a premium to take over a company we knew nothing about and cause it to perform 2 to 2½ times better than it had been, which would have been necessary to get the return on investment we needed," stated Bookout. "We decided we have abundant opportunity in our mainline businesses, and that's where we should stay."

Because of its conclusion that the oil business was an attractive industry on which to concentrate, Shell chose to streamline its operations in the late 1970s, to increase its oil reserves, and to become a low-cost, efficient company. "You have to decide what game you're going to play," said Bookout. "Are you going to play the game that scatters you all over? That means you're playing other people's technology, or their ideas, aren't you?"

As were most large oil companies, Shell was fully vertically integrated from the oil well to the service station. Shell's emphasis on oil-production technology had led to an expertise in enhanced oil recovery and to its becoming an effective and highly efficient oil finder. Developing these skills enabled it to actually increase its oil and gas reserves internally at a time when overall U.S. oil reserves shrank 11%. Bookout in 1986 proudly pointed to the results of his concentration strategy: "In 1976 we had 3.2 billion barrels of reserves. Since then we've used 3.1 billion barrels, and our reserves now stand at 3.9 billion."

SOURCE: T. Mack, "It's Time to Take Risks," *Forbes* (October 6, 1986), pp. 125–133.

Boeing Company's acquisition of around 16% of the stock of Allegis Corporation, the parent of United Airlines, in order to keep a valued customer for its airlines (forward integration).

The vertical growth strategy is quite common in the oil, basic metals, automobile, and forest products industries. As pointed out in Table 7.2, some of its advantages are the lowering of costs and the improvement of coordination and control. It is a good way for a strong firm to increase its competitive advantage in an attractive industry. Although backward integration is usually more profitable than forward integration,[6] it can reduce a corporation's strategic flexibility: by creating an encumbrance of expensive assets that might be hard to sell, it can thus create an exit barrier to the corporation's leaving that particular industry.[7]

A study by Harrigan reveals at least four types of vertical integration

TABLE 7.2

Some Advantages and Disadvantages of Vertical Integration (Vertical Growth Strategy)

ADVANTAGES	DISADVANTAGES
Internal Benefits	*Internal Costs*
Integration economies reduce costs by eliminating steps, reducing duplicate overhead, and cutting costs (technology dependent)	Need for overhead to coordinate vertical integration increased costs
Improved coordination of activities reduces inventorying and other costs	Burden of excess capacity from unevenly balanced minimum efficient scale plants (technology dependent)
Avoid time-consuming tasks, such as price shopping, communicating design details, or negotiating contracts	Poorly organized vertically integrated firms do not enjoy synergies that compensate for higher costs
Competitive Benefits	*Competitive Dangers*
Avoid foreclosure to inputs, services, or markets	Obsolete processes may be perpetuated
Improved marketing or technological intelligence	Creates mobility (or exit) barriers
Opportunity to create product differentiation (increased value added)	Links firm to sick adjacent businesses
Superior control of firm's economic environment (market power)	Lose access to information from suppliers or distributors
Create credibility for new products	Synergies created through vertical integration may be overrated
Synergies could be created by coordinating vertical activities skillfully	Managers integrated before thinking through the most appropriate way to do so

SOURCE: K. R. Harrigan, "Formulating Vertical Integration Strategies," *Academy of Management Review* (October 1984), p. 639. Copyright © 1984 by the Academy of Management. Reprinted by permission.

ranging from **full integration** to **long-term contracts.**[8] For example, if a corporation does not want to have the disadvantages of full vertical integration, it may choose either **taper** or **quasi-integration** strategies. With taper integration, a firm produces part of its own requirements and buys the rest from outside suppliers. In the case of quasi-integration, a company gets most of its requirements from an outside supplier that is under its partial control. For example, by purchasing 20% of the common stock of Intel Corporation, IBM guaranteed its access to 16-bit microprocessors for its personal computers.

DIVERSIFICATION This is the corporate growth strategy in which *different* products or divisions are added to the corporation. These new products may be developed internally or purchased externally, and may be related (concentric) or unrelated (conglomerate) to the corporation's current product line. So that the corporation can reduce its dependence on an industry with low attractiveness, a diversification strategy allows it to move into other industries with greater opportunities. The A. T. Cross Co., for example, decided that further growth in the heavily saturated pen market would be very difficult. It already had more than 50% of the U. S. market share in expensive pens. Rather than diluting its prestige name by attempting to sell inexpensive pens, it chose to diversify into the premium gift business and acquired the Mark Cross, Inc., leather goods stores. As corporations become larger there is a natural tendency for them to diversify into other industries. In the United States, for example, fewer than 15% of the Fortune 500 companies remain largely in a single business.[9] The trend is similar for corporations throughout the world. In the United Kingdom, for example, the percentage of companies that had heavily diversified out of their original business increased from 25% in 1950, to 65% of the total by 1980.[10]

As shown in Table 7.1, there are two types of diversification—concentric and conglomerate.

Concentric Diversification *Concentric diversification* is the addition to a corporation of **related** products or divisions. The corporation's lines of business still possess some "common thread" that serves to relate them in some manner. The point of commonality may be similar technology, customer usage, distribution, managerial skills, or product similarity. Examples of concentric diversification were the internally developed addition of "Eagle Snacks" to Anheuser-Busch's successful line of beers and the external purchase of Nabisco Brands by R. J. Reynolds Industries. In both instances, the new products were complementary to the company's other products and combining the new with the old was likely to provide some product-market synergy that would hopefully increase sales and/or reduce the costs of current products as well as new ones. Concentric diversification is thus most appropriate for companies wishing to take advantage of their competitive position strengths as they diversify out of an unattractive industry.

Conglomerate Diversification *Conglomerate diversification,* in contrast to concentric diversification, is the addition to the firm of **unrelated** products or divisions. Rather than keeping a common thread throughout their corporation, top managers who adopt this strategy are primarily concerned with a return on investment criterion: Will it increase the corporation's level of profitability? The addition may, however, be justified in terms of strategic fit. A cash-rich corporation with few opportunities for growth in its industry might, for example, move into another industry where opportunities are great, but cash hard to find. An example of this strategy was the purchase of Vydec Corporation, a maker of word processors, by Exxon Corporation, the oil company. Another instance of conglomerate diversification might be the purchase by a corporation with a seasonal and, therefore uneven, cash flow of a firm in an unrelated industry with complementing seasonal sales that will level out the cash flow. The purchase of a natural gas transmission business (Texas Gas Resources) by CSX Corporation was considered by CSX management to be a good fit because most of its revenue came in the winter months when railroads go through a seasonally lean period. Conglomerate diversification is thus most appropriate for companies with only average competitive position strengths as they diversify out of an unattractive industry.

Concentric vs. Conglomerate Diversification Beginning with a classic study by Rumelt, a number of researchers have argued that conglomerate (unrelated) diversification into other industries is less profitable than is concentric (related) diversification.[11] Peters and Waterman support this proposition in their book *In Search of Excellence.*

> Our principal finding is clear and simple. Organizations that do branch out (whether by acquisition or internal diversification) but stick very close to their knitting outperform the others. The most successful of all are those diversified around a single skill—the coating and bonding technology at 3M, for example.
>
> The second group, in descending order, comprises those companies that branch out into related fields—the leap from electric power generation turbines to jet engines (another turbine) from GE, for example.
>
> Least successful, as a general rule, are those companies that diversify into a wide variety of fields. Acquisitions, especially among this group, tend to wither on the vine.[12]

Supporting this argument are the recent spinoffs by conglomerate corporations of formerly acquired units. In the past few years ITT, RCA, Gulf & Western, Beatrice Foods, Quaker Oats, General Electric, Exxon, and R. J. Reynolds have sold off major nonrelated holdings.

Nevertheless, studies reported by *Fortune* magazine and by the management consulting firm of Booz, Allen & Hamilton, Inc., found that conglomerate diversifiers not only performed as well as concentric diversifiers, but that over certain periods of time conglomerates actually outperformed industry peers.[13]

It is most probable that concentric and conglomerate diversification are equally valuable strategies for corporate growth, but are successful in different situations.[14] Figure 7.1 suggests that a corporation with a strong competitive position in a particular industry will do better if it diversifies concentrically into a related industry where it can most easily apply its distinctive competence. Corporations with only average competitive positions should thus do better by diversifying into unrelated industries. Leontiades, a well-known scholar in the area, argues that conglomerate acquisitions do not at first appear to be as successful as concentric because the conglomerate acquisition causes an initial reduction in efficiency. (This conclusion, of course, assumes diversification through external means). He states:

> Until a company learns to manage and integrate its acquisitions, it is dependent on autonomous units operating profitably enough to overcome the lack of administrative coordination. This leaves the company vulnerable to unexpected downturns in the new businesses which it cannot directly control nor totally avoid. Over time, the level of administrative control tends to rise. If this aspect of diversification is mastered, and an optimum "family" of businesses emerges, then the fruits of the labor of diversification can be enjoyed.[15]

This argument thus suggests that the real issue may not be concentric vs. conglomerate diversification, but concerns the level of difficulty of managing an acquisition. If the firms are managed with a similar **dominant logic,** they can be integrated quickly and profitably.[16] This concept is exemplified by the comments of F. Ross Johnson, Chief Executive of Nabisco Brands, upon the company's pending acquisition by R. J. Reynolds Industries:

> We studied each other's track records and hit a common road. How we manage our businesses is practically identical. What we believe in—divesting the bad businesses, tight control of the balance sheet, understanding cash flow—is pretty much the same.[17]

EXTERNAL VERSUS INTERNAL GROWTH STRATEGIES Corporations can follow the growth strategies of either concentration or diversification through the internal development of new products and services, or through external acquisitions, mergers, and joint ventures. A study of forty-two large U.S. business firms that had engaged in diversification over a five-year period revealed that 45% diversified through internal means, 19% diversified through external means, and 36% diversified through both internal and external methods. It is interesting that the economic performances of the companies in the three categories were very similar. There appears to be no significant sales or profits advantage to either external or internal growth.[18]

Some of the more common examples of external growth strategies are mergers, acquisitions, and joint ventures.

Mergers A *merger* is a transaction involving two or more corporations in which stock is exchanged, but from which only one corporation survives. Mergers are usually between firms of somewhat similar size and are usually "friendly." The resulting firm is likely to have a name derived from its composite firms. One example is the merging of Allied Corporation and Signal Companies to form Allied Signal.

Acquisitions An *acquisition* is the purchase of a corporation that is completely absorbed as an operating subsidiary or division of the acquiring corporation. Examples are the acquisition by Procter and Gamble of Richardson-Vicks and the purchase of the Chicago Cubs baseball team by the Tribune Company (parent company of the *Chicago Tribune* newspaper and WGN television superstation). Acquisitions are usually between firms of different sizes and can be either "friendly" or "hostile." A friendly acquisition usually begins with the acquiring corporation discussing its desires with the other firm's top management. The top management of the firm to be acquired agrees to work for the acquisition, in return for fair consideration after acquisition. Friendly acquisitions are thus very similar to mergers. Hostile acquisitions, in contrast, are often called "takeovers." The acquiring firm ignores the other firm's top management or board of directors and simply begins buying up the other firm's stock until it owns a controlling interest. The takeover target, in response, begins defensive maneuvers, such as buying up its own stock, calling in the Justice Department to initiate an anti-trust suit in order to stop the acquisition, or looking for a friendly merger partner (as Gulf Oil did with Standard Oil of California when Texas oilman T. Boone Pickens mounted a takeover effort to buy Gulf's stock).

Slang terms are very popular in mergers and acquisitions. For example, a "pigeon" (highly vulnerable target) or "sleeping beauty" (more desirable than a pigeon) might take a "cyanide pill" (taking on a huge long-term debt on the condition that the debt falls due immediately upon the firm's acquisition) so that it can avoid being "raped" (forcible hostile takeover sometimes accompanied by looting of the target's profitability) by a "shark" (extremely predatory takeover artist) using "hired guns" (lawyers, merger and acquisition specialists, and certain investment bankers).[19] To avoid takeover threats, a number of corporations have chosen to stagger the elections of board members (as discussed in Chapter 3), to prohibit two-tier tender offers (the offering of a higher price to stockholders who sell their shares first), to prohibit "green-mail" (the buying back of a company's stock from a "shark" at a premium price), and to require an 80% shareholder vote for approval of a takeover. The ultimate countermeasure appears to be the *poison pill,* a procedure granting present shareholders the right to acquire at a substantial discount a large equity stake in an acquiring company whose offer does not have the support of the acquired company's board of directors.

Joint Ventures A *joint venture* is the strategy of forming a temporary partnership or consortium for the purpose of gaining synergy. Joint ventures occur because the corporations involved do not wish to or cannot legally merge permanently. Joint ventures provide a way to temporarily fit the different strengths of partners together so that an outcome of value to both is achieved.[20] For example, IBM and Sears have formed a joint venture called Trintex to develop and market *videotex*—the sending and receiving of words and pictures to at-home video screens; through this service people can order merchandise, do banking, and carry out other functions. A major innovation in this joint-venture plan is the sending of data to personal computers instead of to special-purpose video-screen terminals. Named "Prodigy," this service costs subscribers $9.95 a month. Sears can use the venture to market its merchandise catalogue and financial services products electronically. Joint ventures are extremely popular in international undertakings because of financial and political-legal constraints. They are also a convenient way for a privately owned and a publicly owned (state-owned) corporation to work together. Joint ventures are discussed further in Chapter 10.[21]

Retrenchment Strategies

Retrenchment strategies are relatively unpopular because retrenchment seems to imply failure—that something has gone wrong with previous strategies.

With these strategies there *is* a great deal of pressure to improve performance. As are the coaches of losing football teams, the CEO is typically under pressure to do something quickly or be fired.

TURNAROUND STRATEGY The turnaround strategy emphasizes the improvement of operational efficiency. It is appropriate when a corporation is in a highly attractive industry and when the corporation's problems are pervasive, but not yet critical. Analogous to going on a diet, a turnaround strategy includes two initial phases. The first phase is **contraction,** the initial effort to reduce size and costs. It typically involves a general cutback in personnel and all noncritical expenditures. Hiring stops, and across-the-board reductions in R&D, advertising, training, supplies, and services are usual. The second phase is **consolidation,** the development of a program to stabilize the now-leaner corporation. An in-depth audit is conducted in order to identify areas in which long-run improvements can be made in corporate efficiency. To streamline the corporation, plans are developed to reduce unnecessary overhead and to make functional activities "cost-effective." Financial expenditures in all areas must be justified on the basis of their contribution to profits. This is a crucial time for the corporation. If the consolidation phase is not conducted in a positive manner, many of the best people will leave the organization. If, however, all employees are encouraged to get involved in productivity improvements, the corporation is likely to emerge from this strategic retrenchment period a much stronger and better organized company.

If the corporation successfully emerges from these two phases of contraction and consolidation, it is then able to enter a third phase, **rebuilding.** At this point, an attempt is made to once again expand the business.[22] For an example of an effective use of the turnaround strategy, see Illustrative Example 7.2.

DIVESTMENT STRATEGY Divestment is appropriate when corporate problems can be traced to the poor performance of an SBU or product line, or when a division or SBU is a "misfit," unable to synchronize itself with the rest of the corporation. Divestment is especially appropriate when a weak SBU is in an industry of low attractiveness (see Figure 7.1). Because over 50% of acquisitions fail to achieve their objectives, it is not surprising that divestment is a popular strategy of corporations that had earlier chosen to grow through external means.[23]

Still another situation appropriate for divestment is that of a division's needing more resources to be competitive than a corporation is willing to provide. Some corporations elect divestment instead of the more painful turnaround strategy. With divestment, top management is able to do one of two things: (1) select a scapegoat to be blamed for all of the corporation's problems, or (2) generate a lot of cash in the sale, which can be used to reduce debt and buy time. The second reason might explain why Pan American chose to sell the most profitable parts of its corporation, the Pan

ILLUSTRATIVE EXAMPLE 7.2

Turnaround Strategy at Toro Company

Top management at Toro Company was astonished when a 1974 marketing survey showed that the brand name of the little lawn-mower manufacturer ranked second only to Hershey chocolate in consumer recognition. Rushing to transform Toro, they broadened both its product lines and distribution system. By 1979 the company had 33,000 new chain-store outlets to sell a stream of new products, such as lightweight snow-throwers and chain saws. Sales of $358 million with earnings of $17.4 million both tripled 1974 levels. "The idea is to make the Toro name an umbrella under which we can market just about anything," said Chairman David T. McLaughlin.

Seeds for disaster had been planted. The pressure to increase sales led to a slide in product quality. New products were rushed to market in the late 1970s and early 1980s before the usual time-consuming development and testing phases were completed. The distribution of mowers and snow-throwers through mass merchandisers like K-Mart and J. C. Penney infuriated Toro's traditional dealer network. Not only were the dealers forced to compete with their own products being sold at lower prices by discounters; they were being stuck with servicing the products the discounters sold! Some dealers refused to service machines they did not sell and actually told prospective customers not to buy a Toro.

The crisis arrived when the two snowless winters of 1979–80 and 1980–81 plunged the company into ten straight quarters of losses. In early 1981, as sales fell from $400 million to $247 million annually, McLaughlin resigned as chairman. Before leaving, he fired 125 managers including Toro's president, John Cantu. The dismissals were probably long overdue. One manager admitted that the firm's staff was that of a billion-dollar company—far too large for a small company like Toro.

Executive Vice-President Kendrick Melrose was named president. The fight for survival began. Dividends were suspended. Melrose acted to cut the work force in half, to 1,800 people; cut sales and administrative costs by 23%; consolidated production to five plants from eight; and suspended production of snow-throwers until sales caught up with inventories, two years later. More importantly, Melrose worked to salvage the dealer network, by stopping sales to discounters of equipment that required servicing. He also improved Toro's inventory-support program, giving independent dealers and distributors more protection from losses when their inventories exceeded a "normal year's" level.

"The toughest decision was to terminate half the employment force," admitted President Melrose. "The second toughest was to go to the half that remained and tell them that not only do we have fewer resources, but we still need greater productivity, and that they're going to have to make some financial sacrifices." That meant no incentive compensation for executives for at least four years, salary freezes and mandatory furlough days for office employees, and wage freezes or reductions for hourly workers. Stringent controls were set in place to keep management aware of inventory levels. "Now we can go through a year with little snow and still be fairly solid," says Mr. Melrose. Embarrassed by Toro's poor-quality image, the new president re-dedicated the company to quality and appointed a vice-president for product excellence.

By 1985, the Minneapolis firm was a much slimmer, more carefully managed, and apparently healthier company. Fiscal 1984 earnings were $8.3 million on sales of $280 million, compared with a modest profit in 1983. Sales have not returned to pre-disaster levels and probably will not for some time. Nevertheless, the dividend has been restored and top management is cautiously optimistic. To keep costs down, some manufacturing is done outside the U.S. Parts are being produced in South Korea, Taiwan, Japan, and Singapore. An assembly plant has opened near Winnepeg, Manitoba. Fabrication joint ventures are under way in New Zealand and Venezuela.

As a result of its successes, Toro management has switched from what it called "a defensive, survival mode" to "a more opportunistic direction." Mr. Melrose put two executive vice-presidents in charge of

(Continued)

ILLUSTRATIVE EXAMPLE 7.2 (Continued)

day-to-day operations so that he could focus on new ventures. According to Melrose, the company is "emphasizing businesses that deliver high margins and don't have a lot of vulnerability on the downside," such as turf irrigation and commercial lawn care equipment. "Long-range planning is something new at Toro," he says. "In the past we didn't spend much time thinking about the future. We thought only about how we're going to get out of the mess."

SOURCE: R. Gibson, "Toro Breaks Out of Its Slump after Taking Drastic Measures," *Wall Street Journal* (January 23, 1985), p. 7. "Toro: Coming to Life after Warm Weather Wilted Its Big Plans," *Business Week* (October 10, 1983), p. 118.

Am Building in New York and Intercontinental Hotels, while keeping its money-losing airline.[24]

CAPTIVE COMPANY STRATEGY   Rarely discussed as a separate strategy, the captive strategy is similar to divestment; but instead of selling off divisions or product lines, the corporation reduces the scope of some of its functional activities and becomes "captive" to another firm. In this manner, it reduces expenses and achieves some security through its relationship with the stronger firm. An agreement is reached with a key customer that in return for a large number of long-run purchases, the captive company will guarantee delivery at a favorable price. At least 75% of its product is sold to a single purchaser, so the captive company can reduce its marketing expenditures and develop long-run production schedules that reduce costs. If supplies ever become a problem for the captive company, it can call on its key customer to help put pressure on a reluctant supplier.

This is a popular strategy in the moderately attractive U.S. auto parts and electronic parts industries for small firms with weak competitive positions. Until the mid-1980s, GM, Ford, and Chrysler each bought from thousands of companies; they preferred to maintain competition between suppliers and backups in case a key parts maker failed. In their quest for higher quality, however, the auto companies have chosen instead to rely on only those companies that could guarantee high quality, low costs, and just-in-time delivery. In order to survive, auto parts firms had to become captive companies. For example, in order to become the sole supplier of a part to GM, Simpson Industries, an engine parts manufacturer in Birmingham, Michigan, agreed to having its facilities and books inspected and its employees interviewed by a special team from General Motors. In return, nearly 80% of Simpson Industries' production was sold to GM through long-term contracts.[25]

LIQUIDATION STRATEGY   A strategy of last resort, used when other retrenchment strategies have failed, an early liquidation can serve stockholders' interests better than an inevitable bankruptcy. To the extent that top management identifies with the corporation, liquidation is perceived as an admission of failure. Pride and reputation are liquidated as well as jobs and financial assets. Nevertheless, this can be the most appropriate strategy for a corporation with a weak competitive position in an unattractive industry.

From their research of companies in difficulty, Nystrom and Starbuck conclude that top management very often does not perceive that crises are developing. When top managers do eventually notice trouble, they are prone to attribute the problems to temporary environmental disturbances and tend to follow profit strategies of postponing investments, reducing maintenance, halting training, liquidating assets, denying credit to customers, and raising prices. They adopt a weathering-the-storm attitude. "A major activity becomes changing the accounting procedures in order to conceal the symptoms."[27] Even when things are going terribly wrong, there is a strong temptation for top management to avoid liquidation in the hope of a miracle. It is for this reason that a corporation needs a strong board of directors who, to safeguard stockholders' interests, can tell top management when to quit.

Evaluation of Corporate Strategies

Before they select a particular corporate strategy, top management must critically analyze the pros and cons of each feasible alternative in light of the corporation's situation. The tendency to select the most obvious strategy can sometimes lead to serious trouble in the long run. The orientation of most top management toward growth strategies has resulted in a strong preference for acquisitions and mergers. In fact, a survey of 236 chief executive officers of the largest 1,000 U.S. industrial firms found that CEOs prefer diversification and acquisition over new product planning and development as a growth strategy.[28] A similar survey of chief financial officers found that the major motive for acquisition of another firm was to generate fast growth.[29] Given these attitudes of strategic managers, it is not surprising that more mergers were announced in the first six months of 1988 than in *all* of 1985. The dollar value of the acquisitions for only half a year exceeded that for *all* of 1984.[30] Growth through external means shows no signs of slacking in the 1990s.

Business (SBU) Strategies

Sometimes referred to as division strategy, business strategy focuses on improving the competitive position of a corporation's products or services within the specific industry or market segment that the division serves. It is a strategy that a division develops to complement the overall corporate strategy.

Porter's Competitive Strategies

Porter, an authority on business level strategies, proposes three generic strategies for outperforming other corporations in a particular industry: overall cost leadership, differentiation, and focus.[31]

1. **Overall cost leadership.** This strategy requires "aggressive construction of efficient-scale facilities, vigorous pursuit of cost reductions from experience, tight cost and overhead control, avoidance of marginal customer accounts, and cost minimization in areas like R&D, service, sales force, advertising, and so on."[32] Having a low-cost position gives an SBU a defense against rivals. Its lower costs allow it to continue to earn profits during times of heavy competition.

   Backward vertical integration (a corporate-level strategy that can also be used at the divisional level) is one route to an overall low-cost position. For example, Humana, Inc., the hospital operator, has moved into the health-insurance field as the low-cost competitor. It is able to underprice Blue Cross, Blue Shield because it controls the source of 60% of all medical bills, the hospital. "The one feature of our product that is clearly understood by employers is that because we own and operate hospitals, we can control costs," states William Werroven, Chief Operating Officer of Humana's group health division.[33]

2. **Differentiation.** This strategy involves the creation of a product or service that is perceived throughout its industry as being unique. This uniqueness can be accomplished through design or brand image, technology, features, dealer network, or customer service. Differentiation is a viable strategy for the earning of above-average returns in a specific business, because the resulting brand loyalty lowers customers' sensitivity to price.

   Examples of the successful use of a differentiation strategy are Walt Disney Productions, Maytag appliances, Mercedes-Benz automobiles, and WordPerfect Corporation. Started in 1980 in Orem, Utah, WordPerfect Corporation chose to compete against Wordstar for the MS-DOS, IBM-compatible word-processing market. To differentiate its WordPerfect software from the competition, it became the only company to offer customers a toll-free help line. At first, the company spent very little on advertising, and sales grew largely through word of mouth. By 1987, WordPerfect had gathered a 30% market share of word-processing programs, a share greater than any of its competitors had.[34]

3. **Focus.** Similar to the corporate strategy of concentration, this business strategy focuses on a particular buyer group, product line segment, or geographic market. This strategy is valued because of a belief that an SBU that focuses its efforts is better able to serve its narrow strategic target more effectively or efficiently than can its competition. Focus does, however, necessitate that a trade-off between profitability and overall market share be made.

   The focus strategy has two variants: *cost focus* and *differentiation focus*. In using cost focus, the company seeks a cost advantage in its target segment; in using differentiation focus, a company seeks differentiation in its target segment. "The target segments must either have buyers with unusual needs or else the production and delivery system that best serves the target must differ from that of the other industry segments."[35] A good example of cost focus is Hammermill Paper's move into low-volume, high-quality specialty papers. By focusing on the quality niche of the market, Hammermill is able to compete against larger companies that need high-volume production runs to reach break-even. Johnson Products, in contrast, has successfully used a differentiation focus by manufacturing and selling hair care and cosmetic products to black consumers. This strategy was most successful when the large cosmetics companies ignored the product preferences of the black community.

Porter argues that, to be successful, a business unit must achieve one of these three "generic" business strategies. Otherwise, the business unit is **stuck in the middle** of the competitive marketplace with no competitive advantage and is doomed to below-average performance.[36] Although research generally supports Porter's contention, there is some evidence that businesses with *both* a low cost and a high differentiation position can be very successful.[37] Before selecting one of these strategies for a particular corporate business or SBU, management should assess its feasibility in terms of divisional strengths and weaknesses. Porter lists some of the commonly required skills and resources, as well as organizational requirements, in Table 7.3.

Functional Strategies

The principal focus of functional strategy is to maximize corporate and divisional resource productivity. Within the constraints of corporate and divisional strategies, functional strategies are developed to pull together the various activities and competencies of each function so that performance improves. For example, a manufacturing department would be very concerned with developing a strategy to reduce costs and to improve the quality of its output. Marketing, in comparison, typically would be concerned with developing strategies to increase sales.

Some typical marketing functional strategies are

- capturing a larger share of an existing market through market saturation and market penetration,
- developing new products for existing markets,
- developing new markets for existing products, and
- developing new products for new markets.[38]

The first and third strategies support a corporate concentration strategy, whereas the second and fourth support a diversification corporate strategy.

TABLE 7.3
Requirements for Generic Competitive Strategies

GENERIC STRATEGY	COMMONLY REQUIRED SKILLS AND RESOURCES	COMMON ORGANIZATIONAL REQUIREMENTS
Overall cost leadership	Sustained capital investment and access to capital Process engineering skills Intense supervision of labor Products designed for ease in manufacture Low-cost distribution system	Tight cost control Frequent, detailed control reports Structured organization and responsibilities Incentives based on meeting strict quantitative targets
Differentiation	Strong marketing abilities Product engineering Creative flair Strong capability in basic research Corporate reputation for quality or technological leadership Long tradition in the industry or unique combination of skills drawn from other businesses Strong cooperation from channels	Strong coordination among functions in R&D, product development, and marketing Subjective measurement and incentives instead of quantitative measures Amenities to attract highly skilled labor, scientists, or creative people
Focus	Combination of the above policies directed at the particular strategic target	Combination of the above policies directed at the particular strategic target

SOURCE: Adapted/reprinted with permission of The Free Press, a Division of Macmillan, Inc. from *Competitive Strategy: Techniques for Analyzing Industries and Competitors* by Michael E. Porter, pp. 40–41. Copyright © 1980 by The Free Press.

Some of the many possible functional strategies are listed in the decision tree depicted in Fig. 7.2. These are some of the many functional strategy decisions that need to be made if corporate and divisional strategies are to be implemented properly by functional managers. For example, once top management decides to acquire another publicly held corporation, it must decide how it will obtain the funds necessary for the purchase. A very popular financial strategy is the **leveraged buyout.** In a leveraged buyout, a company is acquired in a transaction financed largely by debt. Ultimately, the debt is paid with money generated by the acquired company's operations or by sales of its assets. This is what happened when Westray Transportation, Inc., an affiliate of Westray Corporation, purchased Atlas Van Lines. Under the leveraged buyout plan, Atlas stockholders received $18.35 for each share of stock outstanding and the company was taken private by Westray. The money was funded by Merrill Lynch Interfunding, Inc. and Acquisition Funding Corporation. Westray then paid the debt from the operations of its new subsidiary, Atlas Van Lines.[39]

FIGURE 7.2
Functional Strategy Decision Tree

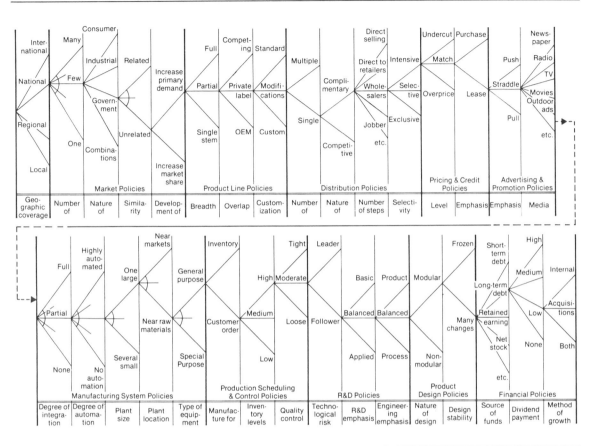

Source: C. W. Hofer, "The Uses and Limitations of Statistical Division Theory" (Boston: Intercollegiate Case Clearing House), no. 9-171-653, 1971, p. 34. Copyright © 1971 by C. W. Hofer. Reprinted by permission.

A functional area that has received a great deal of attention recently in terms of strategy is technology (R&D). Those corporations that are dependent on technology for their success are becoming increasingly concerned with the development of R&D strategies that complement business level strategies.[40] As shown in Fig. 7.2, one of the R&D choices is to either be a **leader** or a **follower.** Porter suggests that making the decision to become a technological leader or follower can be a way of achieving either overall low cost or differentiation.[41] This choice is described in more detail in Table 7.4. An effective use of the follower R&D functional strategy to achieve a low-cost competitive advantage is presented in Illustrative Example 7.3.

TABLE 7.4
Technological Leadership and Competitive Advantage

	TECHNOLOGICAL LEADERSHIP	TECHNOLOGICAL FOLLOWERSHIP
Cost Advantage	Pioneer the lowest-cost product design Be the first firm down the learning curve Create low-cost ways of performing value activities	Lower the cost of the product or value activities by learning from the leader's experience Avoid R&D costs through imitation
Differentiation	Pioneer a unique product that increases buyer value Innovate in other activities to increase buyer value	Adapt the product or delivery system more closely to buyer needs by learning from the leader's experience

SOURCE: Reprinted with permission of The Free Press, a Division of Macmillan, Inc. from *Competitive Advantage: Creating and Sustaining Superior Performance* by Michael E. Porter, p. 181. Copyright © 1985 by Michael E. Porter.

Other functional strategies, such as the location and scale of manufacturing facilities, distribution channels, and the choice of push (promotion) versus pull (advertising) marketing emphasis can only be mentioned briefly in this book. For a detailed discussion of functional strategies, refer to advanced texts in each of the functional areas.

Strategies to be Avoided

There are a number of strategies, used at various levels, that are very dangerous. They might be considered by managers who have made a poor analysis or lack creativity.

Follow the leader. Imitating the strategy of a leading competitor might seem a good idea, but it ignores a firm's particular strengths and weaknesses. The decision by Standard Oil of Ohio to follow Exxon and Mobil Oil into conglomerate diversification resulted in disaster for the company's top management.

Hit another home run. If a corporation is successful because it pioneered an extremely successful product, it has a tendency to search for another superproduct that will ensure growth and prosperity. Like betting on "long shots" at the horse races, the probability of finding a second winner is slight. Polaroid spent a lot of money developing an "instant" movie camera, but the public ignored it.

Arms race. Entering into a spirited battle with another firm for an increase in market share might increase sales revenue, but that increase will probably be more than offset by increases in advertising, promotion, R&D, and manufacturing costs. Since the deregulation of airlines, price wars and rate "specials" have contributed to the low profit margins or bankruptcy of many major airlines.

Do everything. When faced with a number of interesting opportunities, management might tend to take all of them. At first, a corporation

ILLUSTRATIVE EXAMPLE 7.3

Dean Foods Uses a Follower R&D Functional Strategy to Achieve Low-Cost Competitive Advantage

As big food companies battle to build powerful national brand names, Dean Foods Company keeps a low profile by emphasizing a line of copycat private label brands it sells to supermarket chains who want good products at low prices. These increasingly powerful and sophisticated supermarket chains wish to offer their own private label products and to take more control over shelf space and marketing. Dean Foods, located outside Chicago in Franklin Park, Illinois, satisfies the supermarket demands by quickly imitating brand name products and offering them at low cost. "We're able to have the customer come to us and say, 'If you can produce X, Y, and Z product for the same quality and service, but at a lower price and without that expensive label on it, you can have the business,' "

says Howard Dean, President of the company. As a result, Dean's product offerings are typically developed on a shoestring budget with advertising costs far below the industry's average. The emphasis is on rigid cost control and exceptional customer service. Profit in 1986 was $41.1 million on sales of $1.43 billion. The company ranked second to some of the nation's most familiar brand names in the sales of certain foods: Borden's dairy products, Campbell Soups, Vlassic pickles, Carnation's Coffee-mate nondairy creamer, and Kraft's Cracker Barrel aged cheddar cheese.

SOURCE: T. Due, "Dean Foods Thrives On Regional, Off-Brand Products," *Wall Street Journal* (September 17, 1987), p. 6.

might have enough resources to develop each opportunity into a project, but the well soon runs dry as the many projects demand large infusions of time, money, and energy. Convinced that its brand name would serve as an effective umbrella for a whole series of new products, Toro Company quickly ran out of money and time (see Illustrative Example 7.2).

Losing hand. A corporation might have invested so much in a particular strategy that top management is unwilling to accept the fact that the strategy is not successful. Believing that it has "too much invested to quit," the corporation continues to throw good money after bad. Pan American chose to sell its Pan Am Building and Intercontinental Hotels, the most profitable parts of the corporation, to keep its money-losing airline flying. With operating losses of more than $1.4 billion between 1980 and 1987; plus a negative net worth of $68.3 million, $914 million in long-term debt, and $550 million in unfunded pension liability; and one of the industry's oldest jet fleets, Pan American agreed to pay $1.1 billion to Airbus Industries for twenty-eight new jet planes![42]

7.2

SELECTION OF THE BEST STRATEGY

Once potential strategic alternatives have been identified and evaluated in terms of their pros and cons, one must be selected for implementation. By this point, it is likely that a number of alternatives will have emerged as feasible. How is the decision made that determines the "best" strategy?

Choosing among a set of acceptable alternative strategies is often not easy. Each alternative is likely to have its proponents as well as critics. Steiner and Miner suggest using the twenty questions listed below before one strategy is selected over another. Perhaps the most important criterion is the ability of the proposed strategy to deal with the specific *strategic factors* developed earlier in the S.W.O.T. analysis. If the alternative doesn't take advantage of environmental opportunities and corporate strengths, and lead away from environmental threats and corporate weaknesses, it will probably fail. Another important consideration in the selection of a strategy is the ability of each alternative to satisfy agreed-upon objectives with the least use of resources and with the fewest number of negative side effects. It is therefore important to develop a tentative implementation plan so that the difficulties management is likely to face are addressed. Is the alternative worth the probable short-term as well as long-term costs?

A number of techniques to aid strategic planners in estimating the likely effects of strategic changes are available. One of these was derived from the research project on the profit impact of market strategies (PIMS), which was discussed in Chapter 6. From the analysis of data from a large number of business corporations, key factors were identified in regression equations to explain large variations in ROI, profitability, and cash flow. As part of PIMS, reports for a participating corporation's business units show how its expected level of ROI is influenced by each factor. A second report shows how ROI can be expected to change, both in the short and long runs, if particular changes are made in its strategy.[43]

One of the best ways to assess the likely economic impact of each alternative on the future of the corporation is through the construction of

---

TWENTY QUESTIONS FOR USE IN EVALUATION OF STRATEGIES

1. Does the strategy conform with the basic mission and purpose of the corporation? If not, a new competitive arena with which management is not familiar might be entered.

2. Is the strategy consistent with the corporation's external environment?

3. Is the strategy consistent with the internal strengths, objectives, policies, resources, and personal values of managers and employees? A strategy might not be completely in tune with all of these, but major dissonance should be avoided.

4. Does the strategy reflect the acceptance of minimum potential risk, balancing it against the maximum potential profit consistent with the corporation's resources and prospects?

5. Does the strategy fit a niche in the corporation's market not now filled by others? Is this niche likely to remain open long enough for the corporation to return capital investment plus the required level of profit? (Niches have a habit of filling up fast.)

6. Does the strategy conflict with other corporate strategies?

7. Is the strategy divided into substrategies that interrelate properly?

8. Has the strategy been tested with appropriate criteria (such as consistency with past, present, and prospective trends) and by the appropriate analytical tools (such as risk analysis, discounted cash flows, and so on)?

9. Has the strategy been tested by developing feasible implementation plans?

10. Does the strategy really fit the life cycles of the corporation's products?

detailed scenarios. Once these scenarios are adjusted for management's attitude toward risk, pressures from the external and internal environments, and the personal needs and desires of key managers, they are invaluable aids to management's selecting the alternative with the best chance of achieving corporate objectives.

Scenario Construction

Using pro forma balance sheets and income statements, management can construct detailed *scenarios* to forecast the likely effect of each alternative strategy and its various programs on division and corporate return on investment. These scenarios are simply extensions of the industry scenarios discussed in Chapter 4. If, for example, industry scenarios suggest the probable emergence of a strong market demand for certain products, a series of alternative strategy scenarios can be developed. The alternative of acquiring another company having these products can be compared with the alternative of developing the products internally. Using three sets of estimated sales figures (optimistic, pessimistic, and most likely) for the new products over the next five years, the two alternatives can be evaluated in terms of their effect on future company performance as reflected in its probable future financial statements. Pro forma balance sheets and income statements can be generated with spreadsheet software, such as Lotus 1-2-3, on a personal computer.

To construct a scenario, **first** use the industry scenarios discussed earlier in Chapter 4 and develop a set of assumptions about the task environment.

---

11. Is the timing of the strategy correct?

12. Does the strategy pit the product against a powerful competitor? If so, reevaluate carefully.

13. Does the strategy leave the corporation vulnerable to the power of one major customer? If so, reconsider carefully.

14. Does the strategy involve the production of a new product for a new market? If so, reconsider carefully.

15. Is the corporation rushing a revolutionary product to market? If so, reconsider carefully.

16. Does the strategy imitate that of a competitor? If so, reconsider carefully.

17. Is it likely that the corporation can get to the market first with the new product or service? (If so, this is a great advantage. The second firm to market has much less chance of high returns on investment than the first.)

18. Has a really honest and accurate appraisal been made of the competition? Is the competition under- or overestimated?

19. Is the corporation trying to sell abroad something it cannot sell in the United States? (This is not usually a successful strategy.)

20. Is the market share likely to be sufficient to assure a required return on investment? (Market share and return on investment generally are closely related but differ from product to product and market to market.) Has this relationship of market and product been calculated?

SOURCE: Adapted with permission of Macmillan Publishing Company from *Management Policy and Strategy* by George A. Steiner and John B. Miner, pp. 219–221. Copyright © 1977 by Macmillan Publishing Company.

Optimistic, pessimistic, and most likely assumptions should be listed for key economic factors such as the GNP, CPI, and prime interest rate, as well as for other key external strategic factors, such as governmental regulation and industry trends. These same underlying assumptions should be listed for each of the alternative scenarios to be developed.

Second, for each strategic alternative, develop a set of optimistic, pessimistic, and most likely assumptions about the impact of key variables on the company's future financial statements. Forecast three sets of sales and cost-of-goods-sold figures for at least five years into the future. Look at historical data from past financial statements and make adjustments based on the environmental assumptions listed in step one. Do the same for other figures that can vary significantly. For the rest, assume that they will continue in their historical relationship to sales or some other key determining factor. Plug in expected inventory levels, accounts receivable, accounts payable, R&D expenses, advertising and promotion expenses, capital expenditures, and debt payments (assuming that debt is used to finance the strategy), among others. Consider not only historical trends, but also programs that might be needed for the implementation of each alternative strategy (such as building a new manufacturing facility or expanding the sales force).

Third, construct detailed pro forma financial statements for *each* of the strategic alternatives. Using a spreadsheet program on a personal computer, list the *actual* figures from this year's financial statements in the left column. To the right of this column, list the *optimistic* figures for year one, year two, year three, year four, and year five. Go through this same process with the same strategic alternative, but now list the *pessimistic* figures for the next five years. Do the same with the *most likely* figures. Once this is done, develop a similar set of optimistic (O), pessimistic (P), and most likely (ML) pro forma statements for the second strategic alternative. This process will generate six different pro forma scenarios reflecting three different situations (O, P, & ML) for two strategic alternatives. Next, calculate financial ratios and common-size income statements, and balance sheets to accompany the pro formas. To determine the feasibility of the scenarios, compare assumptions underlying the scenarios with these financial statements and ratios. For example, if cost of goods sold drops from 70% to 50% of total sales revenue in the pro forma income statements, this drop should result from a change in the production process or a shift to cheaper raw materials or labor costs, rather than from a failure to keep the cost of goods sold in its usual percentage relationship to sales revenue when the predicted statement was developed.

The result of this detailed scenario construction should be anticipated net profits, cash flow, and net working capital for each of three versions of the two alternatives for five years into the future. Once this is done, the strategist might wish to go further into the future if the strategy is expected to have a major impact on the company's financial statements beyond five years. The result of this work should provide sufficient information upon which forecasts of the likely feasibility and probable profitability of each of the strategic alternatives could be based.

Obviously, these scenarios can quickly become very complicated, especially if three sets of acquisition prices as well as development costs are calculated. Nevertheless, this sort of detailed "what if" analysis is needed for realistic comparisons of the projected outcome of each reasonable alternative strategy and its attendant programs, budgets, and procedures.

Regardless of the quantifiable pros and cons of each alternative, the actual decision will probably be influenced by a number of subjective factors that are difficult to quantify. Some of these factors are management's attitude toward risk, pressures from the external environment, influences from the corporate culture, and the personal needs and desires of key managers.

Management's Attitude Toward Risk

The attractiveness of a particular strategic alternative is partially a function of the amount of risk it entails. The risk is composed not only of the *probability* that the strategy will be effective, but also of the amount of *assets* the corporation must allocate to that strategy, and the length of *time* the assets will be unavailable for other uses. To quantify this risk, a number of people suggest the use of the *Capital Asset Pricing Model* (CAPM). CAPM is a financial method for linking the risk involved in a particular alternative with expected returns on a company's equity.[44] Another technique is the *Arbitrage Pricing Model* (APM), which screens acquisition candidates.[45] Everett proposes a simpler approach for the assessment of the probability of success or failure for a particular strategic alternative; his approach uses a Lotus 1-2-3 spreadsheet.[46]

The greater the amount of assets involved and the longer they are tied up, the more likely top management is to demand a high probability of success. This might be one reason why innovations seem to occur more often in small firms than in large, established corporations.[47] The small firm managed by an entrepreneur is willing to accept greater risk than would a large firm of diversified ownership. It is one thing to take a chance if you are the primary stockholder. It is something else if throngs of widows and orphans depend on your corporation's monthly dividend checks for living expenses.

Pressures from the External Environment

The attractiveness of a strategic alternative will be affected by its perceived compatibility with the key stakeholders in a corporation's task environment. These stakeholders are typically concerned with certain aspects of a corporation's activities. Creditors want to be paid on time. Unions exert pressure for comparable wages and employment security. Governments and interest groups demand social responsibility. Stockholders want dividends. All of these pressures must be considered in the selection of the best alternative. Hicks B. Waldron, Chairman of Avon Products, argues that corporations have duties beyond the maximizing of value for shareholders:

> We have a number of suppliers, institutions, customers, communities. None of them have the democratic freedom as shareholders do to buy or sell their shares. They have much deeper and much more important stakes in our company than our shareholders.[48]

Questions management should raise in their attempting to assess the importance to the corporation of stakeholder concerns are the following:

1. Which stakeholders are most crucial for corporate success?
2. How much of what they want are they likely to get, under this alternative?
3. What are they *likely* to do if they don't get what they want?
4. What is the probability that they will do it?

By ranking the key stakeholders in a corporation's task environment and asking these questions, strategy makers should be better able to choose strategic alternatives that minimize external pressures and maximize the probability of gaining stakeholder support.[49] In addition, top management can propose a political strategy to influence its key stakeholders. Some of the most commonly used political strategies are constituency building, political action committee contributions, advocacy advertising, lobbying, and coalition building.[50]

Pressures from the Corporate Culture

As pointed out in Chapter 5, the norms and values shared by the members of a corporation do affect the attractiveness of certain alternatives. If a strategy is incompatible with the corporate culture, the likelihood of its success will be very low. Footdragging and even sabotage will result, as employees fight to resist a radical change in corporate philosophy.

Precedents from the past tend to restrict the kinds of objectives and strategies that can be seriously considered. The "aura" of the founders of a corporation can linger long past their lifetime because their values have been imprinted on the corporation's members. According to Cyert and March,

> Organizations have memories in the form of precedents, and individuals in the coalition are strongly motivated to accept the precedents as binding. Whether precedents are formalized in the shape of an official standard operating procedure or are less formally stored, they remove from conscious consideration many agreements, decisions, and commitments that might well be subject to renegotiation in an organization without a memory.[51]

In considering a strategic alternative, the strategy makers must assess its compatibility with the corporate culture. If there is little fit, management must decide if it should (1) take a chance on ignoring the culture, (2) manage

ILLUSTRATIVE EXAMPLE 7.4

Changing the Culture at Procter & Gamble

In choosing to emphasize overall low cost as the key competitive strategy for each of its product lines, Procter & Gamble under President Smale is attempting a turnaround strategy of large proportions. By firing people to boost overall management performance, Smale risks undermining the employee loyalty that has been one of the company's greatest strengths. Apparently some board members are unsettled by what they see as a conflict between P&G's time-honored dedication to quality, high-performance products and its new emphasis on controlling costs. Similarly, the drive to move quickly and to take more risks with new products goes counter to the firm's traditional cautious style. Nevertheless, P&G must do something. Because its detergent and consumer paper goods markets are maturing, the company has been unable to attain its cherished goal of doubling its unit volume every ten years. The reason given is that consumers are increasingly responsive to price. The question remains, nonetheless: Will Smale be successful in changing P&G's corporate culture to implement a change from its traditional quality differentiation strategy to one of overall low cost?

SOURCE: "Why Procter & Gamble Is Playing It Even Tougher," *Business Week* (July 18, 1984), pp. 176–186.

around the culture and change the implementation plan, (3) try to change the culture to fit the strategy, or (4) change the strategy to fit the culture.[52] If the culture will be strongly opposed to a strategy, it is foolhardy to ignore the culture. Further, a decision to proceed with a particular strategy without a commitment to changing the culture or managing around the culture (both very tricky and time consuming) is dangerous. Nevertheless, restricting a corporation to only those strategies that are completely compatible with its culture might eliminate from consideration the most profitable alternatives. For an example of an attempt to change a corporate culture in order to implement a change in strategy, see Illustrative Example 7.4.

Needs and Desires of Key Managers

Even the most attractive alternative might not be selected if it is contrary to the needs and desires of important top managers. A person's ego may be tied to a particular proposal to the extent that all other alternatives are strongly lobbied against. Key executives in operating divisions, for example, might be able to influence other people in top management in favor of a particular alternative so that objections to it are ignored.

Such a situation was described by John DeLorean when he was at Pontiac Division of General Motors in 1959. At that time, General Motors was developing a new rear-engined auto called Corvair. Ed Cole, the General Manager of Chevrolet Division, was very attracted to the idea of building the first modern, rear-engine American automobile. A number of engineers, however, were worried about the safety of the car and made vigorous attempts to either change the "unsafe" suspension system or keep the Corvair out of production. "One top corporate engineer told me that he showed his test results to Cole but by then he said, 'Cole's mind was made up.' "[53] By this time, there had developed quite a bit of documented evidence that the car should not be built as designed. However, according to DeLorean,

> . . . Cole was a strong product voice and a top salesman in company affairs. In addition, the car, as he proposed it, would cost less to build than the same car with a conventional rear suspension. Management not only went along with Cole, it also told the dissenters in effect to "stop these objections. Get on the team, or you can find someplace else to work." The ill-fated Corvair was launched in the fall of 1959.
>
> The results were disastrous. I don't think any one car before or since produced as gruesome a record on the highway as the Corvair. It was designed and promoted to appeal to the spirit and flair of young people. It was sold in part as a sports car. Young Corvair owners, therefore, were trying to bend their cars around curves at high speeds and were killing themselves in alarming numbers.[54]

In only a few years, General Motors was inundated by lawsuits over the Corvair. Ralph Nader soon published a book primarily about the Corvair called *Unsafe at Any Speed,* launching his career as a consumer advocate.

7.3
DEVELOPMENT OF POLICIES

The selection of the best strategic alternative is not the end of strategy formulation. Policies to define the ground rules for implementation must now be established. As defined earlier, policies are broad guidelines for the making of decisions. Flowing from the selected strategy, they provide guidance for decision making throughout the organization. Corporate policies are broad guidelines for divisions to follow in compliance with corporate strategy. These policies are interpreted and implemented through each division's own objectives and strategies. Divisions may then develop their own policies that will be guidelines for their functional areas to follow. At General Electric, for example, Chairman Welch insists that GE be Number One or Number Two wherever it competes. This policy gives clear guidance to managers throughout the organization.[55]

Another example of a corporate-level policy is that developed by Ford Motor Company. Concerned with the historic lack of cooperation between Ford U.S. and Ford of Europe, Ford's top management developed a company-wide policy requiring any new car design to be easily adaptable to any market in the world. Previous to this policy, Ford of Europe developed cars strictly for its own market, while engineers in the United States separately designed their own products. The new policy was a natural result of Ford's emphasis on manufacturing efficiency and global integration as a corporation. One result of this new policy was the program to produce the European Sierra and its U.S. counterpart the Merkur. The cost to convert the European Sierra to meet all U.S. safety and emission standards was about one-fourth of what the conversion of previous European models would have cost. The Taurus and Sable models were also engineered for easy conversion to overseas markets.[56]

Some policies will be expressions of a corporation's **critical success factors** (CSF). Critical success factors are those elements of a company that determine its strategic success or failure. They vary from company to company. IBM, for example, sees customer service as its critical success factor. McDonald's CSF is quality, cleanliness, and value. Hewlett-Packard is concerned with new product development.[57] As guidelines for decision making, policies can therefore be based on a corporation's critical success factors. At Lazarus Department Store in Columbus, Ohio, for example, customer service is a critical success factor. Store policies state that the customer is *always* right. Even if a department manager believes that a customer bought a particular shirt from a competitor, the manager is bound by policy to accept the shirt and to give back money to the customer. Lazarus's top management believes that even though a few people might take advantage of the store in the short run, the store will make up for it in the long run with good will and increased market share.

Chaparral Steel, a successful company following a low-cost business strategy with its mini-mills, followed five basic policies to ensure its successful growth through the 1980s:

- Design for maximum labor productivity.
- Design for efficient use of capital.
- Continue to upgrade existing processes.
- Maintain a work environment that nourishes people, innovation, and accomplishment.
- Give priority to the needs of customers and to the threat of foreign producers.[58]

Policies tend to be rather long lived and can even outlast the particular strategy that caused their creation. Interestingly, these general policies, such as "The customer is always right" or "Research and development should get first priority on all budget requests," can become, in time, part of a corporation's culture. Such policies can make the implementation of specific strategies easier. They can also restrict top management's strategic options in the future. It is for this reason that a change in strategy should be followed quickly by a change in policies. Managing policy is one way to manage the corporate culture.

SUMMARY AND CONCLUSION

This chapter has focused on the last stage of the strategy formulation process: generating, evaluating, and selecting the best strategic alternative. It also has discussed the development of policies for implementing strategies.

There are three main kinds of strategies: corporate, business (divisional), and functional. Corporate strategies fall into three main families: *stability, growth,* and *retrenchment.* Epitomized by a steady-as-she-goes philosophy, *stability* strategies are (1) no change, (2) profit, (3) pause, and (4) proceed with caution. The very popular *growth* strategies are (1) concentration, with its sub-strategies of horizontal and vertical growth, and (2) diversification—concentric and conglomerate. Any of these growth strategies can be achieved through internal development or through external acquisition. *Retrenchment* strategies are generally unpopular because they imply failure. They include (1) turnaround, (2) divestment, (3) captive company, and (4) liquidation.

Business or divisional strategies focus on improving the competitive position of a corporation's products or services within a particular industry or market segment. Porter suggests three generic competitive strategies: *overall cost leadership, differentiation,* and *focus.* Functional strategies act to maximize corporate and divi-

sional resource productivity, so that a distinctive competence within an industry will develop. Within any corporation, these three levels of strategy must fit together in a mutually supporting manner so that they form an integrated hierarchy of strategy.

The selection of the best strategic alternative from projected scenarios will probably be affected by a number of factors. Among them are management's attitude toward risk, pressures from the external environment, influences from the corporate culture, and the personal needs and desires of key managers.

As broad guidelines for divisions to follow, corporate policies assure the divisions' compliance with corporate strategy. Divisions may then generate their own internal policies to be followed by their functional areas. These policies define the ground rules for strategy implementation and serve to align corporate activities in the new strategic direction.

DISCUSSION QUESTIONS

1. Is the profit strategy really a stability strategy? Why or why not?

2. Why is growth the most frequently used corporate-level strategy?

3. How does horizontal growth (horizontal integration) differ from concentric diversification?

4. What are the tradeoffs between an internal and an external growth strategy?

5. How is Chapter 11 bankruptcy being used in the United States by major corporations? Is it a strategy?

6. Is it possible for a business unit to follow an overall cost-leadership strategy and a differentiation-through-high-quality-strategy simultaneously? Why or why not?

7. Suggest some methods by which a corporation's culture can be changed.

8. As described in the Integrative Case at the end of this chapter, should CSX in 1986 have continued to grow through external acquisitions or should it have changed its growth strategy to one of internal development?

9. If acquisitions continued to make sense for CSX, as described in the Integrative Case, in what industries should CSX's top management have been looking for attractive acquisition candidates in 1986—railroads, pipelines, trucking, barge lines, ocean freight, airlines, or in some other areas not related to transportation, such as financial services? Give the pros and cons for each industry in terms of their relationship to CSX's mission and growth strategy.

10. From the Integrative Case, what were the pros and cons to CSX of the Sea-Land acquisition?

NOTES

1. M. A. Hitt and R. Duane Ireland, "Corporate Distinctive Competence, Strategy, Industry and Performance," *Strategic Management Journal* (July-September 1985), p. 273.

2. R. E. Winter, "Cincinnati Milacron Starts Third Revamp," *Wall Street Journal* (April 28, 1988), p. 4.

3. W. F. Glueck, *Business Policy and Strategic Management*, 3rd ed. (New York: McGraw-Hill, 1980), p. 290. Glueck uses the term *stable growth* instead of *stability*.

4. R. M. Cyert and J. G. March, *A Behavioral Theory of the Firm* (Englewood Cliffs, N.J.: Prentice-Hall, 1963).

5. D. R. Dalton and I. F. Kesner, "Organizational Growth: Big Is Beautiful," *Journal of Business Strategy* (Summer 1985), pp. 38–48.

6. J. Vesey, "Vertical Integration: Its Effects on Business Performance," *Managerial Planning* (May-June 1978), pp. 11–15.

7. K. R. Harringan, "Exit Barriers and Vertical Integration," *Academy of Management Journal* (September, 1985), pp. 686–697.

8. K. R. Harrigan, *Strategies for Vertical Integration* (Lexington, Mass.: D. C. Heath-Lexington Books, 1983), pp. 16–21.

9. M. Leontiades, *Managing the Unmanageable* (Reading, Mass.: Addison-Wesley, 1986), p. 4.

10. J. Constable, "Diversification as a Factor in U.K. Industrial Strategy," *Long Range Planning* (February 1986), p. 53.

11. R. P. Rumelt, *Strategy, Structure, and Economic Performance* (Cambridge, Mass.: Harvard University Press, 1974).
K. Palepu, "Diversification Strategy, Profit Performance, and the Entropy Measure," *Strategic Management Journal* (July-September 1985), pp. 239–255.
P. Varadarajan and V. Ramanujan, "Diversification and Performance: A Reexamination Using a New Two-Dimensional Conceptualization of Diversity in Firms," *Academy of Management Journal* (June 1987), pp. 380–393.
H. Singh and C. A. Montgomery, "Corporate Acquisition Strategies and Economic Performance," *Strategic Management Journal* (July-August 1987), pp. 377–386.

12. T. J. Peters and R. H. Waterman, Jr., *In Search of Excellence* (New York: Harper & Row, 1982), pp. 293–294.

13. R. Little, "Conglomerates Are Doing Better Than You Think," *Fortune* (May 28, 1984), p. 60.
M. J. Dolan, "In Defense of Conglomerates," *Business Week* (July 29, 1985), p. 5.

14. G. Johnson and H. Thomas, "The Industry Context of Strategy, Structure, and Performance: The U. K. Brewing Industry," *Strategic Management Journal* (July-August 1987), pp. 343–361.

15. M. Leontiades, pp. 62–63.

16. C. K. Prahalad and R. A. Bettis, "The Dominant Logic: A New Linkage Between Diversity and Performance," *Strategic Management Journal* (November-December 1986), pp. 485–501.

17. S. Scredon and A. Dunkin, "Why Nabisco and Reynolds Were Made For Each Other," *Business Week* (June 17, 1985), p. 34.

18. B. T. Lamont and C. A. Anderson, "Mode of Corporate Diversification and Economic Performance," *Academy of Management Journal* (December 1985), pp. 926–936.

19. P. M. Hirsch, "Ambushes, Shootouts, and Knights of the Roundtable: The Language of Corporate Takeovers" (Paper presented to the 40th Meeting of the Academy of Management, Detroit, Mich., August 1980).

20. K. R. Harrigan, "Joint Ventures: Linking For a Leap Forward," *Planning Review* (July 1986), pp. 10–14.

21. For a good summary of guidelines for the formation and management of joint ventures, see P. P. Pekar, "Joint Venture: A New Information System Is Born," *Planning Review* (July 1986), pp. 15–19.

22. D. C. Hambrick, "Turnaround Strategies," in W. D. Guth (ed.), *Handbook of Business Strategy* (Boston: Warren, Gorham & Lamont, 1985), pp. 10.1–10.32.

23. C. J. Clarke and F. Gall, "Planned Divestment—A Five-step Approach," *Long Range Planning* (February 1987), p. 18.

24. For more information on reasons for the divestment of units, see W. R. Fannin, S. Markell, and C. B. Gilmore, "A New Strategic View of Divestitures," in *Handbook of Business Strategy, 1985/86 Yearbook*, edited by W. D. Guth (Boston: Warren, Gorham & Lamont, 1985), pp. 10.1–10.8.

25. J. B. Treece, "U. S. Parts Makers Just Won't Say 'Uncle'," *Business Week* (August 10, 1987), pp. 76–77.

26. R. L. Sutton and A. L. Callahan, "The Stigma of Bankruptcy: Spoiled Organizational Image and Its Management," *Academy of Management Journal* (September 1987) pp. 405–436.

27. P. C. Nystrom and W. H. Starbuck, "To Avoid Organizational Crises, Unlearn," *Organizational Dynamics* (Spring 1984), p. 55.

28. R. Hise and S. McDonald, "CEOs' Views On Strategy: A Survey," *Journal of Business Strategy* (Winter 1984), pp. 81 and 86.

29. H. K. Baker, T. O. Miller, and B. J. Ramsperger, "An Inside Look at Corporate Mergers and Acquisitions," *MSU Business Topics* (Winter 1981), p. 51.

30. B. Burrough, "Takeover Boom Is Expected to Continue Through 1988 After a Strong First Half," *Wall Street Journal* (July 5, 1988), p. 5.

31. M. E. Porter, *Competitive Strategy* (New York: Free Press, 1980), pp. 36–46.

32. Porter, 1980, p. 35.

33. J. B. Hull, "Hospital Chains Battle Health Insurers, But Will Quality Care Lose in the War?" *Wall Street Journal* (February 5, 1985), p. 35.

34. W. M. Bulkeley, "Upstart WordPerfect Corporation Finds Niche," *Wall Street Journal* (April 7, 1987), p. 6.

35. M. E. Porter, *Competitive Advantage* (New York: Free Press, 1985), p. 15.

36. Porter, 1985, p. 16.

37. G. G. Dess and P. S. Davis, "Porter's Generic Strategies as Determinants of Strategic Group Membership and Organizational Performance," *Academy of Management Journal* (September 1984), p. 484.

R. E. White, "Generic Business Strategies, Organizational Context and Performance: An Empirical Approach," *Strategic Management Journal* (May-June 1986), pp. 217–231.

38. F. E. Webster, Jr., "Marketing Strategy in a Slow Growth Economy," *California Management Review* (Spring 1986), p. 94.

39. J. Zaslow, "Atlas Van Lines Agrees to Buyout for $71.6 Million," *Wall Street Journal* (June 25, 1984), p. 10.

40. A. S. Lauglaug, "A Framework for the Strategic Management of Future Tyre Technology," *Long Range Planning* (October 1987), pp. 21–41.

N. K. Sethi, B. Movsesian, and K. D. Hickey, "Can Technology Be Managed Strategically?" *Long Range Planning* (August 1985), pp. 89–99.

41. Porter, 1985, p. 181.

42. C. Hawkins, R. Grover, and A. Bernstein, "Will It Be Kerkorian to the Rescue of Pan Am?" *Business Week* (October 19, 1987), pp. 57–58.

43. S. Schoeffler, R. D. Buzzell, and D. F. Heany, "Impact of Strategic Planning on Profit Performance," *Harvard Business Review* (March-April 1974), pp. 144–145.

44. M. Hergert, "Strategic Resource Allocation Using Divisional Hurdle Rates," *Planning Review* (January-February 1987), pp. 28–32.

D. R. Harrington, "Stock Prices, Beta, and Strategic Planning," *Harvard Business Review* (May-June 1983), pp. 157–164.

45. M. Kroll and S. Caples, "Managing Acquisitions of Strategic Business Units with the Aid of the Arbitrage Pricing Model," *Academy of Management Review* (October 1987), pp. 676–685.

46. M. D. Everett, "A Simplified Guide to Capital Investment Risk Analysis," *Planning Review* (July 1986), pp. 32–36.

47. Peters and Waterman, pp. 115–116.

48. B. Nussbaum and J. H. Dobrzynski, "The Battle For Corporate Control," *Business Week* (May 18, 1987), p. 103.

49. E. Weiner and A. Brown, "Stakeholder Analysis for Effective Issues Management," *Planning Review* (May 1986), pp. 27–31.

50. G. D. Keim and C. P. Zeithaml, "Corporate Political Strategy and Legislative Decision Making: A Review and Contingency Approach," *Academy of Management Review* (October 1986), pp. 828–843.

51. R. M. Cyert and J. G. March, "A Behavioral Theory of Organizational Objectives," *Management Classics,* eds. M. T. Matteson and J. M. Ivancevich (Santa Monica, Calif.: Goodyear Publishing, 1977), p. 114.

52. H. Schwartz and S. M. Davis, "Matching Corporate Culture and Business Strategy," *Organizational Dynamics* (Summer 1981), p. 43.

53. J. P. Wright, *On a Clear Day You Can See General Motors* (Grosse Point, Mich.: Wright Enterprises, 1979), p. 54.

54. Wright, p. 55.

55. M. A. Harris, Z. Schiller, R. Mitchell, and C. Power, "Can Jack Welch Reinvent GE?" *Business Week* (June 30, 1986), p. 67.

56. M. Edid and W. J. Hampton, "Now That It's Cruising, Can Ford Keep Its Foot on the Gas?" *Business Week* (February 11, 1985), pp. 48–52.

57. A. L. Mendlow, "Setting Corporate Goals and Measuring Organizational Effectiveness—A Practical Approach," *Long Range Planning* (February 1983), p. 72.

58. R. T. Jaffre, "Chaparral Steel Company: A Winner in a Market Decimated by Imports," *Planning Review* (July 1986), p. 22.

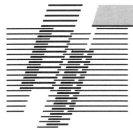

INTEGRATIVE CASE

CSX CORPORATION'S STRATEGIC ALTERNATIVES

In the spring of 1986, CSX Corporation's top management continued to work toward its objective of reaching and exceeding a 15% return on invested capital by 1990. Still following growth strategies aimed at creating America's leading multi-modal transportation system, the corporation's management committee (composed of eleven CSX senior executives and headed by Chairman Hays T. Watkins) pondered alternatives for future growth. The U.S. Senate on February 5, 1986, by a 54–39 vote, had approved the sale of Conrail to CSX's major competitor, Norfolk Southern Corporation. This was no surprise to CSX management, who had supported instead a Morgan Stanley proposal for a public offering of Conrail's stock (in which CSX might secure a minority interest). Nevertheless, the Senate's Conrail bill faced major opposition in the House of Representatives. CSX's management continued to hope for the eventual defeat of the legislation.

CSX closed 1985 in a reasonably strong financial and physical position. Although revenue and operating income were slightly less than they had been in 1984, net earnings increased if one's accounting excluded a special charge for the restructuring of the company's business segments. The issue facing the management committee was planning for future growth given the uncertainty of Conrail's future. In the last couple of years, the company had followed a temporary pause strategy as it worked to digest its recent acquisition of Texas Gas Resources and to make its two rail systems more efficient. How should the corporation continue its growth? Because of its success in forging a multi-modal transportation and natural resource company out of a group of rather diverse acquisitions, top management leaned toward external over internal growth. CSX top management believed that it needed to move quickly, before Norfolk Southern made its next move. Internal growth seemed too slow a method, in the high-stakes chess match being played by U.S. railroads in the 1980s.

CHANGING COMPETITIVE SITUATION

Norfolk Southern had not put all its hopes on the Conrail deal. The ICC had approved in April 1985 Norfolk Southern's acquisition of North American Van Lines—the first purchase of a trucking firm since deregulation. In urging his people to "think like truckers," Robert Claytor, Chief Executive of the Norfolk, Virginia-based railroad, stated that Norfolk Southern wants to "combine the service of trucks with the efficiencies of rail." He went on to say that "the company can begin a new service, when business is usually light, using North American's over-the-road operation. When volume grows, we can then switch the business to rail."[1]

Even after paying $350 million for North American Van Lines, Norfolk Southern had quite a bit left of the $1 billion in cash it had accumulated over the past few years. It had purchased a 19% stock interest in Piedmont Airlines, a 5% interest in Santa Fe Industries, and a 10% interest in Florida's Southeast Banking Corporation.[2] The cash would soon disappear if the Conrail purchase was finally approved by the House. If approval was denied, however, Norfolk Southern would be free to look elsewhere for an investment opportunity. Most in the industry were aware that the five-year agreement restricting Norfolk Southern's ability to increase or sell its stock in Piedmont Airlines would end in January 1987, but, until the Conrail issue was settled, no one would predict what might happen.

SEA-LAND OPPORTUNITY

In April 1986, while CSX's top management was considering possible future directions, a sudden opportunity presented itself. Sea-Land Corporation, one of the pioneer companies in the containerized ocean shipping business, let it be known that it was looking for a "white knight" to help it fight a takeover attempt by Harold Simmons' Contran Corporation. In 1966, Sea-Land became the first U.S. flag carrier to compete in the North Atlantic trade route with containerships and, in 1968, it began commercial service to the Far East. Only a few months after its being incorporated in Delaware in 1969, it was acquired by R. J. Reynolds (now R. J.

Reynolds Industries). In 1984, Reynolds distributed 0.2 shares of Sea-Land common stock in exchange for each share of Reynolds common stock. Sea-Land was once again autonomous.

By 1986, Sea-Land was the largest U.S. containership operation, with a fleet of fifty-eight containerships, averaging seven years of age, serving ports between the continental U.S. and the Far East, Northern Europe, the Mediterranean and the Middle East, Alaska, the Caribbean, and Central America. It had exclusive-use terminals in fifteen ports worldwide, and preferential-use agreements in many others. It operated vessels without federal subsidies and used its own marketing staff. It owned over 100,000 containers. Thanks to deregulation, Sea-Land bought its own double-stack rail cars in 1985 to carry its containers to inland destinations. By stacking two containers on these specially designed rail cars, Sea-Land nearly doubled train capacity and cut rail costs more than 25%. Because the major railroads had no double-stack cars, shipping lines chose to buy their own and contract with rail companies like CSX to haul the cars over the rail company's system.[3]

1985 had been a rather poor year for Sea-Land. Although revenues were 93% of those in 1984, net earnings were only 18% of 1984's because of declining freight rates. (Refer to Tables 7.5 and 7.6 for Sea-Land's financial information.) By April 1986, there appeared to be some firming of rates, but a projected increase in industry capacity of around 14% in 1986 was very likely to stimulate another round of rate cutting. Value Line forecasted that good prospects would develop for the industry by 1990, as additions to the world container fleet slowed and some of the current excess capacity was absorbed. This forecast assumed that a number of the weaker firms would soon leave the business. By cutting personnel costs and other expenses,

TABLE 7.5
Consolidated Statement of Earnings: Sea-Land Corporation
(In Thousands of Dollars)

	YEARS ENDED	
	1985	**1984**
Revenue	$1,634,183	$1,759,207
Expense		
Operating	1,283,976	1,276,646
Selling, general & administrative	249,618	235,346
Depreciation and amortization	105,409	101,351
Total Expenses	1,639,003	1,613,343
Earnings (loss) from operations	(4,820)	145,864
Interest income	28,969	43,196
Interest expense	(45,085)	(44,251)
Other financial income (expense), net	(1,025)	(12,746)
Earnings (loss) before income taxes	(21,961)	132,063
Provision (benefit) for income taxes	(36,163)	51,560
Net Earnings (loss)	$ 14,202	$ 80,503

TABLE 7.6
Consolidated Statement of Financial Position:
Sea-Land Corporation

(In Thousands of Dollars)

	YEARS ENDED	
	1985	1984
Assets		
Current assets		
Cash and short-term investments	$ 10,330	$ 31,236
Accounts and notes receivable (less allowances of $21,858 and $20,454)	164,185	188,963
Materials and supplies	33,357	34,345
Prepaid expenses	10,348	9,097
Total current assets	218,220	263,641
Property and equipment, at cost	2,146,068	1,862,833
Less depreciation and amortization	916,160	832,645
	1,226,908	1,030,188
Capital construction fund	169,102	326,054
Good will	87,735	87,908
Other assets	263,593	103,511
Total assets	$1,965,558	$1,811,302
Liabilities and Shareholders' Equity		
Current liabilities		
Accounts payable and accrued liabilities	$ 215,491	$ 179,132
Notes payable	—	60,000
Current portion of long-term debt	5,927	6,916
Total current liabilities	221,418	246,048
Long-term debt, less current portion	575,196	416,268
Other liabilities	55,408	46,943
Deferred income taxes	325,732	324,192
Shareholder's Equity		
Common stock, $.10 stated value at 12/29/85 and 12/30/84	2,333	2,319
Paid-in capital	230,359	223,485
Cumulative translation adjustments	(602)	(611)
Retained earnings (deficit)	555,714	552,658
Total shareholders' equity	787,804	777,851
Total liabilities and shareholders' equity	$1,965,558	$1,811,302

Sea-Land was attempting to survive a very rocky year, after posting a first quarter loss in March 1986.[4]

Sea-Land's top management and its board of directors were finding it increasingly difficult to fend off a hostile takeover attempt by Harold Simmons. By April, Simmons' Contran Corporation owned around 39% (approximately 9.2 million shares) of Sea-Land's stock and was in the process of being given three seats on the corporation's board at Sea-Land's annual meeting in May. Sea-Land's management was in a serious bind. Because of the weak state of the oceanic shipping business and the fact that 35% of Sea-Land's capitalization consisted of long-term debt, analysts thought it unlikely that any bank would be willing to finance a leveraged buyout by Sea-Land's executives to avoid Simmons' takeover. The only other feasible option was to seek out a friendly merger with a compatible company.

STRATEGIC DECISION POINT

CSX's top management was well aware of Sea-Land's problems with Simmons and wondered if Sea-Land would be a good candidate for acquisition. In its search for growth opportunities, CSX had been studying opportunities in ocean shipping as well as in other areas. Some quiet discussions with Sea-Land executives revealed that Sea-Land might welcome an offer from CSX. By mid-April, Simmons offered $26 for those Sea-Land shares he didn't already own. The company's stock, which had been trading earlier at $23, was now selling for around $25 per share. The question facing the management committee of CSX was what to do about Sea-Land. Would the possible synergies from such a merger more than offset the overcapacity problem in containerized oceanic shipping? It would probably cost $700 million to $800 million to buy all the 26.6 million fully diluted shares (composed of common stock outstanding, plus existing stock options, and the conversion of subordinated notes) of Sea-Land. Was this a good time for CSX to get involved in an international transportation business or should CSX "stick to its knitting" in the U.S.? Some analysts believed that because ocean-container companies were becoming one of the railroad industry's biggest set of customers, railroads would either compete with each other for the business or capture it permanently through acquisition. CSX's management committee did not have much time to decide. Because of Simmons' interest, Sea-Land seemed to be a now or never opportunity.

NOTES

1. L. Abruzzese, "NS Chairman Urges Rails To Be More 'Truck-Like,' " *Journal of Commerce and Commercial* (October 22, 1986), p. 1A(2).
2. J. Cook, "The $1 Billion Holding Action," *Forbes* (December 19, 1983) p. 67.
3. D. Machalaba, "Shipping Lines Find Competitive Edge In Adding Their Own Rail Operations," *Wall Street Journal* (December 26, 1985), p. 3.
4. "Sea-Land," *Value Line Investment Survey,* Part 3: Ratings and Reports, Edition 2 (April 4, 1986), p. 303.

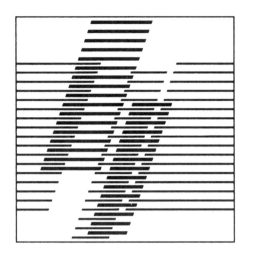

PART FOUR

STRATEGY IMPLEMENTATION AND CONTROL

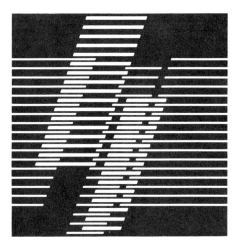

CHAPTER 8

STRATEGY IMPLEMENTATION

STRATEGIC MANAGEMENT MODEL

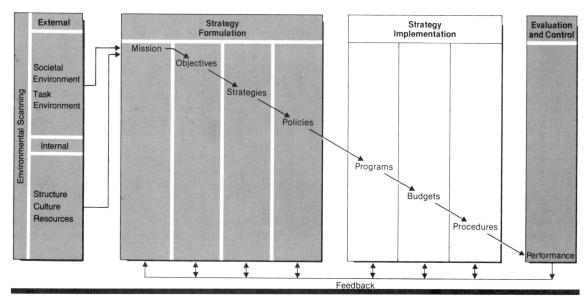

Once a strategy and a set of policies have been formulated, the focus of strategic management shifts to implementation. **Strategy implementation** is the sum total of the activities and choices required for execution of a plan. It is the process by which strategies and policies are put into action, through the development of programs, budgets, and procedures. To begin the implementation process, strategy makers must consider three questions:

Who are the people who will carry out the strategic plan?

What must be done?

How are they going to do what is needed?

These questions and similar ones should have been addressed initially when the pros and cons of strategic alternatives were analyzed. They must also be addressed now before appropriate implementation plans can be made. Unless top management can answer these basic questions in a satisfactory manner, even the best planned strategy is unlikely to have the desired results.

For example, the acquisition of Republic Airlines by Northwest Airlines was a well-conceived, horizontal growth strategy, but it created massive problems when first implemented. Traffic exceeded projections—and overwhelmed Northwest's computer systems. Reservations were lost and passengers were ticketed into the same seats. As ex-Republic workers struggled to learn a new system for baggage transfer, there was a dramatic increase in the number of misplaced bags. Before the merger, 85% of both airlines' flights departed on time. In the first week of the merger, on-time performance plunged to 25%! The U.S. Transportation Department's Consumer

Affairs Division received 4.74 complaints per 100,000 Northwest passengers for the first month of the merged operation—nearly 2½ times the industry average. "We anticipated some problems," said John F. Horn, President of Northwest's parent company, NWA, Inc., "but we had no idea they were going to be the level they were."[1]

Alexander's survey of ninety-three company presidents and divisional managers revealed that the following ten problems were experienced by over half of the group when they attempted to implement a strategic change. These problems are listed in order of frequency of occurrence.

1. More time needed for implementation than originally planned.
2. Unanticipated major problems.
3. Ineffective coordination of activities.
4. Crises that distracted attention away from implementation.
5. Insufficient capabilities of the involved employees.
6. Inadequate training and instruction of lower-level employees.
7. Uncontrollable external environmental factors.
8. Inadequate leadership and direction by departmental managers.
9. Poor definition of key implementation tasks and activities.
10. Inadequate monitoring of activities by the information system.[2]

As shown in Fig. 8.1, poor implementation of an appropriate strategy can result in failure of the strategy. An excellent implementation plan,

FIGURE 8.1

Interaction of Strategy Formulation and Implementation

STRATEGY FORMULATED

		Appropriate	Inappropriate
STRATEGY IMPLEMENTED	Excellent	*Success* Targets for growth, share, profits are met.	*Rescue or Ruin* Good execution may save a poor strategy or may hasten failure.
	Poor	*Trouble* Poor execution hampers good strategy. Management may conclude strategy is inappropriate.	*Failure* Cause of failure hard to diagnose. Poor strategy marked by inability to execute.

however, will not only cause the success of an appropriate strategy; it can also rescue an inappropriate strategy. This is why an increasing number of chief executives are turning their attention to the problems of implementation. Now more than ever before, they realize that the successful implementation of a strategy depends on having the right organization structure, resource allocation, compensation program, information system, and corporate culture.[3]

8.1

WHO IMPLEMENTS STRATEGY?

Depending on how the corporation is organized, those who implement corporate strategy might be a different set of people from those who formulate it. In most large, multi-industry corporations, the implementers will be everyone in the organization except top management and the board of directors. Vice-presidents of functional areas and directors of divisions or SBUs will work with their subordinates to put together large-scale implementation plans. From these plans, plant managers, project managers, and unit heads will put together plans for their specific plants, departments, and units. Therefore, every operational manager down to the first-line supervisor will be involved in some way in the implementing of corporate, divisional, and functional strategies.

It is important to note that most of the people in the corporation who are crucial to successful strategy implementation probably had little, if anything, to do with the development of the corporate strategy. Therefore, they might be entirely ignorant of the vast amount of data and work that went into the formulation process. Unless changes in mission, objectives, strategies, and policies and their importance to the corporation are communicated clearly to all operational managers, there can be a lot of resistance and footdragging. When top management formulates a strategy that challenges the corporation's culture, lower-level managers might even sabotage the implementation. These managers might hope to influence top management to abandon its new plans and return to the old ways. For an example of one company's problems with corporate culture see Illustrative Example 8.1.

8.2

WHAT MUST BE DONE?

The managers of divisions and functional areas work with their fellow managers to develop *programs, budgets,* and *procedures* for the implementation of strategy. A **program** is a statement of the activities or steps needed to accomplish a single-use plan, the purpose of which is to make the strategy action-oriented. For example, top management might have chosen forward vertical integration as its best strategy for growth. It purchased existing retail outlets from another firm instead of building its own. To integrate the new

ILLUSTRATIVE EXAMPLE 8.1

Two Cultures Clash at HNG/InterNorth, Inc.

When InterNorth, Inc., acquired Houston Natural Gas Corporation for $2.4 billion in July 1985, industry analysts predicted that it would soon become a dominant firm in the pipeline industry. The combined company had a good position in growing markets in Southern California and Florida and access to cheap, unregulated Texas natural gas. Unfortunately, the two companies had very different cultures, which created serious implementation problems. Forced to deal with constant infighting, top management couldn't even settle on a name for the company. Even though InterNorth had bought Houston Natural Gas, the temporary name of HNG/InterNorth listed Houston first "because it came off the tongue better," reported Kenneth Lay, Chairman of the corporation. With the help of a New York consulting firm, Lay proposed changing the name to Enteron. Once word spread, however, that the word literally meant the alimentary canal, or digestive tract, Lay became the target of much ridicule. "We know which end of the alimentary canal we are," complained one constituent.

When the merger originally took place, Samuel Segnar, Chairman of InterNorth, agreed that Lay, head of HNG, would serve initially as president and then as chairman of the combined company. Segnar was to serve as chairman until Lay took over the position.

Personnel rivalry throughout the two merged companies, however, created some bizarre situations. From the beginning, there was conflict over which company was to be dominant. To placate both sides, management established dual headquarters in Omaha and Houston. The controller was located in Omaha, while the treasurer had his office in Houston. Matters continued to deteriorate. With the early retirement of Segnar in November 1985, Lay assumed the chairman's position. Lay's decisive, hands-on style conflicted with InterNorth's decentralized approach. Nearly a dozen top executives quit. Noticing the instability of the company, Houston Lighting and Power Company, HNG/InterNorth's biggest customer, cancelled its contract. To try to stem the constant infighting, Lay communicated his desire to form one cohesive company. "Throughout the organization there continues to be too much of the we and they, Omaha versus Houston, and InterNorth or HNG winning or losing." Unfortunately, Lay's attempt to cut costs by eliminating around 10% of the combined workforce did not contribute to improved morale.

SOURCE: J. E. Davis, "A Mega-Pipeline With a Massive Identity Crisis," *Business Week* (April 14, 1986), pp. 65–66.

stores into the corporation, various programs—such as the following—would now have to be developed:

1. A re-structuring program to move the stores into the existing marketing chain of command, so that store managers report to regional managers, who report to the merchandising manager, who reports to the vice-president in charge of marketing.

2. An advertising program. ("Jones Surplus is now a part of Ajax Continental. Prices are lower. Selection is better.")

3. A training program for newly hired store managers as well as for those Jones Surplus managers the corporation has chosen to keep.

4. A program to develop reporting procedures that will integrate the stores into the corporation's accounting system.

5. A program to modernize the stores and to prepare them for a "grand opening."

Once these and other programs are developed, the budget process begins. A **budget** is a statement of a corporation's programs in terms of dollars. The detailed cost of each program is listed for planning and control purposes. Planning a budget is the last real check a corporation has on the feasibility of its selected strategy. An ideal strategy might be found to be completely impractical only after specific implementation programs are costed in detail.

Once program, divisional, and corporate budgets are approved, procedures to guide the employees in their day-to-day actions must be developed. Sometimes referred to as Standard Operating Procedures, **procedures** are a system of sequential steps or techniques that describe in detail how a particular task or job is to be done. They typically detail the various activities that must be carried out to complete a corporation's programs. In the case of the corporation that decided to acquire another firm's retail outlets, new operating procedures must be established for, among others, in-store promotions, inventory ordering, stock selection, customer relations, credits and collections, warehouse distribution, pricing, paycheck timing, grievance handling, and raises and promotions. These procedures ensure that the day-to-day store operations will be consistent over time (that is, next week's work activities will be the same as this week's) and consistent among stores (that is, each store will operate in the same manner as the others). To ensure that its policies are carried out to the letter in every one of its fast-food retail outlets, McDonald's, for example, has done an excellent job of developing very detailed procedures (and policing them!).

8.3

HOW IS STRATEGY TO BE IMPLEMENTED?

Up to this point, both strategy formulation and implementation have been discussed in terms of planning. Programs, budgets, and procedures are simply more greatly detailed plans for the eventual implementation of strategy. The total management process includes, however, several additional activities crucial to implementation, such as organizing, staffing, directing, and controlling. Before *plans* can lead to actual performance, top management must ensure that the corporation is appropriately *organized*, programs are adequately *staffed*, and activities are being *directed* toward the achievement of desired objectives. These activities are reviewed briefly in this chapter. Top management must also ensure that there is progress toward the objectives, according to plan; this is a *control* function that will be discussed in Chapter 9.

Organizing

It is very likely that a change in corporate strategy will require some sort of change in the way a corporation is structured and in the kind of skills needed in particular positions. In a classic study of large American corporations, such as DuPont, General Motors, Sears Roebuck, and Standard Oil, Chandler concluded that changes in corporate strategy lead to changes in organization structure. He also concluded that American corporations follow a pattern of development from one kind of structural arrangement to another as they expand. According to him, these structural changes occur because inefficiencies caused by the old structure have, by being pushed too far, become too obviously detrimental to live with: "The thesis deduced from these several propositions is then that structure follows strategy and that the most complex type of structure is the result of the concatenation [linking together] of several basic strategies."[4] Chandler therefore proposed the following as the sequence of what occurs:

1. New strategy is created.

2. New administrative problems emerge.

3. Economic performance declines.

4. New appropriate structure is invented.

5. Profit returns to its previous level.

Structure Follows Strategy

Chandler found that in their early years, corporations such as DuPont tend to have a centralized organizational structure that is well suited to their producing and selling a limited range of products. As they add new product lines, purchase their own sources of supply, and create their own distribution networks, they become too complex for highly centralized structures. In order to remain successful, this type of successful organization needs to shift to a decentralized structure with several semi-autonomous divisions (referred to as the divisional structure in Chapter 5). This type of structure is also called the *M-form* (for multidivisional structure) by the noted economist, O. E. Williamson.[5]

In his book, *My Years with General Motors,* Alfred P. Sloan detailed how General Motors conducted such structural changes in the 1920s.[6] He saw decentralization of structure as centralized policy determination coupled with decentralized operating management. Once a strategy was developed for the total corporation by top management, the individual divisions, such as Chevrolet, Buick, etc., were free to choose how they would implement that strategy. Patterned after DuPont, GM found the decentralized multi-divisional structure to be extremely effective in allowing the maximum amount of freedom for product development. Return on investment was used as a financial control.

Research generally supports Chandler's proposition that structure follows strategy (as well as the reverse proposition from Chapter 5 that structure influences strategy).[7] Galbraith and Kazanjian propose that the early adoption of an appropriate structure can give a company a competitive advantage.[8] In support of this argument, research indicates that when companies that diversify into unrelated products change from a functional structure to a divisional structure, the companies' rates of return increase. Teece, in particular, found reorganization to generally contribute around 1.2 percentage points to a company's ROA.[9] Research also reveals that the fit between a business-level strategy and the amount of autonomy that corporate headquarters allows the business unit have an effect upon business unit performance.[10]

There is some evidence, however, that a change in strategy might not necessarily result in a corresponding change in structure if the corporation has very little competition. If a firm occupies a monopolistic position, with tariffs in its favor or close ties to a government, it can raise prices to cover internal administrative inefficiencies. This is an easier path for these firms to take than going through the pain of corporate reorganization.[11]

Although it is agreed that organizational structure must vary with different environmental conditions, which, in turn, affect an organization's strategy, there is no agreement about an optimal organizational design.[12] What was appropriate for DuPont and General Motors in the 1920s might not be appropriate today. Firms in the same industry do, however, tend to organize themselves in a similar fashion. For example, automobile manufacturers tend to emulate General Motors' decentralized division concept, whereas consumer-goods producers tend to emulate the brand-management concept pioneered by Procter & Gamble Company. The general conclusion seems to be that firms following similar strategies tend to adopt similar structures.[13] Nevertheless, Galbraith and Kazanjian propose more specific guidelines to better match structure to the strategy:

- Single-business and dominant-business corporations (companies operating primarily in one industry) should be organized in a functional structure. (See Fig. 5.1 in Chapter 5.)
- Related, diversified corporations should be organized into a divisional structure.
- Unrelated, diversified corporations should be organized into a conglomerate (or holding company) structure.[14]

Organic and Mechanistic Structure

Research by Burns and Stalker concluded that a "mechanistic" structure, with its emphasis on the centralization of decision-making and bureaucratic rules and procedures, appears to be well suited to organizations operating in a reasonably stable environment. In contrast, however, they found that successful firms operating in a constantly changing environment, such as those in the electronics and aerospace industries, find that a more "organic" structure, with the decentralization of decision making and flexible procedures, is more appropriate.[15] Studies by Lawrence and Lorsch support this conclusion. They found that successful firms in a reasonably stable environment, such as the container industry, coordinate activities primarily through fairly centralized corporate hierarchies, which place some reliance on direct contact by managers as well as on paperwork directives. Successful firms in more dynamic environments, such as the plastics industry, coordinate activities through integrative departments and permanent cross-functional teams as well as through the hierarchical contact and paperwork.[16] These differences in the use of structural integrating devices are detailed in Table 8.1. The container industry is the most stable; foods, intermediate; plastics, the least stable.

Strategic Business Units

A successful method for the structuring of a large and complex business corporation was developed in 1971 by GE. Referred to as *strategic business units* or SBUs, organizational groups composed of discrete, independent product-market segments served by the firm were identified and given primary responsibility and authority for management of their own functional areas. Recognizing that its structure of decentralized operating divisions was not working efficiently (massive sales growth was not being matched by profit growth), GE's top management decided to reorganize. They restruc-

TABLE 8.1
Integrating Mechanisms in Three Different Industries

	PLASTICS	FOOD	CONTAINER
Percent new products in last 20 years	35%	15%	0%
Integrating devices	Rules. Hierarchy. Goal setting. Direct contact. Teams at 3 levels. Integrating departments.	Rules. Hierarchy. Goal setting. Direct contact. Task forces. Integrators.	Rules. Hierarchy. Goal setting. Direct contact.
Percent integrators/ managers	22%	17%	0%

SOURCE: J. Galbraith, *Designing Complex Organizations.* Copyright © 1973 by Addison-Wesley Publishing Co., Inc. Table on page 111. Reprinted by permission.

tured nine groups and forty-eight divisions into forty-three strategic business units, many of which crossed traditional group, divisional, and profit center lines. For example, food-preparation appliances in three separate divisions were merged into a single SBU serving the "housewares" market.[17] The concept thus is to decentralize on the basis of strategic elements rather than on the basis of size or span of control. As mentioned in Chapter 5, an organization by SBUs is simply another version of the divisional structure.

General Electric was so pleased with the results of its experiment in organizational design that it reported " . . . the system helped GE improve its profitability, and return on investment has been rebuilt to a healthier level. In the last recession, General Electric's earnings dropped much less than the overall decline for the industry generally."[18] Following this lead, other firms such as General Foods, Mead Corporation, Eastman Kodak, Campbell Soup, Union Carbide, and Armco Steel, have implemented the strategic business unit concept. In introducing the concept, General Foods organized certain products on the basis of menu segments like breakfast food, beverage, main meal, dessert, and pet foods.

It is interesting that one of the reasons companies convert to SBUs is to reduce the number of units that top management must monitor. GE's top management found it easier to keep track of forty-eight SBUs than the previous 180 departments. Chief executive officers have limited time and a limited ability for their focus on strategic issues in each of the corporation's many units. This might be one reason why a survey of U.S. Fortune 1000 companies found the mean average number of SBUs in a firm to be thirty regardless of company size.[19]

Typically, once a corporation organizes itself around SBUs, it combines similar SBUs together under a group or sector (as mentioned in Chapter 5). In 1985, Eastman Kodak, for example, reorganized into seventeen business units under three operating groups. This type of reorganization on the basis of markets is a way a **horizontal strategy,** based upon competitive considerations that cut across divisional boundaries, is developed. The group or sector executive therefore is responsible for developing and implementing a horizontal strategy to coordinate the various goals and strategies of related business units. This strategy can help a firm compete with **multipoint competitors**—that is, firms that compete with each other not only in one business unit but in a number of related business units.[20] For example, Procter & Gamble, Kimberly-Clark, Scott Paper, and Johnson and Johnson compete with each other in varying combinations of consumer paper products, from disposable diapers to facial tissue. If (purely hypothetically), Johnson and Johnson had just developed a toilet tissue with which they chose to challenge Procter & Gamble's high-share Charmin brand in a particular district, it might charge a low price for its new brand to build sales quickly. Procter & Gamble might not choose to respond to this attack on its share by cutting prices on Charmin. Because of Charmin's high-market share, Procter & Gamble would lose significantly more sale dollars in a price war than would

Johnson and Johnson with Johnson and Johnson's initially low-share brand. To retaliate Procter & Gamble might thus challenge Johnson and Johnson's high-share baby shampoo with Procter & Gamble's own low-share brand of baby shampoo in a different district. Once Johnson and Johnson had perceived this response by Procter & Gamble, it might choose to stop challenging Procter & Gamble's Charmin brand of toilet tissue in one district so that Procter & Gamble would stop challenging Johnson and Johnson's baby shampoo in a different district.

Matrix Structure

As pointed out in Chapter 5, the matrix structure simultaneously combines the stability of the functional structure with the flexibility of the project organization. It is likely to be used within an SBU when the following three conditions exist:

- There is a need for cross-fertilization of ideas across projects or products.
- Resources are scarce.
- There is a need to improve the abilities to process information and to make decisions.[21]

The matrix structure is appealing but must be carefully managed. To the extent that the goals to be achieved are vague and the technology used is poorly understood, there is likely to be a continuous battle for power between project and functional managers.[22]

Organizing for Innovation

Those corporations that emphasize the latest technology as part of their missions, objectives, and strategies are finding that their structure tends to lag behind their technology. Keen suggests that there is a lag time before a new technology can be fully exploited because more change is expected than a system can handle. An infrastructure needs to be built within a corporation to deal with the implications and impact of rapid technological change.[23] Frohman makes a similar argument: "Many aspects of an organization— from technical talent to reward systems, from climate to equipment—affect the payoff a company will receive from its investments in technology."[24]

A large corporation that wishes to encourage innovation and creativity within its firm must choose a type of structure that will give the new business unit an appropriate amount of freedom with headquarters still having some degree of control. This statement is in agreement with the views of authorities in the area that the entrepreneurial project has to be organized separately from the existing, mainstream organization.[25] This separation is needed because the large, successful corporation tends to have a fairly bureaucratic corporate culture emphasizing efficiency, and thus tends to conflict with the type of loose, often free-wheeling culture that is needed to nurture innovation.

Burgelman proposes, as seen in Fig. 8.2, that the use of a particular organizational design should be determined by the **strategic importance** of the new business to the corporation and the **relatedness** of the unit's operations to those of the corporation.[26] The combination of these two factors results in nine organizational designs for corporate entrepreneurship (or *intrapreneurship*, as it is called by Pinchot).[27]

1. *Direct integration.* If the new business has high strategic importance and operational relatedness, it must be a part of the corporation's mainstream. Product "champions"—people who are respected by others in the corporation and who know how to work the system—are needed to manage these projects. When he was with Ford Motor Company, Lee Iacocca, for example, championed the Mustang.

2. *New product business department.* If the new business has high strategic importance and partial operational relatedness, it should be a separate department, organized around an entrepreneurial project in the division where skills and capabilities can be shared.

3. *Special business units.* If the new business has high strategic importance and low operational relatedness, it should be a special new business unit with specific objectives and time horizons. General Motor's new Saturn unit is one example of this approach.

4. *Micro new-ventures department.* If the new business has uncertain strategic importance and high operational relatedness, it is a "peripheral" project, which is likely to emerge in the operating divisions on a continuous basis. Each division thus has its own new ventures department. Xerox Corporation, for example, uses its SBUs to generate and nurture

FIGURE 8.2
Organizational Designs for Corporate Entrepreneurship

OPERATION RELATEDNESS	Very Important	Uncertain	Not Important
Unrelated	3. Special Business Units	6. Independent Business Units	9. Complete Spin-Off
Partly Related	2. New Product Business Department	5. New Venture Division	8. Contracting
Strongly Related	1. Direct Integration	4. Micro New Ventures Department	7. Nurturing and Contracting

STRATEGIC IMPORTANCE

Source: Reprinted from R. A. Burgelman, "Designs for Corporate Entrepreneurship in Established Firms." Copyright © 1984 by the Regents of the University of California. Reprinted/Condensed from the *California Management Review,* Vol. 26, No. 3, p. 161. By permission of The Regents.

new ideas. Small product-synthesis teams within each SBU test the feasibility of new ideas. Those concepts receiving a "go" decision are managed by an SBU product-delivery team, headed by a chief engineer, who take the prototype from development through manufacturing.[28]

5. *New venture division.* When the new business has uncertain strategic importance and is only partly related to present corporate operations, it belongs in a new venture division. It brings together projects that either exist in various parts of the corporation or can be acquired externally; sizable new businesses are built. R. J. Reynolds Industries, for example, established a separate company, R. J. Reynolds Development, to evaluate new business concepts with growth potential. The development company nurtures and develops businesses that might have the potential to become one of RJR's core businesses.[29]

6. *Independent business units.* Uncertain strategic importance coupled with no relationship to present corporate activities can make external arrangements attractive. Procter and Gamble took this approach when it established a separate unit to manage the uncertain, but potentially major business, created by the synthetic fat substitute, olestra, invented by the company. The company claimed that olestra as a food additive was free of calories and cholesterol, and that it had no serious side effects. While awaiting the Food and Drug Administration's approval for marketing the product, the new unit had to decide which uses of olestra it should reserve for its own products and which it should license.[30]

7. *Nurturing and contracting.* When an entrepreneurial proposal might not be important strategically to the corporation but is strongly related to present operations, top management might help the entrepreneurial unit "spin off" from the corporation. This allows a friendly competitor, instead of one of the corporation's major competitors, to capture a small niche. For example, Tektronix, a maker of oscilloscopes, formed a unit to act as an in-house venture capitalist to its own employees; this relationship allowed the corporation to swap the parent company's operational knowledge for equity in the new company. The arrangement is intended to provide Tektronix with a better return on its R&D expenditures and to help it maintain ties with innovative employees who want to run their own companies.[31]

8. *Contracting.* As the required capabilities and skills of the new business are less related to those of the corporation, the parent corporation may spin off the strategically unimportant unit yet keep some relationship through a contractual arrangement with the new firm. The connection is useful in case the new firm eventually develops something of value to the corporation.

9. *Complete spin off.* If both the strategic importance and the operational relatedness of the new business are negligible, the corporation is likely to completely sell off the business to another firm or to the present employees in some form of ESOP (Employee Stock Ownership Plan). Or the corporation can sell off the unit through a leveraged buyout (executives of the unit buy the unit from the parent company with

money from a third source, to be repaid out of the unit's anticipated earnings). This is what happened to Lifeline Technology, originally a part of Allied Corporation. Lifeline, an inventory management system, had been developed in Allied's new ventures unit (cell #5 in Fig. 8.2). After Allied's merger with Signal Companies in 1985, new ventures that didn't fit into the company's existing businesses were refused further funding. Noting that Lifeline lacked any strategic fit with Allied, Stephen Fields, Lifeline's manager, quit Allied and together with six partners from Allied formed Lifeline Technology to market the product.[32]

Organizing for innovation has become especially important for those corporations in "high tech" industries that wish to recapture the entrepreneurial spirit but are really too large to do so. IBM formed "independent business units," each with its own mini-board of directors. One such IBU produced the company's successful personal computer. IBM spared the personal-computer unit many of the company's usual controls and formalized reporting procedures. Because of this freedom, the original PC moved from preliminary planning to introduction in thirteen months, compared to the years of effort needed for the development of most IBM products. Even Levi Strauss and Company, the clothing manufacturer, is encouraging "in-house entrepreneurs" by financing new fashion-apparel businesses.

Rather than attempting such in-house innovation, a number of corporations are investing venture capital in existing small firms. Wang, for example, purchased a minority interest in InteCom, Inc., a maker of telephone switching equipment. General Motors, Procter and Gamble, and six other companies did the same by buying $20 million of equity in a small artificial-intelligence company called Teknowledge. GM hoped that Teknowledge's expert systems-software would help it to design cars and to prepare factory schedules. Increasingly referred to as *strategic partnerships*, these ventures are similar to Burgelman's nurturing and contracting design (cell #7 in Fig. 8.2) and can be viewed as a form of quasi-vertical integration as well.[33] In such arrangements, it often becomes difficult to tell where one firm begins and the other leaves off!

Stages of Corporate Development

A key proposition of Chandler's was that successful corporations tend to follow a pattern of structural development as they grow and expand. Further work by Thain, Scott, and Tuason specifically delineates three distinct structural stages.[34]

Stage I is typified by the entrepreneur, who founds the corporation to promote an idea (product or service). The entrepreneur tends to make all the important decisions personally, and is involved in every detail and phase of the organization. The Stage I corporation has a structure allowing the entrepreneur to directly supervise the activities of every employee (see Fig.

5.1). The corporation in Stage I is thus characterized by little formal structure. Planning is usually short range or "fire-fighting" in nature. The typical managerial functions of planning, organizing, directing, staffing, and controlling are usually performed to a very limited degree, if at all. The greatest strengths of a Stage I corporation are its flexibility and dynamism. The drive of the entrepreneur energizes the corporation in its struggle for growth. Its greatest weakness is its extreme reliance on the entrepreneur to decide general strategies as well as detailed procedures. If the entrepreneur falters, the corporation usually flounders.

Stage I described Polaroid Corporation, whose founder Dr. Edwin Land championed *Polarvision,* a financially disastrous instant-movie system, while ignoring industrial and commercial uses. Growing concern by stockholders over declines in sales and net income resulted in Dr. Land's resignation from his top management position in 1980 and from the board of directors in 1982. In 1983, analysts reported that Polaroid was in the throes of a "midlife crisis," worrying about its mortality and the loss of Dr. Land's inspiring vision.[35] Polaroid Corporation was, in effect, a Stage II corporation being managed by Dr. Land as if it still were a Stage I corporation.

This is an example of what Greiner calls the *crisis of leadership,* which an organization must solve before it can move into the second stage of growth.[36]

At **Stage II,** the entrepreneur is replaced by a team of managers with functional specializations (see Fig. 5.1). The transition to this state requires a substantial managerial style change for the chief officer of the corporation, especially if the chief officer was the Stage I entrepreneur. Otherwise, having additional staff members yields no benefits to the corporation. At this juncture, the corporate strategy favors protectivism through dominance of the industry, often through vertical or horizontal integration. The great strength of a Stage II corporation lies in its concentration and specialization in one industry. Its great weakness is that all of its eggs are in one basket.

McDonald's, the world's largest food service company, is a Stage II corporation that is concentrating on fast food. Fred Turner, Chairman of the Board, commented in 1984 on the company's specialization in one industry:

> My view is that we can maintain a growth rate in the teens through this decade. And if you believe that, it makes the question of diversification beside the point.[37]

By concentrating on one industry as long as that industry remains attractive, a Stage II company can be very successful. Once a functionally structured firm diversifies into other products in other industries, however, the advantages of the functional structure break down. A crisis of autonomy can develop, in which people managing diversified product lines need more decision-making freedom than top management is willing to delegate to them.

The **Stage III** corporation focuses on managing diverse product lines in numerous industries; it decentralizes decision-making authority. These corporations grow by diversifying their product lines and expanding to cover wider geographical areas. These corporations move to a divisional structure with a central headquarters. Headquarters attempts to coordinate the activities of its operating divisions through performance- and results-oriented control and reporting systems, and by the stressing of corporate planning techniques. The divisions are not tightly controlled, but are held responsible for their own performance results. Therefore, to be effective, the corporation has to have a decentralized decision process. The greatest strength of a Stage III corporation is its almost unlimited resources. Its most significant weakness is that it is usually so large and complex that it tends to become relatively inflexible. General Electric, DuPont, and General Motors are Stage III corporations.

These descriptions of the three stages of corporate development are supported by research.[38] The differences among the stages are specified in more detail by Thain in Table 8.2.

In his study, Chandler noted that the empire builder was rarely the person who created the new structure to fit the new strategy, and that, as a result, the transition from one stage to another is often a painful one. This was true of General Motors Corporation under the management of William Durant, Ford Motor Company under its founder Henry Ford, Polaroid Corporation under Edwin Land, and Apple Computer under its founder Steven Jobs. (See Illustrative Example 8.2.) This difficulty in moving to a new stage is compounded by the founder's tendency to maneuver around the need to delegate by carefully hiring, training, and grooming his/her own team of managers. These managers eventually hold the same beliefs and attitudes as the founder who hired them. In this way a corporation's culture is formed and perpetuated. The team tends to maintain the founder's influence throughout the organization long after the founder is gone.[39] The successors to Ray Kroc, the founder of McDonald's Corporation, promised not to change the fast-food company and to stay true to the founder's vision. This faithfulness gave the hamburger chain a definite strength, but also created a significant roadblock to innovation and change. For example, Mr. Kroc's quick-cooking systems were not geared to the individual service increasingly desired by consumers. More importantly, Kroc's strong emphasis on the continuous expansion of McDonald's hamburger-and-french-fries business kept top management from seriously considering diversification alternatives—even 10 years after Kroc's death! Thain, in Table 8.3, summarizes the internal and external blocks to movement from one stage to another.

Galbraith and Kazanjian propose the existence of a **Stage IV** corporation based on the *matrix* structure. They argue that the matrix is the essential form for diversified multinational corporations.[40] (Refer to Chapter 10 for additional information on multinational corporations.) Others suggest that

TABLE 8.2
Key Factors in Top Management Process in Stage I, II, and III Companies

Function	STAGE I	STAGE II	STAGE III
1. Size-up: Major problems	Survival and growth dealing with short-term operating problems.	Growth, rationalization, and expansion of resources, providing for adequate attention to product problems.	Trusteeship in management and investment and control of large, increasing, and diversified resource. Also, important to diagnose and take action on problems at division level.
2. Objectives	Personal and subjective.	Profits and meeting functionally oriented budgets and performance targets.	ROI, profits, earnings per share.
3. Strategy	Implicit and personal; exploitation of immediate opportunities seen by owner-manager.	Functionally oriented moves restricted to "one product" scope; exploitation of one basic product or service field.	Growth and product diversification; exploitation of general business opportunities.
4. Organization: Major characteristic of structure	One unit, "one-man show."	One-unit, functionally specialized group.	Multiunit general staff office and decentralized operating divisions.
5. (a) Measurement and control	Personal, subjective control based on simple accounting system and daily communication and observation.	Control grows beyond one man; assessment of functional operations necessary; structured control systems evolve.	Complex formal system geared to comparative assessment of performance measures, indicating problems and opportunities and assessing management ability of division managers.
5. (b) Key performance indicators	Personal criteria, relationships with owner, operating efficiency, ability to solve operating problems.	Functional and internal criteria such as sales, performance compared to budget, size of empire, status in group, personal relationships, etc.	More impersonal application of comparisons such as profits, ROI, P/E ratio, sales, market share, productivity, product leadership, personnel development, employee attitudes, public responsibility.

(Continued)

259

TABLE 8.2 (Continued)

Function	STAGE I	STAGE II	STAGE III
6. Reward-punishment system	Informal, personal, subjective; used to maintain control and divide small pool of resources to provide personal incentives for key performers.	More structured; usually based to a greater extent on agreed policies as opposed to personal opinion and relationships.	Allotment by "due process" of a wide variety of different rewards and punishments on a formal and systematic basis. Company-wide policies usually apply to many different classes of managers and workers with few major exceptions for individual cases.

SOURCE: D. H. Thain, "Stages of Corporate Development," *Business Quarterly* (Winter 1969), p. 37. Copyright © 1969 by *Business Quarterly*. Reprinted by permission.

ILLUSTRATIVE EXAMPLE 8.2

Matching the Manager to the Appropriate Strategy and Stage of Corporate Development

What do Apple Computer, Wang Laboratories, Control Data Corporation, Ashton-Tate, Inc. and Lotus Development Corporation have in common—other than heavy involvement in computers and computer software? Answer: All are successful corporations that have recently made or are in the process of making a transition from an entrepreneur-managed Stage I small business to a professionally managed, Stage II corporation. In the case of **Apple Computer,** Chairman and co-founder Steven P. Jobs resigned from the company in 1985 after several years of management turmoil. After only eight years of existence, the two-man start-up had become a $2 billion company with 5,000 employees. The company grew either because of or in spite of spur-of-the-moment decisions by founders Jobs and Stephen Wozniak and fights by staff over competing projects. John Sculley, Jobs' handpicked successor as Chairman at Apple, restructured the company and introduced rules, strict financial controls, and product-development deadlines to go with his strategy of selling Apple Computers to business people. In selecting Sculley one of its "business people of the year," *Fortune* stated:

> What makes him one of the top business people of the year is his success in harnessing Apple's famous combination of blue-jeaned idealism and arrogance—and turning the company, once widely dismissed as a glorified toymaker, into a highly profitable producer of serious computers for the desktops of corporate America.

In the first two months after taking office as President of **Wang Laboratories, Inc.,** in 1986, Frederick Wang, son of founder An Wang, reorganized the company's marketing operation and began implementing a retrenchment strategy. The company had been faltering for two years while the founder had been unable to delegate operating authority for the running of his creation. Even though Wang Laboratories had excellent products, its lack of marketing skills was crippling its growth. "Wang couldn't sell life jackets on the Titanic," said Vincent Flanders, Associate Editor of *Access 87,* an independent magazine for Wang cus-

tomers, in comments on the company's marketing weakness under its founder.

By the time William C. Norris, the founder and Chief Executive Officer of **Control Data Corporation,** resigned from the company in 1986, there was a rising chorus of critics complaining that Norris had stayed too long. Through the late 1960s and 1970s, Control Data had been the world's leading maker of computer peripherals, like disk drives and other data-storage devices. Increased competition during the 1980s cut into the company's sales and profits—to the point that the company was being forced in 1985 to sell some of its businesses to raise cash. Just before Norris resigned, a banker involved with the debt negotiations stated, "They really need outside people—especially in the financial area. There's a sense that this management isn't prepared for the situation."

By the time Edward M. Esber, Jr., became CEO of **Ashton-Tate, Inc.,** in late 1984, most industry analysts had categorized the company as just another one-product software maker that couldn't evolve beyond its beginnings. Under its founder, George Tate, and his successor, David Cole, the company had made dBASE I, II, and III the world's largest selling database management program. Unfortunately, top management had failed to create a stable, well organized corporation. As the new CEO, Esber replaced Cole's charismatic and entrepreneurial one-man rule with a lower-key participatory approach. He also introduced formalized planning, budgeting, and product development procedures. Meetings about new products, once held at the chairman's whim, now took place every other week. Although turnover slowed in the company's managerial positions, the changes did cause the resignation in 1986 of Wayne Ratliff, the programmer who single-handedly wrote dBASE I, II, and most of III. Ratliff said his "distaste" for the corporate environment had been building for more than a year. "Corporations are more interested in keeping the corporation alive than generating quality products," com-

(Continued)

ILLUSTRATIVE EXAMPLE 8.2 (Continued)

mented Ratliff. "Ultimately, I like to sit back and work—write code. But the corporation is like a corpse you have to drag around." In response to the changes at Ashton-Tate and the departure of Ratliff, industry analyst William Shattuck concluded, "Historically, Wayne was a real critical force in the company, but at this stage of the game, given that you're dealing with a much more mature and larger company, the product-development effort is a more controlled, systematic process."

On July 10, 1986, Mitchell "Mitch" Kapor, founder and Chairman of **Lotus Development Corporation,** resigned unexpectedly and handed the chairman's position to Jim Manzi, a marketing-oriented consultant whom Kapor had hired earlier from McKinsey and Company to help manage the growing corporation. Kapor, widely regarded as a software "guru," had developed Lotus 1-2-3, the highly successful spreadsheet program—a product that accounted for more than 70% of the company's operating profits. Kapor had been turning over management responsibilities to

Manzi for the past year, a trend that was capped by Manzi's assumption of the chief executive office in April 1986. Commenting on his resignation, Kapor stated that he had been rethinking his role at Lotus for several months. He said that leaving a large company "is a natural evolution for founders and entrepreneurs." Five years ago, he added, "we were a small band setting out on a great adventure. Now we have 1,200 employees and two million customers. It's a radically different situation."

SOURCES: B. O'Reilly, "Growing Apple Anew For the Business Market," *Fortune* (January 4, 1988), pp. 36–37. A. Beam, "Strong Medicine From the Son of Doctor Wang," *Business Week* (January 19, 1987), p. 33. R. Gibson, "Control Data Betting Smaller Is Better," *Wall Street Journal* (December 3, 1985), p. 6. S. Ticer, "The Dark Horse Who Has Ashton-Tate Galloping Again," *Business Week* (February 10, 1986), pp. 89–92. G. Spector, "Wayne Ratliff, Writer of dBASE, Quits Ashton-Tate," *PC Week* (March 11, 1986), pp. 176 and 178. W. M. Bulkeley, "Kapor, Founder of Lotus Development, Resigns as Chairman of Software Firm," *Wall Street Journal* (July 11, 1986), p. 2.

the further development of corporations will be based on *networks* instead of hierarchies.[41] In such companies, span of communication using information technology can replace span of control. Instead of building large, but cumbersome vertically integrated companies, a number of firms are cultivating strategic relationships with outside vendors, that will give them the flexibility and adaptability they need for success. In arguing for the emergence of the **network organization,** Drake states:

> Organizations will increasingly be seen as flexible networks, expanding and cutting back in response to need. By using subcontractors, a company gains the freedom to cut off contracts or change vendors if the service level doesn't make the grade. Staff can be added or dropped quickly, increasing the firm's flexibility.[42]

The increasing use of joint ventures and quasi-vertical integration strategies, coupled with the popularity of just-in-time delivery using captive company suppliers, supports the proposal of the network organization as a fourth stage of corporate development.

Organizational Life-Cycle

Another approach to a better understanding of the development of corporations is that of the organizational "life cycle."[43] Instead of considering

TABLE 8.3
Blocks to Development

A) INTERNAL BLOCKS STAGE I TO II	STAGE II TO III
Lack of ambition and drive.	Unwillingness to take the risks involved.
Personal reasons of owner-manager for avoiding change in status quo.	Management resistance to change for a variety of reasons including old age, aversion to risk taking, desire to protect personal empires, etc.
Lack of operating efficiency.	
Lack of quantity and quality of operating personnel.	
Lack of resources such as borrowing power, plant and equipment, salesmen, etc.	Personal reasons among managers for defending the status quo.
	Lack of control system related to appraisal of investment of decentralized operations.
Product problems and weaknesses.	Lack of budgetary control ability.
Lack of planning and organizational ability.	Organizational inflexibility.
	Lack of management vision to see opportunities for expansion.
	Lack of management development, i.e., not enough managers to handle expansion.
	Management turnover and loss of promising young managers.
	Lack of ability to formulate and implement strategy that makes company relevant to changing conditions.
	Refusal to delegate power and authority for diversification.

B) EXTERNAL BLOCKS STAGE I TO II	STAGE II TO III
Unfavorable economic conditions.	Unfavorable economic, political, technological, and social conditions and/or trends.
Lack of market growth.	
Tight money or lack of an underwriter who will assist the company "to go public."	Lack of access to financial or management resources.
	Overly conservative accountants, lawyers, investment bankers, etc.
Labor shortages in quality and quantity.	Lack of domestic markets necessary to support large diversified corporation.
Technological obsolescence of product.	"The conservative mentality," e.g., cultural contentment with the status quo and lack of desire to grow and develop.

SOURCE: D. H. Thain, "Stages of Corporate Development," *Business Quarterly* (Winter 1969), pp. 43–44. Copyright © 1969 by *Business Quarterly*. Reprinted by permission.

stages in terms of structure, this approach places the primary emphasis on the dominant issue facing the corporation. The specific organizational structure, therefore, becomes a secondary concern. These stages are *Birth* (Stage I), *Growth* (Stage II), *Maturity* (Stage III), *Decline* (Stage IV), and *Death* (Stage V). The impact of these stages on corporate strategy and structure is summarized in Table 8.4. Note that the first three stages of the organizational life cycle are basically the same as the three stages of corporate development mentioned previously. The only significant difference is the addition of the decline and death stages to complete the cycle.

Miller and Friesen place a *Revival* phase between Maturity and Decline; this reflects how the corporation's life cycle can be extended by innovations in a manner similar to the extension of a product's life-cycle. Nevertheless, revival is not included here as a separate stage because it can occur anytime during a corporation's maturity stage, when a new growth strategy is implemented, or during its decline stage, when a turnaround strategy is being followed.

The Stage IV firm became widespread in the western world during the 1970s and 1980s as many corporations in basic industries such as steel and automobiles seemed to lose their vitality and competitiveness. Most of the product lines of a Stage IV firm are at the mature or declining phase of their product life-cycle. Sales are stagnant and actually declining if adjusted for inflation. An emphasis on company-wide cost-cutting further erodes future competitiveness. The major objective changes from stability to survival. Retrenchment coupled with pleas for government assistance is the only feasible strategy. Chrysler Corporation was a good example of a Stage IV corporation in the early 1980s.

Unless a corporation is able to resolve the critical issues facing it in Stage IV (as Chrysler was able to do), it is likely to move into Stage V, corporate death. This is what happened in the mid-1980s to AM International (pre-

TABLE 8.4
Organizational Life Cycle

	STAGE I	STAGE II	STAGE III	STAGE IV	STAGE V
Dominant issue	Birth	Growth	Maturity	Decline	Death
Popular strategies	Concentration in a niche	Horizontal and vertical integration	Concentric and conglomerate diversification	Profit strategy followed by retrenchment	Liquidation or bankruptcy
Likely structure	Entrepreneur-dominated	Functional management emphasized	Decentralization into profit or investment centers	Structural surgery	Dismemberment of structure

viously known as the Addressograph-Multigraph Corporation), Baldwin-United, and Osborne Computers, as well as many other firms. The corporation is forced into bankruptcy. As in the cases of Rolls Royce and Penn Central, both of which went bankrupt in the 1970s, a corporation might nevertheless rise like a phoenix from its own ashes and live again. The company may be reorganized or liquidated, depending upon the individual circumstances. In some liquidations, the corporation's name is purchased, and the purchasing corporation places that name on some or all of its products. For example, Wordtronix, a maker of stand-alone word processors, acquired the Remington Rand trademark, even though Remington Rand no longer made typewriters. Top management planned to change the Word-tronix name to Remington Rand to give its machines some name recognition in the marketplace.

It is important to realize that not all corporations will move through these five stages in order. Some corporations, for example, might never move past Stage II. Others, like General Motors, might go directly from Stage I to Stage III. A large number will go from Stage I into Stages IV and V. Ford, for example, was unable to move from Stage I into Stage II as long as Henry Ford, I was in command. Its inability to realign itself no doubt contributed to its movement into Stage IV just before World War II. After the war, Henry Ford, II's turnaround strategy successfully restructured the corporation as a Stage II firm. With the death of Henry Ford, II, and the ascent of Donald Peterson to the chairman's position, Ford Motor Company might be ready to diversify and move into a mature Stage III configuration during the 1990s with more decentralized decision making.

Staffing

The implementation of new strategy and policies often calls for a different utilization of personnel. If growth strategies are to be implemented, new people need to be hired and trained. Experienced people with the necessary skills need to be found for promotion into newly created managerial positions. For example, if a firm has decided to integrate forward by opening its own retail outlets, one key concern is the ability of the corporation to find, hire, and train store managers. If a corporation adopts a retrenchment strategy, however, a large number of people may need to be laid off or fired; and top management, as well as the divisional managers, need to specify criteria used in the making of these personnel decisions. Should employees be fired on the basis of low seniority or on the basis of poor performance? Sometimes corporations find it easier to close an entire division than to choose which individuals to fire.

A change in competitive strategy can also have a significant impact on staffing needs. For example, J. C. Penney decided in 1986 to decentralize its purchasing down to the store level so that store managers would have greater opportunity to buy the merchandise most suited to regional needs.

Although it seemed that this strategy would help Penney to better compete with local stores, top management was concerned with implementation. Instead of a corporate buyer purchasing entire lines of merchandise and forcing all stores to carry them, the buyer now presented the items on Penney's satellite television network, and gave local buyers the opportunity to choose all the lines, some of the lines, or none of the lines. Penney's top management and suppliers feared that some local buyers weren't experienced enough to spot potentially popular fashion trends. The job of the corporate buyer had also become riskier. "Their job is going to be selling merchandise on television," said a Penney official. "You may buy good products but might not be able to sell. If the person showing the merchandise turns you off, you as a buyer in Omaha may not go for the line." Although Penney officials denied that a lack of TV skills would cost corporate buyers their jobs, the company considered using video screen-tests to help select future buyers.[44]

Some authorities have suggested that the type of general manager needed to effectively implement a new divisional, corporate, or SBU strategy depends upon the desired strategic direction of that business unit.[45] Illustrative Example 8.3 tells how this approach was followed by the board of AM International in their selecting the corporation's chief executive officer.

Depending on the situation of a specific division, as determined by the GE Business Screen Matrix (Fig. 6.3), the "best" or most appropriate division manager might need to have a specific mix of skills and experiences. Some of these suggested "types" are depicted in Fig. 8.3.

One research study of business executives found that strategic business units with a "build" strategy as compared to SBUs with a "harvest" strategy tend to be headed by managers with a great willingness to take risks and a high tolerance for ambiguity.[46] Another study also found that managers with a particular mix of behaviors, skills, and personality factors tend to be linked with one type of strategy and those with a different mix, to a different type of strategy. For example, SBUs with a stability strategy tend to be run by a manager with a conservative style, a production or engineering background, and experience with controlling budgets, capital expenditures, inventories, and standardization procedures.[47] In summary, there is growing support for matching executive "types" with the dominant strategic direction of a business unit. Unfortunately, there is little available to help top management or the board select the most appropriate manager when a corporation or SBU does not have a specific strategy formulated for that manager to implement. In this instance, the board of directors has no choice; they must search for a person with a proven capability to exercise initiative and leadership in the industry, and hope that the person selected can lead the board and other managers in formulating and implementing a strategy.[48]

Research into the value of selecting a CEO from outside the company as compared to promoting someone already with the company has mixed conclusions. Some studies report that the top performing companies hire

ILLUSTRATIVE EXAMPLE 8.3

AM International Matches the Manager to the Strategy

The board of directors of AM International followed the theory that the general manager should match the firm's desired strategy, when it both hired and fired Joe B. Freeman as the corporation's chief executive officer. Hired originally when the company filed for Chapter 11 bankruptcy in April 1982, Freeman worked hard to turn the firm around. He concentrated on cutting costs, boosting sales, and soothing both creditors and employees. By January 1984, the corporation was beginning to show a profit—and Joe B. Freeman was fired by the board. Looking back on the experience, Freeman admitted that some of the problem had been with his analytically oriented accounting background:

"The company had reached a new phase. My skills had been successful in bringing it to this phase but the board wanted a person with a different set of skills to lead it. . . . [The board wanted] an orientation toward business strategy and people skills. . . . I chose to devote most of my time to managing the company, to working with the creditors, and didn't spend much time on the image side with shareholders and directors."

SOURCE: R. Johnson, "AM International's Ex-Chief Freeman Tells How His Success Got Him Fired," *Wall Street Journal* (August 27, 1984), p. 21.

their CEOs from within; however, other studies report that the percentage of CEOs hired from outside the corporation is higher for prosperous firms than for firms in decline. Another study reports that the incidence of outsiders becoming CEOs of failing (bankrupt) firms is higher than that of solvent firms.[49] Obviously, more research is needed before any clear conclusion can be reached.

There are a number of ways that a continuous development of people for important managerial positions can be ensured. One approach is to establish a sound **performance appraisal system** to identify good performers with managerial potential. A survey of thirty-four corporate planners and human resource executives from twenty-four large U.S. corporations revealed that approximately 80% made some attempt to identify managers' talents and behavioral tendencies, so that they could find a manager with a likely fit to a given competitive strategy.[50] A number of large organizations are using **assessment centers** to evaluate a person's suitability for a management position. Popularized by AT&T in the mid-1950s, corporations such as Standard Oil of Ohio and GE now use them. Because each is specifically tailored to its corporation, these assessment centers are unique. They use special interviews, management games, in-basket exercises, leaderless group discussions, case analyses, decision-making exercises, and oral presentations to assess the potential of employees for higher-level positions. People's promotions into specific positions are based on their performances in the assessment center. Many assessment centers have proved to be highly predictive of subsequent managerial performance.[51]

FIGURE 8.3
The Types of General Managers Needed to Strategically Manage
Different Types of Businesses

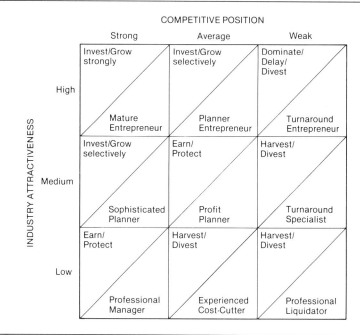

Source: Adapted from C. W. Hofer and M. J. Davoust, *Successful Strategic Management* (Chicago: A. T. Kearney, Inc., 1977), pp. 45 and 82. Used by permission.

The implementation of strategy should be concerned not only with the selection of strategic managers, but also with the selection of the appropriate mix of professional, skilled, and unskilled labor. At IBM, for example, top management decided in 1984 to emphasize software development in its reach for corporate growth objectives. Key divisions were then directed to expand their programming staffs by 20% per year for the next ten years.[52] Research reveals that corporations that pursue related diversification strategies through internal development make greater use of interdivisional transfers of people than do companies that grow through unrelated acquisitions. Apparently, the companies that grow internally attempt to transfer important knowledge and skills throughout the corporation, so that some sort of managerial synergy is achieved.[53]

Directing

To effectively implement a new strategy, top management must delegate appropriate authority and responsibility to the operational managers. People

Incentive Management

To ensure that there is a congruence between the needs of the corporation as a whole and the needs of the employees as individuals, managers should develop an incentive system that rewards desired performance. Research confirms the conventional wisdom that when pay is tied to performance, it motivates higher productivity, and strongly affects both absenteeism and work quality.[59] Corporations have, therefore, developed various types of incentives for executives that range from stock options to cash bonuses. All these incentive plans should be linked in some way to corporate and divisional strategy. Ansoff, an authority on strategic management, proposes that one of the key means of changing corporate culture is by changing formal and informal rewards and incentives.[60] Performance appraisal and incentive systems are discussed in more detail under "Evaluation and Control," Chapter 9.

SUMMARY AND CONCLUSION

This chapter explains the implementation of strategy in terms of (1) *who* the operational managers are who must carry out strategic plans, (2) *what* they must do in order to implement strategy, and (3) *how* they should go about their activities. Vice-presidents of functional areas and directors of divisions or SBUs work with their subordinates to put together large-scale implementation plans. These plans include *programs, budgets,* and *procedures* and become more detailed as they move down the corporate "chain of command."

Strategy is implemented by management through planning, organizing, staffing, and directing activities.

Planning results in fairly detailed programs, budgets, and procedures.

Organizing deals with the design of an appropriate structure for the corporation. Research generally supports Chandler's proposal that changes in corporate strategy tend to lead to changes in organizational structure. The growing use of strategic business units, matrix structures, and entrepreneurial units reflects a need for more flexible structures to manage increasingly diversified corporations. Not only should a firm work to make its structure congruent with its strategy, it should also be aware that there is an organizational life-cycle composed of stages of corporate development through which a corporation is likely to move.

Staffing focuses on the finding and developing of appropriate people for key positions. Without capable and committed managers and staff, strategy can never be implemented satisfactorily. To survey and develop candidates, performance appraisal systems and assessment centers are used by a number of large corporations.

Directing deals with organization-wide approaches that direct operational managers and employees to effect the implementation of corporate, business, and functional strategies. One such approach is Management By Objectives (MBO), which links organizational objectives and the behavior of operational managers. Its ability to tie planning with performance makes it a powerful implementation technique. The proper use of incentives, when integrated with a change in corporate culture or with a goal-centered approach such as MBO, is another method by which effort is directed toward the desired results.

DISCUSSION QUESTIONS

1. Japanese corporations typically involve many more organizational levels and people in the development of implementation plans than do U.S. corporations. Is this appropriate? Why or why not?

2. To what extent should top management be involved in strategy implementation?

3. Does structure follow strategy or does strategy follow stucture? Why?

4. What can be done to encourage innovation in large corporations?

5. Should a corporation's selection of a certain type of person to be a general manager of a division depend on the strategic situation of that particular division? Why or why not?

6. Suppose a successful entrepreneur is creating problems for the corporation by continuing a one-person rule long after it is appropriate. If the founder owns a majority of the stock in the company, what could concerned people (employees, other stockholders, board members, other managers, customers, creditors, among others) do about this Stage I entrepreneur mismanaging his/her own Stage II corporation?

7. Do you agree with the way CSX structured itself for 1986, as described in the Integrative Case at the end of this chapter? What are the pros and cons of the 1986 organization structure depicted in Figure 8.5?

8. Even with the 1986 restructuring as described in the Integrative Case, what implementation problems did CSX still have to overcome? What could have been done to resolve them?

NOTES

1. P. Houston, "Northwest's Merger Has Passengers Fuming," *Business Week* (November 24, 1986), p. 64.

2. L. D. Alexander, "Successfully Implementing Strategic Decisions," *Long Range Planning* (June 1985), p. 92.

3. J. R. Galbraith and R. K. Kazanjian, *Strategy Implementation: Structure, Systems, and Process*, 2nd ed. (St. Paul: West Publishing Co., 1986), p. 108.

P. Miesing, "Integrating Planning with Management," *Long Range Planning* (October 1984), pp. 118–124.

4. A. D. Chandler, *Strategy and Structure* (Cambridge, Mass.: MIT Press, 1962), p. 14.

5. O. E. Williamson, "The Multidivisional Structure," in *Markets and Hierarchies* (The Free Press, 1975), as reprinted in *Organizational Economics* by J. B. Barney and W. G. Ouchi (eds.) (San Francisco, Jossey-Bass, 1986), pp. 163–187.

6. A. P. Sloan, Jr., *My Years with General Motors* (Garden City, N.Y.: Doubleday & Company, 1964).

7. D. Miller, "Strategy Making and Structure: Analysis and Implications for Performance," *Academy of Management Journal* (March 1987), pp. 7–32.

Galbraith and Kazanjian, pp. 13–27.

P. Lorange, *Implementation of Strategic Planning* (Englewood Cliffs, N.J.: Prentice-Hall, 1982), p. 109.

L. G. Hrebiniak and W. F. Joyce, *Implementing Strategy* (New York: Macmillan, 1984), pp. 65–92.

8. Galbraith and Kazanjian, p. 45.

9. R. E. Hoskisson, "Multidivisional Structure and Performance: The Contingency of Diversification Strategy," *Academy of Management Journal* (December 1987), pp. 625–644.

R. E. Hoskisson and C. S. Galbraith, "The Effect of Quantum Versus Incremental M-form Reorganization on Performance: A Time-Series Exploration of Intervention Dynamics," *Journal of Management* (Fall-Winter 1985), pp. 55–70.

D. J. Teece, "Internal Organization and Economic Performance: An Empirical Analysis of the Profitability of Principal Firms," *The Journal of Industrial Economics*, Vol. 30 (1981), pp. 173–199.

10. R. E. White, "Generic Business Strategies, Organizational Context and Performance: An Empirical Investigation," *Strategic Management Journal* (May-June 1986), pp. 217–231.

A. K. Gupta, "SBU Strategies, Corporate–SBU Relations, and SBU Effectiveness in Strategy Implementation," *Academy of Management Journal* (September 1987), pp. 477–500.

11. Galbraith and Kazanjian, p. 24.

12. D. R. Dalton, W. D. Todor, M. J. Spendolini, G. J. Fielding, and L. W. Porter, "Organization Structure and Performance: A Critical Review," *Academy of Management Review* (January 1980), pp. 49–64.

13. Hrebiniak and Joyce, p. 70.

14. Galbraith and Kazajian, pp. 67–68.

15. T. Burns and G. M. Stalker, *The Management of Innovation* (London: Tavistock Publications, 1961).

16. P. R. Lawrence and J. W. Lorsch, *Organization and*

Environment (Homewood, Ill.: Richard D. Irwin, Inc., 1967), p. 138.

17. William K. Hall, "SBUs: Hot New Topic in the Management of Diversification," *Business Horizons* (February 1978), p. 19.

18. "Evolving the GE Management System," *General Electric Monogram* (November-December 1977), p. 4.

19. R. G. Hamermesh, *Making Strategy Work* (New York: John Wiley and Sons, 1986), p. 91.

20. M. E. Porter, *Competitive Advantage* (New York: The Free Press, 1985), pp. 395–398 and p. 322.

21. Hrebiniak and Joyce, pp. 85–86.

22. E. W. Larson and D. H. Gobeli, "Matrix Management: Contradictions and Insights," *California Management Review* (Summer 1987), pp. 131–132.

23. P. G. W. Keen, "Communications in the 21st Century: Telecommunications and Business Policy," *Organizational Dynamics* (Autumn 1981), pp. 54–67.

24. A. L. Frohman, "Technology as a Competitive Weapon," *Harvard Business Review* (January-February 1982), p. 97.

25. P. F. Drucker, *Innovation and Entrepreneurship* (New York: Harper & Row, 1985), pp. 161–170.

J. R. Galbraith, "Human Resource Policies for the Innovating Organization," in *Strategic Human Resources Management*, edited by C. J. Fombrun, N. M. Tichy, and M. A. Devanna (New York: John Wiley and Sons, 1984), pp. 319–341.

P. Strebel, "Organizing for Innovation Over an Industry Cycle," *Strategic Management Journal* (March-April 1987), pp. 117–124.

26. R. A. Burgelman, "Designs for Corporate Entrepreneurship," *California Management Review* (Spring 1984), pp. 154–166.

27. G. Pinchot, *Intrapreneuring, or Why You Don't Have to Leave the Corporation to Become an Entrepreneur* (New York: Harper & Row, 1985) as reported by J. S. DeMott, "Here Come the Intrapreneurs," *Time* (February 4, 1985), pp. 36–37.

28. "How Xerox Speeds Up the Birth of New Products," *Business Week* (March 19, 1984), pp. 58–59.

29. J. T. Wilson, "Strategic Planning at R. J. Reynolds Industries," *Journal of Business Strategy* (Fall 1985), p. 26.

30. R. Koenig, "P&G Establishes Division to Manage Fat Substitute Line," *Wall Street Journal* (September 9, 1987), p. 20.

31. C. Dolan, "Tektronix New-Venture Subsidiary Brings Benefits to Parent, Spinoffs," *Wall Street Journal* (September 18, 1984), p. 31.

32. U. Gupta, "The Perils of a Corporate Entrepreneur," *Wall Street Journal* (September 10, 1987), p. 35.

33. N. W. Miller, "Art of 'Strategic Partnerships' Is Refined by California Firm," *Wall Street Journal* (December 6, 1985), p. 25.

34. D. H. Thain "Stages of Corporate Development,"

The Business Quarterly (Winter 1969), pp. 32–45.

B. R. Scott, "Stages of Corporate Development" (Boston: Intercollegiate Case Clearing House, no. 9-371-294, 1971); and "The Industrial State: Old Myths and New Realities," *Harvard Business Review* (March-April 1973).

R. V. Tuason, "Corporate Life Cycle and the Evaluation of Corporate Strategy," *Proceedings, The Academy of Management* (August 1973), pp. 35–40.

35. W. M. Bulkeley, "As Polaroid Matures, Some Lament a Decline in Creative Excitement," *Wall Street Journal* (May 10, 1983), p. 1.

36. L. E. Greiner, "Evolution and Revolution as Organizations Grow," *Harvard Business Review* (July-August 1972), pp. 37–46.

37. M. J. Williams, "McDonald's Refuses to Plateau," *Fortune* (November 12, 1984), p. 40.

38. N. R. Smith and J. B. Miner, "Type of Entrepreneur, Type of Firm, and Managerial Motivation: Implications for Organizational Life Cycle Theory," *Strategic Management Journal* (October-December 1983), pp. 325–340.

F. Hoy, B. C. Vaught, and W. W. Buchanan, "Managing Managers of Firms in Transition from Stage I to Stage II," *Proceedings, Southern Management Association* (November 1982), pp. 152–153.

K. Smith and T. Mitchell, "An Investigation into the Effect of Changes in Stages of Organizational Maturation on a Decision Maker's Decision Priorities," *Proceedings, Southern Management Association* (November 1983), pp. 7–9.

39. K. G. Smith and J. K. Harrison, "In Search of Excellent Leaders," in *Handbook of Business Strategy, 1986/87 Yearbook,* edited by W. D. Guth (Boston: Warren, Gorham & Lamont, 1986), p. 27.8.

40. Galbraith and Kazanjian, pp. 153–154.

41. J. Child, "Information Technology, Organization, and the Response to Strategic Challenges," *California Management Review* (Fall 1987), pp. 33–50.

R. L. Drake, "Innovative Structures for Managing Change," *Planning Review* (November 1986), pp. 18–22.

42. Drake, p. 22.

43. D. Miller and P. H. Friesen, "A Longitudinal Study of the Corporate Life Cycle," *Management Science* (October 1984), pp. 1161–1183.

J. R. Kimberly, R. H. Miles, and Associates, *The Organizational Life Cycle* (San Francisco: Jossey-Bass, 1980).

44. H. Gilman, "J. C. Penney Decentralizes Its Purchasing," *Wall Street Journal* (May 8, 1986), p. 6.

45. T. T. Herbert and H. Deresky, "Should General Managers Match Their Business Strategies?" *Organizational Dynamics* (Winter 1987), pp. 40–51.

R. Chaganti and R. Sambharya, "Strategic Orientation and Characteristics of Upper Management," *Strategic Management Journal* (July-August 1987), pp. 393–401.

M. Leontiades, "Choosing the Right Manager to Fit the Strategy," *Journal of Business Strategy* (Fall 1982), pp. 58–69.

J. G. Wissema, H. W. Van Der Pol, and H. M. Messer, "Strategic Management Archetypes," *Strategic Management*

Journal (January-March 1980), pp. 37–47.

A. D. Szilagyi, Jr. and D. M. Schweiger, "Matching Managers to Strategies: A Review and Suggested Framework," *Academy of Management Review* (October 1984), pp. 626–637.

46. A. K. Gupta and V. Govindarajan, "Business Unit Strategy, Managerial Characteristics, and Business Unit Effectiveness at Strategy Implementation," *Academy of Management Journal* (March 1984), p. 36.

47. Herbert and Deresky, pp. 43–45.

48. W. F. McCanna and T. E. Comte, "The CEO Succession Dilemma: How Boards Function in Turnover at the Top," *Business Horizons* (May-June 1986), pp. 17–22.

49. D. R. Dalton and I. F. Kesner, "Organizational Performance as An Antecedent of Inside/Outside Chief Executive Succession: An Empirical Assessment," *Academy of Management Journal* (December 1985), pp. 749–762.

R. S. Schuler and S. E. Jackson, "Linking Competitive Strategies with Human Resource Management Practices," *Academy of Management Executive* (August 1987), pp. 207–219.

K. H. Chung, R. C. Rogers, M. Lubatkin, and J. E. Owers, "Do Insiders Make Better CEOs Than Outsiders?" *Academy of Management Executive* (November 1987), pp. 323–329.

K. B. Schwartz and K. Menon, "Executive Succession in Failing Firms," *Academy of Management Journal* (September 1985), pp. 680–686.

50. P. Lorange and D. Murphy, "Bringing Human Resources Into Strategic Planning: System Design Characteristics," in *Strategic Human Resource Management*, ed. C. J. Fombrun, N. M. Tichy, and M. A. Devanna (New York: Wiley and Sons, 1984), pp. 281–283.

51. H. G. Heneman, III, D. P. Schwab, J. A. Fossum, L. D. Dyer, *Personnel/Human Resources Management*, 3rd edition (Homewood, Illinois: Irwin, Inc., 1986), pp. 351–353.

52. M. A. Harris, "IBM: More Worlds to Conquer," *Business Week* (February 18, 1985), p. 85.

53. R. A. Pitts, "Strategies and Structures for Diversification," *Academy of Management Journal* (June 1977), pp. 197–208.

54. P. Shrivastava and W. D. Guth, "The Culture-Strategy Grid," in *Handbook of Business Strategy, 1985/86 Yearbook*, ed. W. D. Guth (Boston: Warren, Gorham, and Lamont, 1985), pp. 2.18–2.19.

55. S. J. Carroll, Jr. and H. L. Tosi, Jr., *Management by Objectives* (New York: Macmillan, 1973), p. 3.

56. M. D. Richards, *Setting Strategic Goals and Objectives*, 2nd ed. (St. Paul: West Publishing Co., 1986), pp. 122–123.

57. E. J. Seyna, "MBO: The Fad That Changed Management," *Long Range Planning* (December 1986), pp. 116–123.

58. Galbraith and Kazanjian, p. 120.

59. E. E. Lawler III, *Pay and Organizational Effectiveness* (New York: McGraw-Hill, 1971).

E. A. Locke, "How to Motivate Employees" (Paper presented at the NATO conference on changes in the nature and quality of working life, Thessaloniki, Greece, August 19–24, 1979.) Cited in E. E. Lawler III, *Pay and Organizational Development* (Reading Mass.: Addison-Wesley, 1981), p. 3.

60. H. I. Ansoff, "Strategic Managment of Technology," *Journal of Business Strategy* (Winter 1987), p. 37.

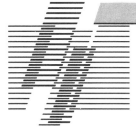

INTEGRATIVE CASE

CSX CORPORATION'S STRATEGY IMPLEMENTATION

In early 1985, CSX Corporation had been composed of a set of independently managed subsidiaries, organized as business groups in transportation and natural resources segments (See Fig. 5.5 in Chapter 5). CSX's top management, however, faced a real problem in the management of these operations so as to gain some synergy. The current organizational chart reflected nothing more than a quick attempt to somehow patch the units together into what was hoped would become one multimodal transportation (and natural resources) company.

CORPORATE CULTURE

Because CSX Corporation had grown from acquisitions, each of the business units had its own distinctive culture and way of structuring its work activities. American Commercial Barge Lines, for example, had a river-going culture that traditionally looked upon the railroad as an enemy, not as something with which to cooperate and to share revenues. Even railroaders from the Chessie and Seaboard systems—

the two rail lines that originally formed CSX—had difficulty working together. From the very beginnings of CSX in 1980, corporate top management had bent over backwards to assure that the company was a true "partnership of equals." Corporate headquarters had been established in Richmond, Virginia, partly because of its closeness to Washington, D. C., and partially because it was halfway between Cleveland (Chessie's headquarters) and Jacksonville (Seaboard's headquarters). Although some integration of activities had been achieved, by and large the two rail systems continued to function autonomously as independent profit centers. Each maintained its own corporate headquarters staff, marketing, and sales teams. Consequently, CSX rail operations were not so efficient as those of its major competitor, Norfolk Southern.

REORGANIZATION

Finally, in December, 1985, the company adopted a plan for the reorganization and restructuring of CSX's business units. The restructuring resulted in a $954 million pre-tax special charge and reduced net earnings in 1985 by $560 million. The special charge included a provision of $327 million for separation pay liabilities, a $533 million write-down to net realizable value of a number of marginal and unproductive assets, and a provision of $94 million related to reorganization expenses, litigation costs, and other claims. The provision for separation pay liabilities was for a workforce reduction of 6,700 employee positions.

The organizational chart was radically altered. The Chessie and Seaboard rail systems were reorganized into three operating units: Distribution Services (marketing/sales), Equipment (freight-car maintenance and management), and Transportation (maintenance and management of track and locomotives). The Chessie and Seaboard systems were fully integrated. No more attempts were made to keep separate identities. Even the famous "Chessie the cat" logo of the old C&O line was eliminated and replaced by the letters "CSX" on all rail equipment. The R.F.&P. continued to be operated separately as a rail link between the old Chessie and Seaboard systems, for legal reasons and because of its ownership of key real estate in the Richmond and Washington, D. C., areas.

CSX's new corporate structure was now composed of four strategic groups—Transportation, Energy, Properties, and Technology. As shown in Figure 8.5, the three rail operating units, plus R.F.&P. and American Commercial Barge Lines, were placed in the **Transportation Group** of CSX. Sea-Land, acquired by CSX in April 1986, was also placed in that segment, even though the merger application was still being considered by the Interstate Commerce Commission. By year-end 1986, ACL and Sea-Land continued to be managed separately, primarily because of ICC anti-trust concerns. Deciding against a presence in air transportation, CSX sold Beckett Aviation.

The **Energy Group** included Texas Gas Transmission, a 6,000-mile pipeline system, and CSX Oil and Gas, an exploration and production unit (formerly Texas Gas Exploration Corporation). By year-end 1986, nearly all of CSX's coal properties and mineral rights had been sold.

The creation of a **Properties Group** signaled a change in the corporation's strategy for real estate and highlighted its potential for growth. Like other railroads, CSX

FIGURE 8.5
CSX Corporation's New Corporate Structure

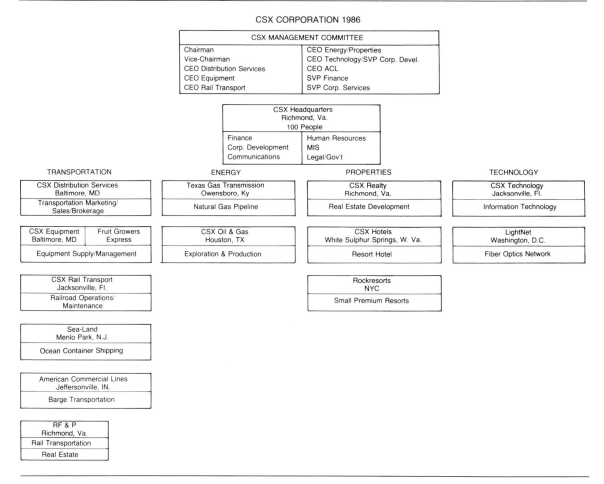

Source: Courtesy of R. Barth Strempek, CSX Corporation.

had historically used real estate as cash in the bank. In the United States, railroads had traditionally either bought or were given (by the government) large areas of undeveloped land on which they placed rails and built transportation depots and maintenance facilities. To finance further expansion, the railroads could then sell unused land. This was the U. S. federal government's approach to encourage nationwide railroad development in the 1800s. CSX's management concluded that although its previous land strategy had provided a good return on its investment for little risk, it offered only a limited opportunity for the company to capitalize on long-term growth prospects in real estate. Consequently, the Properties Group was formed to consolidate a billion-dollar inventory of properties and to examine opportunities in the real estate market. In addition to CSX Realty were CSX Hotels, which owned and operated The Greenbrier resort hotel, and Rockresorts, an April 1986 purchase that owned or managed small premium resorts such as Caneel Bay and Little Dix Bay in the Caribbean, and The Boulders in Arizona. CSX Hotels also had interests in the New Orleans Hilton and the Montgomery, Alabama Sheraton Hotel.

The **Technology Group** included CSX Technology, which combined Chessie Computer Services, Inc. and Cybernetics and Systems, Inc. One of its tasks was to assist other parts of CSX in the development and installation of modern communication and information systems. Examples of its work were an advanced fleet distribution and utilization system developed for CSX Equipment, and a national telemarketing center that provided comprehensive sales coverage to CSX Distribution Services. This telecommunications center enabled CSX sales people to move away from the use of traditional railroad sales techniques to logistics consulting for shippers. These uses of technology were crucial as CSX attempted to better integrate its operations and become a true "one-stop shipper." Also in the Technology Group was Lightnet, a CSX joint venture with Southern New England Telecommunications. It was expected that by the end of 1987 Lightnet would serve more than thirty major U.S. urban markets over its 5,000-mile system, offering customers quality, high-speed data transmission over a cable network.

Impact of Reorganization

Hays T. Watkins, CSX Chairman and Chief Executive Officer, was optimistic about CSX's ability to manage these businesses. In discussing the reorganization, he stated in December 1985 that "the actions will have a very positive effect on future cash flow, earnings, and rates of return."[1] In particular, a $327 million program designed to entice employees to take early retirement, was expected to produce savings of more then $650 million over the next five years. Regarding the Sea-Land acquisition, Watkins predicted a "new era in the transportation industry and a new generation of transportation services." Customers, he said, "want to make one call for the whole haul and we are committed to making that concept a reality around the globe."[2]

Others, however, were not quite so optimistic. Analysts felt that Sea-Land was a risky bet for CSX because it made the corporation even more difficult to manage. Unless CSX could develop the synergy its top management was working toward, lower-cost carriers like Norfolk Southern could threaten CSX's competitive position. The chances were very good that the highly competitive rail-transportation companies in the eastern U.S. would continue to battle for market share for the near future regardless of Conrail's situation. Merging the different cultures of the three rail systems, a barge line, and Sea-Land would certainly be a significant chore. John Snow, who took over as President and Chief Executive Officer of the Transportation Group in 1987, remarked, "My job is to keep peace in the family." Pointing to the American Commerical Lines acquisition, Snow said that the rail-barge combination has helped to change an "atmosphere of suspicion and mistrust" that had undermined efforts to make railroad-to-barge connections. By 1986, the percentage of American Commercial Lines tonnage being transferred to CSX rail lines had increased to 5% from only 2% in 1982.[3]

NOTES

1. D. Machalaba, "CSX Announces Major Restructuring, Will Take $954 Million Pre-Tax Charge," *Wall Street Journal* (December 12, 1985), p. 6.

2. L. McGinley, "CSX's Purchase of Sea-Land Gets Go-Ahead," *Wall Street Journal* (February 12, 1987), p. 4.

3. R. Koenig, "At CSX, Snow Gets His Show on the Road," *Wall Street Journal* (April 8, 1987), p. 36.

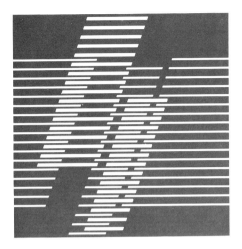

CHAPTER 9

EVALUATION AND CONTROL

STRATEGIC MANAGEMENT MODEL

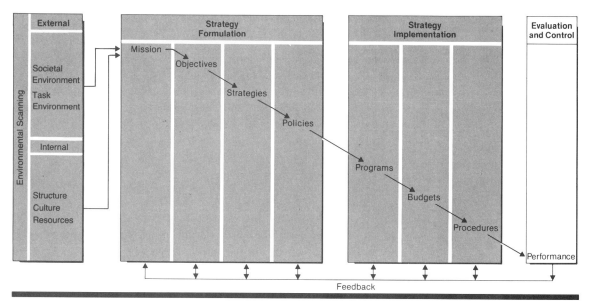

The last part of the strategic management model is the evaluation of performance and the control of work activities. Control follows planning. It ensures that the corporation is achieving what it set out to accomplish. Just as planning involves the setting of objectives along with the strategies and programs necessary to accomplish them, the control process compares performance with desired results and provides the feedback necessary for management to evaluate results and take corrective action, as needed.[1] This process can be viewed as a five-step feedback model, as depicted in Fig. 9.1.

1. **Determine what to measure.** Top managers as well as operational managers need to specify what implementation processes and results will be monitored and evaluated. The processes and results must be capable of being measured in a reasonably objective and consistent manner. The focus should be on the most significant elements in a process—the ones that account for the highest proportion of expense or the greatest number of problems.

2. **Establish standards of performance.** Standards used to measure performance are detailed expressions of strategic objectives. They are *measures* of acceptable performance results. Each standard usually includes a *tolerance range* within which deviations accepted as satisfactory are defined. Standards can be set not only for final output, but also for intermediate stages of production output.

3. **Measure actual performance.** Measurements must be made at predetermined times.

FIGURE 9.1
Evaluation and Control Process

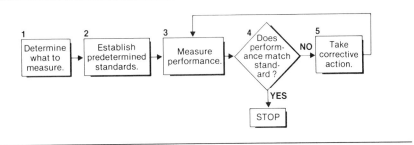

4. **Compare actual performance with the standard.** If actual performance results are within the desired tolerance range, the measurement process stops here.

5. **Take corrective action.** If actual results fall outside the desired tolerance range, action must be taken to correct the deviation. The following must be determined:

   a) Is the deviation only a chance fluctuation?

   b) Are the processes being carried out incorrectly?

   c) Are the processes appropriate to the achievement of the desired standard?

   Action must be taken that will not only correct the deviation, but also prevent its happening again.

The strategic management model shows that evaluation and control information is fed back and assimilated into the entire management process. This information consists of performance data and activity reports (gathered in step 3 of Fig. 9.1). If undesired performance is the result of an inappropriate *use* of the strategic management processes, operational managers must know about it so that they can correct the employee activity. Top management need not be involved. If, however, undesired performance results from the processes themselves, top managers, as well as operational managers, must know about it so that they can develop new implementation programs or procedures.

Lorange, Morton, and Ghoshal, in their book on strategic control, propose three types of control: strategic, tactical, and operational. **Strategic control** deals with the basic strategic direction of the corporation in terms of its relationship with its environment. **Tactical control,** in contrast, deals primarily with the implementation of the strategic plan. **Operational control** deals with near-term corporate activities.[2] Lorange, Morton, and Ghoshal further suggest that just as there is a hierarchy of strategy, there is also a **hierarchy of control,** as depicted in Figure 9.2. At the corporate level, control

FIGURE 9.2
Hierarchy of Control

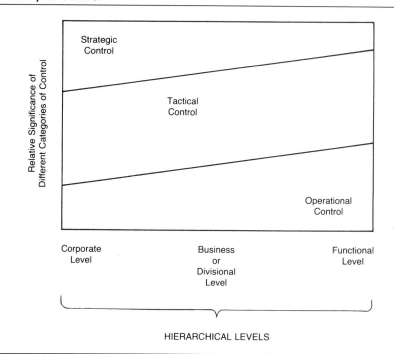

focuses on maintaining a balance among the various activities of the corporation as a whole. Strategic and tactical controls are most important. At the divisional level, control is primarily concerned with the maintenance and improvement of competitive position. Tactical control dominates. At the functional level, the role of control becomes one of developing and enhancing function-based distinctive competencies. Because of the short-term time horizon, operational and tactical controls are most important at this level, with only a modest concern for strategic control.[3]

To help achieve organizational objectives, strategic managers have an obligation to ensure that the entire hierarchy of control is integrated and working properly. As reported by Meredith, according to W. Edwards Deming, the quality-control expert who helped the Japanese build their successful business economy, 85% of the causes of product defects are due to the system within which the worker must perform and only 15% are directly due to the worker.[4] Unfortunately, in the last few decades top management has almost forgotten the importance of strategic control, and when control was called for, they have reverted to more direct tactical and operational control—often becoming crisis management.[5]

9.1

MEASURING PERFORMANCE

Which measures will be used depends on the organizational unit to be measured, as well as on the objectives to be achieved. Some measures, such as return on investment, are very appropriate to evaluating the corporation's or division's ability to achieve a profitability objective. These measures, however, are inadequate for evaluating other objectives that a corporation might want to achieve: social responsibility or employee development, for instance. Different measures are required for different objectives. Even though profitability is the major objective for a corporation, return on investment alone might be insufficient as a control device. ROI, for example, can be computed only *after* profits are totaled for a period. It tells what happened—not what *is* happening or what *will* happen. A firm, therefore, needs to develop measures that predict likely profitability. These are referred to as "steering" or "feed-forward" controls because they measure variables that influence future profitability.

Measures of Corporate Performance

The most commonly used measure of corporate performance (in terms of profits) is return on investment. As discussed in Chapter 2, it is simply the result of dividing net income before taxes by total assets. Although there are a number of advantages to the use of ROI, there are also a number of distinct limitations. Some of these are detailed in Table 9.1.

Other popular measures are earnings per share (EPS) and return on equity (ROE). Earnings per share also has several deficiencies as an evaluation of past and future performance. For one thing, because alternative accounting principles are available, EPS can have several different but equally acceptable values, depending on the principle selected for its computation. Second, because EPS is based on accrual income, the conversion of income to cash can be near term or delayed. Therefore, EPS does not consider the time value of money. Return on equity also has its share of limitations because it is also derived from accounting-based data. Because of these and other limitations, EPS and ROE by themselves are not adequate measures of corporate performance.[6]

Stakeholder Measures

As mentioned in Chapter 4, stakeholders in the corporation's task environment are often very concerned about corporate activities and performance. Each has its own set of criteria to determine how well the corporation is

TABLE 9.1

Advantages and Limitations of ROI as a Measure of Corporate Performance

ADVANTAGES

1. ROI is a single comprehensive figure influenced by everything that happens.

2. It measures how well the division manager uses the property of the company to generate profits. It is also a good way to check on the accuracy of capital investment proposals.

3. It is a common denominator that can be compared with many entities.

4. It provides an incentive to use existing assets efficiently.

5. It provides an incentive to acquire new assets only when doing so would increase the return.

LIMITATIONS

1. ROI is very sensitive to depreciation policy. Depreciation write-off variances between divisions affect ROI performance. Accelerated depreciation techniques reduce ROI, conflicting with capital budgeting discounted cash-flow analysis.

2. ROI is sensitive to book value. Older plants with more depreciated assets have relatively lower investment bases than newer plants (note also the effect of inflation), thus increasing ROI. Note that asset investment may be held down or assets disposed of in order to increase ROI performance.

3. In many firms that use ROI, one division sells to another. As a result, transfer pricing must occur. Expenses incurred affect profit. Since, in theory, the transfer price should be based on the total impact on firm profit, some investment center managers are bound to suffer. Equitable transfer prices are difficult to determine.

4. If one division operates in an industry that has favorable conditions and another division operates in an industry that has unfavorable conditions, the former division will automatically "look" better than the other.

5. The time span of concern here is short range. The performance of division managers should be measured in the long run. This is top management's time-span capacity.

6. The business cycle strongly affects ROI performance, often despite managerial performance.

SOURCE: Table, "Advantages and Limitations of ROI as a Measure of Corporate Performance" from *Organizational Policy and Strategic Management,* Second Edition, copyright © 1983 by The Dryden Press, a division of Holt, Rinehart and Winston, Inc., reprinted by permission of the publisher.

performing. These criteria typically deal with the direct and indirect impact of corporate activities on stakeholder interests. Freeman proposes that top management needs to "keep score" with these stakeholders; it should establish one or more simple measures for each stakeholder category.[7] A few of these measures are listed in Table 9.2.

Value-Added Measures

Assuming that any one measure is bound to have some shortcomings, Hofer recommends the use of three new measures in an evaluation of a corpora-

TABLE 9.2
A Sample Score Card for "Keeping Score with Stakeholders"

STAKEHOLDER CATEGORY	POSSIBLE NEAR-TERM MEASURES	POSSIBLE LONG-TERM MEASURES
Customers	Sales ($ and volume)	Growth in sales
	New customers	Turnover of customer base
	Number of new customer needs met ("tries")	Ability to control price
Suppliers	Cost of raw material	Growth rates of
	Delivery time	Raw material costs
	Inventory	Delivery time
	Availability of raw material	Inventory
		New ideas from suppliers
Financial Community	EPS	Ability to convince Wall Street of strategy
	Stock price	Growth in ROE
	Number of "buy" lists	
	ROE	
Employees	Number of suggestions	Number of internal promotions
	Productivity	Turnover
	Number of grievances	
Congress	Number of new pieces of legislation that affect the firm	Number of new regulations that affect industry
	Access to key members and staff	Ratio of "cooperative" vs. "competitive" encounters
Consumer Advocate	Number of meetings	Number of changes in policy due to C.A.
	Number of "hostile" encounters	Number of C.A. initiated "calls for help"
	Number of times coalitions formed	
	Number of legal actions	
Environmentalists	Number of meetings	Number of changes in policy due to environmentalists
	Number of hostile encounters	Number of environmentalist "calls for help"
	Number of times coalitions formed	
	Number of EPA complaints	
	Number of legal actions	

SOURCE: R. E. Freeman, *Strategic Management: A Stakeholder Approach* (Boston: Ballinger Publishing Company, 1984), p. 179. Copyright © 1984 by R. E. Freeman. Reprinted by permission.

tion's performance results (see Table 9.3). These measures are based on **value added** and are attempts to measure directly the contribution a corporation makes to society. Value added is the difference between dollar sales and the cost of raw materials and purchased parts. Return on value added (ROVA) is a second measure, one that divides net profits before tax by value added and converts the quotient to a percentage. Preliminary studies

TABLE 9.3
Three New Measures of Corporate Performance

Performance Characteristic	SOME TRADITIONAL MEASURES	PROPOSED NEW MEASURES
Growth	Dollar sales, unit sales, dollar assets	Value added[1]
Efficiency	Gross margin, net profits, net profits/ dollar sales	ROVA[2]
Asset utilization	ROI, return on equity, earnings per share	ROVA/ROI

SOURCE: C. W. Hofer, "ROVA: A New Measure for Assessing Organizational Performance," in R. Lamb, ed., *Advances in Strategic Management*, vol. 2 (Greenwich, Conn.: JAI Press, 1983), p. 50. Copyright © 1983 by C. W. Hofer. Reprinted by permission.

[1]Value added = Dollar sales − Cost of raw materials and purchased parts.

[2]ROVA: Return on Value Added = $\dfrac{\text{Net profits before tax}}{\text{Value added}} \times 100\%$.

by Hofer suggest that ROVA tends to stabilize in the range of 12% to 18% for most industries in the maturity or saturation phases of market evolution. Hofer argues that ROVA might be a better measure of corporate performance across various industries than other measures currently in use.[8]

Unfortunately, the major disadvantage of using value added is that the figures are not readily available. There is no way to calculate value added from traditional financial reports in the United States, for example, because of the allocation and application of direct labor, indirect costs, and overhead that become part of the cost of goods manufactured. Nevertheless, authorities on the subject argue that combining value-added measures with traditional performance measures creates a more complete and realistic picture of a corporation's performance.[9]

Shareholder Value

Because of the belief that accounting-based numbers such as return on investment, return on equity, and earnings per share are not reliable indicators of a corporation's economic value, many corporations are using shareholder value as a better measure of corporate performance and strategic management effectiveness.[10] **Shareholder value** (or shareholder wealth) is defined as the sum of dividends plus stock appreciation. It determines if a corporation is earning a rate of return greater than that demanded by investors in the security market. Rappaport, one of the principal advocates of this measure, explains its use:

> What I have termed the "shareholder value approach" estimates the economic value of any strategy as the expected cash flows discounted by the market discount rate. These cash flows in turn serve as the basis for expected shareholder returns from dividends and stock-price appreciation.[11]

A survey of the senior managers of Fortune 500 companies revealed that 30% of their selections of investment proposals are based on their expected contributions to shareholder wealth. The survey also noted that a number of corporations not now using this approach are starting to experiment with value-based techniques.[12]

Performance Objectives

The objectives that were established earlier in the strategy formulation stage of the strategic management process should certainly be used to measure corporate performance once the strategies have been implemented. Drucker, one of the originators of managing by objectives, proposed eight key areas in which overall corporate objectives should be established and monitored:

1. Market standing
2. Innovation
3. Productivity
4. Use of physical and financial resources
5. Profitability
6. Manager performance and development
7. Worker performance and attitude
8. Public responsibility.[13]

Westinghouse Electric Corporation, for example, established a productivity-improvement objective for the entire corporation. Concerned that the company had slipped from the position of number two in the world in its industry, top management decided in 1979 that the firm had to do a better job with the resources it controlled. Consequently, it developed a series of productivity-improvement programs, such as the introduction of quality circles, improved inventory control, and the global location of its manufacturing facilities. To measure the overall impact of these programs upon the corporation, Westinghouse's top management developed a productivity improvement formula:

$$\frac{\text{Constant dollar value } - \text{ Added change}}{\text{Total employee costs}} = \% \text{ P I}$$

Top management established an overall corporate objective for productivity improvement at $6 + \%$ per year. The productivity improvement measure thus became one of the key indicators of corporate performance.[14]

Evaluation of Top Management

Through its strategy, audit, and compensation committees, a board of directors closely evaluates the job performance of the CEO and the top management team. Of course, it is concerned primarily with overall profitability as measured by return on investment, return on equity, earnings per share, and shareholder wealth. The absence of short-run profitability is certainly a factor contributing to the firing of any CEO. The board will also, however, be concerned with other factors.

As shown in Fig. 9.3, the board should evaluate top management not only on quantitative measures, but also on factors relating to its strategic

FIGURE 9.3
Assessing Top Management's Performance

Measure	Excellent	Above Average	Average	Below Average	Poor
Qualitative: Establishing Strategic Direction					
Building Management Team					
Leadership Qualities					
Providing for Succession					
Implementing Strategy					
Employee/Labor Relations					
Technology Leadership					
Board Relations					
Investor Relations					
Community/Gov't Relations					
Quantitative: EPS Over 2–5 years					
Total Return to Shareholders					
Return on Invested Capital					
Return Measure Trends					
Return on Stockholders Equity					
Cash Flow					
Yearly/Quarterly EPS					
Stock Price Performance					
Book Value Performance					
Dividend Payout Ratio					

Source: Suggested by R. Brossy, "What Directors Say About Their Role in Managing Executive Pay," *Directors & Boards* (Summer 1986), pp. 38–40.

management practices. Has the top management team set reasonable long-run as well as short-run objectives? Has it formulated innovative strategies? Has it worked closely with operational managers in the development of realistic implementation plans, schedules, and budgets? Has it developed and used appropriate measures of corporate and divisional performance for feedback and control? Has it provided the board with appropriate feedback on corporate performance in advance of key decision points? These and other questions should be raised by a board of directors as they evaluate the performance of top management.

The specific items that are used by a board to evaluate its top management should be derived from the objectives agreed to earlier by both the board and top management. If better relations with the local community and improved safety practices in work areas were selected as objectives for the year (or for five years), these items should be included in the evaluation. In addition, other factors that tend to lead to profitability might be included, such as market share, product quality, or investment intensity (from the PIMS research discussed in Chapter 6).

Strategic Audits

Used by various consulting firms as a way to measure performance, audits of corporate activities are frequently suggested for use by boards of directors as well as by others in managerial positions. Management audits have been developed to evaluate activities such as corporate social responsibility; functional areas such as the marketing department, divisions such as the international division, as well as to evaluate the corporation itself in a strategic audit (see Chapter 2). The strategic audit is likely to be increasingly used by corporations that have become concerned with closely monitoring those activities that affect overall corporate effectiveness and efficiency. To be effective, the strategic audit should parallel the corporation's strategic management process and/or model.

Measures of Divisional and Functional Unit Performance

Corporations use a variety of techniques to evaluate and control performance in divisions, SBUs, and functional units. If a corporation is composed of SBUs or divisions, it will use many of the same performance measures (ROI, for instance) that it uses to assess overall corporation performance. To the extent that it can isolate specific functional units, such as R&D, the corporation may develop responsibility centers.

Budgets are certainly an important control device. During strategy formulation and implementation, top management approves a series of programs and supporting operating budgets from its business units.[15] During evaluation and control, actual expenses are contrasted with planned expenditures and the degree of variance is assessed. This is typically done on a monthly basis. In addition, top management will probably require *periodic statistical reports* summarizing data on key factors, such as the number of new customer contracts, volume of received orders, and productivity figures, among others.[16]

Evaluating a Division or SBU

At Norton Company, each SBU is evaluated in depth every two years. This evaluation is conducted by the Strategy Guidance Committee, composed of the CEO, the financial vice-president, eight vice-presidents in charge of operations, the controller, assistant controller, vice-president for corporate development, and an assistant vice-president. At the time that the line manager in charge of an SBU comes before the committee with a detailed strategy for each major segment of the unit's operations, the committee is evaluating the unit's performance according to past objectives, and arriving at its strategic position within the corporation and, therefore, its potential.

> The Strategy Guidance Committee looks at a strategic business unit from many viewpoints—return on net assets, return on sales, asset turnover, market share strategy. The committee might test sales growth rate against market growth rate against market share strategy. The committee also looks at competition, relative strengths and weaknesses, and cash generation plotted against market share strategy. It also places the unit on a balloon chart or growth/market share matrix for the entire company, to see how this unit fits in with all the others.[17]

The Strategy Guidance Committee looks at the SBU from all angles and asks a number of penetrating questions. Some of these questions are listed below:

EVALUATION OF A STRATEGIC BUSINESS UNIT AT NORTON COMPANY

- How does this unit contribute to the overall scheme of things?
- Does it help to balance the total?
- Does it increase or decrease the cyclical nature of the company?
- How does it relate to other Norton technologies, processes, or distribution systems?
- How successfully does it compete?
- How is it regarded by its customers and by its competitors?
- Does it hurt or improve the company's image with the investment community?

- What are its mission and mode of operation in terms of build, maintain, or harvest?
- Is its current strategy appropriate?
- Can we win and, if so, how?
- If it has changed its strategy or performance since the last review, why has it changed?
- What does our analysis suggest about the unit's profitability in comparison with similar businesses?

Responsibility Centers

Control systems can be established to monitor specific functions, projects, or divisions. One type of control system, budgets typically are used to control the financial indicators of performance. Responsibility centers are used to isolate a unit so that it can be evaluated separately from the rest of the corporation. Each responsibility center therefore has its own budget and is evaluated on its use of budgeted resources. A responsibility center is headed by the manager responsible for the center's performance. The center uses resources (measured in terms of costs) to produce a service or a product (measured in terms of volume or revenues). There are five major types of responsibility centers. The type is determined by the way these resources and services or products are measured by the corporation's control system:[18]

1. **Standard cost centers.** Primarily used in manufacturing facilities, standard (or expected) costs are computed for each operation on the basis of historical data. In evaluation of the center's performance, its total standard costs are multiplied by the units produced; the result is the expected cost of production, which is then compared to the actual cost of production.

2. **Revenue centers.** Production, usually in terms of unit or dollar sales, is measured without consideration of resource costs (e.g., salaries). The center is thus judged in terms of effectiveness rather than efficiency. The effectiveness of a sales region, for example, is determined by the comparison of its actual sales to its projected or previous year's sales. Profits are not considered because sales departments have very limited influence over the cost of the products they sell.

3. **Expense centers.** Resources are measured in dollars without consideration of service or product costs. Thus budgets will have been prepared for "engineered" expenses (those costs that can be calculated) and for "discretionary" expenses (those costs that can only be estimated). Typical expense centers are administrative, service, and research departments. They cost an organization money, but they only indirectly contribute to revenues.

4. **Profit centers.** Performance is measured in terms of the difference between revenues (which measure production) and expenditures (which measure resources). A profit center is typically established whenever an organizational unit has control over both its resources and its products or services. By having such centers, a corporation can be organized into divisions of separate product lines. The manager of each division is given autonomy to the extent that she or he is able to keep profits at a satisfactory (or better) level. Some organizational units that are not usually considered potentially autonomous can, for the purpose of profit-center evaluations, be made so. A manufacturing department, for example, can be converted from a standard cost center (or expense center) into a profit center: it is allowed to charge a **transfer price** for each product it "sells" to the sales department. The difference between the manufacturing cost per unit and the agreed-upon transfer price is the

unit's "profit." Transfer pricing is commonly used in vertically integrated corporations and can work quite well when a price can be easily determined for a designated amount of product. When a price cannot be set easily, however, the relative bargaining power of the centers, rather than strategic considerations, tend to influence the agreed-upon price.[19] Top management has an obligation to make sure that these political considerations do not overwhelm the strategic ones. Otherwise, profit figures for each center will be biased and provide poor information for strategic decisions at the corporate level.

5. **Investment centers.**   As with profit centers, an investment center's performance is measured in terms of the difference between its resources and its services or products. Most divisions in large manufacturing corporations use huge assets, such as plants and equipment, to make their products, and evaluating their performance on the basis of profits alone can be misleading because it ignores the size of their assets. For example, two divisions in a corporation make identical profits, but one division owns a $3 million plant, whereas the other owns a $1 million plant. Both make the same profits, but one is obviously more efficient: The smaller plant provides the stockholders with a better return on their investment.

The most widely used measure of investment center performance is ROI (see Table 2.1). Another measure, called residual income, is found by subtracting an interest charge from the net income. This interest charge could be based on the interest the corporation is actually paying to lenders for the assets being used. It could also be based on the amount of income that could have been earned if the assets had been invested somewhere else.

Sloan reports that the concept of rate of return on investments was crucial to General Motors' exercise of its permanent control of the whole corporation in a way consistent with its decentralized organization.[20] Donaldson Brown, who came to GM from DuPont in 1921, defined return on investment as a function of the profit margin and the rate of turnover of invested capital. Multiplying the profit margin by the investment turnover equals the percent of return on investment. To increase the return on investment, management can, therefore, increase the rate of capital turnover in relation to sales (that is, increase volume) or increase profit margins (increase revenue and/or cut costs and expenses).[21]

Investment center performance can also be measured in terms of its contribution to shareholder value. One example is given by the CEO of a large corporation:

> We value our businesses by computing the net present value of each unit's equity cash flow, using the appropriate cost of capital. Then we subtract out the market value of assigned debt and arrive at an estimate of the warranted market value of the unit. These techniques allow us to evaluate and rank our units based on their relative contribution to the creation of overall corporate equity value, which is our overall objective.[22]

Most single-business corporations tend to use a combination of cost, expense, and revenue centers. In these corporations, most managers are functional specialists and manage against a budget. Total profitability is integrated at the corporate level. Dominant-product companies, which have diversified into a few small businesses but which still depend upon a single product line for most of their revenue and income, generally use a combination of cost, expense, revenue, plus *profit centers*. Multidivisional corporations, however, will tend to emphasize *investment centers*—although in various units throughout the corporation other types of responsibility centers will also be used.[23]

9.2

STRATEGIC INFORMATION SYSTEMS

Before performance measures can have any impact on strategic management, they must first be communicated to those people responsible for formulating and implementing strategic plans. Strategic information systems can perform this function. They can be computer-based or manual, formal or informal. They serve the information needs of top management.[24] As discussed in Chapter 5, an information system is meant to provide a basis for early warning signals that can originate either externally or internally. These warning signals grow out of the corporation's need to ensure that programs and procedures are being implemented in ways that will achieve corporate and divisional objectives. One of the key reasons given for the bankruptcy of International Harvester was the inability of the corporation's top management to precisely determine its income by major class of similar products. Because of this inability, management kept trying to fix ailing businesses and was unable to respond flexibly to major changes and unexpected events.[25]

As mentioned in Chapter 5, the information system should focus managers' attention on the critical success factors in their jobs. **Critical success factors** are those few things that must go well if a corporation's success is to be ensured. They are typically those 20% of the total factors that determine 80% of the corporation's or business unit's performance. They therefore represent those areas that must be given the special and continuous attention needed for high performance.[26] These critical success factors provide a focal point from which a computer-based information system can be developed. Such an information system will thus pinpoint key areas that require a manager's attention.

The Diversified Products and Services Group of GTE, for example, established in 1984 a formal system, based on critical success factors, to track the implementation of the group's strategic plans. Management referred to this system as their Strategic Tracking System (STS). Charles M. Jones, Vice-President of Administration for GTE Diversified Products relates how it was done:

> We called the things that had to be done well Critical Success Factors (CSFs). The first criteria in defining CSFs was that they had to be very specific and

action oriented. In addition, we developed performance measures for each CSF. Then we set up a monthly STS reporting system, reviewed by the president of Diversified Products. . . .

Each organization developed its own STS reporting process, determining from the various line managers what factors were critical to their particular operation. At the next higher level, these success factors and performance measures were reviewed and the most important were selected as monitors for the monthly report. In theory, and in practice, there's nothing in the STS that general managers don't use to run their businesses, but not everything they use was included.[27]

At the divisional or SBU level of a corporation, the information system should be used to support, reinforce, or enlarge its business-level strategy.[28] An SBU pursuing a strategy of overall cost leadership could use its information system to reduce costs either by the improvement of labor productivity or the utilization of other resources such as inventory or machinery. Another SBU, in contrast, might wish to pursue a differentiation strategy. It could use its information system to add uniqueness to the product or service and contribute to quality, service, or image through the functional areas.[29] American Hospital Supply and both United and American Airlines took this approach to increase their market shares: they offered unique information-systems services to their customers. The choice of the business-level strategy will thus dictate the type of information system that the SBU needs to both implement and control strategic activities. Table 9.4 lists the differences between an information system needed to evaluate and control a low-cost strategy and an information system needed for product differentiation. The information systems will be constructed differently to monitor different activities because the two types of business-level strategies have different critical-success factors.[30]

9.3

PROBLEMS IN MEASURING PERFORMANCE

The measurement of performance is a crucial part of evaluation and control. The lack of quantifiable objectives or performance standards and the inability of the information system to provide timely, valid information are two obvious control problems.[31] Without objective and timely measurements, it would be extremely difficult to make operational, let alone strategic, decisions. Nevertheless, the use of timely, quantifiable standards does not guarantee good performance. The very act of monitoring and measuring performance can cause side-effects that interfere with overall corporate performance. Among the most frequent negative side-effects are a *short-term orientation* and *goal displacement*.

Short-Term Orientation

Hodgetts and Wortman state that in many situations top executives do not analyze *either* the long-term implications of present operations on the strategy they have adopted *or* the operational impact of a strategy on the

TABLE 9.4
Use of Information Systems to Monitor Implementation of Business Strategies

	GENERIC STRATEGIES	
	Low Cost	Product Differentiation
Product Design & Development	Product engineering systems Project control systems	R&D data bases Professional work stations Electronic mail CAD Custom engineering systems Integrated systems for manufacturing
Operations	Process engineering systems Process control systems Labor control systems Inventory management systems Procurement systems Quality monitoring systems	CAM Quality assurance systems Systems for suppliers Quality monitoring systems
Marketing	Streamlined distribution systems Centralized control systems Econometric modeling systems	Sophisticated marketing systems Market data bases Graphic display systems Telemarketing systems Competition analysis systems Modeling systems Service-oriented distribution systems
Sales	Sales control systems Advertising monitoring systems Systems to consolidate sales function Strict incentive/monitoring systems	Differential pricing systems Office/field communications Customer/sales support systems Dealer support systems Customer order entry systems
Administration	Cost control systems Quantitative planning & budgeting systems Office automation for staff reduction	Office automation to integrate functions Environment scanning & nonquantitative planning systems Teleconferencing systems

SOURCE: G. L. Parsons, "Information Technology: A New Competitive Weapon," *Sloan Management Review* (Fall 1983), p. 12. Reprinted by permission of the publisher. Copyright © 1983 by the Sloan Management Review Association. All rights reserved.

corporate mission. They report that long-run evaluations are *not* conducted because executives (1) may not realize their importance, (2) may believe that short-run considerations are more important than long-run considerations, (3) may not be personally evaluated on a long-term basis, or (4) may not have the time to make a long-run analysis.[32] There is no real justification for the first and last "reasons." If executives realize the importance of long-run evaluations, they make the time needed to conduct them. The short-term nature of most incentive and promotion plans, however, provides a rationale for the second and third reasons.

In 1986, according to Sibson and Company, a compensation consulting firm, long-term incentives comprised only 28% of the total annual income of CEOs of large corporations. Although this was an increase from just 15% in 1975, most of the typical chief executive's annual compensation came from salary (46%) and an annual bonus linked to pre-tax profit (26%).[33] A survey of corporate planners and human resource executives from twenty-four U.S. Fortune 500 firms revealed that only about half of the companies attempted to tailor their business-unit managers' incentive systems to the strategic position of the business unit. Fully 90% of the planners and executives that were surveyed reported that their companies were not adequately combining long- and short-term criteria in assessing a business-unit manager's performance.[34]

Table 9.1 indicates that one of the limitations of ROI as a performance measure is its short-term nature. In theory, ROI is not limited to the short run, but in practice it is often difficult to use this measure to realize long-term benefits for the corporation. If the performance of corporate and divisional managers is evaluated primarily on the basis of an annual ROI, the managers tend to focus their effort on those factors that have positive short-term effects. Therefore, division managers often undertake capital investments with early paybacks that will establish a favorable track record for the division. These results are often inconsistent with corporate long-run objectives. Because managers can often manipulate both the numerator (earnings) as well as the denominator (investment), the resulting ROI figure can be meaningless. Advertising, maintenance, and research efforts can be reduced. Mergers can be undertaken that will do more for this year's earnings than for the division's or corporation's future profits. Expensive retooling and plant modernization can be delayed as long as a manager can manipulate figures on production defects and absenteeism. Efforts to compensate for these distortions tend to create a burdensome accounting-control system, which stifles creativity and flexibility, and leads to even more questionable "creative accounting" practices.[35] For example, the manager of Doughtie's Foods' wholesaling operation in Richmond, Virginia, admitted to SEC investigators that he routinely gave false inventory figures to his superiors in order to overstate his division's profits. He admitted that he did it "just to look good." His division had not been doing well and his bosses had been routinely singling him out for criticism at corporate planning meetings.[36]

Goal Displacement

The very monitoring and measuring of performance (if not carefully done) can actually result in a decline in overall corporate performance. A dysfunctional side-effect known as *goal displacement* can occur. This is the confusion of means with ends. Goal displacement occurs when activities originally intended to help managers attain corporate objectives become ends in themselves—or are adapted to meet ends other than those for which they were intended.[37] Two types of goal displacement are *behavior substitution* and *suboptimization*.

Behavior Substitution

Not all activities or aspects of performance can be easily quantified and measured. It can be very difficult to set standards for such desired activities as cooperation or initiative. Therefore, managers tend to focus more of their attention on those behaviors that are measurable than on those that are not.[38] They thus reward those people who do well on these types of measures. Because the managers tend to ignore behaviors that are either unmeasurable or difficult to measure, people receive little to no reward for engaging in these activities. The problem with this phenomenon is that the easy-to-measure activities might have little to no relationship to the desired good performance. Rational people, nevertheless, will tend to work for the rewards the system has to offer. Therefore, employees will tend to substitute behaviors that are recognized and rewarded for those behaviors that are ignored without regard to their contribution to goal accomplishment.[39] A U.S. Navy quip sums up this situation: "What you inspect is what you get." If the evaluation and control system of an auto plant rewards the meeting of quantitative goals while paying only lip-service to qualitative goals, consumers can expect to get a very large number of very poorly built cars!

The most frequently mentioned problem with Management By Objectives (MBO) is that the measurement process partially distorts the realities of the job. Objectives are made for areas in which the measurement of accomplishments is relatively easy, such as ROI, increased sales, or reduced cost. But these might not always be the most important areas. This problem becomes crucial in professional, service, or staff activities in which the making of quantitative measurements is difficult. If, for example, a division manager is achieving all of the quantifiable objectives, but in so doing, alienates the work force, the result could be a long-term drop in the division's performance. If promotions are strictly based on measurable short-term performance results, this manager is very likely to be promoted or transferred before the employees' negative attitudes result in complaints to the personnel office, strikes, or sabotage. The law governing the effect of measurement on behavior seems to be: *Quantifiable measures drive out nonquantifiable measures.*

Suboptimization

The emphasis in large corporations to develop separate responsibility centers can create some problems for the corporation as a whole. To the extent that a division or functional unit views itself as a separate entity, it might refuse to cooperate with other units or divisions in the same corporation if cooperation could in some way negatively affect its performance evaluation. The competition between divisions to achieve a high ROI can result in one division's refusal to share its new technology or work-process improvements. One division's attempt to optimize the accomplishment of its goals can cause other divisions to fall behind and thus negatively affect overall corporate performance. One common example of this type of suboptimization occurs when a marketing department approves an early shipment date to a customer as a means of getting an order and forces the manufacturing department into overtime production for this one order. Production costs are raised, which reduces the manufacturing department's overall efficiency. The end result might be that, although marketing achieves its sales goal, the corporation fails to achieve its expected profitability.

9.4

GUIDELINES FOR PROPER CONTROL

In designing a control system, top management should remember that controls should follow strategy. Unless controls ensure the use of the proper strategy to achieve objectives, there is a strong likelihood that dysfunctional side-effects will completely undermine the implementation of the objectives. The following guidelines are recommended:

1. Control should involve only the minimum amount of information needed to give a reliable picture of events. Too many controls create confusion. Focus on those 20% of the factors that determine 80% of the results.

2. Controls should monitor only meaningful activities and results, regardless of measurement difficulty. If cooperation between divisions is important to corporate performance, some form of qualitative or quantitative measure should be established to monitor cooperation.

3. Controls should be timely so that corrective action can be taken before it is too late. *Steering controls,* controls that monitor or measure the factors influencing performance, should be stressed so that advance notice of problems is given.

4. Long-term as well as short-term controls should be used. If only short-term measures are emphasized, a short-term managerial orientation is likely.

5. Controls should aim at pinpointing exceptions. Only those activities or results that fall outside a predetermined tolerance range should call for action.

6. Emphasize the reward of meeting or exceeding standards rather than punishment for failing to meet standards. Heavy punishment of failure will typically result in goal displacement. Managers will "fudge" reports and lobby for lower standards.

It is surprising that the best-managed companies often have only a few formal objective controls. They focus on measuring the critical success factors—those few things whose success ensures overall success. Other factors are controlled by the social system in the form of the corporate culture. To the extent that the culture complements and reinforces the strategic orientation of the firm, there is less need for an extensive formal control system. In their book, *In Search of Excellence,* Peters and Waterman state that "the stronger the culture and the more it was directed toward the marketplace, the less need was there for policy manuals, organization charts, or detailed procedures and rules. In these companies, people way down the line know what they are supposed to do in most situations because the handful of guiding values is crystal clear."[40]

9.5

STRATEGIC INCENTIVE MANAGEMENT

In an assessment of the strategic planning of large U.S. corporations, Steiner reports that there is a significant overall weakness in corporations' rewarding managers for strategic thinking.[41] His view agrees with the data reported earlier that only around half of the large U.S. corporations link compensation to business unit performance.[42] Traditionally, in the United States the level of compensation for chief executive officers has been a function of CEOs' compensations in comparable firms. Therefore, CEO compensation in the U.S. is related more to the size of the corporation than to the size of its profits. (This is not so much the case in Great Britain, where there is a closer connection between pay and corporate performance).[43] The gap between CEO compensation and corporate performance is most noticeable in those corporations with widely dispersed stock ownership and no dominant stockholder group to demand performance-based pay.[44] This association between firm size and executive compensation, according to Rappaport, can only fuel top management's natural inclination to grow businesses as quickly as possible.[45]

Boards of directors need to take the initiative in the development of long-term controls and corresponding incentive plans. According to Andrews, "The best criterion for appraising the quality of management performance, in the absence of personal failures or unexpected breakdowns, is management's success over time in executing a demanding and approved strategy that is continually tested against opportunity and need."[46]

Executive compensation must be clearly linked to strategic performance—to the management of the corporate portfolio, to the business unit's mission, to short-term financial as well as long-term strategic performance, and to the degree of risk involved in effective and efficient management of a portfolio.[47] One study of over 20,000 managers in fifty-six companies revealed that business units generated higher profits when incentive pay was a larger part of top management's total compensation.[48] A separate study of fifty-eight business units in fifteen different corporations concluded that "the payment of incentive compensation to managers is associated with more profitable businesses of all types."[49]

The following three approaches are tailored to help match measurements and rewards with explicit strategic objectives and timeframes: (1) the *weighted-*

factor method, (2) the *long-term evaluation method,* and (3) the *strategic-funds method.* These approaches can also be combined to best suit a corporation's circumstances.[50]

1. **Weighted-factor method.** The *weighted-factor method* is particularly appropriate for measuring and rewarding the performance of top SBU managers and group-level executives when performance factors and their importance vary from one SBU to another. The measurements used by one corporation might contain the following variations: the performance of high-growth SBUs measured in terms of market share, sales growth, designated future payoff, and progress on several future-oriented strategic projects; the performance of low-growth SBUs, in contrast, measured in terms of ROI and cash generation; and the performance of medium-growth SBUs measured for a combination of these factors. Refer to Table 9.5 for an example of the weighted-factor method applied to three different SBUs.

2. **Long-term evaluation method.** The *long-term evaluation method* compensates managers for achieving objectives set over a multiyear period. An executive is promised some company stock or "performance units" (convertible into dollars) in amounts to be based on long-term perfor-

TABLE 9.5
A Weighted-Factor Approach to Strategic Incentive Management

STRATEGIC BUSINESS UNIT CATEGORY	FACTOR	WEIGHT
High growth	Return on assets	10%
	Cash flow	0%
	Strategic-funds programs	45%
	Market-share increase	45%
		100%
Medium growth	Return on assets	25%
	Cash flow	25%
	Strategic-funds programs	25%
	Market-share increase	25%
		100%
Low growth	Return on assets	50%
	Cash flow	50%
	Strategic-funds programs	0%
	Market-share increase	0%
		100%

SOURCE: Reprinted, by permission of the publisher, from "The Performance Measurement and Reward System: Critical to Strategic Management," by Paul J. Stonich, from *Organization Dynamics,* Winter 1984, p. 51. Copyright © 1984 American Management Association, New York. All rights reserved.

mance. An executive committee, for example, might set a particular objective in terms of growth in earnings per share during a five-year period. The giving of awards would be contingent on the corporation's meeting that objective within the designated time limit. Any executive who leaves the corporation before the objective is met receives nothing. The typical emphasis on stock price makes this approach more applicable to top management than to business unit managers.

3. **Strategic-funds method.** The *strategic-funds method* encourages executives to look at developmental expenses as being different from those expenses required for current operations. The accounting statement for a corporate unit enters strategic funds as a separate entry below the current ROI. It is therefore possible to distinguish between those expense dollars consumed in the generation of current revenues and those invested in the future of the business. Therefore, the manager can be evaluated on both a short- and a long-term basis and has an incentive to invest strategic funds in the future. Refer to Table 9.6 for an example of the strategic-funds method applied to a business unit.

According to Stonich, "An effective way to achieve the desired strategic results through a reward system is to combine the weighted-factor, long-term evaluation, and strategic-funds approaches."[51] To do this, first segregate strategic funds from short-term funds, as is done in the strategic-funds method. Second, develop a weighted-factor chart for each SBU. Third, measure performance on three bases: the pre-tax profit indicated by the strategic-funds approach; the weighted factors; and the long-term evaluation of the SBU's and the corporation's performance. These incentive plans will probably gain increasing acceptance with business corporations in the near future. General Electric and Westinghouse are two firms using a version of these measures.

TABLE 9.6

A Strategic-Funds Approach Applied to an SBU's Profit-and-Loss Statement

Sales	$ 12,300,000
Cost of sales	6,900,000
Gross margin	$ 5,400,000
Operating (general and administrative expense)	− 3,700,000
Operating (return on sales)	$ 1,700,000 or 33%
Strategic funds	− 1,000,000
Pre-tax profit	$ 700,000 or 13.6%

SOURCE: Reprinted, by permission of the publisher, from "The Performance Measurement and Reward System" by Paul J. Stonich, *Organizational Dynamics*, Winter 1984. Copyright © 1984 American Management Association, New York. All rights reserved.

SUMMARY AND CONCLUSION

The evaluation and control of performance is a five-step process: (1) determine what to measure, (2) establish standards for performance, (3) measure actual performance, (4) compare actual performance with the standard, and (5) take corrective action. Information coming from this process is fed back into the strategic control system so that managers at all levels in the hierarchy of control can monitor and correct performance deviations.

Although the most commonly used measures of corporate performance are the various return ratios, measures based on a value-added or shareholder value approach can be of some use. Most corporations also monitor key performance objectives. If a corporation sets goals other than simple profitability or return on investment, it might wish to follow the example of Westinghouse and establish specific performance objectives, such as productivity improvement, for special attention. A stakeholder "scorecard" can also be of some value in the assessment of the corporation's impact on its environment. The strategic audit is recommended as a method by which activities throughout the corporation can be evaluated.

Divisions, SBUs, and functional units are often broken down into responsibility centers to aid control. Such areas are often categorized as standard cost centers, revenue centers, expense centers, profit centers, and investment centers. Budgets and periodic statistical reports are important control devices used in the monitoring of the implementation of major programs in business units.

A strategic information system is an important part of the evaluation and control process. By focusing on critical success factors, it can provide early warning signals to strategic managers. The system can be tailored to the business-level strategy being implemented in the SBU, so that the success of the strategy is ensured.

The monitoring and measurement of performance can result in dysfunctional side effects that negatively affect overall corporate performance. Among the likely side-effects are a short-term orientation and goal displacement. These problems can be reduced if top management remembers that controls must focus on strategic goals. There should be as few controls as possible, and only meaningful activities and results should be monitored. Controls should be timely to both long-term as well as short-term orientations. They should pinpoint exceptions but should be used more to reward than to punish individuals.

Incentive plans should be based upon long-term as well as short-term considerations. Three suggested approaches are the weighted-factor method, the long-term evaluation method, and the strategic-funds method.

A proper evaluation and control system should act to complete the loop shown in the strategic management model. It should feed back information important not only to the implementation of strategy, but also to the initial formulation of strategy. In terms of the strategic decision-making process depicted in Fig. 6.1, the data coming from evaluation and control are the basis for step 1—evaluating current performance results. Because of this feedback effect, evaluation and control is the beginning as well as the end of the strategic management process.

DISCUSSION QUESTIONS

1. Is Fig. 9.1 a realistic model of the evaluation and control process? Why or why not?

2. Why bother with value-added, shareholder value, or a stakeholder's scorecard? Isn't it simpler to eval-

uate a corporation and its SBUs by just using standard measures like ROI or earnings per share?

3. What are the differences between strategic, tactical, and operational controls?

4. What are the pros and cons of using performance objectives to evaluate performance?

5. What is the difference between performance objectives and critical success factors?

6. How much faith can a division or SBU manager place in a *transfer price* as a surrogate for a market price, in measurement of a profit center's performance?

7. Why are goal displacement and short-run orientation likely side-effects of the monitoring of performance? What can a corporation do to avoid them?

8. Is the evaluation and control process appropriate for a corporation that emphasizes creativity? Are control and creativity compatible? Explain.

9. Evaluate the performance of CSX Corporation and that of its key strategic managers as of mid-1987, as described in the Integrative Case at the end of the chapter. Beginning with the formation of CSX in 1980, determine how successfully the corporation's strategic managers have formulated and implemented their strategic plans.

N O T E S

1. L. G. Hrebiniak and W. F. Joyce, *Implementing Strategy* (New York: Macmillan, 1984), p. 195.

2. P. Lorange, M. F. S. Morton, and S. Ghoshal, *Strategic Control* (St. Paul: West Publishing Co., 1986), pp. 11–14.

3. Lorange, Morton, Ghoshal, p. 124.

4. J. R. Meredith, "Strategic Control of Factory Automation," *Long Range Planning* (December 1987), p. 109.

5. Meredith, p. 112.

6. B. C. Reimann and R. Thomas, "Value-Based Portfolio Planning: Improving Shareholder Return," in *Handbook of Business Strategy, 1986/87 Yearbook*, ed. W. D. Guth (Boston: Warren, Gorham and Lamont, 1986), pp. 21.2–21.3.
V. E. Millar, "The Evolution Toward Value-Based Financial Planning," *Information Strategy: The Executive's Journal* (Winter 1985), p. 28.

7. R. E. Freeman, *Strategic Management: A Stakeholder Approach* (Boston: Pitman Publishing Co., 1984), pp. 177–181.

8. C. W. Hofer, "ROVA: A New Measure for Assessing Organizational Performance," in R. Lamb (ed.), *Advances in Strategic Management*, Vol. 2 (Greenwich, Conn.: Jai Press, 1983), pp. 43–55.
C. W. Hofer and D. Schendel, *Strategy Formulation: Analytical Concepts* (St. Paul, Minn.: West Publishing Co., 1978), p. 130.

9. N. E. Swanson and L. A. Digman, "Organizational Performance Measures for Strategic Decisions: A PIMS-Based Investigation," in *Handbook of Business Strategy, 1986/1987 Yearbook*, ed. W. D. Guth (Boston: Warren, Gorham & Lamont, 1986), pp. 17.2–17.4.

10. A. Rappaport, "Corporate Performance Standards and Shareholder Wealth," *Journal of Business Strategy* (Spring 1983), pp. 28–38.

11. A. Rappaport, "Have We Been Measuring Success with the Wrong Ruler?" *Wall Street Journal* (June 25, 1984), p. 22.

12. Millar, pp. 29–30. For more information on shareholder value measures, see A. H. Seed, "Winning Strategies for Shareholder Value Creation," *Journal of Business Strategy* (Fall 1986), pp. 44–51; B. C. Reimann, "Strategy Valuation on Portfolio Planning: Combining Q and VROI Ratios," *Planning Review* (January 1986), pp. 18–32, 42–45; and M. L. Blyth, E. A. Friskey, and A. Rappaport, "Implementing the Shareholder Value Approach," *Journal of Business Strategy* (Winter 1986), pp. 48–58.

13. P. Drucker, *The Practice of Management* (New York: Harper and Brothers, 1954) as reported by M. D. Richards, *Setting Strategic Goals and Objectives* (St. Paul: West Publishing Co., 1986), pp. 16–17.

14. C. C. Borucki and G. D. Childs, "Productivity and Quality Improvement: The Westinghouse Story," in *Strategic Human Resources Management*, ed. C. Fombrun, N. Tichy, and M. A. Devanna (New York: John Wiley and Sons, 1984), pp. 381–401.

15. C. H. Roush, Jr., "Strategic Resource Allocation and Control," in W. D. Guth (ed.), *Handbook of Business Strategy* (Boston: Warren, Gorham, and Lamont, 1985), pp. 20.1–20.25.

16. R. L. Daft and N. B. Macintosh, "The Nature and Use of Formal Control Systems for Management Control and Strategy Implementation," *Journal of Management* (Spring 1984), pp. 43–66.

17. D. R. Melville, "Top Management's Role in Strategic Planning," *Journal of Business Strategy* (Spring 1981), p. 63.

18. This discussion is based on R. N. Anthony, J. Dearden, and R. F. Vancil, *Management Control Systems* (Homewood, Ill.: Richard D. Irwin, Inc., 1972), pp. 200–203.

19. Lorange, Morton, and Ghoshal, p. 69.

20. A. P. Sloan, Jr., *My Years with General Motors* (Garden City, N.Y.: Doubleday, Anchor Books, 1972), p. 159.

21. Sloan, p. 161.

22. Millar, p. 30.

23. J. R. Galbraith and R. K. Kazanjian, *Strategy Implementation: Structure, Systems and Process* (St. Paul: West Publishing Co., 1986), pp. 85–86.

24. J. A. Turner and H. C. Lucas, Jr., "Developing Strategic Information Systems," in W. D. Guth (ed.), *Handbook*

of Business Strategy (Boston: Warren, Gorham and Lamont, 1985), p. 21.2.

25. N. Gross, "Inquest for International Harvester," *Planning Review* (July-August 1987), p. 9.

26. J. Rockart, "Chief Executives Define Their Own Data Needs," *Harvard Business Review* (March-April 1979).
P. V. Jenster, "Using Critical Success Factors in Planning," *Long Range Planning* (August 1987), pp. 102–109.
A. C. Boynton and R. W. Zmud, "An Assessment of Critical Success Factors," *Sloan Management Review* (Summer 1984), p. 17.

27. C. M. Jones, "GTE's Strategic Tracking System," © *Planning Review* (September 1986), p. 28.

28. G. L. Parsons, "Information Technology: A New Competitive Weapon," *Sloan Management Review* (Fall 1983), p. 11.

29. Parsons, p. 11.

30. For other examples of the use of strategic information systems to gain competitive advantage, see J. M. Ward, "Integrating Information Systems Into Business Strategy," *Long Range Planning* (June 1987), pp. 19–29; and B. C. Reimann, "Strategic Management in an Electronic Age: Exploiting the Power of Information Technology," *International Journal of Management* (September 1987), pp. 438–451.

31. Hrebiniak and Joyce, pp. 198–199.

32. R. M. Hodgetts and M. S. Wortman, *Administrative Policy,* 2nd ed. (New York: John Wiley & Sons, 1980), p. 128.

33. L. Reibstein, "Firms Trim Annual Pay Increases and Focus on Long Term: More Employers Link Incentives to Unit Results," *Wall Street Journal* (April 10, 1987), p. 25.

34. P. Lorange and D. Murphy, "Bringing Human Resources Into Strategic Planning: Systems Design Considerations," in *Strategic Human Resources Management,* ed. C. Fombrun, N. M. Tichy, and M. A. Devanna (New York: John Wiley & Sons, 1984), pp. 281–285.

35. J. Dutton and A. Thomas, "Managing Organizational Productivity," *Journal of Business Strategy* (Summer 1982), p. 41.

36. R. L. Hudson, "SEC Charges Fudging of Corporate Figures Is a Growing Practice," *Wall Street Journal* (June 2, 1983), p. 1.

37. H. R. Bobbitt, Jr., R. H. Breinholt, R. H. Doktor, and J. P. McNaul, *Organizational Behavior,* 2nd ed. (Englewood Cliffs, N.J.: Prentice-Hall, 1978), p. 99.

38. J. P. Worthy and R. P. Neuschel, *Emerging Issues in Corporate Governance* (Evanston: Northwestern University Press, 1984), p. 84.

39. S. Kerr, "On the Folly of Rewarding A, While Hoping for B," *Academy of Management Journal* (December 1975), pp. 769–783.

40. T. J. Peters and R. H. Waterman, *In Search of Excellence* (New York: Harper & Row, 1982), pp. 75–76.

41. G. A. Steiner, "Formal Strategic Planning in the United States Today," *Long Range Planning* (June 1983), pp. 12–17.

42. Lorange and Murphy, pp. 283–284.

43. S. P. Sethi and N. Namiki, "Top Management Compensation and Corporate Performance," *Journal of Business Strategy* (Spring 1987), p. 39.
D. Norburn, "GOGOs, YOYOs and DODOs: Company Directors and Industry Performance," *Strategic Management Journal* (March-April 1986), p. 109.

44. L. R. Gomez-Mejia, H. Tosi, and T. Hinkin, "Managerial Control, Performance, and Executive Compensation," *Academy of Management Journal* (March 1987), pp. 51–70.

45. A. Rappaport, "How To Design Value-Contributing Executive Incentives," *Journal of Business Strategy* (Fall 1983), p. 50.

46. K. R. Andrews, "Directors' Responsibility for Corporate Strategy," *Harvard Business Review* (November-December 1980), p. 32.

47. L. J. Brindisi, Jr., "Paying for Strategic Performance: A New Executive Compensation Imperative," in R. B. Lamb (ed.), *Competitive Strategic Management* (Englewood Cliffs, N.J.: Prentice-Hall, 1984), p. 334.

48. H. E. Glass, "The Challenges for Strategic Planning in the Late 1980s and Beyond," in *Handbook of Business Strategy, 1987/1988 Yearbook,* ed. H. Babian and H. E. Glass (Boston: Warren, Gorham, and Lamont, 1987), p. 2.9.

49. A. Giller, "Organizational Characteristics of Successful Business Units," in *Handbook of Business Strategy, 1987/ 1988 Yearbook,* ed. H. Babian and H. E. Glass (Boston: Warren, Gorham, and Lamont, 1987), p. 8.7.

50. P. J. Stonich, "The Performance Measurement and Reward System: Critical to Strategic Management," *Organizational Dynamics* (Winter 1984), pp. 45–57.

51. Stonich, p. 53.

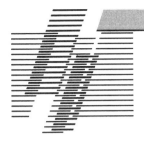

CSX CORPORATION'S EVALUATION OF ITS PERFORMANCE

By mid-1987 a number of environmental issues of significant importance to the rail transportation industry and to CSX Corporation had resolved themselves. Conrail's future was settled at last. Serious opposition in the U.S. House of Representatives to the sale of the U.S. government's 85% of Conrail's stock to Norfolk Southern doomed passage of the Senate's bill. On August 22, 1986, Norfolk Southern's top management, citing tax law changes that made the purchase less attractive, withdrew its bid. After the Conrail Privatization Act of 1986, which restricted other railroads from owning more than 10% of Conrail for a three-year period, was passed, Conrail's stock was sold to the general public in March 1987. Conrail's top management was unwilling, in March 1987, to state publicly if they planned to concentrate on rail operations or diversify into other areas, as CSX and Norfolk Southern had done.[1]

DEVELOPMENTS IN THE RAIL INDUSTRY

In a move to recoup their loss of Conrail, Norfolk Southern's top management made a bid in February 1987 for the 81% of Piedmont Airlines stock that NS didn't already own. Because of Norfolk Southern's sale of its stock (a small minority interest) in Santa Fe Southern Pacific Corporation in 1985, NS appeared to be focusing its future for the time being on multi-modal transportation alternatives in the Eastern United States. Unfortunately for the Roanoke-based company, a bidding war developed around Piedmont, between U.S. Air and TWA. Norfolk Southern dropped out of the bidding and sold much of its stock in Piedmont to U.S. Air for a good profit.

The proposed merger of the Atchison Topeka & Santa Fe Railway with the Southern Pacific railroad was rejected by the Interstate Commerce Commission in a surprise decision in April 1987. Some analysts contended that the insistence by John Schmidt, the Chairman of Santa Fe Southern Pacific Corporation, that the ICC must either approve the entire proposal intact or reject it completely was a primary reason for the ICC's rejection of the merger. Others argued that the decision reflected a movement toward re-regulation in the U.S. This action forced the parent corporation of both railroads to sell at least one of the railroads. In considering the likely sale of either the Santa Fe or the Southern Pacific, analysts wondered if the time was right for an Eastern railroad to create a transcontinental rail system. In response to a question asking if his company might be interested in such an acquisition, Norfolk Southern's new chairman, Arnold McKinnon, told analysts that "we'll look" if one of the Western railroads became available.[2]

Not content to watch other rail companies going multi-modal, Union Pacific Corporation acquired in September 1986 the Overnite Transportation Company. The acquisition of Overnite, the nation's fifth-largest motor carrier of general freight, extended Union Pacific's reach into the Eastern half of the United States. Overnite, headquartered in Richmond, Virginia, had trucking operations in the Northeast, Southeast, and Great Lakes regions. William S. Cook, Chairman and Chief Executive of Union Pacific, explained that the rail company had decided to purchase a trucking firm rather than an Eastern railroad because "the eastern part of the country is more truck oriented." He added that "our studies indicated that it would be a mistake to merge with an Eastern railroad."[3]

CSX'S PERFORMANCE

In reviewing the actions of CSX Corporation over the past few years, Hays T. Watkins, Chairman and Chief Executive Officer of CSX, stated in his letter to the shareholders in the 1986 Annual Report that he was quite pleased with the past performance of the corporation. He was also quite optimistic about CSX's future.

TABLE 9.7

Consolidated Statement of Earnings and Retained Earnings: CSX Corporation

(In Millions of Dollars, Except Per-Share Amounts)

Years Ended December 31,	1986	1985	1984
Operating Revenue			
Transportation	$ 4,803	$ 5,067	$ 5,328
Energy	1,268	1,967	2,303
Other	274	254	269
Total revenues	6,345	7,288	7,900
Operating Expense			
Transportation	4,201	4,404	4,638
Energy	1,131	1,873	2,200
Other	142	130	128
Special charge	—	954	—
Total expenses	5,474	7,361	6,966
Earnings (loss)			
Operating income (loss)	871	(73)	934
Equity in loss of Sea-Land	(2)	—	—
Other income	141	40	33
Interest expense	281	230	242
Earnings (loss) before income taxes	729	(263)	725
Income tax expense (credit)	311	(145)	311
Net earnings (loss)	$ 418	$ (118)	$ 414
Earnings (loss) per share	$ 2.73	$ (.78)	$ 2.80
Retained Earnings			
Balance—January 1	$ 2,741	$ 3,029	$ 2,769
Net earnings (loss)	418	(118)	414
Dividends	(179)	(170)	(154)
Balance—December 31	$ 2,980	$ 2,741	$ 3,029
Per share dividends—common	$ 1.16	$ 1.13	$ 1.04
Common shares outstanding at year-end (thousands)	154,016	152,399	149,566
Average common shares outstanding (thousands)	153,329	151,046	147,608

SOURCE: CSX Corporation, *1986 Annual Report and Form 10-K*, p. 16.

"The programs and plans implemented in the year just past—a transition year as we put our new organization into place—are designed to improve profitability, rates of return and shareholder value through the next decade and beyond." He went on to discuss the operating results of 1986 (see Tables 9.7 to 9.10 for financial results):

TABLE 9.8

Consolidated Statement of Financial Position: CSX Corporation

(In Millions of Dollars)

December 31,	1986	1985	1984
Assets			
Current assets			
Cash and short-term investments	$ 315	$ 187	$ 377
Accounts receivable	1,182	1,299	1,178
Inventories	356	428	458
Other current assets	248	136	124
Total current assets	2,101	2,050	2,137
Investments			
Properties	9,403	9,107	8,987
Investment in Sea-Land	802	—	—
Affiliates and other companies	150	121	137
Other assets	205	198	212
Total investments	10,560	9,426	9,336
Total assets	$12,661	$11,476	$11,473
Liabilities			
Current liabilities			
Accounts payable and other current liabilities	$ 1,511	$ 1,744	$ 1,645
Current maturities of long-term debt	336	208	261
Total current liabilities	1,847	1,952	1,906
Claims and other long-term liabilities	515	598	343
Deferred income taxes	1,903	1,554	1,773
Long-term debt	3,285	2,499	2,302
Redeemable preferred stock and minority interest	238	278	331
Shareholders' Equity			
Common stock, $1 par value	154	152	150
Other capital	1,739	1,702	1,639
Retained earnings	2,980	2,741	3,029
Total common shareholders' equity	4,873	4,595	4,818
Total liabilities and shareholders' equity	$12,661	$11,476	$11,473

SOURCE: CSX Corporation, *1986 Annual Report and Form 10-K,* p. 20.

Earnings for 1986 were $418 million, $2.73 a share, on revenue of $6.3 billion. The 1986 results compare with the $118 million, $.78 per share, net loss reported in 1985. Excluding the special charge announced in the fourth quarter 1985, CSX would have reported earnings of $442 million, $2.92 per share.

Revenue for 1986 ($6,345 million) was down $943 million, 13 percent, from 1985 ($7,288 million). The decline reflects, in part, lower gas transmission revenue due to a change in mix, as substantial sales volumes were replaced by transportation volumes, as well as lower energy prices overall.

In addition, results in 1986 reflect continued weakness in the industrial and agricultural segments of the economy served by rail, increased interest costs associated with the acquisition of Sea-Land, and higher taxes arising from the repeal of investment tax credits retroactive to January 1, 1986.

Transportation results were affected in 1986 by an overall weakness in rail traffic, most notably the decline in the phosphate and fertilizer commodity group, as well as weak export coal loadings. Partially offsetting this were reductions in rail operating expenses, which were cut four percent from 1985 levels, excluding the special charge, as a result of lower fuel costs and aggressive cost controls.

CSX's barge unit, American Commercial Lines, recorded an 89 percent increase, excluding the special charge, in operating income in 1986 over the previous year, led by record coal movements and increases in intermodal tonnages handled jointly and coordinated with the CSX rail units.

Sea-Land had a loss of $2 million on an equity basis for the seven-month period since its acquisition by CSX, but showed improvement in the fourth quarter, reporting earnings of $3 million for the final quarter of 1986.

Energy results were significantly improved by Texas Gas Transmission's record earnings in 1986. CSX Oil & Gas results were impacted unfavorably by lower energy prices.

This was the first reporting year for the company's Technology and Properties groups. The Technology group increased its contribution to income by $17 million as CSX's joint venture in Lightnet, a 5,000-mile fiber optic network, neared completion. In the Properties area, The Greenbrier had a record year and Rockresorts improved its earnings over 1985 and added a new resort, Carambola Beach in the Caribbean, to its list of management properties. Realty earnings were up slightly in 1986, due to stronger fourth quarter results.

Other income increased significantly as a result of two transactions in the fourth quarter of 1986: completion of the sale of nearly all of the company's coal properties and mineral rights and a special, one-time dividend from Trailer Train Company.[4]

NORFOLK SOUTHERN'S PERFORMANCE

Norfolk Southern, in contrast, reported three years of consistently increasing revenues and net profits. Thanks partially to its North American Van Lines acquisition, the corporation's revenues increased from $3.5 billion in 1984 to $4.1 billion in 1986. Its net income increased from $482.2 million in 1984 to $518.7 million in 1986—three years of record net income. In contrast to CSX, NS added to its coal reserves in December 1986 around 225 million tons in West Virginia—reaffirming its commitment to vertically integrated coal mining and transportation. Even with this purchase, NS ended 1986 with cash totaling $724 million and debt comprising less than 15% of capital. In their letter to the stockholders in Norfolk Southern's *1986 Annual Report,* then-Chairman Robert Claytor and Vice-Chairman Arnold Mc-

TABLE 9.9
Business Unit Information: CSX Corporation's Transportation Group
(In Millions of Dollars)

RAIL TRANSPORTATION	1986	1985	1984
Rail revenues			
Merchandise	$2,932	$3,102	$3,195
Coal	1,496	1,570	1,687
Other	149	152	176
Total revenues	4,577	4,824	5,058
Rail expenses			
Labor and fringe	2,246	2,352	2,469
Materials, supplies and other	752	699	736
Fuel	223	368	411
Equipment rent	479	496	504
Depreciation	313	266	280
Special charge	—	844	—
Total expenses	4,013	5,025	4,400
Operating income	$ 564	$ (201)	$ 658
Operating ratio	87.7%	104.1%	87.0%
Property additions	$ 672	$ 903	$ 778
BARGE TRANSPORTATION			
Barge revenues	$226	$243	$270
Barge expenses			
Labor and fringe	48	66	65
Materials, supplies and other	79	88	112
Fuel	26	37	36
Equipment rent	19	13	10
Depreciation	16	19	15
Special charge	—	14	—
Total expenses	188	237	238
Operating income	$ 38	$ 6	$ 32
Property additions	$ 23	$ 30	$ 10
SEA-LAND*			
Revenues	$1,553	$1,634	$1,759
Operating expense	1,601	1,632	1,606
Operating income (loss)	$ (48)	$ 2	$ 153

SOURCE: CSX Corporation, *1986 Annual Report and Form 10-K,* pp. 30, 34, and 35.

*This information is presented on a pro forma basis solely for the purpose of comparative analysis. Sea-Land's earnings are currently included in CSX's earnings on an equity basis from the date of acquisition.

TABLE 9.10

Business Unit Information: CSX Corporation's Energy, Properties, and Technology Groups

(In Millions of Dollars)

ENERGY	1986	1985	1984
Energy revenues			
Gas transmission	$1,070	$1,662	$2,002
Oil and gas	215	307	325
Coal*	21	58	55
Intrasegment eliminations	(38)	(60)	(79)
Total revenues	1,268	1,967	2,303
Energy expenses			
Gas transmission	948	1,556	1,898
Oil and gas	217	328	338
Coal*	4	49	43
Special charge coal*	—	96	—
Intrasegment eliminations	(38)	(60)	(79)
Total expenses	1,131	1,969	2,200
Energy operating income (loss)			
Gas transmission	122	106	104
Oil & gas	(2)	(21)	(13)
Coal*	17	(87)	12
Total operating income	$ 137	$ (2)	$ 103
Energy property additions			
Gas transmission	$ 28	$ 35	$ 41
Oil and gas	51	75	126
Coal*	2	1	1
Total property additions	$ 81	$ 111	$ 168
PROPERTIES			
Operating revenues	$250	$202	$210
Operating expenses	91	57	53
Operating income	$159	$145	$157
TECHNOLOGY			
Computer services			
CSX rail services	$ 88	$ 75	$ 63
Public services	16	12	9
Fiber optic right of occupancy sales	8	5	—
Total revenues	112	92	72

(Continued)

TABLE 9.10 (Continued)

TECHNOLOGY	1986	1985	1984
Computer services			
CSX rail services	88	75	63
Public services	13	9	6
Total expenses	101	84	69
Total operating income	11	8	3
Equity in LIGHTNET®	10	(4)	(5)
Total contribution	$ 21	$ 4	$ (2)

SOURCE: CSX Corporation, *1986 Annual Report and Form 10-K,* pp. 36, 38, and 40.

*Substantially all coal properties were disposed of in December 1986.

Kinnon made the following comment about Norfolk Southern's strategic direction:

> Even as Norfolk Southern works to increase the efficiency and profitability of its railroads, it actively seeks attractive opportunities to strengthen its position in the transportation business and enhance its ability to serve customers. The purchase of North American Van Lines, Inc. in 1985 reflects Norfolk Southern's determination to be the nation's premier provider of transportation services. . . .[5]

THE NEW CSX

Taking advantage of its recent acquisition of Sea-Land, however, CSX altered its mission statement and re-defined itself. In one of a series of advertisements appearing in business publications during 1987, CSX described itself as follows:

> If you think we're just a railroad, take another look.
> We're a lot more. We're Sea-Land, one of the largest container ship lines on earth, serving 76 ports in 64 countries.
> We're also trucks. Barges. Pipelines. Energy resources. Fiber optics. Resorts and property development. And, of course, the railroad. And we're developing new technology to make it all work together.
> We're CSX, the first true global transporter. If you've never heard of one before, it's because there's never been one before. This is a company on the move.[6]

NOTES

1. G. Anders and R. Koenig, "Conrail Offering Raises Record of $1.65 Billion," *Wall Street Journal* (March 26, 1987), p. 4.

2. L. McGinley, J. Valente, and D. Machalaba, "ICC Reaffirms Its Rejection of Merger of Santa Fe, Southern Pacific Railroads," *Wall Street Journal* (July 1, 1987), p. 3.

3. D. Machalaba and L. Williams, "Union Pacific To Buy Overnite For $1.2 Billion," *Wall Street Journal* (September 19, 1986), p. 3.

4. H. T. Watkins, "To Our Shareholders," *1986 Annual Report and Form 10-K,* CSX Corporation, p. 3.

5. R. B. Claytor and A. B. McKinnon, "Dear Stockholder," *1986 Annual Report,* Norfolk Southern Corporation, p. 3.

6. Advertisement, *Business Week* (December 18, 1987), p. 33.

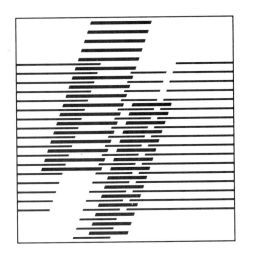

PART FIVE

OTHER STRATEGIC CONCERNS

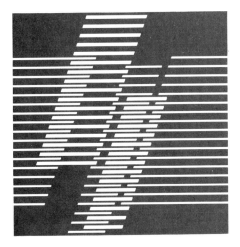

CHAPTER 10

STRATEGIC ISSUES IN MULTINATIONAL CORPORATIONS

STRATEGIC MANAGEMENT MODEL

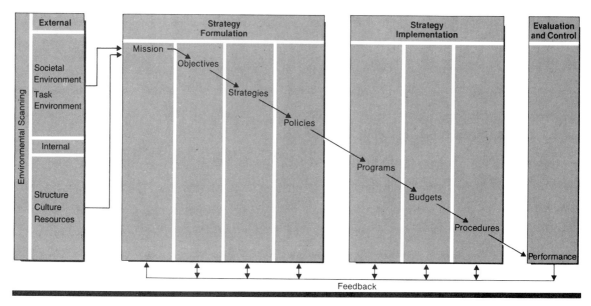

Throughout much of its history, North America has been virtually self-sufficient. During the 1700s and 1800s, the distance between America and Europe encouraged the United States and Canada to develop their own industries. As late as the 1960s, the combined exports and imports of merchandise represented only 7%–8% of the U.S. gross national product—the lowest of any major industrialized nation.[1] A large domestic market, plus a bountiful supply of natural resources and labor, enabled major corporations to grow and become successful while having only a casual interest in "foreign" markets. High tariff laws served to keep the business interests of other countries out of the United States while the infant domestic companies matured.

Since 1960, however, international trade has increased dramatically. In the past quarter-century, the volume of goods traded between all nations has climbed from less than $100 million to around $2 trillion.[2] U.S. exports from 1960 to 1986 increased from $20.6 billion to $217.3 billion—a three-fold increase in constant dollars. At the same time, U.S. imports increased from $16.4 billion to $387.1—a more than five-fold increase in constant dollars.[3] Almost one-fifth of U.S. industrial production is now exported. At least 70% of the goods produced in the U.S. compete with products from other countries.[4]

In the United States alone, there are more than 3,500 multinational corporations (MNCs), 30,000 exporting manufacturers, 25,000 companies with overseas branches and affiliates, and 40,000 firms operating in other countries on an ad-hoc basis. Not only are U.S.-based multinationals increasing their investments in production facilities and companies in other countries, but foreign-based MNCs are also doing the same in the U.S., Canada, and Mexico. In 1983, foreign buyers spent $2.2 billion to buy 116 U.S. companies. In 1987, they spent a record $40.7 billion for 316 companies.[5] The value of U.S. companies and other assets in which Canadians alone hold at least 10% of the equity totals over $100 billion. This total is not surprising: 24% of Canadian corporate assets are owned by foreign investors, many of them U.S. companies or private citizens.[6] International considerations have become crucial to the strategic decisions of any large business corporation.

10.1

THE COMING GLOBAL VILLAGE

In 1965, Marshall McLuhan suggested that advances in communications and transportation technologies were drawing the people of the world closer together. As intercontinental travel times decreased, the world went toward becoming a "global village" of interdependent people.[7] People in all countries were finding themselves affected by huge multinational corporations (MNCs).

In 1984, for example, the Chicago Mercantile Exchange linked with a futures exchange in Singapore in a major step toward global 24-hour financial trading. To increase the number of potential shareholders, an increasing number of corporations are listing their stock at exchanges around the world. R. J. Reynolds Industries, for example, lists its common shares on exchanges in London, Geneva, Zurich, Amsterdam, Dusseldorf, Berlin, Paris, and Brussels. Tokyo is next. Television is rapidly becoming a global phenomenon—linking nations together to watch the Olympics and other high interest events. Ted Turner's Cable Network News was the first truly global television channel, reaching 40% of U.S. homes on cable in 1986 and beaming news to viewers around the world via satellite. CNN's major overseas clients are hotels and government offices in Europe and Japan, but it is also available to homes in Australia and Canada, among other areas.[8] As noted in Illustrative Example 10.1, the modern world is reaching into the most remote locations. We are truly becoming one interdependent global village, with multinational corporations acting as the conduits for the international exchange of information, goods, and services.

Going International

Three basic **reasons** can be listed for business corporations' expanding their operations internationally:

1. To increase their sales and profits, corporations can expand market outlets and exploit growth opportunities. Foreign sales can thus absorb extra capacity and reduce unit costs. They can also spread economic risks over a wider number of markets. For example, realizing that the

ILLUSTRATIVE EXAMPLE 10.1

The Global Village Comes to Borneo

James Sterba, a staff reporter for the *Wall Street Journal,* journeyed to the island of Borneo to search for "civilization's edge." What he found surprised and impressed him:

> An hour by boat from this tiny river port (of Kapit, Malaysia) and five hours by truck over slick mountain trails gets us to three primitive huts occupied by heavily tattooed Iban natives who cut trees for a logging company. Except for the pack of Dunhills that one of the Ibans offer, the 20th century seems distant.
>
> Until a phone rings. The caller is in a motel room in Anaheim, California. He is the logging company's local manager, and he is phoning via satellites and hilltop relay towers to say that his Disneyland vacation is going great. He dialed the jungle direct. . . .
>
> It is a trifle disconcerting to arrive at a village market six hours by longboat from the coast only to find that Australian apples, Chinese pears, and Sunkist oranges got there first; and to travel another two hours to an Iban longhouse—a motel-like structure on stilts—and find that politicians had popped in by helicopter the day before to festoon the place with party banners; and to watch at a tiny river port, the unloading of boxes that contain frozen chicken wings "Made in the U.S.A."
>
> The beginning of the journey was promising enough. . . . River boats remain Borneo's preferred means of transport. In most places, there is no choice because there are no roads or airports. So we hop a water taxi down the Sarawak River, then a tired old longboat back upstream— a sort of mood-setting exercise for the exotica to come. . . .

> Sure enough, around the next bend stands what for Sarawak's 1.5 million residents, most of them villagers, is a pinnacle of exotica that looks as if it got lost on the way to Houston. It is called the Sarawak Plaza Shopping Complex— 10 stories of offices and shops, plus a parking garage and an adjacent Holiday Inn. It is the newest of five such shopping complexes in Kuching.
>
> Since school is out, Sarawak Plaza is bustling with a species of teenager known in suburban America as the "mall rat." Young men—ethnic Chinese, Malays, Ibans—wear baggy trousers and shirts, and their hair is slicked back with styling mousse. Girls with four shades of color between their eyelids and brows flit up and down escalators and in and out of music and video shops (you can rent this year's Oscar-winning "Platoon" for two days at $1.20). . . .
>
> Here we are later in Kapit's only air-conditioned bar, and the town's hot spot, with yesterday's phone call from Anaheim still ringing in our ears. . . . Spend a week in darkest Borneo searching for the edge of civilization and what you find these days are computers and jogging shoes, blue jeans and the latest episode of "L. A. Law". . . . We are confessing failure to a local friend. But he is having trouble hearing because a Malay-Philippino rock band, called D-Illusions and as flat as the draft beer, is belting out a charming 20th-century lyric, "Gimme money, that's what I want."

SOURCE: J. P. Sterba, "Even Deep in Borneo, Civilization Intrudes In All Its Splendor," *Wall Street Journal* (May 5, 1987), p. 1. Reprinted by permission of *Wall Street Journal,* copyright © Dow Jones & Company, Inc., 1987. All Rights Reserved.

market for razor blades in developed countries is stagnant, Gillette is targeting Third World countries. "The opportunities on the blade side really lie in new geography," stated Roderick Mills, Executive Vice-President for Gillette's international business. "In the Third World, there's a very high proportion of people under 15 years old. All those young men are going to be in the shaving population in very short time," he added.[9]

2. To gain competitive advantages, corporations can seek low-cost production facilities in locations close to raw materials and/or cheap labor. They can widen their channels of distribution and access to new technology through joint ventures. Both General Electric and Société Nationale d'Étude et de Construction de Moteurs d'Aviation (SNECMA), the French engine maker, benefited from their joint venture, the forming of CFM International to produce and sell jet engines to airlines.[10]

3. In addition, to secure raw material resources, companies can engage in the worldwide exploration for, and the processing, transportation, and marketing of raw materials. For years, the major rubber companies have owned rubber plantations in Southeast Asia. Oil companies have, of course, gone international for the same reason.

There are a number of **disadvantages,** however, to international expansion. For one thing, the strategic management process is far more complex for a multinational than for a domestic firm. Dymsza lists six limitations to international expansion.[11]

First, the multinational company faces a multiplicity of political, economic, legal, social, and cultural environments as well as a differential rate of change in them.

Second, there are complex interactions between a multinational firm and the multiplicity of its national environments because of national sovereignties, widely disparate economic and social conditions, as well as other factors.

Third, geographical distance, cultural and national differences, variations in business practices, and other differences make communications difficult between the parent corporation and its subsidiaries.

Fourth, the degree of significant economic, marketing, and other information required for planning varies a great deal among countries in availability, depth, and reliability. Furthermore, in any given host country, modern techniques for analyzing and developing data may not be highly developed. For example, an international corporation may find it difficult and expensive to conduct the effective market research essential for business planning.

Fifth, analysis of present and future competition may be more difficult to undertake in a number of countries because of differences in industrial structure and business practices.

Sixth, the multinational company is confronted not only with different national environments but also with regional organizations such as the European Economic Community, the European Trade Area, and the Latin American Free Trade Area, all of which are achieving various degrees of economic integration. The United Nations and specialized international organizations such as the International Bank for Reconstruction and Development, the International Finance Corporation, and the General Agreement on Tariffs and Trade (GATT) may also affect its future opportunities.

The Multinational Corporation

The multinational corporation is a very special type of international firm. Any U.S. company can call itself "international" if it has a small branch office in, say, Juarez or Toronto. An **international company** is one that engages in any combination of activities from exporting/importing to full-scale manufacturing in foreign countries. The **multinational corporation,** in contrast, is a highly developed international company with a deep worldwide involvement, plus a global perspective in its management and decision making. A more specific definition of an MNC is suggested by Dymsza:[12]

1. Although a multinational corporation may not do business in every region of the world, its decision makers consider opportunities throughout the world.

2. A considerable portion of its assets are invested internationally. One authority suggests that a firm becomes global when 20% of its assets are in other countries. Another suggests that the point is reached when operations in other nations account for at least 35% of the corporation's total sales and profits.

3. The corporation engages in international production and operates plants in a number of countries. These plants may range from assembly to fully integrated facilities.

4. Managerial decision making is based on a worldwide perspective. The international business is no longer a sideline or segregated activity. International operations are integrated into the corporation's overall business.

Porter proposes that multinationals operate in world industries that vary on a continuum from multi-domestic to global.[13] **Multi-domestic industries** are specific to each country or group of countries. This type of international industry is a collection of essentially domestic industries, like retailing and insurance. The activities in an MNC's subsidiary in this type of industry is essentially independent of the activities of the MNC's subsidiaries in other countries. In each country the MNC tailors its products or services to the very specific needs of consumers in that particular country. **Global industries,** in contrast, operate worldwide with only small adjustments made by MNCs for country-specific circumstances. A global industry is one in which an MNC's activities in one country are significantly affected by its activities in other countries. MNCs produce products or services in various world locations and sell them with only minor adjustments all over the world. Examples of global industries are commercial aircraft, television sets, semi-conductors, copiers, automobiles, and watches.

10.2

STRATEGY FORMULATION

As described in Chapter 1, the strategic management process includes strategy formulation, implementation, and evaluation and control. In order to formulate strategy, the top management of a multinational corporation must scan both the external environment for opportunities and threats, and the internal environment for strengths and weaknesses.

Scanning the External International Environment

The dominant issue in the strategic-management process of a multinational corporation is the external environment. The type of relationship an MNC can have with each factor in its task environment varies from one country to another and from one region to another. International societal environments vary so widely that a corporation's internal environment and strategic management process must be very flexible. Cultural trends in West Germany, for example, have resulted in the inclusion of worker representatives in corporate strategic planning. Differences in the sociocultural, economic, political-legal, and technological aspects of societal environments strongly affect the ways in which an MNC conducts its marketing, financial, manufacturing, and other functional activities. Some of the variables to be monitored in the various international societal environments are listed in Table 10.1.

Sociocultural Forces

Different sociocultural norms and values have important effects on an MNC's activities. For example, some cultures accept bribery and payoffs as a fact of life, whereas others punish them heavily. In Nigeria the accepted "dash"

TABLE 10.1
Some Important Variables in International Societal Environments

SOCIOCULTURAL	ECONOMIC	TECHNOLOGICAL	POLITICAL-LEGAL
Customs, norms, values	Economic development	Regulations on technology transfer	Form of government
Language	Per capita income	Energy availability/cost	Political ideology
Demographics	Climate	Natural resource availability	Tax laws
Life expectancies	GNP trends	Transportation network	Stability of government
Social institutions	Monetary and fiscal policies	Skill level of workforce	Government attitude toward foreign companies
Status symbols	Unemployment level	Patent-trademark protection	Regulations on foreign ownership of assets
Life-style	Currency convertibility	Information-flow infrastructure	Strength of opposition groups
Religious beliefs	Wage levels		
Attitudes toward foreigners	Nature of competition		Trade regulations
Literacy level	Membership in regional economic associations		Protectionist sentiment
			Foreign policies
			Terrorist activity
			Legal system

(money under the table) ranges from 15% of a multibillion dollar contract to a few naira to get a hotel operator to place a phone call.

Most countries differentiate between "lubrication" or "grease" payments, made to minor officials to expedite the execution of their duties, and large-scale "whitemail" bribes, intended to hide either a violation of the law or an illegal contribution designed to influence government policy. In some countries grease payments are viewed by their citizens as an entitlement—necessary income to supplement low public salaries. Because the dividing line between these two forms of extra payment is indistinct, an MNC must carefully monitor each country's norms and ensure that its actions are in line with local practice. Ethics tend to become pragmatically bound to situations, and the top managers of MNCs may find themselves open to charges of being amoral.

In less developed countries (LDCs), most of the working population can be illiterate. A result is likely to be a shortage of skilled labor and supervisors. Manufacturing facilities that mesh with the technical sophistication of the work force must be designed. If U.S. managers are used in LDCs, they must be aware of the wide variance in working practices around the world and totally familiar with those in the country in which they are stationed. For example, it is common in Europe for employees to get added compensation according to the number of their family members or because of unpleasant working conditions. Finnish paper mill workers get a "sauna premium" for missing baths when they are asked to work on Sunday. Fiji Island miners receive a daily half-hour "sex break" to fulfill their marital obligations.[14] Other examples abound.

Differences in language and social norms will affect heavily the marketing mix for a particular country. Product presentation, packaging, distribution channels, pricing, and advertising must be attuned to each culture. For example, Western cosmetic firms such as Max Factor, Revlon, and Avon have had little success in selling their usual products in Japan. Certain cultural factors affect their sales: in Japan perfume is hardly used; suntans are considered ugly; and bath oil is impractical in communal baths.[15] In contrast, Mr. Donut franchise shops are very successful in Japan, even though there is no coffee and doughnut custom there. Doughnuts are presented as a snack rather than as a breakfast food and located near railroad stations and supermarkets. All the signs are in English in order to appeal to the Western interests of the Japanese.

Even if a product is desired by the public, the literal translation of a product's name and slogan can ruin sales. For example, Pepsi Cola's "Come alive" jingle was translated into German as "Come alive out of the grave."[16] When General Motors introduced its Nova model into Latin America, it believed the name would translate well. Nova means constellation in Spanish. Nevertheless, people began to pronounce it "no vá," which in Spanish means "it does not go."[17] When translated into Spanish, an advertisement for ink by the Parker Pen Company gave the false impression that the product helped prevent pregnancy.[18]

Religious beliefs can also make a significant impact on a country's business practices. For example, to conform with Islamic law, banks in Pakistan stopped paying interest to depositors. The alternative is a profit-sharing and loss-sharing system. Sudan and Iran are also moving toward a totally Islamic banking system.[19] In Japan, each time Mazda manufactures a new car model, a Shinto priest clad in traditional white robe, sandals, and black lacquered hat conducts "honorable purification" rites on the new product with top management in attendance.[20]

Economic Forces

The type of economic system in a country can strongly affect the kind of relationship an MNC can establish with a host country. The managers of an MNC based in a free-market capitalistic country may have difficulty understanding the regulations affecting trade with a centrally planned socialistic country. Licensing, acquisition, and joint ventures may be restricted severely by such a host country. In addition, in most countries inflation and currency exchange rates create further difficulties for an MNC. In Bolivia, for example, the inflation rate during 1985 was 25,000%! After being frozen by the government for a year, prices rose at an annual rate of 545% in Brazil during 1987. Following prices, Brazilian interest rates surged to more than 700%, creating a serious problem for business. An MNC's financial policy in an economy subject to rapid inflation must be altered to protect the firm against inflationary losses. Cash balances must be minimized. Credit terms must be restricted. Prices must be constantly watched. In addition, balance of payments problems in a host country can lead to formal currency devaluations, as occurred in Italy in 1985 and in Mexico throughout the 1980s. Informal currency devaluations, resulting from the "floating" currency-exchange rate, took place in the United States, as well as in some other countries, during the mid-1980s. Such a devaluation leads to an MNC's taking large losses in terms of the assets and profits of its subsidiary in the devaluating country. In addition, a socialistic country may control the prices of the products sold by the MNC in that country but may increase the price of the raw materials it sells to the MNC. This results in a severe profit squeeze as the host government attempts to pass the burden of inflation to "rich" multinational corporations.

Because of these and other economic problems throughout the world, an MNC must be prepared to engage in countertrade and in hedging its foreign currency. **Countertrade** is a modern form of bartering that ranges from relatively simple barter transactions to intricate arrangements that can involve many nations and goods as well as complex financing and credits. Because less developed countries are often unable to pay cash for needed goods, exchanging goods and services is becoming increasingly attractive for them. From 1976 to 1984, countertrade grew from an estimated 2% to 33% of world commerce. For example, Sorimex, a Renault subsidiary, accepts coffee, phosphates, and other commodities in exchange for autos, in agreements with such countries as Colombia, Tunisia, Turkey, Egypt, Rumania, and the People's Republic of China. Almost one-fifth of General Electric's $4 billion in exports in one year were under countertrade contracts. Banks now have countertrade divisions to turn commodities into cash for the bank's commercial customers.[21] Multinational corporations must also deal with fluctuating exchange rates by *hedging* their foreign-currency exposures in the forward foreign-exchange market in which currencies are bought and sold for delivery at specific dates. For example, if a U.S.-based multinational is scheduled to receive 100 million German marks in exchange for machine tools one year from today, it may lose money if the dollar rises in value in relation to that of the mark. Although the 100 million marks is worth 30 million U.S. dollars today, it might be worth only 25 million U.S. dollars next year. To avoid this risk, an MNC may choose to sell marks for dollars in the forward market for delivery in one year. This hedge "locks in" the MNC's dollar revenue at 30 million U.S. dollars regardless of currency fluctuations.

Political-Legal Forces

The system of laws and public policies governing business formation, acquisitions, and competitive activities constrains the strategic options open to a multinational company. It is likely that a particular country will specify guidelines for hiring, firing, and promoting people; it might also mandate employment ratios of "foreigners" to its citizens and restrict management's prerogatives regarding unions. In addition, there are likely to be government policies dealing with ownership, licensing, repatriation of profits (profits leaving the host country for the MNC's home country), royalties, importing, and purchasing. Beyond these, there are likely to be both some sentiment for the establishment of tariff barriers to keep out foreign goods and some strong negative feeling about foreign control by an MNC of the host country's assets.

There are many examples of countries expropriating and nationalizing foreign as well as domestic holdings. In 1981, for example, France, under socialist leader François Mitterand, ordered a number of foreign-owned firms (among them, Honeywell-Bull Computers, ITT-France, and Rouseel-Uclaf Drugs) to sell a large percentage of their stock to the French government. Other countries have passed laws forbidding foreign nationals (including MNCs) from having majority control of firms in key industries. Mexico and India restricted foreign ownership during the 1970s. Canada passed legislation in 1981 requiring U.S. energy companies operating in Canada to sell a majority of their stock to Canadian owners by 1990. Responding to Malaysia's requirement that Malaysians have majority control of rubber plantations, Uniroyal sold its profitable rubber plants to a Malaysian company in 1984 and left the country.[22] A more old-fashioned approach took place in Peru in 1985 when President Perez's police, carrying submachine guns, surrounded the headquarters of HNG/InterNorth Inc.'s Belco Petroleum Corporation and simply took the Omaha energy company's Peruvian assets, worth $400 million.[23]

By the mid-1980s two international trends were evident. One was the desire by a number of countries to sell to private interests previously state-owned firms and to welcome the presence of foreign-owned MNCs. Similar to President Reagan's deregulation of government agencies, this **denationalization** or **privatization** of state-owned corporations was taking place in Canada, Japan, and most Western European nations. Great Britain, for example, sold the assets of Jaguar automobiles and 51% of British Telecom, the telecommunications monopoly. From 1980 to 1988, more than fifty-six state-owned companies from every continent, with total value of more than $90 billion, were sold to private shareholders. Another 2,000 candidates, ranging from Britain's electricity industry and much of France's insurance business, to sugar mills in Mexico and steel mills in Bangladesh, were marked for sale during the early 1990s.[24] Experts predict that state-owned enterprises that become multinational will be increasingly privatized, whether formally or informally. The trend will continue because apart from purely national public services, all state-owned enterprises must expand internationally in order to survive in the increasingly global environment. They cannot compete successfully in other countries if they are forced to follow inefficient home-country government policies and regulations rather than economically-oriented international practices.[25]

The second international trend was an increasing amount of trade barriers, local content regulations, and other **protectionist measures,** designed to help domestic industry compete with foreign competition. Although tariffs world-wide were significantly less during the 1980s than they had been in the 1950s, they remained a favorite defense against imports in developing countries. Taiwan, for example charged a 65% fee on imported autos. Brazil added a 105% tariff to imported wine and sausage. The developed countries often do the same. In an attempt to protect U.S. pasta makers and to retaliate for the Common Market's discrimination against U.S. lemons and oranges, President Reagan in 1985 increased the tariff from about $\frac{1}{10}$ cent to some 10 cents per pound on the price of European noodles. The quota has become very popular as a way to protect home industry without resorting to tariffs. For example, under polite but firm pressure from the European Community, the Japanese agreed to limit their shipments of quartz watches, hi-fi equipment, and computer-controlled machine tools to Europe. Japan, in turn, strictly limited its imports of leather, beef, and citrus fruits. Other protectionist measures are setting product standards at such a level that few foreign products will be acceptable for sale (a favorite in Japan), requiring that government procurement give preference to that nation's own industry (heavily used in the U.S. and France for "national security"), and outright government subsidies to companies in particular industries to help them compete in the international market with artificially lower prices (used worldwide to support local agriculture). Local content regulations, to force foreign companies to manufacture within a particular country at least a part of every product that they sell there, are being generated worldwide. Mexico, for example, requires its six foreign-car manufacturers to use locally produced parts and material equal to half of each vehicle's value. There are examples like these for most nations in the world. Such protectionist and nationalistic tendencies serve to short-circuit the basic logic underlying the economic concept of **comparative advantage** (see Illustrative Example 10.2); the results are higher prices for consumers and inefficient domestic industries.

In order to introduce some stability into international trade, a number of countries have formed alliances and negotiated mutual cooperation agreements. One such agreement is the General Agreement on Tariffs and Trade (GATT) established in 1948 by twenty-three countries. This agreement was formed to create a relatively free system of trading, primarily through the reduction of tariffs. It provides a forum for the negotiating of mutual reductions in trade restrictions. By 1987, ninety-four nations were contracting parties to the GATT. Although the General Agreement covers around 80% of world trade in merchandise, it does not cover a growing trade in services, agriculture, textiles, and investment and capital flows.[26] An example of a political/trade alliance is the European Economic Community (Common Market), which agreed not only to reduce duties and other trade restrictions among member countries, but also to have a common tariff against nonmember countries. This provision was a major factor in encouraging firms from nonmember countries, such as the United States, to locate some manufacturing and marketing facilities inside the EEC to avoid tariffs.

There are also trade associations, such as the Organization of Petroleum Exporting Countries (OPEC), the International Tin Council, and the International Cocoa Organization, which attempt to stabilize commodity supplies and prices to the benefit of their member nations.

Technological Forces

As mentioned in Chapter 4, the question of technology "transfer" has become an important issue in international dealings. Most less developed countries welcome multinational corporations into their nation as conduits of advanced technology and management expertise. They realize that not only will local labor be hired to work for the firm, but also that the MNC will have to educate the work force to deal with advanced methods and techniques. Reich, in his book *The Next American Frontier,* argues that production technologies are rapidly moving from the developed to the developing nations of the world.[27] Countries such as Korea, Hong Kong, Taiwan, Singapore, Brazil, and Spain, which specialized in the 1960s in simple products like clothing and toys, are now mass producing technologically complex products like automobiles, televisions, and ships. At the same

ILLUSTRATIVE EXAMPLE 10.2

The Basics of Absolute and Comparative Advantage in International Trade

Suppose a country presently produces 1 million bushels of corn and 5 million bushels of beans each year. Its people desire more corn. Should it simply plant more corn and less beans? This seems like a reasonable solution until one notes that the soil and water are much better for growing beans than for corn. Each acre planted can produce twice as much bean crop as corn. It takes the same amount of work, and the seeds, fertilizer, and other costs are the same for the farmers regardless of the crop planted. Suppose that the neighboring country has different soil and on every acre planted is able to produce twice as much corn as beans.

The concept of *absolute advantage* in international trade suggests that when both countries are considered, the first country has advantage over the second country in producing beans, but the second has advantage over the first in producing corn. The logical conclusion is that the first country should specialize in producing beans (where it has absolute advantage) and the second should plant only corn (where it also has absolute advantage). The result would be that the first country would produce 7 million bushels of beans each year and *no* corn (with the 2 to 1 advantage of beans to corn, the 1 million bushels of corn would be replaced by 2 million bushels of beans). The reverse would be true in the second country. If the countries are able to trade freely with each other, both countries will be able to have more corn and beans if they each specialize in the crop with which there is advantage, than if both countries try to produce both crops.

Therefore, in answer to the question posed earlier, if a country wants more corn but has an absolute advantage in the production of beans, it should plant more beans. The excess beans can be exported to another country in exchange for more corn than the first country could ever produce with the same resources.

What happens, however, when the first country can produce more corn *and* beans per acre planted than can its neighboring country? Is there any benefit to trade? According to the concept of *comparative advantage*, it still makes sense to specialize as long as the first country is able to grow more of one crop than another crop per acre planted. As an analogy, suppose the best architect in town also happens to be the best carpenter. Would it make sense for him to build his own house? Certainly not, because he can earn more money per hour by devoting all his time to his job as an architect even though he has to employ a carpenter less skillful than himself to build the house. In the same manner, the first country will gain if it concentrates its resources on the production of that commodity it can produce most efficiently. It will earn enough money from the export of that commodity to still import what it needs from its less efficient neighbor country.

SOURCE: J. D. Daniels and L. H. Radebaugh, *International Business: Environments and Operations,* 4th ed. (Reading, Mass.: Addison-Wesley, 1987), pp. 121–129.

---

time, the less developed countries of Malaysia, Thailand, the Philippines, Sri Lanka, and India have taken over the production of clothing, toys, and the like. With Korea and Taiwan on its heels technologically, Japan reduced its steelmaking capacity and began orienting itself in the 1980s beyond consumer electronics toward telecommunications.

Political-legal considerations become important when aerospace firms, with their heavy dependence on government contracts, want to transfer the technology that they developed for military purposes into profitable commercial products sold internationally. General Electric, for example, had a great deal of difficulty forming a joint venture with the French national engine firm SNECMA in the early 1970s. The venture involved the sharing of jet engines developed specifically for the prototype of the B-1 bomber. Although the U.S. federal government refused, for political reasons, to put the B-1 bomber into production, it did not like the idea of GE's selling such advanced technology to another country.[28] The U.S. government has similar fears of semiconductor technology being sold to countries behind the Iron Curtain. The Coordinating Committee for Multilateral Export Controls (Cocom), composed of the fifteen members of the North Atlantic Treaty Organization (NATO) minus Spain and Iceland plus Japan, compiles lists of items that cannot be sold to Communist countries without its approval. This control has created a number of problems for MNCs wishing to sell high-technology products to China.[29]

Another technological issue raised in international trade is the determination of the appropriate technology for use in production plants located in host countries. For example, labor-saving devices (robots, for instance) that are economically justifiable in highly developed countries where wage rates are high, can be more costly than labor-intensive types of production in less developed countries with high unemployment and low wage rates. The knowledge of technology might be so low in a country that the MNC is tempted, to gain operating leverage, to employ very few local people and automate the plant as much as possible. The host country's government, however, faced with massive unemployment, could strongly desire a labor intensive plant.[30] The basic question an MNC might face is whether the benefits to be gained by modifying technologies for the unique conditions of each country are worth the costs that must be incurred.

Assessing International Opportunities and Threats

In searching for an advantageous market or manufacturing location, a multinational corporation must gather and evaluate data on strategic factors in a large number of countries and regions. Because of its global perspective, an MNC might use comparative advantage to its benefit, by making machine parts in Brazil, assembling them as engines in Germany, installing the engines in auto bodies in Italy, and shipping completed cars to the United States for sale. This strategy serves to reduce the risk to the MNC of operating in only one country, but exposes it to a series of smaller risks in a greater number of countries. Therefore, multinational corporations must be able to deal with political and economic risk in many diverse countries and regions.

Some firms, such as American Can Company, develop an elaborate computerized system to rank investment risks. Smaller companies can hire outside consultants like Chicago's Associated Consultants International or Boston's Arthur D. Little, Inc. to provide political risk assessments. Among the many systems that exist to assess political and economic risks are the Political System Stability Index, the Business Environment Risk Index,

Business International's Country Assessment Service, and Frost and Sullivan's World Political Risk Forecasts.[31] (For a summary of Frost and Sullivan's risk index, see the January/February, 1987, issue of *Planning Review*.)[32] Regardless of the source of data, a firm must develop its own method of assessing risk. It must decide upon the most important factors from its point of view and assign weights to each. An example of such a rating method is depicted in Table 10.2.

Scanning the Internal Environment

Any corporation desiring to move into the international arena will need to assess its own strengths and weaknesses. A corporation's chances for success are enhanced if it has or can develop the following capabilities:

1. **Technological lead.** An innovative approach or a new product or a new process gives one a short-term monopolistic position.

2. **A strong trade name.** If a well-known product has snob appeal, a higher profit margin can cover initial entry costs.

3. **Advantage of scale.** A large corporation has the advantage of low unit costs and a financial base strong enough that it can weather setbacks.

4. **A scanning capability.** An ability to search successfully and efficiently for opportunities will take on greater importance in international dealings.

5. **An outstanding product or service.** A solid product or service is more likely to have staying power in international competition.

6. **An outstanding international executive.** The presence of an executive who understands international situations and can develop a core of local executives who can work well with the home office, is likely to result in the building of a strong and long-lasting international organization.[33]

Evaluating Mission and Objectives

Upon assessing its internal strengths and weaknesses and the opportunities and threats present in the international environment, a business corporation must decide upon its level of commitment to national and international markets. Not every firm needs to become a multinational corporation to be successful. Not every MNC needs to aim for high market share throughout the world to be profitable. James Leontiades proposes that a company can take one of four basic approaches, as depicted in Figure 10.1, regarding international competition within an industry; the selection of an approach is based upon a company's **market share objective** and its desired **scope of operations:**[34]

- **Global high share.** As mentioned earlier in this chapter, a global industry is characterized by MNCs having global objectives and a worldwide coordination of resources in interdependent markets. A company desiring global high share in an industry should follow an overall low cost

TABLE 10.2
Example of Weighted Rating of Investment Climate

Factors Listed in Order of Importance	COUNTRY A			COUNTRY B		
	(1) Assigned Weights Considering Importance of Adverse Developments	(2) Rating of Factor from 0 (Completely Unfavorable) to 100 (Completely Favorable)	(3) Weighted Rating (Column 1 × Column 2)	(1) Assigned Weights Considering Importance of Adverse Developments	(2) Rating of Factor from 0 (Completely Unfavorable) to 100 (Completely Favorable)	(3) Weighted Rating (Column 1 × Column 2)
1. Possibility of expropriation.	10	90	900	10	55	550
2. Possibility of damage to property from rebellion or war.	9	80	720	9	50	450
3. Remission of earnings.	8	70	560	8	50	400
4. Governmental restrictions of foreign business compared to domestic-owned enterprise.	8	70	560	8	60	480
5. Availability of local capital at reasonable cost.	7	50	350	7	90	630
6. Political stability.	7	80	560	7	50	350
7. Repatriation of capital.	7	80	560	7	60	420
8. Currency stability.	6	70	420	6	30	180
9. Price stability.	5	40	200	5	30	150
10. Taxes on business (including any discriminatory provisions).	4	80	320	4	90	360
11. Problems of dealing with labor unions.	3	70	210	3	80	240
12. Government investment incentives.	2	0	0	2	90	180
TOTAL WEIGHTED RATING OF INVESTMENT CLIMATE			5,360			4,390

SOURCE: W. A. Dymsza, *Multinational Business Strategy* (New York: McGraw-Hill Book Co., 1972), p. 90. Copyright © 1972 by McGraw-Hill, Inc. Reprinted by permission.

FIGURE 10.1
Four Basic Approaches to International Competition

MARKET SHARE OBJECTIVE

SCOPE OF OPERATIONS

	High	Low
Global	Global High Share	Global Niche
National	National High Share	National Niche

Source: Adapted from J. C. Leontiades, *Multinational Corporate Strategy* (Lexington, Mass.: Lexington Books, 1985), p. 53. Reprinted by permission.

strategy by placing its many operations in those countries where costs are lowest and by using economies of scale. Large MNCs such as IBM, Ford, Philips, and Sony take this approach.

- **Global niche.** Because relatively few companies will have the resources to pursue a global high share objective, most developing multinational corporations will attempt to gain global competitive advantage through specialization of product or market. Using a differentiation competitive strategy, such a corporation might produce a particular type of product or service that global high share MNCs cannot afford to produce. To grow globally, Schlumberger has, for example, offered a variety of specialized services to the oil and computer industries. A company can also follow a focus strategy to satisfy a particular market segment that exists in small numbers in many countries. Rolls Royce automobiles, for example, produces automobiles for the very wealthiest people throughout the world.

- **National high share.** Rather than compete in an international arena for which they are unprepared, many companies choose to concentrate on their domestic market. These firms can be very successful as long as their particular industry remains multi-domestic (in Porter's terms) as compared to global. National barriers to entry are crucial to the preservation of national high share. These barriers, which can range from tariffs to quotas to transportation and communication impediments as well as differences in taste, refer to anything that obstructs the corporation's freedom to transfer and coordinate resources across national borders. Examples of these multi-domestic industries, which exist in every country but are generally unattractive to global competitors, are retailing, distribution, insurance, consumer finance, and caustic chemicals.[35] Norfolk Southern Railroad is a very successful transportation company in the process of achieving national high share in the United States.

- **National niche.** To close off their markets from national high share and global competitors, national niche companies can take advantage of specialization on a national scale. Food (such as barbecue sauce in the U.S.), clothing, and some small-scale handicraft industries often allow a company to achieve a national niche.

If a multinational corporation chooses to achieve global high share, it must be prepared to establish a significant presence in the three developed areas of the world known collectively as **the triad.** Coined by Kenichi Ohmae, Managing Director of the Tokyo office of McKinsey & Company, the three markets of Japan, North America, and Western Europe now form a single market with common needs.[36] Arguing that consumers' behavior is influenced more by their educational background and disposable income than by ethnic characteristics, Ohmae proposes that strategic managers of MNCs must treat the inhabitants of the triad as a single race of consumers with shared needs and aspirations.

Focusing on the triad is essential for an MNC pursuing global high share, according to Ohmae, because close to 90% of all high-value-added, high-technology manufactured goods are produced and consumed in North America, Western Europe, and Japan. Ideally, a company should have a significant presence in each of these regions so that it can produce and market its products simultaneously in all three areas. Otherwise, it will lose competitive advantage to triad-oriented MNCs. No longer can an MNC develop and market a new product in one part of the world before it exports it to other developed countries. According to Ohmae, the previously used "cascade" model of product distribution by stages is being replaced by the "sprinkler" model of simultaneous production and marketing. A personal experience of Ohmae's shows how much of a global village the world has become:

> Recently, . . . when I was showing off my very thin Casio calculator, which fits inside my visiting card case, a Dutchman smiled and pulled out his own, and pointed out that it was even thinner. The latest Casio had been launched simultaneously in all regions of the triad, so that it reached certain parts of the Netherlands faster than a local shop in Japan.[37]

International Portfolio Analysis

To strengthen a firm's competitive position, strategic planning seeks to match markets with products and other corporate resources. Because most multinational corporations manufacture and sell a wide range of products, it is necessary, when management is formulating strategy, to keep track of the country's attractiveness as well as the product's strength. Nevertheless, there is a strong tendency for top management in MNCs to plan around either products or markets, but not both simultaneously.[38]

To aid international strategic planning, Harrell and Kiefer have shown how portfolio analysis can be applied to international markets. As depicted in Fig. 10.2, each axis summarizes a host of data concerning the attractiveness of a particular country and the competitive strength of a particular product.

A **country's attractiveness** is composed of its market size, the market rate of growth, the extent and type of government regulation, and economic and political factors. A product's **competitive strength** is composed of its market share, product fit, contribution margin, and market support. The two scales form the axes of the matrix in Fig. 10.2. Those products falling in the upper left generally should receive funding for growth, whereas products in the lower right are prime for "harvesting," or divesting. Those products falling on the lower left to upper-right diagonal require selective funding strategies. Those falling in the upper-right block require additional funding if the product is to contribute in the future to the firm's profits. Joint ventures or divestitures would be most appropriate if cash is limited. Those falling in the center and lower left blocks are probably good candidates for "milking." They can produce strong cash flows in the short run.[39]

Portfolio analysis might not be useful, however, to those MNCs pursuing

FIGURE 10.2
Matrix for Plotting Products by Country

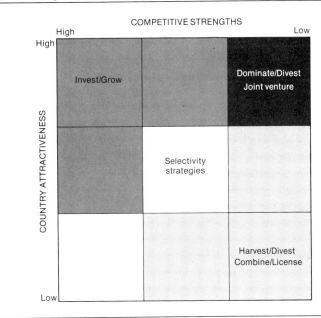

Source: G. D. Harrell and R. O. Kiefer, "Multinational Strategic Market Portfolios," *MSU Business Topics* (Winter 1981), p. 7. Reprinted by permission.

global high share via an overall low-cost competitive strategy. For those MNCs catering to the triad countries, portfolio analysis might be useful only in their considerations of Third World locations. In discussing the importance of global industries, Porter argues against the use of Harrell and Kiefer's recommended portfolio analysis on a country by country basis:

> In a global industry, however, managing international activities like a portfolio will undermine the possibility of achieving competitive advantage. In a global industry, a firm must in some way integrate its activities on a worldwide basis to capture the linkage among countries.[40]

Developing International Strategies

Depending upon its situation and its mission and objectives, a multinational corporation can select from a number of strategic options the most appropriate methods for it to use in entering a foreign market or establishing manufacturing facilities in another country.

Exporting

Exporting is a good way to minimize risk and to experiment with a specific product; it can be conducted in a number of ways. An MNC could choose to handle all critical functions itself, or it could contract these functions to an export management company. To operate in a country such as Japan, which has a series of complex regulations, an MNC could use the services of an agent or distributor.

Licensing

Under a *licensing* agreement, the licensing firm grants rights to a firm in the host country to produce and/or sell a product. The licensee pays compensation to the licensing firm in return for technical expertise. This is an especially useful strategy if the trademark or brand name is well known, but the MNC does not have sufficient funds to finance its entering the country directly. Domino's Pizza, Inc., for example, gave Ernest Higa in 1985 the sole rights to market Domino's pizza in Japan for a share of the receipts. In 1986, Higa's first three stores made more than $1 million in sales.[41] Anheuser-Busch is also using this strategy to produce and market Budweiser beer in Great Britain, Japan, Israel, Australia, Korea, and the Philippines. This strategy also becomes important if the country makes entry via investment either difficult or impossible. Examples are Japan and Eastern European countries. There is always the danger, however, that the licensee might develop its competence to the point that it becomes a competitor to the licensing firm.

Joint Ventures

Joint ventures are very popular with MNCs. Companies often form joint ventures to combine the resources and expertise needed for the development of new products or technologies.[42] The corporation engages in international ownership at a much lower risk. A joint venture may be an association between an MNC and a firm in the host country or a government agency in that country. A quick method of obtaining local management, it also reduces the risks of expropriation and harassment by host country officials. Some of the joint ventures that U.S. firms have made with foreign partners are listed in Table 10.3.

When more than two organizations participate in a joint venture, it is sometimes referred to as a **consortium.** For example, Airbus Industrie, the European producer of jet airplanes, is a consortium owned by four partners from four countries: Aerospatiale of France (37.9%), Messerschmitt-Bokkow-Blohm of West Germany (37.9%), British Aerospace Corp. (20%), and Construcciones Aeronauticas S. A. of Spain (4.2%). Disadvantages of joint ventures include loss of control, lower profits, probability of conflicts with partners, and the likely transfer of technological advantage to the local partner. Joint ventures typically are meant to be temporary, especially by the Japanese, who view them as a way to rectify a competitive weakness until they can achieve long-term dominance in the partnership.[43] For an example of an international joint venture by CSX Corporation, see the Integrative Case at the end of the chapter.

TABLE 10.3
Some International Joint Ventures

Joint Venture	U.S. PARENT	FOREIGN PARTNER	PRODUCTS
New United Motor Mfg.	General Motors	Toyota (Japan)	Subcompact cars
National Steel	National Intergroup	Nippon Kokan (Japan)	Steel
Siecor	Corning Glass Works	Siemens (Germany)	Optical cable
Honeywell/ Ericsson Development	Honeywell	L. M. Ericsson (Sweden)	PBX systems
Himont	Hercules	Montedison (Italy)	Polypropylene resin
GMFanuc Robotics	General Motors	Fanuc (Japan)	Robots
International Aero Engines	United Technologies	Rolls-Royce (Britain)	Aircraft engines

SOURCE: "Are Foreign Partners Good for U.S. Companies?" *Business Week* (May 28, 1984), p. 59. Reprinted from the May 28, 1984 issue of *Business Week* by special permission. Copyright © 1984 by McGraw-Hill, Inc.

Acquisitions

If an MNC wishes to keep total control of its operations, it might want to start a business from scratch or acquire a firm already established in the host country. An *acquisition* has merits because assets can be bought in their entirety rather than on a piecemeal basis. Synergistic benefits can result if the MNC acquires a firm with strong complementary product lines and a good distribution network. Nestlé S. A. of Switzerland, for example, purchased BeechNut (baby foods), Libby, McNeill and Libby (fruit juices), Stouffer (hotels and frozen dinners), Ward-Johnson (candy), Hills Brothers (coffee), and Carnation (evaporated milk) to complement its successful Nescafé, Quik, Nestea, and L'Oreal consumer products. In some countries, however, acquisitions can be difficult to arrange because of a lack of available information about potential candidates. Government restrictions on ownership, such as Canada's requirement that all energy corporations in Canada be controlled by Canadians, also can discourage acquisitions. It can be possible, however, for an MNC to have control of a foreign enterprise even though the MNC cannot attain more than 49% of the ownership. One way is to maintain control over some asset required by the foreign firm. Another device is to separate equity into voting and nonvoting stock so that the minority MNC investor has a majority of the voting stock.

Green-Field Development

If a corporation does not want to buy another firm's existing facilities via acquisition, it may choose a *green-field development,* or the building of a manufacturing facility from scratch. This is usually a far more complicated and expensive operation than acquisition, but it allows the MNC more freedom in designing the plant, choosing suppliers, and hiring a work force. An Italian semiconductor manufacturer, SGS-Ates Componenti Elettronici S. p. A., selected this strategy. According to its Vice-President of Marketing, Richard Pieranunzi: "To find a company that exactly matched our needs would be difficult. And we didn't want to buy other people's problems."[44]

Production Sharing

In a term coined by Peter Drucker, the process of *production sharing* combines the higher labor skills and technology available in the developed countries with the lower-cost labor available in developing countries. Since 1970, U.S. imports under production-sharing arrangements have been increasing at a rate of more than 20% per year.[45] Among the multinational corporations using this strategy are Texas Instruments, RCA, Honeywell, General Electric, and GTE. By locating assembly plants, called *maquiladoras,* in Ciudad Juarez and Tijuana, Mexico, and packaging plants across the border in Texas, these firms are able to take advantage of Mexico's low labor costs. This opportunity was a result of the Mexican government's relaxation of its laws against foreign ownership of factories and its reduction of import taxes on raw materials.

Management Contracts

A large multinational corporation is likely to have a large amount of management talent at its disposal. *Management contracts* offer a means through which an MNC may use part of its personnel to assist a firm in a host country for a specified fee and period of time. Such arrangements are common when a host government expropriates part or all of an MNC's holdings in its country. The contracts allow the MNC to continue to earn some income from its investment and keep the operations going until local management is trained. Management contracts are also used by a number of less developed countries that have the capital but neither the labor nor the managerial skills required to utilize available technology.

Turnkey Operations

Turnkey operations are typically contracts for the construction of operating facilities in exchange for a fee. The facilities are transferred to the host country or firm when they are complete. The customer is usually a government agency of, say, an Eastern European or Middle Eastern country that has decreed that a particular product must be produced locally and under its control. MNCs that perform turnkey operations are frequently industrial equipment manufacturers that supply some of their own equipment for the project and that commonly sell to the host country replacement parts and maintenance services. They thereby create customers as well as future competitors.

Subcontract Arrangements

MNCs might find that, in times of national fervor in the less developed countries, facilities that mine and process raw materials are prime targets for expropriation. Therefore, an MNC can *contract* with a foreign government or local firm to trade raw materials for certain resources belonging to the MNC. For example, several oil-producing countries have made arrangements with oil firms to let the firms take all exploration and development risks in exchange for a share of the sales of the oil produced.

10.3
STRATEGY IMPLEMENTATION

To be effective, international strategies must be implemented in concurrence with national and cultural differences. Among the many considerations of an MNC, three of the most important are (1) selecting the local partner for a joint venture or licensing arrangement, (2) organizing the firm around the most appropriate structure, and (3) encouraging global rather than national management practices.

Partner Selection

Joint ventures and licensing agreements between a multinational company and a local partner in a host country are becoming increasingly popular as a means by which an MNC can gain entry into other countries, especially less developed countries.[46] National policies as well as the complexity of the host country's market often make these the preferred strategies for the balancing of a country's attractiveness against financial risk. The key to the successful implementation of these strategies is the selection of the local partner. In Fig. 10.3, Lasserre proposes a model describing the many variables to be considered by both sides when they are assessing a partnership. Each party needs to assess not only the strategic fit of each company's project strategy, but also the fit of each company's respective resources. Lasserre contends that this process requires a minimum of one to two years of prior contacts between both parties.[47] The fact that joint ventures tend to have a high rate of costly failures suggests that few multinationals use such a careful selection process.[48]

Organizational Structure

Stages of MNC Development

Rarely, if ever, do multinational corporations suddenly appear as full-blown worldwide organizations. They tend to go through three common evolutionary stages, both in their relationships with widely dispersed geographic markets and in the manner in which they structure their operations and programs.

STAGE 1: INITIAL ENTRY The "parent" corporation is attracted to a particular market in another country and seeks to test the potential of its products in this market with minimal risk. The firm thus introduces a number of product lines into the market through home-based export programs, licensing agreements, joint ventures, and/or through local commercial offices. The product divisions at headquarters continue to be responsible for all functional activities.

STAGE 2: EARLY DEVELOPMENT Success in Stage 1 leads the parent corporation to believe that a stronger presence and broader product lines are needed for it to fully exploit its advantage in the host country. The parent company establishes a local operating division or company in the host country, such as Ford of Britain, to better serve the market. The product line is expanded. Local manufacturing capacity is established. Managerial

FIGURE 10.3
Assessing Partners to Implement Joint Venture and Licensing Strategies

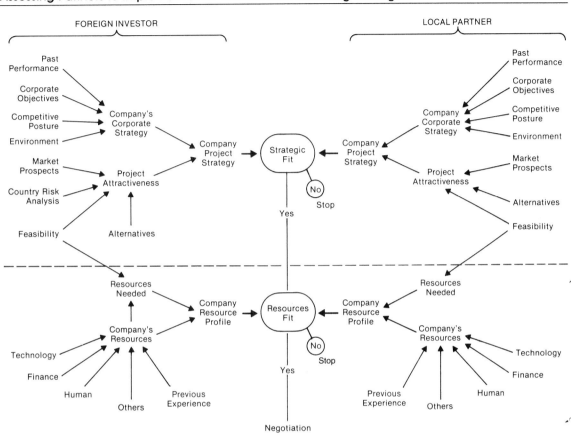

Source: P. Lasserre, "Selecting a Foreign Partner for Technology Transfer," *Long Range Planning* (December 1984), p. 45. Copyright © 1984 Pergamon Press, Ltd. Reprinted by permission.

functions (product development, finance, marketing, etc.) are organized locally. As time goes by, other related businesses are acquired by the parent company so that the base of the local operating division is broadened. As the subsidiary in the host country successfully develops a strong regional presence, it achieves greater autonomy and self-sufficiency.

STAGE 3: MATURITY As the parent corporation becomes aware of the success of its subsidiaries in other countries and the skills of its local managers, it consolidates operations under a regional management organization. It increases the amount of attention given to a wide range of investment opportunities, such as mergers and acquisitions. Although the regional or local company continues to maintain ties with the parent corporation and the product divisions in the home country, it tends to enjoy relative autonomy in terms of local policy-setting and managerial practices. As was the case with the North American Philips Corporation, originally an affiliate of N. V. Philips' Gloeilampenfabrieken, a subsidiary may become a totally separate company with local shareholders and publicly traded stock.[49] Table 10.4 summarizes some of the structural arrangements possible in each stage of MNC development.

Even though most international and multinational corporations move through these stages in their involvement with host countries, any one corporation can be at different stages simultaneously, with different products

TABLE 10.4
International Activity and Structure

Stage	ACTIVITIES OF COMPANY	ORGANIZATION RESPONSIBLE FOR INTERNATIONAL ACTIVITIES	EXECUTIVE IN CHARGE
1	Exports directly and indirectly, but trade is minor.	Export department.	Export manager, reporting to domestic marketing executive.
	Exports become more important.	Export division.	Division manager.
2	Company undertakes licensing and invests in production overseas.	International division.	Director of international operations, usually vice-president.
	International investments increase.	Sometimes international headquarters company as wholly owned subsidiary [of domestic parent company].	President, who is vice-president in parent company.
3	International investments substantial and widespread; diversified international business activities.	Global organizational structure by geographic areas, product lines, functions, or some combination. Also worldwide staff support.	No single executive in charge of international business.

SOURCE: Adapted from W. A. Dymsza, *Multinational Business Strategy* (New York: McGraw-Hill Book Company, 1972), p. 22. Copyright © 1972 by McGraw-Hill, Inc. Reprinted by permission.

in different markets. An example of corporate diversity in international operations is Hewlett-Packard. In the beginning of its international activity, the company exported its products. It used its own staff to oversee exports to Canada, and export management companies (export intermediaries operating on a buy-and-sell basis and providing financing for export shipments) to oversee exports to other countries. These exports were then sold in both cases to middlemen abroad. As sales expanded, Hewlett-Packard took over the exporting functions, opened its own sales office in Mexico, purchased a warehousing facility in Switzerland, organized a wholly owned manufacturing subsidiary in West Germany, and entered into a partly owned venture in Japan.[50]

Centralization versus Decentralization

A basic dilemma facing the globally oriented multinational corporation is how to organize authority centrally, so that it operates as a vast interlocking system that achieves synergy, and at the same time decentralize authority, so that local managers can make the decisions necessary to meet the demands of the local market or host government.[51] To deal with this problem, MNCs tend to structure themselves either along product groups or geographic areas. They may even combine both in a matrix structure.

Typically, multinational corporations do not organize themselves around business functions, such as marketing or manufacturing, unless they are in an extractive raw-materials industry. Basic functions are thus subsumed under either product or geographic units.[52] Two examples of the usual international structures are Nestlé and American Cyanamid. Nestlé's structure is one in which significant power and authority have been decentralized to geographic entities. This structure is similar to that depicted in Fig. 10.4, in which each geographic set of operating companies has a different group of products. In contrast, American Cyanamid has a series of product groups with worldwide responsibilities. To depict Cyanamid's structure, the geographical entities in Fig. 10.4 would have to be replaced by product groups or strategic business units.

The product-group structure enables the company to introduce and manage a similar line of products around the world. The geographic-area structure, in contrast, allows a company to tailor products to regional differences and to achieve regional coordination. Philips, the Dutch electronics firm, recently switched from a geographical structure, oriented to local needs, to a product structure, oriented to global needs. The company's production facilities were small and high-cost because they were designed only for regional markets. The switch to a product structure was believed by top management to be crucial if Philips were to compete effectively with the Japanese MNCs. "We are still weak," stated Dick Snijders, a Director of Corporate Finance at Philips, "because our emphasis is still too much on the national, and we need to achieve much greater economies of scale."[53]

FIGURE 10.4
Geographic Area Structure*

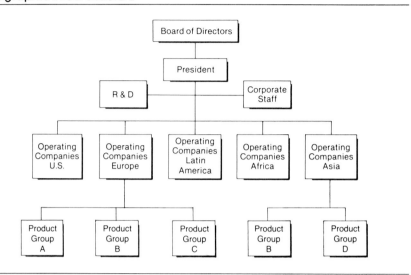

*Note: Because of space limitations, product groups for only Europe and Asia are shown here.

A survey of thirty-seven large, U.S.-based multinational corporations in various industries revealed that 43% used an international division; 35% were organized according to product group; 14% were structured around geographic areas; 5% used a functional structure; and 3% utilized the matrix structure. The international division is much more commonly used by U.S.-based MNCs than European-based MNCs; this is probably a result of the size difference between the domestic markets of the typical U.S.-based and the typical Swiss or British MNC.[54]

Management Practices

As is true of most people from any developed society, managers tend to believe that what works well in their society will work well anywhere. Thus, someone well-schooled in the virtues of MBO, participative decision making, theory Y practices, job enrichment, and management science will have a tendency to transplant these practices without alteration to foreign nations. Unfortunately, just as products often need to be altered to appeal to a new market, so too do most management practices.

In a study of forty different cultures, Hofstede found that he could explain the success or failure of certain management practices on the basis of four cultural dimensions: *power distance, uncertainty avoidance, individualism/ collectivism,* and *masculinity/femininity.*[55] He points out that management by objectives (MBO) has been the single most popular management technique "made in U.S.A." It has succeeded in Germany because the idea of replacing the arbitrary authority of the boss with the impersonal authority of mutually agreed-upon objectives fits the small power-distance and strong uncertainty-avoidance that are dimensions in the German culture. It has failed in France, however, because the French are used to large power distances—to accepting orders from a highly personalized authority. This French cultural dimension goes counter to key aspects of MBO: the small power distance between superior and subordinate, and impersonal, objective goal-setting. This same cultural dimension explains why the French, for whom vertical authority lines are very important, are significantly more reluctant than Americans to accept the multiple authority structures of project management or matrix organization.[56]

Because of these cultural differences, managerial style and practices must be tailored to fit the particular situations in other countries. Most multinational corporations therefore attempt to fill executive positions in their subsidiaries with well-qualified citizens of the host countries. More than 95% of all managers employed by Unilever are "nationals" of the country in which they work.[57] IBM follows a similar policy. This policy serves to placate nationalistic governments and to better attune management practices to the host country's culture. Another approach to staffing the managerial positions of multinational corporations is to use people with an "international" orientation regardless of their country of origin or host country assignment. This approach allows for more promotion opportunities than does Unilever's policy but it can result in a greater number of misunderstandings and conflicts with the local employees and with the host country's government. In addition, it is estimated that anywhere from 25 to 40% of *expatriate* managers (people from a country other than the host country) fail to adjust to the host country's social and business environment.[58] This failure is costly in terms of management performance, operations efficiency, and customer relations. The average cost to the company of repatriating an executive and the family exceeds $100,000.[59] Consequently, to improve their chances of success, multinational corporations are putting more emphasis on intercultural training for those managers being sent on an assignment in a foreign country.[60]

10.4

EVALUATION AND CONTROL

As MNCs increase the scope of their activities around the world, timely information becomes even more important for effective evaluation and control. In evaluating the activities of its international operations, the MNC should consider not only return on investment and other financial measures, but also the effects of its activities on the host country.

Transborder Data Flows

Multinational corporations are increasingly relying on transborder data flow (TDF) and international data networks to coordinate their international operations and control their subsidiaries. TDF, the electronic movement of data across national boundaries, has been made possible by the rapid growth and convergence of new technologies, such as telecommunications and computers. A survey of eighty-nine MNCs concluded that these companies were already dependent on international data flows for their foreign operations and will become even more so in the future. Transborder data flow appears to be a major information-systems issue in multinational corporations. More and more countries are taking steps to control the flow of data across their borders and thus handicap an MNC in its evaluation and control function.[61]

Financial Measures

The three most widely used techniques for international performance evaluation are return on investment, budget analysis, and historical comparisons. In one study, 95% of the corporate officers interviewed stated that they use the same evaluation techniques for foreign and domestic operations. Rate of return was mentioned as the single most important measure.[62] The use of ROI, however, can cause problems when it is applied to international operations: "Because of foreign currencies, different rates of inflation, different tax laws, and the use of transfer pricing, both the net income figure and the investment base may be seriously distorted."[63]

Authorities in international business recommend that the controls used by a globally oriented MNC be different from those used by a multi-domestic MNC.[64] The *multi-domestic MNC* should use loose controls with its foreign units. The management of each geographic unit should be given considerable operational latitude, but be expected to meet some performance targets. Because profit and ROI measures are often unreliable in international operations, it is recommended that the MNC's top management in this instance emphasize budgets and nonfinancial measures of performance, such as market share, productivity, public image, employee morale, and relations with the host country government, to name a few.[65] Multiple measures should be used to differentiate between the worth of the subsidiary and the performance of its management.

An MNC with a *global perspective,* however, needs tight controls over its many units. In order to reduce costs and gain competitive advantage, it is trying to spread the manufacturing and marketing operations of a few fairly uniform products around the world; therefore, its key strategic and operational decisions must be centralized. Its environmental scanning must include research not only into each of the national markets in which the MNC competes, but also into the "global arena" of the interaction between markets. Foreign units are thus evaluated more as cost centers, revenue centers, or expense centers, than as investment or profit centers, because MNCs with a global, high-share perspective do not often make the entire product in the country in which it is sold.

MNC/Host Country Relationships

As multinational corporations grow and spread across the world, nations find themselves in a dilemma. Most countries, especially the less-developed ones, want to have the many benefits an MNC can bring: technology transfer, employment opportunities, tax revenues, and the opportunity that domestic business corporations could be built in partnership with powerful and well-connected foreign-based companies. These countries also fear the problems an MNC can bring. Having welcomed an MNC with tax benefits and subsidies of various types, the host country can find itself in a double bind regarding the repatriation of profits. It can either allow the MNC to export its profits to corporate headquarters—thereby draining the nation of potential investment capital, or it can allow the MNC to send home only a small portion of its profits—thereby making the host country unattractive to other MNCs. For example, research reveals that between 1960 and 1968, profits sent to the United States from Latin America by MNCs exceeded new investment there by $6.7 billion.[66] Host countries also note that MNCs' technology transfer to less-developed countries seldom increases their exports. MNCs also have a tradition of placing business values above the cultural values of the host country.[67] For example, an MNC's need to continue manufacturing operations in order to meet a deadline from the home office may conflict with a country's desire to honor a special event by declaring a holiday.

Given the pros and cons of the multinational corporation's presence in the world, Fayerweather proposes four basic relationships that an MNC can assume with a host country. They range from the positive, *contributing* to the country's development, to the negative, *undermining* the basic culture of the country.[68]

Contributory Relationships

An MNC can act to directly augment or contribute to the goals or achievement of a host nation without any negative effect. In this relationship both the MNC and the local partner (if any) positively help each other as well as their respective countries. Occidental Petroleum's agreement in 1985 with the Bank of China Trust and Consultancy Company and the state-run China National Coal Development Corporation, to develop one of the world's largest open-pit coal mines, has the potential to help all three partners in the relationship plus both countries.[69]

Reinforcing Relationships

The actions of an MNC can reinforce the goals or achievement of a host nation but still tend to have some negative side-effects. This is a somewhat less than ideal relationship. The MNC invests heavily in the country's development and might build the transportation and communication systems so necessary for economic development. Nevertheless, the MNC sends all its profits to its headquarters and its emphasis on its own cultural values sometimes conflicts with the host country's values. This is probably the type of relationship existing between the U.S.-based MNCs that are production-sharing in Mexico and the Mexican government.

Frustrating Relationships

Actions of an MNC can challenge the goals of the nation or impede its immediate functioning in ways to which the nation cannot respond effectively, so that its government is frustrated. Nestlé's aggressive marketing of baby formula to mothers in less-developed countries is an example of this type of relationship. In countries in which breast-feeding is more nutritious and healthier for babies than bottle-feeding (because of the poor quality of water and sanitary conditions), the use of Nestlé's baby formula contributed to babies' malnutrition and other sickness. Because many LDC governments were unable to deal with the situation, church groups from the developed countries plus the United Nations put enough pressure on Nestlé to cause it to stop its aggressive marketing practices in the LDCs.[70]

Undermining Relationships

The effect of an MNC can be to reduce the basic logic (in terms of norms, values, and philosophy) of a nation, so that its functioning is weakened or undermined. MNCs' development of oil resources in the Middle Eastern countries caused a clash between traditional Moslem values and Western values; this clash probably contributed to the Iranian revolution and to disruptions in other Moslem countries. The resulting antagonism from such a relationship is reflected in the following comment by a Third World representative:

> Poor countries have often been swindled out of a decent return for their produce in the name of market mechanism, deprived of their economic independence, seduced by imported life styles, foreign value systems, irrelevant research designs—all in the name of freedom of choice.[71]

To the extent that an MNC fails to contribute to or reinforce the functioning of a host country, it might find its assets expropriated and its home-country management team asked to leave. Those corporations that go to less-developed countries to locate and extract needed raw materials but see the host countries only as something to manipulate and use get pulled into a particular cycle.

First, they are welcomed by the host country as a source of foreign currency, a major employer, a means of upgrading the country's skills, a stimulant to the economy, and a catalyst to attract other investors. *Second,* after a few years, pressure increases on the firm to process in addition to only extracting the material. This often leads to a second phase of investment by the company and more benefits to the country. *Third,* the company is now sufficiently dependent to be vulnerable to a request to have local participation in ownership, either through private parties or directly by the host government. *Fourth,* nationalization advances to a takeout stage after more years of evolving relationships, usually involving compensation for assets and some arrangement of management. *Fifth,* recalling that the primary reason for the original investment was a source of materials, and recognizing that government-owned operations are almost always inefficient, the company is forced to pay increasing prices and turns to alternative sources if they exist.[72]

SUMMARY AND CONCLUSION

A knowledge of international considerations is becoming extremely important to the proper understanding of the strategic-management processes in large corporations. Just as North American firms are becoming more involved every year with operations and markets in other countries, imports and subsidiaries from other countries are becoming more a part of the American landscape. International corporations have been transforming themselves slowly into multinational corporations (MNCs) with a global orientation and flexible management styles.

The dominant issue in the strategic-management process of a multinational corporation is the effects of widely different external environments on the firm's internal activities. A firm's top management must therefore be well schooled in the national differences in sociocultural, economic, political-legal, and technological environmental variables. Data-search procedures and analytical techniques must be used in assessments of the many possible investment opportunities and their risks in world business. Once top management believes that the corporation has the requisite internal qualifications to become multinational, it must then determine the appropriate set of strategies for entering and investing in potential host countries. These may vary from simple exportation, to the formation with other companies of very complex consortiums. The corporation's product portfolio must be constantly monitored for strengths and weaknesses.

Attention must also be paid to the selection of the most appropriate local partner, organizational structure, and management system for a worldwide enterprise. An overall system of control and coordination must be balanced against a host country's need for local flexibility and autonomy. An MNC should use a series of performance indicators so that return on investment, budget analysis, and historical comparisons can be viewed in the context of a strategic audit of operations in the host country. Above all, the top management of a multinational corporation has the responsibility to ensure that the MNC contributes to and reinforces the functioning of the host nation, rather than frustrating or undermining its government and culture.

DISCUSSION QUESTIONS

1. What differentiates a multinational corporation from an international corporation?

2. If the basic concepts of absolute and comparative advantage suggest free trade as the best route to prosperity for all nations, why do so many countries use protectionist measures to keep out imports?

3. Should MNCs be allowed to own more than half the stock of a subsidiary based in a host country? Why or why not?

4. Should the United States allow unrestricted trade between corporations in the United States and communist countries? Why or why not?

5. Discuss the pros and cons of using portfolio analysis in international strategic analysis.

6. There are many disadvantages to the joint venture (loss of control, lower profits, probability of conflicts with partners, and the likely transfer of technological advantage to a partner), plus its typical temporary nature; so why is it such a popular strategy?

7. What are the advantages and disadvantages of using a product-group structure as compared to a geographical-area structure in a multinational corporation?

8. What is the overall impact of multinational corporations on world peace? How do they help? How do they hinder?

9. As discussed in the Integrative Case at the end of this chapter, what are the pros and cons of this joint venture for each of the three involved companies?

NOTES

1. B. D. Henderson, *New Strategies for the New Global Competition* (Boston: Boston Consulting Group, 1981), p. 1.

2. *International Financial Statistics Yearbook,* Vol. LX (Washington, D.C.: International Monetary Fund, 1987), pp. 116–117.

3. *International Financial Statistics Yearbook,* pp. 698–699.

4. D. J. Teece, *The Competitive Challenge* (Cambridge, Mass.: Ballinger Publishing Co., 1987), p. 1.

5. A. Kates, "They Find Bargains in Our Stocks," *USA Today* (January 19, 1988), p. 1B.

6. J. Castro, P. Stoler, and F. Ungeheuer, "The Canadians Came Calling," *Time* (November 17, 1986), p. 68.

7. M. McLuhan, *Understanding Media: The Extensions of Man* (New York: McGraw-Hill Paperbacks, 1965).

8. M. Schrage and D. A. Vise, "Murdock, Turner Launch Era of Global Television," *Washington Post* (August 31, 1986), p. H1.

9. D. Wessel, "Gillette Keys Sales to Third World Tastes," *Wall Street Journal* (January 23, 1986), p. 33.

10. S. Carey and U. Gupta, "GE and CFM Get $2 Billion Order For Airbus Engines," *Wall Street Journal* (July 29, 1987), p. 12.

11. Adapted from W. A. Dymsza, *Multinational Business Strategy* (New York: McGraw-Hill, 1972), pp. 50–51.

12. Dymsza, pp. 5–6.

13. M. E. Porter, "Changing Patterns of International Competition," *California Management Review* (Winter 1986), pp. 9–40. Also in *The Competitive Challenge,* ed. D. J. Teece

(Cambridge, Mass.: Ballinger Publishing Co., 1987), pp. 27–57.

14. J. D. Daniels and L. H. Radebaugh, *International Business: Environments and Operations,* 4th ed. (Reading, Mass.: Addison-Wesley Publishing Co., 1987) p. 766.

15. Daniels and Radebaugh, p. 628.

16. D. Ricks, M. Y. C. Fu, and J. S. Arpan, *International Business Blunders* (Columbus, Ohio: Grid, Inc., 1974).

17. Daniels and Radebaugh, p. 640.

18. D. A. Ricks and V. Mahajan, "Blunders in International Marketing: Fact or Fiction," *Long Range Planning* (February 1984), pp. 78–82.

19. "Banks in Pakistan To Stop Paying Interest in 1985," *Wall Street Journal* (June 18, 1984), p. 23.

20. S. Chang, "The Gods and the U.A.W. Are Smiling: Mazda's New Boss Plans To Make Cars, and Jobs, for Yanks," *People* (February 18, 1985), pp. 90–91.

21. R. T. Grieves, "Modern Barter," *Time* (June 11, 1984) p. 48.

D. B. Yoffie, "Profiting from Countertrade," *Harvard Business Review* (May–June 1984), pp. 8–12, 16.

22. "Uniroyal Sells a Unit for Over $71 Million to Malaysian Concern," *Wall Street Journal* (December 24, 1984), p. 12.

23. J. Ryser and C. A. Robbins, "Garcia Dusts Off An Old Ploy: Expropriation," *Business Week* (January 13, 1986), p. 50.

24. R. I. Kirkland, Jr., "The Death of Socialism," *Fortune* (January 4, 1988), p. 65.

25. J. P. Anastassopoulos, G. Blanc, and P. Dussage, *State-Owned Multinationals* (Chichester, England: John Wiley & Sons, 1987), pp. 180–181.

26. P. Choate and J. Linger, "Tailored Trade: Dealing With the World As It Is," *Harvard Business Review* (January-February 1988), pp. 86–93.

27. R. B. Reich, *The Next American Frontier* (New York: Times Books, 1983).

28. G. W. Weiss, Jr., "The General Electric-SNECMA Jet Engine Development Program" (Boston: *Intercollegiate Case Clearing House,* no. 9-380-739, 1980).

29. J. Mark, "High-Tech Exports to China Still Being Delayed, Despite Eased Rules, U.S. Firms Finding," *Wall Street Journal* (January 3, 1985), p. 16.

30. R. Stobaugh and R. T. Wells, Jr., *Technology Crossing Borders* (Boston: Harvard Business School Press, 1984), p. 4.

31. T. N. Gladwin, "Assessing the Multinational Environment for Corporate Opportunity," in W. D. Guth (ed.), *Handbook of Business Strategy* (Boston: Warren, Gorham and Lamont, 1985), pp. 7.28–7.41.

32. W. D. Coplin and M. K. O'Leary, "World Political/ Business Risk Analysis For 1987," *Planning Review* (January/ February 1987), pp. 34–40.

33. Y. N. Chang and F. Campo-Flores, *Business Policy and Strategy* (Santa Monica, Calif.: Goodyear Publishing, 1980), pp. 602–604.

34. J. Leontiades, "Going Global—Global Strategies vs. National Strategies," *Long Range Planning* (December 1986), pp. 96–104.

35. Porter, (1987), pp. 29–30.

36. K. Ohmae, "The Triad World View," *Journal of Business Strategy* (Spring 1987), pp. 8–19.

37. Ohmae, p. 12.

38. G. D. Harrell and R. O. Kiefer, "Multinational Strategic Market Portfolios," *MSU Business Topics* (Winter 1981), p. 5.

39. Harrell and Kiefer, p. 8.

40. M. Porter, (1986), p. 12.

41. K. Graven, "Tokyo Takeout: Family In Japan Plays Big Role Importing Fast Food From U.S.," *Wall Street Journal* (March 3, 1987), p. 1.

42. J. S. Harrison, "Alternatives to Merger-Joint Ventures and Other Strategies," *Long Range Planning* (December 1987), p. 80.

43. V. Pucik and N. Hatvany, "Management Practices in Japan and Their Impact on Business Strategy," in R. Lamb (ed.), *Advances in Strategic Management,* Vol. I (Greenwich, Conn.: Jai Press, 1983), p. 124.

44. S. P. Galante, "Foreign Semiconductor Firms Try New Strategy in U.S.," *Wall Street Journal* (August 23, 1984), p. 20.

45. K. P. Power, "Now We Can Move Office Work Offshore To Enhance Output," *Wall Street Journal* (June 9, 1983), p. 30.

46. P. Lasserre, "Selecting a Foreign Partner for Technology Transfer," *Long Range Planning* (December 1984), pp. 43–49.

47. Lasserre, pp. 48–49.

48. W. H. Davidson, "Creating and Managing Joint Ventures in China," *California Management Review* (Summer 1987), p. 77.

49. R. L. Drake and L. M. Caudill, "Management of the Large Multinational: Trends and Future Challenges," *Business Horizons* (May-June 1981), pp. 84–85.

50. J. D. Daniels, E. W. Ogram, Jr., and L. H. Radebaugh, *International Business: Environments and Operations,* 2nd ed. (Reading, Mass.: Addison-Wesley, 1979), p. 359.

51. Stobaugh and Wells, pp. 16–17.

52. J. Garland and R. N. Farmer, *International Dimensions of Business Policy and Strategy* (Boston: Kent Publishing Co., 1986), pp. 98–102.

53. G. Turner, "Inside Europe's Giant Companies: Cultural Revolution at Philips," *Long Range Planning* (August 1986), p. 14.

54. J. D. Daniels, R. A. Pitts, and M. J. Tretter, "Organizing for Dual Strategies of Product Diversity and International Expansion," *Strategic Management Journal* (July-September 1985), pp. 223–237.

55. G. Hofstede, "The Cultural Relativity of Organizational Practice and Theories," in *International Business Knowledge: Managing International Functions in the 1990s,* ed. W. A. Dymsza and R. G. Vambery (New York: Praeger Press, 1987), pp. 309–323.

G. Hofstede, "Motivation, Leadership, and Organization: Do American Theories Apply Abroad?" *Organizational Dynamics* (Summer 1980), pp. 42–63.

G. Hofstede, "National Cultures in Four Dimensions: A Research-Based Theory of Cultural Differences among Nations," *International Journal of Management and Organization* (Spring-Summer 1983), pp. 46–74.

G. Hofstede, "The Cultural Relativity of the Quality of Life Concept," *Academy of Management Review* (July 1984), pp. 389–398.

56. G. Inzerilli and A. Laurent, "Managerial Views of Organization Structure in France and the USA," *International Studies of Management and Organization* (Spring-Summer 1983), p. 113.

57. W. C. Kim and R. A. Mauborgne, "Cross-Cultural Strategies," *Journal of Business Strategy* (Spring 1987), p. 30.

58. M. Mendenhall and G. Oddou, "The Dimensions of Expatriate Acculturation: A Review," *Academy of Management Review* (January 1985), pp. 39–47.

59. N. J. Adler, *International Dimensions of Organizational Behavior* (Boston: Kent Publishing Company, 1986), p. 220.

60. P. C. Earley, "Intercultural Training For Managers: A Comparison of Documentary and Interpersonal Methods," *Academy of Management Journal* (December 1987), pp. 685–698.

For more information on dealing with intercultural differences see R. E. Axtell, *Do's and Taboos Around the World*

(Janesville, Wisconsin: The Parker Pen Company, 1985); and P. R. Harris and R. T. Moran, *Managing Cultural Differences*, 2nd ed. (Houston: Gulf Publishing Co., 1987).

61. R. Chandran, A. Phatak, and R. Sambharya, "Transborder Data Flows: Implications for Multinational Corporations," *Business Horizons* (November–December 1987), pp. 74–82.

62. S. M. Robbins and R. B. Stobaugh, "The Bent Measuring Stick for Foreign Subsidiaries," *Harvard Business Review* (September-October 1973), p. 82.

63. Daniels and Radebaugh, pp. 673–674.

64. W. R. Fannin and A. F. Rodrigues, "National or Global?—Control vs. Flexibility," *Long Range Planning* (October 1986), pp. 84–188.

65. A. V. Phatak, *International Dimensions of Management* (Boston: Kent Publishing Co., 1983) p. 139.
Daniels and Radebaugh, p. 674.

66. K. Paul and R. Barbato, "The Multinational Corporation in the Less Developed Country: The Economic Development Model versus the North-South Model," *Academy of Management Review* (January 1985), p. 9.

67. P. Wright, "MNC-Third World Business Unit Performance: Application of Strategic Elements," *Strategic Management Journal* (July-September 1984), pp. 231–240.

68. Adapted from J. Fayerweather, *International Business Strategy and Administration* (Cambridge, Mass.: Ballinger Publishing, 1978), p. 124.

69. "U.S. Oil Firm, China Sign Pact For Giant Mine," *Des Moines Register* (June 30, 1985), p. 3A.

70. J. E. Post, "Assessing the Nestlé Boycott," *California Management Review* (Winter 1985), pp. 113–131.

71. M. Ul Haq, *The Poverty Curtain: Choices for the Third World* (New York: Columbia University Press, 1976) as quoted by Wright, p. 232.

72. F. T. Haner, *Business Policy, Planning and Strategy* (Cambridge, Mass.: Winthrop Publishers, 1976), p. 441.

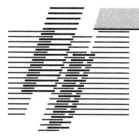

INTEGRATIVE CASE

CSX CORPORATION FORMS INTERNATIONAL JOINT VENTURE

When U.S. Lines Inc. declared bankruptcy in December 1986, industry observers wondered what would become of the firm's twelve giant container ships—often called "superfreighters" or "econships." With the shipping industry suffering from overcapacity in trans-Atlantic shipping, the sale of these twelve ships could only make the glut worse and cut shipping rates even further.

Sea-Land, a unit of CSX Corporation, agreed in February 1988 to purchase all twelve ships for $160 million from the creditors of U.S. Lines. Rather than keep the ships only for its own use, Sea-Land reached an agreement with two other companies to share the superfreighters. Sea-Land's management planned to use all twelve of the ships in trans-Atlantic service between the U.S. and Europe in a space-sharing arrangement with P & O Containers (Trans Freight Lines) Ltd. of the United Kingdom and Nedlloyd Lijnen B.V. of the Netherlands. The superfreighters were to replace twenty-three smaller vessels that the three companies had operated in the Atlantic and would boost their combined capacity less than 4%. The ships were to fly the U.S. flag and operate with U.S. crews.

Industry observers praised the joint venture as a way to improve efficiency in trans-Atlantic shipping. "Hopefully it should take some pressure off rates by boosting the efficiency of the carriers through economies of scale," said Donald Aldridge, a Senior Vice President of the U.S. unit of Hapag Lloyd AG, a West German shipping company. Sea-Land's purchase of the ships and the three companies' sharing agreement were in part defensive measures to keep the giant containerships out of the hands of low-cost competitors who could have started a rate war. "If some Mickey

Mouse operator had bought these ships, anything could have happened," said Frits van Riet, President of the U.S. unit of Nedlloyd, the Dutch company sharing the superfreighters with Sea-Land.

SOURCE: D. Machalaba, "Sea-Land Will Buy 12 Superfreighters Idled by U.S. Lines Inc. for $160 Million," *Wall Street Journal* (February 9, 1988), p. 8.

CHAPTER 11

STRATEGIC ISSUES IN NOT-FOR-PROFIT ORGANIZATIONS

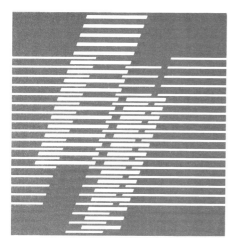

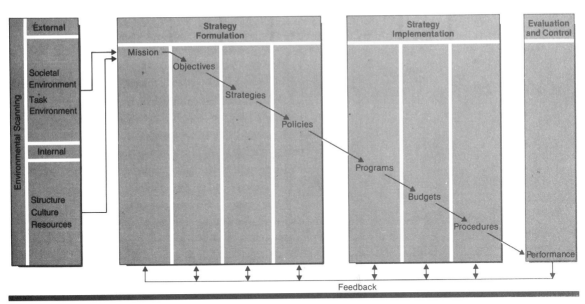

Traditionally, studies in strategic management have dealt with profit-making firms to the exclusion of nonprofit or governmental organizations. The little existing empirical research suggests that not-for-profit organizations are in the initial stage of using strategic management.[1] From their study of 103 not-for-profit organizations, Unterman and Davis conclude: "Not only have not-for-profit organizations failed to reach the strategic management stage of development, but many of them have failed to reach even the strategic planning stages that for-profit enterprises initiated 15 to 20 years ago."[2] Nevertheless, an increasing number of not-for-profits, especially hospitals and colleges, are concerned with strategic issues and strategic planning, even though their use of it might be only an informal process.

A knowledge of not-for-profit organizations would be important even if there were no other reason than the fact that they employ over 25% of those working in the United States and own approximately 15% of the nation's private wealth.[3] Private nonprofit organizations, in particular, represent 5.2% of all corporations, partnerships, and proprietorships in the United States, receive 3.5% of all revenue, and hold about 4.3% of the total assets of business firms. During the 1970s, nonprofit firms increased both in total number and revenues *faster* than did profit-making firms.[4] It is estimated that over one-third of the world's gross product is generated by "non-market" corporations (which include state-owned corporations and regulated utilities).[5] In the United States alone, in addition to various federal, state, and local government agencies, there are about 10,000 not-for-profit hospitals and nursing homes, 4,600 colleges and universities, over 100,000 private and public elementary and secondary schools, almost 350,000 churches and synagogues, plus many thousands of charities and service organizations.[6]

The first ten chapters of this book dealt primarily with the strategic management of profit-making corporations. Scholars and practitioners are concluding, however, that many strategic management concepts and techniques can be successfully adapted to not-for-profit organizations.[7] The purpose of this chapter is, therefore, to highlight briefly the major differences between the profit-making and the not-for-profit organization, so that the effects of their differences on the strategic management process are seen.

11.1

CATEGORIES OF ORGANIZATIONS

All profit-making and not-for-profit organizations can be grouped into four basic categories. In some instances, it is difficult to clearly state where one category leaves off and another begins: "The wide and growing involvement of government in all aspects of life has caused a convergence or blurring of the various sectors."[8] Four categories are as follows:

1. **Private for-profit** businesses depend on the market economy to generate the means of their survival. (These range from small businesses to major corporations.)

2. **Private quasi-public** organizations are created by legislative authority and given a limited monopoly to provide particular goods or services to a population subgroup. (These are primarily public utilities.)

3. **Private nonprofit** organizations operate on public goodwill (donations, contributions, and endowments or government stipends), but are constituted outside the authority of governmental agencies or legislative bodies.

4. **Public** agencies of the government (federal, state, and local) are constituted by law and authorized to collect taxes and provide services.[9]

Typically, the term **not-for-profit** includes private nonprofit corporations (such as hospitals, institutes, private colleges, and organized charities) as well as public governmental units or agencies (such as welfare departments, prisons, and state universities). Regulated public utilities are in a grey area somewhere between profit and not-for-profit. They are profit making and have stockholders, but take on many of the characteristics of the not-for-profit organization, such as a greater dependence on rate-setting government commissions than on customers.

11.2

WHY NOT-FOR-PROFIT?

The not-for-profit sector of the American economy is becoming increasingly important for a number of reasons. *First,* society desires certain goods and services that profit-making firms cannot or will not provide. These are referred to as "public" or "collective" goods because people who might not have paid for the goods also receive benefits from them. Paved roads, police protection, museums, and schools are examples of public goods. A person cannot use a private good unless she or he pays for it. Generally once a public good is provided, however, anyone can partake of it.

Second, a private nonprofit firm tends to receive benefits from society that a private profit-making firm cannot obtain. Preferred tax status to nonstock corporations is given in section 501(c)(3) of the United States Internal Revenue Code in the form of exemptions from corporate income taxes. Private nonprofit firms also enjoy exemptions from various other state, local, and federal taxes. Under certain conditions these firms also benefit from the tax deductibility of donors' contributions and membership dues. In addition, they qualify for special third-class mailing privileges.[10] These benefits are allowed because private nonprofit organizations are typically service organizations, which are expected to use any excess of revenue over costs and expenses to either improve service or reduce the price of their service. This service orientation is reflected in the fact that not-for-profit organizations do not use the term *customer* to refer to the consumer or recipient of the service. The recipient is typically referred to as a patient, student, client, case, or simply "the public."

11.3
IMPORTANCE OF REVENUE SOURCE

The feature that best differentiates not-for-profit organizations from each other as well as from profit-making corporations is their source of income.[11] The profit-making firm depends upon revenues obtained from the sale of its goods and services to customers. Its source of income is the customer who buys and uses the product, and who typically pays for the product when it is received. Profits result when revenues are greater than the costs of making and distributing the product, and are thus a measure of the corporation's **effectiveness** (a product is valued because customers purchase it for use) and **efficiency** (costs are kept below selling price).

The not-for-profit organization, in contrast, depends heavily on dues, assessments, or donations from its membership, or on funding from a sponsoring agency such as the United Way or the federal government. Revenue, therefore, comes from a variety of sources—*not* just from sales to customers/clients. It can come from people who do not even receive the services they are subsidizing. Such charitable organizations as the American Cancer Society and CARE are examples. In another type of not-for-profit organization—such as unions and voluntary medical plans—revenue comes mostly from the members, the people who receive the service. Nevertheless, the members typically pay dues *in advance* and must accept later whatever service is provided whether they want it or not, whether it is what they expected or not. The service is often received long after the dues are paid. Therefore, some members who have paid into a fund for many years leave the organization or die without having received services, whereas newcomers may receive many services even though they have paid only a small amount into it.

Therefore, in profit-making corporations, there is typically a simple and direct connection between the customer or client and the organization. The organization tends to be totally dependent on sales of its products or services to the customer for revenue, and is therefore extremely interested in pleasing the customer. As shown in Fig. 11.1, the profit-making organization (organization A) tries to influence the customer to continue to buy and use its services. By either buying or not buying the item offered, the customer, in turn, directly influences the organization's decision-making process.

In the case of the typical not-for-profit organization, however, there is

FIGURE 11.1
The Effects of Sources of Revenue on Patterns of Client–Organization Influence

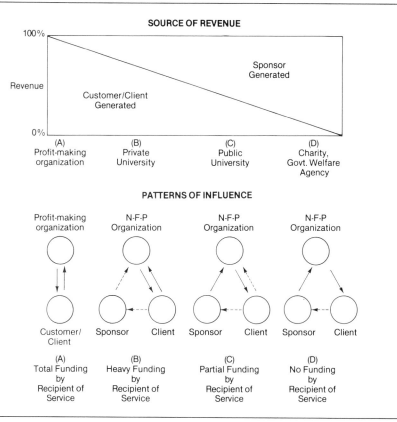

Source: Thomas L. Wheelen and J. David Hunger, "The Effect of Revenue upon Patterns of Client–Organization Influence." Copyright © 1982 by Wheelen and Hunger Associates. Reprinted by permission.

likely to be a very different sort of relationship between the organization providing and the person receiving the service. Because the recipient of the service typically does not pay the entire cost of the service, outside sponsors are required. In most instances, the sponsors receive none of the service but provide partial to total funding of the needed revenues. As indicated earlier, these sponsors can be the government (using taxpayers' money) or charitable organizations, such as the United Way (using voluntary donations). As shown in Fig. 11.1, the not-for-profit (NFP) organization can be partially dependent on sponsors for funding (organizations B and C) or totally dependent on the sponsors (organization D).

The pattern of influence on the organization's strategic decision making derives from its sources of revenue. As shown in Fig. 11.1, a private university (organization B) is heavily dependent on student tuition and other client-generated funds, for around 71% of its revenue.[12] Therefore, the students' desires are likely to have a stronger influence (as shown by an unbroken line) on the university's decision making than are the desires of the various sponsors, such as alumni and private foundations. The sponsors' relatively marginal influence on the organization is reflected by a broken line. In contrast, a public university (depicted in Fig. 11.1 as organization C) is more heavily dependent on outside sponsors, such as a state legislature, for revenue funding. Student tuition and other client-generated funds form a small percentage (typically only 37%) of total revenue. Therefore, the university's decision making is heavily influenced by the sponsors (unbroken line) and only marginally influenced directly by the students (broken line). In the case of organization D in Fig. 11.1, however, the client has no direct influence on the organization because the client pays nothing for the services received. In this type of situation, the organization tends to measure its effectiveness in terms of sponsor satisfaction. It has no real measure of its efficiency other than its ability to carry out its mission and achieve its objectives within the dollar contribution it has received from its sponsors. In contrast to other organizations in which the client contributes a significant proportion of the needed revenue, this type of not-for-profit organization (D) actually might be able to increase the amount of its revenue by heavily lobbying its sponsors while reducing the level of its service to its clients!

Regardless of the percentage of total funding generated by the client, the client may attempt to indirectly influence the not-for-profit organization through the sponsors. This is depicted by the broken lines connecting the client and the sponsor in organizations B, C, and D in the figure. Welfare clients or prison inmates, for example, may be able to indirectly improve the services they receive if they pressure government officials with letters to legislators or, even, by rioting. And students at public universities can lobby state officials for student representation on governing boards.

The key to understanding the management of a not-for-profit organization is thus learning who pays for the delivered services. If the recipients of the service pay only a small proportion of the total cost of the service, it is likely that top management will be more concerned with satisfying the needs and desires of the funding sponsors or agency than those of the people receiving the service. As previous studies indicate, acquisition of resources can become an end in itself.[13]

11.4

CONSTRAINTS ON STRATEGIC MANAGEMENT

Because not-for-profit organizations are truly different from profit-making organizations, there are a number of characteristics peculiar to the former that constrain its behavior and affect its strategic management. Newman and Wallender list the following five constraining **characteristics:**

1. Service is often intangible and hard to measure. This difficulty is typically compounded by the existence of multiple service objectives developed in order to satisfy multiple sponsors.

2. Client influence may be weak. Often the organization has a local monopoly, and payments by customers may be a very small source of funds.

3. Strong employee commitment to professions or to a cause may undermine their allegiance to the organization employing them.

4. Resource contributors—notably fund contributors and government—may intrude upon the organization's internal management.

5. Restraints on the use of rewards and punishments may result from characteristics 1, 3, and 4.[14]

It is true that a number of these characteristics can be found in profit-making as well as in not-for-profit organizations. Nevertheless, as Newman and Wallendar state, the "... frequency of strong impact is much higher in not-for-profit enterprises. ..."[15] As a result, the strategic-management process for any given situation will be different in a not-for-profit organization than in the typical profit-making corporations discussed in earlier chapters.

Impact on Strategy Formulation

The long-range planning and decision making affected by the listed constraining characteristics, serve to add at least four **complications** to strategy formulation.

1. **Goal conflicts interfere with rational planning.** Because the not-for-profit organization typically lacks a single clear-cut performance criterion (such as profits), divergent goals and objectives are likely.[16] This divergence is especially likely if there are multiple sponsors. Differences in the concerns of various important sponsors can prevent top management from stating the organization's mission in anything but very broad terms, if they fear that a sponsor who disagrees with a particular, narrow definition of mission might cancel its funding. In such organizations it is the reduced influence of the clients that **permits** this diversity of values and goals to occur without a clear market check.

2. **An integrated planning focus tends to shift from results to resources.** Because not-for-profit organizations tend to provide services that are hard to measure, they rarely have a net "bottom line." Planning, therefore, becomes more concerned with resource inputs, which can easily be measured, than with service, which cannot. Goal displacement, therefore, becomes even more likely that it is in business organizations.

3. **Ambiguous operating objectives create opportunities for internal politics and goal displacement.** The combination of vague objectives and a heavy concern with resources allows managers considerable leeway in their activities. Such leeway makes possible political maneuvering for personal ends. In addition, because the effectiveness of the not-for-profit organization hinges on the satisfaction of the sponsoring group, there is a tendency for management to ignore the needs of the client while focusing on the desires of the powerful sponsor. This problem is compounded by the fact that boards of trustees are often selected not on the basis of their managerial experience, but on the basis of their ability to contribute money, raise funds, and work with politicians. Their lack of interest in overseeing management is reflected in an overall board-meeting attendance rate of only 50%, compared to 90% for boards of directors of business corporations. Board members of not-for-profit organizations therefore tend to ignore the task of determining strategies and policies—leaving this to the paid (and sometimes unpaid) executive director.[17]

4. **Professionalization simplifies detailed planning but adds rigidity.** In those not-for-profit organizations in which professionals hold important roles (as in hospitals or colleges), professional values and traditions can prevent the organization from changing its conventional behavior patterns to fit new service missions tuned to changing social needs. This rigidity, of course, can occur in any organization that hires professionals. The strong service orientation of most not-for-profit organizations, however, tends to encourage the development of static professional norms and attitudes.

Impact on Strategy Implementation

The five constraining characteristics affect how a not-for-profit organization is organized in both its structure and job design. Three **complications,** in particular, can be highlighted.

1. **Decentralization is complicated.** The difficulty of setting objectives for an intangible, hard-to-measure service mission complicates the delegation of decision-making authority. Important matters are therefore often centralized, and low-level managers are forced to wait until top management makes a decision. Because of the heavy dependence on sponsors for revenue support, the top management of a not-for-profit organization must always be alert to the sponsors' view of an organizational activity. This necessary caution leads to "defensive centralization," in which top management retains all decision-making authority so that low-level managers cannot take any actions to which the sponsors may object.

2. **Linking pins for external–internal integration become important.** Because of the heavy dependence on outside sponsors, a special need arises for people in "buffer" roles to relate to both inside and outside groups. This role is especially necessary when the sponsors are diverse (revenue comes from donations, membership fees, and federal funds), and the service is intangible (for instance, a "good" education) with a broad mission and multiple shifting objectives. The job of a "Dean for External Affairs," for example, consists primarily of working with the school's alumni and raising funds.

3. **Job enlargement and executive development can be restrained by professionalism.** In organizations that employ a large number of professionals, managers must design jobs that appeal to prevailing professional norms. Professionals have rather clear ideas about which activities are, and which are not, within their province. Enriching a nurse's job by expanding his or her decision-making authority for drug dosage, for example, can cause conflict with medical doctors who believe that such authority is theirs alone. In addition, a professional's promotion into a managerial job might be viewed as a punishment rather than as a reward.

Impact on Evaluation and Control

Special **complications** arising from the constraining characteristics also affect how behavior is motivated and performance is controlled. Two problems, in particular, are often noticed.

1. **Rewards and penalties have little or no relation to performance.** When desired results are vague and the judgment of success is subjective, predictable and impersonal feedback cannot be established. Performance is judged either intuitively ("You don't seem to be taking your job seriously") or on the basis of those small aspects of a job that can be measured ("You were late to work twice last month").

2. **Inputs rather than outputs are heavily controlled.** Because its inputs can be measured much more easily than outputs, the not-for-profit organization tends to focus more on the resources going into performance than on the performance itself.[18] The emphasis is thus on setting maximum limits for costs and expenses. Because there is little to no reward for meeting these standards, people usually respond negatively to controls.

11.5
TYPICAL RESPONSES TO CONSTRAINTS

Not-for-profit organizations tend to deal with the complications resulting from constraining characteristics in a number of ways. Although these responses may occur in profit-making organizations as well, they are more typical of not-for-profit organizations.

Select a Dynamic and Forceful Leader

One approach, which is also used in profit-making firms at times, is to appoint a strong leader to the top management position: "The leader has personal convictions about the values to be used in decision making and either has enough power to make important choices, or is so influential that her or his values are accepted by others who make decisions."[19] This manager thus can force a change in the organizational mission and objectives without antagonizing the sponsors; this leader can also direct changes in the organizing and controlling of activities. Father Theodore Hesburgh, past President of Notre Dame University, had enormous influence in shaping the strategic direction of his university. "The very essence of leadership is you have to have a vision," Hesburgh stated. "It's got to be a vision you articulate clearly and forcefully on every occasion. You can't blow an uncertain trumpet."[20] The danger with relying primarily on this approach, however, is that change can occur only from the top down. Rather than accepting the normal risks inherent in making an important decision, low-level managers "play it safe" and either wait for guidance from above to indicate which way "the wind is blowing" or pass the decision upward in the hierarchy.

Develop a Mystique

To integrate the organization's efforts toward the successful accomplishment of its goals, it can develop a "mystique" that dominates the enterprise and attracts sponsors. A strong conviction shared by all employees, as well as the sponsors, about the importance of a particular mission or service objective can also motivate employees to produce unusually high performance and client satisfaction. This sense of mission typically focuses on providing a unique service to a highly visible client group, such as mentally retarded children. Once established, the mystique sets the character and values that decision makers and others are expected to follow. Thus it is similar to the corporate culture discussed earlier. One danger in using mystique to focus activities and to motivate performance is that the mission can move far afield from that desired by the sponsoring groups.

Generate Rules and Regulations

The described constraints can force people in not-for-profit organizations to be concerned more with pleasing the sponsors than with achieving a mission of satisfying the client, and top management's response to this misdirection of efforts might be to generate rules and regulations regarding activities with the client. Minimum standards may be developed regarding the number of contact hours spent with each client, the number of reports completed, and/ or the "proper" method of working. The danger inherent in this approach is that it tends to emphasize form over substance and to confuse looking good and keeping busy with actual performance. Goal displacement develops and feeds upon itself. "Burnout" develops among dedicated employees who might believe that they are being forced to spend too much energy fighting the system rather than helping the client.

Appoint a Strong Board

A board of directors or trustees can help ensure vigilance in setting and monitoring the objectives of the organization. To the extent that the board actively represents the sponsors and special interest groups that determine the organization's revenues, it has a great deal of power: "The potential for control by some not-for-profit boards far exceeds that of the boards of a corporation which represents only the owners."[21] In performing as watchdog over the organization, the board can demand clear-cut, measurable objectives and a mission of client satisfaction. The danger with this approach, however, is that the board might get too involved in operational activities. The board might involve itself not only with strategic matters, but also with operational matters such as hiring, directing, and developing the budget.[22] Nevertheless, like the boards discussed in Chapter 3, not-for-profit boards can range in their degree of involvement in strategic management, from the passive phantom or figurehead boards to the active catalyst type.[23]

Establish Performance-Based Budgets

A fifth approach to dealing with complications in a not-for-profit organization is to institute an information system that ties measurable objectives to budgeted line items. One such system is the *planning, programming, budgeting system* (PPBS) developed by the U.S. Department of Defense. It assists not-for-profit administrators in choosing among alternative programs in terms of resource use. It includes five steps:

1. Specify objectives as clearly as possible in quantitative, measurable terms.
2. Analyze the actual output of the not-for-profit organization in terms of the stated objectives.
3. Measure the cost of the particular program.
4. Analyze alternatives and search for those that have the greatest effectiveness in achieving the objectives.
5. Establish the process in a systematic way so that it continues to occur over time.[24]

Another system is *zero base budgeting* (ZBB). It is a planning process that requires each manager to justify budget requests in detail for each year that a budget is constructed. This procedure serves to avoid the development of annual budgets that are simply based upon the previous year's budget plus a certain percentage of increase. ZBB forces a manager to justify the use of money for old established programs as well as for new ones. The system requires three steps:

1. Identify each activity with a program so that input relates to output.
2. Evaluate each activity by systematic analysis.
3. Rank all programs in order of performance.[25]

Zero base budgeting has been used by the U.S. Department of Agriculture since 1971 and has been employed in nearly a dozen state and local governments as well as other federal agencies, and in over one hundred business firms.[26] Its main value is to tie inputs with outputs and to force managers to set priorities on service programs. It is also a very useful adjunct to MBO, which is being adopted by an increasing number of not-for-profit organizations.

The danger with emphasizing performance-based budgets is that members of an organization become so concerned with justifying the existence of pet programs that they tend to forget about the effects of these programs on achieving the mission. The process can become very political. It gives the appearance of rational decision making, but it can be just another variant of trying to please the sponsors and looking good on paper.[27]

11.6

POPULAR NOT-FOR-PROFIT STRATEGIES

Because the typical mission of the not-for-profit organization is to satisfy an unmet need of a segment of the general public, its objective becomes one of satisfying that need as much as is possible. If revenues exceed costs and expenses, the not-for-profit therefore is likely to use the surplus (otherwise known as "profit") to expand or improve its services. If, however, revenues are less than costs and expenses, strong pressures from both within and without the organization often prevent it from reducing its services. To the extent that management is able to find new sponsors, all may be well. For many not-for-profits, however, there is an eventual limit to contributions with no strings attached. The organization is thus painfully forced to reject contributions from sponsors who wish to alter a portion of the organization's basic mission as a requirement of the contribution.

Because of various pressures upon them to provide more services than the sponsors and clients can pay for, not-for-profit organizations are developing strategies to help them meet their desired service objectives. Two popular strategies are *strategic piggybacking* and *interorganizational linking*.

Strategic Piggybacking

Coined by Nielsen, the term **strategic piggybacking** refers to the development of a new activity for the not-for-profit organization that would generate the funds needed to make up the difference between revenues and expenses.[28] The new activity is related typically in some manner to the not-for-profit's mission, but its purpose is to help subsidize the primary service programs. In an inverted use of portfolio analysis, top management invests in new, safe *cash cows* to fund its current cash-hungry stars, question marks, and dogs.

Although this strategy is not a new one, it has become very popular in the 1980s. As early as 1874, for example, the Metropolitan Museum of Art retained a professional to photograph its collections and to sell copies of the prints. Profits were used to defray the museum's operating costs. Surpluses generated from the sale of food, wine, liquor, and tickets to the Boston Pops performances help support the primary mission of the Boston Symphony Orchestra—the performance of classical music. More recently, various income-generation ventures have appeared under various auspices, from the Girl Scouts to UNICEF, and in numerous forms, from small gift shops to vast real estate developments. The Small Business Administration, however, views this activity as "unfair competition."[29] The Internal Revenue Service advises that a not-for-profit that engages in a business "not substantially related" to the organization's exempt purposes may jeopardize its tax-exempt status, particularly if the income from the business exceeds approximately 20% of total organizational revenues.[30]

Although strategic piggybacks can help not-for-profit organizations self-subsidize their primary missions and better utilize their resources, according to Nielsen, there are several potential negative effects.[31] First, the revenue-generating venture could actually lose money—especially in the short run. Second, the venture could subvert, interfere with, or even take over the primary mission. Third, the public, as well as the sponsors, could reduce their contributions because of negative responses to such "money-grubbing activities" or because of a mistaken belief that the organization is becoming self-supporting. Fourth, the venture could interfere with the internal operations of the not-for-profit organization.

Edward Skloot, President of the New York consulting firm New Ventures, suggests that a not-for-profit organization have five resources before it begins a revenue-earning activity:[32]

1. **Something to sell.** The organization should assess its resources to see if people might be willing to pay for a good or service closely related to the organization's primary activity.

2. **Critical mass of management talent.** There must be enough available people to nurture and sustain an income venture over the long haul.

3. **Trustee support.** If the trustees have strong feelings against earned-income ventures, they could actively or passively resist commercial involvement.

4. **Entrepreneurial attitude.** Management must be able to combine an interest in innovative ideas with businesslike practicality.

5. **Venture capital.** Because it often takes money to make money, engaging in a joint venture with a business corporation can provide the necessary start-up funds as well as the marketing and management support. For example, Massachusetts General Hospital receives $50

million from Hoechst, the West German chemical company for biological research, in exchange for exclusive licenses to develop commercial products from particular research discoveries. The Children's Television Workshop, in partnership with Anheuser-Busch, developed a theme park for young children in Langhorne, Pennsylvania.

Interorganizational Linking

A major strategy often used by not-for-profit organizations to enhance their capacity to serve clients or to acquire resources is developing cooperative ties with other organizations.[33] Not-for-profit hospitals are increasing their use of this strategy as a way to cope with increasing costs and declining revenues. Services can be purchased and provided more efficiently through cooperation with other hospitals than if they were done for one hospital alone. Currently, close to one-third of all nongovernmental not-for-profit hospitals in the United States are part of a *multihospital system,* defined as "two or more acute care hospitals owned, leased, or contract-managed by a corporate office."[34] By belonging to a system, a formerly independent hospital can hope to benefit in terms of staff utilization and management efficiency.

A few of the largest hospital cooperatives are American Healthcare Systems, Inc., an alliance of 1,000 hospitals; Voluntary Hospitals of America, Inc., a league of 480 hospitals; and Consolidated Catholic Health Care, Inc., an alliance of 19 Catholic hospital systems representing 301 institutions. These cooperatives not only pool their members' purchasing orders to reduce costs, they also develop for-profit ventures and access capital markets through investor-owned subsidiaries. Don Arnwine, Chairman of Voluntary Hospitals of America, commented on this trend: "It is time we in the not-for-profit sector got off our duffs and competed."[35]

SUMMARY AND CONCLUSION

Strategic management in not-for-profit organizations is in its initial stages. Approaches and techniques, such as MBO, which work reasonably well in profit-making corporations, are being tried in a number of not-for-profit organizations. Nevertheless, private nonprofit and public organizations differ in terms of their sources of revenue and thus must be treated differently. The relationship between the organization and the client also is more complicated in these organizations. Moreover, not-for-profit organizations have certain constraining characteristics that affect their strategic-management process. These characteristics cause variations in the ways that managers in not-for-profit organizations formulate and implement strategic decisions. Not-for-profit organizations therefore are more likely than profit-making corporations to look for dynamic and forceful leaders who can pull together various constituencies, to develop a mystique about their activities, to generate many rules and regulations regarding the client, to appoint a strong board of directors/trustees to represent sponsoring agencies and special interest groups, and to develop performance-based budgets. As increasing numbers of not-for-profit organizations find it difficult to generate from sponsors the funds they need to achieve key service objectives, they are turning to *strategic piggybacking* and *interorganizational linking* strategies.

Not-for-profit organizations form an important part of society. It is therefore important to understand their reason for existence and their differences from profit-making corporations. The lack of a profit motive often results in vague statements of mission and unmeasurable objectives. This, coupled with a concern for funding

from sponsors, can cause a lack of consideration for the very client the organization was designed to serve. Programs that have little or no connection with the organization's mission can develop. Nevertheless, it is important to remember that not-for-profit organizations usually are established to provide goods and services judged valuable by society, that profit-making firms cannot or will not provide. It is dangerous to judge their performance on the basis of simple economic considerations, because they are designed to deal with conditions under which profit-making corporations could not easily survive.

DISCUSSION QUESTIONS

1. Are not-for-profit organizations less efficient than profit-making organizations? Why or why not?

2. Do you agree that the source of revenue is the best way to differentiate between not-for-profit and profit-making organizations as well as among the many kinds of not-for-profit organizations? Why or why not?

3. Is client influence always weak in the not-for-profit organization? Why or why not?

4. Why does the employment of a large number of people who consider themselves to be professionals complicate the strategic management process? How can this also occur in profit-making firms?

5. How does the lack of a clear-cut performance

measure, such as profits, affect the strategic management of a not-for-profit organization?

6. What are the pros and cons of *strategic piggybacking?*

7. In the past, a number of profit-making businesses such as city bus lines and railroad passenger services have changed their status to not-for-profit as governmental agencies took them over. Recently, however, a number of not-for-profit organizations in the U.S. have been converting to profit-making. For example, more than 20 of the 115 nonprofit Health Maintenance Organizations (HMOs) formed with federal money have converted to for-profit status.[36] Why would a not-for-profit organization want to change its status to profit-making?

NOTES

1. M. S. Wortman, Jr., "Strategic Management: Not-for-Profit Organizations," *Strategic Management*, eds. D. E. Schendel and C. W. Hofer (Boston: Little, Brown, 1979), pp. 353–381.

M. S. Wortman, Jr., "Strategic Management in Voluntary and Nonprofit Organizations: Reality, Prescriptive Behavior and Future Research," in M. Moyer (ed.), *Managing Voluntary Organizations* (Toronto, Ontario: York University, 1983), pp. 146–167.

J. E. Freed, "Relationships Among Indicators of Institutional Viability and Variables Associated with Planning Processes in Small, Independent Liberal Arts Institutions" (unpublished Ph.D. dissertation, Iowa State University, 1987), p. 103.

2. I. Unterman and R. H. Davis, "The Strategy Gap in Not-For-Profits," *Harvard Business Review* (May-June 1982), p. 30.

3. G. Rudney, "The Scope and Dimensions of Nonprofit Activity," in *The Nonprofit Sector: A Research Handbook,* ed. W. W. Powell (New Haven: Yale University Press, 1987), p. 56.

C. P. McLaughlin, *The Management of Nonprofit Organizations* (New York: John Wiley & Sons, 1986), p. 4.

4. D. R. Young, *If Not For Profit, For What?* (Lexington, Mass.: D. C. Heath, Lexington Books, 1983), p. 9.

5. J. Ruffat, "Strategic Management of Public and Non-Market Corporations," *Long Range Planning* (April 1983), p. 74.

6. U. S. Bureau of the Census, *Statistical Abstract of the United States: 1987,* 107th ed. (Washington, D.C., 1986).

7. I. Unterman and R. H. Davis, *Strategic Management of Not-For-Profit Organizations* (New York: Praeger Press, 1984), p. 2.

8. M. D. Fottler, "Is Management Really Generic?" *Academy of Management Review* (January 1981), p. 2.

9. Fottler, p. 2.

10. J. G. Simon, "The Tax Treatment of Nonprofit Organizations: A Review of Federal and State Policies," in *The Nonprofit Sector: A Research Handbook,* ed. W. W. Powell (New Haven: Yale University Press, 1987), pp. 67–98.

11. B. P. Keating and M. O. Keating, *Not-For-Profit* (Glen Ridge, N.J.: Thomas Horton & Daughters, 1980), p. 21.

12. "Revenues and Expenditures of Colleges and Universities, 1981–82," *The Chronicle of Higher Education* (April 4, 1984), p. 14.

13. D. Mott, *Characteristics of Effective Organizations* (San Francisco: Harper & Row, 1972) as reported by H. L. Tosi, Jr. and J. W. Slocum, Jr., "Contingency Theory: Some Suggested Directions," *Journal of Management* (Spring 1984), p. 11.
The contention that the pattern of environmental influence on the organization's strategic decision making derives from the organization's source(s) of income agrees with the work of Emerson, Thompson, and Pfeffer and Salancik. See R. E. Emerson, "Power-Dependence Relations," *American Sociological Review* (February, 1962), pp. 31–41; J. D. Thompson, *Organizations In Action* (New York: McGraw-Hill, 1967), pp. 30–31; and, J. Pfeffer and G. R. Salancik, *The External Control of Organizations: A Resource Dependence Perspective* (New York: Harper & Row, 1978), p. 44.

14. W. H. Newman and H. W. Wallender, III, "Managing Not-For-Profit Enterprises," *Academy of Management Review* (January 1978), p. 26.

15. Newman and Wallender, p. 27. The following discussion of the effects of these constraining characteristics is taken from Newman and Wallender, pp. 27–31.

16. P. C. Nutt, "A Strategic Planning Network for Non-Profit Organizations," *Strategic Management Journal* (January-March 1984), p. 57.

17. Unterman and Davis (1984) p. 174.

18. R. M. Kanter and D. V. Summers, "Doing Well While Doing Good: Dilemmas of Performance Measurement in Nonprofit Organizations and the Need for a Multiple-Constituency Approach," in *The Nonprofit Sector: A Research Handbook,* ed. W. W. Powell (New Haven: Yale University Press, 1987), p. 163.

19. Newman and Wallender, p. 27.

20. E. Bowen and B. Dolan, "His Trumpet Was Never Uncertain," *Time* (May 18, 1987), p. 68.

21. Keating and Keating, p. 130.

22. E. H. Fram, "Changing Expectations for Third Sector Executives," *Human Resource Management* (Fall 1980), p. 9.

23. For more information on the boards of not-for-profit organizations, see C. N. Waldo, *A Working Guide for Directors of Not-For-Profit Organizations* (New York: Quorum Books, 1986); C. A. Anderson and R. N. Anthony, *The New Corporate Directors* (New York: John Wiley & Sons, (1986), pp. 193–220; and R. D. Hay, *Strategic Management of Non-Profit Organizations* (Santa Barbara, California: Kinko's Publishing Group, 1986), pp. 4.1–4.18.

24. Keating and Keating, pp. 140–141.

25. Keating and Keating, pp. 143–144.

26. S. M. Lee and J. P. Shim, "Zero-Base Budgeting—Dealing with Conflicting Objectives," *Long Range Planning* (October 1984), p. 103.

27. M. W. Dirsmith, S. F. Jablonsky, and A. D. Luzi, "Planning and Control in the U.S. Federal Government: A Critical Analysis of PPB, MBO, and ZBB," *Strategic Management Journal* (October-December 1980), pp. 303–329.

E. E. Chaffee, "The Link between Planning and Budgeting," Working Paper, National Center for Higher Education Management Systems, Boulder, Colorado, October 1981, pp. 12–13.

28. R. P. Nielsen, "SMR Forum: Strategic Piggybacking—A Self-Subsidizing Strategy for Nonprofit Institutions," *Sloan Management Review* (Summer 1982), pp. 65–69.

R. P. Nielsen, "Piggybacking for Business and Nonprofits: A Strategy for Hard Times," *Long Range Planning* (April 1984), pp. 96–102.

29. "When Should the Profits of Nonprofits Be Taxed?" *Business Week* (December 5, 1983), p. 191.

30. E. Skloot, "Should Not-For-Profits Go Into Business?" *Harvard Business Review* (January-February 1983), p. 21.

31. R. P. Nielsen, "Piggybacking Strategies for Nonprofits: A Shared Costs Approach," *Strategic Management Journal* (May-June 1986), pp. 209–211.

32. Skloot, pp. 20–24.

33. K. G. Provan, "Interorganizational Cooperation and Decision Making Autonomy in a Consortium Multihospital System," *Academy of Management Review* (July 1984), pp. 494–504.

34. *Directory of Multihospital Systems* (Chicago: American Hospital Association, 1980).

35. T. Mason, "Lifesaving Partnerships For Nonprofit Hospitals," *Business Week* (August 26, 1985), p. 84.

36. D. Wellel, "As HMOs Increasingly Become Big Businesses, Many of Them Convert to Profit-Making Status," *Wall Street Journal* (March 26, 1985), p. 4.

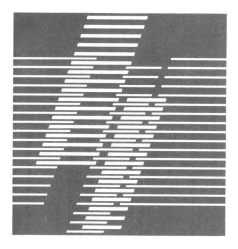

CHAPTER 12

STRATEGIC ISSUES IN ENTREPRENEURIAL VENTURES AND SMALL BUSINESSES

STRATEGIC MANAGEMENT MODEL

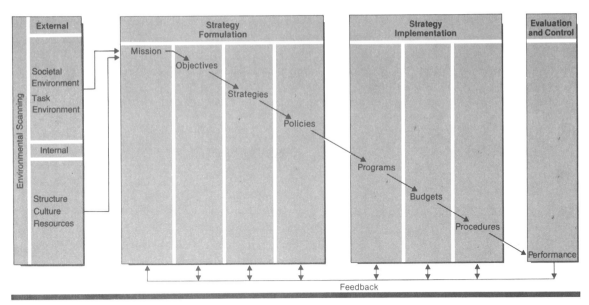

Studies in strategic management have typically dealt with the large, established business corporation to the virtual exclusion of the small business firm. Robinson and Pearce point out in their review of small firm strategic planning that "the state of knowledge pertinent to the strategic management of small and growing firms is woefully inadequate."[1] Except in those instances of an entire industry heavily composed of small entrepreneurial companies that capture the public imagination (like the computer software industry), the strategic management of small firms is rarely considered and rarely discussed in the business press or academic community. There is a tendency to treat these companies as if they were just a smaller version of larger companies and to apply standard strategic management concepts and techniques to their situation. This "little big business" orientation can be a serious mistake. For example, single product companies cannot readily apply portfolio analysis to their situation. Because a large number of small businesses and entrepreneurial ventures have only one product or product line, portfolio theory has little, if any, relevance to their strategy formulation process.

Small business cannot be ignored, however, when strategic management is discussed. Around 99% of the 17 million businesses in the U.S. employ fewer than 100 persons. Small business accounts for approximately half of all U.S. employment. Over 80% of all new jobs created in the U.S. between 1960 and 1985, were created by small businesses. Well over 60% of this total were created by new ventures. Between 1980 and 1988, three million jobs were lost in the Fortune 500 companies while 17 million jobs were created by small businesses.[2] Research reveals that not only do small firms spend almost twice as much of their R&D dollars on fundamental research as do large firms, but also that small companies are responsible for a high proportion of innovations in products and services.[3] For example, 43% of the awards for process and product innovation given over a six-year period by *Food Processing* magazine went to companies with less than $10 million in sales.[4]

Despite the overall success of small businesses, however, every year tens of thousands of small companies go out of business. Even in the best of times a firm has only a 50% chance of survival during its first five years.[5] As shown in Table 12.1, the causes of small business failure (depending upon the study cited) range from inadequate accounting systems to inability to cope with growth. The underlying problem appears to be an overall lack of strategic management—beginning with an inability to formulate a strategy to reach the customer, and ending with a failure to develop a system of evaluation and control to keep track of performance.

TABLE 12.1
Causes of Small Business Failure According to Various Studies

	A GOVERNMENT ANALYSIS	A LARGE ACC'T FIRM	DUN AND BRADSTREET STUDY	BANK OF AMERICA
Inadequate acct'g systems	x	x		
Poor location	x			
Lack of marketing skills	x			
Lack of a capital budget		x		
Inadequate provision for contingencies		x		
Lack of management skills		x		
Excessive inventory		x		
Incompetency			x	
Lack of experience			x	
Neglect			x	
Fraud			x	
Disaster			x	
Poor recordkeeping				x
Reckless money management				x
Lack of formal planning				x
Insufficient marketing talents				x
Indifferent employees				x
Inability to cope with growth				x

SOURCE: M. J. Stanford, *New Enterprise Management* (Reston, Va.: Reston Publishing Company, 1982), p. 4. Courtesy of American Institute of Certified Public Accountants.

Some of the strategic issues that are present in a small, developing company as well as in a large, established firm are:

- What goods or services are to be produced?
- Who is the customer?
- What sources of supply will be used?
- Where will the business be located?
- How much capital is required?
- How will the goods or services be produced?

These are only a few of the many possible strategic decisions with which managers must cope. The small business entrepreneur, however, usually faces them alone. Often defined as a person who organizes and manages a business undertaking, who assumes risk for the sake of a profit, the *entrepreneur* is the ultimate strategic manager. He or she makes all the strategic as well as operational decisions. All three levels of strategy—corporate, business, and functional—are the concerns of this founder and owner-manager of a company.

For these, among other reasons, it is important to understand how strategic management is practiced in small and developing companies as contrasted with large established corporations.

12.1

DIFFERENCE BETWEEN SMALL BUSINESS AND ENTREPRENEURIAL VENTURES

The United States Small Business Administration categorizes a business as small for the purpose of loan qualification if it fits the following criteria:

1. It is **independently** owned and operated.

2. It is not **dominant** in its field.

3. If in **manufacturing,** it has an average employment of no more than 250 employees or a relatively small size within the specific industry (up to 1,500 employees under some circumstances).

4. If in **wholesaling,** its annual sales are no more than $9.5–$22 million, depending on the industry.

5. If in **retailing** or **service,** its annual receipts are no more than $2–$8 million, depending on the industry.

6. If in **construction,** its average annual receipts cannot exceed $9.5 million for the three most recently completed fiscal years for general construction. For special trade construction, the average annual receipts cannot exceed $1 or $2 million for the three most recently completed fiscal years, depending on the industry.

7. If in agriculture, its annual receipts are no more than $1 million.[6]

Although there is considerable overlap between "small business" and "entrepreneurship," the concepts are different. The **small business firm** is defined as any business that is independently owned and operated, not dominant in its field, and does not engage in innovative practices. The **entrepreneurial venture,** in contrast, is any business with primary goals of profitability and growth and can be characterized by innovative strategic practices.[7] The basic difference between the small business firm and the entrepreneurial venture, therefore, lies not in the type of goods or services provided, but in their fundamental views toward growth and innovation. A high percentage of both small businesses and entrepreneurial ventures fit into the first stage of corporate development and the organizational life-cycle, as discussed in Chapter 8. Although all businesses begin life as entrepreneurial ventures and must grow to survive, many owners choose to stabilize their businesses at a particular size of operations and remain indefinitely in either Stage I (entrepreneurial) or II (functional). The primary goal of such a company changes from growth in order to survive, to stability in order to satisfy key needs of the owners/investors, such as lifetime employment for family members or a desire to keep total control in the hands of the entrepreneur.

12.2

USE OF STRATEGIC MANAGEMENT

Sexton, an authority on entrepreneurship, proposes that strategic planning is more likely to be present in an entrepreneurial venture than in the typical small business firm:

> Most firms start with just a single product. Those oriented toward growth immediately start looking for another one. It's that planning approach that separates the entrepreneur from the small-business owner.[8]

The reasons often cited for the apparent lack of strategic management practices in many small business firms are four-fold:

1. **Not enough time.** Day-to-day operating problems take up the time necessary for long-term planning.

2. **Unfamiliar with strategic management.** The small business's CEO may be unaware of strategic management concepts or view them as irrelevant to the small business situation.

3. **Lack of skills.** Small-business managers often lack the skills necessary to begin the strategic decision making process and do not have or wish to spend the money necessary to import trained consultants.

4. **Lack of trust and openness.** Many small-business owner/managers are very sensitive regarding key information about the business and are thus unwilling to share strategic planning with employees or outsiders. For this reason, boards of directors are often composed only of close friends and relatives of the owner/manager—people unlikely to provide an objective viewpoint or professional advice.[9]

Value of Strategic Management

Although many small companies do not use it, strategic management is being practiced by a growing number of small business and entrepreneurial companies. Research shows that strategic planning is strongly related to small business financial performance. For example, a study of 265 entrepreneurs of dry cleaning businesses revealed that firms that had engaged in strategic planning for more than five years significantly outperformed, in terms of revenue growth and net profits, those firms with less than five years of experience in strategic planning.[10] Another study of 135 small businesses in six different industries concluded that firms that engaged in strategic planning had greater increases in both sales and profits over a three-year period than did non-planners.[11]

Degree of Formality in Strategic Planning

Research generally concludes that the strategic planning process should be far more informal in small companies than it is in large corporations.[12] Some studies have even found that too much formalization of the strategic planning process can result in reduced performance![13] It is possible that a heavy emphasis on structured, written plans can be dysfunctional to the small entrepreneurial firm because it detracts from the very flexibility that is a benefit of small size. Nevertheless, there is some evidence that a certain degree of formality and structure in the strategic management process can be very beneficial to the small and developing company. In the study of dry cleaning firms mentioned earlier, companies with written plans (resulting from an analysis of internal strengths and weaknesses, and external opportunities and threats) had higher sales and profits than did those firms with strictly intuitive plans developed by the entrepreneur or no planning process at all. The study concluded that *the process of strategic planning, not the plan itself, was a key component of business performance.*[14]

A study of 220 of the fastest-growing, privately-held companies in the U.S. ranked by *INC.* magazine provided further evidence that some formality in strategic planning is needed as the company grows:

- While one-half of the *INC.* companies did not have a "formal" business plan at start-up, the majority adopted some form of strategic planning once the company was in operation.
- As the companies' sales volume grew, the planning processes became more formal, structured, and participatory. These processes were, however, much less sophisticated than those used by larger corporations.
- The strategic planning activity was more short-run-oriented than that conducted by large corporations.[15]

These observations suggest that new entrepreneurial ventures begin life in Mintzberg's *entrepreneurial mode* of strategic planning (explained in Chapter 6), and move toward the *planning mode* as the company becomes established and wants to continue its strong growth. If, after becoming successfully established, the entrepreneur instead chooses stability over growth, the venture moves more toward the *adaptive mode* so common to many small businesses.

Usefulness of Strategic Management Model

The descriptive model of strategic management, which was presented in Chapter 1 in Figure 1.3 and which prefaces each chapter in the book, is also relevant to entrepreneurial ventures and small businesses. As does the large corporation, the small company must go through (1) strategy formulation, (2) strategy implementation, and (3) evaluation and control. Using an assessment of the company's external and internal environments, top management (often just the CEO/entrepreneur) must first decide the company's mission, objectives, strategies, and policies, and then implement them with the appropriate programs, budgets, and procedures, so that the company's performance meets or exceeds expectations. This basic model holds for both an established small company and a new entrepreneurial venture. As the research mentioned earlier concluded, small and developing companies increase their chances of success if they make a serious attempt to work through the strategic issues imbedded in the strategic management model. The terms used in the process are relatively unimportant. The key is to focus on what's important—that set of managerial decisions and actions that determines the long-run performance of the company. The following list of informal questions can be more useful to a small company than are the more formal terms used by large corporations.

FORMAL	INFORMAL
Define mission	What do we stand for?
Set objectives	What are we trying to achieve?
Formulate strategy	How are we going to get there? How can we beat the competition?
Determine policies	What sort of ground rules should we all be following to get the job done right?
Establish programs	How should we organize this operation to get what we want done as cheaply as possible with the highest quality possible?
Prepare pro-forma budgets	How much is it going to cost us and where can we get the cash?
Specify procedures	In how much detail do we have to lay things out, so that everybody knows what to do?
Determine performance measures	What are those few key things that will determine whether we make it or not? How can we keep track of them?

Usefulness of Strategic Decision-Making Process

As mentioned in Chapters 2 and 6, one way in which the strategic management model can be made action-oriented is to follow the strategic decision-making model presented in Figs. 2.2 and 6.1. The eight steps presented in that model are just as appropriate for small companies as they are for large corporations. Unfortunately, the process does not fit new entrepreneurial ventures. It makes no sense to begin the process with an evaluation of current performance results if the company has not yet started. Likewise, an entrepreneurial venture has no current mission, objectives, strategies, and policies to be evaluated. It must develop new ones out of a comparison of its external opportunities and threats to its potential strengths and weaknesses. Consequently we propose in Figure 12.1 a modified version of the strategic decision-making process; this version more closely suits the new entrepreneurial business.

The *strategic decision-making process for new ventures* is composed of the following eight interrelated steps:

1. **Development of the basic business idea**—a mix of products and/or services having target customers and/or markets. The idea can be developed from a person's experience or it can be generated in a moment of creative insight.

2. **A scanning of the external environment, to locate strategic factors** in the societal and task environments that pose opportunities and threats. The scanning should focus particularly on market potential and resource accessibility.

3. **A scanning of the internal strategic factors** relevant to the new business. The entrepreneur should objectively consider personal assets, areas of expertise, abilities, and experience, in terms of the organizational needs of the new venture.

4. **Analysis of the strategic factors,** in light of the current situation. The venture's potential strengths and weaknesses must be evaluated in light of opportunities and threats.

5. **Decision point.** If the basic business idea appears to be a feasible business opportunity, the process should be continued. Otherwise, further development of the idea should be canceled unless the strategic factors change.

6. **Generation of a business plan** specifying how the idea will be transformed into reality. See Table 12.2 for the suggested contents of a strategic business plan. The proposed venture's mission, objectives, strategies, and policies, as well as its likely board of directors (if a corporation) and key managers, should be developed. Key internal factors should be specified and performance projections generated. The business plan is the last step of a new venture's strategy formulation; it serves as a vehicle through which financial support is obtained from potential investors and creditors.[16]

FIGURE 12.1
Strategic Decision-Making Process for New Ventures

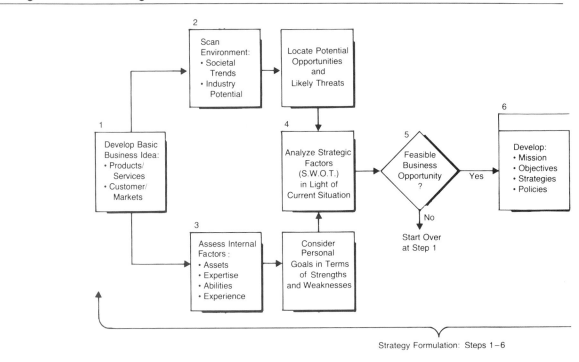

Source: Adapted from Thomas L. Wheelen and Janiece L. Gallagher, *Entrepreneurship and Strategic Management* (New York: McGraw-Hill, 1990). Developed by Thomas L. Wheelen and Charles E. Michaels, Jr. Copyright © 1987 by Thomas L. Wheelen and Janiece L. Gallagher. Reprinted by permission.

7. **Implementation of the business plan,** via the use of action plans and procedures.

8. **Evaluation of the implemented business plan,** through comparison of actual performance against projected performance results. This step leads to step 1(b) of the strategic decision-making process as shown in Figures 2.2 and 6.1. To the extent that actual results are less than or greatly exceed the anticipated results, the entrepreneur needs to reconsider the company's current mission, objectives, strategies and policies, and possibly formulate strategic changes to the original business plan.

12.3

ISSUES IN STRATEGY FORMULATION

A fundamental reason for differences in strategy formulation between large and small companies lies in the relationship between owners and managers.[17] The CEO of a large corporation has to consider and balance the varied needs of the corporation's many stakeholders. The CEO of a small business,

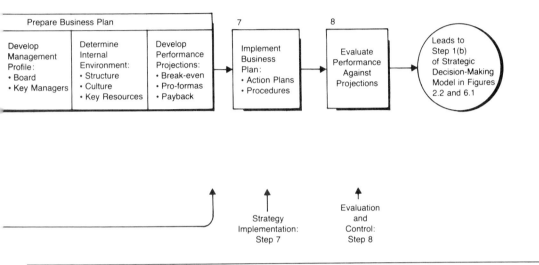

TABLE 12.2

Contents of a Strategic Business Plan for an Entrepreneurial Venture

I. Table of Contents	X. Human Resources Plan
II. Executive Summary	XI. Ownership
III. Nature of the Business	XII. Risk Analysis
IV. Strategy Formulation	XIII. Timetables and Milestones
V. Market Analysis	XIV. Strategy Implementation— Action Plans
VI. Marketing Plan	
VII. Operational Plans—Service/ Product	XV. Evaluation and Control
	XVI. Summary
VIII. Financial Plans	XVII. Appendixes
IX. Organization and Management	

SOURCE: Adapted from Thomas L. Wheelen and Janiece L. Gallagher, *Entrepreneurship and Strategic Management* (N.Y.: McGraw-Hill, 1990). Copyright © 1988 by Thomas L. Wheelen. Reprinted by permission.

however, is very likely to also be the owner—the company's primary stake-holder. Personal and family needs can thus strongly affect the company's mission and objectives and can overrule other considerations. For example, large corporations often choose growth strategies for their many positive side-effects for management as well as for the stockholders. A small company may, however, choose a stability strategy because the entrepreneur is interested mostly in generating employment for family members, providing the family a "decent living," and in being "the boss" of a firm small enough that he/she can manage it comfortably. "Thus in order to understand the goals of a small organization, it is first necessary to understand the motivations of the owner since the two are indistinguishable, certainly in the early days of the firm's start-up."[18]

The basic S.W.O.T. analysis is just as relevant to small businesses as it is to larger ones. As mentioned earlier, portfolio theory is not often relevant to small companies because many of them have only one product or product line. The greatest strength and weakness of the small firm, at least in the beginning, lies with the entrepreneur—the owner/manager of the business. The entrepreneur is *the* strategic manager, the source of product/market knowledge, and the dynamo that energizes the company. That is why the internal assessment of a new venture's strengths and weaknesses focus in Figure 12.1 on the personal characteristics of the founder—his/her assets, expertise, abilities, and experience. Just as an entrepreneur's strengths can be the key to company·success, personal weaknesses can be a primary cause of failure. For example, the reason for the failure of many small retail businesses is the founders' lack of knowledge of retailing skills.[19]

Environmental scanning in small businesses is much less sophisticated than in large corporations. The business is usually too small to justify hiring someone to only do environmental scanning or strategic planning. Top managers, especially if they are the founders, tend to believe that they know the business and can follow it better than anyone else. A study of 220 small, rapid-growth companies reveals that the typical approach to strategic planning includes an analysis of competition (carried out by 60% of the companies), identification of customer requirements (74%), development of detailed resource-allocation plans (65%), analysis of operational strengths and weaknesses (76%), consideration of contingency plans (86%), allowance for control and feedback (70%), and procedures for implementation (86%). Approximately two-thirds of the companies surveyed focus their planning activities in the marketing area, around 20% concentrate on plans for operations, and only 4% focus their planning in the financial area. The majority of the CEOs are actively and personally involved in all phases of the planning process, but especially in the setting of objectives. Only 15% of the companies use a planning officer or form a planning group to assist in the planning process. In the rest of the firms, operating managers who participate in strategic planning only provide input to the CEO, who then formulates the plan.[20]

Sources of Innovations

Drucker, in his book *Innovation and Entrepreneurship*, proposes the existence of seven sources for innovative opportunity that should be monitored by those interested in starting an entrepreneurial venture, either within an established company or as an independent small business.[21] The first four sources of innovation lie within the industry itself. The last three arise in the societal environment. These seven sources are:

1. **The Unexpected.** An unexpected success, an unexpected failure, or an unexpected outside event, can be a symptom of a unique opportunity. For example, at a time in the 1950s when Japanese television manufacturers marketed their products only to affluent people in the cities, Matsushita, a small, undistinguished company, noted that a sizable number of their sets were being bought by farmers who were supposedly too poor to afford TVs. Instead of ignoring this fact as other manufacturers did, Matsushita began to sell their televisions door-to-door in the country. The company soon grew to become a major multinational corporation known for its Panasonic and National brands.

2. **The Incongruity.** A discrepancy between reality and what everyone assumes it to be, or between what is and what ought to be, can create an innovative opportunity. For example, in the 1950s the ocean-going freighter business was believed to be dying. It was assumed that it would be replaced by air freight, to be used for all shipments except bulk commodities. The cost of ocean freight was going up partially because of congestion and pilferage in many ports. To concentrate on competing with air, the industry had emphasized the use of faster, more economical ships using less crew. But loading and unloading problems still overcame any savings. In 1966, however, a new company called Sea-Land Corporation solved the problem: it introduced containerized shipping. Goods could now be packed into large, secure containers at the shipper's warehouse and loaded quickly onto specially-designed containerships. This system reduced time in port and cut costs by 60%. Sea-Land grew to become a dominant force in trans-oceanic shipping and eventually became part of CSX Corporation.

3. **Innovation based on process need.** When a weak link is evident in a particular process, but people work around it instead of doing something about it, an opportunity is present to the person or company willing to supply the "missing link." For example, when a pharmaceutical company's salesman named William Connor decided to start his own business, he looked for a need that was not being fulfilled. Eye surgeons at that time dreaded cutting a particular ligament when they were doing cataract surgery. Unfortunately, the doctors had no choice but to do so. Connor noted that a specific enzyme was known to easily dissolve this particular ligament, but it was not used because it could not be stored for more than a few hours. Through trial and error, Connor found a preservative that would make the enzyme usable. Within a year all eye

surgeons were using his patented compound. Twenty years later, Connor sold his company, Alcon Laboratories, to a multinational company for a substantial amount.

4. **Changes in industry or market structure.**   A business is ready for an innovative product, service, or approach to the business, when the underlying foundation of the industry or market shifts. In 1954, George E. Johnson noted that blacks in the United States wanted to be able to straighten their naturally coarse, thick hair so that they would have more flexibility in hair styling. Even though black consumers were becoming recognized as an important market segment, no established hair care or cosmetics company was interested at the time in developing hair care products specifically for them. Seeing a strong need in a developing market, George Johnson formed what was soon to become the largest manufacturer of personal grooming products for black consumers in the world—Johnson Products Company.

Deregulation in the U.S. and privatization around the world in the 1980s also created innovative opportunities that were used by firms like Texas Air. Small, non-union, entrepreneurial rail lines were born in the U.S., as major unionized rail companies dropped what had been for them unprofitable lines of track. See Illustrative Example 12.1 for one such entrepreneurial venture, the tiny Delaware Otsego Railroad.

5. **Demographics.**   Changes in the population's size, age structure, composition, employment, level of education, and income, can create innovative opportunities. One typical example has been the impact of the WW II "baby boomers" on the U.S. economy in particular. As this large bulge in the U.S. population ages, its interests dominate the marketplace. For example, when this group was in its twenties during the 1970s, products appealing to young adults, such as skiing, beer, rock music, and X-rated movies (to name a few), became very popular. As this group moved into their 30s during the 1980s, their interests shifted to those products and services that would help them balance their developing family and career interests. Day-care centers, family-oriented resorts, and physical fitness centers became popular. The beer-consumption pattern changed from the drinking of cheap beer by the pitcher to the drinking of imported or specialty beers by the glass. Wine coolers replaced six packs. As this group ages, expect increasing interest in health care, cultural activities, travel, and financial security.

6. **Changes in perception, mood, and meaning.**   Innovative opportunities can develop when a society's general assumptions, attitudes, and beliefs change. For example, people's feelings about eating have been shifting from "feeding" (getting down necessary sustenance in the easiest, simplest, and cheapest way) to "dining" (eating gourmet foods in a gracious atmosphere). Because of this shift, gourmet cookbooks and special sections in supermarkets have become very popular. In another example, as families in the developed countries choose to have fewer children, parents tend to spend the same amount on one child as they might have spent on two. Thus baby-carriage manufacturers are able to keep up their sales in dollars while their sales in units drop; they emphasize high-

ILLUSTRATIVE EXAMPLE 12.1

Delaware Otsego Railroad Takes Advantage of Industry Changes and Becomes a Key Small Business in the Northeast

When deregulation in the U.S. changed the competitive environment for railroads, three rail companies emerged as dominant in the Eastern U.S.—Conrail, CSX, and Norfolk Southern. Only one of these, Conrail, had track to New York City. When CSX bought Sea-Land in 1986 and became a global transportation company, it found that ocean-going container ships were using the United States continent as a "land bridge" between the Atlantic and Pacific Oceans; this alternative was cheaper than use of the Panama Canal. To provide rail transportation to and from the west coast for its Sea-Land container traffic, CSX needed access to New York City. To obtain this access, however, CSX had to pay Conrail, a serious rival for containerized traffic, a high fee for the use of its tracks to New York.

Walter Rich saw opportunity in this situation. As the President and CEO of Delaware Otsego Corporation (parent of the small New York, Susquehanna, and Western Railway), he had stitched together unused rail trackage and formed a rail system from New York City to Warwick, New York, and from Binghamton, New York, to Jamesville and Utica, New York. Because he needed track to connect Warwick with Binghamton (his track was in terrible condition), he convinced Conrail in 1982 to grant him rights to use Conrail's track between the two cities. When Sea-Land

failed to reach an acceptable agreement with Conrail on price and terminals, Mr. Rich took advantage of his local freight agreement to break Conrail's monopoly position into New York City. He offered Sea-Land a better deal. Rich's line was able to make a good profit on the traffic even though it had to pay high fees to Conrail. Labor costs were 50% lower than Conrail's because Rich's line was non-union and thus able to operate with smaller crews and less costly work rules.

In 1987 Rich decided to renovate his own decrepit 70-mile stretch of hilly, curvy track between Binghamton and Warwick to avoid Conrail's high fee. Analysts saw it as an audacious but preposterous move. "He's running trains on a Burma Road. The route is long, slow, has stiff gradients, no signals and numerous grade crossings," stated one expert. Nevertheless, Rich was able to proceed partially because of the support of connecting railroads (CSX and Norfolk Southern) eager to find a non-Conrail route to New York City. "We're like a fly on the back of an elephant," confesses Mr. Rich. He went on to say, however, that "within five years we will be very important."

SOURCE: D. Machalaba, "Delaware Otsego Refuses To Be Shunted," *Wall Street Journal* (October 12, 1987), p. 6.

---

quality products with high prices. This move is aided by the trend to two-career families and a high level of divorce—causing parents to spend money instead of time on their children. This trend created a huge market for "educational" products, such as personal computers. Witness the rapid development of Apple Computer—an entrepreneurial success story.

7. **New knowledge.** Advances in scientific and nonscientific knowledge can create new products and new markets. Advances in two different areas can sometimes be integrated to form the basis of a new product. For example, simultaneous developments in computers, communication, and office equipment are being merged to form one new set of products that are able to do what three or more different products did before.

New software firms emerge weekly as new programs are needed to take advantage of technological advancements in computer hardware.

Drucker further proposes **five principles of innovation,** which can help the entrepreneur to take advantage of a source of innovation.[22]

- Begin with an analysis of the opportunities.
- Analyze the opportunity to see if people will be interested in using the innovation. Remember that few people were interested in buying a computer until "user-friendly" software was developed.
- To be effective, the innovation must be simple and clearly focused on a specific need. The "Post-It" note pad was a huge success because, once people saw the removable, self-stick notes in action, they could readily find many uses for the product.
- Effective innovations start small. By appealing to a small, limited market, a product or service requires little money and few people to produce and sell it. As the market grows, the company has time to fine-tune its processes and stay ahead of the emerging competition.
- Aim at market leadership. If an innovation does not aim at leadership in the beginning, it is unlikely to be innovative enough to successfully establish itself. Leadership here can mean dominating a small market niche.

Factors Affecting a New Venture's Success

According to Hofer and Sandberg, there are three factors that have a substantial impact on a new venture's performance. In order of importance, they are (1) *the structure of the industry entered,* (2) *the new venture's business strategy,* and (3) *behavioral characteristics of the entrepreneur.*[23]

Industry Structure

Research shows that the chances for success are greater for those entrepreneurial ventures that enter rapidly changing industries than for those that enter stable industries. In addition, prospects are better in industries that are in the early, high-growth stages of development. There is often less intense competition. Fast market growth also allows new ventures to make a certain number of mistakes without serious penalty. New ventures also increase their chances of success when they enter markets in which they can erect entry barriers to keep out competitors.

PIMS data reveals that a new venture is more likely to be successful entering an industry in which one dominant competitor has a 50% or more market share, than entering an industry in which the largest competitor has less than 25% market share. To explain this phenomenon, Hofer and Sandberg point out that when an industry has one dominant firm, the remaining competitors are relatively weak and are easy prey for an aggressive entrepreneur. To avoid direct competition with a major competitor, the new venture can focus on a market segment that is being ignored.

Two product characteristics of the industry also have a significant impact on a new venture's success. First, a new venture is more likely to be successful when it enters an industry with heterogeneous (different) products than when it enters one with homogeneous (similar) products. In a heterogeneous industry, a new venture can differentiate itself from competitors with a unique product or, by focusing on the unique needs of a market segment, it can find a market niche. Second, a new venture is, according to PIMS data, more likely to be successful if the product is relatively unimportant to the customer's total purchasing needs, than if it is important. Customers are more likely to experiment with a new product if the costs are low and product failure will not create a problem.

Business Strategy

According to Hofer and Sandberg, the key to success in new-venture strategy is (1) to differentiate the product from other competitors in meaningful areas of quality and service and (2) to focus the product on customer needs in a segment of the market, so that a dominant share of that part of the market is achieved. This guideline is in agreement with those of other authorities who argue that a small company cannot successfully follow an overall low-cost strategy because it cannot achieve the economies of scale available to large corporations. Therefore, Porter's focus and differentiation strategies are the most attractive alternatives to small companies who recognize their size and marketing "muscle" limitations.[24] (See the discussion of Michael Porter's competitive strategies in Chapter 7.) Adopting guerrilla-warfare tactics, these companies go after opportunities in market niches too small to justify retaliation from the market leaders.[25] Like the Delaware Otsego Railroad in Illustrative Example 12.1, such a company can operate quite successfully as a "fly on the back of an elephant."

To continue its growth once it has found a niche, the entrepreneurial firm can emphasize continued innovation and pursue natural growth in its current markets. It can expand into related markets in which the company's core skills, resources, and facilities offer the keys to further success. See Illustrative Example 12.2 for one example of such an entrepreneurial company.

Entrepreneurial Characteristics

Hofer and Sandberg propose four behavioral factors as being key to a new venture's success:[26]

1. Successful entrepreneurs are able to identify potential venture opportunities better than are most people. They focus on opportunities—not on problems—and try to learn from failure.

ILLUSTRATIVE EXAMPLE 12.2

The Successful Use of a Differentiation Strategy by a Small Business: Gold Ribbon Concepts

Stephen and David Spencer had been reasonably successful operating a car radio and installation shop called Spencer Sound Systems, which they had started in 1978 in Iowa City, Iowa. After a couple years of barely breaking even, they began earning a healthy profit by installing expensive car stereo equipment—systems sometimes costing $10,000 to $20,000. Soon, they began selling home stereo equipment and moved to a bigger building.

In 1982, the Spencer brothers noticed an innovative opportunity. They began putting most of the company's profits into the development of gold ribbon speakers. The idea of using ribbons in loud speakers, instead of the usual voice coils and cone diaphragms, was not new. Technicians had been experimenting with ribbon designs since the 1920s. Never before, however, had anyone tried to make speaker ribbons with gold.

During the next three years, the brothers spent nearly $1 million on the project before finding their patented technique for making 1-inch-wide gold ribbons on a membrane thinner than a human hair. Combined with other materials, the gold ribbons form what the Spencers call a "transducer" which is then placed inside a padded cabinet. The transducer costs $800 and is sold to serious audiophiles who wish to build their own cabinets. A finished speaker, called *The Gold,*

costs between $3,150 and $7,000.

The speakers have been praised by international stereo magazines. While their product was still under development in 1985, the Spencer brothers were honored at the International Consumer Electronics Trade Show in Chicago. Buyers have come from all over the world to buy the Spencers' version of "high-end" stereo. More than 60% of the first shipment in 1986 was sent to customers in Oslo, Hong Kong, Bangkok, Tokyo, and Sydney. These customers tend to be males earning $30,000–$40,000 annually who like to spend their money on the very best stereo equipment. "Most of our customers are very, very technically oriented," said Stephen Spencer, the 33-year-old Chief Executive of Gold Ribbon Concepts, the speaker side of the Spencer brothers' business.

The Spencers intend to keep plowing profits back into research and development. They plan to create new cabinet designs and gold ribbon car stereo speakers. They may even be able some day to take their speakers home to enjoy. "We are selling them too fast," smiled Stephen. "There haven't been enough for us."

SOURCE: M. Murray, "Audiophiles Strike Gold in Coralville," *Des Moines Register* (January 5, 1986), p. 1.

2. Successful entrepreneurs have a sense of urgency that makes them action-oriented. They have a high need for achievement, which motivates them to turn their ideas into action.

3. Successful entrepreneurs have a detailed knowledge of the key factors needed for success in the industry and have the physical stamina needed to put their lives into their work.

4. Successful entrepreneurs seek outside help to supplement their skills, knowledge, and abilities. Through their enthusiasm, they are able to attract key investors, partners, creditors, and employees. As mentioned in Illustrative Example 8.2, Mitch Kapor of Lotus Development did not hesitate to bring in Jim Manzi as president, because Manzi had the managerial skills that Kapor lacked.

In summarizing their conclusions regarding factors affecting the success of entrepreneurial ventures, Hofer and Sandberg propose guidelines in Table 12.3.

12.4

ISSUES IN STRATEGY IMPLEMENTATION

The implementation of strategy in a small business involves many of the same issues, mentioned in Chapter 8, that concern a large corporation. Programs, budgets, and procedures to make the strategy action-oriented must be developed and used. Resources must be organized so that the work can be done efficiently and effectively; the proper people must be selected for key jobs; and employees' efforts need to be directed toward task accomplishment and coordinated so that the company achieves its objectives and fulfills its mission. The major difference between the large and small company is *who* must implement the strategy. In a large corporation, the implementors are often a very different group of people from those who formulated the strategy. In a small business, the formulators of the strategy are usually the ones to implement it. It is for this reason that the imaginary line between strategy formulation and implementation often becomes blurred in most small businesses.

TABLE 12.3
Some Guidelines for New Venture Success

- Focus on industries facing substantial technological or regulatory changes, especially those with recent exits by established competitors.
- Seek industries whose smaller firms have relatively weak competitive positions.
- Seek industries that are in early, high-growth stages of evolution.
- Seek industries in which it is possible to create high barriers to subsequent entry.
- Seek industries with heterogeneous products that are relatively unimportant to the customer's overall success.
- Seek to differentiate your products from those of your competitors in ways that are meaningful to your customers.
- Focus such differentiation efforts on product quality, marketing approaches, and customer service—and charge enough to cover the costs of doing so.
- Seek to dominate the market segments in which you compete. If necessary, either segment the market differently or change the nature and focus of your differentiation efforts to increase your domination of the segments you serve.
- Stress innovation, especially new product innovation, that is built on existing organizational capabilities.
- Seek natural, organic growth through flexibility and opportunism that builds on existing organizational strengths.

SOURCE: C. W. Hofer and W. R. Sandberg, "Improving New Venture Performance: Some Guidelines for Success," *American Journal of Small Business* (Summer 1987), pp. 17 and 19. Copyright © 1987 by C. W. Hofer and W. R. Sandberg. Reproduced by permission.

Stages of a Small Business's Development

The implementation problems of a small business change as the company grows and develops over time. Just as the strategic decision-making process for entrepreneurial ventures is different from that of established businesses, so do the managerial systems in small companies often vary from those of large corporations. Those variations are based upon their stage of development. The stages of corporate development and the organizational life-cycle discussed in Chapter 8 suggest that all small businesses are either in Stage I or trying to move into Stage II. These models imply that all successful new ventures eventually become Stage II, functionally organized companies. This is not always true, however. In attempting to clearly show how small businesses develop, Churchill and Lewis propose five *sub-stages* of small business development: (a) Existence, (b) Survival, (c) Success, (d) Take-off, and (e) Resource Maturity.[27] (See Table 12.4.) A review of these stages shows in more detail how a company can move through its entrepreneurial Stage I into a functionally-oriented, professionally-managed Stage II of existence.

A. Existence

At this point, the entrepreneurial venture faces the problems of obtaining customers and delivering the promised product or service. The organizational structure is a simple one—like that shown in Figure 5.1 of Chapter 5. The entrepreneur does everything and directly supervises subordinates. Systems are minimal. The owner *is* the business.

TABLE 12.4
Sub-stages of Small Business Development*

A. Existence

B. Survival

C. Success

    1. Disengagement

    2. Growth

D. Take-off

E. Resource Maturity

SOURCE: N. C. Churchill and V. L. Lewis, "The Five Stages of Small Business Growth," *Harvard Business Review* (May–June 1983), pp. 30–50.

*NOTE: These are actually sub-stages within the stages of development discussed in Chapter 8. Thus, small business Stages A through D are really sub-stages of Stage I, entrepreneurial management; whereas Stage E is the first sub-stage of Stage II, functional management. Refer to Table 8.2.

B. Survival

Those ventures able to satisfy a sufficient number of customers enter this sub-stage. The rest of the ventures close when the owners run out of start-up capital. Those reaching the survival stage are concerned about generating the cash flow needed to repair and replace capital assets as they wear out, and to finance the growth to continue satisfying the market segment it has found. At this point in the young company's life, it can be plagued by "problems of prosperity." It is unable to comfortably finance or manage its growth, but it must satisfy an increasing number of customers or else lose them to a competitor.

At this sub-stage, the organizational structure is still simple, but it probably has a sales manager or general foreman to carry out the well-defined orders of the owner. A major problem of many small businesses at this sub-stage is finding a person who is qualified to supervise the business when the owner can't be present but who is still willing to work for a very modest salary. Entrepreneurs usually attempt to use family members rather than to hire an outsider, who lacks the entrepreneur's dedication to the business and (in the words of one owner-manager) "steals them blind." A company that remains in this sub-stage for a long time, will earn marginal returns on invested time and capital (with lots of psychic income!) and eventually go out of business when "mom and pop" give up or retire.

C. Success

By this point the company's sales have reached a level such that the firm is not only profitable, but has sufficient cash flow to reinvest in the business. They key issue at this sub-stage is whether the company should be used as a platform for growth, or as a means of support for the owners as they completely or partially disengage from the company. The company is in transition to a functionally structured organization, but still relies on the entrepreneur for all key decisions.

C(1). DISENGAGEMENT   The company can now successfully follow a stability strategy and remain at this sub-stage almost indefinitely—provided that environmental change does not destroy its niche or poor management reduce its competitive abilities. By now functional managers have taken over some duties of the entrepreneur. A few staff members—usually a controller in the office and a scheduler in the work area—become part of the company's management. The company at this sub-stage may be incorporated, but it still is primarily owned by the founder or founder's family. Consequently, the board of directors is either a rubber stamp for the entrepreneur or a forum for family squabbles. Growth strategies are not pursued, because either the market niche will not allow growth or because the owner is content with a company of the size he/she can still manage comfortably. For example, Fritz Maytag, the owner/manager CEO of Anchor Brewing Company, deliberately chooses to keep his company small.[28]

C(2). GROWTH Like the Spencer brothers in Illustrative Example 12.2, the entrepreneur risks all available cash and the established borrowing power of the company in financing further growth. Strategic as well as operational planning is extensive and deeply involves the owner. Managers with an eye to the company's future rather than for its current situation are hired. It is in this sub-stage that the company avoids creeping bureaucratization and returns to being a risky entrepreneurial venture. Top management begins to view its own role as that of a blocking back in football (eliminating obstacles) rather than that of the quarterback (calling all the plays).[29] The emphasis now is upon teamwork rather than upon the entrepreneur's personal actions and energy.

D. Take-Off

The key problems in this sub-stage are how to grow rapidly and how to finance that growth. The entrepreneur must learn to delegate to the specialized managers who now form the top management of the company. A functional structure for the organization should now be solidly in place. Operational and strategic planning heavily involves the hired managers, but the company is still dominated by the entrepreneur's presence and stock control. Vertical and horizontal growth strategies are being seriously considered as the firm's management debates when and how to grow. This is the point at which the entrepreneur either rises to the occasion of managing the transition from a small to a large company, or recognizes personal limitations, sells his/her stock for a profit, and leaves the firm. The composition of the board of directors changes, from dominance by friends and relatives of the owner, to a large percentage of outsiders with managerial experience, who can help the owner during the transition to a professionally managed company. The biggest danger facing the firm in this sub-stage is the owner's desire to stay in total control as if it were still an entrepreneurial venture, even though he/she lacks the managerial skills necessary to run an established corporation. As pointed out in Chapter 8 in Illustrative Example 8.2, both Steve Jobs of Apple Computer and Mitch Kapor of Lotus Development realized their limitations and brought in someone else to manage the transitions of their firms. William Norris of Control Data, in contrast, had to be forced out.

E. Resource Maturity

It is at this point that the small company has adopted most of the characteristics of an established, large company. It may still be a small- to medium-sized company, but it is recognized as an important force in the industry and a possible candidate for the Fortune 500 someday. The greatest concerns of a company at this sub-stage are (1) controlling the financial gains brought on by rapid growth, and (2) retaining its flexibility and entrepreneurial spirit. The company has now arrived. In the terms of the stages of corporate development and the organizational life cycle discussed in Chapter 8, the company has become a full-fledged Stage II functional corporation.

Transfer of Power and Wealth in Family Businesses

Small businesses are often family businesses. Even though the founders of the companies are the primary forces in starting the entrepreneurial ventures, their needs for personal help and financial assistance will cause them to turn to family members who can be trusted, over unknown outsiders of questionable integrity, who will demand more salary than the enterprise can afford. Sooner or later the founder's spouse and children are drafted into business operations either because (1) the family standard of living is directly tied to the business, or (2) the entrepreneur is in desperate need of help just to staff the operation. The children are guaranteed summer jobs and the business changes from dad's or mom's company to "our" company. The family members are extremely valuable assets to the entrepreneur because they are often also willing, to help the business succeed, to put in long hours at low pay. Even though the spouse and children might have no official stock in the company, they know that they will somehow share in its future and perhaps even inherit the business.

Churchill and Hatten propose that family businesses go through four sequential phases from the time in which the venture is strictly managed by the founder, to the time in which the next generation takes charge.[30]

1. **Owner-managed business.** This is the point that begins at start-up and continues to the entrance of a family member into the business on a full-time basis. Family considerations influence but are not yet a directing part of the firm. At this point, the founder (entrepreneur) and the business are one.

2. **Training and development of new generation.** The children begin to learn the business at the dining table during early childhood and then through part-time and vacation employment. The company is still dad's or mom's, but the children now begin to think of themselves as a small part of the company. The family and the business become one. A key value develops: What's good for the business is good for the family and vice-versa. Just as the entrepreneur ego-identified with the business earlier, the family now begins to identify itself with the business.

3. **Partnership between generations.** At this point, a son or daughter of the founder has acquired sufficient business and managerial competence so that he or she can be involved in key decisions for at least a part of the company. The entrepreneur's offspring has to gain respect from the

firm's employees and other managers and show that he or she can do the job right. Otherwise, the rest of the employees will ignore "Junior" and only pay attention to the founder. Another issue is the willingness of the founder to share authority with the son or daughter. Even the founder may not have sufficient confidence in the child's ability to make company decisions. Consequently, a common tactic taken by sons and daughters in family businesses is to take a job in a large, established corporation in either the same industry or in an industry similar to that of the family business. With a few years of experience in a large respected firm, the son or daughter can return to the family as a successful manager in his/her own right. By that time, the founder might be more willing to view the child as a competent business person.

4. **Transfer of Power.** Instead of the founder's being forced to sell the company when he or she can no longer manage the business, the founder has the option in a family business of turning it over to the next generation as part of their inheritance. Often the founder moves to the position of chairman of the board and promotes one of the children to the position of CEO. This allows the founder to still have an interest in the firm, but not operating responsibility. Unfortunately, some founders cannot resist meddling in operating affairs and unintentionally undermine the leadership position of the son or daughter. Henry Ford I, for example, used his position as Board Chairman to contradict decisions made by his son, the President—Edsel Ford. Because of this intervention, Ford Motor Company floundered through the 1930s until it almost went bankrupt. To avoid this problem, strong-willed entrepreneurs will sell portions of their stock in the company for retirement income. They will make a big ceremony of turning over the reins of power and take an extended vacation. Some will even use the money to start a new venture of their own, to keep their mind occupied and away from what is now someone else's company.

12.5

ISSUES IN EVALUATION AND CONTROL

As a means by which the corporation's implementation of strategy can be evaluated, the control systems of large corporations have evolved over a long period of time, in response to pressures from the environment (particularly the government). Conversely, the entrepreneur creates what is needed as the business grows. Because of a personal involvement in decision making, the entrepreneur has little need for a detailed reporting system.[31] Thus, the founder who has little understanding of accounting and a shortness of cash might employ a bookkeeper instead of an accountant. A formal personnel function might never appear because the entrepreneur lumps it with simple bookkeeping and uses a secretary to handle personnel files. As an entrepreneurial venture becomes more established, it will develop more complex evaluation and control systems, but they are often not the kind used in large corporations and are probably used for different purposes.

Financial statements, in particular, tell only half the story in small, privately-owned companies. The formality of the financial reporting system in such a company is usually a result of pressures from government tax agencies, not from management's desire to have an objective evaluation and control system. Because balance sheets and income statements are not always what they seem, standard ratios such as return on assets and debt/equity are unreliable. Levin and Travis provide five reasons why owners, operators, and outside observers should be wary of using standard financial methods to indicate the health of a small, privately-owned company.[32]

- **The line between debt and equity is blurred.** In some instances, what appears as a loan is really an easy-to-retrieve equity investment. The entrepreneur in this instance doesn't want to lose his/her investment if the company fails. Another condition is that retained earnings seldom reflect the amount of internal financing needed for the company's growth. This account may merely be a place in which cash is left so that the owner can avoid double taxation. To avoid other taxes, owner/managers may own fixed assets that they lease to the corporation. The equity that was used to buy those assets is really the company's equity, but it doesn't appear on the books.

- **Life-style is a part of financial statements.** The life-style of the owner and the owner's family is often reflected in the balance sheet. The assets of some firms include beach cottages, mountain chalets, and automobiles. In others, plants and warehouses that are used for company operations are not shown because they are held separately by the family. Income statements may not reflect how well the company is operating. Profitability is not so important in decision making in small, private companies as it is in large, publicly-held corporations. For example, spending for recreation or transportation and paying rents or salaries above market rates to relatives put artificially high costs on the books of small firms. One privately-held dry cleaning establishment has never made much profit in its years of existence, but has provided the owner with a comfortable living and the owner's children with good paying jobs so that they could go to college. The business might appear to be poorly managed to an outsider, but the owner is acting rationally. The owner/manager wants dependable income or its equivalent with the least painful tax consequences. Because the standard profitability measures like ROI are not useful in the evaluation of such a firm, Levin and Travas recommend return on current assets as a better measure of corporate productivity.[33]

- **Standard financial formulas don't always apply.** Following practices that are in contrast to standard financial recommendations, small companies will often use short-term debt to finance fixed assets. The absence of well-organized capital markets for small businesses, along with the typical banker's resistance to making loans without personal guarantees, leaves the private owner little choice.

- **Personal preference determines financial policies.** Because the owner is often the manager of the small firm, dividend policy is largely irrelevant. Dividend decisions are based not on stock price (which is usually unknown because the stock is not traded), but on the owner's life-style and the trade-off between taking wealth from the corporation and double taxation.

- **Banks combine personal and business wealth.** Because of the large percentage of small businesses that go bankrupt every year, banks' loan officers are reluctant to loan money to a small business unless the owner also provides some personal guarantees for the loan. In some instances, part of the loan may be composed of a second mortgage on the owner's house. If the owner does not want to succumb to this pressure by lenders to include the owner's personal assets as part of the collateral, the owner/manager might be willing to pay high interest rates for a loan that does not put their family's assets at risk.

SUMMARY AND CONCLUSION

Entrepreneurial ventures and small businesses are managed far more informally than are the large, established business corporations discussed elsewhere in this book. Some of the more popular strategic-management concepts and techniques, like portfolio analysis, are not very useful to the typical small-business manager or entrepreneur. As Mintzberg pointed out in Chapter 6, small, rapidly growing companies tend to follow the entrepreneurial mode of strategy formulation—characterized by bold moves and intuitive decisions. The time frame is oriented to the short-run. Once the company has opened its doors, management's concerns are for operations, not for strategic planning. The usual rationale for not engaging in formal strategic management is: "Why should I develop a five-year plan when I don't even know if I'm going to be in business next year?"

Research in this area does support the conclusion that small firms which engage in strategic management outperform those which do not. This does not mean, however, that formal procedures are necessary. *The process of strategic planning, not the plan itself, appears to be a key component of business performance.* The strategic management model that was introduced in Chapter 1 and is used to introduce every chapter in this book is just as useful to small and entrepreneurial companies as it is to large business corporations and

not-for-profit organizations. Even the strategic decision-making process discussed in Chapters 2 and 6 is valuable to existing small businesses. A few adjustments have been made to the model so that it can be applied to new entrepreneurial ventures, as shown in Figure 12.1.

. This chapter presented some issues in strategy formulation that apply to new ventures and small businesses. S.W.O.T. analysis is very useful, but environmental scanning can be much more informal than that performed in large corporations. Peter Drucker proposes seven sources of innovation, which should be carefully monitored by any prospective entrepreneur. Hofer and Sandberg conclude from their research that a new venture's success is largely determined by (1) the industry's structure, (2) the venture's business strategy, and (3) the behavioral characteristics of the entrepreneur.

Although the implementation process for small and entrepreneurial businesses is similar to that used by large corporations, there are some important differences. The primary difference is that in small businesses the person(s) who formulates strategy is usually also responsible for developing implementation plans and carrying them out. Consequently, small business managers tend to make little distinction between formulation and implementation. The stages of growth and development for a small business are also very different from those presented in Chapter 8. Between Stages I and II are five distinct sub-stages that characterize many small companies. The implementation of strategy is also different for those many small companies (and for a few large ones as well) that are privately-held, family businesses. The next generation must always be considered in decisions concerning the staffing of key positions and the company's organization for future growth.

Evaluation and control in small businesses and entrepreneurial ventures is quite different from that practiced by most large, publicly-held cor-porations. For the small operator, the procedures are far less formal and usually result more from the owner/manager's preferences and govern-ment taxation policies than from any strategic considerations. Businesses are often run on a cash basis and have minimum reporting procedures. Again, the rationales often given for what appear to be slip-shod accounting and financial practices

is (1) secrecy (the owner-manager wants to keep everything in his/her head so that neither com-petitors nor tax people can understand the busi-ness), and (2) a lack of concern about the future because of current concerns for survival. For these and other reasons, owners, operators, and out-side observers should be wary of using standard evaluation methods to measure the health of a small, privately-owned company.

In conclusion, this chapter provides the reader with a basic understanding of the differences be-tween large corporations and small businesses in terms of their use of strategic management. En-trepreneurs and top managers of other small busi-nesses live in a very different kind of world from that occupied by their counterparts in large cor-porations. These managers have few resources to draw upon and operate with the knowledge that the difference between success and bankruptcy can be their personal willingness to risk all their possessions on a dream.

DISCUSSION QUESTIONS

1. What are some arguments for and against the use of strategic management concepts and techniques in a small or entrepreneurial business?

2. If the owner/manager of a small company asked you for some advice concerning the introduction of strategic planning, what would you tell the person?

3. In terms of strategic management, how does a new venture's situation differ from that of an ongoing small company?

4. How should a small company engage in environ-mental scanning? To what aspects of the environment should management pay most attention?

5. What considerations should small-business en-trepreneurs keep in mind when they are deciding if a company should follow a growth or a stability strategy?

6. From a small company's point of view, what is the difference between a differentiation and a focus competitive strategy?

7. How does being family-owned as compared to publicly-owned affect the firm's strategic management?

8. What are the pros and cons of using a standard financial reporting system in a small business?

NOTES

1. R. B. Robinson, Jr. and J. A. Pearce, II, "Research Thrusts in Small Firm Strategic Planning," *Academy of Man-agement Review* (January 1984), p. 128.

2. *The State of Small Business: A Report to the President* (Washington, D.C.: U.S. Government Printing Office, 1987), pp. 12–20 and *ABC World News Tonight* (May 6, 1988).

C. W. Hofer and W. R. Sandberg, "Improving New Ven-ture Performance: Some Guidelines for Success," *American Journal of Small Business* (Summer 1987), pp. 11–12.

3. *The State of Small Business: A Report to the President*, p. 117.

4. T. Hall, "When Food Firms Merge, Effects Reach Into

Aisles of Supermarkets," *Wall Street Journal* (June 13, 1985), p. 29.

5. B. C. Vaught and F. Hoy, "Have You Got What It Takes To Run Your Own Business?" *Business* (July-August 1981), p. 2.

6. *The State of Small Business: A Report to the President* (Washington, D.C.: U.S. Government Printing Office, 1985).

7. J. W. Carland, F. Hoy, W. R. Boulton, and J. A. C. Carland, "Differentiating Entrepreneurs from Small Business Owners: A Conceptualization," *Academy of Management Review* (April 1984), p. 358.

8. S. P. Galante, "Counting On A Narrow Market Can Cloud Company's Future," *Wall Street Journal* (January 20, 1986), p. 17.

9. Robinson and Pearce, p. 129.

10. J. S. Bracker and J. N. Pearson, "Planning and Financial Performance of Small, Mature Firms," *Strategic Management Journal* (November-December 1986), pp. 503–522.

11. R. Ackelsberg and P. Arlow, "Small Businesses Do Plan and It Pays Off," *Long Range Planning* (October 1985), pp. 61–67.

12. Robinson and Pearce, p. 130.

13. R. B. Robinson, Jr. and J. A. Pearce II, "The Impact of Formalized Strategic Planning on Financial Performance in Small Organizations," *Strategic Management Journal* (July-September 1983), pp. 197–207.

Ackelsberg and Arlow, pp. 61–67.

14. Bracker and Pearson, p. 512.

15. J. C. Shuman and J. A. Seeger, "The Theory and Practice of Strategic Management in Smaller Rapid Growth Firms," *American Journal of Small Business* (Summer 1986), pp. 7–18; and J. C. Shuman, J. D. Shaw, and G. Sussman, "Strategic Planning in Smaller Rapid Growth Companies," *Long Range Planning* (December 1985), pp. 48–53.

16. For information on preparing a business plan, see S. R. Rich and D. E. Gumpert, "How to Write a Winning Business Plan," *Harvard Business Review* (May-June 1985), pp. 156–163 and C. M. Baumback, *How to Organize and Operate a Small Business* (Englewood Cliffs, N.J.: Prentice-Hall, 1988), pp. 109–112.

17. S. Birley and D. Norburn, "Small vs. Large Companies: The Entrepreneurial Conundrum," *Journal of Business Strategy* (Summer 1985), pp. 81–87.

18. Birley and Norburn, p. 82.

19. Birley and Norburn, p. 83.

20. Shuman and Seeger, p. 14.

21. P. F. Drucker, *Innovation and Entrepreneurship* (New York: Harper and Row, 1985), pp. 30–129.

22. Drucker, pp. 133–136.

23. Hofer and Sandberg, pp. 12–23.

24. P. Wright, "A Refinement of Porter's Strategies," *Strategic Management Journal* (January-February 1987), pp. 93–101.

H. W. Fox, "Strategic Superiorities of Small Size," *SAM Advanced Management Journal* (Winter 1986), pp. 14–21.

25. Birley and Norburn, p. 84.

K. R. Harrigan, "Guerrilla Strategies For Underdog Competitors," *Planning Review* (November 1986), pp. 4–11, 44–45.

26. Hofer and Sandberg, p. 22.

27. N. C. Churchill and V. L. Lewis, "The Five Stages of Small Business Growth," *Harvard Business Review* (May-June 1983), pp. 30–50.

28. F. Maytag, "The Joys of Keeping the Company Small," *Harvard Business Review* (July-August 1986), pp. 6–14.

29. H. H. Stevenson and J. C. Jarillo-Mossi, "Preserving Entrepreneurship As Companies Grow," *Journal of Business Strategy* (Summer 1986), p. 17.

30. N. C. Churchill and K. J. Hatten, "Non-Market-Based Transfers of Wealth and Power: A Research Framework for Family Businesses," *American Journal of Small Business* (Winter 1987), pp. 51–64.

31. Birley and Norburn, p. 85.

32. R. I. Levin and V. R. Travis, "Small Company Finance: What the Books Don't Say," *Harvard Business Review* (November-December 1987), pp. 30–32.

33. Levin and Travas, p. 31.

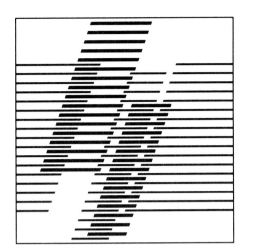

PART SIX

CASES IN STRATEGIC MANAGEMENT

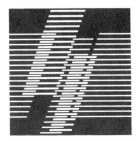

SECTION A
STRATEGIC MANAGERS

CASE 1   Crisis in Geneva

ROLF HACKMANN

BUSINESS BACKGROUND

At 9:00 A.M. Mr. Lansing, Vice-President Europe, is busy already in his Geneva, Switzerland, office, with a sweeping view of the lake and distant mountains. This is the European central office for the Allen Corporation of Chicago, a major producer of over the counter (OTC) pharmaceutical and nutritional products. He is preparing himself to call the Chicago headquarters at 4:00 P.M., which is the start of the business day in the Midwest.

Last week he had received an urgent call from Mr. Davidson, President and CEO of the Allen Corporation, who was concerned about the under-plan performance of his European operations for the first quarter. The profit shortfall for this period is estimated to reach $65,000 because of slower than expected sales, operating expenses that were higher than had been planned, and a constantly rising exchange rate for the dollar. The president seemed well briefed about business details. The rather one-sided conversation emphasized his deep concern for the present situation and its likely impact on the rest of the year. He accused Mr. Lansing of not having a viable business plan to effectively reverse the under-plan performance of his major affiliates in local currency. This would help to minimize the exchange rate problem, which was otherwise accepted as being outside the sphere of influence of both executives.

Mr. Davidson had demanded a return call first thing this morning and specific answers to the following questions:

This case was prepared by Professor Rolf Hackmann of Western Illinois University. This case was presented at the 1986 Workshop of the Midwest Society for Case Research. It also appears in *Annual Advances in Business Cases*, 1986, pp. 77–87, edited by Phillip C. Fisher. Reprinted by permission.

1. What accounted for the soft sales in almost all of the major affiliate markets, and why were sales 5%–9% under local budgets for France, the U.K., and Germany, which together accounted for 72% of all European sales?

2. What was being done to reduce the operating expenses, which were both in excess of local budgets and, because of the low sales, far above approved company guidelines? Mr. Davidson had sarcastically accused Lansing of not being in control of his business at this point.

3. What were the new sales and profits forecasts for the next quarter and the rest of the year, following the first-quarter disaster? Could new product introductions, marketing strategies, or customer groups be expected to compensate for the loss of the first three months? If not, where was he proposing to cut expenses without further hurting business development?

Mr. Lansing had prepared himself well for the afternoon's teleconference with headquarters. In addition to Mr. Davidson, the corporate Vice-President of Finance, the Treasurer, and the Vice-President of Marketing would most likely attend the meeting and have a whole array of uncomfortable questions.

During the past week Mr. Lansing had called in the national managers, with their finance directors and marketing managers, for a business and budget review. After thorough discussions of all related aspects he was confident that he could address the issues in a very constructive manner.

The first two questions could be handled in a very straightforward and factual way that would help to defuse the potentially explosive atmosphere. It was the last one that had caused him quite some difficulty, not so much because he and his associates had suffered from a lack of ideas about the revival of the business, but because certain aspects of their implementation were delicate.

He hoped that against the background of his dismal profit record—his first actually since he had been appointed to his present position—his proposal would be accepted even though it was rather innovative by the standards of his fundamentally conservative company. Actually, it presented the only workable solution to his present predicament as he saw it.

His response to the first question could be that it had been the consensus in hindsight of his European colleagues that the sales budget had been overly optimistic for the first quarter. Everybody from public health authorities to industry sources and retailers had anticipated a recurrence of the strong flu of three years ago. So far it had not materialized and it was unlikely to occur this spring.

Allen's European sales thus were affected by the heavy stocking of cough and cold products with wholesalers and retailers at the end of last year, in anticipation of a strong first-quarter demand. This had helped to produce a record profit performance for the prior year but was now haunting the new budget period.

Another factor depressing to Lansing was the recent increase in interest rates across Europe, which led to tighter inventory policies by the trade. This tightening of inventories could actually provoke product returns, as the channels were grasping for any chance to improve their working capital situation. According to the affiliate managers, the likelihood of actual and sizable returns looked remote despite the company's liberal returns policy. However, they all agreed that the high trade inventories could not be worked off until the middle of the second quarter and so would lead to another poor sales picture for the next three months. After June, sales were expected to return to normal and meet the plan for the rest of the year. The second quarter was expected to produce another profit shortfall which, under the best of circumstances, could be as low as $40,000 and, in the worst-case scenario, might go as high as $54,000.

Expenses in excess of the first-quarter's plan could be defended with effects of the high sales expectations for that period. The overperformance was mainly due to heavy advertising and promotion expenses. Sixty percent of the annual advertising and forty-five percent of the promotion budget had been concentrated in the first three months, to give maximum push to all OTC (non-prescription) health products. The contracting policies of Europe's state-owned T.V. and radio stations required advertisers to prepay air time and did not grant them the right to quick cancellation as was done in the U.S. These funds thus had been committed and were spent. The remaining advertising/promotion budgets offered very little room for significant expense cuts. An area that would allow immediate and substantial corrective action, though, was selling expenses.

The U.K. had hired five new reps plus one district manager on the first of January at a total annual budgeted expense of £128,000 ($193,100), including salary, training, and operating expenses. France had added seven salespeople at the cost of FF 1,840,000 ($241,630) and Germany had expanded its sales force by five reps and one district manager at a total of DM 620,000 ($242,900). (All dollar figures are calculated at the budgeted exchange rates for each currency.) The other European affiliates had also increased their sales forces with a combined expense of only $150,000 for the full year. All positions had been approved in the budget.

In accordance with local labor laws, any or all of the new salespeople in the three big countries could be terminated without cause during a 90-day probation period. Sizable amounts of profit could be produced immediately by slashing salesforce budgets if headquarters really pressed for economy now. Compensating for the projected profit loss of the first half would require the termination of five or six salespeople. This would be only a minor cosmetic surgery if the firings were distributed among the three markets, but Mr. Lansing disliked the idea of even such a small setback for his organizational development plans.

After four weeks of training and a six-month break-in period these people would finally become productive and within two years should contribute average sales of $280,000 per year and a total of roughly $42,000 in operating profit.

Cutting manpower now, after only three months, would not only waste all the money invested so far, but would also make it difficult to reverse the consequences of such a decision if business improved later in the year. Most firms are on annual bonus plans that make salespeople reluctant to change jobs before yearend and forfeit the accrued bonus. One way to overcome this obstacle would be to offer reimbursement of the lost bonus to potential recruits but under present business conditions this did not seem very practical.

DEVELOPING A NEW BUSINESS PLAN	During the discussions with his managers, a line of action had surfaced that would allow Mr. Lansing to retain the sales force expansion and still meet his profit goals for the year, should Mr. Davidson immediately approve the plan that he intended to submit this afternoon.

Over the last couple of years Allen Corporation had successfully introduced a diet product under the trade name Figurella™ in most European markets except France. The French introduction was subject to government approval, a lengthy process required for all drugs and dietary products. Approval was not expected to come before the end of the year. This arrival would be far too late for the all-important summer demand peak for this highly seasonal product, and thus it had not been included in the French budget for the year.

It was Mr. Dedieu, the French manager of Laboratoires Berliot (the Allen subsidiary in Paris), who had come up with a novel and timely solution to the profit problem. He suggested that they proceed with the marketing of Figurella even before summer. In support of his proposal, he had pointed out that sales of the product as a simple food supplement or a quick meal would not require formal government registration procedures.

Although this was a welcome suggestion, he admitted that a problem could arise with trying to position the product in the dietary market without a clear-cut promotional message for weight control. That vital message would, under this plan, not be approved by the authorities. But, according to Mr. Dedieu, this was a minor problem in view of the proposal's advantages, and could be overcome if the product were sold only through pharmacies. Market research had shown that in France, like in other markets of Europe, pharmacists played a significant role in counseling people concerned about their weight but overwhelmed by the multitude of products in the market. This was also the reason why pharmacies accounted for two thirds of the sales of all diet products in France. Heavily promoting the weight-control aspect of Figurella to French pharmacists would help in overcoming or at least minimizing the lack of the diet theme in advertising and promotion. Marketing the product this way would also allow maintenance of better margins and higher retail prices than would result from mass-marketing outlets. These outlets were notoriously unsuited for direct and personal customer counseling. Besides, they tried to attract business strictly on a price basis.

Excluding other channels from the marketing strategy would be unique in this very competitive market, but it would appeal very strongly to the ultraconservative pharmacists who were always jealously protective of their professional status and business interests. Obtaining their full support in the early phases of the marketing program made good business sense by also being consistent with Allen's overall business strategy. Over the years, Laboratoires Berliot had established very close ties with the French pharmacies because of its health-related product lines, and this new product could certainly help to deepen the friendly relations.

Withdrawal of the application for product approval now before the French authorities would thus clear the way for immediate product introduction.

The plan delighted Mr. Lansing because it not only offered a seemingly perfect solution to his present profit crunch, but also presented a legitimate defense of his salesforce expansion in France.

Monsieur Dedieu had come prepared with a complete marketing plan for Figurella. Proposing a May 15 introduction date, which would be right in time for the summer season, he was confident that he could sell 125,000 cans of 500 grams each for the season, as shown in the following list:

May	40,000 cans (initial stocking)
June	20,000
July	20,000
August	20,000
September–December	25,000
Total May–December	125,000

At a wholesale unit price of FF 44.70 ($5.87) excluding VAT (Value Added Tax), this volume would generate sales of FF 5,587,500. Mr. Dedieu had not prepared a profit estimate, because he did not have the details on laid-down costs for the product at his Paris warehouse. Germany as well as the U.K. would be potential supply sources since both countries manufactured the product. Assuming that production costs would be lower in the U.K. than in Germany, he had indicated a preference for English supplies. He had further assumed transportation charges, based on truck delivery, London–Paris or Frankfurt–Paris, to be about the same. As members of the European Community, both countries were exempt from French import tariff levies.

PRODUCT INFORMATION

Figurella is basically a variation of a nutritional supplement developed by Allen Corporation for use by persons debilitated by inadequate food intake because of disease or other medical reasons. The original product is sold under a different trademark and provides accurately measured supplementation of daily nutritional requirements.

Figurella is supplied in 500-gram cans and three different flavors—chocolate, vanilla, and strawberry—to prevent product fatigue in users. Basically the product is milkpowder formulated with added carbohydrates for taste improvement and nutritional balance. Data for the formula in each can are presented in Exhibit 1.1.

The carbohydrates are provided by two sugars: lactose, naturally occurring in milk, and sucrose, added for taste and quick supply of energy. The sucrose content is maintained at 42.5 grams per 100 grams of final powder mixture, and the total carbohydrate content of the formula is 66.4 grams/100 grams. Each 100 grams of powder mixed with about 7–8 ounces of water provides 390 calories. Although it was originally developed to provide additional caloric intake to cases of nutritional deficiencies, the concept of scientifically dosaged nutrition serves the market for weight-control products very well.

The Allen Corporation thus modified the original product slightly and promotes the new product Figurella as a balanced formula for weight loss. The daily regimen consists of one glass of diluted powder each for breakfast and lunch, providing together about 780 calories, plus one regular meal of the customer's choice at night. Such a meal ordinarily should provide another 800 calories, for a daily total of about 1,600 calories—roughly half or even less of what obese people tend to consume. If more rapid weight control is desired, the regular meal may be replaced by one glass of Figurella, for a daily count of 1,170 calories. Such a regimen induces a weight loss of about 1 pound per two days as there is a caloric deficit of 1,800 calories per day for the average adult. (One pound of fat is 3,500 calories.)

One of the three variants presently on the market in the U.K. and Germany, the strawberry formula cannot be sold in France because the coloring agent FDC Red #2 has been banned for some time in the EC (European Community) because of its potentially mutagenic properties.

EXHIBIT 1.1 **Figurella Product Specifications**

	GRAMS/100g	
Protein	23.5	
Fat	3.5	
Carbohydrates	66.4	
Minerals (ash)	4.1	
Moisture	2.5	
	GRAMS/500g	**% OF TOTAL CONTENT**
Milk powder[1]	287.5	57.5
Sucrose	212.5	42.5

[1]Includes 119.5g of lactose

MANUFACTURING COST INFORMATION

According to data from the finance department, production costs for the chocolate and vanilla product in the U.K. amount to £0.981 per can ($1.48) for the chocolate and £0.884 per can ($1.34) for the vanilla flavor. Production costs are 2.5% higher in Germany than in the U.K. for both flavors.

Based on this information and a 50/50 sales split (based on number of cans) between the two flavors, the average cost per finished and French-labeled can is $1.41 from the U.K. and $1.445 from Germany. If there is an average net wholesale price of $5.87 per can in France, the gross margin amounts to $4.46 per can for U.K. and $4.43 per can for German-produced material, before allocation of freight, handling and storage charges. All three countries are EC members and, therefore, no import duties apply.

TRANSPORTATION CHARGES

Transportation expenses for U.K.- and German-produced materials vary only slightly. Based on a standard shipment of 20,000 cans—3333 cartons of six cans each—and a total estimated shipping weight of 15,000 kilograms, these are the estimated total handling and freight charges supplied by freight forwarders, for carriage to Paris.

Inland freight (truck) from Frankfurt	DM 3,060	($1,199)
Barge and inland freight (truck) from London	£1,056	($1,593)

The charges translate to $.06 per can for German supplies and $.08 per can for U.K. Figurella material.

PROFITABILITY PROJECTIONS

The sales forecast of 125,000 cans for France looks realistic and fully in line with introductory sales volumes generated in other markets.

Checking with pharmacists in major population centers indicated a high level of enthusiasm for the new product because of its exclusive sale through pharmacies and the very good profit margin for this type of product. No big difficulties were anticipated for promotion of an official food supplement as a weight-control product.

The consolidated profit picture looks very good and would allow Mr. Lansing to more than compensate for the expected shortfall in the first half. If U.K. supplies were used, unadjusted gross profits of $557,500 would be generated from the sale of 125,000 cans of Figurella, while German supplies would contribute the slightly lower amount of $553,125.

TAX CONSIDERATIONS

With an effective rate of 50% on reported profits, corporate taxes are practically identical for all three nations. (Germany's rate may go up to 56% but that would apply to undistributed profits only and would not apply in this case.) Shifting profits among the three countries, therefore, through intracorporate pricing manipulations would ordinarily only have neutral effects on the overall corporate-tax liability. But Allen Corporation has honed its tax management skills during many years of transfer pricing, involving Swiss corporate intermediaries.

To minimize the impact that high taxes within some countries would have on consolidated corporate profits, the Allen Corporation has set up three trading companies in Switzerland. Each of them is run under a different name, is not readily identified with its owner, and is located in a different city with a different tax structure. The companies are practically one-man organizations (small offices, a manager and a few secretaries, telephones, Telex equipment) and serve the sole purpose of shifting profits among Allen Corporation and its subsidiaries. Some third-party business is occasionally added for window-dressing.

For the purpose of selling Figurella to France, Mr. Lansing has selected Flueli GmbH. in Zug to act as the pro-forma purchaser of the British product. After consulting with his financial director, Mr. Lombardi, he will propose to headquarters that the U.K. subsidiary sell a finished can of Figurella at £1.02 ($1.54) to Flueli and Flueli in turn sell the can for $5.28 to the French subsidiary, with a profit of $3.74 per can going into the Swiss account. Transportation and related charges do not affect this part of the transaction. The French gross profit of $.51 per can (adjusted for transportation charges) will have to cover product introduction and marketing expenses but is not expected to produce a profit for the French operation.

This tax maneuver is going to net $126,412 in extra profit, because the maximum corporate tax rate in Zug is only 22.96%. That portion of the consolidated profits alone more than offsets the profit underperformance forecasted for the first half of the year for all European operations.

Mr. Lansing expects to get quick approval from headquarters for this part of his plan, partly because it promises a substantial and quick recovery of the profit picture, and partly because the payoff depends entirely on the introduction of the product by mid-May, which is only two months away. It presents no unusual business risks and there was unanimous support for it by his European associates.

Sourcing and transfer-pricing decisions invariably lead to resistance by his country's managers who are always quick in suspecting that they are getting an unfair deal. He thus is hearing complaints from the managers in U.K. and Germany, as well as France. Their bonus plan rests on profit performance and any over-plan operating results yield very substantial payoffs over and above base salary.

The German manager resents not having been chosen at least as a partial supplier. His contention is that the minimal production-cost advantage of the British material is more than offset by the stability of German labor relations—the U.K. plant has been the target of wildcat strikes in the past—plus the lower transportation charges.

The English manager wants to have an "arm's length" price equal to his average local net wholesale price of £3.12 ($4.71). Under the proposed pricing, he stands to lose a local profit of £2.1875 per can ($3.30) and claims that the arbitrarily low export price will lead to inquiries by the tax authorities who are always suspecting tax evasion maneuvers by the multinationals.

The French manager, finally, argues that his purchase price is too high to make the product profitable locally, because of the high launching expenses required for salesforce training, distribution, selling, and promotion. He points to the corporate profit guidelines whereby no new product should be introduced with pretax profit margins of less than 25%, which in this case is not going to be realized initially or eventually, because of the high landed (delivered) cost in France.

Mr. Lansing will have to address the issue at some time in the near future because management unrest about bonus prospects can be disruptive. But he does not intend to raise the subject with Chicago today unless specifically asked. If asked, he is prepared to propose allocation of profits on a management basis by splitting the Swiss profits equally between France and the U.K.

PROFIT MAXIMIZATION POTENTIAL

While the Figurella plans for France were being discussed, an interesting and tempting piece of information came up. According to Mr. Dedieu, exports of agricultural surplus products from the European Community (EC) are subsidized by Brussels (the EC headquarters).

In the Figurella case, both the milk powder and the sucrose are eligible for export-support payments based on a rate of ECU 85.86 per 100 kilograms of spray-dried milk powder and ECU 37.78 per 100 kilograms of sugar. (ECU stands for European Currency Unit, which is comprised of a currency basket of the 10-member currencies.)

The sale of 125,000 cans could thus result in subsidies amounting to:

35.94 tons of milk powder	=	ECU 30,858
26.56 tons of sugar	=	ECU 10,034
Total subsidy payment	=	ECU 40,892

Converted at the green (agricultural) rate of £0.618655 per ECU, this is equivalent to £25,298 ($38,348). This would be a tidy extra profit that promises to expand with growing sales of Figurella but there are some caveats.

In order for the sale to Flueli GmbH. to qualify Allen Ltd. for payment of the EC subsidy, the merchandise itself should become a bona fide EC export. But in order to save transportation and handling charges, plus time, Allen Ltd. sells the merchandise to Flueli GmbH. and in a simultaneous transaction Flueli sells the same shipment to Laboratoires Berliot. With two sets of the necessary shipping and insurance documents, commercial invoices, and certificates of origin prepared in the U.K., the shipment does not need to be detoured to Switzerland but goes straight from London to Paris.

From many similar transactions between Allen Ltd. and Flueli GmbH. in the past, a very efficient order-handling procedure has been developed. This allows the use of Flueli GmbH. letterhead stationery and invoice forms by Allen Ltd. order-processing personnel in the London offices. Thus unnecessary mailing delays and transportation expenses are avoided. The blank forms have already been signed before by an authorized Flueli GmbH. official and copies of the whole process are sent to Zug for filing. Without violating any customs procedures, the documents will be processed and stamped at the respective border-crossings and thus legitimate the merchandise so the merchandise has both proof of export from the U.K. to Switzerland—which makes it eligible for the subsidies—and entry as Swiss-owned but EC-produced merchandise into France—which eliminates any import levies.

These "triangle" business transactions are known to be widely practiced as the rewards are so tempting. But they obviously violate ethical and legal

---

EXHIBIT 1.2

Figurella P&L Consolidation (based on U.K. production)
(In U.S. Dollars)

	AMOUNT
Sales	$733,750
Cost of Good Sold (COG)[1]	186,250
Gross Margin (GM)	547,500
Total operating expenses[2]	63,750
Direct operating profit	483,750
Corporate taxes:	
U.K. (50%)	8,125
France (50%)	0
Switzerland (22.96%)	107,338
Total tax liability	115,463
Other income:	
EC export refund	38,348
Total other income	38,348
Net profit adjusted	406,635

[1]The transportation charges London–Paris have been charged to the COG.

[2]French marketing, selling, overhead, and other operating expenses relating to the Figurella introduction have been assumed to be equal to the local gross profit generated by the transfer pricing for simplicity's sake. The purpose of Mr. Lansing's exercise is to demonstrate to top management in Chicago that these profits will at least offset the profit shortage of the first half of the year. This was estimated to range from $105,000 to $119,000.

EXHIBIT 1.3 **Local P&L Data for Figurella**
(In U.S. Dollars)

	UNITED KINGDOM	SWITZERLAND	FRANCE
Price per can	$ 1.54	$ 5.28	$ 5.87
Cost of Good per can	1.41	1.54	5.36[1]
Gross Margin per can	.13	3.74	.51
Gross Margin per dollars	16,250	467,500	63,750
Operating Expenses	0	0	63,750
Direct Operating Profit[2]	16,250	467,500	0
Taxes	8,125	107,338	0
Other Income	38,348	0	0
Net Profit	46,473	360,162	0

[1]Includes handling/freight London–Paris: $.08 per can.

[2]Direct Operating Profit

norms and are thus subject to the EC penal code. Nonetheless, Mr. Lansing intends to ask for headquarter's authorization for this particular aspect of the plan this afternoon, and he will plead that the chances for embarrassment are practically nil.

PROFIT CONSOLIDATION

For the afternoon's discussion Mr. Lansing has prepared the following profit and loss consolidation, which summarizes the effect of the various transactions he will propose.

The data look extremely favorable and should present a pleasant surprise even to Mr. Davidson. They are, above all, very realistic, and Mr. Lansing is confident that approval from Chicago will be forthcoming during his afternoon's business review. After all, the realization of these figures rests entirely on top management's authorization today, as time for the implementation of the whole plan is already running very short.

To be ready for any question that might come up during his presentation, Mr. Lansing has also prepared local P&L data for each country in support of the consolidated P&L figures. A copy of all financial data has been Telexed to Chicago to be in the hands of all participants for this purpose.

The French operating expenses were deliberately set at a level equal to the local gross margin of the product. This neutralizes tax aspects and simplifies the calculation, though it does not account for realistic levels of introductory expenses. Mr. Davidson would probably not be overly interested in precise data on this point as the total package assures him of an extremely positive consolidated profit recovery for Europe. This success will hold true even if he should not approve all parts of the plan as presented.

The Wallace Group

LAURENCE J. STYBEL

Frances Rampar, President of Rampar Associates, drummed her fingers on the desk. Scattered before her were her notes. She had to put the pieces together in order to make an effective sales presentation to Harold Wallace.

Hal Wallace was the President of The Wallace Group. He had asked Frances Rampar to conduct a series of interviews with some key Wallace Group employees, in preparation for a possible consulting assignment for Rampar Associates.

During the past three days, Rampar had been talking with some of these key people and had received background material about the company. The problem was not in finding the problem. The problem was that there were too many problems!

BACKGROUND OF THE WALLACE GROUP

The Wallace Group, Inc., is a diversified company dealing in the manufacture and development of technical products and systems (see Exhibit 2.1). The company currently consists of three operational groups and a corporate staff. The three groups include Electronics, Plastics, and Chemicals, each operating under the direction of a Group Vice-President (see Exhibits 2.2, 2.3, and 2.4). The company generates $70 million in sales as a manufacturer of plastics, chemical products, and electronic components and systems. Principal sales are to large contractors in governmental and automotive markets. With respect to sales volume, Plastics and Chemicals are approximately equal in size, and both of them together equal the size of the Electronics Group.

Electronics offers competence in the areas of microelectronics, electromagnetic sensors, antennas, microwave, and mini-computers. Presently, these skills are devoted primarily to the engineering and manufacture of countermeasure equipment for aircraft. This includes radar detection systems that allow an aircraft crew to know that they are being tracked by radar units either on the ground, on ships, or on other aircraft. Further, the company

This case was prepared by Dr. Laurence J. Stybel. It was prepared for class discussion rather than to illustrate either effective or ineffective handling of an administrative situation. This case is available from and distributed in looseleaf exclusively from Lord Publishing, Inc., One Apple Hill, Suite 320, Natick, Mass. 01760, (508) 651-9955. Lord Publishing cases are protected by U.S. copyright laws. Unauthorized duplication of copyright materials is a violation of federal law. Reprinted by permission.

EXHIBIT 2.1   **An Excerpt from the Annual Report**

To the Shareholders:

This past year was one of definite accomplishment for The Wallace Group, although with some admitted soft spots. This is a period of consolidation, of strengthening our internal capacity for future growth and development. Presently, we are in the process of creating a strong management team able to meet the challenges we will set for the future.

Despite our failure to achieve some objectives, we turned in a profit of $3,521,000 before taxes which was a growth over previous year earnings. And we have declared a dividend for the fifth consecutive year, albeit one that is less than the year before. However, the retention of earnings is imperative if we are to lay a firm foundation for future accomplishment.

Currently, The Wallace Group has achieved a level of stability. We have a firm foothold in our current markets and we could elect to simply enact strong internal controls and maximize our profits. However, this would not be a growth strategy. Instead, we have chosen to adopt a more aggressive posture for the future, to reach out into new markets wherever possible, and to institute the controls necessary to move forward in a planned and orderly fashion.

The Electronics Group performed well this past year and is engaged in two major programs under defense department contracts. These are developmental programs that provide us with the opportunity for ongoing sales upon testing of the final product. Both involve the creation of tactical display systems for aircraft being built by Lombard Aircraft for the Navy and the Air Force. Future potential sales from these efforts could amount to approximately $56 million over the next five years. Additionally, we are developing technical refinements to older, already installed systems under Army Department contracts.

In the future, we will continue to offer our technological competence in such tactical display systems and anticipate additional breakthroughs and success in meeting the demands of this market. However, we also believe that we have unique contributions to make to other markets and to that end we are making the investments necessary to expand our opportunities.

Plastics also turned in a solid performance this past year and has continued to be a major supplier to Chrysler, Martin Tool, Foster Electric, and, of course, to our Electronics Group. The market for this group continues to expand and we believe that additional investments in this group will allow us to seize a larger share in the future.

Chemicals' performance, admittedly, has not been as satisfactory as anticipated during the past year. However, we have been able to realize a small amount of profit from this operation and to halt what was a potentially dangerous decline in profits. We believe this situation is only temporary and that infusions of capital for developing new technology, plus the streamlining of operations, has stabilized the situation. The next step will be to begin more aggressive marketing to capitalize upon the group's basic strengths.

(Continued)

EXHIBIT 2.1 (Continued)

> Overall, the outlook seems to be one of modest but profitable growth. The near term will be one of creating the technology and controls necessary for developing our market offerings and growing in a planned and purposeful manner. Our improvement efforts in the various company groups can be expected to take hold over the years with positive effect on results.
>
> We wish to express our appreciation to all those who participated in our efforts this past year.
>
> Harold Wallace
> Chairman and President

manufactures displays that provide the crew with a visual "fix" on where they are relative to the radar units that are tracking them.

In addition to manufacturing tested and proven systems developed in the past, The Wallace Group is currently involved in two major and minor programs, all involving display systems. The Navy-A Program calls for the development of a display system for a tactical fighter plane; Air Force-B is another such system for an observation plane. Ongoing production orders are anticipated following flight testing. The other two programs, Army-LG and OBT-37, involve the incorporation of new technology into existing aircraft systems.

The Plastics Group manufactures plastic components utilized by the electronics, automotive, and other industries requiring plastic products. These include switches, knobs, keys, insulation materials, and so on, used in the manufacture of electronic equipment and other small made-to-order components found on automobiles, planes, and so forth.

The Chemicals Group produces chemicals used in the development of plastics. They supply bulk chemicals to the Plastics Group and other companies. These chemicals are then injected into molds or extruded to form a variety of finished products.

HISTORY OF THE WALLACE GROUP

Each of the three groups began as a sole proprietorship under the direct operating control of an owner/manager. Several years ago, Harold Wallace, owner of the original electronics company, determined to undertake a program of diversification. Initially, he attempted to expand his market by product development and line extensions entirely within the electronics industry. However, because of initial problems, he drew back and sought other opportunities. Wallace's primary concern was his almost total dependence upon defense-related contracts. He had felt for some time that he should take some strong action to gain a foothold in the private markets. The first major opportunity that seemed to satisfy his various requirements

EXHIBIT 2.2   **The Wallace Group**

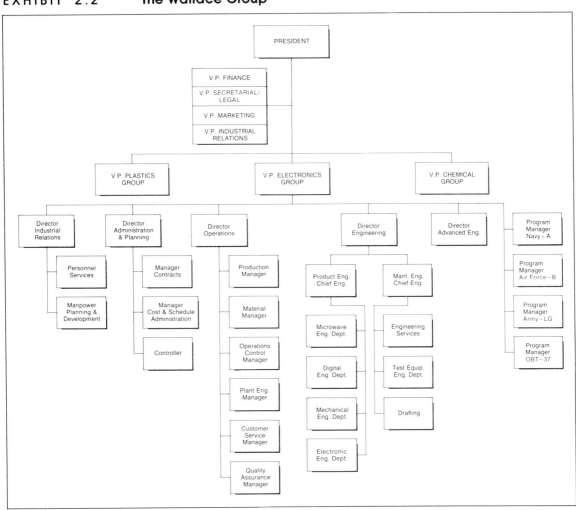

was the acquisition of a former supplier, a plastics company whose primary market was not defense related. The company's owner desired to sell his operation and retire. At the time, Wallace's debt structure was not able to manage such an acquisition and so equity capital had to be attracted. He was able to gather together a relatively small group of investors and form a closed corporation. A Board of Directors was established with Wallace as Chairman and President of the new corporate entity.

With respect to operations, little changed. Mr. Wallace continued direct operational control over the Electronics Group. As holder of 60% of the

EXHIBIT 2.3   **The Wallace Group**

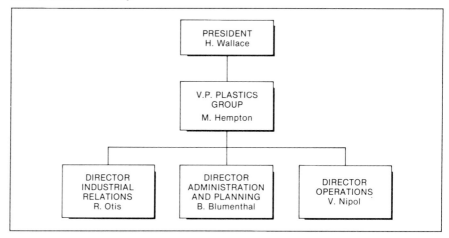

stock, he maintained effective control over policy and operations. However, because of his personal interests, the Plastics Group, now under the direction of a newly hired Vice-President, Martin Hempton, was pretty much left to its own devices except for yearly progress reviews by the President. All Wallace asked for the time being was that the Plastics Group continue its profitable operation, which it did.

Several years ago, Wallace and the Board decided upon further diversification because two-thirds of their business was still defense-dependent. It became known that one of their major suppliers of the Plastic Group, a

EXHIBIT 2.4   **The Wallace Group**

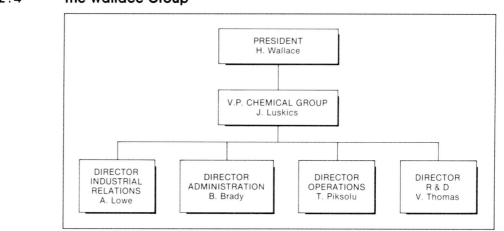

chemical company, was on the verge of bankruptcy. The company's owner, Jerome Luskics, was approached and a sale was consummated. However, this acquisition required a public stock offering, with most of the monies going to pay off debts incurred by the three groups, especially the Chemicals Group. The net result was that Wallace now holds 45% of The Wallace Group, Jerome Luskics 5%, with the remainder distributed among the public.

ORGANIZATION AND PERSONNEL

Presently, Harold Wallace serves as Chairman and President of The Wallace Group. The Electronics Group had been run by LeRoy Tuscher, who just resigned as Vice-President. Hempton continued as Vice-President of Plastics and Luskics served as Vice-President of the Chemicals Group.

Given the requirements for a corporate perspective and approach, a corporate staff has grown up consisting of Vice-Presidents for Finance, Secretarial/Legal, Marketing, and Industrial Relations. This staff has assumed many functions formerly associated with the group offices.

Because these positions are recent additions, many of the job accountabilities are still being defined. Problems have arisen over the responsibilities and relationships existing between corporate and group positions. Most of the disputes have been settled by President Wallace as soon as they appear because of the inability of the various parties to resolve differences among themselves.

CURRENT TRENDS

Presently, there is a mood of lethargy and drift within The Wallace Group. Most managers feel that each of the three groups functions as an independent company. And, with respect to group performance, not much change or progress has been evidenced in recent years. Electronics and Plastics are still stable and profitable, but there does not seem to be growth in either market or profit. The infusion of capital breathed new life and hope into the Chemicals operation but did not relieve most of the old problems and failings that had brought about its initial decline. It was for all of these various reasons that Wallace decided that strong action was necessary. His greatest disappointment was with the Electronics Group, in which he had placed high hopes for future development. Thus, he acted by requesting and getting the Electronics Group Vice-President's resignation. Jason Matthews has been hired from a computer company, to replace LeRoy Tuscher, and joined The Wallace Group a week ago.

Last year, Wallace's net sales were $70 million. On a group basis, this was:

Electronics	$35,000,000
Plastics	$20,000,000
Chemicals	$15,000,000

On a consolidated basis, the financial highlights of the last two years are as follows:

	Last Year	Two Years Ago
Net sales	$70,434,000	$69,950,000
Income (pre-tax)	3,521,000	3,497,500
Income (after-tax)	1,760,500	1,748,750
Working capital	16,200,000	16,088,500
Shareholder's equity	39,000,000	38,647,000
Total assets	59,869,000	59,457,000
Long-term debt	4,350,000	3,500,000
Per Share of Common Stock		
Net income	$.37	$.36
Cash dividends paid	.15	.25

Of the net income, approximately 70% came from Electronics, 25% from Plastics, and 5% from Chemicals.

Selected Portions of a Transcribed Interview with H. Wallace

RAMPAR: What is your greatest problem right now?

WALLACE: That's why I called you in! Engineers are a high-strung, temperamental lot. Always complaining. It's hard to take them seriously.
Last month we had an annual stockholders' meeting. We have an Employee Stock Option Plan, and many of our long-time employees attended the meeting. One of my managers—and I won't mention any names—introduced a resolution calling for the resignation of the President—me!
The vote was defeated. But, of course, I own 45% of the stock!
Now I realize that there could be no serious attempt to get rid of me. Those who voted for the resolution were making a dramatic effort to show me how upset they are with the way things are going.
I could fire those employees who voted against me. I was surprised by how many did. Some of my key people were in that group. Perhaps I ought to stop and listen to what they are saying.
Businesswise, I think we're O.K. Not great, but O.K. Last year we turned in a profit of $3.5 million before taxes, which was a growth over previous years' earnings. We declared a dividend for the fifth consecutive year.
We're currently working on the creation of a tactical display system for aircraft being built by Lombard Aircraft for the Navy and the Air Force. If Lombard gets the contract to produce the prototype, then future sales could amount to $56 million over the next five years.
Why are they complaining?

RAMPAR: You must have some thoughts on the matter.

WALLACE: I think the issue revolves around how we manage people. It's a personnel problem. You were highly recommended as someone with expertise in high-technology human-resource management.

I have some ideas on what is the problem. But I'd like you to do an independent investigation and give me your findings. Give me a plan of action.

Don't give me a laundry list of problems, Fran. Anyone can do that. I want a set of priorities I should focus on during the next year. I want a clear action plan from you. And I want to know how much this plan is going to cost me! Other than that, I'll leave you alone and let you talk to anyone in the company you want.

Selected Portions of a Transcribed Interview with Frank Campbell, Vice-President of Industrial Relations

RAMPAR: What is your greatest problem right now?

CAMPBELL: Trying to contain my enthusiasm over the fact that Wallace brought you in!

Morale is really poor here. Hal runs this place like a one-man operation, when it's grown too big for that. It took a palace revolt to finally get him to see the depths of the resentment. Whether he'll do anything about it, that's another matter.

RAMPAR: What would you like to see changed?

CAMPBELL: Other than a new President?

RAMPAR: Uh-huh.

CAMPBELL: We badly need a management development program for our group. Because of our growth, we have been forced to promote technical people to management positions who have had no prior managerial experience. Mr. Tuscher agreed on the need for a program, but Hal Wallace vetoed the idea because developing such a program would be too expensive. I think it is too expensive *not* to move ahead on this.

RAMPAR: Anything else?

CAMPBELL: The IEWU negotiations have been extremely tough this time around, due to excessive demands they have been making. Union pay scales are already pushing up against our foreman salary levels, and foremen are being paid high in their salary ranges. This problem, coupled with union insistence on a no-layoff clause, is causing us fits. How can we keep all our workers when we have got production equipment on order that will eliminate 20% of our assembly positions?

RAMPAR: Wow.

CAMPBELL: We have been sued by a rejected candidate for a secretarial position on the basis of discrimination. She claimed our entrance qualifications are excessive because we require shorthand. There is some basis for this statement since most reports are given to secretaries in hand-written form or on audio cassettes. In fact, we have always required it and our executives want their secretaries to have skill in taking dictation. Not only is this case taking time, but I need to reconsider if any of our position entrance requirements are, in fact, excessive. I am sure we do not want another case like this one.

RAMPAR: That puts The Wallace Group in a vulnerable position, considering the amount of government work you do.

CAMPBELL: We have a tremendous recruiting backlog, especially for engineering positions. Either our pay scales are too low, our job specs are too high, or we are using the wrong recruiting channels. Kane and Smith (Director of Engineering and Director of Advanced Systems) keep rejecting everyone we send down there as being unqualified.

RAMPAR: Gee.

CAMPBELL: Being head of Human Resources around here is a tough job. We don't act. We react.

Selected Portions of a Transcribed Interview with Matthew Smith, Director of Advanced Systems

RAMPAR: What is your greatest problem right now?

SMITH: Corporate brass keeps making demands on me and others that don't relate to the job we are trying to get done. They say that the information they need is to satisfy corporate planning and operations review requirements, but they don't seem to recognize how much time and effort is required to provide this information. Sometimes it seems like they are generating analyses, reports, and requests for data just to keep themselves busy. Someone should be evaluating how critical these corporate staff activities really are. To me and the Electronics Group, these activities are unnecessary.

An example is the Vice-President, Marketing (L. Holt), who keeps asking us for supporting data so he can prepare a corporate marketing strategy. As you know, we prepare our own group marketing strategic plans annually, but using data and formats that are oriented to our needs, rather than Corporate's. This planning activity, which occurs at the same time as Corporate's coupled with heavy work loads on current projects, makes us appear to Holt as though we are being unresponsive.

Somehow we need to integrate our marketing planning efforts between our group and Corporate. This is especially true if our group is to successfully grow in nondefense-oriented markets and products. We do need corporate help, but not arbitrary demands for information that divert us from putting together effective marketing strategies for our group.

I am getting too old to keep fighting these battles.

RAMPAR: This is an old, long-standing problem?

SMITH: You bet! Our problems are fairly classic in the high-tech field. I've been at other companies and it's not much better. We spend so much time firefighting, we never really get organized. Everything is done on an ad hoc basis.

I'm still waiting for tomorrow.

Selected Portions of a Transcribed Interview with Ralph Kane, Director of Engineering

RAMPAR: What is your greatest problem right now?

KANE: Knowing you were coming, I wrote them down. They fall into four areas:

1. Our salary schedules are too low to attract good, experienced EEs. We have been told by our Vice-President (Frank Campbell) that corporate policy is to hire new people below the salary grade midpoint. All qualified candidates are making more than that now and in some cases are making more than our grade maximums. I think our Project Engineer job is rated too low.

2. Chemicals Group asked for and the former Electronics Vice-President (Tuscher) agreed to "lend" six of our best EEs to help solve problems they are having developing a new battery. That is great for the Chemicals Group, but meanwhile how do we solve the engineering problems that have cropped up in our Navy-A and OBT-37 programs?

3. As you know, Matt Smith (Director of Advanced Systems) is retiring in six months. I depend heavily on his group for technical expertise and in some areas he depends heavily on some of my key engineers. I have lost some people to the Chemicals Group and Matt has been trying to lend me some of his people to fill in. But he and his staff have been heavily involved in marketing planning and trying to identify or recruit a qualified successor soon enough before his retirement to be able to train him. The result is that his people are up to their eyeballs in doing their own stuff and cannot continue to help me meet my needs.

4. IR has been preoccupied with union negotiations in the plant and has not had time to help me deal with this issue of management planning. Campbell is working on some kind of system that will help deal with this kind of problem and prevent them in the future. That is great, but I need help now—not when his "system" is ready.

Selected Portions of a Transcribed Interview with Brad Lowell, Program Manager, Navy-A

RAMPAR: What is your . . .?

LOWELL: . . . great problem? I'll tell you what it is.
I still cannot get the support I need from Kane in Engineering. He commits and then doesn't deliver and it has me quite concerned. The excuse now is that in "his judgment," Sid Wright needs the help for the Air Force program more than I do. Wright's program is one week ahead of schedule, so I disagree with "his judgment." Kane keeps complaining about not having enough people.

RAMPAR: Why do you think Kane says he doesn't have enough people?

LOWELL: Because Hal Wallace is a tight-fisted S.O.B. who won't let us hire the people we need!

Selected Portions of a Transcribed Interview with Phil Jones, Director, Administration and Planning

JONES: Wheel spinning—that's our problem! We talk about expansion, but we don't do anything about it. Are we serious or not?

For example, a bid request came in from a prime contractor seeking help in developing a countermeasure system for a medium-range aircraft. They needed an immediate response and concept proposal in one week. Tuscher just sat on my urgent memo to him asking for a go/no go decision on bidding. I could not give the contractor an answer (because no decision came from Tuscher), so they gave up on us.

I am frustrated because: (1) we lost an opportunity we were "naturals" to win, and (2) my personal reputation was damaged because I was unable to answer the bid request. Okay, Tuscher's gone now, but we need to develop some mechanism so an answer to such a request can be made quickly.

Another thing is our MIS being developed by the Corporate Finance Group. More wheel spinning! They are telling us what information we need rather than asking us what we want! E. Kay (our Group Controller) is going crazy trying to sort out the input requirements they need for the system and understanding the complicated reports that come out. Maybe this new system is great as a technical achievement, but what good is it to us if we can't use it?

Selected Portions of a Transcribed Interview with Burt Williams, Director of Operations

RAMPAR: What is your biggest problem right now?

WILLIAMS: One of our biggest problems we face right now stems from corporate policy regarding transfer pricing. I realize we are "encouraged" to purchase our plastics and chemicals from our sister Wallace groups, but we are also committed to making a profit! Because manufacturing problems in those groups have forced them to raise their prices, should *we* suffer the consequences? We can get some materials cheaper from other suppliers. How can we meet our volume and profit targets when we are saddled with noncompetitive material costs?

RAMPAR: And if that issue was settled to your satisfaction, then would things be O.K.?

WILLIAMS: Although out of my direct function, it occurs to me that we are not planning effectively our efforts to expand into nondefense areas. With minimal alteration to existing production methods, we can develop both end-use products (e.g., small motors, traffic control devices, microwave transceivers for highway emergency communications) and components (e.g., LED and LCD displays, police radar tracking devices, word processing system memory and control devices) with large potential markets.

The problems in this regard are:

1. Matt Smith (Director, Advanced Systems) is retiring and has had only defense-related experience. Therefore, he is not leading any product development efforts along these lines.

2. We have no marketing function at the group level to develop a strategy, define markets, and research and develop product opportunities.

3. Even if we had a marketing plan and products for industrial/commercial application, we have no sales force or rep network to sell the stuff.

Maybe I am way off base, but it seems to me we need a Groups/Marketing/Sales function to lead us in this business expansion effort. It should be headed by an experienced technical marketing manager with a proven track record in developing such products and markets.

RAMPAR: Have you discussed your concerns with others?

WILLIAMS: I have brought these ideas up with Mr. Matthews and others at the Group Management Committee. No one else seems interested in pursuing this concept, but they won't say this outright and don't say why it should not be addressed. I guess that in raising the idea with you I am trying to relieve some of my frustrations.

THE PROBLEM CONFRONTING FRANCES RAMPAR

As Rampar finished reviewing her notes, she kept reflecting on what Hal Wallace had told her:

Don't give me a laundry list of problems, Fran. Anyone can do that. I want a set of priorities I should focus on during the next year. I want a clear action plan from you. And I want to know how much this plan is going to cost me!

Fran Rampar again drummed her fingers on the desk.

Crisis in Conscience at Quasar

JOHN J. FENDROCK

THE CASE SETTING

Universal Nucleonics Company, the parent company for a number of wholly owned subsidiaries, suddenly found itself in the embarrassing position of having to report that its earnings for the year would be substantially lower than had been announced at the end of the previous quarter. Shortly thereafter, a statement appeared in the "Who's News" section of *The Wall Street Journal* reporting that Quasar Stellar Company, one of Universal's subsidiaries, had a new President and a new Vice-President of Finance (replacing the former controller).

As time went on, the financial community learned that Universal had discovered that one of its subsidiaries had been withholding the truth, purposely distorting the facts, or otherwise misrepresenting the situation at hand in its monthly reports to corporate headquarters. By the time Universal had realized the actual condition of Quasar's financial situation, it was too late to correct it without affecting the reported year-end earnings of the parent company.

The two individuals most directly concerned at Quasar—John Kane, President, and Hugh Kay, Controller—had both "resigned." It was generally agreed by the board of directors that there would be no public announcement as to the reasons for the resignations. Privately, however, one director stated flatly that out-and-out fraud was involved; another, more in tune with the times, said that the situation was directly attributable to the pressures to make good and the tendency to have a positive outlook on the outcome of all individual company problems.

Corporate headquarters was vitally interested in finding out why, given the organizational structure of Quasar, no feedback had been received independently of the president-controller monthly statement; whether any of the other executives were involved in the reports either knowingly or unknowingly, willingly or unwillingly; and, finally, what steps could be taken to prevent a recurrence of the situation in the future.

FACT-FINDING TEAM

To resolve these questions, Universal's executive committee decided that a direct approach should be taken. The Executive Vice-President and the Vice-President of Industrial Relations for the corporation would conduct a series of interviews with the Quasar Stellar personnel who might have been involved. Both men were well qualified to appraise the situation. Jim Bowden, the Executive Vice-President, was both an operating and a financial man, having spent a number of years in each area. Hubert Clover, Vice-President of Industrial Relations, was a former professor of industrial psychology at one of the leading business schools.

It was further agreed that each executive would interview different men, compare notes, and then speak with each other's interviewees if the situation so warranted. After studying the organization chart (see Exhibit 3.1), and the company's "Manual of Responsibilities," they decided it would be best to talk to Peter Loomis, Vice-President, Marketing; George Kessler, Vice-President, Manufacturing; and William Heller, Vice-President, Engineering.

<table>
<tr><td>

LOOMIS'S SESSION

</td><td>

The scene opens in a small conference room at Quasar Stellar Company. The first man to be interviewed is Peter Loomis, Vice-President, Marketing, who is known to be outspoken, demanding, and intensely loyal. Loomis is greeted by Hubert Clover.

CLOVER: Pete, as you know, the purpose of our chat is to see if we can learn something from this unfortunate episode that can help to prevent such an occurrence in the future. I would like to get your version of what has happened and any suggestions you may be able to offer as to what can be done to help our planning.

</td></tr>
</table>

EXHIBIT 3.1   Organization Chart of Quasar Stellar Company

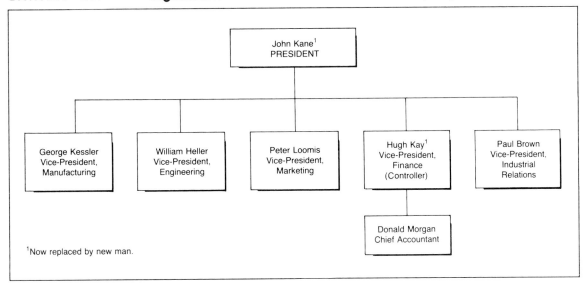

LOOMIS *(defensively):* Well, Hubert, you know I thought very highly of John. I'm certain you are aware that he hired me for this job. I don't mind admitting that I think the decision to fire him was unwarranted and ill advised.

CLOVER: If there is one thing I am certain of, Pete, it is that there is no question of your loyalty to John. I hope that won't bias your outlook. As for John's resignation, perhaps the best I can say is that on the basis of all facts available, the board decided this was the only logical course of action. And if . . .

LOOMIS *(interrupting):* Let me set the record straight on two points. My loyalty to John was based on respect for his abilities—not on personal grounds. And I'm not disagreeing with you, either on the basis of the facts available at the time or on those turned up by the investigation, that the action was not warranted. But I also feel that there was too hasty a collection of facts and an overreaction resulting in his dismissal. What I'm saying is that had a more thorough and penetrating investigation been made, the conclusions would probably have been different.

CLOVER *(attempting to lead the interview back):* I understand your point, Pete, but what are some of the additional facts that you think could have influenced the decision differently?

LOOMIS: You are most likely aware that the failure to receive the Apollo and LEM contracts had significant effects on the overall picture. But when John informally notified headquarters that our chances of receiving these two jobs were less than 50-50, he was told he was just being pessimistic. It was quite evident to him that the board of directors felt these were two prestige jobs that we simply had to get. The trouble was that while we dissipated our efforts on trying to land these low-probability programs, a half-dozen other less known, but perhaps more lucrative, opportunities slipped by.

CLOVER: You say John told headquarters about this. Have you any idea why the so-so probabilities and the alternatives were not openly presented and discussed at the appropriate company board meeting?

LOOMIS: To be frank, the 50-50 chance was an after-the-fact estimate. When the decision was made to pursue the two jobs, because of the pressure from headquarters and knowing what the work could mean to Quasar, I was undoubtedly too optimistic myself. A staff meeting was held in which the two marketing efforts were reviewed in detail.

CLOVER: Who attended that meeting?

LOOMIS: As I recall, there was George Kessler, Bill Heller, Hugh Kay, John, and myself.

CLOVER: Was it unanimously agreed that you should go after the two contracts?

LOOMIS *(shaking his head):* Oh, no! Bill felt very strongly that we should. He thought that the engineering department could gain a heck of a lot by being involved—state-of-the-art stuff. George was against the effort. He argued that production would be severely affected, because these projects would require such a long-term engineering effort before production could start. He wanted more immediate work that would occupy his work force. Hugh was with George. Not only was he worried about overhead and profits, but he had a "gut feeling" that our chances were less than what I forecast. He was right, of course. John was in favor of pursuing the contracts only if we had about a 75% chance of capturing each. John tossed the ball to me when he asked what our chances of getting the jobs were. At the time, I indicated that while I couldn't stick my neck out to 75%, I was willing to guess it would be much closer to 75% than to, say, 50% or even 60%. Considering the attitude at headquarters, the stakes, and my projection, we finally decided to go after both.

CLOVER: Are you saying that you didn't really feel that your chances were as close to 75% as you indicated?

LOOMIS: I believe they weren't. But that isn't to say that I didn't feel they could or should have been.

CLOVER: How long had you been with the company when this meeting took place, Pete?

LOOMIS: Just about nine months. I'm quite sure I know the reason for your question. Actually, I was not as familiar with the company as I should have been to express so strong an opinion on such an important matter.

CLOVER: Obviously, you showed a good deal of enthusiasm . . .

LOOMIS *(interrupting again):* And, I'm afraid you'll have to agree, naiveté. Remember, however, that this is—or at least was—a gung-ho operation. I was anxious to earn my spurs. Those contracts would have put us on the map and made Quasar and Universal household words.

CLOVER: I can certainly understand your decision to go after the big fish, but, once you found that you were out of fishing water, why was headquarters not kept informed of the deteriorating market picture? Wouldn't that have been the logical thing to do?

LOOMIS: Logical, yes, but hardly practical. In retrospect, that is probably what we should have done, but let's go back six months. That's when our fears of a drop in production began to inject themselves. Hugh's warnings about profitability were proving to be only too accurate, and there was nothing that could be pulled in at the last minute to bridge the gap.

CLOVER: Yes, but you must have known very early that your odds were way off.

LOOMIS *(after a pause):* Well, perhaps I did not emphasize that fact strongly enough. I assure you, however, that both George and Hugh did, since their operations were directly and indirectly involved.

CLOVER *(bothered by Loomis's evasiveness):* How, then, was the decision reached not to inform headquarters of this situation? Didn't it bother you to think that there might be adverse effects on employment?

LOOMIS: Once the decision was made to go after the two projects, any reversal could only result in a loss of face and prestige. Like the gambler at the roulette wheel, we plunged deeper—with about the same odds—and lost. I must confess that I had my moments of doubt about our course of action. It was quite clear that people could get hurt, but that too is all part of the game. Frankly, at no time did it occur to me that I had a greater responsibility than the one I had to John. Perhaps this is wrong, but I have always felt that I owe more loyalty to my supervisor than to the company. And besides, I'm not certain to what degree personal morality should enter into business decisions.

CLOVER: Pete, let me ask you one final question. What do you think we might do to prevent this sort of thing from happening again in the future?

LOOMIS: Frankly, I feel that headquarters should give us more independence. For example, if headquarters had not exerted pressure on us to pursue these two contracts, we might have followed a different course. To me, what happened was that headquarters decided on a set course of action, passed the word down, and then—when it became impossible for us to follow through—they looked for scapegoats. Both John and Hugh were sacrificed because of poor headquarters policy.

CLOVER *(rising):* Thanks for a frank and open presentation of your thoughts on the situation, Pete. By the way, Jim Bowden may or may not wish to speak with you, depending on how things go in general. In any event, we'll let you know later. Once again, thanks for your ideas.

LOOMIS: Thanks for asking. I honestly thought this might just be allowed to die on the vine without anyone looking deeper into it.

FOLLOW-UP QUESTIONS

Hubert Clover brooded over his interview with Loomis, scanning his notes in a manner that suggested more sorrow and disappointment than thought. He then decided to summarize his observations and to recommend that Bowden not interview Loomis. But, after reviewing the results of Clover's conversation, Bowden concluded that there was one more thing he wanted resolved: Why had not Loomis, in routine fashion, been put in a position to send a report back to headquarters that would have been at variance with the official statement? Later that afternoon, the two men got together. After exchanging the usual pleasantries and engaging in small talk related to the previous interview, Bowden asked the specific question he had in mind.

BOWDEN: The one thing that puzzles me, Pete, is why you were not able to transmit your misgivings about the possibility of receiving the two contracts directly to the Corporate Vice-President of Marketing.

LOOMIS: Your question, Jim, implies that I was *unable* to do this. Actually, it was always possible, but I was not *required* to do it. However, I was expected to give my observations to John and to support him in any decision he made as to how the information was to be handled.

BOWDEN: Your answer implies to me that you were fully aware that two distorted monthly reports were sent to corporate headquarters. Am I correct in this assumption?

LOOMIS: From what I have said to both you and Jim, there is no doubt that your conclusion is correct. And, to be honest, I was completely aware of the distortions in the reports. I can only repeat what I said earlier this afternoon to Hubert: my loyalty is to my supervisor, and I always support him in his use of information in any way he sees fit.

KESSLER'S INTERROGATION	*The next man to be interviewed was George Kessler, Vice-President, Manufacturing, who was an old-timer by Quasar standards, having been at Quasar for fifteen years. He was known for his outspokenness, integrity, and forcefulness. Clover and Bowden decided that Bowden should conduct the interview with Kessler because there existed a somewhat close relationship between them. As a former operations man, Bowden had taken a direct interest in manufacturing, and he had developed a healthy respect for Kessler. Bowden greeted Kessler, and the two exchanged a few pleasantries.*

BOWDEN: I guess we could keep up the chitchat all day, George, but I'm afraid we've got to get down to business. A fellow in your position must have seen what was coming—how in hell could you let it happen?

KESSLER: I would rather continue reminiscing about old times than get into this. To answer your question, Jim, I saw what was coming; but, to turn the question back to you, how could I possibly have prevented it?

BOWDEN: All right, George, you couldn't have stopped it. Really, what I am asking is this: seeing what was happening, wasn't there something you could have done to raise the storm signals?

KESSLER: You know me well enough to realize that I am not one of the gung-ho types. While I had tremendous respect for John's ability to analyze a situation, I always suspected that he had a streak of the gambler in him. Let's face it; if he had pulled those two jobs out of the hat, he would have been Universal's brightest star.

BOWDEN: Getting back to the point, George, wasn't there some way for you to signal headquarters of what was happening?

KESSLER *(frowning):* You insist on pursuing this point, don't you? Jim, you know as well as I do that I answered directly to John. I'm not going to beat a dead horse; but, without going into details, I think I expressed my views strongly on the approach we were taking. Certainly, I was concerned about a number of things . . . the number of old-time employees who were going to take a beating if this thing fizzled, as it did; what might actually happen to the company overall; and what I owed to myself as well as to John. Taking all these points into consideration, I did what I thought was morally and managerially right, and I don't say that lightly. In expressing my doubts so forcefully, perhaps I did a disservice to everyone I tried to help.

BOWDEN: In what way do you think you performed a disservice?

KESSLER: In short order, I found myself outside of the actual development of the monthly reports. The result was that any influence I might have exerted in determining what information was to be generated for headquarters was cancelled out.

BOWDEN *(nodding):* I appreciate your dilemma, George, and I also respect the position you took. But don't you feel that there might have been some way to get this back to our office?

KESSLER: In weighing my responsibility to the company, corporate headquarters, employees, self, and supervisor, I may possibly have erred in following too narrow a path. It seemed to me at the time, and I feel the same way even now, that with the organizational structure we have, my only approach was to try to change things through the existing framework. My efforts failed. Perhaps I should have been more adventurous and requested—demanded, if you will—an audience with you fellows. But I am certain that if a similar situation arose again, I still would not do this.

BOWDEN: Then let me ask you what you think can be done to prevent this from happening in the future.

KESSLER: To me, there must be an approach that will allow for greater communication between headquarters and the company office. Perhaps the answer lies in having an executive committee sign the monthly report; or possibly having each committee member prepare a short concurrence or dissent report of his own, after the pattern of the Supreme Court; or even a more direct approach of having each manager give an independent report to his respective staff contact at corporate headquarters. The fact is, so long as we have a characteristic line and staff organizational structure, we can only follow the channels of communication that the chief executive officer decides on. No self-respecting manager would consider surreptitiously reporting behind his superior's back.

BOWDEN *(rising and extending a handshake):* George, thanks for your observations. I like your suggestions of a concurrence or disagreement by an executive committee. I hope the next time we have a little get-together it can be under more pleasant circumstances.

HELLER'S INTERVIEW

To some extent, the interview had merely reinforced Bowden's estimation of Kessler. However, he couldn't help feeling a sense of frustration that a man of Kessler's caliber did not find a way to communicate his misgivings to those who could have done something about the developing Quasar problem.

After reading Bowden's notes, Clover concluded there was no need for him to talk with Kessler. Instead, he decided to carry on with the next interview. The final man singled out was William Heller, Vice-President, Engineering, an intense, serious-minded, pipe-smoking engineer whose forte was considered to be R&D, not administrative work. He too was a long-term employee, having been with Quasar over ten years. Clover met him at the door of the conference room and, with a wave of his hand, motioned Heller to a chair.

CLOVER: I suppose the idea of sitting down to discuss this problem is not the most appealing thing to you, Bill. I hope it won't be as painful as realizing that an R&D project is going sour.

HELLER: Since your call a few minutes ago was not completed unexpected, I prepared for this by fixing myself an extra tightly packed pipe of tobacco. It will give me more time to think about your questions.

CLOVER: What can you contribute to our understanding of the things that happened here, and do you have any suggestions as to how they might be prevented in the future?

HELLER: I wonder if you could narrow your question somewhat. Exactly what would you like me to address myself to?

CLOVER: The specific problem, Bill, is this. Do you have an idea why Quasar's deteriorating condition was not reported back to headquarters? Of greatest interest, of course, is the overall condition of the plant operation, but the decline in engineering activity is something you can probably elaborate on in detail. Any light you can shed will be useful.

HELLER: While you have become more specific, I still have a wide-open field. Probably I should first outline what happened to engineering, and from this we might then be able to work into the bigger picture. How does that appeal to you?

CLOVER *(nodding)*: That would be a good start.

HELLER: About a year ago, it became obvious that our engineering activity, including both research and development and general engineering, was going to decline. The decision was made that a joint effort with marketing would be undertaken. After a series of meetings, it was decided to pursue actively and aggressively two relatively large contracts.

CLOVER: Those would be the Apollo and LEM contracts. *(Heller nods assent.)* When you say it was decided that those two contracts would be pursued, what did this imply?

HELLER: It meant that a radically new—for us—course of action was decided on. Always in the past we had operated as a subcontractor to primes on large systems. However, John and Pete took a stand that we were in a position to enter the systems area itself. Frankly, while I had initial skepticism about this approach, John portrayed the picture in optimistic terms. He was convinced that the contracts would be awarded more on the basis of marketing activity than on the engineering proposal, and he was equally confident that Pete's personal contacts would help us in capturing this work. Apparently John knew, or he felt he knew, that Pete had influence with the right people where those two contracts were involved. Thus, while in the past we had been merely keeping our fingers in the pie and hoping to get a piece of the action, it was decided at that point we would go the whole hog after them.

CLOVER: And you agreed with this approach?

HELLER: As I indicated, initially I was skeptical. Our organization is simply not capable of coping with proposals of this size. However, after John and Pete argued their case so persuasively, I was fully in favor of the decision. Actually, I knew it involved a lot of risk, but Quasar stood to benefit greatly if it worked out, and so I went along with them on it.

CLOVER: What did you think the chances were of getting those contracts, Bill?

HELLER (*pausing to light his pipe*): To me, our chances were less than those expressed by Pete, who, as I recall, said he figured them to be closer to 75% than to 60% or so. Frankly, I would have guessed 60% to be the upper limit on our chances for each contract. However, even at that, it seemed like a good risk because, if we had captured but one of them, engineering would have benefited greatly.

CLOVER: And how about the rest of the plant operations?

HELLER: Here, unfortunately, I was shortsighted. While the engineering activity would benefit, in retrospect the company as a whole could conceivably lose if only one, or perhaps even if both contracts were awarded to Quasar. I might add that this point was brought out strongly by George and Hugh. To offset this argument, however, it was pointed out that while a temporary downturn might occur, in about two years Quasar would be hard pressed to satisfy the requirements for the projects. In addition, Quasar would become so well known that interim work would be easy to come by.

CLOVER: Might it not also have worked to Quasar's disadvantage? How can you assume that other companies would be willing to give you work, knowing that it would be short term and that you certainly would give attention to your own contracts once it was time to begin production?

HELLER: Yes, it was an optimistic outlook and probably very shortsighted from a total company point of view.

CLOVER: Even assuming that the decision was a good one when made, why didn't someone recognize it was the wrong course before the entire operation went sour?

HELLER (*puffing on his pipe for a moment*): Now you are in an area that is too deep for me. Once it was decided on to pursue those contracts, my group concentrated its efforts on the technical proposal. We are extremely thin in this area. Therefore, our R&D activity was almost totally devoted to the proposal. Let me add that for approximately a 3-month period, 10- to 12-hour days and 7-day weeks were common for my staff.

CLOVER: But this very activity reduced your effectiveness on current work, did it not, and resulted in costly overruns and delays on contracts already in the house?

HELLER: Unfortunately, yes, but that was not totally unexpected. We attempted to minimize the overruns and delays, but some were certainly inevitable. Since we were trying to maintain our staff, a lot of the added cost went into overhead and project charges as we stockpiled personnel during the initial period when the decline began to manifest itself. Of course, we had to face facts later and let some people go when it became apparent that the plans were not working out.

CLOVER: At that point, why didn't the company reverse itself, abandon its course, and go after some short-term subcontract work? And why didn't you get back to headquarters with your problem?

HELLER: At that point, both John and Pete felt retreat would be impossible. Frankly, I supported them against my better judgment, both because I could see no way to change their attitude, and because I had an obligation to do my utmost in attempting to rectify the situation. Now, then, your other question as to why headquarters was not informed is difficult for me to answer. What can I say?

CLOVER: I would like a frank comment on this point, Bill.

HELLER *(knocking the ashes from his pipe):* Both John and Pete stood high in my book. I don't pretend to be a business manager; rather, I am an engineering manager. The tangibles of engineering are something I grasp and manipulate readily, but the intangibles of business are quite another thing. In retrospect, it's easy to criticize past decisions, but I respect the decisions that were made then. I personally felt there was an obligation to the parent company, but even though I disagreed with the principle of not reporting the situation to headquarters, I accepted it as a business decision.

CLOVER: Then you were aware, were you not, that the reports sent to headquarters distorted conditions at Quasar to such an extent that the status of projects was inaccurately reported, actual and projected earnings were blatantly inflated, and the entire status of the operation was totally misrepresented? How could you have accepted such a situation?

HELLER: If only I could answer you in a manner that might express my feelings at the time. Was I aware of what was going on? Yes, of course, I was. But I didn't *want* to know about it. I will go so far now as to say that I tried *not to know* what was being done. Realistically, once I accepted the basic decision to ride the thing out, I felt stuck with the consequences. There was nothing, as I saw it, that I could do to alter the course taken.

CLOVER: Bill, did you have any opportunity to bring this to the attention of headquarters?

HELLER: Formally, no, of course not. No mechanism existed, or perhaps should never exist, for circumventing top management. On a few occasions I might have had the opportunity to mention to the Corporate Vice-President of Engineering what was happening, but I certainly would not do that.

CLOVER *(shaking his head slowly):* I think you will agree such a situation should never be allowed to exist. Can you offer any suggestions as to how information of such importance to the welfare of both the company and the corporation could be made available to top management without violating any precepts—actual or imaginary?

HELLER: I have given considerable thought to this point. I honestly feel that what gets reported back to headquarters can only reflect what the President sees fit. I would hit the ceiling if I found out one of my project managers was reporting directly or indirectly to the President. By the same token, the President shouldn't have to guard against insurgency in his ranks. The corporation might use an internal audit team composed of knowledgeable personnel to make frequent checks on various phases of the operation. Apart from that, I've no suggestion.

CLOVER: Bill, your pipe's been cold and empty long enough. Thanks for your comments. Hopefully, we won't need another one of these sessions with you.

MORGAN'S OPINIONS

Clover discussed his report with Bowden, and they agreed that another interview with Heller was unnecessary. Then they went over the results of all three interviews in depth. When they had finished, they decided to pursue two additional questions from two other specific areas: (1) why did the accounting people not find a way to report to headquarters? and (2) what was the quality of the morale of the personnel during this period?

Accordingly, Donald Morgan, Chief Accountant, and Paul Brown, Vice-President, Industrial Relations, were invited to sit down with Bowden and Clover, respectively, in two simultaneous sessions. Since both corporate fact finders felt that too much briefing might tend to "lead" the interviews and stifle response, they agreed that the only statement they would make at the start would be to the effect that efforts were being made to prevent a repetition of the Quasar situation in the future.

BOWDEN: Don, you certainly are aware of the upheaval here at Quasar, and I suspect you know pretty well the reasons for it.

MORGAN: Yes, I have a good idea of what's what.

BOWDEN: I wonder if you would care to express your opinions on two specific points. First, why was it not possible to have the information fed back to corporate headquarters once the deteriorating situation began and, second, what might be done to prevent what happened from taking place again?

MORGAN: As standard company policy on reports, we generate our financial statements from whatever information is given to us. Our statements, in turn, are sent to the controller's office, and he does what he sees fit with them. Should we receive instructions from his office to reorganize, let's say, or otherwise manipulate the reports, there is very little we can do but follow instructions. This is particularly true when matters of judgment are involved. Let me give you a for-instance: if a project is reported as being behind schedule by the Program Manager and after review by the Controller's Office it is decided that it is not all that far behind, naturally adjustments are made. Or, say, an expected contract has not yet been received, but management decided to open up a project number anyway and begins accepting charges in anticipation of receiving the job; this too is done. So far as I can see, this is nothing more than exercising management prerogative. I will summarize my position by saying that I do pretty much what I am told. Sometimes I may not like it, but my job is not to set policy or to question decisions. Rather, it is to follow instructions.

BROWN'S OBSERVATIONS

At that point, Bowden decided that he had heard enough and abruptly ended the interview. Meanwhile, Clover was undertaking his interview with Paul Brown.

CLOVER: Paul, can you give any insight into the state of morale during the period when Quasar was apparently falsifying reports to the home office and after it became apparent that a serious problem existed?

BROWN: For a while, everybody acted as if they were on "pot"; everyone was filled with high expectations. To be sure, there were a couple of exceptions. But, in rapid fashion, things began to settle down and disillusionment set in. Many people sensed that there was trouble ahead and that nothing was being done. After a month or two, the exodus began, and, as you know, it still hasn't ceased. I know that some of the managers tried their best to hang onto their key people, but as usual it was just this caliber of individual who could read the writing on the wall and got out while the getting was good. I'm equally certain that a number of the other top people would have left except for loyalty to the company and their fellow employees, their years of company service, and/or other factors. My only other observation on this is that I hope our new president and controller have been selected more for solid, long-range accomplishments than for flashy, short-term results.

The interviews having been concluded, Clover and Bowden are now faced with drafting a series of recommendations on the individuals interviewed and the steps to be taken by Universal Corporation.

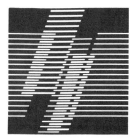

SECTION B

ENVIRONMENTAL ISSUES

The Recalcitrant Director at Byte Inc.: Corporate Legality vs. Corporate Responsibility

DAN R. DALTON · RICHARD A. COSIER · CATHY A. ENZ

Byte Products, Inc., is primarily involved in the production of electronic components that are used in personal computers. Although such components might be found in a few computers in home use, Byte products are found most frequently in computers used for sophisticated business and engineering applications. Annual sales of these products have been steadily increasing over the last several years; Byte Products, Inc. currently has total sales of approximately $265 million.

Over the last six years increases in yearly revenues have consistently reached 12%. Byte Products, Inc., headquartered in the midwestern United States, is regarded as one of the largest volume suppliers of specialized components and is easily the industry leader with some 32% market share. Unfortunately for Byte, many new firms—domestic and foreign—have entered the industry. A dramatic surge in demand, high profitability, and the relative ease of a new firm's entry into the industry, explain in part the increased number of competing firms.

While Byte management—and presumably stockholders as well—are very pleased about the growth of its markets, it faces a major problem: Byte simply cannot meet the demand for these components. The company currently operates three manufacturing facilities in various locations throughout the United States. Each of these plants operate three production shifts (24

This case was prepared by Professors Dan R. Dalton, Richard A. Cosier, and Cathy A. Enz of the Graduate School of Business at Indiana University. This case is also scheduled to appear in the *Journal of Management Case Studies*. Reprinted by permission.

hours per day), seven days a week. This activity constitutes virtually all of the company's production capacity. Without an additional manufacturing plant, Byte simply cannot increase its output of components.

James M. Elliott, Chief Executive Officer and Chairman of the Board, recognizes the gravity of the problem. If Byte Products can not continue to manufacture components in sufficient numbers to meet the demand, buyers will go elsewhere. Worse yet, is the possibility that any continued lack of supply will encourage others to enter the market. The Board of Directors, as a long-term solution to this problem, has unanimously authorized the construction of a new, state-of-the-art manufacturing facility in the southwestern United States. When the planned capacity of this plant is added to that of the three current plants, Byte should be able to meet demand for many years to come. Unfortunately, it has been estimated that it will take some three years to complete the plant and bring it on line.

Jim Elliott believes very strongly that this three-year period is far too long and has insisted that there also be a shorter-range, stopgap solution while the plant is under construction. The instability of the market and the pressure to maintain leader status are two factors contributing to Jim's insistence on a more immediate solution. Without such a move, Byte management believes that it will lose market share and, again, attract competitors into the market.

SEVERAL SOLUTIONS?

A number of suggestions for such a temporary measure were offered by various staff specialists, but rejected by Elliott. It was, for example, possible to license Byte's product and process technology to other manufacturers in the short run to meet immediate demand. This licensing authorization would be short-term, in effect just until the new plant could come on line. Top management as well as the board was uncomfortable with this solution for several reasons. It was thought to be unlikely that any manufacturer would shoulder the fixed costs of producing appropriate components for such a short term. Any manufacturer that would do so, would do so only at a premium to recover its costs. This suggestion, obviously, would make Byte's own products available to its customers at an unacceptable price. It did not seem sensible to pass any price increase to its customers, for this too would almost certainly reduce Byte's market share as well as encourage the entry of further competition.

Overseas facilities and licensing were also considered but rejected as well. When Byte was originally founded and before it became a publicly traded company, it was decided that Byte's manufacturing facilities would be domestic. It was strongly felt by top management that this strategy had served Byte very well; moreover, it was unlikely that Byte's majority stockholders (initial owners of the then privately held Byte) would endorse such a move. Beyond that, however, there was great reticence to foreign license—or make available by any means the technologies for others to produce Byte products, as patent issues could then not be properly overseen. Top management was fearful that foreign licensing would result in essentially giving away costly proprietary information regarding their highly efficient means of product development. There was also the potential for initial low product quality—whether produced domestically or otherwise—especially for such a short-run operation. Any reduction in quality, however brief, would once again threaten Byte's share of this very sensitive market.

THE SOLUTION!

One recommendation that has come to the attention of the chief executive officer could ameliorate Byte's problem in the short run. Certain members of his staff have notified him that there is an abandoned plant currently available in Plainville, a small town in the northeastern United States. Before its closing eight years before, this plant was used primarily for the manufacture of electronic components. As is, it could not possibly be used to produce Byte products, but it could be inexpensively refitted to do so in as few as three months. Moreover, this plant is available at a very attractive price. In fact, discrete inquiries by Elliott's staff indicate that this plant could probably be leased immediately from its present owners, because the building has been vacant for some eight years.

All the news about this temporary plant proposal, however, is not nearly so positive. Elliott's staff concedes that this plant will never be efficient and its profitability will be very low. Even the Plainville location is a poor one in terms of high labor costs (the area is highly unionized); there would be warehousing expenses; and there are inadequate transportation links to Byte's major markets and suppliers. Plainville is simply not a candidate for a long-term solution. Still, in the short run a temporary plant could serve to meet the demand and might forestall additional competition.

The staff is persuasive and notes that there are several advantages: 1) there is no need for any licensing, foreign or domestic, 2) quality control remains firmly in the hands of the firm, and, 3) an increase in the price of the products will be unnecessary. The temporary plant, then, would be used for three years or so until the new plant could be built. At this time, the temporary plant would be immediately closed.

CEO Elliott is convinced.

TAKING THE PLAN TO THE BOARD

The quarterly meeting of the Board of Directors is set to commence at 2:00 P.M. Jim Elliott has been reviewing his notes and agenda items for the meeting most of the morning. The issue of the temporary plant is clearly the most important agenda item. Reviewing his detailed presentation of this matter, including the associated financials, has occupied much of his time for several days. All the available information underscores his contention that the temporary plant in Plainville is the only responsible solution to the demand problems. No other option offers the same low level of risk and insures Byte's status as industry leader.

Having dispensed with a number of routine matters, Jim Elliott turned his attention to the temporary plant. In short order, he advises the eleven-member board (comprised of himself, three additional inside members and seven outside members) of his proposal to obtain and refit the existing plant to ameliorate demand problems in the short run, authorize the construction of the new plant (the completion of which is estimated to take some three years), and plan to switch capacity from the temporary plant to the new one when it is operational. Additional details concerning the costs involved, advantages of this proposal versus domestic or foreign licensing, and so forth are also briefly reviewed.

All the board members except one are in favor of the proposal. In fact, they are most enthusiastic; it seems that the overwhelming majority agree that the temporary plant is an excellent—even inspired—stopgap measure. Ten of the eleven board members seem relieved given that the board was most reticent to endorse any of the other alternatives that had been brought forward.

The single dissenter—T. Kevin Williams, an outside director—is, however, steadfast in his objections. He will not, under any circumstances, endorse the notion of the temporary plant and states rather strongly that "I will not be party to this nonsense, not now, not ever."

T. Kevin Williams, the senior executive of a major nonprofit organization, is normally a reserved and really quite agreeable gentleman. This sudden, uncharacteristic burst of emotion clearly startles the remaining members of the board into silence. The following excerpt captures the ensuing, essentially one-on-one conversation between Williams and Elliott.

WILLIAMS: How many workers do your people estimate will be employed in the temporary plant?

ELLIOTT: Roughly 1,200, possibly a few more.

WILLIAMS: I presume it would be fair, then, to say that, including spouses and children, something on the order of 4,000 people will be attracted to the community.

ELLIOTT: I certainly would not be surprised.

WILLIAMS: If I understand the situation correctly, this plant closed just over eight years ago and that closing had a catastrophic effect on Plainville. Isn't it true that a large portion of the community were employed by this plant?

ELLIOTT: Yes, it was far and away the majority employer.

WILLIAMS: And most of these people have left the community presumably to find employment elsewhere.

ELLIOTT: Definitely, there was a drastic decrease in the area's population.

WILLIAMS: Are you concerned, then, that our company can attract the 1,200 employees to Plainville from other parts of New England?

ELLIOTT: Not in the least. We are absolutely confident that we will attract 1,200—even more, for that matter virtually any number we need. That, in fact, is one of the chief advantages of this proposal. I would think that the community would be very pleased to have us there.

WILLIAMS: On the contrary, I would suspect that the community will rue the day we arrived. Beyond that, though, this plan is totally unworkable if we are candid. On the other hand, if we are less than candid, the proposal will work for us, but only at great cost to Plainville. In fact, quite frankly the implications are appalling. Once again, I must enter my serious objections.

ELLIOTT: I don't follow you.

WILLIAMS: The temporary plant would employ some 1,200 people. Again, this means the infusion of over 4,000 to the community and surrounding areas. Byte Products, however, intends to close this plant in three years or less. If Byte informs the community or the employees that the jobs are temporary, the proposal simply won't work. When the new people arrive in the community, there will be a need for more schools, instructors, utilities, housing, restaurants, and so forth. Obviously, if the banks and local government know that the plant is temporary, no funding will be made available for these projects and certainly no credit for the new employees to buy homes, appliances, automobiles, and so forth.

If, on the other hand, Byte Products does not tell the community of its "temporary" plans, the project can go on. But, in several years when the plant closes (and we here have agreed today that it will close) we will have created a ghost town. The tax base of the community will have been destroyed; property values will decrease precipitously; practically the whole town will be unemployed. This proposal will place Byte Products in an untenable position and in extreme jeopardy.

ELLIOTT: Are you suggesting that this proposal jeopardizes us legally? If so, it should be noted that the legal department has reviewed this proposal in its entirety and has indicated no problem.

WILLIAMS· No! I don't think we are dealing with an issue of legality here. In fact, I don't doubt for a minute that this proposal is altogether legal. I do, however, resolutely believe that this proposal constitutes gross irresponsibility.

I think this decision has captured most of my major concerns. These along with a host of collateral problems associated with this project lead me to strongly suggest that you and the balance of the board reconsider and not endorse this proposal: Byte Products must find another way.

THE DILEMMA

After a short recess, the board meeting reconvened. By this time—presumably because of some discussion during the recess—it became clear that several other board members were not inclined to support the proposal. After a short period of rather heated discussion, the following exchange took place.

ELLIOTT: It appears to me that any vote on this matter is likely to be very close. Given the gravity of our demand capacity problem, I must insist that the stockholders' equity be protected. We cannot wait three years; that is clearly out of the question. I still feel that licensing—domestic or foreign— is not in our long-term interests for any number of reasons, some of which have been discussed here. On the other hand, I do not want to take this project forward on the strength of a mixed vote. A vote of 6–5 or 7–4, for example, does not indicate the board is of anything remotely of one mind. Mr. Williams, is there a compromise to be reached?

WILLIAMS: Respectfully, I have to say no. If we tell the truth, namely the temporary nature of our operations, the proposal is simply not viable. If we are less than candid in this respect, we do grave damage to the community as well as our image. It seems to me that we can only go one way or the other; I don't see a middle ground.

A Problem of Silicosis

FOSTER C. RINEFORT

BACKGROUND OF THE PROBLEM

Frank Rahman, Corporate Safety Director for International Mining and Carbon Corporation, was faced with a complex problem. Rahman was responsible for the prevention and control of work injuries and occupational diseases in the corporation. Recently, he received a copy of the first report of injury reporting a case of class I silicosis at the Emmett, North Carolina plant. The silicosis issue was brought home for Rahman every day. Walter Krutchel, who had built the Emmett plant and run it for over a decade, was now at the corporate headquarters in an office adjacent to Rahman and his silicosis-caused coughing was frequent and loud.

Frank had worked extensively with the Vice-President of the Industrial Group, Norman Dillsworth, and with the other group managers over a period of several years and had visited the Emmett plant within the year. As he tried to put the problem in perspective, Rahman thought about the corporation, its background, and its current financial position. He reviewed the operations and products of the Industrial Group, the Industrial Minerals Division, and the Emmett plant. He then took another look at the corporate safety record to date, including lost workday incidence rates and the lost workday severity rates. He reviewed the causes, symptoms, and effects of silicosis. He knew that he must take appropriate action to deal with this problem. But what should he do?

HISTORY OF INTERNATIONAL MINING AND CARBON CORPORATION

International Mining and Carbon Corporation was incorporated in New York in 1909 as International Mining Corporation. Its operations then consisted of an open-pit phosphate mine in central Florida and several relatively small plants in the southeast United States, where phosphates were combined with potash and some form of nitrogen and were sold in bulk and bagged form to farmers as fertilizer. The company continued to grow moderately within the agricultural fertilizer sector of the economy in the 1920s and 1930s. In the late 1930s, under the leadership of Louis Warren, a mining engineer with banking experience, the company moved its headquarters to Chicago and acquired potash mining leases near Carlsbad, New Mexico. The company opened a mine at this location in 1940. After World War II, the company obtained feldspar and bentonite mining and refining operations,

Prepared by Professor Foster C. Rinefort of Eastern Illinois University. Presented at the 1984 Workshop of the Midwest Society for Case Research. Reprinted by permission.

and built and acquired additional fertilizer plants. Then as the result of an accidental discovery in the company's research laboratories, a food flavor enhancer called "Spice" was produced from sugar beet tops in a plant in San Jose, California. The company continued through acquisitions and growth to expand at a reasonable rate and to show consistent 4%–5% profit as a percentage of sales.

In 1958 Louis Warren's son, Tom, became President and the company began a new era. A new corporate logo was prepared and a motto, "Grow," was developed to provide a statement of the objectives of the organization. A modern corporate headquarters was built in suburban Chicago and a young, capable staff was recruited. Then there followed significant growth in sales and profits, numerous acquisitions, extensive revamping of existing facilities, and the acquisition of a large potash mine that was successfully opened in Saskatchewan, Canada. This era ended in the late 1960s, when an oversupply of chemical fertilizers severely depressed prices and drastically diminished corporate profits.

In the 1970s Nelson Wilson initiated a difficult but successful turnaround period. Richard Langdon, the next Chief Executive Officer, carried on Wilson's work. From 1970 to 1980 sales increased from $588 million to $1,637 million and net earnings grew from $48 million to $146 million (see Exhibit 5.1). During this time the company expanded and further modernized existing facilities, eliminated numerous marginal operations, expanded its important Canadian and Florida mining operations, and built a large nitrogen-producing plant in Louisiana. Through acquisitions the firm expanded further into the industrial chemical and industrial minerals areas, added oil, gas, and coal-producing operations; and became stronger in world markets by purchasing an established New York–based trading company. Since 1981 both sales and net earnings have decreased as the price of primary products has declined on a world basis.

Today (1985) the company employs 9,000 people at 121 locations throughout the world and continues to be a leading producer of chemical fertilizers and fertilizer materials. Thus the corporation is a major factor in the world trade of these products and an important supplier of other industrial chemicals and mineral products.

THE INDUSTRY GROUP

The industry group is an international supplier to heavy industry. It consists of three divisions: Carbon Products, Foundry Products, and Industrial Minerals. The *Carbon Products Division* primarily produces green petroleum coke, a by-product of petroleum refining that is sold to the steel, cement, and electrical utility industries. It also sells graphite furnace electrodes and rods. The *Foundry Products Division* produces sand-bonding resins and oils for automotive and machine foundries. It is a major producer of molding sand additives, bonding clays, facing sands, and refractory mixes, and, in addition, is a manufacturer of foundry core-making machinery. The Foundry

EXHIBIT 5.1 **International Mining and Carbon Corporation**
(Dollars in Millions except Per Share Amounts)

	1984	1983	1982	1981	1980
Revenues	$1,569.9	$1,464.3	$1,621.8	$1,824.2	$1,637.6
Earnings from continuing operations before income taxes	172.7	129.9	197.0	248.7	251.8
Provision for income taxes	60.7	46.8	74.3	97.4	104.4
Earnings from continuing operations	112.0	83.1	122.7	151.3	147.4
Discontinued operations	(30.3)	(2.6)	14.7	2.5	(1.5)
Net Earnings	81.7	80.5	137.4	153.8	145.9
Receivables, net	206.5	179.5	189.0	260.9	238.5
Interest expense	4.7	3.3	4.2	5.4	6.7
Inventory	246.1	253.0	323.7	348.0	297.3
Current assets	613.7	584.7	620.6	618.2	689.5
Current liabilities	326.2	306.7	316.1	358.0	345.4
Earnings from continuing operations[1]	4.17	3.12	4.58	5.54	5.43
Discontinued operations[1]	(1.13)	(.10)	.55	.09	(.05)
Net earnings per share	3.04	3.02	5.13	5.63	5.38
Common dividends[1]	2.60	2.60	2.60	2.46	2.16
Average common shares (in millions)	26.7	26.5	26.7	27.3	27.1
Other Five-Year Data[2]					
Total assets	1,965.6	1,943.9	1,941.9	1,975.2	1,848.6
Working capital	287.5	278.0	304.5	260.2	344.1
Long-term debt, less current maturities	388.1	424.6	441.8	486.3	488.4
Total debt	425.7	459.4	485.7	503.3	500.0
Deferred income taxes	112.7	124.2	125.1	106.1	93.0
Shareholders' equity	1,039.1	1,024.1	1,010.2	975.3	881.3
Invested capital	1,577.5	1,607.7	1,621.0	1,584.7	1,474.3
Number of employees	9,000	8,400	8,400	10,600	10,600

[1]Per share amounts

[2]All figures are in dollars, except number of employees.

Products Division also produces Uniflo, a slag conditioner used by the steel industry, which improves the efficiency of blast furnaces and the quality of the product. This division is a major producer of Bentonite, fireclay, facing sands, shell sand additives, resins for the paint industry, refractory mixes for lining furnace cupolas, and custom-blended moldings and additives.

The third segment, the *Industrial Minerals Division*, is a major miner and processor of feldspar and nepheline syenite materials, which are primarily sold to the glass and ceramics industry. Industrial Minerals Division plants are located in Harwick, Ontario, Canada; Emmett, North Carolina; Brownwood, North Carolina; Rocky River, Virginia; and Whitman, Washington. The Industrial Minerals Division is headed by Charles Lonsbury, a Group Vice-President. He is a mining engineer with a flair for marketing and is young enough to have significant ambitions in the company. His operations manager is Phil Blasevich, a hard worker who worked his way through the Colorado School of Mines. His other principal staff assistant is Walter Krutchel, who supervised the construction of the Emmett, North Carolina, plant and who was its first plant manager until an aggravated case of silicosis forced him to leave the plant or face an early death. The division consists of a 6-person corporate staff, 325 plant-level employees, and 11 salespeople.

THE EMMETT, NORTH CAROLINA MINE AND PLANT

The Emmett open pit mine and plant is located in mountainous western North Carolina, west of the Blue Ridge Parkway. The mine was first opened and operated commercially during World War II. Workers use bulldozers to remove the earthen overburden, pneumatic drills to bore holes into the strata of feldspathic material, dynamite and ammonium nitrate-fuel oil to blast the rock free, and Hough front-end loaders to load the product into heavy-duty trucks for transport to the processing plant. The refining and processing plant was constructed at the bottom of a steep valley two miles from the mine, in the nearest fairly level and accessible site.

When the boulders and slabs of crystalline feldspar arrive at the plant, they are dumped into a pit, picked up by a conveyor belt, and fed into a primary or jaw crusher that breaks them into fist-sized lumps. A secondary crusher and a ball mill further reduce them in size first to the size of marbles and then, as necessary, to powder form. The product is then dried in gas-fired rotary kilns and bagged into forty-pound and eighty-pound bags, or stored in bulk form. The bagged finished product is stored in an adjacent warehouse building and is transported from the plant either by truck or by rail. The Clinchfield Railroad constructed a spur rail line to the plant, so boxcars of bagged product or hopper cars of the product in bulk form can be loaded and sent to customers throughout North America.

Work in the open pit quarry is hard and can be hazardous, particularly during inclement weather. Plant work in the unheated plant is hot and dusty in the summer and bone cold in the winter. In both settings, there are hazards from moving machinery and equipment such as front-end loaders and Clark lift trucks, and from falling or flying chunks or particles of feldspar. Employees face another hazard or risk. Feldspar and napheline syenite are crystalline minerals with unique geological characteristics that make them important in the manufacture of glass and ceramics. When ground, they also produce a dust primarily consisting of crystalline silicon dioxide, or SiO_2. When this dust is inhaled, it collects in the lungs, causing irritation which results in a fibrous hardening of the lungs. This hardening causes the occupational disease pneumoconiosis, or in this case, silicosis. Silicosis progresses from shortness of breath, to wheezing, to coughing, to pulmonary insufficiency, and, finally, to death.

The disease is diagnosed by use of lung x-rays, measurement of vital lung capacity by a spirometer, and medical diagnosis. The quantities of airborne dust can be measured by a Greenberg-Smith or Midget Inpinger or by a grab sample that is later analyzed in an industrial hygiene laboratory. The threshold limit value of pure crystalline SiO_2 is 2.5 million particles per cubic foot of air as calculated by the following formula:

$$\text{Concentration (mppcf)} = \frac{250}{5 + \% \text{ of crystalline } SiO_2 \text{ in airborne dust}}$$

The quantity of SiO_2 in the air can be controlled and reduced in several ways. The best method—also the most expensive—is to totally enclose the dust producing process with an exhaust system that maintains a negative pressure within the enclosure. A slightly less expensive solution is a local exhaust system consisting of a hood, fan, and collector, which can be installed at work stations. Significantly less adequate protection can be provided by installing fans to move and dilute dust concentrations and by mechanically supplying heated make-up air. Dust concentrations can be reduced by adding moisture at any stage of the process, from drilling in the quarry to bagging the finished product in the plant. The least satisfactory—also the least expensive—solution is to provide employees with Mine Health and Safety Administration approved respirators with appropriate filters. Respirators are uncomfortable, particularly in hot weather. They can become ineffective unless they are regularly cleaned and the filters are frequently changed. Workers often will not wear them unless management consistently and vigorously requires their use.

The Emmett plant protects its quarry employees by wet drilling and at the plant, encourages employees to use respirators. It also uses fans to move the air, and uses wet-milling techniques when practical. The plant superintendent is Arby Boone, who is a distant relative of Daniel Boone. He has been at the plant almost since it opened and is well respected by the men. He is completely self-educated. The seventy-two workers at the mine and at the plant are glad to have work because they are aware of their limited marketable skills and the perennial double-digit unemployment in this part of North Carolina. These workers exhibit a rugged mountaineer spirit and clannishness. Alternative local occupations include hunting, fishing, and making moonshine. Many of the workers are related to one another and most have been in this part of the state for several generations. They all suspect that they are getting or will get silicosis at some point, but they are somewhat fatalistic about it, sustained by their fundamentalist religion, their close community, and their fierce pride. They know that if they report formally that they have silicosis and claim workmen's compensation benefits for their disability, they will lose their jobs and will have to live on meager amounts of money. The forty-year-old plant normally operates on very thin profit margins and has lost money at the plant level three of the past five years primarily because of a downturn in the market for glass and ceramic products.

THE PLANT SAFETY PROGRAM

There is a company safety program that this plant has adopted to a reasonable extent (see Exhibit 5.2). Central features of the program are appointment of a parttime safety supervisor; monthly safety inspections by a three-man inspection committee; and a monthly safety committee meeting of inspection committee members, three other supervisors, and the safety supervisor. Other parts of the program are annual safety inspections by an employee of the workmen's compensation insurance carrier, safety posters on the bulletin board, and a provisioned first aid area located near the plant superintendent's office. Excerpts from the Corporate Accident and Fire Prevention Standard Practice Manual are shown in Exhibit 5.3.

The Silicosis Claim

William "Billy" Buchanan was the youngest of a family of six children. His father and two of his brothers had worked at the Emmett mine and mill of

---

EXHIBIT 5.2   **International Mining and Carbon Corporation: Corporate Safety Report, 1984**

	LOST WORKDAY INJURIES	LOST WORKDAY INCIDENCE RATE[1]	DAYS TIME LOST	LOST WORKDAY SEVERITY RATE[2]
Fertilizer Group				
New Mexico Mine	14	1.68	6,490	777.1
Canadian Mine	9	.62	361	24.9
Florida Mine	12	1.28	863	23.1
Florida Chemical	5	.85	152	25.8
Plant Food Division	49	4.51	7,215	661.9
Industry Group	57	3.77	8,451	560.7
Chemical Group	18	1.65	6,504	585.9
Animal Products Group	8	1.24	248	36.6
Headquarters	5	1.61	122	39.1

[1]Lost workday incidence rate is the number of disabling or lost-time work injuries or injuries in which the injured person is unable to work the next scheduled day per 100 full-time employees.

[2]Lost workday severity rate is the number of days lost from disabling work injuries including actual days lost and scheduled changes for deaths, loss of a part of the body, or use of a part of the body per 100 full-time employees.

EXHIBIT 5.3

Excerpts from the Corporate Accident and Fire Prevention Standard Practice Manual

CORPORATE SAFETY POLICY

Safety is the first concern in all company operations. Legal and industrial safety codes, protective equipment and devices, and standard safety practices are regarded as only minimum requirements. Every possible step beyond these minimums should be taken to ensure even greater safety. Each manager or superintendent is charged with the responsibility for the safety and well-being of all employees in the plant or mine under his supervision.

MANAGEMENT RESPONSIBILITY

The responsibility for the control of injuries and fires rests with operating management, from plant manager down to each foreman as a part of their regular management duties.

RESPONSIBILITIES OF THE SAFETY SUPERVISOR

The person designated, whether his title is Safety Supervisor or some other title, has the authority and responsibility for the effective functioning of the accident and fire prevention plan at each plant. . . . Responsibility for the functioning of the plan is carried out by the Safety Supervisor, who provides staff assistance to the production supervisors in filling their responsibilities for the control of unsafe acts or conditions which cause most losses.

INSTRUCTION AND TRAINING OF EMPLOYEES

Because unsafe acts cause most of the accidents, fires, and other insurable losses, the development of safety rules and the thorough indoctrination, instruction, and training of each employee in the safe way of doing his work is the most important part of the plan: wherever a training program is functioning, the safety training required for each job should be incorporated into that program.

THE CORRECTION OF UNSAFE PRACTICES AND CONDITIONS

It is very important to find and correct unsafe practices and conditions before they cause an accident, fire, or other type of loss. Unsafe practices are generally found by Plant Safety Inspection Committees, insurance company representatives, supervisory personnel during the daily operation of their departments, Safety Supervisors, and employees.

SAFETY MEETINGS

The Management Committee is composed of the Plant Manager or Superintendent (in his absence, his assistant), the Safety Supervisor, and other key managerial personnel. . . . The committee would meet once each month and the Safety Supervisor would act as secretary to the group.

MAINTAINING INTEREST

To maintain high interest in safety, something more than monthly safety meetings and inspections is necessary. The following are a few of the activities which are usually most effective.

1. Safety contests.
2. National Safety Council Section contests.
3. Division-wide or inter-departmental safety campaigns or contests.
4. Safety publications.
5. Safety posters.
6. Movies and sound slide films.

FIRST AID

Each plant should have one or more areas where first aid can be administered. Necessary first-aid supplies should be kept in the area. The area should be kept extremely clean and all employees should know where it is located.

International Mining and Carbon for most of their adult lives. Billy's father died of unknown causes when Billy was twelve years old. Billy quit school at age sixteen and was employed by the company when he was eighteen. Twelve years later he employed an attorney from a community located fifty miles east of Emmett in the valley and claimed full disability, or Class I silicosis, under the North Carolina Workmen's Compensation Act. The company, following past practices and industry custom, terminated him, and employed local counsel to fight the claim at every step.

CONCLUSION

Frank Rahman pondered what he should do. He understood the fragile and difficult economics of this plant, this division, and the industry in general. He understood that adverse publicity could cause difficult problems at this plant and possibly trigger a visit from the Mine Health and Safety Administration, U.S. Department of Labor. As a result of his recent visit to the plant, he was painfully aware of its shortcomings regarding employee protection. What should he do?

Brookstone Hospice: Heel or Heroine?

SHIRLEY F. OLSON · SHARON FERGUSON

"To be profit oriented is acceptable for any business but when that profit is given priority over a patient's life . . . well—I've got problems with that," Kathy Bennett tearfully declared. Kathy's anger stemmed from an incident that had taken place earlier in the month. As the nursing supervisor for a large hospice located in the northeastern United States, she had seen many things that she questioned but nothing quite like this latest occurrence.

The hospice with which she was associated employed thirty-five people and operated under the same philosophy as that of all other hospices—its goal was to ensure that the terminally ill patient was as comfortable as possible during the last days of life. Its reason for existence was therefore not to cure in the traditional medical sense but to insure the patient of a relatively pain-free, dignified death. Its mission and purpose as outlined in the company manual was to provide (a) a holistic approach to the dying patients and their significant others (family, friends), (b) assistance in helping the surviving significant others back to an optimal level of functioning, and (c) assistance to health care professionals dealing with dying patients and their significant others.

To achieve that purpose Brookstone's described strategy was to offer care in the last six months of the terminally ill patient's life, with 24-hour, hands-on care if needed, for up to seven days. Otherwise care was limited to two visits per week by the RN and weekly visits from the chaplain and social worker. The hospice doctor made visits as needed. The organization also offered a hot line that patients' families could use for discussing their concerns with the chaplain and for pre-planning the funeral. Brookstone's home health aides were available as the family required for daily duties— patient baths, trips to and from the doctor, to and from the grocery, and light housework. Thus, not only the patient but also the family received services in the form of support from the team. Unlike traditional care, the group members—with the exception of the doctor—continued to visit the family after the death of the patient and thus assured their well-being, as noted in the organization's mission/purpose statement. Team members al-

This case was prepared by Professor Shirley F. Olson of Millsaps College and Ms. Sharon Ferguson, private consultant. It was presented at the North American Case Research Association meeting, 1986. Distributed by the North American Case Research Association. All rights reserved to the authors and the North American Case Research Association. Reprinted by permission of the authors and the North American Case Research Association.

ways attended the funeral and even visited families on the first anniversary of the death, which was a very painful time.

The structure of the organization was quite loose, as was required by the very nature of the work being done. Essentially, all employees were part of matrix-type structures with each patient constituting the center of that matrix. Needless to say, the nurses, chaplains, etc. were associated with more than one patient at any one time, but because the patients' needs were always changing, the components in the matrix also changed rapidly as different members were needed for their particular expertise.

The matrixes were coordinated by an overall administrator, Jim Cole, who prided himself on the flexibility of the organization. Cole went so far as to indicate, "Our people are top-level professionals and need very little managing. I like to leave decisions—to the extent possible—to their discretion. Of course, I still see myself as the final authority. My nurse supervisor coordinates all the RNs and the doctors are coordinated similarly by our in-house physician. The social worker and chaplain also work through the nurse supervisor. My job essentially then is to watch all this happen. So far I've been pretty successful. Just this last year Brookstone grossed $2.5 million. And we are projecting $3.2 this year."

Despite Cole's quick overview of the hospice's structure, Kathy Bennett was one of many to note that although the company procedures manual had a segment devoted to structure, that page was blank. "My team director told me not to ask too many questions about who reported to whom. She said Cole liked the feeling of flexibility and did not want anything about Brookstone to appear bureaucratic. However, I do know that our Chief Team Operator, the Executive Medical Director, and the Marketing Director all answered to Cole. Answering to the Team Operator were the two team directors who directly supervised the RNs, aides, chaplains, and social workers. The hospice MDs reported to the Executive Medical Director, and the marketing representative reported to the Marketing Director." As Kathy noted, "The very nature of the work we do makes us such a close knit group. When you are faced with death every day and sometimes several times a day—you have a much greater appreciation for life and family, and people in general. I've been with this group almost seven years and up until this incident a few days ago, Brookstone has been ideal—not just for me as an employee but for our patients also. Their needs are so great and their time so short. When I leave here every night, I never have to wonder what we accomplished that day. At least that was the case until now."

THE EPISODE

The incident to which Kathy continued to refer involved an 86-year-old man, Sam Gardner, suffering from a malignancy of the kidney. Mr. Gardner had been accepted by Brookstone three weeks earlier and was being visited regularly. On Sunday, February 18, Gardner's daughter, Beverly, had contacted Brookstone's duty nurse saying that her father seemed to be bleeding profusely internally. Although the family had been told that this would happen in the latter stages of the illness, the bleeding was much worse than they had expected and had gone on for almost sixteen hours.

In response, Bennett sent the on-call nurse to the Gardner home to assess the patient's condition. Within minutes of her arrival, the nurse phoned Kathy, the nursing supervisor, and indicated that Mr. Gardner needed to be admitted to a hospital's acute-care in-patient unit. While the nurse was on the phone with Kathy, the family became increasingly hysterical. At one point during the phone conversation Kathy heard Beverly scream out, "I'll call an ambulance myself and take him. We can't just sit here and let him bleed to death while your bureaucratic organization has us on hold."

Realizing the urgency in the duty nurse's voice, Kathy immediately began the procedure for admitting Gardner to Covington General Hospital, the hospital with which Brookstone contracted. The procedure required by Brookstone Hospice was quite lengthy if Gardner was to be admitted to the Hospice Inpatient Unit at Covington General. Specifically:

1. The patient's primary doctor had to be contacted and had to approve admission.
2. The hospice doctor had to be contacted to act as the attending physician; if the patient's primary doctor refused the case, the hospice physician then performed as the primary doctor.
3. The hospital admissions office had to be notified of the incoming patient.

While Kathy was more than familiar with the procedure called for, several factors prevented the protocol from being followed. First of all the primary doctor refused to care for Gardner if he were transported to Covington General, stating that he would treat the patient if and only if he were taken to Catholic Charities Hospital. Brookstone had no contractual agreement with Catholic Charities.

As Kathy attempted to reason with the physician, the patient meanwhile had been placed in an ambulance that sat in the Gardners' driveway and waited for instructions from the duty nurse as to where the patient was to be taken. Kathy desperately continued her telephoning as she sought to follow established procedure, which required that no action on a hospice patient be taken without approval from the hospice's MDs. Despite the efforts she was not able to contact any of the four hospice doctors who were on call that weekend. "I called every answering service, home, and golf course I could think of at the time but to no avail. That went on for at least 45 minutes while my poor patient lay in the ambulance waiting on our 'procedure.' You can only imagine how I felt. Finally in my desperation I gave permission to transport Gardner to the nearest hospital—Covington General (C.G.H.)—and the story goes on from there," Kathy noted.

After Gardner was taken to C.G.H., he went directly to the emergency room where he was assessed by the E.R. physician, C. Wallace. Wallace immediately set Gardner up for urological surgery the following Monday morning. On that Monday, the urologist contacted one of Brookstone's team doctors to discuss the so-called "curative surgery." Brookstone had well-defined policies about how hospice patients were to be treated. Once a patient signed with the hospice, no other health care professional could take any action whatsoever without contacting the hospice. As the procedure manual noted, a paramedic could not even resuscitate a nonbreathing hospice patient until contact was made with Brookstone. Realizing these rules, Wallace knew he faced a battle when he made the call.

Because hospice discouraged curative measures—surgical or otherwise—the hospice physician was forced to discuss the proposed surgery with his superior in the hospice office, before giving the urologist his approval to go ahead with the procedure. Immediately the supervisor vigorously discouraged the proposal—primarily on the grounds that the urologist stated that the surgery would extend the patient's life. Kathy overheard one of the team doctors state, "The man is 86 years old and has cancer. Can't you people understand the situation? That surgery will cost hospice a minimum of $7,800. We—you and me—will pay for that right out of our pockets. We don't want to do that, do we? After all Gardner will be dead anyway in three months. Our purpose is not to extend life but to assure quality life even until death."

Needless to say Kathy could not believe what she was hearing. Affiliated with an organization that she perceived as one of the best in the nation, she suddenly saw Brookstone quite differently in just those few split seconds of that comment.

THE AFTERMATH

"At least something good finally came out of all the madness. Despite the discouragement from the hospice doctors, the Covington General urologist operated anyway. Five days later, the 86-year-old Gardner, who had been diagnosed as having only 3 months to live, was discharged from the hospital—with a prognosis of 3 years or more. Somehow he got my name from his duty nurse and he called me here at the hospice yesterday. His voice was a bit weak but his message was extremely clear. He told me in no uncertain terms that he credited me with saving his life and with giving him 3 years instead of 3 months. Gardner said he knew the chance I took by sending him to Covington General. His call meant everything to me and I could use some good news. The same day he called, I was fired. A medical team doctor and Jim Cole called me in, showed me the surgical bill Brookstone received on Gardner, and informed me that I had seriously violated numerous policies and procedures. As a result my termination was effective immediately. One of the doctors went so far as to remind me of the financial constraints facing the hospice and said, 'Kathy, you know as well as anyone the money difficulty we've been having. Only two weeks ago, our payroll was held up two days because of our cash flow difficulties. That $7,800 we had to pay on Gardner would have gone a long way here in the organization. Yet you saw fit to spend it on a guy who is old and going to die anyway.' "

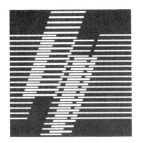

SECTION C

STRATEGIC ISSUES IN LARGE CORPORATIONS

Harley-Davidson, Inc.: The Eagle Soars Alone

STUART C. HINRICHS · CHARLES B. SHRADER · ALAN N. HOFFMAN

In May of 1987, Vaughn Beals, Chief Executive of Harley-Davidson, Inc. and Thomas Gelb, Vice-President of Operations, made a difficult decision. They had turned Harley-Davidson around on a dime and were now poised for continued success with a fine-tuned production process and an exciting new product line. However, in a continued effort to maintain low costs, Beals and Gelb were forced to give a contract for eight electronically controlled machining centers worth $1.5 million to Japanese-owned Toyoda Machine Works. Even though the Toyoda production site for the machining centers was in Illinois, Beals would have preferred to buy from an American company. But he was constrained because of the Japanese company's ability to deliver both high quality and low price.

Beals was well aware of the implications of the decision. He had previously toured several Japanese motorcycle plants during Harley's turnaround and had been impressed with their efficiency and quality. Beals understood the pressure that foreign competition had put on his company, and on other manufacturing-intensive companies in the U.S. as well.

This case was prepared by Lieutenant Commander Stuart Hinrichs and Professor Charles B. Shrader of Iowa State University, and Professor Alan N. Hoffman of Bentley College. The authors would like to thank Linda Zorzi, assistant to V.L. Beals, CEO and Chairman of Harley-Davidson Motor Company, for information she provided in preparing this case. The authors would also like to thank Lieutenant Michael Melvin and Blaine Ballantine of Iowa State University for providing helpful information. Reprinted by permission.

Nonetheless, the decision reflected Harley's commitment to quality and reliability, and also indicated the company's willingness to change with the competitive environment.

Beals and his small management team turned around a company that really symbolized America. Harley-Davidson motorcycles represented freedom and rugged individualism. Beals had put Harley back as the market leader in the super-heavyweight (more than 851cc) motorcycle market. Harley owned 33.3% of that market in 1986 compared to Honda's 30.1%.

EXHIBIT 7.1   **Harley-Davidson's U.S. Market Share, Super Heavyweight Motorcycles (850cc+)**

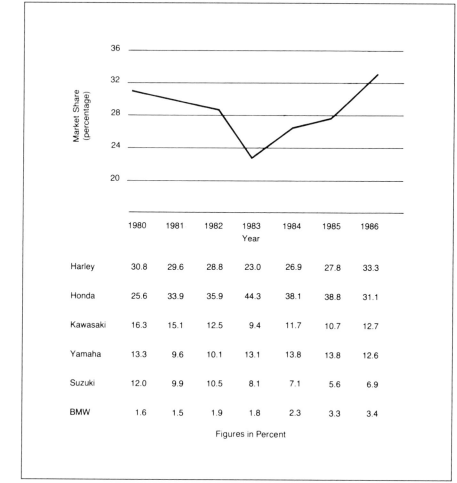

	1980	1981	1982	1983 Year	1984	1985	1986
Harley	30.8	29.6	28.8	23.0	26.9	27.8	33.3
Honda	25.6	33.9	35.9	44.3	38.1	38.8	31.1
Kawasaki	16.3	15.1	12.5	9.4	11.7	10.7	12.7
Yamaha	13.3	9.6	10.1	13.1	13.8	13.8	12.6
Suzuki	12.0	9.9	10.5	8.1	7.1	5.6	6.9
BMW	1.6	1.5	1.9	1.8	2.3	3.3	3.4

Figures in Percent

Source: 1986 *Annual Report*

As of August of 1987, Harley had 38% of the large-cycle market and total company sales were expected to rise from under $300 million in 1986 to over $600 million in 1987[1] (see Exhibit 7.1).

Yet Beals knew that to stabilize that performance, his company needed to diversify. The Milwaukee-based company manufactured motorcycles and motorcycle accessories, as well as bomb casings and other products for the military. In 1986, Harley acquired Holiday Rambler Corporation, a recreational vehicle company. Beals believed that it would fit perfectly with the other businesses, and it was in one industry that was free from Japanese competitors.

Beals knew that Harley had to continue to improve both its production and its human resource management techniques if it was to remain strong competitively. And he also realized that his company's basic product, super-heavyweight ("hog") motorcycles, had the loyal customers and brand image upon which successful competitive and diversification strategies could be built. The company's nonmotorcycle businesses were performing well and the Holiday Rambler acquisition looked promising. Now the challenge Beals faced was how to keep the company moving down the road at high speed.

HISTORY[2]

The Harley-Davidson story began in 1903 when William Harley, aged 21, a draftsman at a Milwaukee manufacturing firm, designed and built a motorcycle with the help of three Davidson brothers: Arthur, a pattern maker employed by the same company as Harley; Walter, a railroad mechanic; and William, a tool maker. At first, they tinkered with ideas, motors, and old bicycle frames. Legend has it that their first carburetor was fashioned from a tin can. Still, they were able to make a three-horsepower, twenty-five-cubic-inch engine and successfully road test their first motorcycle.

Operating out of a shed in the Davidson family's backyard, the men built and sold three motorcycles. Production was expanded to eight in 1904 and in 1906 the company's first building was erected on the current Juneau Avenue site of the main Milwaukee offices. On September 17, 1907, Harley-Davidson Motor Company was incorporated.

Arthur Davidson set off to recruit dealers in New England and in the South. William Harley completed a degree in engineering, specializing in internal combustion engines, and quickly applied his expertise in the company: He developed the first V-twin engine in 1909. He followed this with a major breakthrough in 1912—the first commercially successful motorcycle clutch. This made possible the use of a roller chain to power the motorcycle. The first three-speed transmission was offered in 1915.

During the early 1900s the U.S. experienced rapid growth in the motorcycle industry, with firms such as Excelsior, Indian, Merkel, Thor, and Yale growing and competing. Most of the early U.S. motorcycle companies turned out shoddy, unreliable products. But this was not considered to be true for

Harley-Davidson and Indian cycles. Early continued success in racing and endurance made Harleys favorites among motorcyclists. The company's V-twin engines became known for power and reliability.

During World War I, Harley-Davidson supplied the military with many motorcycles. By virtue of very strong military and domestic sales, Harley-Davidson became the largest motorcycle company in the world in 1918.[3] The company built a 300,000 square foot plant in Milwaukee, Wisconsin in 1922, making it one of the largest motorcycle factories in the world.[4]

In the late 1930s, Harley-Davidson dealt a strong competitive blow to the Indian motorcycle company: it introduced the first overhead-valve engine. The large, 61-cubic-inch engine became very popular and was thereafter referred to as the "Knucklehead." Indian could not make a motorcycle to compete with these Harleys.

Harley introduced major innovations in the suspensions of its cycles in the 1940s. However, in 1949 Harley first met with international competition, from Great Britain. The British motorcycles, such as Nortons and Triumphs, were cheaper, lighter, better handling, and just as fast, even though they had smaller engines.

To counter the British threat, Harley-Davidson further improved the design of the engines, and thereby increased the horsepower of their heavier cycles. The result, in 1957, was what some consider to be the first of the modern superbikes: the Harley Sportster. It was also during the 1950s that Harley developed the styling that made it famous.

As the 1950s drew to a close, new contenders from Japan entered the lightweight (250cc and below) motorcycle market. Harley welcomed the little bikes because it believed that small-bike customers would quickly move to larger bikes as the riders became more experienced. The Japanese cycles proved to have some staying power, however, and Japanese products began to successfully penetrate the off-road and street cycle markets. In the 1960s Japan entered the middleweight (250–500cc) market.

As Harley entered the 1960s, it made an attempt to build smaller, light-weight bikes in the U.S. But the company found it difficult to build small machines and still be profitable. As a result, Harley acquired 50% of Aermacchi, an Italian cycle producer, and built small motorcycles for both street and off-road use. The first Aermacchi Harleys were sold in 1961.[5] The Italian venture endured until 1978, but was never highly successful. Few took Harley's small cycles seriously; some Harley dealers refused to handle them. In the meantime, Japanese cycles dominated the small and middleweight markets. Harley seemed trapped in the heavyweight segment.

In an attempt to expand its production capacity and raise capital, Harley went public in 1965. The company merged with the conglomerate AMF, Inc. in 1969. AMF, a company known for its leisure and industrial products, expanded Harley's production capacity from 15,000 units in 1969 to 40,000 units in 1974.[6] With the expanded capacity, AMF pursued a milking strategy, favoring short-term profits rather than investment in research and development, and retooling. The Japanese continued to improve while Harley began to turn out heavy, noisy, vibrating, laboriously handling, poorly finished machines.

In 1975, AMF failed to react to a serious Japanese threat. Honda Motor Company introduced the "Gold Wing," which quickly became the standard for large touring motorcycles, a segment that Harley had owned. At the time, Harley's top-of-the-line touring bike sold for almost $9,000 while the comparable Honda Gold Wing was approximately $7,000.[7] Not only were Japanese cycles priced lower than similar Harleys, but Japanese manufacturing techniques yielded operating costs that were 30% lower than Harley-Davidson's.

Motorcycle enthusiasts more than ever began to go with Japanese products because of their price and performance advantages. Even some loyal Harley owners and police department contracts were lost. The company was rapidly losing ground both in technological advances and in the market.

Starting in 1975 and continuing through the middle 1980s, the Japanese companies penetrated the big-bore, custom motorcycle market with Harley look-alikes with V-twin engines.[8] The Honda "Magna" and "Shadow," the Suzuki "Intruder," and the Yamaha "Virago" were representative of the Japanese imitations. In a short time the Japanese captured a significant share of the large cycle segment and controlled nearly 90% of the total motorcycle market.[9]

During AMF's ownership of Harley, its motorcycles were strong on sales but relatively weak on profits. AMF did put a great deal of money into Harley and production went as high as 75,000 units in 1975.[10] But motorcycles never seemed to be AMF's priority. For example, in 1978, motorcycles accounted for 17% of its revenues but for only 1% of profits. AMF was more inclined to emphasize its industrial products and services.

THE TURNAROUND[11]

Vaughn Beals served as Harley's top manager during its last six years under AMF control. Beals was uncomfortable with AMF's short-term orientation and unwillingness to confront the problems caused by imports. Consequently, in June of 1981, a subgroup of Harley management, including Beals, completed a leveraged buyout of Harley-Davidson from AMF. To celebrate, Beals and the management team made a Pennsylvania–Wisconsin motorcycle ride, proclaiming, "The Eagle Soars Alone."

Beals knew that reversing the company's momentum would not be easy, especially without the help of the former parent. Indeed, things first began to get worse. Harley suffered its first operating loss in 1981. In 1982, many motorcycles were coming off the assembly line with defects, registrations for heavyweight motorcycles were falling, and the Japanese were continuing to penetrate Harley's market segments. Company losses for the year totalled over $25 million.[12] Several Japanese companies built up inventories in the face of a declining market and engaged in aggressive price discounting.

Beals petitioned the International Trade Commission (ITC) for temporary protection from Japanese "dumping" practices in 1982. He accused the Japanese of dumping large quantities of bikes in the U.S. and selling them for prices much below what they were in Japan. The U.S. Treasury had previously found the Japanese guilty of excess-inventory practices, but the nonpartisan ITC ruled that the practices had not adversely affected the sales of Harley-Davidson motorcycles. Therefore, no sanctions were placed on the Japanese companies. The Japanese continued price competition and many thought that Harley would soon buckle from the pressure.

However, in 1983, with the help of many public officials including Senator John Heinz of Pennsylvania, Harley was able to obtain protection from the excess-inventory practices of the Japanese. In April of 1983, President Reagan, on the recommendation of the ITC, imposed a declining five-year tariff on the wholesale prices of Japanese heavyweight (over 700cc) motorcycles. The tariff schedule was as follows:

    1983   45%
    1984   35%
    1985   20%
    1986   15%
    1987   10%

The effects of the tariff were mixed. Much of the Japanese inventory was already in the U.S. when the tariff went into effect, and prices of those units were not affected. Also, dealers selling Japanese cycles sharply reduced prices on older models, and thus hurt the sale of new bikes.

On the other hand, the tariff signaled that Japanese over-production would not be tolerated, so that Harley would have some breathing room and management would have a chance to reposition the company. Beals and others inside the company felt that the dumping case and the tariff protection helped focus the company on developing its competitive strengths and on improving the production process. They also believed that the tariffs were the result of the government's recognition of Harley's overall revitalization effort. The process of whipping the once proud American company back into shape had begun several years before the tariff went into effect.

IMPROVING PRODUCTION[13]

In the early years Harley had been successfully run by engineers. Beals' background was in engineering as well, and he began to focus on the beleaguered production process. Until 1982, the company used a batch production system that produced only one model at a time. The final line work force would vary from 90–140 people depending on which model was being produced on a given day.

To make the production system more efficient, Beals, Thomas Gelb, and others on the management team, implemented what they called their productivity triad that included the following:

1. An inventory system that supplied materials as needed.

2. An employee involvement and development program.

3. A computer-aided design and manufacturing program.

The Materials As Needed (MAN) system stabilized the production schedule, and helped reduce excess inventory. Under this system, production worked with marketing to make more accurate demand forecasts for each model. Based on these forecasts, precise production schedules were established for a given month and were not allowed to vary by more than 10% in subsequent months. A production method was adopted whereby a different mix of models was produced every day. This was referred to as the "jelly bean" method.

Under the MAN system, Harley also required its suppliers to become more compliant to their quality requirements. Harley offered long-term contracts to suppliers who conformed to the quality requirements and who delivered only the exact quantity needed for a given period of time. Harley also integrated backward into transporting materials from suppliers: when the Harley-Davidson transportation company made scheduled pickups from suppliers, Harley had greater control over the shipments, and was thereby able to cut costs.

Before the 1983 tariff was imposed, Beals, Gelb, and others visited several Japanese motorcycle plants and learned the importance of employee development and employee involvement. As a result, rigorous training programs were developed. By 1986, over one-third of the employees were trained in statistical process control, or the ability to sample and analyze data while performing a job. Set-up times were reduced with the use of ideas gleaned from quality circles—problem-solving sessions between workers, managers, and engineers.

Further improvements in the production process were made by Walter Anderson, senior production engineer, with the help of Harley employees and management. Whereas components had formerly run down straight lines, Anderson organized workers into a series of "work cells." A work cell consisted of a few workers in a small area with all the machines and tools they needed to complete a job. The work cells were often arranged in U-shaped configurations that allowed for intensive work within a cell and reduced the total movement of components through the process. The use of cells also improved employee efficiency, because workers stayed at the same work station all day yet enjoyed variety in their tasks.

Harley also invested heavily in research and development. One payoff of this investment was a computer-aided design (CAD) system developed by the research and development group, that allowed management to make changes in the entire product line while maintaining elements of the traditional styling. The company's R&D group developed a more efficient engine in 1983 and a new suspension in 1984. Harley was soon recognized to be an industry leader in many aspects of production, including belt-drive technology, vibration isolation, and steering geometry. Since 1981, the company had allocated a major portion of its revenues to R&D each year.

Beals' emphasis on production brought big payoffs for the company. Harley's defect rate was reduced to nearly perfect, 1% in 1986. The company also lowered its breakeven point from 53,000 units in 1982, to 35,000 units in 1986.[14] Many companies visited Harley for seminars and advice on how to improve efficiency.

Perhaps one of the greatest indicators of Harley's production turnaround was evidenced through one of their oldest pieces of equipment—a huge, sheet-metal forming machine known simply as the "Tool." The Tool, originally built in Milwaukee but later moved to the York plant in Pennsylvania, was used to forge the "Fat Bob" gas tanks for all the FX and FXR series bikes. There was no operating manual nor maintenance book for the Tool, yet the company still used this old legendary machine to crank out modern, high-quality products (see Exhibit 7.2).

In March of 1987, Vaughn Beals appeared before a Washington, D.C. news conference and offered to give up the tariff protection, which was intended to last until the middle of 1988. Congress praised the announcement

EXHIBIT 7.2   Facilities, Harley-Davidson, Inc.

Type of Facility	LOCATION	AREA (sq. feet)	STATUS
Executive offices, engineering and warehouse	Milwaukee, Wisconsin	502,720	Owned
Manufacturing	Wauwatosa, Wisconsin	342,430	Owned
Manufacturing	Tomahawk, Wisconsin	50,600	Owned
Manufacturing	York, Pennsylvania	869,580	Owned
Engineering test laboratory	Milwaukee, Wisconsin	6,500	Lease expiring 1991
Motorcycle testing	Talladega, Alabama	9,326	Lease expiring 1988
International offices	Danbury, Connecticut	2,850	Lease expiring 1988
Office and workshop	Raunheim, West Germany	4,300	Lease expiring 1989

SOURCE: 1986 *Prospectus,* Dean Witter Reynolds.

and commended the company for its success. President Reagan even visited the York plant in celebration of the event.

CORPORATE STRUCTURE[15]

According to Beals, one of the most important contributions to the company's turnaround was the savings obtained by a drastic reduction in salaried staff, a result of Beals' exposure to the Japanese management systems. The number of managers at each plant was reduced, and each manager was given responsibility for everything at the plant: hiring, operations, productivity, etc.

The number of line employees was also reduced. Line employees were given individual responsibility to inspect products for defects, apply quality-control measures, determine quotas and goals, and make production decisions.

A majority of the company's employees participated actively in quality-circle programs. The quality circles were used not only to improve efficiency but also to address other issues. One such issue was job security. Both the reduction in staff and the increased productivity caused workers to worry about their jobs. However, the quality circles came up with the idea to move some sourcing and fabricating of parts in-house. In-house sourcing made it possible for many employees, who may have otherwise been laid off, to retain their jobs.

Harley's corporate staff was made very lean and the structure was simplified. Top executive officers were put in charge of functional areas. Under top management, the company was basically organized into two divisions—motorcycles and defense. Holiday Rambler Corporation became a wholly owned subsidiary in 1986.

TOP MANAGEMENT[16]

Vaughn L. Beals, Jr. was appointed as the Chief Executive Officer and Chairman of the Board of Directors of Harley-Davidson motor company following the buyout from AMF in 1981. He had originally earned an engineering degree from the Massachusetts Institute of Technology. He worked as a logging-machine manufacturer and as a diesel engine maker before joining AMF in 1975. In 1981, along with one of the grandsons of the founder and twelve other persons, he led the leveraged buyout of the Harley-Davidson Motor Company. He was known throughout the company for his devotion and enthusiasm for motorcycles. He owned a Harley deluxe Electra-Glide and rode it on business trips whenever possible.

Harley's top management always demonstrated their willingness to take a "hog" on the road for a worthy cause. On one occasion, in 1985, Beals and a product designer, William G. Davidson (known as "Willie G"), led a caravan of Harleys from California to New York in an effort to raise money for the Statue of Liberty renovation. At the conclusion of the ride, Beals presented a check for $250,000 to the Statue Foundation.

Beals claimed that his major responsibility was for product-quality improvements. On one occasion, during a business trip, Beals noticed a defect in a 1986 model's seat. He stopped long enough to call the factory about the problem. The workers and test riders, however, had already found and corrected the flaw.

Beals made an all-out effort to keep managerial levels in the company to a minimum. The Board of Directors was composed of six officers, four of whom were from outside the company. The CEO often communicated with everyone in the company through memos known as "Beals'-grams" (see Exhibits 7.3 and 7.4).

Because of the company's success, and in an effort to provide additional capital for growth, Harley went public with an offering of approximately 6 million shares in the summer of 1986. Beals owned nearly 16% of the Harley-Davidson stock, which was then increasing in value.

HUMAN RESOURCE MANAGEMENT[17]

Harley-Davidson employed approximately 2,336 people in 1986. This number was down from that of 3,840 in 1981. Under Chief Executive Beals, the company made great strides in developing a participative, cooperative, less hierarchical work climate. Employees wrote their own job descriptions and actively participated in on-the-job training. Employees learned that they were responsible for not only their own jobs, but for helping others learn as well. Performance was evaluated through a peer review program.

The company developed many career and placement opportunity programs as a response to employees' concern over job security. Harley also entered into a cooperative placement agreement with other Wisconsin unions.

EXHIBIT 7.3   **Board of Directors, Harley-Davidson, Inc.**

Vaugh L. Beals, Jr.
Chairman, President and Chief Executive Officer—Harley-Davidson, Inc., Milwaukee, Wisconsin

Frederick L. Brengel
Chairman and Chief Executive Officer—Johnson Controls, Inc., Milwaukee, Wisconsin

F. Trevor Deeley
Chairman and Chief Executive Officer—Fred Deeley Imports, Richmond, British Columbia, Canada

Dr. Michael J. Kami
President—Corporate Planning, Inc., Lighthouse Point, Florida

Richard Hermon-Taylor
Management Consultant, South Hamilton, Massachusetts

Richard F. Teerlink
Vice President, Treasurer and Chief Financial Officer—Harley-Davidson, Inc., Milwaukee, Wisconsin

SOURCE: 1986 *Annual Report*

EXHIBIT 7.4   **Harley-Davidson Executive Officers**

	AGE	POSITION	YEARS WITH COMPANY[1]	ANNUAL COMPENSATION
Vaughn L. Beals	58	Chairman and CEO	10	$207,217
Richard F. Teerlink	49	Vice-President, Chief Finance Officer	5	$143,375
Jeffrey L. Bleustein	46	Vice-President, Parts and Accessories	15	$118,387
Thomas A. Gelb	50	Vice-President, Operations	21	$132,666
James H. Paterson	38	Vice-President, Marketing	15	$ 95,728
Peter L. Profumo	39	Vice-President, Program Management	17	$129,521

[1]Years with Harley-Davidson or AMF, Inc.

SOURCE: 1986 *Prospectus,* Dean Witter Reynolds.

The company even developed a voluntary layoff program, in which senior workers voluntarily took themselves off in down times to protect the jobs of newer workers. Harley offered sophisticated health and retirement benefits, and has also developed employee wellness and college tuition funding programs.

FINANCIAL PERFORMANCE

Harley was purchased from AMF through a leveraged buyout in 1981, for approximately $65 million.[18] The buyout was financed with a $30 million term loan and $35 million in revolving credit from institutional lenders. AMF also received $9 million of securities in the form of preferred stock. In 1984, the two companies reached an agreement whereby the preferred stock held by AMF was cancelled and subsequent payments were to be made directly to AMF from future Harley-Davidson profits.

In 1985, Harley negotiated an exchange of common stock for forgiveness of a portion of the loans. The company offered $70 million in subordinated notes and $20 million in stock for public sale in 1986. The proceeds from this sale were used to repay a portion of the debt to AMF, to refinance unfavorable loans, to provide financing for the Holiday acquisition, and to provide working capital.

Holiday Rambler Corporation was a privately held company until its acquisition by Harley in 1986. Holiday Rambler performed very well in its first year as part of Harley-Davidson. It had total sales of approximately $257 million through September of 1987, compared to $208 million for the same period in 1986; this was nearly a 24% increase.

Harley-Davidson's net sales and profitability improved during the years 1982 to 1986. Net income and earnings per share fluctuated in that period. The motorcycle division's sales as a percentage of total sales decreased, because of the rapid increase in the defense division. In the years following the 1981 buyout, the company relied greatly on credit for working capital (see Exhibits 7.5, 7.6, and 7.7).

MARKETING STRATEGY

Harley-Davidson's marketing efforts centered around the use of the Harley name. The company emphasized that its name was synonymous with quality, reliability, and styling. Company research indicated a 90% repurchase rate, or loyalty factor, by Harley owners.

Harley's marketing concentrated on dealer promotions, magazine advertising, direct mail advertising, sponsorship of racing activities, and the organization of the Harley Owners Group (HOG). The HOG club had enrolled 77,000 members by 1987, and permitted the company to have close contact with customers. Another major form of advertising was accomplished through the licensing of the Harley name, which was very profitable and served to promote the company's image.

In addition, Harley sponsored or co-sponsored organizations such as the Ellis Island Statue of Liberty Foundation and the Muscular Dystrophy Association.

The company was also the first motorcycle manufacturer to offer a national program of demonstration rides. Some dealers felt the program, introduced in 1984, resulted in a large number of Harley motorcycle purchases.

The company also directed a portion of its marketing expenditures toward expanding the field sales force, in an effort to assist the domestic dealer network. In some areas the sales force developed local marketing programs to train dealers.

THE HARLEY IMAGE

Few companies could elicit the name recognition and brand loyalty of Harley-Davidson. Harley's appeal was based on the thrill and prestige of owning and riding the king of the big bikes. Harleys were known as sturdy, powerful, macho bikes; not for wimps and kids, they were true bikes for the open road, bikes for driving through brick walls!

A worrisome problem with the Harley image, however, was the perceptual connection of Harleys exclusively with "outlaw" groups. The negative "Road Warrior" image affected sales in some areas to such a degree that the

EXHIBIT 7.5

Harley-Davidson, Inc.: Consolidated Balance Sheet
(Dollar Amount in Thousands)

Year Ended December 31	1984	1985	1986
Assets			
Current assets:			
Cash	$ 2,056	$ 9,070	$ 7,345
Temporary investments	—	4,400	20,500
Accounts receivable net of allowance for doubtful accounts	27,767	27,313	36,462
Inventories	32,736	28,868	78,630
Prepaid expenses	2,613	3,241	5,812
Total current assets	65,172	72,892	148,758
Property, plant and equipment, at cost, less accumulated depreciation and amortization	33,512	38,727	90,932
Deferred financing costs	—	2,392	3,340
Intangible assets	—	—	82,114
Other assets	523	81	2,052
	$99,207	$114,092	$327,196
Liabilities and Stockholders' Equity			
Current liabilities:			
Notes payable	$ —	$ —	$ 14,067
Current maturities of long-term debt	2,305	2,875	4,023
Accounts payable	21,880	27,521	29,587
Accrued expenses and other liabilities	24,231	26,251	61,144
Total current liabilities	48,416	56,647	108,821
Long-term debt, less current maturities	56,258	51,504	191,594
Long-term pension liability	856	1,319	622
Stockholders' equity			
Common stock 6,200,000 issued in 1986 and 4,200,000 in 1985	42	42	62
Class B common stock, no shares issued	—	—	—
Additional paid-in capital	9,308	10,258	26,657
Deficit	(15,543)	(5,588)	(717)
Cumulative foreign currency translation adjustment	—	40	287
	(6,193)	4,752	26,289
Less treasury stock (520,000 shares) at cost	(130)	(130)	(130)
Total stockholders' equity	(6,323)	4,622	26,159
	$99,207	$114,092	$327,196

SOURCES: 1986 *Annual report;* 1986 *Prospectus*—Dean Witter Reynolds

EXHIBIT 7.6 — Harley-Davidson, Inc.: Consolidated Statement of Income
(Dollar Amounts in Thousands Except Per-Share Data)

Year Ended December 31	1982	1983	1984	1985	1986
Income statement data:					
Net sales	$ 210,055	$ 253,505	$ 293,825	$ 287,476	$ 295,322
Cost of goods sold	174,967	194,271	220,040	217,222	219,167
Gross profit	35,088	59,234	73,785	70,254	76,153
Operating expenses:					
Selling and administrative	37,510	36,441	47,662	47,162	51,060
Engineering, research and development	13,072	9,320	10,591	10,179	8,999
Total operating expenses	50,582	45,761	58,253	57,341	60,059
Income (loss) from operations	(15,494)	13,473	15,532	12,913	16,096
Other income (expenses):					
Interest expense	(15,778)	(11,782)	(11,256)	(9,412)	(8,373)
Other	(1,272)	188	(311)	(388)	(388)
	(17,050)	(11,594)	(11,567)	(9,750)	(8,761)
Income (loss) before provision (credit) for income taxes, extraordinary items, and cumulative effect of change in accounting principle	(32,544)	1,879	3,965	3,163	7,335
Provision (credit) for income taxes	(7,467)	906	1,077	526	3,028
Income (loss) before extraordinary items and cumulative effect of change in accounting principle	(25,077)	973	2,888	2,637	4,307
Extraordinary items and cumulative effect of change in accounting principle	—	7,795	3,578	7,318	564
Net income (loss)	$ (25,077)	$ 8,768	$ 6,466	$ 9,955	$ 4,871
Average number of common shares outstanding	4,016,664	3,720,000	3,680,000	3,680,000	5,235,230
Per common share:					
Income (loss) before extraordinary items and cumulative effect of change in accounting principle	$ (6.61)	$ .26	$ .79	$ .72	$ .82
Extraordinary items and cumulative effect of change in accounting principle	—	2.10	.97	1.99	.11
Net income (loss)	$ (6.61)	$ 2.36	$ 1.76	$ 2.71	$ .93

SOURCE: 1986 *Annual Report*.

EXHIBIT 7.7	**Harley-Davidson, Inc.: Sales and Income by Business Segment**

(Thousands of Dollars)

	1983	1984	1985
Net sales:			
Motorcycles and related products	$229,412	$260,745	$240,631
Defense and other businesses	24,093	33,080	46,845
	$253,505	$293,825	$287,476
Income from operations:			
Motorcycles and related products	$ 16,513	$ 15,489	$ 9,980
Defense and other businesses	3,566	7,012	9,390
General corporate expenses	(6,606)	(6,969)	(6,457)
	13,473	15,532	12,913
Interest expense	(11,782)	(11,256)	(9,412)
Other	188	(311)	(338)
Income before income taxes, extraordinary items and cumulative effect of change in accounting principle	$ 1,879	$ 3,965	$ 3,163

SOURCE: 1986 *Prospectus*—Dean Witter Reynolds.

company initiated a public relations campaign. They gently attacked the biker image by directing much of their advertising toward young professionals. The message was that Harley-Davidson represented fun, recreation, and reliability. The company heralded the fact that famous professionals such as Malcolm Forbes and Reggie Jackson rode Harleys, and advertisements picturing these celebrities atop their "hogs" further helped the company's image. The campaign seemed to work. More doctors, lawyers, and dentists began to purchase Harleys.

Harley also put tighter controls on licensing its name, ensuring that it was not used in obscene ways. Harley was careful not to alienate their loyal "biker" customers, however. And the company continued to promulgate, even enhance its tough image, through advertising in motorcycle magazines. For example, one ad pictured a group of rather tough looking bikers and had a caption which read: "Would you sell an unreliable bike to these guys? We Don't!" Another ad showed a junkyard filled with scrapped Japanese bikes. The caption was: "Can you find a Harley in here?"

A related problem with its image was that Harley could not attract very many women customers. This was due to the image and to the size of the bikes. Harleys were very big and heavy. The Harley low-rider series was attracting some women customers because the bikes were lower and easier to get on. Notwithstanding this partial success, some Japanese companies introduced smaller, lighter, low-riding, inexpensive, Harley look-alikes in a straightforward attempt to attract women buyers. Honda's "Rebel" (250cc) was one such bike that became fairly successful with women.

Perhaps the most objective indicator of the strength of the image came from an unlikely source—Japan itself! The Japanese made numerous attempts to copy Milwaukee designs.[19] For example, Suzuki's 1987 "Intruder" (1400cc) went to great lengths to hide the radiator—because Harleys were air cooled. Yamaha's "Virago" (1100cc) and Kawasaki's "Vulcan" (1500cc) were V-twin street bikes conspicuously styled in the Harley tradition. Nevertheless, some analysts felt that Japanese imitations only served to strengthen the mystique of the original. The more the Japanese tried to make look-alike bikes, the more the real thing increased in value. Beals agreed. He maintained that Harleys were built to last longer and have a higher resale than other bikes.

DIVERSIFICATION STRATEGY

Harley-Davidson competed in the heavyweight motorcycle market segment since the early years of the company. Heavyweight bikes were divided into three categories: touring/custom, standard street, and performance motorcycles. Harley was never totally successful in building smaller bikes, and at one time Beals was even quoted as saying that Harley would not attempt to build small bikes in the future.

Harley-Davidson had made attempts to diversify throughout its history. However, its current motorcycle product line was very narrow compared to those of its competitors. The company's management thought about breaking out of its narrow niche by expanding into international markets. The largest export markets for Harley were Canada, Australia, and West Germany.

In 1971, Harley attempted to diversify by manufacturing its own line of snowmobiles. The seasonal nature of the business and intense Japanese competition caused the company to abandon the product in 1975.

Another attempt at diversification was the company's purchase of a small three-wheeler firm named "Trihawk" in 1984. Shortly thereafter the company realized it could not make a go of it in this market because of high start-up costs, and the project was terminated.

Under Beals the company moved into the manufacturing of casings for artillery shells and rocket engines for military target drones. Beals set corporate goals to increase the level of defense-related business in an attempt to diversify the company. Thus, the company became very active in making bids for the design and development of defense products. The defense business was very profitable for Harley.

Accessories, bike parts, clothing, "leathers," even furniture associated with the Harley name were big businesses for the company. Brand-name licensing and related accessories generated about as much income as did the motorcycles.

But Beals wanted to move the company into other businesses not related to the rather narrow motorcycle line and not located in an industry with Japanese competitors. He felt Harley needed to diversify in order to be a truly stable performer. That is why Harley acquired the Holiday Rambler Company in December of 1986. Beals saw the fit as a good one because Holiday was a recreational vehicle producer and was what he called "manufacturing intensive" just as Harley was.

Holiday Rambler manufactured premium motorhomes, specialized commercial vehicles, and travel trailers. Holiday employed 2,300 people and was headquartered in Wakarusa, Indiana. Holiday was the largest privately owned maker of recreational vehicles at the time of the acquisition. The company was recognized as one of the leaders in the premium-class motorhome and towable-trailer markets. It ranked fourth, in 1986, in market share in the motorhome market and fifth in towable recreational vehicles. Its products were gaining share in the industry as a whole.

A Holiday subsidiary, Utilimaster, built truck trailers and bodies for commercial uses. The company had contracts with companies such as Purolator Courier and Ryder Truck Rentals. Other Holiday subsidiaries produced office furniture, custom wood products, custom tools, van conversions, and park trailers.

Even with the Holiday acquisition and with the success in defense, Harley looked for other means of diversifying. In September of 1986, a tobacco company purchased a license to test market Harley-Davidson brand cigarettes.

THE FUTURE

The Harley turnaround, in the face of stiff competition, caused the company to be viewed as an example of what can be accomplished by use of modern production and personnel-management techniques. Top management was committed to keeping the company lean and viable. Yet they knew they needed to diversify and change. Beals knew that his company needed to become as tough as its image.

Beals focused his turnaround effort on the internal operating efficiency of the company. Now he needed to provide leadership for a newly acquired subsidiary and plan for growth in the defense division.

He also faced the challenge of breaking the company out of its narrow market segment in its bread-and-butter division: motorcycles. Could he plan for growth and market penetration in the motorcycle industry? Or should he be content with maintaining Harley as a big bike company only?

Since 1903, 150 American motorcycle companies had come and gone. Harley-Davidson Motor Company, with Vaughn Beals at the helm, was the only one that survived. The eagle continued to soar alone.

NOTES

1. Harley-Davidson, Inc., 1986 *Annual Report.*

2. David K. Wright, *The Harley-Davidson Motor Company: An Official Eighty-Year History,* second edition (Osceola, Wisconsin: Motorbooks International), 1987.

3. *Ibid.,* p. 17.

4. *Ibid.,* p. 17.

5. *Ibid.,* p. 35.

6. *Ibid.,* pp. 282–283.

7. "Uneasy Rider: Harley Pleads for Relief," *Time,* (December 13, 1982), p. 61.

8. David K. Wright, *The Harley-Davidson Motor Company: An Official Eighty-Year History,* second edition (Osceola, Wisconsin: Motorbooks International), 1987, pp. 244–262.

9. "Trade Protection: Mind My (Motor) Bike," *The Economist,* (July 2, 1977), p. 82.

10. David K. Wright, *The Harley-Davidson Motor Company: An Official Eighty-Year History,* second edition (Osceola, Wisconsin: Motorbooks International), 1987, p. 281.

11. *Ibid.,* pp. 244–262.

12. Dean Witter Reynolds, *Prospectus,* Harley-Davidson, Inc., July 8, 1986, p. 8.

13. Rod Willis, "Harley-Davidson Comes Roaring Back," *Management Review,* (October, 1986), pp. 20–27.

14. *Ibid.*

15. *Ibid.*

16. Jeff Baily, "Beals Takes Harley-Davidson On New Road," *Wall Street Journal,* (March 20, 1987), p. 39.

17. Rod Willis, "Harley-Davidson Comes Roaring Back," *Management Review,* (October, 1986), pp. 20–27.

18. Dean Witter Reynolds, *Prospectus,* Harley-Davidson, Inc., July 8, 1986, p.10.

19. "Why Milwaukee Won't Die," *Cycle,* (June 1987), pp. 35–41.

Walt Disney Productions—1984

CHARLES B. SHRADER · J. DAVID HUNGER

"It's kind of fun to do the impossible."   WALT DISNEY

As 1984 was drawing to a close, Michael Eisner sat back in his chair, looked out the office window onto the busy Burbank, California streets, and pondered the future direction of Walt Disney Productions. The last few years had been somewhat painful for the company. Except for 1984, net income had declined steadily (see Exhibit 8.1). In 1980, net income had been $135.2 million and earnings per share (EPS) $4.16. Net income fell to $121.5 million in 1981, $100.1 million in 1982, and $93.1 million in 1983. In 1984, however, net income increased (because of an accounting change) to $97.8 million. EPS likewise dropped from $4.16 in 1980, to $3.72 in 1981, $3.01 in 1982, and $2.70 in 1983. EPS was $.61 in 1984 before accounting changes increased the figure to $2.73.

Even though Walt had died some twenty years ago, Eisner could almost feel his presence. Realizing that Disney Productions was an outgrowth of Walt's personal vision, Eisner was faced with making the company stand on its own, without Walt's guidance. The immediate greenmail threat was over but rumors of other takeover attempts persisted. The present relations with the Bass family, who own a large percentage of company stock, have helped stabilize the company. However, with so much ownership outside the Disney family, Eisner contemplated how the company's direction would change.

Should the new direction be toward more and better motion pictures, or toward revitalizing the theme parks? Walt Disney Productions experienced record theme park and box office attendance in 1978–1979. With the opening of EPCOT Center in Walt Disney World during 1982, the future of the company looked bright. Even when faced with gasoline and energy shortages in the late 1970s and early 1980s, the company remained optimistic. For example, the theme of Disney's 1983 annual report was "Looking to New Horizons." Theme park revenues were down in 1984, however, and Eisner knew that the demographic trends looked bad. He also knew that one of Disney's competitors, Taft Broadcasting Company, had recently sold its

This case was prepared by Professor Charles B. Schrader and Professor J. David Hunger of Iowa State University, Ames, Iowa. The authors thank David R. Smith, archivist, Walt Disney Productions–Burbank, and Terry McCorvie, press and publicity director, Walt Disney World, for helpful comments on earlier drafts of this case. This case also appears in the *Case Research Journal*, 1985, pp. 79–122. Reprinted by permission of the authors and the North American Case Research Association.

EXHIBIT 8.1 **Walt Disney Productions, 1980–1984**

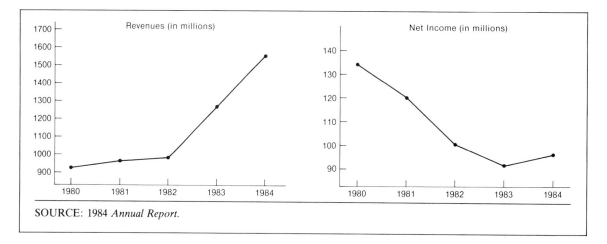

SOURCE: 1984 *Annual Report.*

theme parks in order to concentrate on expanding its communication businesses.

In 1984, Disney Productions had also suffered executive turnover, employee unrest, poor theme park attendance, and lackluster performance in the motion picture division. While top managers and board members were being shuffled, employees and shareholders had become increasingly critical of the company. The Disney image, strongly linked to family entertainment, had come under criticism for being out of date. Attempts to alter the firm's image did not sit well with much of top management. Disney encountered tough competition in its new cable TV and home video businesses. All in all, the events of 1984 caused management and the board of directors to be quite concerned about the future of Walt Disney Productions.

Michael Eisner, CEO only since September 1984, knew he would remember the past few months as a learning experience. With the year of Donald Duck's fiftieth birthday celebration coming to a close, Eisner wondered about the increasing pressure to reduce the corporation's focus on Mickey Mouse and other cartoon characters in order to emphasize more adult-oriented concepts. Did it make sense to put more money into motion pictures and to cut back investment in theme parks? What would Walt think of all the changes going on in his company, especially since it had recently been listed as "excellent" and as one of the best places in which to work?

As he rose pensively from his chair, Eisner picked up his coat and prepared to leave. He looked forward to 1985. It would certainly be an interesting year.

**WALT DISNEY—
COMPANY
HISTORY**[1,2]

"What do you do with all your money?" a friend once asked Walt. Pointing at the studio Walt said, "I fertilize the field with it."

"To the bankers I'm sure he seemed like a wild man, hell-bent for bankruptcy."

Roy O. Disney

Walter Elias Disney was born in Chicago on December 5, 1901. Walt was the fourth son of Elias Disney, a farmer, preacher, and builder, who at one time ran a hotel in Daytona Beach, Florida, only seventy miles from the present Walt Disney World. When Walt was five years old, his family moved from Chicago to a farm in Marceline, Missouri, where Walt spent most of his childhood. Walt loved the orchards and scenery of the farm. It was this memory of Marceline that provided Walt's inspiration for Disneyland's Main Street. Walt developed an interest in drawing. By the time his family moved to Kansas City during his grammar school years, his ambition was to be a cartoonist.

In World War I Walt drove an ambulance for the Red Cross. After the war, Walt returned to Kansas City to look for work as a newspaper cartoonist. Eventually his brother Roy found him a job with the Pesman-Rubin art studio where Walt made drawings for catalogues and advertisements. At Pesman-Rubin, Walt met fellow artist Ubbe ("Ub") Iwerks. Walt and Ub began a friendship that would last throughout Walt's life. After being laid off at the studio, Walt and Ub decided to start their own business. Using borrowed equipment and money, Walt experimented with animation in his brother Herbert's garage. He and Ub made one-minute cartoons called *Laugh-O-Grams* based on popular fairy tales, and sold the cartoons for small fees. With a borrowed $15,000, Walt, Ub, and some other artists incorporated *Laugh-O-Grams* in 1922. Walt sold very few of the cartoons and the business failed one year later.

Early Hollywood Years

The company declared bankruptcy and Walt moved to Hollywood, California. In Hollywood, Walt was turned down both as a director and as an extra. He decided to give animation another try. With the help of Roy and a generous uncle, the Disney Brothers studio was started in 1923. Walt used the profits from his first series to expand the studios and to hire artists and animators, and was continually narrowing his profit margin. Walt hired his friend Ub to work for him in 1924. However, interest in the Disney cartoons started to fade and the Disney Studios needed a creative boost.

In 1926, Charles Mintz, Disney's distributor, suggested a new cartoon about a rabbit. Walt made the animation and Mintz gave the rabbit the name Oswald. With the creation of Oswald the Rabbit, Walt started an animation technique that would stay with him throughout most of his career.

The cartoon characters first were drawn in rough form. The rough animation was then projected and checked many times over in its basic form until Walt okayed the action. After Walt's approval, the final touches and detail were added to the cartoon. This technique vastly improved the quality of the animation and made Oswald a big success.

It was with Oswald that Walt had another influential experience. Oswald was so popular that firms were using him to promote their products. Walt received no royalties from Oswald but saw use of the rabbit as good advertising for his studios. Therefore, he continued to spend time and money perfecting Oswald even after the cartoon was a popular success. Mintz liked the cartoon but was unhappy with the amount of money Walt was spending. Many arguments between Disney and Mintz ensued over financial matters. Finally, after a contract dispute, Mintz kept the rights to Oswald and hired all of Disney's animators (except Ub) to work for him. With Disney Studios now in dire need of a new character, Walt and Ub began work on a new cartoon featuring a mouse. From this time forward, Walt was to maintain close control over his cartoon characters.

In 1928, Walt and Ub created Mickey Mouse. Ub did the drawings and Walt did Mickey's voice. Mickey starred in the first fully synchronized sound cartoon, *Steamboat Willie,* in 1928, and was a huge success. Disney won his first Oscar in 1932, which was followed by an Oscar in 1933 for *The Three Little Pigs.* In the 1930s Disney used his cartoon characters, such as Mickey, Goofy, and Donald Duck, in the merchandising of other products. The company grew despite the Depression and Walt gave his employees a raise even though he received financial advice to the contrary.

During the company's early growth years, Walt's brother Roy acted as financial advisor while Walt was the entrepreneur, or idea man. Roy would try to find a way to finance whatever Walt wanted. Walt reinvested the money in the company as soon as it came in. Walt did no drawing after 1924, but instead, focused on developing his dreams for the company's future.

Becoming a Major Motion Picture Company

Disney made the first feature-length cartoon, *Snow White and the Seven Dwarfs,* in 1937. *Snow White* was a major success. It was with this film that Walt perfected the "multiplane" animation technique. This technique further added to the quality of animation by creating the perception of depth in the cartoon. Subsequent to *Snow White,* the company experienced a spurt in growth. The staff grew from 100 to 750. Disney continued to pour the profits back into the studios, and in 1940, the studio moved to its present home in Burbank.

Also in 1940, Disney made an animated feature called *Fantasia.* Walt was especially proud of this film. *Fantasia* combined animation with classical music in a series of vignettes, such as *The Sorcerer's Apprentice*. It was artistically acclaimed, but was a failure at the box office (until the 1970s, when it became a cult film). *Fantasia* caused the studio to lose a great deal of money. As a result, the banks decided to hold off financing or advancing any more money to Walt. In an attempt to raise needed money, the Disney brothers offered stock to the public for the first time. Walt's major concerns were quality and company growth rather than stockholder returns, so he continued the practice of putting most of the profits back into the company. Walt made a profit-sharing commitment to his employees at this time, but he gave the employees stock instead of cash. The stock was not very valuable in the 1940s so the disgruntled employees went on strike for more money. The employees claimed that they were being used only for Disney's gain. Walt took the strike personally even though it lasted only a short time. As a result of the strike, the Screen Cartoonists Guild was created.

Expansion into Television and Theme Parks

The Disney studio made training films for the government during World War II. In 1950, Disney became one of the first members of the motion picture industry to become involved with television. Disney reached an agreement with ABC TV in 1954 to do weekly programs if ABC in turn would help finance Walt's newest dream, Disneyland. ABC aired a program called *Disneyland,* which was organized around the same themes as the park. For example, a *Frontierland* program might include an episode about Davy Crockett. In 1955, *The Mickey Mouse Club* was first seen on TV. In July of 1955, Disneyland opened in Anaheim, California. (Disney later bought out ABC's interest in Disneyland.) It was also during the early 1950s that Buena Vista Distribution Company was formed to distribute Disney films. These actions were further indications of Walt's desire to hold the rights to his work. Disney used the TV programs and Disneyland to promote his films. During the 1950s the company became financially sound.

In the 1960s Disney experimented with combining animation and live action in films. The successful film *Mary Poppins* was a good example of this process. In 1964, the company formed a subsidiary to acquire land in Florida upon which Walt Disney World would be built. Walt's dream was to build a community of the future in Florida. He died in 1966 before his dream was finished. Roy took over the company after Walt was gone and continued work on Walt Disney World. The Orlando, Florida, theme park opened in October 1971. Unfortunately Roy died in December of that same year. E. Cardon Walker succeeded Roy as President of the company. Walker, who had experience in a variety of Disney operations, had been with the company for thirty-three years prior to being president. It was in 1982, during Walker's administration, that the community of the future (EPCOT), Walt's final dream, was completed.

The Dream Becomes Reality

The growth and creativity of Walt Disney Productions was largely due to Walt Disney himself. Disney was an entrepreneur and a dreamer. His full-

---

EXHIBIT 8.2 | **Walt Disney Productions, Inc.: Consolidated Statement of Changes in Financial Position**
(Dollar Amounts in Thousands)

Year Ended September 30	1984	1983	1982	1981	1980
Cash Provided by Operations					
before Taxes on Income	$364,024	308,369	309,431	316,949	326,504
Taxes received (paid) on income—net	50,012	28,987	(34,649)	(106,144)	(121,822)
Cash provided by operations	414,036	337,356	274,782	210,805	204,682
Cash dividends	40,941	41,100	39,742	32,406	23,280
	373,095	296,256	235,040	178,399	181,402
Investing Activities					
Common stock repurchase	327,679	—	—	—	—
Attractions, property, & net payables	194,142	333,738	614,416	333,407	149,674
Film production & program costs	127,595	83,750	52,295	55,454	68,409
Rights to the Walt Disney name	—	(3,640)	40,000	—	—
EPCOT & Disney Channel start-up costs	—	18,253	19,170	1,907	—
Long-term notes receivable & other	8,542	11,406	26,881	4,023	1,619
	682,296	443,507	752,762	394,791	219,702
	(309,201)	(147,251)	(517,722)	(216,392)	(38,300)
Financing Activities					
Long-term borrowings	421,119	137,500	205,000	110,000	—
Reduction of long-term borrowings	(126,593)	(99,925)	—	—	—
Common stock offering	—	70,883	—	—	—
Common stock issued (ret.) for rights to Disney name & certain equipment	—	(3,640)	46,200	—	—
Participation fees, net of related receivables	6,892	11,169	23,867	24,745	10,361
Collection of notes & other	11,835	35,667	2,030	7,646	1,327
	313,253	151,654	277,097	142,391	11,688
Increase (Decrease) in Cash	4,052	4,403	(240,625)	(74,001)	(26,612)
Cash & short-term invest., beg. yr.	31,294[1]	13,652	254,277	328,278	354,890
Cash & short-term invest., end yr.	$ 35,346	$ 18,055	$ 13,652	$254,277	$328,278

SOURCE: 1984, 1983, & 1980 *Annual Reports.*

[1]Includes $13,239 for Arvida in 1984.

length animated films became the state of the art for the industry. His architectural genius and his landscaping designs have received international acclaim. Disney received 32 Academy awards, 5 Emmy awards, and over 900 citations for his work. All of the company's activities through EPCOT Center were generated by Walt. Walt was fascinated with technology and much of what is seen at other theme parks was originated by Walt at Disneyland. He built a company on the philosophy of providing high-quality entertainment for all ages. Walt once said, "You can't live on things made for children or for critics. I've never made films for either of them. Disneyland is not just for children. I don't play down." When Disney died in 1966, the company's profits were at an all-time high. Walt Disney believed his various businesses were inseparable, so he used his TV programs, Disneyland, and movies to promote one another.

The current Walt Disney Productions is a diversified international company engaged in family entertainment. It operates three major business segments:[3] *Entertainment and Recreation, Filmed Entertainment,* and *Consumer Products.* A fourth segment, *Community Development,* was added upon the purchase of Arvida during 1984. The recreation enterprise includes two major theme parks: Disneyland in California, and Walt Disney World in Florida. The company also produces full-length motion pictures, recorded music, educational media, home video products, and a variety of other consumer products. The company is also involved in real estate development and transportation. The company's financial position is presented in Exhibits 8.2, 8.3, 8.4, and 8.5.

ENTERTAINMENT AND RECREATION

Walt Disney Productions operates two major theme parks: Disneyland in California and Walt Disney World in Florida. The Walt Disney World complex includes EPCOT Center, the Magic Kingdom, three hotels, golf courses, camp grounds, shops, restaurants, a conference center, and other recreational facilities. Walt Disney Productions also receives royalties from Tokyo Disneyland, which is run by a Japanese company. The following is a summary of the recent performance of this business segment:

Entertainment and Recreation (in Thousands)

	1984	Change	1983	Change	1982
Revenues	$1,097,359	+6%	$1,031,202	+42%	$725,610
Operating Income	192,695	−2%	196,878	48%	131,645
Operating Margin	18%		19%		18%
Theme Park Attendance	30,990	−5%	32,692	+42%	22,981

SOURCE: 1984 *Annual Report.*

EXHIBIT 8.3   **Walt Disney Productions and Subsidiaries: Consolidated Financial Statements**

(Dollar Amounts in Thousands Except Per-Share Data)

CONSOLIDATED STATEMENT OF INCOME

Year Ended September 30	1984	1983	1982	1981	1980
Revenues					
Entertainment & recreation	$1,097,359	$1,031,202	$725,610	$691,811	$643,380
Filmed entertainment	244,552	165,458	202,102	196,806	171,965
Community development	204,384				
Consumer products	109,683	110,697	102,538	116,423	99,160
	1,655,977	1,307,357	1,030,250	1,005,040	914,505
Costs and Expenses					
Entertainment & recreation	904,664	834,324	592,965	562,337	515,848
Filmed entertainment	242,303	198,843	182,463	162,180	112,725
Community development	162,158				
Consumer products	55,819	53,815	54,706	65,869	54,632
	1,364,944	1,086,982	830,134	790,376	683,205
Income (Loss) Before Corporate Expenses & Unusual Charges					
Entertainment & recreation	192,965	196,878	132,645	129,474	127,532
Filmed entertainment	2,249	(33,385)	19,639	34,626	48,675
Community development	42,226				
Consumer products	53,863	56,882	47,832	50,564	55,093
	291,033	220,375	200,116	214,664	231,300
Corporate Expenses (Income)					
General & administrative	59,570	35,554	30,957	26,216	21,130
Design projects abandoned	7,032	7,295	5,147	4,598	4,294
Interest expense (income) net	41,738	14,006	(14,781)	(33,130)	(42,110)
	108,340	56,915	21,323	(2,316)	(16,686)
Income Before Unusual Charges, Taxes, & Accounting Change	182,693	163,460	178,793	216,980	247,986
Unusual charges[1]	165,960				
Income Before Taxes & Accounting Change	16,733	163,460	178,793	216,980	247,986
Taxes on income (benefit)	(5,000)	70,300	78,700	95,500	112,800

CONSOLIDATED STATEMENT OF INCOME

Year Ended September 30	1984	1983	1982	1981	1980
Income Before Accounting Change	21,733	93,160	100,093	121,480	135,186
Cumulative effect of change in acct. for investment tax credits[2]	76,111				
Net Income	$97,844	$93,160	$100,093	$121,480	$135,186
Earnings Per Share					
Income before accounting change	$0.61	$2.70	$3.01	$3.72	$4.16
Cumulative effect of acct. change	2.12				
	$2.73	$2.70	$3.01	$3.72	$4.16
Average number of common and uncommon equivalent shares outstanding	35,849	34,481	33,225		

CONSOLIDATED BALANCE SHEET

Year Ended September 30	1984	1983	1982	1981	1980
Assets					
Current Assets					
Cash	$35,346	18,055	13,652	5,869	9,745
Accounts receivable, net of allowances	172,762	102,847	78,968	69,302	50,711
Short term investments				248,408	318,533
Income taxes refundable	60,000	70,000	41,000		
Inventories[3]	312,891	77,945	66,717	59,773	54,648
Film production costs	102,462	44,412	43,850	59,079	61,127
Prepaid expenses		19,843	18,152	15,398	11,438
Total Current Assets	683,461	333,102	262,339	457,829	506,202
Film Production Costs—Non-Current		82,598	64,217	61,561	59,281
Property, plant and equipment					
Entertainment attractions, buildings & equipment	2,413,985	2,251,297	1,916,617	968,223	935,152
Less accumulated depreciation	(600,156)	(504,365)	(419,944)	(384,535)	(352,051)
	1,813,829	1,746,932	1,496,673	583,688	583,101

(Continued)

EXHIBIT 8.3 (Continued)

CONSOLIDATED BALANCE SHEET

Year Ended September 30	1984	1983	1982	1981	1980
Assets (continued)					
Construction & design projects in progress					
EPCOT Center		70,331	120,585	439,858	141,373
Other	94,710	37,859	39,601	29,404	21,658
Land	28,807	16,687	16,379	16,419	16,414
	1,937,346	1,871,809	1,673,238	1,069,369	762,546
Other Assets	118,636	93,686	103,022	21,250	19,378
Total Assets	$2,739,443	2,381,195	2,102,816	1,610,009	1,347,407
Liabilities and Stockholders' Equity					
Current Liabilities					
Accounts payable	$239,992	187,641	210,753	158,516	109,047
Taxes on income	24,145	50,557	26,560	33,057	36,244
Total current liabilities	264,137	238,198	237,313	191,573	145,291
Long Term Borrowings	861,909	346,325	315,000		
Other Long Term Liabilities and Non-Current Advances	178,907	110,874	94,739	161,886	30,429
Deferred Taxes on Income and Investment Credits	279,005	285,270	180,980	89,432	96,889
Commitments and Contingencies					
Stockholders Equity					
Preferred & Common Shares	359,988	661,934	588,250	540,935	537,689
Retained Earnings	795,497	738,594	686,534	626,183	537,109
	1,155,485	1,400,528	1,274,784	1,167,118	1,074,798
Total Liab. & Stockholders Equity	$2,739,443	2,381,195	2,102,816	1,610,009	1,347,407

SOURCES: 1984, 1983, & 1981 *Annual Reports.*

[1]The unusual charges in 1984 were due to adjustments in the carrying values and write downs for several motion picture and television properties.

[2]The company changed its accounting for investment tax credits to the flow-through method in the fourth quarter of 1984.

[3]1984 inventory figure includes real estate.

EXHIBIT 8.4   **Walt Disney Productions and Subsidiaries: Other Financial Data**
(Dollar Amounts in Thousands)

	1984	1983	1982	1981	1980
Entertainment and Recreation					
Walt Disney World					
Admissions & rides	$ 295,921	278,320	153,504	139,326	130,144
Merchandise sales	182,804	172,324	121,410	121,465	116,187
Food sales	177,078	178,791	121,329	114,951	106,404
Lodging	104,779	98,105	81,427	70,110	61,731
Disneyland					
Admissions & rides	110,723	102,619	98,273	92,065	87,066
Merchandise sales	79,260	72,300	76,684	79,146	72,140
Food sales	46,770	45,699	44,481	44,920	41,703
Participant fees, Walt Disney Travel Co., Tokyo Disneyland royalties and other	100,024	83,044	28,502	29,828	28,005
	$1,097,359	1,031,202	725,610	691,811	643,380
Theme park total attendance					
Walt Disney World	21,121	22,712	12,560	13,221	13,783
Disneyland	9,869	9,980	10,421	11,343	11,522
	30,990	32,692	22,981	24,564	25,305
Filmed Entertainment					
Theatrical					
Domestic	$ 70,679	38,635	55,408	54,624	63,350
Foreign	38,182	43,825	64,525	76,279	78,314
Television					
Worldwide	57,479	27,992	44,420	43,672	19,736
Home video and non-theatrical					
Worldwide	78,212	55,006	37,749	22,231	10,565
	$ 244,552	165,548	202,102	196,806	171,965
Community Development					
Residential	$ 53,038	—	—	—	—
Land & commercial property	90,166	—	—	—	—
Resorts & other	61,180	—	—	—	—
	$ 204,384	—	—	—	—

(Continued)

EXHIBIT 8.4 (Continued)

	1984	1983	1982	1981	1980
Consumer Products					
Character merchandise	$ 42,750	45,429	35,912	30,555	29,631
Publications	18,184	20,006	20,821	24,658	22,284
Records & music	33,734	30,666	26,884	27,358	23,342
Educational media	11,509	10,269	15,468	21,148	21,908
Other	3,505	4,327	3,453	12,704	1,905
	$ 109,682	110,629	102,538	116,423	99,160

SOURCE: *1984 Annual Report.*

Disneyland

" . . . the only new towns of any significance built in America since World War II are Disneyland . . . and Disney World . . ."

New York Magazine

Disneyland is located in Anaheim, California, approximately 40 miles south of Los Angeles. The park covers 76.6 acres with a parking facility covering 107.3 acres. There are approximately 40 acres adjacent to the park that Disney has on a long-term lease. Disneyland is the oldest "theme park" in the United States. A theme park differs from an amusement park in that a theme park offers rides, exhibits, restaurants, and shows in the context of an overall theme. For example, Sea World and Marineland are based on oceanographic themes while Disneyland and King's Island are centered around cartoon and movie characters.

When Disneyland opened in 1955, there were 17 attractions; now there are 57. Adventureland, Bear Country, Fantasyland, Frontierland, Main Street, New Orleans Square, and Tomorrowland comprise the seven major areas of the park. Disneyland leases exhibits to corporate sponsors in an attempt to continuously improve and update the park. Corporate sponsors include American Telephone and Telegraph Company, Gulf Oil Corporation, McDonnell Douglas Corporation, Oscar Meyer and Company, and Welch Foods, Inc.[4] Each sponsor pays Disney an annual participation fee for rent and the rights to use the Disney name in advertising the exhibit.

The most significant expansion project of the park in 1983–1984 was the restoration of Fantasyland. The expansion included the use of three-dimensional animation, fiber optics, black light painting, and other special effects to update attractions such as *Alice in Wonderland*.

In each of the park's seven areas there are shops and restaurants with cuisine in keeping with the area theme. For example, *Pinocchio* is the theme of the Village Inn restaurant in Fantasyland. On the average, Disneyland

EXHIBIT 8.5   **Walt Disney Productions, Inc.: Theme Park Information**

	ATTENDANCE	REVENUES
Disneyland		
1976	10,211,000	$122,473,000
1977	10,678,000	140,555,000
1978	10,807,000	158,274,000
1979	10,760,000	177,730,000
1980	11,522,000	207,059,000
1981	11,343,000	222,391,000
1982	10,421,000	225,120,000
1983	9,980,000	220,618,000[1]
1984	9,869,000	236,753,000[1]
Walt Disney World/EPCOT		
1976	13,107,000	$275,386,000
1977	13,057,000	300,515,000
1978	14,071,000	345,638,000
1979	13,792,000	389,623,000
1980	13,783,000	433,377,000
1981	13,221,000	465,436,000
1982	12,560,000	497,445,000
1983	22,712,000	727,540,000[1]
1984	21,121,000	760,582,000[1]

SOURCES: 1980, 1981, 1982, 1983, and 1984 *Annual Reports.*

[1]Estimates based on 1983 and 1984 aggregate data.

restaurants serve 60,000 meals per day or 4,000 people per hour. The park is covered with some 500,000 constantly groomed trees and shrubs. Disneyland is open year-round with its peak season in summer. Other high attendance times are spring school vacation, Easter, Christmas, and other holidays. Financial data for Disneyland are given in Exhibits 8.4 and 8.5

In 1980, Disneyland attracted 11.5 million people, an all-time Disneyland high. Attendance has declined steadily since then. In 1984, for example, attendance was down to 9.9 million. The two Disney theme parks account for 33% of all U.S. theme park attendance. Walt Disney Productions is dependent on theme park attendance for most of its revenue. Therefore, for Disney Productions, the decline in attendance has been painful. Disney officials blame decreases in attendance on high gasoline prices, gasoline shortages, poor economic conditions, changes in U.S. demographics, and poor weather. A harsh winter was blamed for poor attendance during 1983. A low attendance in summer 1984 was blamed on the Olympics held in nearby Los Angeles.

Attendance at Knott's Berry Farm, located in Buena Park in the same county as Disneyland, however, increased by 10% in both 1983 and 1984. Attendance at Sea World in San Diego and Marineland in Los Angeles county did not drop either during that same time.

Knott's Berry Farm is known for restaurants and shops but also has a large section devoted to rides. Knott's reduced their admission price by 20% in 1983–1984. During 1983, Disneyland admission prices increased by 6% and per capita spending was up. Thus Disneyland is in a paradoxical situation. The park has been improved and revenues are up, but attendance and profits are down.

Walt Disney World

"You can see more respectful courteous people at Disney World in one afternoon than in New York in a year."

Wall Street Journal

"If we can bring together the technical know-how of American industry and the creative imagination of the Disney organization—I'm confident we can create right here in Disney World a showcase to the world of the American free enterprise system."

Walt Disney

Walt Disney World, the most advanced entertainment complex in the world, is located 15 miles southwest of Orlando, Florida, on 28,000 acres of land. Walt Disney World is a complete "vacationland" with hotels, resorts, campgrounds, aquatic recreational facilities, sport facilities, and golf courses. There is also a shopping village and a special transportation system. Part of the park is the "Magic Kingdom" theme park located on 100 acres of the complex. EPCOT Center, Walt Disney's "living blueprint" of the future, was opened to the public in 1982. The overall area of Walt Disney World is twice that of Manhattan Island or equivalent to the area of San Francisco.[5] When Disney World originally opened in 1971 there were 35 attractions in the Magic Kingdom; now there are 45. Large corporations, such as Coca Cola Company, also sponsor exhibits at Disney World. A new pavilion at EPCOT Center, "The Living Seas," presented by United Technologies, is now under construction. It will feature the world's largest man-made tropical reef. The Living Seas is scheduled to be completed in January 1986.

The importance of Disneyland and Disney World to the company is in the cash flow they generate. The theme park properties are depreciated over ten years for tax purposes. Maintenance of the parks is a high priority and is performed meticulously.

Partially because of the opening of EPCOT Center in October 1982, Disney World attendance (including EPCOT Center) in 1983 was 22.7 million, topping the original forecast of 20 million. Attendance fell, however, during 1984 to 21.1 million guests. The profit margin at Disney World has slipped to far below that of the smaller and older Disneyland.[6]

Walt Disney World has made an effort to market the recreational and resort aspects of the park by offering vacation packages and by selling three-day passes. In an attempt to appeal to a larger clientele, Disney World is now offering culinary classes, landscaping seminars, technology and transportation seminars, and instruction on other phases of Disney operations.

EPCOT

The acronym EPCOT stands for Experimental Prototype Community of Tomorrow. EPCOT Center, which is located on 600 acres of Walt Disney World land, was opened October 1, 1982. The center consists of two major theme areas: World Showcase and Future World. World Showcase presents the history and culture of countries around the world. In 1984, the "Kingdom of Morocco" was added to World Showcase. Future World explores the challenges and problems facing the world today. Future World exhibits include "Spaceship Earth" presented by the Bell System; "Journey Into Imagination" by Kodak; "Backstage Magic," a computer show sponsored by Sperry Univac; "The World of Motion" presented by General Motors; "Horizons" sponsored by General Electric; and "The Universe of Energy" sponsored by Exxon. Another Future World attraction is "The Land," sponsored by Kraft Foods. This attraction is of particular note because it takes visitors through various earth climates and demonstrates possible agriculture of the future. Food crops can be seen growing in aluminum drums, in salt water, and out of styrofoam—all in an attempt to show the potential alternative food sources of tomorrow.

EPCOT Center was Walt's last dream. He originally planned EPCOT to be primarily funded by sponsors and other interested outside investors much in the same way as Disneyland was financed. However, even though many sponsors have paid millions of dollars toward costs, Walt Disney Productions has been forced to build EPCOT at a cost of approximately $1 billion, a big part of which has had to come from internally generated funds. EPCOT Center was built primarily for adults, to complement the child orientation of Fantasyland and to help attract people to the Walt Disney World complex. EPCOT Center had to close its entrances twice during the peak Christmas season of 1982 when its 6,000-space parking lot was filled. The lot has since been expanded to 9,000 spaces.

Hotels and Land[7]

Walt Disney Productions owns and operates three hotels at Walt Disney World with a total capacity of 1,834 rooms. The largest Disney hotel is the Contemporary Resort with 1,046 rooms, 14 stories, and a 90-foot-high open lobby. The hotel is connected to Walt Disney World's Magic Kingdom by monorail (which runs through the fourth floor concourse of the hotel). Disney World also has the Polynesian Resort hotel and the Golf Resort. The company also operates and owns many villas, townhouses, and campgrounds that are connected with the golf course and other Disney World outdoor recreational facilities. The Disney World hotels run at very high capacity and help make Disney World one of the most popular vacation spots in the world. The company is currently building 541 new rooms at the Polynesian Village Resort, Golf Resort, and Club Lake Villas. See Exhibit 8.6 for hotel occupancy rates.

Disney Productions owns 40 undeveloped acres of land in Anaheim and 28,000 acres in Orlando. The company on the average paid $200 per acre for the undeveloped land. Its worth is now estimated at more than $1,000 per acre.

Transportation[8]

Disneyland and Walt Disney World are known for their monorails and people movers. The monorail system at Disney World is comprised of 10 trains, each with the capacity to travel an average of 45 miles per hour. These trains carry approximately 10,000,000 passengers per year, and have technologically advanced air suspensions that allow smoother rides than those offered by comparable systems. The people movers at Disney World operate at 99.8% efficiency at a cost of 9¢ a passenger mile. In August 1979, Disney accepted a joint contract to build a people mover at the Houston International Airport. The Houston people mover is now complete. Its main advantage is that it has very few belts and gears—the wheels and doors are the only moving parts in the system. Disney's transportation business is conducted in the WED Enterprises Division of the company. Walt often referred to WED as his laboratory (WED stands for Walt's initials to reflect his personal interest in technology). In 1984, Disney contracted with Bombadier Inc. of Canada to build and market people mover and monorail train systems designed by Disney Productions.[9]

Tokyo Disneyland

"From the Emperor down, Japan is presently in the grip of mouse fever!"

Harper's Magazine

EXHIBIT 8.6 **Occupancy Rates: Walt Disney Hotels and Walt Disney World Village**

	1983	1982	1981	1980	1979
Contemporary Resort	99%	96%	99%	99%	98%
Polynesian Village Resort	99%	98%	97%	98%	99%
Golf Resort	96%	89%	94%	96%	95%
Fairway and Club Lake Villas	94–97%		average 81–88%[1]		

SOURCES: 1983, 1982, 1981, 1980, and 1979 *10K Reports.*
[1]1979–1982 average occupancy rate

The biggest Disneyland of all—Tokyo Disneyland—opened April 15, 1983 on 202 acres of landfill in Tokyo Bay, 8 miles from downtown Tokyo, Japan. Walt Disney Productions agreed to invest $2.5 million and to offer technical and strategic advice on the project. The major financing of $600 million, however, came from the Oriental Land Company of Japan. Walt Disney Productions receives 10% of the gate receipts and 5% of other sales. Disney officials are assigned as consultants to ensure the park's profitability.

Tokyo Disneyland is much like its counterpart in Southern California. The Tokyo park has Adventureland, Fantasyland, Tomorrowland, Westernland, and World Bazaar. There is little in the park that is distinctly Japanese, yet approximately 32 million Japanese people live within a 30-mile radius of the park.

The park started off well and attendance surpassed projections for the first year. In 1984, however, attendance has been reported to be off as much as 40% of capacity. The Oriental Land Company has subsequently begun an aggressive advertising campaign.

The Theme Park Industry[10,11]

Amusement parks are a traditional form of American entertainment. Theme parks in particular experienced strong growth in attendance, employment, and income during the early 1970s. For example, 1976 theme park attendance was double that of 1971. Growth, however, slowed to only 1% in 1977. Revenues for parks approached $1.2 billion, with per capita spending of $14 in 1980. In 1981, there was a 1% increase in attendance (87 million visitors), revenues climbed to $1.4 billion, and per capita spending went to $16. From 1981 to 1984 theme park revenues increased but profitability decreased. Total attendance for the industry is growing very slowly. The industry is now facing some difficulties.

Market saturation has become a serious problem. Every metropolitan area in the United States now has a theme park within or very near its boundaries. Fifty percent of those attending theme parks have to travel less than 100 miles to reach their nearest theme park. Therefore, to be successful, a park has to be centrally located and accessible, or it has to attract regional customers. In order to attract regional customers, a park must offer something of special appeal. Disney parks are located at either end of the United States in southern locations that can be kept open all year long. In contrast, over 50% of the country's population is within a day's drive of one of the Six Flags parks. There are five companies that operate more than one park: Walt Disney Productions, which runs Disneyland and Walt Disney World; Bally Manufacturing, which has its Six Flags parks in California, Georgia, Missouri, New Jersey, and Texas; Taft Broadcasting, which operates King's Island in Cincinnati, King's Dominion in Virginia, and Carowinds in North Carolina;* Marriott Corporation, with Great America parks in California

---

*These parks were recently sold.

and Illinois; and Anheuser-Busch, which owns The Dark Continent park in Tampa, Florida, and Old Country in Virginia. In addition, there are successful individual parks, such as Cedar Point, which serves the Cleveland/ Toledo, Ohio metropolitan areas. Exhibit 8.7 lists the twenty-five most popular parks.

Success in this industry is often attributed to repeat customers who return to parks for upgraded rides and attractions, spectaculars, and live shows. To attempt to increase the number of repeat customers, many theme parks cut admission prices and offer special values. Most companies that run theme parks believe that more revenue can be generated by expanding existing parks rather than by building new ones. For example, Six Flags, Inc. adds a new major attraction to its parks about every two years. Building a new park has almost become cost prohibitive.

In the late 1970s industry analysts blamed tapering attendance on gasoline shortages and high gasoline prices. In the 1980s, gasoline prices and quantities available have been relatively stable, yet park attendance has still dropped. Analysts feel that high gas prices might affect only those traveling long distances to parks. Admission prices might be the "real cause" of lower attendance. In order to make money, the parks have to attract large crowds. The crowds come for improved rides and new attractions. The improvements and attractions cost an increasing amount to build, so the parks are forced to raise the admission prices, but the higher price has a dampening affect on demand. Therefore, large theme parks are in a difficult position. They are in a mature industry and the escalating costs of doing business are hampering growth.

Another explanation for the declining growth in amusement and theme park attendance is one of demographics. As the average age of the U.S. population increases and as average family size decreases, fewer people are likely to be interested in the child-oriented themes of the 1960s or in the teenage-oriented thrill rides so popular in the 1970s. The Bureau of Census of the U.S. Department of Commerce projects that the annual rate of population growth will slow from .9% in 1981 to .6% in 2000 and reach zero growth by 2050. With the slowdown in growth, the median age of the U.S. population will increase from 30.3 years in 1981 to 36.3 years in 2000 and 41.6 years in 2050. A summary of U.S. population by age category in Exhibit 8.8 shows these present and projected demographic changes.

Present attendance figures indicate that about half of the people visiting theme parks today are adults. If these parks are to keep their attendance revenues up, analysts of the industry believe that parks will need to further change their entertainment mix. Theme parks may be faced with having to entertain not only children and accompanying adults, but also adults without children.

Another problem facing the industry is intense competition from other forms of entertainment. People now are more active and have interests such as sports and fitness activities. The prospect of going to a theme park to wait in line for a ride may not be appealing to a fast-paced, more adult-

EXHIBIT 8.7   **America's Top 25 Amusement Parks, 1984**

LOCATION	ESTIMATED ATTENDANCE, 1984	% CHANGE FROM 1983
1. Walt Disney World (Orlando, Florida)	22,000,000	−5.0
2. Disneyland (Anaheim, California)	10,000,000	0
3. Knott's Berry Farm (Buena Park, California)	3,500,000	n/a
4. Sea World (Orlando, Florida)	3,050,000	8.8
5. King's Island (Cincinnati, Ohio)	3,000,000	8.0
6. Sea World (San Diego, California)	2,900,000	2.2
7. Busch Gardens Dark Continent (Tampa, Florida)	2,900,000	n/a
8. Magic Mountain (Valencia, California)	2,750,000	9.0
9. Great Adventure (Jackson, New Jersey)	2,600,000	−19.0
10. Cedar Point (Sandusky, Ohio)	2,600,000	n/a
11. Six Flags Over Texas (Arlington, Texas)	2,300,000	−4.0
12. Six Flags Over Georgia (Atlanta, Georgia)	2,100,000	−8.0
13. Opryland U.S.A. (Nashville, Tennessee)	2,060,000	2.2
14. Great America (Santa Clara, California)	2,000,000	n/a
15. Great America (Gurnee, Illinois)	2,000,000	−19.0
16. Busch Gardens Old Country (Williamsburg, Virginia)	1,960,000	0
17. King's Dominion (Doswell, Virginia)	1,880,000	−2.0
18. Santa Cruz Beach Boardwalk (California)	1,800,000	n/a
19. Astroworld (Houston, Texas)	1,700,000	10.0
20. Hersheypark (Hershey, Pennsylvania)	1,604,000	0
21. Darien Lake (Darien Center, New York)	1,410,000	10.0
22. Worlds of Fun (Kansas City, Missouri)	1,366,000	−1.0
23. Six Flags Over Mid-America (Eureka, Missouri)	1,300,000	−7.0
24. Carowinds (Charlotte, North Carolina)	1,138,000	2.0
25. Sea World (Aurora, Ohio)	1,016,000	−8.0

SOURCE: *Amusement Business Magazine* (December 29, 1984) p. 65.

oriented society. Theme parks in the future will very likely need to involve the visitor more in the park experience. Even in the mid-1980s the trend toward water-related rides and activities with a normal side-effect of soaking the participants is beginning to replace traditional thrill rides in popularity.

EXHIBIT 8.8

United States Resident Population and Projected Population Figures

(In Thousands)

	1975	1980	1985[1]	1990[1]	2000[1]
Under 5 yrs.	16,121 (7.5)[2]	16,457 (7.2)	18,462 (7.7)	19,200 (7.7)	17,624 (6.6)
5–17 yrs.	51,044 (23.7)	47,217 (20.8)	44,352 (18.6)	45,123 (18.1)	49,762 (18.5)
18–24 yrs.	27,735 (12.8)	30,091 (13.2)	28,715 (12.0)	25,777 (10.3)	24,590 (9.2)
25–44 yrs.	54,074 (25.1)	63,238 (27.8)	73,779 (30.9)	81,351 (32.6)	80,105 (29.9)
45–64 yrs.	43,794 (20.3)	44,486 (19.6)	44,668 (18.7)	46,481 (18.6)	60,873 (22.7)
Over 65	22,696 (10.5)	25,714 (11.3)	28,673 (12.0)	31,799 (12.7)	35,036 (13.1)
Total	215,464	227,203	238,649	249,731	267,990

United States Average Family Size

	1960	1970	1975	1980	1982
Average size of family	3.67	3.58	3.42	3.29	3.25

SOURCE: *Statistical Abstract of the United States,* 104th edition, 1984, pp. 32, 34, & 47.

[1]Years 1985–2000 contain figures projected on basis of U.S. Census Middle Series (series 14).

[2]Figures in parentheses are percentages of annual totals.

FILMED ENTERTAINMENT[12]

Walt Disney Productions is involved in the making and distribution of theatrical motion pictures, network and cable television, and home video products. In 1983, gross revenues for this segment of Walt Disney Productions totaled $165,458,000; down from $202,102,000 in 1982. In 1984, however, gross revenues for this business segment were up to $244,552,000.

Filmed Entertainment (in Thousands)

	1984	Change	1983	Change	1982
Revenues	$244,552	+48%	$165,458	−18%	$202,102
Operating income (loss)	2,249	+10%	(33,385)	−270%	19,639
Operating margin	1%		−20%		10%

SOURCE: 1984 *Annual Report.*

Theatrical

"It was clear we were in Never-Never Land."
Ronald Miller

Disney's film library is one of the finest anywhere and currently is worth an estimated $500 million. The library, in 1982, contained 25 full-length animated features, 8 true-life adventure films, 118 full-length live action features, and approximately 500 other films on short subjects. In 1979, films accounted for one-fifth of Disney's pretax earnings but lost $33 million in 1983. Disney Productions feels that it is the primary source of family films in the motion picture industry. Nevertheless, recent Disney films have been replaced by *Star Wars* and *E.T.* as the most popular children's movies. The Disney movies have recently been criticized for lack of imagination, creativity, and "clout" at the box office. Full-length animation efforts of other studios, such as *Watership Down* and *The Secret of NIMH*, also seemed to be less than successful in theatre receipts.

Disney makes full-length animated motion pictures, live action movies, and other types of films such as health and safety movies. Walt's personal strategy had been to make films only about stories of proven popularity. He would make a quality film and re-release it about every seven years, and only rarely make sequels. From 1980 to 1983, 50% of Disney's motion picture division revenues came from reissues.[13] One of the company's 1984 objectives was to reissue two or three Disney films a year. Walt also used films to promote his other businesses and generate interest in Disneyland and consumer products, like Mickey Mouse watches.

Although the Disney studios are in the geographic heart of the Hollywood movie industry, Disney has been criticized for being miles away conceptually and behind the times. E. Cardon ("Card") Walker (CEO from 1971 to 1983), once said, "We never were part of the Hollywood scene." Walker at one time wanted Disney to abandon films altogether. The company, however, decided to adapt its motion pictures to changing tastes. Ronald Miller, the chief executive in 1983, wanted to develop more innovative films with wider appeal. In June 1983, Walt Disney Pictures was created as a separate company with Richard Berger as president. Berger was hired from 20th Century Fox and, under the "Touchstone" label, began to produce films for mass audiences.

Disney Productions released a PG-rated film—*Splash*—in 1983. The movie was a tremendous box office success and helped cause Disney's stock price to climb from 50 to 67. *Splash* was produced by Touchstone and starred John Candy, Tom Hanks, and Eugene Levy, all of whom had successful previous endeavors as comedians. The starring actress, Daryl Hannah, also had previous movie experience. Ron Howard of *Happy Days* fame directed the movie.

Some Disney executives, nevertheless, were concerned that Touchstone and *Splash* were not consistent with the Disney image. Other top Disney officials disagreed with hiring top talent from other movie companies because they felt it was giving up too much control of the company. In February of 1984, Disney ran a full-page newspaper ad that was, in effect, a disclaimer for *Splash*. Jack B. Lindquist (Executive Vice-President, Marketing), and James P. Jimirro (Executive Vice-President, Telecommunications) placed the ad to head off expected criticism by the press. People at Disney Productions were worried that Walt might not have approved of Touchstone and PG-rated films. Nevertheless, Touchstone's second release, *Country*, starring Jessica Lange and Sam Shepard, received critical praise in late 1984, and the filmed entertainment segment has set objectives for making ten to twelve Touchstone films a year.

EXHIBIT 8.9   **Motion Picture Industry Sales Data**

BOX OFFICE SALES	
Year	Amount
1983	$3,697,000,000
1982	3,452,000,000
1981	2,965,000,000
1980	2,777,000,000
1979	2,804,000,000
1978	2,665,000,000
1977	2,332,000,000

Domestic Box Office Market Shares: January 1–September 30, 1984

Company	Percent
Paramount	20.9
Warner Bros.	20.7
Columbia	15.5
20th Century Fox	11.5
Universal	7.5
MGM/UA	6.5
Disney	4.8
Tri-Star	4.0
Orion	3.7
Other	4.9
Total	100.0

SOURCE: Estimates for box office sales from aggregate table in *Variety*, January 11, 1984, p. 7; data for domestic box office market shares from *Standard & Poor's Industry Surveys*, 1985, p. L20.

Disney has attempted other nontraditional movies in addition to *Splash*. *Tron,* for example, was intended to improve Disney's creative image, but was a somewhat unsuccessful attempt to make movies primarily for teenagers. *Tron* did, however, lead to an increase of computer simulation in advertising. Other movies, such as *Something Wicked This Way Comes,* failed at the box office and helped cause the stock price to fall. *Never Cry Wolf* was a critical success, but was not successful at the box office, either.

All of Disney's motion pictures are distributed in the United States by Disney's wholly owned subsidiary, Buena Vista Distribution Company. Buena Vista International, another wholly owned subsidiary, distributes Disney films outside the United States.

Disney Productions is not large when compared to other motion picture makers. Disney's market share was 4% in 1980, 1981, and 1982. Universal, on the other hand, had a 30% box office share during that time. Major studios release fifteen movies per year on the average, whereas Disney averages seven releases per year. Box office revenues are shown for the industry and for Disney Productions in Exhibits 8.9 and 8.10.

Television

Disney Productions first aired its TV programs in 1954. It produced forty-eight programs per year for *Walt Disney's Wonderful World* and its predecessor, *Disneyland.* Walt would use the television programs to show off his technological achievements at Disneyland and to demonstrate the animation techniques of his latest movie. In the early 1980s Disney had contracts with CBS and its programs were seen in fifty-eight countries, including Australia, Brazil, Canada, France, Germany, Great Britain, Italy, Japan, Mexico, and

---

EXHIBIT 8.10 **Walt Disney Productions: Motion Picture Revenues**
(In Thousands of Dollars)

	THEATRICAL/DOMESTIC	THEATRICAL/FOREIGN	GROSS REVENUES[1]
1984	$70,679	$38,182	$244,552
1983	38,635	43,825	165,458
1982	55,408	64,525	202,102
1981	54,624	76,279	196,806
1980	63,350	78,314	171,965
1979	49,594	57,288	144,058
1978	69,010	57,912	160,227

SOURCES: 1980 and 1984 *Annual Reports.*

[1]Includes television, video, and other rental revenues.

Spain. The company continues to believe that its TV programs complement its marketing of motion pictures and theme parks. In 1982 TV revenues were $44.4 million, but in 1983 dropped to $27.9 million. Revenues from television, however, climbed back up to $57.5 million in 1984.

The Disney Channel[14]

> "It is a curious thing that the more the world shrinks because of electronic communications, the more limitless becomes the power of the storytelling entertainer."
>
> Walt Disney

The Disney Channel, headquartered in Burbank, was introduced to cable television in 1983. The company entered the cable market because top management believed cable channels have the potential to achieve as much as a 25% profit margin and because most cable channels experience high customer satisfaction. In 1983, approximately 532,000 people subscribed to the Disney Channel. The number jumped to 1,400,000 by September 1984. Disney expected to obtain about 15% of the cable market but was able to get only 7% of cable viewers by mid-1984. James P. Jimirro, Vice-President of Telecommunications, expects the Disney Channel to break even by 1985. The Disney Channel was predicted to lose $15 million in 1983, but only lost $11 million.

Thus Disney claims the cable channel to be a success. It is the fastest growing and has the highest customer-satisfaction rating of any service in the industry. The company feels it has a major asset in instant product identification. A new television business segment has thus been formed at Disney. The Disney Channel is offered on 1,700 cable television systems covering 19 million homes in all 50 states. The company has also purchased several transponders and is optimistic about its future in cable.

Cable operators, however, claim that Disney is too rigid in its marketing strategies. The operators claim that Disney does not know the cable business. For example, they claim that Disney was asked to give the channel away free for two weeks, to develop watching habits in cable-viewing families. The company refused. Other operators complain that the programming is no different than regular TV. Furthermore, Disney offers its own 32-page color magazine, which directly competes with cable operators' magazines. Nevertheless, Cablevision has contracted in 1984 to carry the Disney Channel on its systems for the next ten years. The agreement will pay Disney a minimum of $75 million over the period of the contract.

The format of the Disney Channel is old TV prime time shows, family movies, and original programs. The original programming includes Mouseterpiece Theater, Mousercise, and Good Morning Mickey. The Disney Channel competes with Home Box Office (12.5 million subscribers), Showtime (4.3 million subscribers), and Cinemax (2.5 million subscribers). Analysts report that overall demand for all cable services has been less than

EXHIBIT 8.11

Pay Cable TV Subscribers
(Annual Average in Millions)

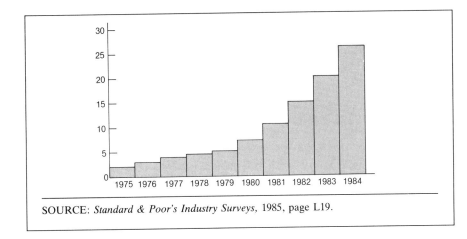

SOURCE: *Standard & Poor's Industry Surveys*, 1985, page L19.

originally forecasted, and that demand for new subscriptions is tapering off. In addition, many companies have failed in the industry.[15] Refer to Exhibit 8.11 for cable industry subscriber data.

Home Video

Disney is also in the home video business, selling video cassettes and video movie discs of such classics as *Dumbo* and *Davy Crockett*. In 1983 *Tron* and *Alice in Wonderland* were released as home videos, and total video sales were $45 million. *Splash, Never Cry Wolf, Robin Hood,* and short cartoons were released in 1984, and their sales totaled $69 million. Prior to 1984, Disney had an exclusive home video distribution agreement with RCA. However, the Sony Corporation fought against the agreement in the courts and won. Disney wanted strict control over the distribution of the videos, to prevent over-exposing its movies and possibly cutting into its motion picture revenue. Disney management now claims that the expiration of the RCA agreement will work to their benefit because it will allow the company to sell movie discs to more companies. Disney home video products are now sold in eighteen countries.

CONSUMER PRODUCTS

The company markets a wide range of consumer products in this business segment. Current revenue and income figures for consumer products are listed below.

Consumer Products and Other (in Thousands)

	1984	Change	1983	Change	1982
Revenues	$109,682	−1%	$110,697	+8%	$102,538
Operating income	53,863	−5%	56,882	+19%	47,832
Operating margin	49%		51%		47%

SOURCE: 1984 Annual Report.

Disney-produced records earned five certified gold records in 1984, and brought the company's total to thirty-one. In character merchandising and publications, Sport Goofy became the official spokesman for the National Federation of State High School Associations. A new "Disney's Fun to Learn Library" was introduced by Bantam Books and several other new Disney books were published by companies such as World Books, Inc. and Simon & Schuster. The company has had cooperative consumer product related agreements with Atari, Coca-Cola, Hasbro Bradley, and Adidas. The educational media division expanded its educational computer software, with learning games using animated graphics. Five computer manufacturers have entered into licensing agreements for the software.

Especially significant in 1984 was the announcement of a complete line of Disney designer sportswear for women, produced by J.G. Hook. Carrying the *Mickey and Co.* label, it will be on display in 2,000 stores throughout the nation. Disney Productions has also made plans to continue producing ice shows such as *Walt Disney's World on Ice* through 1989.

TOP MANAGEMENT AND BOARD OF DIRECTORS[16,17]

Upon Walt Disney's death in 1966, his financially oriented brother Roy took command of the business and continued to carry Walt's ideas forward through the completion of Walt Disney World in Florida. With Roy's death in 1971, E. Cardon ("Card") Walker, a close associate of the Disney brothers since 1938, became president and chief executive officer (CEO) of Walt Disney Productions. A year after the completion of EPCOT, Card resigned his management position but continued as a member of the Board of Directors.

Ronald Miller replaced Card Walker in 1983. A former Los Angeles Rams football player, Miller had worked at Disney since 1957 and had married Walt Disney's daughter Diane. He was forty-eight years old upon becoming the President and CEO of Disney, but served as President only until September 1984. He resigned amidst a series of outside takeover attempts and disagreements with Roy E. Disney, the son of the company's co-founder, Roy O. Disney.

Miller was replaced as Chief Executive Officer by Michael Eisner, President of Paramount Pictures. Frank Wells, previously Vice-Chairman of

Warner Brothers, took over as President and Chief Operating Officer. Eisner's statements upon taking over the president's position at Walt Disney Productions indicated that he planned to make the company's motion picture division more creative and responsive to current trends. His most immediate problem, however, was to deal directly with the kind of acquisition threats that had given Miller so much trouble. Mr. Eisner received a one-time payment of $750,000 and options to purchase 510,000 Disney shares at $57.44 per share upon joining Walt Disney Productions. His annual base salary is $750,000. Mr. Wells received a $250,000 one-time payment and has an annual salary of $400,000.

The Board of Directors of Disney is, according to bylaws, to be comprised of not fewer than nine but not more than fifteen members. There are currently fifteen members on Disney's board. Early in 1984, Roy E. Disney quit the board after two unsuccessful outside takeover attempts. Roy was critical of Ron Miller's managing of the company and was instrumental in forcing Miller's resignation and in the hiring of Michael Eisner as CEO. Roy owns about 5% of Disney shares and runs Shamrock Holdings, Inc. Roy rejoined the company in November of 1984, and assumed both board and management positions. He is now involved with the animation department. Roy is committed to new projects and to putting Disney cartoons on television on Saturday mornings.

The average board member has been serving approximately 9 years and the average age is about 59 years. The current Chairman is CEO Michael Eisner. During 1984, Sharon Disney Lund, a daughter of Walt Disney, and Joseph F. Cullman III, former CEO of Philip Morris, were added to the board. Board members Philip M. Hawley and Robert H.B. Baldwin did not stand for reelection to the board in 1986. Board members and key executives are listed in Exhibits 8.12 and 8.13.

The top management of Walt Disney Productions has been described by analysts as inbred and highly tenured. A number of the managers had actually worked with Walt for as many as twenty years. In addition, Disney family interests appear to have some influence upon strategic decision making and executive succession. This is suggested by Roy E. Disney's disagreements with Ronald Miller and with 1984 news accounts of Walt's widow and one of his daughters hiring advisors so that their interests in the company could be better served.

CORPORATE CULTURE

"We are always asking ourselves, 'What would Walt think?' "
John Mansbridge—art director

Walt Disney's force of personality and obsession with perfection were major ingredients in the building of Walt Disney Productions. Walt's influence on the company has been evaluated by many people as both good and

EXHIBIT 8.12 **Walt Disney Productions: Board of Directors and Top Management, 1984**

Board of Directors	AGE	YEAR JOINED DISNEY	AFFILIATION
Caroline Ahmanson	65	1975	Chairman, Board of Directors—Federal Reserve Bank, San Francisco—12th District
Robert H. B. Baldwin	n/a	1983	Chairman—Morgan Stanley, Inc. (investment bankers)
Charles E. Cobb	n/a	1984	Chairman and CEO—Arvida Corp. (wholly owned subsidiary of Walt Disney Productions)
Joseph F. Cullman III	n/a	1985	Chairman Emeritus—Philip Morris
Roy E. Disney	54	1967	Vice-Chairman—Walt Disney Productions
Michael D. Eisner	n/a	1984	Chairman and CEO—Walt Disney Productions
Philip M. Hawley	58	1975	President and CEO—Carter Hawley Hale Stores, Inc. (retail merchandising)
Ignacio E. Lozano, Jr.	56	1981	Publisher—LA Opinion (newspaper publishing)
Sharon Disney Lund	n/a	1984	Trustee—California Institute of the Arts
Richard A. Nunis	51	1968	Executive Vice-President—Walt Disney World/Disneyland
Donn B. Tatum	70	1957	Chairman of the Finance Committee—Walt Disney Productions
E. Cardon Walker	67	1956	Former CEO—Walt Disney Productions
Raymond L. Watson	56	1974	Chairman of the Executive Committee—Walt Disney Productions
Frank G. Wells	n/a	1984	President and Chief Operating Officer—Walt Disney Productions
Samuel L. Williams	n/a	1983	Partner—Hufstedler, Miller, Carlson & Beardsley (law firm)

Corporate Officers

Michael D. Eisner
Chairman of the Board and Chief Executive Officer

Frank G. Wells
President and Chief Operating Officer

Roy E. Disney
Vice-Chairman of the Board

Michael L. Bagnall
Executive Vice-President—Finance

Carl G. Bongirno
Executive Vice-President—WED

Barton K. Boyd
Executive Vice-President—Consumer Products

Ronald J. Cage
Executive Vice-President—Business Affairs

James P. Jimirro
Executive Vice-President—Telecommunications

Corporate Officers

Jack B. Lindquist
Executive Vice-President—Marketing

Richard A. Nunis
Executive Vice-President—Walt Disney World/
Disneyland

Martin A. Sklar
Executive Vice-President—WED Creative
Development

John J. Cornwell
Vice-President—Management Information Systems

Jose M. Deetjen
Vice-President—Tax Administration and Counsel

Dennis M. Despie
Vice-President—Entertainment

Luther R. Marr
Vice-President—Corporate and Stockholder Affairs

Richard T. Morrow
Vice-President—General Counsel

Peter F. Nolan
Vice-President—Rights/Business Affairs—Consumer
Products

Erwin D. Okun
Vice-President—Corporate Communications

Howard M. Roland
Vice-President—Construction Contract
Administration and Purchasing

Doris A. Smith
Vice-President and Secretary

Frank P. Stanek
Vice-President—Corporate Planning

Donald A. Escen
Treasurer

Bruce F. Johnson
Controller

Leland L. Kirk
Assistant Secretary-Treasurer

Neal E. McClure
Assistant Secretary

Alvin L. Shelbourn
Assistant Secretary

Donald E. Tucker
Assistant Treasurer

Douglas E. Houck
Assistant Controller

Joe E. Stevens
Assistant Controller

SOURCES: 1984 *Annual Report*, 1981 and 1982 *10K Reports*.

EXHIBIT 8.13   **Walt Disney Productions: Subsidiaries and Chief Operating Executives**

DOMESTIC SUBSIDIARIES

Arvida/Disney
Arvida Corporation
Disney Development Company
Charles E. Cobb, Jr., Chairman and
  Chief Executive Officer

Buena Vista International, Inc.
Canasa Trading Corporation
Harold P. Archinal, President

The Disney Channel
Walt Disney Telecommunications
  and Non-Theatrical Company
James P. Jimirro, President

Disneyland
Disneyland Inc.
Lake Buena Vista Communities,
  Inc.
Walt Disney World Company
WED Transportation Systems, Inc.
Richard P. Nunis, President

MAPO
WED Enterprises
Carl G. Bongirno, President

(Continued)

EXHIBIT 8.13   (Continued)

Reedy Creek Utilities Company, Inc.
Ronald J. Cayo, President

United National Operating Company
Walt Disney Educational Media Company
Barton K. Boyd, President

Vista Advertising
Walt Disney Travel Company, Inc.
Jack B. Lindquist, President

Vista Insurance Services, Inc.
Philip N. Smith, President

Vista-United Telecommunications
(a Florida Partnership)
James Tyler, General Manager

Walt Disney Motion Pictures and Television
Walt Disney Pictures
Buena Vista Distribution Company, Inc.
Jeffrey Katzenberg, President

Walt Disney Music Company
Wonderland Music Company, Inc.
Gary Krisel, President

FOREIGN SUBSIDIARIES

Belgium
Walt Disney Productions (Benelux) S.A.
Andre Vanneste

Canada
Walt Disney Music of Canada Limited
James K. Rayburn

Denmark
Walt Disney Productions of A/S Denmark
Gunnar Mansson

France
Walt Disney Productions (France) S.A.
Armand Bigle,
Richard Dassonville,
Dominique Bigle

Germany
Walt Disney Productions (Germany) GmbH
Horst Koblischek

Italy
Creazioni Walt Disney S.p.A.I.
Antonio Bertini

Japan
Walt Disney Enterprises of Japan Ltd.
Matsuo Yokoyama
Walt Disney Productions Japan, Ltd.
Yosaku Seki, Mamoru Morita, Mas Imai

Portugal
Walt Disney Portuguesa Criacoes Artisticas Lda.
Laszlo Hubay Cebrian

Spain
Walt Disney Iberica, S.A.
Enrique Stuyck

United Kingdom
Walt Disney Productions Limited
Dino Troni,
Monty Mendelson,
Terry Byrne,
Keith Bales

SOURCE: 1984 *Annual Report.*

bad. Some saw his obsession with perfection to be what kept the company creative and what set it apart from other film making companies. Others saw Walt's dominant personality as stifling and inhibiting to those who worked for and with him. In 1969, Walt's brother, Roy, told the following story:[18]

> Not long ago, at our Burbank, California, studio, a group of writers were holding a story conference on a new Disney cartoon feature. They were having a tough time agreeing on a story line, and the atmosphere was as stormy as the weather outside. Suddenly, lightning scribbled a jagged streak over the San Fernando Valley and there was a rolling clap of thunder. "Don't worry, Walt," one of the animators quipped, glancing heavenward. "We'll get it right."

Walt Disney's personal style, philosophies, and ideas are still very much a part of the company's way of doing things. John Mansbridge, who was a supervisory art director, says, "We are always asking ourselves, 'What would Walt think?' " Many of Walt's ideas and quotations are found in employee handbooks and training manuals. Pictures and photographs of Walt Disney are common throughout the corporate studios. New employees are educated at the "Disney University" and the informal corporate climate is referred to as the "Disney Democracy." Yet this reverence for Disney has led some to criticize the company for being too "Disney-minded." Until lately, it seemed to some that new ideas and ventures were only undertaken if Walt Disney himself had conceived of them or had approved them.

Walt Disney Productions is considered to be one of the 100 best companies to work for in America.[19] While the company rates only average on pay, benefits, and opportunities to move up in the organization, it rates extremely high on ambiance. Ambiance refers to the attractiveness of the physical work surroundings and to the company's social climate. Disneyland and Disney World are noted for their quality of landscaping, creative architecture, and the cleanliness of the buildings and grounds. Even the studios in Burbank are kept immaculately clean.

The company's image is extremely important at Walt Disney Productions. It is known for creativity and is concerned that the best family entertainment is offered to its customers. Rick Fuess, a Disney training director, states that the purpose of Walt Disney Productions is to make people happy, and that in order to accomplish this purpose, employees must understand their role in creating a world of make-believe. Thus, the employee orientation manual explicitly spells out proper behavior for each job position. The manual also states that the quality and integrity of Disney products must be protected at all costs. Some of the formally written company values include friendliness, public trust, integrity, uniqueness, and quality. The company has dress and moral codes with which employees must comply. An employee can be fired for moral turpitude.

Artists and animators have high status at Disney. They work in specially designed facilities. The creative work groups are kept small. There is constant striving for quality and perfected work. The Disney School of Animation was created to select and train the best and brightest potential young animators.

The organization at Disneyland and Walt Disney World is not thought of in normal terms of departments, personnel, and resources. Instead, the organization is called the "family." Employees are referred to as "cast members," and teamwork and collegiality are the norms. Each person is called by his or her first name. Cast members are encouraged to participate in the generation of ideas. Walt himself once said, "I use the whole plant for ideas. If the janitor has a good idea, I'll use it."

Disney is also very concerned that cast members feel they belong. The company sponsors cast member outings at the parks, employee group travel, regular family film festivals for cast members, and employee softball teams. All these activities are well supported by the employees.

Loyalty to the company was very important to Walt. The management of the company has primarily been kept within the family and within a group of long-time Disney associates. If a friend or family member was loyal and supportive, Walt saw to it that the person was well treated and remembered. Walt also remembered disloyalty. Walt always felt as though he was giving his employees an opportunity they could get nowhere else.

EMPLOYEE RELATIONS

"You can dream, create, design, and build the most wonderful place in the world . . . but it requires people to make the dream a reality."

Walt Disney

Walt Disney Productions employs approximately 30,000 people. The main employment centers are Anaheim and Burbank in California, and Orlando in Florida. In Anaheim, Disneyland employs 5,000 workers during the low season and 8,000 during the peak season. Walt Disney World has 13,000 low-season workers and 16,000 peak-season workers. Other employees work at the company headquarters in Burbank or for the various creative groups.

The company offers its employees pension and deferred compensation, stock option, and stock ownership plans. In 1982, about 1,025,000 options were granted at $20.77 to $64.31 per share. Stock ownership is facilitated by an investment tax credit paid to a trust fund, which is in turn used to buy stock for the employees' benefit. In 1980, approximately 11,600 shares were purchased, while 10,700 shares were purchased in 1981. Disney's aggregate retirement expense was $7,146,000 in 1980; $7,598,000 in 1981; and $9,294,000 in 1982. In general, company benefits are rated as only average.[20]

Pay, however, is rated below the average of other similar companies. The average Disneyland employee in 1984 made $7–10 an hour. Job security and opportunity for advancement are also considered to be somewhat below average at Disney. The low turnover of employees makes chances for advancement few and far between. Overall, Disney is considered to be a good company in which to work. Its heavy emphasis on training and high-quality work makes its employees very attractive to other companies' personnel recruiters.

Management's concern over rising costs and falling profits at Disneyland caused them in late August 1984 to request their employees to accept a wage cut over a period of three years when the current contract expired September 15. Wages were to be reduced by 7% the first year, followed by 5% each of the following two years. A Disney spokesperson said that the pay cut was necessary because of the poor 1984 summer attendance at Disneyland. Unions representing one-third of the workers at the Anaheim theme park rejected the cuts and instead demanded a two-year agreement including a pay increase.

Major strikes had occurred at Walt Disney Productions only three times in its history. In 1940, employees struck over disputes with Walt about profit sharing and pay. In 1970, two dozen talent workers at Disneyland struck for two days over pay. In 1979, 500 maintenance employees at the same theme park went on strike for 13 days over pay issues. These strikes rarely received much media exposure and did little to tarnish the company's image. In contrast, the strike beginning September 25, 1984 by 1,844 Disneyland employees (represented by the Service Employees International Union, the Teamsters Local 88, the Hotel Workers Local 681, and the Bakers Local 324), became a nationwide television event, with network reporters covering every detail.

The striking employees included ride operators, wardrobe workers, food service workers, and ticket sellers. The unions voted in favor of the strike by a 69% majority. Pay was cited as the central issue for the strike. Workers said they walked out to force management into negotiations. In a television interview, a Disneyland employee stated that the employees believed that Disney was different from other firms in the entertainment industry, and should be able to pay them more. Tim Stanley, a ride operator on strike, said, "It had been, basically, a big happy family out here, but now, it's like dad has taken our allowance away and given us more work to do."

On September 26, management offered a new proposal for a two-year wage freeze. The unions rejected the proposal and management said there would be no further negotiations. During this time 3,200 workers stayed on the job and the vacancies created by the strike were filled by temporary employees and by management personnel. A federal mediator tried but was unable to bring the parties together to negotiate. On October 8, management told workers if they did not return to work in one week, they would be replaced. The previous weekend, the striking employees had participated in an evening candlelight vigil, singing "When You Wish Upon a Star." Disneyland employees eventually accepted a wage freeze and returned to work October 17.

At about the same time, Walt Disney World management also asked their employees to accept a wage freeze, but union leaders also threatened to strike. A contract calling for a 3% bonus the first year and a 4% raise the third year was finally approved to replace the one expiring October 1.[21]

On October 23, a total of 200 mid-level and top management personnel at Disney World were fired or demoted following a year-long study to cut costs. Carl Murphy, a labor leader at Disney World, commented on the changes taking place at the theme park:[22]

> Disney's kind of facing reality. The magic's been there years and years and years. Now, they're going to have to become more productive, more efficient.
>
> The company used to be—you were hired in here for life, especially with management. They got fat on management . . . if you were a manager, you had a couple of superintendents under you. You're a superintendent, you had three supervisors under you.

CRISIS IN FANTASYLAND

"Of course we were nervous!"
Ronald Miller

In March 1984, Roy E. Disney, Roy O. Disney's son, resigned from the Board of Directors. This took the company by surprise. At the time, Roy owned 2.3% of Disney shares, and he purchased an additional 500,000 shares immediately after leaving the company. Roy's resignation and large stock purchases started rumors of an anticipated takeover of Disney. Walt Disney Productions was considered to be a good takeover target because of its valuable film library, land holdings, low stock price, and surplus of cash. Aggressive investors could quickly liquidate company assets and make lots of money. As the takeover rumors persisted, Disney's top management tried to protect the company by extending its line of credit and by hiring a consultant who was a takeover specialist.

Takeover Attempt

An investor named Saul Steinberg started acquiring Disney shares in March at a low price and at a rapid rate. By May 1984, Steinberg owned 12.2% of Disney shares and had agreed with Reliance Insurance, an investment group, to make a bid for control of Disney.

Responding to extremely heavy trading of Disney stock, top management moved in June 1984 to purchase Arvida Corporation, a real estate development company based in Boca Raton, Florida. Well known as a premiere planned resort and community development company, its assets included 20,000 acres of prime landholdings in Florida, Georgia, and California. To complete the acquisition, Walt Disney Productions assumed $165 million of debt. Then Standard and Poors lowered its rating of Disney stock. Most analysts believed the acquisition to be an attempt to make the company appear less attractive to possible takeover bids. Disney's top management, however, was thinking of using Arvida to develop the unused property within Walt Disney World.

In an attempt to stop the acquisition of Arvida, Steinberg sued Disney. The courts, however, ruled in Disney's favor and the Arvida acquisition was allowed. Changing his tactics, Steinberg appealed directly to the Disney stockholders to vote to remove those members of the Board of Directors who were in favor of the acquisition. The board responded quickly by voting to change the company's by-laws to make it extremely difficult for a vote to go in Steinberg's favor. In the meantime, Roy E. Disney continued to purchase shares of Disney stock.

Problems with Gibson

Within a week of the June announcement of the Arvida acquisition, Ronald Miller announced top management's decision to also purchase the Gibson Greeting Card Company. A maker of greeting cards and gift wrappings, Gibson has exclusive rights to the cartoon characters of Garfield, Bugs Bunny, and the Road Runner plus the Sesame Street characters. Ron Miller, Disney's president and CEO, believed Gibson to be a good purchase for a number of reasons. It was seen to be a good fit with Walt Disney Productions and would provide new marketing opportunities. It would also have a desired effect of proportionally decreasing Saul Steinberg's shares of stock. The purchase called for an exchange of stock valued at $343 million.

The deal meant that Gibson stockholders would now be Disney stockholders and favorably disposed to Disney's top management. The purchase called for Disney Productions to increase its long-term debt by $30 million. In 1983, Gibson earned $22 million on revenues of $241 million. The 1984 revenues, as of mid-year, were up 30% from the previous year.

Realizing the danger to his plan, Steinberg threatened to acquire 49% of the Disney company. Rumors were flying, but never confirmed, of a possible liaison between Steinberg and Roy Disney. Before the end of June 1984 Disney top management made a deal with Steinberg. In return for a promise that he would never again attempt a takeover against Disney, Steinberg sold his 4,198,333 shares to Disney for $70.83 per share. The stock was selling at the time for around $65 per share and dropped two days later to $50.[23] Included in the agreement was $28 million in expenses that Steinberg had incurred in the takeover attempt. He had paid only approximately $50 per share for the stock, so Saul Steinberg was more than willing to sell his stock to the company for a gain of around $59 million.[24]

With the surprise reinstatement at the end of June 1984 of Roy E. Disney to the Board of Directors, the crisis appeared to be over. Disney's stock price, however, continued to fall and the Board of Directors continued to be nervous. Their fears were realized as the summer wore on. Irwin Jacobs, an investor with a nickname in the financial community of "Irv the Liquidator" from previous takeovers, began buying Disney stock at $47 a share. Once Jacobs controlled 7.7% of the stock, he joined with the Bass family (another large stockholder) to threaten a proxy fight if Disney top management did not drop plans to acquire Gibson Greeting Cards. Over the years Jacobs had developed a reputation of moving in on a company with basic strengths, but weak top management. In August, Jacobs threatened to force a special stockholders' meeting for the purpose of dismantling the company if the Gibson decision was not reversed. In response, Roy Disney vowed publicly to stop Jacobs. Nevertheless, the agreement to buy Gibson was cancelled in August by Disney's top management. Gibson's president, T.M. Conney, publicly criticized Disney's stockholders for thwarting the acquisition. Many Disney stockholders, however, agreed with Jacobs that Disney's top management, in their zeal to escape Steinberg's takeover, had offered more than Gibson was worth. A number were also critical of the large "greenmail" payment made to Steinberg, in the form of buying back the stock at an unrealistically high price.

Management Turmoil

In September 1984, as the labor problems at Disneyland were beginning to surface, Ronald Miller resigned as Disney's president and CEO. Forced to leave by a coalition formed by Roy Disney, Miller received heavy criticism for having not followed Disney traditions. Michael D. Eisner, a Paramount executive, was appointed President and CEO to replace Miller. The Bass family (with the apparent blessings of Roy Disney and Walt Disney Productions top management) doubled their holdings of Disney stock. This act was seen by many as a vote of confidence in the company.

Early in October, the Bass family bought Jacobs' shares of stock for $158.1 million. The Fort Worth, Texas, Bass family now owned approximately 25% of the outstanding shares of common stock. The crisis appeared to be over. The strike at Disneyland had been settled and the takeover attempts by Steinberg and Jacobs had been thwarted. Some analysts, however, were more cynical and referred to Disney Production's friendly overtures to the Bass family as exchanging "one fox for another in the chicken coop."

Roy Disney rejoined the company in November. He announced a desire to revitalize the studio's animation efforts. Stock was now trading for around $57 a share. Meanwhile, the new CEO, Michael Eisner, indicated that he wished to make the motion picture division more creative and more responsive to current trends. The company announced new objectives of producing three to four new family pictures annually, ten to twelve new Touchstone films, plus acceleration of animated feature productions with new releases every eighteen months. As a whole, Disney management vowed to never again become vulnerable to a takeover. Nevertheless, as 1984 came to a close, rumors emerged that Coca-Cola might be interested in buying Walt Disney Productions.

NOTES

1. L. Gartley and E. Leebron, *Walt Disney: A Guide to References and Resources* (Boston: G. K. Hall, 1979) pp. 1–8.

2. R.O. Disney, "Unforgettable Walt Disney," *Reader's Digest* (February 1969) pp. 212–218.

3. *Walt Disney Productions 1983 10K report.*

4. J. Thiel and R.C. Boals, "Walt Disney Productions—1978," in Thomas L. Wheelen and J. David Hunger, *Strategic Management and Business Policy* (Reading, Mass.: Addison-Wesley, 1983) pp. 405–422.

5. D. Walker, "EPCOT 82," *Architectural Design* (1982, Vol. 52)

6. D. Kasler, "Change Is Not a Fantasy," *Tampa Tribune* (Tampa, Fl., November 4, 1984) pp. 1E and 16E.

7. *Walt Disney Productions 1983 10K report.*

8. D. Walker, "EPCOT 82," *Architectural Design* (1982, Vol. 52)

9. *Walt Disney Productions 1984 Annual Report.*

10. *Standard and Poor's Industry Survey,* 1983.

11. R.C. Boals, "A Note on the Theme Park Industry," University of Tennessee, 1979.

12. *Walt Disney Productions 1984 Annual Report.*

13. *Fortune Magazine* (October 4, 1982) p. 66.

14. *Walt Disney Productions 1984 Annual Report.*

15. *Business Week* (July 9, 1984) p. 40.

16. *Walt Disney Productions 1983 10K report.*

17. *Wall Street Journal* (January 16, 1985) p. 7.

18. R.O. Disney, "Unforgettable Walt Disney," *Reader's Digest* (February 1969) pp. 212–218.

19. R. Levering, M. Moskowitz, and M. Katz, *The 100 Best Companies to Work For in America* (Reading, Mass.: Addison-Wesley Publishing Company, 1984)

20. Levering, Moskowitz, and Katz.

21. D. Kasler, "Change Is Not a Fantasy," *Tampa Tribune* (Tampa, Fl.: November 4, 1984) pp. 1E and 16E.

22. Kasler.

23. Kasler.

24. *Fortune Magazine* (October 4, 1982) p. 66.

Anheuser-Busch Companies, Inc. . . . August A. Busch, III

THOMAS L. WHEELEN · JANIECE L. GALLAGER

Sitting in his office on March 15, 1986, Mr. Busch was reviewing his staff's analysis of his first ten-year strategic plan. He was preparing himself for the next day's staff meeting, in which the company's next ten-year strategic plan would be developed. Many changes had been made in the company since its founding more than a century ago. He was proud. Anheuser-Busch had come a long way in its corporate development. Diversification strategies had proven successful and continued growth seemed evident. But, where would the company go within its fast-paced competitive environment? Its primary objective is well-planned and well-managed growth, and the company's long-term diversification strategies of vertical integration, internal development of new business areas, and acquisitions reflect this commitment. Busch stated that "Beer . . . will remain our top priority, as evidenced by substantial future capital commitments." The plan couldn't stop there.

COMPANY HISTORY—AN ENTREPRENEURIAL SPIRIT

In 1852, George Schneider founded the Bavarian Brewery in St. Louis, Missouri. On the brink of bankruptcy in 1857, the brewery was sold to a competitor, who renamed it Hammer and Urban. By 1860, the new company defaulted on a loan to Eberhard Anheuser. Anheuser, a successful soap manufacturer, assumed control of Hammer and Urban and four years later asked his son-in-law, Adolphus Busch, to join the brewery in the position of salesman. Busch, who became the driving force behind the new venture, became a partner (1873), and President (1880–1913) of the brewery. In 1879, the name of the brewery was changed to Anheuser-Busch Brewing Company.

Adolphus Busch was a pioneer in the development of a new pasteurization process for beer and became the first American brewer to pasteurize beer. In 1894, he and Carl Conrad developed a new beer that was lighter in color and body than the previous one. This new beer, Budweiser, gave Busch a

This case was prepared by Professor Thomas L. Wheelen, and Ms. Janiece L. Gallagher, MBA student, of the University of South Florida. Research Assistance was performed by Kelli Anderson, Kim Hart, and Cathy Lee of the University of South Florida at Sarasota. It was presented at the North American Case Research Association Meeting, 1987. Distributed by the North American Case Research Association meeting. All rights reserved to the authors and the North American Case Research Association. Reprinted by permission of the authors and the North American Case Research Association.

national beer, for which he developed many marketing techniques (such as giveaways—tokens and pocketknives), to increase its sales. By 1901, the annual sales of Anheuser-Busch surpassed the million-barrel mark.

In 1913, August A. Busch succeeded his father as president of the company, and served as President through the Prohibition era (1920–1933) to 1934. He led the company into many new diversification endeavors, such as truck bodies, baker's yeast, ice cream, corn products, commercial refrigeration units, and nonalcoholic beverages. With the passage of the Twenty-first Amendment, Anheuser-Busch returned to the manufacture and distribution of beer on a national basis, and in 1934, the company went public.

August A. Busch, Jr., succeeded Adolphus Busch III as President and Chief Executive Officer in 1946. In 1949 Eberhard Anheuser was elected the first Chairman of the Board. August A. Busch, Jr. was elected Chairman in 1956. During his tenure, eight new breweries were constructed and sales increased eleven-fold, from 3 million barrels in 1946 to 34 million barrels in 1974. He also guided the company's pursuit of diversification strategies into real estate, family entertainment parks, transportation, the St. Louis Cardinals baseball team, and can manufacturing. Busch is currently serving as Honorary Chairman of the Board of Anheuser-Busch Companies, Inc., and Chairman and President of the St. Louis National Baseball Club, Inc.

August A. Busch III was elected President in 1974, and Chief Executive Officer in 1975 (see Exhibit 9.1). As of 1986 he is serving as Chairman and President. During his tenure, sales doubled, from 34 million barrels in 1974 to 68 million barrels in 1985. The company has eleven breweries with a total annual capacity of 75.27 million barrels, and under his direction Anheuser-Busch has continued its successful diversification efforts.

August A. Busch III, born on June 16, 1937, is the fifth generation of the Busch brewing dynasty. He started his career hauling beechwood chips out of 31,000-gallon aging tanks. In his youth "Little Augie" was a hell-raiser, but is now a conservative "workaholic" after attending the University of Arizona and the Siebel Institute of Technology, a Chicago school for brewers.

In his ten years of managing the company, Busch has transformed it from a large, loosely run company into a tightly run organization with an emphasis on the bottom line. Busch is known for his tough-mindedness and intensity, his highly competitive nature, and his attention to detail. As Mr. Dennis Long, President of the company's brewing subsidiary, said, "There is little that goes on that he doesn't know something about." Busch, a brewmaster, is known for making unscheduled visits to the breweries at all hours of the day and night. He daily compares beers from different plants and suggests remedies for any variations in look and taste. Mr. Long added, "Let there be no doubt. He's at the helm and he sets the tone."

Encouraging openness and participation from his executives, Busch provides them with plenty of responsibility and freedom, and promotes group decision-making. His Policy Committee is a nine-member forum in which

EXHIBIT 9.1 **Historical Organization Chart**

Steps in Ownership Development

YEAR	FIRM	TYPE
1852–1857	George Schneider	Proprietorship
1857–1858	P. and C. Hammer & Co.	Partnership
1858–1860	Hammer & Urban	Partnership
1860–1875	E. Anheuser & Co.	Partnership
1875–1879	E. Anheuser Co.'s Brewing Association	Corporation
1879–1919	Anheuser-Busch Brewing Association	Corporation
1919–1979	Anheuser-Busch, Inc.	Corporation
1979–(current)	Anheuser-Busch Companies, Inc.	Corporation

Presidents of Anheuser-Busch

NAME	TENURE
Eberhard Anheuser	President of E. Anheuser & Co. from 1860 to July 7, 1875 President of E. Anheuser Co.'s Brewing Association from 1875 to April 29, 1879 President of Anheuser-Busch Brewing Association from April 29, 1879, to May 2, 1880 (death)
Adolphus Busch	President of Anheuser-Busch Brewing Association from May 10, 1880, to October 13, 1913 (death)
August A. Busch, Sr.	President of Anheuser-Busch Brewing Association from December 8, 1913, to November 22, 1919 President of Anheuser-Busch, Inc. from November 22, 1919, to February 13, 1934 (death)
Adolphus Busch III	President of Anheuser-Busch, Inc. from February 22, 1934, to August 29, 1946 (death)
August A. Busch, Jr.	President of Anheuser-Busch, Inc. from September 5, 1946, to April 27, 1971
Richard A. Meyer	President of Anheuser-Busch, Inc. from April 27, 1971, to February 27, 1974
August A. Busch III	President of Anheuser-Busch, Inc. from February 27, 1974, to October 1, 1979 President of Anheuser-Busch Companies, Inc. from October 1, 1979, to present

each member must present an opinion on the current topic or issue and substantiate his position. Mr. Busch feels that "executives do not learn from success, they learn from their failures." What is his philosophy on success? As he states, "The more successful that we become . . . the more humble that we must be . . . because that breeds future success."

During the summer of 1985, Mr. Busch's 21-year-old son, August A. Busch IV was employed in the Corporate Yeast Culture Center at the St. Louis headquarters. Commenting about the succession of his four children, Mr. Busch says, "If they have the competency to do so, they'll be given the opportunity. You learn from the ground up. Those of us who are in this company started out scrubbing the tanks." So the younger August Busch begins his career with Anheuser-Busch.

THE ORGANIZATION	On October 1, 1979, Anheuser-Busch Companies, Inc. was formed as a new holding company (see Exhibit 9.2.)

The new company's name and organizational structure more clearly reflect Anheuser-Busch's mission and diversification endeavors of the past decades. Because each subsidiary of Anheuser-Busch Companies, Inc. has its own Board of Directors and officers, management has gained operational and organizational flexibility. The Policy Committee for Anheuser-Busch Companies, Inc. establishes policies for all the subsidiaries, one of which is Anheuser-Busch, Inc.

For strategic planning purposes, the company is organized into three business segments: (1) beer and beer-related companies, (2) food products companies, and (3) diversified operations. The Board of Directors consists of fifteen members (see Exhibit 9.3). The executive officers of the company are described in Exhibit 9.4.

In 1985, the beer and beer-related business segment contributed 77.3% of the corporation's net sales and 95.8% of the operation revenue. Exhibit 9.5 sketches the eighteen companies that comprise the three business segments, and the financial information for each of the business segments is shown in Exhibit 9.6.

Because of the company's vertical integration strategy, the knowledge of the economics of those businesses has increased, the quantity and quality of supply is better assured, and both packaging and raw materials are more

---

EXHIBIT 9.2   **Anheuser-Busch Companies' Subsidiaries**

Anheuser-Busch, Inc.	Busch Entertainment Corporation
Metal Container Corporation	Busch Properties, Inc.
Busch Agricultural Resources	St. Louis National Baseball Club, Inc.
Container Recovery Corporation	
Anheuser-Busch International, Inc.	Civic Center Corporation
Campbell Taggart, Inc.	St. Louis Refrigerator Car Company
Eagle Snacks, Inc.	
Busch Industrial Products Corporation	Manufacturers Railway Company

EXHIBIT 9.3   **Board of Directors, Anheuser-Busch Companies, Inc.**

DIRECTORS

August A. Busch, Jr.
Honorary Chairman of the Board

August A. Busch III
Chairman of the Board and
President

Richard T. Baker
Former Managing Partner and
present Consultant—Ernst & Ernst
(now Ernst & Whinney); certified
public accountants

Margaret S. Busch
Vice-President—Corporate
Promotions

Peter M. Flanigan
Managing Director—Dillon, Read
& Co. Inc.; an investment banking
firm

Roderick M. Hills
Distinguished Faculty Fellow and
Lecturer, International Finance—
Yale University School of
Management

Edwin S. Jones
Former Chairman of the Board—
First Union Bancorporation (now
Centerre Bancorporation); a multi-
bank holding company

Fred L. Kuhlmann
Vice-Chairman of the Board and
Executive Vice-President of St.
Louis National Baseball Club, Inc.

Vilma S. Martinez
Partner—Munger, Tolles & Olson;
attorneys

Sybil C. Mobley
Dean of the School of Business and
Industry—Florida A&M University

Bernard A. Edison
President and Director—Edison
Brothers Stores, Inc.; retail
specialty stores

James B. Orthwein
Chairman of the Board—Newhard,
Cook & Co. Inc.; an investment
brokerage firm

Walter C. Reisinger
Special Representative—Customer
Relations—Anheuser-Busch
Companies, Inc.

Armand C. Stalnaker
Professor of Management—
Washington University School of
Business

Fred W. Wenzel
Chairman of the Board—Kellwood
Company; a manufacturer of
apparel and home fashions

ADVISORY MEMBER

W. R. Persons
Former Chairman and Chief
Executive Officer—Emerson
Electric Company; a manufacturer
of electrical and electronic
equipment

DIRECTOR EMERITUS

M. R. Chambers
Former Chairman of the Executive
Committee and Director—
INTERCO INCORPORATED

EXHIBIT   9.4   **Executive Officers of Anheuser-Busch Companies, Inc.**

August A. Busch III (age 48) is presently Chairman of the Board, President, Chief Executive Officer, and Director of the company and has served in such capacities since 1977, 1974, 1975, and 1963, respectively. He is also Chairman of the Board and Chief Executive Officer of the company's subsidiary, Anheuser-Busch, Inc. and has served in such capacity since 1979. He serves as a member of the Corporate Office.[1]

Dennis P. Long (age 50) has served as Vice-President and Group Executive of the company since 1979. Also since 1979, he has been President and Chief Operating Officer of the company's subsidiary, Anheuser-Busch, Inc. He serves as a member of the Corporate Office.[1]

Jerry E. Ritter (age 51) has served since 1984 as Vice-President and Group Executive of the company. During the past five years he has also served as Treasurer of the company (1981) and Vice-President, Finance (1981–1983). He serves as a member of the Corporate Office.[1]

Barry H. Beracha (age 44) has been Vice-President and Group Executive of the company since 1976. He is also presently (1988) Chairman of the Board and Chief Executive Officer of two of the company's subsidiaries, Metal Container Corporation and Container Recovery Corporation, and has served in such capacities since 1976 and 1978, respectively. Since 1984 he has served as President of another subsidiary, Metal Label Corporation.

Patrick T. Stokes (age 43) has been Vice-President and Group Executive of the company since 1981. He is also the Chairman and President of Campbell Taggart Inc. He has held these positions since 1985. He was previously Vice-President and Group Executive of the company and served in such capacity from 1981. During the past five years he also served as Vice-President, Materials Acquisition (1980–1981).

John H. Purnell (age 44) has served as Vice-President and Group Executive of the company since 1982. During the past five years he also served as Vice-President, Corporate Planning and Development (1981). He has also been Chairman of the Board and President of two of the company's subsidiaries, Anheuser-Busch International, Inc. and Eagle Snacks, Inc., since 1980 and 1982, respectively.

W. Randolph Baker (age 39) has been Vice-President and Group Executive of the company since 1982. He has also served as Chairman of the Board and President of two of the company's subsidiaries, Busch Entertainment Corporation (since 1979) and Busch Properties, Inc. (since 1978), and Chairman of the Board and Chief Executive Officer of another subsidiary, Busch Creative Services Corporation (since 1983).

Stephen K. Lambright (age 43) has been Vice-President and Group Executive of the company since 1984. During the past five years he has also served as Vice-President, National Affairs (since 1981) and as Vice-President, Industry and Government Affairs (1981–1983).

(Continued)

EXHIBIT 9.4   (Continued)

> **Stuart F. Meyer** (age 52) has served since 1984 as Vice-President, Corporate Human Resources. During the past five years he also served as Vice-President, Employee Relations (1981–1983).
>
> **Raymond E. Goff** (age 40) has been Vice-President and Group Executive of the company since January 1986. Since that time he has also been Chairman of the Board and Chief Executive Officer of two of the company's subsidiaries, Busch Agricultural Resources, Inc., and Busch Industrial Products Corporation. He has also served as Vice-President, Administration of a subsidiary, Anheuser-Busch, Inc. (1981–1985).
>
> ---
> ¹The Corporate Office consists of Mr. Busch, Mr. Long, and Mr. Ritter.

EXHIBIT 9.5   **Anheuser-Busch Companies, Inc.: Segments**

COMPANY	YEAR FOUNDED	ACTIVITIES
Business Segment: Beer and Beer-Related		
1. Anheuser-Busch, Inc.	1852	The world's largest brewer in 1985, selling 68.0 million barrels; has been the industry leader since 1957. Distributes 11 naturally brewed products through 960 independent beer wholesalers and 10 company-owned wholesalers.
2. Busch Agricultural Resources	1962	Processes barley into malt. In 1985, supplied 32% of the company's malt requirements. Grows and processes rice, and can meet 20% of the company's rice need.
3. Container Recovery Corp.	1979	Largest aluminum recycler in U.S.A. in 1985.
4. Metal Container Division	1974	Expected to produce 5.8 billion lids and 5 billion cans in 1986: 35% of the company's requirements and 6.4% of all beverage cans and lids in the U.S.
5. Anheuser-Busch Beverage Group	1985	Responsible for the non-beer beverages. In 1985, acquired two mineral water companies—the Saratoga Spring Co. and à Santé Mineral Water Co. Offers three wine products— Master Cellars Wines, Baybry's champagne coolers, and Dewey Stevens premium light wine coolers.
6. Anheuser-Busch International, Inc.	1981	International licensing and marketing subsidiary. The world beer market is 3.5 times the domestic market.
7. Busch Media Group	1985	In-house agency to purchase national broadcast media time.
8. Promotional Products Group	N/A	Responsible for licensing, development, sales, and warehousing of the company's promotional merchandise.

COMPANY	YEAR FOUNDED	ACTIVITIES
Business Segment: Food Products		
1. Campbell Taggart, Inc.	1982	75 plants and approx. 19,000 employees. Consists of the following subsidiaries: (1) bakery operations, (2) refrigerated products, (3) frozen food products, and (4) international.
2. Eagle Snacks, Inc.	1978	Produces and distributes a premium line of snack foods and nuts. In 1984 began self-manufacturing virtually all of its snack products, and in 1985 purchased Cape Cod Potato Chip Company.
3. Busch Industrial Products Corp.	1927	Leading producer and marketer of compressed yeast in U.S.; also produces autolyzed yeast extract.
Business Segment: Diversified Operations		
1. Busch Entertainment Corp.	1959	Family entertainment subsidiary, with (1) The Dark Continent, (Fla.), (2) The Old Country (Va.), (3) Adventure Island (Fla.), (4) Sesame Place (Pa.), and (5) Exploration Cruise Line—7 ships. In 1985, more than 2.9 million people visited the Dark Continent, and 2.05 million visitors came to The Old Country.
2. Busch Properties, Inc.	1970	Real estate development subsidiary with commercial properties in Va., Ohio, and Calif. Developing a planned community in Williamsburg, Va.
3. St. Louis National Baseball Club, Inc.	1953	St. Louis Cardinals, St. Louis, Mo.
4. Civic Center Corp.	1981	Owns various properties in downtown St. Louis, Mo.
5. Busch Creative Services	1980	Full-service business and marketing communications company, selling its services to Anheuser-Busch and other Fortune 500 companies.
6. St. Louis Refrigerator Car Co.	1878	Transportation subsidiary with 3 facilities. Provides commercial repair, rebuilding, maintenance, and inspection of railroad cars.
7. Manufacturers Railway Co.	1878	The other transportation subsidiary, operates 42 miles of track in the St. Louis area, 525 insulated railroad cars used to ship beer, 48 hopper cars and 77 boxcars. Includes a fleet of 200 trailers.

strongly controlled. In cultivating internally developed businesses such as Eagle Snacks, Anheuser-Busch continues its philosophy of maintaining premium quantity and quality of supply, and control of both packaging and raw materials through self-manufacture. In 1985 Eagle Snacks added plant capacity through the acquisition of Cape Cod Potato Chip Company and through plant expansion.

Another internally developed diversification, Master Cellars Wines, has become part of the newly created Anheuser-Busch Beverage Group. Two

EXHIBIT 9.6

Financial Information for Business Segments
(Dollar Amounts in Millions)

	BEER AND BEER-RELATED	%	PRODUCTS	%	DIVERSIFIED OPERATIONS	%	ELIMINATIONS	%	CONSOLIDATED
1985									
Net sales	$5,412.6	77.3	$1,416.4	20.2	$189.6	2.7	$(18.3)	(0.2)	$7,000.3
Operating income	797.0	95.8	28.5	3.4	6.8	0.8			832.3
Depreciation and amortization expense	161.7	—	53.2	—	21.2	—			236.1
Capital expenditures	416.2	—	103.7	—	36.1	—			601.0
Identifiable assets	3,515.6	—	935.9	—	174.6	—			4,626.1
Corporate assets									495.3
Total assets									$5,121.4
1984									
Net sales	$5,001.7	76.9	$1,343.9	20.7	$169.5	2.6	$(13.9)	(0.2)	$6,501.2
Operating income	728.2	96.5	16.5	2.2	10.0	1.3			754.7
Depreciation and amortization expense	141.1	—	42.3	—	20.0	—			203.4
Capital expenditures	393.1	—	106.7	—	19.4	—			519.2
Identifiable assets	3,214.7	—	811.8	—	128.0	—			4,154.5
Corporate assets									370.2
Total assets									$4,524.7
1983									
Net sales	$4,586.0	76.0	$1,311.9	21.7	$149.3	2.5	$(13.0)	(0.2)	$6,034.2
Operating income	649.9	92.8	47.3	6.7	3.6	0.5			700.8
Depreciation and amortization expense	129.5	—	40.3	—	17.5	—			187.3
Capital expenditures	348.1	—	54.8	—	25.1	—			428.0
Identifiable assets	2,994.1	—	768.6	—	143.7	—			3,906.4
Corporate assets									423.8
Total assets									$4,330.2

other acquisitions were the Saratoga Springs Company and à Santé Mineral Waters bottled water companies.

In 1985, the company became an investor in its first venture capital fund, Innoven, an established fund that has been very successful over the years. With this company, Anheuser-Busch gains exposure to new business areas being developed by the small start-up companies in which Innoven invests capital.

Busch Entertainment in 1985 acquired Exploration Cruise Lines. This six-vessel fleet cruises such areas as Mexico, Tahiti, and Alaska.

The company extended its research and development program with Interferon Sciences, which has been developing and clinically testing both material and recombinant forms of interferon, an anti-viral agent found in the human body. The program has been extended. Planning for the future, Anheuser-Busch will continue its long-term plans for diversification. These efforts are to be maintained as long as they are consistent with the company's objectives.

ALCOHOL ABUSE AND CORPORATE CITIZENSHIP

Anheuser-Busch ". . . is deeply concerned about the abuse of alcohol and the problem of driving while intoxicated. It supports the proposition that anything less than responsible consumption of alcoholic beverages is detrimental to the individual, to society, and to the brewing industry." The company has been a leader in developing programs that support this position.

The TIPS program was developed in 1985 by Health Communications Corporation, Anheuser-Busch, and the Miller Brewing Company to train retail personnel to deal effectively with the patrons who overindulge. Approximately 1,500 Anheuser-Busch wholesaler employees are now certified trainers. Their goal is to train 10,000 servers nationwide.

Anheuser-Busch was the first major brewer to promote on network television the control of alcohol abuse. The company is an active sponsor of SADD (Students Against Drunk Driving), and it developed operation ALERT (Action, Leadership, Education, Responsibility and Training), which serves as an umbrella covering a variety of educational and awareness programs.

In 1985, Anheuser-Busch contributed $11 million to charitable organizations such as the Muscular Dystrophy Association, Job Employment Programs, Urban League Scholarship programs, and the Economic Development Program. It also donated funds for disaster relief to victims of the 1985 Mexico earthquake and West Virginia flood.

LEGISLATION AND LITIGATION

In recent years, Anheuser-Busch has become more active in monitoring and taking positions on issues that could have a major impact on the company. The Industry and Government Affairs Division has expanded in order to identify and respond to such issues with specific programs.

The PUSH Campaign

In 1983, the Reverend Jesse Jackson's campaign PUSH against Anheuser-Busch Companies, Inc., accused the company of discrimination against blacks and encouraged minorities to boycott Anheuser-Busch's products. Using the battlecry "Bud is a Dud," Jackson claimed that the company (1) did not do business with enough minorities, (2) did not hire and promote black employees, (3) did not patronize black-oriented community organizations, and (4) did not have enough black wholesalers in the distribution system. Eventually, Mr. Wayman Smith, Vice-President of Corporate Affairs, was able to make the Reverend Jackson aware of the company's minority hiring and promotion practices, support to minorities throughout the country, and the role of minority suppliers. Anheuser-Busch also agreed to (1) spend $23 million in procurements from minority businesses, (2) spend $8 million on advertising in minority media, (3) spend $10 million in construction performed by minority-owned firms, (4) hold $2 million in certificates of deposit in 41 minority-owned banks, and (5) establish lines of credit for $6 million and deposit $6 million in payroll accounts with 25 of these banks.

The Minimum Drinking Age

The National Minimum Drinking Age Act of 1984 grants the federal government the authority to withhold federal highway funds from states that fail to raise their legal drinking age to 21 by 1986. Currently, forty states have mandated or approved a 21-year-old minimum drinking age.

The Thayer Suit

An insider-trading lawsuit filed by Anheuser-Busch against Paul Thayer, a former director, was resolved in 1985. The suit for $285 million claimed that, during the 1982 acquisition of Campbell-Taggart, Inc., Mr. Thayer leaked information that increased Campbell-Taggart's price before the takeover was complete. Thayer settled SEC civil charges and pleaded guilty to obstructing justice by lying to the SEC. When the suit was resolved, Mr. Thayer's sentence included four years in prison, a $5,000 fine, and the payment of $550,000 in profits earned by others through his tips.

Wholesale Distribution Rights

Anheuser-Busch is also active in the legal issue of allowing distributors to have exclusive wholesale-distribution rights. The state of Indiana is the only state to forbid exclusive-distribution contracts, and 27 states require the contracts. In 1977, the Supreme Court ruled that exclusive contracts can be legal, if the contracts don't hamper competition, but that decisions would be made on a case by case basis. Distributors and brewers say that this court decision has created lawsuits—any wholesaler or retailer can challenge its competitor's exclusive-distribution contracts.

The Malt Beverage Interbrand Competition Act of 1985, which has been cleared by the Senate Judiciary Committee, would preserve the industry's right to sue for antitrust violations. The 140-member U.S. Brewers Association and the 2,000-member National Beer Wholesaler Association have lobbied for the bill, because they believe that it would clarify the existing antitrust law. The bill's opponents, including the Federal Trade Commission, Senator Strom Thurmond (Chairman of the Senate Judiciary Committee), Senator Howard Metzenbaum, and numerous consumer groups, believe that exempting the beer industry from the antitrust laws would increase prices and reduce competition. In fact, the New York Attorney General has filed a class-action lawsuit against Miller, Stroh, Heileman and Anheuser-Busch, and claims that their exclusive agreements with distributors have caused price increases and decreased competition.

Use of "LA" Name

A lawsuit has been filed by G. Heileman Brewing and joined by Miller Brewing Company against Anheuser-Busch's use of "LA" (low alcohol) as a brand name. As in a previous suit by the Stroh Brewery, these breweries claim that this is a generic term. Anheuser-Busch won the Stroh Brewery suit with their claim that LA is a trademark and not a generic term.

COMPETITION

In 1984, there were 92 domestic brewery plants with a total capacity of 232.7 million barrels of beer. Operating at an average 78.7% of capacity, shipments were 178.4 million barrels (see Exhibit 9.7). This is quite a contrast to the 430 brewers in 1850 who produced 750,000 barrels per year. By the end of the 1890s, the number of brewers had grown to 1,169, and over 1,000,000 barrels were produced per year. However, by mid-century the industry had begun to consolidate. In 1954 there were 310 plants and 263 brewers, and by 1963 these numbers had shrunk to 211 plants and 171 brewers. This concentration of the industry continued through the next decade, so that there were 88 plants and 41 brewers in 1980. The top five brewers in the nation accounted for 87.1% of total beer sales in 1985, a 2.6% increase over the previous year.

In 1985, Anheuser-Busch held a 37.1% market share, compared with 35.0% in the previous year, and 23.4% a decade ago. It has set a corporate objective of 40% market share by the late 1980s. As Mr. Long, President and CEO, said, "We have always seen yesterday's success not as our ending point or a conclusion, but as a springboard into tomorrow's challenges."

EXHIBIT 9.7   **U.S. Brewing Industry Capacity and Usage—1984**
(Total Capacity and Shipments in Millions of Barrels)

BREWER	NUMBER OF PLANTS	TOTAL CAPACITY	SHIPMENTS	% OF CAPACITY
Anheuser-Busch	11	66.5	64.0	96.2
Miller Brewing (Philip Morris)	7	54.0	37.5	69.4
The Stroh Brewery	7	32.6	23.9	73.3
G. Heileman Brewing	12	26.5	16.8	63.4
Adolph Coors	1	15.5	13.2	85.2
Pabst Brewing	4	15.0	11.6	77.3
Genesee Brewing	1	4.0	3.0	75.0
Christian Schmidt[1,2]	2	5.0	2.1	42.0
Falstaff Brewing[3]	5	5.0	2.3	46.0
Pittsburgh Brewing	1	1.2	1.0	83.3
All others	41	7.4	3.2	43.2
Domestic total	92	232.7	178.4	78.7

[1]Includes 2.8 million barrels which are tax-free exports and military shipments.

[2]Includes Ohio plant which closed Nov. 1984.

[3]Includes Pearl Brewing Co. and General Brewing Co.

SOURCES: Company Annual Reports; *Modern Brewery Age Blue Book* and *Impact* Databank.

The challenging objective for the 1990s will be a 50% market share. The sales and market-share figures of Anheuser-Busch's competitors are shown in Exhibit 9.8.

Since Philip Morris Company acquired it in 1970, Miller Brewing has been Anheuser-Busch's prime competitor. Miller's market share in 1970 was 4.2% (5.1 million barrels), and it ranked seventh in the industry. The company experienced rapid growth in the 1970s because of the successful introduction of "Lite" beer. Anheuser-Busch countered with two separate strategies. First, the company increased its advertising budgets and took on Miller in head-to-head competition. Then, Anheuser-Busch developed a strategy of flanking Miller's beers in each category with two Anheuser-Busch beers (e.g., Budweiser and Busch flanked Miller High Life in the premium-beer category).

Over the past three years, Miller has introduced eight new brands of beer. Although the company had to mothball its Trenton, Ohio, brewery in 1984, its market share had grown to 20.3% (37.1 million barrels) by 1985, and the company now ranks second in the industry. Miller's sales volume did decline by 1.1 percent in 1985. This decline was attributed to continued weakness in Miller High Life's sales. Miller's other premium beer, Lowen-

EXHIBIT 9.8   **Sales of Leading U.S. Brewers**
(Volume in Thousands of Barrels)

COMPANY	1970 Volume	1970 Market Share (%)	1980 Volume	1980 Market Share (%)	1984 Volume	1984 Market Share (%)	1985 Volume	1985 Market Share (%)	% CHANGE IN VOLUME, 1984–1985
Anheuser-Busch	22,202	18.1	50,160	28.2	64,000	35.0	68,000	37.1	+ 6.3
Miller Brewing	5,150	4.2	37,300	21.0	37,520	20.5	37,100	20.3	− 1.1
The Stroh Brewery	3,276	2.7	6,161	3.5	23,900	13.1	23,400	12.8	− 2.1
G. Heileman Brewing	3,000	2.4	13,270	7.4	16,760	9.2	16,200	8.8	− 3.3
Adolph Coors Co.	7,277	5.9	13,779	7.7	13,187	7.2	14,738	8.1	+11.8
Top 5, total	40,905	33.3	120,670	67.8	155,387	85.0	159,438	87.1	+ 2.8
Other domestic	80,995	68.0	52,830	29.6	20,133	11.1	15,662	8.6	−22.1
Total domestic	121,900	99.3	173,300	97.4	175,500	96.1	175,100	95.7	− 0.2
Imports	900	0.7	4,600	2.8	7,200	3.9	7,900	4.3	+ 9.7
Total	122,700	100.0	177,900	100.0	182,700	100.0	183,000	100.0	+ 0.2

brau, was also competing poorly at this time. However, Miller's profits were up by approximately 17% in 1985 over the depressed profit on 1984.

In 1981, the Stroh Brewery purchased F&M Schaefer and closed their Detroit brewery (7.2 million barrel capacity). On April 27, 1982, the Joseph Schlitz Brewing Company was merged into the Stroh Brewery, and Stroh became the third largest brewer. The company's shipping of 13.1 million barrels in 1985 represents a 12.8% market share and a 2.1% decline in volume sales over the previous years.

G. Heileman Brewing, the United States' fourth largest brewer, has been very effective in competing against Anheuser-Busch in regional markets. It has successfully developed and implemented a strategy of acquiring struggling local brewers at a low cost. After acquiring the new brewery, Heileman reintroduces its brands with an aggressive marketing plan. Anheuser-Busch has countered with a strategy focused on heavy price competition from its Busch brands. Although G. Heileman halted its planned expansion into the Southwest market, the company's market share grew from 2.4% (3.0 million barrels) in 1970 to 8.8% (16.2 million barrels) in 1985. However, the company's earnings from its brewing industry declined by 11% in 1985, and it closed its small Phoenix plant (500,000 barrels).

The fifth largest brewer, Adolph Coors Company, had a 13% volume increase in sales in 1985. This increase was the result of an aggressive expansion into the New England and Illinois markets. Coors's profits from beer increased by 77% from its poor 1984 performance.

Pabst Brewing, the sixth largest brewer, experienced a decline in market share from 6.5% in 1984 to 5.0% in 1985, when the company's new owners aggressively increased prices.

DISTRIBUTION CHANNELS

The company distributes its beer in the United States and the Caribbean through a network of 10 company-owned wholesale operations, employing approximately 1,600 people, and about 960 independently owned wholesale companies (see Exhibit 9.9). The independent wholesalers employ approximately 30,000 people. Canadian and European distribution is achieved through special arrangements with foreign brewing companies.

EXHIBIT 9.9 **National Distribution Map**

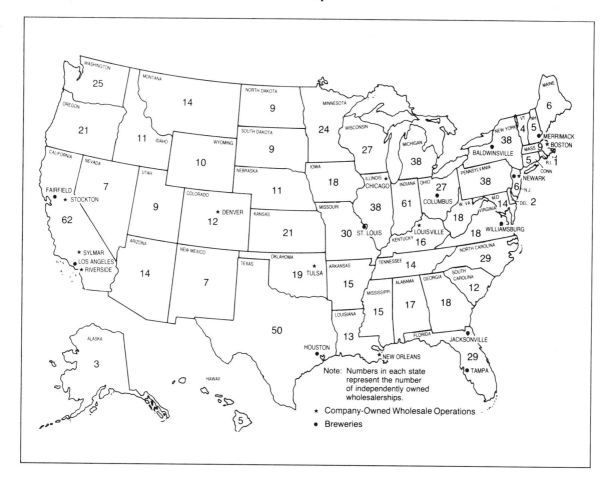

Note: Numbers in each state represent the number of independently owned wholesalerships.

★ Company-Owned Wholesale Operations

• Breweries

Sales volume at the wholesale level ranges from 870 barrels to 1.1 million barrels annually. However, the LA and Busch brands are presently available only in selected markets around the country.

MARKETING, ADVERTISING, AND PRODUCTS	Beer uniquely fits contemporary lifestyles. The five hallmarks of beer as a consumer beverage are convenience, moderation, health, value, and thirst-quenching properties. Each member of the Anheuser-Busch family of eleven beers is positioned to take advantage of this image. Exhibit 9.10 describes the targeted market for each of the company's beers.

There has been a major shift in the consumption of beer by type or class (see Exhibit 9.11). It is expected that per capita beer consumption will decline about 1% or less in 1986, and remain flat throughout the balance of the 1980s. This decline is expected to be accompanied by a 2% rise in beer prices in 1986 and 1987. Also, the Census Bureau projects a drop in the 20–39-year-old age group, a major beer market (see Exhibit 9.12).

Anheuser-Busch has had its beers affiliated with sports for years (see Exhibit 9.13), and is probably the largest sponsor of sporting events, vehicles, and broadcasts. In fact, the company sponsored the 1984 Olympics, and in 1985 spent in excess of $100 million for advertising on television and radio sporting events. Out of a total $522,900,000 spent on advertising in 1985,

EXHIBIT 9.10   Anheuser-Busch Beers

BEER	CLASS	TARGET MARKET
Budweiser	Premium	Any demographic or ethnic group and any region of the country
Bud Light	Light	Young to middle-aged males
Michelob	Super premium	Contemporary adults
Michelob Light	Light	Young, active upscale drinker with high-quality lifestyle
Michelob Classic Dark	Premium dark	Yuppies
Busch	Premium	Consumers who prefer lighter-tasting beer
Natural Light	Light	Beverage to go with good food
LA	Low alcohol	Health-conscious consumers
King Cobra	Malt liquor	Contemporary male adults, aged 21–24
Carlsberg	Lager	Import market
Elephant Malt Liquor	Malt liquor	Consumers who enjoy imported beer

EXHIBIT 9.11

Apparent Beer Consumption by Type
(In Millions of Barrels)

TYPE	CONSUMPTION					% CHANGE, 1983–1984
	1975	1980	1982	1983	1984	
Popular	65.4	30.0	29.5	30.5	38.0	+ 18.0
Premium	71.6	102.3	95.7	94.6	87.0	− 8.0
Super-premium	5.0	11.5	10.8	10.1	9.5	− 5.9
Light	2.8	22.1	32.5	34.1	35.3	+ 3.5
Low alcohol	—	—	—	*	0.8	—
Imported	1.7	4.8	5.8	5.3	7.2	+ 14.3
Malt liquor	3.8	5.5	6.4	8.4	5.8	− 9.4
Ale	N.A.	1.9	1.8	1.7	1.4	− 17.6
Total	150.3	177.9	182.3	183.7	182.8	− 0.5

N.A.—Not available.
*Less than 50,000 gallons.
SOURCE: *Impact* Databank.

EXHIBIT 9.12

U.S. Population Projections

AGE GROUP*	1985		1990		2000	
	Number (thous.)	% of Total	Number (thous.)	% of Total	Number (thous.)	% of Total
Under 5 yrs.	18,453	7.7	19,198	7.7	17,826	6.6
5 to 14 yrs.	33,408	14.0	35,384	14.2	38,277	14.3
15 to 19 yrs.	18,416	7.7	18,968	6.8	18,943	7.1
20 to 24 yrs.	21,301	8.9	18,580	7.4	17.145	6.4
25 to 29 yrs.	21,838	9.2	21,522	8.6	17,396	6.5
30 to 34 yrs.	19,950	8.4	22,007	8.8	19,019	7.1
35 to 39 yrs.	17,894	7.5	20,001	8.0	21,753	8.1
40 to 44 yrs.	14,110	5.9	17,848	7.2	21,990	8.2
45 to 49 yrs.	11,647	4.9	13,980	5.6	19,763	7.4
50 to 54 yrs.	10,817	4.5	11,422	4.6	17,356	6.5
55 to 64 yrs.	22,188	9.3	21,051	8.4	23,787	8.9
65 yrs. & over	28,609	12.0	31,697	12.7	34,921	13.0
All Ages	238,631	100.0	249,658	100.0	267,955	100.0

*Includes Armed Forces abroad.
SOURCE: Department of Commerce, Population Series P–25, as of July 1, 1985.

EXHIBIT 9.13   **Anheuser-Busch's Sports Affiliations**

BUDWEISER	BUD LIGHT	MICHELOB	BUSCH	MICHELOB LIGHT
Horse racing	Triathlon	Lacrosse	NASCAR	
Soccer	Track	Rugby	Auto racing	Skiing
Boxing	Boat racing	Golf	Billiards	Volleyball
Boat racing		Sailing		Tennis

SOURCE: Anheuser-Busch 1986 Fact Sheet.

Anheuser-Busch spent $225,250,000 in television advertising (see Exhibit 9.14). The top fifteen beer advertisers spent a total of $497,163,000 on television advertising in 1985 (see Exhibit 9.15).

Budweiser advertising and sales are very important to Anheuser-Busch, as Bud accounts for more than two-thirds of the company's beer production and one-quarter of the whole domestic market. To promote Bud, Anheuser-Busch began running advertisements exploiting patriotic fervor, the current resurgence in the pride of being an American.

Following this strategy, Anheuser-Busch has fine-tuned the campaign "For All You Do, This Bud's for You" into the very successful "You Make America Work, and This Bud's for You." In 1985, measured media ads and

EXHIBIT 9.14   **1985 Anheuser-Busch Advertising Expenditures**

MEDIUM	EXPENDITURES (THOUS. OF $)
Magazines	$ 13,956
Newspapers	5,611
Newspaper suppliers	327
Business publications	724
Network television	154,503
Sports television	70,747
Network radio	8,929
Sports radio	39,713
Outdoor	5,105
Network cable	16,395
Total Measured Media	$316,011
Total Unmeasured	206,889
Total	$522,900

SOURCE: *Advertising Age*, Sept. 4, 1986.

EXHIBIT 9.15   Top Fifteen Beer Advertisers on Television, 1985

	EXPENDITURES		
	Network	Spot	Total
Anheuser-Busch Cos.	$143,235,200	$ 55,820,000	$199,055,200
Philip Morris Cos. (Miller, et al)	112,641,600	27,337,300	139,978,900
Adolph Coors Co.	18,076,400	33,586,800	51,663,200
Stroh Brewery Co.	31,847,700	8,163,800	40,011,500
G. Heileman Brewing Co.	6,931,300	8,782,700	15,714,000
Brauen Beck & Co.	—	4,160,300	4,160,300
RJR Nabisco, Inc. (Fosters, Moosehead)	90,900	1,198,900	1,289,800
Genesee Brewing Co.	192,000	4,962,500	5,154,500
Van Munching & Co.	6,502,900	9,165,800	15,668,700
S & P Co. (Pabst, Pearl, Hamms)	—	1,847,300	1,847,300
Molson Cos.	99,200	1,800,400	1,899,600
Latrobe Brewing Co.	—	444,500	444;500
Pittsburgh Brewing Co.	—	853,700	853,700
John Labatt, Ltd.	—	567,400	567,400
Masters Brewing Co.	—	929,000	929,000
Total	$329,202,500	$167,961,100	$497,163,600

SOURCE: *Modern Brewery Age,* April 13, 1987, p. 1.

promotions topped $80 million for Bud, the most heavily advertised beer in the United States. Miller also followed the same advertising strategy; however, as Budweiser sales increased, Miller sales decreased.

HUMAN RESOURCES MANAGEMENT

In 1983, Anheuser-Busch established its Office of Corporate Human Resources to focus on human resources activities and issues. Human resource planning has become an integral component of business planning at all levels of the organization.

The company's philosophy concerning its approximately 39,000 employees is that all employees are to be treated with courtesy and respect. The company tries to foster an atmosphere for open, two-way communications. Functioning on a national level, labor–management committees involve employees in issues and decisions that directly affect them and their working conditions. Additionally, in 1985 the beer division introduced "The New A-BI," a communication program to encourage the employees to suggest productivity improvements and cost reductions.

EXHIBIT 9.16

Production Facilities
(Capacity in Millions of Barrels)

BREWERY	YEAR OPENED	1986 CAPACITY	TYPE OF BEER PRODUCED							
			Bud	Bud Light	Michelob Light	Michelob	Busch	Natural Light	LA	Michelob Classic Dark
St. Louis	1880	12.70	X	X	X	X	X	X	X	X
Newark	1951	5.30	X	X	X	X				X
Los Angeles	1954	10.90	X	X	X	X		X	X	X
Tampa	1959	1.80	X	X			X	X		
Houston	1966	9.00	X	X	X	X	X	X		
Columbus	1968	6.30	X	X	X	X	X	X		
Jacksonville	1969	6.60	X	X	X	X	X	X		
Merrimack	1970	2.97	X	X	X	X	X	X		
Williamsburg	1972	8.70	X	X	X	X	X	X	X	
Fairfield	1976	3.90	X	X	X	X		X	X	X
Baldwinsville	1982	7.10	X	X	X	X		X	X	
Total capacity		75.27								

The Teamsters' Union represents approximately 15,600 employees in Anheuser-Busch Companies, Inc. A new labor contract with the International Brotherhood of Teamsters was ratified in 1985 and is effective through February, 1988.

PRODUCTION FACILITIES

Anheuser-Busch has eleven breweries located in nine states, and their annual capacity is 75.27 million barrels of beer (see Exhibit 9.16). A twelfth brewery at Fort Collins, Colorado, is scheduled to be operational in 1988, and its annual capacity will be 5 million barrels. Only the St. Louis plant brews all nine beers.

Productivity continues to be an integral part of Anheuser-Busch's growth strategy. In 1985, Anheuser-Busch, Inc., received the Excellence in Productivity Award from the Institute of Industrial Engineers because of the company's continued commitment to reducing waste and increasing efficiencies. Also, the Williamsburg Brewery received the U.S. Senate's Productivity Award. Capital investment in new and existing plants and equipment resulted in $1.8 billion of cost savings over the past six years. In 1985, Anheuser-Busch's Employee Suggestion Program resulted in $1 million of productivity savings. Nevertheless, productivity is not the sole goal. Anheuser-Busch has an equal commitment to quality because management believes that quality and productivity complement each other.

While many other brewers are shut down or selling their existing facilities and running at lower capacity levels (see Exhibit 9.7), Anheuser-Busch must expand its capacity and operate with a high utilization of existing capacity, in order to meet the increasing demand for its beer. Therefore Anheuser-Busch has developed an extensive expansion and modernization program. For example, the expansion of the Houston brewery, completed in 1985, added 5 million barrels of capacity, and the St. Louis, Newark, and Merrimack plants have been modernized.

The plants that manufacture and recycle cans continue to expand as well. Metal Container Corporation produced 4 billion cans and 2 billion lids in 1985. To meet the company's goals, the Gainesville plant was expanded in 1985; a new Oklahoma City plant, to manufacture ecology-type lids with stay-on tabs, will be completed in 1986; and the Jacksonville, Columbus, and Arnold plants are scheduled for modernization and expansion. In addition, Container Recovery Corporation now has three plants and is the largest recycler in the U.S. As Mr. Busch said, " . . . We intend to adapt our proven management and production abilities to expand over horizons into areas previously uncharted by Anheuser-Busch."

FINANCE

Recently, Standard and Poors raised the bond ratings on $800 million of Anheuser-Busch's senior debt from A + to AA −, in recognition of its improved financial performance. The Busch family owns approximately 23% of the company's stock, and for the fifty-third consecutive year, Anheuser-Busch has paid dividends. Financial data for the company can be found in Exhibits 9.17–9.19.

For the next five years, the company has planned for extensive capital expenditures programs to take advantage of growth opportunities in its three

---

EXHIBIT 9.17   **Consolidated Balance Sheet**
(Dollar Amounts in Millions)

	1985	1984
Assets		
Current Assets		
Cash and marketable securities (marketable securities of $119.9 in 1985 and $69.3 in 1984 at cost, which approximates market)	$ 169.6	$ 78.6
Accounts and notes receivable, less allowance for doubtful accounts of $3.1 in 1985 and $2.8 in 1984	301.7	275.6
Inventories		
Raw materials and supplies	225.4	212.7
Work in process	73.5	65.7
Finished goods	38.8	37.5
Total inventories	337.7	315.9
Other current assets	156.5	106.2
Total current assets	965.5	776.3
Investments and Other Assets		
Investments in and advances to unconsolidated subsidiaries	56.7	42.9
Investment properties	16.5	18.1
Deferred charges and other non-current assets	97.5	87.1
Excess of cost over net assets of acquired businesses, net	99.3	85.3
Total investments and other assets	270.0	233.4
Plant and Equipment		
Land	91.8	85.4
Buildings	1,578.7	1,399.3
Machinery and equipment	3,381.4	2,920.6
Construction in progress	288.9	395.3
Total	5,340.8	4,800.6
Less: Accumulated depreciation	1,454.9	1,285.6
Total plant and equipment	3,885.9	3,515.0
Total assets	$5,121.4	$4,524.7

(Continued)

EXHIBIT 9.17 (Continued)

	1985	1984
Liabilities and Shareholders Equity		
Current Liabilities		
Accounts payable	$ 425.3	$ 338.2
Accrued salaries, wages, and benefits	177.1	150.3
Accrued interest payable	30.1	26.8
Due to customers for returnable containers	33.1	31.8
Accrued taxes, other than income taxes	56.9	43.6
Estimated income taxes	31.3	39.0
Other current liabilities	84.0	66.3
Total current liabilities	837.8	696.0
Long-Term Debt	861.3	835.8
Deferred Income Taxes	961.7	755.0
Convertible Redeemable Preferred Stock (Liquidation Value $300.0)	287.6	286.9
Common Stock And Other Shareholders Equity		
Preferred stock, $1.00 par value, authorized 32,498,000 shares in 1985, 1984, and 1983; none issued	—	—
Common stock, $1.00 par value, authorized 200,000,000 shares in 1985, 1984, and 1983; issued 146,633,977, 48,641,869 and 48,514,214 shares, respectively	146.6	48.6
Capital in excess of par value	90.4	173.2
Retained earnings	2,142.3	1,829.3
Foreign currency translation adjustment	(4.4)	(6.6)
	2,374.9	2,044.5
Less: Cost of treasury stock (8,114,453, 4,692,456 and 358,656 shares in 1985, 1984, and 1983, respectively)	201.9	93.5
	2,173.0	1,951.0
Commitments and Contingencies	—	—
Total Liabilities and Shareholder's Equity	$5,121.4	$4,524.7

business segments. The company is not opposed to long-term financing for some of its capital programs, but cash flow from operations will be the principal source of funds to support these programs. For short-term capital requirements, the company has access to a maximum of $500 million from a bank credit-line agreement.

EXHIBIT 9.18   Financial Summary—Operations

(Dollar Amounts in Millions, Except Per-Share Data)

Eleven Years

	1985	1984	1983	1982	1981	1980	1979	1978	1977	1976	1975
Consolidated Summary of Operations											
Barrels sold	68.0	64.0	60.5	59.1	54.5	50.2	46.2	41.6	36.6	29.1	35.2
Sales	$7,683.3	$7,158.2	$6,658.5	$5,185.7	$4,409.6	$3,822.4	$3,263.7	$2,701.6	$2,231.2	$1,753.0	$2,036.7
Federal and state beer taxes	683.0	657.0	624.3	609.1	562.4	527.0	487.8	442.0	393.2	311.9	391.7
Net sales	7,000.3	6,501.2	6,034.2	4,576.6	3,847.2	3,295.4	2,775.9	2,259.6	1,838.0	1,441.1	1,645.0
Cost of products sold	4,676.1	4,414.2	4,113.2	3,331.7	2,975.5	2,553.9	2,172.1	1,762.4	1,462.8	1,175.0	1,343.8
Gross profit	2,324.2	2,087.0	1,921.0	1,244.9	871.7	741.5	603.8	497.2	375.2	266.1	301.2
Marketing, administrative and research expenses	1,491.9	1,332.3	1,220.2	752.0	515.0	428.6	356.7	274.9	190.4	137.8	126.1
Operating income	832.3	754.7	700.8	492.9	356.7	312.9	247.1	222.3	184.8	128.3	175.1
Interest expense	(93.4)	(102.7)	(111.4)	(89.2)	(89.6)	(75.6)	(40.3)	(28.9)	(26.7)	(26.9)	(22.6)
Interest capitalized	37.2	46.8	32.9	41.2	64.1	41.7	—	—	—	—	—
Interest income	21.3	22.8	12.5	17.0	6.2	2.4	8.4	11.7	7.7	10.3	10.9
Other income (expense), net	(16.9)	(31.8)	(18.8)	(8.1)	(12.2)	(9.9)	5.4	.7	4.1	1.7	1.9
Loss on partial closing of Los Angeles Busch Gardens	—	—	—	—	—	—	—	—	—	(10.0)	—
Gain on sale of Lafayette plant	—	—	—	20.4	—	—	—	—	—	—	—
Income before income taxes	780.5	689.8	616.0	474.2	325.2	271.5	220.6	205.8	169.9	103.4	165.3
Income taxes	336.8	298.3	268.0	186.9	107.8	99.7	76.3	94.8	78.0	48.0	80.6
Income before cumulative effect of an accounting change	443.7	391.5	348.0	287.3	217.4	171.8	144.3	111.0	91.9	55.4	84.7

(Continued)

EXHIBIT 9.18 (Continued)

	1985	1984	1983	1982	1981	1980	1979	1978	1977	1976	1975
Consolidated Summary of Operations											
Cumulative effect of change to the flow-through method of accounting for the investment tax credit	—	—	—	—	—	—	52.1	—	—	—	—
Net income	$ 443.7	$ 391.5	$ 348.0	$ 287.3	$ 217.4	$ 171.8	$ 196.4	$ 111.0	$ 91.9	$ 55.4	$ 84.7
Per share—Primary¹											
Income before cumulative effect of an accounting change	2.84	2.47	2.17	1.99	1.60	1.27	1.07	.82	.68	.41	.63
Cumulative effect of change to the flow-through method of accounting for the investment tax credit	—	—	—	—	—	—	.38	—	—	—	—
Net income	2.84	2.47	2.17	1.99	1.60	1.27	1.45	.82	.68	.41	.63
Per share—Fully diluted	2.84	2.47	2.17	1.96	1.54	1.27	1.45	.82	.68	.41	.63
Cash dividends paid											
Common stock	102.7	89.7	78.3	65.8	51.2	44.8	40.7	37.0	32.0	30.6	28.8
Per share	.73⅓	.62⅔	.54	.46	.37⅔	.33	.30	.27⅓	.23⅔	.22⅔	.21⅓
Preferred stock	27.0	27.0	29.7	—	—	—	—	—	—	—	—
Per share	3.60	3.60	3.60	—	—	—	—	—	—	—	—
Average number of common shares	156.3	158.7	160.5	144.3	136.2	135.6	135.6	135.3	135.3	135.3	135.3

¹Per share data is in $, not millions of $.

EXHIBIT 9.19 Financial Summary—Balance Sheet and Other Information

(Dollar Amounts in Millions, Except Per Share And Statistical Data)

	1985	1984	1983	1982	1981	1980	1979	1978	1977	1976	1975
Balance sheet information											
Working capital	127.7	80.3	175.1	45.8	45.9	26.3	88.1	223.7	175.4	182.1	255.4
Current ratio	1.2	1.1	1.2	1.1	1.1	1.1	1.3	1.8	1.8	2.0	2.5
Plant and equipment, net	3,885.9	3,515.0	3,204.2	2,988.9	2,257.6	1,947.4	1,461.8	1,109.2	952.0	857.1	724.9
Long-term debt	861.3	835.8	961.4	969.0	817.3	743.8	507.9	427.3	337.5	340.7	342.2
Total debt to total debt plus equity	25.9%	27.2%	31.9%	35.4%	42.4%	43.4%	36.0%	36.4%	33.4%	35.8%	36.8%
Deferred income taxes	961.7	755.0	573.2	455.1	357.7	261.6	193.8	146.9	119.1	93.0	74.6
Convertible redeemable preferred stock	287.6	286.9	286.0	285.0	—	—	—	—	—	—	—
Common stock and other shareholders equity	2,173.0	1,951.0	1,766.5	1,526.6	1,206.8	1,031.4	904.3	747.9	673.9	611.9	587.1
Return on shareholders equity	18.9%	18.2%	18.0%	19.9%	19.3%	17.8%	16.9%(2)	15.6%	14.3%	9.2%	15.2%
Total assets	5,121.4	4,524.7	4,330.2	3,902.8	2,875.2	2,449.7	1,926.0	1,648.0	1,403.8	1,268.1	1,202.1
Other information											
Capital expenditures	601.0	519.2	428.0	355.8	421.3	590.0	432.3	228.7	156.7	198.7	155.4
Depreciation and amortization	236.1	203.4	187.3	133.6	108.7	99.4	75.4	66.0	61.2	53.1	51.1
Total payroll cost	1,547.7	1,427.5	1,350.8	853.3	686.7	594.1	529.1	421.8	338.9	271.4	268.3
Effective tax rate	43.2%	43.2%	43.5%	39.4%	33.1%	36.7%	34.6%	46.0%	45.9%	46.4%	48.7%
Price/earnings ratio	14.9	9.8	9.6	11.0	8.9	7.3	7.1	9.8	9.8	18.8	18.1
Percent of pre-tax profit on gross sales	10.2%	9.6%	9.3%	9.1%	7.4%	7.1%	6.8%	7.6%	7.6%	5.9%	8.1%
Market price range of common stock (high/low)	45¾-23⅝	24¾-17⅞	25⅜-19½	23⅝-12⅞	14¾-9¼	10⅜-7	9-6½	9¼-5⅞	8⅜-6¼	12⅞-6⅞	13¼-8⅛

(Continued)

EXHIBIT 9.19 (Continued)

	1985	1984	1983	1982	1981	1980	1979	1978	1977	1976	1975
Pro Forma information, assuming retroactive application of the flow-through method of accounting for the investment tax credit:											
Net income	443.7	391.5	348.0	287.3	217.4	171.8	144.3	121.9	98.3	75.5	89.1
Net income per share:											
Primary	2.84	2.47	2.17	1.99	1.60	1.27	1.07	.90	.73	.56	.66
Fully diluted	2.84	2.47	2.17	1.96	1.54	1.27	1.07	.90	.73	.56	.66
Common stock and other shareholders equity	2,173.0	1,951.0	1,766.5	1,526.6	1,206.8	1,031.4	904.3	800.1	715.1	646.8	601.9
Return on shareholders equity	18.9%	18.2%	18.0%	19.9%	19.3%	17.8%	16.9%	16.1%	14.4%	12.1%	15.6%
Book value per share	15.69	13.81	12.17	10.54	8.86	7.61	6.66	5.91	5.28	4.78	4.45
Effective tax rate	43.2%	43.2%	43.5%	39.4%	33.1%	36.7%	34.6%	40.8%	42.1%	27.0%	46.1%

Apple Computer Corporation, 1987

PHYLLIS FEDDELER · THOMAS L. WHEELEN

On July 20, 1987, John Sculley, the CEO of Apple Computer Corporation, is mulling over a report prepared for him by his marketing department. This report focuses on the computer industry's outlook for the late 1980s, with special emphasis on the recently announced IBM Personal System 2 or PS/2, and Intel's new 80386 microchip.

Apple is a $1.9 billion company that designs, manufactures, sells, and services personal computers (PCs) and related software and peripheral products. The major sources of Apple's customers are homes, businesses, and educational institutions. Although the company is best established in the education segment with the Apple II, it is trying, through its Macintosh product line, to become a more significant competitor in the business markets. Apple also competes internationally, and 26% of its revenues come from outside of the United States. The principal methods of distribution are the independent retail dealer, national retail accounts, and direct sales.

Until recently, experts questioned whether Apple would survive, because of the general slump in the computer industry and Apple's lackluster sales. Even though the company was successfully reorganized in 1985 into a leaner, more profitable organization, some pointed out that cutting costs is not a growth strategy, especially in an innovation-driven industry. Furthermore, it was doubtful that Apple could coexist with IBM, the dominant competitor, in the business market. In 1986, the first "open" Macintosh, designed to provide owners with ease in modification, was introduced. IBM PCs had always been "open."

HISTORICAL BACKGROUND

The company was founded in 1976 by Steve Jobs, who was then 21, and Stephen Wozniak, 26. With only $1,350, raised by the sale of a VW van and an HP programmable calculator, and an order for fifty computers with a selling price of less than $700, the two young men began their business by manufacturing the Apple I in Jobs's garage.

Not long afterward, a mutual friend helped recruit A. D. "Mike" Markkula to help market the company and give it a million-dollar image. Markkula

This case was prepared by Ms. Phyllis Feddeler, MBA student, and Professor Thomas L. Wheelen of the University of South Florida. Copyright © 1987 by Phyllis Feddeler and Thomas L. Wheelen. Reprinted by permission.

533

had successfully managed the marketing departments of two semiconductor companies, Fairchild Semiconductor and Intel Corporation, that had experienced dynamic growth. On January 3, 1977, Apple Computer, Inc., was incorporated. In December 1980 the company went public with an offering of 4.6 million shares of common stock. In May 1981 there was a secondary offering of 2.6 million shares of common stock by approximately 100 selling stockholders, all of whom had acquired their shares through the employee stock plan or private placement.

In the high-growth industry of personal computers, Apple did grow quickly, despite increasing numbers of business failures among competitors. In 1985, Apple was the second-largest competitor, next to IBM, in the PC industry. (See Exhibit 10.1.)

During the years of high growth, the company suffered internal turmoil because of disagreements as to the company's direction, especially in terms of product development. Jobs's pet project, the Macintosh, was consuming an amount of funds disproportionate to the revenues it was bringing in. Internal rivalry grew between the Apple product department and the Macintosh product department. First Wozniak resigned (he now works as a consultant to Apple) and, in September 1985, Jobs resigned and took with him five key managers. Jobs intended to begin another company called Next, Inc. In its subsequent suit against Jobs, Apple claimed that he would use Apple research to build his new company, Next.

When John Sculley (a former CEO of Pepsi-Cola Company, who started working at Apple in May 1983) took over full control, Apple had just suffered its first loss as a public company and had undergone a reorganization that included laying off 20% of its employees. Shipments of Macintosh PCs were only 10,000 per month but the manufacturing capacity was 80,000 per month. Although the Macintosh was easy to use, it was criticized in the business world for being underpowered and overpriced. Sculley, who had no prior experience in the computer industry, knew marketing and personally

---

EXHIBIT 10.1   **Market Share of PC Sales**

	1986 (% OF TOTAL SALES)	1985 (% OF TOTAL SALES)
1. IBM	29.5	40.5
2. Apple	7.3	10.3
3. Compaq	7.0	5.2
4. Zenith	4.2	2.4
5. Tandy	3.4	4.6
6. Commodore	1.9	3.8
7. Other	46.7	33.2

pitched the Macintosh to large corporations such as GE and Eastman Kodak and to software manufacturers, before the improved Macintosh was introduced in January 1986.

MANAGEMENT

Apple is trying to centralize its operations and involve its senior management in day-to-day decisions. Recently, Sculley turned over responsibility of these decisions to Delbert Yocam, the Chief Operating Officer; Sculley could then spend his time on long-term planning. (See Exhibits 10.2 and 10.3 for the Board of Directors and top management.) New high-level management positions include Vice-President of Advanced Technology and Vice-President of U.S. Sales and Marketing. Between September 1986 and the end of 1986, the number of employees had grown from approximately 5,600 to 5,940.

In 1986, the suit against Steve Jobs and his new company was settled.

MICRO-COMPUTER INDUSTRY

There are two types of computer companies, those that follow and those that lead. Leaders are established by developing and producing the best-selling products. The followers wait for the leaders to build their products and then copy or "clone" them.

Since IBM first introduced its PC in 1981, many computer manufacturers have followed their lead. Marketing an innovative computer before IBM has presented its version is risky. If IBM later introduces a comparable machine with proprietary features, the earlier versions may be rendered obsolete and have to be redesigned.

For the past several years the technology industry has been in a slump, but increased earnings for the first quarter of 1987 (see Exhibit 10.4) might indicate that the entire industry is coming out of its recession. Dealer sales rose by 15% in the first two months of 1987 and PC shipments to computer stores rose 19% during the first quarter of 1987. Analysts believe that these strong first-quarter earnings, which contributed to the increases in the stock prices of companies such as IBM, Wang, Prime Computer, Inc., and Apple, also mean that sales will continue to increase.

Important new developments in the personal computer industry include desktop publishing and the recent use of Intel Corporation's 80386 microchip. In desktop publishing, a PC is used to produce low-cost, high-quality printed documents in-house. It was Apple's innovation with the Macintosh. Since the introduction of the Macintosh, however, software developers have been creating desktop publishing programs for the IBM PC, and other companies will be soon to follow.

The 80386 microchip, referred to as the 386, offers to increase the speed, memory, and multitasking capabilities of microcomputers.

In the summer of 1986, Compaq became the first company to market a personal computer with a 386; IBM began marketing its 386 models in April

EXHIBIT 10.2   **Board of Directors and Officers of Apple, Inc.**

BOARD OF DIRECTORS

Peter D. Crisp
General Partner—Venrock
Associates; venture capital
investments

Albert A. Eisenstat
Senior Vice-President, Secretary,
and General Counsel—Apple
Computer, Inc.

A. C. Markkula, Jr.
Chairman—ADM Aviation, Inc.;
private flight service

Arthur Rock
Principal—Arthur Rock & Co.;
venture capital investments

Philip Schlein
Partner—U.S. Venture Partners;
venture capital investments

John Sculley
Chairman, President, and Chief
Executive Officer—Apple
Computer, Inc.

Henry Singleton
Chairman—Teledyne, Inc.;
diversified manufacturing company

OFFICERS

John Sculley
Chairman, President, and Chief
Executive Officer

Delbert W. Yocam
Executive Vice-President and Chief
Operating Officer

Albert A. Eisenstar
Senior Vice-President and General
Counsel

William V. Campbell
Executive Vice-President—U.S.
Sales and Marketing

Michael H. Spindler
Senior Vice-President—
International Sales and Marketing

David J. Barram
Vice-President—Finance, and Chief
Financial Officer

Charles W. Berger
Vice-President—Business
Development

Deborah A. Coleman
Vice-President—Operations

Jean-Louis Gassée
Vice-President—Product
Development

Lawrence G. Tesler
Vice-President, Advanced
Technology

Roy H. Weaver, Jr.
Vice-President—Distribution

Robert W. Saltmarsh
Treasurer

1987. Both of these computers are proving to be quite popular. For instance, by December 1986, Compaq had shipped 10,000 Deskpro 386s and was having trouble keeping up with orders. It is expected that 386 machines will make up around 10% of the entire PC market by the end of 1987, and 25% of the market by 1990. However, one problem with machines using the 80386 microchip is that the machines cannot take full advantage of its

EXHIBIT 10.3   **Executive Officers of Apple, Inc.**

The following information was compiled December 15, 1986.

John Sculley (age 47) joined Apple as President and Chief Executive Officer and a Director in May 1983, and was named Chairman of the Board of Directors in January 1986. Prior to joining Apple, Mr. Sculley was President and Chief Executive Officer of Pepsi-Cola Company, a producer and distributor of soft drink products, from 1977 to 1983. Pepsi-Cola Company is a division of PepsiCo, Inc., of which Mr. Sculley was also a Senior Vice-President. Mr. Sculley is also a director of Communications Satellite Corporation.

Delbert W. Yocam (age 42) joined Apple in November 1979 as Director of Materials, was promoted to Vice-President and General Manager of Manufacturing in August 1981, to Vice-President and General Manager of Operations in September 1982, and in December 1983, was appointed Executive Vice-President and General Manager, Apple II Division. In May 1985, Mr. Yocam was named Executive Vice-President, Group Executive of Product Operations and in July 1985, he was appointed Executive Vice-President and Chief Operating Officer.

Albert A. Eisenstat (age 56) joined Apple in July 1980 as Vice-President and General Counsel; he has also served as Secretary of Apple since September 1980. In November 1985, Mr. Eisenstat was promoted to Senior Vice-President and was elected to the Board of Directors to fill the vacancy created by the resignation of Steven P. Jobs. Mr. Eisenstat is also a director of Adobe Systems, Inc., of Commercial Metals Company, and of Computer Task Group, Inc.

William V. Campbell (age 46) joined Apple as Vice-President of Marketing in June 1983; was appointed Vice-President, U.S. Sales, in January 1984; was appointed Executive Vice-President, Sales, in September 1984; and became Executive Vice-President, U.S. Sales and Marketing in June 1985. Before joining Apple, Mr. Campbell served as Director of Marketing for Eastman Kodak Company (a photographic equipment and supplies manufacturer) from May 1982 to June 1983, and as Account Director for J. Walter Thompson Advertising from January 1980 to May 1982. Mr. Campbell is also a director of Champion Parts Rebuilders.

Michael H. Spindler (age 44) joined Apple as European Marketing Manager in September 1980; was promoted to Vice-President and General Manager, Europe, in January 1984; was named Vice-President, International, in February 1985, and was promoted to Senior Vice-President of International Sales and Marketing in September 1986.

David J. Barram (age 42) joined Apple in April 1985 as Vice-President of Finance and Chief Financial Officer. Prior to his employment with Apple, he was the Vice-President of Finance and Administration and Chief Financial Officer of Silicon Graphics, Inc., a manufacturer of high-performance engineering workstations, from April 1983 to April 1985. From January 1970 to April 1983, Mr. Barram held various positions at Hewlett-Packard Company, a diversified electronics measurement and computer equipment manufacturer; his most recent position there was Group Controller of the Technical Computer Division.

(Continued)

EXHIBIT 10.3 (Continued)

Charles W. Berger (age 32) joined Apple in April 1982 as Treasurer and was appointed Director of Strategic Sales in June 1985. In September 1986, Mr. Berger was appointed Vice-President of Business Development. Prior to joining Apple, Mr. Berger served as Assistant Treasurer at Rolm Corporation, a wholly-owned subsidiary of IBM Corporation that manufactures computerized telephone switches and digital telephones, and President of Rolm Credit Corporation.

Deborah A. Coleman (age 33) joined Apple in November 1981, initially as Controller and subsequently as Director of Operations of the Macintosh Division. Ms. Coleman was promoted to Director of Manufacturing in June 1985, to Vice-President of Manufacturing in November 1985, and to Vice-President of Operations in October 1986. Before joining Apple, Ms. Coleman served as a financial manager and cost-accounting supervisor at Hewlett-Packard Company.

Jean-Louis Gassée (age 42) joined Apple in February 1981 as General Manager of Seedrin S.A.F.L., a wholly-owned subsidiary of the company. In May 1985, Mr. Gassée became Director of Marketing of the Macintosh Division, and in June 1985, he was named Vice-President, Product Development.

Lawrence G. Tesler (age 41) joined Apple in July 1980 as a senior member of the technical staff. Beginning in October 1980, he was appointed Project Supervisor, Lisa Applications Software; in August 1981, Section Manager, Lisa Applications Software; in February 1983, Consulting Engineering and Manager of Object-Oriented Systems. Prior to Mr. Tesler's promotion to Vice-President of Advanced Technology in October 1986, Mr. Tesler served as Director of Advanced Development from July 1986 to October 1986.

Roy H. Weaver, Jr. (age 54) joined Apple in September 1980 as U.S. Distribution Manager. In April 1981, he was Director of Distribution and Service Operations, and in April 1982, he was promoted to General Manager of Distribution and Service. In September 1982, he was appointed Vice-President and General Manager of the Distribution, Service, and Support Division; in September 1984, Vice-President, Field Operations; and in June 1985, Vice-President, Distribution.

Robert W. Saltmarsh (age 36) joined Apple as Assistant Treasurer in November 1982 and was promoted to Treasurer in October 1985. Between November 1978 and November 1982, Mr. Saltmarsh worked for Data General Corporation, a minicomputer manufacturer, first as European Treasury Manager and then as Corporate Treasury Manager.

capabilities until software catches up with the new technology, which might take several years.

Other than the microprocessor itself, software is becoming one of the most important parts of a computer. Companies such as Lotus and Microsoft develop software programs specifically for a particular computer model.

In April of 1987, IBM came out with its new product line, called the

EXHIBIT 10.4   **1987 First-Quarter Sales**

	SALES (MILLIONS OF DOLLARS)		PERCENT CHANGE
	1986	**1987**	
Apple	$409	$575	+41.0
Digital	1,928	2,410	+25.0
IBM	10,127	10,682	+ 5.5
Intel	280	395	+41.0
National Semiconductor	324	398	+23.0
NCR	961	1,122	+17.0

SOURCE: Quarterly reports of these companies.

Personal System 2, or PS/2. Designing in part to discourage clonemakers, IBM incorporated custom microchips, and doubled the amount of software that will have to be written to make clone machines 100% compatible with PS/2. Those companies that use the Micro Channel to connect personal computers to mainframes (in other words IBM's top mainframe customers, or about half of the market) are expected to purchase the PS/2. However, sales of IBM compatibles were up more than 10% in the first five months of 1987, so many customers might not yet be inclined to switch over to the PS/2.

FORECAST OF DEMAND

Overall computer sales are expected to grow in 1987. Some experts predict that the growth rate for microcomputers will range from 7% to 10%, as shown in Exhibit 10.5. Others expect the microcomputer market to grow by

EXHIBIT 10.5   **Projected World-Wide Sales**

BUSINESS COMPUTERS (BILLIONS OF DOLLARS)		MICRO SALES (BILLIONS OF DOLLARS)		LAN EQUIPMENT (BILLIONS OF DOLLARS)	
Year	Sales	Year	Sales	Year	Sales
1990	50.0	1990	47.9	1991	3.02
1988	45.7	1988	38.9	1990	2.49
1986	40.6	1986	32.0	1989	2.05
1984	37.6	1984	24.4	1988	1.64
1982	28.1	1982	6.8	1986	.92

SOURCE: Kimball Brown, *Dataquest.*

only 3% because of indecision in the business markets about IBM's new products. For example, PC unit growth in major corporations was 100% from 1981–1984, but this growth could slow to only 48% in 1987 because companies are waiting to see how good the IBM PS/2 products are.

Currently, the hot topic in the personal computer market is the 80386 microchip, which is manufactured by Intel Corporation.

The second hot issue, desktop publishing, is becoming so popular that dozens of companies are finding ways to adapt PCs to provide this option. It is expected that the sales of publishing systems for machines that are based on IBM and IBM-compatible computers will exceed the sales of the Macintosh in 1987. The market is growing very quickly, though, and Macintosh sales will probably grow by 70%.

Corporate capital-equipment spending in the U.S. is projected to increase at an average annual rate of 8.8% in the last three quarters of 1987 compared to just 4.2% in 1986. However, the demand for Apple computers in the business environment depends on Apple's ability to convince its customer corporations' MIS managers and the people who actually buy computers, that the Macintosh line offers more than any competing machines can offer. In corporations, large multiple-computer sales are not awarded on price alone, but also on value and performance. Many business people think that Apple does not provide the necessary support to corporations, but the company plans to improve their support before 1988. Buyers of large computers will also require a 25% increase in computing capacity in 1987.

The home computer market is projected to reach $34.5 billion wholesale in 1987. Twenty percent of consumers plan to purchase a computer in 1987 or 1988, and half of those intend to spend less than $1000. Currently, there are approximately 2.5 to 3 million units of IBM computers in homes. Many people, try as they might, cannot yet justify the purchase of a home computer, as evidenced by a 1985 survey that found that 76.7% of shoppers did not know what they would do with a home computer if they purchased one.

Networking is becoming increasingly important in the business market. Computer customers are being drawn to networks at an accelerating pace as software improves and technical difficulties subside. Access to a Local Area Network (LAN) makes computing easier for the average customer and places the complex issues on the shoulders of somebody more technically competent. Currently, only about 6% of the 13 million PCs installed in U.S. corporate offices are or were connected to a LAN. That percentage is expected to more than double by 1990. The number of networks installed worldwide is expected to be 220,000 by the end of 1987, up from 52,000 in 1984. As shown in Exhibit 10.5, worldwide sales of networks could hit $3.02 billion by 1990. The leaders in networking shipments in 1986 are shown on the following page.

1986 Shipments

Terminal Network, Units		PC Network, Units	
Digital Equipment	3,750	Boyell	8,200
Proteon	1,220	3 Com	8,200
Wang	850	IBM PC Net	7,500
Xerox	750	Fox	3,800
Ungermann-Bass	450	Orchid	3,150
		IBM Token-Ring	1,200

DEC was the first computer giant to capitalize on network demand when they set up dozens of three-member teams with representatives from sales, service, and software, to push local networking. Many computer companies are now working on expanding their product lines to include networking. For example, in the past year DEC, AT&T, Hewlett-Packard, and Apple have all introduced new network products and regrouped their sales forces to go after the business market. Major computer makers are moving into this $1.5 billion market, which had been dominated by such independents as Ungermann-Bass, Novell, 3Com, and Fox Research. Future network wars are possible. Tandem Computers, Inc., for example, has teamed with Boeing Company's computer services division, to sell factory networks. IBM also has joined with Microsoft Corporation, a software company, which is designing software to link the new PS/2 computers together. IBM's #1 corporate priority of late has been the networking market.

MARKET SEGMENTS

Apple's objectives are to excel in the business markets, where computer sales are growing fastest, but not get dragged into the low-priced end of the computer industry. To achieve these objectives, it plans to exploit and develop the communications talents of the Macintosh family.

There are three types of companies that use Apple computers. First are the technical and aerospace corporations (such as DuPont, Hughes Company, Chevron, Motorola, General Dynamics, and Plessey–British telecommunications), which use the Macintosh for computer-aided design and other technical uses. Second, there are service companies (such as Arthur Young; Peat, Marwick, Mitchell; and Seafirst Bank's Seattle branches), which have many employees who are computer illiterate. In these companies use of the Macintosh reduces training costs. Third are the groups (such as Knight-Ridder and marketing departments of GE) that need the desktop-publishing capabilities provided by the Macintosh and the LaserWriter.

Two thirds of the one million Macintoshes that have been sold are in the business marketplace, and 27% of these units are in companies having fewer than 100 employees, 37% are in companies having 100–999 employees, and the remaining 36% are in companies with more than 1,000 employees.

International markets are becoming more important as the computer revolution is just beginning in many countries. Apple's goal is to become multilocal by providing products tailored to each market, wherever it may be. In the United Kingdom, for example, Apple Centres, or satellite stores dedicated exclusively to selling Apple desktop solutions, provide business dealers with showcase locations in high traffic areas. In Japan, Kanjitalk systems of software give Macintosh the three traditional Japanese alphabets, in addition to English, so Japanese users are provided immediate access to a powerful library of Macintosh software.

In the consumer segment, Apple has historically experienced increased sales during the Christmas season, especially with the Apple IIc.

At this time, no one customer of Apple accounts for 10% of net sales.

Apple currently has no material U.S. government contracts, but plans to expand its sales efforts to the government. It has a separate thirty-person sales group that hopes to snare some of the estimated $1.6 billion federal microcomputer market.

COMPETITION

The market for the design, manufacture, sale, and servicing of personal computers and their related software and peripheral products is highly competitive. It has been characterized by rapid technological advances in both hardware and software development—advances that have substantially increased the capabilities and applications of personal computers. The principal competitive factors in this market are the product's quality and reliability, the relation of its price to its performance, the manufacturer's marketing and distribution capabilities, the quality of service and support, the availability of hardware and software accessories, and corporate reputation.

Many companies, such as IBM Corporation, Compaq Computer Corporation, AT&T Company, Tandy Corporation, Hewlett-Packard Company, Commodore Corporation, Atari Corporation, and various Japanese and Asian manufacturers, some of which have considerably greater financial resources than those of Apple, are very active in the personal computer market. In particular, IBM Corporation must be considered to be dominant in that market. In office automation and information processing, Apple competes directly with the companies mentioned and with other large domestic and foreign manufacturers, such as Digital Equipment Corporation and Wang Corporation.

IBM

Approximately 10 million IBM PCs and compatibles are in the business world, but for the first time since the PC was hatched in an obscure lab in

Florida six years ago, the company is focusing its full technological and marketing expertise on its PCs. This focus could pose a critical threat to Apple. Before the introduction of the IBM PS/2, IBM's various PCs outsold the Macintosh by a 5 to 1 ratio in all businesses. In the largest corporations, IBM and IBM-compatible machines accounted for more than 75% of the PCs in use. If corporations perceive the new IBM PCs to be similar to the Macintosh, then the distinctive quality of the Macintosh will be reduced.

With its new PCs, IBM is aggressively attempting to regain its momentum in the PC industry. Evidence of a strong marketing approach is seen in the name "Personal Systems," which underscore the PCs' role as partners with IBM mainframes and midrange computers in corporate networks. Some competitors complain that in its marketing of the PS/2, IBM has implied that only they will perform such tasks as sharing complex software with IBM mainframes across companywide networks. IBM's commitment is also seen in research and development. About half of the technology being put into the new machines is being developed by IBM (vs. one fifth in 1981). On the 32-bit machine, 80% is IBM technology.

IBM's market share went below 30% in 1986 because of the PC clonemakers, such as Compaq, Tandy, and Korea's Daewoo. For the PS/2, IBM did not switch to totally proprietary hardware and software, which would have made it harder for its competition to clone the products, because it also would have made it harder for customers to tailor the new PCs to their businesses and so would have limited PC sales. In an effort to stave off clonemakers, IBM did design a new way of sending graphic images to a screen and embedded that software in custom microchips. The machine's design also doubles the amount of software needed to make a clone 100% compatible with a new IBM PC. Thus, in the time it takes cloners to duplicate the PS/2, IBM will have put $50 million in ads behind its new machines, and will keep the clones from reaching IBM's best corporate customers. Another competitive edge for the new PS/2 will be the efficiency of its manufacture. IBM PS/2 machines are based on circuit boards designed to be assembled at IBM's Austin, Texas, factory, a model of advanced automation, and are very cheap to make. Final assembly takes less than a minute.

The company introduced four new machines: two replacements for its PC/AT and one for its basic PC, plus a 32-bit machine that is as powerful as a small minicomputer. At the low end of IBM's new line is the Model 30, which in 1987 sold for $1,695. Like Apple's Macintosh, the Model 30 creates elaborate graphics, synthesizes music, and stores data on disks only 3 1/2 inches across. The new system, in fact, looks like a ringing endorsement of Apple's designs. But the price is no lower than that of a Macintosh and far above that of the Macintosh-like Apple IIGS. Experts feel that if IBM had priced the Model 30 at $1,000 or less that it would undoubtedly be successful. Higher up in the line are three machines, Models 50, 60, and 80, which cost from $3,600 to $11,000. All eventually will use new software and hardware accessories for easy communication with IBM mainframes. The best-received PS/2 appears to be the Model 50, which is a desktop system that is twice as fast as IBM's older, top-end PC/AT and, at $3,845, is regarded as competitively priced with the most powerful AT-compatibles.

Some disadvantages of the new IBM Personal System/2 are that (1) it uses a different kind of floppy disk so it is difficult to transfer programs and files from previous IBMs to the new machines; (2) it can't use the add-in circuit cards designed for existing PCs. (A new feature, called the Micro Channel, is used for connecting circuit cards and accepts only add-ons designed specifically for it, so existing PC circuit cards are obsolete); and (3) powerful software that will let the new PC use its power won't exist for a year after introduction.

The software for both the PC/AT and the new PS/2 is not sophisticated enough to take full advantage of the power of their chips—or to deliver the productivity that is promised with the new operating systems. Once these promised capabilities are realized, the machines will be able to perform several tasks at once and handle the voluminous software instructions and graphics needed to make PCs nearly as easy to use as typewriters.

Microsoft's new operating system for the three-year-old IBM PC/AT should be ready by 1988. Also ready in 1988 should be another operating system for a new generation of extremely powerful, 32-bit personal computers. Based on Intel Corp.'s new 386 microchip, these are now being introduced by IBM and others.

Windows, a Microsoft software program to be built into new operating systems, will be sold with every new IBM PC, except the most basic model. Windows uses graphics similar to those of Apple's Macintosh and will simplify the commands needed to operate the new PCs and therefore make them much easier to use.

Another software company, Lotus, will produce a spreadsheet, called 1-2-3/M, for IBM minicomputers and mainframes. Over the next decade, Lotus and IBM will jointly develop and market products for a full range of computers.

Dealers have complained that not only do they have to upgrade sales and support staffs (in the computer stores), but they are also required to invest the time and money needed for their staff members to gain expertise in at least one specialized computer application, such as accounting. Dealers can't offset such costs by selling the high-profit hardware upgrades that went with older IBM PCs. Many additional functions are built into the new PS/2 models, and there is very little opportunity to add disk drives or monitors, which formerly were a major source of revenue.

In May 1987, 15% of PC sales in U.S. computer stores were PS/2 models, but two thirds of those were the PS/2 Model 30, which does not include the advanced PS/2 features.

International Data Corp. surveys show that 52% of corporate computer buyers may delay making major purchasing decisions immediately following the PS/2 introduction.

round in the low-priced computer battle in 1986; its Leading Edge model already has snared a 5% share of the home computer market. Another example is Multitech Industrial Corporation, a Taiwan-based firm that has been making computers for years and could become a legitimate rival to Japanese, Korean, and U.S. multinational corporations. The company's most recent offering is an IBM PC/AT compatible computer using Intel Corp's new 32-bit 80386 microchip. The machine hit the U.S. and European markets months before IBM brought out its first 80386-based machine. To successfully expand overseas, Multitech has adopted the name of Acer Technologies for its products and is launching a $5 million ad campaign to sell the name to consumers and computer distributors.

Other companies that offer competition, especially in the less-than-$1,000 market, include Blue Chip, United Kingdom-based Amstrad (PC 1512), Commodore International (PC 10-1 and PC 10-2), Atari (PC), and Franklin Computer (PC 8000).

PRODUCTION

The raw materials essential to Apple's business are generally available from multiple sources. Certain components, such as power supplies, integrated circuits, and plastic housings, are obtained from single sources, although Apple believes that other sources for such parts are available. New products often utilize custom components that are available only from a single source upon initial introduction of the product. Although Apple generally qualifies other sources after the product is introduced, the inability to obtain components fast enough to satisfy demand for the new product can cause significant delays in product delivery. The Apple IIGS encountered such delays during the fourth quarter of 1986.

Apple's foreign operations consist of three manufacturing facilities in Ireland and Singapore. In the United States, the company has four manufacturing facilities.

In general, Apple sells its products directly to customers, who typically purchase products on an as-needed basis and frequently change delivery schedules and order rates. For this reason, Apple's backlog of orders at any particular date might not represent its actual sales for any succeeding period.

MARKETING

William V. Campbell, Apple's Executive Vice-President for U.S. Sales and Marketing, says, "We've been dragged to our mission kicking and screaming. We've put together a business advisory panel. No longer do we put out technology for technology's sake." Marketing and distribution expenses were $477 million or 25% of sales in 1986. In 1986 more was spent in sales and marketing programs than in advertising and merchandising (excluding increases related to the Apple IIGS rollout and a new television campaign).

One goal is to increase international sales from 36% of total sales. There has been strong growth in newer markets, including Spain, Sweden, Holland, and Belgium. Sales in Japan are also rising to reflect the initial success with Kanjitalk. The largest international markets are France, Canada, and Australia.

PRODUCTS

Apple has two computer families, the Apple II and Macintosh families. The Apple II, the company's original line, has a large customer base in the education and home markets. There are three Apple II models, the IIC, IIE, and the IIGS. The Macintosh line has four models, the Macintosh 512K, Macintosh Plus, Macintosh SE, and Macintosh II. Macintosh is targeted towards the business markets.

The Apple Line

Apple IIc

Introduced late in the 1986 fiscal year, the updated IIc can provide up to one megabyte of memory, which enables users to work with sophisticated software programs.

Apple IIGS and Apple IIe

The IIGS was introduced in September 1986 and is a high-end model, featuring a 16-bit microprocessor, high-resolution color graphics, advanced sound capabilities, and up to one megabyte of internal memory. Although the IIGS is praised for its speed and graphics, production problems slowed sales during the Christmas quarter of 1986, when the company usually earns more than one third of its annual profit. Some experts complain that what is being done on the GS can be accomplished just as well on a II Plus, IIe, or IIc. They say that about the only thing that can't be done with the old Apple II that can be done with the new GS is high-resolution color graphics. Color graphics are a bonus, but for routine, everyday tasks, they aren't really necessary. Apple IIe users can buy an upgrade kit that will give their computers all Apple IIGS capabilities.

The Macintosh Line

The Macintosh is an extremely user-friendly computer that makes use of graphic icons (pictorial representatives of function) and a mouse device, which allows a user to enter commands without touching the keyboard. Apple relies on the Macintosh for more than half of its revenues and earnings. In 1985, Apple sold 100,000 Macintoshs to businesses with annual revenues of more than $100 million. Sales of 175,000 surpassed Apple II sales for the first time in 1986. The prediction for 1987 is 325,000. As of

1986, the Macintosh had about 7% of total sales to the business market. Shipments of the Macintosh doubled in 1986, while worldwide PC shipments rose only 9%. Approximately one million Macintoshs have been sold; nearly two thirds of those sales were in the business marketplace. Companies with fewer than 100 employees comprise 27% of sales, 37% are in companies with 100–999 employees, and 37% in companies with more than 1,000 employees.

Desktop publishing, which Macintosh pioneered, is a method for printing typeset-quality documents. Approximately 50,000 Macintosh publishing systems were sold in 1986 and sales of accompanying printers grossed around $150 million.

Microsoft's Excel, a spreadsheet program, enables the Macintosh to go head-to-head with an IBM PC running Lotus's 1-2-3. In large companies, desktop-publishing enthusiasts have helped Apple sell the Macintosh for other uses. Since people began trying other Macintosh software, including the Excel spreadsheet, a lot of Lotus users have transferred their files. Some claim that the Macintosh increases productivity faster than do other computers because it is easier to use. Apple makes software developers conform to a single set of commands, so that once an operator has mastered those commands, it is relatively easy to learn another Macintosh software package.

Apple still owns the rights to Macintosh's built-in programs, so it can't be cloned the way the IBM PC can.

Macintosh Plus

Introduced in January 1986, the Mac Plus has a high-speed socket that limits the means by which hardware options can be connected. Thus Apple is courting companies whose add-on options can help sell the Macintosh—companies such as Radius Inc., whose 15-inch screen for the Macintosh Plus has scored big. Along with the LaserWriter Plus printer, this model opened the door for Apple in business. In fact, the two are seen as the standard for the rapidly growing desktop publishing market.

Macintosh 512K Enhanced

The 512K Enhanced was introduced in the early spring of 1986 and is a more affordable version of the Macintosh Plus. Now that the Macintosh Plus is selling to corporations and Apple has introduced a new model of the Macintosh, prices on the 512K Enhanced are falling to around $4,100. That makes it less expensive than the new IIGS and about the same price as the Atari 1040ST.

Macintosh SE

To get into the corporate MIS department, Apple has created Macintosh II and the Macintosh SE, which embrace MS/DOS, Unix, Ethernet, token ring, and all else dear to the heart of the corporate PC user. The new "open" Macintosh is designed to be flexible enough that its owners can customize it, and thus this Macintosh will eliminate one of business customers' largest objections to the old "closed" Macintosh. For instance, the machine has several card slots, so owners can customize a machine simply by plugging in circuit cards to give it new functions, such as high-resolution graphics.

The Macintosh SE, with prices ranging from $2,898 to $4,500, is intended to become the Macintosh line's staple for office use. It is an enhanced version of the flagship Macintosh Plus and uses the same, relatively slower Motorola 68000 microprocessor, but has room for the add-on features, such as extra speed or memory, demanded by customers.

SE stands for System Expansion. The Macintosh SE is equipped with an internal slot for add-in cards and with two internal disks, one of which can be a 20-megabyte SCSI (Small Computer Systems Interface) hard drive. With Dayna's DaynaFile, a disk drive that connects directly to the Macintosh via an SCSI port and acts as an external 5-1/4-inch drive, it is possible to access such IBM compatible files as Lotus 1-2-3, dBase III, or WordPerfect as though they had been created on a Macintosh disk.

Macintosh II

The Macintosh II costs up to $12,000 and has a 13-inch color screen, four megabytes of internal memory, and an 80-megabyte hard disk. It combines advanced color graphics with computational muscle rivaling machines with three times the price. With this machine, Apple beat IBM to the 32-bit generation, because it features Motorola Corp.'s 68020 chip and thereby presents a direct challenge to the high-powered 385 PCs. Larry Magid, Senior Analyst at the Sybold, San Jose, California, says, "There no longer is an excuse for not buying a Mac. Now it's a matter of which machine is more suited to your application, to your environment. The Mac II is a credible second standard computer in the corporate area."

Other Products

The *AppleTalk* local-area network can link as many as thirty-two computers and peripheral devices. The company claims that *AppleTalk,* one of Apple's most successful new products in 1986, is the first and only network solution that is as easy to learn and use as Macintosh itself. There is an *AppleTalk* network connection built into every new Macintosh and Apple IIGS. This network "configures" itself so that linking computers, printers, and other peripherals becomes extremely simple and economical. As of 1986 there are over 200,000 *AppleTalk* networks in place. However, some people see LANs as the next bottleneck for Apple in the corporate world. *AppleTalk* is fine for small groups (eight or fewer machines) but might not be adequate if hundreds of machines need to be connected.

The *LaserWriter* and *LaserWriter Plus,* introduced January 1986, are high-resolution laser printers.

New peripherals include Hard Disk 20SC, Apple II-compatible UniDisk 3.5-inch 800K disk drive, ImageWriter II printer, and Apple Personal Modem.

The company announced in 1986 that it is creating a new software subsidiary to develop critical programs for its Apple II and Macintosh computers. This new subsidiary should also open up new areas of exploration for smaller vendors. William V. Campbell, who will be President of the new company, denies an anti-Microsoft strategy, but a highly placed Apple insider says one goal was to make Apple less dependent on Microsoft, which sells 50% of the software bought each year for Apple's Macintosh. Like IBM, Apple sees Microsoft aiding the enemy, because Microsoft's Windows program can turn another PC into a Macintosh look-alike. In 1986, the worldwide software sales were $27 billion.

One future worry about Apple's product line is that the Macintosh won't be unique for long. Graphics options for the IBM PC are moving fast, and dozens of companies are finding ways in which PCs can be adapted for desktop publishing. It is predicted that sometime in 1987, sales of desktop publishing systems based on IBM and IBM-compatible computers will start to exceed sales on the Macintosh. Even though the market is growing so quickly that Apple's own desktop publishing sales will increase by 70% in 1987, the Macintosh may lose some of its edge.

RESEARCH AND DEVELOPMENT

Apple's design principle is, "No matter how powerful or sophisticated the system, keep it simple to set up and operate." R&D expenses in 1986 increased to $128 million or 6.7% of sales, from $73 million or 3.8% of sales in 1985. The company plans to increase its research budget by 30%, to $166 million, or about 7% of projected sales in fiscal 1987. These funds went to significant additions to the engineering staff, to increases in prototype materials and tooling, and to the purchase of other equipment and proprietary design software that can shorten product development cycles. In March 1986, the company installed a $15.5 million Cray X-MP/48 supercomputer from Cray Research Inc. One of the largest and most powerful scientific supercomputers in the world, the Cray can simulate new computer architectures and operating systems in three months to one year less that was ever before possible.

Current programs include a collaborative effort with the National Geographic Society and LucasFilm Ltd. to explore the effective use of optical technologies (video and compact disks) for the Apple II line in education. These devices can store vast amounts of information, including still and moving images and stereo sound, and still allow easy interaction.

Apple University Consortium brings universities and countries together to share and explore the integration of technology and education. The United States has 32 consortium members.

Apple's Office of Special Education represents the company's commitment to work with educational institutions and human services organizations, to identify and assist the computer-related needs of disabled persons.

PROMOTION

For the fiscal year 1986, advertising expenditures were $157,833. This figure is down from $187,457 in 1985 and $179,739 in 1984. This total includes both salaries and other costs of in-house advertising, graphic design, and public relations departments, as well as the costs of advertising in various media and employing outside advertising agencies.

Recent ads call the Macintosh "the computer for the rest of us." Another slogan, "The Power to be Your Best," focuses on people and how Apple products help them realize their full potential. Consumers who are a bit more educated about computers now want to know precisely how a computer will solve real problems in their work and their lives. In response to these consumers, image ads are out.

DISTRIBUTION

Apple has distribution facilities in the U.S., Europe, Canada, and Australia. In 1986 the U.S. dealer organization was trimmed by 25% and sales per dealer location increased by 15%. A field sales force gave the best service to those dealers with the best performance.

Apple's strategy is to carefully select its dealers and restrict distribution of the more complex products to the most sophisticated outlets, which will attract business customers. For example, Businessland Inc. sells both IBM and Apple products to large corporations. The dealer's most important characteristic is that it markets Apple machines effectively.

However, Apple is up against the direct-sales forces of IBM and DEC, and many experts think that it's not possible to sell in the business market without a direct-sales force. Through a national accounts program, Apple has been trying to convince the heads of information services and data processing departments of how Apple products differ and why those differences are important to business. Between 1985 and 1987, more than twenty companies have put Apple on their approved vendor list.

Mass merchants, such as Target Stores, The Wiz, Toys 'R' Us, Wal-Mart, K-Mart, and Jamesway Corp., have been selling home computers since the late 70s and early 80s ushered in Commodore's 64 and Atari's 600 XL and 130 XE. This competition may cause some concern to Apple's retailers. It is most likely, though, that the middle market outlets such as Radio Shack will suffer more than will the specialty retailers at the hands of the discounters selling clones, since the specialty retailers are geared toward businesses.

Approximately 4,500 dealers sell computers. During 1985, about 7% dropped out of the business because their profit margins were down. Apple and IBM (51% of computer store sales) requalify their dealers to be sure

EXHIBIT 10.6

Apple Computer: Consolidated Statements of Income— Nine Year Summary

(Dollars and Shares in Thousands, Except Per Share Amounts)

	1986	1985	1984	1983	1982	1981	1980	1979	1978
Net Sales	$1,901,898	$1,918,280	$1,515,876	$982,769	$583,061	$334,763	$117,126	$47,867	$ 7,883
Costs and expenses:									
Cost of sales	891,112	1,117,864	878,586	505,765	288,001	170,124	66,490	27,450	3,960
Research and development	127,758	72,526	71,136	60,040	37,979	20,956	7,282	3,601	597
Marketing and distribution	476,685	478,079	398,463	229,961	119,945	55,369	12,619	8,802	1,170
General and administrative	132,812	110,077	81,840	57,364	34,927	22,191	7,150	2,080	609
Total costs and expenses	1,628,367	1,778,546	1,430,025	853,130	480,852	268,640	93,541	41,933	6,336
Operating income	273,531	102,768	85,851	129,639	102,209	66,143	23,585	5,933	1,547
Interest and other income, net	36,187	17,277	23,334	16,483	14,563	10,400	567	0	0
Income before taxes on income	309,718	120,045	109,165	146,122	116,772	76,543	24,152	5,933	1,547
Provision for income taxes	155,755	58,822	45,130	69,408	55,466	37,123	12,454	860	754
Net income	$ 153,755	$ 61,895	$ 64,055	$ 76,714	$ 61,306	$ 39,420	$ 11,698	$ 5,073	$ 793
Earnings per common and common equivalent share	$ 2.39	$ .99	$ 1.05	$ 1.28	$ 1.06	$ .70	$ .24	$ .12	$ .03
Common and common equivalent shares used in the calculations of earnings per share	64,315	61,895	60,887	59,867	57,798	56,181	48,412	43,620	31,544

SOURCE: Apple Computer Annual Report, 1986, p. 38; Annual Report, 1984, p. 38; Annual Report, 1983, p. 16; and Annual Report, 1981, p. 16. *Note*: The financial data was expanded to include the years 1981–1978.

that only the best carry products such as the Macintosh II and the most powerful models of the new IBM PS/2 line. Of Apple's 2000 dealers, 300 have been chosen to carry the top-of-the-line Macintosh II. Apple is expected to allow 800 more to carry the Macintosh II. Apple feels that the fewer the stores carrying the product, the higher the profit margins. Dealers who aren't allowed to carry the best products will have to compete in the high-volume discount business—almost a guarantee of thin margins for these retailers.

FINANCIAL POSITION

Apple relies on funds from operations ($273 million in 1986; $102 million in 1985) to meet its liquidity needs. It also uses proceeds from the sale of common stock ($46 million in 1986 vs. $22 million in 1985) under the company's stock-option and employee stock-purchase plans, and related tax benefits ($9 million in 1986 vs. $23 million in 1985). In 1986, Apple had $576,215,000 in cash and no debt. See Exhibits 10.6 and 10.7 for detailed information.

EXHIBIT 10.7

Apple Computer, Inc.: Consolidated Balance Sheets
(Dollar Amounts in Thousands)

	SEPT 26, 1986	SEPT 25, 1985	SEPT 28, 1984
Assets			
Current assets:			
Cash and temporary cash investments	576,215	$337,013	$114,888
Accounts receivable	263,126	220,157	258,238
Inventories	108,680	166,951	264,619
Prepaid income taxes	53,029	70,375	26,751
Other current assets	39,884	27,569	23,055
Total current assets	1,040,934	882,065	687,551
Net property, plant and equipment	107,315	90,446	75,868
Other assets	11,879	23,666	25,367
	1,160,128	936,177	788,786
Liabilities and Shareholders' Equity			
Current liabilities	328,535	295,425	255,184
Deferred income taxes	137,506	90,265	69,037
Shareholders' equity	694,087	550,177	464,565
	1,160,128	936,177	788,786

Apple stock was the most active OTC issue of 1986; it rose 18 1/2 points on $7.71 billion of volume and finished the year at 40 1/2. Prior to 1987 its record price was 63 1/4—that level was reached in 1983 after its all-time low of 10 3/4 only a year earlier. Apple's stock traded over the counter on the NASDAQ. Officers and directors control about 11% of the outstanding common, while institutions hold approximately 60%. The largest investor (as of December, 1986) is Citicorp with 4.7 million shares, followed by Atalanta/Sosnoff Capital, which has 2.2 million. There are about 35,000 shareholders of record. As of 1986 there were about 65 million shares outstanding. Apple stock has risen to close to $80 in 1987.

On April 23, 1987, Apple announced its first-ever quarterly dividend of $.12 per share. The company also announced a 2-for-1 stock split. This makes Apple one of the first Silicon-Valley–based computer and electronics concerns to pay a dividend. Mr. Sculley called the dividend "an expression of our confidence" in Apple's long-term future. Apple plans to continue paying this dividend quarterly.

Tandy, Inc.

SEXTON ADAMS · ADELAIDE GRIFFIN

The Tandy Corporation, which controls the largest number of retail electronics outlets in the world, and produces over $2.4 billion in sales was, as of 1984, "the world's leading distributor of electronic technology to the individual."[1] The span of products sold through the Tandy system is almost overwhelming, ranging from sophisticated computer and telecommunicative systems at one extreme to diodes and transistors at the other. The incredible size Tandy has achieved becomes that much more amazing when one considers its humble beginnings only a short time ago.

With any organization that has experienced extraordinary early growth, the environmental forces facing the firm and the resulting choices made in response to those forces, require constant review, and Tandy is no exception. Tandy presently faces many challenges in many new markets. How these challenges are met will determine whether Tandy can maintain its past growth rate and remain a "star" or simply become another company "has been."

HISTORY

Since 1960 the Radio Shack chain had grown from a small, money-losing, Boston-based company to an electronics powerhouse whose after-tax income rivals those of the country's largest retailers. The man who oversaw much of that transformation was Charles Tandy, a Harvard Business School dropout who converted common sense, salesmanship, and employee motivation into a spectacular business success.

Tandy had practice at turning local operations into national ones. During the 1950s he had turned his family's small leathercraft business, Tandycrafts, Inc., into a national chain. He then sold Tandycrafts to a leather and sportswear company, but shortly afterward reacquired it, along with the leather and sportswear firm, in a proxy fight.

In 1960, Tandy bought an option of 51% of Radio Shack stock. He paid $5,000 cash and took out a $300,000 loan for the option, which allowed him to purchase the stock at book value. Book value, as the auditors later determined, was a negative $1.5 million. The loan was later converted to

This case was prepared by Paul Trobaugh, Greg Dufour, Michelle Little, Alex Blair, Sally Dehaney, and Alan Moore under the supervision of Professor Sexton Adams, North Texas State University and Professor Adelaide Griffin, Texas Woman's University. Reprinted by permission.

stock, and Charles Tandy was left with control of Radio Shack on a personal investment of only $5,000.

Some would say that the purchase of a losing proposition at any price is not a bargain. There was little doubt that Radio Shack was a losing proposition. In addition to its huge debts, the chain had posted a $4.0 million loss the year before Tandy took control. Tandy, however, felt that the firm, which at the time was selling electronic equipment to ham operators and other electronic buffs, would complement his recent acquisition of the Electronic Crafts Company of Fort Worth. In addition, Tandy was attracted by the chain's $9.0 million annual sales and by the high quality of its personnel, a characteristic that he considered essential for growth in the electronics area.

Charles Tandy set out to prove his doubters wrong "with a vengeance." The first order of business was to reduce the ailing firm's accounts-receivable balance. Radio Shack had a policy of selling on a no-money down, two-years-to-pay basis, which had resulted in a large number of bad debts. Tandy quickly eliminated this problem by hiring a legal team to "go after Radio Shack's dead beats."

Also of concern to Tandy was the excessive number of products offered and the high inventory levels. Using aggressive, direct-mail advertising campaigns and sidewalk sales, Tandy reduced inventory and whittled the product lines down from over 25,000 to just 2,500. Products that had a low turnover were cut, as well as those that generated anything less than a 50% gross profit margin. Radio Shack was eventually left with a relatively small group of diverse, but highly profitable products.

Tandy also decided to eliminate brand name items; larger profits could be made by marketing private-label merchandise. He was particularly successful in negotiations with Japanese manufacturers, who at that time were actively seeking an opening into U.S. markets.

Tandy felt that the company's overhead costs should be spread out over as many stores as possible. That belief led to the rapid expansion of Radio Shack's retail outlets. In less than ten years, the company was opening new stores at the rate of one per day. By 1969, the firm was ready to begin producing its own goods, and the first of twenty-six manufacturing plants was built.

But the development of Radio Shack was not Tandy's only concern during the 1960s. The company acquired, developed, and eventually spun off Color Tile, Inc. and Stafford Lowden, Inc., a printing firm. Tandycrafts and Tandy Brands were also spun off. The Radio Shack division, however, remained, and became one of the world's leading distributors of technology to the individual consumer.

The firm was more than ready for the CB radio boom of the mid-1970s. "As consumers stampeded to get the chance to say 'breaker one nine,' Tandy saw its net income rise from $26.8 million in 1975 to $69 million in 1977, a

157% increase.''[2] But CB's proved to be a passing fad and "Tandy had to scramble in 1977 to switch from its heavy commitment to CB manufacturing.''[3]

In 1977 the firm began developing its first home computer. Tandy was among the first companies to enter that market, and the move was to provide much of the firm's growth in the early part of the eighties.

MANAGEMENT

Tandy had an extremely young management team who relied, for the most part, on Charles Tandy's tried and true management techniques. In 1983 the average age of the company's vice-presidents was forty-eight, and more than two-thirds had spent fifteen years or more with Tandy.

Charles Tandy

Charles Tandy had been described as the "founder, architect, and driving force behind the corporation that bears his name.''[4] Tandy was still a strong influence at Tandy more than five years after his death. According to one source, "even today, Radio Shack executives characterize their performance by saying, 'Charles Tandy would have been proud of what we've done.' ''[5]

Tandy's rise to the top closely paralleled that of his company. "He had no hobbies, no children," said one Tandy executive. "He ate, drank and slept business, from dawn until as late as anyone was willing to talk about his business with him." Executives described him as "larger than life . . . throwing off boundless energy, laughing into his ever-busy phone, while waving a 30-cent cigar with his free hand . . . .''[6]

Tandy, in his own unique style, "set the rules and pattern successors have carried on since he died. . . ." Among his favorite Tandyisms were, "You can't sell from an empty wagon" (a conviction that led the firm to stock high levels of inventory in its retail outlets); "Who wants dividends when they can have capital gains?" (thus the firm never paid dividends, but used all earnings for growth); and "If you want to catch a mouse, you have to make a noise like a cheese" (the philosophy that justified an exceptionally large advertising budget). He also emphasized gross profit: "Tandy never entered a market or sold a product without a 50% gross margin.''[7]

Vertical integration was another important part of Tandy's management philosophy. Everything from production to distribution to retailing to advertising was kept in-house whenever possible. By 1982, one observer was moved to remark, "No retailer—not even Sears—has that kind of vertical integration.''[8]

Charles Tandy's real genius was in motivation. Store managers were offered large bonuses and profit sharing plans based on their store's performance. Former chairman Phil North recounted, "Charles would call the employees into a room when it was time to hand out the bonus checks. He wouldn't let them out until they bought Tandy stock.''[9] He was so successful at convincing employees to invest in the company that today nearly 25% of Tandy's stock is estimated to be owned by employees.

Charles Tandy's fatal heart attack could hardly be said to mark the end of an era at the Tandy Corporation. "I miss him," says one executive, "but the company won't, because he taught enough people to do it right."[10] Another observer agrees, "Tandy's personal influence on the development of the corporation cannot be understated. He developed a top management team that understood and appreciated his business philosophy."[11]

Journalist Harold Seneker described Tandy's death: "Charles D. Tandy, 60, lay down for a nap one Saturday afternoon in November and never got up. He couldn't have timed his passing much better if he had planned it." The firm's directors and top officers were in Fort Worth for a stockholders' meeting, and by the time the stockmarket opened on Monday they had decided on their course of action—business as usual—and on Charles Tandy's successor, Phil North.[12]

Phil North

Phil North was named President and Chairman of Tandy when his long-time friend and business associate, Charles Tandy, passed away. As a young man, North had been a reporter on his family's newspaper, the *Fort Worth Star Telegram*. During World War II, he served as General Douglas MacArthur's personal press secretary. In 1964, Tandy convinced him to invest $100,000 in his firm, and in 1966, North became a member of Tandy's Board of Directors.

North was less than delighted by the prospect of taking control of the firm. "I'd rather be perfecting my duplicate bridge or seeing friends around the world," he said. He agreed to accept the position only "to provide a smooth transition of management for an interim period," saying that it was "one of the last things I can do for Charles, and by God, I'm going to do it."[13]

North, who described himself as "the company philosopher," was described by others as "Charles Tandy's alter ego." Determined to carry on the Tandy philosophy, he said, "We will achieve the goals Charles set."[14]

As soon as it was practical, North relinquished the presidency to John Roach, and in 1982 Roach also took over as Chairman of the Board. Phil North returned to his position as a director, and presumably, to his bridge.

John Roach

John Roach, Chairman and CEO, took charge of Tandy Corporation at the age of forty-three. Roach was born and raised in Texas, as were the majority of Tandy's executives, and had received his MBA from Fort Worth's Texas Christian University. Roach came to Tandy in 1967 as a data processing specialist and embarked on what was to become his pet project, the development of a home computer. Ten years later, after rapidly rising within the firm, his project was complete. One day in early 1977 Charles Tandy came down to his office to see it and was hooked. The computer was a resounding success and Roach's future with the company assured.

In spite of his youth, Roach was awarded the 1982 Chief Executive of the Year Award by Financial World. Roach's management philosophy smacks of Tandy's: "We are continuing to build Tandy's business on the strong fundamentals that have yielded extraordinary operating results for a retailer in one of the most competitive segments of the retail industry. Our basic philosophies of private label merchandising, strong promotion . . . convenient locations, vertical integration and the institutionalization of individual entrepreneurship truly make Tandy and Radio Shack unique."[15]

The Executive Vice-Presidents

Roach's two primary executives in the Radio Shack division are Bernard Appel, Executive Vice-President for Marketing, and Robert Keto, Executive Vice-President for Operations (see Exhibit 11.1). Appel, who had been with Tandy for twenty-four years, was also strongly committed to the Tandy philosophy. As Appel puts it, "Charles Tandy was a genius."[16] Appel's

EXHIBIT 11.1   **Tandy Corporation's Organizational Chart**

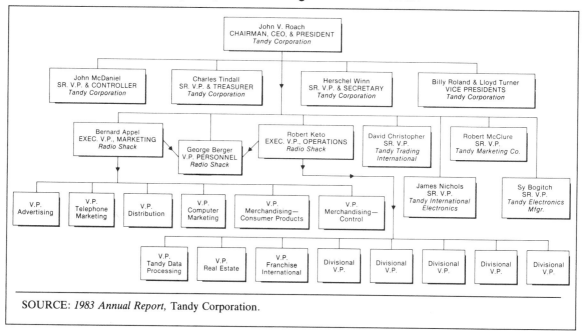

SOURCE: *1983 Annual Report,* Tandy Corporation.

approach, like Tandy's, was that "our own product line, sold through our own distribution system via our own marketing plan . . . will enable us to remain the Number One retailer of electronics to the world."[17] Robert Keto added, "Providing our customers with products they want at a convenient location and then giving them the after-the-sale service they have come to expect, is why Radio Shack continues to be the leader in consumer electronics." Keto was forty-two years old in 1983 and had been with Radio Shack for nineteen years.[18]

MARKETING

The Tandy marketing effort was a reflection of the size and diversity of the company as a whole. The marketing effort cannot be discussed in terms of stores alone, because to do so would drastically oversimplify the nature of the organization. As a result this section is subdivided into two sections: internal and external. Each of these is in turn further subdivided into stores and products. In this way, the major internal operations and external forces affecting those operations are singled out for thorough analysis.

Internal

Store Operations

John Roach described the Tandy Store concept better than anyone else when he said, "Tandy is a distribution system for the products of technology. Sometimes we are innovators, sometimes not, but we do have the capability to move a lot of products."[19] As of 1983 the Tandy distribution system was comprised of more than 6,400 individual stores.

Of these 6,400 stores approximately 4,300 are corporate owned and managed; some 2,000 are privately franchised. In fiscal 1983 Tandy opened the 500th full-service computer center worldwide. More than 400 of these are in the United States. In addition to the stand-alone Computer Centers, more than 775 Radio Shack stores have Computer departments. Six hundred of these are in the United States. Through expansion of both stand-alone Computer Centers and computer departments within Radio Shack stores, Tandy anticipated having more than 1,400 computer centers and computer departments by the end of 1984. For many retail organizations, this number of stores would be considered unmanageable. However, Tandy had always considered a large number of stores crucial to their strategy of insuring distribution.

Although generally lost in the intense interest in computers, Tandy has always been primarily a full-line electronics retailer. As Exhibit 11.2 illustrates, the lines carried by Tandy stores have ranged from computers to diodes and almost everything in between. Again, reviewing Exhibit 11.2, significant trends appear in this data. The first, and most notable, was that computers and computer-related sales were steadily becoming a much larger

EXHIBIT 11.2 **Worldwide Warehouse Shipments (Unaudited)**

Class of Products	Year Ended June 30				
	1983	1982	1981	1980	1979
Radios, phonographs, and televisions	8.6%	9.4%	11.6%	12.1%	13.3%
Citizens band radios, walkie-talkies, scanners, and public address systems	4.9	6.0	6.8	9.3	13.2
Audio equipment, tape recorders, and related accessories	18.2	21.5	25.4	29.5	33.8
Electronic parts, batteries, test equipment, and related items	13.2	13.9	14.5	15.8	16.4
Toys, antennas, security devices, timers, and calculators	12.5	12.0	14.1	12.6	10.3
Telephones and intercoms	8.0	6.5	5.8	5.6	3.5
Microcomputers, software, and peripheral equipment	34.6	30.7	21.8	15.1	9.5
Total	100.0%	100.0%	100.0%	100.0%	100.0%

SOURCE: *1983 Annual Report,* Tandy Corporation.

and more substantial part of the business. Along with this growth, areas of historical strength (such as stereos and CBs) had become much less significant. Second, telephone and telephone-related sales, while not substantial, had been growing very rapidly.

As a result of these trends, Tandy aggressively pursued both the computer and the telecommunications business. Exhibit 11.3 provides a breakdown of computer-related sales by product group. Although telecommunications was still in its infancy, Tandy pursued the same formula for these lines of business as it did for computer systems. That formula consisted of providing full line "Tandy" computer or telephone centers in large metropolitan areas (thereby disassociating these products from the Radio Shack name) and using add-on departments in those areas too small to support free-standing specialty stores. The free-standing store was typically about 3,000 square feet and incorporated a sales area, training room, repair service, storage space, and offices. A typical staffing arrangement includes a store manager, one manager trainee, three full-time sales representatives, a full-time instructor, and a repair service technician.

The altering of traditional merchandise lines was tied directly to changes taking place in Tandy's customer base. In the past, Tandy was essentially a consumer electronics "hobby shop," which catered to electronics hobby buffs. This group represented a substantial customer base. The Tandy of 1984, however, was moving toward the commercial consumer of computer and telecommunications products. This move resulted in the customer base being segmented into two broad classes: consumer and commercial.

EXHIBIT 11.3	Computer-Related Sales by Product Group (Unaudited)		
		Year Ended June 30	
	1983	1982	1981
Model I/III/4	28.1%	27.2%	30.5%
Model II/12/16	21.4	25.7	25.3
Color computers	9.8	7.2	3.3
Portable/pocket computers	3.1	2.5	2.7
Printers	16.5	16.7	17.5
Software	9.2	8.5	7.5
Other	11.9	12.2	13.2
Total	100.0%	100.0%	100.0%

SOURCE: *1983 Annual Report,* Tandy Corporation.

Tandy experienced problems with this shift in customer groups stemming from its carefully developed image as an electronics hobby shop. Commercial customers tended to view Radio Shack equipment as more appropriate to the home than to the office. For this reason new computer and telecommunications products were marketed under the brand name of Tandy rather than Radio Shack. In addition, free-standing computer and telephone stores carried the name "Tandy" instead of Radio Shack.

One of Tandy's great strengths had been their ability to hold customers through heavy, targeted advertising. At the core of the advertising program was the direct mail catalog. Each month Radio Shack sent a 24-page pamphlet (32-page in November and 48-page in December) to more than 25 million previous customers. The mailing list used for these mailings had been assembled over many years at checkout centers in Radio Shack stores all over the United States. The objective of the catalogs was that the "complex nature of the electronic equipment and gadgetry sold through the Radio Shack stores is distilled and presented in an easy-to-understand form."[20] This philosophy was apparent in the manner that computers were marketed through the catalog. The catalogs stressed a computer for every walk of life, for every use, whether it be a computer for the home or business. This was done in a style that stressed plain English and deemphasized technical descriptions. The catalogs also served to standardize (or police) pricing in all stores (franchised or company owned), and promote Radio Shack's nationwide distribution and service network.

Although catalogs were the primary advertising vehicle, they were still only a part of the program. Catalogs were closely linked to free-standing inserts and ROP (Run Of the Paper) newspaper advertising. Free-standing inserts consisted of eight- or twelve-page inserts circulated at least fifteen times per year. Magazines played an increasing role in advertising to more specialized markets, such as computer and telecommunications users. Television was considered the least important medium, and was used primarily for status or "class" exposure.

An in-house agency named Radio Shack National Advertising Agency was responsible for all advertising programs. This agency, which employed 145 people and took up one floor of the corporate headquarters, was given the company's total advertising budget of over $160 million. Notes Bernard Appel, Executive Vice-President of Marketing, "Keeping the agency inside allows us to have tighter control and ultimately better input over our advertising. It would also be much more costly to go outside."[21] Although the agency was in-house, its relationship to the company was similar to that of an outside agency, with the client being Radio Shack. All of the advertising for a product was the responsibility of the buyer. The buyer acted as the client and the agency had to obtain his approval.

The total cost of advertising was $199.1 million in 1983, a 23% increase from the expenditure of $160.9 million in 1982. For the first time since 1979 the percentage increase in advertising expense was greater than the sales increase. Even so the advertising expense as a percent of sales had been declining since 1979. This percentage was 9.4%, 9.0%, 8.1%, 7.9%, and 8.0% in 1979, 1980, 1981, 1982, and 1983, respectively.

The merchandising of the Radio Shack stores was guided primarily by information gathered at the store level. One type of information previously noted was the customer names that supported the mailing list. An even more critical type of information was that gathered through the Radio Shack operating system (SOS). Through this system, each retail store was able to transmit its daily sales, financial data, payroll, inventory, and merchandise orders. This system has served to provide up-to-date merchandising data, streamline stores and central office accounting and warehouse operations. Through a joint venture with Citibank Tandy began offering a national credit card good for purchases of more than $225.00 at all Radio Shack stores nationwide. This provided a new source of information on large credit purchasers.

Tandy put this information to good use judging by the financial status of its stores. Year-to-year sales gains of 22%, 20%, 22%, 14%, and 15% were recorded in 1983, 1982, 1981, 1980, and 1979. This sales growth came from four areas: the expansion of the store system, increases in sales of old stores, new product categories, and international operations. As can be seen from Exhibit 11.4, none of these gains were at the expense of gross profit or general overhead expenses.

Gross profit as a percent of sales remained steady for fiscal 1983 and 1982 after four years of increases. Factors that favorably influenced the gross profit were the continuing increase in the volume of self-manufactured products and the increase in manufacturing profits. The factors that limited gross margins were adverse conditions in international operations, caused by the strong dollar and by foreign market restrictions.

EXHIBIT 11.4   **Profit and Expenses Trends at Tandy**

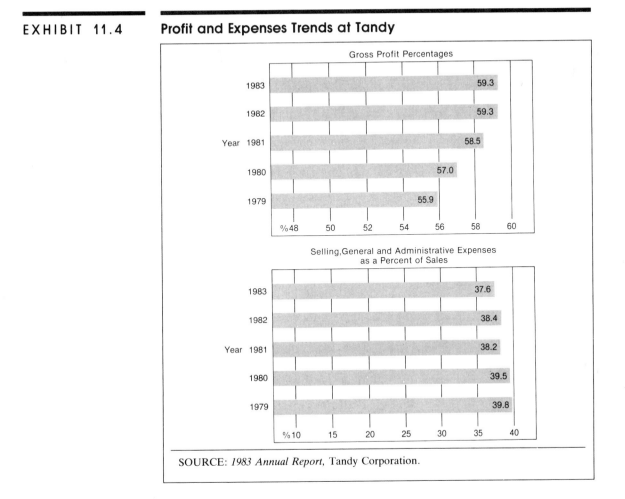

SOURCE: *1983 Annual Report,* Tandy Corporation.

Through a continuous improvement in financial position, Tandy had become a retail powerhouse rivaling the traditional giants of the industry.

As can be seen from Exhibit 11.5, Tandy's return on equity was still one of the highest of the nation's retail giants.

Products

The primary strategy Tandy had pursued was to develop the largest retail distribution system in the electronics industry. The distribution system Tandy developed became enormous, and presented both opportunities and problems. One way that Tandy had chosen to capitalize on these opportunities and cope with these problems had been through self-manufacturing.

Tandy produced some products within all of the product categories sold in the Radio Shack stores. The percentage manufactured in-house varied by

EXHIBIT 11.5 **Financial Information for Retail Chains**

	TWELVE MONTHS ENDING	TOTAL SALES (MILLIONS)	RETAIL INCOME (MILLIONS)	RETURN ON EQUITY
K Mart	10/28/81	$15,759	$232	9.9%
JC Penney	1/31/82	11,860	156	12.9
Sears, Roebuck	12/31/81	27,357	285*	6.6
Tandy	12/31/81	1,886	200	40.8
Toys R Us	11/01/81	687	36	19.4
Wal Mart	1/31/82	2,445	83	27.9

SOURCE: *Forbes,* March 1982.

*After capital gains and before unassigned corporate costs of $108 million.

product line, the largest concentration being in the area of computers and related peripheral devices. One area of rapidly increasing production was that of telephone and telecommunications equipment. This was particularly true of those product areas that combined the features of computer and telephone equipment. In addition to production in-house, a large number of products were manufactured under contract, in production facilities not owned by Tandy. These products carried private labels, such as Realistic.

Tandy saw many opportunities in self-production. The first was the positive effect that manufacturing in-house had on gross profit. As can be seen from Exhibit 11.4 gross margins had been increasing in direct relation to the percentage of private label merchandise sold through the Radio Shack stores. The percentage of private-label merchandise was limited, however. Since the early 1980s, Tandy had been building mainly computer-manufacturing capacity and President John Roach estimated that because of this Tandy might get up to 65% self production, but no further.[22] Margins were assisted through both the ability to control vendor profit, and the ability to develop products designed to fit the unique needs of the Radio Shack stores. One of the major advantages of in-house production was the result of one of the problems arising out of maintaining a large distribution system. The sheer size of the Tandy system made it difficult to find suitable suppliers, and manufacturing in-house reduced Tandy's dependence on outside suppliers. Other advantages were obvious. Tandy had the ability to keep in close contact with technological developments. Tandy had continuous merchandising input to help it guide and quickly implement product development. In summary, Tandy had reduced its overall dependence on outside suppliers and increased its control over the products sold in Radio Shack stores.

Tandy also experienced a number of disadvantages with this system. One of the more substantial was its attempting to play the dual role of both manufacturer and retailer. As Equil Juliussen, computer marketing analyst, states, "If you have your manufacturing hat on, you want as many outlets as possible; but if you have your retail hat on, you may not, since you could be taking sales from our own stores."[23] This had never been a problem until Tandy became heavily committed to computers. Computer sales had become such a substantial portion of the business in terms of retail and manufacturing sales, that neither one could be thought of as subservient to the other.

Tandy, in late 1983, realizing that more outlets were needed in order to maintain market share in computers, began for the first time using independent distributors. Sixty distributors were signed up, who would sell to over 2,000 retail outlets. Although the move had been promoted as "experimental," Tandy management had clearly become aware that they would have to expand distribution if they were to maintain their position in the computer market. Tandy was being slowly forced into a position of having to set priorities. "The company could be forced to choose which role is more important if its competitors pushed strategies of heavily discounting their computers to win customers, and aggressively pursuing the highly profitable software and peripheral markets."[24]

Radio Shack's computer and electronic equipment prices had been traditionally thought of as low, compared to competitors' prices. Radio Shack's low pricing strategy was developed in 1977 when the TRS-80 was first brought into the market. The primary reason Tandy chose a low pricing strategy was that in order to sell through their Radio Shack stores, the computers' prices had to be in line with its other consumer electronic products. It was in Radio Shack's strategy to keep the TRS-80 at a reasonable price ($599.95) so that their current customers could afford to buy one.

Since that time, however, competition in the home and personal computer market had become intense. This had served to place extreme pressure on gross margins which had placed Tandy in a serious dilemma. Tandy's strategy had always been to drop lines that did not produce at least a 50% gross margin. Tandy was now far too dependent upon computer systems to simply drop them. This problem was not acute when Tandy never had to compete head to head with the products in non-Radio Shack stores. However, with wider distribution, Tandy no longer had this luxury. This problem was further aggravated by the fact that costs have not come down as fast as prices, and that Tandy had a high manufacturing cost. As one article on the subject points out, "It seems no accident that the home computer company with the highest prices in the U.S.—Tandy—also performs most of its assemblies in the U.S."[25] This situation had the effect of forcing price discounting on the independent retailers that were now carrying Tandy computers. This had been unheard of in the past and had the effect of putting more price pressures on Tandy products in Radio Shack stores.

The name "Radio Shack" corresponded with a hobby-shop image in the minds of many consumers. This was a desirable image for most of the product areas that Tandy serves. However, computer systems was not one of those areas. To many computer buyers, Tandy maintained the image of a peddler of cheap electronic goods. The TRS-80 model 16 was developed primarily to counteract this image. The unit, which initially cost $4,999, was aimed at the sophisticated user, such as large corporations. In further moves to change their image, Tandy replaced the Radio Shack name with Tandy, on all computer products and full-service computer stores. Probably more important was the manner in which Tandy modeled themselves after IBM, which emphasized support and systems as selling points. This area had needed improvement, which had become especially apparent to independent retailers who had complained of weak and indecisive support from Tandy.

External

Stores

Tandy, as discussed earlier, marketed a wide range of electronics products. These products essentially fell into four general areas: consumer electronics (radios, stereos, etc.); electronic components (diodes, transistors, etc.); computer-related (computers and peripheral devices); and telephone-related (telephones and related peripheral devices). The first two of these product areas were entered when they were considered high-growth markets. As these markets began to mature and stagnate, efforts were made to replace them with products aimed at new growth markets. It was at this time that Tandy entered the computer market. When that growth in the computer markets began to slow and competition became more intense, Tandy began to invest in the development of telephone and telecommunications equipment. This was the pattern that led to the market structure facing Tandy, in addition to providing a basis on which to understand its retail competition.

Tandy's original product line was electronic components aimed at the home electronics buff. These components were carried in all Radio Shack stores except those that were full-line computer or telephone stores. Competitors in this area were generally small independent retailers or small regional chains.

The next market was that for consumer electronics. This category covered a wide range of products, from expensive component stereos to walkie-talkies. These products were carried in all stores except those devoted exclusively to computers or telephone systems. Tandy's primary competition in this market could generally be considered the large mass merchandising chains such as Sears, Penney, and Target on the one hand, and the large stereo/electronics specialty chains such as Pacific Stereo, on the other.

The next market, and the one that was responsible for the strongest recent growth and largest percentage of total sales, was that for computers and related equipment. Tandy faced strong competition in three areas: mass merchandisers, computer specialty stores, and manufacturers who sold directly.

It was estimated that in 1983 there were approximately 20,000 mass merchandisers selling low-priced home computers (less than $1,000). As a result, margins on these units had been squeezed to the point where most computer specialty stores were being forced out of this market into professional business systems.

The strongest competition for Tandy came from computer specialty stores. In 1982 there were an estimated 1,800 computer dealers in the United States, who controlled over 50% of the microcomputer market. It was expected that in 1988 this number would grow to over 6,500 stores, who would control 35% of the products in the personal computer market alone. As the number of stores grew, their makeup was also changing, as can be seen in Exhibit 11.6. Independent retailers were gradually losing ground as chains began to dominate the market. The largest of the competing chains was Computer Land (over 500 franchised stores), followed by Sears (over 100 stores), IBM (over 60 stores), and Computer Craft (over 30).

This trend toward chains was being motivated by shifts in market structure. Smaller stores were having a difficult time competing with the same recognition, buying power, capital-formation abilities, and advertising power of the larger chains. In addition, there was a shift toward standardization and a deemphasis on technology, in favor of marketing, value-added services, and price cutting. This translated into retail chains that operated on minimum margins, maintained outside sales personnel, and provided high levels of service.

One chronic problem of many chains and independent wholesalers alike was lack of adequate cash flow. High-ticket merchandise coupled with a high-growth market had created severe cash flow problems for many dealers. Tandy had not had any serious difficulties with this problem.

Tandy was meeting the competition from other computer retail organizations in several ways. Tandy's primary strategy was to blanket the nation with a large number of stores, in order to guarantee stable national distribution. As of 1983 Tandy had 412 free-standing computer centers, and 632 Radio Shack stores containing computer departments; it also planned to add 100 centers and 50 combined stores by the end of the year. In order to further enhance distribution, Tandy had signed up at least 60 distributors to market its computers to independent retailers. Aware of the need to sell to corporate customers directly, Tandy had begun the formation of a direct field sales force. This sales force had embarked upon a campaign of seminars and direct mail advertising to data processing managers, in order to acquaint professional users with the capabilities of Tandy equipment. Last, Tandy was beginning to provide comprehensive service in terms of repair and training throughout the entire Tandy store system.

The last market, and the one in which Tandy saw the potential for further growth, was that for telephones and related equipment. Tandy was, at this time, considered the largest independent retailer of telephones in the United States. Telephones were marketed through all Tandy stores except computer

EXHIBIT 11.6 **Computer Chains vs. Independent Retailers, 1982–1983**

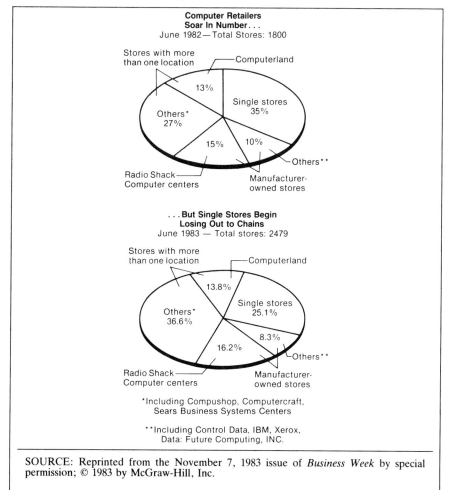

**Computer Retailers
Soar In Number . . .**
June 1982 — Total Stores: 1800

Stores with more than one location — Computerland

13%

Single stores 35%

Others* 27%

15%   10%

Others**

Radio Shack Computer centers   Manufacturer-owned stores

**. . . But Single Stores Begin
Losing Out to Chains**
June 1983 — Total stores: 2479

Stores with more than one location — Computerland

13.8%

Single stores 25.1%

Others* 36.6%

8.3%

Others**

16.2%

Radio Shack Computer centers   Manufacturer-owned stores

*Including Compushop, Computercraft,
Sears Business Systems Centers

**Including Control Data, IBM, Xerox,
Data: Future Computing, INC.

SOURCE: Reprinted from the November 7, 1983 issue of *Business Week* by special permission; © 1983 by McGraw-Hill, Inc.

centers. In 1984, Tandy opened a group of experimental telephone centers designed to carry nothing but telephone equipment. The telephone centers were designed to fulfill a similar role to that of the stand-alone computer centers, in that they carried lines (such as business phones and key systems) that were appropriate to the small business user.

Tandy's interest in telephones was based on two factors. The first was that the telephone market was projected to reach over $5 billion annually by the latter part of the decade. The second was that developing technology was giving the telephone substantial new capabilities that would include integration with such devices as personal computers and home electronics.

Last, telephones and related products were the fastest growing segment of Tandy's business.

Tandy was not alone in its interest in this market. AT&T already had over 461 phone centers and had announced plans to open more in major Sears mall locations. GTE was also a major retailer through freestanding phone centers, as were most other national mass merchandisers.

Products

The consumer electronics industry, of which Tandy was a part, represented an estimated $20 billion dollars in 1983. Tandy's sales, while dominated by the computer, had shown comfortable growth in nearly all "traditional" product areas. Only two areas will be reviewed in depth: computers and telecommunications. Computers are included because they dominate sales and their markets had become substantially more competitive; telecommunications, because this market represented future growth.

COMPUTER SYSTEMS   The conditions facing Tandy in the computer markets were the result of its two markets: home and small business.

The vast majority of people for whom a home computer is a necessity already owned a computer. As a result, the order of the day was to create a mass market for home computers. Atari's Senior Vice-President of Marketing, Ted Vass, put the situation clearly when he said, "The people who pioneered this field were technology-oriented. But now the essence of the business is consumer marketing."[26] The drive toward mass merchandising accurately described the nature of the home computer market in 1984.

The most significant factor that faced both the home and the small-business computer markets was intense competition. The inner workings of most small computers were the same, with key ingredients provided by the same handful of suppliers. Much of the software was also the same. Although manufacturers had tried to distinguish themselves by providing innovative features, these were rapidly copied by competitors. The result was that no computer really had a substantial technological advantage. Therefore, the real differences were found in price, service, compatibility, distribution networks, and image.

"Clearly, the industry had grown out of its initial, entrepreneurial stage and is reaching for maturity," said David Lawrence, an analyst with Montgomery Securities in San Francisco.[27] With the change from an entrepreneurial to a mature market, the critical factors for success also changed. To succeed, personal computer makers would need to monitor these critical areas:

1. **Low cost production:**   as personal computer hardware became increasingly standardized, the ability to provide the most value for the dollar greatly influences sales.

2. **Distribution:** only those makers that could keep their products in the customer's line of sight would survive.

3. **Software:** computer sales would suffer unless a wide choice of software packages was offered to increase the number of applications.[28]

In summary, the market became saturated with undifferentiated manufacturers, crowded distribution channels, and heavy price discounting. Therefore, even though worldwide sales were expected to grow from $6.1 billion in 1982 to $21 billion in 1986, there was little doubt that a shakeout would gradually occur over the next three to five years. By 1986, it has been predicted that there could be only one dozen micro-computer vendors left.

Exhibit 11.7 provides an overview of the general position Tandy held as compared to the competition.

Tandy's strengths were guaranteed distribution, financial muscle, and service through Radio Shack stores. However, as Cleve G. Smith, an analyst for the Yankee Group, says, "Tandy's advantage in distribution has disappeared"; he further stated that "the company will slip to fourth this year (1982) in home computer sales."[29] Tandy also had two notable weaknesses, in that it lacked a national outside sales force and that it had relied entirely on in-house programmers for software development. Moving to correct these deficiencies, Tandy began to staff full-line computer centers with field sales personnel, in addition to allowing software companies to sell products under the Tandy name. Finally, Tandy had begun to respond to price pressures by reducing prices on many items, particularly those that are more price-sensitive, such as low-priced home computers.

Tandy's largest competitor was without a doubt IBM. In fact, it could be said that IBM had virtually defined the competition. As can be seen from Exhibit 11.7, it had no obvious weaknesses. IBM was known for its aggressive marketing, superb sales force, financial power, and an impeccable brand image. By combining all of these abilities it had created one of the most incredible marketing success stories of this century, the introduction of the IBM-PC. As Exhibit 11.8 illustrates, the growth of the PC had been nothing less than phenomenal.

Following the introduction of the PC, IBM had introduced the PC Jr. With both of these IBM had followed a strategy of aggressive distribution and pricing, designed to make them the dominant producer in these markets. Declares David G. Jackson, President of Altos Computer Systems, "IBM is moving faster than anything I've ever seen. It is being absolutely predatory."[30]

New sales, however, did not necessarily represent the whole picture, as Exhibit 11.9 demonstrates. IBM, while certainly a powerful new force, was far behind in terms of units in place.

The success of the IBM PC was unseating Apple Computer from the number one spot in personal computers. Apple (referring again to Exhibit 11.7) had many areas of weaknesses, the primary one being its inability to

EXHIBIT 11.7 Competition in Personal Computers

	CURRENT STRENGTHS							
	Applications Software	Brand Image	Depth of Management	Financial Muscle	Low-cost Production	National Sales Force	Retail Distribution	Service and Support
Apple Computer	*	*					*	
Atari (Warner)	*	*		*			*	
Commodore International					*		*	*
Digital Equipment			*	*	*	*		
Fortune Systems	*							
International Business Machines	*		*	*	*	*	*	*
Japan Inc.			*	*	*			
Radio Shack (Tandy)	*	*		*			*	*
Texas Instruments			*	*	*		*	*

SOURCE: Reprinted from the November 22, 1982 issue of *Business Week* by special permission; © 1982 by McGraw-Hill, Inc.

NOTE: *Business Week* interviewed more than forty leading hardware, software, and peripheral equipment makers; industry consultants; and analysts to come up with a list of expected survivors and their current strengths.

EXHIBIT 11.8

Which Companies Are Taking the Biggest Byte of the Pie?

	PERSONAL-COMPUTER MARKET SHARES			
	1980	1981	1982	1983
Apple	29.3%	41.8%	28.5%	22.0%
IBM	0%	5.0%	22.2%	28.0%
Tandy	37.6%	22.5%	10.1%	7.0%
Hewlett-Packard	5.3%	6.1%	4.7%	3.5%
Commodore	15.9%	10.6%	3.6%	3.5%
Franklin	0%	0%	2.5%	3.5%
Others	11.9%	12.6%	20.2%	29.0%

Reprinted with permission from the March 5, 1984 issue of *Advertising Age.*
Copyright 1984 by Crain Communications, Inc. Source: *Dataquest.*

come up with a cohesive product and marketing strategy. However, under the direction of its new President John Sculley, who resigned as President of Pepsi-Cola to join Apple, these flaws were being rapidly corrected. Apple brought out a whole new series of products aimed directly at IBM, and cut prices and redirected its marketing efforts onto current lines.

Of the remaining competition, the most significant fell into the area of inexpensive home computers. These makers included Commodore, Atari, and Texas Instruments. Of this group, Commodore was probably the most significant to Tandy. Of the larger computer manufacturers, Commodore alone had yet to be scathed in the home-computer price wars. This success had largely resulted from the low production costs Commodore enjoyed in the Far East. Atari, following suit, had completely eliminated its assembly operations in the United States and hoped to achieve cost parity through the use of foreign assembly operations.

These computer manufacturers had been at the forefront of the effort to mass merchandise home computers. They had pursued this effort through extensive distribution, low levels of service, and heavy price discounting. It was because of these companies that Tandy decided to begin using independent distributors, and a more flexible pricing policy.

Telecommunications

Arthur D. Andersen expected the world telecommunications market to grow from $40 billion in 1980 to about $87.5 billion by the end of the decade.[31] The telephone market alone in 1982 was growing at a rate of 40% per year.

Quite understandably, U.S. manufacturers and those abroad were rapidly moving into what was shaping up to be a very lucrative market.

At the heart of this growth were three factors: the breakup of AT&T, the high demand for new service, and new technology. The breakup of

EXHIBIT 11.9   **Comparison of Computer Companies by Number of Installed Units**

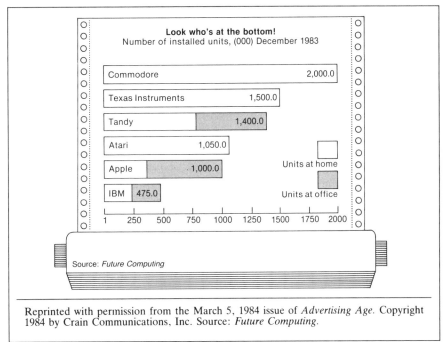

Look who's at the bottom!
Number of installed units, (000) December 1983

Commodore — 2,000.0
Texas Instruments — 1,500.0
Tandy — 1,400.0
Atari — 1,050.0
Apple — 1,000.0
IBM — 475.0

Units at home
Units at office

250   500   750   1000   1250   1500   1750   2000

Source: *Future Computing*

Reprinted with permission from the March 5, 1984 issue of *Advertising Age.* Copyright 1984 by Crain Communications, Inc. Source: *Future Computing.*

AT&T provided an opening for new competitors in what was once a monopolistic market. Second, much of the future demand would be for services aimed at moving computer data. Last, new technology was providing systems for applications never before possible.

Tandy focused on two markets in this industry: the basic telephone, and data systems. Tandy pursued the first market area through products such as telephones, pagers, answering machines, and the like. More focus, however, was being placed on combining computer and communications technologies into a "symbiotic connection."

Tandy already faced competition from an array of large corporations. The most significant of these was AT&T. Already AT&T had distribution of its products through 4,500 retail stores and at least half of their sales were made through another group of mail order houses, and catalog companies.

In addition, AT&T was developing an entirely new line of small office, data, and computer systems, all of which integrated telecommunications and data-processing functions.

The potential of this market had not been lost on IBM, which had bought a 15% interest in Rolm Corporation, a maker of telecommunications equipment. Thanks to the IBM connection Rolm was the safe choice of buyers of telecommunications equipment, the way the phone company used to be. This development, of course, placed Tandy in direct competition with IBM in the telecommunications market as well as the computer market.

The International Telephone & Telegraph Corporation (ITT) was the second largest telephone company in the world; in 1982 it had a net income of $702.8 million and a 21% market share in the total electronics industry. ITT was aggressively pursuing the market because of the void created by the deregulation of AT&T. Unlike Tandy, ITT was known for its aggressive pricing policies, and in addition, spent over $750 million in telecommunications research in 1982.

PRODUCTION

Tandy operated twenty-nine wholly owned factories in the United States, Asia, and Canada, that produced products for Radio Shack stores. Other products were manufactured under contract by independent producers and sold under private labels through Radio Shack stores.

The company had been consistently increasing the percentage of products made internally. However, John Roach, the President and CEO, forecasted that Tandy might get up to 65% self-production, but no further. This was due to the fact that most self-production was dedicated to computer-related products, and there was a limit to the total percentage of these that could be economically produced in-house. Another reason was the criteria applied to an in-house production decision. If Tandy could not offer the best possible product at competitive prices and make an adequate profit, merchandising would be from the outside sources. If the decision was made to produce in-house, the sampling and quality control procedures were the same as outside vendors were required to follow.

Private Label Merchandise as a Percentage of Total Sales		
1981	**1982**	**1983**
Less than 50%	54%	57%

One of the major problems with this arrangement had been the conflict between the needs of the retail and the manufacturing operations. This conflict was strengthened when Tandy had begun selling to independent distributors. In response to this problem Tandy moved the top management of its International Manufacturing Operations into Tandy Division. The latter was eventually split, and one half was given responsibility for the manufacturing of all products sold through the Radio Shack store chain, and the other half was given responsibility for products sold to the general retail market. These divisions were called Tandy Electronics Manufacturing and Tandy Marketing Company, respectively.

Although Tandy's greatest strength was its distribution system, manufacturing operations were taking on much greater importance. Tandy was thus constantly on the lookout for manufacturing plants that it could acquire, in order to improve its already high degree of vertical integration and ability to capture additional manufacturing margins. For example, on September 27, 1983, Tandy announced its intentions of acquiring Datapoint's half of a joint disk-manufacturing venture. In fiscal 1982, videotape-manufacturing capabilities were added through the purchase of the domestic portion of the Consumer Products Division of Memorex. The international operations of this division were being acquired on a country-by-country basis. Also, Tandy has agreed to a joint manufacturing venture with Matra S.A. of France in order to produce micro-computers. On August 18, 1983, Tandy made public its plans to acquire O'Sullivan Industries, Inc., a subsidiary of Conroy Inc. O'Sullivan was a manufacturer of consumer electronic stands, racks, desks, and accessories.

These production facilities were supported by the efforts of two major design centers: one in Fort Worth and one in Tokyo. These design centers, along with those attached to specialized production facilities, were responsible for all product design, from car radios to computers. These groups included not only hardware designers but also a 180-person team engaged in software development for the Tandy computer line.

Even with this R&D capability Tandy did not strive to be an innovator, as was revealed by the fact that R&D costs were considered financially "immaterial." The Tandy product-design effort was set up to create applications, not technologies.

One of the major tasks of these groups was to reduce production costs. This had become a substantial problem in recent years because of the strong dollar and high domestic production costs. Most of Tandy's computer products came from domestic plants, which were considered to be high-cost production facilities. At the same time these products were competing against imports (Commodore), which had a price advantage because of the strong dollar.

WORKING CAPITAL

In 1983 operations generated $321 million in working capital, an increase of over 23% from 1982 (see Exhibit 11.10). The amount of working capital generated in 1983 was approximately twelve times that of 1974.

Tandy utilized its working capital for capital expansion, and did not issue any long-term debt in 1983. The total capital-expansion budget for 1983 was $75 million. This included the expansion of manufacturing facilities, the opening of 350 new retail stores, and the remodeling of 600 existing retail stores.

EXHIBIT 11.10

Working Capital Provided by Operations
(In Millions of Dollars)

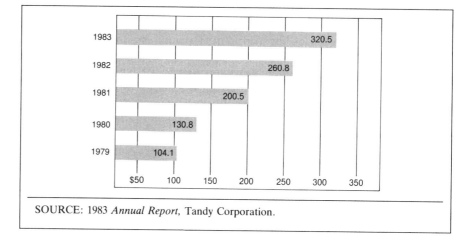

SOURCE: 1983 *Annual Report,* Tandy Corporation.

Cash Flow

In 1983 Tandy's net income increased by 24.3% on a sales increase of 21.8%. Tandy had recorded similar gains, such as the one in 1976 when sales increased 40% because of the CB-radio craze. The lowest sales increase Tandy had experienced since 1973 was in 1978, when sales grew only 12% after the CB-radio craze ended (see Exhibits 11.11 and 11.12).

The effect of the CB-radio craze is shown through an Operational Cash Flow (OCF) analysis that was performed by Paul Pappadio, a professional analyst. Pappadio defined OCF as net income, plus depreciation, plus changes in working capital, less investments in property, plant and equipment, and debt. OCF can be thought of as the uncommitted cash Tandy has on hand at the end of the year.[32]

Through his analysis, Pappadio found that in 1977, when the CB-radio craze ended, Tandy's OCF fell to negative $30 million. In the years following, because Tandy rebounded by entering the microcomputer market, its OCF rose to a high of $70 million. Pappadio also found that in 1982 Tandy's OCF fell again to negative $78.5 million. Pappadio credits this drop to the accumulation of huge inventories.

In response to this OCF analysis, Garland Asher, a Tandy financial officer, stated that putting cash into inventory, rather than simply holding it, makes it earn a better return and that this therefore is the better strategy. Substantiating this conclusion, Asher stated that in 1982 Tandy's after-tax return on non-cash assets was 25.5%. Further, Asher concluded that the

EXHIBIT 11.11

Ten-Year Consolidated Statements of Income, Tandy Corporation and Subsidiaries

(In Thousands of Dollars Except Per-Share Amounts)

Year Ended June 30

	1983	1982	1981	1980	1979	1978	1977	1976	1975	1974
Net sales[1,2]	$2,475,188	$2,032,555	$1,691,373	$1,384,637	$1,215,483	$1,059,324	$949,267	$741,722	$528,286	$411,241
Other income	38,109	28,657	15,697	11,360	11,403	5,629	3,763	2,649	3,963	2,153
	2,513,297	2,061,212	1,707,070	1,395,997	1,226,886	1,064,953	953,030	744,371	532,249	413,394
Costs and expenses:										
Cost of products sold	1,008,187	826,842	701,777	594,841	535,549	491,509	434,031	331,400	249,006	198,067
Selling, general and administrative, net of amounts allocated to spun-off operations in fiscal 1976 and prior	930,244	780,378	645,934	546,325	484,249	403,173	350,878	270,308	204,107	158,792
Depreciation and amortization	38,679	29,437	23,288	19,110	17,121	13,879	11,140	8,034	7,392	5,461
Interest expense, net of interest income and interest allocated to spun-off operations in fiscal 1976 and prior	8,905	1,168	15,454	25,063	28,466	30,260	15,192	7,282	14,044	8,544
	1,986,015	1,637,825	1,386,453	1,185,339	1,065,385	938,821	811,241	617,024	474,549	370,864
Income from continuing operations before income taxes	527,282	423,387	320,617	210,658	161,501	126,132	141,789	127,347	57,700	42,530
Provision for income taxes	248,761	199,302	151,015	98,423	78,272	59,986	69,970	63,066	29,078	20,669
Income from continuing operations	278,521	224,085	169,602	112,235	83,229	66,146	71,819	64,281	28,622	21,861
Loss from discontinued operations, net of income taxes	—	—	—	—	—	—	(2,777)	—	(1,820)	(7,072)

(Continued)

EXHIBIT 11.11 (Continued)

Year Ended June 30

	1983	1982	1981	1980	1979	1978	1977	1976	1975	1974
Net income before income from operations spun off	278,521	224,085	169,602	112,235	83,229	66,146	69,042	64,281	26,802	14,789
Income from operations spun off, net of income taxes	—	—	—	—	—	—	—	3,243	7,794	5,657
Net income	$ 278,521	$ 224,085	$ 169,602	$ 112,235	$ 83,229	$ 66,146	$ 69,042	$ 67,524	$ 34,596	$ 20,446
Income (loss) per average common share and common share equivalent:										
Continuing operations	$2.67	$2.17	$1.65	$1.12	$ .81	$ .69	$ .54	$ .44	$ .20	$ .13
Discontinued operations	—	—	—	—	—	—	(.02)	—	(.01)	(.04)
Spun-off operations	—	—	—	—	—	—	—	.02	.05	.03
Net income	$2.67	$2.17	$1.65	$1.12	$ .81	$ .69	$ .52	$ .46	$ .24	$ .12
Average common shares and common share equivalents outstanding	104,335	103,395	102,578	103,644	106,004	96,136	132,336	144,824	145,408	169,992

SOURCE: 1983 *Annual Report*, Tandy Corporation.

[1]Per share amounts restated for two-for-one stock splits in May 1981, December 1980, June 1978, and December 1975.

[2]Fiscal 1983 and 1982 amounts reflected the adoption of FAS No. 52, Foreign Currency Translation.

EXHIBIT 11.12

Consolidated Balance Sheets, Tandy Corporation and Subsidiaries

(Dollar Amounts in Thousands)

	JUNE 30	
	1983	1982
Assets		
Current assets:		
Cash and short-term investments	$ 279,743	$ 167,547
Accounts and notes receivable, less allowance for doubtful accounts	107,530	83,616
Inventories	844,097	670,568
Other current assets	31,928	27,000
Total current assets	1,263,298	948,731
Property and equipment, at cost:		
Consumer electronics operations, net of accumulated depreciation	194,004	158,678
Tandy Center, net of accumulated depreciation	63,616	66,317
	257,620	224,995
Other assets	60,990	53,918
Total	$1,581,908	$1,227,644
Liabilities and Stockholders' Equity		
Current liabilities:		
Notes payable	$ 55,737	$ 24,942
Accounts payable	64,640	63,641
Accrued expenses	115,054	92,125
Income taxes payable	50,668	52,160
Total current liabilities	286,099	232,868
Notes payable, due after one year	15,482	20,642
Subordinated debentures, net of unamortized bond discount	122,938	122,666
Store managers' deposits	8,490	9,306
Deferred income taxes	17,682	18,886
Other non-current liabilities	10,345	10,599
Total other liabilities	174,937	182,099
Stockholders' equity:		
Preferred stock, no par value, 1,000,000 shares authorized, none issued or outstanding	—	—
Common stock, $1 par value, 250,000,000 shares authorized with 105,645,000 shares issued	105,645	105,645

(Continued)

EXHIBIT 11.12   **(Continued)**

	JUNE 30	
	1983	**1982**
Liabilities and Stockholders' Equity		
Additional paid-in capital	68,111	39,627
Retained earnings	969,626	691,105
Foreign currency translation effects	(16,297)	(12,317)
Common stock in treasury, at cost, 976,000 and 1,789,000 shares, respectively	(6,213)	(11,383)
Total stockholders' equity	1,120,872	812,677
Commitments and contingent liabilities	—	—
Total liab. & stockholders' equity	$1,581,908	$1,227,644

SOURCE: 1983 *Annual Report,* Tandy Corporation.

success of the company lay largely in the fact that its customers were never faced with empty shelves.[33]

International Financial Markets

The strength of the U.S. dollar in the 1981–1983 period affected Tandy in three major ways. First, foreign-produced products imported into the United States carried a favorable price advantage. In fact, Robert Miller, Vice-President of Merchandising, Consumer Products, said, "The strong U.S. dollar, improved technology, and manufacturing efficiencies, continue to bring our customers more advanced products at lower retail prices."[34]

Second, the strong dollar raised the costs of Tandy's exported products in the international markets. This means that exported American-made products carried a price disadvantage abroad.

Finally, the profits generated by the international division were greatly reduced by currency-translation charges. These charges reflect the costs of translating foreign-currency-denominated profits into U.S. dollars. In 1983, the international division yielded $527 million of profits but lost over $590 million in foreign-currency translation.

NOTES

1. 1983 10-K Tandy Corporation, p. 2.

2. Borenstein, Paul, "Can Tandy Stay on Top?" *Forbes,* April 11, 1983, p. 43.

3. *Ibid.*

4. *Business Week,* "A Computer That Builds Radio Shack Image," February 1, 1982, p. 23.

5. Appel, Bernard, *Marketing and Media Decisions,* "Advantages of Being Self Contained," Spring 1982, special, p. 71.

6. Seneker, Harold, "What Do You Do after You Bury the Boss?" *Forbes,* March 3, 1979, p. 7.

7. Rudnitsky, Harold, and Mach, Toni, "Sometimes We Are Innovators, Sometimes Not," *Forbes,* March 29, 1982, p. 66.

8. *Ibid.*, p. 68.

9. Seneker, p. 7.

10. Rudnitsky and Mach, p. 66.

11. Appel, p. 71.

12. Seneker, p. 118.

13. *Forbes*, "Tandy Man," December 11, 1978, p. 118.

14. *Ibid.*

15. 1983 *Annual Report*, p. 3.

16. Appel, p. 71.

17. 1983 *Annual Report*, p. 5.

18. *Ibid*, p. 15.

19. Rudnitsky and Mach, p. 66.

20. 1983 *Annual Report*, p. 14.

21. Madeleine and Dreyfack, "Do It Yourself," *Marketing and Media Decisions*, May 1983, p. 60.

22. Rudnitsky and Mach, p. 68.

23. *Business Week*, August 30, 1983, p. 30.

24. *Business Week*, "Rivals Crowd Tandy's Computer Niches," August 30, 1982, p. 30.

25. Halper, Mark, "Losses Mount in Home Computers as Suppliers Assess 2nd. Half," *Electronic News*, p. 60.

26. "Computer Marketing: No Longer Fun and Games," *Advertising Age*, March 5, 1984, M-1.

27. "Painful Adolescence: A Hot Market Meets a Shake-Out," *Electronic Business*, December 1983, p. 30.

28. *Business Week*, "The Coming Shakeout in Personal Computers," November 22, 1982, p. 74.

29. *Business Week*, "Rivals Crowd Tandy's Computer Niches," August 30, 1982, p. 28.

30. *Business Week*, "Personal Computers and the Winner is IBM," October 3, 1983, p. 78.

31. "World Telecommunication: Study II 1980–1990," A. D. Little, Inc., Cambridge, MA.

32. "Tandy to Acquire Datapoints Half of Disk Venture," *Electronic News*, September 27, 1983, p. 16.

33. *Ibid.*

34. *Ibid.*

VLSI Technology, Inc.

WILLIAM H. DAVIDSON · STEPHEN J. SCHEWE

In February 1983, Alfred J. Stein was reviewing the position of VLSI Technology (VTI) prior to its initial public stock offering. Mr. Stein, who had been President of Arrow Electronics before joining VTI, had just completed his first year as Chairman and CEO of the new company. VTI had been formed in 1979 by Jack Balleto, Dan Floyd, and Gunnar Wetlesen, all of whom had left Synertek Corporation after it was acquired by Honeywell.

VTI was formed to design and manufacture custom VLSI chips. VTI also marketed advanced, circuit-design tools under the name "User-Designed VLSI." These software design tools were intended to shift the function of designing complex integrated circuits from semiconductor makers to original equipment manufacturers themselves. If such a shift occurred, VTI had the potential to grow at a tremendous rate over the next few years. Al Stein's chief concerns were how to encourage the adoption of VTI's services and how to prepare for and manage the company's future growth. His most immediate concern, however, was the stock market's assessment of VTI's prospects.

VTI—THE CONCEPT

Al Stein leaned forward in his chair and spoke softly but intently:

> We have dedicated ourselves uniquely to this business; our whole strategy is based on being a fully integrated "custom" house. We are marketing our design tools and providing training programs to systems companies so they can design their own chips. Other companies in our business want to do custom designs internally. We are of the opposite opinion; we think that industry resources, that is, IC designers, are extremely limited. We want to give the design responsibility to the much larger number of systems engineers. If they design more chips than they have in the past, we hope to reap the benefits by producing those designs in our silicon foundry.

VTI was incorporated on August 1, 1979, in San Jose, California. The founders proposed to greatly reduce lead times for delivery of custom circuits. They planned to slash design time and costs through automation of the design process. VTI's software tools permitted an electrical engineer working at a terminal to design a circuit in graphic form using conventional electrical engineering symbols. The engineer specified the circuit elements and their relationships. The software package then verified the integrity of the circuit design and its efficiency. Once the design was complete, the software package converted the graphic representation into digital code that specified the precise layout of the semiconductor chip.

VTI licensed its design tool software to its customers under agreements that grant the customer a non-transferable, non-exclusive right to use the software for a fixed fee ranging from $58,000 to $160,000. The tools are used on the DEC VAX family of minicomputers or with Apollo Computer workstations (see Exhibit 12.1). A version for IBM mainframe systems was also being developed.

VTI's activities did not end with the completed design. They also planned to provide "quick turnaround" fabrication capability for prototypes and volume production of custom integrated circuits. The digital code generated by the software package would be fed into VTI's wafer fabrication facility to manufacture prototypes and later final products in volume.

ROM OPERATIONS

While anticipating growth in custom chip sales, VTI commenced production of read-only memories (ROMs) in 1982. ROMs were standard products typically manufactured in large volumes. A ROM differed from a RAM, the other primary memory product, in that the data in the ROM was permanently encoded. Data in a RAM is lost when the electric current is turned off. ROMs are typically encoded by the manufacturer. Because

---

EXHIBIT 12.1

VTI User-Designed Software* and Function

CIRCUIT DESIGN PROCESS	CORRESPONDING SOFTWARE
System design	*CELL COMPILERS—Automatic implementation of system building blocks.
Logic design	*VNET—Language to describe logic method. *VSIM—Logic simulator to check function.
Circuit design	*SPICE—Circuit simulator to check performance.
Physical design	*STICKS—Symbolic design for unique cells. *GEOMETRIC EDITOR—Direct creation and modification of layout data base. *PLOT—Graphic output of layout data base.
Verification	*EXTRACT—Circuit extractor to regenerate logic network from implementation. *VSIM—Logic simulator to verify function. *DRC—Design rule check for compatibility with design process.

*Starred software indicates names that have been trademarked by VTI.

ROMs can be uniquely programmed (i.e., can have a unique combination of positive and negative charges within a standard grid), they have some of the characteristics of custom chips. During 1982, the company derived 76% of its revenues from ROM sales to five consumer-product manufacturers. Sales to these customers were primarily for use in home video game cartridges. VTI's largest customers were Mattel, Inc. and Coleco Industries, Inc., which accounted for approximately 52% and 17% of revenues, respectively.

VTI contracted with independent companies for most of the fabrication, assembly, and test of its read-only memories. These arrangements enabled the development cash flows and important customer relationships to become established before the opening of VTI's wafer fabrication facility in November 1982. Dan Floyd, Vice-President of Programmable Memory Operations (ROMs), planned to continue using subcontractors for his orders, while VTI's fabrication facilities would be used to produce high-performance custom circuits designed with the company's software tools.

CUSTOM INTEGRATED CIRCUITS

I think there are a lot of parallels in this business with the last major electronics revolution, which centered around the microprocessor. A lot of engineers felt the need to learn and use the microprocessor to avoid being pushed aside by younger engineers coming out of college. It's another opportunity/threat.

Wes Patterson, VTI's Director of Systems Marketing, was discussing the complicated motivations of potential customers as they decided whether to switch from standard to custom integrated circuits. Although custom circuits had long been available, standard chips accounted for well over 95% of all semiconductor sales.

This usage pattern was due to the higher design costs and longer lead times for custom products. Manufacturing realities also limited the development of custom-chip usage. The key issue in semiconductor manufacturing had long been the yield of usable chips for a wafer of silicon. Semiconductor manufacturing was a delicate process that required expensive equipment operating at precise tolerances. This process did not reward adjustments of machinery to accommodate the production of multiple devices. Fabrication lines usually were set up for large batches of one standard device. Producers invested in research to develop new, more complex devices suitable for wide application, and in plant and equipment designed for long production runs of standard components. These pressures have shaped competitive strategies that emphasize aggressive pricing of standardized components to maximize volume and minimize costs. These industry characteristics had proven extremely attractive to Japanese competitors, who had made major inroads into the U.S. semiconductor market. Japanese suppliers had captured over half of the U.S. market for the latest generation of RAM products (64K units) and were expanding their activities in other high-volume, standardized product segments.

Custom chips began to have an impact in the semiconductor market only in the late 1970s. The custom-chip market was stimulated by development of the microprocessor at Intel in 1970. When combined with read-only memory containing a software program, the microprocessor became a device that could be tailored to specific applications. With customized ROM, microprocessors ran products ranging from handheld toys to automobile ignition systems and microcomputers. Although flexible, microprocessors themselves were still standard components; they became less effective as higher levels of performance were demanded. Dedicated devices designed for single applications proved to be far more efficient than microprocessors. Although programmable microprocessors have some of the characteristics of custom chips, primary custom products were gate arrays, standard cells, and full custom chips.

Gate arrays are preprocessed layers of silicon containing thousands of logic gates. A gate is an on/off switch in a logic circuit or a bit of information in a memory product. The bottom layers of a gate array are of standard configuration; the top one to three layers are unique for each application. The top layers specify how gates in the other layers will be interconnected to fit a customer's specific requirements. This approach offers superior performance in some applications over microprocessors; gate arrays, however, use silicon space inefficiently. Some of the gates produced in preprocessing will not be wired in the final design. One executive estimated that gate array designs typically waste at least 20% of a chip's gates in this way. Nonetheless, gate arrays have provided fast and flexible system design. IBM gave the technology instant credibility when it used gate arrays in its 4300 series computers in 1978, and more recently in its high-end 308X mainframes. Gate arrays offer quick turnaround time; makers can develop prototypes from customers' specifications in twelve weeks. Systems designers in industries with extremely short product lives such as data processing or computer peripherals favor this approach; they can achieve higher density and lower cost than with standard chips. Gate array manufacturers also claim that their technology requires less design time than do full custom approaches.

Standard cells can provide a more economical solution than gate arrays for users less constrained by product design deadlines. These cells are complete functional blocks drawn from a computerized "library"; they include logic functions, memories, processors, and peripheral components. These cells are put into position and connected on a silicon chip in a process similar to the putting of standard components onto a printed circuit board. Standard cells are more efficient than gate arrays because only necessary functions are included in the design. If standard cells and gate arrays are the same size, the greater density of standard cells will allow for higher operating speed. Furthermore, because of smaller size, standard cells will realize higher yields and lower unit fabrication costs. These benefits must be weighed against the lower development costs for gate arrays; for a typical application, standard cells become more attractive at higher production volumes. (See Exhibit 12.2.)

The Structured Design Approach for Full Custom Chips

Developments in circuit design methodology in the late 1970s reduced the time and cost needed to design a custom VLSI circuit. A design methodology known as "Hierarchical VLSI" was developed by Professor Carver Mead of Cal Tech and Lynn Conway of the Xerox Research Center in Palo Alto. Their approach applied systems concepts to circuit design. It could be used by application engineers to lay out a simplified "floor plan" of a circuit and then to lay out individual cells in detail using design tools. Using these tools, a systems engineer could improve circuit density, increase the number of functions on a chip, and reduce the number of components needed in a system. For example, the Apple II+ had 110 components on its printed circuit board; the next generation Apple IIE was redesigned with VLSI technology to use only thirty-one components. Custom chips become more attractive with larger unit requirements. Exhibit 12.3 shows an estimate of user economics for a state-of-the-art 20,000 logic gate system.

The user-designed chip had lower development costs because of the new availability of computer-aided design (CAD) tools, and made more efficient use of silicon, so material and overhead costs were cut.

EXHIBIT 12.2   **User Economics for a 2,000-Gate Application: Standard Cells vs. Gate Arrays**

	GATE ARRAY	STANDARD CELLS
Tooling costs	$10,000	$40,000
Other development costs	30,000	40,000
Total development costs	$40,000	$80,000
Chip capacity, 4-inch silicon wafer	198 chips	265 to 380 chips
Yield	5%	7–9%
Chip yield	9.9 chips	18.6 to 34.2 chips
Cost of wafer fabrication	$100	$100
Cost per chip processed	$10.10/chip	$2.92 to $5.38/chip
Breakeven requirements	5,571 to 8,475 units	

SOURCE: *Electronics*, February 10, 1983.

EXHIBIT 12.3	User Economics for a 20,000-Gate Application: Standard, Semi-Custom, and Custom		
	STANDARD PARTS	SEMI-CUSTOM (GATE ARRAY)	USER-DESIGNED
Number of chips	1,667	27	13
Number of circuit boards	33	2	1
Development cost	$165,000	$550,000	$395,000
Total Cost for 10,000 units	$56 million	$15.2 million	$8.7 million

SOURCE: *Dataquest,* December 1982.

Past Objections to Custom Circuits

Although the economics appeared attractive, certain risks attended the use of custom chips. The design process in the past had been subject to frequent errors in manually performed procedures, such as verifying circuit design or the debugging of prototypes. Intricate devices such as VLSI logic circuits ran the risk of eating up man-years of design resources when traditional methods were used. Skilled IC design engineers available to complete these designs were scarce; there were only about 2,000 IC engineers in the United States, compared to 200,000 or more systems-level engineers. The supply situation promised to become worse in the future; the American Electronics Association projected demand for 51,300 electrical engineers in 1985. At the same time, product lives have shortened as OEMs push to use the latest chips in their systems and thereby increase demand.

In the past, potential users of custom chips have had three alternative solutions to these problems. To obtain chips, they could develop an internal or "captive" production capability, acquire a minority interest or complete ownership of an existing IC manufacturer, or request custom service from one of the large semiconductor manufacturers. The first option had been widely pursued; the industry had witnessed a dramatic surge of new entrants in the past twenty-five years. While some were ventures formed to exploit new technology, others were large users of chips who formed their own in-house or "captive" suppliers of semiconductors. Captive production of integrated circuits was estimated to have accounted for one third of total U.S. production in 1980 and 90% of all custom-chip production. (See Exhibit 12.4.)

The relative advantages of vertical integration were being debated hotly in the industry. Recently, Hewlett-Packard used its captive operations to develop a 32-bit microprocessor for use in its 9000 series of minicomputers. Development took $100 million and five years; the device will be used only

EXHIBIT 12.4

Number of Integrated Circuit Manufacturers, U.S. Market

YEAR	MERCHANT MANUFACTURERS	CAPTIVE MANUFACTURERS
1960	27	6
1965	44	11
1970	92	18
1975	108	31
1980	95	60
1983	107	65

Top 10 U.S.-Based Captive Suppliers of Integrated Circuits

COMPANY	ESTIMATED 1982 PRODUCTION (MILLIONS OF DOLLARS)
IBM	2100
Western Electric	385
Delco (General Motors)	185
Hewlett-Packard	160
NCR	70
Honeywell	70
DEC	60
Burroughs	40
Data General	30
Tektronix	25

SOURCE: *Integrated Circuit Engineering.*

in HP products. In an interview with Electronic News, George Bodway, the General Manager of HP's Computer Integrated Circuits Division, explained that HP's device would provide a substantial lead over competitors because no equivalent product was available from merchant vendors.

Many companies have acquired semiconductor makers; major recent purchasers of chip manufacturers included GE (Intersil), Honeywell (Synertek), and IBM (30% investment in Intel). For others, the choice was to request service from the semiconductor houses like Motorola, TI, and Intel. Douglas Fairbairn, VTI's Director of User-Designed VLSI software, explained that large amounts of demand were not being satisfied by such manufacturers because of economic pressures.

> In the past, only customers who needed a very high volume of product could get someone to design a chip for them—say, 10,000 units and up. Below 10,000 it was not cost effective to use scarce engineering talent.

VTI's managers believed that their long-term profitability depended on their convincing users to give VTI high-volume fabrication contracts for custom chips. Wes Patterson said:

> We believe we can get the silicon business, which is the nice difference between our strategy and just being a tools company. When the guy designs a circuit that hits his own market niche and sells by the hundreds of thousands, we get to participate in that success.

To aid in securing fabrication runs, the company planned to provide a steady stream of enhancements to its proprietary design tools. As Wes explained:

> We plant a hook in these tools that brings the guy back to our foundry in the form of what we call a cell compiler library. The library contains a set of specific circuit functions. It uses parameters to provide an exact fit for the guy's requirements; nobody else can do that. The cell compiler and other enhancements can further cut design time by a factor of 3 or 4 times. To obtain a license for the enhancements, we ask for a commitment of the production from designs done with these tools, typically 80% in the first year and decreasing after that.

In 1982, ROM sales provided 76% of VTI revenues; design tools and foundry operations made up the balance. By 1985, VTI's management hoped to reverse that ratio, so that design tools and custom foundry runs would generate 60%–80% of sales. ROM sales were expected to continue expanding at 15% per year.

PROGRAMMABLE MEMORY OPERATIONS

"We see ROMs as our lead horse and our cash cow," commented Dan Floyd, Vice-President, Programmable Memory Operations. VTI's ROM business addressed a broad segment of the market and emphasized high performance and density. The company offered five types of ROMs: standard 32K and 64K, "fast" 64K and 128K, and a 256K device. The majority of sales came from the standard 32K and 64K products. In addition, VTI designed "custom" ROMs, which incorporated random access memory and logic onto the same chip with the ROM circuitry.

The logistics of selling ROMs were relatively easy, because there was a small number of significant potential customers. According to Wes Patterson, the business was based on close relationships and assurance of delivery.

> The customers knew they had our attention and that we'd jump through hoops for them. The big companies can't turn on a dime and deliver product (ROMs) inside four weeks.

VTI expanded these relationships through joint design projects for custom logic chips. The ROM strategy also meshed nicely with the tiny sales force of seven, which could cover the major customers without difficulty.

Besides generating revenues, the ROM business provided pressure for the company to improve technological processes and reduce costs. Gunnar Wetlesen, Vice-President of Wafer Fabrication, said:

> No company has been able to develop state of the art processes for building logic unless they are also in the memory business. They need the volumes and densities to keep the technologies current. The learning curve is nothing more than continuous experimentation on a fixed data base of production runs; the more runs you have, the more opportunities to reduce costs.

VTI's manufacturing policy to date had been to subcontract ROM production in a complicated international network. After chips were designed internally, masks for the photolithography process were produced under subcontract by U.S. specialty houses. Completed masks were then flown to Japan for wafer fabrication by Ricoh, and to Korea for assembly and test. At the end of the processing, completed chips were drop-shipped to customers. This strategy allowed VTI to accept ROM contracts before completing its own processing facilities and helped to fund custom chip research and development.

Now that VTI's own wafer-processing facility had begun operations, Floyd expected to move the most sophisticated segment of the ROM business to it. The 128K and 256K chips would be used to drive the process technology; shared benefits would accrue in the costs, quality, and capacity of custom production. A separate line within the "clean room" where the chips were fabricated would be maintained for quick turnaround of custom prototypes; this line would have only four operations in common with the rest of the facility. Floyd hoped to add a packaging operation next to the wafer processing facility in 1983. The standard "jelly bean" ROMs like the 32K and the 64K would continue to be subcontracted.

COMPETITION— ROMs

Competition in the ROM market was intense because of a large number of established competitors and readily available substitutes. VTI competed with over thirty ROM suppliers, including Synertek, a division of Honeywell founded by current members of VTI management; National Semiconductor; NEC; American Microsystems (a division of Gould); and General Instrument. Competition was based on price. Many competitors had shared costs with other product lines; entry decisions could be made on an incremental basis. Exhibit 12.6 shows projected prices for ROMs for the next three years.

In many low-volume applications, and in products requiring software revisions, erasable programmable memories (EPROMs) had replaced ROMs. EPROMs can be reprogrammed in the field: ultraviolet light was used to erase previous instructions. These circuits are generally more expensive than

EXHIBIT 12.6

Price Forecast for ROMs

Product	1982	1983E	1984E	1985E
32K	$2.21	$1.53	$1.07	$0.82
64K	4.42	3.06	2.14	1.64
128K	8.86	6.12	4.28	3.28
256K	NA	12.24	8.56	6.56

ROMs, however, and ROMs are thus more likely to be used in consumer products in which the circuit features are not alterable by the user. Although price is an important competitive factor in this market, service and delivery are also important because ROMs cannot be sold from inventory; they must be manufactured to meet the customer's pattern or program.

Mask ROMs, supported by the toy and game markets, were expected to grow from $414.7 million in 1982 to $492.9 million in 1983, an increase of 19%. Sales had increased 22.6% in 1982. It was estimated that five producers (TI, Motorola, Intel, National, and Advanced Micro Devices) held 53% of the $869 million ROM and EPROM market.

COMPETITION—SEMICUSTOM

Nearly 100 companies were currently competing in the semicustom IC market. Gate-array and standard cell-design approaches continued to battle for market acceptance as the industry standard; as explained above, each had specific strengths and shortcomings. Six firms currently offering cell-library design: American Microsystems, startups International Microelectronic Products and Zymos, Synertek, NCR's Microelectronics Division, and Harris Corporation's Semiconductor Division. No Japanese suppliers had yet announced standard cell libraries in the United States. Fifty to sixty companies compete in the gate-arrays market, including industry giants such as Motorola, Texas Instruments, Toshiba, and Fujitsu. Gould's American Microsystems was the largest company devoted exclusively to custom semiconductor devices and was a major participant in gate arrays.

Competition—Custom Design Tools

Competition among manufacturers of integrated-circuit-design tools was intense. The market consisted of several large manufacturers of CAD workstations (IBM, Calma/GE, Applicon/Schlumberger, Computervision) and dozens of software suppliers who offered packages to run on these machines. Most of these companies were small startup ventures concentrating on the simulation and verification aspects of chip design. These companies included

Avera, CADTEC, CAE Systems, Daisy Systems, Mentor Graphics, Metheus, and Valid Logic Systems.

The natural progression of the industry was toward further integration of the design process within one system. Although VTI's system of design tools had not yet gained significant commercial acceptance, its approach was unique in that it integrated most stages of the design process. The user could construct an electrical engineering diagram with the aid of a sophisticated graphics package and cell library. VTI's system automatically tested, optimized, and converted the electrical engineering diagram to a semiconductor circuit design. The user could then transmit the resulting data via VTINet to the fabrication facility. Although VTI's system was unique, management believed they had only a nine-month lead on the competition. New packages were being offered weekly.

In its custom design business, the company competed with many large custom circuit manufacturers, as well as the internal design centers of several original equipment manufacturers. In addition, the custom design process competed with the gate array, standard cell, and field-programmable devices (microprocessors with ROMs) mentioned before.

COMPETITION— SILICON FOUNDRIES

In the latest survey published in VLSI Design, a trade journal for the industry, thirty-eight companies reported that they were offering silicon foundry service, up from twenty-six the year before. Competitors included small startups like VTI, successful semicustom chip makers like American Microsystems that specialized in gate arrays, and established standard components manufacturers. The commitment of these firms to the concept of the silicon foundry was unclear in January 1983. The larger houses seemed to be searching for ways to fill capacity idled by the recession, while many of the smaller firms did not yet have a complete processing facility. Wes Patterson exclaimed,

> The competitor that scares me to death is Intel. They've got the foundry, the technology and the sales force, and they still have enough entrepreneurial spirit to go after this market. Motorola and TI don't.

Intel had recently concluded an agreement with Zymos to buy a cell library for its newest high-performance fabrication process. According to press reports, they hoped that the agreement would generate new business from small volume users for its silicon foundry, while the company could avoid having to invest in design support operations.

Al Stein believed that his company's emphasis on quick turnaround time, its advanced software and design capability, and its fully integrated service-oriented approach provided it a distinct market advantage.

> There are CAD companies that sell the design tools, and companies that just do wafer processing. We're a one-stop shop.

RESEARCH AND DEVELOPMENT

VTI has spent $4.2 million on research and development since its founding, including $3.3 million in 1982. Major areas of emphasis include

- Advanced software design tools for integrated circuits,
- Advanced networking and communications to provide an interface between customers and the VTI silicon foundry,
- Read-only memory circuits, and
- Semiconductor manufacturing processes.

The company's research expenditures were focused on increasing circuit density and quickening turnaround time. During 1983, VTI planned to expand its VTINet capabilities to include transmission and processing of custom circuit data bases, and remote inquiry systems to allow customers to track jobs in progress.

HUMAN RESOURCES

At the end of 1982, VTI employed 193 people: 62 in research and development; 20 in manufacturing engineering; 76 in manufacturing; 18 in marketing; and 17 in general management and administration. Al Stein saw his major task as managing this group of highly talented and diverse people:

> The success of any organization, whether it's a high technology company or a football team, is dependent on the people you have in your company. My major efforts are directed at putting together a highly talented group of people who work together well and get the job done.

In turn, Al Stein's move to VTI as Chairman and Chief Executive Officer in February 1982 brought an important level of business and financial credibility to the company. VTI was founded by Jack Balletto, Gunnar Wetlesen, and Dan Floyd. The positions and backgrounds of the company's officers are shown in Exhibit 12.7. According to Doug Fairbairn, Vice-President of User Designed VLSI and a co-founder, Stein's strengths were his business skills and his track record:

> He's doing here the same things that made him successful at TI and Motorola. He's concentrating on getting product out. He's burdening the company with a minimum amount of overhead for things like administration, and he's demanding absolute perfection, or as close to it as he can, from everybody in the company. Al is well-respected by the financial community and his presence has focused a lot of attention on us. There's a perceived quality of assumed success rather than assumed failure.

FINANCES

VTI had grown at a rapid pace: revenues were $82,404 in 1980; $552,553 in 1981; and $21,229,251 in 1982. Net revenues in 1981 resulted primarily from course fees and rentals from the related videotaped lecture series. The sharp

EXHIBIT 12.7   **VLSI Technology Inc.: Officers and Directors**

NAME	AGE	POSITION AND BACKGROUND
Alfred J. Stein	50	Chief Executive Officer, President, and Chairman of the Board. With VTI since March 1982. Previously CEO Arrow Electronics, 1981–1982; Corporate V-P of Motorola, Assistant Gen. Mgr. (Semiconductor Group), Gen. Mgr. (Integrated Circuits Division), 1977–1981; various positions with Texas Instruments, most recently Corporate VP, 1958–1976. Also Director of Tandy Corporation, Applied Materials, Inc.
John G. Balletto	42	Senior Vice-President and Director. President and CFO, VTI, 1979–1983; Director of Marketing, Synertek, 1973–1979; Assistant to President, Ricoh Electronics, various positions at Fairchild Camera and Instrument, 1962–1973.
Daniel W. Floyd	42	Vice-President, Programmable Memory Operations, and Director. With VTI since 1979. Previously Vice-President of Manufacturing, Synertek, 1973–1979; Director of Wafer Fabrication, American Microsystems, and Director of Standard Products, Harris Semiconductor, 1963–1973.
Gunnar A. Wetlesen	35	Vice-President, Wafer Fabrication, Technology, and Foundry Activities; and Director. With VTI since 1979. Previously Director of Technology Development, 1974–1979, and Director of Memory Products, 1976–1979, Synertek; Manager of Process Technology, American Microsystems, 1968–1974.
Douglas G. Fairbairn	34	Vice-President, User-Designed Technology. With VTI since December 1980. Research Staff, Xerox Corporation's Palo Alto Research Center, 1972–1980.
Kenneth A. Goldman	33	Vice President, Finance; CFO and Secretary. With VTI since 1981. Previously Group Controller, Consumer Products Group, 1979–1981, Manager of Budgeting and International Planning, 1977–1979, Memorex Corporation; Controller of MOS Division, Fairchild Camera and Instrument and other positions, 1974–1977.

NAME	AGE	POSITION AND BACKGROUND
Ronald C. Kasper	40	Vice-President, Sales. With VTI since 1981. Previously Managing Director, European Sales, 1978–1981, and Western Area Sales Manager, 1976–1978, Synertek; various sales positions, Electronic Memories and Magnetics, 1967–1976.
David C. Evans	58	Director. President, CEO, and Chairman of the Board, Evans and Sutherland Computer Corporation, 1968–present. Previously Director of Engineering, Research and Development, Bendix Corporation.
William R. Hambrecht	47	Director. President, CEO, and Director of Hambrecht and Quist, 1968–present. Also Director of ADAC Laboratories, Auto-trol Technology, Computer and Communications Technology, Evans & Sutherland, Granger Associates, Magnuson Computer Systems, NBI, People Express Airlines, Silicon General, and Xidex Corporation.
James J. Kim	47	Director. Chairman of AMKOR Electronics, Inc., and President of The Electronics Boutique, 1978–present.
William J. Perry	55	Director. Senior Vice-President of Hambrecht & Quest, 1981–present. Undersecretary of Defense for Research and Engineering, 1977–1981; President and Chief Executive Officer, ESL, Incorporated (now a division of TRW), 1964–1977. Also director of ARGO Systems, Avantek, and Technology for Communications International.

increase in revenues realized in 1982 resulted from initial sales of ROM circuits, which accounted for 76% of revenues. VTI's management expected another sizeable increase in sales in 1983. The company's design tools were first offered to customers in 1982, and the first production runs from custom chips designed with the VTI design methods were expected at the end of 1983. These revenue gains were accompanied by heavy expenses resulting from the staffing of engineering teams, product development, and marketing activities during 1981, and large capital expenditures and startup costs for the wafer processing facilities in 1982. As a result of these expenses, VTI had lost a total of $3.6 million during its first three years of operations. Exhibits 12.8, 12.9, and 12.10 show the income statements, balance sheets, and statement of sources and uses of VTI, for the years 1980–1982.

EXHIBIT 12.8 **VLSI Technology, Inc.: Statement of Operations**

	YEARS ENDED		
	December 31, 1980	December 31, 1981	December 26, 1982
Net revenues	$ 82,404	$ 552,553	$21,229,251
Cost and expenses:			
Cost of sales	73,811	139,942	14,238,656
Wafer processing start-up	—	—	2,761,547
Research and development	—	809,257	3,319,959
Marketing, general and administrative	32,453	1,229,198	3,299,819
Operating costs and expenses	106,264	2,178,397	23,619,981
Operating income (loss)	(23,860)	(1,625,844)	(2,390,730)
Interest income	2,010	151,666	831,057
Interest expense	—	(3,456)	(530,302)
Net income (loss)	$ (21,850)	$(1,477,634)	$(2,089,975)
Income (loss) per common share	$(.01)	$(.72)	$(.53)
Weighted average common shares outstanding	1,563,000	2,054,600	3,967,507

Funding needs were expected to remain high in the foreseeable future. VTI's business strategy required a large up-front investment in equipment for the silicon foundry and in development outlays for the design tools. The company's operating plan estimated that $20 million would be required in plant and equipment investment over the next eighteen months. Rapid technological changes in chip fabrication and circuit-design software indicated the need for sustained development expenditures and equipment investments of this magnitude. Dataquest estimated that the industry was becoming more capital intensive each year and projected an increase in net plant over sales to 70% by 1985.

Cash flows from custom chip fabrication would increase slowly because of the long development cycle typical of VTI's OEM customers. Industry observers compared the development cycle to a "two-year wheat crop": the OEMs needed additional time for the design and development of new systems after receiving working prototypes of the custom chips; volume production runs that generated large demand for foundry services would

EXHIBIT 12.9   VLSI Technology, Inc.: Balance Sheet

	YEARS ENDED	
	December 31, 1981	December 26, 1982
Assets		
Current assets		
Cash and cash equivalents	$ 757,928	$10,552,577
Accounts receivable, net of allowance for doubtful accounts, and customer returns of $338,000 in 1982	99,212	4,246,640
Inventories	—	1,093,304
Prepaid expenses and other current assets	49,220	58,375
Preferred stock subscriptions receivable due within 1 year	8,016,000	—
Total current assets	8,922,360	15,950,896
Plant and equipment		
Machine equipment	17,287	874,788
Leasehold improvements and equipment leased under capital leases	577,676	12,424,381
	594,963	13,299,169
Accumulated depreciation and amortization	(26,801)	(993,666)
Net plant and equipment	568,162	12,305,503
Deposits and other assets	119,220	49,286
Total assets	$9,609,742	$28,305,685
Liabilities and Shareholders' Equity		
Current liabilities		
Accounts payable	$ 390,925	$ 5,914,776
Accrued liabilities	197,977	1,377,640
Deferred income	147,628	761,845
Current portion of capital lease obligations	31,144	1,009,866
Total current liabilities	767,674	9,064,127
Noncurrent obligations under capital leases	318,135	10,783,129
Shareholders' equity		
Series A Preferred Stock, no par value; 6,000,000 shares authorized;		
Issued: 6,000,000 in 1982, 1,200,000 in 1981	1,973,750	9,989,750
Subscribed: 4,800,000 in 1981	8,016,000	—
Series B Preferred Stock, no par value; 2,600,000 shares authorized;		
Issued: 598,803 in 1982	1,000	1,976,102
Common Stock, no par value, 30,000,000 shares authorized;		
Issued: 4,874,464 in 1982, 2,504,000 in 1981	50,080	99,449
Retained earnings (deficit)	(1,516,897)	(3,606,872)
Total shareholders' equity	8,523,933	8,458,429
Total liabilities and shareholders' equity	$9,609,742	$28,305,685

EXHIBIT 12.10 **VLSI Technology, Inc.: Statement of Changes in Financial Position**

	YEARS ENDED		
	December 31, 1980	December 31, 1981	December 26, 1982
Working capital was applied to:			
Net loss from operations	$ 21,850	$1,477,634	$ 2,089,975
Less charges to operations not involving the current use of working capital—depreciation and amortization	—	(26,801)	(966,865)
Total working capital applied to operations	21,850	1,450,833	1,123,110
Additions to plant and equipment	—	594,963	12,704,206
Increase in deposits and other assets	—	119,220	(69,934)
Total working capital applied	21,850	2,165,016	13,757,382
Working capital was provided by:			
Issuance of common stock	2,500	17,580	49,369
Issuance of preferred stock	971,750	1,002,000	9,991,002
Preferred stock subscribed	9,018,000	(1,002,000)	(8,016,000)
(Increase) decrease in preferred stock subscriptions receivable due after one year	(8,016,000)	8,016,000	—
Issuance of warrant	—	1,000	100
Increases in noncurrent obligations under capital leases	—	318,135	10,464,994
Total working capital provided	1,976,250	8,352,715	12,489,465
Increase (decrease) in working capital	$1,954,400	$6,187,699	$(1,267,917)
Increase (decrease) in working capital by component:			
Cash and cash equivalents	$ 984,025	$ (238,684)	$ 9,794,649
Accounts receivable	13,203	86,009	4,147,428
Inventories	—	—	1,093,304
Prepaid expenses and other current assets	—	49,220	9,155
Preferred stock subscriptions receivable due within one year	1,002,000	7,014,000	(8,016,000)
Accounts payable	(26,328)	(364,597)	(5,523,851)
Accrued liabilities	(18,500)	(179,477)	(1,179,663)
Deferred income	—	(147,628)	(614,217)
Current portion of capital lease obligations	—	(31,144)	(978,722)
Increase (decrease) in working capital	$1,954,400	$6,187,699	$(1,267,917)

only occur at "harvest," once the product was in the market. When volume orders for foundry business came in, VTI would have a comfortable margin; variable costs were estimated at only 20–30% of costs.

For a startup venture, VTI had experienced unusual success in obtaining funds during its early years. Originally, funding was provided in December 1980 by sales of preferred stock to five venture capital firms and Evans and Sutherland Computer Corporation. The venture capitalists were among the most successful firms in the business, including Hambrecht and Quist; Rothschild; Advanced Technology Ventures; and Kleiner, Perkins, Caufield & Byers. A list of major shareholders is given in Exhibit 12.11. William Hambrecht and William Perry of Hambrecht and Quist were directors of the company. Further funding was provided by capitalized leases and favorable terms by customers and suppliers. With the assistance of Bendix Corporation, VTI leased the first $13.6 million of equipment and leasehold improvements associated with its facilities. Bendix also purchased Series B preferred stock from VTI. At the end of 1982, VTI's unused sources of funds consisted of $10.553 million in cash and equivalents, $3.5 million in net available capital lease financing, and $500,000 in research and development funds available from Bendix. In addition, the company possessed $2.7 million in tax carryforwards, including net operating losses, investment tax credits, and research and development credits.

EXHIBIT 12.11

VLSI Technology, Inc.:
Major Shareholdings

	NUMBER[1]	% OWNED
Evans & Sutherland Computer Corporation	1,800,000	15.7%
Advanced Technology Ventures	1,154,791	10.1
Accounts advised by Rothschild	1,154,791	10.1
The Bendix Corporation	908,267	7.9
Olivetti Realty	598,803	5.2
Kleiner, Perkins, Caufield & Byers II	577,545	5.0
Officers and directors (11 total)[2]	3,125,869	27.2
Other shares[3]	2,153,201	18.8
Total shares outstanding	11,473,267	100.0

[1]Includes all common stock and all preferred shares; preferred is convertible into common; the preferred is convertible into common at a price of $1.67 per share. Cost basis for the common is $0.025 per share.

[2]Major individual shareholders include Alfred J. Stein, 936,889 shares; John G. Balletto, 500,000 shares; Daniel W. Floyd, 500,000 shares; and Gunnar Wetlesen, 485,000 shares.

[3]Includes shares beneficially owned and held in trust.

EXHIBIT 12.12   Statistics on Selected Initial Public Offerings

	GALILEO ELECTRO-OPTICS	QUANTUM CORP	ARGO SYSTEMS, INC.	IMAGIC	ALTOS COMPUTER SYSTEMS	SYSTEMS & COMPUTER TECHNOLOGY CORP.	CONVERGENT TECHNOLOGIES INC.	VTI, INC.
Date offer filed	12/28/82	11/9/82	10/27/82	11/3/82	10/14/82	10/5/82	4/14/82	
Line of business	Manufacturer of electro-optic components	Designs and mfg. rigid disk drives	Designs and mfg. elec. re-connaisance systems	Designs and mfg. home entertain-ment systems	Designs and mfg. micro-computer systems	Provides ap-plication software products and services	Manufactures computer systems	Custom i/c vendor
Financial Information (In Thousands of Dollars Except Per-Share Data)								
Revenues	14,268	29,968	32,187	35,044	57,443	26,792	19,692	21,229
Net income	774	4,928	2,462	6,108	6,359	3,225	1,881	−2,090
Earnings per share	.57	1.13	1.08	.43	.55	.29	.15	−.53
Total assets	8,187	18,448	28,014	29,352	27,033	12,166	20,247	9,610
Shareholders' equity	1,060	13,981	9,442	8,597	14,553	8,337	13,165	−3,607
Offering Data								
Underwriter	L.F. Roths-child	Morgan Stanley	Hambrecht & Quist	Merrill Lynch	L.F. Roths-child	L.F. Roths-child	L.F. Roths-child	L.F. Roths-child
Securities offered	700,000 com.	2.5 million com.	606,390 com.	2.7 million com.	3.3 million com.	2.58 million com.	4 million com.	3 million com.

EXHIBIT 12.12 (Continued)

	GALILEO ELECTRO-OPTICS	QUANTUM CORP	ARGO SYSTEMS, INC.	IMAGIC	ALTOS COMPUTER SYSTEMS	SYSTEMS & COMPUTER TECHNOLOGY CORP.	CONVERGENT TECHNOLOGIES INC.	VTI, INC.
Price range	$8.00–$10.00	$20.50	$16.00–$18.00	$15.00–$17.00	$21.00	$16.50	$12.00–$15.00	$10.00–$12.00
Value of offering	$7 million	$51.25 million	$10.915 million	$45.9 million	$69.3 million	$42.57 million	$60 million	$36 million
P/E ratio	17.5x	18.1x	16.7x	39.5x	38.2x	56.9x	100.0x	negative
Offerings as a % of pro forma shares outstanding	38.4%	28.1%	22.2%	16.9%	23.3%	20.2%	20.8%	20.7%
Mkt. value at initial price	$18.22 million	$182.34 million	$49.272 million	$272.3 million	$297.0 million	$210.8 million	$288.7 million	$173.7 million
Aftermarket								
Bid on 1/21/83 (Day before VTI filed offering)	NA	24.75	34.75	NA	26	NA	NA	
% Change from initial price		18.3	104.4		23.8			

PUBLIC OFFERING

VTI filed for a public offering of common stock on January 25, 1983. The preliminary prospectus estimated that three million shares would be sold at a price between $10 and $12 per share. VTI said the proceeds would be used for capital expenditures and working capital. Currently, 11.5 million shares were outstanding.

Al Stein recognized that VTI's growth potential depended on his company's access to the capital markets:

> We need to raise a good amount of additional capital if we're going to grow at this rate. We think a public offering is the way to go because Wall Street is enthusiastic and our financial performance to date has been better than expected.

New registrations for initial public offerings had surged to a 1982 peak of 31 in the month of December; in the first 11 months of 1982, 186 companies had gone public, raising more than $1.1 billion. Industry participants believed that the market would continue to strengthen; for example, Morgan Stanley announced plans to manage the initial public offering for Apollo Computer in early 1983. Other new issues rumored to be imminent included offerings for the robotics manufacturer, Automatix; Diasonics, Inc., a supplier of ultrasound imaging systems to radiologists and cardiologists; and desktop-computer maker Fortune Systems. Exhibit 12.12 lists selected statistics on recent public offerings.

THE FUTURE

1983 would be an important year for VTI. Stein still saw the company as being in its startup phase; the wafer processing facility would require several quarters to reach efficient operation and would cause continued losses. The company also needed to build acceptance for its design tools, and to lessen its dependence on the ROM business, add customers for custom chips. "The thing that's holding us back is a few solid references," said Wes Patterson. "That cycle takes a couple of years. We won't have testimonials from our earliest customers until the end of 1983."

To reach its goal of 1000 customers by 1986, VTI needed to firmly publicize its claimed advantages in cost and performance. As Gunnar Wetlesen explained:

> The design cost, production cost, and performance are all dynamic and must achieve a new equilibrium now that CAD techniques are on the scene. It takes time to realize what's happening and switch over.

Stein was confident that VTI was in the right place at the right time:

> A little semiconductor company has to find a strategy and a market niche so that it's not competing with the Motorolas, TIs and Fairchilds. There's no way

from a financial or people-resources point of view that it can compete successfully with such companies. You have to have something unique. I think we do indeed have something that is different and that will, over time, change the whole semiconductor industry.

Multicon, Incorporated . . . Robotics

DAVID W. ROSENTHAL

John E. Clark, Executive Vice-President of Multicon, Inc. shook his head and smiled as he walked off the second tee. His ball had hooked badly into the trees and high rough on the left side of the second hole, and his next shot would be a difficult one. "There's no doubt about it," he said, "As little as I have played, I can't just come out and put the ball in the fairway. This is only the second time I've been out this year, but I guess that I can't complain. . . . Business has been so hectic since the 'split' that I just haven't had time to work on my game."

Clark referred to the split that had removed Multicon from divisional status as part of Murphy Controls Company over a year before. "We're still completing the move to become an independent company now," said Clark, eyeing his golfball and measuring the approach to the green with a harsh stare. "As a matter of fact, there are some shifts in ownership and organization that are going to take place shortly, and they will really put us in a position to move!" Falling silent, Clark hesitated momentarily, considering which club to use for his next swing. His hand paused briefly on his pitching wedge, the correct club for simply playing his ball back to the fairway, but quickly settled on his 2-iron. Undaunted by the brow of the hill over which his ball would have to rise and the trees it would have to negotiate on its way to the green some 200 yards distant, Clark slashed at the ball.

"Our biggest difficulty, other than financing, of course, is a strategic issue. It is an extremely complex situation," commented Clark as he walked toward the green. "Multicon has made a good name for itself as a 'systems house' putting together 'turn-key' robotics installations for manufacturing concerns. But we are good at both general-purpose robotics and vision systems." Clark's second shot had rattled into the trees to the right of the green, and he now had to make an almost impossible shot just to put his ball on the green and keep it there. "The question facing us now is, should we continue in robotics or should we specialize in vision systems?" Clark's third shot rolled quickly down the sloping green, past the hole, and off into the fringe some 25 feet away.

This case was prepared by Professor David W. Rosenthal of Miami University. It was presented at the North American Case Research Association Meeting, 1985. Distributed by the North American Case Research Association. All rights reserved to the author and the North American Case Research Association. Reprinted by permission of the author and the North American Case Research Association.

As he lined up his lengthy putt, Clark noted, "The big advantage of staying with robotics is that we have developed some great expertise in a variety of applications. That's 'money in the bank.' At the same time, vision systems are really state-of-the-art, and there are only a few companies in the country that have our knowledge and proven abilities in that area. We'd be awfully hard to touch in a couple of years." Clark settled himself over his putt, stroked the ball, and watched motionless as it "broke" to his right and settled some 18 inches from the hole. After his "tap-in" for a bogey five, Clark commented, "Guess I'll have to settle for bogey. . . . My practice time is unlikely to get any better for the foreseeable future."

COMPANY DEVELOPMENT

Multicon had begun in mid-1982 as a division of Murphy Controls Company, Inc. Murphy Controls Company was a small Cincinnati-based distributor of industrial control devices. At that time it was apparent that the programmable controls distributed by the company lent themselves to networking with industrial microcomputers and that an increasing need for appropriate software was developing. The Multicon Division was formed to improve Murphy's position in this business.

John E. Clark, then a regional manager with Automatix, a Boston-based firm in robotics and machine vision, was hired to manage the new division with help from Roscoe C. Forche, a member of the Murphy Controls engineering staff.

"I won't say that those were the 'good old days,' because they weren't," said Forche. "Business was tight, the economy was lousy. We were right in the depths of the recession, and capital expenditures on machinery were at a low point. Start-up problems were the rule rather than the exception. Still, we had a good base to work from, and we knew for certain that the market would improve."

In the twelve-month period ended December 31, 1983, the division had achieved sales of $929,000 and an after-tax profit of $71,000. Multicon, Inc. was created as of January 1, 1984, to take over the operations of the division. In calendar year 1984, Multicon generated sales of $1,903,000 and an after-tax profit of $58,000. Additional financial information may be found in Exhibits 13.1, 13.2, and 13.3.

The executives of Multicon expected the company to generate billings of $3.21 million in the calendar year 1985 on the basis of existing bookings and as a result of an evaluation of outstanding proposals. The company currently held a $450,000 line of credit with local banks and anticipated additional capital requirements of $150,000 plus an increase in bank debt to cover up a total of $850,000 in working capital. The company was expected to generate a pre-tax profit of $287,000 for 1985 if sufficient working capital could be secured; but despite the excellent record of growth, local banks were not enthusiastic about increasing the company's debt position.

EXHIBIT 13.1 **Comparative Income Statement**

	1983	1984
Sales	$928,921	$1,903,349
Cost of Sales:		
Materials	$626,015	N.A.
Program Development	$ 81,332	N.A.
Total	$707,347	$1,513,768
Gross Profit on Sales	$221,574	$ 389,581
Operating Expenses:		
Wages and Benefits	$ 62,175	$ 152,402
Travel and Sales Promotion	23,173	72,323
Shop Expense	8,755	N.A.
Depreciation, Rent, Insurance	12,511	20,968
Utilities and Telephone	6,918	11,343
Supplies	N.A.	13,782
Interest	N.A.	21,754
Other	14,195	31,547
	$127,727	$ 324,119
Income before provision for federal income taxes	$ 93,847	$ 65,462
Provision for federal income taxes	$ 23,298	$ 7,200
Net Income	$ 70,558	$ 58,262

ORGANIZATION

By June 1985, the Multicon organization had grown to include seventeen people. Ronald P. Barker, 44, was the President and Chief Executive Officer of both Murphy Controls Company and Multicon. At Multicon his duties principally related to overall supervision and, increasingly, finances. John E. Clark, 31, was Executive Vice-President and was responsible for all marketing, engineering, manufacturing, and administrative activities. Increasingly, Clark found himself in the role of CEO as Barker retreated to managing the parent company, Murphy Controls Company.

The engineering functions of the business were overseen as a whole by Roscoe C. Forche, 31, from his position as Vice-President of Engineering. Forche controlled all technical matters in all functional areas of the firm, and reported to Clark in a staff relationship. Also reporting to Clark were Terrell Zielesnick, Manager of Applications Engineering, and Geoff D. Plum, Manager of Project Engineering. Generally, Zielesnick was responsible for the sales development engineering, while Plum was responsible for the design and actual building of the systems. An organization chart and brief biographies of the officers are shown in Exhibits 13.4 and 13.5.

EXHIBIT 13.2   **Balance Sheet—Calendar Year 1984**

Current Assets:

Cash	$ 746
Accounts Receivable, Net	253,102
Receivables from affiliate	49,668
Inventories	192,741
Costs and Profits in Excess of Billings on Uncompleted Contracts	263,692
Other	346
Total Current Assets	$760,295

Property and Equipment:

Furniture and Fixtures	$ 47,652
Shop Equipment	4,928
Leasehold Improvements	3,725
Automobile	8,865
	$ 65,170
Less Accumulated Depreciation	8,770
	$ 56,400
Deferred Organization Costs, Net	$ 8,989
Total Assets	$825,684

Current Liabilities:

Notes Payable	$110,000
Trade Accounts Payable	364,944
Accrued Payroll and Other	30,625
Advance Payments from Customers	62,822
Deferred Income Taxes	12,600
Total Current Liabilities	$580,991

Shareholder's Equity:

Common stock, no par value, 100,000 shares authorized, 60,000 shares issued and outstanding, stated at	$ 500
Paid-in Capital	186,231
Retained Earnings	57,962
	$244,693
Total Liabilities and Shareholder's Equity	$825,684

PRODUCTS   Multicon operated in computer-aided manufacturing (CAM) in two principal markets: machine vision and industrial robots. The company has acted as a "systems house" connecting a variety of manufacturers with end users. The term "value-added reseller" was also used to describe the types of activities conducted by Multicon.

EXHIBIT 13.3

Statement of Changes in Financial Position for the Year Ended December 31, 1984

Sources of Cash:	
Operations—	
Net income	$ 58,262
Expenses not requiring an outlay of cash—	
Deferred income taxes	12,600
Depreciation and amortization	8,169
Cash provided by operations	$ 79,031
Increase in—	
Notes payable	$ 85,000
Trade accounts payable	262,293
Accrued payroll and other	30,625
Advance payments from customers	62,822
Total sources of cash	$519,771
Uses of Cash:	
Additions to property and equipment	$ 53,046
Deferred organizational costs	6,754
Dividends paid	300
Increase in—	
Trade accounts receivable	156,281
Receivables from affiliate	72,957
Inventories	254,341
Other	346
Total uses of cash	$544,025
Decrease in cash	$(24,254)
Cash, beginning of period	25,000
Cash, end of period	$ 746

Clark described Multicon's business as being similar to that of a good stereo salesperson:

> When a customer visits a good stereo salesperson, they are asked about their needs, the amount of money they wish to spend, the types of music they listen to, and how they wish to listen. Perhaps even the type of furniture and housing they have can play a role. Having gained an understanding of the client's needs, the salesperson, using his knowledge of the available equipment in the market, can help to pick out the most appropriate kind of speakers, a turntable from another manufacturer, an amplifier from a third company, and so forth.
>
> A systems house brings together the best robotic or vision components for a particular job, writes programming to enable the assembled components to

EXHIBIT 13.4 **Organizational Chart—June, 1985**

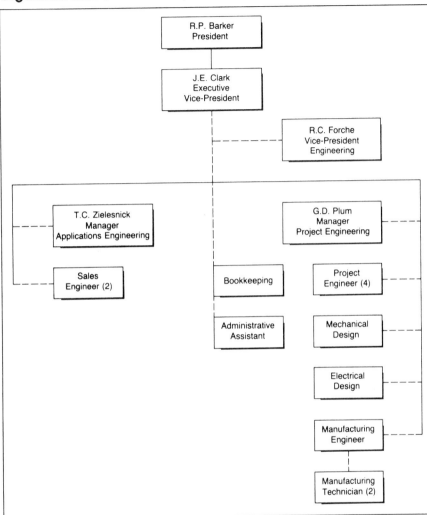

do the work, develops instructions and training for the users, installs the equipment, and troubleshoots the whole thing until it is running smoothly. In short, a manufacturer who wishes to install a robotic assembly would make use of a systems house to hand over an operational set of equipment, "turn-key" system.

The Multicon company provided one-, two-, and three-dimensional vision systems for machine guidance, part sorting, inspection, and gauging. Inte-grating hardware from the major vision-systems manufacturers with application engineering, software, optics, lighting, and peripheral devices, the company offered operational systems for industrial users. As of June 1985, the company had successfully installed more than twenty-five vision systems. Primary suppliers of vision systems to Multicon were Automatix Autovision Systems, and Opcon 20/20 Systems.

In the industrial robot area, Multicon had focused its efforts on assembly, sophisticated parts-handling, and special processes. The company offered turn-key robot cells including hardware, software, and peripherals such as end-of-arm tooling, sensor integration, parts delivery systems, and controls. Multicon was a designated Systems Application Center for Hitachi America, Ltd., and acted as a Systems Integrator Reseller for Cincinnati Milacron.

The company had designed and installed a number of systems for a broad spectrum of applications, including a vision system for the high-speed inspection of consumer products' packaging, labeling, and content; a machine vision system, with custom optics and lighting, to inspect for casting flaws

---

EXHIBIT 13.5 **Executive Biographies**

John E. Clark

Co-founder and Executive Vice-President

Age 32

BBA Marketing, University of Cincinnati, Cincinnati, Ohio, 1976

1976–1980   Sales Engineering positions with Honeywell and Texas Instruments

1980–1982   Regional Manager, Automatix, Inc. a Boston based start-up company in the field of machine vision and robotics

1982–1983   Manager, Multicon division of Murphy Controls Company

1984–present   Executive Vice-President, Multicon, Inc.

Charter member of Robotics International and Machine Vision Association of Society of Management Engineers (SME).

Roscoe C. Forche

Co-founder and Vice-President Engineering

Age 31

BS and MS, University of Cincinnati, Cincinnati, Ohio, 1975 and 1977

1978–1982   Sales Engineer and Manager Technical Services, Murphy Controls Company

1982–1983   Chief Engineer, Multicon Division of Murphy Controls Company

1984–present   Vice-President Engineering, Multicon, Inc.

Charter member of Robotics International and Machine Vision Association of SME.

Geoff D. Plum

Manager, Project Engineering

Age 35

BSC and MBA, University of Louisville, Louisville, Kentucky, 1973 and 1980

1968–1980   General Electric Company, various positions including Manufacturing Engineer, Production Supervisor, and Advanced Manufacturing Engineer

1980–1985   Cincinnati Milacron, Industrial Robot Division, Supervisor of Application Development

1985–present   Multicon, Inc., Manager, Project Engineering

Charter member Robotics International of SME.

Terrell Zielesnick

Manager, Applications Engineering

Age 35

SEE, Ohio State University, Columbus, Ohio, 1977

MBA, University of Cincinnati, Cincinnati, Ohio, 1985

1976–1980   Goodyear Atomic Corporation, Electrical and Project Engineer

1980–1981   Ziel-Blossom and Associates, Electrical Engineer

1981–1984   Crouse Hinds Company, Supervisor Applications Engineering

1984–present   Multicon, Inc., Manager, Applications Engineering

Member, Institute of Electrical and Electronic Engineers; Member, Robotics International of SME; and Registered Professional Engineer, Ohio

in the bores of machined parts; a machine vision system for the detection of welded seams in rolled steel; and robot cells for the loading of lead fittings into the die cavity of injection-molding machines.

OPERATIONS

Multicon sales took place on a project basis. Sales leads came from direct contact, trade show activities, presentations to industry associations, and referrals from manufacturers and customers. John Clark both oversaw the sales activities of the two individuals who called on prospective customers and made sales calls himself.

Once a potential customer contact had been established, the Multicon executives and engineers took great pains to determine that the prospective customer had a definite and viable need for a robotic or machine vision system and that Multicon possessed the expertise to deliver an operational solution. Multicon often required that samples of the customer's product be made available and that engineering documentation such as a floor layout exist.

As Terrell Zielesnick, who provided pre-sale engineering support, noted:

> The worst thing that can happen is for a customer to have a misconception about his needs and our capabilities. If a clear problem is not defined, we won't attempt to develop a proposal. It is not uncommon to find "customers" who are simply looking for a free education, or who have heard about this new-fangled robotics stuff and figure that it is about time to jump into it. It takes us a long time and a lot of effort to develop a well reasoned proposal to solve a specific problem. We can't afford to waste our energies on too many unaccepted proposals. Besides, the well defined projects are difficult enough!

Generally, a Multicon sales engineer visited the prospective customer's site and, by reviewing its technical and commercial content, attempted to qualify the project further. He attempted to determine whether it was a project Multicon was competent to do, whether the project was funded, who the competition might be, and why the customer wanted to do the project. The particulars were then reviewed by Clark and Zielesnick, who authorized further development and a feasibility study, possibly including a customer-funded demonstration.

Pricing was the responsibility of the marketing group, headed by John Clark. Once a proposal was written, it was submitted for review to a committee composed of Clark, Forche, Zielesnick, and Plum. A proposal was not submitted to a customer until it was approved by that group. Once a proposal was accepted, the project was transferred to the engineering and production departments. Typically, a project manager was appointed to shepherd the project through engineering, design, and production. The final step in the process consisted of a demonstration and acceptance by the customer at the Multicon facility. Multicon employees then followed the project into the customer's location for installation, start-up, testing, and training.

As a value-added remarketer, Multicon marked up the price of the hardware that it sold as part of its systems. While the actual markups varied from supplier to supplier, and even from product to product, the company set 30% as a target markup. Increasingly, however, robotics hardware was being marked up only an average of about 15% while vision systems hardware continued to average roughly 30%. Considerable downward pressure appeared to be building on prices of robotics equipment. In the installation of most systems, testing, software development controls, training, and set-up costs added from half to twice the cost of the hardware alone. Estimating these labor-intensive functions was difficult and they added considerable risk to the pricing process. Should a particular job be quoted at too large a price, the customer would be unlikely to contract for the system; but if the price were too low, difficulties in the engineering or applications process could actually result in a loss for Multicon.

THE ROBOTICS INDUSTRY

In 1985, the robotics industry was in a state of rapid change. Technological advances during the previous ten years, and growing capability to apply the benefits brought by robotic automation, had brought the industry to a new level of sophistication. Even the definition of an industrial robot had changed dramatically in just a few years. While old definitions had focused on the ability of a robot to accomplish "3-D tasks" (Dumb, Dirty, and Dangerous) to the advantage of human workers, the new definition focused on flexibility. In 1985, the Robotic Industries Association (RIA) defined an industrial robot as

> a reprogrammable, multifunctional manipulator designed to move material, parts, tools or specialized devices through variable programmed motions for the performance of a variety of tasks.

Although industrial robots had been invented some twenty-five years before, the real growth in installation and use of robots in industry had only begun in the early 1980s. At that time, industry analysts eagerly developed forecasts for market growth reaching yearly sales of $2 billion by 1990. Individual companies predicted their own sales to be as high as $1 billion by 1990 and loudly proclaimed their projections to the press.

By 1985, however, it had become obvious that the industry had not grown at the pace predicted earlier. A variety of reasons were commonly cited as constraints to the adoption of robots. Central among these were the economic recession of the early 1980s, unrealistic expectations about the capabilities of robots brought on by popular movies such as "Star Wars," lack of government support in the form of tax incentives for installation, and labor demands for the maintenance of employment levels. Actual installations and sales figures for the industry are shown in Exhibits 13.6 and 13.7.

The purchase and installation of a robotic manufacturing cell was often emotional, because of a variety of fears. To counter these fears industry sources referred to the following points:

1. Most current robot installations involved the selection of a robot over another form of equipment, not the replacement of a person.

2. Robots in factories generally performed the hazardous, boring, demoralizing, and repetitive tasks, and thus allowed the removal of workers from dangerous environments.

3. The increased productivity offered by robots could pave the way to a shorter work week, higher pay, and better working conditions.

4. Higher productivity could mean fewer jobs lost to overseas manufacturers in competitive industries.

Industry analysts and participants had anticipated that after the economic recession ended, there would be an industry shakeout, which would reduce the number of competitors in the market. The shakeout had not yet occurred

EXHIBIT   13.6

Shipments by U.S.-Based Robot Suppliers

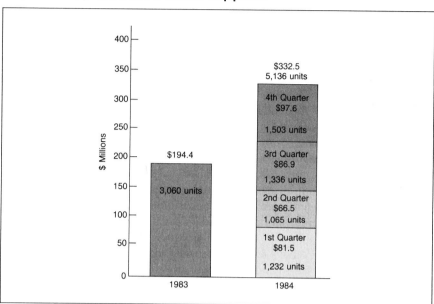

EXHIBIT   13.7

U.S. Robot Population
(Installed Base)

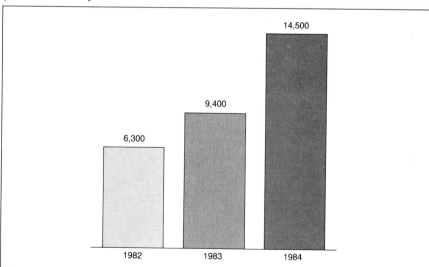

in June 1985, but there were indications that many companies were on the brink of insolvency. John Clark described the situation:

> We're also starting to see, not the demise of the industry, but that the industry troubles are starting to have an effect. Only three years ago, everybody forecasted the industry as being just absolutely successful, with high growth rates, good profitability, and every major company wanted it. GE got into it, Westinghouse got into it, Caterpillar bought into Advanced Robotics. GM bought into GM—Fanuc (GMF). Just this year, Ford bought into American Robotics. Everybody thought it was just nirvana.
>
> But, now in 1985, the headaches are starting to show. Outside of GMF, whose numbers are suspect because they're part of GM and you can't get a handle on them, everybody's losing money. *Everybody's* losing money. I think that's starting to have its toll. People look at GE, you know, as an illustration of the problems in the industry. They had huge corporate resources, a lot of commitment, big hoopla, and they have not been a major factor in the market. . . . And they've been in it for four or five years.
>
> One of the main problems with the industry today is that in 1980 everybody believed the forecasts. In 1980 numbers were banging around like you wouldn't believe. The problem is that because everyone believed the forecasts, they built capacity and staffed to meet that inflated view of demand. Now the industry is plagued by overcapacity. Many companies went so far as to buy inventory, almost on speculation. Now they have literally hundreds of robots stuck in warehouses. They have to sell them off cheap, and I think that generates a lot of pressure. A guy is running a profit center and he's getting killed by having this inventory tie up his capital. I think that's part of the crash coming, the reductions in pricing, just to correct the initial forecast errors.
>
> The shakeout's started. I think the economy's as good as it's going to get for a couple more years. And I think that, if anything, from a capital equipment standpoint, it may even be on the downside. GMF's market presence in automotive goods, which is the biggest user of robotics to date, is being felt by the rest of the robot community. And I think if you put those two things together, people've been living on high hopes for a little bit too long and the reality is starting to close them down. Some people are just plain running out of money.

The robotics industry was characterized in two ways: by the applications for which robots were purchased, and by the companies who manufactured (or assembled) the robots. The major industrial applications had been in the automotive industry, primarily in the area of spot welding. Estimates of industry sales going to automotive spot-welding applications ranged as high as 60%. Other automotive applications included are welding, materials handling, painting, stamping, and metal working. Automotive applications as a whole were estimated to account for as much as 80% of robot sales. Other applications included parts manufacturing, injection molding, and materials handling. A list of major U.S. robotics firms and their estimated market shares for 1983 and 1984 are shown in Exhibit 13.8.

EXHIBIT 13.8   **U.S. Robot Manufacturers' Estimated Share of Market 1983–1984**

	SHARE OF MARKET	
	1983	1984
Cincinnati Milacron	17%	17–20%
Westinghouse/Unimation	15%	6–7%
GMF Robotics	9%	30–35%
DeVilbiss	9%	4%
Automatix	7%	7%
Others	43%	27–36%

THE MACHINE-VISION INDUSTRY

Machine-vision systems ranged in complexity from simple television-camera–computer hookups to sophisticated, laser-based, three-dimensional robotic controls. The basic concept of a vision system was to digitize an image, and thus provide a source of data for a computer's software package to interpret. In simple terms, a television camera would take a digital picture of a brightly lit scene: it would break the image into thousands of individual points or cells called "pixels." Each pixel would be assigned a numeric value between 0 and 63, according to the pixel's level of brightness or darkness. A microcomputer attached to the system would then be capable of interpreting the numeric data from the image, according to a set of programmed instructions.

A simple illustration of an application might be a vision system that determines whether an assembly line has a part on it at a given location. The vision system would "view" the location and register a constant level of brightness when no part was present. As a part was delivered to that point, the level of brightness would change, so the numeric value of the pixels in the image would change and the computer would recognize that a part had arrived.

Similar to the early predictions regarding the robotics industry, estimations of market size and growth in the machine-vision area varied widely during 1985. Estimates of the 1984 machine-vision market ranged from $40 million to $80 million, with 50–210 companies participating. Estimates for market growth ranged from 50% per year to an optimistic doubling each year, which yielded market-size projections of $1 billion by 1990. The range of market projections is illustrated in Exhibit 13.9.

The machine-vision market in 1985 was dominated by a group of five companies controlling up to 80% of the sales in the area. The remainder of the market was divided among many smaller firms. The market was characterized by many small start-up companies with limited product lines and

EXHIBIT 13.9   **Machine-Vision Industry Market Estimates, 1985**

	MARKET ESTIMATE	
	Companies	Dollars
1980	30	NA
1981	NA	NA
1982	NA	NA
1983	NA	$35 M–$84 M
1984	50–120	$75 M–$80 M
1985	150	$150 M
—		
1987		$480 M
—		
1989		$455 M
1990		$800 M–$1 B

NOTES: (1) NA: Not available; (2) M = million; (3) B = billion.

capabilities. The five major companies and their estimated 1985 market shares are shown in Exhibit 13.10.

John Clark described the market:

> There is no barrier to entry. None. Any halfway bright person could go to Digital Equipment Corporation and buy an O.E.M. computer, say, for about $5,000 and from any number of companies buy an interface board that lets a camera "talk" to the computer, and go to any video store and buy an off-the-shelf camera that's used for security surveillance or something, put it all in a cabinet that costs a couple hundred bucks, and he's got a vision system. It doesn't do much, and it's not very sophisticated, but he's a player in the market! That is what is happening right now. The market is just full of "mom and pop" companies, little guys with a garage. It's a mess.

EXHIBIT 13.10   **Machine-Vision Industry's Estimated 1985 Market Shares, by Company**

COMPANY	ESTIMATED SHARE
Automatix	20–22%
View Engineering	20–22%
Machine Vision International (MVI)	14–15%
General Electric	5–10%
Diffracto	8–10%
Others	33–21%

The purchase of a vision system was often less emotional than the purchase of a robot. While considerable publicity had surrounded the job-displacement issue with robots, little pressure had been felt by the vision industry. Decisions to purchase vision systems tended to be made at lower levels of management than did robot-purchase decisions, as plant managers apparently did not require the reassurance of upper-management support as they did with robot installations.

Zielesnick suggested that purchasers of visions systems were less sensitive because the systems often did the job better than the currently used processes:

> A good example is label inspection. Picture dishwashing liquid bottles coming by. You are sitting in a chair in front of a conveyor and the bottles are coming by at the rate of five a second, 300 a minute. On the other side of the conveyor is a mirror, and your job is to look at both the front of the bottle, and in the mirror, at the back of the bottle. You are supposed to identify those bottles that have torn labels or labels that are misplaced by more than a sixteenth of an inch. That's a lousy job, and you probably aren't doing it very well.

Competition in the vision-systems market focused on product characteristics, particularly computing speed and power, development of software packages and decision logic, and expertise in on-site engineering elements such as lighting and lenses. Increasingly, manufacturers of vision systems were relying on systems houses for programming and on-site engineering functions in the channel of distribution.

THE CURRENT DECISION: INTERVIEW WITH JOHN CLARK

"The thing that makes our strategic decision so difficult is that we have some compelling reasons to stay with robotics, and at the same time we have strong reasons to go with vision systems. With our resources, I'm not sure that we can afford to do both. . . . At least, not well."

Robotics

"Currently our sales are roughly 60% robotics, and 40% vision. A robot system is worth anywhere from $60,000 to $120,000 in sales to us on the average. A vision system can go anywhere from $20,000 to $200,000 with an average installed price of about $75,000. When we started the year we were shooting for 40% robotics and 60% vision, but it just hasn't worked out that way. With a small company like ours, a single large order can make a dramatic shift.

"Our position in the robotics industry is at once a problem and an advantage. We are one of a number, probably less than 100, of systems houses in the country. In terms of skills and experience that number falls to about 50. But, that number is growing and the robot manufacturers are encouraging it. We are software- and controls-oriented, but other systems houses are positioned at the metal-fabricating end of the business. They can actually design a system and build the conveyors to actually create a production line. Our stated policy is that we don't want to get into metal working. We have a good skill set and we have good people, but we will be competing with companies that can provide the metal side, too.

"Another problem with the robotics business is the margins. The robot manufacturers aren't giving us the margins that we need right now. Fifteen percent is typical. If you look at a robot cell that cost $100,000 installed, there is probably a $60,000 robot in there. At 15%, that generates a nice volume, but it is actually a cash burden. We actually have to go out and buy that piece of equipment. If we have to carry it for 90 or 120 days while we put all the pieces together, and program it, and put it into the customer's plant, and start it up . . . all before we get paid, that 15% margin almost doesn't cut it. That may change. We are trying to force the robot manufacturers to change, but I just don't know.

"Robotics is very, very service oriented. There is nothing wrong with that, but the big leverage comes from having a product to sell. Our role in the robotics business is strictly service: design engineering, drafting, mechanical engineering, electrical engineering, training, and start-up. There is no proprietary product that Multicon will own. When you place a robot cell, sure you gain the expertise and knowledge of that application, but the next placement, even for the same application, will require a completely new set of services. You can't just plug it in. . . . There's no 'product' opportunity there.

"On the positive side, the robot market is growing at 50 or 60% per year, and it will continue for a lot of years. We are in a very, very good start-up service. The market is more mature than the vision market, so we think that a robot is easier to sell than a vision system right now. The industry has already gone through the pains of education and establishing its worth. Our overall marketing costs are lower in robots than in vision. Further, we have a good name in the business, and we have great expertise.

"A key to success for us has been our people. We've got good access to robotics engineers, and there is a shortage of robotic and machine vision engineers in the marketplace. Still, we have been able to hire key people, and we will be able to attract more, particularly in robotics."

Machine Vision

"We are early, early in the machine-vision cycle or phase of development. We are one of a very, very select few machine-vision systems houses in the country. There may be three or four people like us, but I've only identified one. I'm sure that there are others, but there aren't many. Because of that, we can establish a very strong market identity, and that is very important.

"We have established some good relationships, probably stronger relationships with our machine-vision vendors than we have with our robot vendors. They are embracing us just a little bit tighter for a whole variety of reasons, but that is a definite plus.

"Probably the major advantage for vision is that it gives us the opportunity to become product driven. There are real opportunities to develop proprietary packages based around a piece of machine-vision hardware, that become 'products' out in the market. Our first is a label inspection package. The consumer products packaging community doesn't want to buy a vision system for label inspection, they want to buy something to inspect labels, and they want the vision system to be 'transparent.' They don't want to have to fool with it. Their product comes through the test space, and good product is passed through, and bad product is kicked out. We have a standard system that will do that with standard design, standard manufacture, standard software, standard lighting. We'll still have to customize it a little, but we can tell a customer that we can or cannot do the job in about an hour.

"Machine vision is a higher risk going in than robotics for every project. The initial contact on a new application is riskier from our standpoint. We may look at it, we may evaluate it, and say that we can do it. Our assumptions and evaluations may not be as accurate in vision. It's easier to be off, and at that point we are pumping a lot of unforeseen resources to finish a commitment made to the customer. That is a risk.

"A big problem in machine vision is that it is difficult for us to find people to work on it. It is a skill that is not in the market, so you kind of have to 'home grow' it. There is a significant cost in finding people and in training them to contribute. We should be hiring people six months to a year before we really need them. We need to invest the $50,000 to $70,000 per head in educational costs to get them up the learning curve. Right now, that is a problem for us.

"Another major concern is that the machine-vision manufacturers won't always be willing to rely on service groups like us. As they get more sophisticated in their applications software it will become much easier to tell the vision system to do something. Users won't need a systems house to design, program and install a system. It is the old 'user friendly' issue. The more the manufacturers invest in research, the less important our role as just an applier will become."

CONCLUSION

Clark smiled as he stood over his golf ball on the right side of the fairway on the par-five eleventh hole. For one of the few times today he had driven the ball straight and long. Looking toward the green, he reached for his 3-wood. Despite the long distance to the green and the pond guarding the approach, Clark intended to take the risky shot rather than "laying up" with an iron. After taking a practice swing, he addressed the ball and smoothly stroked what had to be his best shot of the day.

"Well, we'll see," laughed Clark, replacing his club in his bag. The result of the shot was not visible, since the pond was out of sight over a ridge in the fairway and the green too far to see a ball clearly. "There are only so many opportunities, and you have to do the best with them that you can!"

Piper Aircraft Corporation

THOMAS L. WHEELEN · J. DAVID HUNGER · MOUSTAFA H. ABDELSAMAD

HISTORY

In 1928, William T. Piper and Ralph Lloyd were partners in the drilling and selling of crude oil in Bradford, Pennsylvania. During that year, Mr. Lloyd invested $400 in Piper's behalf (without Piper's knowledge) in a new venture and made a similar investment for himself. This new venture was the Taylor Aircraft Company of Bradford, Pennsylvania. At the time of the investment, Piper knew absolutely nothing about aircraft and in fact felt that they were unsafe. He was certainly unaware that this $400 investment would lead him into an era in which he would be known as the "Henry Ford of Aviation."[1]

For the next nine years, Taylor Aircraft struggled financially as its first airplane, the Chummy, fought to take a foothold in the light airplane market. To keep the company afloat, William Piper was forced to invest more and more money from his oil holdings. During this period the aviation industry was dominated by larger aircraft tailored for the airlines. With the flight of Charles Lindbergh in a light aircraft, the Spirit of St. Louis, Piper saw potential for an owner-flown, small aircraft market. As Piper saw it, the key was to make the airplane easy to operate and inexpensive to own. By the end of 1934 this philosophy had begun to pay off as Taylor Aircraft finally made a profit.

In 1935, Piper bought out the original founder of Taylor Aircraft, C. G. Taylor, and took complete control of the company. Piper renamed the Taylor Cub the J-2 Cub, an airplane that would eventually make the company the top manufacturer of light airplanes.

In 1937 the Bradford plant burned down. This growing aircraft manufacturing company needed a new site and a new name. In that same year the Taylor Aircraft Company ceased to exist, and Piper Aircraft Corporation began at a new site in Lock Haven, Pennsylvania, on the banks of the West Branch of the Susquehanna River. The new plant site, previously an old silk mill next to the airport, was still in use in 1983.

From the corporate headquarters in Lock Haven, the original plan of building an inexpensive airplane that was easy to fly continued to be the

This case was prepared by Professor Thomas L. Wheelen of the University of South Florida, Professor J. David Hunger of Iowa State University, and Moustafa H. Abdelsamad, Dean, of Southeastern Massachusetts University from research by David Dunmore, Linda Montgomery, and John Westerman of the University of South Florida and Wayne Wylie of Piper Aircraft Corporation. Copyright © 1986 by Thomas L. Wheelen and J. David Hunger.

Source: Thomas L. Wheelen, J. David Hunger, and Moustafa H. Abdelsamad, "Piper Aircraft Corporation," *Journal of Case Research*, 1986, Vol. 6, pp. 32–59. Reprinted by permission of the authors and North American Case Research Association.

company's mission as the leadership of Piper Aircraft changed hands from father to sons. It was not until the mid-1950s that Piper Aircraft began to turn away from the light, single-engine aircraft to its first twin-engine plane, the Apache. This was Piper's first attempt to break the Cub image of the company. But William Piper still believed that the light airplane market was the best niche for the company. Even though he had no knowledge of the aircraft business when he first started, William Piper's original idea had been to introduce flying to the ordinary individual through flying lessons. Piper hoped that, as people learned more about flying, they would eventually want to purchase their own airplanes.

THE GENERAL AVIATION INDUSTRY

General Aviation Aircraft in 1984 were basically divided into four categories. From the smallest to the largest they were (1) single-engine piston, (2) multi-engine piston, (3) turbo-prop, and (4) jets. (See Exhibit 14.1.) Each category was divided into classes. In the single-engine piston category the classes were the basic two-seater trainer, the narrow-body four-seat single, the wide-body six-seat single, and the wide-body cabin-class six-seat single. In the twin-engine piston category were the wide-body six-seat light twins and the wide-body six- to eight-seat cabin-class twins. Piper refers to multi-engine aircraft as twin-engine. All of the turbo-props were considered by Piper to be wide-body cabin-class, but seating varied from seven to eleven. The last category was the business (civil) jet.

EXHIBIT 14.1 **U.S. General Aviation Aircraft**
Shipments by Type of Aircraft

| | TYPE OF AIRCRAFT | | | | | |
YEAR	Single-Engine	Multi-Engine	Turbo-Prop	Jet	TOTAL	TOTAL FACTORY BILLINGS
1983	1,811	417	321	142	2,691	$1,469,504,000
1982	2,871	678	458	259	4,266	$1,999,463,689
1981	6,608	1,542	918	389	9,457	$2,919,947,000
1980	8,640	2,116	795	326	11,877	$2,486,182,900
1979	13,286	2,843	637	282	17,048	$2,164,973,000
1978	14,398	2,634	548	231	17,811	$1,781,245,400
1977	14,057	2,195	428	227	16,907	$1,488,114,000
1976	12,783	2,120	359	187	15,449	$1,225,483,000
1975	11,439	2,116	305	196	14,056	$1,032,900,000
1974	11,562	2,135	250	219	14,166	$ 909,400,000

SOURCE: *General Aviation Statistical Databook*, 1983 Edition.

The markets for these categories varied with price and usage. In the single-engine category, the classes up to the wide-body six-seat single were mostly used for training and sport flying. The cabin-class singles up to light twin-engine aircraft were targeted for wealthy individuals and small companies. The cabin-class twins up to the turbo-props were primarily for the corporate market.

In the early 1970s the single-engine plane dominated the civil aviation market. However, by the mid-1970s the demand by business for a larger aircraft resulted in a shift in emphasis toward the cabin-class twin and turbo-prop airplanes. (See Exhibits 14.1–14.3.)

Since the industry shifted to producing and selling more of the larger and more expensive corporate airplanes, its net billings (which represent amounts invoiced from the factory to its distributors or directly to dealers) continued to grow for three years after total unit shipments began to decline in 1978. (See Exhibits 14.4 and 14.5.) Beginning in 1974, the average net billings per unit were $64,168 on 14,166 units shipped. By 1983 the average net billings per unit were $546,265 on 2,691 units shipped. Exhibits 14.1, 14.2, and 14.3 reflect the increasing role of twin-engine and turbo-prop aircraft during the late 1970s.

During the 1970s, private aircraft had become a major source of transportation for the business community. Since 1970 the general aviation fleet had almost doubled to 200,000 aircraft. By 1990 the fleet was projected to grow by 50% to 300,000. About 90% of general aviation sales were for business purposes.

Even though the corporate aircraft was becoming more popular, this asset

---

EXHIBIT 14.2   **Unit Shipment by Type, as Percentages of Total Unit Shipments[1]**

	SINGLE-ENGINE	MULTI-ENGINE	TURBO-PROP
1984E[2]	71.54%	16.26%	12.20%
1983	71.05	16.36	12.59
1982	71.65	16.92	11.43
1981	72.87	17.00	10.12
1980	74.80	18.23	6.88
1979	79.24	16.96	3.80
1978	81.90	14.98	3.12
1977	84.27	13.16	2.57
1976	83.76	13.89	2.35

SOURCE: Extrapolated from *General Aviation Statistical Databook,* 1983 Edition.

NOTES: [1]Indicates less jets. [2]Indicates that E means estimated.

EXHIBIT 14.3   **Market Trends[1]**

	SINGLE-ENGINE UNITS	% CHANGE	MULTI-ENGINE UNITS	% CHANGE	TURBO-PROP UNITS	% CHANGE
1984E[2]	2,200	+21.48%	500	+19.90%	375	+16.82%
1983	1,811	−36.92	417	−39.30	321	−29.91
1982	2,871	−56.55	678	−55.45	458	−50.11
1981	6,608	−23.52	1,542	−27.13	918	+15.47
1980	8,640	−34.97	2,116	−25.57	795	+24.80
1979	13,286	− 7.72	2,843	+ 7.93	637	+16.24
1978	14,398	+ 2.43	2,634	+20.00	548	+28.04
1977	14,057	+ 9.97	2,195	+ 3.54	428	+19.22
1976	12,783	+11.75	2,120	+ 0.19	359	+17.70

SOURCE: Extrapolated from *General Aviation Statistical Databook*, 1983 Edition.

NOTES: [1]Indicates excluding jets. [2]Indicates that E means estimated.

EXHIBIT 14.4   **General Aviation Unit Shipments/Billings**

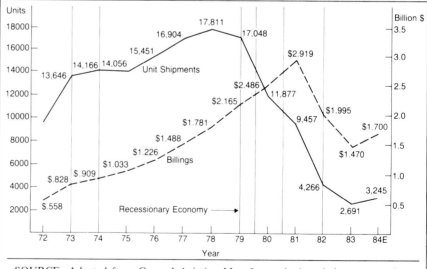

SOURCE: Adapted from General Aviation Manufacturer's Association presentation, January 1984.

NOTE: Data for 1984 (shown as 84E) was *forecast data* presented in January 1984. Forecast was later revised.

EXHIBIT 14.5

General Aviation Manufacturer's Association Domestic Billings and U.S. Corporate Profits

(In 1972 Dollars)

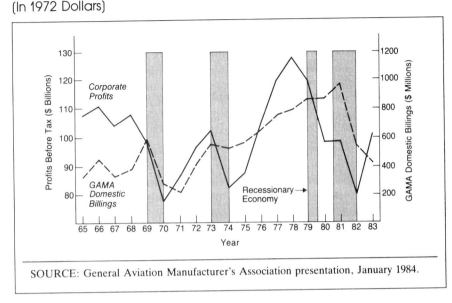

SOURCE: General Aviation Manufacturer's Association presentation, January 1984.

was not income-producing for the purchaser. Planes were paid for typically with excess cash flow, which made the corporate aircraft sensitive to economic conditions, especially inflation and interest rates. Between 1979 and 1982 was a period of high interest rates and inflation. The prime rate during this period went as high as 21%, while inflation reached a peak of 14%.

These factors had a pronounced effect on the general aviation manufacturers' pre-tax profits (as can be seen in Exhibit 14.5). These profits, as stated in 1972 dollars, dropped to less than $80 billion by 1982. Exhibit 14.4 shows that aircraft shipments from the factories declined sharply from an industry high of 17,811 units in 1978 to 2,691 units in 1983.

ORGANIZATIONAL STRUCTURE

Piper Management

From its inception through the 1960s, Piper Aircraft was run as a family business by Bill Piper, Sr.; Tony Piper; Bill Piper, Jr.; and Howard "Pug" Piper. Even though the Board of Directors typically consisted mainly of persons from outside the company, the direction of the company had been primarily set by Bill Piper, Sr.

In January 1969, when Bill Piper, Jr. was the President of the company, he received a call from Herbert J. Siegle, President of Chris-Craft Industries, who announced that Piper Aircraft was being targeted for takeover by Chris-Craft.[2] Neither had any knowledge that this conversation would start a fight for control of the company. A takeover battle for Piper soon erupted between Chris-Craft and Bangor Punta Corporation. During 1969, Bangor Punta was able to acquire an approximate 51% interest in Piper. Chris-Craft owned a lesser percentage of stock. The fight for control was not finally settled until 1977, when the United States Supreme Court awarded control of Piper Aircraft to Bangor Punta.

In 1969, Bill Piper, Sr. died. By this time, members of the Piper family were no longer affiliated with the company. Between 1969 and 1977, Piper's Board of Directors was evenly split between Bangor Punta and Chris-Craft. After 1977, Bangor Punta controlled the board.

Piper's new parent company, Bangor Punta Corporation, which had several other holdings, had a policy of decentralization. This meant that each of its divisions was allowed to operate almost independently. As quoted from the President of Bangor Punta, David W. Wallace:

> We must avoid like a plague having centralized headquarters. These divisions of ours are operated in most instances by the entrepreneurs who founded them and operated them successfully for many years.[3]

The 1983 Board of Directors of Piper Aircraft was made up of the following five people:

David W. Wallace: President of Bangor Punta Corporation. Mr. Wallace had been with Bangor Punta since 1967 with a background in law and a law degree from Harvard Law School.

David H. Street: Senior Vice-President and Treasurer of Bangor Punta Corporation. Mr. Street had come to Bangor Punta in 1978. His previous experience had been in the banking industry.

Max E. Bleck: President and Chief Executive Officer of Piper Aircraft. Mr. Bleck had come to Piper in 1976 as Senior Vice-President—Manufacturing Operations. He had been appointed President and Chief Operating Officer in 1979 and then promoted to President and Chief Executive Officer in 1980. Mr. Bleck's background prior to Piper had been in manufacturing and production with Cessna Aircraft.

Alfred J. Koontz, Jr.: Vice-President—Finance of Piper Aircraft. Mr. Koontz had come to Piper in 1975 from the accounting firm of Price Waterhouse and Co.

Dudley Phillips: Senior Vice-President and General Counsel of Bangor Punta Corporation.

Besides Max Bleck and Al Koontz, the top management of Piper included Robert Dickerson, Executive Vice-President and Chief Operations Officer. (See Exhibit 14.6.) Mr. Dickerson had been hired in 1980. His previous background had been in manufacturing and engineering at Cessna Aircraft.

EXHIBIT 14.6   Piper Aircraft Corporation: Summary Chart of Organization

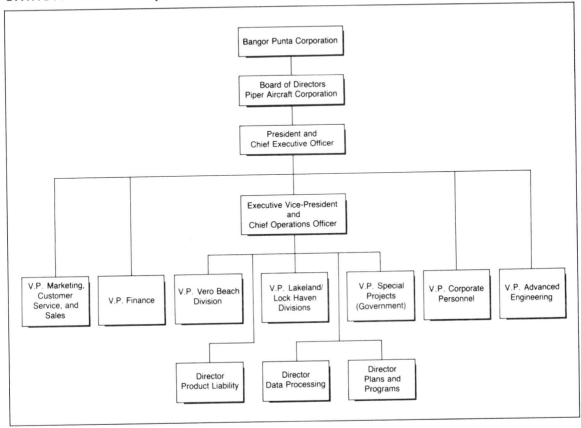

Bangor Punta Management

In 1983, Bangor Punta was a diversified company composed of the following four business segments in addition to Piper Aircraft:

Smith & Wesson: manufactured and marketed a line of quality handguns; law enforcement, military, and public-security equipment; shotguns; and knives. Smith & Wesson also conducted a training academy and an armorer's school for law enforcement agencies.

Recreational Products: manufactured and sold, in the United States, Canada, and Europe, a broad product line of marine products and recreational vehicles. Marine products included aluminum runabouts, cruisers, and fishing boats, as well as fiberglass powerboats. Recreational vehicles included van conversions and camping trailers. Jeanneau also manufactured the Microcar, a small, two-seat, powered vehicle.

Agriculture: served the agricultural market through Producers Cotton Oil Company, an integrated grower, processor, warehouser, and merchandiser of cotton and its related by-products.

Industrial Products: manufactured and marketed ovens and furnaces for the can manufacturing and building products industries.[4]

Bangor Punta's Board of Directors consisted of ten members, three of whom were outside the company.

MARKETING

Domestic Market

Piper's niche in the aircraft industry had traditionally been in the light, single-engine market. Nevertheless, in the mid-1970s the company began to emphasize the twin-engine piston market. Piper's marketing strategy was directed at the business community, where the airplane was beginning to become an important business tool. By the end of 1976, Piper had produced over 2,000 aircraft of its Navajo line (a cabin-class, twin-engine) and held a 70% share of sales in the market.

A new marketing strategy was beginning to take hold in 1977. Piper was putting more emphasis on increasing the market share of its twin-engine, piston and turbo-prop lines. (See Exhibits 14.7 and 14.8.) Piper also introduced a new trainer airplane, the Tomahawk. As stated in the September 30, 1977, year-end financial statement of Bangor Punta:

> (A student pilot training program) is the foundation of effective general aviation marketing. One in every three student pilots will eventually buy a plane. A majority of these purchases will be from the manufacturer of the plane in which the student trained.

By 1979, Piper's market share in the single-engine market had begun to decline, and total emphasis was shifted to the twin-engine piston and turbo-prop planes, which provided higher margins. With the Cheyenne and cabin-class twin-engine lines, Piper had developed its new niche in the industry.

In the 1980s, Piper began developing new planes for the commercial aviation market, specifically the small commuter-aircraft segment. In 1981, Piper introduced two nine-passenger models, the T1020 and T1040. These aircraft were hybrids of Piper's cabin-class twin-engine, Chieftain, which was very popular with the commuter industry. By 1985, Piper held 25% of the commuter aircraft market for planes with nine seats or less, and thereby accounted for the largest portion of aircraft in the commuter industry.

Government Contracts

In the late 1970s, Piper began to submit bids for government contracts for the first time since World War II. In September 1981 the Department of Defense awarded Piper a $12 million contract for operational demonstration

EXHIBIT 14.7 Market Share Trends[1]

	1977	1978	1979	1980	1981	1982	1983
Single-Engine							
Piper Aircraft	26.70%	25.70%	30.80%	21.74%	22.99%	21.46%	25.83%
Beech Aircraft	5.25%	4.80%	5.12%	6.72%	7.50%	7.80%	8.50%
Cessna Aircraft	57.34%	56.93%	51.59%	62.06%	59.73%	60.74%	52.95%
Other Manufacturers	10.71%	12.44%	12.49%	9.48%	9.78%	10.00%	12.72%
Twin-Engine							
Piper Aircraft	41.70%	44.09%	46.72%	44.44%	45.43%	45.80%	41.46%
Beech Aircraft	15.51%	13.61%	18.44%	18.80%	20.13%	16.55%	21.73%
Cessna Aircraft	29.76%	35.53%	31.54%	36.63%	34.38%	36.53%	35.03%
Other Manufacturers	10.71%	12.44%	3.29%	.13%	.06%	.11%	1.77%
Turbo-Prop							
Piper Aircraft	15.30%	18.15%	23.99%	21.22%	20.23%	12.19%	17.43%
Beech Aircraft	48.34%	44.46%	46.70%	46.15%	45.34%	47.08%	42.51%
Cessna Aircraft	—	9.26%	7.73%	9.81%	15.34%	18.02%	18.35%
Other Manufacturers	36.36%	28.13%	21.58%	22.81%	19.09%	22.54%	21.71%
Total Share							
Piper Aircraft	28.43%	28.10%	33.26%	25.82%	26.53%	24.77%	27.36%
Beech Aircraft	7.85%	7.26%	8.87%	11.28%	12.96%	14.01%	14.57%
Cessna Aircraft	51.98%	52.48%	46.62%	54.31%	51.55%	51.45%	46.06%
Other Manufacturers	11.74%	12.16%	11.25%	8.59%	8.96%	9.77%	12.01%

SOURCE: Extrapolated from Bangor Punta Financial Statements and GAMA Handbook for 1983.

NOTE: [1]Based on fiscal year ending September 30.

EXHIBIT 14.8 Unit Shipments per Category[1]

	1977	1978	1979	1980	1981	1982	1983
Single-Engine							
Piper Aircraft	3,619	3,760	4,249	2,065	1,707	762	526
Beech Aircraft	712	699	707	638	557	277	173
Cessna Aircraft	7,772	8,290	7,117	5,894	4,435	2,157	1,078
Other Manufacturers	1,452	1,812	1,723	900	726	355	259
Total Units	13,555	14,561	13,796	9,497	7,425	3,551	2,036
Twin-Engine							
Piper Aircraft	922	1,066	1,376	1,007	765	410	187
Beech Aircraft	343	329	543	426	339	245	98
Cessna Aircraft	658	859	929	830	579	320	158
Other Manufacturers	228	164	97	3	1	1	8
Total Units	2,211	2,418	2,945	2,266	1,684	876	451
Turbo-Prop							
Piper Aircraft	69	100	149	160	178	73	57
Beech Aircraft	218	245	290	348	399	282	139
Cessna Aircraft	0	51	48	74	135	109	60
Other Manufacturers	164	155	134	172	168	135	71
Total Units	451	551	621	754	880	599	327
Total Share							
Piper Aircraft	4,610	4,926	5,774	3,232	2,650	1,245	770
Beech Aircraft	1,273	1,273	1,540	1,412	1,295	704	410
Cessna Aircraft	8,430	9,200	8,094	6,798	5,149	2,586	1,296
Other Manufacturers	1,940	2,131	1,954	1,075	895	491	338
Total Units	16,217	17,530	17,362	12,517	9,989	5,016	2,814

SOURCE: Extrapolated from Bangor Punta Financial Statements and GAMA Handbook for 1983.

NOTE: [1]Based on fiscal year ending September 30.

of the Enforcer aircraft, a lightweight turbo-prop, close-support aircraft. The first year's funding of $5.8 million initiated Piper to defense work. The aircraft was designed after the World War II P-51 Mustang and could reach speeds of over 350 knots.

Piper did not expect the U.S. Air Force to purchase many of the aircraft. The company did believe that many third-world countries still flying old P-51's would be very interested in the Enforcer. As predicted, many countries in South and Central America as well as the Middle East showed great interest in this plane.

Competition

Piper's main competition has always been Beech Aircraft and Cessna Aircraft. Exhibit 14.9 shows the billings of the fourteen largest manufacturers of general aviation aircraft. Like Piper, both Beech and Cessna had been founded in the early 1930s, but their orientation had always been with the higher-priced, big single- and twin-engine aircraft.

EXHIBIT 14.9

Summary of Manufacturers' Net Billings for Shipments of General Aviation Aircraft
(Dollar Amounts in Thousands)

	NET BILLINGS			
	1983	1982	1981	1980
Ayres Corporation	$ 2,247	$ 4,031	$ 8,654	$ 7,491
Beech Aircraft	250,228	320,188	619,727	514,604
Bellanca	NA	NA	NA	2,910
Cessna Aircraft	362,545	531,877	895,679	783,518
Fairchild Aircraft	77,486	87,602	NA	NA
Gates Learjet	198,130	423,053	436,070	298,557
Gulfstream Aerospace	436,353	446,442	303,818	156,018
Lake Aircraft	3,204	2,018	4,165	4,424
Maule Aircraft	1,647	1,895	1,805	2,052
Mooney Aircraft	NA	NA	NA	NA
Piper Aircraft	135,238	179,008	368,846	335,465
Rockwell International	NA	NA	150,765	252,589
Schweizer Aircraft	2,427	3,349	717	NA
Swearingen	NA	NA	129,783	108,652
Total	$1,469,504	$1,999,463	$2,919,947	$2,486,182

SOURCE: General Aviation Manufacturers Association, *Summary of Shipments of General Aviation Airplanes*, 1983.

Exhibits 14.7 and 14.8 give sales data for the three aircraft manufacturers. Beech, which had always relied on larger, high-margin aircraft, introduced its first turbo-prop, the King Air, in 1965. Beech continued to dominate the turbo-prop market in 1983.

In contrast, Cessna was the overall dominant force in general aviation. Its dominant market niche was the single-engine market; it held at least a 50% share from 1976 through 1983. Nevertheless, it has also recently begun to emphasize the high-margin, turbo-prop line.

Even though both Beech and Cessna were strong in 1983 in both the single-engine and turbo-prop markets, Piper was committed to expand its market share in each of these categories. In 1983, Piper introduced six new models to its product line, more than any of its competitors. In its turbo-prop line, Piper introduced three models: Cheyenne 1A, Cheyenne IIIA, and Cheyenne IV. (See Exhibit 14.10.) Two models were phased out. In the single-engine, wide-body line, Piper added the new pressurized Malibu. The Mojave was added to the cabin-class, twin-engine line. The Aerostar 700P was introduced to the light twin-engine line.

EXHIBIT 14.10   **Piper Aircraft Corporation: 1984 Models by Class**

	PLANT LOCATIONS		
	Lock Haven, PA	Vero Beach, FL	Lakeland, FL
Single-engine trainer	Tomahawk	Archer II Warrior Dakota	
Single-engine wide-body		Saratoga[1] Malibu	
Light twin-engine		Seneca III Aerostar	
Cabin-class			Navajo Navajo C/R Chieftain Mojave[3] T1020[2]
Turbo-prop	Cheyenne IA Cheyenne IIXL T1040[2,3]		Cheyenne IIIA Cheyenne IV T1040[2,3]

NOTES: [1]There are four variations in the Saratoga line.

[2]T1040—commuter model.

[3]Parts of the T1040 and Mojave are built in Lakeland, FL, and the aircraft are finished in Lock Haven, PA.

Distribution

Piper's distribution system was based on a combination of three-tier and two-tier systems. The three-tier system flowed from the factory to the wholesale distributor and then to the dealer. The two-tier system began at the factory and went directly to the dealer. The two-tier system was the most common one in the industry. Some of the dealerships were factory owned. The factory directly served four types of dealers: the basic single-engine dealer, the twin-engine dealer, the single- and twin-engine dealer, and the turbo-prop dealer. The distributor in the three-tier system was an independent business contracting with independent dealers. Dealers who were not under a distributor were contracted directly by the factory.

In 1983, Piper established the Piper Airline Division to sell commuter aircraft direct from the factory to the customers. Even though the Airline Division was set up as a factory dealer, it did not enjoy many of the benefits other Piper dealers had. Specifically, the Airline Division could not take trade-in aircraft or get subsidy financing from Piper Acceptance Corporation.

Dealers were contracted at the beginning of each model year, October 1. To stay at a certain dealer level, they had to commit to buy a certain number of airplanes through the model year to September 30. If a dealer failed to meet its commitment, it could be downgraded or have its dealership terminated.

Foreign Distribution

There were thirty-six Piper piston distributors and twenty-four turbo-prop distributors outside the United States. These distributors also acted as dealers.

Piper's foreign unit sales and billings are shown here.

	1983	1982	1981	1980
Units	208	311	764	1,134
Billing	$34,037,267	$48,146,369	$85,837,053	$96,620,842

Export sales for the industry as a whole are provided in Exhibit 14.11.

PRODUCTION

Facilities

One very important variable that Piper used to determine production levels was the annual dealers' commitment. Between 1979 and 1983, when the economy went through two recessionary periods, dealers became backlogged with inventory. This situation affected Piper at all levels of production.

EXHIBIT 14.11   Domestic and Export Sales of General Aviation Aircraft

	SALES BY UNITS		EXPORT % OF PRODUCTION	FACTORY NET BILLINGS ($ MILLIONS)	% OF TOTAL BILLINGS
	Domestic	Export			
1983[1]	2,158	533	19.8%	318.9	21.7%
1982	3,104	1,162	27.2	650.2	32.5
1981	7,187	2,270	24.0	749.0	25.6
1980	8,322	3,555	30.0	756.4	29.9
1979	13,053	3,995	25.5	600.9	27.9

SOURCE: *General Aviation Statistical Databook,* 1983 Edition.
NOTE: [1]Extrapolated from GAMA.

During fiscal year 1979, Piper had six plants in operation. These were in Lock Haven, Pennsylvania; Lakeland, Florida; Vero Beach, Florida; Santa Maria, California; Quehanna, Pennsylvania; and Renovo, Pennsylvania. Exhibit 14.10 shows 1984 model production by plant location. The Quehanna and Renovo plants manufactured additional parts, which were supplied to the main manufacturing plants. The Santa Maria plant produced only the Aerostar line.

Piper began to lay off workers in 1981. By 1983, Piper had reduced the number of plants to four. The plants in Renovo and Santa Maria were closed down so as to better utilize space in Piper's other plants. Besides closing plants, Piper reduced production and employment at the remaining plants. Exhibit 14.12 shows the effect on average employment.

Piper's Lock Haven plant was unionized. Its two Florida plants were currently nonunion. Although Florida was a right-to-work state, unionization problems could occur if layoffs continued.

Technology

Piper Aircraft has made significant strides to keep up with technological changes in the general aviation industry. One key example was the new single-engine Malibu. This aircraft had been totally computer designed inside and out to give the passengers maximum comfort and the pilot the best handling characteristics. The Malibu was the world's first cabin-class pressurized single-engine aircraft in the industry. Production of the Malibu for 1984 was sold out before 1983 ended.

One important factor in Piper's favor was its emphasis on the use of engines specifically designed for its aircraft. Both the Malibu and the new Cheyenne IV (the industry's first 400-mph turbo-prop) had engines designed specifically for them. The new Cheyenne IV's engine not only produced

EXHIBIT 14.15   **About Lear Siegler, Inc.**

OPERATIONS

Lear Siegler is a broadly based manufacturer of components, assemblies and systems for consumer, industrial and military customers the world over. LSI's most important sales objective is to establish and maintain a leading market position for each product line.

Headquartered in Santa Monica, California, LSI operates 45 divisions and subsidiaries in 25 states and 10 foreign countries. For effective management and control of these diverse facilities, the Company's operations are divided into six major business segments, each under the direction of a corporate vice president.

LSI plays a vital role in upgrading American and allied defenses and in increasing the efficiency of commercial aircraft. The Company's aerospace activities are highly diversified among military and commercial programs, domestic and foreign sales and new and retrofit equipment.

Lear Siegler is the largest designer and manufacturer of material handling systems for industrial facilities, warehouses and distribution centers. It is also the leading manufacturer of gear cutting, honing and finishing machines.

The Company produces professional sound equipment and computer terminals and printers, and in telecommunications, it manufactures telephone line treatment equipment and test equipment.

LSI is a leading manufacturer, wholesaler and retailer of automotive replacement glass, and it makes and distributes the most complete line of replacement disc brake linings in North America.

The Company manufactures original equipment components, such as truck and trailer air suspension systems and brake products for heavy trucks, as well as automotive seating assemblies in the United States, Canada, Mexico, Germany, and France. Its principal agricultural products are grain handling equipment and specialized tillage equipment.

Lear Siegler's commercial products are directed toward specific markets influenced primarily by consumer spending and housing starts. They include heating and air conditioning units, furniture components and pre-engineered structural steel buildings.

OBJECTIVES

The key to successful management is the adoption and observance of certain fundamental principles. In the case of Lear Siegler, these have been stated in the following primary objectives:

To continually improve the quality and effectiveness of management through the selection, development and utilization of outstanding people.

To encourage, foster and stimulate the development and growth of new products and new markets to insure internal growth.

To satisfy customer needs with a marketing program, based on sound marketing research, that provides quality products, properly serviced and competitively priced.

(Continued)

EXHIBIT 14.15   (Continued)

> To identify and pursue acquisitions in high-growth markets.
>
> To maximize profitability and return on investment under any economic conditions through better utilization of resources, a constant surveillance of operations and strict financial controls.
>
> To recognize changing economic conditions and to redeploy affected assets.
>
> To achieve annual productivity improvement in all divisions.
>
> ## STRATEGIC PLANNING
>
> LSI's strategic planning program contributes significantly to the growth, competitive position and financial performance of the Company. An essential part of this program is an annual evaluation of the Company's more than 200 product lines by management at all levels of the organization. This analysis includes a review of the competitive standing of each product line, the economic conditions affecting its performance and other market and operational factors. Goals and strategies are then developed for each.
>
> ## ACQUISITION STRATEGY
>
> LSI's acquisition program is broad in interest and flexible in approach. It is designed to accelerate growth, improve earnings and complement the Company's product base.
>
> Lear Siegler is interested in companies with strong profit, product and market positions; a record of growth and a favorable outlook; a demonstrated ability to generate earnings with an attractive return on investment, and capable management which will remain with an organization.
>
> ## MANAGEMENT DEVELOPMENT
>
> The Company's management development program provides regular assessment of LSI's overall management situation; realistic projections of the Company's anticipated management needs; procedures to adequately identify, motivate, monitor and reward management; formalized job rotation; techniques to identify and accommodate managers who demonstrate potential; and orderly and timely top management succession.
>
> ## PRODUCTIVITY
>
> Lear Siegler recognizes that increasing the Company's productivity significantly improves its competitive position in the marketplace. The corporate office provides leadership, motivation and encouragement and closely monitors the progress of the program at every Company facility.
>
> LSI has proceeded on the premise that the people who know most about their jobs and how to improve them are the employees themselves. Numerous valuable and often ingenious suggestions on how to improve a process, add value to a product or simplify a task have been implemented.

SOURCE: *This Is LSI* (Santa Monica, CA: Lear Siegler, Inc., 1983), pp. 2–3. Reprinted by permission.

LEAR SIEGLER ACQUIRES PIPER

On December 12, 1983, Bangor Punta and Lear Siegler top managements agreed on a merger of their two companies, and Bangor Punta was brought into Lear Siegler. According to its second-quarter report dated December 31, 1983, Lear Siegler stated that:

> Bangor Punta represented the right company at the right time. Our aerospace and defense contracting experience and our financial resources will allow Bangor Punta's businesses to accelerate product and marketing development programs. Each of the company's operations has demonstrated the ability to achieve leadership in the markets it serves and to maintain its tradition of excellence during the difficult economic times of the recent past.

Lear Siegler was organized into the following six business segments:

- Aerospace
- Material handling/machine tools
- Electronics
- Auto service products
- Auto/agricultural
- Commercial products

Exhibit 14.14 contains relevant financial information on Lear Siegler before the merger. Information about Lear Siegler's operations, objectives, strategic planning, acquisition strategy, management development, and productivity is provided in Exhibit 14.15.

Top executives of Piper Corporation wondered whether they would lose the autonomy that Bangor Punta had previously allowed them in managing the company. Given Lear Siegler's objectives, would Lear Siegler tolerate Piper's recent poor financial performance, especially the losses of the past two years? Piper's managers were also concerned that Piper's product identity and image might be lost within the dominant corporate identity of Lear Siegler.

NOTES

1. Devon, Francis, *Mr. Piper and His Cubs*, The Iowa State University Press, Ames, Iowa, 1973, p. 8.

2. *Ibid.*, p. 219.

3. *Ibid.*, p. 228.

4. Bangor Punta Corporation, *1983 Annual Report*, p. 43.

Springfield Remanufacturing Corporation

CHARLES BOYD · D. KEITH DENTON

Salespeople desperately tried to generate new orders. The company's President John Stack stated that he had enough work for the remaining employees through August, but that he needed a "big play" by September. Stack considered whether to lay off employees (SRC had never had a layoff) or to avoid the layoff and risk the financial stability of the corporation. A dejected Stack noted, "I guess we will find out if we mean what we say—we'll show them the numbers—we'll see."

FORMATION OF THE COMPANY

On February 1, 1983, after nearly three years of rumors and frustration, the financially troubled International Harvester (IH) sold one of its last remaining diesel engine and engine-component remanufacturing operations as part of its turnaround strategy. International Harvester needed to do something because of its $4 billion debt load and $1.6 billion in operating losses. During a depressed truck and farm economy, the corporation was seeking answers to its troubles. Therefore, it decided to sell the Springfield plant and four other parts-remanufacturing centers. The sale of its Springfield, Missouri, facility marked the end of its remanufacturing activities but not the end of its troubles. International Harvester later sold its Farm Division in order to save its Truck Division, and the firm later reorganized as NAVISTAR.

The Springfield Remanufacturing Company (SRC) employed 171 workers at the time of the sale. It was originally meant to be sold to Dresser Industries, a major customer of the plant, despite the fact that the plant's employees had a bid on the table to purchase the company. When negotiations with Dresser broke down in December, 1982, employees of the firm began to consider forming their own company. Springfield Remanufacturing Corporation was the result of these discussions, when two months later

This case was prepared by Professors Charles Boyd and D. Keith Denton of the Southwest Missouri State University. It was presented at the North American Case Research Association meeting, 1987. Distributed by the North American Case Research Association. All rights reserved to the authors and the North American Case Research Association. Reprinted by permission of the authors and the North American Case Research Association.

employees obtained financing from the Bank of America in San Francisco. The company and the 68,000-square-foot plant was bought from International Harvester by a group of thirteen employees for approximately $7 million, borrowed at three percentage points above the prime rate. The plant's assets provided enough collateral so that the employees did not have to give the lender any of the equity in the firm.

Twelve of these new owners were former employees and managers of International Harvester at the plant. The thirteenth was Don McCoy, the controller of the International Harvester division of which the Springfield plant was part. President of the new corporation was John P. (Jack) Stack, who had previously been Plant Manager. Stack and the other twelve owners decided to broaden the ownership of the new corporation through an employee stock-ownership program. As former employees were rehired, the owners decided to set aside each year a portion of the corporate earnings to buy some of the company's unissued stock. This stock would then go into a trust fund for workers. The Employee Stock-Ownership Plan (ESOP) was greeted with enthusiasm. Foreman Joe Loeber noted, "It added a little incentive to know you're working for your own future and not just the other guy's. Everybody's excited." The managers owned shares of stock and signed an agreement that the corporation would issue shares of stock directly into the ESOP. Thus the ESOP became the vehicle for employee ownership of the firm.

Stack and other management realized that the plant's future lay outside of International Harvester. He noted, "We were really different. International Harvester employees were normally represented by United Auto Workers and the Springfield plant wasn't." As early as two years before the actual sale, local management at the Springfield plant had submitted a bid for the plant that was not given serious consideration by International Harvester. A year later a more detailed plan had been submitted but again was rejected. In five weeks they closed the deal.

The day after the sale, Springfield Remanufacturing Corporation brought back thirty of former International Harvester employees and increased their employment by thirty per day until most of the original employees were back. When Springfield Remanufacturing Corporation started business they had signed up 60 percent of their old customers. Before the sale, they had $10 million in sales of parts for construction equipment, another $7 million for farm equipment, and $3 million for trucks.

On February 1, 1983, Jack Stack, President of Springfield Remanufacturing Corporation, issued a news release stating that the new firm would remain in Springfield and would continue to be a major rebuilder of diesel engines, injection pumps, water pumps, and other engine components. The news release noted that Springfield Remanufacturing Corporation would be a supplier of remanufactured engines and engine components to International Harvester's agricultural equipment and truck dealers.

The news release, like the news about the International Harvester sale of the Springfield facility, did not tell the whole story about this unique situation. It was no secret that many of International Harvester's manufacturing facilities had suffered from abrasive employee-management relations. When Jack Stack had arrived at the facility four years before the eventual sale, the employees were on the verge of forming a union and the company was running behind production schedule. Stack was sent from International Harvester headquarters and given six months to straighten out the problems at the plant or close it.

Stack called a meeting with all employees and "begged" them to give him and his team a chance to change things. He promised to listen, and he promised change. The employees agreed to give him a chance. The union election was scheduled for March 10; this gave Stack two months to win over the employees. Stack won the election as over 75 percent of the employees voted in favor of management over the union.

Management's relations with employees began to change. There were better human relations, better communications, and better cooperation. Three topics were emphasized to the employees: safety, housekeeping, and quality. Statistical measures for these three activities were developed by management and taught to the employees. Eventually the employees were taught about costs and profits. Data were graphed, kept updated, and posted in prominent places within the plant. As a result, employees became very goal-oriented. Stack commented

> You've got to have an enemy to have a team. If you can set that enemy outside your organization and declare what that enemy is, that's the unifying factor behind the whole organization.

So such things as safety problems and quality rejects became the enemy, and improving performance in these areas became the employees' goals. As a result, the organization's efficiency and effectiveness improved dramatically.

One year later production was up 30%. By June, 1984, the facility had become the "best" of the outside firms performing remanufacturing work for International Harvester. They had remained profitable during the time that similar facilities had been losing money.

Several programs that Stack and others started during this time were given credit for helping turn things around. One of these is the Quality of Work Life (QWL) program, in which employees analyze and propose solutions to organizational problems. They had also formed small employee groups, known as quality circles, that were used to make the plant more efficient and productive. Innovative approaches were also used. For example, when International Harvester imposed a wage freeze, the QWL group decided to go to a flex-time schedule, with a four-day, ten-hour per day week. This saved employees money on transportation and lunches and reduced absenteeism, by giving workers an extra day off so they could take care of personal business.

METEORIC RISE

The rise of Springfield Remanufacturing Corporation from the ashes of International Harvester was almost immediate and profound. Its success did not go unnoticed by the news media. Several articles on its success were written, and the firm was featured in an issue of *INC* magazine. A television documentary by PBS was to be aired during the fall of 1987.

During 1984, Springfield Remanufacturing Corporation increased its sales by 20%, to $15.5 million. A year later business increased by 40% to $23 million in sales, and 100 employees were added to the payroll to bring total employment to 225.

In one year they remanufactured 2,500 engines, and in two years of operation the firm had warranty returns averaging less than 1%. Springfield Remanufacturing Corporation's customers included Ingersol-Rand, J.I. Case, Dresser Industries, and International Harvester.

A red-letter day for Springfield Remanufacturing Corporation came in April, 1985, two years after their formation, when Springfield Remanufacturing Corporation announced that they had received a contract from General Motors to remanufacture 15,400 5.7-liter, V-8 diesel engines for GM's Oldsmobile Division. There are about 1.5 million General Motor cars in service powered by the 5.7-liter engine. General Motors decided to subcontract the remanufacturing of these engines because daily demand had stabilized at a level that its management considered no longer justified the plant space it had devoted to the remanufacturing. It ceased production of the 5.7-liter diesel engine a week prior to signing the contract with Springfield Remanufacturing Corporation. The volume of Springfield Remanufacturing Corporation's work was expected to slowly decrease as the cars powered by the 5.7 are taken out of service over time.

Lee Shroyer, Marketing Manager, said that the contract could mean forty new jobs in Springfield and sixty new jobs at a satellite operation in the nearby community of Willow Springs. With this contract Springfield Remanufacturing Corporation became the first company to be named as an authorized engine rebuilder for General Motors. The three-year contract was expected to be worth $40 million to Springfield Remanufacturing Corporation. A Springfield Remanufacturing Corporation manager stated, "We should continue to work with General Motors as long as we can maintain their quality and safety requirements and I don't see any problem with that." With this new business, 1985 sales were expected to exceed $30 million.

Because of this new business, additional fixtures, tooling, jet sprays, and new arrangements to improve the flow of materials were made in the Springfield plant. To accommodate the increase in business, Springfield Remanufacturing Corporation needed a new building. In May, 1985, management secured an additional building in Willow Springs, a small town seventy miles from Springfield. Stack expected to be turning out 5 engines per day by mid-May and 125 per day by November. By November they expected to employ 75 people and employ 150 after two years.

Reasons for Success

Springfield Remanufacturing Corporation's 40% growth rate did not come by accident. It would not have received the General Motors contract if it did not turn out extremely high-quality products. Stack noted that a remanufactured or recycled assembly is 30%–40% the price of a new one, so there is a lower inventory-carrying cost for the original equipment manufacturer (OEM) customer. Springfield Remanufacturing Corporation's product warranties are as good as or better than those of a new product. Fewer than 1% of its products are returned for any reason—the industry average is 6%. Some of its products are guaranteed to be delivered within forty-eight hours. Within the industry it has some of the best warranties, lowest cost, and highest reliability. During recent years, Springfield Remanufacturing Corporation experienced almost a 400% growth in business, and a 5% decrease in overhead cost. This growth occurred despite the depression in the agriculture and construction industries.

Springfield's success is built on at least four ingredients: Jack Stack, the charismatic and thoughtful president; a very capable management team; a positive philosophy toward employees; and employee ownership. Stack is the visionary who keeps the company focused on its objectives and clearly believes in his management style. Stack is complemented by those around him. Mike Carrigan, Vice-President of Production, is a self-confessed "pack rat" who totally understands the production process. He is always looking to improve methods of operation and reduce waste. He would much rather fix what he has than buy something new. He seems ideally suited to this recycling work. Gary Brown, the Human Resources Manager, likewise understands the personnel function and knows what kind of people Springfield Remanufacturing Corporation is looking for. Both Brown and Carrigan say there are two types of people—competitive and noncompetitive ones. They look for the competitive "hungry" ones. The ones who like to win, who like to compete and who are interested in self-improvement.

Springfield Remanufacturing Corporation tries to maximize its people. Management spends a great deal of time trying to cultivate an air of trust and openness between people. Stack noted, "There's not a financial number our employees don't know or have access to." Managers conduct weekly meetings with employees in which they go over the business, including financial statements, operating income, profits, losses, assets, liabilities and other financial figures. All employees may not know or understand all the financial figures, but they are aware that the figures are available. They do know what each department contributes and costs the company. Stack has been quoted as saying, "We teach them about finance and accounting before we teach them how to turn a wrench."

Management at Springfield Remanufacturing Corporation also tries to make work "fun." They are constantly setting standards for direct and indirect labor and then try to make "games" out of achieving results. These games are set up so employees understand what is needed and have both incentives and rewards. A popular phrase around the company is STP—GUTR (Stop The Praise—Give Us The Raise). Springfield Remanufacturing Corporation pays employees a sizeable bonus if its quarterly financial goals are met. Winning at the "game" is based on an employee's ability to save labor and/or material cost. Some employees at the plant receive as much as 12% of their salary in bonus money. Employees also receive cash payments for suggestions that save the company money. When safety goals were met, insurance money refunded to Springfield Remanufacturing Corporation was used to purchase gifts of appreciation.

Springfield Remanufacturing Corporation also practices a decentralized-participative style of management in which managers try to push decision-making down to the lowest level. Employees and first-line supervisors are encouraged to take on new tasks. For example, most supervisors "adopt" an area outside their supervisory area. One supervisor may be in charge of controlling costs for chemicals ranging from solvents to "white-out" type-writer-correction fluid. Another supervisor may be in charge of all plant abrasives. Management at Springfield Remanufacturing Corporation believes that this system teaches everyone the value of cooperation and makes its employees better at communicating and persuading, because they must convince others outside their area to control costs in their "adopted" area. Of course all of these programs are enhanced because of the ESOP. It is not someone else's business, it's theirs.

MARKETING CONCEPT

Springfield Remanufacturing Corporation fills a market niche in which the OEM is the customer. The marketing concept is simple and straightforward. Diesel engines are usually employed in trucks, earth-moving equipment, and other types of "workhorse" applications in which these engines labor daily under heavy strain. Because of this heavy usage, vital engine parts eventually break down, and the user must either purchase an entirely new piece of equipment, have the engine repaired, or have the engine or its major components rebuilt. The first option is often passed up because of the very high expense of purchasing an entirely new piece of equipment. Each of the other two options requires the services of a firm that either builds or repairs engine components. This market niche is known as the aftermarket.

To compete against the OEM company that originally built a particular engine component, most firms in the engine or automotive aftermarket offer their own repair service or replacement part. Therefore, the OEM loses market share in the aftermarket. The distinctive difference of Springfield Remanufacturing Corporation is that it seeks to restore a portion of this lost market share to the OEM, and serves as the OEM's contracted provider of aftermarket engine components. It provides the OEM with a replacement engine or engine component. Because of this service, the OEM is spared the tremendous costs of real estate, plant, and equipment investments that would be incurred in it doing its own remanufacturing work. Springfield Remanufacturing Corporation incurs these expenses for the OEM and sells a quality remanufactured product, built to exacting specifications, that will cost the OEM customer less than a component it had built itself. In addition, new engines or components are available when needed because they are produced in quantity rather than individually prepared upon demand. This means that the end user can get a failed piece of equipment up and running again much quicker and at a lower cost than might otherwise be possible.

An example will help illustrate the advantages Springfield Remanufacturing Corporation can offer to an OEM customer. Suppose a truck operated by a commercial carrier is put out of commission by the failure of the fuel-injection pump. The trucking company is likely to inquire to the OEM regarding the problem. The OEM may be able to offer a new replacement pump for $580. The trucking company may instead buy a new or rebuilt pump at a lower price from a competing company in the aftermarket. Another alternative would be to have the failed pump repaired, but this would entail more downtime for the truck and thus lost revenue to the trucking company. If the OEM had a contract with Springfield Remanufacturing Corporation, however, the OEM would have a high-quality remanufactured fuel-injection pump, with the same warranty as a new pump, to sell to the trucking company for $300.

Because of its remanufacturing operations, Springfield Remanufacturing Corporation is able to offer value to its OEM customers in a number of ways:

1. Preserving part of the OEM's market share in the automotive aftermarket.

2. Providing the OEM more total profitability over the entire life of the engine.

3. Preventing costly investment in plant and equipment for remanufacturing operations. (These operations cannot be performed on an OEM's existing production lines.) These savings become even more important when the OEM must continue to supply components for an engine that has gone out of production.

4. Because Springfield Remanufacturing Corporation uses an efficient job-shop operation, it is able to sell its products to its OEM customers at a relatively low price. This saves the OEM customer money and lowers its inventory-carrying cost.

Springfield Remanufacturing Corporation sales personnel visit OEM engine and equipment builders around the country and try to explain to their management teams how Springfield Remanufacturing Corporation can add value to their operations in the above-listed ways. The sales personnel try to make them aware of all the costs they must incur *after* they have sold their products. These costs include warranties, return parts, labor, and inventory-carrying costs. They try to explain how Springfield Remanufacturing Corporation can minimize these costs and increase the OEM's total profitability and share of the aftermarket.

| SHORT-TERM FORECASTS FOR THE AUTOMOTIVE AFTERMARKET[1] | The success of the automotive aftermarket is highly dependent upon the rate of new-car sales and the number of older vehicles in service. By knowing these figures, aftermarket companies can estimate the size of the "pipeline" of new-to-aging cars that represents the size of their market. |

SHORT-TERM FORECASTS FOR THE AUTOMOTIVE AFTERMARKET[1]

The success of the automotive aftermarket is highly dependent upon the rate of new-car sales and the number of older vehicles in service. By knowing these figures, aftermarket companies can estimate the size of the "pipeline" of new-to-aging cars that represents the size of their market.

The 1987 outlook for the U.S. automobile industry has been summarized as follows:

> For 1987, U.S. car and truck output is projected to decline about five percent from the 11.5 million units estimated for 1986, even if no lengthy strikes occur when UAW contracts expire next fall. Following an estimated 12 percent decline in 1986, profits for 1987 may recede another 20 percent or so, despite efficiency gains. This relatively unfavorable outlook reflects lower unit volume, mounting competition, a less favorable sales mix, costly sales incentive programs, and plant closing costs.

While 1987 sales are projected to be 5% lower than 1986 sales, it should be remembered that 1984–1986 sales were well above the long-term U.S. sales trend for this industry.

The average age of vehicles on the road is particularly important to Springfield Remanufacturing Corporation and other firms in the automotive aftermarket, because their business comes from the wearout of vehicle parts and components. The following table reveals that the average age of American-produced cars and trucks in use has increased during recent years:

| Year | Average Age (years) | |
	Passenger Cars	Motor Trucks
1985	7.6	8.1
1984	7.5	8.2
1983	7.4	8.1
1982	7.2	7.8
1981	6.9	7.5
1980	6.6	7.1
1979	6.4	6.9
1978	6.3	6.9
1977	6.2	6.9

Major replacement-parts supplier Federal-Mogul Corporation estimates that sales of automotive aftermarket parts will grow by approximately 2.6% in real terms over the next few years. General Motors estimates a 2.5%–

3.0% real growth rate. The Motor and Equipment Manufacturers Association (MEMA) estimates a 3.3% average compound growth rate in the number of vehicles in operation through 1990.

| **A TURNING POINT** | Four years after its initial formation, Springfield Remanufacturing Corporation was enjoying its success. Financial information is provided in Exhibits 15.1, 15.2 and 15.3. The firm was by now sufficiently diversified into the industry's market niches, which Stack referred to as the "four cylinders": |

1. Construction equipment,
2. Agricultural equipment,
3. Trucks,
4. Automobiles.

EXHIBIT 15.1 **Springfield Remanufacturing Corporation and Subsidiary: Consolidated Balance Sheets**

	JANUARY 25, 1987	JANUARY 26, 1986	JANUARY 27, 1985	JANUARY 29, 1984
Assets				
Current Assets:				
Cash	$ 50,082	$ 13,584	20,597	316,688
Trade accounts receivable, less allowances for doubtful accounts	2,237,471	3,184,409	2,098,321	2,547,771
Inventories	9,230,828	10,451,968	8,055,556	9,514,189
Prepaid income taxes	—	—	—	298,200
Prepaid expenses and other current assets	32,637	37,875	39,826	48,645
Total current assets	11,551,018	13,687,836	10,214,300	12,725,493
Property, buildings and equipment	2,244,519	1,905,348	669,177	291,043
Total Assets	$13,795,537	$15,593,184	$10,883,477	$13,016,536
Liabilities and Stockholders' Equity				
Current Liabilities:				
Notes payable	$ 383,658	$ 2,677,195	$ 2,526,557	7,141,616
Accounts payable	3,867,352	5,825,521	2,661,636	1,907,233
Accrued contribution to employee stock ownership trust	—	521,011	413,510	—
Income taxes payable	363,340	47,000	—	—
Other current liabilities	1,211,717	900,450	771,721	727,954
Current portion of long-term debt	358,533	309,002	297,280	10,006
Total current liabilities	6,184,600	10,280,179	6,670,704	9,786,809

EXHIBIT 15.1   (Continued)

	JANUARY 25, 1987	JANUARY 26, 1986	JANUARY 27, 1985	JANUARY 29, 1984
Liabilities and Stockholders' Equity				
Excess of net assets acquired over cost	786,710	1,573,420	2,360,129	3,146,838
Long-term debt	2,537,874	1,317,522	1,126,922	43,377
Deferred income taxes	10,000	34,000	—	—
	9,519,184	13,205,121	10,157,755	12,977,024
Stockholders' Equity:				
Class A Common Stock, voting, par value $.10 per share, 1,500,000 and 500,000 shares authorized, 1,140,000 and 500,000 issued and outstanding	114,000	50,000	50,000	50,000
Class B Common Stock, nonvoting, par value $.10 per share, 10,000,000 and 1,000,000 shares authorized, 1,984,500 and 541,500 shares issued and outstanding	198,450	54,150	51,000	50,000
Additional paid-in capital	603,300	124,365	5,100	—
Retained earnings	3,688,114	2,159,548	619,622	(60,488)
Treasury stock, at cost	(327,511)	—	—	—
Total Liab. and Stockholders' Equity	4,276,353 $13,795,537	2,388,063 $15,593,184	725,722 $10,883,477	39,512 $13,016,536

Customers had been added so rapidly to each "cylinder" during the four-year period that Stack decided it was time to consolidate the company's gains. The 1987 financial plan was prepared in August 1986, completed in October, and approved in November. The strategy for 1987 would be to seek no new customers. Instead, the sales and marketing operation would be reorganized and would concentrate on enhancing service to Springfield Remanufacturing Corporation's present customers. There had not seemed to be time to do that during the four previous years of rapid growth; this year the company would take the time.

But from November 1986 to February 1987, several significant changes occurred at General Motors: the $700 million payoff to Ross Perot, a huge stock buyback, and continued competitive problems in the automobile market. And what happened to General Motors was important to Springfield Remanufacturing Corporation, because 50 percent of Springfield Remanufacturing Corporation's business was with General Motors during 1986. In April 1987, General Motors notified Springfield Remanufacturing Corpo-

EXHIBIT 15.2   **Springfield Remanufacturing Corporation and Subsidiary: Consolidated Statements of Earnings**

	JANUARY 25, 1987	JANUARY 26, 1986	JANUARY 27, 1985	JANUARY 29, 1984
Net sales	$37,937,498	$27,818,322	$23,976,808	$16,347,600
Cost of goods sold	30,864,793	23,766,826	20,696,029	13,420,229
	7,072,705	4,051,496	3,280,779	2,927,371
Gain (loss) on disposal of inventory	(2,229,765)	115,138	—	—
Gross Profit	4,842,940	4,166,634	3,280,779	2,927,371
Operating expenses:				
Selling, general and administrative	2,850,189	2,570,828	2,158,463	2,826,165
Contribution to employee stock ownership trust	706,216	521,011	419,610	—
Interest	442,039	597,462	798,305	948,403
	3,998,444	3,689,301	3,376,378	3,774,568
	844,496	477,333	(95,599)	(847,197)
Nonoperating income:				
Amortization of excess of net assets acquired over cost	786,710	786,709	786,709	786,709
Other, net	331,295	351,884	—	—
	1,118,005	1,138,593	786,709	786,709
Earnings (or loss) before income taxes	1,962,501	1,615,926	691,110	(60,488)
Income taxes	350,000	76,000	103,000	—
Earnings (or loss) before extraordinary item	1,612,501	1,539,926	588,110	(60,488)
Extraordinary item—tax benefit from utilization of loss carryforward	—	—	92,000	—
Net earnings (or loss)	$ 1,612,501	$ 1,539,926	$ 680,110	($ 60,488)

ration that it would need 5,000 fewer engines from the firm during 1987 than it had previously planned. To Springfield Remanufacturing Corporation, this cutback meant 50,000 manhours, or 25% of its 1987 business.

Fortunately, Springfield Remanufacturing Corporation had moved six months previously from remanufacturing diesel engines exclusively to also remanufacturing gasoline engines. The firm began remanufacturing thirty gasoline engines per day for Chrysler in February 1987, and later began

EXHIBIT 15.3	**Springfield Remanufacturing Corporation and Subsidiary: Consolidated Statements of Changes in Financial Position**			
	JANUARY 25, 1987	**JANUARY 26, 1986**	**JANUARY 27, 1985**	**JANUARY 29, 1984**
Source of Funds				
Operations:				
Earnings (loss) before extraordinary item	$1,612,501	$1,539,926	$ 588,110	($ 60,488)
Charges (credits) to operations, not requiring outlay of working capital:				
Amortization of excess net assets acquired over cost	(786,710)	(786,709)	(786,709)	(786,709)
Depreciation	499,901	247,408	97,057	30,349
Increase (decrease) in deferred income taxes	(24,000)	34,000	—	—
Funds provided by (used in) operations	1,301,692	1,034,625	(101,542)	816,848
Additions to long-term debt	2,688,500	489,500	1,500,000	60,275
Extraordinary item—tax benefit from utilization of loss carryforward	—	—	92,000	—
Contribution of common stock to employee stock ownership trust	706,216	121,500	6,100	—
Excess of net assets acquired over cost	—	—	—	3,933,547
Sale of treasury stock	258,073	—	—	—
Disposals of property, buildings and equipment	—	51,495	—	—
Proceeds from sale of common stock	—	915	—	100,000
Decrease in working capital	—	135,939	—	—
	$4,954,481	$1,833,974	$1,496,558	$4,093,822
Application of Funds				
Reduction and current maturities of long-term debt	$1,468,148	$ 298,900	$ 416,455	16,898
Additions to property, buildings and equipment	839,072	1,535,074	475,191	321,392
Purchase of treasury stock	688,500	—	—	
Increase in working capital	1,958,761	—	604,912	2,938,684
	$4,954,481	$1,833,974	$1,496,558	$3,276,974

(Continued)

EXHIBIT 15.3 (Continued)

	JANUARY 25, 1987	JANUARY 26, 1986	JANUARY 27, 1985	JANUARY 29, 1984
Analysis of Working Capital Changes				
Increase (decrease) in current assets:				
Cash	$ 36,498	($ 7,013)	($ 296,091)	$ 316,688
Trade accounts receivable	(946,938)	1,086,088	(449,450)	2,547,771
Inventories	(1,221,140)	2,396,412	(1,458,633)	9,514,189
Prepaid income taxes	—	—	(298,200)	298,200
Prepaid expenses and other current assets	(5,238)	(1,951)	(8,819)	48,645
	(2,136,818)	3,473,536	(2,511,193)	12,725,493
Increase (decrease) in current liabilities:				
Notes payable	(2,293,537)	150,638	(4,615,059)	7,141,616
Accounts payable	(1,958,169)	3,163,885	754,403	1,907,233
Accrued contribution to employee stock ownership trust	(521,011)	107,501	413,510	—
Income taxes payable	316,340	36,000	—	—
Other current liabilities	311,267	139,729	43,767	727,954
Current portion of long-term debt	49,531	11,722	287,274	10,006
	(4,095,579)	3,609,475	(3,116,105)	9,786,809
Increase (Decrease) in Working Capital	$1,958,761	($ 135,939)	$ 604,912	$ 2,938,684

remanufacturing them for General Motors too. This new business helps cushion the blow from the loss of General Motor's diesels, but is not nearly enough. It is clear that Springfield Remanufacturing Corporation will have to work hard for new business during 1987; it cannot be the year of concentrating on customer enhancement that Stack had hoped it would be.

By early June, 1987, Springfield Remanufacturing Company had responded to the situation with an increased attrition rate from its 400-person work force. During the past six months, forty-three positions had been terminated: twenty for performance reasons, the rest voluntarily. Still no layoff program has been instituted, but time is running out. Stack's "big play" has to come soon. He wonders, "What options are available, what will be the effect of my actions?"

NOTES

1. The data reported in this subsection were obtained from Standard & Poor's *Industry Surveys,* April, 1987, pp. 75, 80, and 85.

Comdial Corporation

Per V. Jenster

March 1986 was a critical month for Comdial Corporation of Charlottesville, Virginia, a $100 million manufacturer of telecommunications equipment. Ted B. Westfall, Chairman and Chief Executive Officer of Comdial Equipment, was faced with the problem of guiding the firm in a volatile market with intense competition. Mr. Westfall had served as Chairman of the Board since September 1981 and Chief Executive Officer of the company since December 1981. He was a consultant to ITT from 1975 until September 1982 and served as Executive Vice-President and Director of ITT from 1964 to 1974. Capacity utilization at Comdial was down to 40% and the firm had been forced to lay off 900 of its 2,200 employees over the past year. After two years of substantial losses, Comdial was burdened with a debt-to-equity ratio of over 130%.

A team of independent analysts had identified four possible alternatives that could see the company through this trying period of industry shake-out. One option was to carve out a high-quality, high-service marketing niche, which emphasized the firm's proven reliability and customer service along with a "Made in America" pitch to a growing market of small-business customers.

A second and more drastic alternative was to liquidate domestic manufacturing operations and move its production to the Far East, to take advantage of lower labor costs there. The firm could then continue to market to the more price-sensitive residential market as well. This course, though radical, would allow the company to achieve lower manufacturing costs, while continuing to capitalize on its superior knowledge and technological expertise.

A third option was to go after the large, business-system market. The high margins and massive scale of operations in this arena were quite attractive.

The final alternative involved reshaping Comdial's mission, and broadening the firm's operations to include the manufacture of other specialized plastic products. Such a shift would help utilize its excess capacity, and enable the firm to scale back its communications production toward its more successful product lines. All four options appeared risky, but feasible. What

This case was prepared by Professor Per V. Jenster with assistance from S. Barnes, Bierly K. Gothie, M. Park and L. Wilt of the McIntire School of Commerce, University of Virginia. Reprinted by permission.

would it take to pilot Comdial back down the road to sustained growth and profitability?

COMPANY HISTORY	Comdial was formed in 1977 as a telephone-equipment concern. Its first goal was to reduce the cost of push-button telephone-set dialers and improve their functions. By 1982 the company completed development of a state-of-the-art dialer and was preparing to build a plant to complete telephone sets and to develop distribution channels for them. At the same time, General Dynamics announced that it would leave the telephone business and sell off its divisions that were producing such equipment. Taking advantage of this opportunity, Comdial bought the two divisions—Stromberg-Carlson telephone set division, located in Charlottesville, Virginia; and American Telecommunications Corporation (ATC) in Upland, California. Stromberg-Carlson manufactured high-quality standard telephone sets and key systems and provided a large telephone-refurbishment service. ATC was a leading manufacturer of character and decorator telephone sets.

In February of 1982, Comdial acquired R&G Communications, a large telephone refurbishing company. In June of that year, in order to develop expertise in operating its own distribution channel, the company acquired a telephone retail chain. In late August, the firm acquired an 80% interest in Scott Technology Corporation, a development-stage company researching a device that automatically allowed small telephone systems to select the cheapest long-distance carrier. The company made a major overseas commitment in January 1984 to invest in HPF, the second-largest telephone producer in France. Another overseas interest was the development of a credit card verification terminal in conjunction with British Telecom. Comdial also negotiated at that time for highly automated factory facilities in South Wales.

By the beginning of 1982, Comdial had reached the position of fourth-largest domestic manufacturer of telephone sets. However, the strong position of the firm changed dramatically in late 1982 after AT&T announced that it would reorganize its retail distribution of telephone equipment. Sales by Comdial to Bell Phone Centers dropped from $53 million in 1982 to $13 million a year later. Because these sales produced the highest margins, the effect on earnings was substantial.

The new Bell Regional Companies were legally forbidden to market new telephone equipment in 1983. The restriction was lifted after the January 1, 1984, divestiture of AT&T and this was seen as a major opportunity for Comdial, as it hoped to supply the seven Regional Bell Operating Companies (RBOCs) with telephone equipment. However, the retail telephone market was severely affected by heavy overstocking, primarily with imported products. Sales to the RBOCs dwindled as the regional companies failed to gain a strong position as distributors in the home phone market. As a consequence, during 1984 Comdial closed down its ATC operations in El Monte, California, and its manufacturing facilities in Upland, California, and put these properties up for sale. In addition, Comdial reduced its retail operations, American Phone Centers, from nineteen stores to eleven stores, in accordance with a change in primary focus from residential sales to small-business sales. Further responding to its challenging economic position, Comdial sold its overseas interest in HPF as well as its interest in the project with British Telecom.

INDUSTRY AND COMPETITION

The telecommunications industry, including telephone manufacturing, had experienced a dramatic increase in competition, changing distribution channels, and rapid technological innovation. The number of long-distance carriers and manufacturers of telephone systems had increased dramatically, and so differentiation strategies based on cost, quality, and services offered had grown.

The telephone manufacturing industry of 1985 could be broken down into three basic markets: (1) standard telephones, used by households and small businesses, (2) telephone systems for small businesses, and (3) large network systems, ranging in size from a few hundred lines to more than one hundred thousand lines. International Telephone and Telegraph (ITT) had emerged as the leader in the network systems market, but also made significant sales to the household and small business markets.

Comdial faced strong competition from two other domestic manufacturers as well, GTE and AT&T. AT&T marketed network systems to Bell Telephone companies, various long-distance carriers, and private businesses. AT&T was also established in the highly competitive and price-sensitive standard telephone business, but was shifting its concentration to multifunctional home telecommunications systems. The Canadian Northern Telecom was also a rival in the systems market.

In addition, Comdial was facing increased competition in the standard telephone business from companies in the Far East; this competition was having an adverse effect on revenues because of reduced prices and volume. These low-cost products from the Far East were introduced in 1983 and quickly gained market share. Although the quality of these products was initially very poor, it had since been upgraded to meet or surpass that of domestic products yet remained significantly cheaper. Traditional products sold through supply distributors had been largely displaced by imports. Furthermore, to take advantage of the cheaper labor, domestic manufacturers had shifted much of their production overseas. ITT imported from a Spanish subsidiary; AT&T had shifted manufacturing operations to Singapore; and GTE was purchasing products made in the Far East.

Rapid changes in technology and the pressure of increased competition (which resulted in price wars and intensive cost-cutting efforts) had produced a shakeout in the industry—the profitable suppliers were becoming entrenched while the nonprofitable ones were disappearing.

OPERATIONS

Comdial currently operated with 1300 employees in a 500,000-square-foot facility in Charlottesville, Virginia. Only 40% of capacity was being utilized; production of 25,000–30,000 phones per week was down from 60,000–70,000 phones per week in 1983. Of the phones being produced, 12,500 were pushbutton models.

In 1985, the company had opened a new plant in the Shenandoah Valley. In order to utilize their excess capacity, Comdial was subcontracting for the Electrolux Corporation; basically, Comdial molded plastic for them. This was viewed as a possibly continuing trend, as there were several other subcontracting proposals on the drawing board.

In manufacturing its telephone terminal equipment, the corporation fabricated metal parts, molded plastics by use of injection machines, and automatically sequenced and inserted semiconductors onto printed wiring boards. Final assembly and testing was performed on mechanized conveyor lines. These processes required machinery costing more than $100,000.

Like the machinery, raw materials came from many suppliers. These materials included raw plastic powder, ABS plastic, steel, aluminum, and nylon. Transformers, wiring boards, receivers, microphones, capacitors, diodes, and other hardware were typically purchased from suppliers, as it would have been too costly for Comdial to manufacture them. Upon arrival, all materials were thoroughly inspected by specification engineers to ensure top quality. The company had not experienced any significant production problems or delays due to shortages of materials or components.

All materials inventories were stored in the Charlottesville facility, and levels were kept as low as possible. A 30-day supply of raw materials and a two-day work-in-process inventory were maintained. Finished goods were shipped as soon as they were completed.

PRODUCTS

Comdial manufactured a full line of single and multi-line telephones. Beginning in 1985, it began supplying a variety of business systems, ranging from ones with two central office trunks (a circuit between two exchanges) and four telephones, to ones with twenty central office trunks and eighty telephones.

Comdial's line of single-line telephones included the standard desk, wall, and rotary models, and a standard desk telephone with a message-waiting flash and a flash for access to Private Branch Exchange. A PBX (Private Branch Exchange) is a switching exchange located on a site and used by that site. Also included was the "Maxplus" line of desk and wall phones, with such features as speakerphone, message waiting, and the "Voice Express." The latter was a full-featured autodialer/speakerphone that could be used as a single-line telephone or with a IA2 Key system (a telephone system that could be programmed to automatically dial selected numbers, its features normally included line pickup, hold, recall, and intercom).

Comdial's multi-line telephones included both the standard six-, ten-, twenty- and thirty-button phones used behind IA2 key systems, with a variety of new features, and a new line of six- and ten-button phones for use with the IA2 key systems with features such as TAP (transfer access phone) and speakerphone.

Comdial's business systems included the "Maxplus II," a two-trunk system using central office or PBX power, which provided all the features of a IA2 key system except intercom. "Maxplus III" was a three-trunk and one-intercom system with all the functions of the standard IA2 system. One of the most popular was the "Executech Key System," which ranged in size from three central office trunks and eight phones to fourteen trunks and thirty-two phones. The standard system was already full-featured; speakerphone was the only option. Comdial produced 200 of these systems per week.

"Westars" was a hybrid Key/PBX system that featured a least-cost routing and message accounting system at a competitive price, and "Tracs" was a least-cost routing and message accounting system designed to be added to already existing key systems and PBX's.

MARKETS

Comdial marketed to both the residential and small business areas. It sold most of its products through independent distributors, who sold to interconnects (sellers to final users who installed systems), and through independent telephone companies for lease or resold to end users. The company also sold smaller quantities directly to the government and to manufacturers of PBX equipment. Comdial distributed residential telephone products primarily through the Regional Bell Operating Companies (RBOCs) with whom it acquired contracts in 1984. The company had wide distribution for its business systems through ten of the major distributors of telecommunications equipment. In addition, Comdial had its own retail operation, American Phone Centers.

Comdial's sales were made monthly through short-term purchase orders issued by customers. The company also had long-term supply contracts with some of the RBOCs, although these contracts were non-exclusive.

Comdial was the only American manufacturer of single-line systems that were used in both residential and business products. In the past, the company's business product line had been mostly limited to the standard single-line telephones and multi-line telephone terminals for use with the key service units. The trend recently, however, had been away from plain old telephones (POTS) to more sophisticated, high-tech products. The company had also shifted its primary focus to the small-business product lines because of the deluge of cheaper foreign-made systems in the residential market.

In order to compete more effectively, Comdial had the current marketing strategy of focusing on innovation, and developing phones with more features. The emphasis was on quality and customer service rather than price. By using a push-pull strategy emphasizing its quality product, competitive pricing, custom features, and prompt delivery, Comdial hoped to increase distribution channels and customer loyalty.

By March 1986, Comdial held 20%–25% of the market for traditional phone products and about 10% of the key system market. There was great opportunity for growth in the telecommunications industry, especially with key system products. Figures from Dataquest Inc. (1986) indicated that industry spending would increase more than 28% between 1985 and 1987, and over 38% of total sales would be attributed to key systems, PBX, and automatic call distributors.

LABOR

In 1985, Comdial reduced the number of its employees from approximately 2200 to 1300; most of the cuts were from the manufacturing area. With these cuts, manufacturing employees currently outnumbered indirect or support personnel by a ratio of 3.5 to 1.

Wages for Comdial employees varied according to the task performed. On average, assembly workers were paid $5.65 per hour, and product specialists earned $9.00 per hour. Since these wages were relatively low for the Charlottesville area, an incentive plan was in effect. If a worker produced 124% of a set quota, he/she was paid 125% of the base salary. The employees viewed the quota as very achievable, as 90% of them exceeded the standard. The wages in the Shenandoah facility were, on average, $1 less per hour than at the Charlottesville facility. As a result, the most labor-intensive operations were performed at the Shenandoah site. While it could generally be said that Comdial operated with one shift, the capital-intensive machines operated with three shifts, so that fuller, more efficient usage was achieved.

Labor at Comdial was non-unionized; the last major attempt to organize a union occurred five years ago. At that time, the workers voted the union down by a margin of 5 to 1. Based on the employees' actions, Comdial believed that its employee relations were generally satisfactory, and the company had experienced no work stoppages.

FINANCIAL POSITION

Comdial Corporation had suffered substantial operating losses since the divestiture of AT&T and the subsequent loss of sales to the Bell System. In 1982, the Bell System, Comdial's largest distributor, accounted for nearly one third of the company's sales. Comdial sustained operating losses of approximately $39.5 million in 1984 and a further net loss of $30.5 million in 1985, as seen in Exhibits 16.1, 16.2, and 16.3.

EXHIBIT 16.1   Selected Financial Data

(Dollar Amounts in Thousands, Except Per Share Data)

Year Ended December 31	1981	1982	1983	1984	1985
Selected Consolidated Statements of Operations Data					
Net sales	6,669	56,909	141,860	118,705	85,196
Cost of sales	5,211	39,298	105,473	116,911	84,999
Gross profit	1,458	17,611	36,387	1,794	197
Marketing, administrative and general expenses	3,175	10,644	22,151	23,446	17,372
Engineering, research and development	710	2,330	7,421	6,918	3,268
Earnings (loss)[1]	(4,035)	(665)	1,147	(39,423)	(30,500)
Earnings (loss) per share[1]	(0.69)	(0.08)	(0.07)	(2.53)	(1.76)
Weighted average shares outstanding	5,840	8,746	15,635	15,569	17,278
Selected Consolidated Balance Sheet Data					
Working capital	3,882	30,246	36,087	41,141	(8,281)
Total assets	7,829	76,512	134,934	112,157	77,118
Short-term borrowings	350	359	36,200	8,768[2]	43,905[2]
Long-term debt	490	27,259	1,979	45,426	1,788
Stockholders' equity	3,100	29,589	79,135	43,097	20,074

[1]Before extraordinary credit.

[2]Includes current maturities on long-term debt.

Cost-cutting efforts in 1985 were successful in decreasing inventories from $43,025,000 on December 31, 1984, to $37,946,000 on September 27, 1985. However, the company's current ratio declined from a high of 3.1 on March 29, 1985 to a low of 0.98 at the end of the third quarter, and the quick ratio dropped to 0.35 from 1.07. Profitability continued to decline in 1985, and stockholders' equity had dropped from $79 million at year-end 1984, to $36.4 million at the close of the third quarter, 1985. Comdial had managed to reduce its long-term debt from $49.4 million on December 31, 1984, to under $7 million after three quarters in 1985.

EXHIBIT 16.2   **Consolidated Statements of Operations: Comdial Corporation and Subsidiaries**

(Dollars in Thousands Except Per Share Amounts)

Year Ended December 31	1985	1984	1983
Net sales	$ 85,196	$ 118,705	$ 141,860
Cost and expenses:			
Cost of sales	84,999	116,911	105,473
Engineering, research and development	3,268	6,918	7,421
Marketing, administrative and general	17,372	23,446	22,151
Minority interest in subsidiary	—	—	(98)
	105,639	147,275	134,947
Earnings (loss) from operations	(20,443)	(28,570)	6,913
Other income (expense)			
Equity in loss from Semiconductor operations	(2,429)	(4,682)	(4,384)
Equity in loss from European operations	—	(455)	(733)
Gain on disposal of European operations	4,537	—	—
Loss on disposal of Upland facility	(3,601)	—	—
Interest expense	(7,761)	(6,066)	(1,144)
Other income (expense)	(803)	350	2,541
Earnings (loss) before income taxes and extraordinary credit	(30,500)	(39,423)	3,193
Income taxes	—	—	2,046
Earnings (loss) before extraordinary credit	(30,500)	(39,423)	1,147
Extraordinary credit—benefit from tax loss carryforward	—	—	1,615
Net earnings (loss)	$ (30,500)	$ (39,423)	$ 2,762
Net earnings (loss) per common share and common equivalent shares (1983)			
Before extraordinary item	$ (1.76)	$ (2.53)	$ .07
Extraordinary item	—	—	.11
	$ (1.76)	$ (2.53)	$ 0.18
Weighted average common shares outstanding and common equivalent shares (1983)	17,278	15,569	15,635

EXHIBIT 16.3

Consolidated Balance Sheets: Comdial Corporation and Subsidiaries

(Dollars in Thousands Except Par Value)

December 31	1985	1984
Assets		
Current assets		
Cash and short term investments	$ 3,758	$ 968
Accounts receivable (less allowance for doubtful accounts: 1985-$2,172; 1984-$2,806)	11,715	17,509
Inventories	30,112	42,682
Prepaid expenses and other current assets	1,002	2,746
Total current assets	46,587	63,905
Investment and advances—subsidiaries	—	7,029
Property, plant and equipment—net	25,481	30,563
Assets held for disposition	1,199	9,800
Other assets	3,851	860
Total assets	$77,118	$112,157
Liabilities and stockholders' equity		
Current liabilities:		
Accounts payable	$ 4,613	$ 5,020
Accrued payroll and related expenses	1,897	1,765
Plant close-down accrual	—	1,592
Other accrued liabilities	4,244	5,313
Income taxes payable	209	306
Current maturities on long-term debt	43,905	8,768
Total current liabilities	54,868	22,764
Long-term debt	1,788	45,426
Minority interest and other long-term liabilities	388	870
Stockholders' equity:		
Common stock $0.01 par value and paid-in capital:		
Authorized 25,000 shares; issued 17,975 and 15,979 shares, respectively	98,331	91,249
Other	(1,397)	(1,792)
Accumulated deficit	(76,860)	(46,360)
Total stockholders' equity	20,074	43,097
Total liabilities and equity	$77,118	$112,157

Global Marine, Inc.

James W. Clinton

"You would not want to stay in this business if you expected the price of oil to drop," asserted David Herasimchuk, Vice-President for Market Development, Global Marine, Inc. Saudi Arabia's decision in the fall of 1985 to increase crude oil production caused oil prices to drop dramatically and led to widespread unprofitability and disarray within the international offshore oil and gas drilling industry. However, optimism is endemic to the industry, and most independent offshore oil and gas drilling contractors at the beginning of 1986 believed the worst was over.

CORPORATE ORGANIZATION

Global Marine, Inc. (GMI), a member of the international offshore oil and gas drilling industry, has three subsidiaries: Global Marine Drilling Company, Challenger Minerals, Inc., and Applied Drilling Technology. The corporate headquarters and the headquarters of subsidiaries are located in Houston, Texas. The corporate organization of Global Marine, Inc., is shown in Exhibit 17.1.

THE 1977 SEVEN-YEAR STRATEGIC PLAN

C. Russell Luigs became CEO of Global Marine, Inc., in 1977. Global Marine's offshore drilling capability at that time was limited entirely to eight ocean-going drillships that were becoming technologically obsolete. The choice facing Luigs and Global Marine was either to maintain an existing conservative philosophy of bidding for drilling contracts with obsolete and, therefore, inferior equipment; or take the high-risk option and develop a world-wide ability to drill in any offshore environmental conditions and thereby become a major factor in the industry. Russ Luigs, with the consent and encouragement of the Board, embarked upon the high-risk alternative. Global Marine's expansion strategy for the 1980s locked the company into large capital commitments with high penalties if rig construction contracts were canceled.

Global Marine diversified at first into semi-submersibles and then into jackups. (See the next section for a description of drilling equipment.) Global

This case was prepared by Professor James W. Clinton of the University of Northern Colorado. This case was presented at the 1986 Workshop of the Midwest Society for Case Research. It also appears in *Annual Advances in Business Cases*, 1986, pp. 197-214, edited by Philip C. Fisher. Reprinted by permission.

EXHIBIT 17.1   **Organization Chart, Global Marine, Inc., 1986**

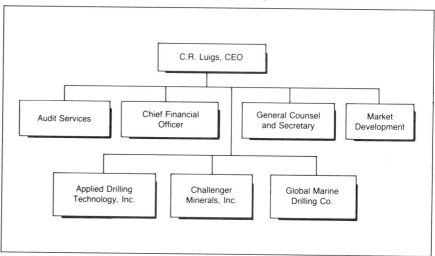

Marine's 1981 budget provided for an inventory of fifty-two offshore drilling rigs. In 1981, however, David Herasimchuk, Global Marine's Director of Market Development, noted that (1) rigs were being delivered to contractors at three times the rate of 1978, (2) shipyards were able to deliver two jackups a month, and (3) delivery rates of jackups implied a 27% increase in jackups for 1981 and a 29% increase in jackup inventories in 1982. Herasimchuk concluded that any change in year-to-year demand of less than 25% could create a serious oversupply of jackup rigs and reduce the day rates charged for offshore drilling as much as 50%. At the time, however, there was a lack of unanimity within the industry concerning the outlook for offshore oil drilling; the industry's rig-utilization rates averaged above 95% between mid-1979 and mid-1982, and within the industry the rule is that new rig construction is justified when the utilization rate is above 95%.

Note that construction lead-times for jackups normally was about two years and could be as little as eighteen months. At the height of the rig construction boom in 1981, lead times were three years. By adding together existing inventories of offshore drilling rigs and anticipated additions to inventory, the supply of rigs is known. Industry analysts can then forecast what demand is necessary, so that day rates stay within a profitable range.

In April 1982, Global Marine's management concluded that the industry's expansion plans were overly ambitious and reduced the company's offshore-drilling-rig construction program by about one-third; a target of thirty-five rigs was set. Global Marine decided also not to order any more 250-foot jackups and to order a 300-foot jackup only if the company had a firm contract for its use. Global Marine thus canceled delivery of all jackups that it was possible to cancel, and deferred delivery of some jackups until 1984, in anticipation that the industry's cycle would peak once again, as it had in the past, at a later date.

GLOBAL MARINE DRILLING COMPANY (GMDC)

GMDC, Global Marine's largest subsidiary, is engaged in offshore oil-drilling operations throughout the world. GMDC, as of the end of 1985, operated thirty-four offshore drilling rigs capable of operating in a variety of marine environments. The entire fleet possessed the capability to drill in any ocean—from shallow water in the Gulf of Mexico, to 2,500-foot depths off the coast of Spain, to the icecaps of the Arctic. The fleet consisted of twenty-one jackups, seven drill ships, five semi-submersibles, and one Arctic submersible.

Drilling Equipment

Rigs used to drill offshore for oil and gas are sturdier than land-based rigs because the former are subjected to greater stresses. GMDC uses a variety of rigs in offshore drilling operations. The most frequently used rigs (and the sequence in which they generally are utilized) are (a) jackup rigs, (b) drillships, (c) semi-submersibles, and (d) fixed platforms.

Jackups

The jackup rig is so named because steel legs located at the three corners of the rig are extended (jacked) down to the ocean floor to provide a stable drilling platform, or raised up above the main platform of the rig so that the rig can be towed to another drilling site. Jackups generally drill in water depths of 15–375 feet and can drill to a depth of up to 25,000 feet. Jackups are used both for exploration and field-development drilling.

Some jackups are cantilevered so that they can drill over a fixed ocean platform without putting weight on the platform—thus permitting the fixed platform to be lighter and, therefore, less costly.

Drillships

Drillships are ocean-going vessels that, unlike most jackups and semi-submersibles, do not require towing. Drillships typically operate in water depths up to 1,500 feet and can drill to a depth of about 25,000 feet. Drillships are self-contained rigs configured to the shape of a ship. Drillships are used for deepwater exploration in moderate environments and in remote areas. They possess the advantage of mobility and are able to carry the large loads necessary for remote drilling operations.

Most moored ships and semi-submersibles are limited to drilling in water depths between 600 and 1,500 feet. Dynamically positioned ships and semi-submersibles operating without a mooring system are generally capable of drilling in depths of 3,000 to 6,000 feet.

Semi-submersibles

Semi-submersible, ocean drilling rigs are mobile and float in the water on very large pontoons submerged below the ocean's surface; these provide stability to the platform floating on the pontoons above the water. Semi-submersibles drill in water depths to about 1,500 feet and can drill to a depth of 25,000 feet. Semi-submersible rigs operate in most of the same areas in which drillships are used and are preferred for deepwater drilling in hostile seas.

Fixed Platforms

If an offshore operator drills a successful exploratory well, a platform rig might next be used to drill additional, developmental wells in the oil field. The platform can only be justified economically, however, if the oil field is large.

GMDC's Drill-Rig Inventory and Utilization

GMDC owns all of its rigs now in service except for one jackup rig, the Glomar Main Pass II, and the Concrete Island Drilling System (CIDS), which are under long-term lease. All rigs owned by GMDC are subject to mortgages except for the Glomar Platform I, the Glomar Biscay I, and the Glomar Adriatic VIII.

The average age of GMDC's fleet of rigs is six years, compared to an industry average of nine years. GMDC operates a modern rig training and drilling-simulation center in Houston, Texas. Drilling crews receive periodic refresher training as part of the company's objective of developing the most highly skilled crews in the industry.

Global Marine recognized in 1982 that offshore oil and gas drilling was below earlier forecasts. The company therefore delayed delivery of three semi-submersible rigs and one drillship and canceled orders for four jackup rigs. The company also agreed to reduce its drilling rate charged to customers if those customers agreed either to use Global Marine rigs in the future or to extend existing drilling contracts.

During 1985 the company concluded seventy-one drilling contracts and contract extensions. As of January 1, 1986, drilling contracts for thirty-one of the company's thirty-four rigs were due to expire during 1986. For 1987, rigs were presently contracted for only 3% of their availability. Utilization rates of the company's rigs for the last eight years and the rate estimated for 1986 are shown on the following page. (Utilization rate is computed by dividing the number of days a rig earned revenues by the total number of days the rig was available for work.)

	1986*	1985	1984	1983	1982	1981	1980	1979	1978
Number of rigs in fleet at end of year	32	34	35	32	28	28	18	14	11
% utilization	30%	91	92	92	93	100	100	98	91

*Estimated.

Arctic Exploration

Global Marine also designs and develops state-of-the-art offshore oil drilling technology and other oil-service equipment. The company has developed a new concept to replace arctic drilling platforms that are used only one time. There is great interest in a mobile drilling platform for Arctic operations because a $140-million dry hole in the Arctic involves a platform costing about $85 million, which has to be abandoned because it was permanently constructed on the drilling site. This costly approach was labeled the "gravel island" concept. Global Marine's concept involves the use of a concrete and steel island capable of operating in water depths of 35–52 feet, with a maximum drilling depth of 25,000 feet. The island can be ballasted (temporarily seated on the ocean floor), deballasted (prepared for towing), moved, and used again.

Global's portable island, labeled the Concrete Island Drilling System (CIDS), was first used by Exxon in November 1984 to explore an area near Prudhoe Bay. CIDS is 300 by 300 feet, and was constructed in Japan. CIDS is intended to replace gravel islands, constructed in shallow waters in the Arctic, that cannot be moved. The company presently is researching a more advanced concept for a mechanism that can operate in deeper Arctic waters. Approximately twenty United States and Canadian oil companies are potential customers for Global Marine's Arctic drilling equipment.

THE OFFSHORE OIL AND GAS DRILLING INDUSTRY

Current Situation

At the beginning of 1986, international oil and gas drilling contractors were engaged in offshore drilling operations in the North Sea, the Mediterranean Sea, Southeast Asia, South America, and the Gulf of Mexico. Contractors were experiencing reduced demand for their offshore drilling rigs and profit margins were narrowing or nonexistent. The entire industry was exceedingly competitive.

Offshore, a publication about the offshore oil and gas industry, reported in June 1985 that 550 rigs of a total 742 available rigs were working, 8 were en route to drill sites, and 184 were idle. This compared to 1984 figures of 539 working, 170 idle, and 8 en route. In addition to these 742 mobile offshore drilling rigs, approximately 100 other drilling rigs were located in Eastern-bloc Communist countries or positioned in Lake Maracaibo, Venezuela (an unusually placid body of water not subject to stresses encountered in the open sea).

Most offshore oil and gas drilling rigs are owned by independent contractors. Some foreign governments that control nationalized oil companies operate their own rigs, and several major international oil companies maintain equity positions in offshore drilling rigs, so they can influence rig design related to their specialized needs.

Historical Background

The offshore oil and gas drilling service industry was born out of the desire by international oil companies to concentrate on those areas they knew best and from which they expected the greatest profit—purchase or lease of oil and gas properties, transporting, refining, and marketing of petroleum and petroleum by-products. Independent offshore-drilling contractors provided and operated drilling rigs at locations selected by the international oil companies' own geologists. Contractors absorbed the risk of low rig utilization in exchange for rates that returned a satisfactory profit—when and if most drilling rigs were under contract.

Post-World War II

Since the end of World War II, the offshore oil drilling industry has experienced a succession of boom and bust cycles that led contractors to conclude that if demand for rigs was depressed, recovery and future prosperity were not far off. The fortunes of the offshore oil and gas industry are inextricably tied to the international oil and gas industry. When demand for oil and gas is high, and prices paid for oil and gas are similarly high, the world's major oil companies exert strong demand for offshore mobile drilling rigs. The reverse is also true—low oil and gas demand coupled with low prices reduce the demand for drilling rigs.

1970–1979

Some major oil producers anticipated a constant increase in oil prices due to the expected steady growth in consumer demand. Natural gas was in short supply during the 1970s, and the shortage culminated in 1978 in widespread media publicity about aged widows freezing to death because they were unable to pay large utility heating bills. This unacceptable human suffering led the federal government to halt construction of new utility plants using natural gas and effectively limit new construction to nuclear and electricity-generating facilities.

1979–1981

Between 1979 and 1981, demand for offshore drilling rigs drove daily rental rates (day rates) up to record levels and encouraged substantial increases in construction of new drilling rigs.

1983

DECLINING DEMAND FOR NATURAL GAS A combination of factors led to a major decline in demand for natural gas in 1983. In addition to federal restrictions on natural gas utility plants, the United States experienced a recession. American consumers also proved more adept at conserving gas and oil than the industry had anticipated. Meanwhile, the United States was shifting from a production to a service economy, requiring less energy per employee, and the traditionally high consumers of energy, "the smokestack industries," were depressed as a result of increased low-priced foreign competition.

Gas pipeline companies had commonly committed themselves to fifteen- to twenty-year long-term contracts for gas deliveries when both demand and prices were high, and demand was expected to increase steadily. The decline in demand for gas forced many pipeline companies to renege on long-term contracts because they could not sell the gas at the prices or volumes at which they had agreed to buy. Many of these canceled contracts are still under litigation.

EXPANDED AVAILABILITY OF FEDERAL OFFSHORE LEASES James Watt, Secretary of the Interior, further complicated the nature of the natural gas industry and its economics. Secretary Watt eliminated the previous practice of major oil and gas companies, of proposing certain tracts of acreage for drilling and negotiating a price directly with the government. Secretary Watt introduced an area-wide leasing system in 1983 that opened offshore areas to competitive bidding. Watt's more liberal attitude toward the development of America's energy resources produced a five-fold increase in acreage leased for a five-year period for oil and gas exploration.

NEW DRILLING RIG CONSTRUCTION Addition of new rigs to the world-wide inventory lowered utilization rates for mobile offshore drilling units from approximately 100% in 1981 to a low of 74% in August, 1983. At the same time, day rates declined as much as 75%.

BUYING VERSUS EXPLORING FOR OIL AND GAS RESERVES Oil and gas exploration in the United States, both on and offshore, declined 23% during 1983. Of oil companies surveyed in 1983, 40% increased reserves by acquiring producing oil and gas properties or companies; this method reflects a belief that oil obtained through purchase was cheaper than oil obtained through exploration and development.

1983–1984

Offshore oil and gas drilling rose late in 1983 and the signals were that a recovery was underway. However, at about this time, T. Boone Pickens, President of Mesa Petroleum, threatened takeover of several oil companies. Other major oil companies followed his lead and several giant mergers took place. Many oil companies became apprehensive that they too might be takeover targets. To avoid takeover, their managements increased financial leverage; thus the companies became less attractive to raiders, but their amount of funds available for oil and gas exploration and drilling was also reduced. To placate shareholders considering sale of their stock to unfriendly raiders, managements increased cash flow to shareholders through formation of royalty trusts, and thus further curtailed drilling plans.

1985

By February 1985, utilization rates for all types of offshore drilling rigs had risen to 84%. Along with the increase in utilization rates, day rates also rose by about 50% during the same period. Major oil companies, however, reduced worldwide exploration so that offshore rig utilization declined steadily through the year to 81% at yearend. Rig utilization in the Gulf of Mexico declined even further to 75%, as of January 1, 1986. The decline in rig utilization caused a concurrent decrease in day rates.

Despite the declining demand for offshore drilling rigs, as of May 1985, there was a total of fifty-three new offshore drilling units under construction worldwide: eighteen jackups, thirty-two semisubmersibles, two drillships, and one submersible.

In December 1985, George Gaspar, an oil and gas industry analyst, forecast oil prices in 1986 to decline $1–$2 per barrel from 1985's average price of $27.50 per barrel. Oil prices were forecast to continue to fall $1–$2 per barrel through 1988 before reversing direction.

A positive factor for the domestic offshore drilling industry was that about 2,000 leases of offshore drilling tracts bought by oil companies for $6.4 billion were due to expire between 1986 and 1988. The oil companies must drill before the leases expired or lose the leases.

INFLUENCES ON OIL AND GAS EXPLORATION AND PRODUCTION

Oil and gas exploration and production are influenced by a variety of factors that include (a) governmental regulation of production, (b) availability of government offshore lands for drilling, (c) prices for competitive fuels, (d) seasonal variations in demand, (e) investment tax credits and other regulations that either encourage or discourage oil exploration and production, (f) attempts by the Organization of Petroleum Exporting Countries (OPEC) to administer prices and establish a single worldwide price, and (g) efforts by individual nations to increase their market share of total oil production, regardless of price.

Oil Supply

The world supply of oil is generated by OPEC and non-OPEC countries. OPEC is an international cartel that attempts to control supply, and thus the price of oil. However, OPEC's members squabble among themselves concerning their fair share of oil production and, by secretly selling more than their allotted share, some members thus increase the supply and tend to reduce the price of oil. As non-OPEC countries compete to sell their supply and acquire larger market share, OPEC becomes less influential. Up to 90% of the increase in non-OPEC oil production since 1978 is derived from offshore wells. Offshore oil production represents 28% of total world production. Non-OPEC oil production was two-thirds of world-wide oil production in 1985, compared to only one-third of world-wide production in 1975. If both OPEC and non-OPEC countries reduce supply, however, prices will rise and offshore drilling outside of the Persian Gulf becomes attractive. Low-priced oil makes exploration of many offshore drilling areas uneconomical.

Oil Demand

Demand for oil is related to price and to various factors of alternative forms of energy—the price of these alternatives, and their compatibility with environmental laws and regulations. Oil is the more popular energy source because it burns more cleanly than does coal. When consumers conserve use of petroleum, demand for oil routinely declines.

Supply of Drilling Rigs

The number of offshore drilling rigs available in the industry and their ability to drill in the specific environment for which they are needed are the major factors affecting day rates for offshore rigs. When demand for drilling rigs falls below the supply of rigs, day rates fall rapidly and drilling contractors compete to keep their rigs busy.

The Cost of Money

The offshore drilling industry is capital intensive because of the high cost of drilling rigs. If drilling contractors borrow money at high interest rates, they are committed to long-term debt repayment of interest and principal, possible only if owned drilling rigs are leased enough so that utilization rates are high. When day rates decline, contractors are squeezed and profitability is difficult. The more modern the drilling fleet, the higher the company's fixed payments and the greater its vulnerability to a decline in day rates.

Foreign Tax Rates

Offshore oil exploration budgets of the major oil companies typically followed fluctuations in oil prices. High oil prices, however, led foreign governments who were hosting drilling rigs to raise tax rates on recovered oil, and several years thereafter, oil exploration decreased.

The U.S. Federal Debt

Some industry analysts suggest that the ballooning size of the U.S. federal debt soon will lead to a new tax on oil, lead to additional consumer conservation, and reduce the need for offshore oil exploration.

Costs of Exploration Vary

Exploration, drilling, and development costs for offshore oil vary widely throughout the world. In the Persian Gulf, the total cost to find and develop a barrel of oil was $1 per barrel in 1984. U.S. major oil companies at other foreign offshore locations incurred a $7 per barrel cost, up to and including development of the drill site location. In the continental United States, onshore drilling costs were $12 per barrel. Offshore drilling in the North Sea near the United Kingdom was $14 per barrel. Additional costs depend upon the tax structure of the country or state in which the drilling takes place. One industry expert estimates that a drop from $30 to $20 per barrel would decrease the number of drillable offshore prospects by about 25%.

RISKS AND ENVIRONMENTAL HAZARDS

Offshore drillers experience hazards and difficulties their land-based competitors do not have to contend with. Offshore oil spills near resort areas can inflict substantial damage upon beaches, the tourist trade, and sea life, and can cause major environmental harm. The spill of oil from a well being drilled from an offshore platform in the Santa Barbara Channel off the California coast in 1969 led to a 10-year moratorium on all drilling off the California coast and stricter state regulation of subsequent offshore drilling operations. Owners and operators of offshore facilities on the Outer Continental Shelf of North America, moreover, are liable for damages and for the cost of removing oil spills for which they are responsible.

Since 1970, only one oil spill has released more than 10,000 barrels of oil into the environment. That spill was the result of a ship's anchor being dragged across a seabed and rupturing an oil pipeline. Between 1975 and

1982, the U.S. Department of the Interior reports that total oil spillage related to offshore drilling in federally leased waters amounted to about 17,000 barrels of oil—only 0.07 of 1% of total oil produced.

When drilling for oil, drillers pump "mud" to the bottom of the well bore, to raise rock chips cut by the drill bit from the well, and control well pressure and avoid "blowouts." Mud is a mixture of clay, barite, water, and several concentrated chemicals. Most mud does not pose a threat to the environment. According to the National Academy of Sciences, natural seepage from the earth accounts for 15% of the oil that reaches the world's water surfaces. Runoff from onshore industry generates additional oil pollution. In contrast, offshore drilling operations in U.S. waters account for .05 of 1% of oil pollution of the world's oceans.

Drilling for oil and gas involves the hazard of a blowout, an uncontrolled high-pressure flow of oil or gas from a well bore, that can catch fire and destroy a rig. Offshore rigs are also susceptible to collisions while they are being towed or positioned for drilling. Rigs under tow have sometimes run aground and some rigs have been destroyed or severely damaged by hurricanes, storms, tidal waves, and typhoons.

Global Marine, Inc., experienced a major maritime disaster on October 25, 1983 when its drillship, the Glomar Java Sea, capsized and sank during Typhoon Lex in the South China Sea. All eighty-one persons aboard the drillship are presumed dead. The Glomar Java Sea was valued at $35 million. The National Transportation Safety Board (NTSB) determined that the ship sank due to a structural failure. The NTSB also stated,

> Contributing to the structural failure was the decision that the drillship would remain anchored with all nine anchors, which subjected the vessel to the full force of the storm. Contributing to the large loss of life was the failure of the master and Atlantic Richfield Company and Global Marine management personnel to remove nonessential personnel from the Glomar Java Sea.

Oil drilling contractors who operate in foreign locations encounter additional risks from (a) expropriation, (b) nationalization, (c) foreign exchange restrictions, (d) foreign taxation, (e) changing political conditions, (f) foreign and domestic monetary policies, and (g) foreign government regulations that give preferential treatment to local contractors or require foreign contractors to employ local citizens or purchase supplies locally.

CHALLENGER MINERALS, INC. (CMI)

Global Marine's second major subsidiary, CMI, is engaged in both onshore and offshore oil and gas exploration. The company's primary exploration and development areas are in the Gulf of Mexico and onshore within four states in the U.S.

A CMI customer for natural gas has refused delivery of a minimum quantity of gas previously contracted for. Gas intended for such delivery is produced at CMI's Weatherford properties in Oklahoma. The Weatherford properties were the source of slightly over one-half of CMI's oil and gas revenues for 1984. Because of this customer's refusal to accept delivery, CMI has been forced to reduce or close down approximately one-half of the company's current production capacity. Global Marine has filed suit against Southern Natural Gas Company (SONAT) for failure to honor its gas purchase contract and is attempting to require SONAT to accept delivery of such gas. CMI is claiming damages of about $99 million.

Another major CMI customer also has refused to accept future delivery of gas previously contracted for. During 1984, CMI evaluated seventeen of the company's leased drilling areas and determined that declining oil prices and a reduction in the properties' production potential lowered the properties' value. Consequently, CMI charged $73 million against 1984 income. In 1983, CMI made a similar charge of $26.9 million.

APPLIED DRILLING TECHNOLOGY, INC. (ADTI)

ADTI, Global Marine's third major subsidiary, provides offshore turnkey drilling services; that is, ADTI guarantees a customer a specified fixed cost for drilling a well, which includes all supervision and management, necessary equipment, material, and personnel. ADTI drilled four turnkey wells in 1985 compared to ten drilled during 1984, and has completed a total of forty-one turnkey wells since 1980. Through 1984, ADTI performed 75% of all offshore turnkey drilling in the Gulf of Mexico.

MARKETING

Global Marine maintains sales offices at nine overseas locations: Aberdeen, Scotland; Anchorage, Alaska; Cairo, Egypt; Calgary, Alberta; Jakarta, Indonesia; London, England; Port Gentil, Gabon (west-central Africa); Singapore; and Siracusa, Sicily. Global·Marine also operates offices in Bakersfield and Los Angeles, California, and Lafayette and New Orleans, Louisiana.

Global Marine's potential customers are relatively few, numbering about fifty-seven major oil and gas companies, and include affiliates of major oil companies. A customer's buying decisions vary from total control at the company's headquarters to delegated decision-making in the field. In between, the field manager makes his recommendation to headquarters and usually his choice is confirmed.

Global Marine's field representatives are expected to develop a relationship with each potential customer; by assuring them that Global Marine is capable of performing a wide range of drilling requirements, they thus establish trust and confidence in Global Marine. Because many of the drilling contractors have similar capabilities, the difference between winning and losing a contract can depend upon the nature of the relationship between Global Marine's representatives and their customer contacts.

Global Marine develops a profile of each customer, noting the customer's concerns and preferences, which are incorporated within the bid the company makes to secure a drilling contract. Global Marine develops similar information about competitors: it accumulates information about what they paid for their rigs, the length of existing contracts, availability of rigs for bidding, and what competitors bid on contracts either awarded or lost.

Bidding of contracts varies among competitors: some bid low to keep their rigs busy; others insist upon a minimum return on investment and will not contract for less; still others bid to maintain a target market share. Some bidders, prior to 1985, might even bid at a higher than expected price, anticipating the low bidders to drop out because of other jobs.

The first step toward obtaining a contract is to get on the qualified-bidders list maintained by customers. Usually each company identifies about a dozen or so drilling contractors as qualified to drill for offshore oil and gas.

FINANCE

Global Marine lost $220 million in 1985 on revenues of $360.7 million, compared to a loss of $91.2 million in 1984 on revenues of $385.8 million. (See Exhibit 17.2.) Contributing to the 1985 loss was a charge of $102 million, made because of a lowered revaluation of the company's oil and gas properties—associated with a major decline in oil and gas prices. (See Exhibit 17.3.) The previous six years, Global Marine earned a profit.

To conserve cash, Global Marine reduced its 1985 capital expenditures to $36 million, a decline of $348 million from the previous year's $384 million capital expenditures.

Global Marine suspended dividend payments on both common and preferred stock in May 1985. On July 1, 1985, Global Marine suspended interest and principal payments (which amounted to approximately $240 million per year) on substantially all long-term debt and is, therefore, in default on most of its long-term debt. As a result, debt formerly identified as long-term has been reclassified as current debt. Between 1980 and 1983, Global Marine spent approximately $1.3 billion on capital expenditures. Expenditures were financed from a variety of sources, which were (a) current operations, (b) two stock issues that raised $178 million, (c) a convertible subordinated debenture issue of $100 million, (d) two subordinated debenture issues of $201 million, (e) $361 million received from subsidized or government guaranteed financing in support of shipyard deliveries, (f) a special lease transaction, (g) $168 million from the sale of tax benefits, (h) secured and unsecured loans from banks, and (i) $100 million from United States Title XI government guaranteed bonds secured by three of the company's previously unencumbered drilling rigs. (See Exhibit 17.4 for a summary of key 1981–1985 data.)

Some of Global Marine's creditors require their approval before the company can borrow additional funds. Another creditor restriction requires

EXHIBIT 17.2 **Consolidated Statement of Changes in Financial Position, Global Marine, 1983–1985**

(Dollar Amounts in Millions)

	1985	1984	1983
Cash from operations			
Net income (loss)	$(220.0)	$ (91.2)	$ 49.3
Non-cash charges	192.2	111.5	109.2
Cash from operations	(27.8)	20.3	158.5
Changes in working capital[1]			
Accounts receivable	5.2	(13.3)	26.7
Materials and supplies	1.5	12.9	(5.7)
Other current assets	1.9	(0.3)	(3.1)
Current maturity of long-term debt	—	—	—
Accounts payable	(18.0)	12.4	(8.2)
Accrued liabilities	56.0	1.4	16.9
Change in working capital	46.6	10.1	26.6
Net cash from operations	18.8	33.4	185.1
Cash required to expand operations			
Capital expenditures	(35.9)	(384.0)	(332.1)
Disposal of properties	4.6	3.3	23.2
Equity investment	—	—	(17.5)
Other, net	(12.3)	.1	(8.2)
Total	(43.6)	(380.6)	(334.6)
Cash before financing	(24.8)	(347.2)	(149.5)
Financing activities			
Long-term borrowing	7.3	241.6	393.6
Reduction in long-term debt	(63.8)	(110.5)	(130.3)
Sale-leaseback of drilling rig	—	77.8	—
Preferred/common stock dividends	(6.6)	(23.9)	(8.6)
Sale of preferred stock	—	—	107.6
Other	(3.4)	4.5	79.3
Cash from financing	(66.5)	$ 189.5	441.6
Increase (Decrease) in cash	(91.3)	$(157.7)	$292.1

[1]Excludes cash, short-term investments, and current maturities of long-term debt.

the company to maintain a minimum of $428.7 million in shareholders' equity.

The company's ability to pay its maturing debt obligations depends largely upon the extent to which rigs are contracted out and the rates obtained for these contracts. Because most of the company's drilling contracts are short-

EXHIBIT 17.3

Consolidated Balance Sheet, Global Marine, 1983–1985
(Dollar Amounts in Millions)

As of December 31	1985	1984	1983
Assets			
Cash	$ 11.1	$ 4.3	$ 3.3
Short-term investments	78.7	176.8	335.5
Accounts receivable	59.5	64.7	51.4
Materials and supplies	24.3	25.8	38.7
Prepaid expenses	10.6	4.9	6.9
Deferred income taxes	—	7.6	5.3
Total current assets	$ 184.2	$ 284.1	$ 441.1
Rigs and drilling equipment (less accumulated depreciation)	$1,260.3	$1,324.6	$ 972.0
Rigs under construction	—	—	80.3
Oil and gas properties			
Subject to amortization	90.2	168.7	222.5
Not subject to amortization	—	15.1	85.7
Net properties	1,350.5	1,508.4	1,360.5
Other assets	38.3	54.3	42.5
Total assets	$1,573.0	$1,846.8	$1,844.1
Liabilities			
Current maturity of long-term debt	$ —	$ 97.8	$ 83.5
Accounts payable	30.6	48.6	36.2
Accrued liabilities	30.2	71.5	70.1
Long-term debt reclassified due to default	1,087.7	—	—
Related accrued interest	97.3	—	—
Total current liabilities	$1,245.8	$ 217.9	$ 189.8
Long-term debt	—	$1,035.0	$ 902.9
Other long-term liabilities	25.5	22.6	18.7
Deferred income taxes	—	21.6	76.2
Deferred credits	11.1	34.6	28.3
Total long-term debt	$ 36.6	$1,113.8	$1,026.1
Shareholders' Equity			
Cumulative convertible preferred stock	$ 115.0	$ 115.0	$ 115.0
Common stock	4.1	4.0	3.9
Additional paid-in capital	211.8	209.8	207.9
Retained earnings	(40.3)	186.3	301.4
Total shareholders' equity	$ 290.6	$ 515.1	$ 628.2
Total liabilities and equity	$1,573.0	$1,846.8	$1,844.1

EXHIBIT 17.4

Five-Year Review of Operations, 1981–1985, Global Marine
(Dollar Amounts in Millions Except Per-Share Data and Dividends)

Year ended	1985	1984	1983	1982	1981
Revenues:					
Marine drilling	$360.7	$385.8	$421.2	$421.0	$324.2
Oil and gas	17.9	20.6	22.3	24.4	16.3
Other energy services	—	0.2	3.5	10.3	11.9
Total Revenues	$378.6	406.6	447.0	455.7	352.4
Net Income (loss)	(220.0)	(91.2)	49.3	85.0	79.8
Shareholders' equity	$290.6	$515.0	$628.0	$476.0	$394.0
Net Income (loss) per common	($7.27)	($3.35)	$1.52	$2.71	$2.61
Dividends paid per common share	$.06	$.24	$.24	$.23	$.175

term in nature, annual cash flow is difficult to project. The decline in Global Marine's 1985 drilling revenues was attributed to lower rates at which the company's drilling rigs were leased to customers under new contracts.

Global Marine currently has sixty-eight claims, totaling $208.5 million, pending in connection with the loss of the Glomar Java Sea (discussed earlier under industry hazards). Five other claims have been settled by Global Marine. An additional five lawsuits, seeking $240 million in damages, have been filed against the company. Global Marine is confident that existing insurance covers pending lawsuits and claims against the company.

COMPETITIVE FINANCIAL PERFORMANCE

The financial performance of major competitors in the offshore drilling industry for the period 1981–1985 appears in Exhibit 17.5. David Herasimchuk of Global Marine offered the following comments about several offshore drilling contractors:

> Rowan Drilling Company and the Offshore Drilling and Exploration Company (ODECO) are financially conservative. Rowan finances capital investments primarily from operations.
>
> Atwood Oceanics, 41% of which is owned by Helmerich and Payne, is conservatively managed and does not order offshore drilling rigs constructed on speculation. The company has equipment that tends to be obsolete. The company's financial condition, however, is excellent. Atwood has accumulated cash while using older rigs and invested profits in major oil companies—its customers—rather than purchase high technology offshore drilling equipment.

EXHIBIT 17.5	**Financial Performance, Selected Offshore Drilling Contractors, 1981–1985** (Dollar Amounts in Millions)				
	1985	**1984**	**1983**	**1982**	**1981**
Global Marine, Inc.					
Revenues	$378.6	406.6	447.0	455.7	352.4
Net Income	(220.0)	(94.9)	49.3	85.0	79.8
Book Value: Common	$ 5.34	12.86	16.13	15.15	12.81
Ocean Drilling and Exploration Company (ODECO)					
Revenues	$633.8	698.6	811.7	979.6	892.2
Net Income	33.7	65.8	119.4	191.9	175.0
Book Value: Common	$ 16.30	16.34	16.31	15.05	12.09
Reading & Bates Corporation					
Revenues	$236.7	329.2	431.1	516.8	530.5
Net Income	(83.2)	18.7	38.2	73.3	93.4
Book Value: Common	$ 7.87	15.36	15.21	14.80	13.07
Rowan Companies, Inc.					
Revenues	$272.5	198.4	206.5	400.4	369.0
Net Income	3.8	4.2	21.9	119.4	111.8
Book Value: Common	$ 10.61	10.66	10.66	10.54	8.23
Zapata Corporation					
Revenues	$288.7	421.3	443.0	537.1	413.0
Net Income	(63.9)	26.1	52.5	103.9	81.7
Book Value: Common	$ 19.05	23.21	22.65	20.90	18.30
Helmerich and Payne					
Revenues	$192.0	192.6	208.1	338.2	287.6
Net Income	18.5	21.4	47.8	75.7	75.3
Book Value: Common	$ 17.01	16.63	16.12	14.54	12.04

SOURCE: *Value Line*, June 13, 1986, pp. 1868–1878.

MANAGEMENT   Corporate Officers

C. Russell Luigs, 52, is Chairman of the Board, President, and Chief Executive Officer. Luigs was elected President and CEO in May, 1977. He has served as Chairman since 1982. Luigs previously was President and a director of U.S. Industries, a diversified manufacturing and service company, from 1974 to 1976.

Jerry C. Martin, 53, Senior Vice-President and Chief Financial Officer, joined Global Marine in 1979 and was elected to his present position in May, 1985. Other officers include:

James T. Goodwyn, Jr., 57, President, Challenger Minerals, Inc. (joined Global Marine in February, 1985)

Gary L. Kott, 43, President, Global Marine Drilling Company (joined Global Marine in 1978 and appointed to present position in 1979)

Thomas E. Short, 57, President, Applied Drilling Technology, Inc. (1979)

Robert E. Sleet, 39, Vice-President and Treasurer (joined Global Marine in April, 1985)

David A. Herasimchuk, 43, Vice-President, Market Development (August, 1980)

John G. Ryan, 33, Senior Vice-President, Secretary and General Counsel

James C. Schmitz, 37, Vice-President, Tax and Government Affairs.

Board of Directors

The Board of Directors includes Chairman Luigs and the following members:

Retired (1985) Senior Vice-President William R. Thomas

Donald B. Brown, 58, an oil and gas consultant (elected to the board in 1982)

Edward J. Campbell, 56, President and Chief Executive Officer, Newport News Shipbuilding, a Tenneco subsidiary (elected in 1981)

Hubert Faure, 65, Senior Executive Vice-President, United Technologies Corporation (elected in 1984)

John M. Galvin, 52, Senior Vice-President, Aetna Life and Casualty (joined the board in 1979)

Warren F. Kane, 61, private consultant and recently retired President of Baker Drilling Equipment Company, a subsidiary of Baker International Corporation (elected in 1982)

Lynn L. Leigh, 59, Chairman, President, and Chief Executive Officer, Summit Oilfield Corporation (elected to the board in 1981)

William C. Walker, consultant to the petroleum industry (1985).

Anti-takeover Actions in 1985

The Board of Directors was concerned in 1985 about the possible vulnerability of Global Marine to takeover by a larger company. Therefore, several anti-takeover provisions were proposed for inclusion in the company's certificate of incorporation. These proposals would (1) divide the Board of Directors into three classes serving staggered three-year terms, (2) allow the board's size to range from a minimum of three to a maximum of fifteen directors, (3) require stockholder actions to be initiated only at a stockholders' meeting to which all stockholders were invited, (4) permit incumbent directors to fill any vacancies on the board, and (5) increase the stockholder vote required to change, amend, or repeal company bylaws from a majority to 80% of the stock available for voting.

REEVALUATING GLOBAL MARINE'S FUTURE DIRECTIONS

Russ Luigs joined Global Marine in 1977 and shortly thereafter introduced a seven-year plan intended to place the company in a position of preeminence within the industry. During most of those years, Global Marine experienced profitability and record growth in assets and revenues. However, 1985 was a watershed year for Global Marine. The company's $1 billion investment in state-of-the-art technology had indeed brought Global Marine to a leadership position among offshore oil and gas drilling contractors, but its cash flow was insufficient to pay off the company's indebtedness.

Luigs might well reflect on those factors critical to success and survival in the offshore drilling industry. He had driven Global Marine to the cutting edge of offshore drilling technology and assembled a fleet of rigs capable of meeting any customer's needs, no matter what the environment. His organization personified the concept, "The Customer is King."

In an industry renowned for risk, Russ Luigs had taken no more than a conventional approach and pursued a strategic course of action that neither he, his board of directors, nor his creditors perceived as excessively risky. Was the price of industry leadership too high? Should he and could he have acted differently? What basis was there to indicate that an alternative course of action would have led to a more favorable set of circumstances?

Global Marine, Inc., as of January 1, 1986, had no seven-year strategic plan for the future. The company's primary objective was survival, as stated by Mr. Luigs in the company's 1985 Annual Report. Although hindsight indicated that the company could have pursued less ambitious objectives, Global Marine's current concerns were what actions and circumstance might combine to preserve the company as an independent entity in the international offshore oil and gas drilling industry.

Pioneer Hi-Bred International, Inc.

J. DAVID HUNGER · DEBORAH READING · DAVID SAVERAID
MARRETT VARGHESE · LARRY MAXWELL

Perhaps Henry Agard Wallace will not be remembered as Vice-President of the United States under Franklin D. Roosevelt or as the Progressive Party's candidate for President in 1948, but the legacy he left to agriculture will never be forgotten. Chiefly responsible for the development of hybrid corn seed, Wallace provided the impetus for a doubling of American corn yields per acre in the last forty years. As an Iowa high school student, Wallace produced the famous Copper Cross variety of corn seed in 1924, and sold all fifteen bushels to finance his genetic experiments. In 1926, Wallace and a few friends founded the world's first hybrid seed company, the Hi-Bred Corn Company, to market the results of his research. Around 1936, Pioneer was added to the company name.

The native Americans who first domesticated corn had simply saved the best ears from the healthiest plants to plant the next spring. The typical American corn grower continued to use this same breeding method through the 1800s. This time-honored program cost little to implement and generally provided good results over the years. By around 1870, however, average U.S. corn yields had leveled off at twenty-six bushels per acre. Fifty years later, in the 1920s, corn growers harvested only about twenty-eight bushels of grain for every acre planted.[1]

Henry Wallace forged an agreement during the Great Depression of the 1930s with a Des Moines real estate agent, Roswell Garst, to distribute Pioneer's hybrid corn seed to the nation's skeptical farmers. The Garst-Pioneer relationship, cemented by a 1930 handshake, was to continue for more than half a century.

Garst returned to his native Coon Rapids, Iowa, taking with him Wallace's latest hybrid corn varieties. Unimpressed by tales of the hybrid's superiority over naturally produced seeds, farmers took Garst up on what they considered a sure bet. Any farmer planting Pioneer's hybrids alongside his own seed could harvest the results and pay Pioneer half the value of the difference between the two yields. To the farmer's surprise, Pioneer's hybrids outproduced generic seeds by twenty bushels to the acre.

This case was prepared by Professor J. David Hunger, Deborah Reading, David Saveraid, Marrett Varghese, and Larry Maxwell of Iowa State University. This case was presented at the 1985 Workshop of the Midwest Society for Case Research. Copyright © 1985 by J. David Hunger. Reprinted by permission.

As of January 1985, Wallace's corn company, known as Pioneer Hi-Bred International, Inc., provided more than a third of the nation's seed corn. More than half the farmers in the Corn Belt bought their hybrid corn seed from Pioneer.

THE HYBRID SEED INDUSTRY

A hybrid seed is the first-generation cross between two or more inbred or "parent" strains. A corn inbred is produced when the ear shoots of corn plants are covered with inverted paper bags so that no stray pollen from other corn plants can fall on the silks. Later, these bags are removed, and the female silks are pollinated by hand from the male tassels of the same strain. Bags are then replaced on the ear shoots to prevent further pollination from unwanted corn plants. The best ears are saved for the next year's seed. This self-pollination process is repeated until the unbred ears become uniform, although small, with the good traits of the inbred strain being firmly fixed in the seed. The crossing of two such inbred parent strains produces a hybrid seed that, when planted, grows into a large and vigorous plant.[2]

Interestingly, hybrids do not reproduce themselves with the same vigor. Although an estimated 90% of all corn and sorghum plus a small but growing proportion of other grains produced in the United States grow from hybrid seed, farmers cannot harvest their hybrid-grown crops, plant the resulting seeds, and expect the next generation to exhibit its parents' characteristics. Hybrids can be produced only from two or more inbred parent strains. These inbreds can be genetically engineered to increase yields, resist insects and diseases, withstand strong wind, and retain a desired moisture content in the kernels. Because of the necessity to use genetically engineered parent strains to produce hybrid seed, the modern farmer must look each year to companies like Pioneer to provide, at a price, the desired seed for planting.

By 1984 the only major field crops to be commercially successfully hybridized were corn and sorghum. Sunflower, still a minor crop, was also a hybrid. Corn, the United States' largest and most valuable crop, alone accounted for approximately $1.5 billion in sales out of an estimated $5 billion U.S. seed market. The hybrid corn seed market was felt by many, however, to be a mature business with low potential for growth. As a result, firms in the seed industry were trying to develop economically practical hybrids of wheat, soybeans, and cotton—each of which could become a billion-dollar seed market.

Unlike hybrid corn, the seeds of wheat, soybeans, and cotton could be saved from one year's crop and planted the following season. Therefore even though acreage devoted to corn and soybeans were roughly equal in size, the lack of a successful soybean hybrid resulted in much smaller annual sales of soybean seed than of corn. Nevertheless, in the early 1980s an estimated 65% of planted soybean seed came from the previous year's crop, compared to about 85% one decade earlier. Farmers were apparently willing to accept higher seed costs in exchange for better yields and stronger disease resistance.

Owing to its nature, wheat has been difficult to hybridize on a commercial scale. Believing that the potential of adding 20% or more to wheat yields have made wheat hybrids worth pursuing. Pioneer breeders have been developing several varieties for the U.S. market. James Windish, Director of Monsanto Corporation's plant-sciences business group, was very optimistic about wheat and soybean hybrid development. (Monsanto had bought DeKalb's wheat operation in 1982 and Hartz Seed Company's soybean seed business in 1983.) "We feel very strongly that in the 1990s, some combination of wheat and soybean breakthroughs will generate $300 million to $500 million in annual revenue for Monsanto."[3]

As a minor crop, hybrid sunflower seeds were a fairly recent commercial development, as 95% of the oil-type sunflower crop were grown from hybrids in 1977 compared to only 15% in 1974. Some people were optimistically comparing its stage of development in the 1980s to that of hybrid corn in the 1940s.[4] Pioneer's hybrid sunflower program, however, was not expected to result in Pioneer brand sunflower seed for several years.

MANAGEMENT PHILOSOPHY

Henry Wallace founded Pioneer on four principles:

- produce the best possible products,
- deal honestly and fairly with customers, vendors, and employees,
- sell vigorously, but without misrepresentation, and
- give service to customers.[5]

The current Chairman of the Board, Thomas N. Urban, described Pioneer's primary mission in a November 7, 1984, letter to the stockholders as "the same as it has been since the company's founding—making the production of food more efficient through the science of genetics."

Pioneer's traditional concern for its primary customer, the American farmer, was shown by its willingness during the 1930s depression to carry the debt of its customers on its books rather than demanding payment. Pioneer's top management believed that profits could be recovered, but customer loyalty could not. During the unusually poor growing year of 1978, Pioneer absorbed a 20% earnings drop rather than raise its prices above the 4.5% increase previously announced. "To raise prices further than we had originally set wouldn't have been justified," remarked then-Chairman, Dr. William L. Brown. "We're not in business for a year or two, but for the long-run."[6] In light of the 1984 depressed farm economy, Pioneer management elected not to raise seed prices for the 1985 growing season.

In comparison with business corporations in many other industries, Pioneer has a long-term time horizon. This orientation derived from its beginnings in the hybrid seed business. It typically takes ten years to develop new proven and accepted products from research. It takes fifteen to twenty years to develop new breeding techniques and to prove them in actual crops. This is generally slow, tedious work and rewards only those with persistence. Thomas Urban acknowledged this key part of the company in his remarks to the annual Pioneer stockholders' meeting of January 24, 1984. He was being promoted to the office of Chairman of the Board, replacing the retiring Chairman, Dr. William L. Brown.

> We are not only preparing for 1985 but for the years beyond as well. We are continuing to emphasize our research programs. We have not lost sight of the fact that Pioneer is research driven.

Pioneer continued in 1985 to be a successful, closely held corporation with its headquarters in Des Moines, Iowa. Although it became publicly held in 1973, "insiders" still controlled 70% of the 31,926,527 outstanding shares of common stock in 1984.[7] Wallace family and other heirs owned or controlled around 27% of the stock. Four members of the founding families served on Pioneer's Board of Directors: Robert B. Wallace, John P. Wallace, Owen Newlin, and Thomas N. Urban. In repeated statements in the 1982, 1983, and 1984 Annual Reports, the board announced its strong desire to keep Pioneer an independent company. This was apparently in response to the large numbers of mergers and acquisitions taking place in the seed industry. For a listing of board members, refer to Exhibit 18.1.

Top management was composed of Thomas N. Urban, Chairman and President, and seven other members of the Executive Committee. (See Exhibit 18.2.) Because of promotion from within, the average tenure at Pioneer of a member of the Executive Committee was twenty-five years. Firmly in charge of the corporate reins in 1985, Tom Urban had joined Pioneer in 1960 after earning an MBA from Harvard University. After serving a term from 1968 to 1971 as Mayor of Des Moines, he assumed the positions of President of the Illinois-Wisconsin Division in 1971, Corporate Vice-President in 1974, President in 1979, and Chief Executive Officer in 1984. Vice-Presidents Owen Newlin, Charles Johnson, and Carrol Bolen split responsibilities for overseeing thirteen of the sixteen corporate units. Newlin monitored the Eastern, Plains, and Southwestern Divisions, as well as Pioneer Hi-Bred Limited (Canada). Bolen handled the Illinois-Wisconsin, Cereal Seed, Soybean Seed, and Turf and Forage Divisions. As Vice-President of Finance and Treasurer, Johnson monitored the Central Division, Farm Information Management Systems, Green Meadows Limited, and Norand Corporation, plus the Administrative Services Group. Dr. Duvick was in charge of the research activities of the Plant Breeding and Microbial Genetics Divisions. Dr. Sehgal managed the Pioneer Overseas Corporation. Mr. Cleary served as Director of Corporate Information, and Mr. Porter as Secretary and Corporate Counsel.

EXHIBIT 18.1   **Board of Directors, Pioneer Hi-Bred International, Inc.**

C. Robert Brenton, President, Brenton Banks

Robert B. Wallace, National Co-Chairman, Population Crisis Committee/
Draper World Population Fund
Stock ownership: 15.4%

Thomas N. Urban, President and Chairman
Stock ownership: 0.8%

Fred W. Weitz, President and CEO, The Weitz Corporation

Clifford L. Peterson, Retired Senior Vice-President—Finance, Deere and
Company

Dr. Donald N. Duvick, Vice-President—Research, Director, Plant Breeding
Division

John P. Wallace, President, Wallace Hatchery, Inc.

Raymond Baker, Retired Director of Corn Breeding
Stock ownership: 3.18%

Dr. Ray A. Goldberg, Moffet Professor of Agriculture and Business,
Harvard University

Simon Casady, Retired Secretary, Chairman of the Executive Committee,
United Central Bancshares
Stock ownership: 0.84%

Dr. Owen J. Newlin, Vice-President
Stock ownership: 9.5%

Robert J. Fleming, President, National By-Products, Inc.
Stock ownership: 0.37%

Charles S. Johnson, Vice-President—Finance and Treasurer

Raymond Lutjen, Retired Vice-President—Finance

SOURCE: Pioneer Hi-Bred International, *1984 Annual Report.*

With many successful years in the hybrid seed business, Pioneer's top
management saw little need to diversify the company's product line beyond
related offerings. Nonseed products contributed only about 9% to Pioneer's
sales in 1984, sharply contrasting with the 66% provided by the diversified
operations of the company's chief competitor, DeKalb Ag Research. Even
before its 1982 merger with Pfizer, DeKalb had been involved in the breeding
of swine and larger chickens, livestock marketing, commodity futures brokerage, oil and gas exploration, mining, oil well servicing, and irrigation
systems, in addition to seeds.

EXHIBIT 18.2 **Officers and Executive Committee, Pioneer Hi-Bred International, Inc.**

NAME/EDUCATION	AGE	TITLE	YEARS WITH PIONEER
Thomas N. Urban[1] MBA, Harvard	50	Chairman and President	22
Owen J. Newlin[1] Ph.D., University of Minnesota Plant Breeding	56	Vice-President	29
Charles S. Johnson[1] B.S., Iowa State University Business	46	Vice-President—Finance and Treasurer	19
Carrol D. Bolen M.S., University of Illinois Agronomy	46	Vice-President	19
Donald N. Duvick[1] Ph.D., Washington University Plant Breeding	60	Vice-President—Research	33
Suri Sehgal Ph.D., Harvard Plant Breeding	50	Vice-President; President, Pioneer Overseas Corporation	21
Gordon McCleary B.S., University of Illinois Journalism	56	Director of Corporate Information	26
Dale L. Porter J.D., Drake University	59	Secretary and Corporate Counsel	32

SOURCE: Pioneer Hi-Bred International, *Leaders of Pioneer,* 1984.

NOTE: [1]Indicates member of the Board of Directors.

According to former Chairman Dr. William L. Brown, in an interview in 1980, Pioneer's long-term growth will come from its diversification within the seed business. "If we were diversified, management time would be taken away from our major business and I can't help but think that would adversely affect our seed operations."[8] President Urban echoed these thoughts when he agreed that the company may not reduce its dependence on corn for a decade or more. "We would rather live or die on our ability to research new seed products than hedge that with an acquisition to provide earnings to offset any failure in research."[9]

In addition to a conservative attitude toward diversification, management philosophy encouraged decentralized decision-making, promotion from within, and the placement of maximum responsibility on each employee for performance of individual tasks. Some analysts felt that this decentralized management style allowed Pioneer's researchers free rein, and accounted for the firm's renowned creativity. The company has been proud of this laissez-faire relationship with its employees, which encourages initiative, creativity, and productivity. A member of Pioneer's Board of Directors remarked: "Employee attitudes are particularly important since many employees are in direct contact with the end users of our products."[10]

HUMAN RESOURCES

Pioneer directly employed 2,947 nonunionized employees in 1984, an increase of 10% over 1983. Scientists, engineers, and research support staff comprised 6% of the total work force.

The Department of Human Resources, according to Chairman Urban, was created at Pioneer in 1981 to "increase job satisfaction and further increase the productivity of our already productive people."[11] This new department was put in charge of two-year training and employee development programs, meetings to improve communication between levels of the company, management seminars, individualized job performance audits, and workshops on enhancing teamwork within Pioneer.

ORGANIZATION

Pioneer organized itself primarily around its product lines and geographic areas.[12] Key staff responsibilities were handled by the *Administrative Services Group* headed by Vice-President Charles Johnson with the assistance of the Corporate Controller, the Human Resources Director, and the President of Pioneer Data Systems. Pioneer Data Systems, in particular, provided data/information processing services for all units of the corporation. In addition to the Administrative Services Group were seven geographic units and eight product units. Except for the Plant Breeding Division, each unit was managed by a person with the title of President.

The seven geographic units were as follows:

- *Central Division:* produced Pioneer seed corn and marketed it along with Pioneer-developed wheat, alfalfa, soybeans, and other forages, plus sorghum and silage inoculants in Iowa, Minnesota, Missouri, the Dakotas, and eight western states. It operated seed corn production plants, soybean seed conditioning plants, and hard red spring wheat plants.

- *Eastern Division:* produced and marketed Pioneer corn, wheat, and soybean seed in much of the eastern and southern United States. Besides operating seed corn plants, it marketed silage inoculant and alfalfa and sorghum seed.

- *Illinois-Wisconsin Division:* produced and marketed Pioneer corn, soybean, and wheat seed. It also marketed sorghum, alfalfa, and forage seed, as well as silage inoculants produced by other Pioneer divisions.

- *Plains Division:* marketed pioneer seed and silage inoculant in Kansas, Nebraska, and Colorado. It also had some production facilities.

- *Southwestern Division:* marketed Pioneer corn, sorghum, soybean, wheat, and alfalfa seed in Texas, Oklahoma, and New Mexico. In addition to producing Pioneer soybean and wheat seed, it produced the total supply of sorghum seed marketed worldwide by Pioneer.

- *Pioneer Hi-Bred Limited:* a wholly owned subsidiary of Pioneer Hi-Bred International, it produced and marketed Pioneer corn and soybean seed in Canada. It also sold alfalfa, sorghum seed, and silage inoculants produced by other Pioneer divisions.
- *Pioneer Overseas Corporation:* marketed Pioneer corn, sorghum, and alfalfa seed plus silage inoculants outside North America. It also conducted its own research program for the development of corn hybrids for overseas markets. The division's President, Dr. Suri Sehgal, also served as Vice-President on Pioneer's Executive Committee.

The eight product units were as follows:

- *Cereal Seed Division:* produced parent seed for Pioneer wheat varieties, for production and marketing by the geographic units.
- *Soybean Seed Division:* produced parent seed for Pioneer soybean varieties, for production and marketing by the geographic units.
- *Turf and Forage Seed Division:* produced and procured forage seeds, such as alfalfa, for distribution by the geographic units and other channels.
- *Plant Breeding Division:* engaged in genetic research in corn, sorghum, soybeans, wheat, alfalfa, and sunflowers. Within the division, each crop had its own breeding department. The division's director, Dr. Donald Duvick, also served as Vice-President of Research on Pioneer's Executive Committee.
- *Microbial Genetics Division:* developed and produced bacterial inoculants to hasten the fermentation process that turned forage into a storage form for year-round animal feed. It was also researching bacterial intestinal-tract treatments for livestock. Its products were marketed by the geographic units.
- *Norand Corporation:* a wholly owned subsidiary of Pioneer, it developed, manufactured, and marketed microprocessor-based data handling systems for a variety of businesses, including wholesale and retail distributors, route truck operators, and field salespeople.
- *Farm Information Management Services Division:* marketed on-farm computer systems, educational packages, and specially developed computer software to farmers.
- *Green Meadows, Ltd.:* developed Pioneer-owned real estate for residential and commercial usage.

SEED PRODUCTION

To produce marketable hybrid corn seed, Pioneer planted a record 270,000 acres of parent inbreds in 1984; two parent strains alternated in rows of four. Because corn plants contained both male and female characteristics, the female parent was detasseled (Pioneer employed 80,000 temporary workers for this task in 1984), and the male plant left intact. Pollination crossed the two inbred parents to form the desired hybrid offspring. Seed produced in this manner generated fully half the fourfold increase in American corn yields over the last four decades. Without special characteristics bred into the plants, some parts of the country currently under production could not grow crops at all.

Some of Pioneer's seeds were grown in Florida, Texas, and Chile, where climatic conditions allowed the production of several generations in a single season. Even so, Pioneer experienced shortages of some popular new varieties of soybeans and forages because of uncooperative weather conditions in 1983.

Pioneer typically contracted with 2,000 farmers to produce its hybrid seeds, and paid them the market price for grain on the date of delivery. Some of these relationships dated back over a quarter of a century. However, this producton method required that Pioneer release its proprietary plant materials to the very farmers who bought its products. By planting Pioneer's parent varieties without crossing them, the astute agriculturalists could easily create their own breeding stock. This necessary release of trade secrets has been compared to Kentucky Fried Chicken's turning its recipe and ingredients over to every fry cook in the chain.[13] Because of a Pioneer lawsuit, however, hybrid seed corn producers were made liable for any proprietary inbreds planted to produce parent seed rather than hybrid crosses.[14]

Pioneer offered 115 varieties of hybrid seed corn, bred for different maturities and weather conditions, at three of the company's North American divisions. Ten of these 115 strains provided two-thirds of total corn seed sales in 1984. Two new varieties of hybrid wheat seed were developed by the Cereal Seed Division for the 1984 season. The Soybean Seed Division produced twenty-one varieties of soybeans, five of them new in 1984. The Turf and Forage Division developed two new alfalfa strains for 1985, which increased the plant's ability to return nitrogen to soil previously planted with nutrient-grabbing corn plants. In addition, the Southwestern Division introduced three new lines of sorghum seed in 1984.

PRODUCTION FACILITIES

Pioneer's production facilities were extensive and far-flung in 1985, and overall plant age was estimated at four years.[15] Twenty-four plants in North America conditioned commercial seed, a process requiring harvesting and drying before the first frost destroyed germination potential. Corn seeds underwent husking, sorting, and a six-month drying period before storage in one of Pioneer's facilities. Nine million bushels of bulk seed and 17.8 million 50-pound bags of corn could be warehoused in Pioneer's massive storage buildings. Corn dryers with a combined capacity of 1.9 million bushels were filled an average of eight times per season. Parent seed corn was conditioned at four plants in Iowa, Texas, Indiana, and Ontario, Canada. Separate production facilities were located in Spain, Brazil, Italy, India, and Austria.

Three unused seed-conditioning plants had been leased from competitors to handle 1984's bumper crop. Mr. James Ansorge, Financial Relations Manager at Pioneer, did not anticipate a recurrence of undercapacity problems in the next few years because of completion in fiscal 1984 of the new facilities at Mt. Pleasant, Iowa, and the remodeling of facilities at Marengo, Iowa, and Donipan, Nebraska.

Sorghum seed was conditioned at Pioneer's Plainview, Texas plant. Forage seeds were prepared in Idaho, California, and Minnesota. As part of Pioneer's move toward the sale of multiple seed products, plants in Iowa, Illinois, Ohio, North Dakota, North Carolina, Nebraska, Indiana, Michigan, and Ontario, Canada, have been redesigned to condition a mix of corn, wheat, and soybean seeds.

Microbial culture research took place at Pioneer's Oregon and Iowa facilities, while plant breeding and biotechnology research were undertaken at the Johnston, Iowa, headquarters. Field research on plant breeding was conducted at forty-five stations in the United States and Canada and at an additional twenty locations throughout the world. Finally, Cedar Rapids, Iowa, was the site of Pioneer's production and distribution of data-handling systems through its Norand subsidiary.

NORAND CORPORATION

Pioneer acquired the Norand Corporation in October 1976 to develop, manufacture, and market electronic-information systems. Pioneer purchased Norand from George Chadima and his associates for $2.2 million. Mr. Chadima remained at Norand as Director of Research and Development, Executive Vice-President, and Chairman of Norand's board. The subsidiary was then managed by Arnold Sunde, who left what then became Pioneer Data Systems to become Norand's President.

Initially, Norand hoped to quickly boost its sales and earnings with the aid of Pioneer's abundant cash reserves. Pioneer's top management realized almost immediately, however, that drastic changes were needed. "We closed it after 30 days, shut it down, and started all over again," said Pioneer's Chairman, Thomas Urban. "They were at the low end of the market with their small inventory machine and we could see that the trend was for lower and lower prices in that market. So we decided to go for the high end of the market."[16] Norand's field sales and systems engineering staff have similarly been reorganized and expanded.

Norand's portable Route Commander computer, used by beer, soft drink, dairy and snack food delivery people, was the industry's standout in 1984 despite its premium price. The company's A-line buttonless cash registers have been installed in 823 Winchell Donut Shops and 814 Long John Silver's restaurants. Norand's big breakthrough came when Pepsico's Pizza Hut, Inc. signed a contract for $40 million of A-line equipment for its nearly 2,000 restaurants. Norand was also in the running for a contract with Southland Corporation, owner of 7,400 7-Eleven convenience stores. The

A-line equipment being tested in 1984 at 7-Elevens listed at $17,000 per store according to David Karney, Southland's Manager of Management Information Services in Dallas. A final decision on installation throughout Southland's chain was to be made during 1985.

Despite Pioneer's initial investment of $18 million in expansion funds and Norand's steadily increasing revenues, the subsidiary has accumulated more than $42 million in operating losses over the last seven years. Yet Pioneer has been patient with its subsidiary. "They are used to eight to ten year cycles in their seed corn hybrid development. But at the same time, it's true that they would have liked to have seen a little less investment cost," remarked one analyst.[17] Norand recently completed a $2.6 million expansion to its headquarters and has hired 150 new employees, bringing its total employment in Cedar Rapids to 550. Half of the unit's products are made at the Cedar Rapids plant. The rest is subcontracted to other manufacturers in the United States and Mexico. Norand contributed positively to Pioneer's profits in 1984 with $875,000 in net income. According to Charles Johnson, Vice-President of Finance and Treasurer, Norand in 1985 had well over 90% of the installed route distribution base.

IBM, NCR, and a growing number of other companies were developing and selling systems to battle Norand's A-line. Service has been one of the strong points of the computer giants and one of the primary factors clients considered in choosing between competing systems.

Thomas Urban assessed the strategic importance of Norand:

There is a lot of synergy in microbiology, biotechnology, genetic engineering, and computers. Our association with Norand has put us five to ten years ahead of our competition on the market side. By the end of 1985, we'll have 4,000 Norand portable computers with our seed salesmen. That product wouldn't even exist probably until 1990 if we hadn't made it, and it gives us the most efficient sales representative system in the seed business. What we want to do is put new products together to fit markets that we understand better than anyone.[18]

GREEN MEADOWS, LTD.

Pioneer's Green Meadows, Ltd. subsidiary has been developing 529.5 acres of company-owned land in Johnston, Iowa, a suburb of Des Moines. No longer required for agricultural research, the land has sprouted homes, townhouses, apartments, shops, recreational facilities, a retirement home, and a convalescent home for children. Although development has lagged along with the depressed Des Moines real estate market, 1982 marked the opening of Village Square shopping center in Green Meadows. The Pioneer Overseas Corporation, Microbial Products Division, Employee Relations Department, and a Hy-Vee grocery store leased space in the new development.

FARM INFORMATION MANAGEMENT SERVICES

Developed in 1983, the Farm Information Management Services (FIMS) Division strove to bridge the gap between farmer and computer terminal. Pioneer's "Information Cultivation" program offered seminars, farm-friendly software, and a support system designed to help farmers make timely and accurate decisions regarding their operations. The package included an IBM personal computer, monitor, printer, and software to help a farmer examine the available alternatives as well as potential results of various actions. Also available were swine-production, corn-production, farm-accounting, and education-support packages developed by Pioneer. Newsletters, classroom instruction, local meetings, and a toll-free hotline were part of the FIMS support package. Pioneer hoped that its experience with its internal data processing division, Pioneer Data Systems, would help it introduce FIMS to Iowa, Minnesota, and North Dakota in early 1985. Pioneer planned to expand quickly into other markets as soon as it had the necessary support staff in place.[19]

The consulting firm of Frost and Sullivan estimated that microcomputer and computer service sales to the farming industry will reach $104,232,000 per year by 1987. Spending on farm-related computer services, fueled by decision support systems, was expected to grow 24% per year through 1987. Total hardware unit sales for the period were projected at 94,000 units and dollar sales were projected to increase 15% per year.[20] To set the company apart from competitors, Pioneer's computer marketing strategists planned to offer a complete record-keeping and analysis system plus after-purchase service and support.

FINANCE

Although 1983 was a poor year for Pioneer, the company rebounded strongly in 1984. Pioneer rang up $554.9 million in seed corn sales, $12.5 million in sorghum seed, $45.4 million in soybean seed, and $12.1 million in cereal seeds, as well as forage, microbial products, and information products sales, totaling over $700 million. (See Exhibit 18.3.) Forages, the discontinued cotton seed operations, and the fledgling Farm Information Management Services suffered losses. However, corn's 27% contribution margin served to finance the development of the new and/or less successful lines. Overall, profits increased nearly 60% from 1983 to 1984. (See Exhibits 18.4 and 18.5 for financial statements.)

Seed sales and profits were typically high in the second and third quarters (December through May), and activity in the first and fourth quarters (June through November) was slow. In 1984, net income for the second and third quarters totaled $91,716,402, while a combined loss of $22,565,719 occurred in quarters one and four. Pioneer established a company borrowing record in 1984 by arranging $243 million in short-term credit to cover unusually high inventory levels.

EXHIBIT 18.3 Net Sales and Contribution by Product: Pioneer Hi-Bred International, Inc.
(In Thousands of Dollars)

Year Ended August 31	1984		1983		1982		1981		1980	
	Total	%	Total	%	Total	%	Total	%	Total	%
Net Sales										
Agricultural seeds:										
Corn	$554,991	77.5	$376,142	74.4	$454,458	81.5	$382,883	80.1	$329,796	81.3
Sorghum	12,453	1.7	10,332	2.0	8,687	1.6	8,226	1.7	6,295	1.6
Soybeans	45,399	6.3	31,225	6.2	22,447	4.0	22,307	4.7	15,899	3.9
Forage	27,770	3.9	37,037	7.3	29,363	5.3	29,893	6.3	29,104	7.1
Cereal	12,107	1.7	8,624	1.7	9,386	1.7	6,100	1.3	3,116	.8
Cotton	684	.1	1,373	.3	2,073	.4	1,650	.3	3,233	.8
	$653,404	91.2	$464,733	91.9	$526,414	94.5	$451,059	94.4	$387,443	95.5
Electronic information systems										
Norand	$ 54,800	7.7	$ 31,698	6.3	$ 22,103	3.9	$ 15,871	3.3	$ 11,381	2.8
Pioneer Data Systems	—	—	—	—	—	—	2,899	.6	2,691	.7
Farm Information Management Services	28	—	—	—	—	—	—	—	—	—
	$ 54,828	7.7	$ 31,698	6.3	$ 22,103	3.9	$ 18,770	3.9	$ 14,072	3.5
Other	7,829	1.1	9,003	1.8	8,881	1.6	8,166	1.7	4,369	1.0
Total Net Sales	$716,061	100.0	$505,434	100.0	$557,398	100.0	$477,995	100.0	$405,884	100.0

Contributions (Loss)

	Amount	%	Amount	%	Amount	%	Amount	%	Amount	%
Agricultural seeds										
Corn	$151,899	123.4	$103,632	133.9	$150,972	107.9	$125,825	103.7	$129,547	114.5
Sorghum	2,257	1.8	1,917	2.5	2,501	1.8	2,150	1.7	899	.8
Soybeans	1,792	1.5	2,477	3.2	3,055	2.2	2,948	2.4	2,182	1.9
Forage	(617)	(.5)	1,728	2.2	1,344	1.0	2,221	1.8	1,023	.9
Cereal	52	—	(37)	—	1,316	.9	837	.8	(179)	(.2)
Cotton	(437)	(.4)	1,312	(1.7)	(299)	(.2)	(623)	(.5)	10	—
	$154,946	125.8	$108,405	140.1	$158,889	113.6	$133,358	109.9	$133,482	117.9
Electronic information systems:										
Norand	$ 875	.7	$ (5,506)	(7.1)	$ (5,845)	(4.2)	$ (7,426)	(6.1)	$ (9,644)	(8.5)
Pioneer Data Systems	—	—	—	—	—	—	144	.1	348	.3
Farm Information Management Services	(1,463)	(1.2)	—	—	—	—	—	—	—	—
	$ (588)	(.5)	$ (5,506)	(7.1)	$ (5,845)	(4.2)	$ (7,282)	(6.0)	$ (9,296)	(8.2)
Other	(6,277)	(5.1)	(1,851)	(2.4)	(421)	(.3)	295	.3	(1,260)	(1.1)
Total Contributions	$148,081	120.2	$101,048	130.6	$152,623	109.1	$126,371	104.2	$122,926	108.6
Indirect Expense	(24,943)	(20.2)	(23,702)	(30.6)	(12,766)	(9.1)	(5,052)	(4.2)	(9,753)	(8.6)
Pretax Earnings from Continuing Operations	$123,138	100.0	$ 77,346	100.0	$139,857	100.0	$121,319	100.0	$113,173	100.0

SOURCE: Pioneer Hi-Bred International.

EXHIBIT 18.4

Pioneer Hi-Bred International, Inc.: Income Statements

Year Ended August 31	1984	1983	1982	1981	1980
Net Sales	$716,061,483	$505,433,624	$557,397,642	$477,995,165	$405,884,401
Cost of Goods Sold	401,834,761	281,264,434	291,280,906	257,654,570	198,667,674
Gross Profit	$314,226,722	$224,169,190	$266,116,736	$220,340,595	$207,216,727
Operating Expenses:					
Selling	$140,693,527	$104,765,746	$100,563,089	$ 85,087,756	$ 76,375,321
General and Administrative	37,280,265	31,099,363	24,563,042	17,665,478	15,853,029
	$177,973,792	$135,865,109	$125,126,131	$102,753,054	$ 92,228,350
Operating Income	$136,252,930	$ 88,304,081	$140,990,605	$117,587,541	$114,988,377
Financial Expense (Income)	13,115,366	10,957,884	1,133,253	(3,731,582)	1,815,021
Income before provision for income taxes and equity in net income (loss) of unconsolidated subsidiaries	$123,137,564	$ 77,346,197	$139,857,352	$121,319,123	$113,173,356
Provision for Income Taxes	56,656,161	32,527,680	67,808,796	59,651,214	56,026,114
Income before equity in net income (loss) of unconsolidated subsidiaries	$ 66,481,403	$ 44,818,517	$ 72,048,556	$ 61,667,909	$ 57,147,242
Equity in net income (loss) of unconsolidated subsidiaries	2,659,280	(1,094,119)	(444,438)	1,783,775	97,648
Net Income	$ 69,140,683	$ 43,724,398	$ 71,604,118	$ 63,451,684	$ 57,244,890
Earnings per Common Share	$ 2.17	$ 1.37	$ 2.24	$ 1.99	$ 1.80

SOURCE: Pioneer Hi-Bred International, Inc.

EXHIBIT 18.5 **Pioneer Hi-Bred International, Inc.: Consolidated Balance Sheets**

Year Ended August 31	1984	1983	1982	1981	1980
Current Assets					
Cash	$ 5,754,402	$ 1,724,827	$ 14,107,044	$ 18,116,420	$ 11,417,319
Marketable securities	18,684,951	6,489,833	3,393,253	16,440,833	60,182,539
Receivables:					
Trade	44,701,282	40,525,360	29,661,624	18,506,807	14,378,185
Other	2,000,090	4,390,434	29,206,450	20,769,078	2,144,227
Inventories	213,685,893	271,543,088	199,920,862	121,947,657	130,095,924
Prepaid expenses	8,499,573	9,146,510	7,625,968	9,004,211	6,835,214
Deferred income tax charges	16,280,133	—	—	—	—
Total current assets	$309,606,324	$333,820,052	$283,915,201	$204,785,006	$225,053,408
Investments and Other Assets					
Equity in and advances to unconsolidated subsidiaries	31,667,274	22,789,754	21,804,413	14,015,118	8,516,233
Other	5,832,895	6,450,676	5,605,657	5,163,961	3,779,253
	$ 37,500,169	$ 29,240,430	$ 27,410,070	$ 19,179,079	$ 12,295,486
Property and Equipment					
Land and land improvements	$ 27,488,426	$ 25,161,381	$ 18,334,359	$ 14,993,901	$ 11,972,255
Buildings	125,679,659	117,626,822	77,874,232	66,040,455	58,541,329
Machinery and equipment	139,383,892	118,025,252	85,083,977	69,809,689	58,200,752
Construction in progress	28,094,209	20,502,555	65,598,619	34,844,771	12,113,618
	$320,646,186	$281,316,010	$246,891,187	$185,688,816	$140,827,954
Less accumulated depreciation	83,075,018	69,232,322	56,502,596	47,697,358	41,401,814
	$237,571,168	$212,083,688	$190,388,591	$137,991,458	$ 99,426,140
Intangibles					
Goodwill	$ 2,589,086	$ 3,805,794	$ 4,657,706	$ 5,538,601	$ 6,379,367
Other	1,197,741	3,810,994	6,424,247	—	—
	$ 3,786,827	$ 7,616,788	$ 11,081,953	$ 5,538,601	$ 6,379,367
Total Assets	$588,464,488	$582,760,958	$512,795,815	$367,494,144	$343,154,401

(Continued)

EXHIBIT 18.5 (continued)

Year Ended August 31	1984	1983	1982	1981	1980
Current Liabilities					
Commercial paper and line of credit borrowings	$ 62,082,640	$133,979,669	$ 66,676,069	$ —	$ —
Current maturities of long-term debt	2,911,072	3,436,750	2,873,801	2,266,569	31,390,043
Accounts payable, trade	26,635,647	23,702,736	18,969,514	17,429,221	13,122,256
Accrued liabilities:					
Salaries and wages	10,326,595	6,933,584	8,919,097	4,340,350	2,032,517
Dividends	6,385,305	5,746,987	5,745,943	4,149,380	3,827,359
Property and withholding taxes	5,698,588	4,252,003	3,834,914	2,571,758	2,741,605
Other	4,157,218	2,877,222	1,963,531	3,102,372	1,540,765
Income taxes payable	36,750,532	14,702,909	42,087,310	30,297,891	34,763,206
Deferred income tax credits, net	—	921,156	3,968,948	2,725,714	514,189
Total current liabilities	$154,947,597	$196,553,016	$155,039,127	$ 66,883,255	$ 89,931,940
Long-term Debt	$ 17,826,328	$ 19,389,350	$ 14,747,879	$ 7,937,308	$ 9,881,940
Deferred Income Tax Credits	$ 22,120,150	$ 14,552,070	$ 10,070,936	$ 7,184,975	$ 5,890,000
Stockholders' Equity					
Common, $1 par value; authorized, 70,000,000; issued 32,084,606 shares[1]	$ 32,084,606	$ 32,084,606	$ 32,078,806[1]	$ 16,116,053	$ 16,104,228
Additional paid-in capital	9,870,357	9,861,065	9,806,746	9,769,377	9,556,809
Retained earnings	360,375,271	315,498,753	294,761,762	259,867,536	212,053,993
Cumulative translation adjustment	(7,144,579)	(4,189,636)	(3,445,081)	—	—
	$395,185,655	$353,254,788	$333,202,233	$285,752,966	$237,715,030
Less:					
Cost of treasury stock	(303,644)	(264,360)	(264,360)	(264,360)	(264,360)
Unearned compensation[2]	(1,311,598)	(723,906)	—	—	—
	$393,570,413	$352,266,522	$332,937,873	$285,488,606	$237,450,670
Total liabilities and stockholders' equity	$588,464,488	$582,760,958	$512,795,815	$367,494,144	$343,154,401

SOURCE: Pioneer Hi-Bred International, Inc.

[1] Stock split two for one on March 19, 1982.

[2] Forfeitures by employees of stock tendered under compensation plan.

Pioneer financed its growth primarily through internal sources, although $242 million in credit lines was available for seasonal and long-term borrowing in 1985. The company had increased its dividend every year since beginning dividends as a publicly held corporation in 1974. On August 31, 1984, 3,125 individuals and organizations held the 31,926,527 outstanding shares of common stock. Although 10,000,000 shares of preferred, cumulative stock have been authorized, none had been issued through 1984. Pioneer stock ranged in price from $23.25 in the third quarter of 1984 to a high of $32.25 in the second, having split two for one on March 19, 1982.

MARKETING

Pioneer's marketing system, developed in the 1930s by Roswell Garst, had evolved into the finest farmer-as-salesman network in the seed industry. Pioneer distributed seed primarily to farmers who sold it to other farmers on a part-time, commission basis. Over 5,000 such entrepreneurs were employed during 1984, some earning as much as $30,000 in a single year. A 1982 survey of Iowa farmers by *Wallace's Farmer* magazine concluded that 93.5% of all seed corn sold in Iowa was purchased from farmer-dealers. (See Exhibit 18.6.) To accommodate local buying habits in the southern states, Pioneer distributed through seed dealers.

The 1982 survey also indicated that 10.6% of Iowa farmers canceled or returned part of their 1982 seed corn order, up from 5.7% in 1979. Pioneer typically recorded sales as income when the customer took physical possession of the goods, not when the order was placed. Unopened bags of seed could be returned to Pioneer at any time for a full refund. Financing was provided independently by the farmer-dealer at his own risk.

During 1984 the average fifty-pound bag of Pioneer seed corn sold for approximately $70. Because seed typically represented less than 5% of a farmer's total costs, growers were willing to pay higher prices for genetically

---

EXHIBIT 18.6   **Sources of Hybrid Seed Corn in Iowa 1976–1982**

	% 1976	% 1979	% 1982
Farmer-dealer	97.1	96.8	93.5
Seed store	6.2	6.7	8.8
Direct from seed company	6.9	5.2	9.4
Elevator	6.5	4.9	6.8
Farm center	1.2	2.2	2.1
Co-op store	.5	.9	NA
Buying group	.9	.2	.8

SOURCE: *Wallace's Farmer* magazine, "1982 Seed Corn Soybean and Field Seed Survey Report."

engineered hybrids that achieve increased yields. U.S. farmers spent $3,993 million on seed during 1982, while fertilizer costs totaled $9,024 million.[21]

According to Dr. Donald Duvick, Pioneer's Vice-President—Research, seed corn varieties remained in use an average of seven years (nine years for soybeans) before gradual replacement by "seeds believed to be better for several reasons, including enhanced yields and resistance to disease."[22]

Results of the 1982 *Wallace's Farmer* magazine survey indicated that 89.9% of Iowa farmers selected seed primarily for its yield performance. (See Exhibit 18.7.) The introduction of a new, higher-yielding hybrid can therefore have a dramatic, long-term effect on sales. Analysts believed that the emphasis on disease resistance over increased yields by DeKalb-Pfizer Genetics, Pioneer's main competitor in hybrid corn, had cost DeKalb-Pfizer dearly in the marketplace. Yields consistently 5% higher than those provided by DeKalb allowed Pioneer to pull ahead by twenty market share points in the 1970s. Company-sponsored field tests in 1983 indicated that Pioneer seed outproduced the competition by 6.9 bushels per acre. However, independent tests performed by Iowa State University placed Pioneer seed corn first in only two of Iowa's seven agricultural districts. The highest yields in the other five districts were generated by Stauffer Seeds, Renze Hybrids, Wilson Hybrids, Crows Hybrids, and Lynnville Seeds. None of these, however, had the highest yield in more than one district.[23] Despite the university's findings, Pioneer brand corn and alfalfa seeds continued in 1982 to be Iowa's front runners in terms of market share at 62.9% and 17.0%, respectively. Pioneer's soybean seed ranked second in its share of the Iowa market at 17.7% compared to Northrup King's 25.4%. (Information is provided only on Iowa because it typically ranks first among the fifty states in terms of acres planted in corn, and provides approximately one-sixth of the total U.S. corn acreage in 1984.)

EXHIBIT 18.7

Factors Considered in the Purchase of Seed Corn in Iowa, 1976–1982

	% 1976	% 1979	% 1982
Corn performance	86.1	86.3	89.9
Company well known	23.1	20.7	21.9
Service is good	17.0	17.3	22.1
Dealer is friend	15.5	15.2	11.6
Price	13.4	12.5	17.2
University corn test	8.3	8.6	13.2
Private company research	NA	NA	9.3
Dealer widely known	6.0	6.3	5.4
Company sales incentive	NA	2.6	1.5

SOURCE: *Wallace's Farmer* magazine "1982 Seed Corn Soybean and Field Seed Survey Report."

Seed sales have tended to be highly seasonal. In past years, farmers placed their orders between July and December. During the 1980s, however, they have tended to delay their purchase decisions until August and sometimes were not fully committed until January.[24] During "Pioneer Days" each February, Pioneer dealers invited their customers for informal visits to settle their seed orders over a cup of coffee. At this time, early payment discounts encouraged customers to purchase and pick up seed for the following planting season.

Although the number of U.S. farms has been decreasing, the United States Statistical Reporting Service discovered an upward trend in average farm size from 420 acres in 1975 to 433 acres in 1982.[25] Larger farming operations tended to demand larger order volumes, special financing, and appointments for sales calls. Many analysts believed the days of informal, low-key marketing to be coming to an end.[26]

Until 1983 the agreement between Wallace and Garst had meant that the Garst Seed Company was Pioneer's exclusive distributor in western Iowa, Missouri, Colorado, Kansas, and Nebraska. With the termination of that agreement, Pioneer assumed complete control of the distribution of Pioneer brand products in the United States. In July 1982, Pioneer formed its Plains division with Kansas, Nebraska, and Colorado. The remaining ex-Garst territories of Missouri and western Iowa became the responsibility of the Central Division.

David Grieve, President of Pioneer's Plains Division, indicated in an interview that the total area formerly served by Garst represented 20.2% of the total U.S. corn acres in 1982. Pioneer's new Plains Division contained 12.2% of the U.S. corn acres in 1984. Nevertheless, recent water shortages, combined with the rising cost of energy needed to pump available irrigation water, are likely, according to Mr. Grieve, to result over the next decade in a gradual decline in acres devoted to corn in the Plains area. "Those acres will likely shift to more water-efficient crops such as sorghum and wheat," predicted Grieve.

In terms of overall market share, Pioneer's share of the U.S. market for its seed corn was approximately 35% in 1984. The next five companies' total share was slightly over 24%. The market shares of other seeds were, however, far below that of corn. The company estimated its share of the hybrid sorghum seed market in 1984 at half that of the leader. The branded wheat and soybean seed concept was new and ill-defined. Pioneer claimed a growing although not significant share of these growing markets.[27] Analysts estimated Pioneer's soybean market share at 3% compared to 10% by the leader, Asgrow Seeds. Overall, Pioneer captured a 12% share of the $5 billion seed market in 1984, compared to DeKalb-Pfizer Genetics' 4%.

Similarly, market shares of Pioneer's fledgling bacterial products and cotton seeds were not dramatic. Pioneer bowed out of hybrid cotton seed production in 1983, stating that "it appeared unlikely that (the market for premium cotton planting seed) would grow large enough to support the kind of commitments to research and production we make in our other seed products."[28] Cotton research expenditures for 1980–1983 had totaled $1,260,000.

The company's cattle-breeding operations had been sold in 1976. Management felt poor bull performance reflected negatively on Pioneer's seed corn business. Pioneer divested its thirty-year-old Hy-Line and Indian River poultry concerns for book value (about $13 million) in 1978.[29] Although poultry had been a major Wallace family concern, created by Henry Wallace and run by his son, the division had consistently lost money.

Pioneer's print-media advertising budget of $2,132,121 ranked it thirteenth among agricultural advertisers for 1983. The typical agricultural concern spent 42.1% of its advertising budget on print media. Pioneer employed radio and television spots, trade shows, point-of-purchase devices, cooperative advertising schemes, newspaper and business publication advertisements (see Exhibit 18.8 for an example), outdoor displays, direct mail, premiums, catalogs, and directories to advertise its products. Each August, Pioneer hosted "Expo Days," during which neighboring farmers gathered to examine first-hand the various hybrids planted in a local Pioneer test plot. This two- to three-day event enabled farmers to discuss the performance of various hybrids with their neighbors as well as with Pioneer personnel. It was not unusual for farmers to receive a hat or jacket with the familiar green Pioneer logo, either at this event or when seed was purchased from the local farmer-dealer.

Word-of-mouth has been extremely important in seed marketing, because seed stocks are largely bought on faith. Their real merit could not be judged until the crop was "in the bin." Pioneer management believed that "there is no better advertising and no better selling aid than good performance by the product. We spend much more on research to improve our products than we spend to advertise them in the conventional ways."[30]

RESEARCH AND DEVELOPMENT

In-house research and development efforts were given most of the credit for Pioneer's dominance in the seed corn industry. Over the last five years, Pioneer budgeted an average of 3.7% of sales for research. (See Exhibit 18.9.) The Plant Breeding Division had been established to conduct independent research in corn, sorghum, soybean, wheat, alfalfa, and sunflower breeding. Within the division, each crop had its own breeding department.

Improved stress tolerance has been a major contribution of Pioneer plant breeders. By reducing the effects of stress on plants, researchers have been able to develop hybrids and strains that are capable of increased yields under a variety of conditions. Specific resistance to plant diseases, parasites, and adverse weather have been bred into Pioneer's hybrids.

Modern biotechnology was expected to allow Pioneer's researchers to make rapid progress in stress tolerance. One of the Department of Biotechnology's major goals was to allow plant breeders to transfer desired genes

EXHIBIT 18.8   Example of Pioneer Hi-Bred International, Inc., Advertisement

Numbers you know...
Numbers you know you should try.

It happens almost every year. Just when you think Pioneer can't come out with new and better hybrids than the ones you planted last spring, they do. Next year is no exception. The best Pioneer® brand hybrids you can plant on your farm include some "old and familiar" numbers ... and some "brand new". Hybrids like these:

3978

A hybrid that northern corn growers have come to know and trust, because it offers yield and drydown advantages that few competitive corns in this maturity can beat. **3978** performs very well on your better soils, and on "slower" peat ground, too.

3881 NEW

This exciting, new hybrid is about the same maturity as 3978, but with even higher yield potential. Better stalks and roots, and very good head smut tolerance are other reasons why you'll want to make **3881** part of your "new generation" team of Pioneer® brand hybrids.

3803 NEW

A hybrid that's a lot like 3906 for strong, dependable agronomic traits, but with even faster field drydown. You'll especially like the extended kernel "fill" period that enables **3803** to make the most of the season. Push your populations to boost yields even more.

3906

A full-season hybrid with the defensive agronomic traits it takes to maintain top plant health, and the yield punch it takes to be the "backbone" of your corn program. **3906** has strong stalks and roots, and the ability to turn higher populations into extra yield.

The Limitation of Warranty and remedy appearing on the label is part of the terms of sale.

Pioneer is a brand name; numbers identify varieties. ®Registered trademark of Pioneer Hi-Bred International, Inc., Des Moines, Iowa, U.S.A.

SOURCE: *Farm Journal*, January 1985. Reprinted courtesy of Pioneer Hi-Bred International, Inc., Des Moines, Iowa.

EXHIBIT 18.9 **Pioneer's Research and Development Expenditures, 1980–1984**

(Dollar Amounts in Thousands)

PRODUCT	1980	1981	1982	1983	1984
Corn	$ 8,255	$ 9,635	$13,309	$15,859	$19,015
Sorghum	763	843	912	1,428	1,395
Wheat	832	956	1,160	1,754	2,110
Soybeans	641	843	1,041	1,780	2,109
Alfalfa	405	632	773	1,239	1,123
Cotton	245	280	314	421	0
Sunflowers	51	141	182	219	258
Computer Systems	645	547	529	733	843
Microbial Cultures	632	780	825	1,297	1,331
Total	$12,469	$14,657	$19,045	$24,730	$28,184

SOURCE: Pioneer Hi-Bred International, *1984 Annual Report* and *1982 Annual Report.*

directly into breeding material. This accomplishment could dramatically increase the rate of genetic selection.

In the Biotechnology Research Department, the Plant Breeding Division's newest unit, bioengineers worked to develop techniques for manipulating genes at the molecular level. Pioneer's scientists hoped to eventually move nitrogen-fixing genes from legume bacteria to corn, thus substantially reducing fertilizer requirements. However, this gene-splicing technique was considered by Pioneer to be a distant possibility.

The Corn Breeding Department, the largest subsection of the Plant Breeding Division, worked from twenty-five strategically located research stations. Each research station conducted location-specific yield tests at approximately fifteen outlying sites. Pioneer corn breeders continuously strove to develop hybrids that produced more harvestable bushels per acre than strains currently available.

A three-year study conducted by Pioneer researchers compared hybrids developed over the past fifty years with those in use in the 1980s. The study found annual yield improvements to average 1.4 bushels per acre. Modern hybrids were found to produce superior yields in both high- and low-fertility environments, yielding fifty more bushels per acre than the seed corn farmers planted fifty years ago.[31]

The goal of the Microbial Genetics Division in 1985 was to develop three new marketable products by 1987. This would bring to six the number of products in Pioneer's microbial genetics line. Silage and alfalfa inoculants and a bacterial digestive-tract treatment for livestock were already in Pioneer's product arsenal.

Gene splitting and microbial genetic research were becoming the targets of increasing controversy. Some public interest groups felt that mutant strains of potentially harmful organisms could result from attempts to develop organic herbicides and insecticides. While Pioneer lauded microbial genetic research as the newest tool whose application might result in advances even more exciting than those related to computer technology, some environmentalists feared that human-made genes could migrate and "create havoc."[32] Public opposition was successful in halting a major corn genetic research project at Stanford University. The University of Pennsylvania was in court in 1984 defending its right to perform genetically related experiments.

INTERNATIONAL ACTIVITIES

Through a network of subsidiaries, joint ventures, and independent distributors, Pioneer Overseas Corporation (POC) marketed Pioneer products in more than sixty countries outside North America. The majority of POC business in 1984 involved hybrid corn and sorghum seeds. In 1983, international sales contributed $18.7 million (24%) of total pre-tax income, a significant increase from a 10% contribution in 1982. In 1984, POC enjoyed an 8% increase in dollar sales and a 17% increase in unit sales over those of 1983. Nevertheless, the 1984 pre-tax contribution declined because of the relative strength of the dollar in international trade and abnormally high production costs due to the 1983 drought. Total unit sales of corn seed outside North America rose by 3% in 1984 over 1983; most of the increase came from Latin America. Nearly two-thirds of Pioneer's international sales were made in Europe. Although Asia's sales accounted for less than 5% of Pioneer's overseas sales, future growth in Asian corn seed demand was expected to grow as Oriental diets began to include more grain-fed meats.

Dr. William L. Brown, past Chairman of Pioneer, summarized Pioneer's situation in international activities in a 1984 speech to stockholders:

> Over the years the principal foreign markets for our products have been identified, effective and dedicated organizations are now in place in most of those marketing areas and breeding programs in areas where U.S. hybrids are not adapted are beginning to generate superior products.[33]

Nevertheless, in 1985, Pioneer was not as strong internationally as it was in North America.

COMPETITION

Traditionally, other than two to three major corporations the U.S. seed corn market has been the province of small, family-controlled companies. Nearly all of the 600-member companies of the American Seed Trade Association had sales in the range of $3 million to $10 million annually.[34] The lifeblood of these small firms was the propagation and sale of seeds developed by university and government experiment stations. These small, private seed companies conducted little to no research on their own. The industry's complexion, nevertheless, was changing.

In the last decade, more than 100 of these smaller companies have been acquired by large chemical and drug conglomerates with enormous research budgets. Developments in biotechnology have meant that instead of planting seeds and selecting those with desirable characteristics, scientists can now identify those traits in test tubes. "It takes 12 years to develop a classically bred variety; we think we can do the same thing (with biotechnology) in six years," predicted James E. Windish, director of Monsanto's plant-sciences business group.[35]

In place of the independent, family-owned seed companies, the industry has been consolidating behind giants like Monsanto, Sandoz, Celanese, and Ciba-Geigy. (See Exhibit 18.10.) Ownership of plant materials vital to the development of new strains has been attracting these bioresearch giants to private seed companies. Perhaps more important, the established hybrid companies occupied the front lines of the seed business. Without the channels provided by such experienced firms, the production, field testing, and marketing of new hybrids would be difficult for an acquiring company to perform.

L. William Teweles, seed company broker, predicted in 1984 that the

---

EXHIBIT 18.10   **Seed Companies and Their Parents**

SEED COMPANY	PARENT ORGANIZATION
Asgrow O's Gold	Upjohn
Burpee	ITT
Harris	Celanese
Trojan Dekalb	Pfizer
Blaney Farms Prairie Valley	Stauffer
Ferry Morse	Purex
ACCO	Cargill
Jacques Keystone	Agrigenetics
Funk Seeds International Louisiana Ring Around Products	Ciba-Geigy (Switzerland)
Northrup King	Sandoz (Switzerland)
Wilson Hybrids	LaFarge Coppee (France)
DeKalb Wheat Jacob Hart Soybeans	Monsanto
Lynnville Seeds	Lubrizol

major food companies would also begin snapping up smaller seed companies as a means to produce and test improved hybrids of grains used in common food products. Most new entrants were enchanted by Pioneer's profit margins approaching 30% in corn. They recognized it as the industry leader in marketing and research. Teweles estimated that varieties produced by new genetic techniques would add $6.8 billion in sales to the industry by the end of the century.[36]

Commenting on the influx of multinational chemical companies into the seed industry, Pat R. Mooney, author of *Seeds of the Earth,* remarked, "Certainly the distribution mechanism for seeds and crop chemicals are the same and companies might be tempted to advertise the two products in package deals for farmers."[37] Pioneer's Dr. Duvick, Vice-President—Research, countered, "I doubt if such packages will ever be practical. Farmers are too individualistic to accept a complete package as long as they are free to choose."[38] Nevertheless, marketing efforts by seed-selling multinationals were becoming intense. Of 1983's top five seed advertisers, four were global conglomerates: Monsanto, Upjohn, Ciba-Geigy, and Stauffer. The fifth was Pioneer.[39]

Occidental Petroleum had planned to introduce the first hybrid cotton seed (and a hybrid rice seed it had received from the Chinese government during oil drilling negotiations) through its Ring Around Products subsidiary.[40] However, Ciba-Geigy's Funk Seeds International purchased the Dallas-based Ring Around Products in December 1984 to complement its new $7 million plant science and technology research facility in North Carolina.

Upjohn's operations combined agricultural chemicals with hybrid seed marketing in 105 countries of the world. Upjohn recently purchased O's Gold Seeds of Parkersburg, Iowa, to augment the pea, bean, sweet corn, field corn, sorghum, and soybean seed operations of its Asgrow Seed Company.

Stauffer Chemical's agricultural operations accounted for 16% of its $1,505.7 million in total sales for 1984. Stauffer continued to streamline its seed business through the consolidation of manufacturing and sales operations.

Mr. James Ansorge, Financial Relations Manager for Pioneer, denied in an interview feeling any widespread competitive pressure from these major corporations. He believed their entry into the industry was too recent and that they had too narrow a range of products to pose any immediate nationwide threat. Pioneer executives were aware, however, that the major attack, if and when it came, would be launched in the lucrative Midwestern Corn Belt market.

THE PIONEER-GARST "DIVORCE"

On May 18, 1983, Garst Seed Company and Pioneer Hi-Bred International issued a joint public statement. It read:

Following the settlement, both companies will compete with one another. Pioneer will begin serving all of the area heretofore served by Garst; Garst intends to expand the area in which it operates. In the future Garst will be offering for sale its own brands of product produced from other than Pioneer breeding material.[41]

Thus ended the cooperative relationship forged by a Henry Wallace/Roswell Garst handshake fifty-three years before.

When Pioneer became publicly held in 1973, the company's outlook on profit and control changed. Henry Wallace had died in 1963. The Board felt that Garst's market share in the lucrative Western Corn Belt of Western Iowa, Missouri, Colorado, Kansas, and Nebraska, was not increasing as rapidly as was Pioneer's in the rest of the nation. Upon Roswell Garst's death in 1977, Pioneer's management voted to terminate the unwritten distributor agreement with Garst at Pioneer's June 17, 1977, meeting. (The Wallace-Garst handshake had been made into a written contract in 1932. A new agreement was signed in 1940; when it lapsed in 1955, the two companies continued the relationship with no written contract in force.)

The Garst & Thomas Seed Company (Roswell Garst and Charles Thomas teamed up in the mid-1930s) was Pioneer's only distributor. Garst & Thomas regularly sold about 20% of all Pioneer's corn and grew 1.5% of Pioneer's seed. Alone, it was the third largest corn dealer in the country. The decades-old arrangement called for Garst to pay Pioneer a 7% royalty on all Pioneer seed produced, sold, and delivered by Garst (not to exceed half of Garst's net profits) and to reimburse Pioneer for the cost of parent seed production. In 1981, Pioneer netted $1.94 on each bag of hybrid corn seed sold by Garst, while Pioneer salesmen brought in profits of $7.88 per bag.[42] Pioneer's Board, citing smaller profit margins on the 20% of Pioneer's market held by Garst and diverging management styles of the two firms, signed a letter of intent with Garst & Thomas Seed Company on October 13, 1980, outlining Pioneer's offer to buy Garst & Thomas for $18 million.

The situation changed in 1982 when the Garst family bought out the Thomases for $24.5 million. Disturbed by the loss of the Thomas family's stabilizing influence and by a lack of progress in the sales talks, Pioneer's CEO, Thomas Urban, served the new Garst Seed Company with an ultimatum on August 31, 1981: "You are hereby notified that the relationship which has existed between us is terminated as of August 31, 1983. Please take notice and govern yourselves accordingly."[43] Despite the prior sales agreement, Pioneer would not deliver products to the new Garst Seed Co. after August 31, 1983. The Garsts responded with an April 9, 1982, request for an injunction to forbid Pioneer from terminating the relationship, claiming that (1) Garst could not survive without Pioneer seed stock, (2) no good reason existed for termination, and (3) ten years, not two, was a reasonable period to allow Garst to develop its own parent seed stock. If the injunction were to be denied, Garst sought $140 million in damages. Pioneer soon responded with an injunction of its own.

Pioneer management discovered that 125 bags of proprietary parent seed had been removed from the Garst Seed Co. warehouses and stored in the basement of David Garst's residence. During the course of courtroom testimony, it became clear that the Garsts planted the 125 bags, not to produce more hybrid seed as agreed, but to create more parent stock. Pioneer filed suit on July 25, 1982, for the return of any parent inbreds in Garst's possession. Because corn reproduced itself 200 times each season, the 125 bags of seed could produce 25,000 bags of parent corn. With 25,000 bags of parent seed, Garst could harvest as much hybrid seed as Pioneer could, and have parents left in reserve.

In fighting the injunction, Garst claimed partnership with Pioneer, and cited their long history together, plus Garst's participation in Pioneer's research and testing, aid to Pioneer's sorghum program, and investment of $250 million earned from the sale of its Oklahoma sales group to Pioneer, allegedly in return for the right to sell the resulting wheat seed.

In a marathon hearing, Judge Thomas Smith of Carroll County, Iowa District Court, denied the Garst injunction request after sixty-four days and 10,000 pages of testimony. Judge Smith ruled that "Pioneer should not be forced to deal with a company that has said it wants to become a major competitor. An injunction continuing the relationship would be impossible to enforce because of the level of ill feelings between the Garsts and Pioneer." The judge further ordered the return of any and all "kidnapped" Pioneer genetic plant material in the Garsts' possession, claiming they had "acted with unclean hands" in retaining the parent seed.[44]

Before the suits and countersuits could be brought to trial, however, Garst and Pioneer issued their joint statement resolving the issue. The resolution outlined the following points: (1) Garst was terminated as Pioneer's distributor; (2) Garst agreed to return all plant-breeding material to Pioneer; (3) after the Spring 1983 season, Garst could no longer produce Pioneer seed but might sell any leftover Pioneer seed corn, sorghum, and wheat under the Garst name until July 1, 1985; and (4) Garst must pay service charges to Pioneer for any retained inventory.[45]

The battle moved out of the courts and into the marketplace. Chairman Urban commented that "the full impact of the change in distribution won't be felt until fiscal 1985."[46] Garst lost eighteen out of thirty-two sales managers to Pioneer soon after the breakup. Garst, vowing to position itself as the number two seed corn producer, increased its print advertising budget by 97%, to $349,681 and began recruiting sales representatives in earnest.[47] Garst established six research centers, including one on Oahu, Hawaii, where it was growing three generations of breeding material per year. Research headquarters were under construction in 1985 in Slater, Iowa. Garst signed a breeding material sharing agreement with Coop de Pau, Europe's third largest seed corn company, and it purchased Clyde Black and Son Seeds to obtain its proprietary lines. Garst described its research program as "one of the largest and most productive in the industry."[48]

BREEDERS' RIGHTS

According to former-Chairman Brown, less developed nations have accused the major seed companies of collecting the world's plant genetic resources mainly from third world countries, storing these resources in the form of seeds in gene banks in the developed countries, and refusing to make them available to the developing nations from which they originally came. It has further been alleged that the seed companies took unfair advantage of the third world through their use of plant patents, plant breeders' rights, and the private exploitation of improved varieties of plants.[49] Those making the accusations demanded the free exchange of plant genetic material, regardless of breeders' rights, a development that could quickly bankrupt the seed companies. Although this movement was not a large one in 1984, support appeared to be growing throughout the less developed countries of the world.

This disregard for breeders' rights was bemoaned by Dr. Brown. "There was a time when the proprietary nature of lines and hybrids was respected by the competitor. This seems no longer to be true."[50] Chairman Urban echoed this concern as he pointed out a "rather peculiar turn in the competition in the seed corn business. We are selling against corn hybrids that look amazingly like those we have developed. The 'lookalike' problem has been building over the past five years or so."[51] The 1970 Plant Variety Protection Law provided some recourse against lookalike seeds, but techniques for identifying germ plasm had yet to be legally recognized.

OTHER FACTORS AFFECTING THE HYBRID SEED INDUSTRY

The hybrid seed corn market was relatively mature in 1985. Growth came only from increases in the number of corn acres planted. The government's policy has had a profound effect on crop acreage in recent years. One such effect stemmed from the 1983 Payment in Kind (PIK) program. In return for idling a portion of their cropland, farmers were paid with government surplus corn and wheat. Part of a broad acreage-reduction strategy, PIK sought to reduce agricultural surplus while increasing farm income. So successful was this strategy that corn acreage planted fell 27% in 1983. (See Exhibit 18.11.) Pioneer strongly supported the acreage reduction policy as being beneficial to the American farmer, although the resulting drop in corn plantings reduced Pioneer's profits 39%.

In addition to government policy, commodity prices, energy and fertilizer supplies, plant diseases, and, of course, the weather all influence the hybrid seed industry's profitability. In 1983, drought nearly doubled Pioneer's seed production costs and reduced seed production to 47% of normal. September 1984 freezes damaged a portion of that year's crop.

A doubling of per capita high-fructose corn sweetener consumption (see Exhibit 18.12), spurred by the recent switch from sugar to 100% corn sweetener in major soft drink formulations, and expanding production of ethanol for fuel use, provided incentives for corn growers. The federal tax

25. *Agriculture Yearbook* (Washingto partment of Agriculture), p. 381.

26. "De Kalb-Pfizer Genetics Works t *Agri Marketing* (January 1983).

27. *1983 Annual Report,* Pioneer Hi-l Inc., p. 24.

28. *Ibid.*, p. 4.

29. "A Sustained Harvest," *Forbes* (p. 122.

30. *The Long Look* (Des Moines, Iow International, Inc., 1981), pp. 3–4.

31. *Pioneer in Applied Genetics* (Des oneer Hi-Bred International, Inc., 1983),

32. P. A. Bellew, "Agricultural Res Noticed, Grows Controversial," *Wall Stre* ber 21, 1984), pp. 1, 17.

33. "Remarks of Thomas N. Urban ɛ Brown," Annual Shareholders Meeting (F ternational, Inc., January 24, 1984), p. 1ɛ

34. "The Biotech Big Shots Snapping ι panies," *Business Week* (June 11, 1984), |

35. *Ibid.*

36. *Ibid.*

37. G. Anthan, "Multinational Corpo into Seed Business," *Des Moines Register*

38. *Ibid.*

39. "Top 150 Print Advertisers over *Agri Marketing* (December 1983), p. 40.

EXHIBIT 18.11

Planted Acreage of Selected U.S. Crops
(In Millions of Acres)

YEAR	CORN	WHEAT	SOYBEANS	SORGHUM
1975	78.7	74.9	54.6	18.1
1976	84.6	80.4	50.3	18.1
1977	84.3	75.4	59.0	16.6
1978	81.7	66.0	64.7	16.2
1979	81.4	71.4	71.6	15.3
1980	84.0	80.6	70.0	15.6
1981	84.2	88.9	67.8	16.0
1982	81.9	87.3	71.5	16.1
1983	60.1	76.8	63.5	11.8
1984	81.8	82.6	65.2	14.8

SOURCE: United States Department of Agriculture, Crop Reporting Board.

credit for refiners who mixed alcohol with their gasoline increased from 50 to 60 cents per gallon of alcohol on January 1, 1985.[52] In addition, tariffs on imported fuel alcohol increased to 63 cents per gallon.

Although farm prices were depressed and farm exports suffered from the strong dollar, Pioneer's Urban predicted permanent surpluses in U.S. grain bins. He estimated that research will provide average yields of 145 bushels per acre by the year 2000, an increase of 26% over yields achieved in 1982.[53]

U.S. agricultural policy in the 1980s focused on the use of price supports and acreage reductions to offset excess supply. However, economists and

EXHIBIT 18.12

U.S. Per Capita Consumption of Corn Sweeteners
(In Pounds)

YEAR	HIGH-FRUCTOSE	GLUCOSE	DEXTROSE	TOTAL
1974	3.0	17.2	4.9	25.1
1975	5.0	17.5	5.0	27.5
1976	7.2	17.5	5.0	29.7
1977	9.5	17.6	4.1	31.2
1978	12.1	17.8	3.8	33.7
1979	14.9	17.9	3.6	36.4
1980	19.2	17.6	3.5	40.3
1981	23.3	17.8	3.5	44.6
1982	26.7	18.0	3.5	48.2

SOURCE: U.S. Department of Agriculture.

consı
incre
with
beco
begu
1985.
coulc
wors
Farm
farm
Th
begu
impr
to pr
suppe
to ma
survi
and r
Pione
most

1. *Pioneer in Applied Genetics*
oneer Hi-Bred International, Inc., 19

2. *Grains: Production, Processir*
Ill: Board of Trade, 1977), pp. 14–1!

3. "The Biotech Big Shots Snapp
panies," *Business Week* (June 11, 19!

4. C. H. Davenport, "Sowing the
2, 1981), pp. 9–10, 33.

5. *The Long Look* (Des Moines,
International, Inc., 1981), p. 3.

6. "A Sustained Harvest," *Forl*
pp. 120, 122.

7. *The Value Line Investment Su*
p. 1493.

8. "Seed Corn's Long, Hot, Brui
Week (August 25, 1980), pp. 52–56.

9. *Ibid.*

10. *1984 Annual Report,* Pioneer
Inc., p. 6.

11. "Remarks of Thomas N. Urk
Brown," Annual Shareholders Meetir
ternational, Inc., January 24, 1984), |

12. The information on Pioneer'ː
was taken from *Leaders of Pioneer* (
oneer Hi-Bred International, Inc., 19

CASE 19

Xerox Corporation: Proposed Diversification

J. DAVID HUNGER · THOMAS CONQUEST · WILLIAM MILLER

In the autumn of 1982, David Kearns was facing some difficult problems as the new Chief Executive Officer of the Xerox Corporation. His company had recently posted a 39% drop in third quarter earnings. This was Xerox's fourth quarterly decline in a row and the picture didn't appear any brighter for the current quarter. Much of the profit decline had been attributed to narrow profit margins brought on by steep price-cutting on many copier models in response to increasing competition, especially from the Japanese. In addition, profits had been reduced by the severance costs of trimming its work force; by the strength of the dollar, which eroded the dollar values of sales made abroad; and particularly, by the sluggish economy. Xerox had been forced to reduce its work force by 2,174 in 1981, down to 120,981 people worldwide. This was the first such reduction in the company's history. Further reductions occurred in 1982 and more were predicted for the coming year. Kearns had watched Xerox's share of the plain paper copier market slip from 95% in the early 1970s to about 45% in 1982. In addition, Xerox stock, which had traded for as high as $172 in 1972, was selling for less than $40 in 1982.

Xerox's attempt to lessen its dependence on the competitive copier market, by moving into the broader office-automation arena, had proved less than spectacular. The Office Products Division has had only one profitable quarter in its seven-year history and racked up losses last year totaling approximately $90 million. Kearns recently admitted to analysts that he did not expect the unit to be profitable until 1984.[1] The division had recently been reorganized in an attempt to more effectively deal with some of these problems. Shortly after the reorganization, however, two of the key executives of the Office Products Division resigned to form their own company. Industry reaction to these resignations and Xerox's proposed acquisition of an insurance company has given rise to reports that Xerox may be somewhat less than enthusiastic about the office-automation marketplace and its strategies to garner a piece of the market.

This case was prepared by Professor J. David Hunger, Thomas Conquest, and William Miller of the College of Business, Iowa State University, Ames, Iowa as a basis for class discussion rather than to illustrate either effective or ineffective organizational practices. Copyright © 1984 by J. David Hunger. Presented at the 1984 Workshop of the Midwest Society for Case Research. This case also appears in C. F. Douds (ed.), *Annual Advances in Business Cases, 1984* (Chicago: Midwest Case Writers Association, 1983), pp. 203-242 and *Journal of Management Case Studies,* Vol. I, No. 1 (Spring 1985), pp. 13-35. Reprinted by permission.

Wall Street analysts were puzzled over Xerox's recent offer to acquire Crum & Forster, an insurance holding company, for about $1.65 billion in cash and securities. The proposed acquisition thrusts Xerox, with a mixed record in diversification efforts, into the property-casualty insurance field, where it has no experience. Kearns has defended the proposed acquisition by saying that it could eventually produce a lot of cash, which Xerox needs to support its vigorous research efforts in its core businesses. He maintained that Xerox's entry into the insurance business would not alter its commitment to the office-automation market, nor would it sap resources from Xerox's basic business.[2] Some analysts felt, however, that the acquisition might have been a defensive move to counter a rumored offer by GTE in late summer 1982 to acquire Xerox Corporation. The offer had apparently been made on a very quiet, friendly basis. The mere presence of such an offer, nevertheless, might have prompted top management to more seriously consider making itself less attractive to an acquiring firm by diversifying out of the high-tech industry and by taking on more debt.[3]

HISTORY

Xerography, from the Greek words for "dry" and "writing," is basically a process that uses static electricity to make copies instantly on plain paper. Every office worker today takes it for granted, but it took Chester Carlson, a patent attorney and amateur physicist, several years of dabbling in his kitchen to discover the fundamental principles of what he called "electrophotography." By 1927 he had enough of a process to patent it, and he set up a small lab behind a beauty parlor in Astoria, Long Island, to pursue his experiments. His breakthrough came on October 22, 1938, when he duplicated a glass slide on which he had written: "10-22-38 ASTORIA."

Selling his process was more difficult and frustrating than inventing it. During the next six years Carlson was turned down by more than twenty companies, including such notables as IBM, RCA, and General Electric. Finally, in 1944, the Battelle Memorial Institute, a nonprofit research organization in Columbus, Ohio, became interested. It signed a royalty-sharing contract with Carlson and began to develop the process. In 1947 Battelle entered into an agreement with a small photographic paper company in Rochester, New York, called Haloid, giving the company the right to develop an "electrophotography" machine. Chester Carlson joined Haloid as a consultant.

Haloid's president, Joseph C. Wilson, had grown up with the business. His grandfather had been one of the company's founders in 1906, and his father had worked for the firm from the start. As Haloid and Battelle continued to develop electrophotography, Wilson decided that the process needed a more distinctive name. A Greek scholar from Ohio State University suggested "xeros" (dry) and "graphien" (writing) to form the word "xerography." The machine itself, they decided, would be called Xerox.

Haloid introduced its first copier in 1949, but it was slow and complicated. Haloid found the early models to be better for making lithography masters than for copying documents, but management was sure they were on the right track. In 1958, they changed the name of the company to Haloid Xerox, and in 1959 the firm marketed the first dependable, easy-to-use document copier. The 914 copier, so named because it could copy sheets as large as 9 × 14 inches, was very successful, and within three years the company was ranked among the FORTUNE 500. In 1961, management changed the name of the company to Xerox.

Between 1959, when Xerox introduced the world's first convenient office copier, and 1974, its sales exploded from $33 million a year to $3.6 billion; its profits mushroomed from $2 million to $331 million; and the price of its stock soared from $2 a share to $172. The company had grown by 100 times in fifteen years. In that same short period, photocopying machines dramatically transformed the nature of office work. Xerography made carbon paper and mimeograph machines obsolete and drastically reduced typing time. By year-end 1970, Xerox held a dominant position in the world-wide office plain-paper copier marketplace with more than a 95% share of the market.

This monopolistic market share was seriously eroded in the 1970s because of increased competition from many sources. Xerox had built its business by creating the plain-paper copying market and then protecting it with a solid wall of patents, a classic entry barrier to keep out competition. In 1975, however, the company signed a consent decree with the Federal Trade Commission. The decree forced Xerox to license other companies wanting to use its process. The seventeen-year patent protection was also expiring and Xerox's technology could be used by anyone. Recognizing the mature state of the reprographics industry, Xerox has positioned itself, through both horizontal and vertical integration, to become a major competitor in the *Office of the Future* marketplace. In 1981, Xerox executives stated to stockholders in the company's annual report that the overriding corporate objective over the next decade is to be one of the leading companies in providing productivity to the office. "In order to accomplish this," asserted top management, "Xerox must maintain and strengthen its position of leadership in reprographics—as we refer to our total copying and duplicating business—*and* emerge from the 1980's as a leading systems company that is a major factor in automating the office."[4]

MANAGEMENT

David T. Kearns, who had served previously as President and Chief Operating Officer of Xerox, succeeded C. Peter McColough as Chief Executive Officer in May 1982. McColough, who had joined Xerox in 1954 and served as chief executive since 1968, continued as Chairman of the Board. Other key executives and related information are shown in Exhibit 19.1. Xerox's top management has generally been promoted from within. Outside help

EXHIBIT 19.1   Xerox Corporation: 1982 Top Management

NAME	TITLE	YEARS WITH XEROX	JOBS PRIOR TO XEROX	EXPERTISE
D. T. Kearns*	Chief Executive Officer	11	IBM: Vice-President of Data Processing	Marketing
W. F. Glavin*	Executive Vice-President	12	IBM: Vice-President Operations	Operations
W. F. Souders*	Executive Vice-President	18		Marketing
J. V. Titsworth*	Executive Vice-President	3	Control Data: Executive Vice-President, Systems	
M. H. Antonini	Group Vice-President	7	Eltra Corp., Group Vice-President	Operations
			Kaiser Jeep International, Vice-President	
R. D. Firth	Group Vice-President	13	IBM: Various Positions	Personnel
M. Howard*	Senior Vice-President, Chief Financial Officer	12	Shoe Corp. of America, Vice-President	Finance
F. J. Pipp	Group Vice-President	11	Ford Motor Co.	Manufacturing
R. M. Pippitt*	Senior Vice-President	21		Marketing
R. S. Banks	Vice-President & General Counsel	15	E. I. Dupont, Attorney	Legal Affairs
E. K. Damon	Vice-President & Secretary	33		Accounting
S. B. Ross	Vice-President & Controller	16	Macmillan Publishing Co., C.P.A. Harris, Kerr & Forster, Accountant	Finance
J. S. Crowley*	Executive Vice-President	5	McKinsey & Co., Sr. Partner and Director	Administration
J. E. Goldman*	Senior Vice-President	14	Ford Motor Co.	Engineering

SOURCE: Xerox *Form 10-K Annual Report,* 1981.

*Also serve on the Board of Directors.

has been recruited when the company has had to deal with significant changes in strategy or the introduction of new products.

There are nineteen directors on the Xerox board, eight of whom are officers of the corporation. The eleven outside directors include a retired Executive Vice-President of Xerox, two university professors (one from Europe), the Chairman of the Board of Prudential Insurance, a retired Chairman of American Express, the President of the Children's Television Workshop, a Managing Director of Deutsch Bank AG, the Chairman of an investment firm, a President of a university, and two partners in a Washington-based law firm. Together, the corporation's directors and officers own about 1% of the common stock of the firm.

The corporation introduced an executive long-term incentive plan in 1976 under which approximately 5.4 million shares of common stock have been reserved for issue. In December 1981, the Board of Directors amended the plan to provide for the issuance of incentive stock options as defined in the Economic Recovery Tax Act of 1981. Under the plan, eligible employees may be granted incentive stock rights, incentive stock options, non-qualified stock options, stock appreciation rights, and performance unit rights. Performance rights entitle the employee to receive the value of the performance unit in cash, in shares of common stock, or a combination of the two at the company's discretion. The value of a performance unit is determined by a formula based upon the achievement of specific performance goals. Performance unit rights are payable at the end of a five-year award period.

BUSINESS SEGMENTS

Although Xerox Corporation is organized around a set of groups and divisions, it primarily defines itself in terms of its various businesses. Xerox's principal business segment is reprographics, consisting of the development, manufacture, and marketing of xerographic copiers and duplicators, electronic printing systems, and providing related service. Another significant segment is paper, consisting primarily of the distribution of paper related to reprographic products. The other business segments include electric typewriters, word processors, small computers, facsimile transceivers, toner and other supplies, and publishing education-related materials. Estimated revenues and profits for each product line are shown in Exhibit 19.2.

Reprographics

Xerox manufactures and markets reprographic equipment for lease or purchase. Leasing accounted for over 55% of the company's revenues in 1981. The revenues and profits from this segment depend principally on the number of units of xerographic equipment leased and the usage of these units. In 1981, the Reprographics segment accounted for 72% of revenues.

Copiers

Copying machines have been and still are the largest segment of Xerox's business. However, Xerox has experienced problems in this segment over the past few years. Increased competition from IBM and Kodak in the medium-volume market and Japan in the lower-volume market has significantly decreased Xerox's market share. Competing now with 40 companies selling at least 240 different models, Xerox's share of the plain-paper copier industry in the United States has dropped from 67% to 43% over the past

EXHIBIT 19.2

Xerox Corporation: Estimated Revenues, Operating Profit, and Operating Margins by Product Line, 1981

(Dollar Amounts in Millions)

PRODUCT LINE	REVENUES	OPERATING PROFIT	OPERATING MARGIN (%)
Copiers			
Rentals	$4,805	$ —	—
Sales	1,135	—	—
Paper & supplies	795	—	—
Total	6,735	1,400	20.8
Office products			
Word processing & small computers	310	(22)	—
Facsimile	95	11	11.6
Total	405	(11)	—
Peripherals			
Printing	125	(15)	—
Xerox computer services	90	10	11.1
Shugart	200	25	12.5
Century data	110	10	9.1
Diablo	130	13	10.0
Versatec	75	7	9.3
Kurzweil	5	0.5	10.0
Total	735	50.5	6.9
Other products			
Publishing	320	30	9.4
WUI	175	26	14.9
Other	310	25	8.1
Total	805	81	10.1
TOTAL	$8,680	1,520.5	17.5

SOURCE: *Xerox: A Strategic Analysis* (New York: Northern Business Information, Inc., 1982), p. 6.

five years. The market, however, has grown in terms of total revenues from $2.8 billion in 1976 to $7.5 billion in 1981. Competitors imported more than a million units into the country in 1981. Analysts expected this number to increase by 50% in 1982.[5] Xerox faces similar competition worldwide. Current estimates of market share data are presented in Exhibit 19.3.

"We really should have been thinking about the market on a much broader basis," says Kearns.[6] Xerox ignored the low-cost, coated-paper copier that

EXHIBIT 19.3

Xerox Corporation: Estimated Copier Revenues and Market Share by Geographic Area, 1981

AREA	MARKET SIZE	XEROX REVENUES (MILLIONS OF $)	XEROX MARKET SHARE
U.S.	7,350	$3,160	43%
Europe	4,900	2,200	45%
Japan	1,510	620	41%
Canada	725	410	56%
Other	—	525	—

SOURCE: *Xerox: A Strategic Analysis* (New York: Northern Business Information, Inc., 1982), p. 79.

dominated the world copier market before Xerox introduced the first plain-paper copier. But the coated-paper copiers served a market much larger than anyone knew. Xerox has clearly fought back to regain some if its lost market share. It has cut prices on its lower-volume models, concentrating on cutting costs to improve profit margins, and decentralizing the management of the reprographics group to enable managers more timely and market-oriented decision-making. Two desktop copiers, the 2350 and 2830, were introduced in 1982 with a selling price of around $3,500 each. A new line of low- and medium-volume copiers will be introduced in January 1983 labeled the "10" series. These copiers will be imported from Fuji Xerox Co. in Japan. "If you can't beat 'em, join 'em," states Peter McColough.[7] To help lower costs, Xerox will also bring in parts and subassemblies from the Japanese affiliate. Production of the new 10 series costs between 40% and 50% less than earlier machines.

Another technique used by Xerox to stay competitive is called "competitive benchmarking." This means looking carefully at the lowest priced competing copier, determining exactly how it is being produced for less, and developing a plan to make and sell a competitive product.

In large copiers, Xerox still dominates the industry with a 70% market share. This is due mainly to Xerox's large and experienced sales and service staff. Japanese companies currently lack extensive service support and are not seen to offer Xerox much competition in the high-priced copier market in the near future. Xerox has many models in this market with high output rates and sorting capabilities. Prices range from $25,000 to $125,000.

In a maturing market with high competition, Xerox management realizes that the copier segment will not provide growing profits in the long run as the company would like. This realization underlies the company's diversification into office automation. Eugene C. Glazer of Dean Witter Reynolds states, "Eventually the company won't make it if they have to depend only on copiers."[8] In the company's annual report, David Kearns notes, "To continue to succeed in the face of strong competition, Xerox must undergo major and lasting change." Robert D. Firth, however, President of the Reprographics group, maintains, "Our copier business is and will remain the main business of Xerox for the projectable future."[9]

Electronic Printing

Listed under Peripherals in Exhibit 19.2, this segment became a dominant product line in 1977, with the introduction of the 9700 electronic printer. Until March 1982, the electronic-printing segment reported to U.S. copier operations in Rochester. Now established as the Printing Systems Division, it reports directly to corporate headquarters in Stamford, Connecticut. The traditional computer-printout method has been impact printing, with ink ribbons and mechanical printing heads on 11 × 17-inch fan-fold computer paper. Although this printing serves many purposes, Xerox management believes that for periodic reports, forms, proposals, or other information stored on electronic computer data files, non-bulky and clear printouts would be a better alternative. With its electronic printer, Xerox has combined computer technology, lasers, and xerography to design a printer that can print exceptionally clear text on standard 8½ × 11-inch paper. In addition, this printer can print graphics, which cannot be done on most traditional printers, and it has multiple copy and sorting capabilities as well. Xerox management sees electronic printing as playing a large role in the company's future. Customers seem to agree. Jack Jones, Vice-President of the Southern Railway System, states that "the quality of the print is such that everybody is enthusiastic about the smaller page."[10]

In 1980 Xerox developed the 5700 printing system. Priced at $66,000, this unit is designed to be used in an office environment, whereas the 9700 is geared more toward a computer room. The 5700 has the same basic technology as the 9700, but is extremely easy to use and has a touch-control screen to eliminate operator confusion. It can also be connected to Xerox's Ethernet network system, which can link a printer to various word processors or computer terminals on the network. A lower-priced model with many of the same features as the 9700 and 5700 has been released on a limited basis. The 2700, priced at $19,000, is marketed for the small business that can't afford some of the more expensive models.

Xerox has approximately 40% of the global market for electronic printing—slightly behind IBM, with Honeywell a distant third in market share. The market in electronic printing may soon be crowded with heavy competition from Japanese companies, such as Canon and Fujitsu. It is also a market in which new technology can change things drastically. Ink-jet printing and heat-transfer processes are already being considered as printing alternatives.

Currently, electronic printing accounts for only 15% of the $8.7 billion computer-printing market. Predictions for electronic printing are for a $5.8

billion market by 1986. According to Robert Adams, president of Xerox's Printing Systems Division, "The majority of information generated from host computers and word processors will someday be produced by electronic printers."[11] Although Xerox revenues in 1981 from electronic printing were estimated at $125 million by Northern Business Information, Inc., a New York-based research firm, the newly established Printing Systems Division was hoping for $300 million in revenues in 1982 and $2 billion annually in revenues by 1987.[12]

Office Products

The Office Products Division (responsible for electronic typewriters, word processors, and facsimile telecopiers) and the Office Systems Division manufacture and market information processing equipment for use in the *Office of the Future*. Although office products accounted for only 10% of the company's revenues in 1981, the commitment was made several years ago to steer Xerox away from a copier-only company to an information company capable of supplying many types of office information and equipment. Current estimates of market share data for both divisions are provided in Exhibit 19.4.

The 860 Information Processing System, first marketed in 1979, is a word-processing workstation with full text-editing capability. It is medium priced and designed for use by professional and clerical personnel. It has limited programming capability. Xerox introduced its 8010 Star Professional workstation in 1981 for a price of $17,000. It is designed for use by managers and professionals to perform word and data processing tasks with a minimum of training. Its ease of use makes it very desirable for the preparation of presentations and reports.

In 1981, the 820 Information Processor was developed to service a broad range of needs. It can be used as a limited professional workstation for small businesses that cannot afford the Star. It can also be used as a business

EXHIBIT 19.4 **Xerox Corporation: Estimated Office Products Revenues and Market Share by Geographic Area, 1981**
(Dollar Amounts in Millions)

SEGMENT	U.S. MARKET SIZE	U.S. XEROX SHARE	XEROX REVENUES		
			U.S.	International	Total
Word processing	1,386	13%	180	115	295
Facsimile telecopiers	165	30%	50	45	95
Small business systems	1,300	1%	10	5	15

SOURCE: *Xerox: A Strategic Analysis* (New York: Northern Business Information, Inc., 1982), p. 115.

or personal computer or a word processor. Prices for the microcomputer system start at $3,000 and options for word processing capability bring the price up to $6,500. These prices make the model very competitive with the Apple II or Radio Shack TRS Model III personal computer and also with the IBM Displaywriter and Wang Wangwriter word processors. Xerox also introduced in 1981 a new line of electronic typewriters, called Memorywriters, and an inexpensive (under $1,000) personal computer.

Probably the biggest gamble that Xerox is taking in the office product segment is its *Ethernet* concept. Ethernet is a communication network, designed for short physical distances (intra-building), that will connect many pieces of office equipment by coaxial cable together into one information system. This concept allows several word processors or professional work-stations to use common databanks or printing facilities that are in different physical locations within the building. Xerox's marketing strategy is to force its Ethernet network as an industry standard so that all manufacturers of office equipment will be pressured to make their equipment compatible.

Peter McColough describes the development this way: "We can go into your company and tell you that you don't have to stick with Xerox. You can go to DEC, Intel, or anybody else. The IBM approach says: "We'll put our system in there with IBM equipment, but you won't be able to get much else.""[13] This compatibility argument is an extremely effective marketing tool for customers leery of total commitment. The automated office product market is highly competitive and expanding. Major competitors include IBM, Wang, Exxon, Hewlett-Packard, and dozens of smaller companies.

Many problems currently face Xerox's office product divisions. Contributions to profits have been nonexistent for the last several years. Although Xerox has intentionally sacrificed profits to get a jump on competitors, the new products are not selling as management had hoped they would by this time. Of the 300 Ethernet system installations planned for 1981, only 45 were completed. Marketing may be to blame. The company acknowledged that the 820 had met with little success in the retail sales environment because many had perceived the machine as an entry into the home computer market, not the office. Software development problems created delays for the full-scale production of the 8010 Star. In addition, the country's prolonged recession has prevented companies from making commitments in office automation.

Disagreements between top management and division management resulted in the resignations of Donald Massaro, President of Xerox Office Systems, and David E. Liddle, Vice-President. The 39-year-old Massaro had founded Shugart Associates, a leading computer-memory manufacturer that had been acquired by Xerox in 1977. Liddle, a 10-year Xerox veteran, had worked closely with Massaro to develop the Star and Ethernet. In an interview with *Business Week,* Massaro asserted that he resigned because he wanted complete control of Xerox's office systems effort. He conceded, however, that in a corporation like Xerox in which 75% of the revenues and almost all the profits came from copiers and duplicators, "it was frustrating trying to get the attention of top management."[14] Analysts felt that Massaro's resignation was an expected result of the battle between the "old Xerox," epitomized by the conservative East Coast copier group, and the "new Xerox," epitomized by the freewheeling California-type entrepreneurial Massaro. A consultant who had worked extensively with Xerox suggested that a real schism had developed. "The copier people didn't like the idea they were being used as a cash cow and Xerox's office systems people could spend all this money without making any."[15]

In a report from Strategic, Inc., before the Office Products Division was split, the company's President, Michael Killen, boldly predicted, "Xerox will fail because the Office Products Division will fail; and the Office Products Division will fail because Ethernet will fail."[16] Killen's rationale is that Ethernet is built on base-band modulation techniques, which limit information over the network to interactive data. Broad band modulation techniques, on the other hand, although more complex with which to interface components, allow video and voice communications as well as interactive data.

Ethernet may not become the formal industry standard supported by the Institute of Electrical and Electronics Engineers. Much squabbling is still going on over this issue. Hewlett-Packard, for example, has dropped its support of Ethernet in favor of the slightly different IEEE 802 proposed local-area-networking (LAN) standard. Nevertheless, Xerox's management plans to continue working to get Ethernet accepted by the industry as an informal standard even though IBM is said to be working on its own version of Ethernet.

Many people continue to believe that Ethernet is a viable system. John W. King, an industry analyst, says, "Ethernet is alive and well and has excellent prospects through the 1980s." King sees Ethernet and broad band networks working together.[17] Many new electronic components have been developed to simplify connecting equipment to Ethernet. Digital Equipment Corporation (DEC) and Intel agreed to a joint venture with Xerox in May 1980. DEC's role was to provide design expertise in the area of communication transceivers and computer networks. Intel provided expertise in integrated circuits for communications functions. Because Xerox has based all its products in the office segment around Ethernet, its future is of vital strategic importance.

Other Segments

Xerox is one of the largest distributors in the world of standard-cut sheet paper used for writing, typing, copying, and other office needs. In addition, it also distributes many types of office chemicals for use with its machines.

Xerox's peripheral subsidiaries are generally composed of acquisitions that helped to vertically integrate the company. Shugart Associates manufactures floppy disk drives, Diablo Systems, Inc. manufactures daisy wheel printers (a substitute technology for IBM's famous typewriter ball), Century Data Systems manufactures rigid disk drives, Versatec manufactures electrostatic printers and plotters, and Kurzweil makes optical scanners. Xerox Computer Services was established in 1970 as an outgrowth of its Scientific Data Systems acquisition and offers timesharing and software packages. Other products and services include published materials, information services, medical systems, and a credit service.

MARKETING

In the past, Xerox has traditionally been a single-product company, selling copiers to large businesses through its own sales and service force. This has changed over the past several years as it has diversified its product lines and redefined its customers. All the company's product lines have been revamped to offer a wide range of products, not only to larger companies, but to smaller businesses as well. With the advent of Ethernet, a systems approach to marketing has become necessary.

To better meet the distribution problems associated with the company's new concepts, Xerox is experimenting with new distribution techniques. Independent distributors and dealers have been contracted to sell products not only to end users, but also to Original Equipment Manufacturers (OEMs) who resell the products as part of a larger system. These distribution channels reduce the company's expenses, thereby increasing profit margins while unburdening the company's own sales force. Xerox also plans to use retail chains as well as its own retail stores to reach small business people. It has already opened approximately thirty retail stores throughout the United States and management has plans to open more nationwide. All outlets are named *The Xerox Store* and are designed to make the small business person comfortable in a store with a familiar name and reputation. In addition to selling Xerox's equipment, these retail outlets also carry brand name equipment of other manufacturers (including competitors) for home and office use. Most of this other equipment complements Xerox's own product line. This supermarket approach includes the selling of Apple Computers, Hewlett-Packard calculators, Matsushita dictating machines, as well as a host of other products.[18]

Xerox is also using new promotions as part of its marketing strategy. To better compete with Japanese firms for the small business person's dollar, management has cut prices on many products. Mail order and telephone campaigns are also being used to reach smaller firms. For the larger customers, Xerox has been offering quantity discounts as an incentive to buy total systems.

According to industry analysts, Xerox has three major marketing strengths. First, its sales and service staff is the largest in the industry. These people have excellent sales skills and are well known in most major companies.

Second, the company has large financial resources to fund challenging new product developments. No other company, with the possible exception of IBM, could have tackled the highly complex Star workstation project. Third, the Xerox name is a household word, and gives the business person a feeling of confidence when it comes to getting the product serviced.

If there is any weakness in the company's marketing department, analysts agree it is its lack of expertise in marketing complex office products and systems. There is apparently a world of difference between marketing stand-alone copying machines and marketing technically more involved information handling and processing systems. In addition, retailing is a new field for Xerox and one in which it has no previous experience. There appears to be some confusion among customers as to the purpose of several particular products. For example, Xerox's efforts to sell the 820 to the retail market through Xerox stores as well as distributors has been costly and somewhat ineffective. Jack Darcy, Senior Vice-President of Kierulff Distributors, an independent distributor who sells equipment from many manufacturers to industrial users, says: "There is such a difference in the mentality to run a successful retail operation and to run a successful industrial business. At Kierulff, we're pointing our effort totally toward the industrial. Xerox, as I understand it, is a consumer product. We're not interested."[19]

FINANCIAL

Consolidated income statements and balance sheets for the 5-year period of 1977–1981 are shown in Exhibits 19.5, 19.6, and 19.7. Although Xerox's management considers the firm to be strong financially, it can be seen that both revenues and profits have been increasing at a decreasing rate. From 1964 to 1974, net income had grown 24% a year on 30% annual revenue gains. From 1975 to 1981, revenues increased 15%, compounded annually, while earnings for the same period increased by slightly over 12% a year. In the first nine months of 1982, Xerox's net income was $370 million, down 24% from the same period the year earlier. Revenues were $6.24 billion, slightly down from $6.28 billion during the same period in 1981.

Data outlining Xerox's common-stock performance is given in Exhibit 19.8. The company's stock, which made millionaires of several early investors, has recently traded as low as $27 per share, bringing its P/E ratio to an all-time low. In addition, Xerox stock reacted negatively, falling over $3 per share, to the news of the proposed acquisition of Crum & Forster. Investment analysts have recently advised customers to postpone purchases of Xerox stock "until current operations show some sign of life."[20]

Xerox attributes much of the earnings decline to greatly reduced profit margins, as shown in Exhibit 19.9. The company's after-tax profit margin in the third quarter of 1982 was equal to 4.7% of sales, down from 7.9% a year earlier. In the first nine months of 1982, the profit margin was 5.9% compared with 7.7% in 1981. Xerox top management attributes the squeeze on profit margins to several factors:

EXHIBIT 19.5   **Xerox Corporation: Consolidated Income Statements 1977–1981**
(Dollar Amounts in Millions, Except Per-Share Data)

	1981	1980	1979	1978	1977
Operating revenues					
Rentals and services	$5,279.6	$5,151.6	$4,606.3	$4,130.5	$3,713.8
Sales	3,411.4	3,044.9	2,390.1	1,887.5	1,368.2
Total operating revenues	8,691.0	8,196.5	6,996.4	6,018.0	5,082.0
Costs and expenses					
Cost of rentals & services	2,269.5	2,167.5	1,905.0	1,691.6	1,477.1
Cost of sales	1,570.8	1,435.6	1,075.1	770.6	579.8
Research & development	526.3	435.8	378.1	311.0	269.0
Selling, administrative, & general	3,095.0	2,882.1	2,432.9	2,089.0	1,760.9
Total costs & expenses	7,461.6	6,921.0	5,791.1	4,862.2	4,086.8
Operating income	1,229.4	1,275.5	1,205.3	1,155.8	995.2
Other income less interest expense	(49.5)	3.6	1.7	(64.6)	(82.4)
Income before income taxes	1,179.9	1,279.1	1,207.0	1,091.2	912.8
Income taxes	454.4	611.8	587.2	528.0	440.5
Income before outside shareholders' interests	725.5	667.3	619.8	563.2	472.3
Outside shareholders' interests	127.3	102.4	104.8	86.7	68.3
Net income	$ 598.2	$ 564.9	$ 515.0	$ 476.5	$ 404.0
Average common shares outstanding	84.5	84.4	84.1	84.1	83.9
Net income per common share	$ 7.08	$ 6.69	$ 6.12	$ 5.91	$ 5.15

SOURCE: *Moody's 1982 Industrial Manual*, p. 4672 and *1981 Annual Report*, Xerox Corporation, p. 29.

1. Increased competition has forced price reductions on many copier models, especially in the low-volume segment where competition has been the fiercest. Reductions of up to 27% have been seen on many models.

2. Increased revenues have occurred in the low-volume copier segment, in which margins are traditionally lower. (See Exhibit 19.10.)

3. There have been increasing expenditures for research and development, and capital expenditures. In 1981, Xerox spent $526 million and $1.4 billion for these items, respectively. Of the 1981 total for capital expenditures, $1.1 billion was for additions to rental equipment and related inventories, and the balance was for additions to land, buildings, and equipment.

4. Revenues and net income from foreign operations represented 44% and 41%, respectively, of the company's 1981 total. Because of the strong dollar, it is estimated that foreign-currency translations created a $64.5

EXHIBIT 19.6   **Xerox Corporation: Consolidated Balance Sheets 1977–1981**

(Dollar Amounts in Millions)

	1981	1980	1979	1978	1977
Assets					
Current assets					
Cash	$ 45.2	$ 86.8	$ 42.2	$ 57.7	$ 73.3
Bank time deposits	234.0	228.8	267.7	412.0	338.4
Marketable securities	148.0	207.3	447.7	269.8	280.3
Trade receivables	1,245.3	1,163.8	1,120.4	927.5	731.0
Receivable from Xerox credit corp.	178.2	196.3	—	—	—
Accrued revenues	403.3	376.8	259.3	211.3	191.6
Inventories	1,131.9	1,090.2	785.8	601.8	525.3
Other current assets	230.2	210.0	180.5	158.7	128.7
Total current assets	3,616.1	3,560.0	3,103.6	2,638.8	2,268.6
Trade receivables due after one year	245.5	199.4	274.2	216.2	104.9
Rental equipment & related inventories	1,905.1	1,966.8	1,736.4	1,501.2	1,397.7
Land, buildings, & equipment	1,438.7	1,410.4	1,222.3	1,111.3	1,029.2
Investments, at equity	319.6	226.6	105.7	67.9	63.2
Other assets	149.4	150.6	111.4	137.7	183.0
Total assets	$7,674.4	$7,513.8	$6,553.6	$5,765.7	$5,046.6
Liabilities and Shareholders' Equity					
Current liabilities					
Notes payable	$ 224.2	$ 208.4	$ 96.3	$ 64.5	$ 109.6
Current portion of long-term debt	96.3	80.0	40.2	52.4	57.5
Accounts payable	340.2	315.8	325.1	273.2	209.4
Salaries, profit-sharing, other accruals	909.9	907.3	689.5	600.7	475.1
Income taxes	346.5	425.4	426.0	328.8	232.3
Other current liabilities	163.7	147.8	102.2	81.3	61.7
Total current liabilities	2,080.8	2,084.7	1,679.3	1,400.9	1,145.6
Long-term debt	869.5	898.3	913.0	938.3	1,020.0
Other noncurrent liabilities	145.0	133.0	127.9	97.2	46.1
Deferred income taxes	247.0	142.7	110.4	62.7	—
Deferred investment tax credits	108.9	85.6	70.1	63.2	59.6
Outside shareholders' interests in equity of subsidiaries	495.6	539.5	431.5	349.0	315.2
Shareholders' equity					
Common stock, $1 par value authorized 100,000 shares	84.3	84.3	83.9	83.8	80.1

	1981	1980	1979	1978	1977
Liabilities and Shareholders' Equity (continued)					
Class B stock, $1 par value authorized 600,000 shares	.2	.2	.2	.3	.3
Additional paid-in capital	306.0	304.9	286.8	286.0	257.3
Retained earnings	3,500.1	3,155.4	2,866.2	2,501.3	2,142.0
Cumulative translation adjustments	(150.1)	98.8	—	—	—
Total	3,740.5	3,643.6	3,237.1	2,871.4	2,479.7
Deduct class B stock receivables	12.9	13.6	15.7	17.0	19.6
Total shareholders' equity	3,727.6	3,630.0	3,221.4	2,854.4	2,460.1
Total Liabilities and Shareholders' Equity	$7,674.4	$7,513.8	$6,553.6	$5,765.7	$5,046.6

SOURCE: *Moody's 1982 Industrial Manual,* p. 4673 and *1981 Annual Report,* Xerox Corporation, pp. 30–31.

million loss to Xerox in 1981. If unfavorable currency impacts were excluded, international revenue growth would have been 13 percent in 1981 over 1980, slightly higher than domestic growth.

5. The reduction of overhead cost the company $63 million in severance costs in 1981.

RESEARCH AND DEVELOPMENT

The Xerox research and development program is directed mostly to the development of new and improved copying and duplicating equipment and supplies, facsimile and digital communications equipment, computer peripheral equipment and services, as well as to the development of new products and capabilities in other areas related to the broad field of information systems.

The company's Palo Alto Research Center (PARC), established in Palo Alto, California in 1969 by then-President Peter McColough, was to provide the technology Xerox needed to become "an architect of information" in the office. Flourishing under a hands-off policy by corporate headquarters, PARC soon developed an excellent reputation within the research community. The Center developed technology in computer-aided design, artificial intelligence, and laser printers. Xerox's ability to design custom chips for use in future copiers comes largely from PARC. Nevertheless, analysts contend that Xerox has been unable to really take advantage of PARC's research on computerized office systems, its original reason for being. Arguing that Xerox's sheer size slows decision-making, analysts state that the corporation has trouble translating first-rate research into profitable products. It is simply unable to move quickly into small, fast-changing markets.

EXHIBIT 19.7

Xerox Corporation: Business Segment Data, 1979–1981*

(Dollar Amounts in Millions)

	1981	1980	1979
Reprographics			
Rentals and services	$4,974.2	$4,840.9	$4,313.1
Sales	1,419.2	1,224.1	990.6
Total operating revenues	6,393.4	6,065.0	5,303.7
Operating profit	1,355.6	1,326.1	1,243.0
Identifiable assets	5,172.2	5,212.4	4,544.9
Depreciation	717.9	718.6	664.6
Capital expenditures	1,202.3	1,108.0	1,004.0
Paper			
Operating revenues (sales)	554.5	573.6	446.4
Operating profit	34.9	44.2	34.9
Identifiable assets	202.6	220.9	185.5
Depreciation	8.0	8.3	7.7
Capital expenditures	11.0	13.1	11.3
Other Businesses			
Rentals and services	449.3	409.1	357.1
Sales	1,437.7	1,247.2	953.1
Transfers between segments	37.4	34.0	16.6
Total operating revenues	1,924.4	1,690.3	1,326.8
Operating profit	107.8	124.7	106.1
Identifiable assets	1,511.2	1,398.0	1,171.5
Depreciation	96.8	98.3	90.3
Capital expenditures	188.1	192.4	179.7

SOURCE: *1981 Annual Report,* Xerox Corporation, p. 36.

*Figures do not sum to data in consolidated income statements because of various adjustments and expenses due to foreign currency gains and losses and general expense items not included in this exhibit.

Loose management by headquarters also may have encouraged PARC to go into the development of products that were not necessarily in line with the corporation's needs. For example, PARC worked in the mid-1970s to develop the Alto, a computer with some of the attributes of a personal computer, which was supposed to serve as a research prototype. Alto and its software became so popular inside Xerox that some researchers began to develop it as a commercial product. This put PARC into direct conflict with Xerox's product development group, which was developing a rival machine called the Star. Because the Star was in line with the company's expressed product strategy of developing complete office systems, the Alto

EXHIBIT 19.8 Xerox Corporation: Stock Performance, 1973–1982

	1982	1981	1980	1979	1978	1977	1976	1975	1974	1973
High price ($)	41.8	64.0	71.8	69.1	64.0	58.8	68.4	87.6	127.1	170.0
Low price ($)	27.1	37.4	48.6	52.6	40.5	43.1	48.8	46.4	49.0	114.8
Book value ($)	46.45	44.11	42.90	38.29	34.72	30.76	27.30	23.97	22.14	18.89
Earnings per share ($)	—	7.08	7.33	6.69	5.77	5.06	4.51	3.07	4.18	3.80
P/E ratio	—	7.1	8.2	9.0	8.9	9.9	13.2	20.8	22.3	39.0
Dividends per share ($)	3.00	3.00	2.80	2.40	2.00	1.50	1.10	1.00	1.00	.90
Earnings yield (%)	—	14.1	12.2	11.1	11.2	10.1	7.6	4.8	4.5	2.6
Dividend yield (%)	—	5.9	4.7	4.0	3.9	3.0	1.9	1.6	1.1	0.6
Common shares (million)	84.55	84.51	84.48	84.14	80.24	80.37	79.83	79.57	79.24	27.17

SOURCE: *Value Line Investment Survey*, November 12, 1982.

EXHIBIT 19.9

Xerox Corporation: After-Tax Margins, 1967–1982

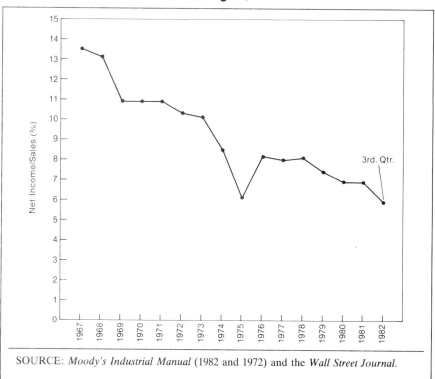

SOURCE: *Moody's Industrial Manual* (1982 and 1972) and the *Wall Street Journal.*

EXHIBIT 19.10

Xerox Corporation: Copier Revenues and Operating Profit by Market Segment, 1981

(Dollar Amounts in Millions)

SEGMENT	REVENUE ($)	OPERATING PROFIT ($)	OPERATING MARGINS (%)
Low volume	2,020	300	14.9
Medium volume	2,265	700	30.9
High volume	1,835	365	19.9
Paper & supplies	795	70	8.8
TOTAL	6,915	1,435	20.8

SOURCE: *Xerox: A Strategic Analysis* (New York: Northern Business Information, Inc., 1982), p. 80.

was ignored by top management and emphasis was placed on the Star and the Ethernet concept. The conflict between PARC and Xerox's top management has resulted in a number of researchers leaving PARC for firms such as Atari and Apple.

Jack Goldman, Xerox's former research chief, suggests that a big company like Xerox wants every product to be a "home run" in order to justify the costs of marketing and development. Another former employee says that top management "followed the big-bang strategy. They wanted to build absolutely the best office system instead of taking things bit by bit."[21]

In 1981, Xerox incurred $526 million in research and development expenses, approximately 6% of total revenues. Less than $35 million went to PARC. The 6% of total revenues represents less than the average percentage of research and development to sales of some of Xerox's major competitors (Hewlett-Packard, 9.7%; Apple Computer, 6.3%; Burroughs, 6.5%; Commodore, 5.9%; Digital Equipment Corp., 9.0%; Honeywell, 7.0%; IBM, 5.5%; Wang, 7.5%; CPT, 5.0%).[22]

OPERATIONS AND INTERNATIONAL

Xerox's principal xerographic facilities are located on a 1,047-acre site owned in Webster, New York, a suburb of Rochester. Corporate headquarters were moved to Stamford, Connecticut, in 1969 in order that corporate attention would be given not only to xerography, but to xerography overseas, to computers, data processing, education and other extensions of activity generated by acquisitions, mergers, and related research. The Office Products Division, recently reorganized into Office Products and Office Systems, is located in Dallas, Texas. The Office Systems Division, located in Palo Alto, California, is responsible for marketing local, network-based office systems to end users. In forming these two divisions, Xerox retained centralized marketing, sales, and manufacturing functions with the Office Products Division in Dallas.

Xerox's largest interests outside the United States are the Rank Xerox Companies—composed of Rank Xerox Limited of London, England, Rank Xerox Holding B.V. of the Netherlands and their respective subsidiaries—and the other subsidiaries jointly owned by Xerox and the Rank Organization. Approximately 51% of the voting power of Rank Xerox Limited and Rank Xerox Holding B.V. is owned directly or indirectly by Xerox and 49% is owned directly or indirectly by the Rank Organization Limited. The earnings of the Rank Xerox Companies are allocated according to an agreement between Xerox and the Rank Organization. For 1981, approximately 66% of the earnings of Rank Xerox was allocated to Xerox. Rank Xerox Limited manufactures and markets most xerographic copier/duplicator products developed by Xerox. Its manufacturing operations are located principally in the United Kingdom.

Fuji Xerox Co., Ltd., of Tokyo, Japan, equally owned by Fuji Photo

Film Co., Ltd., of Japan and by Rank Xerox Limited, manufactures in Japan various copiers, duplicators, and supplies, which are marketed in Japan and in other areas of the Far East. They are also marketed by Xerox in the United States and by Rank Xerox Limited in Europe.

THE PROPOSED CRUM & FORSTER ACQUISITION	In September 1982, Xerox announced an agreement to acquire Crum & Forster, an insurance holding company, for about $1.65 billion in cash and securities. Crum & Forster, the nation's fifteenth largest property-casualty insurer with a 1981 premium volume of $1.6 billion, is largely involved in writing insurance for businesses. In 1981, it drew 83% of its premiums from commercial insurance lines. Its biggest line is workers' compensation insurance, which generated 28% of premiums last year. Other lines include commercial casualty, commercial automobile, multiple-peril and fire insurance. In 1981, its operating income was $171 million, up 17% over 1980. Its net income of $176 million increased 24 percent over 1980. (See Exhibits 19.11 and 19.12.) This increase in net income, however, was due almost entirely to an increase in net investment income of $270 million. Pre-tax underwriting losses of over $70 million were somewhat larger than in 1980. (See Exhibit 19.13.) In effect, although insurance premiums were insufficient to cover claims and expenses, interest from the investment of these premiums enabled the firm to make a profit. In the first half of 1982, Crum & Forster's operating profit was down 30% to $64.8 million ($2.25 per share) from $92.1 million ($3.24 per share) a year earlier.

Xerox offered $55 for each Crum & Forster share, and gave holders the choice of receiving either cash or a combination of Xerox common and a new Xerox preferred stock. At $55 per share, Crum & Forster shareholders will receive about 1.7 times book value, which was $32.33 per share in June, 1982. The Xerox offer is double the pre-offer price and 40% above the stock's fifteen-year high price.

Xerox plans to finance the cash part of the acquisition, about $800 million, through existing revolving-credit agreements and short-term bank loans, and will not touch any cash holdings set aside for its office-products businesses. Xerox claims that the acquisition will be self-funding, in that interest costs associated with the takeover will be covered by Crum & Forster's earnings.[23]

Responding to industry puzzlement over Xerox's choice of diversification, Kearns has cited the following reasons for the acquisition:

- Xerox believes that the property-casualty insurance lines offer the best growth opportunities in the insurance business. Crum & Forster's lines aren't heavily dominated by a few industries, as in auto coverage.
- Xerox perceives the acquisition to be an expansion of Xerox's commercial financial services, pioneered by Xerox Credit Corporation. Formed in 1979, Xerox Credit is expecting to report a profit of about $35 million in 1982, about double 1981's profits.

EXHIBIT 19.11   **Crum & Forster and Subsidiaries: Consolidated Statement of Income for the Years Ended December 31**
(All Amounts Except Per Share Stated in Thousands)

	1981	1980	1979	1978	1977
Income					
Net premiums written	$1,624,614	$1,660,636	$1,585,022	$1,436,061	$1,283,149
Increase (decrease) in unearned premiums	15,522	(4,473)	50,742	69,891	60,210
Premiums earned	1,609,092	1,665,109	1,534,280	1,366,170	1,222,939
Net investment income	270,199	220,957	171,967	132,526	103,400
Commission income	45,203	44,306	38,280	26,564	11,870
Rental income on operating properties	591	627	541	876	566
Total income	1,925,085	1,930,999	1,745,068	1,526,136	1,338,775
Expenses					
Losses	954,844	988,041	881,070	769,907	722,228
Loss expenses	173,907	187,377	183,995	144,423	131,252
Acquisition costs	496,328	507,847	450,936	400,257	339,075
General expenses	65,505	46,315	39,843	26,102	17,509
Dividends to policyholders	62,940	55,371	26,866	24,622	21,895
Total expenses	1,753,524	1,784,951	1,582,710	1,365,311	1,231,959
Operating income before federal and foreign income taxes	171,561	146,048	162,358	160,825	106,816
Provision for (recovery of) federal and foreign income taxes:					
Current	593	3,497	1,032	11,991	1,107
Deferred	(5,185)	(8,911)	13,275	22,912	20,615
Operating income	176,153	151,462	148,051	125,922	85,094
Net realized capital (losses) gains	(160)	(19,790)	(5,968)	(6,627)	4,385
Discontinued operations		9,886	1,265	979	1,135
Net income	$ 175,993	$ 141,558	$ 143,348	$ 120,274	$ 90,614
Earnings Per Common Share					
Primary:					
Operating income	$6.16	$5.39	$5.36	$4.69	$3.23
Net realized capital (losses) gains	(.01)	(.70)	(.22)	(.25)	.17
Discontinued operations		.35	.04	.04	.04
Net income	6.15	5.04	5.18	4.48	3.44

(Continued)

EXHIBIT 19.11 (Continued)

	1981	1980	1979	1978	1977
Fully Diluted:					
Operating income	6.02	5.26	5.20	4.52	3.11
Net realized capital (losses) gains	(.01)	(.68)	(.21)	(.24)	.16
Discontinued operations		.34	.04	.04	.04
Net income	6.01	4.92	5.03	4.32	3.31
Cash and Accrued Dividends Per Share					
Preferred Series A	2.40	2.40	2.40	2.40	2.40
Common	1.54	1.35	1.15	.905	.80

SOURCE: *1981 Annual Report*, Crum & Forster, p. 19.

EXHIBIT 19.12 Crum & Forster and Subsidiaries: Consolidated Balance Sheet at December 31

(Dollar amounts in Thousands)

	1981	1980
Assets		
Fixed maturities		
Bonds, at amortized cost (market $1,648,849 and $1,575,439, respectively)	$2,376,859	$2,118,257
Preferred stocks, at amortized cost (market $87,705 and $93,895, respectively)	120,344	119,976
Equity securities		
Preferred stocks, at market (cost $28,486 and $36,383, respectively)	21,486	27,746
Common stocks, at market (cost $350,119 and $286,841, respectively)	413,016	455,070
Short-term investments, at cost (market $270,139 and $361,459, respectively)	270,136	361,472
Investment in real estate (net of accumulated depreciation of $13,702)		15,417
Cash	11,689	9,740
Receivables:		
Premiums (net of allowance for uncollectible accounts of $6,245 and $6,019, respectively)	439,356	372,904
Other	192,008	99,294
Equity in assets of insurance associations	5,204	8,339
Acquisition costs applicable to unearned premiums	144,939	146,919
Land, buildings, and equipment used in operations (net of accumulated depreciation of $40,832 and $38,492, respectively)	75,591	65,249
Other assets	89,480	60,602
Total assets	4,160,108	3,862,985

	1981	1980
Liabilities		
Unearned premiums	661,759	646,237
Unpaid losses	1,672,510	1,510,458
Unpaid loss expenses	402,978	300,645
Dividends to policyholders	65,189	54,320
Accounts payable and accrued liabilities	314,981	295,496
Mortgages payable	19,372	12,104
Deferred federal and foreign income taxes		
Unrealized appreciation of equity investments	16,984	46,571
Other	60,945	65,338
Other liabilities	22,000	12,312
Total liabilities	3,236,718	3,003,481
Stockholders' Equity		
Preferred stock (liquidating value $4,804 and $5,467, respectively)	480	547
Common stock (issued 28,487,085 and 28,071,639 shares, respectively)	17,804	17,545
Additional paid-in capital	39,175	31,858
Retained earnings	827,084	649,911
Net unrealized appreciation of equity investments	38,913	115,021
Less treasury stock at cost (4,000 and 16,000 shares, respectively)	(66)	(378)
Total stockholders' equity	923,390	859,504
Total liabilities and stockholders' equity	$4,160,108	$3,862,985

SOURCE: *1981 Annual Report,* Crum & Forster, p. 20.

- The acquisition will provide investment income that Xerox needs to support its vigorous research efforts in copiers, duplicators, electronic typewriters, and other office equipment.
- Xerox foresees a reduction of its tax rate during the down phase of the insurance cycle. Crum & Forster's current underwriting losses, which totaled $110 million before taxes in the first half of 1982, offers potential tax benefits to Xerox. The insurer currently pays relatively little in taxes and says its effective federal income tax rate has ranged from 12% to 14% of operating profit.[24]

Xerox watchers, however, wonder whether the company has lost confidence in its office automation business. Amy Wohl, president of Advanced Office Concepts Corp., responded to the announcement by saying, "This says Xerox doesn't feel its current set of investments gives enough return."[25] "My hunch," says office automation analyst Patricia Seybold, "is that office products may never be profitable for them. They've lost momentum."[26] Kearns, however, disagrees: "This is a very aggressive strategy to grow this business more rapidly with two market segments very different from each

EXHIBIT 19.13

Crum & Forster and Subsidiaries: Business Segments
(Dollar Amounts in Thousands)

	1981	1980	1979
Revenues			
Workers' compensation	$ 443,086	$ 431,257	$ 376,349
Casualty	304,454	358,882	357,622
Automobile—commercial	171,586	175,714	161,874
Automobile—personal	167,493	166,699	137,989
Commercial multiple-peril	218,389	217,564	208,049
Fire and allied	133,056	171,154	164,255
Homeowners'	96,246	85,532	77,722
Marine	95,169	79,781	69,743
Fidelity and surety	25,816	23,666	18,957
Investments	277,931	229,383	178,064
Other	591	627	541
Total	1,932,817	1,940,259	1,751,165
Operating Profit (Loss)			
Workers' compensation	14,241	2,796	(1,935)
Casualty	9,615	(10,431)	12,386
Automobile—commercial	(17,342)	(12,602)	1,760
Automobile—personal	(20,671)	(15,568)	(11,842)
Commercial multiple-peril	(44,775)	(7,303)	3,141
Fire and allied	(6,912)	(5,952)	6,084
Homeowners'	(8,265)	(9,291)	(3,284)
Marine	(1,324)	(6,978)	(8,781)
Fidelity and surety	2,937	2,919	3,148
Investments	270,199	220,957	171,967
Other	591	627	541
Total	198,294	159,174	173,185
General corporate expenses	(26,733)	(13,126)	(10,827)
Operating income before federal and foreign income taxes	$ 171,561	$ 146,048	$ 162,358

SOURCE: *1981 Annual Report*, Crum & Forster, p. 29.

other." As he explains it, Xerox management believes that they can maintain their total commitment to office automation and still diversify into a self-funding, high-growth area. "We concluded we could leverage the balance sheet at this time to branch out to other areas for a better return to our shareholders."[27]

Xerox, however, has had a mixed record in previous diversification attempts. In 1969, for example, the company purchased Scientific Data Systems (SDS), a manufacturer of mainframe computers, for 10 million shares of Xerox stock worth approximately $908 million. Hoping to compete with IBM, Xerox management hoped that SDS's expertise in computers would be worth giving the SDS stockholders a 73% premium over the stock's market price. Renamed Xerox Data Systems (XDS), the new division's sales fell below $100 million in 1970 and failed to show a profit. By 1972, XDS had lost $100 million before taxes. Losses ranging from $25 to $44 million annually continued until 1975 when the company wrote off the division at an $84 million loss. After six years of effort, XDS still had less than 1% of the mainframe computer market. Analysts reported that Xerox management had been surprised by the lack of R & D capability in Scientific Data Systems.[28]

In 1979, Xerox purchased Western Union International (WUI), an international communications carrier, for $212 million. This represented Xerox's first entry into telecommunications and operations in a regulated environment. Before it purchased WUI, Xerox already had a proposal before the Federal Communications Commission for a domestic data-communications network called XTEN. This project was subsequently canceled because Xerox felt that the funds could be better used elsewhere. In December 1981, Xerox announced that it had reached an agreement to sell WUI to MCI Communications Corp. for $185 million, a $27 million loss. Other recent acquisitions, such as Shugart Associates, have been of a smaller nature, less than $50 million, and represent Xerox's attempt to diversify, both horizontally and vertically, in the information-processing industry in order to bolster its position in the office-automation marketplace.

Just as the current recession has had a negative impact on Xerox's business, the weak economic climate has hurt the insurance industry. Pressures on pricing have cut underwriting profits for property and casualty insurance companies and, with interest rates declining, investment profits may drop. In the last quarter of 1982, the industry looked forward to record underwriting losses offset by record income from investments. Insurers in recent years have been willing to cut their rates and write policies at a loss in order to generate policyholders' premiums for investment activities. Analysts fear, however, that the industry's underwriting losses may be growing faster than its investment income.[29]

On the other hand, declining interest rates have several positive effects on the insurance business. First, the bonds that comprise the bulk of the companies' portfolios are worth more when rates come down. Second, the insurers' reserves for future claims liabilities are likely to be adequate when interest rates (and by association, inflation) are low. Third, low interest rates raise the prospect of an end to the destructive three-year price war still raging in the industry. Finally, with rates coming down, general economic prospects might brighten enough to increase demand for insurers' services.

Once a turnaround in pricing occurs, industry analysts expect profits to show strong growth over the next three to five years. Between 1975 and 1979, after the last recession, industry profits increased almost eight times.

The rebound is not expected to be as strong this time, but considerable growth is predicted. Lower inflation, reduced interest rates, and generally improved economic conditions are predicted to boost the demand for insurance by the mid-1980s.[30]

In reaction to the announcement of the proposed acquisition of Crum & Forster by Xerox, Moody's Investors Service lowered its ratings of several debt issues of Xerox. Moody's said its action "reflects the anticipated additional claim on existing cash flow in support of debt to be issued to acquire Crum & Forster, and the effect of competitive conditions in the company's key markets."[31]

THE OFFICE OF THE FUTURE

The high costs of management, professional, and clerical workers, in combination with continued favorable trends for electronic systems capabilities and costs, establishes Office Automation as a major growth market in the 1980s. The powerful, basic reason for automating offices is that white-collar salaries are a huge and intractable cost of doing business. In 1980, 60% of the $1.3 trillion paid out for wages, salaries, and benefits in the United States went to office workers. Meanwhile the prices of electronics have been falling. Computer memory has become cheaper at a compound annual rate of 42% over the last five years, and the price of the logic chips that give computers their intelligence has dropped about 28% a year.

Although in theory office automation makes sense, the market has not developed as quickly as vendors had hoped. According to Wang Laboratories, only 60 or so of the largest industrial corporations have acquired as many as 100 office workstations. A much smaller number have linked them into pervasive networks. Demand has simply developed more slowly than anyone thought it would a few years ago. The current market is so narrow that profits may not appear for years.[32]

Vendors give many reasons for the slow growth of this market. First of all, the recession has cut back capital-spending plans of many organizations. Second, the lack of convincing studies on the savings associated with office automation has heightened customers' reluctance to purchase. Third, in developing automation for managers and professionals, there is a problem in specifying exactly what steps or processes these individuals go through in doing their jobs. Fourth, top management does not yet feel comfortable with a computer terminal on their desks. Fifth, the confusion over which networking system, broad-band or base-band, will prevail, has made buyers slower to purchase networks. Finally, despite the universal desire of business people to find better ways of doing work, office automation remains poorly understood.[33]

Dataquest, Inc., a California-based market research firm, estimates that U.S. shipments of equipment that can be linked to form electronic offices should grow 34% a year through 1986. Total revenues are predicted to grow between $12 and $15 billion by 1986.[34] Exhibit 19.14 describes the predicted growth in the U.S. market for office automation equipment.

This anticipation of a "booming" market for office automation has brought dozens of companies into the competition. AT&T, IBM, and Xerox have declared the market a key to their futures. In 1981, the top three minicomputer companies—Digital Equipment, Hewlett-Packard, and Data General—launched office automation systems within 30 days of one another. The most successful vendors court the end user and are actually encouraged to do so by most corporate customers. Buyers will designate "preferred" vendors, but leave the final decisions to the line managers and secretaries who have to use the gear. Analysts see IBM, Wang, Digital Equipment, and Xerox as being in the best position to capture large pieces of the growing market. Yet there appear to be enough profitable niches to reward any company that can fill a particular customer's need.

Xerox's thrust in office automation has been in directing its equipment to professionals and managers, and in selling complete systems. Its strategy in gaining a share of this market has the following characteristics:

- sacrifice profits for market share until the mid-1980s;
- aim automation at the executive rather than at clerical workers;
- design machines with a multitude of uses;
- provide buyers with the opportunity to use the best available equipment from a range of suppliers;
- be the first to enter new markets;
- make products easy and nonfatiguing to use.

Although the traditionally routine tasks have been automated so far, manufacturers of this equipment must reach beyond the secretary to managers and professionals, for office automation to reach its true potential. These individuals account for 80% of the white-collar salaries. The more complex products, such as professional workstations and intelligent copiers,

---

EXHIBIT 19.14   **The U.S. Market for Office Automation Equipment**

(Dollar Amounts in Millions)

	1981	1986
Word processors	$2,200	$6,000
Electronic typewriters	275	1,200
Professional workstations	5	250
Intelligent copiers	185	900
Digital PBX's	220	4,100

SOURCE: Dataquest, Inc., *Fortune*, May 3, 1982, p. 184.

may not come into their own for some time. Analysts estimate that in 1985 only 6% of managers and professionals are likely to be using sophisticated workstations.[35]

NOTES

1. *Electronic News* (Oct. 4, 1982), p. 22.

2. *Time* (Nov. 1, 1982), p. 67, and *Wall Street Journal* (Sept. 22, 1982), p. 3.

3. *Datamation* (February 1983), pp. 90–98.

4. *1981 Annual Report,* Xerox Corporation, p. 3.

5. *Sales and Marketing Management* (Feb. 8, 1982), p. 24.

6. *Forbes* (July 7, 1980), pp. 40–41.

7. *Ibid.*

8. *Sales and Marketing Management* (Feb. 8, 1982), p. 24.

9. *Ibid.*

10. *Infosystems* (January 1981).

11. *Ibid.*

12. *Business Week* (Aug. 23, 1982), p. 80, and *Xerox: A Strategic Analysis* by Northern Business Information, Inc. (New York, NY: January, 1982), p. 156.

13. *Forbes* (July 7, 1980), pp. 40–41.

14. *Business Week* (Oct. 18, 1982), p. 134M.

15. *Datamation* (February 1983), p. 92.

16. *Infosystems* (February 1982), p. 26.

17. *Mini-Micro Systems* (February 1982), p. 18.

18. *Business Week* (April 21, 1980), p. 130.

19. *Electronic News* (Dec. 7, 1981), p. 18.

20. *Value Line* (Nov. 12, 1982), p. 1128.

21. *Fortune* (Sept. 5, 1983), pp. 97–102.

22. *Value Line* (Nov. 12, 1982), pp. 1055, 1085, 1087, 1089, 1098, 1102, 1103, 1113, and 1115.

23. *Wall Street Journal* (Sept. 22, 1982), p. 24.

24. *Ibid.*

25. *Business Week* (Oct. 4, 1982), p. 52.

26. *Ibid.*

27. *Ibid.*

28. *Electronics* (Mar. 29, 1981), p. 86.

29. *Wall Street Journal* (Dec. 30, 1982), p. 20.

30. *Value Line* (Oct. 22, 1982), p. 637.

31. *Wall Street Journal* (Oct. 1982).

32. *Fortune* (May 3, 1982), p. 176.

33. *Ibid.*

34. *Ibid.*

35. *Ibid.*

Federal Express Corporation

SEXTON ADAMS · ADELAIDE GRIFFIN

Federal Express proved the virtue of persistence with the right product in a growing market. In 1985 the company held a $1.2 billion share of the $3 billion overnight-delivery industry, which it had originally created. Most, if not all, of the credit went to the founder and Chairman of Federal Express, Frederick W. Smith.[1] He had taken an idea originally developed in a college term paper, for which he was awarded a "C," and gone on to change the way America did business. In the process he added a new cliché to the language: "when it absolutely, positively has to be there overnight."[2]

INDUSTRY

Within the aerospace and air transport industry, Federal Express became a leader in only a few short years.[3] While its main competitors had been around for two decades, satisfied with the traditional air-freight-forwarding market share they occupied, Federal took the market by storm and "changed the rules of the game."[4]

Federal Express laid claim to being the founder of the small package/document express market. Constantly expanding into areas of new services and extended service areas, this sector experienced phenomenal growth in the late 1970s and early 1980s.

Markets for all classes of cargo movement, from heavyweight to documents and letters, grew in 1984. Firms involved in cargo movement included all-cargo air carriers, traditional air-freight forwarders, passenger airlines, ground transportation companies, and air couriers. Although air-freight movement in general experienced a profitable year in 1984, the small-package express-shipping sector continued its five-year annual growth rate of 20%.[5]

Competitors that were directly involved in the small package/document express market included Federal Express, Emery Air Freight, Purolator, the United Parcel Service (UPS), and the United States Postal Service. Through 1983 and 1984, price and service innovations abounded as participants struggled to gain a competitive edge.[6] This sector of the air-cargo industry was characterized by price wars, constant cost-cutting strategies, and innovative marketing plans. To keep in the running for the growing

This case was prepared by R.J. Balhorn, Beverly Bowen, Jane Shouse, Steve Spencer, and Carey Spriggs under the supervision of Professor Sexton Adams, North Texas State University, and Professor Adelaide Griffin, Texas Woman's University. Reprinted with permission.

market, most competitors felt an urgent need to earmark large capital investments for future expansion.[7]

Regulatory authority for participants in this industry was provided by the Federal Aviation Act of 1958, the Civil Aeronautics Board (CAB), and the Federal Aviation Administration (FAA). When the CAB was in existence, its authority related to the economic aspects of air transportation. The FAA's regulatory authority, however, related primarily to the safety aspects of air transportation, including aircraft standards and maintenance. Ground transportation services were exempt from regulation by the Interstate Commerce Commission; but because of the use of radio and communication equipment in ground and air units, Federal Express operations were subject to regulation by the Federal Communications Act of 1934. Finally, as of May 1984, Federal Express was in compliance with all regulations of the Environmental Protection Agency with regard to smoke emissions.[8]

HISTORY

Fred Smith was Chairman and Chief Executive Officer of the Memphis-based Federal Express Corporation, an air cargo firm that specialized in door-to-door overnight delivery, using its own planes. Smith originated his revolutionary idea for his firm in the 1960s while majoring in economics and political science at Yale. He had a close acquaintance with aviation; he had earned a pilot's license at age fifteen and pursued his flying hobby while a student at Yale. During this same period, such companies as IBM and Xerox were already flying material out of airports not far from Yale's Connecticut campus.[9]

Smith spelled it all out in an overdue economics paper. To cut cost and time, packages from all over the country would be flown to a central point, there to be sorted, redistributed, and flown out again to their destinations. The flying would be done late at night when air lanes were comparatively empty. Airports used would be in sizable cities; and trucks would carry packages to their final destinations, whether in those cities or in smaller communities. Equipment and documents from anywhere in the United States could be delivered anywhere else in the United States the next day.[10]

Smith was thinking not only of parts and contracts, but also of canceled checks. His concept, he thought, could be sold to the Federal Reserve to cut down on the float, the period between receipt of a check and collection of funds. A general, commercial-delivery system could be built on that basis. When the time came to create his company years later, his ambition to serve the Federal Reserve and his desire for an impressive name with broad geographical connotation led him to the name "Federal Express." The Fed turned down his contract bid, but it now has its own check-delivery system, which Smith said was patterned after his operations.[11]

After college, Smith served two tours of duty in Vietnam, first as a platoon leader and then as a reconnaissance pilot. Upon returning home he decided to give his air express idea a try. Starting with $4 million that he had inherited, he chose Memphis as a home base. A company study showed that Memphis was near the center of business shipping in the continental United States, and its airport was closed only an average of ten hours per year because of adverse weather conditions. The airport offered long runways, a large abandoned ramp, and a pair of inexpensive World War II hangars.[12]

Of course, $4 million was not much for starting a company that needed an entire fleet of planes. Smith had to have more funds. He went to New York and Chicago and brought Wall Streeters to Memphis. His knowledge of the air-freight field impressed investors; at the end of the year he had managed to raise a whopping $72 million in loans and equity investment.

Then Federal Express, which had been marking time operating a charter service, got down to its present business. Serving thirteen airports, it began transporting packages of under 70 pounds in April 1973. The first night's package total was eighteen. Volume picked up rapidly, and service was extended. Federal Express was an overnight success, but not for long. OPEC's inflation of fuel prices sent costs up faster than revenues were growing, and by mid-1974 the company was losing more than $1 million per month.[13]

Smith went back to his disappointed investors for more money to keep the company growing until revenues could catch up with expenses. Bankruptcy was a real possibility. After being turned down many times, Smith was able to raise $11 million, which was enough to get Federal Express over the hump. Federal Express, which lost $27 million in its first two years, went $3.6 million into the black in 1976 on $75 million in revenues. It has remained on the upswing ever since.[14]

Federal's short-term goals included increased surface productivity, telecommunications, and international expansion. Federal Express also considered the possibility of going into the passenger business. Chairman Smith considered this option "awfully tempting." All of Federal's big jets were easily convertible between freight-container pallets and passenger seats, and these jets were used an average of only 4.7 hours out of every 24. Nevertheless, the return on investment from carrying passengers would have been far below what it was from carrying small packages, and the chance of planes being delayed and out of position for the nightly race to deliver packages on schedule was too great. "Nothing," said Smith, "can be allowed to impair our primary business."[15]

MANAGEMENT/ PERSONNEL

Fred Smith—Entrepreneur

Fred Smith was a man of integrity, whose charisma enabled him to motivate investors and employees to believe in his dream. His drive was mainly attributed to the scars that he carried from his military service, feelings so strong that Smith himself stated that Federal Express was a creature of Vietnam, and he would not have had the same perspective if not for his experiences there.[16]

As a true entrepreneur, Smith never threw in the towel. When the Arab embargo on oil in 1974 forced fuel costs sky high, Smith ran to investors, courting them for more money. When outdated CAB regulations made it impossible for Federal to expand into the larger aircraft it needed, Smith went to Washington and lobbied for deregulation of the airlines. When the U.S. Postal Service relaxed its regulations against private delivery of extremely urgent mail, Smith jumped at the opportunity and began testing the overnight letter service.[17]

And Smith did it with style. To win support from prominent Capitol Hill figures, he wined and dined them. To win the confidence of investors, he was always prepared with thorough market and economic analyses to support his ideas.[18] Unfortunately, by the late 1970s, Federal Express had grown too large for the wheeler-dealer, entrepreneurial approach to running an organization. But Smith believed that some principles remained the same in managing a $1.2 billion operation as in a $1.2 million operation:

> One of the biggest principles is that you've got to take action. Most large organizations reach a static point. They cannot take any action, because there are all types of barriers to doing so. There are institutionalized barriers that weren't there when the company was considerably smaller. What changes is your knowledge and your appreciation of how to deal with those institutional barriers, to eliminate them or use them to your advantage in achieving those changes. There are myriad number of changes that have to take place in the management style for the company to continue growing.[19]

Corporate Giants

Smith's colleagues also had the same "fighter pilot attitude" toward Federal Express. They were all former pilots and entrepreneurs; and although most thought his idea very strange, each one had the "right stuff" needed to make Federal Express fly.[20] From day one, the camaraderie and loyalty exhibited by employees of Federal Express was strong—strong enough to hold Federal together and transform it from an "entrepreneurial crusade" (us against them) to a respected corporate strength. (See Exhibit 20.1 for Federal's organizational chart.)

The year 1979, however, brought much change to Federal's ranks. President Art Bass, one of the initial crusaders, decided to leave and took five vice-presidents with him, all but one of whom had been with Federal from the start. The reason for their departure was shocking to some but easily understood by Smith. Federal had matured, and Bass and his colleagues felt they lacked the ability to adapt their entrepreneurial perspectives to management of a mature operation. Smith replaced his elite few with managers who were more comfortable with the traditional corporate organization, but he maintained associations with Bass and the others in a think-tank type of

EXHIBIT 20.1   **Federal Express Organizational Chart**

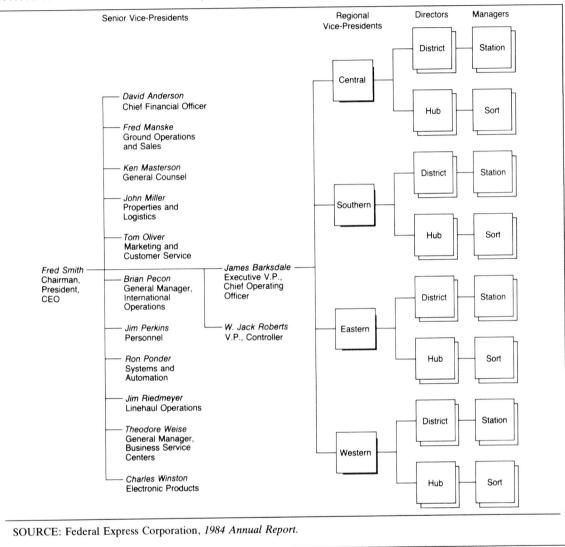

SOURCE: Federal Express Corporation, *1984 Annual Report.*

arrangement.[21] Their only responsibility, as far as Smith was concerned, was to think about the future of Federal.

Federal's Backbone

Dedication to professional, faultless service enabled Federal to "get it there overnight." From the beginning, Federal was a people organization. With an employee force of over 24,000, management felt a strong responsibility to provide an array of training programs, to support the image it wanted to portray.[22] For example, training for the ZapMail service, when it was first introduced, included courses for over 18,000 employees.[23] In addition to a thorough training program, Federal boasted of an active file of 45,000 applicants for positions ranging from pilot to courier and made the claim that this was an indication of the attractiveness of the company's policy and benefits.[24] One general benefit offered by Federal was paying full college tuition for college students working at the hub. These policies supported Federal's commitment to maintaining the image of professionalism and stability.

When the company hired an employee, it was viewed as a long-term investment. To minimize the necessity to furlough any employee, Federal scheduled part-time employees, so that operations could expand or contract according to traffic levels.[25] Smith, though, was exceedingly canny about labor. By employing part-time college students who would come and go as their education progressed, Federal set up a buffer between its operations and the entrance of unions to the hub.[26] This approach also allowed Federal Express to keep its labor costs low, lower than those of any company in the industry.[27]

Recruiting

Because of Federal's reputation of being a leader in its industry, it never had any difficulty in finding qualified people to uphold that image. Unfortunately, the old tactics used to fill Federal's ranks did not work when it came time for Federal to staff its ZapMail operation in 1984. The ZapMail operation required high-tech professionals who could go out to a client and sell them on the new, revolutionary service, but the ads Federal was running were not attracting this type of candidate. Federal had to target its advertising to a new, young professional crowd who were looking for career opportunities on the leading edge of technology.[28] And it worked.

Hundreds of qualified candidates were recruited, all because Federal targeted its advertising to a specific audience. But not only did Federal change its recruiting approach, it also restructured its compensation plan for the ZapMail sales force. ZapMail salespeople received low base salaries. Commissions were based solely on the number of machines installed in offices. Federal's management felt that this would help make ZapMail grow at a faster rate.[29]

OPERATIONS   Federal Express provided an overnight, door-to-door, express delivery service for high-priority packages and documents. In essence, two industries were merged to accomplish this: aviation and pickup/delivery trucking service. Federal Express services were available Monday through Saturday from 145 airports in the United States, Canada, Puerto Rico, Europe, and the Far East. Approximately 90% of the U.S. population was served through an intricate ground/air network—Smith's brainchild, the hub and spoke system.

Hub and Spoke

The service operation that made Federal Express unique in its field was its central sorting facility located in Memphis, Tennessee. The key factor was that every package and letter transmitted by Federal passed through the center in Memphis, where it was sorted and dispatched to the points of delivery across the country and internationally.

The operations at the hub had been fine-tuned for maximum efficiency. The central sorting process occurred in the middle of the night under "time bomb" pressure.[30] An executive gazing out over the bustling hub said, "If they decide to sit down for an hour, we're dead."[31] All during the day, packages had been collected in sorting facilities and local offices in 300 cities. Once transported to the local airports, the packages were flown to Memphis, where all planes arrived about midnight. The planes were directly unloaded into a giant warehouse of elaborate conveyor belts; there they were frantically sorted and loaded back into the planes headed for their intended destinations. By 3 A.M. the planes were ready to depart for sorting facilities located at the local airports, where couriers would then transport packages to local offices and then on to the receiver—and all of this happened overnight!

Contact with couriers was maintained through the use of Digitally Assisted Dispatch Systems (DADS). The system, installed in over 70% of Federal's vehicles, enabled the company to leave dispatch information in couriers' vans even when unoccupied. In late 1984, hand-held DADS units were introduced to help eliminate duplicated routes, retraced steps, and other inefficiencies.[32] This prototype microprocessor maintained constant data and voice contact between the courier and dispatcher even if the courier was on the upper floor of an office building, as foot couriers often were.

COSMOS, Federal Express's computer network for dispatch entry and tracking, used a satellite and telephone network to locate a customer's shipment at any time as it passed through six electronic gates during transit. Each parcel was bar-coded so that movement could be monitored and recorded at every step of the journey. Thus the whereabouts of a package, not just the paperwork, could be recalled in an instant.[33]

Facilities

Federal Express leased its facilities at the hub from the Memphis-Shelby County Airport Authority. These facilities consisted of a central sorting facility, aircraft hangars, flight training and fuel facilities, warehouse space, and a portion of the administrative offices.[34] Off-airport facilities in Memphis were also leased and consisted of Federal Express headquarters, PartsBank operations, and other administrative offices.[35]

City station operations were located in 300 cities throughout the United States, Canada, Puerto Rico, Europe, and the Far East. These stations were leased for 5- to 10-year periods. In 1984 a station and service-center expansion program was begun that included the construction of Business Service Centers and the installation of unmanned Overnight Delivery Counters, to supplement the city stations and to provide improved access to services in high-density areas.[36]

Equipment and Vehicles

Federal operated almost 10,000 delivery vehicles; approximately 2,000 of these were leased. Other vehicles owned by Federal included mainly ground support equipment, cargo loaders, transports, and aircraft tugs.[37] As of July 31, 1984, Federal owned fifty-eight aircraft and an inventory of spare engines and parts for each type. The company was committed to purchase eleven additional aircraft to be delivered in 1985–1987.[38] Deposits and payments to be made according to these agreements were

$ 98,700,000 in 1985,

$169,800,000 in 1986,

$105,800,000 in 1987.

PRODUCT LINES On a domestic level, Federal Express offered three basic services: Priority One, ZapMail, and Standard Air, a 1- to 2-day package and document delivery service. Additionally, Federal provided special handling for dangerous goods and restricted articles, an air-cargo charter service, and an inventory-parts shipment service. Through the use of expanded direct service and exclusive agents, Federal Express could also deliver documents and custom-cleared packages internationally to areas in Canada, Puerto Rico, Western Europe, the Far East, and Australia.[39]

Priority One

Priority One, an overnight door-to-door delivery of business goods, absolutely, positively guaranteed a 10:30 A.M. next morning delivery. In either the sender's packaging or that of Federal Express, time-sensitive letters, boxes, and tubes up to 150 pounds in weight, 62″ in length or 120″ in length and girth combined could be shipped to almost any location in the contiguous states.[40] Couriers were used for pickup and delivery, or customers could bring packages and documents to self-service centers or Federal Express

Business Service Centers. Permitting face-to-face customer contact, these staffed storefront facilities were located in high-traffic, high-density areas. Over 300 of the centers were planned to be in place by the end of fiscal 1985.[41]

Rates for overnight letters were $11.00 if delivered to a drop-off location by the sender and $14.00 if picked up by a courier. Courier-Pak boxes and tubes were subject to a five-pound or $34.00 minimum charge, while Courier-Pak envelopes were priced at a two-pound or $25.00 minimum. Schedules indicating price per pound then applied for parcels over the minimum weight. Up to 40% discounts were offered to qualified shippers.[42]

Standard Air

Standard Air gave the same array of service features offered under Priority One, except that packages were scheduled for delivery no later than the second business day after pickup. At approximately one-half the Priority One rates, Standard Air was promoted as, "when it has to be there, but doesn't have to be there overnight."[43] Many packages arrived the next business day, making this 1- to 2-day service an economical alternative for time-pressured shippers.

Charter/PartsBank

Beyond delivering packages, Federal offered two unique services to serve the larger distribution needs of U.S. business. The first, Air Cargo Charter, allowed the charter of McDonnell DC-10s, Boeing 727s, or Dassault Falcons on either a one-time or contractual basis. Subject to availability, aircraft could be chartered twenty-four hours per day, seven days per week. The second, PartsBank, arose from the need for the speedy handling of critical inventories. Combining a parts warehouse system with an overnight airline, PartsBank allowed companies to place time-sensitive inventory such as computer parts, medical supplies, and electronic components in Federal's Memphis PartsBank warehouse. A toll-free telephone call to PartsBank could have the item shipped immediately.[44]

ZapMail

An answer to electronic mail, ZapMail was conceived approximately seven years before its 1984 introduction, but it evolved into a major product because of indications of strong demand.[45] Users could call to request the service, and within an hour a courier arrived to pick up the document. Then the courier delivered the document to the nearest input station, where the document was inserted into a scanner, digitized, and sent over the Federal Express network to the receiving station. There it was printed and delivered to the recipient by courier. Total elapsed time from initial call to delivery time was two hours. If the sender took the document to a Federal Express Business Service Center, ZapMail delivery was accomplished in one hour. In contrast to electronic mail, ZapMail was an electronically transmitted document rather than just a message. Therefore charts, contracts, invoices, artwork, etc., could be reproduced into high-resolution copies. Original documents would be either forwarded to the recipient or returned to the sender by 10:30 A.M. the next business day.[46]

ZapMail charges were $25 for the first twenty pages and $1 per page after twenty pages. If it was sent from a Service Center, the cost was reduced by $5.00.[47] For a leasing fee of approximately $200 per month, a frequent user could have a ZapMail terminal placed in his or her office with no installation or maintenance fees.[48]

Although much had been staked on the success of ZapMail, initial results were disappointing. Several marketing and operational problems had hindered the initial launch of the project, but optimism remained high for the long term.

From an operational standpoint, there had at first been a delay, later resolved, in the installation of dedicated long-distance lines by AT&T. More recently, in the second stage of the project—that of placing on-premises terminals (ZapMailers) with volume users—there was a one-month delay from installation of the software required for the simultaneous transmission of documents to multiple destinations. Thus the targeted goal of 3,000 ZapMailers in place by the end of May 1985 was in doubt. As of the end of January 1985, slightly over 700 orders for the machines had been placed.[49]

On the marketing front, management noted that it had been perhaps overly optimistic in relying on its market research indicating a pent-up need for the new service. ZapMail shipments were averaging about 3,200 per day, far below the 20,090–30,000 needed to reach the initial projected break-even level twelve to eighteen months after startup.[50] It had become clear that the marketing approach that had been effective for small packages was not working in the same-day market. Part of the problem rested in consumer education. As with its overnight express service, Federal needed to get potential customers to understand exactly what was being offered and how to use it. The company had overestimated the ease with which its customer base could be educated about the benefits of ZapMail. It set about rectifying the problem.

Stressing how the new service should be used as a part of the business routine rather than merely in emergencies, Federal began pumping an additional $10 million into its planned advertising budget.[51] Anticipating difficulty in convincing prospects of the necessity for on-premise ZapMailers, Federal equipped its sales force with preprogrammed Radio Shack calculators. These were to be used to run a comparison of the prospect's current communications systems cost (based on estimated activity levels) with that of a comparable ZapMailer system.[52] Federal targeted the following industries as having the highest potential, at least initially, for ZapMailer installations:

Legal	Banking
Accounting	Manufacturing
Consulting	Advertising
Retail	Commercial and Financial Printing
Insurance	Government[53]

In spite of its initial difficulties, ZapMail was highly regarded by analysts in the investment community, who believed that it would become an unqualified success once the glitches involved with any new product were resolved. Further, Federal's management indicated that possible future enhancements to ZapMailers might include the ability to communicate with word processors and personal computers.[54] Speculation was that Federal intended to be a major player in the "office of the future" through the use of ZapMailers. By connecting word processors and personal computers to the ZapMail network, Federal could leverage its ability to capture office-document traffic once the software was developed to do so.

International Operations

Federal Express also delivered Courier-Pak envelopes and packages up to seventy pounds to many international locations. Because of distance and time differences in the areas served, time of day and delivery varied. For the areas that they did not serve, Federal Express offered a Worldwide Referral Service that could arrange delivery to additional locations.[55]

In an effort to expand outside North America, in fiscal 1984, Federal acquired Gelco Express International, a world-wide, on-board courier service with offices in London, Amsterdam, Paris, Brussels, Hong Kong, Tokyo, and Singapore. In 1985 the Gelco operation was to be absorbed into the system with the Federal Express name and identity.[56]

Preparing at home for international service, Federal opened an international customer-service department with multilingual representatives. An added effort by Federal was made to give special attention to customs and cultures of the international markets.[57] But critics abroad said that running a domestic service in the United States was entirely different from operating an international one because it required a different expertise, and a common market approach could not be taken. Competition was growing in the international market as well as the U.S. market, so analysts felt that Federal could have problems promoting itself in Europe with only the experience of a small European courier for guidance.[58]

**MARKETING/
ADVERTISING**

The image of Federal Express was one of an innovator. Smith and his colleagues had created a demand for small-package express delivery and then cleverly set out to satisfy that demand. Smith, in analyzing Federal Express, stated that Federal was selling time, and people who save time in their daily routines and functions are more effective.[59] Once the message was heard, the public immediately altered their perspective from "get it there as soon as possible" to "get it there overnight."

Smith spared nothing to get the message across. Federal Express needed dramatic advertising to reach an indifferent world that needed to know about Federal Express.[60] Tom Oliver, Senior Vice-President of Marketing and Customer Service, said, "At the outset the advertising was oriented toward explaining the network system . . . focusing on the difference in Federal's system from their competitors." However, people could not understand how this strange combination of airplanes, hubs, and couriers could keep the boss from yelling.[61] The public just wanted to trust that Federal would do what it claimed to do, no matter how they did it.

After much effort, Federal did get the message across and won award after award for its clever spots. In the "motor-mouth" businessman; the pitch, "Federal Express. When it absolutely, positively has to be there overnight"; or the man uprooting a phone booth as the announcer says "Federal Express is so easy to use, all you have to do is pick up the phone," it was easy to appreciate the humor, and that was what Oliver wanted.[62]

But not everyone felt that Federal's humorous ads were of benefit to the company's objective. Competitors and advertisers alike felt that Federal ads often offended the little guy. Also, although attention-getters, the ads left no message as to what Federal really offered.[63] Unaffected by criticisms hurled at its campaigns, Federal believed that another factor—price—was not as important as dramatizing the problem people have in getting fast, sure, easy delivery. Cost of delivery was important to people only after they were sure it would get to the destination when they wanted it to.[64]

Federal's marketing plan for ZapMail also came under fire by industry analysts. The original ZapMail marketing plan was ill-conceived; no one really understood what ZapMail was.[65] But because of the newly recruited sales force for ZapMail and new leasing plans as an alternative to purchase of the machines, analysts believed that ZapMail would evolve into a tool necessary for business activities.

COMPETITION

Federal Express Corporation was a major competitor in the time-sensitive package delivery or courier industry. It faced stiff competition from such firms as Purolator Courier Corporation, Emery Air Freight Corporation, UPS, and the U.S. Postal Service.

Purolator Courier Corporation

Purolator said that its packages were "overnight, not overpriced," and the company mandated that each package be delivered the next business day or on some other time-sensitive schedule. Most packages weighed less than five pounds and each was picked up and delivered door to door, either on call or on a scheduled basis.[66]

In 1984 Purolator had two major products that were designed to make its door-to-door courier services easy and economical. Customers could send two ounces (up to ten pages) of important documents anywhere in the continental United States at a very low price with the PuroLetter. The PuroPak could handle as much as two pounds of documents for delivery across town or across the country, and the customer was automatically billed at the lowest applicable rate. Very low rates applied up to 300 miles or between certain pairs of cities, and a competitive rate was applied for longer distances. A related product, called the PuroPak Box, offered a very low rate for one- to six-pound shipments.[67]

To enable the movement of shipments over long distances for next-day delivery, Purolator operated an air network with its central hub located in Columbus, Ohio. However, major volume constraints and operating inefficiencies were being experienced at the Columbus facility. To alleviate this problem and in anticipation of future growth needs, Purolator had a continuing program to upgrade terminal facilities. A major, new air-hub facility was under construction in Indianapolis, Indiana, that, upon its completion in 1986, would have a capacity of 125,000 packages per night.[68]

Purolator Courier, Ltd., the company's Canadian subsidiary, offered courier services to over 6,000 cities and towns in the ten provinces of Canada. Partly because of sluggish growth in the Canadian economy, operating results of this subsidiary had been mediocre. Management had concentrated on improving operating efficiency and modestly expanding terminal facilities.[69]

The management of Purolator Courier Corporation saw the company as "the most economical national supplier of overnight package delivery." To aggressively exploit this position, Purolator planned to capitalize on its large fleet of airplanes and ground delivery vehicles, all supported by an aggressive advertising campaign. As the U.S. and Canadian economies continued to improve, management expected Purolator to continue its record growth.[70]

For a comparison of Purolator and its competitors, see Exhibits 20.2 and 20.3.[71]

Emery Air Freight

Emery was one of the largest domestic air-cargo carriers and was a major competitor in the international field as well. The company maintained 165 offices, fifty-three of which were outside the United States in twenty-seven different countries and territories. In another forty-two countries, agents acted on the company's behalf.[72]

Emery could provide overnight door-to-door delivery of any size, any weight package or shipment to over 56,000 cities and towns in North America. The company also had 24- to 72-hour door-to-door service to various cities around the world. Emery offered a variety of overnight delivery

EXHIBIT 20.2   **Sales Revenues of Federal Express and Selected Competitors, 1983**

(In Thousands of Dollars)

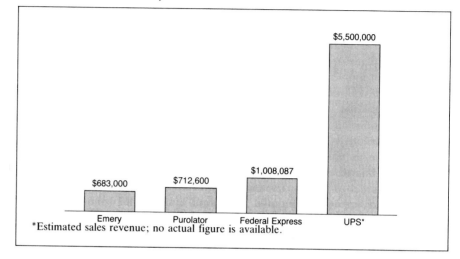

*Estimated sales revenue; no actual figure is available.

services including Same Day, A.M., P.M., Day 2, and the five-ounce Emery Urgent Letter.[73]

According to management, Emery's goal was to have "the lowest cost, highest quality, world-wide transportation system." To achieve this goal, Emery had spent large sums for expansion of existing facilities and the modernization of existing aircraft as well as the acquisition of new aircraft. In addition, the company had made major capital investments in state-of-the-art technology to foster its future business growth. For example, a $20 million expansion of its "superhub" terminal facility in Dayton, Ohio, was begun in March 1984 and was completed at year's end. This expansion increased the company's handling capacity to almost 2 million pounds per night, up from 1.7 million pounds. A major capital improvement at the Dayton facility in 1983 was the installation of an automated envelope-sorting system that was capable of handling 10,000 Emery Urgent letters or envelopes per hour.[74]

Emery had maintained a special "heavyweight" niche in the package delivery business. Its unique ability to deliver heavy air cargo the next day gave the company a competitive edge during the recent economic recovery. Approximately 45% of the company's seventy-pound traffic had a next-morning delivery requirement. This ability was particularly useful to large companies that often required cargo-transportation services for shipments of any size, weight, or shape. This "heavyweight" service was restricted to customers who purchased over $1 million of air cargo transportation services per year.[75]

EXHIBIT 20.3   ### Numbers of In-Service Aircraft and Vehicles of Federal Express and Selected Competitors, 1983

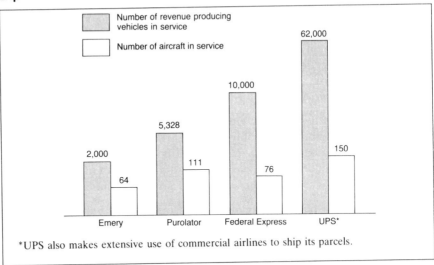

*UPS also makes extensive use of commercial airlines to ship its parcels.

Emery suffered a sharp drop in earnings per share in 1982, but made a strong recovery in 1983 and 1984. Historically, Emery had shown consistent growth in earnings per share, and dividends had been paid without interruption since 1952.[76]

United Parcel Service

United Parcel Service (UPS) was a giant in package delivery, its only competitor in terms of volume being the U.S. Postal Service. No other company could match its basic claim that it could deliver a package in two days anywhere in the continental United States if the customer was willing to pay the price. UPS had long had a reputation for dependability, productivity, and efficiency that was admired by customers and envied by competitors.

Building upon the success of its basic business, UPS entered the overnight package-delivery market late in 1982. Any UPS customer that was currently served by daily pickups could make use of this overnight delivery service. Rates were usually 50% lower than those charged by Federal Express.[77]

UPS occupied a very strong position in the transportation industry. It was the largest single private shipper on most railroads, owned a large fleet of airplanes, and also shipped packages on other airlines. In addition, it owned a huge fleet of delivery trucks. (See Exhibit 20.3.) Its drivers were unionized and called on some 600,000 offices, factories, and stores each day.[78]

Financially, UPS was solid, with earnings that had more than quadrupled from $76.1 million in 1978 to $331.9 million in 1982. During this same period, revenues doubled, going from $2.8 billion in 1978 to $5.2 billion in 1982. Very few companies in any industry could match this earnings and productivity record.[79]

U.S. Postal Service

The U.S. Postal Service had been a competitor in the overnight-package delivery business for a number of years. With its Express Mail next-day service, the Postal Service could ship packages weighing up to seventy pounds and guarantee delivery to the addressee the next day. To make use of this service, customers simply took their packages and letters to the Express Mail window at the post office. Shipments were delivered to the addressee by 3:00 P.M. of the following day. The addressee also had the option of picking up the package personally as early as 10:00 A.M. of the next business day. All shipments were guaranteed to arrive on time; if they did not, the customer could obtain a full refund. According to Postal Service statistics, 95% of all shipments did arrive on time.[80]

The U.S. Postal Service also offered package pickup from the customer's place of business, but only on a planned, regularly scheduled basis. A single, flat charge was made per pickup, regardless of the number of packages or letters the customer might be sending.

The Express Mail Service could ship packages and letters to almost any major metropolitan area in the United States. Also available on an international basis, Express Mail Service served major cities in the United Kingdom, Australia, Brazil, Hong Kong, Japan, Belgium, France, and the Netherlands.[81]

FINANCIAL SITUATION

Federal Express did not become a financial success overnight. It took four years and $70 million in venture capital before the first profitable period in late 1975. The company nearly went bankrupt several times during that four-year drought because the venture-capital market was in a profound depression of its own.

In 1975, new capital was $10 million (versus $3 billion in 1983), and the initial offering in 1974–1975 raised only $32 million (against $5.5 billion in 1984). Federal Express was constantly asking banks, corporations, and venture capitalists for new loans and equity participations. Ultimately, the company survived as over a dozen equity groups participated in three major rounds of financing. In his desperate search for money, Smith had to give up virtually all his equity in his company. (He eventually recaptured a substantial portion in later refinancings.)

Throughout the bad times, however, Smith earned the undying loyalty of the people who worked for him. "He was a fantastic motivator of people," said Charles Tucker Morse, the company's first General Counsel. "I have not worked since in a situation so intense and so free of politics."[82]

Financial results for fiscal 1984 were gratifying, despite the considerable expense incurred to improve existing service and to introduce a new electronic document-transmission product. Revenues increased by 42% to $1.4 billion. Net income totaled $115 million, or $2.52 per share; these were gains of 30% and 24%, respectively, over $89 million, or $2.03 per share, in fiscal 1983. (See Exhibits 20.4 and 20.5.)[83]

EXHIBIT 20.4

Federal Express: Consolidated Financial Highlights for Year Ended May 31

(In Millions of Dollars Except Per Share and Other Data)

	1982	1983	1984
Operating Results			
Express service revenues	$803,915	$1,008,087	$1,436,305
Operating income	119,466	150,737	165,208
Income before income taxes	131,080	150,216	152,260
Net income	78,385	88,933	115,430
Earnings per share	$ 1.85	$ 2.03	$ 2.52
Average shares outstanding	41,788	43,316	45,448
Financial Position			
Working capital	$ 79,669	$ 89,878	$ 72,226
Property and equipment, net	457,572	596,392	1,112,639
Long-term debt	223,856	247,424	435,158
Common stockholders' investment	350,319	503,794	717,721
Other Operating Data			
Average daily package volume	125,881	166,428	263,385
Average pounds per package	6.5	5.8	5.5
Average revenue per pound	$ 3.81	$ 4.02	$ 3.80
Aircraft fleet at end of year:			
McDonnell DC-10-10s	4	6	6
McDonnell DC-10-30s	0	0	4
Boeing 727-100s	31	38	35
Boeing 727-200s	0	0	12
Dassault Falcons[1]	32	32	0
Average number of full-time equivalent employees during year	10,092	12,507	18,368

[1]As of May 31, 1984, the company removed its Dassault Falcons from scheduled operations. Ten of the aircraft had been disposed of at that date; and as of July 31, 1984, twelve were under contract for sale. The company was evaluating plans for the ultimate disposition of the remaining fleet.

EXHIBIT 20.5

Federal Express: Consolidated Statement of Income
(In Thousands of Dollars)

	1982	1983	1984
Express Service Revenues	$803,915	$1,008,087	$1,436,305
Operating Expenses			
Salaries and employee benefits	320,345	419,644	622,675
Depreciation and amortization	56,353	77,421	111,956
Fuel and oil	69,282	71,262	93,520
Equipment and facilities rental	46,116	59,115	89,775
Maintenance and repairs	38,795	44,083	59,482
Advertising	25,302	34,558	39,345
Other	128,256	151,267	254,344
Total expenses	684,449	857,350	1,271,097
Operating Income	119,466	150,737	165,208
Other Income (Expense)			
Interest expense	(15,933)	(23,451)	(36,350)
Interest capitalized	2,852	5,831	11,851
Interest income	11,994	9,679	13,166
Gain on aircraft sales	7,318	4,224	2,463
Other	5,383	3,196	(4,078)
	11,614	(521)	(12,948)
Income Before Income Taxes	131,080	150,216	152,260
Provision for Income Taxes	52,695	61,283	36,830
Net Income	$ 78,385	$ 88,933	$ 115,430
Earnings per Share	$ 1.85	$ 2.03	$ 2.52
Average Shares Outstanding	41,788	43,316	45,448

Other extraordinary expenses incurred during 1984 were to expand the network geographically and to add Business Service Centers in high-density, downtown areas. Also, increasing customer use of volume discounts and the relatively rapid growth of the lower-priced Overnight Letter and Standard Air Services resulted in a decline in the yield, or average revenue, per package. This trend exceeded the impressive decrease in operating costs per package achieved during the fiscal year.

Management expected the trend in declining yields to reverse because of three policy changes, made during fiscal 1984, that produced higher than average yields. The first change was increasing the per package weight limit from 70 to 150 pounds. The second change was to introduce a Saturday pickup for Monday morning delivery service. The third and most important change was to charge by the pound rather than the package for multi-package shipments. Management hoped the third policy change would enable the company to enter the high-revenue air-freight market for the first time.[84]

Federal Express had a fiscal 1984 current ratio of 1.28:1, which had declined from 1.5:1 in fiscal 1983. One of the reasons for this decline was the 1984 implementation of ZapMail. To maintain its large credit agreements with banks and other lenders, the company had been relatively conservative with its financial policies. It had not paid any dividends on common stock throughout its incorporated history and maintained minimum levels of working capital and certain financial ratios. The stock price showed consistent growth and split three times since the company went public in 1978. As of May 31, 1984, there were 46,386,287 shares of common stock. The 1983 and 1984 comparative balance sheets are shown in Exhibit 20.6.[85]

The company was determined to grow and expand its services geographically, as is shown by the large increases in capital expenditures during the three years prior to 1985 (see Exhibit 20.7). The bulk of these expenditures were for additional aircraft and additions and improvements to ZapMail equipment. Some of these capital funds had been internally generated; others were proceeds from loan agreements, tax-exempt bond issues and equity offerings. The commitment to growth had a significant effect on the company's cash and working capital. On May 31, 1984, both had suffered declines of 64% and 20%, respectively, from the previous year.

LEGAL SITUATION	Federal's only threat of liability due to litigation involved its ZapMail product. Federal was sued in November 1984 by Zap Legislative Courier Service of Albany, New York, for alleged trademark infringement over the use of the name ZapMail. A judge ruled that the company could seek unspecified monetary and punitive damages from Federal Express. As of May 1985 a trial date had not been set.[86]

OUTLOOK	**Industry**

Andrew B. Kim, a stock analyst for F. Eberstadt & Co., Inc., predicted that, from a stock market standpoint, investors perceived that the profit-margin squeeze would intensify as downward pressures on prices increased, especially if a downturn in the economy materialized. Kim also felt that the rapid increase in demand for the services of the air express and freight industry had been partly due to price reduction but, on the other hand, felt that investors were asking why the companies were all cutting prices when demand was so strong.[87]

Large frequent shippers had become relatively more sensitive to pricing than before. But the quality of service was still the dominant variable for both frequent and infrequent shippers. Federal Express's 400,000 customer base at that time included many infrequent shippers.[88]

EXHIBIT 20.6

Federal Express: Consolidated Balance Sheet for Fiscal Year Ended May 31

(In Thousands of Dollars)

	1983	1984
Assets		
Cash	$ 204	$ 2,190
Short-term investments	105,233	35,500
Net receivables	124,841	207,256
Inventories	16,203	39,725
Prepayments, etc.	18,690	43,465
Total current assets	265,171	328,136
Property, plant, and equipment	817,650	1,427,281
Accumulated depreciation and amortization	(221,258)	(314,642)
Net property, plant, and equipment	596,392	1,112,639
Construction funds in escrow	47,839	32,168
Equipment deposits and other	82,315	52,862
Total assets	991,717	1,525,805
Liabilities and Equity		
Current debt maturity	12,171	22,001
Notes payable	15,912	0
Accounts payable	59,047	129,960
Accrued liabilities	88,163	103,949
Total current liabilities	175,293	255,910
Long-term debt	247,424	435,158
Deferred income tax	59,094	112,439
Total liabilities	481,811	803,507
Preferred stock ($1 par)	6,112	4,577
Common stock ($.1 par)	2,197	4,639
Paid-in surplus	222,782	321,768
Retained earnings	278,815	391,314
Total equity	509,906	722,298
Total liabilities and equity	991,717	1,525,805

The industry's rapid consolidation had invited temporary pricing instability that resulted more from the service-mix change than actual price cutting. Once product lines were broadened, it was expected that future pricing would be essentially dictated by the differential in the cost structures of the six or seven major participants. The barrier to entry was expected to grow higher, not only in terms of capital requirements, but also in terms of

EXHIBIT 20.7

Federal Express: Capital Expenditures
(In Thousands of Dollars)

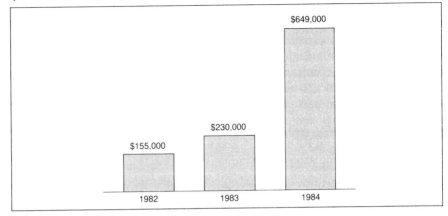

service capability in the full range of markets being served. These markets included four-hour courier service, extended delivery, short-haul trucking, and international forwarding.

Federal Express

Looking at product differentiation, Fred Smith was worried about the startup difficulties of Federal Express's electronic mail service. He blamed these on the painfully slow process of educating the users, even the sophisticated customers.[89]

However, the possibility still remained that the predicted demand for ZapMail did not actually exist. Startup losses had already dramatically exceeded projections, and volume was significantly below expectations. Considering the enormous capital investment involved in the project, Federal was determined to make ZapMail a success and was placing a large stake of the company's future on the service. In view of the enormity of the challenge and the complexity of the logistical problems, historical experience suggested that such a revolutionary new service would need both time and effective marketing to generate volume.

NOTES

1. Eugene Linden, "Frederick W. Smith of Federal Express: He Didn't Get There Over Night," *INC.* (April 1984), p. 89.

2. *Ibid.*, p. 89.

3. *Standard & Poors Industry Surveys* (December 6, 1984), p. A36.

4. Geoffrey Colvin, "Federal Express Dives into Air Mail," *Fortune* (June 15, 1981), p. 107.

5. *Standard & Poors Industry Surveys*, p. A36.

6. *Ibid.*, p. A36.

7. *Ibid.*, p. A36.

8. *10K Report*, Federal Express Corporation, May 31, 1984.

9. Henry Altman, "A Business Visionary Who Really Delivered," *Nation's Business* (November 1981), p. 50.

10. *Ibid.*, p. 50.

11. *Ibid.*, p. 50.

12. Colvin, pp. 106–108.

13. Altman, p. 54.

14. *Ibid.*, p. 54.

15. "Federal Express Rides the Small Package Boom," *Business Week* (March 31, 1980), p. 111.

16. "Creativity with Bill Moyers: Fred Smith and the Federal Express," PBS *Video*, 1981.

17. "The Memphis Connection," *Marketing & Media Decisions* (May 1982), p. 62.

18. *Ibid.*, p. 63.

19. Katie Hafner, "Fred Smith: The Entrepreneur Redux," *INC.* (June 1984), p. 40.

20. *Ibid.*, p. 40.

21. Colvin, p. 107.

22. *1984 Annual Report*, Federal Express Corporation, p. 13.

23. *Ibid.*, p. 13.

24. *1982 Annual Report*, Federal Express Corporation, p. 14.

25. *Ibid.*, p. 14.

26. Colvin, p. 107.

27. *Ibid.*, p. 108.

28. Rick Stoops, "How Federal Express Recruited for a New High-Tech Image," *Personnel Journal* (August 1984), p. 16.

29. "Federal Express Readdresses ZapMail," *Sales and Marketing Management* (March 11, 1985), p. 26.

30. *Ibid.*

31. Colvin, p. 107.

32. *Ibid.*, pp. 6–7.

33. *Ibid.*, p. 9.

34. *10K Report*, Federal Express (May 31, 1984), p. 9.

35. *Ibid.*, p. 10.

36. *Ibid.*, p. 10.

37. *Ibid.*, p. 9.

38. *Ibid.*, p. 10.

39. *1984 Annual Report*, Federal Express Corporation, p. 1.

40. *Service Guide*, Federal Express Corporation, (October 1, 1984), p. 19.

41. *1984 Annual Report*, Federal Express Corporation, p. 10.

42. *Service Guide*, p. 19.

43. *Ibid.*, p. 23.

44. *Ibid.*, p. 27.

45. *Air Freight Progress Report* (New York: Morgan Stanley Investment Research, January 21, 1985), p. 1.

46. *Service Guide*, p. 17.

47. *Air Freight Progress Report* (New York: Morgan Stanley Investment Research, November 19, 1984), p. 1.

48. *Research, Federal Express*, Morgan Keegan & Company, Inc. (November 28, 1983), p. 4.

49. *Air Freight* (January 21, 1985), p. 1

50. *Ibid.*, p. 1.

51. *Ibid.*, p. 1.

52. *Research, Federal Express*, Morgan Keegan & Company, Inc. (February 14, 1985), p. 4.

53. *Ibid.*, p. 4.

54. *Ibid.*, pp. 3–4.

55. *Service Guide*, p. 162.

56. *1984 Annual Report*, Federal Express Corporation, pp. 14–15.

57. *Ibid.*, p. 14.

58. Sean Milmo, "British Air Couriers Welcome U.S. Entrant," *Business Marketing* (April 1984), p. 9.

59. *Ibid.*

60. *Ibid.*

61. "The Memphis Connection," p. 62.

62. *Ibid.*, p. 128.

63. Hank Seiden, "The Delivery Doesn't Fly," *Advertising Age* (October 31, 1983), p. M66.

64. "The Memphis Connection," p. 62.

65. "Federal Express Readdresses ZapMail," p. 26.

66. "Introduction," *1982 Annual Report*, Purolator Courier Corporation.

67. *Ibid.*

68. *Standard & Poors N.Y.S.E. Stock Reports*, p. 1885.

69. *1982 Annual Report*, Purolator Courier Corporation, p. 10.

70. *Ibid.*, p. 8

71. *Standard & Poors N.Y.S.E. Stock Reports*, p. 1885.

72. *Ibid.*, p. 827.

73. "Introduction," *1983 Annual Report*, Emery Air Freight.

74. *Ibid.*, p. 3

75. *Ibid.*, p. 13.

76. *Standard & Poors N.Y.S.E. Stock Reports*, p. 827.

77. "Behind the UPS Mystique: Puritanism and Productivity," *Business Week* (June 6, 1983), p. 66.

78. *Ibid.*, p. 66.

79. *Ibid.*, p. 66.

80. "Express Mail Next Day Service," *U.S. Postal Service Pamphlet Notice 43* (July 1977), p. 2.

81. *Ibid.*, p. 6.

82. *INC.*, Linden, p. 89.

83. *1984 Annual Report,* Federal Express Corporation.
84. *Ibid.*
85. *Standard & Poors Industry Report,* p. 2551.
86. *Wall Street Journal* (December 28, 1984), p. 33.

87. *Research Notes,* F. Eberstadt & Co., Inc. (May 3, 1984), p. 1.
88. *Ibid.,* p. 2.
89. *Ibid.,* p. 2.

Hershey Foods Corporation

JOYCE P. VINCELETTE · THOMAS L. WHEELEN · J. DAVID HUNGER

INTRODUCTION

Hershey Foods Corporation and its subsidiaries engaged in 1985 in the manufacture and distribution of food and food-related items. Since the early 1960s, Hershey Foods had grown from a firm with one plant, a few chocolate products, and sales of $185 million to a multiplant, multiproduct corporation with sales of $1.8 billion in 1984. In addition to becoming a major domestic producer of chocolate and confectionery products, the company operated a chain of restaurants, manufactured and distributed pasta products, operated a coffee service plan, and managed various types of international operations.

To lessen its dependence on chocolate, Hershey began to diversify in the 1960s, but it was not until William Dearden took over as Chief Executive Officer in 1976 that diversification was emphasized as a distinct strategy. When Dearden took office, he made strategic planning his first priority. He charged a corporate planning committee to develop a strategic plan for the company covering the period from 1976 to 1985. The resulting plan for Hershey to become more of a major, diversified, international food and food-related company included the following four strategies:

1. To capitalize on the considerable growth potential in existing brands and products in current markets.

2. To introduce new products.

3. To expand the distribution of long-established, well-known brands into new domestic and foreign markets.

4. To make acquisitions and other types of alliances, both in the United States and elsewhere in the world.

Richard A. Zimmerman was selected by Hershey's board to succeed Dearden as Chief Executive Officer in 1984 and as Chairman of the Board in March 1985. Dearden continued to serve on Hershey's Board of Directors. One of Zimmerman's first priorities in his new position was to assess Hershey

This case was prepared by Professor Joyce P. Vincelette and Professor Thomas L. Wheelen of the University of South Florida, and Professor J. David Hunger of Iowa State University. Initial research was performed by the following MBA students: Marie Anderson, Peggy Gallup, Patty Gibbs, Michael Hall, and Glenn Wilt of the University of South Florida. This case was presented at the North American Case Research Association meeting, 1986. Reprinted by permission of the authors and the North American Case Research Association. Copyright © 1986 by Joyce P. Vincelette, Thomas L. Wheelen, and J. David Hunger. It is also scheduled to appear in the *Journal of Management Case Studies*.

Food Corporation's performance from 1976 to 1985 in light of Dearden's strategic plan. New strategic plans for the next five years also needed to be developed for presentation to the Board of Directors.

HISTORY

Milton S. Hershey dreamed of making candy, but he had many setbacks before he achieved success. His formal education ended at the fourth grade. As a teenager, Hershey worked as an apprentice to a confectioner in Lancaster, Pennsylvania. When he was nineteen, he set out on his own to make penny candy. After business failures in Philadelphia, Chicago, and New York, Milton Hershey finally found success, at the age of forty, making caramels in Lancaster. He sold his caramel business for $1 million in 1900, at age forty-two.

Milton Hershey had traveled to the World's Exposition in Chicago in 1893 and had seen some chocolate-making equipment on exhibit. At that time, only the rich were able to afford chocolate. It was Hershey's conviction that the world was ready for an inexpensive chocolate confection. He purchased chocolate-manufacturing equipment from Germany and began manufacturing chocolate candies. In 1894 he turned out the first Hershey bar, which was made of solid chocolate and sold for a nickel. When the caramel business was sold, Mr. Hershey retained the right to manufacture chocolate, and rented space from his former company. The chocolate business grew, and by 1901, sales were $622,000. Additional manufacturing space was required. Several locations were considered, but Milton Hershey finally decided to build his chocolate factory in Derry Church, Pennsylvania, where he had been born. Derry Church was renamed "Hershey" in 1906 in his honor.

This location was chosen for the Hershey Chocolate Company to capitalize on the availability of fresh milk, which was essential to its two basic products—milk chocolate and almond chocolate bars. By streamlining production methods and gearing output to large standardized quantities sold at moderate prices, the company achieved immediate success. Production in the new factory began in 1905; by 1911, sales had reached $5 million. Hershey became the Henry Ford of the confectionery field, with one major difference: Hershey had no serious competition for over forty years.

Milton Hershey built not only a company, but also a storybook town with street lights shaped like Hershey kisses. Mr. Hershey used to consider the company, the town, and its inhabitants as a large farm of which he was the owner. If the residents wanted or needed something, such as a bank, they asked him and he built it. Among other things, he built two hotels (Hotel Hershey and the Hershey Lodge), an airport, a sports arena, a half-dozen golf courses, and amusement park, a zoo, a public garden, a monorail, and a professional hockey team called the Hershey Bears.

Because Milton and Catherine Hershey were unable to have children, they founded in 1909 the Milton Hershey School for orphan boys. (Girls have been admitted since 1976.) The school, through the Hershey Trust, owned 100% interest in the company until 1927, when approximately 20% of the stock was sold to the public. In the same year, Hershey was incorporated under the laws of the state of Delaware as the Hershey Chocolate Company. When Hershey went public in 1927, Mr. Hershey thought that investors might be concerned about a company that owned things like a zoo and a hockey team. Until 1927 the administration of the company, the town, and the school were intermingled. At this time, all was reorganized, and the Chocolate Corporation acquired all the chocolate properties; Hershey Estates, now the Hershey Entertainment and Resort Company (known as HERCO), owned the amusement park, the hotels, and the hockey team, among other properties; and the Hershey Trust Company continued to oversee the funds of the Milton Hershey School. In 1985, HERCO was owned entirely by the Hershey Trust but had no legal ties to Hershey Foods. The Milton Hershey School received 100% of the profits of HERCO. The orphanage, through the Hershey Trust, still owned 50.1% of the Chocolate Corporation. Dividends from Hershey stock were the orphan school's biggest source of income.

Many people have wondered about an orphanage having as much control as it did at Hershey. As a Hershey officer admitted, "That place is sitting there with the power to remove all the directors of this company if it wanted to. It could do whatever it wants."[1] The orphanage, nevertheless, never wanted to do much more than collect its quarterly checks and educate children. It never traded its stock. Thus, Hershey Foods people tended to look on the school as nonthreatening.

Though Milton Hershey died in 1945, the company maintained much of his conservative philosophy. This included treating all employees fairly and with dignity; providing employees with good working conditions, competitive wages, and rewards according to performance; maintaining quality standards for all ingredients; and tasteful advertising. See Exhibit 21.1 for Hershey's statement of Corporate Philosophy.

In 1968, Hershey adopted a new name, Hershey Foods Corporation, to reflect its broadened product line, represented by the following acquisitions:

1963—H. B. Reese Company (peanut butter candies)

1967—San Giorgio Macaroni, Inc. (pasta)

1967—Delmonico Foods (pasta)

1967—Cory Food Services, Inc. (coffee service)

1977—Y & S Candies (licorice)

1978—Procino-Rossi (pasta)

1979—Skinner Macaroni Company (pasta)

1979—Friendly Ice Cream Corporation (informal restaurants)

1982—Petybon Industries Alimenticias Ltd. (Brazil) (pasta and biscuits)

1984—American Beauty Macaroni Company (pasta)

EXHIBIT 21.1   Statement of Corporate Philosophy[1]

Hershey is in business to make a reasonable profit and to enhance the value of its stockholders' investment, pursuing a policy of profitable growth by further diversifying into other food and food-related business and/or such businesses which offer significant opportunity for growth.

1. All employees should be treated fairly and with dignity, provided with good working conditions and competitive wages, rewarded according to performance. To the fullest extent possible, promotions should be made from within the corporation.

2. Sincere commitment to Hershey's Affirmative Action Program with an obligation to follow it in both the spirit and letter of the law.

3. Results oriented, with all employees given the opportunity to express individual initiative and judgment.

4. Each employee should strive to improve the communications relating to his or her area of responsibility in order to successfully conduct the business of the corporation.

5. Individual and company relationships conducted on the basis of the highest standards of conduct and ethics. Success of the business depends upon the character and integrity of people working in a spirit of constructive cooperation.

6. Provide customers and consumers with products of consistent excellent quality at competitive prices which insure an adequate return on investment.

7. Inherent responsibility to be a good neighbor and to support community projects. All employees encouraged to take an active part in improving the quality of community life.

8. Responsibility to conduct operations within the regulatory guidelines and in a manner that does not adversely affect our environment.

It is imperative to conduct operations throughout our entire organization which cause these philosophies to become a way of life.

[1]This was adopted in 1975 and reaffirmed in 1983.

STRATEGIC MANAGERS

As of March 1, 1985, there were eleven Directors; seven of them from outside the corporation represented the fields of investment banking, public accounting, industrial manufacturing, and education.

The Chairman of the Board and Chief Executive Officer was Richard A. Zimmerman, age 53. A graduate of Pennsylvania State University in 1953, Zimmerman did graduate work at Florida A & M University. He joined Hershey Foods Corporation in 1958 as an Administrative Assistant. After that he held a number of positions at Hershey, including President of Cory Food Services, Inc. between 1971 and 1974. He was named President and

Chief Operating Officer in 1976. He was a member of the Board of Directors of a number of organizations including the Hershey Trust Company. He was also a member of the Board of Managers of the Milton Hershey School.

Also effective March 1, 1985, the Board selected Kenneth L. Wolfe, Senior Vice-President and Chief Financial Officer, to be President and Chief Operating Officer. Wolfe had joined Hershey in 1967 and had been promoted to a number of positions in the Finance Division. In 1984 he was named Senior Vice-President and Chief Financial Officer and was selected to the corporation's Board of Directors. Wolfe held a bachelor's degree from Yale University and a master of business administration in finance from the University of Pennsylvania. Exhibit 21.2 details the structure of Hershey Foods Corporation.

Each of Hershey's divisions operated as a strategic business unit. Joseph P. Viviano was President of Hershey Chocolate Company, replacing Earl J. Spangler, who retired in 1985; David Conn was President of Hershey Canada Inc.; Robert Gaudrault was chairman and CEO of Friendly Ice Cream Corporation; and L. William Chiles was President and CEO of Cory Food

EXHIBIT 21.2   Hershey Foods Corporation: Organizational Chart

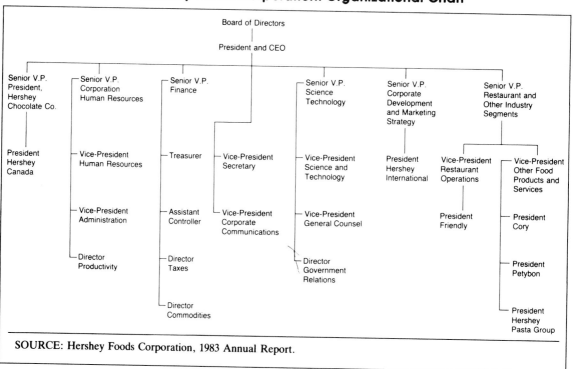

SOURCE: Hershey Foods Corporation, 1983 Annual Report.

Services. In 1984 the company's pasta operations were renamed the Hershey Pasta Group with C. Mickey Skinner as President and CEO.

HUMAN RESOURCES

As of December 31, 1984, Hershey Foods Corporation had a total of 15,200 full-time employees, many of whom were covered under collective bargaining agreements. In addition, Friendly Ice Cream Corporation employed approximately 18,000–23,000 restaurant personnel on a part-time basis. The company considered its employee relations to be good even though there had been a three-week strike at the main chocolate plant in Hershey in November 1980. Hershey Foods believed that its continued growth depended on its ability to manage effectively its human resources. Its stated goal was "to create a challenging, but satisfying, work environment and to provide employees with the opportunity to contribute and share in the future success of the corporation."[2]

To assist in meeting this goal, a number of human-resource-management programs have been established since 1977. Hershey initiated a formal, systematic human-resources-planning and organizational review process to improve the corporation's ability to project its future organizational needs and labor requirements. In addition, management launched a long-range planning program designed to identify the appropriate organizational structure, skills, and employee training and development needs for the next three years.

Critical to the overall planning and development program was the initiation of a new Corporate Management Succession Process. The major thrust of this activity was the identification and development of candidates for key management positions. A top management committee, chaired by the Chief Executive Officer, was set up to provide the necessary guidance in this effort.

BUSINESS SEGMENTS

Hershey Foods Corporation operated in three business segments: *Chocolate and Confectionery Products; Restaurant Operations;* and *Other Food Products and Services.* Operations in the Chocolate and Confectionery segment involved the manufacture and sale of a broad line of chocolate and confectionery products. The principal product groups were bar goods, bagged items, baking ingredients, chocolate drink mixes, and dessert toppings. The Restaurant Operations segment operated restaurants and manufactured certain products sold in those restaurants. The Other Food Products and Services segment was involved in the manufacture and sale of pasta products in the United States and Brazil and in the operation of a coffee service plan for U.S. and Canadian businesses and institutions. In addition, Hershey was involved in a number of other ventures both within the United States and internationally. Exhibit 21.3 presents net sales, operating income, identifiable assets, and other information for the three business segments.

Chocolate and Confectionery Products

Hershey Chocolate Company

Despite an aggressive diversification program, the Hershey Chocolate unit still furnished 16% of the nation's chocolate and accounted for 80% of the operating profits and 68% of the sales of Hershey Foods Corporation in 1984. Hershey Foods' profits have dropped only twice in the past 10 years, in 1973 and 1977, two years when cocoa prices skyrocketed.

Hershey Chocolate Company's strategic plan was first developed in 1976 and remained essentially the same in 1985. Two of the company's principal strategic objectives were to achieve compounded annual real growth in operating income and to continue its market leadership position in chocolate and confectionery products. According to Earl J. Spangler, former President, the principal strategies to achieve these objectives were to (1) increase annual sales of existing products, (2) develop new products, (3) acquire new businesses, and (4) develop special markets.

MANAGEMENT Earl J. Spangler retired as President of Hershey Chocolate Company on January 1, 1985, after 34 years of service to the company. Joseph P. Viviano was named as his successor. Viviano also served as a Senior Vice-President of Hershey Foods.

Viviano began his career in 1960 when he joined his family's pasta business, Delmonico Foods, Inc., in Louisville, Kentucky. Hershey acquired Delmonico in 1966. Viviano was named Vice-President of Operations in 1968 and promoted to President in 1972. After the merger of Delmonico with San Giorgio Macaroni, Inc. in 1975, he was appointed President of the combined companies. In 1979 the pasta division was again enlarged with the acquisition of Skinner Macaroni Company, and Viviano became President of the newly formed San Giorgio-Skinner Company.

PRODUCTS Hershey Chocolate Company produced a broad line of chocolate and confectionery products. The principle product groups formed two major categories: *Confectionery Products,* including goods such as Hershey Chocolate Bars, Kisses, and Peanut Butter Cups; and *Grocery Products,* including cocoa syrup, chocolate chips, and chocolate milk, among other goods.

To increase the sales of existing products, Hershey Chocolate Company has restructured and expanded its consumer sales force to over 470 men and women. This restructured sales force created substantial incremental sales volume. Six of Hershey's traditional products—Hershey's Milk Chocolate Bars, Hershey's Almond Bars, Kisses, Syrup, Mr. Goodbar, and Reese's

EXHIBIT 21.3

Hershey Foods Corporation: Financial Statistics by Industry Segments
(In Thousands of Dollars) For the Year Ended December 31

	1984	1983	1982	1981	1980	1979	1978	1977	1976
Net sales									
Chocolate and confectionery	$1,287,100	$1,159,065	$1,081,558	$1,015,106	$ 929,885	$ 822,813	$678,652	$586,882	$526,822
Restaurant operations	427,122	383,543	335,836	302,908	274,297	224,072	0	0	0
Other food products and services	178,284	163,497	148,342	133,137	131,107	114,410	89,228	84,345	75,138
Total net sales	$1,892,506	$1,706,105	$1,565,736	$1,451,151	$1,335,289	$1,161,295	$767,880	$671,227	$601,960
Operating income									
Chocolate and confectionery	$ 195,810	$ 179,253	$ 154,805	$ 142,648	$ 118,435	$ 99,880	$ 79,143	$ 69,834	$ 86,898
Restaurant operations	41,770	39,428	34,279	29,309	25,567	23,322	0	0	0
Other food products and services	4,804	4,692	4,947	7,250	51,482	6,397	5,061	4,528	5,005
Total operating income	$ 242,384	$ 223,373	$ 194,031	$ 179,207	$ 149,150	$ 129,599	$ 84,204	$ 74,362	$ 91,903
General corporate expenses	22,464	18,208	14,629	11,763	10,190	7,742	4,981	3,491	2,299
Interest expense (income)—net	10,349	15,814	7,859	12,512	14,100	17,764	(2,683)	(509)	357
Income before taxes	209,571	189,351	171,543	154,932	124,860	104,093	81,906	71,380	89,247
Less: Income taxes	100,889	89,185	77,375	74,580	62,805	50,589	40,450	35,349	45,562
Discontinued operations	0	0	0	0	0	0	0	(5,300)	(1,112)
Net income	$ 108,682	$ 100,166	$ 94,168	$ 80,352	$ 62,055	$ 53,504	$ 41,456	$ 41,331	$ 44,797
Identifiable assets:									
Chocolate and confectionery	$ 580,586	$ 552,422	$ 528,194	$ 445,815	$ 333,232	$297,296	$241,070	$221,928	$222,541
Restaurant operations	273,356	251,781	234,860	223,265	219,196	207,125	0	0	0
Other food products and services	152,747	84,964	83,345	63,446	62,553	63,886	50,450	47,023	44,325
Corporate	115,878	94,777	58,355	96,921	69,491	38,892	130,484	127,202	65,004
Total identifiable assets	$1,122,567	$ 983,944	$ 904,754	$ 829,447	$ 684,472	$607,199	$422,004	$396,153	$331,870

(Continued)

EXHIBIT 21.3 (Continued)

	1984	1983	1982	1981	1980	1979	1978	1977	1976
Depreciation:									
Chocolate and confectionery	$ 17,636	$ 14,393	$ 10,225	$ 9,554	$ 8,469	$ 7,389	$ 6,574	$ 5,702	$ 5,439
Restaurant operations	18,874	17,066	15,574	14,379	10,015	10,283	0	0	0
Other food products and services	5,524	4,597	3,670	2,675	2,671	2,185	1,720	1,789	1,755
Corporate	1,079	1,218	1,212	957	741	658	556	504	345
Total depreciation	$ 43,113	$ 37,274	$ 30,681	$ 27,565	$ 21,896	$ 20,515	$ 8,850	$ 7,995	$ 7,539
Capital additions:									
Chocolate and confectionery	$ 37,508	$ 51,779	$ 77,074	$ 57,504	$ 27,061	$ 29,472	$ 26,586	$ 22,381	$ 17,227
Restaurant operations	41,885	35,751	28,005	22,098	24,468	20,965	0	0	0
Other food products and services	5,574	7,462	7,022	5,525	6,141	2,233	4,420	3,014	1,754
Corporate	2,082	10,252	4,635	6,546	1,359	3,767	6,419	2,140	1,741
Total capital additions	$ 87,049	$ 105,244	$ 116,736	$ 91,673	$ 59,029	$ 56,437	$ 37,425	$ 27,535	$ 20,722

SOURCE: Hershey Foods Corporation Annual Reports, 1984, 1983, 1980, 1978, and 1976.

Peanut Butter Cups—had a compound annual growth rate of more than 11% in dollar sales between 1979 and 1983. Together these brands accounted for almost $600 million in sales in 1982.

The impetus behind Hershey Chocolate Company's strategies of developing new products and acquiring new businesses had been the need to lessen the impact of the cocoa bean on its overall business. In addition, Hershey's diversification efforts coincided with a shift in consumer tastes away from its traditional, predominantly chocolate candies. In 1963, predominantly chocolate products accounted for 80% of the candy division's sales; in 1983 the figure was down to 46%. America's candy eaters, once lovers of solid milk chocolate, seemed to prefer snacks that combined chocolate, nuts, and wafers. "People want a more complex, more interesting texture," said James F. Echeandia, a candy industry consultant in Orlando, Florida.[3] In 1985, more consumers appeared to be concerned about the nutritional value of the snacks they ate.

One way Hershey has been diversifying is through acquisition, as in the case of Y & S Licorice Products, which Hershey acquired in 1977. Hershey has also been broadening its product line through line extensions, such as Hershey's Big Block, which was introduced in 1980 at 50 cents, and through internally developed new products, many of which contained significantly less chocolate, such as Reese's Pieces, and Whatchamacallit in the moderately priced area and the Golden Almond Bar, Hershey Golden Almond Solitaires, and Skor in the luxury chocolate line. Skor was manufactured at the Hershey plant under license from Hershey's Swedish affiliate, AB Maribou. Skor was the most popular chocolate/toffee brand in the United States in 1984.

A number of new products have been introduced into regional markets as the foundation for future growth of new products. These included Reese's Pieces Peanut, the Golden Pecan Bar, and Take Five, a wafer bar layered with peanut butter creme and covered with milk chocolate, which was introduced and positioned as a light but satisfying adult snack. Hershey's management was now looking to Take Five to make important future contributions.

Responding to the $250 million granola industry, Hershey was courting health-conscious consumers with a product containing little or no chocolate— New Trail Granola Bars. Introduced nationally in late 1983 after almost two years in test markets, New Trail Bars had already captured by 1985 a sizable chunk of the rapidly expanding granola market. New Trail Bars came in six flavors (only two of which contained chocolate), and other varieties were planned. Hershey officials, who promoted New Trail as a snack, initially feared that a strong link with the Hershey name would make consumers think of the bars as candy. But the product has been so successful that Hershey has moved its name, previously in small print on the back of the package, to a prominent spot on the front.

New ground was broken in 1983 with Hershey's first franchised product, Hershey Chocolate Milk. The Company licensed the Hershey trademark for use on the milk carton and sold its own formulation of powdered chocolate-flavor mix to licensed dairies with market areas covering all fifty states. The dairies had full responsibility for producing the chocolate milk and selling it to retailers. Hershey promoted the product with consumer advertising and ensured that rigorous quality standards were met by the dairies. Hershey had become the largest selling national distributor of branded chocolate milk in the United States by 1985.

New product introductions have not always gone smoothly. Sales of Hershey's Whatchamacallit, a chocolate-covered crisped rice bar, have been slipping. Hershey's entry into the ready-to-spread frosting market, a four-product "Frostin" line, was not successful and was withdrawn in 1983 after two years. Hershey claimed that it was a victim of line and price promotion and could not compete with brands that had cake mixes to complement their frosting lines.

Internationally, Hershey was following the joint venture and licensing approach with already well-established food and confectionery companies. In 1983, Hershey was selling Kit Kat, Rolo, and After Eight under license from Roundtree Mackintosh of Great Britain and licorice products under license from Bassets of Great Britain. Hershey's rights under these agreements were extendable on a long-term basis at the company's option, subject to minimum sales limitations. As of 1985, these requirements have been substantially exceeded. In 1983, Kit Kat was one of the fastest growing major brands in the confectionery industry. In 1984 the Marabou Milk Chocolate Roll, which was imported from AB Marabou, Sweden, was successfully marketed on a nationwide basis.

Sales of new chocolate and confectionery products from 1980 to 1984 have increased from 5% to 22% of total unit sales. While lessening the company's dependence on chocolate, the new snacks have also added some variety to Hershey's line of products. Company officials believed that people rarely buy the same candy twice in a row. "All we can hope to do is get on your menu," said John H. Dowd, Vice-President for New Business Development in Hershey's confectionery division.[4]

To achieve their fourth growth strategy of developing special markets, a separate business unit, the Special Markets Department, was established in 1979 and assigned the responsibility for the sale of special confections, fund-raising projects (of the type in which scouting and school groups participate), food service, institutional products, and industrial products.

CONSUMERS   Candy consumption in the United States hit a peak of 20 pounds per person per year in the late 1960s. Factors such as price rises, substitute products, and an increasing concern for health and nutrition combined to cause consumption to diminish to 16.7 pounds per person per year in 1984. This per capita consumption of chocolate was about half that in England and Western Europe.

MANUFACTURING AND DISTRIBUTION   The success of Hershey's new products, coupled with the continued growth of its traditional products, caused Hershey Chocolate Company plants to run at full capacity. The Company took steps to remedy this situation with the construction of a new plant in Stuarts Draft, Virginia. This $90 million, 458,000-square-foot facility began production in October 1982. This plant increased Hershey's capacity for the production of recently introduced products as well as provided for the manufacturing needs of future products.

For many years the Hershey Chocolate Company's main plant in Hershey served as the primary distribution center in the East; it served volume customers as well as field warehouses strategically located throughout the continental United States, Hawaii, Puerto Rico, and Canada. New products and production facilities created a strain on the Hershey Plant to store finished product, mix inventories, and ship orders.

The need for a facility to perform these functions became obvious. After much study a 65-acre site in New Kingston, Pennsylvania, was selected. This location was 20 miles west of the main manufacturing facility in Hershey. Construction of an Eastern Distribution Center began in November 1982, and the 435,000-square-foot, $16 million facility became fully operational in November 1983. The site for the distribution center was chosen for its centralized location in relation to the company's eastern manufacturing facilities and for its prime access to major interstate highways and railroad systems.

Hershey's products were distributed in the United States and abroad through a network of thirty-two field warehouses and by direct shipment to customers from the manufacturing plants. Location of customers and the quantity ordered determined the method of shipment and warehousing. Hershey's customers included convenience stores, grocery chains, independent grocery wholesalers, candy and tobacco distributors, syndicate stores, drug chains, and vending machine operators. These formed the link between Hershey and the consumer.

In 1985, finished goods moved from the manufacturing plants to the Eastern Distribution Center for storage and mixing. This center served as the stock replenishment point for twenty-four field warehouses, the Western Distribution Center, and volume customers located east of Colorado. The Oakdale, California, plant, serving as a distribution center in the West, replenished the western field warehouses and supported direct shipments to volume customers.

The field warehouses serviced most customers who placed orders for less than 25,000 pounds of product. They were commercial warehouses that provided temperature-controlled storage space in the major market areas.

The field warehouses gave Hershey the ability to deliver in temperature-controlled trucks an order to any of their less-than-truckload customers within 48–72 hours of receipt. To improve customer service and information turnaround, as well as to enhance inventory control and reduce operating costs, Hershey computerized its field-order–processing and inventory-control system.

MARKETING AND SALES Hershey's leadership in the chocolate and confectionery industry was based on three criteria: high quality of product, mass distribution, and optimum consumer value consistent with earning a profit in the competitive marketplace.

Hershey confectionery products were sold to some 65,000 wholesalers and retailers in 20,000 cities and towns by its sales and marketing forces. The field sales organization totaled over 470 full-time sales representatives and over 200 part-time sales merchandisers throughout the United States and Canada. This was a conventional selling organization in which sales representatives sold to the customer directly and then contacted retail outlets to draw the product out of customer warehouses.

The United States was divided into six sales divisions, twenty-four sales regions, and ninety-six districts, each with its own district manager. Canada was divided into six districts with independent wholesalers.

Hershey used the brand-manager concept of marketing management. The brands manager and the new-products manager were responsible for the development of the total marketing plan for the profitable growth of their assigned brands. They worked under the direction of the marketing manager, who along with the managers of marketing research and packing development, reported to the divisional Vice-President for Marketing. Exhibit 21.4 depicts a partial marketing and sales structure of Hershey Chocolate Company.

An innovative concept introduced by its Sales Department in 1983 was the retail merchandising force. This sales force of part-time people has enabled Hershey to economically expand its coverage of smaller retail outlets such as convenience stores. Before the formation of this retail merchandising force, Hershey's sales representatives did not have time to cover these outlets and concentrated on mass-merchandising outlets such as supermarkets. The additional part-time sales coverage resulted in Hershey's capability to improve the position and salability of its products in previously uncontacted retail outlets.

For the purpose of developing special markets, the Special Markets Department was established in 1981 and assigned the responsibility for the sale of specialty confections, fund-raising projects, food service, and institutional and industrial products. To exploit the growth opportunities in these special market categories, Hershey developed an institutional broker network of over sixty brokers to sell to its special market customers. This selling organization has been very effective, as is shown by special-markets sales growth since 1976 of over 230%.

EXHIBIT 21.4 **Hershey Chocolate Company: Marketing and Sales Structure**

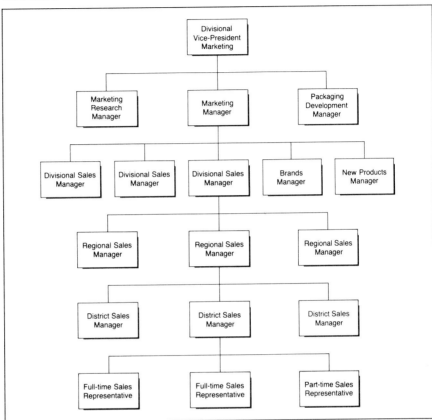

COMPETITORS In the $5 billion a year candy business, one percentage point of market share represents approximately $50 million in sales. In response to industry pressures, chocolate and confectionery-product manufacturers resorted to producing more chocolate-coated candies and reducing the sizes of bars while increasing prices to the retailer. Many retail stores sold similar sizes or types of candy at one price to avoid confusion, regardless of small wholesale price differences.

In November 1980, Mars, Inc. broke industry tradition: It increased candy bar size without increasing price. The 10% weight increase resulted in a 50% increase in sales. Mars' market share increased from 37% to 46%. Hershey's share decreased from 28% to 26% while Curtiss, Peter Paul Cadbury, D. L. Clark, and Nabisco suffered even more, because most of the market expansion went to Mars.

Confectionery companies change the prices and weights of their products from time to time to accommodate changes in the cost of manufacturing (including the cost of raw materials), the competitive environment, and profit objectives. In September 1981, Mars increased its bar prices to 30 cents retail. Hershey did not and advertised that it had not raised prices and was not responsible for the higher prices stores were charging. Most other candy makers followed Mars' lead, and most stores charged the same higher price to avoid confusion and pocketed the difference.

In March 1982, Hershey increased its price to 30 cents and increased the weight of its bars by 35%. In December 1983, Hershey increased its price to 35 cents, a 17% wholesale price hike reflecting the increase in cocoa prices to about $1.20 per pound. Mars increased its bar prices to 35 cents in April 1984. Exhibit 21.5 details these price/weight changes.

By 1983, industry analysts estimated that Hershey and Mars were "locked in a head-to-head confrontation." Hershey's Marketing Department estimated the market share to be 33% for each firm. Six of the twelve top-selling bars were made by Mars. Hershey made four. The remainder of the top candy manufacturers included Standard Brands, Nestle, and Cadbury. Exhibit 21.6 lists the top-selling candy bars of 1983.

EXHIBIT 21.5   Hershey and Mars Price and Weight Changes

YEAR	MARS (SNICKERS)			HERSHEY (PLAIN)		
	Ounces	Price	Cost/oz.	Ounces	Price	Cost/oz.
1921				1.0	.05	5.0 cents
1930	2.5	.05	2.0 cents			
1968	1.16	.05	4.3	.75	.05	6.7
1969	2.3	.10	4.3	1.5	.10	6.7
1973	2.3	.15	6.5			
1976 (Jan.)	2.3	.20	8.7	1.2	.15	12.5
1976 (Dec.)				1.35	.20	14.8
1977				1.2	.20	16.7
1978	2.3	.25	10.9	1.2	.25	20.8
1980 (Apr.)				1.05	.25	23.8
1980 (Oct.)	1.69	.25	14.8			
1980 (Nov.)	1.8	.25	13.9			
1981 (Sept.)	1.8	.30	16.7			
1982	1.8	.30	16.7	1.45	.30	20.7
1983 (Dec.)				1.45	.35	24.1

SOURCES: 1921–1981: *Washington Post,* May 17, 1981: 1976–1982: *Washington Post,* July 11, 1982; and 1982–1983: Hershey Foods Corporation, *1983 Annual Report.*

EXHIBIT 21.6   **National Candy Buyers' Survey of the Top Ten Candy Bars,[1] 1983**

RANK	BRAND	MANUFACTURER	1977 RANK
1	Snickers	Mars	1
2	M & M Peanut	Mars	3
3	M & M Plain	Mars	4
	Reese's Peanut Butter Cup	Hershey	2
4	3 Musketeers	Mars	5
5	Hershey Almond	Hershey	7
	Milky Way	Mars	6
6	Hershey Plain	Hershey	9
7	Kit Kat	Hershey	8
8	Almond Joy	Peter Paul Cadbury	
9	Mars Bar	Mars	
10	Mounds	Peter Paul Cadbury	

SOURCE: *Candy Industry* (May 1983), pp. 52–58.

[1]Because this survey was based on a regional basis (Northeast, Southeast, North Central, South Central, Mountain, and Pacific), national rankings were derived by summing regional rankings.

To battle Mars, Hershey had been regularly adding new confectionery products containing less chocolate. Mars made some aggressive moves of its own. To expand sales, it had started a campaign trying to convince customers that candy was an acceptable snack food rather than a cause of tooth decay, acne, or obesity. Mars paid about $5 million to sponsor the 1984 summer and winter Olympic games and promoted Snickers and M & M products as the "official snack foods" of the Olympics. In addition, Mars has been known in the industry for its aggressive sales force.

INDUSTRY FORECASTS   The confectionery industry anticipated changing demographics between 1985 and 1990. The under-18 age group, the dominant consumption group, will be shrinking; senior citizens will be growing in numbers; and the 35–54 age group, the main buyers of boxed chocolates, will be the dominant age group. Hershey's research revealed some important facts about the candy consumer. Consumers tended to make their purchases from a menu or roster of ten to twelve bars and never to buy the same bar twice in a row. In addition, the heavy users (six or more bars in thirty days), who made up 24.6% of the population, consumed 68.5% of all the candy sold. The light users represented 66.4% of the population and consumed 31.5% of the candy.

Research also indicated that traditional meal patterns have changed considerably with today's busy lifestyles. More and more people eat when they can and when they choose. Snacking has become an acceptable way of eating for both children and adults. Because of the changing eating patterns, consumers' taste preferences have shifted away from the traditional, predominately chocolate bar to a combination bar that is a more nutritionally balanced snack.

In 1983, there were two noteworthy trends. First, per capita consumption of candy had been increasing since 1981, reversing an earlier trend, even though overall consumption declined at a compound annual rate of 0.9% between 1972 and 1983. Specifically, per capita consumption increased 2.5% in 1981, 3.7% in 1982, and 2% in 1983. In 1983, U.S. per capita consumption of all chocolate and nonchocolate candies, including imports, reached approximately 17.0 pounds. In 1984, per capita consumption of chocolate was 16.7 pounds. The most significant increase was in the consumption of imported candy, which reached 0.65 pound per capita in 1983, an increase of 8% over 1982. The second trend concerned the gain in popularity of ultra-expensive chocolate candies. In 1983, assortments of these ultra-expensive chocolate candies secured a larger share of the presentation-box candy market. These costly chocolates, which featured elaborate packaging and exotic ingredients, were usually available in a select group of retail outlets, such as department stores, and sold for about $18.00 per pound and up. In comparison, most domestic chocolate assortments, which were widely available, sold for $5.00–$7.00 per pound. To respond to this trend, Hershey had introduced the Golden Almond Bar and Skor and was researching and test marketing other products for inclusion in this product line.

Halloween has always been an important season for the sale of confectionery products, especially in the bar goods segment. In 1982, Halloween retail candy sales dropped between 10% and 25%, depending on area, because of the Tylenol scare and copycat product tampering. Halloween sales traditionally accounted for $1.5 billion of an annual industry total of $5.4 billion. In 1983 the industry mounted a consumer education program and made arrangements for a Halloween Hotline to the National Confectioners Association and the Chocolate Manufactures Association in order to "nip in the bud" possible erroneous reporting. In addition, drug manufacturers introduced new, more secure, tamper-resistant packaging. Also in 1983, President Reagan signed into law a bill that defined willful adulteration of food products as a felony, with severe penalties attached. Because of these efforts, Halloween sales of candy in 1983 increased but had not regained 1981 levels.

Hershey Canada, Inc.

After thirty years of exporting its products through wholesale candy brokers in Canada, Hershey established its Canadian operation in 1963, with the opening of a 250,000-square-foot chocolate-making plant in Smith Falls, Ontario. This operation was augmented in late 1977 when Hershey acquired

U.S.-based Y & S Candies, Inc., which included a 125,000-square-foot licorice plant in Montreal that became part of Hershey Canada, Inc. after the acquisition. By 1981 the Canadian operation was achieving record sales and substantial increases in tonnage in the chocolate, grocery, and licorice areas; new products accounted for over 25% of consumer sales. During 1981, Hershey's Canadian chocolate and confectionery operations were re-organized and transferred to a wholly owned subsidiary, Hershey Canada, Inc. In addition, a new company headquarters office was opened in Toronto to house the entire administrative and financial staffs.

In addition to introducing into the Canadian market several of the products for which Hershey was well known in the United States, Hershey Canada has also developed some unique products of its own, designed particularly for the Canadian market. These have included Brown Cow and Strawberry Cow, both cold milk modifiers, and Top Scotch, a butterscotch-flavored ice cream topping. In addition, Hershey Canada introduced in 1983 a completely new chocolate, which was designed, after extensive consumer testing, to satisfy the taste of the Canadian consumer. Hershey Canada implemented other significant changes in its business during 1983. The package graphics on the Hershey Bar line were completely redesigned; the weight of Reese's Peanut Butter Cups and Special Crisp were increased by 23% and 20%, respectively; bar prices were increased from $0.40 to $0.45 to match the competition; and part-time sales merchandisers were added to the company's sales organization.

In 1984, Hershey Canada, Inc. achieved record sales, and operating income improved substantially in comparison with 1983. The sales increase in 1984 came almost totally from volume increases on established products and the introduction of new products, as selling prices remained at the approximate levels of 1983. To take advantage of available plant capacity, a program to supply selected products to the United States was developed and implemented in the second half of 1984. This program was a major contributor to Hershey Canada's favorable operating results in 1984.

Restaurant Operations

Friendly Ice Cream Corporation

In 1979, Hershey Foods acquired the Friendly Ice Cream Corporation for $164 million ($75 million in debentures and $89 million in cash) and entered the restaurant industry. At that time, Friendly was a nonfranchised chain of 613 ice cream and sandwich shops located in the New England, Middle Atlantic, and Midwestern states. At the time of purchase it was vertically integrated, with two plants and products distributed in its own refrigerated trucks.

By the end of 1984, 707 family or mall restaurants, located in sixteen states, were in operation. The space in shopping centers was held under lease, while 68% of the freestanding sites were owned by Friendly. Essentially, all of Friendly's units were concentrated in suburban areas. Exhibit 21.7 lists the shops by state. A second O'goodies! ice cream dip shop was opened in 1984. At O'goodies shops, customers could create their own sundaes and ice cream flavors, as well as obtain a variety of beverages and made-on-the-premises baked products. This concept was in a development and testing phase to determine its viability as a growth vehicle.

Friendly's plants at Wilbraham, Massachusetts, and Troy, Ohio, manufactured the ice cream and most of the syrups and toppings used in its units. Most of the meat used was processed in the Wilbraham plant and was shipped to the units in frozen form. Most of the other food and supplies were also furnished by these plants and distributed to each unit by a company-operated fleet of refrigerated trucks. A limited number of other items—mostly milk, baked goods, eggs, and produce—were purchased from local sources designated by Friendly's purchasing department. Friendly also maintained its own real estate, engineering, construction, carpentry, decorating, design, and maintenance departments. Approximately 10,400 square feet of additional production and office space was added to Friendly's

EXHIBIT 21.7

Friendly Ice Cream Shops

State	1979	1980	1983	1984[1]
Connecticut	75	73	74	75
Delaware	3	3	3	3
Illinois	4	4	4	4
Indiana	4	3	2	2
Maine	5	5	5	6
Maryland	22	23	24	29
Massachusetts	182	187	179	179
Michigan	15	9	9	8
New Hampshire	11	11	12	13
New Jersey	48	49	60	64
New York	117	123	134	153
Ohio	76	78	82	89
Pennsylvania	37	42	46	53
Rhode Island	5	5	5	7
Vermont	3	4	4	5
Virginia	6	9	13	14
Total	613	628	656	709

SOURCE: Friendly Ice Cream Executive Office Pamphlet, June 1985.

[1]Number of stores as of June 1985, less those under construction.

Wilbraham, Massachusetts, headquarters in 1983, and new production equipment was installed, to enhance the company's capacity for the production of ice cream pies and extruded products such as Wattamelon Roll.

Between 1981 and 1984 a number of programs to improve productivity and customer service have been undertaken. Standardized and expanded menus were introduced for all restaurants, field sales supervision was realigned along geographic lines, sharp increases were made in promotional expenditures, and advances were made in prefabricated restaurant-building techniques. In addition, significant capital investment for future growth was being made through the Restaurant Modification Program. By 1985, Friendly was in the process of modifying its restaurants from ice cream and sandwich shops to informal family restaurants serving high-quality, moderately priced menu items such as spaghetti.

"We have tried to strengthen the conviction of what we want Friendly to be," said Mr. Zimmerman. "Friendly has something special: the fourth meal. Everyone else has breakfast, lunch and dinner. We have a snack portion. We do a lot of business after eight o'clock at night, and it's not hamburgers, it's ice cream."[5]

Other Food Products and Services

Hershey Pasta Group

The history of Hershey's involvement in the pasta business began in 1967 with the acquisition of San Giorgio Macaroni Company of Lebanon, Pennsylvania, from the Guerrisi family. This brand was a familiar name in Central Pennsylvania, but distribution was limited mostly to the Pennsylvania, Washington, D.C., and New York areas. In the same year, Hershey acquired Delmonico Foods of Louisville, Kentucky, from the Viviano family. The Delmonico brand distribution was mostly in Kentucky, Ohio, and parts of West Virginia. The two pasta companies were consolidated into one in 1975 under the name San Giorgio Macaroni Company, Inc.

In 1978, San Giorgio acquired the Procino-Rossi Company of Albany, New York, a third family-owned business with a high-quality Italian-oriented brand. Sales of P & R were limited to upper New York state.

The pasta division acquired the Skinner Macaroni Company of Omaha, Nebraska, in 1979 for 398,680 shares of Hershey stock. Acquired from the Skinner family, this brand was sold predominantly in the southwestern and the southeastern parts of the United States and represented Hershey's first departure from an Italian-oriented brand name.

By 1981, San Giorgio was the fastest growing pasta brand in the United States, with a 10% market share (worth $800 million at retail) that was second only to Mueller, with a 16% market share. Record sales and operating income were achieved in both 1982 and 1983, as well as additions to operating capacity. The company marketed its products under several brand names, including San Giorgio, Skinner, Delmonico, P & R, and Light 'N Fluffy as well as certain private labels, to chain grocery stores, grocery wholesalers, convenience stores, and food distributors.

Hershey Foods Corporation announced on September 21, 1984, that it had reached an agreement with The Pillsbury Company for the purchase of American Beauty Macaroni Company, a division of Pillsbury. Under the agreement, Hershey purchased certain assets of the American Beauty business, including three plant facilities, fixed assets, inventories, and trademarks. American Beauty was a full-line, consumer-branded, dry pasta company, which conducted its business mostly in the central, southwestern, and western United States.

According to Richard A. Zimmerman, Hershey's President and Chief Executive Officer, "This acquisition is consistent with the company's stated objective of expanding its business into geographical areas where essentially it does not market its pasta products."[6]

This acquisition moved Hershey into the number one market-share position in branded pasta sales in the United States. To better reflect the character of the consolidation of Hershey's five strong regional brands, the company's pasta operations were renamed the Hershey Pasta Group in 1984.

Annual per capita consumption of pasta increased from 8.6 pounds in 1975 to almost 11 pounds in 1985 and was still growing. By comparison, Italians ate an average of 66 pounds of pasta per year in 1985. In the same period, pasta dollar sales in the United States grew by over 170%. Between 1980 and 1985, dry pasta sales grew at three times the growth rate of other dry groceries in supermarket sales and dry pasta continued to be one of the leading food categories in the grocery store. Much of this growth has gone to Italian imports. In waging an attack on the Italian imports and attempting to increase pasta consumption, U.S. pasta makers stressed quality, cut costs, and developed new products such as low-calorie, high-protein pasta.

Research also showed that pasta, relative to other carbohydrates, was inexpensive, and the long-term projections of high meat prices indicated a continued strong pasta market through 1990. The branded pasta industry as a whole was expected to reach a billion-dollar sales level at retail by the mid-1980s.

Cory Food Services, Inc.

Cory Food Services, Inc. was a Chicago-based provider of one of the largest coffee-service plans for businesses and institutions in the United States and Canada. The company provided and serviced its own brewing equipment in locations to which it sold and delivered coffee and other related products. In addition to coffee services, Cory provided allied product services such as hot tea, hot soup mixes, and hot cocoa and leased water-treatment units, microwave ovens, and compact refrigeration units. Cory was acquired in 1967 for $25 million and in that year became a wholly owned subsidiary of Hershey Foods.

The state of the economy affected Cory more than it did Hershey's other businesses. A depressed economy led to cutbacks in coffee use through layoffs and subsequent reduction in consumption. High inflation reduced expenditures for coffee. Hot summers have a depressing effect on coffee consumption. Because of weather and economic conditions in coffee-bean–growing countries, there were wide fluctuations in the prices of green coffee beans. In addition, customers' perceptions toward lowered caffeine consumption have changed dramatically since the coffee-service concept was introduced in the mid-1960s. Annual per capita consumption in the United States had declined from 39.2 gallons in 1964 to 32.8 gallons in 1972 and to 26.4 gallons in 1982.

In 1978, Cory withdrew from the consumer products market. In addition, Cory disposed of its manufacturing operations, because of reduced profitability in the manufacture of brewing equipment and other appliances. In 1979 a major market survey revealed that Cory had the largest market share and a lower account turnover than the industry average; but by 1980, Cory was experiencing a decrease in its consumer base. Cory President George E. Wilber, Jr. resigned in September 1980; Ogden C. Johnson, the corporation's Vice-President of Science and Technology, assumed the additional responsibility of Acting President of Cory until a new president was selected.

L. William Chiles was appointed President and Chief Executive Officer of Cory in 1981. Sales in 1981 were hampered by inflation, unemployment, and decreased per capita consumption of coffee, although sales of allied products (tea, soup, canned juices, and leases of water treatment units, microwave ovens, and compact refrigeration units) showed growth. By 1982 the significant issues were considered to be the need for more effective sales and marketing programs, management training and compensation, restructured product pricing, and the addition and expansion of new lines of business such as a line extension to include gourmet coffees. By 1983, financial results were well below expectations because of competitive price pressures and hot summer months. At this time the field management structure was completely reorganized, and sales and customer service were separated, in an attempt to maximize productivity and focus management expertise in these areas.

To place greater emphasis on Cory's expertise with large accounts and its national service capability, a new sales team to focus on major account development and service was formed in 1984. These customers were particularly valuable to Cory because their high-volume purchases did not require a proportionate investment in brewers and related equipment. Another major change in 1984 was the revision of the sales force compensation plan, in an effort to improve the quality of the sales force.

Hershey International, Ltd.

The Hershey approach has been to form joint ventures with partners abroad who were willing to risk their own capital and who had strong, well-established businesses and a good knowledge of local market conditions. As with its domestic markets, Hershey's international investments and commercial activities concentrated primarily in the chocolate, confectionery, and pasta areas.

In 1977, Hershey staffed an International Department to actively pursue joint ventures, licensing, and export opportunities. In 1978, Hershey's investment and development activities in the international field expanded considerably. Special emphasis was placed on Brazil, which is larger than the United States in area and had half the population of South America. In 1981, all non-Canadian business interests were grouped into a new subsidiary company, Hershey International, Ltd., so that the monitoring, control, and reporting of international operations was strengthened. Despite a worldwide poor economy, exports were profitable in 1982, and joint ventures were profitable in local currencies, although Hershey experienced losses on foreign-exchange adjustments. By 1983, industry-wide profits were hurt by poor economic conditions worldwide, weak foreign currencies, and severe financial problems in South America and Latin America.

Hershey International, Ltd's sales and operating income in 1984 increased significantly over those of the previous year, in spite of the continuing high inflation levels and depressed economic conditions prevailing in two of the company's largest foreign markets, Brazil and Mexico. Export sales in 1984 surpassed the previous year's level despite the continued high value of the U.S. dollar. Marketing programs supporting these export sales activities were monitored closely and adapted as was necessary to meet local competition.

In the U.S. market, Hershey was working closely with three European manufacturers of chocolate and confectionery products: Roundtree Mackintosh of York, England, for the sales and/or manufacture of Kit Kat, Rolo, and After Eight; P. Ferrero of Alba, Italy, for the test marketing of its Kinder line; and Bassets of Great Britain for the importation and distribution of high-quality licorice products.

PETYBON INDUSTRIAS ALIMENTICIAS LTDA. (BRAZIL) Petybon was originally a 40% joint venture between Hershey Foods Corporation and S. A. Industrias Reunidas F. Matarazzo of Sao Paulo, Brazil. This joint venture was formed in 1979 to manufacture and distribute pasta, biscuits, and margarine products, and to sell cooking oils, flour, candles, and soap manufactured by the Food Division of Matarazzo and other companies. Hershey purchased the remaining 60% for $13 million in 1982.

A. B. MARABOU (SUNDBYBERG, SWEDEN) Marabou was the leading chocolate and confectionery manufacturer in Sweden, and manufactured and distributed a complete line of chocolate and confectionery products. In 1977, Hershey acquired a 20% interest for direct investment and a joint research partnership for the exchange of production technology and know-how. In addition, Hershey began to import Marabou's fine-quality boxed chocolates into the United States. In 1979, Marabou completed the acquisition of Goteborgs Kex, Sweden's leading cookie and cracker producer. In 1983, Marabou expanded through the acquisition of Maarud, Norway's leading snack food producer. Marabou experienced significant growth in sales and earnings in 1984, supported by demand for its high-quality chocolate, confectionery, snack, and biscuit items and its continued export growth.

CHADLER INDUSTRIAL DA BAHIA S.A. (BRAZIL) In 1978, Hershey purchased 22.5% interest in this Brazilian processor of cocoa beans. Hershey agreed to provide technical assistance and quality-assurance inputs, to improve the quality and yield in the conversion of cocoa beans to semiprocessed products such as chocolate liquor, cocoa butter, and cocoa powder. By 1980, a plant expansion was completed. Chadler Industrial operations lost money in U.S. dollars between 1981 and 1983 but showed significant improvements in sales and earnings in 1984, because of more attractive conditions in world export markets for cocoa powder and cocoa butter.

NACIONAL DE DULCES (MEXICO) In 1978, Hershey initiated a 50% joint venture with Anderson Clayton & Co., S.A. High startup and financing costs associated with the opening of a new plant in Guadalajara burdened sales and profits through 1982, but 1983 saw improved results of operations despite the weakened Mexican economy and high interest rates. Two new products were introduced in 1983; and on the basis of improved operating performance and the long-range potential for chocolate and confectionery products in Mexico, both partners agreed to increase capital structure to provide additional funds for repair and replacement of production equipment and for working capital. In 1984, sales and operating income increased over the 1983 levels.

PHILIPPINE COCOA CORPORATION (PHILIPPINES) In 1978 was signed a product-licensing agreement that covered trademark, know-how, and technical assistance in the growth, production, and processing of cocoa beans, and the production and quality control of derived products. This agreement was approved by the Philippine government in 1980. In 1981 a 30% joint venture to provide technical assistance for the improvement of cocoa growing and processing, was made. In 1982, sales and profits increased, with the completion of a new cocoa-processing plant and the first phase of an experimental farm for cocoa beans. Although 1983 brought slightly reduced sales and earnings, a new cocoa-processing operation, making possible the production of Hershey's Cocoa and other cocoa products, was completed. In addition, several new low-priced, bite-size chocolate items and hard candies were introduced. During 1984, locally produced Sweetened and Unsweetened Cocoa Powder were introduced, along with a new line of high-quality lollipops and the first locally produced, real milk-chocolate confectionery product. During this year the Philippine Cocoa Corporation showed growth in earnings, restructured its debt, and completed a major reorganization program.

FUJIYA CONFECTIONERY COMPANY (TOKYO)   Fujiya was a leading manufacturer of chocolate and confectionery products, snack foods, beverages, ice cream, and bakery products. It also had a number of restaurant operations. Expecting a substantial increase in export sales of finished products and bulk to Japan, Hershey entered into trademark-license and technical-assistance agreements with Fujiya in 1979. These agreements gave the company the exclusive right to import, manufacture, and sell Hershey products in the Japanese market. Sales and earnings began expanding in 1980; and by 1983, Fujiya was manufacturing Hershey's Syrup in Japan and had introduced Hershey's Hellos (the international brand name for Reese's Pieces).

INDUSTRIAS DE CHOCOLATE LACTA, S.A. (BRAZIL)   In 1980 the company entered into a joint venture partnership (no direct equity participation) with Lacta, Brazil's leading chocolate and confectionery company, to explore industrial and marketing projects in chocolate and confectionery.

RAW MATERIALS

The unique quality and flavor of Hershey's chocolate products were the result of the skillful blending of several basic ingredients, among which were cocoa beans, milk, sugar, almonds, and peanuts.

Cocoa beans were imported from West Africa, which accounted for approximately three-fifths of the world's crop, and from South American equatorial regions. Ghana was the largest supplier, followed by Nigeria and Brazil. Cocoa trees thrived only in tropical areas, within twenty degrees north or south of the equator, where the balance of temperature, rainfall, and soil conditions was precisely right. Cocoa beans were not uniform in quality and/or flavor, and the various grades and varieties were reflective of the different agricultural practices and environmental conditions found in the growing areas.

To meet its manufacturing objectives, Hershey bought a mix of cocoa beans. These beans were shipped to facilities in Hershey, Pennsylvania; Oakdale, California; and Canada for storage until needed. The main storage facility in Hershey had a capacity of more than 90 million pounds, enough for about five and one half billion Hershey bars.

The cocoa beans were the major raw material used in the production of Hershey's chocolate and confectionery products and as such, had the greatest impact on the cost of the candy bar. Cocoa beans had demonstrated wide price fluctuations that could be attributed to a variety of factors. These included weather and other conditions affecting crop size, the consuming countries' demand requirements, the producing countries' sales policies, speculative influences, international economics, and currency movements.

World output of cocoa exceeded demand between 1977 and 1981. Between 1982 and 1984, production fell below demand because drought, severe winds, and brush fires damaged the crop; world stocks were reduced. Speculation on the extent of damage to West African crops caused cocoa prices to jump from $1,900 per ton in 1983 to more than $2,700 per ton in 1984. The price of the cocoa bean jumped 184% between 1973 and 1984 and that increase forced some manufacturers to shift to more cocoa substitutes and extenders in their products. Exhibit 21.8 provides information on the prices of raw materials.

To minimize the effect of cocoa-bean price fluctuations, Hershey forward-purchased quantities of cocoa beans and cocoa products, principally chocolate liquor and cocoa butter, and bought and sold cocoa futures contracts. Hershey held memberships on the Coffee, Sugar and Cocoa Exchange, Inc. in New York and on the London Terminal Market Association. In addition, Hershey maintained West African and Brazilian crop-forecasting operations.

Fresh whole milk was vital to Hershey. Milk was purchased daily from more than 1,000 farms in the vicinity of Hershey's plants and was shipped directly to those plants in bulk tankers. The Hershey storage silos had a capacity of more than 300,000 gallons. Every day, Hershey used enough milk to supply all the people in a city the size of Salt Lake City. From 1973 to 1984 the price of milk rose 206%.

Sugar was another important raw material. In the East, most of the sugar was derived from cane and imported through eastern ports. The Oakdale plant used both beet and cane sugar processed in California. Because of the

---

EXHIBIT 21.8 **Prices of Raw Materials**

(In Dollars per Pound)

YEAR	REFINED CANE SUGAR	COCOA	CORN SYRUP	PEANUTS
1984	.31	1.32	N.A.[1]	.241
1983	.32	1.08	N.A.	.256
1982	.30	0.92	.2670(E)[2]	.249
1981	.31	1.09	.1507	.162
1980	.41	1.35	.1441	.251
1979	.23	1.60	.1082	.206
1978	.21	1.74	.1044	.212

SOURCES: 1984: *Commodity Yearbook;* 1982–1983: Production, Consumption and Sales Values, *Current Industrial Reports—Confectionery* 1982; 1978–1981: Standard & Poor's *Industry,* January 1983.

[1]N.A. means that information was not available.

[2]E means that estimates were based on the 1984 *U.S. Industrial Outlook* and the 1984 *Commodity Yearbook.*

import quotas and duties imposed by the Agriculture and Food Act of 1981, which support the price of sugar, sugar prices paid by U.S. users were substantially higher than prices on the world sugar market.

Hershey was the largest user of almonds in the United States, all of which were grown in California. Peanuts, primarily from the southern and southwestern states, were another important raw material. Market prices of peanuts and almonds were determined in the fourth quarter of the year, after the harvest of these crops. The prices per pound of peanuts between 1978 and 1984 can be found in Exhibit 21.8.

Pasta products were made from semolina flour milled from durum wheat. This wheat was a specialized, hard wheat grown almost exclusively in North Dakota. Recent crops had been excellent. Prices were reasonably stable.

General manufacturing costs have also escalated. Energy and wage costs increased by 495% and 112%, respectively, from 1975 to 1984.

RESEARCH AND DEVELOPMENT

Between 1978 and 1984 Hershey increased its spending from $2,786,000 to $9,942,000 on research activities, which involved the development of new products, improvements in the quality and safety of existing products, and improvement and modernization of production processes.

In November 1979, Hershey's 114,000-square-foot, $7.4 million Technical Center was completed. This center was considered to be the most complete and advanced research facility in the U.S. confectionery industry. This facility enabled Hershey to centralize many of its research and engineering operations, and contained offices, libraries, an auditorium, animal-testing facilities, and a pilot plant.

To facilitate the development and implementation of ideas, a reorganization of the company's technological and scientific functions into one unit took place in 1978. The resulting Department of Science and Technology consisted of four sections: *Research, Product and Process Development, Engineering,* and *Equipment Design and Development.*

The *Research Section* was responsible for developing new knowledge on issues that would keep the company competitive in its current businesses and provide for future growth. This section conducted nutritional research on Hershey products and developed one of the largest data banks in the world on the nutritional properties of chocolate and cocoa. In addition, research was conducted on tooth decay, chocolate allergies, and acne. This section was also responsible for ensuring that materials received from foreign countries met the company's quality specifications.

The *Product and Process Development Section* was responsible for investigating long-range product opportunities and consumer trends. The goal of this section was to provide Hershey's business segments with new products. Between 1978 and 1984 a number of new products and product modifications were introduced. Of these, eleven new products were for the Chocolate and Confectionery Division, four were for the Restaurant Division, and three were for the Other Food Products Division. New products introduced from 1980 to 1984 accounted for 22% of 1984 sales volume. Also being developed were new and improved chocolate-processing techniques to better control the products' quality and ingredient usage while conserving energy and maintaining the unique flavor and texture of Hershey's chocolate. In addition, a major thrust has been toward developing new products with a lower chocolate content.

The goal of the *Engineering Section* was to provide engineering support to assist in moving new products into production. The major responsibility of the *Equipment Design and Development Section* was to improve existing manufacturing systems. Newly designed equipment and manufacturing processes could be tested in a 8,500-square-foot pilot plant.

Hershey was continuously developing programs to improve the quality of its raw materials. Major programs involved efforts to improve the growing, harvesting, processing, and shipment of cocoa beans from farm to factory. The company's Agribusiness Department, a branch of the Science and Technology Department, was attempting to prove that modern organizational and production methods could be successfully applied to cocoa.

One project in this area involved Hershey's 1978 purchase of Hummingbird Hershey, Ltd., a cocoa farm located in the Central American nation of Belize. Another project involved a joint venture in Costa Rica. The purposes of these ventures were to demonstrate the feasibility of commercial cocoa production in the Western Hemisphere and to demonstrate the utilization of modern agricultural techniques in the growing of cocoa.

ADVERTISING AND PROMOTION

For 68 years, Hershey did not advertise in mass consumer media. This attitude toward advertising had been based on the philosophy of the founder, Milton S. Hershey. He believed in point-of-purchase advertising and always said, "Give them quality. That's the best kind of advertising there is."[7] He believed that the best advertising was word-of-mouth endorsements from satisfied customers and good representation in retail outlets. By the middle 1960s, however, there was increased competition in the confectionery industry, coupled with the fact that young people were accepting advertising as an aid to discretionary purchasing. As new Hershey products were developed, it became necessary, to make profitable production feasible, to achieve mass distribution in a relatively short time. Without mass consumer advertising, Hershey was operating at a competitive disadvantage, and its new products' record was suffering as a consequence. These environmental changes brought a policy change in 1968, when Hershey announced its intention to initiate a consumer advertising program for its confectionery and grocery products.

Hershey learned a valuable lesson the hard way in 1974 when the price of cocoa beans soared and Hershey's advertising budgets were cut. Its chief competitor, Mars, continued full-scale advertising; and, for the first time in its history, Hershey was number two. Then Hershey became aggressive in both product advertising and product promotion. Hershey promoted to the trade (grocery chains, wholesalers, vendors, etc.) with promotions usually expressed in cents or dollars off the regular price of a box, case, etc. of its products. It also promoted to the consumer through point-of-sale promotions such as coupon and premium offers. In addition, it used television and radio forms of consumer advertising as well as advertising in newspapers, magazines, and other forms of printed media.

Promotional spending rose to $178 million in 1984 from $76 million in 1979. Hershey increased its advertising budget from $9.5 million in 1975 to $79.1 million in 1984. Sales during this period increased from $576 million to $1.9 billion.

According to then-President Dearden, in 1983 Hershey had recaptured the number one spot, but no official statistics were available, because Mars was secretive about its results. Under Dearden, Hershey Kisses were heavily promoted, and its sales tripled. The biggest success came through an accident of sorts. The Mars Company was approached by producers who offered to use M & M's in the movie *E.T.* When Mars refused the offer, the producers approached Hershey. After Hershey executive Jack Dowd, Vice-President for New Business Development, reviewed clips of the movie to ensure that it was not a monster movie, Hershey agreed to let them use Reese's Pieces in the film. Hershey also agreed to invest $1 million in a joint promotion with MCA, the film's distributor, over six weeks coinciding with the opening of the movie. Sales of the previously steady but unspectacularly selling candy increased 150% in the two weeks following *E.T.*'s release in June 1982; there followed an overall increase in sales of 80% over those of 1981. Furthermore, movie theaters started carrying the candy, whereas before they had refused. In 1982, Hershey negotiated a new agreement with Universal Studios to secure the rights to continue promotion of Reese's Pieces as E.T.'s favorite candy.

In 1984, Hershey Chocolate Co. became the first candy account for the Black Entertainment Network Cable System, Washington, D.C., with a multi-year, million-dollar advertising commitment. Hershey had been using other cable spots since 1980.

Hershey has always been concerned about the content of its advertising, as well as the type of program it supported. Its ads were constantly reviewed by child psychologists and public affairs specialists to make sure that they were not misleading and could not be misunderstood. Hershey did not indulge in advertisements that compared its products with those of a competitor, and advertising agencies were instructed not to position its ads on programs that featured sex or violence. Exhibit 21.9 outlines Hershey's advertising philosophy.

EXHIBIT 21.9 **Hershey's Advertising Philosophy**

Simply stated, Hershey's advertising philosophy will observe the following guidelines:

1. *Honest*
   We will make no false or devious claims.

2. *Ethical*
   We will not degrade competition. We will not produce advertising whose tone or claims would offend or mislead. We will advertise in good taste.

3. *Respectful of Consumers' Intelligence*
   We can entertain and amuse, but never at the expense of truth. We will inform consumers of the merits of our products, but we will not take unfair advantage of our audience's lack of sophistication or technical background in presenting those merits.

4. *Effective*
   Hershey's advertising must be effective, while adhering to the above criteria.

Our intent is not just to be "legal" but to be as honest and ethical in our dealings with our unseen audience as we are with our direct customers—and as we would expect others to be with us.

SOURCE: Hershey Foods Corporation, College Packet, December 9, 1983.

Hershey voluntarily began printing nutritional information on its labels in 1973 and for several years was the only manufacturer in the chocolate and confectionery industry to provide this customer service.

FINANCES

Hershey Foods Corporation's sales and earnings have improved yearly between 1978 and 1984. This period paralleled the existence of Hershey's strategic plan. During this time, sales grew at a compound annual rate of 16.0%, income from operations at 17.6%, and net income at 14.8%. Financial information is presented in Exhibits 21.3, 21.10, and 21.11.

In 1984, Hershey successfully completed its equity expansion program, to provide flexibility for growth as a major, diversified food company. Because of the company's unique ownership by the Milton Hershey School, it was necessary to devise a proposal that would allow the company to issue additional common stock while meeting the majority stockholder's desire to maintain voting control of the company. Stockholders approved and adopted amendments to the company's Certificate of Incorporation increasing the authorized shares of Common Stock from 50,000,000 to 150,000,000 and authorizing 75,000,000 shares of a new Class B Stock with greater voting power but lesser dividend rights. Under the amendments, holders of the Common Stock and the Class B Stock would generally vote together without

EXHIBIT 21.10 Hershey Foods Corporation: Consolidated Balance Sheet
(In Thousands of Dollars)

	1984	1983	1982	1981	1980	1979	1978	1977
Assets								
Cash and short-term investments	$ 87,917	$ 73,091	$ 34,503	$ 53,879	$ 48,906	$ 17,185	$111,756	$117,248
Accounts receivable—(net)	$ 80,977	56,456	65,129	56,241	45,964	37,423	31,787	27,008
Inventories	$ 185,953	194,666	178,585	151,890	113,701	106,078	65,611	61,950
Other current assets	$ 30,474	12,392	13,411	25,020	12,796	9,564	7,505	6,258
Total current assets	$ 385,321	336,605	291,628	287,030	221,367	170,250	216,659	221,202
Property/plant/equipment	$ 901,719	794,667	729,275	597,981	515,030	462,745	265,261	231,334
Less depreciation and amortization	259,110	219,546	189,361	157,797	135,589	113,480	94,481	88,164
Net property	$ 642,609	575,121	539,914	440,184	379,441	349,265	170,780	143,170
Goodwill	79,252	51,307	52,609	53,911	55,214	56,516	18,056	17,771
Investments and other assets	15,385	20,911	20,603	25,675	28,450	31,168	16,509	14,004
Total assets	1,122,567	983,944	904,754	806,800	684,472	607,199	422,004	396,153
Liabilities								
Accounts payable	$ 96,378	67,107	61,971	48,085	52,498	51,636	43,696	55,650
Accrued liabilities	85,558	68,269	55,944	57,033	40,415	36,208	20,855	14,154
Accrued income taxes	14,247	10,287	11,399	10,006	17,107	7,546	9,864	13,345
Current portion of long-term debt	6,770	5,971	19,579	2,131	1,640	8,436	—	—
Total current liabilities	202,953	151,634	148,893	117,255	111,660	103,826	74,415	83,149
Long-term debt	150,316	127,990	140,250	158,182	158,758	143,700	35,540	29,440
Other long-term liabilities	—	22,367	9,350	—	—	—	—	—
Deferred income taxes	108,370	85,916	73,766	61,699	52,504	38,943	27,660	23,896
Common stock	31,337	31,337	15,669	15,669	14,160	14,159	13,745	13,730
Additional paid-in capital	54,006	54,006	54,006	54,006	2,259	2,255	2,169	2,083
Foreign currency adjustments[1]	(7,265)	(2,154)	—	—	—	—	—	—
Retained earnings	582,850	512,848	462,820	399,989	345,131	304,316	268,475	243,855
Total liabilities and stockholders' equity	$1,122,567	$983,944	$904,754	$806,800	$684,472	$607,199	$422,004	$396,153

SOURCE: Hershey Foods Corporation Annual Reports, 1984 and 1980.

[1]1983 restated to reflect the adoption of SFAS #52, "Foreign Currency Translations," January 1, 1983.

EXHIBIT 21.11

Hershey Foods Corporation: Eight-Year Consolidated Financial Summary

(All Dollar and Share Amounts Are in Thousands Except Market Price and Per Share Statistics)

	1984	1983	1982	1981	1980	1979	1978	1977
Summary of Earnings								
Net sales	$1,892,506	1,706,105	1,565,736	1,451,151	1,335,289	1,161,295	767,880	671,227
Cost of sales	$1,293,446	1,168,109	1,084,748	1,015,767	971,714	855,252	560,137	489,802
Selling, general and administrative	$ 379,140	332,831	301,586	267,930	224,615	184,186	128,520	110,554
Interest expense	$ 15,291	16,766	11,441	15,291	16,197	19,424	2,620	2,422
Interest (income)	$ (4,942)	(952)	(3,582)	(2,779)	(2,097)	(1,660)	(5,303)	(2,931)
Income taxes	$ 100,889	89,185	77,375	74,580	62,805	50,589	40,450	35,349
Income from continuing operations	$ 108,862	100,166	94,168	80,362	62,055	53,504	41,456	36,031
Gain related to disposal of discontinued operations	—	—	—	—	—	—	—	5,300
Net income	$ 108,682	100,166	94,168	80,362	62,055	53,504	41,456	41,331
Net income per share	3.47	3.20	3.00	2.81	2.19	1.89	1.51	1.51
Dividends paid per share of common stock	$ 1.24	1.10	1.00	.875	.75	.675	.6125	.57
Dividends paid per share of Class B stock	$ .315	—	—	—	—	—	—	—
Average number of shares of common stock and Class B stock outstanding during the year	31,337	31,337	31,337	28,643	28,320	28,306	27,484	27,444
Net income as a percentage of net sales	5.7%	5.9%	6.0%	5.5%	4.6%	4.6%	5.4%	5.4%
Financial Statistics								
Capital additions	$ 87,049	105,244	116,736	91,673	59,029	56,437	37,425	27,535
Depreciation	$ 43,113	37,274	30,681	27,565	24,696	20,515	8,850	7,995
Advertising	$ 79,169	68,852	64,046	56,516	42,684	32,063	21,847	17,635
Current assets	$ 385,321	336,605	291,628	309,677	221,367	170,250	216,659	221,202
Current liabilities	$ 202,953	151,634	148,893	134,035	111,660	103,826	74,415	83,149
Working capital	$ 182,368	184,971	142,735	175,642	109,707	66,424	142,244	138,053
Long-term debt	$ 125,236	127,990	140,250	158,182	158,758	143,700	35,540	29,440
Stockholders' equity	$ 660,928	596,037	532,495	469,664	361,550	320,730	284,389	259,668
Total assets	$1,122,567	983,944	904,754	829,447	684,472	607,199	422,004	396,153

(Continued)

EXHIBIT 21.11 (Continued)

	1984	1983	1982	1981	1980	1979	1978	1977
Return on average stockholders' equity	17.3%	17.8%	18.8%	19.3%	18.2%	17.7%	15.2%	16.8%
After-tax return on average invested capital	13.5%	13.8%	14.3%	13.9%	12.8%	14.3%	13.0%	14.2%
Stockholders' Data								
Outstanding shares of common stock and Class B stock at year-end	31,337	31,337	31,337	31,337	28,320	28,318	27,491	27,460
Market price of common stock								
At year-end	$ 38⅝	31⅝	28¼	18	11¾	12⅜	10⅜	9 15/16
Range during year	$41¼–28¼	35–24⅜	29¾–16¼	20½–11½	13–10	13¼–8⅝	11¾–9¼	11 3/16–8 5/16
Number of common stock and Class B stockholders at year-end	16,729	16,467	16,033	16,817	17,774	18,417	18,735	19,964
Employee Data								
Payrolls	$ 368,164	340,944	305,651	273,097	253,297	227,987	112,135	99,322
Number of full-time employees at year-end	15,200	14,310	13,600	12,450	12,430	11,700	8,100	7,660

SOURCE: Hershey Foods Corporation *Annual Reports*, 1984 and 1980.

[1]All shares and per share amounts have been adjusted for the two-for-one stock split effective September 15, 1983.

[2]Financial statistics include certain reclassifications that have been made to the December 31, 1982 and 1981 consolidated financial statements.

regard to class on matters submitted to the stockholders, including the election of five-sixths of the Board of Directors; the Common Stockholders would have one vote per share and the Class B Stockholders, ten votes per share. The Common Stockholders, voting separately as a class, were entitled to elect one-sixth of the board of directors. With respect to dividend rights, holders of the Common Stock were entitled to cash dividends 10% higher than those declared and paid on the Class B Stock. To put this differential into effect during the fourth quarter of 1984, Hershey declared an increase in fourth quarter dividends to common shareholders to 35 cents per share. Dividends on Class B Stock remained at 31.5 cents per share.

To implement the amendments, Hershey offered shares of Class B Stock to all holders of Common Stock on a share-for-share basis in late 1984. At December 31, 1984, there were 26,235,110 shares of Common Stock and 5,102,002 shares of Class B Stock outstanding. Hershey Trust Company, as Trustee for the Milton Hershey School, owned 10,642,831 shares of the Common Stock and 5,051,001 shares of the Class B Stock as of December 31, 1984.

NOTES

1. *The New York Times* (July 22, 1984), p. 5.

2. *1979 Annual Report,* Hershey Foods Corporation.

3. *Second Quarter Report,* Hershey Foods Corporation, 1984.

4. *The Wall Street Journal* (July 11, 1984), p. 33.

5. *The New York Times* (July 22, 1984). p. 4F.

6. *Third Quarter Report,* Hershey Foods Corporation, 1984, p. 4.

7. *1983 Annual Report,* Hershey Foods Corporation, p. 5.

Johnson Products Company, Inc., A Turnaround Strategy

THOMAS L. WHEELEN · CHARLES E. MICHAELS, JR. · ROBERT L. NIXON ·
JANIECE L. GALLAGHER

GEORGE E. JOHNSON— ENTREPRENEUR

In 1954, George E. Johnson estimated it would take $500 to get his new product, Ultra Wave Hair Culture, a hair straightener for black men, to the marketplace. The first loan officer that he approached was not impressed with his new product. The loan officer said, "You've got a good job, you've been there ten years, why blow it? If your boss finds out that you're in business, you might lose your job and then you can't pay us back." Mr. Johnson was very disappointed, but he did not give up. He went to another bank and told the loan officer that he wanted to go to California on vacation and needed a $250 loan. The loan was granted. With this loan, Johnson, his wife, Joan, his brother, John, and a friend, Dr. Herbert Martini, a chemist, started Johnson Products on February 15, 1954. The company was organized as an Illinois corporation in 1957, but in 1969, its state of incorporation was changed to Delaware. On December 10, 1969, it became the first black-owned company to be publicly held.

George E. Johnson began his career as a door-to-door salesman in Chicago for Fuller Products, which made cosmetics for blacks. Some time later, he had an opportunity to work as an assistant chemist with Dr. Herbert Martini in the lab at Fuller Products. During the ten years Johnson worked with Martini, he learned the foundations upon which he built his own cosmetics business.

Johnson started the Johnson Products Company after he became aware that many blacks were unhappy with their naturally coarse, thick hair. These blacks wanted their hair straightened so that they could have more flexibility in their hair styling. The beginning of Johnson Products can be traced back to a particular day on which Johnson met a barber who had visited the managers at Fuller Products and sought help in formulating an improved hair straightener. Fuller Products was not interested, but Johnson was.

A special note of thanks to Professor Neil H. Snyder of the McIntire School of Commerce at the University of Virginia. Dr. Snyder authored "Johnson Products Company, Inc.," and co-authored "Johnson Products, Inc. . . . The Challenges of the 1980s." The first case appears in *Strategic Management and Business Policy,* first edition, and the second case appears in the second edition of that book.

This case was prepared by Professors Thomas L. Wheelen, Charles E. Michaels, Jr., and Robert L. Nixon, and Janiece L. Gallagher, MBA Student, of the University of South Florida. Copyright © 1987 by Thomas L. Wheelen. Reprinted by permission.

Johnson spoke with the barber, Orville Nelson, about his problem and, to explore the matter further, later visited his shop. At the shop, Johnson found customers standing in line to have their hair straightened, but the straightener being used simply did not work. Johnson and Nelson formed a short-lived partnership by putting up $250 each in capital, and Johnson sought Dr. Martini's assistance in identifying the problem with existing hair straighteners.

To obtain as much information as he could about the demand for hair straighteners, Johnson visited many owners of beauty shops with black clientele; there he hoped to discover "their perceptions of the market." He found that the problem was universal: blacks wanted a hair straightener that worked. Mr. Johnson was quoted as saying, "Black beauticians used a hot comb and grease on the hair of black women. Dr. Martini and I agreed that the smoke was bad for the health and the grease was no good for the hair, so we worked on a process to eliminate the smoke and grease and came up with a cream press permanent, cream shampoo and Ultra-Sheen that could be applied at home between visits to the beauty shop." Using a hot comb technique, a client had to redo the hairstyle constantly, because rain or moisture would destroy the arrangement.

Although Johnson was not the first to enter the market for black hair care products, his company became a leading firm because of his efforts to satisfy the needs of the black consumer. However, the "black revolution" of the 1960s brought the Afro and a dilemma. Mr. Johnson said, "I didn't know if it was a fad or not, so I took a wait-and-see attitude until I was sure it was a trend. Then we developed Afro Sheen for the natural. But, I always felt the natural wouldn't last. It's too monotonous, and sure enough, women are moving from it."

Historically a vigorous, competitive manufacturer of hair care products and cosmetics, Johnson Products also became an important black institution and a growing American business. In 1971, Johnson Products Company, Inc. became the first black-owned firm to be listed on the American Exchange. Through innovative product development and promotional techniques, it rapidly became one of the success stories of American business in the 1960s and early 1970s.

The Johnson story might have ended one day in October 1964 when a devastating fire swept through the plant on Green Street in Chicago and virtually destroyed all of the production facilities. Instead of abandoning the business, George E. Johnson and his employees salvaged what they could and, with the help of suppliers and Fuller Products Company, the company was operating from temporary headquarters within a week.

Growth of the company was steady but certainly not spectacular until product innovations in 1965 ushered in a period of rapid sales growth. In four years (1971–1975) gross sales increased from $13 million to $39 million. However, since 1975 the firm has experienced a series of setbacks.

Its first attempt to move beyond the ethnic market through an expensive men's cologne, "Black Tie," was a disaster. This failure was attributed to improper distribution channels, and poor shelf space and displays at retail establishments. Coinciding with this setback was the mounting pressure exerted by major competing firms, primarily Revlon, which viewed the fast-growing ethnic market as an untapped well.

In February of 1975, the firm's public image was seriously damaged when it felt obligated to sign a consent order issued by the Federal Trade Commission requiring that warning labels be placed on its best-selling hair straightener, Ultra Sheen Permanent Creme Relaxer. Although its competitors also used the damaging chemical, sodium hydroxide, in their products, they were not compelled to take similar action until twenty months later.

Compounding these problems were the generally poor state of the economy and the high level of black unemployment in the late 1970s and early 1980s. The company experienced its first operating loss in 1980, and has sustained losses of $14,839,000 on sales of $254,585,000 over the past seven fiscal years (1980–1986). Only in 1981 and 1983 did the company post a profit (see Exhibit 22.9).

On April 4, 1986, the company hired a management consulting firm, Buccino & Associates, to help develop and implement a turnaround strategic plan. Some of the consultants' recommendations resulted in immediate retrenchment tactics—that is, the work force was cut back from 558 to 431 employees, and the salaries of the remaining employees were cut 10%–20%. These actions, combined with others, resulted in annualized savings of approximately $3.5 million.

Would the stockholders be pleased with this news? On December 1, 1986, George E. Johnson and his staff were finalizing his remarks to the shareholders for the Annual Meeting on December 10, 1986. Excerpts from those remarks are presented in Exhibit 22.1.

COMPANY HIGHLIGHTS		
	1954	Company founded with one product, Ultra Wave Hair Culture
	1957	Ultra Sheen Conditioner and Hair Dress introduced
	1958	Ultra Sheen line entered professional beauticians' market
	1960	Ultra Sheen line introduced in retail market
	1964	Fire destroys production facilities
	1965	Ultra Sheen No-Base Creme Relaxer introduced
	1966	Completed first phase of new headquarters
	1968	Afro Sheen products introduced
		Established The George E. Johnson Foundation
	1969	Sponsored its first nationwide TV special, ". . . and Beautiful"
	1969	First black-owned company to become publicly held
	1970	Ultra Sheen cosmetics introduced

EXHIBIT 22.1

Excerpts of Remarks Made to Shareholders at the Annual Meeting, by President George E. Johnson, December 10, 1986

I feel somewhat better today about where we are as a company than I did last year at this time. I don't mean to imply that we are out of the woods by any stretch of the imagination. What I am saying is that we made some genuine advances last year in several key areas and that the road before us is perhaps a little less rocky than a year ago.

I said last year that we would be biting many bullets to achieve "must" goals, that we were guardedly optimistic about being able to push forward and that we would do so by taking carefully measured steps. In a nutshell, that was pretty much the scenario for fiscal 1986. One significant measure of our progress is that our basic hair care products business turned profitable in the fourth quarter compared with a sizeable loss in the same quarter a year earlier.

Reaching that point took a great deal of soul searching as we tried to figure out how to curtail even further the outflow of cash so vitally needed for day-to-day operations. Although expenses had been reduced sharply in the previous year, it wasn't enough. We needed to cut at least $3 million more.

To accomplish this we took the extremely difficult step last April to eliminate 20% of the work force, and followed that with 10%–20% across-the-board salary reductions. These actions, together with others, resulted in annualized savings of approximately $3.5 million. Some of this is reflected in the 56% drop in our fiscal 1986 loss compared with fiscal 1985.

There was deep concern that cutting more staff would tend to impede operational efficiency. But just the opposite happened. We were able to tighten many functions, eliminate others and become a more cohesive organization, thanks to the responsive attitudes of all of our people.

The most encouraging aspect of this $3.5 million savings is that we will continue to benefit by approximately that amount in the current year, which means that hair care products operations should be profitable even if sales remain at fiscal 1986 levels. We are anticipating better than that.

In working out our turnaround strategy, we had objective input from Buccino & Associates, Inc., a management consulting firm with excellent credentials for aiding companies in situations such as ours. They started with us last April and completed their assignment last month.

Another area of urgency last year that took a great amount of management time was the replacement of our short-term debt with a flexible long-term financing arrangement that also would include more dollars for working capital. The additional money was critical if we were to generate and maintain forward momentum.

It was with considerable satisfaction that we concluded, late last October, a fully secured three-year credit agreement, including renewal options, with a national financing institution that provided us with a total of $10 million in the form of a $4-million term loan and a $6-million revolving credit. Approximately $6 million of the loan proceeds were used immediately to repay existing bank debt. The balance will be available for us to draw on as needed to operate the business.

(Continued)

EXHIBIT 22.1 (Continued)

To increase further our cash resources, we entered into an agreement with a real estate developer to sell approximately eleven acres of unneeded Chicago headquarters property, including a 200,000-square-foot office and warehouse building for $2.7 million. To date, we have received two non-refundable deposits amounting to $500,000. We expect to net $2.5 million from the sale and immediately use $1.6 million to reduce our term debt. The balance will be available for working capital.

The major factor affecting our hair care products sales continues to be intensive competition. There has been no let up. In fact, general market companies have been making noises that they expect to gobble up our industry. I don't foresee that ever happening, but the infighting could get even rougher, which might lead to a small shakeout in the industry.

Changing hair fashions, to some extent, also have had an effect on our business. Until about two years ago, curly hair was the rage and our Classy Curl hair curl kits generated good sales. But as most of you well know, fashion can be fickle. What is in vogue one day can become old hat the next, and that is what happened in most parts of the country to the curly hair look. This of course, has been eating into our hair curl kit sales.

But the bright side is that the fashion pendulum has swung back to relaxed hair stylings, and that can be good for Johnson Products because relaxer and conditioner and hair dress products traditionally have been our strengths. Ultra Sheen brand, long our mainstay, is widely known and through the years has generated considerable loyalty among users. And we continually have added attractive products to the line such as Ultra Sheen Light Conditioner and Hair Dress, which is just going into distribution.

Gentle-Treatment No-Lye Conditioning Relaxer is our best seller as well as one of the leaders among all products in the retail marketplace. A testimony to its quality is its consistent growth in popularity since its introduction in 1981. Moreover, we have been taking full advantage of the selling power of the brand name by marketing a variety of products under the Gentle-Treatment label. Extending the line even more with quality items is an ongoing priority.

Because of Gentle-Treatment's success, we moved to expand the brand's base of customers with the introduction last August of Gentle-Treatment Xtra, which is a stronger formulation that should have great appeal to the large percentage of potential users with hard-to-relax hair. I'm delighted to report that up to this time, sales of both the regular and Xtra formulas have been exceeding expectations. Even more encouraging is that we already have received a number of reorders for Xtra, and it appears that these sales have not been at the expense of the original product.

Our sights this year are set on improving business with the professional beautician. This group is very important to us not only because of the products they buy but because they can be instrumental in motivating consumers to buy our products in their salons or at other retail outlets. Our premium-priced Ultra Sheen's Precise brand is a staple in hair salons, and we are moving to make our more modest-priced Bantu products even more attractive by offering the brand as a hair care system.

In order to achieve sales goals we will need a consistently strong performance from our sales force, and we believe that in its current form it can deliver what we expect. The restructuring of the entire sales organization in fiscal 1986, when we established profit centers and began concentrating in geographic areas representing our main marketplaces, gave us a realistic operating concept. Moreover, we improved the caliber of individual sales representatives last year and initiated intensive ongoing sales training programs designed to help each one deal more effectively with and sell to both the retail and professional markets.

At the management level, we made a move that should enable the field staff to understand its role more clearly as it relates to the marketing process. Essentially, we combined the marketing and sales functions under the direction of a single officer. These were individual responsibilities before, and we found that there often were communication breakdowns between the two that taxed efficiency. Under the new arrangements, sales and marketing activities, which are closely interrelated, are being carried out with a greater understanding by all concerned of the potential ramifications each of these vital functions has on the other.

As for advertising and promotion, our plans mainly include pushing important brands and using carefully selected media that experience has shown to be especially effective for us. The advertising and promotion budget this year will be about 21 percent higher than last year's expenditure.

Last year we entered the private-label manufacturing business as a way of putting our expertise and excess plant capacity to profitable use. Although we made a variety of products for several large companies, our volume was disappointing. However, we continue to be enthused about the potential for developing this kind of business and we are working hard to do so. A number of proposals are currently under review by prospective customers. We believe that some will result in contracts.

A management change in our international division augurs well for its future. Plans to improve these operations include more European promotions and the establishment of more distributors or licensers in the Caribbean, Central and South America, and in selected African countries.

The Debbie's School of Beauty Culture subsidiary also contributed to fourth quarter profitability, and its losses for the full year were lower than for the previous year. Although enrollments trended slightly downward, collection action against students' accounts previously written off, contributed to our increase in total revenue. At this point enrollments appear to be relatively stable.

In summary, our position and prospects today certainly are slightly better than a year ago for the following reasons: our break-even point has been reduced substantially, we have sorely needed working capital, the hair care fashion trend is favoring our relaxer products, several new products could do very well, our sales organization is stronger and better trained, coordination between sales and marketing has improved, and every individual in the company is striving to accelerate a complete turnaround.

But even with all these positives, the yellow caution light still signals brightly, telling us we must continue to act prudently and take carefully measured steps as we inch forward to achieve our goals.

Thank you.

1971 Began sponsorship of "Soul Train," nationally syndicated TV show

First black-owned company listed on American Stock Exchange

1972 Established The George E. Johnson Educational Fund

1973 Completed third phase of new headquarters

1975 Entered men's fragrance market with "Black Tie" cologne and splash-on

Started exporting to Nigeria

Acquired the Debbie's School of Beauty Culture—5 salons

1979 Cosmetics lines were reformulated

Acquired Freedom Distributors, which distributed the company's and competitors' products on the eastern seaboard

1980 Established Johnson Products of Nigeria as a manufacturing subsidiary, with a 40% interest

Introduced Ultra Sheen Precise, first of 42 innovative product lines

1981 Overseas expansion by establishing a sales and service center in Eastbourne, England

Introduced new products Gentle Treatment, Tender Treatment and Bantu Curl

1982 Established Debbie Howell Cosmetics, direct sales line in key black market areas

Introduced 19 new products

Formed Mello Touch Labs, Inc. to manufacture, market and distribute a line of consumer products

1983 Introduced two lines of cosmetics, Ultra Sheen and Moisture Formula

Sold Freedom Distributors

1984 Introduced Metra Star Curls for men

Two additional Debbie Schools of Beauty Culture were opened in Texas and Georgia

1985 Restructured the marketing and sales organization
Two new products were introduced—a unique exothermus hair curling system and deep penetrating conditioner. They were sold to both the professional and retail markets

Signed Michael Jordan of the Chicago Bulls to a multi-year endorsement contract

1986 Excel Manufacturing Company, Inc. was formed as a private label arm of the company

STRATEGIC MANAGERS

George E. Johnson (age 59) serves as the Chairman of the Board and President. Mr. Johnson's business affiliations include board positions with Commonwealth Edison Company, Metropolitan Life Insurance Company, American Health and Beauty Aids Institute (Chairman) and the Cosmetic, Toiletry and Fragrance Association. He is also a member of a number of civic, charitable, professional, and social organizations.

Dorothy McConner (age 57) serves as the Executive Vice-President; Vice-President, Administration; and Corporate Secretary. She was elected a Director of the company in 1979. Mrs. McConner has been with the company for approximately twenty-five years and was selected *Blackbook*'s 1975 Businesswoman of the Year.

David N. Corner (age 56) joined the company in December, 1979 as Vice-President, Finance; and Chief Financial Officer. Before joining this company, he was with Libby, McNeil & Libby, Inc., most recently as Vice-President, Finance; and Treasurer.

Marilynn J. Cason (age 43) was elected Vice-President in 1977 and was promoted to Vice-President, International, in 1986. She also served as Corporate Counsel. She has been responsible for the Nigerian operations for the past three and one-half years. Before joining the company in 1975, she spent three years as an attorney for Kraft, Inc., and three years as an associate attorney with the Denver law firm of Dawson, Nagel, Sherman and Horwald.

Tehsel S. Dhaliwal (age 45), with the company since 1973, served previously as Director of Manufacturing Operations. He was promoted to Vice-President of Operations in 1983.

Joan B. Johnson (age 57), wife of George E. Johnson, shared in the founding of the company in 1954. She presently serves as Treasurer and Director.

Danny O. Clarke (age 37) serves as Vice-President and Controller, a position he has held since 1984. He has served as Internal Auditor, Assistant Controller, and Controller since joining the company in 1977. Prior to joining the company, he was General Accounting Manager for a division of Container Corporation of America.

Sylvia J. Wynn (age 45) was promoted to Vice-President, Marketing and Sales in 1986. Having held similar positions with major brand products for Avon, Gillette, and Playtex, she joined the company as a marketing manager in 1983. A year later she was appointed Marketing Director.

Each executive officer was last elected as such on August 31, 1986, and shall serve until a successor is appointed and qualified. Mr. Clarke was appointed as Vice-President in March 1984 and Ms. Wynn in March 1986. Deborah A. Howell serves as President of Debbie's School of Beauty Culture, which has been a wholly owned subsidiary since 1975.

The three internal directors are George E. and Joan B. Johnson and Dorothy McConner. The outside directors are the following persons.

Alvin J. Boatte (age 57) has served as President of the Independence Bank of Chicago, Illinois, and became its Chairman of the Board in 1980. He has served as a Director of this company since 1969.

Melvin D. Jefferson (age 63) is owner and President of Superior Beauty and Barber Supply (Detroit, Michigan), a full-service distributor of beauty and hair care products. He has served as a Director of this company since 1969.

Jesse L. Howell (age 58) serves as Executive Vice-President of Debbie's School of Beauty Culture, Inc. (a wholly-owned subsidiary of the company since 1975). He has served as a Director of the company since 1977.

Mr. John T. Schriver, a Director of the company, resigned in 1986.

OWNERSHIP

Because of their direct and indirect ownership of shares of the company's stock, Mr. George E. Johnson and Mrs. Joan B. Johnson may be deemed to be controlling persons of the company for the purposes of the federal securities law. As shown in Exhibit 22.2, the Johnson family controls 60.8% of the company.

EXECUTIVE COMPENSATION

The eleven officers and directors were paid a total of $1,061,697 in cash compensation in 1985. In 1986, the fourteen officers and directors received $751,833 in cash compensation. The outside directors were paid a fee of

EXHIBIT 22.2   **Stock Ownership**

TITLE OF CLASS	NAMES AND ADDRESSES OF BENEFICIAL OWNERS	NUMBER OF SHARES BENEFICIALLY OWNED	% OF CLASS
Common stock	George E. Johnson, Trustee of personal trust[1] 95 Brentwood Drive Glencoe, Illinois 60022	1,989,475	49.9
Common stock	Joan B. Johnson, Trustee of personal trust[2] 95 Brentwood Drive Glencoe, Illinois 60022	180,000	4.5
Common stock	Joan B. Johnson, Trustee for children[1,2]	254,000	6.4
Common stock	Total shares owned by George E. and Joan B. Johnson	2,423,475	60.8

As of November 3, 1986, directors and officers of the company (eleven persons in all) beneficially owned the following shares:

Common stock	. . .	2,456,950[3]	61.6

[1]Mrs. Johnson disclaims beneficial ownership in these shares.

[2]Mr. Johnson disclaims beneficial ownership in these shares.

[3]Includes 1,800 shares under options exercisable within 60 days.

$5,000 in 1985 and $2,500 in 1986. Below are the 1985 and 1986 salaries of the key company executives.

| | CASH COMPENSATION | |
	1985	1986
George E. Johnson	$195,200	$177,750
Dorothy McConner	95,400	86,961
David N. Corner	97,886	89,227
Tehsel S. Dhaliwal	N/A	80,685
Jesse L. Howell	144,846	100,539

SUBSIDIARIES AND FACILITIES

The company's corporate offices and manufacturing facilities are located in a building held by it in fee; this building is on a twelve-acre tract at 8522 South Lafayette Avenue, Chicago, Illinois. The building encompasses approximately 64,000 square feet of office space and 176,000 square feet for manufacturing and warehousing purposes.

To support its continued growth, the company acquired additional property adjacent to the South Lafayette facilities at 87th Street and Dan Ryan Expressway in November 1974, at a cost of $1,100,000. This property consists of approximately eleven acres of land (compared to the twelve-acre tract of the old facility) and a 200,000 square foot building. This building currently houses warehousing, selected administrative offices of the company, and the administrative offices of Johnson's subsidiary, Debbie's School of Beauty Culture, Inc. The remainder of the building is under lease.

Johnson Products distributes its retail products mostly through national and regional drug, grocery, and mass merchandising chains. In 1979, it acquired Freedom Distributors, which distributed both the company's and its competitors' products on the eastern seaboard. It sold Freedom in 1983.

Its professional product lines are sold to beauty salons and barber shops. The company's wholly-owned subsidiary, Debbie's School of Beauty Culture, operates thirteen beautician-training facilities throughout the country. In 1977, Johnson Products Company purchased a Chicago building of 12,000 square feet. This facility now houses one of Debbie's schools. The other twelve locations are leased. The locations and terms of the leases are outlined in Exhibit 22.3.

The school's staff currently includes approximately 100 administrative personnel and instructors who direct a 1500 hour course completed over nine and one half months. The curriculum includes the subjects: anatomy, hairdressing, hair weaving, personal appearance, skin and nail care, shop management, and product education.

Since its acquisition in 1975, Debbie's has operated profitably each year with the exception of fiscal 1982 and 1985. Its poor performance in that

EXHIBIT 22.3 **Facilities of Johnson Products**

LOCATION	APPROXIMATE SQUARE FOOTAGE	LEASE EXPIRES[2]
Chicago, Illinois	25,000	December 31, 1986[1]
Chicago, Illinois	15,000	December 31, 1986[1]
Chicago, Illinois	5,000	December 31, 1986[1]
Harvey, Illinois	9,000	December 31, 1986
East St. Louis, Illinois	12,000	December 31, 1986
Detroit, Michigan	7,200	December 31, 1986
Birmingham, Alabama	28,000	October 31, 1988
Indianapolis, Indiana	10,000	December 31, 1986
Atlanta, Georgia	5,000	July 31, 1989
Houston, Texas	10,000	January 31, 1987
St. Louis, Missouri	6,100	July 31, 1987
Houston, Texas	8,100	July 10, 1990

[1]The Chicago leases that expire in December, 1986 are renewable at the option of Debbie's. In addition, Debbie's operates one Ultra Precise Beauty Boutique in Chicago with approximately 2000 ft[2]. Although the lease expired on September 30, 1986, the Company expects that the new lease will be negotiated on terms comparable to those for similar situations.

[2]Total operating expense for leases in fiscal years ended August 31, 1986, 1985, and 1984 was $457,000, $347,000 and $229,000, respectively.

year was attributed to the economic recession and curtailment in federal funding for certain types of education. In 1983, Debbie's graduated a record 1000 students, compared to the previous class of 455 students. Revenues and profits increased substantially. Fiscal year 1984 was another excellent year as enrollments increased by 25% over those of the previous year and generated an equal percentage increase in both revenues and income. In 1985, however, Debbie's revenues were off about $1.5 million from the $5.5 million of fiscal 1984, and it suffered a net loss for the year. The decline was attributed to the reduction in the number of students entering and completing the school's programs.

Competition from other schools providing the same course of study has increased sharply. To combat a sharp drop in enrollments, top management was freed from many administrative functions in 1986 so that they could concentrate on attracting new students. Although enrollment still trended slightly downward, aggressive collection against students' accounts previously written off in 1985 ($1.4 million) contributed to an increase in total revenue. Enrollments seem to have stabilized, and Debbie's loss in 1986 was less than it had been the previous year.

Debbie's also operates a salon division, which consists of three Ultra Precise Beauty Boutiques in Chicago, one of which is situated in a Sears department store. All of Debbie's schools and salons use Johnson Products predominately.

In 1982, Debbie's established Debbie Howell Cosmetics, a direct-sales organization to promote Johnson's new line of cosmetics. This division currently employs consultants in about thirty cities that the firm believes to be key black-consumer markets. Losses in its first year of operation (approximately $147,000) were due primarily to start-up costs. The parent company is optimistic about the future of the direct sales endeavor because it believes that this sales technique has proven to be successful for companies such as Avon and Mary Kay Cosmetics. There are plans to expand further in existing markets, and in other key black-consumer market areas, but this organization still remains relatively small.

In October, 1983, Mellow Touch Labs, Inc. was formed to manufacture, market, and distribute a line of consumer products. Mello Touch shares common manufacturing, marketing, and distribution facilities, as well as resources, with the parent company.

In March 1986, Excel Manufacturing Company, Inc. was formed as a private label arm of the company. It manufactures to the customers' specifications a broad base of products, ranging from medicated gels to lotions, to hair, skin and baby care products. Like Mellow Touch it shares common facilities and resources with the parent company.

INDUSTRY AND COMPETITION

In 1986, consumers spent $8.615 billion on toiletries and cosmetics. (See Exhibit 22.4) While continued gains are expected for years ahead, the industry's real growth rate is expected to fall to an annual increase of 2%–3%. This growth is well below that experienced in the 1960s and 1970s. The decline is attributed to the fact that the rate of women entering the labor force is now lower, indicating that the trend of the 1960s and 1970s for multi-income families may have run its course and stabilized.

One of the fastest growing market segments in the toiletries and cosmetics industry is the ethnic market, consisting of an estimated 40 million blacks, Hispanics, and other minorities. Minority women are estimated to spend three times more per person on cosmetics than white women, and it is estimated that 30% of Johnson's sales are accounted for by minorities other than blacks. The market for ethnic hair care products has become a $1 billion industry growing by approximately 11% annually, while the ethnic toiletries and cosmetics market is growing at an annual rate of 20%.

In the 1984 U.S. Census, the black population was approximately 28.9 million with a median age of 27.8. Although in 1979 the 25–34 age group had accounted for 14.1% of the black population, by 1987, this had increased to 17.7% (see Exhibit 22.5). With these shifts in population, black consumers are experiencing an increase in their disposable incomes greater than that of the population at large. Between 1972 and 1979, blacks' aggregate income

EXHIBIT 22.4 Selected Financial Information on Competitors

COMPANY	SALES¹					PROFIT¹				
	1986	1985	1984	1983	1982	1986	1985	1984	1983	1982
Alberto-Culver	$ 435.4	368.6	348.6	313.7	320.4	13.3	7.9	4.5	3.9	6.6
Avon Products	2,883.1	2,470.1	3,141.3	3,000.1	3,000.6	158.7	128.2	181.7	164.4	196.6
Gillette	2,818.3	2,400.0	2,288.6	2,183.3	2,239.0	184.7	159.9	159.3	145.9	135.1
Helene Curtis	400.1	360.8	370.3	330.4	243.2	10.3	8.9	2.7	10.4	3.6
Noxell Corp.	438.8	382.1	349.5	304.3	261.9	37.1	32.4	28.3	23.2	18.5
Redkin Labs	103.2	108.5	101.4	86.3	84.6	2.0	8.4	8.3	6.4	6.5
Industry total	8,615.0	7,388.0	7,789.2	7,305.0	7,111.1	540.0	466.9	490.4	448.9	440.0

COMPANY	NET PROFIT MARGIN (%)					OPERATING MARGIN (%)				
	1986	1985	1984	1983	1982	1986	1985	1984	1983	1982
Alberto/Culver	3.1%	2.1%	1.3%	1.3%	2.1%	8.3%	7.8%	5.0%	5.1%	6.0%
Avon Products	5.5	5.2	5.5	5.5	6.6	13.8	12.6	14.7	13.6	15.7
Gillette	6.4	6.7	7.0	6.7	6.0	18.4	19.5	18.7	18.1	17.7
Helene Curtis	2.6	2.5	0.7	3.2	1.5	8.0	7.8	3.1	8.3	5.2
Noxell Corp.	8.5	8.5	8.1	7.6	7.1	17.3	17.5	16.0	14.5	13.7
Redkin Labs	1.9	7.7	8.2	7.4	7.6	7.0	16.2	16.8	15.7	16.2
Industry total	6.3	6.3	6.3	6.2	6.2	16.0	15.7	15.4	14.9	15.4

¹These figures are stated in million of dollars.

EXHIBIT 22.5   **Demographics of the Black Population**

AGE	1978	1979	1980	1981	1982	1983	1984	1985
Labor Force by % of U.S. Population								
16–19	8.8	8.4	8.0	7.5	7.3	6.6	7.6	6.8
20–24	16.0	16.1	15.8	16.0	16.3	15.4	16.7	14.7
25–34	28.0	28.6	29.5	31.0	30.8	32.8	31.4	31.8
35–44	19.4	19.5	19.7	20.0	20.3	21.3	20.7	22.3
45–54	15.8	15.7	15.6	14.5	14.2	13.8	13.8	14.0
55–64	9.2	9.1	9.0	9.0	9.0	8.7	8.2	8.4
65 +	2.8	2.6	2.4	2.0	2.1	1.8	1.4	2.1
Mean Income of U.S. Blacks								
14–24	$ 6,673	$ 7,738	$ 7,898[1]	$10,350[1]	$10,487[1]	$ 2,111[1]	$10,387[1]	N/A
25–34	11,815	12,916	14,018	15,079	16,256	16,092	16,956	N/A
35–44	14,021	15,277	16,788	18,350	19,172	21,385	22,459	N/A
45–54	14,983	16,933	18,013	19,286	19,812	25,809	28,215	N/A
55–64	11,976	14,741	16,301	17,089	18,093	19,527	18,135	N/A
65 +	8,363	8,713	10,472	10,650	11,566	14,161	12,042	N/A
Number of Blacks as % Total of U.S. Population								
16–19	9.3[2]	9.1[2]	11.3[4]	10.8[4]	10.5[4]	9.0[4]	9.3[4]	9.6[4]
20–24	14.4[3]	13.5[3]	10.3	10.5	10.5	9.7	9.8	9.9
25–34	14.5	15.0	17.1	16.6	17.0	18.0	17.7	17.8
35–44	10.3	10.4	10.2	10.3	10.6	11.9	11.7	11.5
45–54	9.0	9.0	8.6	8.4	8.3	8.0	8.6	8.3
55–64	7.1	7.1	7.2	7.1	7.1	7.6	7.6	7.2
65 +	7.8	7.9	7.9	7.9	8.0	9.2	9.2	8.1

SOURCE: Statistical Abstracts of U.S., 1984, 1985, 1986 and 1987.

[1]These figures represent the age category of 15–24.

[2]These figures represent the age category of 14–17.

[3]These figures represent the age category of 18–24.

[4]These figures represent the age category of 15–19.

expanded 194%, from $30 billion to $88.2 billion, and in 1983, it almost doubled again to $170.3 billion. With statistics like these the ethnic consumer is being sought after as never before.

As the disposable income of the ethnic consumer increases, competition in the industry has become fierce. Johnson Products' large competitors include: Revlon, with Realistic hair straightener and Polished Amber lines; Avon with its Shades of Beauty and Earth & Fire lines of makeup products for black women; Cosmair's L'Oreal of Paris, which has a product line called Radience that consists of hair colors and formula hair relaxers; and Alberto Culver.

By 1984, the market penetration of the larger national companies may have peaked, but Johnson Products is still in fierce competition with 50 or more black-owned regional firms, most of which make only one or two brands. Examples of these companies are M & M Products Company with its product Sta-Sof-Fro; and Pro-Line, a small but innovative black hair care firm that has introduced new products such as Perm Repair and Cherry Fragrance Oil Shampoo. Fueling the competitive fires is the fact that the innovative product offerings of the 1960s and 1970s have seemed harder to develop in the 1980s (see Exhibit 22.6). A few imaginative products producing above-average growth have been introduced, but the sales advances are closely tied to the increase in consumers' disposable income.

A major shift in the industry occurred when computerized inventory-management techniques were introduced at the retail level. Use of this technique permanently reduced the amount of stock needed on hand to sustain the particular dollar-level of sales, and resulted in a fierce battle for market share and shelf space. Because the production of innovative products

---

EXHIBIT 22.6 **Major Product Lines Introduced Since 1980**

	YEAR INTRODUCED
Professional Lines	
Ultra Sheen brand	
Precise Conditioning Relaxer	1980
Precise Curl System	1980
Precise No-Lye Relaxer	1983
Bantu Curl brand (8 products)	1981
Ultra Sheen II	1983
New shampoo	1985
Retail Lines	
Afro Sheen brand	1980
Ultra Sheen brand	
Natural Body Formula	1980
Ultra Sheen No-Lye Relaxer	1983
Pump-dispensed conditioner and hair dress	1985
Classy Curl brand	1980
Tender Treatment brand	1980
Gentle Treatment brand	1981
Gentle Treatment Instant Conditioner	1983
Super Setting Lotion	1983
No-Lye Condition Relaxer	1983
Extra-No-Lye Conditioning Creme Relaxer	1985

is expensive and risky, companies have been forced to defend their traditional offerings. Therefore, to increase their sales, the personal health care manufacturers are increasing their advertising and promotional budgets on a yearly basis.

INTERNATIONAL SUBSIDIARIES	After ten and one-half years with the company, Marilynn Cason was elected Vice-President, International in 1986. She had been serving as Vice-President and Corporate Counsel, yet for much of her time in the past several years she was deeply involved with international operations.

In 1980, the executives of the company made the strategic decision to establish Johnson Products of Nigeria as the first American company to manufacture hair care products in Nigeria. The company holds a 40% interest in this business venture with Nigerian partners representing various segments of the nation's business community. Mr. Johnson said of the Nigerian investment:

> We have been exporting to Nigeria since 1975, but actually our products have been sold there since the 1960s. Consequently, we have excellent corporate and product name recognition. . . . By manufacturing in Nigeria we are taking what we believe is the best approach to building on our well-established reputation and maximizing the opportunities available in a developing country.

The company's investment in Nigeria was $1.6 million. The facilities include a 36,000 square foot manufacturing and warehousing building located just outside the capital of Lagos. An additional 18,000 square foot facility is available if expansion is deemed necessary.

Optimism about the potential profitability of this venture waned as major losses were incurred. First-year losses totalled $380,000. These were attributed to extremely heavy living costs in accommodating a team of Johnson Products representatives from headquarters who supervised the setting up of the plant and the early stages of operations. Ms. Cason was a member of the team and managed the operation for three and one-half years. Total losses in fiscal 1981 were $466,000. In fiscal 1982 losses were $1,802,000 which included a $1,557,000 write-down of investment and advances to this subsidiary. However, in 1985 and 1986 it was a profitable operation.

Many difficulties have plagued the operations from the start. Problems first stemmed from smuggling activities, which forced Johnson Products of Nigeria, Ltd. to compete with its own product being sold on the black market at prices well below retail. Then in 1981, in an effort to stave off illegal imports, the Nigerian government severely restricted the flow of goods entering the country. The Nigerian plant, manufacturing more than 30 different products under Ultra Sheen and Afro Sheen brands, was forced to suspend operations on several occasions because of difficulties in receiving shipments of raw materials and other goods.

In 1983, Nigeria remained the largest market in black Africa, as well as the one most likely to provide business opportunities for American firms in the medium- and long-term. One of the main problems for the past few years centers around the Nigerian government's lack of foreign exchange. This causes prolonged delays in the acquisition of raw materials even when import licenses have been granted. Although it is believed that the basic raw-materials problem will not be resolved in the immediate future, the company will maintain some degree of production in the country. Basically, Nigeria is an untapped ethnic consumer market with approximately 100 million people and an annual growth rate in excess of 3%.

In continuing its overseas expansion, Johnson Products established a sales and service center in Eastbourne, England (40 miles south of London) in October, 1981. It is essentially a low-overhead central distribution center for the Great Britain and Western European markets, primarily France, Germany, Belgium, and Holland. This 3,000 square foot facility has allowed the company to offer a broader range of its professional and retail products to that area. In fiscal 1983, this distribution center "made a positive contribution" toward profit, according to corporate records. Personal income in England experienced an increase in 1985 that prompted an approximate 2% growth in personal consumption. These markets are to be supported by an expanding advertising and promotion campaign.

Although competition is very intense throughout the Caribbean markets, the company has distributors in Haiti and in Puerto Rico, Johnson's biggest market in the Caribbean area. In 1981, the company entered into its first licensing agreement with a Jamaican manufacturer. Johnson Products supplies the raw materials as well as technical and marketing support, and in turn it receives a royalty for services. The company is waiting for approval of a similar licensing agreement in Trinidad.

The company's future emphasis will be on opening new markets in those Central and South American countries that have the fewest import restrictions. Management is also exploring the business opportunities in several other African countries.

Despite continued expansion, international sales in 1986 decreased by 10.5%. Below is the breakdown of sales in the United States and international markets.

	SALES (MILLIONS OF DOLLARS)					
	1986	1985	1984	1983	1982	1981
United States	$32,956	$36,069	$39,366	$43,624	$40,933	$40,933
International	1,586	1,772	2,161	2,151	1,514	2,690

PRODUCTS

Johnson Products currently manufactures over 100 different products, more than 50 of which have been developed since January 1980. Most of these have been matched by similar new products from Johnson's competitors.

Before the introduction of Ultra Sheen Precise in 1980, the company admits, it had not offered a single innovative new product in over 15 years. Because of this lack of innovation, the firm's public image had waned and its reputation among professional beauty operators had faltered. Each product introduction in the following four years was designed to portray the firm as an industry innovator, "personally concerned with solving the beauty problems of black consumers."

According to Mr. Johnson, "In assessing why our business [1980] had slacked we learned several things. For one, we were no longer thought of as an innovative, sophisticated organization. We found also a low level of loyalty from professional beauticians and salon operators. In addition, there was an apparent lack of understanding among many large retail buyers that Johnson Products is a large, substantial organization."

He also cited other problems, including:

1. Increased competition from large and small regional competitors.
2. Competition for shelf-space allocations.
3. Changes in the buying habits of the consumer, due to economic conditions.
4. Bad times in the economy caused retailers to carry smaller inventories, causing higher frequencies of stock-out conditions and loss of customer goodwill.

Johnson's product lines fall into two categories, those marketed to the professional industry and those sold to the general public. (See Exhibit 22.6.) Hair care products accounted for 86%, 89%, and 86% of net sales and other operating revenue in 1984, 1985 and 1986, respectively. The firm also manufactures two lines of cosmetics, Ultra Sheen and Moisture Formula. Retail sales to the general public is the company's largest segment.

MARKETING AND SALES

In March 1986, Ms. Sylvia J. Wynn was named Vice-President, Marketing and Sales, and the two functions of marketing and sales that were previously directed by two individuals were combined. Mr. Johnson said, "Combining the two areas was a practical move because they were closely related. . . . Decisions now are being made with a full awareness of their overall ramification on both areas. An important by-product of this change has been a pairing down and better utilization of our sales force, along with a keener understanding among the field staff of marketing and promotional strategies." In the past, the company found that often there were communication breakdowns between the two officers who directed marketing and sales and these breakdowns caused inefficiencies in these areas.

A restructuring of the entire sales force was accomplished in fiscal 1986. Three sales zones were established as profit centers. A support system to provide marketing and other support services to each zone was developed. According to management this should facilitate the selling process.

A top priority in 1985 was to get more shelf space by getting closer to the individual who decides which products get what shelf space. To do this the company initiated an intensive, ongoing sales-training program designed to help each sales person to deal more effectively with and sell to both the retail and professional markets. Utilizing a salesperson to call on both markets was a departure from previous practices; sales representatives have stronger retail selling backgrounds. This training program also promotes the careful monitoring of each salesperson's results.

On September 1, 1986, the company initiated a new sales commission program that would enable salaries to double when specific sales goals are met. Response to the plan by the staff has been positive and encouraging.

Marketing strategies have also been redirected to a more intense concentration on key customer groups. In addition to focusing on the company's broad national needs, marketing will be doing even more to develop attractive promotions directed specifically toward distributors and major retailers, and to provide support to the three zone offices, which are "closer to our customers and have a better understanding of their customers."

The company has experimented with several extensive promotional campaigns. The "Win A Date" contest offering a male and female winner each a weekend date in Jamaica with the two Classy Curl models, was used in the Classy Curl campaign. In promoting the Gentle Treatment Conditioning Creme Relaxer the "Great Model Search" was conducted. More than 7000 consumers entered this contest, and the winners were used as models in promotional campaigns in 1983. The 1983 tour also featured the Gap Band.

Soon after these promotions, an A. C. Nielson audit survey was conducted; it showed an increase of market share in both product categories. The "Great Model Search" program, now entitled "Gentle-Treatment Model Search," draws thousands of entries annually. Each contestant must show proof of product purchase. The highlight of the 1986 contest will be a 17-city promotional tour by the 1986 winner.

In 1985, Michael Jordan, the Chicago Bulls basketball team's superstar, was signed to a multi-year contract for his endorsement of selected products. At this time, the company is working to develop a suitable program in which he can participate effectively.

One of the company's product development goals for the 1980s was to increase professional market share. The professional-sales market segment currently constitutes about 15% of the firm's total hair care business, and this decade has seen sales in this segment increase between 15% and 20% annually. The first market introduction in 1983 was the Precise No-Lye Relaxer. This has been followed each year by improved versions of earlier lines' Ultra Sheen II and Bantu. Special promotions and training programs are being aimed at the professional market segment with this goal in mind.

In 1982, Johnson Products commissioned a study to research consumer opinions and/or perceptions of the company. The study showed that there were (1) a high level of name recognition (93%), (2) a feeling that its products guarantee quality (68%), and (3) a belief that the firm is reliable and trustworthy (70%).

Drastic cuts in advertising expenditures were made in 1985 and 1986, as shown in Exhibit 22.7. The company has found that even though reports indicate that its advertising is still being well received and effective in attracting customers to its products, quite often, when customers go to buy, the item they want is out of stock.

The frequent lack of retail shelf space for the large number of black hair care products is a major problem for the industry. It is further complicated as new companies enter the regional markets. The competition from large companies such as Revlon, Avon, and Fashion Fair, still in pursuit of the ethnic dollar, has added a new facet to the problem. It is further complicated by competition from 50 small regional manufacturers, who enter into the regional markets with a restricted product line yet compete for the same shelf space.

RESEARCH AND DEVELOPMENT

Since January 1980, the Johnson Products Research Center has introduced, for both the retail and professional markets, more than 50 new products and line extensions. These new products accounted for more than 80% of sales in 1985, compared to 60%, 48%, and 36% in 1983, 1982, and 1981, respectively.

One significant aspect of the company is its capability to perform basic scientific research; this capability has enabled Johnson Products to develop

EXHIBIT 22.7   **Advertising and Promotion Expenditures, 1975–1986**

YEAR	DOLLARS	PERCENTAGE OF NET SALES
1986	$ 5,384,000	18
1985	5,986,000	18
1984	10,031,000	20
1983	7,226,000	16
1982	7,467,000	18
1981	8,076,000	17
1980	7,243,000	21
1979	6,019,000	18
1978	6,211,000	17
1977	5,731,000	18
1976	5,608,000	14
1975	4,498,000	12

unique technologies for the production of a variety of beauty products. During the past few years the company has received several patents for products presently on the market and several other patents are pending.

The Johnson Products Research Center is considered to be the largest laboratory of its kind devoted exclusively to the research and development of beauty care products for black consumers. In 1984, a staff of thirty-four technicians and scientists, representing a variety of scientific disciplines, worked with the latest sophisticated equipment in a 7,000 square foot research laboratory. By 1986, the staff had been reduced to 20, and expenditures for research and development were the lowest since those of 1976. (See Exhibit 22.8.) Approximately one third of the research and development manhours are spent on quality control; the rest are spent on new product development and the improvement of existing products. In-house capabilities are supplemented through the use of outside consultants and technical services, in the developing of concepts, designing of packages, and researching the characteristics of ethnic skin and hair.

FINANCE

During the seven fiscal years 1980–1986 the company's losses in seventeen of the twenty-eight quarters totalled $14,839,000 on sales of $254,585,000. Johnson Products was profitable only in 1981 and 1983. During the last three of those years, the company lost money in nine out of twelve quarters.

To reduce expenditures and costs in the past seven years, several cost cutting programs have been implemented. In 1982, total staff was reduced by approximately 10% through an increase in employee productivity and

EXHIBIT 22.8   **R & D Expenditures**

YEAR	R & D EXPENDITURES
1986	$693,000
1985	840,000
1984	818,000
1983	799,000
1982	868,000
1981	870,000
1980	782,000
1979	690,000
1978	763,000
1977	739,000
1976	525,000
1975	467,000

the elimination of certain job functions. The turnaround strategic plan for 1986 has resulted in a reduction in the number of employees by approximately 20%, to 431 employees. Salaries of the remaining employees were cut by 10%–20%. The company also started to perform some previously contracted services (e.g., building maintenance and silk-screening of plastic bottles) in-house.

During the last quarter of 1986 the company lost $2,154,000. George E. Johnson told the shareholders, "Fiscal 1986 could mark the end of a series of substantial losses. Our cautious optimism is based on a number of actions that lifted a great amount of pressure from management, enabling us to concentrate fully on building profitable sales." He went on to say, "Our primary objective last year was to find new ways to stem the outflow of sorely needed cash in our hair care products business without affecting our ability to produce and sell quality products." The company was able to reduce its losses by 56% over those of 1985, but sales for 1986 were reduced by $3,769,000 or 11.2%. The impact of the company's financial condition is reflected in the company's stock price. It has varied from high of $20.625 in 1976 to low of $1.75 in 1986 (see Exhibit 22.9).

The company owns a 40% interest in Johnson Products of Nigeria, Ltd. Because of the significant operating losses at Johnson Products of Nigeria, Ltd. and other external factors, the Johnson investment and advances to the Nigerian operation were written down in 1982. Previously, Johnson's 40% interest in this venture was carried at acquisition cost adjusted for equity in losses through July 31 of each year. Fiscal year 1986 was a profitable year for the Nigerian operation. Because this affiliate is still in operation, Johnson may be required in the future to advance significant amounts of working capital to this venture. The company's total export shipments to twenty-two foreign countries, including Canada, provided less than 10% of consolidated revenue for 1986.

To strengthen its financial position, the company negotiated a fully secured $10 million refinancing package with a national financial institution. The arrangement provided the company a $4 million term loan and revolving credit of up to $6 million, based on available collateral. The company also has a firm offer to buy eleven acres and 200,000 square feet of Johnson Products' office and plant space at the 87th Street and Dan Ryan Expressway facility, for $2.7 million. Management expects to net $2.5 million and use $1.5 million to reduce the company's $3.8 million long-term debt. The remainder would be used for working capital.

The company's financial information is shown in Exhibits 22.9–22.12.

EXHIBIT 22.9 Johnson Products Company: Financial Review, 1978–1986

(In Thousands of Dollars Except Per Share Data, Percentages, and Employee Data)

Years Ended August 31	1986	1985	1984	1983	1982	1981	1980	1979	1978
Summary of Operations									
Net sales	$29,811	$33,580	$35,589	$40,937	$39,177	$43,197	$32,294	$31,337	$37,246
Other operating revenue	4,731	4,261	5,938	4,838	3,270	3,710	2,842	1,801	1,416
Total net sales and other operating revenue	34,542	37,841	41,527	45,775	42,447	46,907	35,136	33,138	38,662
Cost of sales	13,243	15,169	15,419	16,649	18,191	19,528	15,250	12,291	14,854
Selling, general and administrative (exclusive of advertising and promotion)	17,028	20,283	21,055	18,490	19,122	17,866	16,773	14,657	13,776
Advertising and promotion	5,384	5,986	10,031	7,226	7,467	8,076	7,243	6,019	6,211
Equity in losses and write-down of investment in Nigerian affiliate	—	—	—	—	1,802	466	380	—	—
Interest expense (income), net	870	917	624	424	414	48	(270)	(450)	(416)
Income (loss) before income taxes	(1,983)	(4,514)	(5,602)	2,986	(4,549)	923	(4,240)	621	4,237
Income taxes (benefit)	—	—	(1,519)	1,358	(926)	538	(1,861)	300	2,000
Net income (loss)	(1,983)	(4,514)	(4,083)	1,628	(3,623)	385	(2,379)	321	2,237
Net income (loss) per share	(.50)	(1.13)	(1.03)	.41	(.91)	.10	(.60)	.08	.56
Dividends per share	—	—	—	—	—	—	.18	.36	.36
Other Financial Data									
Research and development expenses	693	840	818	799	868	870	782	690	763
Current assets	14,915	16,768	19,694	19,894	20,082	20,112	18,573	18,658	22,632
Current liabilities	8,584	13,369	11,983	7,186	9,022	6,683	5,396	2,989	5,510

Working capital	6,331	3,399	7,711	12,708	11,060	13,429	13,177	15,669	17,122
Property, net	8,068	8,891	9,120	9,210	9,133	8,988	9,062	9,400	9,346
Total assets	23,517	26,598	29,850	29,785	29,659	30,860	29,205	29,886	33,505
Capital lease obligations	16	111	221	299	—	—	—	—	—
Shareholders' equity	11,150	13,118	17,646	21,715	20,062	23,660	23,257	26,355	27,433
Shareholders' equity per share	2.80	3.29	4.43	5.46	5.05	5.96	5.86	6.63	6.87
Capital expenditures	302	754	803	987	1,076	791	528	1,008	864
Ratios									
Income (loss) before income taxes to net sales and other operating revenue	(5.7%)	(11.9%)	(13.5%)	6.5%	(10.7%)	2.0%	(12.1%)	1.9%	11.0%
Net income (loss) to net sales and other operating revenue	(5.7%)	(11.9%)	(9.8%)	3.6%	(8.5%)	.8%	(6.8%)	1.0%	5.8%
Return on average shareholders' equity	(16.3%)	(29.3%)	(20.7%)	7.8%	(16.6%)	1.6%	(9.6%)	1.2%	8.2%
Advertising and promotion to net sales and other operating revenue	15.6%	15.8%	24.2%	15.8%	17.6%	17.2%	20.6%	18.2%	16.1%
Average common and common equivalent shares outstanding (000s)[1]	3,987	3,984	3,982	3,980	3,973	3,972	3,972	3,976	3,995
Stock price range (high)	4	6½	11	11⅜	3½	5⅛	5⅜	6¾	11¼
Stock price range (low)	1¾	2¼	3	3⅛	2	2⅛	2⅛	3½	8⅞
Sales per share (dollars)	7.35	8.28	6.78	11.50	10.68	11.81	8.85	8.34	9.73
Number of employees	431	558	540	550	540	568	563	516	553

SOURCE: 1986 *Annual Report*, and *Value Line Investment Survey*, April 19, 1985, p. 821.

[1]Common equivalent shares consist of Class B common shares for the years 1974 through 1976.

EXHIBIT 22.10 | **Johnson Products Company: Consolidated Balance Sheets**

Years Ended August 31	1986	1985
Assets		
Current assets:		
Cash	$ 996,000	$ 455,000
Receivables:		
Trade, less allowance for doubtful accounts of $425,000 in 1986 and $300,000 in 1985	9,112,000	9,118,000
Other	120,000	502,000
Refundable income taxes	—	30,000
Inventories	4,112,000	5,897,000
Prepaid expenses	575,000	766,000
Total current assets	14,915,000	16,768,000
Property, plant and equipment	19,052,000	19,147,000
Less accumulated depreciation and amortization	10,984,000	10,256,000
	8,068,000	8,891,000
Other assets:		
Cash value, officers' life insurance	166,000	435,000
Investments	244,000	244,000
Miscellaneous receivables	124,000	260,000
	534,000	939,000
Total assets	23,517,000	26,598,000
Liabilities and Shareholders' Equity		
Current liabilities:		
Short-term loans	2,269,000	6,293,000
Accounts payable	3,082,000	4,403,000
Current maturities of long-term debt and capital lease obligations	329,000	113,000
Accrued expenses	2,200,000	2,064,000
Income taxes	248,000	371,000
Deferred income	456,000	125,000
Total current liabilities	8,584,000	13,369,000
Long-term debt	3,767,000	—
Capital lease obligations	16,000	111,000
Shareholders' equity		
Capital stock:		
Preferred stock, no par; authorized 300,000 shares; none issued	—	—
Common stock, $.50 par; authorized 7,504,400 shares; issued 4,052,722 shares	2,027,000	2,027,000

Years Ended August 31	1986	1985
Liabilities and Shareholders' Equity (continued)		
Additional paid-in capital	628,000	627,000
Retained earnings	8,849,000	10,832,000
Treasury stock, 65,560 shares in 1986 and 68,140 shares in 1985, at cost	(354,000)	(368,000)
	11,150,000	13,118,000
Total liabilities and shareholders' equity	$23,517,000	$26,598,000

EXHIBIT 22.11

Johnson Products Company: Consolidated Statements of Operations, 1984–1986

Years Ended August 31	1986	1985	1984
Net sales	29,811,000	33,580,000	35,589,000
Other operating revenue	4,731,000	4,261,000	5,938,000
	34,542,000	37,841,000	41,527,000
Cost and expenses:			
Cost of sales	13,243,000	15,169,000	15,419,000
Selling, general and administrative expenses	22,412,000	26,269,000	31,086,000
	35,655,000	41,438,000	46,505,000
Loss from operations	(1,113,000)	(3,597,000)	(4,978,000)
Interest expense, net	870,000	917,000	624,000
Loss before income taxes	(1,983,000)	(4,514,000)	(5,602,000)
Income taxes	—	—	(1,519,000)
Net loss	(1,983,000)	(4,514,000)	(4,083,000)
Net loss per common and common equivalent share	$ (.50)	$ (1.13)	$ (1.03)

EXHIBIT 22.12   **Johnson Products Company: Consolidated Statements of Shareholders' Equity**

Years Ended August 31, 1986, 1985, and 1984	COMMON STOCK	ADDITIONAL PAID-IN CAPITAL	RETAINED EARNINGS	TREASURY STOCK	TOTAL SHAREHOLDERS' EQUITY
Balance, August 31, 1983	$2,027,000	$649,000	$19,430,000	$(391,000)	$21,715,000
Net loss			(4,083,000)		(4,083,000)
Compensation arising from restricted stock plan		11,000			11,000
Exercise of stock options		(7,000)		11,000	4,000
Other			(1,000)		(1,000)
Balance, August 31, 1984	$2,027,000	$653,000	$15,346,000	$(380,000)	$17,646,000
Net loss			(4,514,000)		(4,514,000)
Compensation arising from restricted stock plan		(15,000)			(15,000)
Exercise of stock options		(11,000)		12,000	1,000
Balance, August 31, 1985	$2,027,000	$627,000	$10,832,000	$(368,000)	$13,118,000
Net loss			(1,983,000)		(1,983,000)
Compensation arising from restricted stock plan		(14,000)			(14,000)
Exercise of stock options		(13,000)		14,000	1,000
Other		28,000			28,000
Balance, August 31, 1986	$2,027,000	$628,000	$ 8,849,000	$(354,000)	$11,150,000

CASE 23

American Greetings

DAN KOPP · LOIS SHUFELDT

"We're in touch" and the corporate rose logo identify the world's largest publicly owned manufacturer of greeting cards and related social-expression merchandise, American Greetings (AG). In 1981, President Morry Weiss announced the formulation of a corporate growth objective to achieve $1 billion in annual sales by 1985, which would represent a 60% increase over 1982 sales of $623.6 million. The battle for market-share dominance between the two industry leaders, Hallmark and American Greetings, had escalated and intensified. Previously, the two leading firms peacefully coexisted by having mutually exclusive niches. Hallmark offered higher-priced, quality cards in department stores and card shops, and American Greetings offered inexpensive cards in mass-merchandise outlets. However, in 1977 American Greetings formulated a growth strategy for its attack of the industry leader and its niche.

THE GREETING-CARD INDUSTRY

In 1985, Americans exchanged more than 7 billion cards—around thirty per person, marking the highest per capita card consumption ever. And with the average retail price per card of a dollar, that made "social expression" a multi-billion dollar business. According to the Greeting Card Association, card senders gave 2.2 billion Christmas cards, 1.5 billion birthday cards, 850 million valentines, 180 million Easter cards, 140 million Mother's Day cards, 85 million Father's Day cards, 80 million graduation cards, 40 million Thanksgiving cards, 26 million Halloween cards, 16 million St. Patrick's Day cards, and about 10 million Grandparent's Day cards. Everyday, non-occasion cards now account for a large proportion of all industry sales, and they're on the rise. People living in the northeast and north-central parts of the country buy more cards than average, and Southerners 30 percent fewer. People who buy the majority of them tend to be between 35 and 54 years of age, come from large families, live in their own homes in the suburbs, and have an average household income of $30,000. Changes in society—demographic and social—are fueling the growth of alternative cards. These changes have included increases in the numbers of

- blended families,
- single-parent households,

This case was prepared by Professors Dan Kopp and Lois Shufeldt of Southwest Missouri State University. It was presented at the North American Case Research Association Meeting, 1987. Distributed by the North American Case Research Association meeting. All rights reserved to the authors and the North American Case Research Association. Reprinted by permission of the authors and North American Case Research Association.

- working women,
- divorces and remarriages, and
- population segments that traditionally have included the heaviest greeting-card users—35- to 65-year-olds. (Note that the baby boom generation is approaching the peak card-purchasing age).

Women purchase over 90% of all greeting cards. Women enjoy browsing and shopping for cards, and tend to purchase a card only if it is appropriate, when the card's verse and design combine to convey the sentiment she wishes to express. However, because an increasing number of women are working, these women are shopping less frequently and buying less impulse merchandise.

The growth rate for the industry has been 5%–6% annually over the past several years. Sales of unorthodox cards aimed at 18–35-year-old baby boomers have grown 25% per year. However, sales of greeting cards for the past few quarters have been lackluster. The industry is mature; sales are stagnant at about 7 billion units. According to *Chain Store Age,* the channels of distribution have been moving away from specialty stores to mass merchants. Now, department stores are cutting back square footage and dropping cards altogether. Mass market appeal now has a growth area— one-stop shopping. In addition to diversifying into other areas, Hallmark has been pushing its Ambassador line through mass merchants such as Wal-Mart and Target.

American Greetings is concentrating on the social expressions business; it has launched a massive, national television advertising campaign to firmly position itself in all aspects of the greeting-card industry. On the other hand, Hallmark, whose recent acquisitions are unrelated to the social expressions industry, is shifting its emphasis. Irvine O. Hockaday, Hallmark's CEO, said recently that he prefers outside businesses to contribute 40% of total Hallmark revenues, instead of the 10 percent they now contribute. Cards accounted for 64% of American Greetings' 1985 sales. According to some industry experts, Hallmark is now playing follow the leader in card innovations and character licensing.

An overall slowdown in retail traffic has resulted in reduced sales. Generally, there is a soft retailing environment. The retailing industry is over-stored and promotion-oriented, so retailers might have to ask greeting-card suppliers for lower prices to assist them in keeping their margins from shrinking. Retailers are losing their loyalty to manufacturers that supply a full line of products—cards, gift wrap, etc.—and are looking instead for the lowest-cost supplier of each, according to Kidder, Peabody & Company. The competition in the industry has become and will continue to be intensified, especially in the areas of price, sales promotion, distribution, and selling.

More new cards have been introduced in 1986 than in any other previous year, according to the Greeting Card Association. More "feelings" type of cards, such as the In Touch line by American Greetings, have been introduced. Because men buy only 10% of all cards sold, they are the prime target for many of the new types of cards.

Hallmark and American Greetings are experimenting with different styles, are fabricating novel reasons for people to buy their wares, and using new technology that enables cards to play tunes or talk. According to *Time,* Hallmark offers 1,200 varieties of cards for Mother's Day, while American Greetings boasts of 1,300. The product ranges from a traditional card with a picture of flowers and syrupy poetry for $1 or less, to a $7 electronic version that plays the tune, "You are the Sunshine of My Life."

Hallmark has introduced several lines of personal-relationship-oriented cards, commemorating such milestones as the wedding anniversary of a parent and a stepparent. In 1984, Hallmark introduced its Honesty Collection, which has been discontinued, with messages that reflected the nature of modern day relationships. In May of 1985, American Greetings's primary competitor brought out its Personal Touch line of cards, with intimate, conversational prose displayed on the front and with no message inside. The Greeting Card Association found that 83% of all card senders do something—add a snapshot or a newspaper clipping or jot a note—to personalize a card, and Hallmark has been quick to supply a vehicle that takes advantage of this opportunity.

Forbes has reported that there are more than 400 firms in the greeting card industry, but the two major ones, Hallmark and American Greetings, control approximately 75% of the market. Gibson Greetings is the third major firm in the industry. Approximate market shares (in percentages) for the three industry leaders have been as follows.

Company	1985	1984	1977
Hallmark	40–45%	45%	50%
American Greetings	30–35	33	24
Gibson	8–10	NA	5

Analysts expect American Greetings to keep increasing its market share. Over the last five years, the unit growth rate at American Greetings has been 4%–5% per year, against an industry-wide growth rate of 1%–2%. Industry expert, E. Gray Glass, III of Kidder, Peabody & Company, has indicated that American Greetings has been showing good growth, at 15% or better annually. Furthermore, *Chain Store Age* has projected that American Greetings will continue to take some of Hallmark's market share, but that it will take a long time for American Greetings to pass it.

New York Times has reported that Hallmark has been successful in free-standing card shops, which account for about 40% of all greeting cards sold. Fastest growth for American Greetings has been in big drugstores and supermarket chains. Growth has been slower at variety stores, traditional department stores, and gift shops, which account for about 30% of American Greetings sales.

According to *Investor's Daily,* American Greetings and Hallmark have been increasing their market shares at the expense of smaller card companies, which have been forced out of the market because of the high costs of selling, distributing, and marketing, as well as their lack of extensive computerized inventory-monitoring systems, which only large companies can afford. Industry analysts, however, have predicted that small firms, with a focus niche and geographic area, will continue to enter the industry and can be profitable.

Richard H. Connor, American Greetings' Executive Vice-President, stated that the company has been gaining ground on Hallmark, although he wouldn't say by how much:

> If you compare the businesses that are similar with both companies, we are closing the gap. Between the both of us, we have 75 percent of the market, and some of our growth must be at their expense.

Both Hallmark and American Greetings are being challenged by Gibson, which is the fastest growing company in the industry. Gibson scored a coup with Walt Disney Productions when they secured the rights to use Mickey Mouse and his friends, who previously had been featured by Hallmark. Gibson also has licensed Garfield the Cat and Sesame Street characters, but Hallmark's line of Peanuts cards remains one of the industry's most successful.

| **HISTORY OF AMERICAN GREETINGS** | The story of American Greetings is one of the "American Dream" of an immigrant from Poland, who came to the land of promised opportunity to seek his fortune. Jacob Sapirstein was born in 1884 in Wasosz, Poland, and because of the Russian-Japanese war of 1904, he was sent, along with his seven brothers and one sister, by his widowed mother to live in America. |

Jacob, also known as J.S., began his one-man business buying postcards made in Germany from wholesalers and selling them to candy, novelty, and drug stores in Cleveland in 1906. From a horse-drawn card wagon, the small venture steadily flourished.

J.S. and his wife, Jennie, also a Polish immigrant, had three sons and a daughter; all three sons became active in their father's business. At the age of nine, Irving, the oldest, kept the family business afloat while J.S. was recovering from the flu during the great epidemic of 1918. The business had outgrown the family's living room and was moved to a garage at this time.

J.S. had a basic philosophy of service to the retailer and a quality product for the consumer. He developed the first wire wall rack as well as rotating floor stands, as more attractive, convenient displays. In the 1930s the Sapirstein Card Company began to print its own cards so that the quality of its product was ensured. The name of the company was changed to American

Greetings Publishers to reflect the national stature and functioning of the company. Their first published line of cards under the American Greetings name, the Forget Me Not Line, went on sale in 1939 for a nickel. One card, which remains the company's all-time best seller, was designed by Irving.

The company saw great expansion throughout the 1940s, as loved ones found the need to communicate with World War II soldiers. The most significant effect of this need was the widespread use of greeting cards by the soldiers. In the past, cards had been primarily utilized by women; thus the expansion to the male market was a significant breakthrough for the card industry.

The 1950s marked the first public offering of stock and the name change to American Greetings Corporation. Ground was broken for a new world headquarters, and the way was set for expansion to world markets. The company made connections with several foreign markets and acquired a Canadian plant.

In 1960, J.S. stepped down at the age of 76. His son Irving succeeded him as President. Under Irving's leadership and with the assistance of his brothers, Morris and Harry Stone (all three brothers had changed their names from Sapirstein, meaning sapphire, to Stone in 1940 for business reasons), the company has continued to expand into gift wrapping, party goods, calendars, stationery, candles, ceramics and perhaps, most importantly, the creation of licensed characters.

Expansion into these related items has somewhat diminished American Greetings' recession-proof profits. Greeting-card sales typically increase during recessions as people refrain from buying gifts and instead remember others with a less expensive card. The supplemental items now constitute one third of the company's sales, not enough to seriously jeopardize American Greetings during down economies, but enough to greatly augment the company's sales during good economic times.

American Greetings' world expansion became a major pursuit throughout the 1960s and 1970s. Morry Weiss, a grandson-in-law of J.S., became the new President of American Greetings in 1978, as Irving continued to act as the CEO and Chairman of the Board of Directors. Morris Stone continues to serve as Vice-Chairman of the Board, and Harry Stone remains as an active board member. (See Exhibit 23.1.)

OBJECTIVES

In 1981, at the first national sales meeting ever held by American Greetings, President Morry Weiss announced the formulation of a major corporate objective: to achieve $1 billion in annual sales by 1985. During fiscal 1985, American Greetings strengthened its position as a leader in the industry; that year marked the seventy-ninth consecutive year of increased revenue— total revenue increased to $945.7 million, while net income increased to $74.4 million. This record of success represented a:

EXHIBIT 23.1 **Corporate Directory**

BOARD OF DIRECTORS

Jacob Sapirstein
Founder

Irving I. Stone[1]
Chairman,
Chief Executive Officer

Morris S. Stone[1]
Vice-Chairman

Morry Weiss[1]
President,
Chief Operating Officer

Hugh Calkins[2]
Partner
Jones, Day, Reavis & Pogue
(attorneys-at-law)

Herbert H. Jacobs
personal investments
and consultant

Frank E. Joseph[2]
Attorney and Secretary
Kulas Foundation
(philanthropic foundation)

Millard B. Opper[2]
Retired Chairman of
Canadian Operations

Albert B. Ratner[2]
President
Forest City Enterprises, Inc.
(real estate, construction
and retail operations)

Harry H. Stone[2]
President
Courtland Management, Inc.
(personal investments)
Chairman
Barks Williams Oil

Milton A. Wolf
Former United States
Ambassador to Austria
(personal investments)

Morton Wyman[1]
Executive Vice-President

CORPORATE OFFICERS

Irving I. Stone
Chairman
Chief Executive Officer

Morris S. Stone
Vice-Chairman

Morry Weiss
President
Chief Operating Officer

Richard H. Connor
Executive Vice-President
American Greetings Division

Morton Wyman
Executive Vice-President

Rubin Feldman
Senior Vice-President

Henry Lowenthal
Senior Vice-President
Chief Financial Officer

Packy Nespeca
Senior Vice-President
Corporate Trade Development

Al J. Stenger
Senior Vice-President
International & Subsidiary
Operations

Dale J. Beinker
Vice-President
International

Raymond P. Kenny
Vice-President
Strategic Planning

Ralph L. White
Vice-President
Chief Human Resource Officer

Allan J. Goodfellow
General Counsel & Secretary

John M. Klipfell
Controller

Eugene B. Scherry
Treasurer

AMERICAN GREETINGS DIVISION

Richard H. Connor
Executive Vice-President

William E. Schmitt
Group Vice-President—
Marketing

Robert C. Swilik
Group Vice-President
Manufacturing

James Van Arsdale
Group Vice-President—
Operations

H. David Bender
Vice-President
Information Services

Edward F. Doherty
Vice-President—Manufacturing/
Everyday Division

James H. Edler
Vice-President
Materials Management

John T. Fortner
Vice-President—Manufacturing/
Seasonal Division

Edward Fruchtenbaum
Vice-President
Marketing Administration

David J. Gamble
Vice-President
Inventory and Quality Control

Gary E. Johnston
Vice-President—Creative

David R. Ledvina
Vice-President
Computer Operations

William R. Mason
Vice-President
General Sales Manager

William R. Parsons
Vice-President—Chain Sales

Ronald J. Peer
Vice-President—Field Sales

Joy E. Sweeney
Vice-President—Primary
Product Management

Kenneth J. Valore
Vice-President—Finance

Gordon Van Over
Vice-President—Consumer
Product Management

George A. Wenz
Vice-President
National Accounts

SOURCE: American Greetings
[1]Member of Executive Committee
[2]Member of Audit Committee

- 300% increase in total revenue during the past 10 years,
- 613% increase in net income during the past 10 years, and
- 315% increase in dividends per share in the past 10 years, with two increases in fiscal 1985.

According to Morry Weiss, President and Chief Operating Officer,

American Greetings today is positioning itself for transition from a greeting card company to a total communications company. For years, American Greetings was thought of only as a greeting card maker. That narrow description no longer applies to the world's largest, publicly-owned manufacturer of greeting cards and related social-expression merchandise. Today we are diversified into other major product lines, including gift wrap, candles, stationery, ceramics, party goods, and calendars. In addition, we lead the industry in licensing characters, such as Holly Hobbie, Ziggy, Strawberry Shortcake, Care Bears and Care Bear Cousins, which are featured on thousands of retail products and on television and in motion pictures.

Irving Stone, Chairman of the Board and Chief Executive Officer added,

American Greetings is aggressively pursuing growth in their core business, concentrating specifically on increasing market share and unit volume, and continued margin. We'll grow through our retailers by providing the programs that will generate sales and make the greeting card department the most profitable area in their store. We'll grow through our consumers by understanding their needs and providing them with products they want and enjoy buying. We'll grow by constantly improving our operations and productivity through creativity, innovation, and technology.

He further added,

We expect growth and are planning for it throughout the corporation. In the past four years we have invested heavily in increased capacity, plant expansion, new equipment, and new technology. Almost two years ago, we completed an equity offering that substantially strengthened our financial position; an additional offering is not expected in the near future. Today we see no problem financing our growth while at the same time increasing our dividends.

A flurry of acquisitions occurred in the 1980s. A full list of subsidiaries, as well as American Greetings' international operations, is displayed in Exhibit 23.2.

EXHIBIT 23.2 **International and Subsidiary Operations**

UNITED STATES

A.G. Industries, Inc.
Cleveland, Ohio
Charles H. Nervig, President

AmToy, Inc.
New York, New York
Larry Freiberg, President

Drawing Board Greeting Cards, Inc.
Dallas, Texas
Selwin Belofsky, President

Plus Mark, Inc.
Greeneville, Tennessee
Ronald E. Clouse, President

The Summit Corporation
Berlin, Connecticut
Robert P. Chase, President

Those Characters From Cleveland, Inc.
Cleveland, Ohio
John S. Chojnacki, Thomas A. Wilson, Co-Presidents

Tower Products Company, Inc.
Chicago, Illinois
Melvin Mertz, President

CANADA

Carlton Cards Ltd.
Toronto, Ontario
William L. Powell, President and Chairman of Canadian Operations

Plus Mark Canada
Toronto, Ontario
Richard L. Krelstein, President

Rust Craft Canada, Inc.
Scarborough, Ontario
Gary Toporoski, Vice President, Managing Director

CONTINENTAL EUROPE

Richard C. Schulte
Director of Operations

Grako Oy
Helsinki, Finland
Risto Pitkanen, Managing Director

A/S Muva Grafiske Produkter
Oslo, Norway
Aage Dahl, Managing Director

Muva Greetings B.V.
Heerlen, The Netherlands
Huub Robroeks, General Manager

Susy Card
Hamburg, West Germany
Charles Wightman, Managing Director

MEXICO

Felicitaciones Nacionales S.A. de C.V.
Mexico City, Mexico
Antonio Felix G., President

MONACO

Rust Craft International S.A.
Michel Bourda, Managing Director

UNITED KINGDOM

Rust Craft Greeting Cards (U.K.) Ltd.
Dewsbury, England
David M. Beards, Managing Director and Chairman of U.K. Operations

Andrew Valentine Holdings Ltd.
Dundee, Scotland
Alistair R.L. Mackay, Managing Director

Celebration Arts Group Ltd.
Corby, England
W. George Pomphrett, Managing Director

Denison Colour Ltd.
Guiseley, England
Brian Holliday, Managing Director

SOURCE: American Greetings

MARKETING STRATEGIES

Product

American Greetings produces a wide product line, including greeting cards, gift wrap, party goods, toys and gift items. Greeting cards accounted for 66% of the company's 1986 fiscal-year sales. The percentage breakdown of sales by major product categories is as follows:

Everyday greeting cards	37%
Holiday greeting cards	29
Gift wrap and party goods	18
Consumer products (toys, etc.)	7
Stationery	9

It is the belief of American Greetings that one of the keys to increased sales is to have a product line that offers a wide variety and selection of cards, such that a consumer can always find the right card for that special person. Each year American Greetings offers more new products than ever before. The creative department produces over 20,000 different designs to ensure the wide selection.

American Greetings' creative staff is one of largest assemblages of artistic talent in the world. The department has over 400 designers, artists, and writers who are guided by the latest research data available from computer analysis, consumer testing, and information from the company's sales and merchandising departments. Careful monitoring of societal changes, fashion and color trends, and consumer preferences provides further guidance to product development. American Greetings also gives uncompromising adherence to quality—in papers, inks, and printing procedures.

American Greetings pioneered licensing and now dominates the industry of character licensing. Their strategy has been to maximize the potential of their creative and marketing expertise. Holly Hobbie was the first licensed character, in 1968; Ziggy followed in 1971, and Strawberry Shortcake in 1980. When introduced, Strawberry Shortcake was the most popular new character in licensing history. Sales for Strawberry Shortcake will soon exceed $1 billion in retail sales, a revenue larger than that of any other character. In 1983 American Greetings introduced Care Bears and Herself the Elf. When the products were launched, General Mills and twenty-three licensees were supported by an $8 million advertising and promotional campaign, including a half-hour animated television special. The Care Bears license identifies ten adorable cuddlies, each with a sentimental message on its tummy.

Another licensing creation, Popples, added a new dimension to a field crowded with lookalikes. Popples literally "pop out" from a plush ball to a lovable, furry playmate. A plush toy that folds into its own pouch, the Popples enables children to make its arms, legs, and fluffy tail appear and disappear at will. Another new and under-cultivated market is being reached by two new toys from AmToy: My Pet Monster and Madballs. They were the hits of 1986's Toy Fair show. These creatures are designed to delight the millions of young boys who prefer the bizarre to the cuddly. Forty companies initially signed up to manufacture other products such as clothing, knapsacks, and books featuring the characters. American Greetings and Mattel together spent about $10 million promoting the characters, including a half-hour Popples television special. The licensed product industry is $50 billion strong.

According to *Forbes*, all of American Greetings' licensed characters have not been successful. One flop, Herself the Elf, was perceived by retailers as being too much like Strawberry Shortcake; it also missed the Christmas season because of production problems. Another failure was Get Along Gang, which tried to appeal to both little girls and boys.

Distribution

American Greetings distributes its products through 90,000 retail outlets located throughout the free world; this number has increased from 80,000 in 1983. Additionally, there has been growth in those channels of distribution in which American Greetings is dominant. Consumers have been seeking greater convenience shopping and one-stop shopping, channels in which the company is strong—chain drugstores, chain supermarkets, and mass merchandise retailers. Thirty-nine percent of American Greetings's sales went to drug stores; the remaining sales (in order of rank) were to mass merchandisers, supermarkets, stationery and gift shops, variety stores, military post exchanges, combo stores (food, general merchandise and gift items), and department stores. During the last five years, sales to drug, variety, and department stores as a percentage of total revenue have declined, while sales to supermarkets, mass merchandisers, combo stores, and military post exchange units have increased; sales to stationery and gift shops have remained constant.

Promotion

In 1982, American Greetings became recognized nationwide, first through television commercials and then through a new corporate identity program. The new logo is now featured prominently at retail outlets; the updated corporate rose logo is now a standard and highly recognizable feature greeting American Greetings customers on all product packaging, store signage, point of purchase displays, and even their truck fleet. The year-round advertising campaign included the promotion of the major card-sending holidays and non-seasonal occasions during daytime and prime-time television programming.

Supporting marketing is a promotional generator out of which flow seasonal and special displays, special signs, sales catalogues, national television advertising, media and trade journal exposure, television programming, and special events featuring American Greetings' exclusive characters. Results can be seen in increased support for American Greetings' sales personnel, greater consumer awareness, improved relations with retail dealers, greater visibility within the financial community, and improved relations with employees and communities in which plant facilities are operating.

The aim of American Greetings' national consumer-advertising and public-relations programs is to remind people to send cards, in that one of the company's chief competitors is consumer forgetfulness. American Greetings is the only company in the industry to sponsor national consumer retail promotions. These consumer-directed programs serve to establish brand identity and generate retail-store traffic.

In 1983 American Greetings employed 1,600 full-time salespeople, in addition to 7,000 part-timers; all of these have been directed through fifteen regional and sixty-six district sales offices in the United States, the United Kingdom, Canada, Mexico, and France. The company employs a large force of retail store merchandisers who visit each department at regular intervals, and ensure that every pocket in every display is kept filled with appropriate merchandise.

The American Greetings sales force is meeting the unique and challenging needs of their customers; no other company in the industry has sales and marketing personnel assigned to specific channels of distribution. This sales organization gives retailers the advantage of working with specialists who understand their markets, their customers, and their specific marketing needs.

The success of American Greetings' aggressive marketing programs is explained by William E. Schmitt, Group Vice-President, Marketing:

First we have the creativity to develop the best products in the industry. Every year we prove this with new characters, new card lines, and other products and programs that attract consumers and increase sales for our customers and ourselves. Second, we have a close relationship with our customers. The retailer support programs we offer—including terms, display fixtures, advertising and merchandising programs, promotion support and inventory controls—are unsurpassed in the industry.

Programs are tailored to help individual retailers plan their greeting-card locations, department sizes, and displays. American Greetings shows the retailers how to merchandise innovative ideas and enhance visibility by means of proven promotional programs.

Computer technology is helping American Greetings' sales people to project retailers' needs better, and this ability has resulted in improved sell-through of the product at retail. MIS, the data-processing unit for American Greetings, is playing a vital role in the increasing of sales of American Greetings' products at the retail level. In 1984, the company began implementing a computer-to-computer reordering system that allows retail accounts to control their inventories and turnaround time; that data is electronically transferred to American Greetings' headquarters data center.

Good retail presentation is a key to card sales; American Greetings has created a unique identification for the greeting-cards department. It is called the Total Retail Environment, and it uses a completely planned and coordinated approach that integrates display cabinets, signage, lighting, product packaging, and even products to create a stunning new American Greetings look. The purposes of this new system are to establish greater consumer awareness of the American Greetings card department, to provide a distinctive look and appeal, and to provide an attractive and enjoyable place in which customers like to shop.

American Greetings also possesses the most favorable terms-of-sale program in the industry. To improve the retailer's return on inventory investment, the company has successful merchandising plans, retail-store merchandisers, and computerized inventory controls. American Greetings also sports a Direct Product Profitability (DPP) concept, to evaluate productivity and space allocation for products in stores. To take gross margin and return on inventory investment analysis a step further, DPP reflects revenue after allowances and discounts and subtracts all costs attributable to the product, including labor and freight. American Greetings' sales people can then demonstrate to retailers that their greeting-card department returns a high rate of profit for the space allocated.

Richard H. Connor, American Greetings Executive Vice-President recently announced,

> To increase market share, American Greetings revamped its sales force and created one sales department that specializes in independent retail accounts and another sales department that specializes in selling to retail chains. A third

department will stock and service all types of accounts. This will give greater selling strength where it's needed and lowers our selling costs.

American Greetings has created a New Retail Communications Network (RCTN), which conducts research that will better enable the company to identify the products appropriate to the needs of their customers. Data are compiled by the monitoring of product sales and space productivity from a chain of nationwide test stores that encompass all demographic and geographic variables and represent all channels of distribution. The RCTN then interprets data as it would apply to an account's specifications, including type of store, size, location, and consumer profile. This total merchandising approach to achieving maximum sales and space potential is unique in the industry.

PRODUCTION STRATEGIES

American Greetings has forty-nine plants and facilities in the United States, Canada, Continental Europe, Mexico, Monaco, and the United Kingdom.

American Greetings has been concerned with reducing its production costs, in order to remain the industry's lowest cost producer through efficient manufacturing operations and still maintain quality and service to their customers. According to Robert C. Swilik, Group Vice-President, Manufacturing,

> Improved control of our manufacturing process through planning and scheduling enable us to improve productivity, reduce manufacturing costs and reduce inventory. Increased productivity is the result of our growing sense of shared responsibility. The relationship between management and the work force is excellent.

Quality improvements have been consistently made. Some of the major improvements have been:

1. Upgraded die cutting and embossing capabilities with the purchase of nine high-speed Bobst presses costing $1 million each.

2. Added capacity to the hot stamping and thermography operations.

3. Streamlined order filling in both everyday and seasonal operations.

4. Completed a 200,000-square-foot warehouse addition to the Osceola, Arkansas, plant and began operations on an addition to the Ripley, Tennessee, plant, which increased its capacity by 20%.

5. Installed a Scitex system that will dramatically improve product quality and increase productivity; new electronic pre-press system enables creative department to interact with manufacturing at the creatively crucial pre-press stage.

6. Installed additional high-speed and more powerful presses to further improve quality of die cutting and embossing at the Bardstown, Kentucky, plant; a 300,000-square-foot addition is also planned.

7. Installed new computer graphics system called Via Video for design and layout functions for a variety of in-house publications and brochures. (This gives the artist freedom to create while quickly and inexpensively exploring options and alternatives, thus increasing productivity.)

PERSONNEL STRATEGIES

American Greetings currently employs over 20,000 people in the United States, Canada, Mexico, and Europe.

According to Morry Weiss, American Greetings is deeply concerned about management succession:

> Our young executives are being developed to succeed retiring senior officers. Last year, more management movement occurred than in any of the preceding five years. The Stone family built and developed the company. However, managing this dynamic business today presents challenges beyond the capability of any one or two persons. Thus, over the past ten years, the management of American Greetings has been changing from a singular head to a broad based management group. We have broadened decision making authority. Each business unit has been given stretch goals and responsibility for achieving those goals. Units are preparing strategic plans and are vying for corporate resources based upon projections of growth and profitability.

According to Robert C. Swilik, Group Vice-President,

> Relationship between management and the work force is excellent. We have never had a strike in any of our plants, and we plan to work on keeping that harmonious spirit alive. We will expand an employee involvement program that brings all levels of employees into greater participation.

MANAGEMENT

In 1983, American Greetings underwent a major management restructuring to permit top officers of the company more time to concentrate on strategic planning. The company was reorganized, from a centralized structure to a divisional profit-center basis. Each division has its own budget committee, and an executive management committee comprised of five senior executives approves the strategic plans for all the divisions. Strategic plans are established in one-, three-, ten-, and twenty-year time frames. Corporate American Greetings maintains strict budgetary and accounting controls.

The basic, domestic greeting-card business was placed under the American Greetings Division. Foreign and U.S. subsidiaries and the licensing division have become a second unit, with corporate management a third. Restructuring has allowed corporate management to step back from day-to-day operations and focus on the growth of American Greetings beyond the $1 billion annual revenue.

According to Irving Stone:

The prime function of corporate management is to plan and manage the growth of the entire corporation, developing capable management and allocating corporate resources to those units offering the greatest potential return on investment. Greeting cards has been our basic business for 78 years and remains today our largest business unit; there are smaller business units, which complement the greeting card business and are deserving of our attention.

American Greetings is composed of the following divisions.

The *American Greetings Division* encompasses the core business of greeting cards and related products, including manufacturing, sales, merchandising, research, and administrative services. It produces and distributes greeting cards and related products domestically. Some products are distributed throughout the world by international subsidiaries and licensees.

Foreign and Domestic Subsidiaries encompasses two wholly owned companies in Canada, four in the United Kingdom, six in Continental Europe, and one in Mexico. Licensees use American Greetings designs and verses in almost every free country in the world. Subdivisions include:

> ***Canadian Operations:*** Carlton Cards and Rust Craft, two companies.
>
> ***United Kingdom Operations:*** British are largest per capita senders of greetings cards in the world. Three American Greetings companies in the UK—Rust Craft, Celebration Arts and Andrew Valentine.
>
> ***Continental European Operations:*** five companies wholly owned.
>
> ***Those Characters From Cleveland:*** licensing division of American Greetings. Characters and new television series, The Get Along Gang.
>
> ***Plus Mark:*** began producing Christmas promotional products such as gift wrap, ribbon, bows, and boxed Christmas cards in an industry selling primarily to mass merchandisers.
>
> ***AmToy:*** sells novelties, dolls, and plush toys.
>
> ***AG Industries:*** produces display cabinet-fixtures in wood, metal, or plastic for all American Greetings retail accounts and a growing list of external clients.

Exhibit 23.1 provides a corporate directory of management personnel and their divisional assignments.

FINANCE STRATEGIES

Exhibits 23.3–23.5 contain relevant financial information of American Greetings. The financial condition of American Greetings has been exemplary over the years. However, the company's financial performance in 1986 was disappointing, with revenue growth estimated to be at 7% and earnings similar to those of 1985. American Greetings's revenue and earnings growth rates for the previous five years had increased at compound annual rates of 17% and 29%, respectively. American Greetings's stock declined sharply after the disappointing financial report.

EXHIBIT 23.3 American Greetings: Consolidated Statements of Financial Position
(Dollars in Thousands)

Year Ended February 28 or 29	1986	1985	1984	1983	1982
Assets					
Current Assets					
Cash and equivalents	$ 26,853	$ 66,363	$ 62,551	$ 19,950	$ 3,367
Trade accounts receivable, less allowances for sales returns of $57,382 ($42,198 in 1985) and for doubtful accounts of $3,378 ($2,900 in 1985)	240,471	173,637	146,896	148,018	131,996
Inventories:					
Raw material	59,343	59,197	48,738	47,636	53,515
Work in process	60,179	53,728	43,929	54,756	52,214
Finished products	181,237	152,543	139,275	122,167	97,221
	300,759	265,468	231,942	224,559	202,950
Less LIFO reserve	76,552	71,828	63,455	59,345	55,051
	224,207	193,640	168,487	165,214	147,899
Display material and factory supplies	26,826	20,809	11,532	12,245	11,724
Total inventories	251,033	214,449	180,019	177,459	159,623
Deferred income taxes	36,669	33,016	26,517	24,847	18,014
Prepaid expenses and other	6,228	4,795	4,187	3,524	2,057
Total current assets	561,254	492,260	420,170	373,798	315,057
Other Assets	47,085	31,634	34,820	32,866	22,063
Property, Plant and Equipment					
Land	7,523	6,822	6,621	5,427	3,380
Buildings	165,241	143,671	133,868	118,598	110,479
Equipment and fixtures	222,718	182,101	158,507	133,731	115,927
	395,482	332,594	298,996	257,756	229,786
Less accumulated depreciation and amortization	130,519	108,591	95,092	83,745	75,052
Property, plant and equipment—net	264,963	224,003	203,904	174,011	154,734
Total assets	$873,302	$747,897	$658,894	$580,675	$491,854

Liabilities and Shareholders' Equity

Current Liabilities					
Notes payable to banks	$ 15,921	$ 4,574	$ 4,647	$ 29,836	$ 4,564
Accounts payable	66,685	56,840	52,302	40,568	39,016
Payrolls and payroll taxes	28,675	26,761	23,160	16,914	17,224
Retirement plans	11,697	12,612	10,362	7,405	5,696
State and local taxes	2,763	2,796	2,811	2,448	3,278
Dividends payable	5,317	4,622	3,304	2,641	1,918
Income taxes	18,988	27,465	23,672	8,841	12,177
Sales returns	23,889	21,822	17,795	16,423	9,241
Current maturities of long-term debt	4,786	4,359	6,432	6,998	6,531
Total current liabilities	178,721	161,851	144,485	132,074	99,645
Long-Term Debt	147,592	112,876	119,941	111,066	148,895
Deferred Income Taxes	64,025	47,422	28,972	21,167	15,530
Shareholders' Equity					
Common shares—par value $1:					
Class A	29,203	28,835	28,397	27,896	12,293
Class B	2,982	3,046	3,070	3,080	1,413
Capital in excess of par value	93,055	87,545	80,428	76,851	37,690
Cumulative translation adjustment	(16,801)	(13,688)	(9,158)	(7,179)	(3,829)
Retained earnings	374,525	320,010	262,759	215,620	180,217
Total shareholders' equity	482,964	425,748	365,496	316,368	227,784
Total liabilities and shareholders' equity	$873,302	$747,897	$658,894	$580,675	$491,854

SOURCE: American Greetings

851

EXHIBIT 23.4   **American Greetings: Consolidated Statements of Income**
(Thousands of Dollars Except Per Share Amounts)

Years Ended February 28 or 29, 1986, 1985, and 1984

	1986	1985	1984	1983	1982	1981
Net sales	$1,012,451	$919,371	$817,329	$722,431	$605,970	$489,213
Other income	23,200	26,287	22,585	20,252	17,634	9,059
Total revenue	1,035,651	945,658	839,914	742,683	623,604	498,272
Costs and expenses:						
Material, labor and other production costs	416,322	377,755	339,988	310,022	276,071	222,993
Selling, distribution and marketing	308,745	274,095	246,456	217,022	179,021	140,733
Administrative and general	131,928	123,750	112,363	96,012	76,494	61,033
Depreciation and amortization	23,471	18,799	15,507	13,890	12,752	10,863
Interest	19,125	15,556	16,135	24,086	21,647	13,548
	899,591	809,955	730,449	661,032	565,985	449,170
Income before income taxes	136,060	135,703	109,465	81,651	57,619	49,102
Income taxes	61,635	61,338	49,807	37,069	24,776	22,587
Net income	$ 74,425	$ 74,365	$ 59,658	$ 44,582	$ 32,843	$ 26,515
Net income per share	$2.32	$2.35	$1.91	$1.54	$1.20	$ .97

SOURCE: American Greetings

EXHIBIT 23.5 American Greetings: Selected Financial Data
(Thousands of Dollars Except Per Share Amounts)

Years Ended February 28 or 29	1986	1985	1984	1983	1982	1981	1980	1979	1978	1977	1976
Summary of Operations											
Total revenue											
As reported	$1,035,651	$945,658	$839,914	$742,683	$623,604	$498,272	$427,469	$373,487	$315,644	$277,985	$255,770
Adjusted for general inflation*	1,035,651	979,399	906,904	827,715	737,611	650,499	633,535	615,852	560,333	525,318	511,223
Material, labor and other production costs	416,322	377,755	339,988	310,022	276,071	222,993	190,135	161,654	131,769	118,252	114,190
Depreciation and amortization	23,471	18,799	15,507	13,890	12,752	10,863	10,070	8,453	7,544	6,982	6,328
Interest expense	19,125	15,556	16,135	24,086	21,647	13,548	9,716	5,911	3,935	5,423	4,970
Net income											
As reported	74,425	74,365	59,658	44,582	32,843	26,515	25,638	22,911	19,926	16,787	14,601
Adjusted for specific inflation*	63,630	63,860	52,298	34,817	21,349	17,495	23,024	—	—	—	—
Net income per share											
As reported	2.32	2.35	1.91	1.54	1.20	.97	.94	.84	.73	.62	.53
Adjusted for specific inflation*	1.98	2.02	1.67	1.20	.78	.64	.84	—	—	—	—
Cash dividends per share											
As reported	.62	.54	.40	.31	.27	.26	.25	.22	.19	.15	.13
Adjusted for general inflation*	.62	.56	.43	.35	.32	.34	.37	.36	.34	.28	.26
Fiscal year end market price per share											
As reported	35.62	33.06	23.69	18.69	9.63	5.50	5.69	5.75	5.25	4.69	5.07
Adjusted for general inflation*	35.05	33.75	25.16	20.60	11.03	6.87	7.99	9.12	9.08	8.68	9.83
Purchasing power gain from holding net monetary liabilities*	1,843	1,438	1,784	4,739	9,366	9,391	9,750	—	—	—	—
Increase (decrease) in value of assets adjusted for specific inflation compared to general inflation*	(5,642)	(16,067)	(10,605)	2,693	(4,981)	(15,935)	9,625	—	—	—	—
Translation adjustment*	(3,653)	(5,881)	(2,289)	(4,701)	(3,867)	—	—	—	—	—	—
Average number of shares outstanding	32,059,851	31,629,418	31,240,455	28,967,092	27,352,342	27,314,594	27,302,686	27,293,376	27,292,036	27,292,484	27,292,484

(Continued)

853

EXHIBIT 23.5   (Continued)

Years Ended February 28 or 29	1986	1985	1984	1983	1982	1981	1980	1979	1978	1977	1976
Average consumer price index	322.2	311.1	298.4	289.1	272.4	246.8	217.4	195.4	181.5	170.5	161.2
Financial Position											
Accounts receivable	$240,471	$173,637	$146,896	$148,018	$131,996	$114,051	$ 76,629	$ 67,651	$ 54,634	$ 48,920	$ 53,258
Inventories	251,033	214,449	180,019	177,459	159,623	133,836	112,279	98,075	71,581	53,741	52,581
Working capital	382,533	330,409	275,685	241,724	215,412	167,772	135,443	119,421	98,188	90,308	99,643
Total assets	873,302	747,897	685,894	580,675	491,854	433,204	344,395	305,746	256,297	247,503	233,572
Capital additions	61,799	43,575	46,418	33,967	26,720	22,768	34,516	25,205	20,586	7,630	15,150
Long-term debt	147,592	112,876	119,941	111,066	148,895	113,486	75,994	54,845	45,929	41,855	66,048
Shareholders' equity											
As reported	482,964	425,748	365,496	316,368	227,784	205,550	186,043	167,168	150,242	135,370	122,608
Adjusted for specific inflation*	642,767	602,350	559,395	518,955	432,781	422,991	421,248	—	—	—	—
Shareholders' equity per share	15.01	13.35	11.62	10.18	8.31	7.52	6.81	6.12	5.51	4.96	4.49
Net return on average shareholders' equity	16.5%	19.2%	17.8%	17.1%	15.4%	13.7%	14.6%	14.5%	14.0%	13.0%	12.5%
Pre-tax return on total revenue	13.1%	14.4%	13.0%	11.0%	9.2%	9.9%	11.2%	12.0%	13.3%	11.7%	10.2%

SOURCE: American Greetings.

*In average fiscal 1986 dollars.

According to the research department of the Ohio Company, the reasons for the change in sales and revenues were attributed to:

1. Weak retail environment—decline in retail traffic.

2. Heavy investment in display fixtures—intense competition has forced larger investment than anticipated.

3. Reduced licensing revenues—short lifecycle of products and greater competitive pressures reduced licensing revenues.

4. Increased accounts receivables and inventory due to slower collections and weak ordering by retailers.

5. Increased interest expense due to increased accounts-receivable and inventory levels.

Irving Stone remarked about the company's finances:

> In Fiscal 1986, the retailing picture was a rapidly changing mosaic, featuring a generally poor environment marked by a substantial drop-off in store traffic. As a result, sales of many of our products, which are dependent upon store traffic and impulse buying, fell below our expectations. Nevertheless, total revenue increased for the eightieth consecutive year, primarily due to increased greeting card sales. This is a proud record which few business enterprises can match. While this increase established a new corporate revenue milestone, it did not meet our performance goals, and earnings were flat for the first time in ten years.

FUTURE OF AMERICAN GREETINGS

Although American Greetings has had significant growth in the past, events in its external environment are clouding the long-term picture.

Again, from Irving Stone:

> We foresee opportunities to expand our business and profitability. Recent management restructuring provides key officers with the time necessary to concentrate on long term strategic planning in order to identify specific opportunities, seize upon them and transform them into bottom line results. Much growth potential lies ahead in our basic greeting card business, both domestically and internationally. We will strengthen our growing number of subsidiaries, improve efficiency and increase productivity. Sales increases and expanded distribution in all channels of trade are key objectives. Licensing will continue to flourish, extending our horizons further and further.

Morry Weiss further added:

> Our future growth plans: aggressively pursuing growth in our core business, concentrating specifically on increasing market share and unit volume, and continued margin improvement.

However, according to William Blair and Company, American Greetings' earnings growth will moderate significantly from the high earning growth rate over the past five years. This is due in part to cyclical factors in the economy, but also because of slowdowns in expansion of market share, licensing revenues, and more intense competition. Furthermore, there are two conflicting trends for American Greetings' operating margins: gains should be made from increased productivity, but the increasing competitive nature of the industry with increased promotion might well erode such productivity increases.

Furthermore, according to industry expert, E. Gray Glass, III of Kidder, Peabody, & Company, there are some positives in the industry such as demographics and promising Christmas sales. However, major concerns exist, which include

- aggressive price competition, which was only modest in the past (markup for greeting cards is 100 percent between factory and retail outlet).
- high account turnover, as retailers look for most profitable lines and card companies fight intensely for large chain retail accounts. (American Greetings recently acquired the Sears account while Hallmark secured Penney's.)
- increased cost pressures, due to increasing advertising and distribution (racks, point of purchase, etc.) costs. (Hallmark will spend in excess of $40 million in television and magazine ads for Hallmark merchandise and benefits of sending cards. American Greetings will spend $33 million.)
- market share gains at the expense of other firms; these gains come at high cost to the winner.
- growth rate of past five years will not be matched over the next five years.
- new, viable, and growing competitors will emerge.
- investment decisions will have to be made more carefully.
- speculation exists that Hallmark may be formulating some counterattack strategies.

Merrill Lynch recently reduced American Greetings' earnings estimates for fiscal 1987 and 1988 because of many factors: the above conditions, the difficulties in production of the Christmas line and its shipment to retailers, and higher-than-expected new business expenses. Needless to say, the Executive Committee of American Greetings is concerned about the future growth potential and is in the process of formulating long-term objectives and strategies.

CASE 24

Kmart

DONNA BUSH · JOE THOMAS

S.S. Kresge "five- and ten-cent stores" were founded by S.S. Kresge in 1897. On April 15, 1912, the Company became S.S. Kresge Company of Delaware. In Michigan, 1966, the Company incorporated as S.S. Kresge Company. The "Kmart" name was adopted on May 17, 1977. Kmart is the country's second largest retailer, operating a portfolio of retailing businesses. Headquartered in Troy, Michigan, the firm had sales of $22.4 billion and income from continuing retail operations of $756 million for its fiscal year ending in 1986.

On January 23, 1974, Kmart Corporation operated 2,400 retail stores; 2,215 were in the United States and 185 were in Canada. At the end of 1985, Kmart operated a total of 3,848 retail stores. Of these stores, 2,332 were general-merchandise stores consisting of Kmart discount department stores, Kresge variety and Jupiter limited-line discount stores. The remaining stores are part of the Specialty Retailing Group, consisting of Pay Less Drug Stores Northwest, Inc., Walden Book Company, Inc., Builders Square, Inc., Designer Depot, Bargain Harold's Discount Limited, Big Top, Furr's Cafeterias, Inc., and Bishop Buffets, Inc.

STORE IMAGE

Kmart began a move in 1983 to upgrade the image and profitability of Kmart. Through advertising, remodeling, and upgrading of merchandise, Kmart has attempted to increase the intrinsic quality of Kmart merchandise. Moving to what Kmart calls the "look of the '80s" entailed a fine tuning of merchandise. Designer label and brandname merchandise were added and the quality of private-label merchandise was enhanced. The intent is to offer shoppers an expanded market basket of merchandise, which will also expand Kmart's profit margin.

To promote the upgraded image, Kmart raised its advertising budget for 1984, the first full year of the program, to $480 million. This increase represented an 18% increase over 1983's advertising budget and about 3% of 1984 sales. Some Kmart divisions spent a larger percentage of sales on advertising. For example, Glen Shanks, Director of Designer Depot, Kmart's

This case was prepared by Donna Bush, Graduate Assistant, and Professor Joe Thomas of University of Central Arkansas. This case was presented at the 1986 Workshop of the Midwest Society for Case Research. It also appears in *Annual Advances in Business Cases: 1986*, pp. 235–246, edited by Philip C. Fisher. Reprinted by permission.

thirty-store, off-price apparel chain, stated that Designer Depot spent 6% of sales on advertising. Other divisions such as Garment Rack and Kmart Auto Parts Center spent at similar levels.

Capital expenditures were not neglected either. In 1984 Kmart spent $430 million on capital improvements and $130 million to remodel Kmart stores.

Kmart's store of the future will reflect a shift to designer labels, brand-name merchandise, and upscale private labels. Over 900 Kmart stores will be affected by this upward shift. The ultimate prototype will be a combination of 8,500-square-feet or 40,000-square-feet stores. Fashion fixtures are in and bargain tables are out as departments, such as the Home Care Center, Kitchen Korner, Bed and Bath Shop, Nutrition and Health Care Center, and Home Electronics Center, take on a store-within-a-store status. Cherry-picked assortments are displayed with fashionable, department store techniques, so Kmart can compete with specialty and department stores.

In the remodeled units, multi-tiered glass cases house upscale giftware in the front of the stores. Apparel and electronic departments have been carpeted and mass-merchandise pipe fixtures have been replaced with waterfall and cube fixtures. Finger racks and freestanding walls provide a backdrop, highlighted by graphics in some cases, for Kmart's private-label merchandise. A neon stripe outlines the electronic department. A partial race track pattern with outlined aisles has been installed to improve the flow of traffic.

Kmart's goal is to increase sales—not to diversify revenues to any large extent. Managers are expected to assess consumer demand and then invest corporate resources so that market share improves in *each* of the several hundred merchandise categories sold. Kmart's strategy calls for improving productivity by achieving higher turnover and greater sales per square foot. The annual turnover rate for Kmart is presently 4.25 annually, but the corporate target in the five-year plan is 5.5.

The corporate thinking at Kmart relies heavily on good communications in a human chain that runs from store manager to district manager to regional manager. Although 80% of Kmart's merchandise is standardized on a national basis, store managers are free to fine-tune 10%–20% of the mix in an effort to appeal directly to local markets.

The Kmart customer is the person who works and lives near the store. Even though Kmart is upgrading, it still plans to remain within its customers' price range. For example, Kmart will sell cardigans in the $17 to $24 range. In the past Kmart would have sold the cardigans for $15 to $17. The objective behind upgrading is to expand the upper end of its market, not to abandon the lower end. Kmart officials feel that the people who bought in the middle will step up while lower-priced merchandise will still be available for the customer who buys in the lower price range.

In order to win customers over to the more ego-intensive items, Kmart advertising themes have changed from loss leaders in print advertising to higher ticketed groups of upscaled merchandise. In television advertising, for example, Kmart is moving away from advertisements for individual items and is promoting the Kmart name and a more positive store image. Kmart bought a $10 million television campaign tied to the 1984 Olympic Games.

Bernard Fauber, Kmart's Chairman, has called for 5%–6% annual sales increases over the next four years, with sales per square foot reaching $200 by 1988, even though the chain is no longer in the expansion mode. Kmart built only seventy-one new stores in 1983, compared to a five-year average of 178 units per year. Sales per square foot have already topped $200 in the specialty departments such as the Kitchen Korner, the Home Care Center, home electronics, cameras, and jewelry. These departments have undergone expensive remodeling and remerchandising. Larry Paukin, Chairman and CEO of Kmart Apparel, claims that the remodeling and remerchandising have raised sales in his department by 40%.

Kmart is facing increased competition as more and more retailers, like Wal-Mart, are moving into its territories. Some financial experts feel that low-cost retailers such as Wal-Mart are better able to weather cyclical dips in consumer demand. Industry research done by the University of Oklahoma showed before-tax profits per square foot of selling area at other discounters to be considerably higher than those earned by Kmart. For example, Target earned $12.09 versus $10.99 at Wal-Mart and $6.90 at Kmart.

Kmart has also expanded its in-store home-improvement product offerings and reorganized them into mini-home-center modules. Kmart was guided by customer surveys and market research. The research found that people are getting more involved in do-it-yourself activities and that they want to go to one place to purchase all the products needed to complete the project. In particular, Kmart brought together hardware, plumbing and other products that previously might have been located in different departments. Inventories of building materials—roofing, insulation, and dimensional lumber, for example—were expanded, and, in many cases, relocated from storage areas. In combination, these moves essentially turned the home-improvement modules into 8,000- to 12,000-square-foot mini-home-centers within the Kmart store.

Sears officials say that they probably will not parallel the moves made at Kmart, because Sears is limited in how extensively it can tie in with do-it-yourself consumer trends. However, Sears has done some rearranging and remerchandising in this area. In contrast, J.C. Penney Company has backed away from the home improvement market. J.C. Penney has eliminated those product lines in order to provide additional space for more fashionable lines of merchandise, which its research showed is what customers would expect to find in department stores in regional shopping malls. This is where most J.C. Penney stores are located.

HOME CENTERS OF AMERICA

In August, 1984, Kmart paid $90 million for Home Centers of America, a nine-store Texas chain of home improvement stores based in San Antonio. These stores, located mostly in Texas and Illinois, operate under the name of Builders Square. Kmart hopes this acquisition will enable it to become a dominant factor in the home-improvement market by the end of 1986. Kmart also hopes to increase overall corporate sales by 5% through its Builders Square acquisition.

Kmart Chairman Bernard Fauber reorganized top management by grouping Builders Square into a separate specialty operating division. The 80,000- to 100,000-square-foot "retail warehouse home-improvement stores" will cater to a different market than do Kmart's in-house home centers. The Kmart in-house centers cater to the one-day or weekender projects, whereas Builders Square stores will feature products for more extensive, more elaborate projects. Builders Square stores will provide expertise and special guidance for customers. Kmart intends to initiate special training programs to teach its employees to provide this kind of service.

In October, 1984, Kmart opened in Chicago its first three Builders Square stores outside of Texas. It also turned a redundant Kmart store in Tulsa into a Builders Square. Kmart eventually plans to convert 10% of all existing Kmart stores into Builders Square stores. Detroit and Cleveland are next on Kmart's list for new sites. Kmart had thirty Builders Square warehouses open by the end of 1985 and planned to open fifty new units in 1986. Plans are to eventually operate a minimum of 125 Builders Square stores.

The Builders Square outlets in Chicago are 80,000–100,000 square feet— typically two to three times larger than local competitors. Each store carries around 35,000 items in stock worth $2.5 million. These items range from sink elbows to snow cats, and from $2'' \times 4''$ lumber to T-squares. Having a high level of specialist staffing means that those stocks will have to be turned over eight times per year for the stores to break even. The average building-materials business in the U.S. turns its stock four times per year.

To move stock quickly, Kmart sells around 10% of its stock at near cost. Because Kmart purchases in large quantities, it can keep those costs low. Competitors already moan that Builders Square can sell dry-wall panels, for example, at a lower price than they can buy it. The rest of Builders Square stock is sold at above-average markups for the industry. Builders Square stores have caused a price war in Chicago. For example, Gee Lumber, Courtesy, Handy Andy, Forest City and other regional chains are cutting prices and plugging lines of housewares and motor accessories that Builders Square stores do not carry. However, a serious problem confronts Kmart in that the Builders Square warehouse needs a market area of 70,000 households. While Kmart managers state that there is the potential for 400 stores the size of Builders Square, industry authorities argue that only seventy-two cities in the U.S. are large enough to provide the needed market size.

The home-improvement industry is growing so rapidly (19% per year in unit sales since 1974) that major companies such as Payless Cashways and the Atlanta-based regional chain Home Depot (the leader) are buying smaller, weaker companies like the Texas-based Bowater chain, which sold out to Home Depot in December, 1984. Home Depot's Chairman, Bernard Marcus, plans to tackle Kmart headon by opening four stores in Houston and four to six in Detroit. Detroit is close to Kmart headquarters in nearby Troy.

OTHER SUBSIDIARIES AND ACQUISITIONS	Kmart's largest diversification to date has been the $509 million acquisition of Pay Less Drug Stores in 1985. At the end of 1985, Pay Less operated 183 stores in Oregon, Washington, California, Idaho, and Nevada, and 41 additional units were scheduled for opening in 1986. Kmart management sees drug stores as replacements for the variety stores, for many frequently made, small purchases. Stores of 25,000 square feet or more are required to provide the variety needed to meet such customer needs. With stores ranging in size from 25,000 to 80,000 square feet, Pay Less is one of the leaders in the large variety-drug store format.

In 1984, Kmart paid $294 million for Waldenbooks. This purchase price was twenty-four times the company's fiscal 1983 earnings. Waldenbooks is the nation's largest bookstore chain and had sales of $417.8 million in the year ended January 28, 1984. Waldenbooks stores maintain a wide variety of titles and can quickly obtain, through their Quicktrac special order system, any title not carried in stock. Waldenbooks has also developed marketing niches through book clubs emphasizing mystery, romance, science fiction, and children's books. Besides books, video and audio tapes and computer software are also sold through Waldenbooks. Though all Kmart stores also sell books, Kmart has no plans to integrate Waldenbooks and its own bookselling operations. Kmart plans to appoint someone to act as a liaison between the two companies.

It should be noted that Kmart's only internally developed subsidiary is Designer Depot. Initially, Designer Depots were directed to the higher end of the price spectrum. Designer Depot has now moved back to more mid-range-priced merchandise, contributing to what Kmart managers feel is an "increased consumer perception of value." Designer Depot's refusal to sell seconds and irregulars also gives them a distinct, but unprofitable niche within the off-price apparel field. After several years in the developmental phase, Kmart feels that this subsidiary is now positioned to begin contributing to corporate profits.

Kmart expects its new specialized retailing group (consisting of Pay Less Drug Stores, Waldenbooks, Home Centers of America, Furr's and Bishop's cafeteria chains, Bargain Harold's, Big Top, Designer Depot, Garment Rack and Accent) to ring up more than a fifth of total company sales by 1987 or 1988. This group does not include financial and insurance services or Kmart Trading Services.

Kmart's strategy is to buy or develop hot new retailing concepts and expand them rapidly for market dominance. Frederick Stevens, Executive

Vice-President of Specialized Retailing, states that by providing quality and value to the customer, Kmart is looking for domination of the retail market. Kmart is still seeking more emerging specialty retailing companies. Kmart will not rule out any type of company, except for grocery stores and drugstores, as a possible acquisition target.

Managers of newly acquired companies are usually retained, with only a single parent-company executive placed as a liaison. The managers even select their own ad agencies.

Exhibit 24.1 shows the expansion of Kmart's operations in the U.S. and Canada for 1984 and 1985. Waldenbooks, with 955 outlets in 1985, will be expanded at the rate of seventy to eighty stores annually for the next five years. Home Centers of America (Builders Square) nearly doubled its size to fifteen stores in 1984 and did double that number of stores to a total of thirty stores in 1985. Designer Depot added twenty-one outlets in 1985 although it continues to lose money. The cafeteria operations will add a net of six restaurants in 1985 to Bishop's current 31 and Furr's 124 restaurants. Kmart has also dabbled in two experimental pizza-video parlors, but closed them after eighteen months.

Kmart's turn to diversification for growth comes as its top competitor, Sears, is reemphasizing general merchandising and cutting back its fledgling

EXHIBIT 24.1   Kmart's Expansion Activities, by Number of Stores

	1983	1984			1985		
		Acquired	Opened	Closed	Acquired	Opened	Closed
Kmart							
U.S.	2041		21	7		18	11
Canada	119		2	3			
Kresge/Jupiter							
U.S.	144			24			24
Canada	58						2
Waldenbooks		860	41	3		68	11
Builders Square		9	6			15	
Pay Less					171	12	
Designer Depot	30		22			21	
Bargain Harold's					56	17	
Big Top	8		42	1		11	5
Other	147	—	29	7	—	2	10
Total	2547	869	163	45	227	164	63

overseas trading operations. Wal-Mart, another leading discounter, is moving to "deep" discounting and has achieved much of its growth serving small markets that Kmart has abandoned as too small.

INTERNATIONAL OPERATIONS

Kmart has operated in a number of international markets, including Mexico, Canada, Europe, and the Far East. Because of a variety of cultural, business, and economic conditions, not all of these operations have been successful. In September, 1981, Kmart acquired a 44% interest in a joint venture with the Gentor Group of Monterrey, Mexico, to operate a retail subsidiary in Mexico. Losses for the operation exceeded $31 million through 1985. A formal plan was announced in January, 1986, to discontinue these operations because of "prevailing business and economic conditions in Mexico (that) combined with the reduced value of the Mexican peso, adversely affected the joint venture's earnings and cash flow potential." Also, the company's wholly owned insurance subsidiary was discontinued. These decisions resulted in an after-tax charge against 1985 corporate earnings of $250.0 million and resulted in $1.90 charge against earnings per share.

Kmart operates its overseas markets differently than it does its marketing activities in the U.S. For instance, Kmart has no stores located overseas. Kmart brand merchandise is sold primarily through other retailers.

Overseas operations are handled through Kmart Trading Services (KTS), which was formed in 1982 to promote sales of U.S. goods in overseas markets. KTS is separate from and in balance with Kmart's large import operations. One of KTS's biggest successes has been increasing the trade between the Far East and Europe. KTS also is importing foreign goods to the U.S., especially components and materials for Kmart's U.S. vendors. In general, Kmart labels merchandise from the U.S. and elsewhere with a Kmart brand name. Kmart has a $300,000 ad campaign in Taiwan as a test aimed at developing consumers' awareness of Kmart brand goods. KTS was formed after 1981 legislation was passed to encourage exports. KTS resembles Sears' World Trade service, which was also formed in 1982.

FINANCIAL SERVICES

Kmart is letting Sears, Roebuck and Company, and other retailers take the lead in offering financial services, and plans to overtake them later. This is consistent with Kmart's diversification strategy of looking for retailing trends that can be rolled out quickly. Jon Hartman, corporate financial management analyst, states that this strategy is much like a runner holding back until the end of the race before sprinting past front-running opponents.

Looking for successful formulas that can be adopted quickly, Kmart will test several in-store financial service programs. Kmart is considering full-service branch banking, real estate services, consumer lending, and discount brokerage services. Kmart intends to test different ideas in different regions of the country. For example, the company plans to sell an insurance program in 100 Florida and Texas stores. Kmart feels that success in retailing depends on the company's knowing the makeup of local markets.

Advertising for the pilot programs will be handled through the agencies of the financial companies with which Kmart joins forces. However, Kmart's marketing and advertising departments will oversee ad strategy of all pilot programs, to ensure compatibility.

Kmart intends to lease floor space to the financial services marketers, for a combination of a flat fee and a percentage of sales volume. (A similar arrangement has been made for the leasing of Kmart footwear departments to Meldisco, a subsidiary of Melville Corporation.) Kmart feels that sales from its financial services must be at least $200 a square foot by the end of calendar 1986 to justify the floor space devoted to the new venture. Leasing departments is unlike Sears' full integration of its Financial Network.

MANAGEMENT (PERSONNEL)

Most of the candidates in Kmart's manager-training program are college recruits. Kmart has an annual training budget of $20 million. The management trainees' salaries start at $15,500. These trainees eventually make up 70% of the chain's store managers—the remainder advance from the stores. Of the 2,047 store managers employed by Kmart, 121 are female. There are no female district or regional managers. Average store managers make about $46,000 a year; however, some make over $100,000 while the low end of the scale is $32,000.

Robert A. Dewar, Chairman of the Finance and Executive committees, says Kmart has found it difficult to bring M.B.A.s into a structured store-operations program. Therefore, Kmart prefers to provide the opportunity for M.B.A. training, often at night, to those who have already joined the company. When M.B.A.s are brought into the organization, they are placed in staff functions, not in line jobs. Mr. Dewar also says that Kmart hires people regardless of their college education—or lack of it. According to Mr. Dewar, "Kmart rewards initiative, imagination, and hard work."

Kmart believes strongly in promoting from within. Kmart management believes that this builds loyalty. The majority of Kmart's senior executives in merchandising and operations advanced through the store's training programs. Kmart wants the people who work for it to know that if they perform, they will be given the opportunity to grow with the company.

In the last five years, Kmart has added 4,000 people to the payroll. Five years ago the mix of full-time to part-time employees at the store level was 80% to 20%, respectively. The mix has changed to a 55/45% mix. Increasing the portion of part-time employees reduces the cost of benefits for the company and accounts for the corporate goal of 40% full-time and 60% part-time employees. Kmart also limits other benefits employees receive.

Kmart store employees do not receive a discount. For the most part Kmart is nonunion, with the exception of some of its warehousing and distribution operations. Payroll represents 15.5% of sales.

FINANCIAL

Selected financial information concerning the recent performance of Kmart for fiscal 1984, 1985, and 1986 is provided in Exhibits 24.2 and 24.3.

EXHIBIT 24.2 **K-mart: Consolidated Statements of Income**
(In Millions of Dollars Except Per Share Data)

	FISCAL YEAR ENDED		
	January 29, 1986	January 30, 1985	January 25, 1984
Sales	$22,420	$21,096	$18,598
Licensee fees and rental income	225	207	191
Equity in income of affiliated retail companies	76	65	57
Interest income	24	40	38
	22,745	21,408	18,884
Cost of merchandise sold (including buying and occupancy costs)	16,181	15,260	13,447
Selling, general and administrative expenses	4,845	4,428	3,880
Advertising	567	554	425
Interest expense:			
Debt	205	147	84
Capital lease obligations	191	193	189
	21,989	20,582	18,025
Income from continuing retail operations before income taxes	756	826	859
Income taxes	285	327	366
Income from continuing retail operations	471	499	493
Discontinued operations	(250)	—	(1)
Net income for the year	$ 221	$ 499	$ 492
Earnings per common and common equivalent share:			
Continuing retail operations	$3.63	$3.84	$3.81
Discontinued operations	(1.90)	—	(.01)
Net income	$1.73	$3.84	$3.80

EXHIBIT 24.3

Kmart: Consolidated Balance Sheets

(In Millions of Dollars Except Per Share Data)

	FISCAL YEAR ENDED	
	January 29, 1986	January 30, 1985
Assets		
Current assets:		
Cash (includes temporary investments of $352 and $294, respectively)	$ 627	$ 492
Merchandise inventories	4,537	4,588
Accounts receivable and other current assets	363	231
Total current assets	5,527	5,311
Investments in affiliated retail companies	293	188
Property and equipment—net	3,644	3,339
Other assets and deferred charges	527	220
Investments in discontinued operations	—	204
Total assets	$9,991	$9,262
Liabilities and Shareholders' Equity		
Current liabilities:		
Long-term debt due within one year	$ 15	$ 2
Capital lease obligations due within one year	76	74
Notes payable	127	235
Accounts payable—trade	1,908	1,917
Accrued payrolls and other liabilities	548	362
Taxes other than income taxes	218	200
Income taxes	198	99
Total current liabilities	3,090	2,889
Capital lease obligations	1,713	1,780
Long-term debt	1,456	1,107
Other long-term liabilities	345	163
Deferred income taxes	114	89
Shareholders' equity	3,273	3,234
Total liabilities and shareholders' equity	$9,991	$9,262

SECTION D

STRATEGIC ISSUES IN ENTREPRENEURIAL AND SMALL BUSINESSES

CASE 25

Dakotah, Inc.

DIANE HOADLEY · PHIL FISHER

In May of 1987, Dakotah, Inc. appeared to be on the brink of a new era of growth and profitability. The South Dakota-based manufacturer of bedcoverings and associated textile home furnishings had enjoyed record sales of over $13 million in 1986 and record after-tax profits of nearly $400,000. Its products, marketed from a posh showroom in New York City, were widely recognized by department-store buyers and consumers alike as the top of the line in textile home furnishings.

Dakotah was an employee-owned company headquartered in the small (population 2,400) town of Webster, South Dakota. It had seven plants, located in small towns in three counties in the northeastern corner of South Dakota with a combined population of 24,448.

HISTORY OF DAKOTAH, INC.

In 1970, George Whyte was 21, an age when many of his peers were thinking about finishing college and finding a job, but Whyte was worried about pigs. As a VISTA (Volunteers in Service to America) volunteer, Whyte had encouraged the farm families of rural northeastern South Dakota to partic-

---

This case was prepared by Professor Diane Hoadley and Professor Phil Fisher at the University of South Dakota. It was presented at the 1987 Workshop of the Midwest Society for Case Research. Reprinted by permission.

ipate in an economic development program called, "Pigs for Pork." The federal government gave farmers bred sows to raise and eventually sell at market. When the price of pork plummeted, the program failed. Raising the pigs cost more than their market value. The program had done nothing to improve the distressed economic condition of farmers in this depressed region.

Undaunted, Whyte hit upon another idea. He had noticed the farm wives making beautiful handcrafted quilts. His grandmother had made quilts and he knew something of their value. He turned his attention to the talent and skill of the women of the families who were participating in the "Pigs for Pork" program, and realized that this might be the opportunity he was looking for. Whyte convinced the wives and daughters of these farmers that they could successfully produce and sell their handcrafted items. Whyte and Bob Pierce, who headed the Northeast South Dakota Community Action Program, collected hand-sewn quilts, afghans, pillows, shawls, and a variety of other items from the women in a three-county region of northeastern South Dakota. Armed with these samples Whyte and Pierce flew to the East coast in an attempt to market the products to department-store buyers.

They failed miserably. They flew first to Washington, D.C., engaged a hotel suite, got out the telephone book and contacted the department stores listed in the Yellow Pages. "Oh God, it was awful!" exclaimed Whyte recounting the events. No one even came to look at the products. Whyte and Pierce then flew to New York City and repeated the process, with the same discouraging results. They knew that the circumstances required more aggressive tactics, so they put their samples in a trunk and marched unannounced into the office of the quilt buyer for one of New York's leading department stores. They were promptly removed by the store's security guards.

On their way back to South Dakota, discouraged but still hopeful, they stopped at Dayton's, a department-store chain based in Minneapolis. There they saw the assistant buyer for the drapery and bedspread department. He, too, was not interested in the handicraft products being shown, but he put Whyte in contact with a leading, independent manufacturers' representative in New York City, Park B. Smith.

Smith flew to South Dakota in September of 1971, liked what he saw, made some suggestions for design changes, and negotiated a contract with Whyte to produce a line of samples to show in the November home-furnishings market in New York. Twice a year, in November and May, buyers gather on Fifth Avenue in New York City and preview new home-furnishing merchandise and to place orders for the products that will appear in their stores.

The South Dakota farm women had from Labor Day to November 5 to style and produce their first product line. The women focused on quilts and pillow shams and succeeded in having a line of samples ready for the market. This time the products received a better reception from the department store buyers. *Home Furnishings Daily*, the home furnishings industry trade journal, ran a front page article stating that "Dakotah has the freshest design ideas in the last 100 years in bed covers." Over $50,000 in orders were placed at that first show.

Back in South Dakota, a $54,000 Small Business Administration loan provided the capital to purchase sewing machines and fabric enough to fill the orders, but working capital was still inadequate. The Webster, South Dakota, Junior Chamber of Commerce raised $1,600 to buy fuel oil; the local Isaac Walton League donated the use of their building; and Whyte and the women worked for six months without pay until they delivered their first shipments of products to the buyers. They organized as the Tract Handicraft Industries Cooperative and the firm was off and sewing.

In 1986 this employees cooperative, reorganized as an employee-owned corporation in 1976, had sales of almost $14 million, employed over 400 employees, and was considered to be the Mercedes-Benz of the bed-covering industry.

MARKETING

Dakotah manufactured and wholesaled textile home-furnishings products in four major categories: bed coverings (bedspreads, comforters, etc.), which accounted for 50% of sales; pillows (including decorator pillows), which made up 40% of sales; window treatments (curtains, draperies, etc.), which were 5% of sales; and miscellaneous items (shower curtains, napkins, placemats, wall hangings, etc.), which accounted for the remaining 5% of sales. Approximately 50% of these items were sold in department stores, 40% to mass and catalog merchants (Spiegels was the largest single customer), 5% to bed and bath specialty stores, and 5% to the hotel and motel industry. Dakotah also operated its own factory outlet store in Webster. Dakotah products were distributed in all fifty states and the company had a small amount of export sales.

Dakotah was a very small producer in a large industry. Manufacturers' sales in the textile home-furnishings industry were estimated at $3.9 billion in 1985; of this amount, sales of bedspreads and bed sets were $375.7 million. (This total did not include sheets and pillowcases, for which sales were estimated at $813.5 million.) The largest competitor was Spring Mills, with total sales of $1,505 million, 64% of which were in textile home furnishings. Another major competitor was Fieldcrest Cannon with sales of $1,083 million. The industry was becoming increasingly concentrated in the face of pressure from foreign competitors. Major developments had been the acquisition of Burlington Industry's sheet and towel division by J. P. Stevens, Fieldcrest's purchase of Cannon, and West Point Pepperell's purchase of Cluett Peabody. Firms chose acquisitions as a means of expanding their product lines and avoiding the risk and cost of establishing new brand names. Well established brand names were considered important in succeeding against imports. Another industry response to foreign competition was the increased use of automated production techniques. All large producers used a relatively high degree of automation to produce both fabrics and finished goods. In spite of these developments, the textile industry averaged net profits of only .32% of sales in 1986.

In the face of such competitive pressures, Dakotah had succeeded in establishing strong brand identification. George Whyte explained how this was done: "Dakotah sells a lot of sizzle. Once you create the image, the product sells itself. So we have invested a great deal of time and money in creating an image." Dakotah's major thrust to create an image began in 1976, when the newly incorporated company contracted with a consulting firm that specialized in the development of corporate identities. The consulting firm's first recommendation was to change the name of the products from Dakotah Handcrafts by Tract, and the name of the organization from Tract Handcraft Industries Cooperative, Inc. to just Dakotah. The company and its products are now identified by the name Dakotah, written in distinctive script.

The next step in creating the Dakotah image was to develop a magnificent company showroom in the midst of the home-furnishing market in New York City. Much time and money were spent in finding the right location and creating a suitable ambience. Finally a space became available on the ground floor of the textile market building, located on Fifth Avenue between 30th and 31st Streets. The building houses offices for several textile and home furnishing manufacturers. Whyte created a spacious and dramatic office that rivals the office of any chief executive officer for a Fortune 500 company.

The New York showroom and offices were owned by a Dakotah subsidiary, Dakotah USA. Employees as well were technically employees of the subsidiary. Sales were under the management of Neil Zuber, Vice-President of Sales. Zuber ran the New York showroom and coordinated the selling activities of eleven independent sales representatives, each assigned an exclusive geographical area. John Panarello, the Vice-President of National Accounts, sold to the large department stores and catalog merchants.

Great care was taken so that the Dakotah name written in its characteristic script was the only trademark to appear before the public. Whyte also insisted that the Dakotah name accompany catalog layouts of the products, a practice reserved for a few select designers such as Bill Blass and Ralph Lauren.

Whyte believed that Dakotah's principal strength was its ability to create high-fashion, uniquely designed items. Dakotah focused on designs that created an upscale, contemporary look. The first designs came from Whyte and other staff members. By 1982, Whyte recognized the need to hire a professional designer and asked one of Park Smith's former employees, Belinda Ballash, to join the Dakotah company. Working out of her office in Pacific Palisades, California, Ballash supplied Dakotah with designs reflecting the most up-to-date trends from the West coast. In May of 1987,

Whyte hired another designer housed on the East coast to provide designs reflecting East coast trends. The designers were employees of Dakotah USA. Although Dakotah products were styled to reflect the current fashion taste, which, in 1987, was returning to a "country" look, Whyte believed that Dakotah's emphasis would remain on products with contemporary styling. Whyte's attention to creating a unique look for the Dakotah products had been successful. Dakotah had always had difficulty filling its orders; it sometimes runs months behind orders and, at other times, does not allow its sales representatives to take new orders for periods of up to two months. In 1987, Whyte negotiated a licensing agreement with The Spring Mills Company, the leading manufacturer of sheets and pillow cases, for use of Dakotah designs for a new line that would feature the Dakotah name. Whyte believed that similar licensing agreements would be negotiated with manufacturers of other home-furnishing products.

In 1986, Whyte decided to move Dakotah into the hospitality market. The company had sold furnishings to hotels and motels on a limited scale furnishing suites for the Hyatt corporation. Whyte was convinced that more appealing interior furnishings would improve occupancy rates. His first major deal was with the Super 8 Motel company. The Super 8 company, headquartered in Aberdeen, South Dakota, fifty miles from Webster, was a motel franchise chain with over 400 budget motels in the United States and Canada. After testing guest responses to some of the products, Super 8 agreed to purchase bedspreads, wall hangings, and pillow ensembles. Dakotah became the exclusive supplier of bedcoverings to the corporate-owned motels, and a recommended supplier for the franchises.

With this success, Whyte planned to pursue the hospitality industry vigorously. In 1987, these sales were being handled by a two-person telemarketing effort located at the Webster headquarters. Initial results had been very encouraging. Company plans were for hospitality sales to be 15% of sales by 1988, 30% in 1989, 40% in 1990, and 50% of sales by 1991.

MANUFAC-TURING

Dakotah bedcoverings were unique in that they were made with a technique called appliqué. In appliqué, decorations are created by the application of cut pieces of one material onto the surface of another. Manufacturing processes at Dakotah were a mixture of skilled hand work and highly automated processes. The decorative pieces of fabric were bound to the surface of the background material with adhesive, then outlined with zigzag stitching, which was done manually by guiding the fabric through a sewing machine. This process was labor-intensive and required considerable skill. Other manufacturing processes, such as the decorative stitching at the edges of the bedcoverings, were performed by computer controlled machines.

Dakotah operated seven plants in six small towns, all in northeastern South Dakota. Two plants were located in Webster, S.D. Webster 1 employed forty-five people, who were engaged in the initial measurement and cutting of all fabric used in the other plants. Webster 1 also produced the batting or fiber fill used to give bulk to the bedspreads. Batting production was highly automated. It was made from bales of purchased fibers that were fed into hoppers. These fibers were then woven into rolls of batting 40 yards long, in one continuous automated process that could be adjusted to vary the width and thickness of the batting.

Dakotah had recently acquired a computer controlled, laser fabric cutter that would be used to cut the pieces of cloth used in the appliqué. Patterns would be fed into the computer, which would lay out the pieces on the fabric so as to minimize waste. Additional benefits from the laser cutter would be reduced labor, and increased capacity; the laser cutting would also bind the edges and eliminate the ravelling that sometimes occurred with the current method, which employed a hand guided, power driven, circular blade.

Webster 2 was located a block away from Webster 1 and included the company's administrative offices. This plant did the finishing and shipping for all products except pillows. In the final step of the manufacturing process, the decorated top of the bedspread and the underside fabric were placed on large frames with the batting in between. Large, computer-controlled quilting machines sewed the three layers together. These machines also could be programmed to sew decorative designs on the bedspreads. Some bedspreads without appliqué were decorated entirely by the quilting machines. Appliquéd coverings were then outlined and embellished with stitching, a process in which the coverings were again manually guided through a sewing machine. The operators in this operation were the most highly skilled in the plant. The process required not only manual dexterity, but also keen memory, as the operators sewed the designs from memory. Webster 2 employed 80 people in manufacturing.

Other Dakotah plants were located in Veblen, S.D. (population 322), where 93 people produced and shipped pillows; Wilmot, S.D. (population 492), where shams, or decorative pillow coverings, were produced and 43 people were employed; Eden, S.D. (population 126), where draperies and bedskirts were made, and 36 people were employed; Pierpont, S.D. (population 165), where appliqués were bound to the coverings and 30 people were employed; and Sisseton, S.D. (population 2,717), where hanging samples used as point of purchase displays were made. Thirteen people were employed here. Several of these plants had the versatility to perform the skilled hand-stitching operations used in making bedspreads and other products. Approximately 90% of the employees in manufacturing were women.

Company executives believed that Dakotah had an important competitive edge in manufacturing skills. While design changes were important in retaining the distinctive look of the Dakotah products, protection from copying came largely from the fact that the appliquéd designs were difficult to manufacture and Dakotah had more expertise in the appliqué processes than any one else. Only one competitor made appliquéd products. It was also a difficult process to automate or mechanize. As one manager put it, "We have an edge in marketing and design. Survival depends on success in manufacturing."

Manufacturing operations were under the management of Ed Johnson. As a teenager Johnson had been employed by the Northeast South Dakota Community Action Program and one of his jobs had been to help the newly formed Tract Handcraft Industries Cooperative move from its first quarters to a larger building. At that time, Bob Pierce recommended him for a permanent job with the cooperative. Johnson started as a delivery boy and had grown with manufacturing operations, as the company converted from exclusively handcrafted to automated processes.

Johnson, 32, was youthful appearing, soft spoken, and articulate. Other company executives gave him credit for solving production problems that had given the company a reputation for not being able to meet promised delivery dates. Previously the company had employed manufacturing managers with experience in textile manufacturing. While they had provided the needed technical expertise, Whyte's judgement was that they had lacked the right approach to managing people. "They came from a different school of thought. Theirs was the whip and chain approach." Despite the fact that Dakotah was an employee-owned company, there had been a serious attempt to unionize the company in 1984.

Johnson's technical experience had come from his working at many jobs within Dakotah manufacturing, taking home study courses, attending seminars, but "mostly trial and error learning." He saw his major tasks as maintaining efficiency and meeting delivery commitments.

Improvements in efficiency were sought through continued automation and careful upgrading of equipment. Once the potential use of the laser fabric cutter had been identified, for example, the company had spent a year in evaluating it before making the purchase. Some of the company's equipment was over ten years old and Johnson believed that improved equipment was important in enabling the company to meet the demand for its products. One company executive estimated that, in 1986, the company had turned away from two to four million in sales and company sales representatives were quoting delivery dates of six months. He said, "People can build a house faster than they can get the bedspreads." Continued automation was constrained by capital requirements. For example, the laser cutter had cost $300,000. Dakotah had invested over $3 million in plant and equipment during the five years prior to 1987 and planned to invest well over $1 million in 1987.

PERSONNEL	The Personnel and Human Resource Manager for Dakotah, Inc. was Jim Nixon. He was responsible for employee recruitment, selection, orientation, and training. Nixon also was responsible for drafting personnel policies and procedures and for administering the compensation and benefit plans.

Nixon described recruitment as an ongoing source of concern. "The company is under a lot of pressure to fill openings," he explained. "We usually have more job openings than applicants. Sometimes I think we hire every warm body that applies for a job." In fact, Dakotah hired approximately 70% of all applicants for work. Dakotah's labor force was recruited from the entire northeastern region of South Dakota and about forty miles into the southern edge of North Dakota.

Employees were trained by their supervisors. Nixon provided supervisory training either through in-house training or off-site seminars. He had the most success with the in-house training, as supervisors were reluctant to participate in off-site training.

Nixon joined Dakotah in July of 1984 shortly after the unsuccessful union attempt to organize employees at six Dakotah plants. Complaints of favoritism and arbitrary actions were among the reasons that prompted the attempt to bring in a union. Nixon believed that the union drive failed because the workers were reluctant to bring in an outside organization to represent their interests. Nixon's first priority when starting his job was to spend time in the plants, listen to the problems of workers, and institute corrective actions as quickly as possible.

Among changes brought into being were formalization of performance appraisals, a policy of posting job openings in the plants, and advertising of openings in the local media. Nixon was also responsible for testing applicants for color perception, manual dexterity, or other skills required for the job. Applicants for manufacturing positions were interviewed by Nixon, the plant supervisor, and Ed Johnson; the plant supervisor made the final decision.

The manufacturing employee turnover for 1984 was 64%, compared to an industry average of approximately 10%. The 1985 rate was 38%, and the 1986 rate was 26%. Nixon's goal was to reach the industry turnover rate by 1988. The drop in the turnover rate was attributed to two factors. One factor was improved hiring and supervisory practices. The other was that the company had reduced seasonal layoffs.

Manufacturing workers at Dakotah were paid an average of $4.51 per hour. A skilled worker, such as a fabric cutter or an appliqué stitcher, could make as much as $4.92. The base wage was 20% to 30% below the manufacturing wages paid in larger eastern South Dakota cities such as Watertown or Sioux Falls, but well above the $1.50 per hour labor costs of Korean and Taiwanese textile manufacturers. The clerical staff was paid at rates similar to those paid in Sioux Falls. Top managers at Dakotah were paid salaries substantially below industry averages.

A company document on corporate objectives set the following goals for "our people": to have wages equal to industry standards by 1988 and above industry standards by 1989, to have fringe benefits equal to industry standards by 1990 and above industry standards by 1991, to have employee turnover lower than industry averages by 1990, to have employee absenteeism lower than industry averages by 1990, and to have reportable injuries lower than industry averages by 1989. The same document called for the establishment of "associate teams" consisting of members from direct labor, office staff and management. Teams to be established in 1987 were a communication team, a compensation and benefits team, a quality team, and a training, education, and safety team.

EMPLOYEE OWNERSHIP	Employee ownership rights in Dakotah were exercised through ownership of two classes of stock. Class A stock had exclusive voting power, but no rights to dividends or to share in the distribution of assets. Ownership of Class A stock was limited to those who owned any amount of Class B stock, and no stockholder could own more than one share of Class A stock. This arrangement, in effect, provided that each stockholder had equal voting power regardless of the size of their investment in the company. At the end of 1986, 168 employees (of a total work force of 412) held shares of Class A stock.

Class B stock was non-voting but entitled the holder to participate in dividends and to hold one share of Class A voting stock. No individual employee could own more than 5% of the outstanding shares of Class B stock.

Employees participated in company ownership in two ways, an employee stock-purchase plan and an employee stock-bonus plan. The stock-purchase plan provided that any employee who completed 1,000 hours of service was granted an option to purchase up to 100 shares of Class B stock. After the first 1,000 hours of service an employee was entitled to purchase one share for each ten hours of service. This option to buy could be exercised immediately, usually through payroll deductions, or at any time during the year in which the options were earned or during the next calendar year. The purchase price for any year was the book value of the stock as of December 31 in the previous year. During 1986 employees purchased 6,501 shares of Class B stock for $35,430. In 1985 they had purchased 2,040 shares for $10,547. The current stock-purchase plan had been revised in 1985 to encourage greater employee purchases. Formerly employees had been required to purchase stock in blocks of 100 shares, for cash. This requirement made participation difficult. The company had nearly 300 shareholders in 1976; by 1985 the number had dwindled to 80. A total of 112 employees had begun their participation in company ownership since the revision.

The stock-bonus plan was for retirement benefits. It was first established in 1976, and amended in 1980 to conform to the provisions of the Employee Retirement Income Security Act. The Dakotah Board of Directors declared stock contributions to the plan in years when company profits were sufficient. Stock dividends were valued at "fair market value." For 1986, the directors had paid a dividend of 37,202 shares with an estimated value of $250,000. This represented approximately 9% of the aggregated salaries of those employees eligible to participate in the plan. Eligibility in the plan was limited to employees with at least 1,000 hours of service during their initial year. Employees with at least 500 hours in subsequent years participated in the plan, but vesting rights were earned only in years in which employees worked at least 1,000 hours.

When employees left employment at Dakotah, they were required to sell their stock acquired through the Employee Stock Purchase Plan. The selling price was book value. Other employees had first right of refusal and if no employee exercised their right of purchase, the company would repurchase the stock. Most stock was repurchased by the company. In 1986 the company repurchased 39,886 shares of stock from twenty-four employees. At the close of 1986 there were 346,032 shares of Class B stock outstanding.

FINANCE

The Chief Financial Officer at Dakotah was Richard Engel. Engel was a C.P.A. and had an M.B.A. from an eastern business school. Prior to joining Dakotah he had been employed in New York by Dakotah's public accounting firm and Dakotah was one of his accounts. In 1980, he told George Whyte that he planned to leave public accounting. When Whyte suggested that he join Dakotah, his first reaction was "Sure, if you move it to New York." Eventually he agreed to come for two years and by 1987 had been in Webster, South Dakota, for more than six years.

"The concept of this company is to make jobs," Engel said. "So we try to control the cost of the product through mechanization, experimentation, and heavy investment." Engel saw the employee ownership concept as being of mixed benefit. It gave employees a sense of commitment, but it severely limited its access to capital. Currently Dakotah had $1,250,000 in outstanding long-term notes. This included approximately $65,000 in a revolving, working capital loan financed at 1% above the prime rate, and the rest in the form of a six-year loan secured by machinery and equipment and at 1½% above the prime rate. At one time the company had paid 4½% over prime. (For financial statements see Exhibits 25.1 and 25.2.)

When asked about the company's improved performance in 1986, Engel attributed it to several factors. The recruitment of more experienced middle managers, significant investments in machinery and equipment, better cost controls, and the development of new markets such as the hotel and motel industry were all judged to have been significant. Some of these initiatives began as early as 1983 and the benefits began showing up at the bottom line in 1986.

Dakotah had formal five-year goals for profit and growth. These were a sales growth of 15%; a net pre-tax earning on sales of 4% in 1987, rising to 12% by 1991; and an average rate of return on stockholders' equity of 15%. "If we want to grow," Engel said, "we have to look to external equity. We can support 10% growth but 25% will require more. We have reached

EXHIBIT 25.1

Dakotah, Inc., Balance Sheets, 1980–1986

	1986	1985	1984	1983	1982	1981	1980
Assets							
Current assets							
Cash	$18,171	$16,372	$25,558	$3,207	$81,629	$81,447	$12,162
Accounts receivable less allowance for doubtful accounts	1,718,731	1,337,006	1,635,032	1,912,920	1,278,584	1,289,537	1,325,765
Merchandise inventory	1,994,279	2,352,272	2,405,746	3,103,208	1,769,199	1,448,964	1,207,482
Prepaid income tax		66,441	80,114	115,392	12,880	29,398	35,915
Other current assets	16,094	12,686	7,239	25,142	17,587	3,831	19,413
Total current assets	3,747,275	3,784,777	4,153,689	5,159,869	3,159,879	2,853,177	2,600,737
Property, plant and equipment—less accumulated depreciation	1,732,239	1,415,983	1,640,582	1,780,827	1,325,579	904,634	775,438
Other assets	9,270	9,190	11,010	11,830	22,770	19,420	19,420
Total assets	5,488,784	5,209,950	5,805,281	6,952,526	4,508,228	3,777,231	3,395,595
Liabilities and Stockholders' Equity							
Current liabilities							
Notes payable—bank	264,537	1,124,104	1,487,241	1,849,604	511,720	927,856	839,111
Capital lease obligations	20,886	19,140	17,718	16,336	14,868	21,700	21,700
Notes payable—other				31,153	49,593	92,654	101,385
Accounts payable	828,303	632,589	747,876	1,394,598	853,646	632,225	632,650
Income tax payable						16,607	8,891
Other current liabilities	408,935	286,303	199,188	277,395	174,971	86,174	122,278
Total current liabilities	1,522,661	2,062,136	2,452,023	3,569,086	1,604,798	1,777,216	1,726,015

(Continued)

EXHIBIT 25.1 (Continued)

	1986	1985	1984	1983	1982	1981	1980
Long-term debt							
Notes payable—bank	1,250,000	870,000	1,140,000	1,210,000	880,000	—	—
Capital lease obligations	391,088	412,154	430,821	448,337	465,364	475,398	496,347
Notes payable—other						70,541	89,930
Total long-term debt	1,641,088	1,282,154	1,570,821	1,658,337	1,345,364	545,939	586,277
Stockholders' equity							
Common stock	1,159,383	936,382	926,434	927,435	927,948	928,999	679,448
Contributed capital	13,207	13,207	13,207	13,207	13,207	13,207	13,207
Retained earnings	1,152,445	916,071	842,796	784,461	616,911	511,870	390,648
Total stockholders' equity	2,325,035	1,865,660	1,782,437	1,725,103	1,558,066	1,454,076	1,083,303
Total liabilities and stockholders' equity	5,488,784	5,209,950	5,805,281	6,952,526	4,508,228	3,777,231	3,395,595

EXHIBIT 25.2 Dakotah, Inc., Income Statements, 1980–1986

	1986	1985	1984	1983	1982	1981	1980
Sales	$14,085,870	$11,708,748	$13,729,250	$12,300,726	$9,124,241	$10,721,784	$9,628,706
Less returns and allowances	410,329	645,166	605,621	479,567	344,014	472,897	487,616
Net sales before discounts	13,675,341	11,063,582	13,123,629	11,821,159	8,780,227	10,248,887	9,141,090
Less discounts	0	2,659	7,928	7,908	8,647	14,473	17,912
Net sales	13,675,541	11,060,923	13,115,701	11,813,251	8,771,580	10,234,414	9,123,178
Cost of goods sold							
Merchandise inventory	2,352,272	2,405,746	3,103,208	1,769,199	1,448,964	1,207,482	1,251,553
Purchases	4,721,640	3,642,072	4,551,872	5,326,805	3,532,998	4,227,009	3,576,734
Freight in	141,341	123,026	164,711	238,175	207,934	191,943	195,760
Direct labor	2,350,930	2,206,586	2,478,520	2,769,484	1,591,026	1,820,766	1,615,935
Employee fringe benefits							98,877
Payroll taxes	228,861	197,406	213,148	330,376	140,935	155,466	119,257
Cost of goods available for sale	9,795,044	8,574,836	10,511,459	10,434,039	6,921,857	7,602,666	6,858,116
Less merchandise inventory—end of year	1,994,279	2,352,272	2,405,746	3,103,208	1,769,199	1,448,964	1,207,482
Cost of goods sold	7,800,765	6,222,564	8,105,713	7,330,831	5,152,658	6,153,702	5,650,634
Gross profit	5,874,776	4,838,359	5,009,988	4,482,420	3,618,922	4,080,712	3,472,544
Operating expenses							
Manufacturing	1,574,785	1,349,893	1,276,410	1,023,828	729,888	601,535	462,506
Selling	1,844,953	1,656,810	1,831,548	1,788,532	1,393,449	1,772,059	1,254,170
Shipping	371,997	323,299	379,414	336,820	340,730	275,127	312,128
Financial	254,921	326,000	480,412	308,677	218,372	216,027	311,236
General and administrative	1,148,188	1,060,443	937,439	920,559	758,941	722,736	617,110
Total operating expenses	5,194,844	4,716,445	4,905,223	4,378,416	3,441,380	3,587,484	2,957,150
Income from operations	679,932	121,914	104,765	104,004	177,542	493,228	515,394
Royalty income, net	—	—	—	—	—	—	4,330
Provision for income taxes	40,423	25,966	7,328	(83,951)	40,949	52,607	34,299
Contribution to employee stock bonus plan	250,000	—	—	—	—	250,000	371,213
Net income	$ 389,509	$ 95,948	$ 97,437	$ 187,955	$ 136,593	$ 190,621	$ 114,212

the limit of debt financing." Engel recognized that going outside the limits of employee ownership for equity capital was a departure from an important company policy. "One thing I have learned is that some things are sacred." Employee ownership was one of those things.

COMMUNITY IMPACT

Because the original purpose of Dakotah, Inc. had been to provide jobs for rural families, the casewriters, in making some determination of the impact it had made in Webster, interviewed community leaders. Webster's Mayor, Mike Grosek, a supermarket owner, described his assessment. "Over the last three or four years the agricultural economy has been deteriorating. We are all fighting to just survive. Dakotah is an important part of Webster now because it employs so many women from the rural area. It gives them a second income to support the groceries and clothing their families need while their husbands are struggling on the farm. In some cases, it is a primary source of income."

Other community leaders supported Grosek's views. They pointed out that employment at Dakotah had enabled people to remain in their home communities when otherwise they would have had to go elsewhere for employment. They believed that the retail businesses in Webster and other communities in which Dakotah plants were located had remained healthier than those in other farming communities in the region.

Some perspective on Dakotah's impact on improving the economic situation in northeastern South Dakota, can be gained by a reference to the following statistics for Day County. In 1970, the unemployment rate for Day County, the county in which Webster is located, was 2.8% compared to 3.9% for the state of South Dakota as a whole. The labor participation rate, that is, the percentage of individuals aged 16 and older who were part of the labor force, was 33.3%. Individuals not participating in the labor force would include students not employed, housewives, retirees, individuals who have given up looking for work, and people who do not need to work. In 1986, the unemployment rate for Day County was 5% compared to 4.6% for the state, and the labor force participation was 43.4%. In 1970, census figures showed that 859 women were employed in Day County. For 1986 the number was estimated to be 1218. Dakotah employed approximately 230 people in Day County. According to the U.S. Department of Commerce, Bureau of Economic Analysis, the multiplier factor for textile manufacturers in South Dakota was 1.42. The 1970 census indicated that the population of Day County was 8,713 people; the 1985 estimated census was 7,852 residents; this population decline was typical for rural South Dakota counties over this period.

DAKOTAH'S FUTURE

Dakotah had begun as a manufacturing company established to create jobs in northeastern South Dakota. Over the years the focus of the company had shifted from manufacturing to marketing. "It is our forte," explained Whyte. He believed that marketing opportunities through licensing and franchising could allow the company to grow to a $100 million company over the next ten years.

Licensing possibilities included such products as wall and floor coverings, a more extensive line of window treatments, as well as other textile products. A franchised chain of Dakotah stores would allow the company greater access to a larger number of consumers. Both of these alternatives would allow the company to increase its revenues with a relatively small capital investment.

Dakotah was beginning to consider other markets. In 1986, Dakotah quietly began selling pillows to Wal-Mart, a large discount chain. Sales were $1.5 million with $2.5 million expected in 1987. The possibilities for increased sales through discount outlets raised the possibility that overseas manufacturing of Dakotah designs might be considered.

Finally, the capital limitation of confining equity ownership to employees was recognized as an obstacle to growth. Perhaps employee ownership was no longer "sacred." However, it was a decision with far reaching consequences. "The intent is still to create jobs," Whyte said. "The concept of employee ownership has not changed yet."

Home Shopping Network (A), Initial Stock Offering

THOMAS L. WHEELEN · CHARLES E. MICHAELS, JR. · MELTON L. MARTIN, JR.
JANIECE L. GALLAGHER

On the floor of the American Stock Exchange on May 13, 1986, Mr. Roy Speer and Mr. Lowell W. Paxson, co-founders of Home Shopping Network (HSN), were awaiting the opening bell. Their company was making its first public stock offering of 2,000,000 shares. The initial price was $18 per share.

A NEW COMPANY AND NEW INDUSTRY

The Home Shopping Network concept began in late 1977, when co-founder and President Lowell "Bud" Paxson owned radio station WWQT/WHBS (FM) in Clearwater, Florida. He had owned radio stations in Newark, N.J., Waterbury, Conn., Sarasota, Fl., and Jamestown, N.Y., as well as a UHF television station in Jamestown. Having owned a record store, he had some retail experience and about thirty years' experience in the radio business. Now, under his guidance, WWQT/WHBS was suffering severe advertising revenue problems.

Bud accidentally found that he could make more money by selling merchandise over the air than he could by selling traditional advertising time. One of the station's clients had been unable to pay for his advertising and paid the station with name-brand electric can openers. Bud Paxson sold these can openers over the airwaves to listeners, who then came by the station and picked up their purchases.

Sometime later, after an unsuccessful day of sales calls, Paxson came back to the station convinced there was a better way to generate revenue. As he said, "I knew the value of radio advertising and its ability to motivate people." Within a week he was selling to his radio listeners merchandise that he had obtained from distressed or overstocked merchants. Paxson himself got behind the studio mike to hawk electronics, gifts, and housewares at prices far below retail.

The program was such a success that he created a full program day, from 6 A.M. to 8 P.M., revolving around direct sales. When a listener called to purchase an item, he could talk with the host announcer and get information

This case was prepared by Professor Thomas L. Wheelen, Professor Charles E. Michaels, Jr., and Melton L. Martin, Jr., and Janiece L. Gallagher, MBA students, at the University of South Florida. Copyright © 1987 by Thomas L. Wheelen. Reprinted by permission of the copyright holder.

on the item while their conversation was broadcast live on the air. Because of the small size of the local radio audience, neither the local merchants nor national advertisers felt threatened, and the station was thus able to gain the time and revenues it needed for survival.

In July 1982, Bud Paxson approached Vision Cable in Clearwater, Florida, about its carrying his program, the Bargaineer Club. This program, offered by the Home Shopping Channel Inc., was simultaneously broadcast live on the radio and cable television for the first six months.

The initial cable offering was 14,000 homes, but the program quickly spread to three adjoining cable systems in Pinellas and Pasco counties, with 145,000 subscribers. About the time the program went on cable, Bud Paxson sold his broadcast interest.

In order for the company to grow and expand, Mr. Paxson had to have an infusion of money and management expertise into the Home Shopping Channel. In July 1982, Mr. Roy Speer, entrepreneur, made a $500,000 investment in the company for a 60% controlling interest.

Mr. Speer, who graduated from Southern Methodist University in 1956 with a business degree, earned a law degree from Stetson College of Law. Mr. Speer feels that "the law is the best toolbox when you go into business." Speer, who has been involved with many successful entrepreneurial ventures over the years, served as a Florida Attorney General. His companies built over 15,000 houses, and he owns Aloha Utilities, a private utility serving Speer's real estate development in Pasco County, Florida.

In 1981, Mr. Speer lost half his wealth when the Arab oil embargo wrecked his massive investment in oil and gas drilling rigs in Texas. When a venture flops, it is a Speer habit to "act quickly and cash out." In 1982, he brought his money and expertise to Home Shopping Channel.

Initial advertising for the Home Shopping Channel was achieved through a two-color self-mailer. Bill stuffers were also placed in monthly cable bills, and direct-response advertisements appeared in local newspapers of areas served by the cable.

When it came to selling merchandise, Paxson found that cable TV worked better than radio. The customer-interactive format was maintained on television, and, to keep the viewers' interest, games were played and prizes were given away to the winners. There was no format for merchandise to be sold, so a viewer was induced to continue watching so as not to miss anything. The management realized that the more the program was watched, the greater the sales would be.

Purchases were made either with cash or a credit card, and "Club members" received their merchandise in person at seven pick-up points called "Home Shopping Marts." The pick-up point was assigned to the customer's zip code, so that a member never had to drive more than six miles to pick up his merchandise.

Revenues for the period April 23, 1982, to December 31, 1982, were $898,000 and there was a net loss of $202,000. In 1983, sales were $3,639,000 with a profit of $259,000. The sales for fiscal year 1984 increased to $10,819,000 with a profit of $359,000.

In 1985, Paxson and Speer were making plans to expand the program to Fort Lauderdale, Florida, but these plans were scrapped by management. Paxson said, "We could do it (go national) for the same money." Mr. Speer insisted that, for the company to be successful on a national basis, three key elements would be required. The company would need to increase its staff with operators, to acquire sufficient telephone lines, and most important, it would need a computer system with the capacity to respond to customers' needs instantly. He believed that buyers who were burned the first time would not return.

On July 1, 1985, the Home Shopping Network was formed. At that time, the Home Shopping Channel went national and was merged into Home Shopping Network. On February 26, 1986, Home Shopping Network was reincorporated and recapitalized. Mr. Speer used "the law of large numbers" to predict the expected buyer's profile on a national basis. That is, he took the buying profile of customers in the Tampa Bay area and multiplied it by expected national market figures to draw a profile of a national customer.

STRATEGIC MANAGERS

The officers and directors of Home Shopping Company are described below.

Roy M. Speer (age 53), Chairman of the Board and co-founder of the company, has served as the Chief Executive Officer of the company since 1985. Since 1966, Mr. Speer has been engaged in real estate and industrial development in Florida. Since 1966 he has owned and operated Aloha Utilities, Inc., a water supply and distribution/sewer collection, treatment, and disposal company. From 1977 to 1982, he was involved in the ownership and management of radio stations in Florida, and from 1979 until 1986, he was a partner in the law firm of Speer and Olson, HSN's General Counsel. He has been a director of the company since it commenced operations in 1985, and has devoted more than three quarters of his business time to the management of the company.

Lowell W. Paxson (age 51), President and co-founder of the company, has served as the Chief Operating Officer of the company and its predecessors since 1982. From 1957 to 1982, Mr. Paxson was the owner and operator of eight AM/FM and television broadcast licensees in New York, Connecticut, and Florida. From 1957 through 1973, he owned and managed several retail operations, including art galleries and record stores. He has been a Director of the company since it commenced operations in 1985.

J. Patrick Michaels, Jr. (age 41) has been since 1973 Chairman of the Board of Communications Equity Associates, a firm providing financial and other services to the cable television and related communications industries. Mr. Michaels also serves as Chairman of Atlantic American Cablevision, of Gulfstream Cablevision of Pasco County, and of Silver King Broadcasting,

Inc. Mr. Michaels has been involved with the cable television industry since 1968 and has been a director of HSN since 1986.

Nando DiFilippo, Jr. (age 38) is a Senior Vice-President, General Counsel, and Secretary of Baltimore Federal Financial, F.S.A. Prior to joining Baltimore Federal Financial, F.S.A. in 1985, Mr. DiFilippo was a partner in the Washington, D.C., office of the law firm of Baker and McKenzie. He has been a Director of the company since 1986.

Franklin J. Chu (age 30) is a Vice-President in the Investment Banking Division of Merrill Lynch Capital Markets. From 1980 through 1986, he was a Vice-President of Drexel Burnham Lambert, Incorporated. He is a director of Autotote Systems, Inc., and he has been a Director of HSN since 1986.

Richard M. Speer (age 24) (son of Roy M. Speer) is the Vice-President—Operations. He has been employed by the company and its predecessors in a variety of capacities since 1983. He graduated from Southern Methodist University in 1983 with a degree in Business Management.

Richard W. Baker (age 40) is the Treasurer and Secretary of the company. He has been employed by the company and its predecessors since 1984. Prior to his employment with HSN, he was engaged in private practice as a certified public accountant for more than three years. Mr. Baker was previously employed by Price Waterhouse & Company and is a member of the Florida and American Institutes of Certified Public Accountants.

The officers are elected by the Board of Directors and serve at the pleasure of the Chairman of the Board. The members of the Board of Directors serve for a term of one year and until their successors are elected.

The company had 982 employees on February 28, 1986.

The executive compensation during the eight-month period ended August 31, 1985 was:

Name	Position	Cash Compensation
Roy M. Speer	Chairman of the Board	$107,000
Lowell W. Paxson	President	$107,000
All executive officers		$256,000

Home Shopping Network has employment agreements with Mr. Speer and Mr. Paxson (see Exhibit 26.1). However, the company has not adopted a plan or policy regarding the compensation of Directors who are not officers of the company.

The holders of common stock have the right to elect 25% of the Board of Directors. As to the election of the remaining 75% of the directors, the holders of Class B common stock are entitled to 10 votes for each Class B share, and the holders of the common stock are entitled to one vote per share. There are no cumulative voting rights.

Mr. Roy Speer is the holder of all the Class B shares. This ownership enables him to exercise control over the major corporate actions, such as

EXHIBIT 26.1   **Employment Agreements**

> Mr. Speer has entered into a five year employment agreement, renewable automatically for additional three year terms, which provides for a base salary of $250,000 per year and the use of a Company car. Either the Company or Mr. Speer may terminate the employment agreement upon 180 days notice prior to the expiration of the initial or any subsequent term. Under the terms of the employment agreement, Mr. Speer may not compete with the Company for a period of five years following termination of his employment unless terminated by reason of death, long-term illness, disability or other incapacity. Additionally, the employment agreement prohibits Mr. Speer from disclosing information relating to the business and practices of the Company. In the event that Mr. Speer's employment is terminated without cause, the Company will retain Mr. Speer during the five year noncompetition period as a consultant at 100% of his base salary; however, if Mr. Speer's employment is terminated with cause, he will earn 50% of his base salary as a consultant for the Company during the noncompetition period. The employment agreement also provides a death benefit of one year's salary. Mr. Paxson has signed an employment agreement under terms similar to Mr. Speer's employment agreement with an annual base salary of $215,000.

SOURCE: *The Prospectus of Home Shopping Network,* Merrill Lynch Capital Markets (May 13, 1986), p. 23.

dissolution or liquidation, merger, reorganization, sale of substantial assets, and an amendment of the Certificate of Incorporation. Thus, Mr. Speer can block any takeover attempts, and currently he may elect 75% of the board.*

Exhibit 26.2 lists the business relationships between Home Shopping Network and other individuals and companies.

THE BUSINESS[†]   General

The Company is a specialty retailer that markets a variety of consumer products by means of live, customer-interactive, televised sales programs

---

*This control exists because as long as at least 3.8 million shares of Class B Common Stock remain outstanding, the approval of the requisite majority of the Class B Common Stock and Common Stock, each voting separately as a class, is required for approval of such major corporate action. Thus, Mr. Speer, both before and after this offering, will be able to block any takeover attempt directed at the company. Moreover, the Board of Directors of the company has the authority to issue preferred stock of the company with preferences, rights, and qualifications that could be useful in the prevention of a takeover of the company. In the event that less than 3.8 million shares of Class B Common Stock are outstanding, each such share is entitled to vote ten votes, voting together with the Common Stock, and each share of Common Stock will have one vote.

†This entire section, *"The Business,"* is taken directly from the *Prospectus of Home Shopping Network,* Merrill Lynch Capital Markets (May 13, 1986), pp. 15–20.

EXHIBIT 26.2   **Business Relationships and Certain Transactions Relating to Home Shopping Network**

1. The founders of the Company are Roy M. Speer and Lowell W. Paxson. In connection with the formation of the Company and in consideration of the extension of credit, financial guarantees and the payment of $500 in cash, Mr. Speer and Mr. Paxson were issued 1.2 million and 800,000 shares, respectively, of common stock of the Company. Subsequently, these shares were split 3.75 to one. In February 1986, Home Shopping Channel's, Inc. was merged into the Company. In connection with the merger, and on the same basis as unaffiliated shareholders, certain trusts established for the benefit of Mr. Speer's family and Mr. Paxson's family received 250,000 and 150,000 shares of the Company's stock, respectively, in exchange for an equal number of shares of Home Shopping Channel's, Inc. In connection with the reincorporation of the Company in Delaware in February 1986 and a subsequent recapitalization, Mr. Speer's shares of the Company's stock were converted into 2,812,524 shares of Common Stock and 4,026,576 shares of Class B Common Stock of the Company. Mr. Paxson's shares of the Company's stock were converted into 4,559,400 shares of Common Stock of the Company based upon a conversion rate of 1.53 shares of Common Stock of the Company for each share of Common Stock previously held. The Speer family trust received 382,500 shares of Common Stock and the Paxson family trust received 229,500 shares of Common Stock. Mr. Speer and Mr. Paxson have been paid cash compensation and other benefits as employees of the Company and have entered into employment agreements with the Company. (See "Employment Agreements," Exhibit 26.1.)

2. From time to time, the Speer family trust has lent funds to the Company and its predecessors. As of August 31, 1985, the outstanding loan amount was $233,334, which amount was subsequently repaid in full. The loan, which was payable on demand, bore interest at the rate of two percent over the prime rate. In addition, Mr. Speer and his wife, from time to time, have lent money to the Company and received interest at market rates. The amount of these loans, which have subsequently been repaid in full, did not exceed $60,000.

3. During 1986, Drexel Burnham Lambert Incorporated was retained by the Company as its financial adviser. Franklin J. Chu, a director of the Company, was then a Vice President of that firm.

4. On May 20, 1982, Home Shopping Channel's, Inc. entered into a two year equipment lease agreement with the Speer family trust pursuant to which television equipment was leased from the trust for a rental of $6,500 per month plus applicable sales tax. On May 25, 1984, the Company renewed the equipment lease for an additional five years, terminating June 19, 1989 on the same terms and conditions as the original lease. Upon termination of the lease, the Company has an option to purchase the equipment for $19,000.

5. On June 21, 1985, the Company entered into two agreements with Interphase, Inc. ("Interphase") whereby Interphase agreed to lease certain computer equipment and certain television equipment to the Company for a period of 36 months. The Company agreed to pay $26,665 per month, plus sales tax, for the lease of the computer equipment and $12,250 per

(Continued)

EXHIBIT 26.2 **(Continued)**

month, plus sales tax, for the lease of the communication equipment. Both agreements provide for increases in lease payments as a function of increases in the prime rate. Roy M. Speer is the sole shareholder, President, and a Director of Interphase.

6. On June 21, 1985, the Company and one of its predecessors entered into agreements with Pioneer Data, Inc. ("Pioneer") whereby Pioneer agreed to provide computer advice and certain software programs and personnel used by the Company for an indefinite period beginning on July 1, 1985. In return, the Company agreed to pay Pioneer 1% of the Company's gross profit, as defined. Pioneer also agreed to lease certain computer equipment to the Company for a period of 36 months commencing July 1, 1985 at a rental of $12,774 per month. Richard M. Speer is the President and sole shareholder of Pioneer. Roy M. Speer is a Director of Pioneer.

7. In June 1985, Interphase was retained by the Company to construct a television studio at its leased premises in Clearwater, Florida for which Interphase was paid $98,803.

8. On August 1, 1985, the Company borrowed $378,452 from Interphase to be used for the payment of a deposit under a transponder lease agreement, leasehold improvements and additional working capital. In consideration of which, the Company executed a promissory note whereby the Company promises to pay to the order of Interphase the sum of $378,452 in equal monthly principal installments of $10,513, plus interest at prime plus two percent (prime being set as "Barnett Bank Prime").

9. On November 1, 1984, the Company (through its predecessor) assumed the lease of Home Shopping Medical Center of Clearwater, Inc. at 1563 U.S. Highway 19 South in Clearwater, Florida for use as the Company's accounting and data processing center. In consideration of leasehold improvements made by Home Shopping Medical Center of Clearwater, Inc., the Company executed a 33 month promissory note whereby it agreed to pay to the order of Home Shopping Medical Center of Clearwater, Inc. the sum of $243,000 with interest at the rate of 10% per annum; the note requires monthly payments of $8,453 (principal and interest) commencing November 1, 1984. Home Shopping Medical Center of Clearwater, Inc. subsequently changed its name to Western Hemisphere Sales, Inc. ("Western Hemisphere"). Richard M. Speer is the sole shareholder of Western Hemisphere. Roy M. Speer is the President and a Director of Western Hemisphere.

10. Merchandise that is unusable for sale by the Company is sold by Western Hemisphere at prices designated by the Company for a commission of 15% of the proceeds.

11. Merrill Lynch Capital Markets has agreed to pay an amount of not more than $75,000 to one of its consultants as a fee relating to the introduction of Home Shopping Network, Inc. to Merrill Lynch Capital Markets. Pursuant to an agreement between Communications Equity Associates and the consultant of Merrill Lynch entitled to the aforementioned fee. Communications Equity Associates will receive 100% of such fee. J. Patrick Michaels, Jr., a director of the Company, is the Chairman of the Board and a controlling person of Communications Equity Associates.

12. J. Patrick Michaels, Jr. is also the Chairman of the Board and a controlling person of Gulfstream Cablevision of Pinellas County, Inc. and Gulfstream

Cablevision of Pasco County, Inc. (together "Gulfstream"). Gulfstream operates cable systems which carry the Company's programming service.

13. On September 8, 1982, certain Texas banks filed Chapter 7 involuntary bankruptcy proceedings against Roy M. Speer arising out of a commercial dispute involving oil rig leasing and drilling corporate ventures in which Mr. Speer and two other individuals were guarantors. On petition of Mr. Speer, the proceedings were converted to a Chapter 11 (reorganization) proceeding, and a final order approving a plan of reorganization was entered on July 24, 1985. The plan has been fully satisfied. At no time during the proceedings were Mr. Speer's existing credit arrangements with other banks adversely affected by these proceedings.

14. All future transactions, as well as modifications to existing agreements between the Company and its officers, directors or stockholders holding 5% or more of the Company's voting securities will be on terms no less favorable to the Company than could be obtained from unaffiliated third parties and shall be subject to the approval of a majority of the outside directors of the Company. Moreover, the Company does not plan to use related parties for the construction of future leasehold improvements. The outside directors are Messrs. Michaels, DiFilippo and Chu.

SOURCE: *The Prospectus of Home Shopping Network*, Merrill Lynch Capital Markets (May 13, 1986), pp. 23–24.

broadcast over its own networks. The copyrighted sales programs, which are in a distinctive format, use the spontaneity of live television, viewer participation, club membership and quality products at bargain prices to attract viewers and promote sales. The programs are broadcast twenty-four hours a day, 7 days a week via satellite to cable systems and satellite dish receivers and feature a wide variety of merchandise, such as jewelry, housewares, china, appliances and electronics. At February 28, 1986, approximately six million homes throughout the United States could receive part or all of the Company's round-the-clock broadcasts of its original program, HSN 1. HSN 1 is broadcast from a newly constructed studio located in the existing building in which the Company's headquarters are located. A second twenty-four hour program service, HSN 2, offering higher-priced, innovative merchandise, began broadcasts on March 1, 1986 and on that date reached approximately two million homes in which HSN 1 could also be viewed.

National Cable and Satellite Market

The following table shows, by year, the growth in basic cable television subscribers. Such growth has been generated from increases both in subscribers to existing cable systems and newly constructed systems.

Year	U.S. Television Households	Basic Cable Subscribers	Basic Cable Subscribers as a Percent of TV Households
1985	86,000,000	36,120,000	42%
1984	84,600,000	32,994,000	39%
1983	83,500,000	30,300,000	36%
1982	82,800,000	28,200,000	34%

SOURCE: *The Cable File* published by International Thomson Communications, Inc.

As of December 1985, industry sources indicate that an additional 1.7 million households own home satellite dishes, enabling these households to watch the Company's programs. As of February 28, 1986, the Company estimates that the Company's program was broadcast to approximately six million households. (See "Business—Cable Operators and Satellite Dishes.")

The Home Shopping Club™ Programs

The Company's primary marketing concept is its twenty-four hour television programming, "The Home Shopping Club." The distinctive format of The Home Shopping Club is intended to promote sales through a combination of product information, price information, entertainment and the creation of confidence in the Company and its products, thus promoting customer loyalty and repeat purchases. The same format is used on both HSN 1 and HSN 2.

The Home Shopping Club program is divided into segments. Each segment is broadcast live with an experienced host. The host presents the merchandise one product at a time and conveys to the viewer information relating to the product including price, quality, uses and attributes. Viewers place orders with the Company's telephone operators by calling a toll-free number. The Company maintains more than 400 WATS lines to handle incoming orders and in February 1986 acquired automatic call distributing equipment to enable the Company's operators to handle a greater volume of orders efficiently. Show hosts engage callers in on-the-air discussions regarding the Club, the currently featured product and the caller's previous experience with the Company and its products. The distinctive format creates a spontaneous and entertaining program. A first-time purchaser of merchandise receives a complimentary membership in the Home Shopping Club. The Club stimulates customer loyalty by providing the customer with incentives to purchase additional items from the Company. The Company, at February 28, 1986, had approximately 235,000 Club members.

Distribution and Data Processing

The Company is committed to the rapid delivery of merchandise to customers. The Company ships merchandise ordered on HSN 1 and HSN 2 from its distribution facility in Clearwater, Florida, typically within forty-eight hours after receipt of an order. Delivery is generally made via United Parcel Service within seven to ten days of an order. The Company is currently considering plans to further reduce the time between receipt of an order and delivery of merchandise.

The Company has also decided to expand its distribution capacity by the addition of four warehouse and distribution facilities placed in geographic locations in which distribution via United Parcel Service can be accomplished more quickly and inexpensively.

To facilitate the processing of customer orders, the Company has purchased a state-of-the-art mainframe computer system and has computerized many of its operations. Over a five year period, the Company has developed with the assistance of Pioneer Data, Inc. a proprietary software program which allows the computer system to maintain customer records, control inventory, facilitate credit checks and payments and process customer orders. The Company maintains alternate sources of power for its computer and studio facilities. Pioneer Data, Inc. has furnished the Company and its predecessors with the use of certain computer facilities, software, programmers and supervisory personnel for use in the continuing development and improvement of the computer system utilized by the Company. A number of the programs used by the Company are based upon programs originally developed by Pioneer Data, Inc.

Customer Service and Return Policy

The Company believes that satisfied customers will be loyal Club members who will purchase from the Company on a regular basis. In order to assure customer satisfaction, the Company delivers its products quickly and has customer service personnel available from 9:00 a.m. to 12 midnight, local time, seven days a week to help any customer with a complaint or problem. The Company maintains in excess of 75 toll-free telephone lines to enable customers to contact the customer service department with any complaints or questions.

As part of the Company's customer service policy, the Company maintains a return policy under which a customer may, within thirty days of purchase, return for any reason an item purchased from the Company for a refund of the full purchase price and the original shipping and handling costs for the returned item. The customer pays only the cost of shipping the item back to the Company. An allowance for returned merchandise is provided as a percentage of gross sales based upon prior experience. Although there can be no assurance that future refunds will match the Company's experience, the experience of the Company's national sales program for the six months ended February 28, 1986 indicates that the rate of refunds (including returns, breakage, inventory discrepancies and undeliverable goods) varies from month to month between 9 and 18 percent of sales. Higher return rates are generally experienced when the Company offers a larger percentage of expensive items, such as jewelry, in a given month. For the quarter ending February 28, 1986, based upon management's analysis of Company data, the Company believes that approximately 80% of its sales were to repeat customers. The Company attributes the high level of repeat customers to the quality of the products that it offers, the club atmosphere of the programs and the Company's customer service efforts.

The Company does not function as a manufacturer's representative for warranty claims on any of the products which it sells. Customers must communicate directly with a manufacturer regarding the failure of a product to conform with a manufacturer's specifications.

Merchandise that is unusable for sale via The Home Shopping Club is sold by Western Hemisphere Sales, Inc., a related party company, for a commission of 15% of the amount realized. Such sales were less than 1% of the total sales of the Company in the six month period ended February 28, 1986.

Product Strategy and Purchasing

The Company believes that a primary factor contributing to the success of its business is its ability to locate and take advantage of opportunities to purchase large quantities of quality merchandise at prices which reflect substantial discounts from wholesale prices. The Company's buyers purchase merchandise from more than 1,500 suppliers throughout the world and continually seek opportunities created by manufacturers' overproduction and close-out circumstances, the overstock inventory of wholesalers and retailers, as well as other sources. The Company's experience and expertise in buying merchandise from such suppliers has enabled it to develop relationships with many manufacturers and wholesalers who offer some or all of their close-out merchandise to the Company prior to attempting to dispose of it through other means. By selling their inventories to the Company, suppliers can reduce warehouse expenses and avoid the sale of products at concessionary prices through their normal means of distribution. The Company has no long-term purchase commitments with any of its suppliers, and, historically, there have been various sources of supply available for each category of merchandise sold by the Company.

The Company's primary sources of merchandise are manufacturers, distributors, importers, barter agents and professional finders. The Company is continually developing new sources of supply, through advertising in commercial and trade publications and through both direct mail solicitation of suppliers and direct contact with these sources of supply. The Company's experience in purchasing large quantities of merchandise and management's ability to respond promptly to purchase opportunities have enabled the Company to develop a reputation as a leading purchaser of such goods, giving it access to a broad range of possible suppliers. In many cases, the Company has developed valuable sources from which it obtains certain lines of merchandise on a continuing basis.

In addition to the Company's purchases of manufacturers' overproduction and closeout opportunities, wholesaler and retailer inventory overstocking and other sources, approximately 20% of the Company's sales are realized from sales of items, such as jewelry, certain toys and briefcases manufactured to the Company's order, in the United States and abroad. The Company typically provides a domestic or foreign manufacturer with product specifications and pricing requirements for items to be manufactured for the Company. The Company anticipates that the percentage of sales attributable to items manufactured to order will increase in the future.

The products sold on HSN 2 are generally more expensive and consist, to a greater degree, of brand name and specially manufactured products. Certain innovative products, such as stereo systems, leather products, computers and distinctive curios, many of which are offered on HSN 2, are purchased from the current stocks of major brand name manufacturers. Nevertheless, the strategy and purchasing policies of HSN 2 are modeled after those of HSN 1. The Company's experience with HSN 2 is limited, and no prediction can be made as to future profit margins.

Transmission and Programming Distribution

The Company produces HSN 1 and HSN 2 in separate studios located in Clearwater, Florida and transmits or "uplinks" the program signals to transponders on domestic communications satellites owned by RCA. The satellites consist of a number of transponders which receive signals transmitted from terrestrial stations and, in turn, retransmit those signals so that they can be received by satellite receiving stations throughout the United States. The Company's sales programs are potentially available to all cable companies in the United States which have the proper satellite receiving facilities. Local cable operators generally distribute the Company's signal to their customers as part of their basic cable service. Additionally, a majority of home satellite dish receivers are able to receive the Company's transmissions via the domestic communications satellites carrying the Company's signals.

The Company has secured rights to use of transponders on RCA's domestic communications satellites Satcom IIIR (used by HSN 1 and HSN 2) and Satcom IV (used by HSN 2). The Company subleases transponder time on Satcom IV from Home Box Office, Inc. ("HBO") and on Satcom IIIR from The Learning Channel, Inc. The Company's transponder subleases are subject to a tariff filed with the FCC (the "Tariff") which generally sets forth the terms and nature of the service provided by RCA to its lessees.

In particular, under the terms of the Tariff and the HBO sublease, the Company is provided with transponder time twenty-four hours a day, seven days a week through December 31, 1989 on a protected, non-preemptible basis as defined in the Tariff. The Company's protected, non-preemptible status provides the Company transponder time on Satcom IIIR or Satcom IV or on RCA's "protection satellite" which would provide additional transponder capacity in the event of the failure of Satcom IIIR or Satcom IV. After 1989, the Company may opt, subject to RCA's consent, to assume HBO's position as the primary lessee of the transponder on Satcom IV. Under the terms of The Learning Channel, Inc. sublease, the Company is provided with transponder time between 4:00 a.m. and 4:00 p.m. (Eastern Time), seven days a week on Satcom IIIR through April 30, 1987 on a protected, non-preemptible basis. Prior to January 1, 1987 the Company may opt, subject to RCA's consent, to assume The Learning Channel Inc.'s position as the primary lessee of the transponder on Satcom IIIR.

The Company leases additional transponder time on Satcom IIIR directly from RCA as customer of record pursuant to the terms of the Tariff. The Company leases from RCA a total of twenty-four hours of transponder time daily, seven days a week through December 31, 1988 on a protected, non-preemptible basis. The term of the Company's transponder lease on Satcom IIIR may be extended for an additional eight years, through December 31, 1996. RCA has estimated that the useful lives of Satcom IIIR and IV will run through 1992. The terms of any extensions of the leases will be subject to the terms of the Tariff as then in force.

The Company believes that it will be in a position to avail itself of future technological developments in the satellite communications and cable television industries and thereby maintain the appropriate level of service to cable operators carrying the Company's programs.

Cable system operators receive the Company's signal and, in turn, redistribute the signal to cable subscribers as part of their cable service. Generally, there is no additional charge for distribution of the Company's programs. The terms of the Company's agreements with cable operators typically prevent operators from carrying the Company's program for an additional monthly fee.

Cable Operators and Satellite Dishes

The Company has entered into agreements with a number of cable system operators to carry HSN 1 or both HSN 1 and HSN 2. The Company also is in the process of negotiating agreements with additional cable system operators. The Company employs a policy whereby only cable operators which agree to carry HSN 1 may carry HSN 2. Both HSN 1 and HSN 2 may be received by any cable company in the United States with the proper satellite receiving equipment. The total number of cable subscribers who could receive HSN 1, at February 28, 1986, was approximately 4.3 million, of which approximately 52% were subscribers to cable systems that had contracted to carry the Company's programs. The Company is in the process of negotiating agreements with operators of the remaining cable systems. As of March 1, 1986, when HSN 2 began operation, the Company believes that HSN 2 reached approximately 2 million homes.

The Company's agreements with cable operators to carry the sales programs generally provide that the cable operator will receive a percentage of the net sales of merchandise sold to customers located within the cable company's service area in return for receiving and distributing to its customers the Company's sales programs as part of the cable operator's basic cable service. The percentage of net sales received by cable operators varies from 1% to 5% depending upon the number of years an operator has carried the Company's programs, the number of cable subscribers that actually receive the programs and the percentage that this number represents of the cable operator's total subscribers. Cable operators which carry both HSN 1 and HSN 2 generally receive a higher percentage of net sales than those operators which carry only HSN 1. By compensating its cable system operators directly on the basis of sales in a systems operating area for distributing its programming, the Company feels that additional cable operators will distribute the Company's programming, thereby providing the Company access to a greater number of viewers.

Although there is variation among the various agreements with cable operators, a typical agreement provides for an initial term of one year which is automatically renewable for subsequent one year terms. In general, the agreements may be terminated by either party ninety days prior to the end of their terms and encourage a local operator to assist the promotional efforts of the Company by carrying commercials regarding the Company and distributing the Company's advertising circulars to their customers.

The Company's Affiliate Relations Department is in the process of negotiating cable affiliation agreements with a number of cable multiple system operators ("MSO's"). There can be no assurance that the Company will be able to reach agreement with these cable systems on terms and conditions that the Company considers appropriate. Moreover, there are channel capacity constraints with respect to certain cable systems, and even if the Company is able to reach agreement with these MSO's, the Company may not be guaranteed channel access in all of the cable systems managed by an MSO. Under such circumstances, the Company may be provided access to cable channels only as they become available. Since MSO's serve approximately 80% of all cabled homes, the growth of the Company may be limited by the availability of channel capacity on MSO's cable systems that do not currently carry the Company's programs.

The Company's programs may be received by households in the United States furnished with the appropriate satellite dish receiving equipment. The Company estimates that at February 28, 1986, approximately 1.7 million homes were capable of receiving the Company's programs by means of satellite dish receivers. The Company seeks to attract owners of satellite dish receivers to watch its programs through a variety of marketing and promotional techniques.

While a number of cable television programmers plan to "scramble" their broadcasts to prevent unauthorized viewing of their programming by owners of satellite dish receivers, the Company has no present intention to scramble the signals for either of its two programs. Thus, owners of satellite dish receivers will not need to purchase a decoder to watch either HSN 1 or HSN 2.

Unless the Company decides to establish a marketing system through which owners of satellite dish receivers could be charged for receiving the Company's programs, satellite dish owners will be able to receive those programs at no charge without incurring liability under either the Communications Act or the Copyright Act. The Company plans not to establish such a marketing plan.

Expansion Strategy

The Company believes that it can expand sales by increasing its viewership in cable areas in which the Company's programs are currently distributed and by enlarging the number of cable operators which carry its programs. The Company employs eight people in its Affiliate Relations Department who are responsible for negotiating contracts with cable operators and securing channel availability. No assurance can be given that these negotiations will be successful. Furthermore, the Company believes that future increases in the number of satellite dish receivers will contribute to an increase in the number of homes which receive the Company's programs. The Company hopes to achieve increased penetration in the cable market in which the Company's programs are currently available through additional promotional and marketing efforts directed at households which currently receive HSN 1 and HSN 2, but are not Club members.

On March 1, 1986, the Company inaugurated HSN 2, "Innovations in Living," which utilizes the same program format employed by HSN 1, but offers a variety of innovative products that are generally more expensive than those offered on HSN 1. In contrast to HSN 1, the products sold on HSN 2 are higher priced, innovative products some of which are purchased directly from brand name manufacturers.

The Company also intends to engage in shared revenue advertising in which the Company will direct market merchandise on cable and broadcast television stations and to develop its capacity for mail order retailing by acquiring or forming a mail order subsidiary. No negotiations for acquisition of such a company are occurring.

To accommodate the expected growth of the Company and to further expedite the delivery of products to customers, the Company plans to purchase regional warehouse and distribution facilities from which customer orders will be shipped via United Parcel Service. The regional warehouse and distribution facilities will be linked by computer to further enhance speed of product delivery.

Competition

The Company operates in a highly competitive environment.‡ It is in direct competition with businesses which are engaged in retail merchandising and cable programming. In particular, the Company, as a cable programmer, competes for channel space with other programmers and, as a retailer, competes most intensely with direct marketing retailers such as mail order companies and companies that sell from catalogues and other discount, volume retail outlets.

No other retailer at this time markets merchandise solely by means of a live, nationally televised sales program broadcast 24 hours a day. A number of other entities are engaged in direct retail sales businesses which utilize television in some form and which target the same markets in which the Company operates. Some of the Company's competitors are larger and more diversified than the Company. The Company cannot predict the degree of success with which the Company will meet competition in the future.

[*Author's note:* Modern Satellite Network shut down its "Home Shopping Show" after six years. Adams-Russell decided last year not to mount the "Cable Shop," touted to be a full-time shopping and informational service. Two years ago the UTV Network proposed a daily feature called "Easy Shopping." The UTV concept didn't excite financial backers, and the program was never developed. On May 1, 1986, Cable Value Network was formed as a co-operative test venture between Minneapolis-based C.O.M.B., Inc. (Closeout Merchandise Buyers, Inc.) and Tel-Communications, Inc. (TCI) of Denver, the largest cable company in the country. It initially broadcast 88 hours per week to TCI's six million subscribers and plans to expand to 24 hours per day soon. To challenge Home Shopping, Cable Value Network is offering cable operators equity in the company.

Government Regulation

The Federal Communications Commission ("FCC") does not directly regulate provision of programming services to cable television systems or satellite dish receivers. The FCC, however, has and exercises regulatory authority over cable television systems and satellite service and facility providers.

The FCC grants licenses to construct and operate uplink equipment, which transmits signals to satellites. These licenses are generally issued without a hearing if suitable frequencies are available. The Company presently operates transportable uplink equipment leased from a third party, which has temporary authority from the FCC to transmit signals from the Company's location. The Company has applied for a license for operation of its present transmission facilities on a permanent basis. Upon grant of the license, the Company intends to purchase the leased facilities currently in place and convert same into the Company's permanent transmission facility. There can be no assurances, however, that the FCC will grant the Company's application for licensing of permanent transmission facilities.

The FCC has jurisdiction over satellite service and facility providers. It is presently the policy of the FCC, however, to treat domestic satellite service providers, such as RCA, as forborne common carriers. Accordingly, the FCC does not set the rates of such carriers. Further, the FCC does not require these carriers to file tariffs, and if such carriers have tariffs on file, it allows them to withdraw those tariffs. The FCC has recently asked Congress to amend the Communications Act to authorize the FCC to prohibit forborne carriers from filing tariffs and to require them to withdraw tariffs already on file. RCA is currently required to provide service on terms and conditions that are just, reasonable and non-discriminatory, and is subject to complaints filed with the FCC pursuant to the Communications Act. RCA would still be subject to these requirements and the complaint process even if its tariffs were withdrawn.

Under current FCC policy, forborne carriers are not subject to the market exit provisions of Section 214 of the Communications Act. RCA may, therefore, cease providing communication services to customers on short notice. The Company has no reason to believe that RCA has any intention to cease providing transmission services.

Trademarks, Tradenames and Copyrights

The Company has registered and is currently registering its marks as they are developed and used. The Company believes that its trademarks are a primary marketing tool. The Company's trademarks have been filed for registration with the United States Patent and Trademark Office and some have been issued on the Principal Register. The initial term for such registration is twenty years. The Company has entered into secrecy agreements with Mr. Speer, Mr. Paxson and its computer personnel. The Company's televised sales programs are copyrighted.

Properties

The Company or its subsidiaries lease space in the Tampa Bay area for its administrative offices, studios, computer and broadcasting facilities, distribution center and warehouses.**

****Author's note:* The actual 16 different facilities were listed individually in the Prospectus. It listed (a) the location, (b) function, (c) square footage, (d) current annual rent and (e) expiration date of lease.

THE STOCK OFFERING

[*Author's note:* On May 13, 1986, the first public offering of HSN stock was made. Of the 2,000,000 shares of common stock offered, 1,600,000 were being sold by Home Shopping Network, Inc., and 400,000 shares were being sold by the two co-founders (see Exhibit 26.3). The offering price was $18 per share.]

[The forty-six underwriters, acting through their representative, Merrill Lynch, Pierce, Fenner & Smith, Incorporated, agreed to purchase the 2,000,000 shares. The underwriters agreed to reserve a maximum of 130,000 shares of common stock for offering and sale at the public offering price, to certain officers and employees of the company and to certain other persons designated by the company. The company also granted the underwriters a thirty-day option on an additional 300,000 shares.]

[The net proceeds to the company from the stock sale were estimated to be $26,272,000 ($30,299,200 if the underwriters' over-allotment option is exercised in full).]

EXHIBIT 26.3 Principal and Selling Stockholders

NAME AND ADDRESS OF BENEFICIAL OWNER	BENEFICIAL OWNERSHIP OF COMMON STOCK PRIOR TO THIS OFFERING		Number of Shares of Common Stock Being Sold[1]	BENEFICIAL OWNERSHIP OF COMMON STOCK AFTER OFFERING[1]	
	No. of Shares	Percent of Class		No. of Shares	Percent of Class
Roy M. Speer[2] 1529 U.S. 19 South Clearwater, FL 33546	2,812,524	34.3%	240,000	2,572,524	26.2%
Lowell W. Paxson[3] 1529 U.S. 19 South Clearwater, FL 33546	4,559,400	55.6%	160,000	4,399,400	44.9%
J. Patrick Michaels	—	—	—	—	—
Nando DiFilippo, Jr.	4,590	.1%	—	4,590	.1%
Franklin J. Chu	—	—	—	—	—
All officers and directors as a group (7 persons)	7,507,864	91.5%	400,000	7,107,864	72.5%

[1]Assuming the Underwriters' over-allotment option is not exercised.

[2]Does not include 382,500 shares of Common Stock held by Richard W. Baker, Trustee under the Intervivos Trust Agreement dated January 1, 1967 with Roy M. Speer for which Mr. Speer disclaims beneficial ownership. All or any portion of the shares of Class B Common Stock beneficially owned by Mr. Speer may be converted at any time into an equal number of shares of Common Stock of the Company. Upon conversion of Class B Common Stock, Roy Speer would own 6,839,100 shares of Common Stock or 55.9% prior to this offering and 6,599,100 shares or 47.7% after this offering (assuming the Underwriters' over-allotment option is not exercised).

[3]This number excludes 229,500 shares of Common Stock held by Lowell W. Paxson as Trustee under a Trust Agreement dated January 4, 1981 with Barbara A. Paxson and 4,361 shares owned by Barbara A. Paxson for which Mr. Paxson disclaims beneficial ownership.

(Continued)

EXHIBIT 26.3   (Continued)

The following table sets forth current information relating to the beneficial ownership of the Company's Class B Common Stock:

TITLE OF CLASS	NAME AND ADDRESS OF BENEFICIAL OWNER	BENEFICIAL OWNERSHIP	PERCENT OF CLASS
Class B Common	Roy M. Speer 1529 U.S. 19 South Clearwater, FL 33546	4,026,576	100%

Description of Capital Stock

The authorized capital stock of the Company consists of 30,000,000 shares of Common Stock, $.01 par value; 4,026,576 shares of Class B Common Stock, $.01 par value; and 500,000 shares of Preferred Stock, $.01 par value. A total of 8,204,244 shares of Common Stock and 4,026,576 shares of Class B Common Stock are presently outstanding. All of the shares of Common Stock presently outstanding are fully paid and non-assessable and the shares of Common Stock being sold by the Company will be fully paid and non-assessable. Giving effect to the sale of shares of Common Stock offered hereby (exclusive of the over-allotment option), there will be 9,804,244 shares of Common Stock outstanding at the close of this offering. No Class B Common Stock is being sold pursuant to this offering.

SOURCE: *The Prospectus of Home Shopping Network,* Merrill Lynch Capital Markets (May 13, 1986), p. 25.

[The use of the proceeds are as follows: (1) approximately $5.5 million for general corporate purposes including the acquisition of warehouse and distribution facilities in Waterloo, Iowa, and St. Petersburg, Florida, (2) approximately $6.0 million to purchase new computer equipment, (3) $1.4 million for reducing existing debt and capital leases, (4) approximately $4.0 million for the acquisition of corporate headquarters and studio facilities, (5) approximately $1.0 million for the purchase of additional uplink and broadcast equipment, and (6) approximately $1.0 million for pre-opening expenses for the new warehouses. The remainder of the sale's proceeds will be used to finance inventories at existing warehouses.]

FINANCIAL INFORMATION   The financial statements for the company are shown in Exhibits 26.4, 26.5, and 26.6.

EXHIBIT 26.4 Home Shopping Network, Inc. and Subsidiaries, Consolidated Statements of Earnings[1]

	YEARS ENDED DECEMBER 31,		EIGHT MONTHS ENDED AUGUST 31,		SIX MONTHS ENDED FEBRUARY 28,	
	1983	1984	1984 (Unaudited)	1985	1985 (Unaudited)	1986
Net sales	$3,639,043	$10,819,210	$5,135,616	$11,141,371	$8,285,910	$63,861,838
Cost of sales	1,716,857	5,993,900	2,602,161	6,344,656	4,999,476	38,175,269
Gross profit	1,922,186	4,825,310	2,533,455	4,796,715	3,286,434	25,686,569
Operating expenses						
Selling and marketing	508,129	1,549,184	837,043	1,822,917	1,025,545	7,654,505
Engineering and programming	452,976	1,702,525	806,108	1,531,794	1,158,381	3,011,408
General and administrative	594,421	780,405	428,062	1,117,073	756,613	1,799,107
Depreciation and amortization	33,390	169,360	105,515	328,853	95,768	686,917
	1,588,916	4,201,474	2,176,728	4,800,637	3,036,307	13,151,937
Operating profit (loss)	333,270	623,836	356,727	(3,922)	250,127	12,534,632
Other income (expenses)						
Interest income	—	11,891	7,162	4,614	4,834	190,768
Interest expense	(49,582)	(68,994)	(30,745)	(92,154)	(39,485)	(145,798)
Miscellaneous	(22,910)	(73,469)	1,555	23,146	(73,472)	19,148
	(72,492)	(130,572)	(22,028)	(64,394)	(108,123)	64,118
Earnings (loss) before extraordinary item and income taxes	260,778	493,264	334,699	(68,316)	142,004	12,598,750

EXHIBIT 26.4 (Continued)

	YEARS ENDED DECEMBER 31,		EIGHT MONTHS ENDED AUGUST 31,		SIX MONTHS ENDED FEBRUARY 28,	
	1983	1984	1984 (Unaudited)	1985	1985 (Unaudited)	1986
Income taxes (benefit)						
Currently payable	105,000	119,000	79,000	184,000	14,000	5,691,000
Deferred	—	15,000	12,000	(268,000)	3,000	69,000
	105,000	134,000	91,000	(84,000)	17,000	5,760,000
Earnings before extraordinary item	155,778	359,264	243,699	15,684	125,004	6,838,750
Extraordinary item						
Tax benefit of utilization of net operating loss carry-forward	103,000	—	—	—	—	—
Net earnings	$ 258,778	$ 359,264	$ 243,699	$ 15,684	$ 125,004	$ 6,838,750
Earnings per common share						
Earnings before extraordinary item	$ .01	$ .03	$ .02	$ —	$ .01	$ .56
Extraordinary item	.01	—	—	—	—	—
Net earnings	$ .02	$ .03	$ .02	$ —	$ .01	$ .56

SOURCE: *The Prospectus of Home Shopping Network*, Merrill Lynch Capital Markets (May 13, 1986), p. F-4.

The original, accompanying notes were deleted.

EXHIBIT 26.5 Home Shopping Network, Inc. and Subsidiaries, Consolidated Statements of Changes in Financial Position

	YEARS ENDED DECEMBER 31,		EIGHT MONTHS ENDED AUGUST 31,		SIX MONTHS ENDED FEBRUARY 28,	
	1983	1984	1984 (Unaudited)	1985	1985 (Unaudited)	1986
Sources of working capital						
From operations						
Net earnings before extraordinary item	$155,778	$ 359,264	$243,699	$ 15,684	$125,004	$6,838,750
Charges to earnings before extraordinary item not using working capital						
Depreciation and amortization	33,390	169,360	105,515	328,853	95,768	686,917
Deferred income tax	—	15,000	12,000	—	3,000	158,300
Loss on disposal of assets	—	—	—	—	—	47,630
Working capital provided from operations exclusive of extraordinary item	189,168	543,624	361,214	344,537	223,772	7,731,597
Working capital provided by extraordinary item	103,000	—	—	—	—	—
Working capital provided from operations	292,168	543,624	361,214	344,537	223,772	7,731,597
Proceeds from issuance of long-term debt	58,500	272,548	34,933	568,260	249,918	857,656
Increase in obligations under capital leases	—	75,014	75,014	1,180,120	28,868	96,405
Proceeds from sale of assets	—	3,618	—	—	—	7,173
	350,668	894,804	471,161	2,092,917	502,558	8,692,831

(Continued)

EXHIBIT 26.5   (Continued)

	YEARS ENDED DECEMBER 31,		EIGHT MONTHS ENDED AUGUST 31,		SIX MONTHS ENDED FEBRUARY 28,	
	1983	1984	1984 (Unaudited)	1985	1985 (Unaudited)	1986
Applications of working capital						
Increase in other noncurrent assets	6,578	42,991	33,110	69,438	12,940	1,678,070
Additions to property and equipment	68,827	1,156,330	619,637	1,675,090	639,211	4,677,482
Payments on long-term debt including changes to current maturities	34,610	145,240	45,919	266,613	168,529	660,440
Payments on obligations under capital leases including changes to current maturities	—	53,370	33,221	429,078	28,010	213,854
	110,015	1,397,931	731,887	2,440,219	848,690	7,229,846
Increase (Decrease) in Working Capital	240,653	(503,127)	(260,726)	(347,302)	(346,132)	1,462,985
Working capital (deficit) at beginning of period	(220,078)	20,575	20,575	(482,552)	(150,331)	(829,854)
Working capital (deficit) at end of period	$ 20,575	$ (482,552)	$(240,151)	$ (829,854)	$(496,463)	$ 633,131

SOURCE: *The Prospectus of Home Shopping Network,* Merrill Lynch Capital Markets (May 13, 1986), p. F-6.

| EXHIBIT 26.6 | Home Shopping Network, Inc. and Subsidiaries, Consolidated Balance Sheets |

	DECEMBER 31, 1984	AUGUST 31, 1985	FEBRUARY 28, 1986
Assets[1]			
Current assets			
Cash	$ 319,473	$ 404,500	$ 6,807,631
Accounts receivable, less allowance for doubtful accounts of $20,000, $17,000 and $15,000	65,899	103,999	302,161
Inventories	722,749	1,608,394	7,011,823
Deferred income tax	—	268,000	357,300
Other	42,995	159,562	326,547
Total current assets	1,151,116	2,544,455	14,805,462
Property and equipment—at cost			
Computer and broadcast equipment	—	220,846	3,967,603
Equipment under capital leases	75,014	1,255,134	1,363,345
Furniture and other equipment	794,633	833,689	1,168,916
Vehicles	59,797	150,513	153,273
Leasehold improvements	389,798	534,150	945,066
	1,319,242	2,994,332	7,598,203
Less accumulated depreciation and amortization	209,257	538,110	1,170,323
	1,109,985	2,456,222	6,427,880
Other assets			
Transponder rights (net of accumulated amortization of $35,896)	—	—	1,471,755
Deferred offering costs	—	—	171,896
Other	72,292	141,730	140,253
	72,292	141,730	1,783,904
Total assets	$2,333,393	$5,142,407	$23,017,246
Liabilities and Stockholders' Equity[1]			
Current liabilities			
Notes payable	$ 263,611	$ 570,567	$ 235,000
Current maturities of long-term debt	118,419	302,460	490,840
Current portion of obligations under capital leases	36,917	385,717	403,946
Accounts payable	769,988	1,688,753	6,380,586
Accrued liabilities	325,733	349,312	971,217
Income taxes payable	119,000	77,500	5,690,742
Total current liabilities	1,633,668	3,374,309	14,172,331
Long-term debt, less current maturities	275,399	577,046	774,262
Obligations under capital leases, less current portion	21,644	772,686	655,237
Deferred income taxes	15,000	15,000	173,300

EXHIBIT 26.6 (Continued)

	DECEMBER 31, 1984	AUGUST 31, 1985	FEBRUARY 28, 1986
Commitments and contingencies	—	—	—
Stockholders' equity			
Preferred stock—authorized 500,000 shares, $.01 par value; no shares issued and outstanding	—	—	—
Common stock—authorized 30,000,000 shares, $.01 par value; issued and outstanding 8,204,244 shares	82,042	82,042	82,042
Class B—common stock—authorized, issued and outstanding, 4,026,576 shares $.01 par value	40,266	40,266	40,266
Retained earnings	265,374	281,058	7,119,808
Total liabilities and stockholders' equity	387,682	403,366	7,242,116
	$2,333,393	$5,142,407	$23,017,246

SOURCE: *The Prospectus of Home Shopping Network,* Merrill Lynch Capital Markets (May 13, 1986), p. F-3.

¹The original, accompanying notes were deleted.

CASE 27

Inner-City Paint Corporation

DONALD F. KURATKO · NORMAN J. GIERLASINSKI

HISTORY

Stanley Walsh began Inner-City Paint Corporation in a run-down warehouse, which he rented, on the fringe of Chicago's "downtown" business area. The company is still located at the original 1976 site.

Inner-City is a small company that manufactures wall paint. It does not compete with giants such as Glidden and DuPont. There are small paint manufacturers in Chicago that supply the immediate area. The proliferation of paint manufacturers is due to the fact that the weight of the product (fifty-two and one-half pounds per five-gallon container) makes the cost of shipping great distances prohibitive. Inner-City's chief product is flat white wall paint sold in five-gallon plastic cans. It also produces colors on request in fifty-five-gallon containers.

The primary market of Inner-City is the small to medium-sized decorating company. Pricing must be competitive; and until recently, Inner-City had shown steady growth in this market. The slowdown in the housing market combined with a slowdown in the overall economy caused financial difficulty for Inner-City Paint Corporation. Inner-City's reputation had been built on fast service: it frequently supplied paint to contractors within twenty-four hours. Speedy delivery to customers became difficult when Inner-City was required to pay cash on delivery (C.O.D.) for its raw materials.

Inner-City had been operating without management controls or financial controls. It had grown from a very small two-person company with sales of $60,000 annually in 1976, to sales of $1,800,000 and thirty-eight employees in 1981. Stanley Walsh realized that tighter controls within his organization would be necessary if the company was to survive.

EQUIPMENT

Five mixers are used in the manufacturing process. Three large mixers can produce a maximum of 400 gallons, per batch, per mixer. The two smaller mixers can produce a maximum of 100 gallons, per batch, per mixer.

Two lift trucks are used for moving raw materials. The materials are packed in 100-pound bags. The lift trucks also move finished goods, which are stacked on pallets.

This case was prepared by Dr. Donald F. Kuratko, from the College of Business, Ball State University, and Dr. Norman J. Gierlasinski from the School of Business, Central Washington University. It was presented at the 1984 Workshop of the Midwest Society for Case Research. It also appears in *Annual Advances in Business Cases, 1984*, pp. 243–251, edited by Charles Douds. Reprinted by permission.

A small testing lab ensures the quality of materials received and the consistent quality of their finished product. The equipment in the lab is sufficient to handle the current volume of product manufactured.

Transportation equipment consists of two 24-foot delivery trucks and two vans. This small fleet is more than sufficient because many customers pick up their orders to save delivery costs.

FACILITIES

Inner-City performs all operations from one building consisting of 16,400 square feet. The majority of the space is devoted to manufacturing and storage; only 850 square feet is assigned as office space. The building is forty-five years old and in disrepair. It is being leased in three-year increments. The current monthly rent on this lease is $2,700. The rent is low in consideration of the poor condition of the building and its undesirable location in a run-down neighborhood (south side of Chicago). These conditions are suitable to Inner-City because of the dusty, dirty nature of the manufacturing process and the small contribution of the rent to overhead costs.

PRODUCT

Flat white paint is made with pigment (titanium dioxide and silicates), vehicle (resin), and water. The water makes up 72% of the contents of the product. To produce a color, the necessary pigment is added to the flat white paint. The pigment used to produce the color has been previously tested in the lab to ensure consistent quality of texture. Essentially, the process is the mixing of powders with water, then tapping off of the result into five- or fifty-five-gallon containers. Color overruns are tapped off into two-gallon containers.

Inventory records are not kept. The warehouse manager keeps a mental count of what is in stock. He documents (on a lined yellow pad) what has been shipped for the day and to whom. That list is given to the billing clerk at the end of each day.

The cost of the materials to produce flat white paint is $2.40 per gallon. The cost for colors is approximately 40%–50% higher. Five-gallon covered plastic pails cost Inner-City $1.72 each. Fifty-five-gallon drums (with lids) are $8.35 each.

Selling price varies with the quantity purchased. To the average customer, flat white sells at $27.45 for five gallons and $182.75 for 55 gallons. Colors vary in selling price, because of the variety in pigment cost and quantity ordered. Customers purchase on credit and usually pay their invoices in 30 to 60 days. Inner-City telephones the customer after 60 days of nonpayment and inquires when payment will be made.

MANAGEMENT

The President and majority stockholder is Stanley Walsh. He began his career as a house painter and advanced to become a painter for a large decorating company. Mr. Walsh painted mostly walls in large commercial buildings and hospitals. Eventually, he came to believe that he could produce a paint that was less expensive and of higher quality than what was being used. A keen desire to open his own business resulted in the creation of Inner-City Paint Corporation.

Mr. Walsh manages the corporation today in much the same way that he did when the business began. He personally must open *all* the mail, approve *all* payments, and inspect *all* customer billings before they are mailed. He has been unable to detach himself from any detail of the operation and cannot properly delegate authority. As the company has grown, the time element alone has aggravated the situation. Frequently, these tasks are performed days after transactions occur and mail is received.

The office is managed by Mrs. Walsh (Mr. Walsh's mother). Two part-time clerks assist her, and all records are processed manually.

The plant is managed by a man in his twenties, whom Mr. Walsh hired from one of his customers. Mr. Walsh became acquainted with him when the man picked up paint from Inner-City for his previous employer. Prior to the eight months he has been employed by Mr. Walsh as plant manager, his only other experience has been that of painter.

EMPLOYEES

Thirty-five employees (twenty workers are part-time) work in various phases of the manufacturing process. The employees are nonunion, and most are unskilled laborers. They take turns making paint and driving the delivery trucks.

Stanley Walsh does all of the sales work and public relations work. He spends approximately one half of every day making sales calls and answering complaints about defective paint. He is the only salesman. Other salesmen had been employed in the past, but Mr. Walsh felt that they "could not be trusted."

CUSTOMER PERCEPTION

Customers view Inner-City as a company that provides fast service and negotiates on price and payment out of desperation. Mr. Walsh is seen as a disorganized man who may not be able to keep Inner-City afloat much longer. Paint contractors are reluctant to give Inner-City large orders out of fear that the paint may not be ready on a continuous, reliable basis. Larger orders usually go to larger companies that have demonstrated their reliability and solvency.

Rumors abound that Inner-City is in difficult financial straits, that it is unable to pay suppliers, and that it owes a considerable sum for payment on back taxes. All of the above contribute to the customers' serious lack of confidence in the corporation.

FINANCIAL STRUCTURE

Exhibits 27.1 and 27.2 are the most current financial statements of Inner-City Paint Corporation. They have been prepared by the company's accounting service. No audit has been performed, because Mr. Walsh did not want to incur the expense it would have required.

FUTURE

Stanley Walsh wishes to improve the financial situation and reputation of Inner-City Paint Corporation. He is considering the purchase of a computer to organize the business and reduce needless paperwork. He has read about

EXHIBIT 27.1

Balance Sheet for the Year Ended June 30

CURRENT ASSETS		
Cash	$ 1,535	
Accounts receivable (net of allowance for bad debts of $63,400)	242,320	
Inventory	18,660	
Total current assets		$262,515
Machinery and transportation equipment	47,550	
Less: accumulated depreciation	15,500	
Net fixed assets		32,050
Total assets		$294,565
CURRENT LIABILITIES		
Accounts payable	$217,820	
Salaries payable	22,480	
Notes payable	6,220	
Taxes payable	38,510	
Total current liabilities		$285,030
Long-term notes payable		15,000
OWNERS' EQUITY		
Common stock, no par, 1,824 shares outstanding		12,400
Deficit		(17,865)
Total liabilities & owners' equity		$294,565

EXHIBIT 27.2   **Income Statement for the Year Ended June 30**

Sales		$1,784,080
Cost of goods sold		1,428,730
Gross margin		$ 355,350
Selling expenses	$ 72,460	
Administrative expenses	67,280	
President's salary	132,000	
Office manager's salary	66,000	
Total expenses		337,740
Net income		$ 17,610

consultants who are able to quickly spot problems in businesses, but he will not spend more than $300 on such a consultant.

The solution that Mr. Walsh favors most is one that requires him to borrow money from the bank, which he will then use to pay his current bills. He feels that as soon as business conditions improve, he will be able to pay back the loans. He believes that the problems Inner-City is experiencing are due to the overall poor economy and are only temporary.

Southern Cabinet Company

TIMOTHY M. SINGLETON · ROBERT McGLASHAN · MIKE HARRIS

Mike Norris leaned back in his chair and stared alternately between the computer screen's spreadsheet and the view through the front window of his suburban home. The view out the window was only a blur, however, as Mike's attention and energy were focused on the information in front of him on the screen. The numbers were a profit-cost-volume analysis of Southern Cabinet Company (SCC), a manufacturer of kitchen and bathroom cabinets located in a large metropolitan area in the Sunbelt. The President and Chairman of the Board of the small firm was Mike's father-in-law, Bill Martin. Mike and Bill had often discussed the business over the years when convenience and time permitted. Mike's interest was now more serious, however, as he was considering an offer by Bill to go to work in the business. Mike was a recent M.B.A. graduate; Bill's formal education did not extend beyond high school. But they were both impressed that they often came to the same conclusions regarding various aspects of the business, despite their different analytical approaches and perspectives.

Southern Cabinet Company was founded in 1956 by Bill Martin, the current President and Chairman of the Board. In the early days, there were times when Bill was literally the only employee of the company. By 1984 there were 32 people in the shop and six full-time office personnel, including Bill's wife, Laura. SCC builds kitchen and bathroom cabinets for new residential construction only, including townhouses and condominiums. Several characteristics of SCC are believed to make it unique with respect to the competition:

1. The product, although not strictly a custom cabinet, is of better quality than that built by its major competitors.
2. The price of SCC's products is slightly higher than the competition.
3. SCC is smaller (in sales volume) than its competitors.
4. SCC builds a wider variety of cabinet sizes and types than its competitors, and offers over 800 unique pieces.

Prepared by Timothy M. Singleton, Robert McGlashan, and Mike Harris of the University of Houston-Clear Lake. This case was presented at the North American Case Research Association Meeting, 1984. Distributed by the North American Case Research Association. All rights reserved to the authors and the North American Case Research Association. Reprinted by permission of the North American Case Research Association and Timothy M. Singleton.

5. SCC does not carry a finished goods inventory; that is, cabinets are manufactured only after they are ordered by the customer.

RECENT BUSINESS HISTORY	The nature of SCC's operations changed rather dramatically in the past four years. (See Exhibits 28.1 and 28.2.) Even with relatively good economic fortune in many areas of the Sunbelt, many builders and SCC's competitors were hurt badly due to a combination of high interest rates and heavy debt. In contrast, SCC had its best years ever during the early 1980s recession. Operations provided the cash flow to support an increase in sales, and the computer acquired in 1980 handled the additional administrative and management burden necessary for support of the increased volume.

PLANT OPERATIONS	SCC manufactures cabinets with three different wood finishes, although all contain certain common wood products for the shelves and back. The manufacturing process begins after an order has been received, the dimensions of the kitchen at the construction site have been carefully measured, and the order is placed on a schedule. A list of individual pieces (cabinets) that make up the order is produced by the sales department, using a detailed hand drawing of the installation site. This list is entered into a computer program, and "cutting lists," output from the computer, are given to various departments in the plant. These lists describe the parts that must be cut for a particular job order that may contain several work orders. (For example, one job can entail building cabinets for several kitchens.)

Although there are many steps in the assembly-line-like manufacturing procedure, there are a few key steps that can give one a feel for the process. There are six major departments. One cuts the parts for the face frame, the frame that fits to the front of the body of the cabinet. A second department, the Cutting Department, cuts parts for the body of the cabinet. Some of the cut parts require finishing in the Sanding Department; then they are gathered in one location, so that an audit can be made, to verify that all the parts necessary for completion of the work order have been produced. The collection of parts is then moved to the Assembly Department. The cabinets are assembled with staple guns and glue, and the Hardware Department installs the drawer guides and doors. The assembled cabinets are then placed on a dolly and moved to the Paint Department. After they are stained and finished, cabinets are stacked until the customer can take delivery.

All the manufacturing processes are relatively simple tasks, and, with the exception of painting, require no special skills. Most of the labor is unskilled, and from time to time workers can be shifted from one job to another if a

EXHIBIT 28.1   Balance Sheet

(Fiscal Year Begins October 1)	1979	1980	1981	1982	1983	1984 (YEAR TO DATE, APRIL 30)
Assets						
Current assets						
Cash	$ 53,314	$152,524	$236,391	$277,507	$264,094	$ 308,489
Accounts receivable	221,582	160,568	213,671	175,917	248,592	238,887
Merchandise inventory (doors and hardware)	121,419	116,902	180,070	180,886	195,020	214,635
Prepaid expenses	12,789	22,341	20,040	19,044	22,333	23,440
Total	409,104	452,335	650,172	653,354	730,039	785,451
Fixed assets (net)						
Land & building	—	—	—	—	90,941	153,508
Office furniture	3,359	16,915	13,126	25,088	32,695	28,646
Plant equipment	18,662	17,360	22,386	22,490	16,926	15,528
Auto equipment	7,406	47,709	39,215	32,063	21,477	14,766
Other	467	1,582	500	5,000	—	—
Total	29,894	83,566	75,227	84,641	162,039	212,448
Other assets (Including prepaid tax)	1,710	54,027	10,321	24,331	563	45,055
TOTAL ASSETS	440,708	589,928	735,720	762,326	892,641	1,042,954
Liabilities						
Current liabilities						
Accounts payable	76,718	34,282	36,993	30,759	31,824	34,898
Notes payable	35,164	15,281	13,677	13,229	6,745	6,196
Accrued wages, sales commissions, and salary bonuses	46,879	77,995	113,800	74,720	92,935	9,705
Other	6,859	57,523	29,472	12,859	18,768	11,182
Total current liabilities	165,620	185,081	193,942	131,567	150,272	61,981
Long-term liabilities	594	28,518	15,235	2,804	—	—
Net Worth						
Capital stock	14,590	14,590	14,590	15,000	15,000	15,000
Treasury stock	—	—	—	410	410	410
Capital surplus	28	28	28	28	28	28
Retained earnings	162,448	256,183	358,096	460,449	548,926	724,404
Net profit, year to date	97,428	105,528	153,829	152,068	178,005	241,131
Total	274,494	376,329	526,543	627,955	742,369	980,973
TOTAL LIABILITIES AND NET WORTH	$440,708	$589,928	$735,720	$762,326	$892,641	$1,042,954

EXHIBIT 28.2   Income Statements

(Fiscal Year Begins October 1)	1979	1980	1981	1982	1983	1984 YEAR TO DATE APRIL 30, 1984
Sales	$1,541,133	$1,414,931	$1,913,990	$1,914,553	$1,967,429	$1,514,975
Cost of sales	1,195,531	998,568	1,304,707	1,414,781	1,393,861	1,059,338
Gross profit	345,602	416,363	609,283	499,772	573,568	455,637
Operating expenses						
Office and administration	143,262	116,075	138,489	181,542	208,178	134,016
Selling and advertising	48,551	48,092	60,935	62,306	76,023	59,214
Delivery expense	55,585	42,907	63,082	60,101	47,651	36,321
Total operating expense	247,398	207,074	262,506	303,949	331,852	229,551
Net profit from operations	98,204	209,289	346,777	195,823	241,716	226,086
Installation income (Exp)	(776)	415	2,344	1,455	1,371	3,669
Other administrative income	8,341	7,017	8,819	24,153	19,128	11,377
Net operating profit	105,769	216,721	357,940	221,431	262,215	241,132
Incentive bonuses*	16,694	68,090	112,111	69,362	84,210	—
Net profit for federal taxes	89,075	148,631	245,829	152,069	178,005	241,132
Provision for federal taxes	15,911	43,101	91,998	47,871	59,986	—
Net profit after taxes	$ 73,164	$ 105,530	$ 153,831	$ 104,198	$ 118,019	$ 241,132

*Office personnel bonuses based on net operating profit.

worker quits or is ill. Many of the workers in the plant have been with the company over ten years, and a few for over twenty years. Though the average pay is about $6.50 per hour, all workers in the plant participate in a piece-count bonus program on a weekly basis. Starting at 500 pieces, the entire crew receives extra pay for each piece produced. The incremental pay for each extra piece increases gradually for each 100 pieces up to 1,000. For 1,000 pieces and up, the incremental pay per piece is constant. Mike has noted in looking over the past few months' production and pay statistics that the unit labor cost decreases despite the bonus pay until production reaches around 800 to 900 pieces per week. At that point, overtime pay expense begins to be incurred which offsets the benefits of increased volume, and unit labor costs begin to increase. The increase in pay at 1,000 pieces, not counting overtime, is $100 per week per employee if the employee has perfect attendance for the week.

CAN'T LIVE WITH 'EM, BUT CAN'T LIVE WITHOUT 'EM

Like most small companies that have been initiated to the uses of microcomputers and minicomputers, SCC has had its share of problems. Overall, however, SCC has benefited significantly from the use of first a microcomputer and now its Texas Instruments minicomputer. The primary use continues to be the creation of "cutting lists" for use in the plant, as mentioned previously. The accounting system has gradually been placed on the computer over the past year with limited success. The accounting package was built from scratch by Bud Melman, assistant to Linda Sharp (Bill and Laura's administrative assistant), who happens to have extensive programming experience but little actual accounting experience. In fact, to facilitate the program's development Bud took a course in accounting. Most of the "bugs" seem to be out of the system at this point, though occasional problems still lead Laura to have little confidence in the system. A further potential problem with the software is that it is written in a language called TPL, which is unique to Texas Instruments systems, and consequently the average programmer who has developed business software has never heard of TPL. This makes modifying the software much more difficult than it would be if it were written in a more common language. In addition, TPL is not an easy language to use in "database" development, a feature that usually makes business software development much easier. Mike has also noticed that the current software is not documented. There is no explanation within the code the programmer had developed, so a subsequent programmer's attempts to modify the current software will not be easy. SCC's latest system, however, does have a new operating system with the ability to run COBOL, a common computer language used in business. SCC has currently invested about $50,000 in computer hardware and software in the past four years. The question now is what to do about the current software, particularly the accounting software.

KEY PEOPLE AT SCC

If entrepreneurs tend to "march to their own drummer," Bill Martin is no exception. He was born in a small Southern town in 1920. Despite being brought up in what some call a "Bible Belt" region, Bill did not care much for the local religion. He developed an interest in other religious philosophies through the years, as well as an interest in movies and film making. Bill still has color film of Hawaii that he took during the Second World War when he was stationed at Hickam Field. He was learning to fly B-17s when the Japanese attacked in 1941, and later piloted a B-17 with the 8th Air

Force over Germany. In the past ten years, he has produced two full-length films of the homemade variety, and if not for the demands of the business, which he also continues to enjoy, Bill would gladly spend more time with the movie equipment and other hobbies.

Bill had acquired experience in the construction industry while he was growing up and decided to start his own business; he was motivated primarily by a desire to be his own boss, rather than to make a lot of money. Bill runs the company in what most would consider a very relaxed manner, and with an "open door" policy. If he ever gets very excited about anything, he disguises it well. Most people would probably describe him as patient and deliberate. Bill is not at all impulsive, and likes to mull things over carefully before making decisions—a habit that for the most part seems to have served him well.

Laura Martin, Bill's wife of forty-three years, handles the accounting and office administration. Laura seems to enjoy the work as much as Bill and often serves as a sounding board for office and plant employees who discuss business as well as personal matters. Laura is from Bill's home town, and left home after high school to marry Bill in Hawaii in 1941.

Harry Wood, 42, holds the title of Vice-President of Sales, and has been with the company for over ten years. He has an assistant, but Harry does all the direct selling to the customer. Harry has a knack for satisfying the customer before and after the sale, and an excellent ability to qualify potential customers. Bad debts were less than one-half of 1% of sales in 1983.

Linda Sharp, 32, serves as an administrative assistant to Bill and Laura. Linda does a little of everything, and through the years has gradually assumed more and more administrative responsibility around the office. She has consistently done a good job and demonstrated talent in many areas, including public relations. Harry has even mentioned that he would like to have her in sales. Linda now has an assistant, but she still often handles the front desk and other general office duties, such as answering the phone. Linda has been with the company for eight years, and she and Harry are considered to be loyal and invaluable employees.

The key people in the plant have been with the company over twenty-five years. Jim Mayo, 70, manages the materials flow and performs maintenance on most of the plant's equipment. Despite his age, Jim seems to have more energy than almost anyone in the plant. Oscar Wyatt, 58, is general shop foreman and supervises the lead people who oversee the six departments in the plant.

Mike Norris, 34, has worked for six years as a senior systems engineer for an aircraft simulator manufacturer and has a Masters degree in mathematics as well as an M.B.A. Mike's previous experience around construction has been limited to part-time work for a painting contractor during summers when he was an undergraduate student. His recent experience is primarily in software design of various aircraft systems, and he has approximately three years' experience as a department supervisor with fifteen people. His duties now include customer contact, report generation, planning, hiring new employees, and employee evaluation. He began the M.B.A. program at a local university primarily as a diversion from the normal day to day activities and because he felt it was a good use of his extra time. As he began to accumulate hours in the business program, he began to think more seriously about changing careers and going to work for Southern Cabinets.

RECENT DEVELOPMENTS

Sales have been growing steadily over the years; the last five years' sales history is shown in the operating statements in Exhibit 28.2. Though sales leveled off in 1983, projected sales for the current fiscal year are around $2.5 million. The average price per piece in 1983 was around $63, and the volume was 31,000 pieces. Bill sees a lack of space to store the finished product (a recurring problem) as a hindrance to the increase of sales much beyond current levels. Though the customer takes delivery fairly soon after the order is completed, more sales mean more product to store at one time, and this can be particularly troublesome during winter if the weather is bad and the customer cannot take delivery readily. Bill leases space on a monthly basis, to help alleviate this problem. This leads to increases in fixed as well as variable costs that need to be carefully analyzed. Recent cost of the leased storage space was $1,000 per month. This high level of business is a new experience for SCC, and it has not been necessary until recently to give these problems close attention.

The lease on the current building has increased dramatically over the past two years from $3,500 to $5,600 per month, and the current lease runs out within six months. Seeing these problems coming on, Bill bought three acres of land near the present building a little over a year ago for $90,000 with the intention of eventually building his own facility. Architectural and engineering plans have been completed, bringing the total current investment to $150,000. The cost of the new building is estimated at around $800,000, down from about $1 million in the original estimate. In addition to solving the problems with space (the new building plans show an increase of 40% in floor space), the new building includes plans for a conveyor that will more efficiently transfer the assembled products to the paint department, and greatly simplify the paint department operations. Materials handling and storage, scheduling, and a myriad of other problems would also be alleviated with the extra space in the shop. A 40% increase in floor space will also satisfy a need for increased office space. The computer, which is housed in a 6-foot-tall cabinet, and a printer currently occupy a space of less than 75 square feet that also serves as a coffee room and lunch-time gathering place for plant employees who use a microwave oven in the same room. In addition, all employees share two restrooms that are located in the office portion of the building.

To finance the new building, Bill will have to borrow heavily and believes that he ought to hold on to as much cash as possible, to provide a safe level of working capital necessary to support current or increased sales levels. The monthly payment on the new building with a thirty-year loan is expected to be around $10,000. Bill has not borrowed any money for about three years and has not aggressively sought a loan, but he foresees no serious problem in getting the money. His major concern is whether to actually go ahead with the building at the present time. Business for the current year could produce an increase in profit from operations of around 100%, with an increase in sales volume of 25%. Prospects for the next fiscal year are considerably more uncertain, with many economists predicting a downturn in housing starts. Complicating the decision are strong indications that the land Bill purchased for the building may have tripled in value because of rapid development of surrounding property. The land might be worth more in the long run without a building on the property.

In past years, Bill has often wished the company had the financial and physical capacity to carry some finished inventory. He has always considered this a very risky business, however, because it would require more debt than he wanted or could carry, or because of the space limitations mentioned previously. The average material cost in a piece in 1983 was about $24 out of a total variable cost per piece of around $32. The $32 includes variable selling and administrative costs as well as manufacturing costs. Bill's work force is rather stable throughout the year despite rather wide fluctuations in production, and Mike compiled these cost figures assuming direct labor as a fixed cost. Clearly, it would not be possible to carry inventory on every cabinet. A decision would have to be made about which cabinets to build for the finished goods inventory. Complicating this decision is the fact that SCC uses several types of paint finishes on the cabinets, so it would seem to be impractical to store the cabinets in a completely finished condition. A considerable portion of the assembled cabinets, however, are shipped without paint finishing.

Several factors intrigued Mike about leasing extra space as a temporary measure rather than building a new facility, as well as possibly carrying some finished goods inventory:

1. Harry Wood has indicated that if the price of the product was a little more in line with the competition, sales could increase significantly.

2. The current work force, which in 1984 has shown the capacity to produce 60% over the average 1983 monthly production, might be more efficiently utilized if the work were spread more evenly over the year, so that the level at peak activity decreased with the potential of increased overall production.

3. It appears that profit from operations could increase substantially with only a moderate increase in sales volume from current levels.

4. Customer uncertainty concerning SCC's ability to provide the product quickly and reliably would be reduced.

Mike is uncertain about the desirability of financing extra inventory for other reasons:

1. A more sophisticated inventory control system, which might affect current computer software needs, would have to be implemented.

2. Sales volume across the industry is highly dependent on swings in the economy, and it might be difficult to avoid getting stuck with unwanted inventory.

3. The sudden growth in the level of operations is beginning to strain the administrative capacity of management.

The current, successful profit picture might indicate that SCC should only seek to maintain current sales level while the entire organization adjusts to the growth in the level of operations—adopt a temporary philosophy of "If it ain't broke, don't fix it." If operations continue to produce similar results over the next year or two, the financial flexibility of the company will be greatly enhanced.

TO SELL OR NOT TO SELL

On a recent trip to the plant, Mike was asked by Bill to sit in on a meeting between Bill and Charlie White, a local business broker. Charlie had in the past discussed with Bill the possibility of selling the business. Though Bill was not considering the idea seriously, he liked Charlie, and was interested in what he had to say about the value of the business. In particular, on this day, Charlie was bringing some figures that he had analyzed with the help of a "young man" with a degree in finance. Mike had done his own analysis, and was interested that Charlie had valued the business from the point of view of projected cash flow as well as current asset value. Mike's figures closely matched Charlie's in measuring the estimated present value of cash flow. There was apparently an interested buyer who had seen the last five years' operating statements and had ideas about continuing the cabinet operation as well as using the equipment for other purposes. Though the tax consequences for Bill of a sale had not been analyzed, the amount mentioned was sufficient enough to provide Bill and Laura with a comfortable retirement. The figure mentioned did not include the current cash in the business, which Bill would keep, nor did it allow for the appreciation of the land Bill had purchased the year before. Bill and Laura, however, feel they would have a hard time being comfortable with the retired life. Laura has often said the business "keeps us young." Furthermore, they are naturally concerned about the fate of some of the people in the plant who have been loyal to them for almost three decades.

WHAT'S NEXT?   Bill Martin wants to continue operating SCC for several years. He currently sees SCC as being on the threshold of becoming a much larger company if some of the opportunities and obstacles described above are handled skillfully. Though there seem to be strong indications that SCC may have found a niche in the market with builders who seek to put extra quality in their homes, the size and stability of this market are uncertain. Meanwhile, Bill and Laura have the feeling that a company must change and grow, if it is to remain viable.

UMC, Inc.

ALBERT O. TROSTEL

UMC, Inc. has gone through a very turbulent period during the past five years. On June 26, 1981, it filed for bankruptcy under Chapter 11 of the bankruptcy law. A year later the court finally confirmed a plan of reorganization whereby all the unsecured debts would be paid off in full in twenty equal quarterly installments, beginning on November 1, 1982. As a part of getting the creditors to agree to the reorganization, the President of UMC, Terry Tomann, had to upgrade the quality of his management and install controls to prevent the runaway loss of control in assets that the company had experienced in the several years prior to the filing for bankruptcy. Now, in the summer of 1986, as UMC approaches completion of repaying those debts, Terry Tomann and the rest of management, as well as the directors, are debating how the company should proceed.

HISTORY

To 1981

Under the name of Ultra Machining Company, UMC, Inc. began operation in 1968 in a western suburb of Minneapolis. Initially the company operated out of the garage of Terry Tomann, UMC's President and owner. Its business has been to provide precision machining services to customers in the computer, aerospace, and medical instruments businesses, and to general industrial markets in which the manufacturer requires precision components to be machined out of difficult metals.

UMC's operations expanded rapidly: net sales increased from $574,000 for the fiscal year ending March 31, 1974, to $4,513,000 for the year ended March 28, 1980. (See Exhibit 29.1.) During this period, sales growth was spectacular, with annual volume increases in excess of 50% not uncommon. Unfortunately, as often happens when an entrepreneur with technical skills experiences the rapid growth of his organization, UMC's expansion was uncontrolled and unplanned, more the result of meeting whatever a customer seemed to desire rather than of any well-thought-out concept of what the company did well. Increased demand drove increased acquisition of ma-

This case was prepared by Professor Albert O. Trostel of the College of St. Thomas. It was presented at the North American Case Research Meeting, 1986. Distributed by the North American Case Research Association. All rights reserved to the authors and the North American Case Research Association. Reprinted by permission of the author and the North American Case Research Association.

EXHIBIT 29.1　　UMC, Financial Statements, 1976–1986
(Dollar Amounts in Thousands)

INCOME STATEMENT	1986	1985	1984	1983	1982	1981	1980	1979	1978	1977	1976
Income											
Net sales	$4,299	$3,491	$2,676	$2,791	$4,049	$4,052	$4,513	$3,293	$2,013	$1,192	$608
Cost of sales	$3,408	$2,785	$2,440	$2,232	$3,247	$3,597	$3,627	$2,587	$1,738	$933	$519
Gross profit	$891	$706	$236	$559	$802	$455	$886	$706	$275	$259	$89
Percent of gross profit	20.7%	20.2%	8.8%	20.0%	19.8%	11.2%	19.6%	21.4%	13.7%	21.7%	14.6%
Operating expenses											
Sales & promotion	$75	$51	$41	$58	$106	$157	$131	$116	$56	$38	$20
General and administration	$336	$281	$353	$378	$443	$380	$271	$262	$97	$94	$79
Total operating expenses	$411	$332	$394	$436	$549	$537	$402	$378	$153	$132	$99
Earnings from operations	$480	$374	($158)	$123	$253	($82)	$484	$328	$122	$127	($10)
Other income (expenses)											
Gain on sale of equipment	$6	$19	$11	($3)	($74)	$3	$0	$0	$0	$0	$0
Interest income	$2	$1	$0	$4	$8	$1	$0	$1	$2	$0	$0
Interest expense	($156)	($196)	($185)	($189)	($201)	($285)	($194)	($110)	($36)	($16)	($13)
Miscellaneous	$9	($46)	$0	$11	$39	$8	$0	$0	$0	$0	$0
Total other income	($139)	($222)	($174)	($177)	($228)	($273)	($194)	($109)	($34)	($16)	($13)
Earnings pretax	$341	$152	($332)	($54)	$25	($355)	$290	$219	$88	$111	($23)
Income taxes	$140	$60	($13)	($5)	$5	($157)	$55	$27	$0	$0	$0
Net before extra	$201	$92	($319)	($49)	$20	($198)	$235	$192	$88	$111	($23)
Extraordinary	$78	$56	$0	$0	$0	$0	$0	$0	$0	$0	$0
Net after extraordinary	$279	$148	($319)	($49)	$20	($198)	$235	$192	$88	$111	($23)

(Continued)

EXHIBIT 29.1 (Continued)

BALANCE SHEET	1986	1985	1984	1983	1982	1981	1980	1979	1978	1977	1976
Assets											
Current assets											
Cash	$5	($61)	($5)	$51	$170	$0	$12	$68	$16	($11)	($7)
Accounts receivable	$174	$346	$329	$198	$270	$460	$519	$577	$330	$215	$73
Inventory¹	$839	$311	$276	$342	$368	$340	$380	$198	$75	$0	$0
Other	$79	$51	$40	$57	$83	$206	$97	$31	$13	$3	$1
Total current assets	$1,097	$647	$640	$648	$891	$1,006	$1,008	$874	$434	$207	$67
Property & equipment											
Building	$615	$607	$605	$606	$606	$606	$514	$227	$212	$48	$48
Shop equipment	$2,114	$2,063	$2,060	$1,857	$1,844	$2,386	$2,046	$1,340	$824	$385	$248
Other	$146	$109	$125	$107	$113	$103	$71	$52	$40	$40	$33
	$2,875	$2,779	$2,790	$2,570	$2,563	$3,095	$2,631	$1,619	$1,076	$473	$329
Accumulated depreciation	($1,782)	($1,556)	($1,382)	($1,158)	($916)	($870)	($589)	($370)	($214)	($156)	($117)
Net property & equipment	$1,093	$1,223	$1,408	$1,412	$1,647	$2,225	$2,042	$1,249	$862	$317	$212
Other assets	$19	$19	$16	$6	$0	$0	$0	$0	$5	$0	$0
Total assets	$2,209	$1,889	$2,064	$2,066	$2,538	$3,231	$3,050	$2,123	$1,301	$524	$279

Liabilities and Stockholders' Equity

Current liabilities

Accounts payable	$162	$97	$179	$77	$91	$522	$410	$312	$178	$61	$39
Accrued expenses	$190	$145	$168	$104	$133	$121	$92	$126	$24	$10	$2
Deferred revenues	$321	$33	$0	$0	$0	$0	$0	$0	$0	$0	$0
Current portion long term debt	$333	$352	$310	$253	$329	$481	$270	$190	$0	$15	$23
Notes payable	$98	$277	$292	$135	$265	$505	$244	$228	$42	$9	$4
Other	$33	$0	$0	$0	$5	$78	$33	$63	$0	$0	$0
Total current liabilities	$1,137	$904	$949	$569	$823	$1,707	$1,049	$919	$244	$95	$68
Deferred income tax	$51	$9	$5	$15	$15	$15	$85	$66	$0	$0	$0
Long term debt	$545	$800	$1,081	$1,134	$1,303	$1,132	$1,342	$799	$675	$200	$91
Equity	$476	$176	$29	$348	$397	$377	$574	$339	$382	$229	$120
Total liabilities & equity	$2,209	$1,889	$2,064	$2,066	$2,538	$3,231	$3,050	$2,123	$1,301	$524	$279

The inventory for the end of fiscal 1986 is $414,000 higher than normal because one large customer has held up shipments. These parts are mostly completed and sitting in the finished goods inventory. UMC has received progress payments, which are reflected in the "deferred revenues" current liability. That $414,000 is on the books at its cost value, which is approximately 55% of its sales value. Management of UMC anticipates the customer will request shipment of this entire inventory during the first half of fiscal 1987.

chinery to meet that demand; the machinery was acquired just for that one application. UMC took on a variety of different kinds of work that dictated a similarly wide variety of machines, and the utilization of any one machine was therefore quite vulnerable to any change in a customer's demand. When business conditions did weaken, UMC suddenly could not keep all that machinery busy. Fiscal year ending March 31, 1981 showed a loss of $198,000 and by June of 1981 the company was in bankruptcy court.

John Giere, the head of Production, describes the situation in the Twin Cities (Minneapolis and St. Paul) during these years as follows.

> Control Data really set this town on fire [for machining companies]. They created a tremendous demand, and it was possible to be in business simply by being good at machining. It really didn't take business skills. Now that CDC and MPI (Magnetic Peripherals Incorporated, a joint venture of Control Data and Honeywell) are not doing so well there are a lot of companies here dying.

1981 to Present

In the years since the bankruptcy agreement, the firm has gone through two major periods. In the first, Terry sold off some of his equipment to raise cash and reduce financing costs, hired professional managers, engaged consultants on quality control and planning, reorganized the management of the company, and established a true outside board of directors. The company seemed to make some progress initially, but with the continuation of the recession into 1983, he had to pull back more, simply to survive. To cut way back on his overhead, he cut back on the work force, jettisoned the general manager he had hired nineteen months before to upgrade his management, converted the sales manager to a commission representative, discharged all but two of his board and deferred plans for further hiring. Those draconian cuts finally reduced the break-even point to a level of sales that UMC could maintain, and since that time the company has been moderately profitable. Actually, fiscal 1986, the most recently completed year, was much more profitable than shown because of some very conservative accounting of one job that was completed but held up for shipment.

The rest of this case will describe those two periods in greater detail. That description will give the reader a more thorough sense of the nature of UMC today.

NATURE OF THE BUSINESS

UMC is what one would describe as a job shop, supplying other manufacturers. Its mixture of machinery and people gives it particular capabilities for the production of parts for its customers on a job basis. UMC produces no final products; all of its products are components that go into the manufacture of something else.

The possibility for business starts when a manufacturer designs some product for which the making of certain parts will require specialized skills, skills that manufacturer does not have. Alternatively, the company has been purchasing the part from one or several other suppliers and, to reduce its costs, would like to find a vendor who can give some combination of a lower price and higher quality. In either case, the job shop is really an extension of the manufacturing capability of the customer.

The first step in the process of obtaining new business is for the purchasing agent of the customer to give the job shop a print and an indication of the quantities desired by delivery date. The purchasing agent knows about the job shop because of past experience or sales calls that have occurred. Brochures, often left off in previous sales calls, describe the job shop's capabilities and are often very useful at this time. In some companies the design engineers talk with job shop sales people; in which case they advise the buyer to ask for quotations. The sales task for the job shop in this phase of the solicitation is to convince the purchasing agent and/or the engineers that this job shop has the requisite skills.

For UMC, Terry makes most of the sales calls that develop new business. There is a manufacturers' representative who calls on customers in the region around Minnesota, but not much of the new business is attributable to his efforts. Bill, the General Manager until 1983, occasionally visited customers. Birchard, Controller, and Giere today occasionally visit established customers and both of them have frequent telephone contact with customers on issues of delivery and quality.

Once UMC has the invitation to quote, someone analyzes the specifications on the print, develops a procedure to make the part, estimates the costs of making the part, and makes a quotation of price and delivery capability. At UMC the engineers' job is to perform this function of making estimates and quotes, but Terry is in on all the quotes at some stage in the process. Often, however, he does the entire quotation job himself. Delivery commitments are difficult to make at this stage because the order is not in hand, but production control can make at least a tentative commitment of production capacity. Because delivery is a part of the quotation, there is pressure on production to over-promise production capacity, just as airlines are under pressure to overbook.

Sometimes the purchasing agent merely accepts the lowest bid. At other times the purchasing agent may consider other factors such as reputation for quality and dependability of delivery. In any event, the buyer determines whether the quotation is attractive and if so, places an order. At this time UMC makes a commitment of production capacity to a delivery schedule, but even at this time the customer's requirements for delivery are subject to significant change.

Those factors of attractiveness can cover a wide range of characteristics, depending on the customer's needs. Obviously, the price must be competitive, but if the firm has an especially good reputation for meeting the requirements of the customer, price can become much less important. Also, strategic considerations can result is a supplier getting the business even though neither the reputation nor the price is the best. For example, a customer might want to make sure that there are competent machinists close to his plant and would therefore favor suppliers that are located close by in hopes that in time the proximity will provide better service. Customers who are moving rapidly in state-of-the-art technology need to have suppliers that are very responsive and willing to devote special attention to solving their particular problems. Speed in solving those special problems may yield business. In any case, because of the wide range of reasons a job shop like UMC can win business, it cannot possibly be all things to all customers. It must determine what it does best and do it well.

As one can see from the above discussion, different job-shop machinists can compete with different collections of skills. On the other hand, there are certain abilities that all of them must have in order to survive. In the first place, they must know their costs, so that they do not bid themselves into a losing position or lose the business by overpricing. Second, they must be able to deliver when they say they will. Third, the parts must meet the customers' specifications.

In the spring of 1982 Terry recruited an outside Board of Directors. That Board consisted of a consultant and an executive recruiter with whom he was working, a President of an electronic component company, and a college professor with business management experience in family-held companies. Terry and the recently recruited General Manager were the two inside Board members. As the board began its work, it was important to acquaint the members with the company. In June of 1982, Terry wrote the following memorandum to the Board to assist the members in understanding the company.

We must know who we are before we can determine our competition.

UMC is a medium-sized, precision machining job shop, well diversified, meaning we have a good variety of different machining capabilities. Our quality is good, but our machining expertise on a scale from 1–10 ranks about 7.5. We have good personnel, but in almost all departments we lack the "top-notch individuals". From past experience with good shops, usually 2–3 people out of every 10 will be considered top-notch. We do have personnel that can be developed, primarily through more experience and outside exposure, but we are about 2–3 years away from these people being fully developed.

To strengthen UMC's position without better people, we must create an atmosphere of being part of the total picture. This will keep them more involved with UMC's goals and put us in a more competitive picture with our customers.

It appears as if we could be part of our own competition. Recent years of uncontrolled growth has forced us into a pattern of no growth, even a significant cut-back. During this no-growth time we find ourselves unable to purchase equipment which would make us more productive and competitive.

Our main competition comes from other precision machining job shops similar to UMC with annual sales ranging from $2–15 million. Small shops aren't likely to receive large, long-run contracts which are our bread and butter. Large shops lose their ability to turn a job around in a fair amount of time. The customer finds himself being less important and not getting the attention that he wants. Maybe one reason for the lack of attention shown a customer in a larger shop is that they usually have some of their own products and feel more independent.

Some of our competitors will tool up for a customer's part at their own expense and devote their own machinery for a long period, taking the risk that the job will last and pay them back.

Other competition comes from customers' in-house machining capabilities. However, customers that are very large usually are unable to run their in-house machining facilities profitably, and are therefore not considered real competitors. Medium- to small-sized customers usually run a profitable machining facility because management is much closer to the action.

We occasionally lose business because a customer's part was converted over to plastic molding, stamping, powdered metal, castings, etc. More competition comes from laser machining. Eight years after the introduction of the laser, the high-powered laser is considered a machine tool that is capable of improving productivity.

A 1980 Delphi survey published by SME indicates that between 1980 and 1990 the number of U.S. companies implementing CAD/CAM (Computer-aided design/Computer-aided manufacture) will jump from 10% to 25%. This rapid advancement has created an urgent need to educate persons on successful applications of CAD/CAM technology. Robotics is another area of competition that is growing rapidly. It has the ability to increase production significantly.

Keeping up with new technology is going to be much more of a problem in the future than it is now. When you are a small shop, the customer doesn't usually expect you to keep current with the latest technology. When you are a large concern going after the large-volume jobs, it is expected by the customer that you will find more efficient means of producing their products. If you do not, you will eventually lose their business. That is why it is most important to have an engineering group that has an experienced background, is eager to be exposed to the latest technologies, and will sit down in brainstorming sessions periodically to find ways to reducing costs for the customer and UMC.

The following comments come from the notes of one of those directors, made after the first several directors' meetings in 1982.

The company has business consisting of a very large number of individual items, although there seems to be a high concentration in the top business. Three customers with rather few parts numbers account for 80% of the business. . . . A great deal of the cost of making a part seems to depend on the skill and attention to detail of the individual machinist. The shop is non-union and Terry has made it clear that the company's continued survival depends on their being able to continue that way. . . . They do not really know where they are making their money. The cost system is not very good. It appears that they make their bids based on some calculation of burden rates by machine center that Terry developed manually, but whatever company cost system that they have is not used at all. Some recently acquired software has not come up to expectations, but they do not even have a person knowledgable in cost on the payroll who could install such a system. . . . There is a fair amount of concern expressed about their quality. They were running a quality seminar while we were there. . . . They also expressed concern for their lack of ability to deliver on time, and realized that on-time delivery was an important aspect of quality. . . . The organization is very much in flux as they work out the division of responsibilities between Bill, the new "General Manager," and Terry. Dean (one of the outside Directors who knows Terry) commented that Terry is the kind of person who wants to get into everything.*

Two years later, one year after the severe cutback in overhead in the fall of 1983, Terry and the Directors took another look at the nature of UMC's business. Although there had been significant progress in the intervening time in the establishment of a cost system, the nature of the business was very much the same as it had been in 1982. In one of these meetings Terry talked about the business as he saw it and the two other Directors and John Birchard, the Controller, noted his comments and added their observations. In the second meeting they invited a retired purchasing executive to comment on UMC from the customer's perspective. The following sections are taken from the minutes of those meetings.

Directors' Meeting of December 7, 1984

An attempt was then made to describe common characteristics of UMC's major current customers, including "Process Control," "Jet Engine Sub 2," "Computer," "Munitions," "Industrial 1," and "Flight Control."† The general characteristics noted were (1) large company, (2) computer/aerospace/defense industries, (3) long-run jobs, not short-run, prototype work, (4) close tolerances and/or complex operations, and (5) tough materials such as stainless steel.

It was noted that most of our major customers will not put work into the "small" shops, effectively eliminating 75% of our competition from this marketplace. A brief breakdown of competitors in the machining industry was given, as follows:

- Little guy—Five–ten employees. There is a large number of this kind of shop.

- Medium guy—Approximately thirty employees. This is a very critical stage for machining companies, as they experience severe growth pains.

Author's note: Bill was an engineer approximately Terry's age who had spent most of his career in the engineering departments of companies considerably larger than UMC. He came to UMC from a company that manufactures telecommunications components and was also a member of the Governor's Council on High Technology.

†Customers' names are disguised in this case, but each has a name corresponding to its principal industry. See Exhibits 29.4 and 29.5 for more information on the major customers.

- Big guy—100 plus employees. There are rather few firms in this category, but they tend to be the most profitable.
- UMC—Sixty employees.

UMC's long-run jobs can be generally described as "tough jobs" in that they have multiple operations, close tolerances, and tough materials to work with. Terry noted that this description fits about 80% of UMC's work.

The question of "how do you get new orders from new customers" was briefly addressed. It was important to (1) be persistent (As a rule of thumb it took eight contacts with a buyer prior to any action.), and (2) contact new purchasing agents soon after changes are made. It was generally agreed that successfully opening a new account of the caliber of our existing major customers was worth a lot, at a minimum of $250,000 in sales annually. With this knowledge, it seems that UMC's sales effort should be carefully targeted and managed. While no effort was made to specify exactly which companies UMC should set as targets, it was noted that in the computer industry, there are a number of large, reputable companies that are not customers of UMC.

We then turned to alternative methods UMC might adopt in developing new accounts. Either we develop a relationship with a manufacturer's representative who services the area that we have established as an expansion area, or Terry can pack his bags and do the calling himself. This was seen as not a good method since the follow-up needed to open a new account was considered impossible. . . .

Terry expressed a concern [about a concerted program to develop new business]. If we get the new business, how can we fit it into our already loaded machines? Which comes first, new business or machining capacity? It was noted that information regarding the capacity situation must be available in order to determine the need for additional equipment. . . . There seem to be two different kinds of sales solicitation: (1) planned sales in which we seek on a long-term basis to get certain kinds of jobs for certain kinds of machines. These will tend to be longer-run jobs and have longer lead times (enough time to purchase a machine if necessary), and (2) fill-in sales, used to fill in gaps in capacity utilization. These will have short lead times and smaller quantities, and we would sell only where we have an identified capacity. UMC's goal would seem to be to increase the portion of its business that could be called "planned sales."

Directors' Meeting, December 12, 1984

The major source of information was a retired buyer. The buyer made the following comments about his ex-employer, a large, multinational company:

- Their buyers are engineers trained in purchasing.
- The buyers are given performance goals in quality, delivery, and price.

They must find suppliers which support the company's projects, and their salary increases are tied directly to the performance of the suppliers.

- They favor dealing with employees of the suppliers, not with independent sales reps.

- They will work with a supplier to ensure that projects are moving on schedule. They will often work with a supplier to get a job placed in his shop, even though the initial quoted price might be high, if the buyer has a good feeling about the supplier's ability to perform and wants to place the work there. In dealing with government contracts, buyers are under considerable pressure to take the lowest bid, although they may go with a slightly higher price if they can provide support for that decision.

- Military specifications and requirements are more rigid than for most civilian work. Where many of UMC's customers may accept parts not produced to specifications (through the use of deviations) we and the government are much less tolerant of mistakes and require more "perfect" parts. . . .

- They are not likely to start doing their own machining because they have very high overhead, whereas UMC's overhead is lower. . . .

- UMC is seen as a producer of "moderately sophisticated" components. Military aircraft parts with tolerances measured in 0.0001 inches are tighter than normal for UMC, although UMC does run some pretty tight work. Many shops are capable of producing more sophisticated parts than UMC.

- In general, it is difficult for a company like UMC to break into the supplier group for a large company. The most effective method of advertising and soliciting new accounts is through word-of-mouth advertising by satisfied customers. A good brochure showing current capabilities is important.

Another ex-buyer who had bought from UMC had the following comments on the market for machining.

The requirements of the customers vary over a wide range. On one end of the spectrum are the very large companies with extensive design capability on their staff and who manufacture a product in a volume large enough to require fairly steady production. This company is going to require from its supplier mostly the ability to produce to the required quality level at the lowest possible cost. The supplier does not participate much in the design process, but rather quotes on a drawing supplied by the customer. Because the supplier will have an extended run and because fractions of a cent can have a significant impact on whether that supplier will get the business, that supplier will tend to have two characteristics. First, it will be larger in order to handle the volume and secondly, it will be more specialized in order to most efficiently use its engineering staff on the one hand and its production staff on the other. Such a supplier will be strong on process engineering talent which will be able to reduce the requirements specified in the drawing to process sheets and routings that will represent accurately what the company can do. Production people, then, must have the requisite skills to consistently accomplish according to specifications at the lowest possible cost.

At the other end of the spectrum are the customers that require very short runs. Sometimes these are aerospace companies, but medical technology companies would also fall into this category. These companies seldom order in quantities above a few hundred parts, often much less than that, maybe even three or four pieces at a time. These companies tend to depend much more on the process engineering capability of the supplier and that company's ability to convert functional specifications (rather than a highly specified drawing) into a finished product quickly. A supplier to this sort of customer will tend to be a smaller shop and will need to rely on the skills of the technicians and operators to make the adjustments necessary to making a good product "on the fly." Because there are so few parts, the customer is not likely to be very price sensitive. For example, in aerospace work performance is primary, and price is quite secondary. Volumes are likewise very low. What that customer needs are the skills and the flexibility to produce the required quality and make it available quickly.

Consequently, at the extremes there are two distinctly different kinds of suppliers based on two very different customer requirements. At the one end will be the large shop with elegant control systems and a high level of specialization and at the other end will be the small shop that trades off the ability to produce at the lowest cost for flexibility and responsiveness. When our business changed (i.e., the customer's business) from one requiring that special ability for the short runs to one requiring regular, longer runs, we found that we had to assemble a whole new set of suppliers. The small machining companies that had been supplying us told us that they simply were not interested in that longer-run business.

Independent machining companies have an additional threat to their business. Not only do the customers constantly evaluate whether it is cheaper to do the machining themselves, but the changes in technology and thinking on organization of manufacturing is driving down the volume at which a company will consider doing the work in house. The machines are getting smarter, which means that the customer does not have to have such skilled people to start making the parts. That customer can purchase much more of the skill that the outside supplier traditionally sold simply by buying one of these smarter, computer-controlled machines. Secondly, with the onset of "cellular manufacturing," companies are setting up several fairly self-contained units which operate on lower volumes rather than require a large volume on one specialized machine. Consequently, they start considering making rather than buying at a much lower volume.

To be true, not all companies are driven to resolve the "make versus buy" decision in favor of buying a machine and making. Even though the numbers may look very favorable for making, some customers, as a matter of policy, will simply not want to invest in that kind of specialized technology. For example, a medical instruments company may determine that to pay attention to machining technology might be a diversion from paying attention to the medical technology, which is their true lifeblood.

One of the most difficult aspects in analyzing this business has been to describe just what is UMC's business. As one can see from reading the minutes, there is a kind of a chicken and egg dilemma. On the one hand, it is very difficult to solicit business for current delivery if the company does not have the equipment in the shop that can run that business efficiently enough to allow the company to bid competitively. On the other hand, without a sense that there is significant demand for a certain capability, it is extremely risky to invest in new machinery. How then should such a company manage its search for new business and its upgrading of technology? More expensive machinery like the Mori-Sieki enables UMC to lower its costs and improve its quality, but one piece of business is seldom enough to justify the best new machine. Consequently, UMC can reduce its risk by acquiring new machines that can take on some of the business already in house, thereby producing a general improvement in quality and cost. To what degree, then, should a company like UMC search for new business on the basis of what its present business would require in improved machines and to what degree should UMC buy machines for business that it does not presently have but believes will be good in the future?

As a beginning to understanding where the capabilities of this company might lie, Exhibit 29.2 is a listing of the machines that UMC has ("Major

---

EXHIBIT 29.2

Major Facilities

CNC LATHES

(1) Mori-Sieki SL-1A; 6000 rpm spindle, 12 station turret, CRT, and tailstock.

(1) Mazak Tape Lathe; 22″ chucking, 14 station, shaft work up to 4′ with CRT. (M-4)

(1) Mazak Tape Lathe; 22″ chucking, shaft work up to 6′ long. (M-4)

(1) Mazak Tape Lathe; 3-L, 20″ chucking.

(1) Mazak Tape Lathe; 2-L, 12″ chucking.

(1) Hardinge HNC, super-precision chucker.

(2) Hardinge Automatic Chucker.

MANUAL LATHES

(2) Fuji Automatic Lathes, 12″ swing.

(2) Mazak Automatic Chucker, 12″ swing.

(4) Hardinge Chuckers.

(1) Hardinge high-precision toolroom lathe.

(1) Tudor Engine Lathe, 15″ swing, 41″ between centers.

(1) Webb Engine Lathe, 10″ swing, 36″ between centers.

CNC MILLING MACHINES

(1) Matsuura MC-760V, vertical machining center; complete with high-speed spindle, full <u>4th axis</u> capability, and 30 tool magazine.

(1) Matsuura MC-500V, vertical machining center; complete with 20 tool magazine, 6000 rpm spindle, and Erickson Model 400 rigid clamp indexer.

(1) Mazak V-5 machining center with 24 station tool changer.

(2) Acroloc machining center with 12 station tool changer.

(2) Bridgeport, with Bandit CNC tape controller.

(1) Wells Tape, 500 G.E. N/C controlled vertical milling machine with <u>4th axis</u>.

MANUAL MILLING MACHINES:

(6) Bridgeport milling machines with digital readouts

(2) Horizontal milling machines.

SUPPORT EQUIPMENT:

(1) Myford between-center grinder.

(1) Tool and cutter grinder.

(1) Marvel power saw, 12″ × 16″ full-automatic.

(1) Horizontal broach, 75 ton, 6′ stroke.

(3) Drill presses, with multiple drill heads.

(2) Bank's of four ½″ drill presses; various other single spindle drill presses.

(4) Leadscrew tappers.

(1) 6′ dia., vibrating tumbler.

(1) 18″ dia., vibrating tumbler.

INSPECTION EQUIPMENT:

(1) Cordax 1000 coordinate measuring machine with XYZ axis and MPP2 computer.

(1) Scherr-Tumico optical comparator, 14″.

(1) Scherr-Tumico optical comparator, 30″.

(1) Bendix profilometer.

(1) Rockwell hardness tester.

(1) Mitutoyo comparator.

(2) Master gage block sets.

(3) Compter gages.
Bendix electronic gaging.
Diatest bore gages.
Bendix Sheffield air gages.

A partial list of special alloy metals commonly used at UMC, Inc. for the aerospace, missile, aircraft, chemical, and other associated industries is as follows:

Astroloy

Hastelloy X

Inconel 625

(Continued)

EXHIBIT 29.2 (Continued)

> Incoloy 700
> Incoloy 800
> Nickel 200
> Titanium
> Waspaloy
> Greek Ascoloy
> Tantalum
> Assorted other stainless high temperature alloys.

Facilities") and Exhibit 29.3 gives some further information on the capabilities of the principal machines. These machines essentially describe the capabilities of UMC. The other machines and equipment are quite common and merely support the major capabilities. Exhibit 29.4 lists the fiscal 1986 sales by customer and Exhibit 29.5 shows the detail for the past three months. Finally, Exhibit 29.6 shows the information on the key management personnel.

RECENT DEVELOPMENTS

Over the past three years the company has made some significant progress in its cost and its scheduling systems in addition to stemming the losses. Birchard has computerized the cost system so that the engineers have much more detailed and current information on how jobs are doing compared to their quotes. The engineers weren't very enthusiastic about this information at first because the data that came off of the computer was not exactly comparable to that which they had manually generated previously. However, the new system did result in an orderly accounting of all the costs. Birchard also moved into the production control area about ten months ago, and for the first time the company has been able to describe with some accuracy how the backlog of business affects each machining center and where openings for "fill-in business" might lie. The system is manual, simply displaying the load on a large board readily available to everyone in the plant, but with the high concentration of business in a relatively few parts numbers, it is quite effective.

The outlook for business is mixed, however. For the next few months there is enough on the books to ship between $250,000 and $300,000 per month, enough to break even. It has lost some of the "Munitions" business, but there is a feeling that that loss is really a blessing in disguise because it will force management to think through just what business it should develop.

EXHIBIT 29.5 **Detail of Shipments to Major Customers, Final Quarter, Fiscal 1986**

CUSTOMER	PART NUMBER	SALES JANUARY	SALES FEBRUARY	SALES MARCH	TOTAL
Medical	5967	($1,452)	$0	$0	($1,452)
	6038	$0	$0	$420	$420
		($1,452)	$0	$420	($1,032)
Jet engine sub 1	3832	$0	$0	$11,320	$11,320
Jet engine sub 2	5315	$70,832	$20,123	$0	$90,955
	5928	$17,093	$13,831	($4,175)	$26,749
	5932	$22,378	$0	$0	$22,378
	5944	$1,117	$2,375	$5,579	$9,071
	5382	$0	$9,007	$0	$9,007
	5929	$0	$32,073	($1,031)	$31,042
	5933	$0	$735	$0	$735
	6018	$0	$11,692	$0	$11,692
	5943	$0	$0	$16,024	$16,024
		$111,420	$89,836	$16,397	$217,653
Jet engine sub 3	5936	$323	$0	$0	$323
	5973	$0	$0	$1,071	$1,071
		$323	$0	$1,071	$1,394
Munitions	5316	$51,787	$260,311	$260,086	$572,184
	5575	$37,328	$26,846	$25,717	$89,891
	5979	($1,893)	$1,880	($112)	($125)
	5999	$2,715	$0	$0	$2,715
	5622	$0	($1,337)	$0	($1,337)
	5627	$0	($1,084)	$0	($1,064)
		$89,937	$286,616	$285,691	$662,244
Computer	5540	$72,618	$50,054	$64,728	$187,400
Military aircraft sub	5893	$720	$1,440	$720	$2,880
	5938	$3,492	$2,328	$2,701	$8,521
		$4,212	$3,768	$3,421	$11,401
Automotive supplier	5429	$0	$4,687	$0	$4,687
	5947	$0	$3,980	$0	$3,980
		$0	$8,667	$0	$8,667
Aerospace	5294	$0	$0	$3,059	$3,059
Flight control	5854	$1,024	$0	$0	$1,024
	5945	$4,371	$0	$0	$4,371
	5956	$2,742	$0	$0	$2,742

(Continued)

EXHIBIT 29.5 (Continued)

CUSTOMER	PART NUMBER	SALES JANUARY	SALES FEBRUARY	SALES MARCH	TOTAL
	5974	$4,697	$5	$4,697	$9,399
	5976	($41)	$0	$0	($41)
	5982	$1,222	$0	$0	$1,222
	5991	$1,745	$0	$1,747	$3,492
	5996	$39,709	$0	$0	$39,709
	5998	($29)	$0	($363)	($392)
	6001	$2,977	$0	$0	$2,977
	6003	$3,162	$0	$0	$3,162
	6005	$7,024	$3,504	$0	$10,528
	6007	$19,061	$0	$0	$19,061
	5841	$0	$1,820	$0	$1,820
	5853	$50	$0	$0	$50
	5894	$0	$2,063	($27)	$2,036
	5930	$0	$5,229	$0	$5,229
	5963	$0	$2,562	$0	$2,562
	5983	$0	$6,183	$0	$6,183
	5994	$0	$27	($27)	$0
	6008	$0	$2,673	$0	$2,673
	6004	$0	$3,528	$0	$3,528
	5995	$0	$0	($2,928)	($2,928)
	6000	$0	$0	$4,913	$4,913
	5860	$0	$0	$1,126	$1,126
		$87,714	$27,594	$9,138	$124,446
Avionics	5498	$3,525	$2,182	$1,772	$7,479
	5638	$0	$1,554	$0	$1,554
		$3,525	$3,736	$1,772	$9,033
Process control	3416	$4,852	$3,558	$0	$8,410
	4822	$3,273	$2,277	$0	$5,550
	4959	$3,100	$0	$0	$3,100
	5242	$2,309	$0	$0	$2,309
	5288	$975	$0	$0	$975
	5478	$1,472	$2,760	$3,896	$8,128
	5571	$497	$0	$497	$994
	5572	$1,301	$2,602	$1,301	$5,204
	5858	$814	$651	$650	$2,115
	5992	$681	$0	$0	$681
	4525	$0	$1,218	$1,386	$2,604
	4822	$0	$2,846	$0	$2,846
	5957	$0	$7,058	$0	$7,058

CUSTOMER	PART NUMBER	SALES JANUARY	SALES FEBRUARY	SALES MARCH	TOTAL
	5972	$0	$607	$607	$1,214
	5200	$0	$0	$2,016	$2,016
	6023	$0	$0	$4,767	$4,767
	6024	$0	$0	$6,318	$6,318
		$19,274	$23,577	$21,438	$64,289
Industrial 2	5676	$6,167	$3,900	$0	$10,067
Aircraft parts	5527	$0	$0	$12,729	$12,729
Other		$22,851	$28,321	$20,328	$94,296
Sales for month		$400,840	$506,228	$431,846	$1,338,914

EXHIBIT 29.6   **Key Personnel**

NAME	AGE	YEARS W/ COMPANY	POSITION	BACKGROUND	EDUCATION
Terry Tomann	48	18	President	Machinist. Started business in garage	High School; Numerous seminars on management and planning.
John Birchard	36	3	Controller Treasurer	Accounting Controller	MBA
John Giere	35	1	Production manager	Machinist Process engineering	Attended college
Dale Erickson	48	12	Quality Ctrl. manager	Machinist	High School; Votech
Kerry Barnard	31	9	Engineer	Machinist	High School; Votech courses in manufacturing
Bob Pepin	32	15	Engineer	Machinist Foreman	High School; Votech courses in management
Ken Antl	32	1	Engineer	Engineer w/ customer Engineer w/ service	High School; Votech courses in manufacturing
Randy Hatcher	30	9	Foreman	Machinist	High School; Votech courses in manufacturing and supervision
Pat Tomann	28	3*	Night Foreman Will be salesperson	Machinist	High School; Votech course in supervision

*Has worked part-time from the time he was a boy.

STRATEGIC PLAN

In the middle of June of 1986, Terry had just received a call from one of the two remaining directors asking how he was doing on the written strategic plan that he had promised for the next meeting of the Board of Directors in July, just four weeks away. The schedule that Terry had set for himself was to have a written draft by now, a draft that he would circulate to John Birchard and John Giere for comment and discussion. The Director had sounded perturbed when Terry had to report that all he had were some notes from Giere (Exhibit 29.3) and figures Birchard had assembled (Exhibits 29.4 and 29.5). He realized that with all the time that the two remaining Directors had put into helping him turn the business around, and with the possible negative effect on his relations with the bank if they were to resign in disgust, he had to pull something together quickly, even if it meant postponing getting started on training for the Twin City Marathon and working through the next several weekends. (Additional information on the machining industry is found in Exhibit 29.7.)

EXHIBIT 29.7 **Notes on Machining**

> There are two principal kinds of machine tools at UMC, lathes and milling machines. Lathes are machines that cut away material (i.e., machine) by turning the piece worked upon against the tool. The cutting tool remains relatively still, moving around in order to be properly positioned relative to the work piece and feeding in as it cuts metal away. One can use a lathe if the part is round on any axis. Milling machines, on the other hand, hold the work piece relatively fixed and the tool moves over the part. The tool turns with a cutting action to remove the metal. Just as the tool moves into the spinning work piece on a lathe, the work piece on a milling machine, held in place on the table, can be moved around so that it is properly positioned relative to the tool. In general, lathes are used for round parts and milling machines are used for complex shapes or flat parts, but the mills are becoming so accurate and sophisticated that they can make some very fine round shapes too.
>
> In any event, the purpose of machining is to cut away metal to more precise dimensions than are possible in the various casting or molding processes. Obviously, one is wasting metal by cutting it away, but that is the only way of obtaining sufficient precision and quality of finish in many instances. Conversely, if it were possible to obtain sufficiently accurate dimensions in the original shaping of the part, no machining would be necessary at all. Consequently, as technology of fabrication and materials changes, it is always possible that certain products that required machining at one time would no longer require it. For example, plastics that are precision-molded have taken some of these applications. Automotive carburetors that once required machining are now rapidly molded in seconds out of thermoplastics.

There are three kinds of controls on the machine tools, CNC (Computerized Numerically Controlled), NC (Numerically Controlled), and manual. The computerized numerically controlled machines have a computer that the operator can program or edit right on the machine. Consequently, the operator can instruct the machine exactly how to machine the part from the beginning of the process to the end, or he can merely edit a program that the engineers had previously developed if some modifications in the process are necessary. The numerically controlled machine, on the other hand, is controlled by a tape that the engineers develop. The operator has limited capability to change the instructions to the machine that are in the tape. Finally, the manual machines require operator skill to control the machine. The tool or the piece is fed with a screw or a hydraulic feed mechanism under the direct control of the operator.

Each machine requires a different set of skills. The manual machine requires great manual skills and experience to accomplish good work. The CNC machines, on the other hand, require numerical skills that the old-time skilled machinists sometimes do not have. The NC machines require the least skill of the three. The machinist must be able to set up the job correctly and to recognize if something is running improperly.

One of the more difficult challenges for a job-shop machining company is to define just what the capabilities are in terms that will allow a sales person to identify what kind of business to seek. The parameters that are of interest for describing the kinds of parts that a machinist can make are as follows:

- The tolerances. These are usually described in a range plus or minus thousandths of an inch. In UMC's case the usual range is from 0.0001 (one-tenth of a thousandth) to 0.010 (one-hundredth) of an inch, although very few parts go to 0.0001 inch.

- Metals with which they work. Aluminum is very easy to machine. Heat treatable steel is more difficult, but stainless steel or some of the very hard, "space age" alloys such as titanium are much more difficult to machine. All of the metals listed in the UMC capability listing, "Major Facilities" (Exhibit 29.2), would be considered hard-to-machine metals.

- Size of the part. Most of UMC's parts would fit within a five-inch square envelope. Such an envelope does not place a minimum on the size of the part. A job shop like UMC will run parts significantly smaller than the envelope if the volumes can justify putting a number (e.g., fifty) pieces in a fixture and running them all at the same time. In addition, there are some short-run jobs that run outside these size limits. On these jobs cost tends to be a less important consideration in successful bidding.

- Volume of the run. With very small runs the company must be extremely flexible and skilled to switch from one part to another rapidly without making errors. With very large runs it is possible to reduce the labor cost through heavy investment in special equipment and robotics. In UMC's case it does not seem to be able to make extremely small runs profitably or to reduce costs low enough to get the really large (5000–10,000 and up) piece orders.

Because there is a ready aftermarket for machine tools, new machines are relatively easy to finance. A lender has minimum risk using one of these

(Continued)

EXHIBIT 29.7 **(Continued)**

machine tools as collateral for a loan and leasing companies are willing to purchase and lease one of these machines to a company even though the financial strength of the company might be quite weak. For example, in 1985 a leasing company was willing to lease the Mori-Sieki and the Matsura machines to UMC despite its obviously weak financial condition. While this situation helps UMC to have modern machinery, it also enables competition to have similarly modern machinery.

Patton Septic Tank

L. K. WILLIAMS · ROBERT E. MEADOWS

INTRODUCTION

Patton Septic Tank, a manufacturer of metal septic tanks, opened for business in the spring of 1983 in a small rural community located in Appalachia. Ben Patton, 62, founded the business after his hardware business filed for a debt restructuring bankruptcy. Ben had had a variety of business experiences before starting his septic tank business. He had sold insurance and had operated a small farm, but the majority of his career was spent building residential homes.

Based upon this experience in home construction, Ben opened a hardware store in 1978, but after a few good years, the business did not survive the recession that took place in the housing industry during the early 1980s. Poor management of inventories and accounts receivables also contributed to the business failure. The hardware store had no accounting system to control inventories and incurred unknown losses from being charged for inventory never received and through inventory theft. Also, Ben assumed that individuals would pay him back and extended credit to too many individuals during this period. Unfortunately, Ben was left holding nearly $170,000 in unpaid receivables, and had little hope of collection.

These circumstances left Ben with little to show for the hard work and money he had invested. Deeply in debt, Ben decided to start a business to manufacture septic tanks. Ben thought that two of his major problems in the hardware business, inventory control and accounts receivable control, would be more manageable in the metal septic-tank business. His judgment was based on the fact that the raw-materials inventory came in four-by-eight-foot sheets of metal and the finished goods inventory would consist of the metal septic tanks. Both inventories would be easier to track than the inventory in the hardware store. Because Ben would be selling tanks to businesses and collecting on delivery, he should have very few, if any, receivables.

In order to start the business, Ben designed his septic tanks and developed the manufacturing process. Ben's design was superior to the septic tanks then being sold in the state of Tennessee. The design was so impressive that the state adopted Ben's design as the new standard in the state. Ben believed that the new design would increase the expected life of a septic tank from its present twenty years to twenty-five (or more) years.

This case was prepared by Professor L. K. Williams of Tennessee Technological University, and Professor Robert E. Meadows of Morehead State University. It was presented at the 1987 Workshop of the Midwest Society for Case Research. It also appears in *Annual Advances in Business Cases, 1987*, pp. 300–307, edited by Cyril Ling. Reprinted by permission.

MANUFAC-TURING

Patton manufactures tanks in three sizes: 500-gallon, 750-gallon, and 1,000-gallon. Some 400-gallon tanks and a few water tanks were also made; however, the state now prohibits 400-gallon tanks. Sheets of four-by-eight-foot, fourteen-gauge steel are used as the primary raw-material component for the tanks. Ben can purchase steel delivered for $14.75 per 100 pounds, less a 2% discount. The price has increased from $12.50 per 100 pounds over the last year, because of increasing fuel prices. A 500-gallon tank requires 346 pounds of steel; a 750-gallon tank requires 427 pounds of steel; and a 1,000-gallon tank requires 534 pounds of steel. Every tank, regardless of size, requires two plastic baffles, pipe and coating—all of which cost approximately $5.00 total per tank. Each tank requires two circular ends, which are cut out with a cutting torch. The sheets of steel are rolled into a cylinder to provide the body of each tank. Workers then assemble the tank by arc welding the circular ends to the body. To allow entrance and exit of sewage, a plastic baffle is placed on each end of the tank. Also, an access lid is installed on the cylindrical body of each tank to allow a servicing entrance after the tank is installed underground. After assembly, tanks are put on an overhead hoist that is used to dip the tanks in a tar-like coating. The coating is one-eighth of an inch thick. After coating, the tanks sit out to dry until ready for shipment.

The building within which Ben makes septic tanks is an aluminum structure that he had built in 1981 for $14,000, and measures sixty by forty feet. The building is neither heated nor air-conditioned. A large cooling fan sets in one wall and is used in the summer months. Half of the building has a concrete floor while the other half is gravel.

LABOR

The unemployment rate in the county in which the company is located runs extremely high. Most of the laborers that work for Ben are not highly motivated and seem to require constant supervision. Ben has noted that production sharply increases when either he or his son oversees the activities at the shop.

The company has two eight-hour shifts, of five workers on each shift. Ben pays his laborers on a piece rate as if they were independent contractors. This saves him from having to withhold taxes or pay payroll taxes. Ben has discussed this treatment of his laborers as independent contractors (instead of employees that the company would have to make payroll deductions and pay payroll taxes) with an attorney. The attorney stated that the company's situation is in a "grey area" of the law that could be treated either way. If the federal and/or state government would ever question Ben's treating his laborers as independent contractors, the company might be required to pay a substantial amount of unpaid payroll taxes and/or penalties.

For every tank smaller than 1,000 gallons, the laborers are paid $20; they receive $37 for every 1,000-gallon tank. The crew working on those tanks will split the total received. The length of time it takes a five-man crew to manufacture a given tank is dependent upon the size of the tank. Exhibit 30.1 lists the time normally required to make each tank.

MARKETING

Because hardware and home-supply stores served as the primary retailers of metal septic tanks, Ben developed a marketing strategy to break into the regional metal septic-tank market—he called on prospective buyers person- ally. He carried a prototype of a 500-gallon tank in the back of his pickup truck and showed it to the individuals upon whom he called. In addition, Ben would take with him the design specifications of the tank.

At the time Ben started his septic tank business, the region of Appalachia in which he was located was serviced almost exclusively by a larger and more established manufacturer of septic tanks—Webster's Welding. Web- ster's was located across the state, 150 miles west of Ben's shop. Webster's manufactured metal septic tanks, metal gates, and other metal goods. Web- ster's would deliver tanks to buyers in a minimum load of eighteen tanks. Ben gained many buyers by allowing his customers to purchase any size load of tanks at a time. The inventory-costs savings of carrying fewer septic tanks enticed many buyers to Ben even though he was a newcomer. How- ever, the risk of being serviced by a new supplier caused many potential buyers to be cautious of Ben. These were mostly larger hardware and home- supply stores that could handle large loads and did not want to risk Ben's inability to meet their inventory demands. However, after becoming more established, Ben did receive orders from bigger stores.

Ben would also receive customer orders by phone. Because Ben did not have a personal or business telephone, he would write down his son Steve's home phone number on a piece of paper and give it to customers to call in orders. Ben would miss orders when no one was at Steve's or when one of Steve's children would incorrectly take an order.

Ben priced his tanks at anywhere from five to ten dollars less than did his major competitor, Webster's Welding. He did not want, nor could he afford, to get into a price war with Webster's. However, Ben wanted to

EXHIBIT 30.1

Manufacturing by Tank Size

TANK SIZE (IN GALLONS)	NORMAL MANUFACTURING TIME
400	55 Minutes
500	60 Minutes
750	65 Minutes
1,000	90 Minutes

offer small price incentives to penetrate the market. Exhibit 30.2 shows the current wholesale and retail price of Ben's 500-, 700-, and 1,000-gallon tanks.

OTHER SEPTIC TANKS

In Ben's present marketing and service region, 70% of all septic tanks sold are made of metal. Eighteen percent are made of cement and 12% from plastic. Ben feels that the plastic tanks, which sell for approximately $100 per tank higher than metal tanks, are on their way out because a high percentage of them collapse shortly after being installed. On the other hand, cement tanks, which will last a lifetime, are becoming more popular. Like the plastic tanks, the cement tanks are priced higher than the metal tanks. The increased demand for cement tanks has allowed manufacturers to become more price competitive; e.g., in 1985, a 1,000-gallon cement tank was priced at retail at approximately $500, but in 1986 the same tank sold for close to $300. Presently, a move is underway to persuade the state legislature to prohibit the use of the steel septic tanks and only to allow cement tanks. Ben judges that the likelihood of a legislative ban is low.

SALES

In spite of the difficulties of breaking into a market, sales have been very good and in the major sector of the state in which Ben sells tanks, the company has nearly 80% of the market share. Ben has always been optimistic about the success of the company even though a student consulting team from a nearby regional state university advised Ben against going into the septic tank business, because of a lack of demand for septic tanks in the area of Appalachia in which he was located.

In Exhibit 30.3, sales revenues and units sold (by size) for the company for each year since Ben started the business are listed. Ben does not keep extensive records of expenditures and often deals in cash; however, he knows that the business has been profitable because he has been able to pay off over $50,000 in debts in the last three years, while drawing funds out of the business for his living expenses. Ben estimates that total costs

EXHIBIT 30.2   **Current Wholesale and Retail Price List**

TANK SIZE	WHOLESALE PRICE	RETAIL PRICE
500-gallon	$115	$150
750-gallon	$160	$195
1,000-gallon	$210	$260

EXHIBIT   30.3   **Sales Revenues and Units Sold**

YEAR	REVENUES	400-GAL	500-GAL	750-GAL	1000-GAL	WATER TANKS	LIDS
1983*	$ 53,122	41	268	60	32	4	2
1984	$131,228	104	617	157	73	7	11
1985	$213,199	194	1075	228	98	27	6
1986	$202,865	109	1061	260	112	20	48

*April through December.

(manufacturing and operating) will run between 75% and 80% of sales. The business profits are protected from taxes because of their being offset by the losses carried over from the hardware business. Ben noted that, "If I had begun this septic tank business three years ago, instead of the hardware business, I would now be sitting good financially." The company's balance sheet, as of December 31, 1986, is shown in Exhibit 30.4. (Assets are shown at their estimated fair market value.) Statements of net receipts are shown in Exhibit 30.5.

FINANCING

Ben had trouble arranging financing after his problems with his prior business. This inability to find funding caused the company cash-flow problems. Frequently, Ben drove to Cincinnati, Ohio, or Detroit, Michigan to purchase steel with the small amounts of cash he had. Because he purchased steel in

EXHIBIT   30.4   **Patton Septic Tanks, Balance Sheet, December 31, 1986**

Assets	
Cash	$ 6,000
Accounts receivable	4,500
Land	15,000
Building and improvements	17,000
Machinery and tools	16,200
Trucks	6,000
Total assets	$64,700
Liabilities and equity	
Notes payable	$13,000
Ben Patton's equity	51,700
Total liabilities and equity	$64,700

EXHIBIT 30.5 **Patton Septic Tank, Statement of Revenues and Costs for the Years Ended 1985 and 1986**

	1985	1986
Sales	$213,199	$202,865
Cost of metal	80,422	82,044
Cost of manufacturing labor	36,490	37,600
Depreciation	3,070	3,070
Other labor (Steve Patton salary)*	20,000	22,000
Gasoline, welding material, etc.	24,182	17,781
Total expenses	164,164	162,495
Net Revenues	$ 49,035	$ 40,370

*Steve delivers most of the tanks and oversees production whenever he is not delivering tanks.

small quantities, Ben paid higher prices per pound for the steel than he would have had to pay if he had been able to purchase in larger quantities.

In December of 1985, Ben found himself needing money to produce tanks for the spring busy season. In addition, Ben needed cash for personal expenditures to get through the winter slow season. He sought help from the Small Business Administration (SBA) through the Small Business Development Center at the nearby state university. The SBA helped to arrange an immediate loan through a local bank and a line of credit for working capital. This loan arrangement provided a shot in the arm for the business. It helped the company purchase steel in large enough quantities that it could be delivered to the company and quantity discounts could be taken. Ben could then spend more time selling and overseeing the production of tanks.

PROBLEMS

Although Ben had weathered many problems, the company had been very profitable. In 1985, Ben had yet another serious problem with the state agency that regulated sewage treatment. The agency required Ben to recall several of his tanks because the metal was not properly coated on the inside. Ben complied with the agency requirements; however, the situation was very costly for the company. Ben had to pick up the recalled tanks, haul them back to the plant, fix them, and return them to the supplier. During the thirty-day recall period, the state agency blocked the sale of his tanks until they were satisfied that the problem was corrected. Ben felt the incident caused some loss of credibility with his customers and was upset because he felt that his company was being singled out while other septic tank manufacturers, especially Webster's, were let alone by the state agency although their tanks were substandard too.

PRODUCTION

In the slow production period during the winter of 1986–1987, Ben pondered how his business could grow and prosper in the future. Ben judged that with the vast untapped areas in the state, he could sell all the tanks that he could manufacture and he searched for ways to increase the company's manufacturing ability. However, he did not want to expand too quickly and assume a lot of debt.

One option open to Ben was to increase to three shifts and operate year-round. However, this would require a large commitment of money for labor, and meant that he would have to hold inventory instead of producing to order. Another option was to create another assembly line that could be established in the present building. He thought that with two assembly lines, he could produce two times as many tanks as were presently being produced. Ben estimated the cost of the equipment necessary for an additional assembly line to be between $10,000 and $12,000. The total would require external financing.

Ben also thought that more automation in the construction process would increase output. This could be done with an unknown substantial outlay of funds for improved machinery. Ben thought that he could then get by with fewer workers. However, he did not know exactly how many fewer.

Ben also thought about starting one or two new plants, one east and one west of the present plant. A new plant, similar in size and construction to the present building, would cost approximately $43,000. By having more manufacturing plants, less travel would be required for the delivering of tanks. However, Ben thought that if production could be increased, by whatever means, he could reduce travel and delivery expenditures by storing tanks at distribution centers around the state.

Whatever the future holds, Ben would like to slow down from the rigorous pace that he and his wife, Jean, have been keeping for the last few years. He hopes that his oldest son, Steve, 41, can manage more and more of the business in the immediate future, and allow him and Jean to travel around servicing customers and thereby concentrate on the company's public relations.

CASE 31

Christian's

THOMAS L. WHEELEN · MOUSTAFA H. ABDELSAMAD · JEFF CURRY ·
DEAN SALPINI · ART SCIBELLI · GORDON SHANKS

BACKGROUND

In the Spring Semester of 1984 four seniors at the University of Virginia were trying to decide whether they should invest in Christian's Restaurant, a small eating establishment located several miles from the university's campus in Charlottesville, Virginia.

The four students—Jeff Curry, Dean Salpini, Art Scibelli, and Gordon Shanks—were all business majors who had become involved with Christian's as the result of a management course entitled "Entrepreneurship" in which they were enrolled. The objective of this course was for the students to "set up a new company that is completely researched in all phases of the business (location, services, finance, and so on) and submit the written business plan for evaluation." The four students had decided to work together on the project at the beginning of the semester and had quickly begun investigating potential business ventures in the Charlottesville area.

The group's first idea centered on the opening of a seafood restaurant. Art believed that a restaurant offering the same product as a local chain of seafood houses near his home in Northern Virginia could prove highly successful in Charlottesville. These restaurants offered fresh seafood for relatively moderate prices in a family-type atmosphere and additionally featured several "all you can eat" items on their menu. Art had gotten in touch with one of the owner-founders of the chain, Mr. Easby-Smyth, and the group had gone to Northern Virginia to meet with him and discuss their idea.

The meeting with Mr. Easby-Smyth had produced two conclusions: Charlottesville was probably too small a market to support the size of restaurant the group had originally considered, and the amount of money involved would make the project infeasible for the group. Mr. Easby-Smyth had informed them that the cost of building and outfitting a seafood house of 6,000 square feet would be approximately $300,000. The group had no desire

This case was prepared by Jeff Curry, Dean Salpini, Art Scibelli, and Gordon Shanks, under the supervision of Professor Thomas L. Wheelen, University of South Florida, and Professor Moustafa H. Abdelsamad, Southeastern Massachusetts University. This case was presented at the North American Case Research Association Meeting, 1984. Copyright © 1985 by Thomas L. Wheelen and Moustafa H. Abdelsamad.

to enter into an investment of this magnitude and was also aware of the great deal of difficulty they were sure to encounter in trying to raise the capital for such a venture.

The students still felt a smaller seafood restaurant might be successful in Charlottesville, though, and began searching for an already existing building that would be suitable for their restaurant. Ideally, they would find a restaurant that was selling out and could easily be converted for their purposes. Then news of the Happy Clam reached them.

The Happy Clam was a new seafood restaurant opening up on Route 29 North, the main highway leading from Charlottesville. One visit to the new restaurant confirmed that not only was it located in the general area the group had hoped to locate in, but it was also offering the same basic product mix as they had hoped to offer. In addition, the restaurant's owner had already successfully opened an identical seafood house in nearby Fredericksburg, Virginia.

Up to this point, the area had contained no restaurant similar to the one that the students conceived. Now, however, they were faced with a direct competitor who had proven he could be successful in the seafood business. It was at this point, as the students reconsidered their strategy, that Art visited a local realtor and found out about Christian's.

Christian's was a small restaurant specializing in sandwiches for lunch, and specialty dishes for dinner (see dinner menu, Exhibit 31.1). It was being sold as an ongoing business to include the name Christian's. The students met with the realtor handling the sale, William Page, who arranged a meeting with the owners of Christian's.

Peter and Mary Tarpey, a young couple from the New York area, along with a University of Virginia professor who acted as a silent partner, were the owners of Christian's. The students met with Page and the Tarpeys as arranged on a Wednesday afternoon, and the group sat down at a table in Christian's to answer each other's questions and discuss the possible purchase.

Mary Tarpey first showed the group a handwritten profit and loss statement for the period from June 13, 1983, to October 31, 1983 (see Exhibit 31.2). She explained how some of the expenses were direct payments to the banks and were being written off as business expenses, such as car payments and a life insurance policy, and need not be incurred by a new owner. She also showed the students monthly sales figures for the period of January 1983 to October 1983, as verified by a local CPA firm (see Exhibit 31.3), as well as a list of assets owned by Christian's (see Exhibit 31.4).

The Tarpeys defined their target market as "young professional." By this, they meant persons in the eighteen- to thirty-five-year age group who worked in the area and came to Christian's for the menu's variety and the quality of food. They stated that these people eat out about twenty-two times per month for lunch and dinner, and their strategy was to try to get them at Christian's five days a month. The Tarpeys also quoted the average lunch check as being $3.76 and the average dinner check amounting to $5.92.

EXHIBIT 31.1 | **Dinner Menu**

Soups	Wines
French Onion $1.50	By the glass $1.25
Cream of Asparagus $1.25	½ Litre $3.25
Vegetable $1.00	Full Litre $5.75
Split Pea or Lentil $1.00	Champagne Cocktail $1.25

Entrées
(Served with Salad & Bread)

Beef Bazaar $4.25
Marinated beef, onions & green peppers broiled & served on rice

Broccoli Casserole $3.25
Broccoli, tomatoes, onions & eggs topped with cheese

Lobster Scampi $4.25
Langostinos broiled in herb butter & served on rice

Syrian Chicken $3.85
Marinated chicken in pita bread with lettuce, tomatoes

Sausage Lasagne $4.25
An Italian dish that speaks for itself!

Omelet special $3.95
Large dinner omelet filled with pepperoni and provolone cheese

Crêpes $3.75
Chicken Divan or Sauteed Mushrooms

Desserts

Ginger Sherbet	$.75
Homemade Pecan Pie	$1.00
Cheesecake	$1.25
Carrot Cake	$1.25
Coffee or Tea	$.35
Soft Drinks	$.50
Beer	$.75

The Tarpeys also answered questions concerning Christian's daily operations and suppliers. One of the important issues raised was that of a transition period. The group hoped to hire an experienced, full-time manager for the restaurant, and the Tarpeys agreed that they would stay on for a period of two weeks or so to help train the manager and show him the cost-control and portion-control procedures they had used. In addition, the Tarpeys stated that the whole employee staff had expressed their willingness to stay with the restaurant after an ownership change. The group viewed these two factors as distinct assets.

EXHIBIT 31.2 | **Christian's Profit and Loss Statement**
(June 13, 1983–October 31, 1983)

Sales		$100,000.00
Cost of Sales		
Beer and Wine	$2,688.30	
Food	29,189.60	
		31,877.90
		$ 68,122.10
Gross Profit		
Operating Expenses		
Paper	$1,079.88	
Insurance		
Store	600.00	
Car	150.00	
Health	460.00	
Workmen's Compensation	950.00	
Employment Commission	360.00	
Laundry, Linen	483.25	
Licenses	250.00	
Sales Tax (State)	4,000.00	
Repairs Maintenance	250.00	
Rent	2,500.00	
Rubbish Removal—City	448.50	
Salaries & Wages	20,000.00	
Payroll Taxes	6,000.00	
Utilities	4,000.00	
Loan Payment	1,150.00	
Equipment Payments	1,150.00	
Life Insurance	625.00	
Car Payment	1,095.00	
Maintenance	950.00	
Lease Dishwasher	448.50	
Advertising	2,750.00	
Business Association Dues & Expenses	450.00	
Administrative Salaries	5,000.00	
TOTAL		55,150.13
Income before Taxes		$ 12,971.97

NOTE: This was a handwritten statement provided by the owners.

EXHIBIT 31.3   **Sales Information**

BROWN AND JONES COMPANY
CERTIFIED PUBLIC ACCOUNTANTS
CHARLOTTESVILLE, VIRGINIA 22906

January 9, 1984

Peter Tarpey
Christian's, Inc.
1703 Allied Lane
Charlottesville, Virginia 22901

Dear Peter:

As per your request, enclosed are sales figures for Christian's, Inc., for the ten months ending October, 1983 as filed on your monthly Virginia sales tax returns.

January 1983	$18,543.30
February 1983	19,085.43
March 1983	18,097.54
April 1983	19,984.20
May 1983	20,422.71
June 1983	21,836.37
July 1983	19,304.76
August 1983	22,231.69
September 1983	20,002.19
October 1983	20,588.86

If you need sales figures for November, 1983 and December, 1983, you will have to get these amounts from worksheets in your files. Let me know if I can be of further assistance.

Yours truly,

Thomas L. Brown
Certified Public Accountant

TLB/d

P.S.: The sales figures for November, 1983 are: $19,300.00

    TLB

EXHIBIT 31.4   **Additional Information Provided by Thomas L. Brown**
(September 27, 1983)

Attached is a schedule of fixed assets owned by Christian's, Inc., and the estimated market value of each. Since a purchaser of these would have a cost basis for depreciation and useful life different from that of Christian's, Inc., this information is not provided.

21 Tables	$ 525
43 Chairs	430
2 Banquettes	100
6 Church Pew Benches	120
Small Refrigerator	300
Walk In Box	1,500
Ice Machine	100
NCR Cash Register	150
3 Toasters	225
Jordan Box	250
Fogle Refrigerator	1,200
Hobart Slicer	1,000
Hobart Microwave	1,000
Sandwich Box	200
Stainless Prep. Table	100
Deep Fat Fryer	75
Steam Table	75
Stainless Prep. Table	125
3 Butcher Block Chef Tables	300
Small Hobart Slicer	200
3 Basin Sinks	75
Universal Freezer	100
Sears' Freezer	75
Stereo System	150
Curtains	100
Pots, Pans, Flatware, China, Glassware	600
Placemats, Salt and Pepper Mills	100
New Sign	2,000
TOTAL FIXED ASSETS	$11,175

Should you desire additional information in this matter, please contact Peter Tarpey and the data will be forthcoming.

Another important issue was the future plans of the Tarpeys. As it turned out, the Tarpeys would be opening a new restaurant in a shopping center being built three-quarters of a mile from Christian's. Peter Tarpey explained that the restaurant was to be more dinner-oriented than Christian's. He described it as an "Irish cafe with French food," which would serve more expensive meals than Christian's and also serve liquor, which Christian's did not feature. Tarpey estimated that by his moving and opening a new restaurant, Christian's might lose at most 5% of its customers.

A second meeting was held with the Tarpeys at a later date, during which more of the group's questions were answered. A new lease would have to be renegotiated by any new owner in August 1984, which would be substantially higher than the current one. The students had questions about Christian's specific suppliers and asked to see the restaurant's books, but the Tarpeys wanted some sort of firm commitment on the group's part before more information about Christian's would be given out.

The price being asked for Christian's was $57,750 and the students estimated that they could put up about $17,500 of their own capital. Because the rest would have to be financed by a loan of some sort, Jeff visited several banks to discuss terms. One of the banks he visited told him that they loaned money for a restaurant only if it was going to be family owned and operated. At Sovran Bank, Jeff got a more positive response. The loan officer there stated that the bank would loan up to 70% of the purchase price, fully collateralized. The interest rate would be 14 or 15%.

At this point, the group decided to evaluate their objectives and "take stock" of the situation. They hoped to run the restaurant as absentee owners and have the full-time manager handle daily operations. Art's immediate plans included law school in September, although he was still unsure which law school he would be attending. Dean planned on going to work in Northern Virginia after graduation, and Jeff and Gordon would be returning to the University of Virginia in the fall to complete their degrees.

The students' families, from whom they hoped to borrow some of the initial equity capital, all had reservations about the venture. Most of the doubt centered on the policy of running the restaurant as absentee owners. The families also wondered if it was wise for the students to make such an investment at this time in their careers when their futures were so undecided.

By now it was March 24, and the students knew a decision would have to be made very soon. A call to William Page had confirmed the rumor that another party had entered the scene and was seriously considering buying Christian's. A meeting was called at which the group planned to decide their next move.

At the meeting, the students decided that some sort of comprehensive analysis of the information they had gathered was necessary. Then, with the analysis in front of them, they felt they would be able to reach the best conclusion.

The group decided to break up the information into sections, with Jeff concentrating on the finance, Dean on the marketing, and Gordon and Art on the operations. When they got back together on March 31 (one week away) to put all the results together, the decision would have to be made.

MARKET ANALYSIS

Although Mr. Tarpey assured the group of the existence and loyalty of a definite market for Christian's, it was felt that a marketing survey would strengthen the group's understanding of this market. Using the survey form shown (see Exhibit 31.5), the survey was conducted among eighty-eight people who were customers at competitive restaurants. The competition was determined from an assessment based on a number of factors, including location, clientele, product offering, and Mr. Tarpey's estimates. Christian's, however, was not included because the group felt that their regular clientele might bias the results in favor of the restaurant.

From the results of the survey, it was discovered that most people were aware of Christian's, but were not being drawn down there to eat. In addition, only 7% of those who had eaten at Christian's did so at least five times/month, so their repeat business seemed to be lacking. Of those who ate there regularly, most people seemed to prefer the lunch period (60%), as opposed to the dinner period, as Mr. Tarpey had claimed would occur. Analysis of the various factors involved with Christian's showed that location was the most significant problem, with 64% of the respondents rating it below average. However, a study of traffic-flow patterns in Charlottesville around the McIntyre Road area, where Christian's is located, revealed that 20% of the whole day's traffic passed Christian's between 11:00 A.M. and 2:00 P.M. Price and service seemed to be average and comparable to other restaurants in most respondents' minds.

The most significant factors in a person's decision to eat at Christian's were the menu's variety and the food's quality. Most of those who had eaten at the restaurant named specific food items as their main reason for coming. This also accounts for the major form of advertising that Christian's used, which seemed to be "word-of-mouth" advertising from satisfied customers. As far as changes in Christian's were concerned, most respondents favored the introduction of seafood into the menu (81%), whereas the same percentage felt that having live entertainment would be a mistake.

One of the problems that might confront the group was the introduction of Mr. Tarpey's new restaurant down the street from Christian's. Because he had already developed a loyal clientele, the group was afraid of losing them to his new restaurant, although Mr. Tarpey assured the group that only 5% of the market would be affected. According to the survey, the figure to determine those customers that would be lost through a change in management was approximately 6.8%, a little higher than Mr. Tarpey's estimate.

EXHIBIT 31.5 **Marketing Survey**

Hello, we are students doing a research study on Christian's restaurant. Could you *please* take a little time to help us to fill out our survey and help make Christian's a better place to eat. Thank you for your cooperation. (The key results of the survey are summarized below.)

1. Have you ever eaten at Christian's?   YES 50%   NO 50%

   If NO, have you heard of it?   YES 59%   If No, no further questions. 41%

   If YES, how often do you eat there?

   Less than 5 times a month   93%

   5 times a month   5%

   More than 5 times a month   2%

2. Which meal do you usually eat at Christian's?

   Lunch 59%   Dinner 32%   Both 9%

3. How would you rate Christian's on these factors:

	POOR	FAIR	AVERAGE	ABOVE AVERAGE	EXCELLENT
Location	29.5%	34%	32%	4.5%	
Food Quality			23.3%	53.5%	23.3%
Price	4.5%	11%	61.5%	16%	7%
Service		14%	48%	33%	5%
Atmosphere	9%	11.4%	41%	34%	4.6%
Menu Variety		5%	33%	45%	17%
Cleanliness	9.5%	9.5%	36%	33%	12%

4. What is the main reason(s) you eat at Christian's? Answers varied; most were complimentary.

5. How did you hear about Christian's?

   TV 2%   Radio 12%   Newspaper Ads 10.6%   Friends 58%

   Drove By 5.8%   Other (please specify) 11.6%

6. Would you like to see the following at Christian's?

	YES	NO
More Vegetarian Dishes	44%	56%
More Seafood	81%	19%
More Take-out Variety	48%	52%
Live Entertainment	19%	81%

7. An informal survey of age was conducted.

Although there were no direct questions addressing demographics on the survey, respondents were asked to place themselves in one of the three age brackets: eighteen to thirty-five, thirty-five to fifty, and over fifty. Age of the customer was thought to be important in the students' decision to purchase Christian's, so that the target market could be firmly established.

EXHIBIT 31.6 **The Charlottesville Market**[1]
(In Thousands of Dollars)

YEAR	RETAIL SALES	EATING & DRINKING[2]	POPULATION	HOUSEHOLDS[3]
1978	153,995	N.A.[4]	38.8	13.8
1979	176,731	N.A.	38.7	14.0
1980	224,588	N.A.	39.0	14.2
1981	235,679	17,882	39.1	14.7
1982	251,766	19,753	38.9	14.7

NOTES: [1]Data provided by Virginia State Planning Service. [2]*Eating and Drinking Places:* This is a broad classification which includes any establishment selling prepared food or drink. Caterers, lunch counters, and concession stands are included as well as restaurants. [3]*Households:* All people occupying a single housing unit whether related or not. Includes single persons living alone. [4]N.A.: not available.

Overall, it was found that 60% of those interviewed were between eighteen and thirty-five years of age, while 31% fell into the thirty-five to fifty bracket. Further analysis showed that 98% of those who presently eat at Christian's were within the eighteen- to fifty-year age range. Those customers who were over fifty, therefore, figured to be an insignificant number of Christian's target market. Therefore, Mr. Tarpey's claim of "young professionals" as being his primary customers seems to have been supported through this age-group data.

As can be seen from Exhibit 31.6, sales for eating and drinking establishments in 1982 were 10.5% above those of 1981, while total retail sales increased only 6.8% for the same period. Households also seemed to be forming at a faster rate than the total population was growing. In addition, the Virginia State Planning Office projections show that the twenty- to thirty-four-year-old segment has shown disproportionate increases, which could explain the faster formation of households. These same figures also show that the twenty-five to thirty-nine-year-old age group will increase 17% between 1980 and 1985. In Albemarle County, in which Charlottesville is located, this increase will be almost 32%.

These growth figures were considered important because of the number of people who drive into Charlottesville's central business district (C.B.D.) from the county who use McIntyre Road as a major artery. The C.B.D. itself was also considered to be important, because a large part of Christian's clientele came from there. Over $2,000,000 had been privately invested in downtown since 1982; thus the C.B.D. appeared to be booming. Another important development was the county's move of their executive offices into the old Lane High School building, located down the street from Christian's. This decision would increase Christian's target market, because these people seemed to fit the characteristics of their clientele.

ADVERTISING AND PROMOTION

Christian's present advertising program was very sporadic, with a yearly expenditure of only $2,750. Mr. Tarpey spoke of occasional spots on television that he had used, along with local radio stations and the major newspaper in Charlottesville. However, Dean and the other members of the group felt that the effectiveness of this program was lacking.

OPERATIONS

The students were aware of their lack of experience in the restaurant business, and because the daily operations of Christian's had gone smoothly in the past, they did not plan any significant changes upon their taking over.

The entire employee staff had stated they would be willing to remain at Christian's after the ownership change, and Peter and Mary Tarpey agreed they would stay on for a transition period to "show the ropes" to the new manager.

The students had realized early in their involvement with Christian's that they would need to hire a full-time manager for the restaurant were they to purchase it. It was determined that they would want someone with experience in restaurant management from the Charlottesville area. Their realtor had informed them he knew of a man who fit this description and had expressed interest in the opportunity, but the group was unable to get in contact with him before the week ended.

The group planned on putting the manager in charge of general daily operations, to include ordering, cost control, hiring, firing, scheduling, and any other operations-related duty. The students planned on doing the bookkeeping themselves. They planned to pay the manager a salary of approximately $12,000, plus a commission based on the bottom-line figure. This commission would be approximately 11%.

It was determined that the following employees would be needed to operate Christian's:

> 1 manager @ $12,000 salary plus commission
>
> 3 cooks @ $5.00/hour
>
> 1 grillman @ $4.75/hour
>
> 2 countermen @ $4.25/hour
>
> 2 prep men @ $4.25/hour
>
> 2 dishwashers @ $4.25/hour
>
> 2 cashiers @ $4.25/hour
>
> 12 waitresses @ $1.50/hour plus tips

Employees were to be allowed free drinks and half-price meals while working.

Under the students' ownership, Christian's would continue to buy its food supplies from institutional food distributors from Richmond, Virginia, who delivered to Charlottesville. In addition, they would obtain their beer from local distributors and their soft drinks from local bottling companies.

In the past, inventory had turned over approximately once a week. Normal credit terms of suppliers had been net thirty days.

The marketing survey had indicated that Christian's menu was one of its strongest points, so the group planned few changes. The lunch menu featured over forty sandwiches along with omelets, salads, and chili. The dinner menu featured specialty dishes such as beef bazaar and Syrian chicken (see Exhibit 31.1).

In the past, Christian's had varied its dinner menu daily. The students would plan to vary it weekly, and if one combination proved particularly popular, it would be used again at a different time.

Approximately 15% of Christian's gross sales came from beer sales. The restaurant carried mainly premium and foreign beers, in keeping with its target market of young professionals.

INVESTMENT

Benefiting from knowledge they had obtained in a business law course the previous semester, the group decided to establish Christian's as a Subchapter S corporation. This business form was chosen because of the tax advantages and flexibility it would allow the group; the business would be taxed as a partnership, but would retain the limited liability of a corporation, to protect the shareholders. Because income-tax rates for individuals in this case are substantially lower than for a corporation, the group felt that this form would offer them the best return on their investment.

LEASE

At the time of negotiations, Christian's was paying Allied Realty, the owner of the shopping plaza in which the restaurant was located, a base rent of $350 per month plus an additional percentage of gross sales (4%) not exceeding a total monthly rental of $500 per month. However, this lease would expire on August 1, 1984, and a new lease would have to be renegotiated by the new purchaser.

The new rent terms would be considerably higher than those experienced by previous owners and would consist of a minimum payment of $600 per month or 4% of sales (whichever is higher), not to exceed $750 per month. Because Christian's historical monthly sales have averaged approximately $20,000, this would mean payments of $750 per month. In addition, there would be an additional requirement that if gross sales exceeded $60,000 in any quarter, the restaurant would pay 3% of sales exceeding this amount.

Fortunately, the group was informed by its realtor, Henry Brasswell, that it might be possible to negotiate a less expensive lease, so that average monthly payments would be between $650 and $700 per month. Because the outcome of such negotiations was uncertain at the time, however, the group used a figure of $750 per month in developing pro forma statements for the business.

INCOME STATEMENTS

An examination of the 1983 sales uncovered two major factors that had to be considered in the development of pro forma income statements. First, the monthly sales figures supplied by the CPA firm indicated a seasonal fluctuation in sales (see Exhibit 31.7). The effect of this fluctuation on the cash flows of the restaurant and its ability to meet its debts had to be determined. Secondly, the revenue growth of this restaurant would be limited by its capacity. Jeff needed to establish how close to capacity the restaurant was operating currently. Lunch and dinner sales should be considered separately. Lunch projections would be based on 260 days per year (52 weeks × 5 days) while dinner should be based on the full 312 days during which the restaurant was open. The current owners had already estimated the average check at each meal. The restaurant seated fifty-six people.

In order to get an idea of the expenses that the new management could face, Jeff then took the handwritten income statement provided by Mrs. Tarpey and attempted to adjust it. Several of the perquisites the Tarpeys enjoyed had been discussed during the meeting at Christian's. Excessive long-distance calls and the car payments could be eliminated. The new management would have to add the manager's salary and bonus. A 10% annual bonus on pre-tax profits would be offered to motivate the manager to run a tight ship. These expenses had to be separated into variable and fixed expense categories to determine a break-even point. The new estimates were in line with those found in a book entitled *Restaurant Finance*.

EXHIBIT 31.7

Seasonality Index—1983 Sales
(100 = 19,945)

MONTH	SALES	ACTUAL SEASONALITY
Jan	$18,543	93
Feb	19,085	96
Mar	18,097	91
Apr	19,984	100
May	20,423	102
Jun	21,836	109
Jul	19,304	97
Aug	22,231	111
Sep	20,002	100
Oct	20,589	103
Nov	19,300	97
Dec	18,948*	95*

*Assumed

Jeff was certain sales in the first year could be maintained at the current level if there was effective advertising. Forecasted sales for the second year are based on expanding lunch sales to capacity. Projections for years three through five assume that the restaurant will operate at capacity for both lunch and dinner. Increased sales will be achieved through advertising.

THE BANK LOAN

With the income statements prepared, Jeff approached the Sovran Bank to discuss the terms of a loan (see Exhibits 31.8 and 31.9). The bank was willing to set the monthly payments at a level that could be met by the cash flows of the restaurant, as long as the maturity of the loan did not exceed ten years. It appeared that five years would be an acceptable maturity. This loan would entail monthly payments of approximately $1,000.

The bank would accept 50% of the book value (approximately the $11,175 listed as market value by the CPA firm) of the assets as collateral but demanded that the balance be fully collateralized also.

The loan officer was concerned that the purchase price was too high and that an excessive amount of goodwill would be involved in the new business. He was also concerned that none of the new owners had any experience with operating a restaurant. With this in mind, he wanted to know more about the manager and cook.

EXHIBIT 31.8   **Pro Forma Income Statement**
(In Thousands of Dollars)

	YEAR			
For the Year Ended July 31	Two	Three	Four	Five
Net Sales				
Lunch	$120.0	$120.0	$120.0	$120.0
Dinner	144.0	152.0	152.0	152.0
Total	$264.0	$272.0	$272.0	$272.0
Variable Expenses (68%)	(180.0)	(185.0)	(185.0)	(185.0)
Operating Margin (32%)	$ 84.0	$ 87.0	$ 87.0	$ 87.0
Fixed Expenses	(40.8)	(40.9)	(42.4)	(42.4)
Earnings before Interest	$ 43.2	$ 46.1	$ 44.6	$ 44.6
Interest	(3.9)	(2.9)	(1.9)	(1.0)
Earnings before Bonus (EBB)	$ 39.3	$ 43.2	$ 42.7	$ 43.6
Bonus (.10 × EBB)	3.9	4.3	4.3	4.4
Taxable Earnings	$ 35.4	$ 38.9	$ 38.4	$ 39.2

EXHIBIT 31.9

Pro Forma Balance Sheet
(In Thousands of Dollars)

For the Year Ended July 31	YEAR					
	Initial	1	2	3	4	5
Assets						
Current assets						
Cash and securities	.30	10.70	20.70	20.70	34.60	27.70
Inventory						
Beer and wine (.04 month)	.80	.80	.90	.90	.90	.90
Food (.36/month)	7.20	7.20	7.90	8.20	8.20	8.20
Total current assets	8.30	18.70	29.50	29.80	43.70	36.80
Fixed assets	22.30	22.30	22.30	27.30	27.30	32.30
Accumulated depreciation	0.00	4.40	8.80	13.20	17.60	22.00
Net fixed assets	22.30	17.90	13.50	14.10	9.70	10.30
Intangibles						
Goodwill	35.20	35.20	35.20	35.20	35.20	35.20
Accumulated amortization	0.00	3.52	7.04	10.56	14.08	17.60
Net goodwill	35.20	31.68	28.16	24.64	21.12	17.60
Organization costs	.50	.40	.30	.20	.10	0.00
Total assets	66.30	68.68	71.46	68.74	74.62	64.70
Liabilities						
Current liabilities						
Accounts payable	7.60	7.60	7.90	8.20	8.20	8.20
Note payable	1.00	0.00	0.00	0.00	0.00	0.00
Total current liabilities	8.60	7.60	7.90	8.20	8.20	8.20
Long-term note	40.25	32.20	24.10	16.10	8.00	0.00
Total liabilities	48.85	39.80	32.00	24.30	16.20	8.20
Equity						
Stock	17.50	17.50	17.50	17.50	17.50	17.50
Retained earnings	0.00	11.38	21.96	26.94	40.92	39.00
Total equity	17.50	28.88	39.46	44.44	58.42	56.50
Total liabilities and equity	66.35	68.68	71.46	68.74	74.62	64.70

EVALUATING THE PURCHASE PRICE

Because several people had expressed concern over the price that the owners were asking, the partners wanted to decide the proper value of the restaurant. They agreed that this should be based on the present value of the income stream that the restaurant could generate. In light of the fact that eight out of ten restaurants fail, the partners selected 25% as the hurdle rate that would be used to discount future earnings. The set-up costs should not exceed the present value of the income stream. The partners wanted to include the eventual sales price or liquidation value of the restaurant at the end of five years in the computation of the present value. Assuming various levels of sales would establish a proper price range. The set-up costs included the $57,750 asking price and $500 organizational expense for legal and accounting fees. Because this was an ongoing concern, they would not have to invest significant additional working capital.

CONCLUDING REMARKS

On March 31, at the final meeting to discuss the prospects of purchasing Christian's, the group members were fully aware of the implications such a decision would have. It was generally agreed that such an endeavor provided potential for optimum managerial skill and experience in the business world, though none of the group members was certain that this was the route he wanted to take. Faced with exams in the coming weeks, time pressure from the realtor, and the knowledge that at least one other party was interested in purchasing Christian's, the group set out to make their decision, which for better or worse would affect their immediate futures.

The students were informed by the present owners that they must reach a decision quickly because other purchasers were interested in the same business opportunity.

Austad's

PHIL FISHER · JAMES TAYLOR

In 1982 the Austad Company, the world's largest retailer of golfing equipment, was attempting to extend its product lines. Located in Sioux Falls, South Dakota, and selling primarily by direct mail, the company had achieved sales of over $18 million in 1979, averaging over 20% growth in sales from 1974 to 1979. Sales had not increased in 1980 and 1981, however; and although profits had improved, the company founder and President, Oscar Austad, believed that a change in emphasis was needed.

> We don't want to be a sporting goods operation or an athletic supply house. We want to cater to a more affluent society that is looking for material needed for leisure time activities. We think people are going to have more time and money and we're going to get into things that will simply be called leisure time activities. This could involve some phase of travel, for example. Golf is, of course, a big part of that and always will be.

Austad's 1982 Summer catalog had sixty-four full-color pages of leisure-time equipment. The first thirty pages were devoted to golf clubs, bags, balls, shoes, accessories, and clothing. The catalog also featured running shoes, jogging suits, T-shirts, sportswear, tennis equipment, exercise equipment, lawn games, footballs, basketballs, baseball and softball gloves and bats, water skis, inflatable boats, fishing gear, and hiking and camping equipment.

Several factors were thought to have contributed to the lack of sales growth in 1980 and 1981. By increasing the number of regular mailings and decreasing the number of sale catalogs, Austad's had changed its mix of catalog mailings. Also, the economic recession had generally depressed sales of sports equipment. (See Exhibit 32.1.)

A third factor, and the major reason for Austad's product line extension, was that demand for golfing equipment was growing more slowly than was demand for equipment associated with other leisure-time activities. High real-estate prices discouraged the expansion of golf courses at a time when facilities for and interest in other leisure time activities were increasing rapidly. (See Exhibit 32.2.)

This case was prepared by Professor Phillip C. Fisher and Professor James Taylor of the University of South Dakota. It was presented at the 1985 Workshop of the Midwest Society for Case Research. Reprinted by permission.

EXHIBIT 32.1

U.S. Factory Sales of Selected Categories of Sports Equipment, 1974–1982

(In Millions of Dollars)

Equipment Year	1974	1976	1978	1980	1982
Golf	327	339	366	399	385
Fishing	220	238	268	325	318
Exercise and Playground	180	266	260	305	258
Tennis	N.A.	N.A.	114	119	135
Bowling	N.A.	N.A.	101	120	102

SOURCE: U.S. Department of Commerce, *Statistical Abstract of the United States*, 1978–1984.

COMPANY HISTORY

Mr. Austad started his business in 1963. Then employed as an insurance claims adjuster, he began selling golf-club tubes by mail. (Golf-club tubes are plastic cylinders that fit over golf club handles, to protect them while they are carried in a golf bag.) The business operated out of the basement of his Sioux Falls home. He reached his customers—golf pro shops and sporting goods stores—by way of a one-page mimeographed price list. A

EXHIBIT 32.2

Selected Statistics of Recreational Activity in the U.S., 1960–1980

Activity	1960	1965	1970	1975	1980
Fishing licenses sold (millions)	23	25	31	35	35
Hunting licenses sold (millions)	18	19	22	26	27
Tennis participants (millions)	5	N.A.	11	29	32(1979)
Tennis courts (thousands)	N.A.	N.A.	N.A.	130	160(1979)
Amateur Softball Playoffs (millions)	8	13	16	26	30
Golfers (millions)	4	8	10	12	13
Golf courses (number)	6,385	8,323	10,188	12,306	12,849
Retail sales of sports equipment and durable toys ($ billion)	2	2.9	5.1	9.7	13.8

SOURCE: U.S. Department of Commerce, *Statistical Abstract of the United States*, 1978–1984.

year later, with additional golf accessories added to his product line, he moved the operation to the upper floor of a warehouse and hired his first employee, Sharon Stahl. Miss Stahl processed orders, typed labels, answered the telephone, and waited on walk-in customers. Austad packed orders after the end of his working day as a claims adjuster. In 1965, with the business still growing, Austad, then 43 with a young family to support, quit his job and gave undivided attention to the business.

His sole supplier at this time was Kroyden, a Chicago-based golf equipment manufacturer (now the Ram Golf Corporation). Kroyden was owned and managed by Mr. Austad's brothers-in-law, who extended inventory financing to him. "They didn't want to see their sister starve," Austad explained.

While the business grew during the early years, Mr. Austad recognized factors that would limit its progress. He believed that many of his pro shop customers were indifferent merchandisers and poor credit risks. Sporting goods stores sold relatively little golf equipment. Dissatisfied with available channels, he decided to try direct-mail selling. He developed his own mailing lists from the Yellow Pages of telephone books. His first mailing was to banks, and subsequent mailings were to doctors and lawyers. All were successful in generating orders. An ample inventory enabled the company to fill orders and ship them within twenty-four hours. That and the company's emphasis on satisfying the customer led to repeat orders and growth of the mailing list through customer referrals.

After four years the business, now with eight employees, outgrew the warehouse loft, and in 1969 the company purchased a 36,000-square-foot building on the outskirts of Sioux Falls. Additions to the building brought it to 131,000 square feet by 1978; it included the warehouse, offices, and a large display room for walk-in retail sales. In 1982, Austad's had 170 employees; sixty of these were part-time employees.

Originally, customers ordered by mail. In 1974 the company installed its first WATS line to answer requests for information or complaints. Soon customers began requesting orders while they were on the phone, and in 1975, Austad's began accepting credit-card-billed telephone orders. Sales in 1975 increased by 58% over 1974, and the company currently has 16 WATS lines to receive calls from all states except South Dakota, Alaska, and Hawaii. In 1982 the company took orders from 7:00 A.M. to 8:00 P.M. Central Time on weekdays and during reduced hours on Saturdays and Sundays. Austad planned to increase the service to seven days, twenty-four hours when demand made it profitable.

Financial statements are shown in Exhibits 32.3, 32.4, and 32.5.

| **ORGANIZATION AND MANAGEMENT** | Seated in his large paneled office, wearing a golf shirt (although he admitted that he rarely played golf) and bright red slacks, Oscar Austad explained the principles that had brought his company to its present position. |

EXHIBIT 32.3 **The Austad Company: Condensed Statement of Operations**

(For the Years Ended December 31, 1974, through 1981)

	NET SALES	COST OF SALES	GROSS PROFIT	EXPENSES, INCLUDING FEDERAL INCOME TAX AND NET OF OTHER INCOME	NET INCOME (LOSS)
1974	$ 5,747,077	$ 4,343,058	$1,404,019	$1,273,206	$130,813
1975	8,869,593	6,484,509	2,385,084	2,089,159	298,925
1976	11,109,017	7,638,855	3,470,162	2,967,021	503,141
1977	13,722,558	8,878,712	4,843,846	4,022,079	821,767
1978	13,958,600	10,526,506	3,432,094	3,595,065	(162,971)
1979	18,656,353	12,678,905	5,977,488	5,728,198	249,250
1980	18,109,103	12,424,841	5,684,262	5,606,410	77,852
1981	18,148,246	10,471,236	7,677,010	6,959,364	717,646

NOTE: The Austad Company operated as a sole proprietorship of Oscar M. Austad from 1963 through 1973. The above summary reflects the results of operations of the company since incorporation.

I had some definite ideas on a business. I knew nothing about the mail order business, but I had dealt enough with other companies that I could tell the things that pleased me and the things that irritated me. I also felt that too many companies, even giant companies, were not customer conscious enough. They weren't determined enough to make sure that everyone was treated fairly. If they goofed up an order or a customer, they would just shrug and let it go at that and figure who cares if we lose one customer, we have a million others! I've always looked upon this as like a snowball rolling down a hill, you lose a customer and he starts telling others, then you are going in the wrong direction. On the other hand, if you get a satisfied customer and he is talking it up, there is no limit to how much good you can do. This is why one thing I wanted to do was to not *just* make sure we were being fair with everyone, but if we did goof something up and got a customer mad at us, probably with good reason, to me it was a golden opportunity that we shouldn't pass up; that we should turn that man around from being one of our severest critics to being one of our biggest boosters. This has happened time and time again. We don't ignore complaints.

The type of situation which has occurred is a customer gets in touch with us by letter or telephone and says he was promised an order by a certain date and it came late and something was shipped wrong, etc., and he has had it, and he is mad, and he says "Take me off your mailing list, I'll tell all my friends to never buy from you again." We look on this as a challenge. I get back to these personally by phone or letter. I admit the mistake, I don't try to soft pedal it. He is right and we are wrong, and we admit it. However,

EXHIBIT 32.4

The Austad Company: Statement of Income and Retained Earnings

(For the Years Ended December 31, 1981 and 1980)

	1981	1980
Gross sales	$18,351,286	$18,263,090
Less refunds and allowances	203,040	153,987
Net sales	18,148,246	18,109,103
Cost of goods sold	10,471,236	12,424,841
Gross profit	7,677,010	5,684,262
Selling, general, and administrative expenses	6,193,043	5,045,623
Income from operations	1,483,967	638,639
Other income (expense):		
Interest expense	(764,344)	(593,950)
Investment income	335,153	—
Other income	107,870	53,163
	(321,321)	(540,787)
Income before provision for federal income taxes	1,162,646	97,852
Provision for federal income taxes	445,000	20,000
Net income	717,646	77,852
Retained earnings, beginning	1,820,377	1,742,525
Retained earnings, ending	$ 2,538,023	$ 1,820,377

EXHIBIT 32.5

The Austad Company: Balance Sheet

(December 31, 1981 and 1980)

	1981	1980
Assets		
Current assets:		
Cash and savings	$102,979	$129,117
Trade accounts receivable	115,563	98,742
Merchandise inventory	7,263,534	7,732,567
Prepaid postage and other	11,009	28,571
Refundable federal income taxes	—	85,231
Marketable securities at cost, net of allowance for decline in market of $10,280 in 1980	—	1,777
Total current assets	$7,493,085	$8,076,005

	1981	1980
Assets		
Property and equipment:		
Land	15,000	15,000
Buildings and building improvements	1,491,598	1,479,614
Equipment and fixtures	483,741	374,646
Vehicles	68,378	49,019
	2,058,717	1,918,279
Less accumulated depreciation	740,796	613,653
Net property and equipment	1,317,921	1,304,626
Total assets	$8,811,006	$9,380,631
Liabilities		
Current liabilities:		
Current portion of long-term debt	$ 84,031	$ 76,305
Notes payable, bank[1]	1,600,000	2,650,000
Trade accounts payable	3,086,147	3,753,388
Prepaid customer orders	24,334	49,464
Accrued liabilities:		
Payroll, property and sales taxes	61,873	42,977
Salaries and wages	96,368	51,079
Interest and other	62,788	57,326
Employees' pension contribution	66,691	50,000
Federal income taxes payable	445,031	—
Total current liabilities	5,527,263	6,730,539
Long-term debt, net of current portion above	696,319	780,314
Total liabilities	6,223,582	7,510,853
Stockholders' Equity		
Capital stock—$1 par value, 500,000 shares authorized, 44,817 shares issued and outstanding	44,817	44,817
Additional paid-in capital	4,584	4,584
Retained earnings	2,538,023	1,820,377
Total stockholders' equity	2,587,424	1,869,778
Total liabilities and stockholders' equity	$8,811,006	$9,380,631

[1]Notes payable, bank consists of a revolving loan agreement with a limit of $4,500,000 due monthly at the current prime rate.

when we are right and he is wrong we don't try to change the facts either. We explain what happened and what can be done to make amends, and give him a lot of choices. And even if he doesn't buy from us anymore and wants to sent the order back for a refund, we'll send him one or two dozen golf balls with his name on them, just for the inconvenience it has caused him. We don't ask for anything in return. Every time, without exception, we get a contact from that customer. He apologizes for complaining in the first place, says please don't take his name off the mailing list. Some have even asked for catalogs to pass out among their friends.

I think in the mail order business the image of the company must be one where the customer trusts us and knows he'll get a fair and proper adjustment.

The best source of names we have is from customers who send us names. We encourage it by including a place on back of order blanks for that. They give us at least 100,000 good names a year. These are not only the best names, most productive, but they are free.

The Austad Company was organized into three functional groups: finance, marketing, and operations. The Austad organizational chart is shown in Exhibit 32.6 as it appeared in company documents.

EXHIBIT 32.6   Austad's Organizational Chart

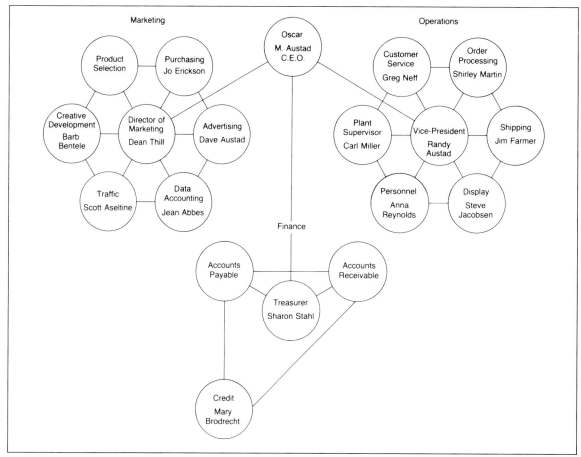

Mr. Austad had somewhat reluctantly had the chart drawn at the urging of his sons, Randy and Dave, and the cluster form reflects his general dislike for hierarchy and bureaucratic institutions. Top managers included Sharon Stahl, his first employee, who was responsible for financial functions; Randy Austad, Oscar's eldest son, who managed operations; and Dean Thill, Director of Marketing.

The Austad Company promoted from within when possible. Its operational employees were not unionized, and company management believed that the performance of the work force was excellent. Seven of the 15 people listed on the organizational chart were women, Mr. Austad commented:

> I have worked with a lot of companies that I felt discriminated against women. I learned a long time ago that women can do anything men can do and they usually try a little harder. I don't know of any company that has treated all employees as fairly as we have. At least half of our supervisors happen to be female. I think a lot of companies are missing the boat by not using this talent because they feel it has got to be a man to do this or that. We don't discriminate against men, we just look at what people can do whatever sex they may be.

Commenting on this, Treasurer Sharon Stahl said, "If you work here you have a golden opportunity. Oscar has always felt that if you will try harder he will give you a chance."

The Austad Company enforced a no-smoking rule that applied to all areas of its building, including customers in the retail display area. Oscar Austad was Chairman of the Board of Trustees of Action on Smoking and Health (ASH). A Washington-based organization that Austad described as the legal arm of the nonsmoking community, it was instrumental in securing segregated smoking and nonsmoking seating on airlines.

Mr. Austad was active in other community and national affairs. He had served in the South Dakota State Senate, was on the Board of Regents for Augsburg College, which he had attended, was a Director of a local bank, and in 1982 was serving as President of the Center on National Labor Policy, a conservative research and lobbying organization affiliated with the National Right-to-Work Committee.

MARKETING

Austad's purchased its products directly from manufacturers and sold them directly to consumers, although a small percentage of sales were still made to pro shops and other retail outlets. Most manufacturers sold to Austad's on terms of net in 90 days; a few gave even longer terms. Direct volume buying at prices as low as those charged to wholesalers allowed Austad's to sell at prices it believed to be very competitive. Austad's also preferred to sell products that were unique. Golfing equipment included clubs, balls, and bags sold under Austad's house brand, Senator (Mr. Austad has served as a South Dakota state senator). Beginner's golf equipment and some accessories were sold under the Austad's name. Austad's also carried such well-known brand names as McGregor, Ram, Spalding, and Wilson, but these products were often specially manufactured for Austad's and were to some degree unique. For example, there were many Jack Nicklaus clubs on the market, but the one called Jack Nicklaus "Classic" was exclusive with Austad's.

In Mr. Austad's opinion, competition for sales of golf equipment comes primarily from traditional outlets such as golf club pro shops, sporting goods stores, and department store chains. Austad's offered a wider product selection and typically sold at lower prices than these retailers. Discount stores also carried limited lines of golf equipment, but Mr. Austad believed that with a few exceptions they had not merchandised it successfully. Some had recently discontinued carrying golf equipment. There were other mail-order competitors, but Mr. Austad believed that lack of experience and inadequate financing had as yet prevented them from being serious competitors.

New products were added to the Austad line after evaluation by a committee that was headed by Oscar's son, Dave. Criteria for selecting new products included consistency with the leisure-time-equipment concept and potential profitability. In 1980, shortly after completing his B.S. in Business Administration at Augustana College, a private college in Sioux Falls, Dave initiated a study of profitability by product line. Product lines were expected to cover both direct costs and allocated overhead. As a result of this analysis, some product lines such as billiard equipment were dropped. Some other nongolfing product lines such as tennis equipment were considered only marginally profitable.

Until 1981, Austad's mailed one catalog a year but ran numerous sales using small flyers. An analysis of sales indicated that customers would wait for the flyers to do their buying, so in 1981, Austad's reduced the number of sales flyers and changed the catalog mailings to four per year: An Early Bird catalog in January, a Summer catalog in March, a Fall catalog in August, and a Christmas catalog in October. The new schedule of mailings helped the company in two ways. First, suppliers that had formerly been asked to guarantee prices for eighteen months were now asked only for four-month guarantees and therefore sold to Austad's at somewhat lower prices. Second, it improved average selling prices, because customers purchased more goods at regular prices.

The Austad Company's catalog mailing list contained nearly one million names. In addition to catalog mailings, the company also placed ads for particular products and for catalogs in about 100 different magazines and newspapers. These ads brought some orders for products and requests for catalogs, but whether they would result in long-term profits was as yet unclear.

The Austad Company had conducted research on the demographics of its customers. While evenly distributed across age groups from 18 to 64, the average Austad customer was unique in several ways: 70% had college degrees, the average income in 1982 was $36,000, most were married with no children, and 80% were golfers.

The survey also indicated that customers had a very favorable image of the company. Dave Austad discussed the survey's results:

> In a survey last year I mailed 5,000 questionnaires to our recent customers—those who ordered in the last year—just to get perceptions of how they feel about Austad's—about how they rate our service, quality, or merchandise, delivery time—we came out very positive on that. People who buy from us enjoy us a lot, and they tell others. Seventy percent of our customers heard about us from friends or relatives, which I think is a great tribute. I think that is the reason we have been successful. Even though he started out without long range plans, Dad still had the perception that we want to be here for a long time, that we don't want to get one sale then drop them, we want to continue to nurture those who buy from us once and continue to buy from us in the future. I think that is why we were successful.

The demographic analysis and the analysis of profitability had led to a gradual shift in selection of products. Dave Austad went on to say, "We and our customers perceived us as a discount house and our margins were too low." Current product-line selection criteria were expected to result in a shift in the company's image to that of a specialty retailer with unique merchandise. New product lines were added incrementally. A few products in the new line were offered and tested before Austad's would commit itself to the full line. New market targets were fashion-oriented, active, sports and fitness enthusiasts. The order-processing system at Austad's was entirely manual, but most orders were shipped within 24 hours of receipt, and each order received quality-control checks at every stage in the processing system.

Customer service representatives manned the 16 WATS lines and took about one-half of Austad's sales orders. They manually filled out order forms as the orders were taken. They were also responsible for making credit checks. Austad's placed great emphasis on fraud detection and believed that its phone service representatives had been effective in the minimizing of this problem.

Completed order forms from the customer service department and orders received by mail were sent to the Order Processing Department, where mailing labels were typed, numbered, and filmed for recording. Each order and the accompanying label were checked before being sent to the warehouse.

At Austad's spacious warehouse, order "pickers" manually assembled the orders. The assembled orders were checked against the order and packed for shipping. At the shipping department, invoices were prepared and checked against the order before shipping, and the shipping order forms were filmed once more.

Dave Austad commented on changes which were occurring in the company's operations:

> I see my father as an entrepreneur. He is the type of person who is successful when he can handle the whole process himself. He's a "doer." He saw that there was a market for selling golf clubs. He had the idea of going through phone books and picking out doctors and lawyers. He typed up labels, sent

out flyers—he had total control over the company. We are coming to the point where dad has a difficult time controlling everything. We can't do some of the old ways—inventory, for example. On Saturday night after watching a TV show he would go through his inventory book in about two hours and decide what he needed. Now we have about 7,000 sku's [stock keeping units] and there is no way we can do that. Interest rates were much lower then and if he could get a quantity discount he would get a sizable supply. We can't do that now. We have systems now for determining economic order point, what lead times are needed, etc. We are past the point where we must get into formal procedures. We have made greater changes since last year than at any time in the past. We went on the Vandemark System about eight months ago. Since then we have not seen the large inventory surpluses of the past. This system is a manual system that we use since we don't have our system on computer yet.

Austad's eldest son, Randy, had the major responsibility for designing and managing operations. He had visited several other mail-order companies and studied their operations. Randy was preparing to convert manual operations and record keeping to a computerized system. Various vendors had been contacted and were making proposals. Conversion was to be implemented on a step-by-step basis and completed in early 1983.

FUTURE DIRECTIONS

The Austads were not completely satisfied with the results of their product-line extension. While sales of nongolf-related equipment had reached 32% of revenues by 1982, few nongolf products were earning adequate profits. The Austads wondered if the use of a single catalog and mailing list was the best strategy. Since 80% of their customers were golfers and much of the catalog was devoted to golf equipment, clothing, and accessories, it was possible that their other products were not being directed to the right market or being shown to the best advantage.

Although the retail display room had originally been intended as a convenience to local customers, the Austads found that increasing local advertising increased sales for this outlet. These sales had grown to slightly more than 10% of total sales, and the Austads were seriously thinking about opening other retail outlets. Other mail-order companies, such as Eddie Bauer, had done this successfully. One approach being considered would be to open stores in major cities in areas having their highest mail-order sales. Here they would presumably already have a base of loyal customers. This option would concentrate their stores in the upper Midwest. Another option under consideration was to open several stores in a single state, preferably a large, high-growth Sun Belt state such as Texas. This would simplify distribution and place stores in growing markets. It would also minimize the company's requirements for the collection of sales taxes, because direct-mail retailers are required to collect sales taxes only on shipments to states in which they have retail facilities.

The Austads were confident of the company's ability to continue to succeed in direct mail retailing of golf equipment and accessories. They were less certain, however, of which direction to take for the achievement of continued growth.

APPENDIX 32.1

Direct Marketing

The appeal was low prices when Aaron Montgomery Ward developed his first catalog in Chicago in 1872 and Richard Sears sold watches with a mailing list of 20,000 railroad station agents. Small towns in the United States had few stores that carried much beyond basic general merchandise, which was placed on sale with a relatively high markup to cover business costs and low volume of sales. Only 27% of the population lived in cities then.

Other "mail-order" establishments were selling seed and sporting goods. By 1912, in Freeport, Maine, L. L. Bean started selling rubber-bottomed shoes for outdoorsmen; also in sporting goods, Orvis in Manchester, Vermont, and Seattle's Eddie Bauer were in business.[1]

In 1913, "mail order" received help when the parcel post system of the U.S. Postal Service was established.[2]

Mail-order retailers numbered around 2,500 by 1918. In the 1930s and 1940s, many retailers discontinued their mail-order operations because of the spread of chain stores to smaller cities and the spread of hard-surface roads that made these smaller cities accessible to rural and small town citizens.[3]

By the early 1970s the direct-mail or mail-and-telephone-order retailers numbered around 8,000 and never achieved more than 1.3% of total U.S. retail sales.[4]

In 1982, more than five billion catalogs were sent to U.S. households. Each household received an average of forty catalogs in 1982. The $40 billion in consumer sales by mail order represented 4% of retail sales in 1982 and sales were growing at a rate of 15% a year—five times faster than other retail sales. Predictions have been made that 20% of total retail sales will be by mail-order retailers by 1990.[5]

The mail-and-telephone-order business, also known as direct marketers, takes several forms:[6]

1. *Mail-order catalog:* The seller mails a catalog to a list of potential customers. These mailing lists are often developed by and sold to the companies by mailing-list brokerage houses.

2. *Direct response:* The seller runs an ad in a newspaper, a magazine, on radio, or on TV. The buyer writes or phones the address or number in the ad, places an order for merchandise, and/or asks for a catalog.

3. *Direct mail:* The seller sends a mail piece—letter flyer or foldout—to people whose names appear on special mailing lists, which usually represent prospects for the product the company is marketing.

4. *Telephone selling:* Sellers use telephones to solicit orders for specific items such as subscriptions to a magazine, home repair service, or contributions to fund drives at the old alma mater.

(Continued)

APPENDIX 32.1 **(Continued)**

The rise in the direct marketing business has attracted the attention of ad agencies that formerly did not seek direct marketing business.

The agencies now promote direct marketing because they can offer both advertising and selling in one operation, with completely traceable, countable, measurable and bankable reactions from the market.[7]

The reasons for the increased sales of direct marketing firms are mainly environmental changes and lifestyles. Shopping in retail stores has become a hassle to many. Herding children in stores, carrying heavy packages a block across parking lots, attempting to get assistance in a self-service mass merchandising "one-stop convenience" store makes the sedentary buying in the home from a catalog look better than ever before. Lester Wunderman of Young and Rubicam's direct-marketing group comments:

He (the retailer) uses fewer and less-well trained clerks, stocks only fast-turnover or high-markup products, insists they be well pre-advertised, offers no credit, sells cash and carry—your cash and your carry. The retailer dehumanizes the whole process of shopping. The manufacturer increasingly carries the burden and expense of selling. And the consumer is offered more and more self-service—a euphemism for no service at all.[8]

Direct marketing is expanding partly because more retailers are starting catalog operations and finding store-traffic building, suggesting a synergy in the two operations. Also, many marketers find that featuring an 800 phone number in their ads for direct ordering produces immediate sales.

Direct-marketing agencies and branches of regular ad agencies have developed over the past few years. These agencies offer direct marketing services, including research, design, printing, and distribution. These agencies develop information about the demographics of buyers, and help in the identifying of market segments. "Most major ad agencies now have some internal or subsidiary direct marketing capabilities—or are working to acquire some."[9]

Concerning lifestyles, the changing role of women, as more are employed with less time to shop, helps account for at-home shopping. The rise in the number of working women also means more two-income families and thus more family money to spend and less time to spend it.

Technology has helped direct marketing. The industry would be handicapped without the computer, the credit card, and the telephone. The industry has also given opportunity to seventy-five mailing-list brokers. The service of WATS 800 lines and 24-hour-a-day order taking has made direct marketing the most convenient way to shop. It is also the only way many shoppers can get access to merchandise of an unusual, even exotic nature. Few would be able to find some of the merchandise other than through direct marketing even if they knew it was available.

The future of direct marketing may include shopping from the TV set with two-way videotex, which will allow a shopper to view items and their descriptions and order instantly.

N O T E S

1. "Catalog Cornucopia," *Time* (Nov. 8, 1982), p. 76.

2. Richard M. Clevett, *Marketing Channels* (Homewood, Il.: Richard D. Irwin, Inc., 1954), p. 62.

3. Phillip Kotler, *Principles of Marketing,* 2nd ed. (Englewood Cliffs, N.J.: Prentice-Hall, Inc., 1983), pp. 398–399.

4. E. Jerome McCarthy, *Basic Marketing,* 6th ed. (Homewood, Il.: Richard D. Irwin, Inc., 1978), p. 341.

5. "Catalog Cornucopia," p. 73.

6. Kotler.

7. Walter McQuade, "There's a Lot of Satisfaction (Guaranteed) in Direct Marketing," *Fortune* (April 21, 1980), p. 111.

8. *Ibid.*

9. Len Strazewski, "Taking the Best of Both Scenes," *Advertising Age* (March 7, 1985), p. 16.

Urschel Laboratories, Inc.

WILLIAM E. SCHLENDER

INTRODUCTION Since 1910 Urschel Laboratories has grown to be the dominant producer of equipment for food processing, technically referred to as precision size reduction. Size reduction is done by machines designed to perform a variety of operations, including slicing, dicing, strip cutting, julienne cutting, shredding, comminuting, granulating, homogenizing, emulsifying, and mincing. The market for size-reduction equipment includes such firms as suppliers to restaurants and hotels, fast food chains, manufacturers of food products (such as canning companies), potato chip makers, and similar industries.

As of the end of 1986, Urschel Laboratories is a privately held corporation, wholly owned by the Urschel family. The company is headquartered in Valparaiso, Indiana, and has annual sales of approximately $40 million. Top management executives are Urschel family members. Despite its market domination in the United States and its evident success in foreign countries, the company's current plans are to remain a privately held corporation, and no major change in rate of growth is projected. Management believes in generating the needed financing internally. Although Urschel follows conservative pricing policies related almost entirely to production costs, and customer service is given the highest priority, management does not see itself as a market-oriented firm, but rather prefers to describe itself as a product-oriented enterprise.

The creative force behind the development, production, and management of Urschel Laboratories resides in the Urschel family, which combined invention and entrepreneurship to produce a product that has been widely used in the food processing industry, and more recently in pharmaceutical, chemical, and cosmetic industries as well. Because of the heavy emphasis that management places upon quality in both the manufacturing processes and the performance of the end product, Urschel has gradually moved toward a high degree of vertical integration. The company manufactures the equipment used in producing size-reduction-machine parts, assembles the final product, and performs the marketing functions in domestic and foreign markets.

This case was prepared by Professor William E. Schlender of Valparaiso University. It was presented at the 1986 Workshop of the Midwest Society for Case Research. It also appears in *Annual Advances in Business Cases,* 1986, pp. 395–415, edited by Phillip C. Fisher. Reprinted by permission.

COMPANY HISTORY

In 1910 William E. Urschel founded the company that was to become Urschel Laboratories. Born and raised on a farm in Indiana, he graduated in 1901 from Valparaiso University with a major in fine arts. He then journeyed west to Idaho and Montana, and worked in such diverse jobs as postal service, government surveying, and prospecting for gold. After several years, he returned to do further study in fine arts at Valparaiso University and later in Chicago, where he also worked as a designer of hand-painted china.

Gooseberries were grown in considerable volume in Indiana at that time, and in 1907 Mr. Urschel returned to Valparaiso and began experimenting with the Gooseberry Snipper, a machine that he invented to remove the stems and blossom ends from gooseberries. The result was the Urschel Gooseberry Snipper Factory. The gooseberry snipper was the first of more than ninety patents eventually held by William Urschel, and the machine was soon sold in many parts of the world. As the firm flourished and inventions were produced, the business rapidly became an experimental laboratory for the development of machinery for the canning industry. Eventually the name of the firm was changed to Urschel Laboratories. As the dominant producer of precision size-reduction-equipment for food, Urschel continues to place a heavy emphasis on development of new kinds of processing machinery.

In the company's earlier years the smaller food-processing machines were manufactured in the Valparaiso factory. Patents covering inventions for larger machines were licensed to other manufacturers. William Urschel was more interested in experimentation and development than in manufacturing. He cared little about making money beyond an amount necessary to carry on experimental work and felt that management of money took time away from the work he enjoyed. So absorbed was he in innovation and experimental work that he frequently neglected to arrange for other firms to produce his inventions because of the time such contact and negotiating work involved. Mr. Urschel decided early not to enlarge the manufacturing facilities of Urschel Laboratories, because he believed that such enlargements would interfere with his experimental and development work.

The inventive trait was encouraged in William Urschel's three sons, Joe, Gerald, and Kenneth, who entered the business in the 1930s. Joe Urschel gave this account of how William Urschel taught his three sons to be inventors.

> By the time we boys were 12 years old, we could run all the machine tools, make patterns for the foundry and make molds in the foundry. Then, father began to teach us how to invent. There were some rules. When we were to design a better machine than those made by others, we were never to determine how the other machines operated. This knowledge could prejudice our thinking and prevent us from creating designs from our own brains. Also, we were not to discover the selling price of these other machines. Such knowledge could

cause us to cheapen our own product. We were encouraged to conceive of many diverse methods that were not conventional. Sometimes each of us would take our drawing boards into different rooms to work on a new idea, then afterward we would compare our drawings to determine who had the best solution.

Upon entering the business, the three sons began inventing and developing a full line of machinery for performing the various kinds of processing operations used for size reduction. The "take-off" phase of Urschel Laboratories occurred with greatly increased production in the late 1930s. Differentiated models of machines to perform the various functions were developed.

Joe R. Urschel served as President of Urschel Laboratories until 1984, and currently presides as Chairman of the Board and Chief Executive Officer. He has been the chief spokesman for the company and the author of corporate policy statements, as well as of most general communications to employees.

Joe Urschel studied engineering at the University of Wisconsin for three years. Entering with advanced standing in some courses, he decided after several years that he had learned all he would from the available offerings and returned to Urschel Laboratories. In addition to heading up management of the Urschel enterprises, his interests involved him in a number of diverse activities. In 1974 he authored and published a book entitled *Sophisticated Electronics For Fun*. In it he set forth a step by step guide to the "how to" of modern electronics, and gave "complete tried and proven plans" for the building of electronic slot machines, electronic clocks with chimes, a juke box with no moving parts, and a "complete game to test your skills against the computer." This avocation some years later led to the establishment of Indiana Information Controls Inc., a subsidiary established to provide data-processing services to business firms, particularly banks located in several states.

Joe and Gerald Urschel together hold about seventy patents for Urschel products and represent much of the driving force behind the development of the technology of Urschel size-reduction equipment. Kenneth Urschel chose to channel his creative talent toward the planning of the company buildings, design of layout, and acting as architect for such structures as the computer facility.

Machines generally can be adapted to produce different sizes of processed foods or other materials. An illustrated catalog distributed by Urschel details size-reduction of food products from "Almonds" to "Zucchini." For each product, the catalog lists, in order of suitability, the type of machine to be used, along with the degrees of size-reduction possible, summary instructions for the machine's use, its capacity of production, and similar information. Additional technical information about Urschel precision size-reduction equipment is offered upon request.

Experience with applications of Urschel machines has been detailed extensively in trade magazines such as *Food Engineering International* and *Processed Prepared Foods*. Processing of food has taken such forms as slicing, dicing, and strip-cutting of vegetables and fruits for canning, freezing and dehydration; preparing vegetables for salad bars in fast-food restaurants; dicing and chopping meat for hamburger; flake-cutting of meat for reconstituted steaks and stew meats; and size reduction of peanuts for peanut butter. Other examples of foods prepared with Urschel machines and reported on are mustard, ketchup, pizzas, and cheese products.

Eventually the company entered the foreign market, and export of Urschel machinery grew to such a volume that sales of machines for export exceeded in some years domestic market sales. With increasing sales volume and production operations, Urschel found it necessary to relocate to the northern section of Valparaiso, where the company acquired several hundred acres of undeveloped land. This became the site of Urschel Laboratories, Indiana Information Controls, and Urschel Development Corporation.

At the end of 1986, management estimated that 90% of all commercial size-reduction of food was done on Urschel equipment. In some lines, such as commercial potato chips, the estimate approximates 99%. Personnel employed by Urschel Laboratories totaled approximately 200.

PROCESSING TECHNOLOGY

Urschel Laboratories produces about forty different models of food processing machines. They are unique in that all employ continuous motion operation, permitting free and uninterrupted flow of products through the machines, and thus contributing to their high capacities and gentle action on the food products.

Because Urschel produces a full line of machinery for slicing, dicing, strip cutting, julienne cutting, shredding, comminuting, granulating, homogenizing, emulsifying, and mincing operations, the design of each model is directed toward the effective application of one or more of the above operations. As the manual *How To Cut Food Products* details in its cataloging of various food products for size reduction, particular models are prescribed for the desired processing of a product. For example, potatoes may be processed on any one of fourteen different models depending on the shape and dimensions into which the slices or cubes are to be cut. Some machines may be adapted for different operations by variation in the type and setting of cutting blades.

The bulk of the company's business is the production of machines for cutting up fruits and vegetables. Quoting Joe Urschel:

> One of the models, the potato chip slicer, is important to food processors because it is the first machine manufactured that could cut potato chips at very high capacity and yet make a uniform slice thickness that is necessary to

make a quality potato chip. In slicing, dicing and strip cutting of all kinds of fruits and vegetables, Urschel machines have higher capacities in tons per hour than any previously built machines; they also cut the product more accurately, and they create less tearing and mashing of the product. An Urschel machine, for example, is able to dice a soft product like avocados at the rate of several tons per hour without mashing them. We also discovered that the best way to slice pickles is one slice at a time. Older types of slicers built by other firms made all the slices at one time, resulting in many mashed and broken slices. In our machine, pickles are sliced one slice at a time, but at 600 slices per second.

Illustrative of the operating principle of a number of models is the dicing machine shown in *How to Cut Food Products,* and described in Exhibit 33.1. Food products are fed to the machine through a hopper and then impelled past several sets of cutting blades that result in cubes or three-dimensional cuts of selected sizes. Portion control is achieved in a variety of food dishes—fresh canned or frozen—so that the use of exactly measurable portions is permitted.

A different operation is illustrated by the Model SPS Slicer, which uses a horizontal cutting design to prepare cream-style corn for canning. The operating principle and distinctive features of this high-precision machine makes possible the production of up to ten tons of sliced corn per hour.

Perhaps the most advanced size-reduction machine produced by Urschel Laboratories is the Comitrol®* Comminuting Machine. It is described in a company booklet as having "helped to revolutionize controlled size-reduction techniques. Its unique, precision-cutting principle has proved to be a processing breakthrough . . . handling a constantly expanding variety of applications in the Food, Pharmaceutical and Chemical Industries."

The size-reduction process is actually a high-speed centrifugal cutting operation. Centrifugal force impels the meat or other food product at very high rotational speeds against a stationary cutting head made up of closely spaced, precision-honed shearing edges or blades. As the centrifugal impelling force moves the product against the cutting edges of the blades a uniformly cut product results. The cutting or size-reduction, using the principle of incremental shear, can be varied ranging from slicing or dicing in fairly large pieces down to producing particles of ingredients in a pharmaceutical paste ointment; or a cutting head could reduce peanuts to sizes that permit production of crunchy peanut butter, or alternatively, peanut butter of a very creamy consistency.

Flaking and Forming Meat Products

A major application of Urschel machines has been in the flaking and forming of meat products. In this process a Comitrol machine, for example, slices

---

*Comitrol® is a registered trademark of Urschel Laboratories, Inc.

EXHIBIT 33.1   **Urschel Dicing Machine, Machine Descriptions**

MACHINE DESCRIPTIONS

MODELS G, GK and H
MODELS G-A, GK-A and H-A

These models operate exactly alike. The Model G makes straight cuts in the smaller size range. The Model H makes straight cuts in the larger size range. The Model GK is for making both crinkle and straight cuts.

The performance of these machines is outstanding because of gentle cutting action and high capacity.

OPERATING PRINCIPLE

Products to be cut are fed through a hopper into the center of the rotating impeller. Centrifugal action of the impeller blades causes the product to move in a circular path along the inner surface of the slicing case. An adjustable slicing gate at the top of the case allows the product to move outward with relation to the edge of the slicing knife. Distance between the end of the slicing gate and the knife edge determines slice thickness. As slices emerge, cross cut knives move downward producing strips or French fry cuts. Strips move without interruption across the top surface of the slicing knife holder into circular knives. Strips are then cut transversely by the circular knives to form cubes or three dimensional cuts of selected size.

This advanced cutting principle has distinct advantages over previously used methods. Many products tend to crack parallel with the knife edge during slicing. This is particularly true of brittle root vegetables which may have been stored at low temperatures. Cross cut knife edges of G, GK and H machines are parallel with the edge of the slicing knife so that slicing strains are relieved as strips are cut, and before actual cracking can occur.

Product damage is further reduced by moving slices in a single plane from first cut to last. The crushing and impact which accompanies rapid changes in direction is eliminated and makes gentle, high speed cutting a reality.

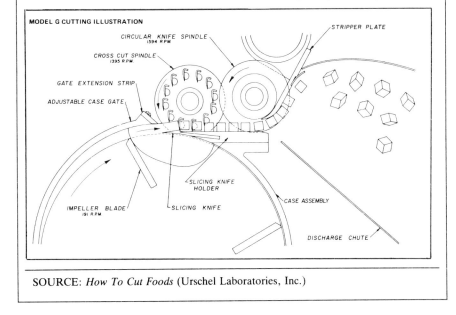

MODEL G CUTTING ILLUSTRATION

CIRCULAR KNIFE SPINDLE 1594 R.P.M.

CROSS CUT SPINDLE 1395 R.P.M.

GATE EXTENSION STRIP

ADJUSTABLE CASE GATE

STRIPPER PLATE

SLICING KNIFE HOLDER

SLICING KNIFE

IMPELLER BLADE 191 R.P.M.

CASE ASSEMBLY

DISCHARGE CHUTE

SOURCE: *How To Cut Foods* (Urschel Laboratories, Inc.)

meat into paper-thin flakes. They are then blended and reformed or refabricated into "logs" or loaves, which are then used to make steaks, roasts, patties, and other shapes. Examples of meat products made by flaking and forming are beef, pork (including boneless ribs), lamb, poultry and fish.

Although the flaking and forming of meat products was introduced in the early 1940s, early processing methods were uneconomical. Processing was done by cutting, chopping, grinding or slicing. These required that meat be kept within a narrow temperature range—if too cold it could chip, if too warm it would not flake or slice at all. Furthermore, only high-lean, low-fat content with a minimum of connective tissue could be used. Thus the raw material costs for higher quality meats added to the total cost.

Flaking by the Urschel process retains the meat's flavor juices because there is no grinding or crushing involved. Also, the thin flaking process lends itself ideally to effective size-reduction and integration of connective tissue, bone and gristle, and thus converts these waste products into edible ingredients of the final product. The Urschel process readily uses fresh or frozen meats, utilizes more of the parts of meat that formerly had to be discarded, yet results in flavor improvement because basic juices of the meat are retained. Also, because Urschel machines operate at a faster rate and at cooler temperatures than did other methods, food products are exposed for less time and absorb less heat, and thus further retain flavor.

Pharmaceuticals

The comminuting process by Comitrol machines is also used for particle size-reduction for ingredients in ointment. Previously, typical particle size-reduction has been accomplished by the passing of ointment ingredients through a three-roll mill until the proper particle size was achieved.

An account of particle size-reduction at Marion Laboratories illustrates the machine's application and advantages. The firm manufactures a topical ointment for heart patients. The ointment is applied directly to the skin above the heart area, and the active ingredients are absorbed slowly over time. Previous processing was done by the passing of the ointment through a three-roll mill. The Urschel comminuting process was credited with resulting in: (1) finer particles, (2) longer shelf life, with no sign of deterioration or separation, (3) faster production time, (4) less exposure time, reducing risk of contamination, (5) 50% reduction in cleaning time, (6) immediate start-up time vs. twenty-minute start-up time for the previous three-roll mill process.[1]

SELF-CONSTRUCTED MANUFACTURING EQUIPMENT

Urschel management has encouraged design suggestions from customers, who also have often set standards as to how size-reduction machines should be made. In its efforts to provide the kind of products that would meet customer requirements, Urschel found that suppliers could not meet its requirements for capital equipment used to manufacture size-reduction machines. The company therefore gradually assumed the task of making virtually all its own production equipment. For example, the company set up its own foundry operation to assure a supply of parts that meet specifications of quality and dimension.[2] It also developed its own computer controls for production and quality control processes.

THE QUALITY FACTOR

Several factors account for Urschel's heavy emphasis on quality as being perhaps the single most important ingredient in the success formula of Urschel Laboratories. First, from the beginning William Urschel preferred experimentation, innovation, and improvement of machines and equipment over producing them. He manufactured the processing machines only when he could not find other manufacturers to do the production. When the next generation of the family began to develop high-speed cutting equipment, other firms were unable to produce the caliber of production equipment that would perform satisfactorily.

Second, Campbell Soup Company contracted in 1938 to purchase food processing machinery from Urschel. Campbell's specifications were extremely stringent. The various parts of a machine had to be built with such accuracy that if a part needed replacement it could be replaced with total accuracy in the five minutes allowed between work shifts. Urschel's products met the requirement and Campbell has continued to be one of the largest customers of Urschel equipment to the present, and accounts for more than 400 food-processing machines.

A third factor playing a part in Urschel's strict policy on quality is the firm's experience in World War II. When Urschel was instructed by the government at the outset of World War II to convert from manufacturing food-processing machinery to making equipment for the war effort, management found itself competing for business in an unfamiliar area of machine-shop operations. It bid on contracts thought to be within the company's capabilities but found the field crowded with competitors looking for the "easy" jobs. Management decided to change its strategy to bidding on only the most difficult of jobs. The results in the words of Joe Urschel:

> We were surprised to find that we were awarded all the contracts to complete these jobs. We discovered that we could do this type of work and that during the war, we did not make a single part or machine that was rejected as being out of specifications. We established a reputation for producing the highest quality workmanship and we soon had all the work that our shop could accomplish. Suddenly, one day we were ordered by Washington to stop building war machines and to begin building Model B Dicers for the dehydrated food industry. We were placed on a high priority basis for building this equipment throughout the remainder of the war. We had learned a lesson in building the machines of war. We were best equipped to compete with machinery that other manufacturers could not build or did not wish to build. Based upon this principle, we have developed a highly sophisticated manufacturing operation dedicated toward excellence in both machine design and in the finished product. Rather than becoming sloppy in our workmanship, we have continued to

tighten our specifications on all the parts that we manufacture. At various times in our history, we have purchased castings from foundries in bronze, cast iron and stainless steel. As we continued to tighten our specifications, we rejected more and more castings purchased from outside foundries. We have now brought almost all this work into our own foundries. It would seem that our costs would be higher in our foundries than by purchasing from outside sources, but the added quality produced in our own operation has paid off in more efficient machine operations and in the added quality to the finished parts. We have produced parts in our stainless steel foundry that no outside source would attempt. At one time, most of our heat treatment was accomplished outside. Great benefit has been made by bringing this operation into our own shop where we have complete control and are able to accomplish what no outside source is able to offer. The same situation has come about in the making of special nuts and bolts and in many other parts that were once produced outside our operation.

Thus the emphasis on quality extends to the company's assuming virtually complete control of the processing technology (including making the production equipment), and manufacture of parts as well as the final product.

Joe Urschel defines the precise nature of quality and its contribution to the effectiveness and economy in a competitive product, in the following communication to Urschel employees:

> Quality may mean different things to different people. In our business, quality means that machines and repair parts meet the requirements of our customers; that is all; no more and no less. . . .
>
> If a great amount of work has gone into a part to make it look beautiful, this has nothing to do with quality. This extra work will be picked up off the time cards and will be added to the price of the part. The customer will be paying a price for something he does not require. The next day after the part goes into operation in the customer's plant, the part will no longer look beautiful and no real good will have been accomplished.
>
> Many of our parts are expensive and parts certainly should not look shoddy. However, it is most desirable to have parts look good in the first place rather than to have to expend extra work to make them look satisfactory. . . .

Quality As Each Employee's Responsibility

At Urschel Laboratories each employee is made individually responsible for the quality of his or her operation. This is in line with Urschel's philosophy of placing responsibility and trust in each individual employee. Urschel Laboratories has no inspection department. Each machine operator inspects his or her own parts and is responsible for correcting any defects. As a way of discouraging the sacrifice of quality for quantity production, no employees are paid on a piecework basis.

Each machinist is responsible for keeping his own work area clean. It is customary at the end of the work week to stop production for one-half to one hour so that machinists may clean their machines and work areas. Management believes that this practice instills employees' pride in their machine and in the parts produced.

| **MARKETING AND SALES** | Urschel Laboratories considers itself to be a product-oriented firm as against one that is sales-oriented. Its expansion has been achieved over the years with little emphasis on advertising and sales promotion. |

> For the most part, expanded sales have come about through word-of-mouth advertising. Most of our customers have been in the canning and freezing business. It is known that people in other businesses can use our equipment but do not know we exist and do not know our equipment. A sales organization can expand our sales into these other businesses.†

Sales personnel are expected to be instrumental in (1) finding new uses for equipment presently being manufactured, (2) finding new fields of use for equipment presently being manufactured in which a machine's modification can result in increased sales, and (3) bringing to management an idea for an entirely new machine that can be sold in large quantities and will be compatible with our manufacturing operation.

Company policy is for ideas for (2) and (3) above to be brought directly to management rather than to the engineering department. Decisions regarding such proposals or suggestions involve design and tooling requiring high financial outlays; thus management will first want to determine their feasibility.

Sales subsidiaries, with sales offices in a number of principal cities, have been set up in several countries. (Urschel has no plans to establish manufacturing facilities in other countries. Management feels that it has not been able to duplicate the production skills and other resources to make machines of the quality produced in Valparaiso. By the same reasoning management does not foresee any formidable competition in the kind of technology and quality that have made Urschel a success.) Total annual dollar volume of sales in 1986, including original equipment and aftermarket sales, approximated $40 million. Over a ten-year period, annual export sales have totaled in excess of 40% of total sales; the figure for 1986 through August is tending to be closer to 30%. Management reported that domestic sales have again been on the rise. Total sales continue to increase at a consistent rate of 11%–12% per year.

In recent years sales have been made to Eastern-bloc countries of Europe, and a 1985 exhibit staged in the People's Republic of China resulted in a significant number of sales.

---

†Sales personnel, as well as all other personnel not directly engaged in operating production equipment in the plant, including executives, are considered to be in staff positions. Their total effort is to assist the production people to become more effective.

In addition to an extensive offering of standard machines, Urschel Laboratories will produce to specific customer requirements. Thus on two recent occasions, the company has been asked to accommodate producers of potato chips, each of whom wanted size-reduction machines with special kinds of cuts. A special machine was designed for a canner of pickle products for which a special process was desired. Such machines are sometimes one-of-a-kind units.

Price Determination and Policy

Urschel Laboratories establishes its products' prices by continually and thoroughly checking costs of making the constituent parts. An increase in cost of manufacture of a part is reflected in the selling price. If the cost of producing the part is reduced the sales price is reduced accordingly. As Joe Urschel states, "If the cost of making a part goes up or goes down, this has little effect on company profits, but it does have a great effect on the selling price of that part."

Urschel management does not believe in increasing the selling price of a machine each year by a given percentage, or in simply charging what the traffic will bear. Quoting Joe Urschel:

> In some instances machines have saved the customers so much money that the savings made in one or two weeks by the customer would pay for the price of the machine. Some people have suggested that we could have charged several times as much for these machines. We have good reason to believe that this is a poor policy. We attempt to make approximately the same profit on all machines. More profits are made on part sales than on machine sales, but here again we do not attempt to take advantage of the customers by overcharging. Many customers will know when they are being appreciably overcharged and will go to almost any extent to buy elsewhere, even though they may have to buy an inferior product.

For a recent three-year period the company made no price increases for machines or parts. Keeping the selling price of products and parts fairly stable is one reason Urschel Laboratories has had little competition, and why Urschel was able to maintain full employment for its workers through the years, including a particularly severe recession in the 1980s. Management is also aware that some European manufacturers are attempting to become competitive with Urschel. Rather than make possible the lowering of prices by reducing wages and fringe benefits, Urschel's policy is to concentrate on more efficient methods of reducing time and amount of work involved in making machine parts.

Sales of Urschel machines tend to vary little with economic conditions, according to the management.

Aftermarket Sales and Service

The high volume of sales of Urschel equipment over the years had resulted in the need to provide replacement parts for machines. In addition to its impact upon total sales, management considers the replacement market a means of maintaining sales volume and employment during economic recession. Management is also aware that other makers of parts are attempting to enter into competition in providing repair parts for Urschel machines. To protect its aftermarket sales, management states its policy is to (1) continue to maintain and improve quality, (2) develop new methods to reduce production time so prices can be lowered, and (3) carry a full inventory so as to permit prompt delivery of parts to customers.

Urschel Laboratories places heavy emphasis on providing effective service to users of its products. The company's policy is to furnish service anywhere in the world within twenty-four hours of receiving the order. Parts are furnished for virtually all Urschel machines in use. Parts and service have been supplied for machines that have been in operation for fifty or more years. Thus the company carries an extensive inventory.

As part of its service policy the company produces video tapes detailing the maintenance procedures of the various machines. These enable the user company to perform a significant part of its maintenance. Tapes are prepared in a number of languages to accommodate foreign users of Urschel machines.

Approximately 65% of total sales represents aftermarket, or replacement parts, sales.

FINANCIAL POLICIES

Urschel Laboratories follows a policy of operating on internally generated funds. In the first year of Urschel's operation, Mr. William Urschel borrowed $500, which he repaid after one year. No other funds have been borrowed except on one occasion when the company borrowed against a certificate of deposit. As Joe Urschel recalls,

> Father often stated that the difference between borrowing at 6 percent and loaning money at 6 percent was 12 percent, and that could be a good profit. That kind of thinking is not popular today in the business world, but the truth of the statement is as valid today as it was then. The present management holds to this principle, and we do not buy until we can pay cash without the burden of a loan.

When the company relocated after World War II in order to expand, the Urschels were unable to find a lending institution to construct the building. The company finally completed a move to a building (redesigned to contemporary needs) in 1957. The new building having depleted the company's cash, management of resources became especially critical. The firm's practice of discounting its invoices and other conservation methods proved effective in meeting cash needs. Management prides itself on keeping a high credit rating, which management views as another way of conserving funds. Plant expansion since 1957 has continued as funds have become available from internal sources. Today Urschel Laboratories covers 121,000 square feet of floor space.

PERSONNEL

Urschel Laboratories places a heavy emphasis on the selection and development of its employees. The personnel department does the initial screening of applicants and administers tests, or arranges for tests to be administered by a test consultant. Past work history of the applicant is also made a part of the work record. The attitude of the company with respect to its rigorous selection process is apparent in the following company communication:

> A large number of people are interviewed for each person who is selected for employment. This procedure is followed for every type of job in the company. Various tests are given to prospective employees and psychological evaluation is made of each to project the capabilities of that particular prospect. For those to be employed in the shop, a mechanical aptitude test is given which has proven to be extremely accurate in its projection. Our methods of hiring through these procedures has had considerable criticism. It has been pointed out that we miss hiring some good people through errors in the testing procedure or because of personal prejudices of those in the personnel department. This is probably a fact. But, we are quite certain that we miss hiring a great many more people who are completely unqualified for the jobs to be filled. Also, we do know that we have hired some highly qualified people through the testing procedure that we would never consider hiring through a personal interview. In our company, the personnel department does not hire. They only make reports to the individual who will have that person in his department. In the shop, the foreman has the authority to either hire or reject a recommended applicant. We feel certain that because of our hiring procedure, our productivity is much higher than other shops and because of this we are able to pay much higher wages. Because we pay higher wages, we are able to keep these qualified people.

Management's reliance on tests is further evidenced by its practice of administering mechanical-aptitude tests in screening of sales personnel, because these individuals are expected to be fully familiar with the operating characteristics of complex Urschel machines.

The company makes available to all employees an employee handbook that gives a brief history and philosophy of Urschel Laboratories, company policies, compensation system, and other conditions of employment. Department supervisors participated in formulating the general rules covering employment. The introduction to the handbook contains the statement that "Conditions of employment as stated are intended to work in the best interest of the greatest majority of employees and any rule which does not benefit the greatest majority will be changed." Specific topics covered include probationary period, pay schedule, absences and tardiness, telephone calls, safety rules, fringe benefits, time clock and time cards, and wages.

The handbook includes a complete set of job descriptions, wage structure, and the system for determining wages. For each factory job the handbook carries summary descriptions and detailed duties. The merit-wage range for each job includes ten merit-step increases from beginning wage to the top range. The supervisor periodically reviews each employee to determine rate changes. Each employee is given a Wage Computation Table for use in computing wages whenever a general wage increase is made.

A point system of job evaluation is used, with each job rated on the basis of skill, responsibility, effort, and job work conditions.

Training

New employees are given on-the-job training, which is generally the responsibility of the department supervisors. The company also has a policy of tuition remission to employees who successfully complete outside programs or courses of study when these are approved by the company.

Management personnel are made familiar with operations throughout the company. Bob Urschel, current President and son of Joe Urschel, spent six years working in the plant, including a stint as a shop manager. Two other children of Joe Urschel are presently working in various departments of the company preparatory to their assuming further management responsibilities.

Employee Motivation

Urschel eschews company-provided benefits ordinarily classed as paternalistic, such as recreational activities and company stores. Management's stated policy is to provide comfortable work areas and the best of machine tools and measuring instruments to insure quality performance. Other than occasionally providing uniforms for sports teams organized by employees, for example, the company does not provide recreational activities.

Management traditionally has been skeptical about participation in seminars on motivating employees, but in recent years has been sending foremen and other managers to such seminars. It has been highly selective in the choice of such programs, however. Management's objective is to provide each employee an opportunity to "develop a feeling of human dignity."

> A number of companies attempt to sell us motivational posters to hang on the walls of our shop. They are supposed to motivate the employees toward safety, higher production or better quality. We feel that they do just the opposite. The employee may ask himself, "Why is the boss putting up a thing like that!" Employees do not wish to be preached to on the job. Employees

often consider such posters as an insult to their intelligence and to their integrity. It has been discovered that the only kind of motivation that is of any value is self-motivation. This condition is achieved by employing only those people who are self-motivated.

It is probably fortunate and it is probably no accident that all the people in management who are related to operation of the shop have worked many years in the shop and know from experience what problems can exist there.

Discharge/Separation

Urschel management prides itself on the basic honesty and trust among its employees. "They do not steal from the company and they do not steal from each other. In the shop, they do not lock their tool boxes and many do not lock their tool boxes even when away on vacation." This description appears in a company publication. On the rare occasions when an employee is found to be involved in a theft, he or she is warned and given a second chance before being discharged. When an employee does become a problem, management attempts to give assistance. In most cases management feels that such efforts are futile and the employee is terminated. In fact, management feels that employees have often been kept on the payroll longer than they should have been, but holds that it was partially to blame also and, therefore, "owed them something." When an employee is terminated because management feels he or she is unqualified but has been kept on for some time, the employee is given "a substantial severance pay" based upon length of time employed.

Urschel Laboratories has had no layoffs since the 1940s. During two periods since then when production declined, working hours in the shop were reduced below forty hours per week, but employees were paid for a full forty-hour week. Management explains that this is good business because it protects the employees' financial security and avoids losing valued employees. Turnover of employees for all reasons is close to zero.

BASIC MANAGEMENT AND ORGANIZATIONAL CONCEPTS

The management's philosophy is one of reliance on the individual job holder to assume responsibility in his job. Joe Urschel explains:

> We have more or less permitted people to go their own way. This has probably made it difficult for some of the employees. But, right or wrong, this is the way it was. It is believed that the use of authority has been minimal throughout the organization. On several occasions over the years, I have had employees come to me and say that if I would give them the authority over another person or a group of persons, that more could be accomplished. My response has been something to the effect that authority is earned and not given. If people earn the respect of others, then they do not need the authority to accomplish their purposes. As the organization has grown over the years,

the shop was broken down into various departments. It was necessary to appoint foremen. Foremen were selected by attempting to observe what individual was most helpful to others when they had problems with their machining operations. The foremen in our shop are not there to boss people around and to drive them. The foreman's job is to provide sufficient inspection of parts being made so that an employee will not unwittingly make mistakes, provide help to those who need it, to schedule an even flow of work in his department and to use good judgment in recommending merit wage increases. The foremen and the shop superintendent work out merit wage increases together. By funneling all these wage increases through the superintendent, wage rates between departments are prevented from getting out of balance. Unless some outstanding trouble arises, each department is permitted to run itself. Management decisions are often carried to a low level of authority. For instance, when a new machine tool or other piece of equipment is to be purchased, foremen carry great weight in making the selection and often the men under them are consulted. Sometimes a foreman is given the responsibility of making the final decision. Much of what is accomplished in the company is accomplished without any management; people simply use their good judgment and do their jobs.

The Urschel management style is generally that all those who spend a part of their time in managing activity also have some working specialty at which they spend time. "Even the foremen and shop superintendent spend a small amount of their time in supervision of people. Most of their time is spent in planning work schedules, in studying methods of improving production and in studying ways to improve quality."

Exhibit 33.2 shows the formal organizational structure of Urschel Laboratories. Organizational relationships throughout the company reflect an informal environment, however; employees in the shop address Joe Urschel by his first name. Periodically, Mr. Urschel sends newsletters to all employees. These are sent to the employees' homes so that their spouses will be kept informed about company matters also. The newsletters cover information such as business conditions as they may affect the company, improvements in fringe benefits, new uses of equipment by customers, and similar topics that should be of interest to employees.

The use of meetings for coordination and communication is encouraged throughout the organization. The company Board of Directors meets once a month, chiefly to review the last month's operations. Major decisions are infrequently made at these meetings, however; decisions of major import are more often made "in a more casual manner by various members of management at whatever time it is necessary to make such decisions." Meetings of foremen, once used to set production schedules, are now used to disseminate pertinent management information and discuss matters of mutual concern. Meetings of small groups of people may be called to discuss a project underway. Meetings of the entire company's personnel are sometimes held on the shop floor to feature awards for service, announce campaigns such as United Fund, or simply to communicate company information of concern to all members of the organization.

EXHIBIT 33.2 **Urschel Organization**

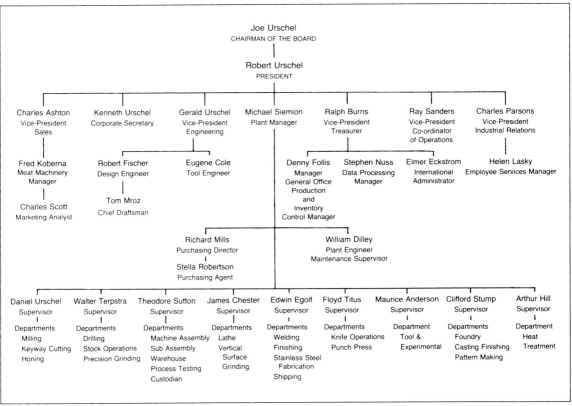

Any shop department may hold a dinner once a year which is paid for by the company. At these meetings any employee can bring up particular job problems or complaints, make suggestions for work improvement, or make any other comments. Such information is recorded and then brought to the attention of an appropriate member of top management. Management attempts to respond to each individual communication with an explanation or a decision.

The management of Urschel Laboratories does not follow a structured long-range plan for the company's future. Company growth as such is not a quantified long-run objective. The company's philosophy and policy is perhaps best expressed by Joe Urschel's views on company growth and future expectations:

> In our country there seems to be a philosophy that bigness is better and the bigger a company can grow, the better it is. In many companies there seems to be a goal of growth for growth's sake. We have never had any desire to

grow big. We have had the opportunity to do so. We could have copied other people's equipment as other companies do. We could have then put on three shifts of people instead of the one shift that is our standard work day. Some of the people who have viewed our operation have been appalled at the number of machine tools that are not in operation, and some are appalled that this equipment sits idle for two shifts a day. They say that we should take in outside work to keep our machine tools operating. If we did this we would become a job shop that experiences feast or famine in orders received, and this would interfere in our production of food processing machines wherein we make our profit. And, we must ask ourselves what is the object of growth for growth's sake. Even if we were to make more profit through such a venture, which is doubtful, we find that we can eat only so much and we do not need more money for the pleasures of life. Our company has grown from its small beginning to its present size only because people in the food industry brought their problems to us and we needed to expand our operation to solve their problems. This is the only legitimate reason we can understand for the growth of a company.

TECHNOLOGY CHANGES, AUTOMATION AND COMPUTERIZATION

Urschel Laboratories has been receptive to making changes whenever advantages of quality, quantity, time and expense can be realized. Management considers its greatest asset to be the Urschel reputation for the production of a quality product. Quality has been advanced by the adoption of new metals, new methods, and new processes as these have been discovered. Joe Urschel observed that,

> sometimes the process of increasing the quality of parts is expensive and can add to the cost of these parts. This added cost can be offset by automating the processes for making the parts so that the amount of labor in making them is reduced. . . . Many of the patents on our equipment have expired and this makes it possible for others to copy our machines. Because of our quality, and because we can keep our selling prices low through automation, we have virtually no competition in this country.

To determine when the production of parts reaches a sufficiently high volume to justify automation, Urschel conducts continuous study of all processes. Much of the automation is built into special machine tools that Urschel designs and builds in its own shop. These in turn are controlled by computers that are also entirely designed and built by Urschel.

The use of robots has been introduced into some stages of the production process. For example, a robot is in operation in the stainless steel foundry. Stainless steel castings are made by the investment casting process, also referred to as the lost wax process. The robot used in this operation performs with more consistency than can a human being and thus produces a better product. Quality rather than labor-saving is the chief reason for Urschel's use of robots.

Urschel Laboratories has used computer applications in various aspects of business operation since 1963. Manufacturing operations were among the first to be programmed into the computer, and computer usage is credited with having a strong impact on reduction of manufacturing costs. Inventory control is computerized and inventory is updated four times each week. Computer programs calculate and print out reports of manufacturing costs, schedule inventory replacement, and produce a print-out for the shop foremen twice a week for use in scheduling their department work load.

While the computer is used for all accounting functions and for various activities of the sales department, the manufacturing operation has first priority on the use of the computer in event of any question as to which department shall be serviced.

SUBSIDIARIES

Indiana Information Controls, Inc.

Indiana Information Controls, Inc. is a wholly owned subsidiary formed to provide data-processing services to a number of business firms, particularly banks located in several states. About 115 banks have contracted with the firm for data-processing services. Management credits the accuracy and timeliness of its service for its competitive success.

Indiana Information Controls was established in 1966 in response to requests from potential customers for such assistance. The Urschels felt that the need for developing these information-processing services could be met by the resources already existing at Urschel Laboratories, as well as by the personal avocational interests of the Urschels.

Initially, Joe Urschel composed all contracts with customer banks. Personnel functions are supplied by the personnel department of the parent company. The company policy is determined by a Board of Directors, composed of the same individuals as those on the board of Urschel Laboratories. Urschel Information Controls employs 166 people.

Urschel Development Corporation

The Urschel Development Corporation is another wholly owned subsidiary, established to build Vale Park Village. It was formed because Urschel Laboratories had acquired a considerable tract of land when it moved to its present location in north Valparaiso. The subsidiary's basic objective was to establish Vale Park Village, a development of about 250 acres with an apartment complex of 298 apartments.

Urschel Development Corporation is headed by Joe Urschel, whose chief ongoing function as President is concerned with planning and selling land in Vale Park South. Its personnel number six to eight employees at any one time.

THE FUTURE OF THE COMPANY

As Joe Urschel noted earlier, Urschel Laboratories' management does not value growth for growth's sake, and providing for customers' needs is the only acceptable basis for growth. Management considers itself a unique organization with respect to its product and its method of operation. There are no specific plans for diversification into other product lines. Such diversification as is represented by Indiana Information Controls or the Urschel Development Corporation has occurred because available resources were matched to market opportunities: Urschel's inventive ability to develop a data-processing service in response to requests from bankers in the first instance, and land in excess of company business needs being used to fill expanded need for housing.

As noted earlier, Urschel's sales are approximately $40 million annually; sales have experienced approximately 11%–12% growth annually for the last fifteen years and management projects a similar growth rate in the future. Much of the company's sales are expected to be in replacement of parts (approximately 65% of sales are for replacement). Competitors have attempted entry into the market, even to the extent of giving away their machines or selling them at one-third of Urschel's price simply to gain a foothold in the parts supply market. Management feels that the unique design of its machines and the emphasis on quality and reliability in the component-materials manufacturing process and the final product make it exceedingly difficult for competitors to duplicate the custom-built approach to turning out an Urschel product. Joe Urschel notes that a number of design patents are at the point of expiring, but that so far other firms simply have not been able to mount effective competition through reproducing Urschel machines even when licensed to do so. Thus management is reasonably confident of its continued preeminence in the market.

At present Urschel Laboratories has three major sales subsidiaries located in England, France and Japan, with sales offices in many principal cities. In April of 1985 Robert Urschel headed a group of Urschel sales and technical personnel to China, and management was optimistic about developing a market in that area. Urschel has also staged an exhibit in Australia, with demonstrations of Urschel machine capability to government agencies as well as business prospects. Information on Urschel machines has been prepared in eleven different languages, including Chinese and Russian. As Third World countries continue to develop they will become prospects for sales contracts.

The extent to which the distinctive philosophy that has characterized Urschel Laboratories through its seventy-five years of operation will continue to influence the objectives, policies, and "personality" or "culture" of the company for some years to come may be inferred by the following comments of Joe Urschel, Chairman of Urschel, concerning its future.

> The company is owned entirely by the Urschel family. Insofar as my brothers and I are concerned, we could sell the company and retire for the remainder

of our lives at some vacation spot. All of us enjoy working and we have no intention of doing this. Perhaps some people would believe that we should not care what happens to the company after we are gone. We do care and that is one of the reasons for what is written here. Many companies have come to us with offers to purchase our company. We have had as many as three offers in a two-day period. We simply tell all of them that we are not interested in their offers. The vice-president of a very large international company was given a tour of our plant. This man had been in charge of a machine shop at one time. His company is noted for purchasing large numbers of other companies. After viewing our operation, the man said, "It is evident that the success of this business is due to a meticulous attention to detail and if our company would buy your company, we would wreck it within a year." This was an honest man. What he told us was what would happen to our company with the sale to almost any other company.

Several years ago we considered that we could best perpetuate our company by selling a part of the common stock in our company to the general public. In this way, when each of us died, a definite market price would be established for our stock, and we could pass most of it onto our children. We would keep the majority of the stock so that we and our children would have control of the company. We went through the process of what is known as "going public" up to the final steps. We stopped before the final step because we discovered that we would not have the complete freedom in operating our company that we thought we would have and we learned of other consequences that were completely unacceptable to us. We believe that "going public" would be an unhealthy venture for the company. We have since learned of other ways that we can perpetuate the life of the company through various agreements which my brothers and I have made with the company.

While William Urschel's three sons, Joe, Gerald, and Kenneth remain active in the business, third-generation members have begun assuming active management of the company. Robert Urschel, son of Joe Urschel, was named President in 1984. Bob attended Hamline University for three years. His early exposure to company activities were also his initial training as a member of the organization. Working with his father, Bob also pursues such collateral interests as building electronic mechanisms as well as independent projects of an innovative nature. Joe Urschel's other son, Daniel, and daughter, Elena Pilgrim, are also currently working through various departments of the company as part of their managerial development.

Just as the third generation of Urschels were encouraged to become actively interested in the organization, so the fourth generation are being encouraged at an early age to visit and observe the shop operations at Urschel Laboratories, in the hope that they, too, will develop an identity with the family-managed company.

In addition to owning and managing a major corporation in the northwest Indiana area, Urschel family members take an active part in community civic activities and as members of service organizations, or as prime movers of projects benefiting the community.

NOTES

1. Keiser, James D., "Capacity Increased, Time Cut With Change to 15 HP Mill," *Chemical Processing,* July 1981.

2. "The Story of How Urschel Machines Are Made" in *Urschel Laboratories,* a booklet published by Urschel Laboratories, Inc. in 1984.

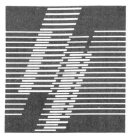

SECTION E

STRATEGIC ISSUES IN MULTINATIONAL CORPORATIONS

AB Volvo (Sweden)

JYOTI N. PRASAD · HANS J. BOCKER · MEGAN E. SUTTON ·
FAZAL J. SEYYED

On March 26, 1986, Pehr G. Gyllenhammar, the C.E.O. and Chairman of Sweden's largest company, AB Volvo, gave a last-minute glance at the statement he was going to make to the press releasing Volvo's 1985 annual report. He knew that the press would be eager to ask him questions about the recent resignations of the President of Volvo Group, Haken Frisinger, and some other top officials of Volvo; that questions would be raised about the increased dividends for the Volvo stockholders for 1986 when the labor unions are asked to hold their demands for increased wages; and also that concerns would be raised about the impact of the recent assassination of Swedish Prime Minister Olof Palme on Volvo's future plans. Gyllenhammar mentally prepared himself for all the probing questions he was about to face in the afternoon's conference. He wondered that, in search for not-so-bright aspects of the company's operations, probably most of the people would not care to notice that AB Volvo, which employed over 67,000 people and generated 13% of Sweden's GNP, had earned a record profit, equivalent of about one billion U.S. dollars, in 1985.

This case was prepared by Professors Jyoti N. Prasad, Hans J. Bocker, Megan E. Sutton, and Fazal J. Seyyed of Western Illinois University. It was presented at the 1986 Workshop of the Midwest Society for Case Research. It also appears in *Annual Advances in Business Cases,* 1986, pp. 1–25, edited by Phillip C. Fisher. Reprinted by permission.

HISTORY OF AB VOLVO

Volvo, incorporated in 1915 as a subsidiary of AB Svenska Kullagerfabriken, SKF, commenced business in 1926, assembling cars and trucks, and became an independent company in 1935. From the late 1930s there has been steady development of the company's automotive business, and Volvo has grown into a diversified group with integrated manufacturing operations.

The Volvo company was founded by Gustaf Larson, an engineer, and Assar Gabrielsson, an economist who rose so quickly within the Swedish ball-bearing company SKF that by the age of 32, he was the company's International Sales Manager. As a young fellow working in England, Larson got to know William Morris, who at the time was designing a small car. Returning to Sweden, Larson earned his engineering degree and went to work for SKF. But it was not until after he left the firm that he met Gabrielsson in 1924. The two began work on a test series of ten cars—one sedan and the rest touring cars. The prototypes were finished under Larson's direction in 1926, and Gabrielsson convinced SKF to set up a new automotive company named Volvo. Gabrielsson remained at the helm of Volvo until 1956.

The first Volvo rolled off the line at a plant on the island of Hisingen, Gothenberg, on April 14, 1927. That year Volvo's sixty-six workers built 297 cars, more American in style than European. The first series OV 4, featured long leaf springs front and rear, and a four-cylinder engine that developed 28 horse-power and was capable of taking the car to 55 m.p.h. However, Volvo quickly discovered that its market lay in selling covered sedans, and in 1929 it introduced a new model, PV 651, equipped with a six-cylinder engine. The company sold 1,383 cars that year, enough to generate its first profit.

The company expanded its product line in the 1930s to include trucks and seven-passenger taxis. In the middle of the decade, a revolutionary Volvo was introduced: the PV 36, with smoother, more aerodynamic lines and the first Volvo body made completely of steel. However, the car did not gain popularity and it took a long time to sell the 500 units of the limited series that the company had built.

In late 1936 the company introduced a small, inexpensive car with similar styling, the PV 51, and it proved a big hit. The little car still couldn't compete in price with some of the imports of the day, but Swedish buyers had come to trust Volvo's quality, and the new model helped propel the company to nearly double its sales in 1937.

During World War II Volvo became Sweden's number one defense contractor. It built special vehicles for the Swedish Army despite widespread parts shortages. Remaining in the defense business to this day, Volvo supplies engines built by its Volvo Flygmotor unit for Saab airplanes for both civilian and military use. Other Volvo Flygmotor engines, developed independently and in conjunction with General Electric, are also designed for military and civilian craft.

In the fall of 1944, about 150,000 people showed up for the Volvo Exhibition in Stockholm to see the PV 444 prototype, Volvo's postwar model. Nearly 2,300 signed orders for the car. Those who held orders for the first shipment were able to sell them, shortly afterwards, for twice what they had paid originally.

Mainly because of the eventual success of the little PV 444, Volvo auto production topped its truck and bus output for the first time in 1949. By 1953 the PV 444 was Sweden's top selling car. It was about this time that Volvo introduced fixed repair prices and five-year guarantees against auto damage in Sweden. In 1960 Volvo set up its own Swedish insurance company and issued all Volvo owners the guarantees.

The first Volvo sports car, a roadster called P 1900, went into production in 1956 with a fiberglass-reinforced plastic body. It failed completely. Only 67 were sold. The next—and last—time Volvo ventured into the sports-car market was in 1961 when the P 1800, a two-seat coupe, was introduced.

Although a handful of cars had been exported to California in 1955, Volvo's real push into the U.S. markets came in 1957. Its directors decided that the company's need for growth was more compelling than their reservations about entering the highly competitive U.S. market. By 1960, however, 20% of Volvo's production was going to the United States. Today the U.S. is Volvo's largest market—even bigger than Sweden. Volvo has the second-highest European brand sales in the U.S., close behind Volkswagen. Only one tenth of all Volvos manufactured today are destined for the Swedish market.

Canada also proved to be a good market. In 1963, to satisfy local-content rules, Volvo started manufacturing in Nova Scotia. It was Volvo's first fully owned plant outside Sweden, and was soon followed by the opening of a plant in Belgium.

The first U.S.-bound cars were the trusty PV 444. The PV was thoroughly updated in 1958, and remained in production until the end of 1965. When the last PV sedan rolled off the Gothenberg line, 440,000 units had been built over its lifetime. PV station wagons stayed in production until 1969. The 121/122 model enjoyed a similarly long lifespan. The series was in production from 1956 until 1970, almost 15 years. But it was the 144 series, introduced in 1966 as the PV replacement, that gave Volvo its reputation for safety. The company had been the first to introduce three-point seatbelts (1959), laminated windshields in the 1950s, front disc brakes, and orthopedically designed seats in the 1960s.

The company further enhanced its safety reputation by developing the Volvo Experimental Safety Car in 1972. This was a very favorable year for the company in other respects. Volvo bought 33% of the Netherlands' DAF Car Division, and opened the Volvo technical center. The DAF car was redesigned, the Holland company renamed Volvo Car BV, and its new model called the Volvo 66, which once more brought the Volvo name to a small car. Meanwhile, the Swedish cars were moving upscale; the 144 had evolved into the 200 series, combining safety with greater luxury. To celebrate its fiftieth birthday Volvo commissioned the 262, a luxury coupe, designed by Bertone. But the company's real drive into the luxury segment came in 1982 with the introduction of the 760 GLE. But Volvo hasn't abandoned its once-successful niche. As of mid-1986 a replacement for the Dutch small car is in the works, and is expected to be headed for Volvo's top market, the United States.

In the 1970s Volvo undertook decentralization of its management responsibility and expansion of its marketing organization. During this period, the Company also introduced and implemented new production technologies, built plants in key market areas and developed further the quality, reliability and safety of its products. In addition, Volvo has identified the heavy vehicle industry as an area of increased strategic importance. Toward the end of the period, Volvo entered into a number of cooperation agreements with other companies and, in 1980, formed Volvo Energy Corporation, to engage in hydrocarbon exploration, development, investment, and related activities, which the company had also identified as an area of strategic importance.

The transport equipment area dominated the Group's business until 1981. In 1981 AB Volvo acquired all of the capital stock of Beijerinvest AB, a publicly traded Swedish holding company with interests in energy, industrial, food, trading, and financial businesses. However, in recent years, Volvo has disposed of some Beijerinvest interests that had no immediate connection with the company's major business lines, and has regrouped others into distinct business segments. Volvo has also made a number of strategic acquisitions of, and investments in, companies that complement the Volvo Group's industrial base and others that implement its developing emphasis in the energy business. Certain investments in shares of Swedish companies held by Volvo have been disposed of and other major investments acquired.

Volvo's international growth has been substantial. Production facilities abroad have been established and expanded through a joint-venture truck and bus assembly plant in Brazil in the late 1970s, and the acquisition in 1981 of most of the truck manufacturing assets of White Motor Corporation in the United States. North America, and Western Europe, especially the Nordic Area, are the Group's most important markets. Marine engines, oil rigs, factory automation equipment—even beer—now fall under the Volvo umbrella. The offshoot of a ball-bearing company is today Sweden's largest company, employing 67,857 people and among the world's largest fifty companies in terms of business operations and profitability.

AB VOLVO: BUSINESS OPERATIONS

Volvo as an industrial group has operations in three principal areas: transport equipment, energy, and food. Volvo products are sold throughout the world and 84% of the Group's sales are to customers outside Sweden. (See Exhibits 34.1–34.6.) Part of its concentration on foreign markets is wholly or partially owned plants in the following countries, among others: Denmark,

EXHIBIT 34.1

AB Volvo: Operating Income by Sector[1]
(In SEK Millions)

	1985	1984	1983	1982	1981
Cars	6,138	5,737	4,805	1,801	736
Trucks & buses	981	1,236	437	1,260	1,075
Construction equipment	—	190	164	158	136
Marine & industrial engines	330	351	316	187	118
Aircraft engines, etc.	187	133	99	113	139
Industrial equipment	—	—	233	226	188
Energy	(146)	(22)	(1,175)	3	(15)
Food	167	152	174	128	89
Discontinued operations	(364)	(202)	—	—	—
Other operations	170	(39)	(111)	(81)	(15)
Total	7,463	7,536	4,942	3,795	2,457
Corporate Expenses	(988)	(908)	(440)	(460)	(491)
Total operating income	6,475	6,628	4,502	3,335	1,966

SOURCE: *Annual Report,* AB Volvo, 1985, p. 8.

[1]*Author's Note:* Throughout the text and in the exhibits, various financial information have been presented either in U.S. dollars or in Swedish kronor. Due to basic differences in U.S. and Swedish accounting principles, one has to be careful when computing and interpreting ratios or attempting to convert them into one single currency. However, for the advantage of U.S. analysts, AB Volvo recently has started the practice of reporting its financial information based on U.S. accounting principles.

EXHIBIT 34.2

AB Volvo: Income Before Allocations, Taxes and Minority Interests, by Geographical Area
(In SEK Millions)

	1985	1984	1983	1982
Sweden	5,820	6,260	4,015	1,945
Nordic area (excluding Sweden)	139	117	72	76
Other Europe	313	208	270	281
North America (losses)	1,077	877	(591)*	102
Other Countries	253	185	13	36
Total	7,602	7,647	3,779	2,440

*Includes losses of SEK 1,067 Million on energy operations.

SOURCE: *Annual Report,* AB Volvo, 1985, p. 8.

EXHIBIT   34.3

AB Volvo: Sales by Products
(In SEK Millions)

	1985	1984	1983	1982	1981
Cars	34,549	30,304	26,262	18,109	13,569
Trucks	16,642	15,219	11,576	10,793	8,209
Buses	1,672	1,336	1,131	1,028	1,030
Marine & industrial engines	2,262	2,238	2,011	1,508	1,308
Construction equipment	—	2,851	2,664	2,203	2,277
Aircraft engines, etc.	1,426	1,152	957	919	590
Industrial equipment	—	—	3,625	2,967	2,118
Energy & trading	21,514	27,737	46,030	33,512	14,638
Food	5,393	4,947	4,429	3,171	1,889
Other operations	2,738*	1,268	775	1,414	2,389
Total	86,196	87,052	99,460	75,624	48,017

*Includes construction equipment sales of SEK 887 Million.
SOURCE: *Annual Report,* AB Volvo, 1985, p. 5.

EXHIBIT   34.4

AB Volvo: Sales by Market
(In SEK Millions)

	1985	1984	1983	1982	1981
Sweden	12,023	10,958	12,233	10,728	9,341
Nordic area (excluding Sweden)	6,211	5,418	5,025	4,207	3,835
Europe (excluding Nordic area)	16,789	16,258	15,849	12,206	9,298
North America	24,102	20,513	15,380	9,817	5,560
Other markets	6,573	6,988	6,146	5,959	5,678
Total (excluding oil trading)	65,698	60,135	54,633	42,917	33,712
Oil trading	20,498	26,917	44,827	32,707	14,305
Total	86,196	87,052	99,460	75,624	48,017

SOURCE: *Annual Report,* AB Volvo, 1985, p. 5.

EXHIBIT 34.5

AB Volvo: Assets by Sector
(In SEK Millions)

	1985	1984	1983	1982
Cars	14,267	11,795	11,493	10,255
Trucks & buses	9,687	8,679	8,705	8,898
Construction equipment	—	2,377	2,353	2,355
Marine & industrial engines	1,378	1,569	1,322	1,182
Aircraft engines, etc.	2,034	1,672	1,585	1,562
Industrial equipment	—	—	3,409	2,586
Energy & trading	2,152	4,818	5,337	4,906
Food	2,047	1,842	1,788	1,529
Other	6,696	2,759	2,695	2,286
Discontinued operations	420	279	—	—
Corporate assets*	24,112	22,118	14,819	10,706
Total	62,793	57,629	53,506	46,265

SOURCE: *Annual Report,* AB Volvo, 1985, p. 10.
*Consists of investments, restricted deposits in the banks, and receivables.

Belgium, the Netherlands, France, Austria, Great Britain, the United States, Canada, Peru, Brazil, Iran, Thailand, Malaysia, and Australia.

Volvo's growth and development have occurred primarily in the transport-vehicle field, which continues to form the base of the Group's operations. The activities include the production of cars, of commercial vehicles such as trucks, buses and construction equipment, and of marine, industrial and aircraft engines.

In the energy business, Volvo is active in oil trading as well as prospecting and recovery of oil and gas through associated companies.

EXHIBIT 34.6

AB Volvo: Assets by Geographical Area
(In SEK Millions)

	1985	1984	1983	1982
Sweden	39,657	37,370	33,900	30,169
Nordic area (excluding Sweden)	2,106	1,866	1,980	2,012
Europe excluding Nordic area	8,610	6,673	8,232	6,010
North America	10,507	10,336	7,921	6,455
Other countries	1,913	1,384	1,473	1,629
Total	62,793	57,629	53,506	46,275

SOURCE: *Annual Report,* AB Volvo, 1985, p. 8.

The food companies are coordinated through Provendor Food AB. These firms produce and market frozen and preserved foods based on farm products and fish, as well as cured meat products, butchered meat, and mineral water. Industrial operations are supplemented by strategic shareholdings in listed companies.

Volvo Cars

The Cars operating sector is composed of the activities of Volvo Car Corporation, the production of components within Volvo Components Corporation, marketing handled by Volvo's sales subsidiaries, and the spare parts business. (See Exhibit 34.7.)

Development and manufacture of Volvo cars in the 200 and 700 series are parts of this sector. Most of the cars are assembled in Sweden and in Belgium, but assembly also takes place in Canada, Thailand, Malaysia, Australia, and other countries. The largest markets for Volvo cars are in North America, the Nordic countries, and the other countries of Western Europe. The Volvo 300 series is produced at Volvo Car BV in the Netherlands, of which Volvo Car Corporation owns 30%.

Sixty years ago Volvo was not building cars but was manufacturing ball-bearings. A decade ago the company's cars were considered means of solid transportation, but were far from being deemed luxury items. But today Volvo builds some of the most sophisticated luxury automobiles in the world.

Volvo Trucks

Within its Trucks operating sector, Volvo designs, manufactures and markets forward-control and normal-control heavy trucks for long-distance and forest transport, construction work, tanker, and bulk transport. It also makes medium-size trucks for local distribution service and light long-distance traffic.

EXHIBIT 34.7

AB Volvo: Automotive Production (Absolute Number of Cars, Trucks, and Buses Including Chassis, Produced)

	1985	1984	1983
Cars: 200/700 series	288,100	270,600	266,800
Cars: 300 series	109,000	108,900	105,600
Trucks	41,200	40,800	34,300
Buses and bus chassis	3,220	3,240	3,410
Total units	441,520	423,540	410,110

SOURCES: *Moody's International Manual*, 1985, Vol. 2. *Annual Report*, AB Volvo, 1985.

Assembly takes place mainly in Sweden, Belgium, Great Britain, the United States, Brazil, and Australia. There is a substantial market potential for Volvo trucks in all parts of the world.

On August 15, 1986, Volvo and GM announced their plans to merge their heavy truck operations in the United States. The joint venture with 65% of ownership by Volvo will be called the Volvo GM Heavy Truck Corporation, and will be based on Volvo's wholly owned U.S. subsidiary, Volvo White Truck Corporation, in Greensboro, North Carolina, and the heavy-duty-truck operations of GM's Truck and Bus Group in Pontiac, Michigan. General Motors has agreed to pay an estimated $50 to $75 million for its stake in the venture, which is expected to become fully operational in two years. Under the joint venture, the manufacturing operations would be based at Volvo/White's three existing plants in Virginia, Ohio, and Utah. The estimated U.S. market for heavy trucks in 1986 was 115,000 units, against 140,000 units in 1985.

Volvo Buses

Within its Buses operating sector, Volvo develops, manufactures and markets bus chassis, components, and complete buses. Volvo is one of the leading bus manufacturers in the Organization for Economic Cooperation and Development (OECD) countries. Assembly and production takes place in twelve countries; most of the production occurs in Sweden. Volvo manufactures approximately 8% of all buses of more than twelve tons gross weight produced in the OECD.

Construction Equipment

Volvo BM designs, manufactures, and markets wheel loaders, articulated dump trucks, rigid dump trucks, and excavator loaders, and is one of Europe's leading construction-equipment companies. Volvo BM has a substantial share of the world market for articulated dumpers and is further increasing its percentage of the market for wheel loaders.

An arrangement has been reached for Volvo BM to merge with the Clark Michigan Company in the United States, so that it can obtain benefits in the areas of product development, production, and marketing of construction equipment.

Marine and Industrial Engines

The Marine and Industrial Engines operating sector is composed of the development, design, manufacture, and conversion of diesel and gasoline engines, as well as marine transmissions and industrial components. The products are used in leisure and commercial craft, in materials-handling vehicles, construction equipment, etc., or as power sources for generators and pumps. Volvo Penta engines are sold in most markets throughout the world.

Aircraft Engines, etc.

Volvo Flygmotor's operations include the development and production of jet engines and components for military and civil aircraft and space projects, as well as the manufacture of hydraulic machinery, transmission systems, and heaters. The long-term objective is to replace a diminishing military work-load with civil projects. The focus is on creating balance among the three large areas of operation: products for defense, civil aviation, and other civil applications.

Energy

STC Scandinavian Trading Company AB is one of the larger independent, oil-trading companies in the world. In recent years its operations have been broadened to include other types of international trading.

Volvo Energy has concessions in the North Sea and owns interests in Saga Petroleum a.s. (recovery of oil and gas in the North Sea), and in accommodation and service platforms. Volvo also has, through its subsidiary Volvo North America Corporation, substantial interests in the Hamilton Oil Corporation.

Food

This product group is comprised of a number of manufacturers, who are well known in Sweden for such food products as preserved and frozen vegetables, meat and potato products, preserved fish products, processed meat and sandwich foods, chopped meat, and mineral water. The operations of various companies are coordinated through Provendor Food AB.

TROUBLE IN PARADISE

Pehr Gyllenhammar Story

Pehr G. Gyllenhammar became head of Volvo in 1971 at the age of 36 after marrying the daughter of the carmaker's boss. (See Exhibit 34.8.) Before that he was chief of Sweden's largest insurer, Skandia, where he succeeded his father.

But Gyllenhammar is more than a rich man's son and another rich man's son-in-law. Volvo has thrived under his stewardship. On sales of just $3.5 billion, its car business pulled out about $700 million in operating earnings in 1984. That's a 20% return on sales. Using U.S. accounting principles, about $400 million dropped to the bottom line, almost a 100% profit gain

EXHIBIT 34.8   **AB Volvo: Management Team**

Chairman of the Board of AB Volvo and C.E.O. of the Volvo Group:
Pehr G. Gyllenhammar

Vice-Chairmen of the Volvo Board:
Tore Browaidh
Lennart Johansson

Members of the Volvo Board:
Ulf Laurin
Sven Hulterstrom
Mats Israelsson
Sven Agrup
Nils Holgersson
Goran Johansson
Curt Nicolin
Stig A.L. Svensson
Haken Frisinger

Deputy Members of the Board:

Egon Kajsjo   Ulf G. Linden
Olle Ludvigsson   Hans-Eric Ovin

Secretary to the Board:
Claes Beyer

Group Executive Committee:

Pehr G. Gyllenhammar, Chairman & C.E.O.
Haken Frisinger, Vice-Chairman
U.G. Linden, Executive Vice-President
Gosta Renell, Executive Vice-President
Bo Ekman, Senior Vice-President
E.G. Knappe, Senior Vice-President

SOURCE: *Annual Report,* Volvo AB, 1985.

over 1983. AB Volvo as a group earned record profits of $860 million in 1984, and a staggering $1 billion in 1985. In 1985, Volvo sales increased to a record 392,600 cars, including the Dutch-built Volvo 340/360 series (which, in fact, has produced lower results than had been expected. Sales totals in 1985 surpassed 1984 figures by 6,600 units.

However, trouble for Gyllenhammar had begun popping up in late 1982. Gyllenhammar was seen as the man most likely to succeed Swedish billionnaire Marcus Wallenberg as head of the Wallenberg empire. The Wallenberg financial empire controls major financial institutions, and the Saab-Scania cars and airplane manufacturing operations in Sweden. The Swedish billionnaire wanted Gyllenhammar as his heir rather than his own son, Peter Wallenberg. But after the death of Marcus Wallenberg in September 1982, Peter Wallenberg made his move to take revenge. The power struggle was compounded when Volvo bought 25% shareholdings in two Wallenberg companies: Atlas Copco, the engineering group of which Peter Wallenberg is the chairman; and Stora Kopparberg, the paper manufacturer. Peter Wallenberg retaliated by buying into Volvo. Furthermore, the animosity between the two men was intensified by a fight over the chairmanship of Skandinaviska-Enskilda Bank, Sweden's biggest commercial bank. Its chairmanship was traditionally seen as the Wallenbergs' throne. The position went to bank insider Curt Olsson, although both Wallenberg and Gyllenhammar were candidates. They blamed each other for allowing the chairmanship to slip into the hands of a third party.

Finally a settlement was arranged: Peter would sell off his Volvo stock, and Volvo would sell shares it held in divisions of the Wallenberg empire. Volvo made $190 million in that exchange. With that and auto profits, Volvo found itself to have accumulated $1.6 billion in cash and securities at its disposal in 1984.

Gyllenhammar has successfully run Volvo for over fifteen years, and turned it into Sweden's biggest company. (See Exhibits 34.9–34.11.) Sales in 1983 of SEK 99.46 billion and a pretax profit of SEK 3.8 billion, represent a dramatic increase from sales of SEK 19.2 billion in 1978. (Sales in 1984 were down to SEK 87.05 billion). Gyllenhammar is a respected industrialist in Europe as well as in his home country. Nobody doubts that he is a man of vision, but many of those visions have spurred criticism lately. For example, in recent years some of the moves by Gyllenhammar were obstructed or undermined because of his different way of thinking and his leadership style.

In 1983 Volvo's Board successfully blocked Gyllenhammar's plan to issue $100 million of equity in America late in 1984. However, Gyllenhammar asked the Swedish government for permission for Volvo's restricting articles of association to be changed so that the company could raise more foreign capital. In December 1984, in spite of the Volvo Board's opposition, Gyllenhammar was able to list Volvo shares on the Paris Bourse, and on the over-the-counter market in the United States via the NASDAQ system.

In retaliation to the Volvo Board's refusal to sell stock in the United States in 1984–1985, Gyllenhammar replaced three outside directors with Volvo executives of his own choice. To strike back, rebellious stockholders thwarted his extraordinary proposal to sell 40% of Volvo's share capital to the Norwegian government in exchange for a share of Norway's oil fields in the North Sea. But Volvo later bought into North Sea and U.S. oil properties. These investments ultimately led to losses totaling $143.5 million.

EXHIBIT 34.9   **AB Volvo: Income Accounts**

(In SEK Thousands)

Year Ending December 31	1985	1984	1983	1982	1981
Sales	86,196,000	87,052,000	99,460,000	75,624,000	48,017,000
Cost of sales	70,388,000	72,062,000	85,774,000	70,992,000	45,039,000
Selling, general & admin exp	7,608,000	6,960,000	7,611,000		
Depreciation	1,725,000	1,402,000	1,573,000	1,297,000	1,012,000
Operating income	6,475,000	6,628,000	4,502,000	3,335,000	1,966,000
Divs. rec. & sale of secur. net	110,000	138,000	86,000	195,000	132,000
Foreign exchange gain (loss)	759,000	(551,000)	(226,000)	(721,000)	(246,000)
Interest income	2,223,000	2,052,000	1,768,000	1,333,000	1,040,000
Interest expense	1,802,000	1,803,000	2,185,000	1,897,000	1,467,000
Inc. after financial inc. & exp.	7,765,000	6,464,000	3,945,000	2,245,000	1,425,000
Extraordinary income	—	1,363,000	—	235,000	—
Provision for employee bonus	(163,000)	(180,000)	(166,000)	(40,000)	—
Inc. bef. alloca. taxes & min. int.	7,602,000	7,647,000	3,779,000	2,440,000	1,425,000
Allocat. to untaxes reserves	3,330,000	(4,384,000)	(2,981,000)	(1,348,000)	(704,000)
Inc. bef. taxes & min. int.	4,272,000	3,263,000	798,000	1,092,000	721,000
Provision for taxes	1,713,000	1,624,000	752,000	508,000	222,000
Minority interests	(13,000)	(74,000)	158,000	(88,000)	(46,000)
Net income	2,546,000	1,565,000	204,000	496,000	453,000

SOURCES: *Moody's International Manual*, 1985, Vol. 2. AB Volvo, *Annual Report*, 1985.

The investment in the Dutch carmaker, DAF, intended to give Volvo a cheap entry to the market for small cars, also proved a failure.

A proposed merger between Volvo and its main competitor Saab-Scania, the other Swedish car and truck manufacturer, fell through when it was blocked by the Saab-Scania management.

There are signs of growing discontent within and outside the company, which employs 10% of the Swedish workforce and accounts for 13% of the country's gross national product. Some stockholders and analysts are increasingly wary of Gyllenhammar's management style. Stockholm's stock exchange is hitting new highs, but in the month of February 1986 the price of Volvo B shares—the restricted voting shares available to foreigners—had dropped from $50 to $42.

In early 1986, Volvo was tarnished by its close association with Egyptian-born Refaat El-Sayed, who controlled Fermenta, a Swedish biotech and

EXHIBIT 34.10 **AB Volvo: Balance Sheets**

(In SEK Thousands)

December 31	1985	1984	1983	1982¹	1981
Assets					
Cash in banks	4,202,000	5,713,000	6,000,000	3,583,000	785,000
Temporary investments	10,192,000	6,187,000	5,625,000	3,667,000	4,691,000
Accounts receivable	11,244,000	13,265,000	10,706,000	10,528,000	8,546,000
Inventories	16,044,000	15,462,000	15,415,000	14,341,000	11,580,000
Total current assets	41,682,000	40,627,000	37,746,000	32,119,000	25,602,000
Restricted dep. in Bank of Sweden	2,823,000	1,762,000	264,000	221,000	208,000
Long term receivables & loans	1,209,000	1,213,000	1,670,000	996,000	618,000
Intangibles	620,000	419,000	576,000	523,000	1,832,000
Property, plant & equipment net	9,565,000	8,199,000	10,056,000	8,960,000	8,385,000
Investments	6,894,000	5,409,000	3,194,000	3,456,000	—
Total assets	62,793,000	57,629,000	53,506,000	46,275,000	36,645,000
Liabilities and stockholders' equity					
Accounts Payable	6,340,000	6,510,000	6,100,000	5,701,000	4,708,000
Advances from customers	1,024,000	1,015,000	1,052,000	1,101,000	1,070,000
Bank loans	6,595,000	6,074,000	7,553,000	5,768,000	4,088,000
Other loans	3,674,000	3,757,000	3,263,000	2,109,000	1,967,000
Other current liabilities	9,223,000	8,710,000	8,663,000	6,805,000	5,333,000
Total current liabilities	26,856,000	26,066,000	26,631,000	21,484,000	17,388,000
Notes payable, mortgage loans	4,032,000	4,566,000	4,932,000	6,577,000	4,333,000
Subordinated loans	677,000	673,000	764,000	802,000	862,000
Bond loans	2,710,000	1,871,000	2,016,000	1,287,000	1,227,000
Provision for pension	1,866,000	1,895,000	1,974,000	1,790,000	1,644,000
Det. taxes	—	—	—	448,000	449
Untaxed reserves	17,738,000	14,973,000	10,832,000	7,846,000	6,458,000
Minority interests	116,000	229,000	757,000	732,000	451,000
Share capital (Kr 50)	1,940,000	4,940,000	1,733,000	1,698,000	1,394,000
Reserves	2,585,000	2,854,000	2,651,000	2,257,000	1,389,000
Retained earnings incl. yrs net inc.	4,273,000	2,362,000	1,194,000	1,354,000	1,030,000
Shareholders equity	8,798,000	7,356,000	5,530,000	5,309,000	3,813,000
Total liabilities and stockholders' equity	62,793,000	57,629,000	53,506,000	46,273,000	36,643,000
Net current assets*	14,826,000	14,561,000	11,115,000	10,635,000	8,214,000

¹Adjusted to reflect effective from 1980, change in accounting principles for translating the financial statements of foreign subsidiaries to Swedish Kronor.

*Reflects total current assets—total current liabilities

SOURCES: *Moody's International Manual,* Vol. 2, 1985; and AB Volvo, *Annual Report,* 1985.

EXHIBIT 34.11   **AB Volvo: Balance Sheets***

(In SEK Millions)

	UNDER SWEDISH ACCOUNTING PRINCIPLES			UNDER U.S. GAAP		
	1985	1984	1983	1985	1984	1983
Current assets	41,682	40,627	37,746	41,575	40,451	37,626
Restricted deposits in Bank of Sweden	2,823	1,762	264	2,823	1,762	264
Property, plant & equipment (net)	9,565	8,199	10,056	10,171	9,019	9,887
Investments	6,894	5,409	3,194	7,358	5,479	3,250
Other assets	1,829	1,632	2,246	2,306	1,632	2,246
Total Assets	62,793	57,629	53,506	64,233	58,343	53,273
Current liabilities	26,856	26,066	26,631	26,783	26,102	26,128
Long-term liabilities	9,285	9,005	9,706	9,285	9,005	9,706
Deferred taxes	—	—	—	10,245	9,147	6,758
Untaxes reserves	17,738	14,973	10,832	—	—	—
Minority interests	116	229	757	116	593	810
Shareholders' equity	8,798	7,356	5,580	17,804	13,496	9,871
Total liabilities & equity	62,793	57,629	53,506	64,233	58,343	53,273

SOURCES: AB Volvo *Annual Report,* 1985; and *Moody's International Manual,* 1985, Vol. 2.

*Balance sheets under Swedish accounting principles: adjusted to conform with U.S. GAAP (Generally Accepted Accounting Principles)

chemical company. In January of 1986 Volvo and Fermenta agreed to a $556 million joint-venture that would have made them the undisputed leaders of biotech in Sweden. But in February 1986, El-Sayed admitted that he had lied about holding a doctoral degree in biochemistry from the University of California at Davis, and he resigned as Fermenta's chairman. In March 1986 Volvo canceled its venture with Fermenta and admitted that it had lent an estimated $35 million to El-Sayed to finance purchases of Fermenta stock. Meanwhile heavy trading in Fermenta stock prompted an investigation on behalf of the twenty-two bankers and industrialists governing the Stockholm Stock Exchange. In May of 1986 they voted unanimously to fine Volvo $267,000 and Fermenta $152,777. Pehr Gyllenhammar denounced the action by the Swedish Exchange and called exchange President Bengt Ryden "meddlesome." He also said that he had broken no rules and threatened to sue the exchange's governing body. The Fermenta affair, however, made Gyllenhammar suffer a setback in prestige.

Gyllenhammar suffered another blow in early 1986. That happened when, along with Volvo President Haken Frisinger and twenty-eight other top Swedish executives, he became embroiled in a political and media controversy over a stock-market investment that netted them large gains. The government subsequently launched an investigation into the practice—quite common by Swedish standards—whereby executives are given a chance to buy stock of their own company while denying it to small stockholders. Three years ago, a Volvo subsidiary, Sonesson, acquired a privately held medical company, Leo. When Sonesson decided two years ago to issue a separate and private stock for Leo, it offered the thirty executives shares at the same favorable price it had paid for them. In 1985 the stock was then listed on the exchange for the first time. Sales of the shares opened at considerably higher prices, which allowed the executives gains that in some cases reached millions of dollars. The transaction was revealed in the press the day before the traditional annual Volvo press conference to announce the results of the first nine months of 1985. Reporters centered their questions more on Gyllenhammar's business ethics than on the financial results of Volvo. The questions angered Gyllenhammar, who declared that his honor was worth more to him than any private profit. He said he would sell his shares at their original price to the cancer research fund set up in the name of the Volvo founder, Assar Gabrielsson. The massive press coverage that followed snowballed into a political dispute concerning the so-called pilot practice that allows executives to make such profits while small stockholders in a company do not have such an opportunity. In the wake of the *Leo Affair* as it was called, the Sonesson Chairman resigned, and an executive of the bank that financed the executives' stock purchases—and who had bought stock for himself—was fired. The press also reported a rift between Gyllenhammar and Frisinger because Frisinger refused to forsake his profits, which were substantially larger than Gyllenhammar's. The affair got so hot that the late Socialist Prime Minister Mr. Palme subsequently ordered an official investigation into what occurred and how a similar situation could be avoided in the future. A three-person commission was quickly set up to start its official investigation beginning early 1986. Among other things, the findings may result in tax implications for Gyllenhammar when the question will be addressed as to whether Gyllenhammar's donation of his share would be tax-exempt.

In the wake of the above incident, another shock came when both Volvo President Haken Frisinger and Executive Vice-President Ulf Linden resigned effective in 1987. It came as a hard blow to Volvo because the 60-year-old Frisinger gets the credit for turning the car division around. From declining sales and a reputation for poor quality ten years ago, Volvo has jumped to leadership in the U.S. market for imported luxury cars. Linden, 37, was Gyllenhammar's troubleshooter and responsible for Volvo's recent diversification into biotech. Frisinger agreed to take early retirement but will continue to advise Volvo on international matters. He wishes to be based outside Sweden. Linden will remain a director of AB Volvo and work part-time with issues related to financial development and strategic projects. Their respective replacements will be Gunnar Johansson, currently in charge of the aerospace engine division, Volvo Flygmotor, and Lennart Jeansson, Volvo Car Corporation's Director of Purchasing.

In April 1986, Volvo experienced labor trouble. It occurred when Volvo raised dividends in the wake of its record profits for 1985. The action resulted in protests from labor unions, which had been told to be more moderate in their wage requests than ever before in order to help the government fight inflation. Volvo's profits in 1985 amounted to approximately $1 billion, compared with the former record profit of roughly $860 million in 1984. Dividends, which were stipulated to be frozen at around $.76 per share, were raised to about $1.12, which led analysts to believe that if other important industries follow Volvo's lead, the annual round of labor negotiations in 1986 could be one of the toughest ever.

In spite of all the commotion, Gyllenhammar has proven that he can make things work. Although in 1984 European analysts were skeptical about his continuation as Volvo chief, Gyllenhammar is holding on and pursuing his goals. The Volvo insiders call him "the Emperor." He has been called "colorful," "ambitious," a "master builder" who is "a law unto himself," with "remarkable instinct for survival," and who will "recover and remain." A debonair and impeccable dresser, Gyllenhammar seems to enjoy his celebrity status. He is well known and is an essential figure within the international directors' circuit, including United Technologies, (Henry) Kissinger Associates, and Chase Manhattan Bank's International Advisory Committee.

Gyllenhammar's Grand Strategy

Gyllenhammar has used the Volvo Group's successes to acquire businesses in and diversify into areas unrelated to automobiles, such as pharmaceuticals and biotechnology. After his skirmish with Wallenberg, from which Gyllenhammar emerged unscathed, he announced: "For the first time in our history, we have not only reached a size but also have the equity position where we have real freedom." And Gyllenhammar plans to use this affluence and freedom to promote active diversification in the years to come.

Gyllenhammar figures that Volvo's car business has peaked and now it will serve only as a cash cow. The worldwide car business is going to grow only 2% per year, and the big Volvo-like cars aren't as popular in Europe as they used to be. Volvo builds only 390,000 cars per year, and 100,000 of them are low-profit runabouts picked up in acquisitions at times when it looked as if oil prices were headed through the roof. That leaves Volvo's car profits dangerously dependent on the U.S. market situations. Here Volvo sales are pushing 100,000, and Americans are willing to pay $20,000 for top models. The strong dollar made the profits even better than the unit sales gains. Besides, Gyllenhammar knows that European governments will continue subsidizing companies like Renault and Fiat, the Japanese manufacturers will remain unbeatable, and that Americans eventually will come back with a vengeance in the auto-market should the dollar recover. The answer to such a complex situation, Gyllenhammar thinks, lies in "diversification." Gyllenhammar says that he does not have any ambition to push the auto division in faster growth and expanding capacity, except through Volvo's own moderate "natural" growth rates.

THE ACQUISITIONS BY VOLVO

Alarmed by the devastating effects of the oil crisis of the early 1970s and its threat to the world auto industry, Gyllenhammar has been intent on hedging Volvo's bets by its buying into industries unrelated to autos. (See Exhibit 34.12.) Even so, vehicles and engines still accounted for two-thirds of Volvo's sales in 1985, as well as more than 90% of its profits of $1 billion.

In 1981 Volvo acquired Sweden's giant investment outfit Beijerinvest and its sizable oil-trading unit, Scandinavian Trading Company. Overnight this transaction almost doubled Volvo's revenue. Gyllenhammar planned on entering a business that would be countercyclical to the auto industry and offer more growth potential.

But oil was just one of Gyllenhammar's targets. With the Beijerinvest merger, Volvo also acquired, and plans to expand in, a group of Scandinavian food companies—herring, pickles, and mineral water. Gyllenhammar believes that although it is not a dramatic enterprise, it has a safe cash flow and is a good balance against Volvo's other businesses, which tend to fluctuate rather widely with economic upturns and recessions.

EXHIBIT 34.12   **AB Volvo Acquisitions Since 1983***

1. STC Scandinavian Trading Company AB
2. STC Venture AB
3. Hamilton Oil Corporation
4. Investment AB Beijer
5. Volvo Car Corporation
6. Saga Petroleum a.s.
7. AB Catena, Wilh Sonesson AB, Atlas Copco AB and Stora Kopparbergs Bergslags AB
8. Consafe AB
9. Protorp Forvatnings AB and AB Cardo
10. Volvo BM AB
11. AB Custos
12. Pharmacia AB

---

*For details of each acquisition and its implications please refer to *Moody's International Manual*, 1985, Vol. 2, p. 3311.

According to a report in April 1986, Volvo finally succeeded in taking over the widely diversified Sonesson concern after a tough struggle. Sonesson is heavily involved in machines, communications, pumps, drugs, and biotechnology. Because of this acquisition, Volvo will now be able to regroup its biotech holdings on an international scale. Because Volvo is already a 40% shareholder with the firm Pharmacia (drugs, pharmaceuticals, diagnosis equipments), those divisions of Sonesson that do not fit into the new restructuring concept of the biotech area will most likely be sold off by Volvo. This will happen primarily because Volvo's top management had already developed a concept of how to structure and develop its own biotech empire, after a takeover attempt on Fermenta failed in January of 1986. In bidding for Sonesson, Volvo had gradually expanded its offer from an original 30% to the eventual 80% of all shares. But to reach the critical limit of 90% at which, according to Swedish laws, the remaining shareholders can be forced to turn their shares in and accept a reasonable offer—and the company thus acquired could officially be run as a full subsidiary of the parent company— Volvo had to convince the South Swedish firm Crafoord to sell its 12.9% of Sonesson shares. This seemed to fail because of tax reasons, because Crafoord owned the Sonesson shares for a period of less than two years. In Sweden, any share sale within two years of its purchase is subject to a massive speculation tax, and in this case, Crafoord would have suffered a total loss of 70 million SEK after everything was settled.

In any case, to circumvent the tax dilemma a two-tiered strategy was chosen in April, 1986. First, the tax-free Crafoord foundation, which is a member of the Crafoord concern, sells its Sonesson shares first to Volvo, tax-free of course. With that purchase, Volvo just passes the critical 90% share limit. The remaining Sonesson shares, normally heavily taxable, could be obtained through the legal handover order. But if anyone is legally forced to sell his shares to the 90% holder, the two-year waiting period is not applicable. This is because "force" is not considered "speculation," in which case the shareholder has a choice. In the event of such a forced sale only a small tax will be applicable.

ATTITUDE OF THE SWEDISH GOVERNMENT TOWARD VOLVO

Although acquisitions are getting tougher for Gyllenhammar in socialist-ruled Sweden, the realistic socialists know that free enterprise lays the golden eggs. Therefore they avoid total strangulation of business but still place endless restrictions on industry in general. For example, exchange controls prohibit Volvo from using any of its domestic earnings for investments abroad; those funds must stay home. So overseas activities have to be financed with capital raised overseas. Volvo could acquire more Swedish companies, but it is so big in Sweden already that this might be politically unwise. Moreover, after the tragic assassination of Swedish Prime Minister Olof Palme, Swedish industry will need to monitor the future trends with extra caution.

For Gyllenhammar it has been a different ballgame, however. He and Volvo have always been favorites of the Swedish government. In fact, Volvo is receiving massive government support for its building an auto assembly plant in Uddevalla, a city fifty-five miles north of Gothenburg with a struck shipyard. Critics have accused the government of eating out of Pehr Gyllenhammar's hands, but neither of the parties has admitted to any complicity in making a deal that pours millions of public dollars into the project at a time when Volvo has achieved record profits. Apart from that, Volvo has already been promised that it can use about $1.38 billion of set-aside profits without taxation, for different plant projects around Gothenberg.

THE VOLVO IMAGE

Recently, serious-minded readers of such publications as *The Wall Street Journal, The Financial Times* of London, *Le Monde,* and *Institutional Investor* have been looking at Volvo's heavily allegorical fairy tales, written and illustrated in children's-book fashion, appearing as dramatic three-page spreads in fourteen countries. The moral of each tale was lent a concrete dimension by the real-life facts and figures on the diversified automaker. One senior Volvo official commented: "We wanted to expose our values, our philosophy, our way of doing business, not just facts. We asked ourselves, 'What is the oldest form to communicate wishes and values? Fairy tales.' "

The ads, early in 1985, were the centerpiece of a broad, international investor-relations campaign meant to convey the message that Europe's nineteenth largest company has become much more than merely a car maker. One senior official of Volvo North America observed that a few years ago in the United States over half of the general population didn't recognize that Volvo was a Swedish company or that it was also a large truck and marine-power manufacturer. Some thought that Volvo made motorcycles, while others believed that it was a Japanese or German company. In fact, autos account for only 40% of Volvo's worldwide revenues.

Investor image-building, both domestic and foreign, has become an urgent priority for Volvo because of its push to diversify internationally. Early in 1985 Volvo announced a joint venture to manufacture off-road trucks and other types of heavy construction equipment with Clark Equipment Company of the United States.

Although fully 90% of Volvo's sales are generated outside Sweden, roughly the same proportion of its shares are held within the country, mostly by insurance companies and other institutions that are all but saturated with Volvo stock. Under Swedish law a foreign investor may hold only up to 40% of a Swedish company's capital. Adding extra impetus to the desire to broaden the shareholder base was Gyllenhammar's run-in with Peter Wallenberg in 1984.

Volvo has already had a headstart in raising its profile among foreign investors. Its shares have long been listed abroad—on both the West German bourse and the London Stock Exchange since 1974, and on Norway's exchange since 1979. But despite deriving 40% of its revenues from the U.S., Volvo waited until late 1983 to offer its shares directly to American investors in the form of unsponsored over-the-counter American depositary receipts (ADRs). The company followed up with sponsored shares in 1984, the same year Volvo obtained a listing on the Paris bourse.

Although the late 1984 ADRs weren't exactly snapped up by the market, by early 1985 Volvo had some 3 million shares outstanding in the U.S (compared with 78 million in Sweden), and had further plans to cultivate U.S. investors. The company had scheduled a series of high-powered road shows in 1985 to introduce the company's senior management to U.S. analysts. The first of these—timed to follow the Volvo Masters Tennis Tournament in New York's Madison Square Garden in January of 1985—featured five top executives, including Volvo's chief, Pehr Gyllenhammar.

In 1984 Volvo had budgeted just under $1 million for advertising each of the three fairy tales featured in the initial three-month campaign. Volvo Group Treasurer Holmstrom commented that he was aware that the U.S. investment community was familiar with Volvo. But, in addition to that familiarity he wanted them to know the company's finances, its aims, its philosophy, and that it is not only successful, profitable and international, but is also a social laboratory.

EXHIBIT 34.13

1985 Top Selling Imports in the U.S.A.
(Units Sold)

1.	Toyota	620,047
2.	Nissan	575,166
3.	Honda	552,389
4.	Mazda	211,093
5.	Subaru	178,175
6.	Volvo	104,267
7.	BMW	87,857
8.	Mercedes-Benz	86,903
9.	Audi	74,061
10.	Mitsubishi	49,734
11.	Saab	39,264
12.	Isuzu	26,953
13.	Porsche	25,306
14.	Jaguar	20,528

SOURCE: *Automotive News* (January 13, 1986), p. 1

Volvo's Marketing in the U.S.

Out of the total 11,042,658 cars (which includes domestics, foreign-based domestics, and foreign) sold in the U.S. in 1985, Volvo had a market share of 104,267 units. (0.94%). (See Exhibits 34.13–34.14.) But, in 1985, out of a total of 2,837,963 imports sold in the U.S., Volvo had a market share of 3.7%. This statistic shows that Volvo has plenty of elbow room yet, for the positioning of its autos in U.S. markets.

In 1986, it appears that in the United States Volvo has positioned itself squarely in the center of the family-car segment in spite of heavy and increasing competition. Volvo anticipates better sales results in 1986, compared to 1985. It recently introduced an entry into the over-$30,000 luxury segment—the 780 series. Although it won't be available until the fall of 1986 for marketing as a 1987 model, the 780 will give the company a full range of cars from the base 240DL, priced at $14,615, to the $30,000+ level.

EXHIBIT 34.14   **New Car Sales in Europe**
(In Thousands)

	1985	1986*
Austria	227	250
Belgium	350	360
Denmark	139	131
Finland	132	133
France	1,810	1,902
Greece	71	74
Ireland	58	66
Italy	1,672	1,658
Netherlands	476	461
Norway	128	126
Portugal	96	91
Spain	528	570
Sweden	249	225
Switzerland	253	266
United Kingdom	1,770	1,732
West Germany	2,295	2,546
Total	10,254	10,591

SOURCE: DRI Europe, in *Automotive News* (January 13, 1986), p. E8
*Projected figures

The decision to offer the 780 also gives Volvo one of the broadest model ranges, in terms of market price. It is apparent that the company is pursuing repeat buyers and trying to keep them climbing into Volvos as they rise through income brackets.

REFERENCES

Bayless, P., "Volvo Draws a Moral for Investors," *Institutional Investor* (May 1985), pp. 133–34.

Berss, M., "The Master Builder," *Forbes* (November 19, 1984), pp. 242–43.

Bjorklund, S., "Volvo Brass Embroiled in Stock Fray," *Automotive News* (January 13, 1986), p. 7.

Borsen-Zietung (Frankfurt, W. Germany: 80, April 26, 1986), p. 5.

Done, Kevin, "Volvo GM to Link Truck Operations in North America," *Financial Times* (London: August 16, 1986), p. 1.

Feast, R., "Volvo Becomes European High Roller," *Automotive World News* (May 21, 1984).

"Higher Dividend at Volvo Stirs Labor Protests," *Automotive News* (April 21, 1986), p. 30.

Kaja, J. "How Solid is Sweden's Prosperity?" *Institutional Investor* (March 1985), pp. 224–31.

Kapstein, J., "A Slap on the Wrist Leaves Volvo Smarting," *Business Week* (June 16, 1986), p. 52.

Kapstein, J., "Volvo's Emperor Faces Rebellion in the Ranks," *Business Week* (March 31, 1986), p. 45.

Krebs, M. "The Doomsayers," *Automotive News* (January 13, 1986), p. E4.

Moody's International Manual (1985), Vol. 2.

Russell, J., "Uncommon Market," *Automotive News* (March 10, 1986), pp. E20–E23.

"Sweden Helps Volvo Build Plant," *Automotive News* (February 25, 1985), p. 20.

"Two Volvo Chiefs to Leave in 1987; Successors Named," *Automotive News* (January 27, 1986), p. 6.

"Volvo: A Company on a Fast Roll—Upward," *Automotive News* (October 30, 1985), p. 404.

"Volvo Moving Ahead with Product Plans," *Automotive News* (February 24, 1986), p. 12.

"A Wrench of the Wheel," *The Economist* (April 14, 1984), p. 76.

Cotton Belt Exporters

PAUL N. KEATON · PATRICIA A. WATSON-KUENTZ

While John Welch was growing up in Texas, he was an excellent student. His parents and teachers thought of him as "college capable"; in fact, he never seriously considered any option other than college. He chose his major in marketing because one of his goals was, in his own words, "not to get stuck in Civil Service like my dad did. Private industry is the place for me where I have more of an opportunity to be promoted on my own merits and not necessarily on seniority." John entered college and, as usual, did well scholastically.

As college graduation neared, John began to interview with a number of companies. The college placement counselor advised John to make a list of aspects that he would find desirable or undesirable in a job. One of the items on his list was that the company and its product or goal had to be socially justifiable. This item had come to mind because many of his class-mates were going to work for oil companies. John believed that in spite of the oil companies' slightly higher pay scale, he would not want to work for a company that made its money selling a non-renewable resource.

Another of the items on his list was that he wanted to travel in his job. His family had traveled in the United States on vacations when he was a child and he had been to Mexico and Canada, but he wanted to see something of other parts of the world. Although John did not care to live in another country, he did think that a job which took him periodically to other countries for short trips would be desirable.

One day during the spring semester of his senior year, John talked with one of his marketing professors, Dr. Mayfield, about his career goals, and Dr. Mayfield suggested that perhaps John should look into the exporting business. Dr. Mayfield said he had a friend in Memphis who was a vice-president in a cotton exporting firm, Cotton Belt Exporters. Things fell into place and John received and accepted an offer of a job in the firm.

For the first couple of years, John's responsibilities included traveling throughout the southern United States and California buying cotton from farmers and gins, but the company promised that once he had proven himself in a couple of positions he would be promoted into a position where he would be dealing directly with people in foreign countries. After about six

Prepared by Professor Paul N. Keaton of the University of Wisconsin-La Crosse and Ms. Patricia A. Watson-Kuentz. Presented at the 1982 Workshop of the Midwest Society for Case Research. Reprinted by permission.

years and two positions with the firm, he was promoted to Manager of Export Sales to Japan.

It took John some time to become accustomed to dealing with Japanese businesspeople, but in doing so he became fascinated by the differences in customs. He learned to understand that just because a Mr. Tanaka said "yes" while John was talking to him, he did not mean that he agreed to what was being said—instead, he meant merely that he understood what was being said. Each trip to Japan was a learning experience.

John also became acquainted with the mechanics of selling cotton to Japan. He learned that disagreements between cotton sellers in the United States and cotton buyers in Japan were arbitrated to a large degree by two associations, one in the United States (the American Cotton Shipping Association) and one in Japan (the Cotton Trade Association). The two associations agreed on many rules for trade but when their rules conflicted, the cotton contracts themselves specified which rules would apply.

On one trip to Japan, John heard rumors from importers that the Cotton Trade Association was contemplating some rule changes in the near future that could affect the company's ability to trade with Japan. He paid a visit to the Association but his usual contact was on vacation in Hawaii, so he had to see another gentleman, Mr. Kodama. Mr. Kodama said that he knew little about the pending changes but he intimated that, although he was a busy man, for a small fee he could probably find out "many" details. John left the office promising to get back to Mr. Kodama.

John considered his options. He decided that although he had never approved of payment for such information, the urgency of the situation and the probable need for immediate action dictated that he should make the payment. The next day he returned to Mr. Kodama's office with an envelope containing 22,170 yen (equivalent to about $100 U.S.) which was, from his experience, the going rate for such payments.

Mr. Kodama told John that a middle-level government official, Mr. Nakamura, was pressuring the cotton importing people to diversify their source of cotton in order to reduce Japan's dependency on any one country. The Association reacted by considering rule changes that would encourage importers to buy from sources other than their largest ones. Because the United States was the largest supplier of cotton to Japan, this action was certain to reduce the total amount of cotton it could sell to Japan.

John checked with his company, and his boss approved John's suggestion that he do some lobbying while he was in Japan. After obtaining the appropriate introductions John arranged to have lunch with Mr. Nakamura. At the restaurant, John explained his company's situation, and gave Mr. Nakamura facts about the promise of larger crops in the United States, reduced prices because of technological advances in production, improved strains of cotton, and so on. After much discussion, Mr. Nakamura indicated that, having given some thought to the specifics of the problem, he believed he might be able to see John's side of the argument.

Later in the conversation, Mr. Nakamura began to discuss the increasing cost of living, especially since his son had been admitted to Harvard. He wondered if John's company might see fit to give the boy some type of scholarship. According to the Harvard catalog, his son would need about $20,000 per year to attend school. Mr. Nakamura subtly (but unmistakably) intimated that financial aid to his son might help him see the cotton situation more clearly.

John found himself in a dilemma. He had rationalized the payments for information, but somehow this situation seemed different.

The Standard Oil Company: British Petroleum Loses Patience

J. DAVID HUNGER

The members of the Special Committee of Standard Oil's Board of Directors were in a quandary. It was April 14, 1987. The committee had only nine days in which to decide what to recommend to the minority stockholders regarding the offer by British Petroleum (BP) to buy the 45% of Standard's shares BP did not already own. British Petroleum was offering $70 a share, but the committee worried that the price was too low. A report to the Special Committee prepared by First Boston Corporation argued that the shares not owned by BP had an acquisition value of at least $85 per share—significantly higher than BP's offer.

The Special Committee, composed of the seven outside members of Standard's Board of Directors, had been unable to decide upon a recommendation. Because of differing valuations of the company, the committee had proposed that Standard's Board not take a position on British Petroleum's offer until April 23—only five days before BP's offer expired. Douglas Danforth, Committee Chairman, knew that the matter could be delayed no longer. What should the committee recommend?

BACKGROUND

Standard Oil of Ohio was officially established as an independent firm in 1911, when the United States Supreme Court ordered the giant Standard Oil Trust to divest itself of holdings in thirty-three other companies. The largest, Standard of New Jersey, became the successful Exxon Corporation. Standard Oil of Ohio, in contrast, was established as a one-state marketer with an obsolete and inadequate refining capacity. Even though it continued to operate under the original Standard Oil charter signed by J. D. Rockefeller in 1870, the company owned no crude oil and no pipelines. Its assets were only $6.6 million, consisting of Rockefeller's original Cleveland refinery, some storage tanks, and wagons. Reduced to the status of buying and selling other companies' oil, Standard of Ohio concentrated on marketing gasoline to the developing automobile market. Its red, white, and blue *SOHIO* signs shone from attractive service stations located on the most desirable intersections throughout Ohio. It also marketed in contiguous

This case was prepared by Professor J. David Hunger of Iowa State University. Copyright © 1987 by J. David Hunger. It was presented at the 1987 Workshop of the Midwest Society for Case Research. Reprinted by permission.

states under the name "Boron." Standard's marketing expertise made the firm a very strong competitor. Nevertheless, until 1970, Standard Oil of Ohio, or Sohio, as it referred to itself, was a very minor player in the global petroleum industry.

In 1970, Sohio exchanged a special stock interest, equal to about a 25% stake in Standard Oil, to acquire British Petroleum's U.S. interests, which included large Alaskan holdings believed to contain rich deposits of oil. This gave Sohio a 50% share of what became the 1.5-million-barrel-per-day Prudhoe Bay oil field. The company also took over management of the Sinclair/BP operation, which ranged from Texas to New England. In return, the British company obtained two seats on Sohio's fifteen-person Board of Directors, a voice in Sohio's spending plans, a healthy infusion of cash in the form of dividends from Sohio, and an experienced U.S. marketer for its Alaskan oil. Based on a formula tied to Prudhoe Bay crude oil production, the gain for British Petroleum (BP) was a 53% majority interest in Standard and a third seat on its Board of Directors by 1978.

The huge cost of environmental battles plus inflation increased the price of the Prudhoe Bay oil pipeline from its initial 1971 estimate of $900 million to $9.3 billion at completion in 1978, and Sohio was forced to borrow approximately $4.6 billion to pay its share of construction costs. Fortunately, world oil prices began to soar with the 1973 OPEC oil embargo. The bold gamble paid off when the oil started flowing from Alaska. Sohio suddenly found itself in 1978 among the major oil companies; it ranked ninth in total assets. Prudhoe Bay, however, accounted for 80% of its assets, about 97% of its oil production, and more than 85% of its profits. Standard Oil of Ohio became the holder of one of the largest U.S. oil reserves, as well as one of the largest companies in the United States. By 1981, Sohio's earnings of $1.95 billion were more than 46 times its profits of ten years earlier.

Realizing that the flow of oil coming from Prudhoe Bay was likely to decline in the late 1980s, and with it the huge annual cash profits, the top management of Sohio set in motion in 1978 a two-pronged strategy of (1) expanding oil and gas exploration, and (2) diversifying into energy-related industries. Spending billions of dollars for exploration rights, the company began actively searching for oil in the lower forty-eight states and the Gulf of Mexico. From 1977, when Sohio spent only $20 million on exploration, to 1982, when its exploration/production capital expenditure budget was $1.96 billion, Standard attempted to find enough oil that it could reduce its heavy dependence on Prudhoe Bay. It increased its exploration staff from 60 in 1977 to nearly 1,000 by the end of 1983. Seeking to expand beyond its current operations, Standard acquired in 1984 Truckstops Corporation of America, with its facilities along interstate highways in fifteen states, and Gulf Oil Corporation's refining and marketing properties in the eight south-eastern states of Kentucky, Tennessee, Alabama, Mississippi, Georgia, Florida, South Carolina, and North Carolina. The company also spent money on a number of unprofitable ventures as well as some that might be profitable in the long run.

Disappointing Kennecott Acquisition

By far, however, the company's two largest investments, Kennecott and Mukluk, have been unsuccessful. In 1981, Sohio purchased the nation's largest copper producer, Kennecott Corporation, for $1.77 billion. Unfortunately for Sohio, the price of copper soon began to drop precipitously as foreign copper producers began to oversupply the world market. Attempting to stem Kennecott's losses, Standard acted to close Kennecott's abrasive operations (part of Carborundum, which Kennecott had earlier purchased) as well as to cut back and modernize copper operations. Even with these cost-cutting moves, by end-1985 Kennecott had lost a total of $702 million since its purchase by Sohio.

The twelve major U.S. copper producers were operating in 1985 at 59% of capacity and were in danger of going out of business. By keeping output high, Third World competitors, such as Chile (where ore was twice as rich in copper as that pulled from most U.S. mines) kept prices around 67 cents per pound in 1985 (about half the 1980 prices) versus the 82-cents-per-pound average cost of U.S. production. Nevertheless, in 1985, Sohio's top management decided to spend $400 million on a three-year modernization program of Kennecott's Bingham Canyon mine in Utah. The stated goal was to make Kennecott profitable by 1989: the cost of copper production was to be reduced from 75 cents to around 45 cents per pound. Sohio's top management might have had little choice because the estimated costs of closing the Bingham mine were anywhere from $500 million to $5 billion—depending on environmental and severance-pay requirements.[1]

Costly Mukluk Exploration

Realizing that it needed a big oil strike to replace the $6 billion in annual revenues from Prudhoe, Sohio invested heavily in a prospect called *Mukluk* in the Beaufort Sea. After an estimated cost of $1.7 billion for leases and drilling fourteen miles off Alaska's north coast, the exploratory well was found on December 3, 1983, to contain water, not oil. Even though this was the most expensive "dry well" in history, Sohio's top management continued to push for continued exploration both in Alaska and in the lower forty-eight. "Because we want to replace Prudhoe, we need to do some elephant-hunting," said Richard Bray, head of Sohio's exploration and production unit. "But because most times you don't bag one, you also need to go after rabbits, squirrels, anything that's out there."[2]

Unfortunately, after spending nearly $5 billion on exploration and leases from 1980 to 1985, the company had replaced only a little more than one third of the oil it had produced during that time. In early 1986, it was estimated that output from Prudhoe Bay would begin to decline approximately 11% to 12% beginning in 1988. "If they had gone out three or four years ago (1982–1983) and bought an independent oil company, they would have been in a substantially better position," stated Lawrence Tween, an oil analyst for Kidder Peabody and Company.[3] During the fourth quarter of 1985, Sohio finally cut its aggressive oil exploration budget by $200 million and reduced its exploration personnel by 600 employees.

Sohio Becomes Standard Oil

In February, 1986, Sohio changed its name to "The Standard Oil Company." This appeared to reflect its desire to become more like the company John D. Rockefeller had founded 116 years before. In their February 19, 1986, letter to shareholders and employees, Alton Whitehouse, Chief Executive Officer and Chairman of the Board, and John Miller, President and Chief Operating Officer stated:

> We are the original Standard Oil Company, founded by John D. Rockefeller in Cleveland in 1870. All other Standard Oil Companies that were a part of The Standard Oil Trust have either disappeared entirely or have changed their corporate names. Standard Oil also says plainly that we are primarily in energy, a field where we have attained major stature and where we intend to remain and continue to grow. It is a strong corporate name with a proud heritage and we plan to use it widely.

In a speech to security analysts in early February of 1986, Whitehouse reported that he had succeeded in streamlining the company's work force and asserted that "we're ready to handle the worst."[4] Taking over from Charles Spahr in 1978 as Chief Executive Officer, Alton W. Whitehouse, Jr. had worked hard to transform Sohio from a small regional marketer/refiner into a major integrated oil company. Coming to the company in 1968 as the firm's first Chief Legal Counsel, Whitehouse represented Sohio in the negotiations with British Petroleum. He subsequently became Sohio's President in 1970 and its Vice-Chairman in 1977. Admitting his lack of technical knowledge of the oil industry, Mr. Whitehouse divided the company into business groups and delegated most operating responsibility to the unit heads.

Explaining why the company's net income had dropped from $1.5 billion in 1984 to $308 million in 1985, Whitehouse stated that income had been reduced by $1.86 billion before tax ($1.15 billion after tax) in the fourth quarter of 1985. The charges against earnings reflected a reevaluation of assets, the cost of the continued shutdown of the Utah Copper Division during modernization, as well as expenses related to staff reductions (some 1,300 positions had been eliminated). "In 1985, total operating income before special charges was almost equal to that of 1984, as the combination of higher sales volumes of Alaskan crude oil and significant gains in refining and marketing income balanced the effects of lower crude oil prices and higher exploration expenses," reported Whitehouse and Miller.[5]

British Petroleum Takes Charge

With almost no warning, however, Standard Oil's parent company, British Petroleum, decided to assert itself in the affairs of Whitehouse's company. Since BP had acquired control of the company in 1970, it had allowed Standard to operate independently of BP. Under the 1970 pact, BP had been limited initially to two, then to three members of Sohio's Board of Directors. By 1986, however, Sir Peter Walters, Chief Executive of British Petroleum Company, and his top aides decided that BP's hands-off policy had to change. The precipitous drop in oil prices, coupled with Standard's $1.8 billion pre-tax writeoff in 1985 of Kennecott and coal assets, triggered the action. "There were a number of disappointments in the past few years," said Sir Peter. "Looking back at those, and the testing time ahead for oil prices, we felt we had to strengthen management for all shareholders' benefits."[6] Informed by Sir Peter of BP's plan to take over managerial control of Standard Oil, Alton Whitehouse reluctantly resigned his position as CEO at Standard's February 27, 1986, meeting of its Board of Directors.

Robert B. Horton, an executive with British Petroleum and a Standard Oil Board member, succeeded Whitehouse as Chairman and Chief Executive Officer of Standard Oil on April 1, 1986. Frank Mosier, Standard's Executive Vice-President, succeeded John Miller as President and Chief Operating Officer. The functions of Chief Vice-President/Chief Financial Officer and of Executive Vice-President for Engineered Products, Chemicals, Metallurgical Products and Technology were filled by BP executives, John Browne, and Colin Webster, respectively, brought to Cleveland from London. Described as a workaholic, CEO Horton had experience at turning around two problem BP units: a $2.8 billion chemical subsidiary and a tanker company. Concerned with Standard's failure to successfully reinvest the cash from Prudhoe Bay, Horton was faced with the prospect of recommending to the Board either that Standard continue trying to replace Prudhoe Bay oil or that the company be shrunk. "If I have somewhat of a reputation as a hatchet man, it's perhaps because I've never been reluctant to admit it when I made a mistake," asserted Horton. "It's really best at that point to cut your losses and move on."[7]

THE U.S. OIL INDUSTRY

1986 had been another difficult year for the U.S. oil industry. United States oil demand of 16 million barrels per day was still far below peak demand of 19 million barrels per day in 1978. The "spot" or non-contract price for West Texas Intermediate, the barometer of U.S. oil prices, dropped from $30 per barrel in October 1985 to $10 per barrel in March 1986, and stayed below $18 for the rest of the year. Standard Oil's 1986 budget had been based on an oil price of $18 per barrel. The company's total cost of producing and transporting Alaskan crude oil to refineries ranged between $11 and

$12 per barrel.[8] Other oil companies faced the same problem. An industry composite of the twenty-nine largest fuel companies in the United States by *Business Week* revealed a 26% decline in dollar sales and a 24% decline in dollar profits in 1986 from 1985.[9] The National Petroleum Council estimated that approximately 150,000 jobs, roughly 25% of the total, were lost in the oil industry in 1986, as U.S. oil production dropped by 700,000 barrels per day, or about 6%, even though demand was rising nearly 3%. "America's oil industry has been devastated by this price skid, and the devastation continues," reported Fred Hartley, Chairman of Unocal Corporation.[10]

Problems with Diversification

A number of the major integrated oil companies have found the industry-wide problems to be aggravated by their experiences in diversifying outside the energy-related field. Standard Oil's poor experience with its Kennecott acquisition was paralleled by Mobil's problems with its cash-hungry Montgomery Ward subsidiary, Atlantic Richfield's difficulties with its Anaconda mining unit, Ashland Oil's unsuccessful move into insurance, and Exxon's string of bad investments. In particular, Exxon's purchase of Reliance Electric in 1979 for $1.2 billion had been selected by *Fortune* as one of the decade's seven worst mergers. The list of oil firms diversifying out of oil during the 1970s had become quite a long one by 1980. Nevertheless by 1986, most of these non–oil-related acquisitions had been sold or were in the process of being sold as companies began to concentrate once again on the oil/energy business.

Threat of Takeovers

Adding to the pressures facing the major oil firms in the 1980s was the increasing threat of being taken over by another firm. The acquisition of Conoco by DuPont, Cities Service by Occidental Petroleum, Getty Oil by Texaco, Superior Oil by Mobil, and Gulf Oil by Chevron (Standard Oil of California) shook the industry. In addition, Royal Dutch/Shell acquired the remainder of its 64.9%-owned U.S. subsidiary after a lengthy stockholder lawsuit. Pennzoil's dissatisfaction with having lost Getty Oil to Texaco led to a successful lawsuit against the winner and to Texaco's surprising declaration of Chapter 11 bankruptcy in April 1987.

Also in early 1987, Amoco (Standard Oil of Indiana) outbid both Exxon (Standard Oil of New Jersey) and TransCanada Pipelines for Canada's Dome Petroleum. Canadian Energy Minister Marcel Masse was concerned with Amoco's purchase, because of the Canadian government's commitment to its goal of increasing Canadian ownership in the oil and gas sector from its then current 48% level to 50%. The purchase of Dome by Amoco, the fifth largest U.S. oil company in terms of revenue, reduced Canadian ownership in the industry to about 40%.[11]

Forces leading to the intense merger activity included undervalued stock prices, high cash positions, and declining U.S. oil reserves. The world demand for refined oil products was projected to grow at a rate of only 1%–2% annually for the rest of the 1980s, and stocks of the big oil firms were trading at substantial discounts to the value of the wealth they had amassed to date. The huge cash flows coming from the production and sales of oil and gas reserves were generally far larger than could be prudently spent on new drilling prospects. After noting the bad experiences of Mobil, Sohio, Ashland Oil, and Exxon, among others, in investing outside of the energy industry, and considering the depressed nature of coal and nuclear energy, almost all of the large firms had been raising their dividends and buying back their own stock. Purchasing one's own stock served several functions. Assets were acquired with excess cash at low risk without a takeover premium. By the reduction of stock outstanding, earnings per share was increased. The company's stock price was also supported.

The average cost of finding oil was around $12 per barrel, and U.S. oil companies reduced their exploration spending by 40% in 1987 from 1986. Many U.S. oil operators insisted in April 1987 that they would not resume much domestic exploration until the price of oil increased from its current $18 per barrel to $25 per barrel.[12] (See Exhibit 36.1 for a summary of current reserves of representative companies.)

EXHIBIT 36.1 **Year-End Oil and Natural Gas Reserves of Representative U.S. Integrated Petroleum Corporations**

	OIL VOLUMES (MILLIONS OF BBLS.)		GAS VOLUMES (BILLIONS OF CU. FT.)	
	1985	1986	1985	1986
Amerada	692	458	1,882	1,936
Amoco	2,769	2,424	15,137	15,375
Atlantic Richfield	2,931	2,927	7,065	6,895
Chevron	3,831	3,513	9,994	10,081
Exxon	6,733	6,512	29,723	29,430
Mobil	2,366	2,460	20,687	20,479
Occidental	963	752	2,703	3,258
Pennzoil	111	98	961	900
Phillips	901	718	4,883	5,144
Standard Oil	2,648	2,406	7,219	7,308
Sun	848	796	3,174	2,917
Texaco	3,333	3,225	8,869	8,165
Unocal	751	752	6,189	6,073

SOURCE: *Value Line Investment Survey*, Part 3: Ratings and Reports, Edition 3, Volume 42, Number 29 (April 10, 1987), p. 402.

It therefore made sense for oil firms to supplement their exploration activities by the buying of other companies' reserves. Noting that the industry was not heavily concentrated by Federal Trade Commission and Justice Department standards, the U.S. Congress in March 1984 had rejected a proposed eleven-month moratorium on further oil-industry mergers. A green light was thus given to further merger activity for the foreseeable future.

STANDARD OIL'S OPERATIONS

The Standard Oil Company ended 1986 with a loss. In his first official letter in February 1987 to the shareholders and employees, Robert Horton reported:

> It was a terrible year; we reported a net loss of $345 million after special and extraordinary charges of $844 million net of tax. Even before these charges, our earnings fell some 66 percent to $499 million, largely because our average oil price was only $13.83 per barrel in 1986, compared with $26.43 per barrel in the previous year. And things would have been worse if our downstream oil and non-oil businesses had not generally put in good performances.

(Financial and operational data for Standard Oil are presented in Exhibit 36.2 through 36.4.) Having spent a year of pruning the exploration portfolio,

EXHIBIT 36.2

Statement of Income, Standard Oil Company
(Millions of Dollars, Except Per-Share Amounts)

Year Ended December 31	1986	1985	1984
Revenues			
Sales and operating revenue	$ 9,219	$13,002	$11,692
Excise taxes	803	816	559
	10,022	13,818	12,251
Costs and expenses			
Costs of products sold and operating expenses	4,903	6,156	5,406
Taxes other than income taxes	1,368	1,817	1,579
Depreciation, depletion and amortization	1,158	927	796
Oil and gas exploration expenses, including amortization of unproved properties	926	1,101	704
Selling, general and administrative expenses	954	943	728
Unusual items (write down or disposal of properties in coal, metals, and exploration)	1,079	1,699	90
	10,388	12,643	9,303

(Continued)

EXHIBIT 36.2   (Continued)

Year Ended December 31	1986	1985	1984
Income (loss) before interest, income taxes, and extraordinary item	(366)	1,175	2,948
Interest expense	(335)	(396)	(374)
Interest income	93	97	132
Income (loss) before income taxes and extraordinary item	(608)	876	2,706
Income taxes	297	(568)	(1,218)
Income (loss) before extraordinary item	(311)	308	1,488
Extraordinary item—loss on early payment of some debt, net of income taxes	(34)	—	—
Net income (loss)	$ (345)	$ 308	$ 1,488
Per share of common stock			
Income (loss) before extraordinary item	$ (1.32)	$ 1.31	$ 6.14
Extraordinary item	$ (.15)	—	—
Net income (loss)	$ (1.47)	$ 1.31	$ 6.14
Cash dividends	$ 2.80	$ 2.80	$ 2.65
Average number of common and equivalent shares outstanding (millions)	235	235	242
Statement of retained earnings			
Balance at beginning of year	$ 7,628	$ 7,977	$ 7,128
Net income (loss)	(345)	308	1,488
Cash dividends			
Common	(305)	(305)	(306)
Special	(352)	(352)	(333)
Balance at end of year	$ 6,626	$ 7,628	$ 7,977

SOURCE: *1986 Annual Report,* Standard Oil Company, p. 41.

cutting capital expenditures, reducing overhead, selling off some businesses, and modernizing others, Horton next presented in the February 1987 letter his plan for surviving the oil prices that he believed would average only $15 per barrel:

Our strategy for Standard Oil has four simple rules:

- First and foremost, we are an oil company.
- Diversify in moderation only. Non-oil must fit, be competitive, and be profitable.
- Keep our financial position strong.
- Manage for profitability, not for size or growth for its own sake.

EXHIBIT   36.3

Balance Sheet, Standard Oil Company
(In Millions of Dollars)

Year Ending December 31	1986	1985
Assets		
Current assets		
Cash, including time deposits of $6 and $37	$ 138	$ 120
Marketable securities at cost, which approximates market	275	235
Accounts receivable, less allowances of $20 and $17	861	1,611
Refundable federal income taxes	771	—
Inventories (current cost—$1,429 and $2,247)	1,200	1,437
Net investment in operations to be divested	127	—
Prepaid expenses and deferred charges	83	92
Total current assets	3,455	3,495
Property, plant and equipment		
Petroleum		
Exploration and production (successful-efforts accounting method)	13,733	13,502
Refining and marketing	2,130	1,998
Coal	501	962
Metals mining	1,396	2,114
Chemicals	468	461
QIT	279	219
Other business	290	420
Corporate and other	454	460
	19,251	20,136
Less accumulated depreciation, depletion and amortization	7,434	7,001
	11,817	13,135
Other noncurrent assets		
Investments in unconsolidated affiliates	218	291
Receivables	333	390
Prepaid expenses and deferred charges	132	197
	683	878
	$15,955	$17,508
Liabilities and Shareholders' Equity		
Current liabilities		
Notes payable	$ 318	$ 72
Current maturities of long-term obligations	101	328
Accounts payable	974	1,568

(Continued)

EXHIBIT 36.3   (Continued)

Year Ending December 31	1986	1985
Liabilities and Shareholders' Equity		
Accrued income and other taxes	365	413
Accrued interest	134	113
Other	554	733
	2,446	3,227
Long-term obligations and accruals		
Long-term debt	2,951	2,962
Capital lease obligations	325	343
Accruals and reserves	1,152	1,300
	4,428	4,605
Deferred income taxes	2,061	1,658
Shareholders' equity		
Capital stock		
Common—$1.25 stated value, 300 million shares authorized, shares issued—122,498,893 and 122,337,553	154	154
Special—stated value 1,000 shares authorized and issued	25	25
	179	179
Additional paid-in capital	822	818
Retained earnings	6,626	7,628
Common stock in treasury, at cost—13,626,248 shares and 13,623,050 shares	(607)	(607)
	7,020	8,018
	$15,955	$17,508

SOURCE: *1986 Annual Report*, Standard Oil Company, pp. 42–43.

EXHIBIT 36.4   **Operating and Other Statistics, Standard Oil Company**

	1986	1985	1984	1983	1982
Petroleum					
Crude oil and natural gas produced (net), bbl./day					
Alaska	706,400	699,700	617,900	594,800	676,700
Lower 48 states	20,200	20,000	16,500	17,200	18,200
Foreign	—	—	—	—	—
	726,600	719,700	634,400	612,000	694,900

	1986	1985	1984	1983	1982
Produced natural gas sold (net), thous. of cu. ft./day	154,400	110,100	87,600	95,600	90,700
Refinery runs, bbl./day	622,800	597,500	405,700	393,700	360,100
Refinery capacity (yr-end), bbls./calendar day	656,000	656,000	456,000	456,000	456,000
Refined petroleum products sold, bbls./day	644,500	604,200	410,800	404,700	370,900
Marketing retail outlets[1]	8,100	8,200	3,050	3,175	3,550
Nonpetroleum					
Acrylonitrile produced, mill. lbs.	840	830	760	660	590
Ilmenite ore shipped, thous. tons	3,000	2,780	2,040	1,700	2,030
Coal sold, thous. tons	15,400	13,900	14,400	10,700	10,900
Produced copper sold, thous. tons	181	189	310	316	268
Operating results					
Revenues (mill. $)	$10,022	$13,818	$12,251	$11,958	$13,490
Income (loss) before extraordinary item (mill. $)	$ (311)	$ 308	$ 1,488	$ 1,512	$ 1,879
Net income (loss) (mill. $)	$ (345)	$ 308	$ 1,488	$ 1,512	$ 1,879
Return on average capital employed	(1.3)%	3.8%	12.4%	13.2%	17.2%
Ratio of earnings to fixed charges	. . .[2]	2.6	6.0	5.7	5.3
Per share of common stock					
Income (loss) before extraordinary item	$ (1.32)	$ 1.31	$ 6.14	$ 6.14	$ 7.63
Net income (loss)	$ (1.47)	$ 1.31	$ 6.14	$ 6.14	$ 7.63
Dividends paid	$ 2.80	$ 2.80	$ 2.65	$ 2.60	$ 2.55
Market price, high/low	$ 52/40	$ 56/40	$ 51/40	$ 59/35	$ 42/26
Other data					
Avg. # shares outstanding (mill.)	235	235	242	246	246
Shareholders of record of common stock	52,100	55,300	59,900	62,800	63,300
Employees	39,700	42,100	44,200	44,000	49,800
Wages, salaries, employee benefits (mill. $)	$ 1,419	$ 1,627	$ 1,593	$ 1,510	$ 1,612
R&D expense (mill. $)[3]	$ 125	$ 158	$ 148	$ 135	$ 96
Oil and gas exploration expenses (mill. $)	926	$ 1,101	$ 704	$ 834	$ 486

SOURCE: *1986 Annual Report*, Standard Oil Company, p. 63.

[1]Includes outlets supplied by jobbers, automobile dealers, marine dealers, etc.

[2]Earnings for 1986 were inadequate to cover fixed charges. The amount of the deficiency in total adjusted earnings was $679 million.

[3]Includes research and development expense funded at both the corporate and business segment levels, and expenses associated with synthetic fuels and other alternate energy development projects.

Business Segments

The Standard Oil Company in 1987 was composed of seven business segments: Exploration and Production, Refining and Marketing, Chemicals, Metals Mining, Coal, QIT, and Other Businesses. (Exhibit 36.5 presents information on these business units over a five-year period.)

Exploration and Production was responsible for finding and developing crude oil and natural gas for the company. These activities were typically referred to in the industry as "upstream" operations. At year-end 1986 Standard's proved developed and undeveloped reserves of crude oil, condensate, and natural gas liquids were 2.4 billion barrels plus 7.3 trillion cubic feet of natural gas. According to *Value Line,* the after-tax present value of Standard's combined oil and gas reserves using low year-end 1986 prices was $3.4 billion.[13] Weak prices continued to rule out building the costly pipelines needed to bring the natural gas to market. Exploration spending during 1986 was $331 million, about one-third of that spent during 1985, but $31 million more than that planned for 1987. Exploration activities were to focus on northern Alaska, the Gulf of Mexico, and Oklahoma's Anadarko Basin. Top management's new strategy was to increase operating efficiency and to reduce costs of the upstream business. Based on its forecast that crude oil prices would average $15 per barrel in 1986 dollars for the rest of the decade, top management wanted to ensure the company's profitability while maintaining its ability to take advantage of attractive acquisitions.

Refining and Marketing was responsible for all "downstream" operations, such as transporting and trading crude oil, refining the oil into gasoline and diesel fuel, and marketing products and services to the general public. Because wholesale and retail product prices fell less rapidly in 1986 than did crude oil prices, operating income was $436 million in 1986, up from $351 million in 1985. About 29% of the 1986 operating income, however, was contributed by the former Gulf Oil properties which Standard had bought from Chevron. Standard's four refineries had an above-average ability to maximize production of the more profitable light products, such as gasoline and diesel fuel. They operated at 92% capacity in 1986, compared to the industry average of 84%. Seeking more operating efficiency, management cut the number of company-operated stations in Ohio by 16% from 1983 through 1986 while increasing retail gasoline sales by 10%. To make up for the reduction of full-service stations, Standard introduced PROCARE automotive service centers in Ohio metropolitan areas. Management planned to expand the number of PROCARE centers in Ohio and western Pennsylvania from 72 in 1986 to 100 by 1988. The company also planned to add to its 1986 total of forty-one truckstops in nineteen states. Management hoped to expand its presence in the Southeastern states and was "particularly interested in acquiring a presence on the West Coast."[14]

Chemicals, in comparison with other Standard businesses, was relatively small, but profitable. The unit produced and marketed two lines of com-

EXHIBIT 36.5   **Business Segment Data, Standard Oil Company**
(In Millions of Dollars)

	1986	1985	1984	1983	1982
Revenues					
Petroleum	$ 7,959	$11,425	$ 9,480	$ 9,438	$10,875
Coal	465	437	465	361	346
Metals mining	178	270	482	619	557
Chemicals	475	551	643	516	554
QIT	337	303	257	198	213
Other businesses	708	857	909	827	953
Corporate and other	(28)	23	15	(1)	(8)
Intersegment eliminations	(72)	(48)	—	—	—
	$10,022	$13,818	$12,251	$11,958	$13,490
Income (loss) before interest, income taxes and extraordinary item					
Petroleum					
Exploration/production	$ 13	$ 2,442	$ 2,954	$ 2,848	$ 3,647
Refining and marketing	436	351	200	453	390
	449	2,793	3,154	3,301	4,037
Coal	(255)	(518)	61	21	(1)
Metals mining	(342)	(851)	(160)	(91)	(187)
Chemicals	57	39	45	(7)	(22)
QIT	110	80	41	16	34
Other businesses	(151)	(98)	(33)	(173)	(32)
Corporate and other	(234)	(270)	(160)	(158)	(132)
	$ (366)	$ 1,175	$ 2,948	$ 2,909	$ 3,697
Assets					
Petroleum					
Exploration/production	$ 8,677	$ 9,608	$ 9,366	$ 8,536	$ 8,023
Refining and marketing	2,469	2,949	2,079	1,803	1,568
	11,146	12,557	11,445	10,339	9,591
Coal	376	679	1,131	1,103	1,113
Metals mining	1,289	1,729	2,317	2,174	2,240
Chemicals	347	402	495	536	576
QIT	458	365	318	341	359
Other businesses	390	736	715	713	874
Corporate and other	1,949	1,040	1,066	1,156	1,263
	$15,955	$17,508	$17,487	$16,362	$16,016

(Continued)

EXHIBIT 36.5 (Continued)

	1986	1985	1984	1983	1982
Capital expenditures					
Petroleum					
Exploration/production	$ 1,121	$ 1,535	$ 1,633	$ 1,795	$ 1,996
Refining and marketing	185	489	247	151	120
	1,306	2,024	1,880	1,946	2,116
Coal	53	74	51	23	168
Metals mining	101	98	176	156	202
Chemicals	10	13	23	20	69
QIT	68	80	19	12	6
Other businesses	42	81	58	58	65
Corporate and other	38	114	122	83	82
	$ 1,618	$ 2,484	$ 2,329	$ 2,298	$ 2,708

SOURCE: *1986 Annual Report,* Standard Oil Company, p. 62.

modity chemicals, acrylonitrile (used to create plastics and fibers) and nitriles, as well as nitrogen products and benzene. Operating income equalled $57 million in 1986, $2 million less than the previous year once unusual charges were excluded from the 1985 figures. More than 90% of the worldwide acrylonitrile capacity used technology licensed from Standard Oil, so the company planned to emphasize the licensing of this technology to developing countries. The company thus seemed to have a competitive advantage in a small segment within the very competitive, but growing, world chemical industry.

Metals Mining was composed of the Bingham Canyon copper mine in Utah, the last operating remnant of Kennecott Corporation. One of Robert Horton's first acts as Standard's Chairman and CEO was to tie the $400 million modernization program to wage concessions by the United Steelworkers. Although the Bingham Canyon mine was closed in March 1985, operations began again piecemeal in September 1986, as modernization proceeded. Standard sold its Ray Mines Division in Arizona and Chino Mines Company in New Mexico, as well as some other properties, in November 1986, for approximately $160 million. Although metals mining recorded a loss of $342 million in 1986, if unusual charges associated with the sale of the Ray and Chino copper mines were excluded, operating income would have been $11 million. When the modernization of Bingham Canyon was completed in 1988, it was to have the capacity to produce 185,000 tons of copper, 260,000 ounces of gold, two million ounces of silver, and eight million pounds of molybdenum annually. Its production costs were expected to be the lowest in the U.S. and in the lowest quartile among free-world producers. Nevertheless, the market demand for copper was expected to remain poor to moderate, although prices could rise as mines continued to be closed in the U.S. and third-world producers stopped adding to their mining capacity.

Coal was composed of the Old Ben Coal Company, a business that recorded an operating loss of $255 million in 1986. This loss included, however, $300 million worth of unusual charges related to the disposal of undeveloped coal properties and to the closing of the high-cost Kitt Mine in West Virginia. As a result of asset sales and writedowns, net coal assets were $200 million (706 million tons) at the end of 1986. The unit's plans to reduce costs and improve productivity included moving the coal headquarters from Lexington, Kentucky, to Standard headquarters in Cleveland, and reducing its staff by 37%. The unit's overall productivity improved from 17.8 tons per man-shift in 1985 to 21.8 tons in 1986. Nevertheless, the situation facing the coal industry continued to be one of worldwide over-capacity and declining prices.

QIT was the shortened form of the Canadian-based "Qit-Fer et Titane, Inc." As the leading producer of titanium dioxide slag, QIT's operating income was $110 million in 1986, up $30 million from 1985. Titanium dioxide slag was used to make white pigments for paint, paper, plastics, ceramics, and textiles. With demand consistently increasing over the past ten years, titanium dioxide pigments had replaced nearly all other white pigments in the world. Since QIT was the low-cost producer of this slag (because of its technological expertise and its access to abundant raw materials) the demand for QIT's slag had grown faster than overall pigment demand. A moderni-zation and construction program, to expand the company's slag production capacity by 25% by 1988, was in process. The company also was the major supplier of high-purity iron (generated as a coproduct in QIT's proprietary process of making titanium dioxide slag) to the ductile-iron casting industry.

Other Businesses of Standard Oil were its Engineered Materials Company and its Chase Brass and Copper Company. This segment recorded an operating loss of $151 million in 1986 compared to a loss of $98 million in 1985. Results for 1986 included unusual charges of $140 million for various divestitures and losses totaling $12 million from the businesses divested. Operating income from Engineered Materials increased from $30 million in 1985 to $36 million in 1986. Its principal products were high-temperature ceramic-fiber insulation, advanced refractories, polyester resins and panels, and molten-metal pumping systems. The outlook for structural and electronic ceramics appeared to be very bright. Chase Brass and Copper, in contrast, reported an operating loss of $10 million in 1986 compared to a $4 million loss in 1985. Chase's new copper and brass narrow-strip mill was completed just in time for declining prices in brass and copper items.

Strategic Managers

The Board of Directors of Standard Oil was composed of fifteen members in 1987 (see Exhibit 36.6). Butler, Hartigan, and Keep were representatives of British Petroleum's 55% interest in the company. (The percentage had

EXHIBIT 36.6   **Board of Directors, Standard Oil Company**

E. E. Bailey[2,3,5]
Dean, Graduate School of
Industrial Administration, Carnegie-
Mellon University

R. A. Bray
Executive Vice-President

E. J. P. Browne
Executive Vice President and Chief
Financial Officer

D. W. Buchanan Jr.[2,3]
Retired President—Old Ben Coal
Company

B. R. R. Butler[4]
Managing Director—The British
Petroleum Company p.l.c.
(International Oil Company) and
Chairman BP Exploration Company
Limited (subsidiary of The British
Petroleum Company p.l.c.)

D. D. Danforth[2,4]
Chairman of the Board and Chief
Executive Officer—Westinghouse
Electric Corporation (diversified
electrical company)

W. J. De Lancey[1,2,4]
Retired Chairman of the Board and
Chief Executive Officer—Republic
Steel Corporation (steel
manufacturer)

J. T. Gorman[2,4]
President and Chief Operating
Officer—TRW, Inc. (diversified
high-technology company)

J. J. Hangen[1,2,3]
Retired Chairman of the Board and
Chief Executive Officer—Appleton
Papers Inc. (paper manufacturer)

I. G. S. Hartigan[1]
President—BP North America Inc.
(subsidiary of the British Petroleum
Company p.l.c.)

R. B. Horton[1]
Chairman of the Board and Chief
Executive Officer

K. R. Keep[5]
Director Technical—BP
Exploration Company Limited
(subsidiary of The British
Petroleum Company p.l.c.)

C. F. Knight[2,4]
Chairman of the Board and Chief
Executive Officer—Emerson
Electric Co. (electrical and
electronic products and systems
manufacturer)

F. E. Mosier
President and Chief Operating
Officer

J. C. E. Webster[5]
Executive Vice-President

SOURCE: *1986 Annual Report,* Standard Oil Company, p. 64.

Committee Memberships as of January 31, 1987:

[1]Member of Executive Committee

[2]Member of Special Committee

[3]Member of Audit Committee

[4]Member of Compensation Committee

[5]Member of Contributions Committee

increased from 53% because of Standard's purchase of its own stock from 1983 to 1985.) Browne, Horton, and Webster were executives of Standard Oil who had previously served in managerial positions with British Petroleum. Mosier and Bray were also executives of Standard Oil. Of these eight inside or management Directors, Mosier had served seven consecutive years on the Board. Horton had served on the Board since 1983. Bray and Webster had served one previous year. For the other four inside Directors, 1986 was their first year on the Board.

The remaining seven Directors were outside or non-management–related members of the Board. D. W. Buchanan, Jr. was a retired president of Old Ben Coal Company. The other six outside directors with no past connections with the company were Bailey, Danforth, De Lancey, Gorman, Hangen, and Knight. Of the seven, Bailey, Buchanan, Hangen, and Knight had served for at least the previous four years. These seven outside Directors formed a Special Committee established by the Board in April 1986. This committee was given the task of monitoring Standard Oil's relationship with British Petroleum and advising the Board with regard to that relationship and all joint Standard-BP transactions and ventures.

Standard Oil's top management was composed of five people in 1987. Robert B. Horton, Chairman of the Board and Chief Executive Officer, was 47 years old. Before 1986 he had served as a Managing Director (similar to Executive Vice-President) of British Petroleum with responsibility for finance, planning, and the company's operations in the Western Hemisphere. Frank E. Mosier, President and Chief Operating Officer, was 56 years old. Before 1986, he had served as Standard Oil's Executive Vice-President overseeing downstream petroleum, metals mining, and corporate planning. He had joined Sohio in 1953 and had been primarily involved with the downstream petroleum business. Richard A. Bray, Executive Vice-President with responsibility for exploration and production, coal, and external affairs, was 55 years old. Since joining Standard Oil in 1982, he had been in charge of exploration and production. Prior to that time, he had held a variety of exploration and production offices during twenty-four years with Exxon. E. John P. Browne, Executive Vice-President and Chief Financial Officer, was 39 years old. Before 1986, he had served as Group Treasurer of British Petroleum and Chief Executive of BP Finance International. J. Colin E. Webster, Executive Vice-President responsible for chemicals, metals mining, industrial products companies, research and development, and ventures, was 50 years old. Before 1986, he had served as President of BP North America, Inc.

THE BRITISH PETROLEUM COMPANY p.l.c.

Registered originally in the United Kingdom on April 14, 1909, as the Anglo-Persian Oil Company, Ltd. to develop newly discovered oil resources in Persia (now Iran), British Petroleum or BP as it was commonly known, grew to become one of the most successful and powerful multinational oil companies. Along with Exxon, Royal Dutch/Shell, Mobil, Texaco, Chevron, and Gulf, British Petroleum was one of the famed "Seven Sisters"—the major integrated multinationals that engaged in every stage of petroleum operation throughout the world and controlled around 70% of the world's oil trade until the OPEC oil embargo in 1973. Led by Sir Peter Walters, Chairman of the Board since 1981, BP worked hard to overcome one of the most outmoded refining and marketing networks in the industry. According to *Business Week,* Sir Peter's concentration on quiet profitability during the 1980s transformed BP into a pacesetter for the industry.[15] In contrast to Standard Oil's management, BP's top management had not hesitated to get rid of businesses that failed to perform profitably.

BP Operations and Ownership

Besides its widespread oil and gas operations, in 1987 BP had interests in chemicals and plastics, animal feeds and agricultural seeds (including its 1986 purchases of the U.S. firms Purina Mills and Edward J. Funk and Sons), minerals mining, coal, marine shipping, detergents, and computer software. Until 1977, 68.3% of British Petroleum stock had been owned by the British Government and the Bank of England. Over time, various sales of stock by the government reduced the percentage to 31.6% (578,496,892 shares) by end-1986. On March 18, 1987, the British government announced plans to sell its remaining shares, valued at $8.51 billion, by March 31, 1988.[16] BP shares were listed on the stock exchanges in the U.K., the U.S., Canada, Switzerland, France, West Germany, and the Netherlands.

Following the profit patterns of other oil companies in 1986, BP's profits of 817 million pounds sterling were 49% less than those in 1985, primarily because of the dramatic drop in oil prices. (See Exhibits 36.7 and 36.8 for BP's financial data.) Oil production averaged 718,000 barrels per day in 1986 compared with 694,000 barrels in 1985. BP management estimated, however, that oil production would fall to 620,000 barrels per day by 1990. Estimated net proved reserves of crude oil stood at 2,252 million barrels in 1987 compared to Standard Oil's 2,406 million barrels. Oil from the United Kingdom (primarily the North Sea), which comprised 55% of BP's total proved reserves, had showed a steady decline since 1984. This was a significant problem for British Petroleum because the oil and gas business accounted for 84% of BP's operating profit in 1986 and 95% in 1985 (when oil prices had been higher). Exploration in offshore China and Brazil during the 1980s had proved disappointing, although some oil had been found in New Guinea and in Ecuador.

BP's Bid for Standard Oil

Only eight days after the British government had announced its intention to sell its remaining shares in British Petroleum, the top management of BP announced a 28-day tender offer to begin April 1, 1987 for the 45% of

EXHIBIT 36.7   **Summarized Group Income Statements, British Petroleum Company**

(In Millions of Dollars)

	1986	1985	1984	1983	1982
Turnover	39,941	53,281	50,830	49,219	51,300
Operating expenses	37,229	48,551	46,440	45,020	47,418
	2,712	4,730	4,390	4,199	3,882
Other income	1,155	1,039	837	800	1,246
Replacement cost operating profit	3,867	5,769	5,227	4,999	5,128
Realised stock holding gain (loss)	(1,724)	(323)	162	(217)	120
Historical cost operating profit	2,143	5,446	5,389	4,782	5,248
Interest expense	735	749	760	841	1,214
Profit before taxation	1,408	4,697	4,629	3,941	4,034
Taxation	62	1,797	1,911	1,845	1,930
Profit after taxation	1,346	2,900	2,718	2,096	2,104
Minority shareholders' interest	145	823	840	780	851
Profit before extraordinary items	1,201	2,077	1,878	1,316	1,253
Extraordinary items	(467)	(1,207)	(399)	251	(7)
Profit for the year	734	870	1,479	1,567	1,246
Distribution to shareholders	944	809	734	666	647
Retained profit/(deficit) for the year	(210)	61	745	901	599
Earnings per ordinary share	$0.66	$1.14	$1.03	$0.72	$0.69
Replacement cost profit					
Historical cost profit before extraordinary items	1,201	2,077	1,878	1,316	1,253
Realised stock holding (gain) loss less minority interest	1,414	284	(185)	158	(156)
Replacement cost profit before extraordinary items	$2,615	$2,361	$1,693	$1,474	$1,097

SOURCE: *1986 Annual Report*, British Petroleum Company, p. 57.

Standard Oil it did not already own. It offered to pay $70 for each of the approximately 105.8 million shares, for a total of $7.4 billion. The bid was the largest ever for a British company and the largest in the United States since Chevron's $13.23 billion acquisition of Gulf in 1984. If it succeeded, the offer would make BP the third largest oil company in the world behind Exxon and Royal Dutch/Shell.

At a London news conference on March 26, Sir Peter Walters said that BP's management wanted to eliminate the minority holding to make expansion easier in the U.S.—"an important focal point of our future strategy." In the past, Sir Peter added, BP had been hampered by a cumbersome dual-board structure and potential competitive conflicts with Standard in its planning of U.S. opportunities. David Simon, Chief Financial Managing

EXHIBIT 36.8 **Summarized Group Balance Sheets, British Petroleum Company**

(In Millions of Dollars)

	1986	1985	1984	1983	1982
Fixed assets	26,464	26,442	24,636	24,857	25,110
Stocks and debtors	11,788	14,181	12,367	13,218	14,878
Liquid resources	3,743	3,198	2,685	1,327	2,560
Total assets	41,995	43,821	39,688	39,402	42,548
Creditors and provisions excluding finance debt	14,615	17,121	13,048	12,394	13,158
Capital employed	27,380	26,700	26,640	27,008	29,390
Financed by:					
Finance debt	7,506	7,438	8,187	7,928	10,588
Minority shareholders' interest	5,115	4,895	5,063	5,105	4,795
BP shareholders' interest	14,759	14,267	13,390	13,975	14,007
	27,380	26,700	26,640	27,008	29,390

SOURCE: *1986 Annual Report*, British Petroleum Company, p. 59.

Director of BP, said that a combination of the two companies "cleared the ground for" major acquisitions of oil reserves or downstream operations in the U.S. "Much of what BP can do, we feel it can do in the U.S.," added Sir Peter Walters. Walters stressed that his goal in taking full ownership of Standard was not to make BP larger but to make it more efficient and profitable by its focusing on low-cost production. Referring to past relations with Standard Oil, he pointed out that "we were either missing tricks because our joint overheads were too high, or we were pursuing different paths."[17] The last point was a reference to the tendency of Standard's previous CEO, Alton Whitehouse, to act independently of BP and to ignore the parent company's advice. For example, when Standard purchased a concession in 1985 to prospect for oil in Qatar, a Middle East state where BP had considerable exploration experience, BP's top managers first learned of the purchase when they read it in the newspapers.[18]

According to BP's David Simon, the company planned to fund about one third of the stock purchase from its own cash, another third would come from commercial paper, and the remainder from bank borrowings. "We would intend to (repay the bank loans) from the joint cash flow of the combined companies," stated Simon. Rodney Chase, BP Group Treasurer, said that BP's debt to total capital would increase from 33% to 44%, but would be back in the high 30s within a year of the purchase. The price for Standard's shares, set at $70, had been based upon top management's assumption of an inflation-adjusted crude oil price of $18 per barrel through the end of the century. This was an increase over the $15 per barrel price both BP and Standard had used during 1986 for planning purposes, said Simon.[19]

Upon BP's announcement on March 26, the price of Standard Oil stock rose $6.50 on the New York Stock Exchange to $71.375 on a volume of 5.5 million shares. Just hours after BP's bid was announced, a class-action suit was filed in Cleveland on behalf of Standard's minority stockholders. The suit argued that BP was offering "a fraudulently low and unfair price" for the stock. This action was reminiscent of Royal Dutch/Shell's attempt in 1985 to buy the remaining 30.5% of the U.S. Shell stock it didn't own. In that instance, the parent company's offer of $55 a share faced a similar class-action suit. Royal Dutch/Shell was forced to raise the bid twice to $60 a share because of protests from Shell's minority shareholders and outside directors. After much delay, the terms were finally approved in a Delaware court.[20]

In response to a question if BP might increase its offer, Sir Peter Walters uttered a flat "no" and said that unlike Royal Dutch/Shell, BP wasn't proposing a merger. British Petroleum was simply buying Standard's stock in the open market and only had to follow full disclosure rules. Therefore, Standard's board did not need to place an independent valuation on the company. In addition, Sir Peter stated that under BP's interpretation of Ohio corporate law, British Petroleum could force minority shareholders to accept the $70 offer if BP's current 55% stake in Standard Oil reached 90%. The shareholders of British Petroleum were to vote on BP's action at a special April 22 meeting.

STANDARD OIL'S RESPONSE

British Petroleum had presented its plans to purchase Standard Oil's remaining stock at a special Standard Oil board meeting on March 9, 1987. The Special Committee of outside directors established to monitor Standard-BP relations gave BP a guarded response. The committee's Chairman, Douglas Danforth, asked Sir Peter to postpone the offer for one or two months so that the committee could have adequate time to review the offer. BP replied negatively. The Committee hired First Boston Corporation to examine the offer. In an April 3 letter to the Committee, First Boston contended that BP's offer did not include a premium over Standard's current stock market price, because Standard's stock would have been trading at $70 even without BP's bid. It concluded that Standard Oil stock was worth at least $85 a share. After first announcing that it would issue a statement on BP's offer on April 14, the Special Committee of outside board members decided to postpone its recommendation until April 23. The committee did, however, ask shareholders to wait until the committee made its report to Standard's board before tendering their shares to BP. The tender offer was due to expire on April 28, unless it was extended by BP.

The wide gap between First Boston's valuation of Standard Oil and that of Goldman, Sachs, & Company, which had prepared the BP offer, created a war of words between the two investment banking firms. In addition to differences in the amount of probable reserves in Prudhoe Bay and in the future operating income of Standard's refining and marketing business, the two valuations differed on the future price of oil. BP's offer was based on a forecasted 1988 price of $18 per barrel for West Texas Intermediate crude oil, adjusted for an expected 5% annual rate of inflation through the end of the century. First Boston, in contrast, took into account three possible oil-price scenarios, ranging from a starting price of $17.25 per barrel with modest price escalation, to $20 per barrel with rapid escalation.[21] British Petroleum labeled First Boston's calculations "ill-founded" and "seriously flawed."

The eight inside Directors of Standard Oil were in a rather difficult position. The three representatives of BP on the Board obviously had to support BP's offer. The three top executives of Standard Oil who had been placed there by BP were caught between the two sides. Horton, as an ex-Managing Director of British Petroleum and a likely candidate to run BP some day, was bound to provoke criticism as the Chairman of Standard Oil. Directors Mosier and Bray had no past connections with BP, but obviously depended on Horton and BP executives for their future with Standard Oil. The discussions that took place during April between the committee of seven outside directors and top management of British Petroleum suggested that the outside directors were not willing to go along with BP's $70 per share offer.

What should the board recommend to the minority stockholders of Standard Oil? A failure by BP to obtain the stock or a drawn-out legal battle could hurt the British government's plan to sell its 32% stake in BP in the fall of 1987. Because one of the members of BP's thirteen-member Board of Directors was appointed by the British government, this was no small concern to BP's top management. This situation worked to the benefit of Standard's special board committee as it deliberated on what to recommend.

THE FUTURE PRICE OF OIL

Every oil company and industry analyst appeared to have a different estimate of the future price of oil. Many believed that the price was bound to increase significantly. Exxon, for example, assumed in 1987 that the price of oil would stay flat in constant dollar terms for a few years and then rise faster than the rate of inflation. In a speech delivered to the Australian Petroleum Exploration Association on March 22, 1987, Donald McIvor, an Exxon Senior Vice President, said that "the price of oil must rise significantly again before too long." He noted that the world had been using oil at rates of 20–25 billion barrels per year since 1970 while discoveries had been accumulating at only 10–25 billion barrels per year. "Most major consuming countries, including those with substantial production of their own, will ultimately come to depend heavily on Middle East oil."[22] In general agreement with this view, the U.S. Department of Energy forecast a $33 per barrel price in constant dollars by the year 2000. Data Resources, Inc., an economic forecaster, estimated a $32 constant-dollar price ($64 with likely inflation) by the end of the century.

A case could be made, however, for a reasonably constant oil price. For example, Arlon Tussing, an energy economist, predicted that oil prices in constant dollars were "likely to remain within a range of $10 a barrel and $20 a barrel for the rest of this century." As for the longer term, he expected technology to push energy prices not up but down. Tussing argued that increases in the price of oil would cause large switches to natural gas and coal as substitutes. Unlike the situation in the early 1970s, oil was "no longer the indispensable fuel," said Tussing. For example, many industrial energy users in 1987 were equipped with dual or triple fuel capacity and could choose oil, gas, or coal, depending on the price. At prices much above $20, Tussing said, oil loses almost the entire global bulk-fuels market to other energy sources.[23]

A report issued in February 1987 by the National Petroleum Council proposed two possible trends for future oil prices. One trend began at $18 per barrel in 1986, with growth at a constant dollar rate of 5% per year to $36 in the year 2000. The second trend started at $12 per barrel in 1986 and grew at a constant dollar rate of 4% per year to $21 by the year 2000. The report also warned that the percentage of U.S. consumption that came from imports could increase from 33% in 1986 to 48% by 1990 if crude oil prices remained near 1986 levels and could even rise to 66% of consumption by the end of the century. The report further warned that the U.S. could face a return to the oil crises of the 1970s, when the combination of political problems in the Mideast and high American dependence on imported oil created shortages.[24]

These varying estimates regarding the future price of oil were reflected in the different valuations of Standard Oil by Goldman, Sachs and Company (BP's financial adviser) and First Boston Corporation (financial adviser to the special board committee of Standard Oil). According to Goldman, Sachs and Company, a $1 change in the per barrel price of oil had the effect of changing the value of Standard Oil's proved oil and gas reserves by an amount equivalent to approximately $4 per share of common stock.[25]

NOTES

1. A. Sullivan and J. Valentine, "U.S. Copper Industry Is Ill and Getting Sicker," *Wall Street Journal* (June 18, 1985), p. 6.

G. Stricharchuk, "Sohio Predicts It Can Weather Oil-Price Plunge," *Wall Street Journal* (February 6, 1986), p. 11.

D. Cook and W. Glasgall, "Is Sohio Getting In Shape for a Buyout?" *Business Week* (December 16, 1985), pp. 28–29.

2. G. Brooks, "After Mukluk Fiasco, Sohio Strives to Find, or Perhaps to Buy, Oil," *Wall Street Journal* (April 19, 1984), p. 22.

3. G. Putka, R. E. Winter, and G. Stricharchuk, "How and Why BP Put Its Own Commanders at Standard Oil Helm," *Wall Street Journal* (March 7, 1986), p. 8.

4. Stricharchuk.

5. A. W. Whitehouse and J. R. Miller, "Letter to Shareholders and Employees," *1985 Annual Report*, The Standard Oil Company, p. 2.

6. Putka, Winter, and Stricharchuk, p. 1.

7. D. Cook, "Will Horton Have to Take a Hatchet to Standard Oil?" *Business Week* (May 12, 1986), p. 79.

8. Stricharchuk.

9. "The Top 1000 U.S. Companies Ranked by Industry," *Business Week* (April 17, 1987), p. 134.

10. M. Potts, "Concern Grows Over Rise in U.S. Oil Imports," *Washington Post* (March 8, 1987), p. H3.

11. B. Richards, J. McNish, and L. Zehr, "Amoco Agrees to Buy Dome Petroleum Ltd," *Wall Street Journal* (April 20, 1987), p. 2.

P. Berkowitz, "Canada Says It Would Place Conditions on Dome Petroleum Purchase by Amoco," *Wall Street Journal* (April 24, 1987), p. 41.

12. J. Tanner and Y. Ibrahim, "Price Stability Encourages Oil Industry," *Wall Street Journal* (April 28, 1987), p. 6.

13. "Petroleum (Integrated) Industry," *Value Line Investment Survey*, Part 3: Ratings and Reports, Edition 3 (April 10, 1987), p. 402.

14. *1986 Annual Report*, The Standard Oil Company, p. 15.

15. S. Miller and D. Cook, "Why BP Is Going All Out For All of Standard Oil," *Business Week* (April 13, 1987), p. 50.

16. "The British Petroleum Company p.l.c.," *Moody's Industrial Manual*, Vol. 1, A-1, 1986, p. 1072.

G. Putka and R. E. Winter, "British Petroleum Bids $7.4 Billion for the Rest of Standard Oil Stock," *Wall Street Journal* (March 27, 1987), p. 2.

17. Putka and Winter.

18. Putka, Winter, and Stricharchuk, p. 8.

19. Putka and Winter, pp. 2 and 16.

20. G. Anders, "Standard Holders File Suit to Block BP in Effort to Replay Shell Case," *Wall Street Journal* (March 27, 1987), p. 2.

21. M. W. Miller and R. E. Winter, "British Petroleum's Standard Bid Spurs Price Dispute," *Wall Street Journal* (April 7, 1987), pp. 3 and 28.

22. J. Tanner, "Exxon Official Sees a Significant Rise in Price of Oil as Inevitable Before Long," *Wall Street Journal* (March 23, 1987), p. 7.

23. A. Bayless, "A Bear in the Oil Patch," *Wall Street Journal* (April 28, 1987), p. 34.

24. M. Potts.

25. *The Standard Oil Company*, Special report prepared by Goldman, Sachs and Company for British Petroleum, April 21, 1987.

SECTION F

STRATEGIC ISSUES IN NOT-FOR-PROFIT ORGANIZATIONS

The National Jazz Hall of Fame

CORNELIS A. DE KLUYVER

Mr. Robert Rutland, founder of the National Jazz Hall of Fame, poured himself another drink as he listened to some old jazz recordings and thought about the decisions facing him. Established about one year ago, the National Jazz Hall of Fame (NJHF) had achieved moderate success locally but had not yet attracted national recognition. Mr. Rutland wondered how much support existed nationally, what services the NJHF should provide and for whom, and what the NJHF should charge for those services. He also thought about other jazz halls of fame and their implications for the NJHF. Although he had engaged an independent consultant to find some answers, the questions still lingered.

JAZZ

The word *jazz*, according to Dr. David Pharies, a linguistics scholar at the University of Florida, originally meant *copulation*, but later identified a certain type of music. By combining Black spirituals, African rhythms, and Cajun music, jazz music began in New Orleans in the early 1900s amid the march of funeral bands; Dixieland jazz became the sound of New Orleans.

Jazz traveled from New Orleans, a major trade center, on river boats and ships and reached St. Louis, Kansas City, Memphis, Chicago, and New York. Musicians in these cities developed local styles of jazz, all of which remained highly improvisational, personal, and rhythmically complex. Over the years, different sounds emerged—swing, big band, be-bop, fusion, and others—indicating the fluidity and diversity of jazz. Jazz artists developed their own styles and competed with one another for recognition of their musical ability and compositions. Such diversity denied jazz a simple definition, and opinions still differed sharply on what exactly jazz was. It was difficult, however, to dispute Louis Armstrong's statement that "if you have to ask what jazz is, you'll never know."

ORIGINS OF THE NATIONAL JAZZ HALL OF FAME

Mr. Rutland, a history professor at the University of Virginia, which is in Charlottesville, discovered that renovation plans for the city's historic district excluded the Paramount Theatre, a local landmark. The Paramount was constructed in the 1930s and used as a performance center and later as a movie theatre. It was closed in the 1970s and now was in danger of becoming dilapidated. Alarmed by the apparent lack of interest in saving the Paramount, Mr. Rutland began to look for opportunities to restore and eventually use the theatre. The most attractive option to him was to establish a jazz hall of fame that would use the theatre as a museum and performance center; this would capitalize on the theatre's name, because the Paramount Theatre in New York City was a prominent jazz hall during the 1930s and 1940s. Mr. Rutland mentioned his idea—saving the theatre by establishing a jazz hall of fame—to several friends in Charlottesville. They shared his enthusiasm, and together they incorporated the National Jazz Hall of Fame and formed the Board of Directors in early 1983. A few prominent jazz musicians, such as Benny Goodman and Chick Corea, joined the NJHF National Advisory Board. The purpose of the NJHF was to establish and maintain a museum, archives, and concert center in Charlottesville, to sponsor jazz festivals, workshops, and scholarships, and to promote other activities remembering great jazz artists, serving jazz enthusiasts, and educating the public on the importance of jazz in American culture and history.

THE FIRST YEAR'S EFFORTS

Immediately after incorporation, the Directors began their search for funds that they could use to save the Paramount and to establish the NJHF, and soon encountered two difficulties. Philanthropic organizations refused to make grants because no one on the Board of Directors had experience in a project like the NJHF. In addition government agencies such as the National Endowment for the Arts and the National Endowment for the Humanities considered only organizations in operation for at least two years. However, some small contributions came from jazz enthusiasts who had read stories about the NJHF in *Billboard,* a music industry magazine, and in the Charlottesville and Richmond newspapers.

By mid-1983, the Board of Directors discovered that to save the Paramount at least $600,000 would be needed, a sum too large for them to consider. They decided, however, that out of their love for jazz they would continue to work to establish the NJHF in Charlottesville.

Despite these setbacks, Mr. Rutland and the other directors believed that the first year's activities showed promise. The NJHF sponsored three concerts at local high schools. The concerts featured such jazz greats as Maxine Sullivan, Buddy Rich, and Jon Hendricks and Company, and each concert attracted more than 500 people. Although the NJHF lost some money on each concert, the Directors thought that the concerts succeeded in publicizing and promoting the NJHF. In addition, a fundraiser at a Charlottesville country club brought $2,000 to the NJHF, and Mr. Rutland started the NJHF newsletter. The collection of objects for the museum was enlarged, and Louis Armstrong and Duke Ellington were posthumously inducted into the NJHF. At the end of the first year, enthusiasm among Board members was still high, and they believed that the NJHF could survive indefinitely, albeit on a small scale.

BUT A HALL OF FAME IN CHARLOTTES-VILLE . . .

Mr. Rutland believed that a hall of fame could succeed in Charlottesville, though other cities might at first seem more appropriate. More than 500,000 tourists annually were attracted to Charlottesville (1980 population: 40,000) to visit Thomas Jefferson's home at Monticello, James Monroe's home at Ash Lawn, and the Rotunda and the Lawn of the University of Virginia, where total enrollment was 16,000. Mr. Jefferson had designed the Rotunda and the buildings on the Lawn and supervised their construction. The Virginia Office of Tourism promoted these national landmarks as well as the city's two convention centers. In addition, 13 million people lived within a three-hour drive of Charlottesville. If Charlottesville seemed illogical for the hall of fame, Mr. Rutland reasoned, so did Cooperstown, New York, home of the Baseball Hall of Fame and Canton, Ohio, location of the Professional Football Hall of Fame. He thought that successful jazz festivals in such different places as Newport, Rhode Island, and French Lick, Indiana, showed that location was relatively unimportant for jazz. Moreover, a Charlottesville radio station recently switched to a music format called "Memory Lane," which featured classics by Frank Sinatra, Patti Page, the Mills Brothers, the Glenn Miller Orchestra, and numerous others. The station played much jazz, and won the loyalty of many jazz enthusiasts in the Charlottesville area. The success of "Memory Lane" indicated to Mr. Rutland that the Charlottesville community could provide the NJHF with a base of interest and loyalty. Most important, Mr. Rutland believed that he and his friends possessed the commitment necessary to make a jazz hall of fame succeed.

. . . AND HALLS OF FAME IN OTHER CITIES?

Although no national organization operated successfully, several local groups claimed to be *the* Jazz Hall of Fame, as *Billboard* magazine reported in the following articles. From "Hall of Fame in Harlem," by Sam Sutherland and Peter Keepnews (April 28, 1984):

> CBS Records and the Harlem YMCA have joined forces to establish a Jazz Hall of Fame. The first induction ceremony will take place on May 14 at Avery Fisher Hall, combined with a concert featuring such artists as Ramsey Lewis, Hubert Laws, Ron Carter, and an all-star Latin Jazz ensemble. Proceeds from the concert will benefit the Harlem YMCA.
>
> Who will the initial inductees be, and how will they be chosen? What's being described in the official literature as "a prestigious group of jazz editorialists, critics, producers, and respected connoisseurs" (and, also, incidentally, musicians—among those on the panel are Miles Davis, Dizzy Gillespie, Cab Calloway, Max Roach and the ubiquitous Dr. Billy Taylor) will do the actual selecting, but nominations are being solicited from the general public. Jazz lovers are invited to submit the names of six artists, three living and three dead, to: The Harlem YMCA Jazz Hall of Fame, New York, NY 10030. Deadline for nominations is May 1.

From "One, Two, Many Halls of Fame?" by Sam Sutherland and Peter Keepnews, *Billboard,* (May 19, 1984):

> Monday night marks the official launch of the Harlem YMCA Jazz Hall of Fame (Billboard, April 28), a project in which CBS Records is closely involved. The Hall's first inductees are being unveiled at an Avery Fisher Hall concert that also includes performances by, among others, Sarah Vaughan and Branford Marsalis.
>
> The project is being touted as the first jazz hall of fame, a statement that discounts a number of similar projects in the past that never quite reached fruition. But first or not, the good people at CBS and the Harlem YMCA are apparently in for some competition.
>
> According to a new publication known as JAMA, the Jazz Listeners/ Musicians Newsletter, Dizzy Gillespie—who also is a member of the Harlem YMCA Jazz Hall of Fame committee—"promised in Kansas City, Mo. to ask musicians for help in establishing an International Jazz Hall of Fame" in that city. The newsletter quotes Gillespie, whom it describes as "honorary chairman of the proposed hall," as vowing to ask "those musicians who were inspired by jazz"—among them Stevie Wonder, Quincy Jones and Paul McCartney (?)—to contribute financially to the Kansas City project, which, as envisioned by the great trumpeter, would also include a jazz museum, classrooms and performance areas.
>
> Is there room for two Jazz Halls of Fame? Do the people involved in the New York City project know about the Kansas City project, and vice versa? (Obviously Gillespie does, but does anyone else?) Remember the New York Jazz Museum? Remember the plaques in the sidewalk on 52nd Street (another CBS Records brainchild)?
>
> The notion of commemorating the contributions of the great jazz musicians is a noble one. It would be a shame to see the energies of the jazz community

get diverted into too many different endeavors for accomplishing the same admirable goal—which, unfortunately, is what has tended to happen in the past.

Also from *Billboard* (May 26, 1984):

> Also noted: the first inductees in the Harlem YMCA Jazz Hall of Fame (Billboard, May 19) have been announced. The posthumous inductees are, to nobody's great surprise, Louis Armstrong, Duke Ellington, Count Basie, Charlie Parker, and—a slight surprise, perhaps—Mary Lou Williams. The living honorees are Roy Eldridge, Dizzy Gillespie, Miles Davis, Ella Fitzgerald and Art Blakey.

The New York Jazz museum (which the May 19, 1984 article referred to) was established in the early 1970s but quickly ran out of money and was closed a few years later. In the early 1960s, a jazz museum was established in New Orleans, but, because of insufficient funds, all that remained was the Louis Armstrong Memorial Park, the site of an outdoor jazz festival each summer. Tulane and Rutgers universities each possessed extensive archives containing thousands of phonograph records, tape recordings, posters, books, magazines, journals, and other historic pieces and memorabilia. Neither university, however, considered its archives a hall of fame.

OTHER HALLS OF FAME

The more prominent halls of fame in the U.S. were the Baseball, the Professional Football, the College Football, and the Country Music Hall of Fame. These and many other halls of fame were primarily concerned with preserving history by their collecting and displaying memorabilia, compiling records, and inducting new members annually.

Mr. Rutland visited most of the other halls of fame and learned that they were usually established by a significant contribution from an enthusiast. In the case of the Country Music Hall of Fame, some country music stars agreed to make a special recording of country hits and to donate the royalties to the organization.

Mr. Rutland was especially interested in the Country Music Hall of Fame because of similarities between country music and jazz. Country music, like jazz, had a rich cultural history in America, and neither type of music was the most popular in the U.S.

The Country Music Hall of Fame (CMHF) was established in 1967 in Nashville after a cooperative fundraising effort involving the city, artists, and sponsors. By 1976, the CMHF included a museum, an archive, a library, and a gift shop. More than one-half million people visited the CMHF in 1983, partly because of the nearby Grand Ole Opry, the premier concert hall for country music and origin of the Grand Ole Opry cable-radio broadcasts. Of the CMHF's $2.1 million annual budget, 85% came from admissions, 10% from sales at the gift shop and by mail, and 5% from donations.

In the past two years, the CMHF had formed the Friends of Country Music, now more than 2,000 people who each donated $25 per year and who received a country music newsletter every three months and discounts on CMHF merchandise.

THE NATIONAL ASSOCIATION OF JAZZ EDUCATORS

Mr. Rutland was uncertain how much and what type of support he could get from the National Association of Jazz Educators. This organization, with 5,000 members, primarily coordinated and promoted jazz education programs.

Performance programs were normally offered through music departments. Most high schools and colleges had bands that played a variety of jazz arrangements as part of their repertoire. Band conductors usually had a music degree from a major university and belonged to the National Association of Jazz Educators.

Most of the jazz appreciation courses offered in schools throughout the U.S. treated jazz as a popular art form, as a barometer of society, rather than as a subject of interest in itself. Some educators believed that jazz greats such as Louis Armstrong and Duke Ellington should be honored not as jazz musicians, but as composers like George Gershwin and Richard Rogers. Indeed, a prominent jazz historian told Mr. Rutland that jazz might benefit more from breaking down this distinction between jazz artists and composers than from reinforcing it.

THE NATIONAL SURVEY

To get some of the answers to his many questions, Mr. Rutland engaged an independent consultant who conducted two surveys; the first was a national survey and the second a tourist survey. For the national survey (Appendix 37.A), the consultant designed a questionnaire to gauge the respondent's level of interest in both jazz and the concept of a National Jazz Hall of Fame, and to determine the respondent's demographics. A sample size of 1,300 was used and the mailing covered the entire continental United States. The mailing list, obtained from the Smithsonian Institution in Washington, DC, contained names and addresses of people who had purchased the "Classic Jazz Record Collection," as advertised in *Smithsonian* magazine. Of the 1,300 questionnaires, 440 were sent to Virginia residents and 860 to residents of other states so that both statewide and national data were obtained. Of the questionnaires that went to other states, the majority was targeted toward major cities and apportioned according to the interest level for jazz in each city, as indicated by the circulation statistics of *Downbeat*, a jazz magazine. Of the 860 questionnaires sent to the other cities, 88 were sent to residents of Chicago, 88 to Detroit, 83 to New York City, 60 to San Francisco, 56 to Philadelphia, 56 to Washington, DC, 52 to Los Angeles, 46 to Charlotte, 46 to Miami, 45 to Dallas, 42 to Atlanta, 42 to Houston,

30 to Denver, 28 to Kansas City, 28 to New Orleans, 28 to St. Louis, 27 to Boston, and 15 to Seattle. Of the 1,300 questionnaires, 165, or 12.7%, were returned.

As shown in Exhibit 37.1, 79% of the respondents were 35 years of age or older, 73% were male, and the majority were well-educated, professionals, and had an annual income of more than $50,000. Of interest also was that 75% of the respondents contributed $200 or more per year to different non-profit organizations. Because the sample included a large number of record buyers of age 50 or older, the consultant weighted the survey results with age data obtained from the Recording Industry Association of America, so that the survey's results would be representative of all jazz-record buyers.

The survey also showed in Exhibit 37.2 that swing was the most popular form of jazz, followed by Dixieland, and then more traditional forms of jazz, from which the consultant concluded that a nostalgic emphasis should gather support from jazz enthusiasts of all ages, and that later, the National Jazz Hall of Fame could promote more contemporary forms of jazz.

As for services, the survey suggested in Exhibit 37.3 that respondents most wanted a performance center or concert hall. A museum and seminars were also popular choices. The consultant was surprised by the strong interest in information about jazz recordings, because the average respondent did not buy many records. A newsletter was rated relatively unimportant by most respondents. Most gratifying for Mr. Rutland was that respondents on average were willing to contribute between $20.00 and $30.00 per year to the National Jazz Hall of Fame, with a weighted average contribution of $23.40.

EXHIBIT 37.1   **National Survey Results: Demographics of Respondents**

	PERCENTAGE OF RESPONDENTS	PERCENTAGE OF ALL RECORD BUYERS*	CENSUS DATA**
Age—35+	79	37	43
Sex—Male	73	82	49
Education—College Grad. +	54	24***	31
Job—Professional	57	26	22
Income—$50,000+	50	23	7
Non-profit contr.—$200/year+	75		

*Source: Consumer Purchasing of Records and Pre-recorded Tapes in the U.S., 1979–1983, Recording Industry Association of America.

**Source: U.S. Department of Commerce, Bureau of the Census, 1982.

***Source: Simmons Market Research Bureau, 1982.

EXHIBIT 37.2   **National Survey Results: Preferences for Different Styles of Jazz**

Type of Interest	PERCENTAGE OF RESPONDENTS ANSWERING WITH A 4 OR 5 RATING	WEIGHTED PERCENTAGE OF RESPONDENTS ANSWERING WITH A 4 OR 5 RATING
General interest in music	62	71
Dixieland	62	70
Swing	87	81
Traditional	63	66
Improvisational	41	48
Jazz rock	25	47
Fusion	15	9
Pop jazz	27	53
Classical	68	73

EXHIBIT 37.3   **National Survey Results: Preferences for Services Offered**

	PERCENTAGE OF RESPONDENTS ANSWERING WITH A 4 OR 5 RATING	WEIGHTED PERCENTAGE OF RESPONDENTS ANSWERING WITH A 4 OR 5 RATING
Service		
Performance Center	70	83
Concert Hall	66	79
Artist Seminars	50	62
Nightclub	52	57
Museum	57	57
Tourist Center	42	48
Audio-Visual Exhibitions	57	55
Shrine	55	52
Educational Programs	48	51
Record Information	71	69
History Seminars	38	54
Member Workshops	25	34
Lounge	37	45
Financial Support		
at $10.00/year	17	13
at $20.00/year	30	26
at $30.00/year	15	25
Number of Contributors	62	64

THE TOURIST SURVEY

In addition to conducting the National Survey, the consultant developed a questionnaire (Appendix 37.B) and interviewed approximately 100 tourists to the Charlottesville area at the Western Virginia Visitors Center near Monticello. About 140,000 tourists stopped at the center annually to collect information on attractions nearby and throughout the state. The respondents came from all areas of the country, and most were traveling for more than one day. Almost 70 percent said they liked jazz, mostly Dixieland and big band, and more than 60 percent indicated they would visit a Jazz Hall of Fame. The average admission they suggested was $3.50 per person.

THE CONSULTANT'S RECOMMEN-DATIONS

The consultant limited his recommendations to the results of the two surveys. Therefore, the question of whether the efforts in other cities to establish a National Jazz Hall of Fame would make the Charlottesville project infeasible was still unresolved. In a private discussion, however, the consultant intimated that "if the other efforts are as clumsily undertaken as many of the previous attempts, you will have nothing to worry about." He thought it was time that a professional approach was taken toward this project. Specifically, he made three recommendations:

1. Launch a direct-mail campaign to the 100,000 people on the Smithsonian jazz mailing list. The focus of the mailing should be an appeal by a jazz great such as Benny Goodman that a contributor becomes a Funding Sponsor of the National Jazz Hall of Fame. He estimated that the cost of the campaign would range between $25,000 and $30,000; however, with an average contribution of $25.00 per respondent, a response rate of only 2 percent would allow the National Jazz Hall of Fame to break even.

2. Appoint a full-time executive director with any funds exceeding the cost of the mailing. The principal responsibilities of the executive director would be to organize and coordinate fund-raising activities, to establish a performance center and museum, and to coordinate the collection of memorabilia and other artifacts.

3. To attract tourists and other visitors, promote the National Jazz Hall of Fame at strategic locations around Charlottesville. The Western Virginia Visitors Center was a prime prospect in his view for this activity. He calculated that 50,000 tourists annually at $3.00 each would provide sufficient funds to operate and maintain the National Jazz Hall of Fame.

The consultant also identified what he considered the critical elements for his plan's success. First, the National Jazz Hall of Fame should be professional in all of its services and communications to jazz enthusiasts. Second, the Executive Director should have prior experience in both fund-raising and direct mail; he should have a commitment to and love for jazz, as well as administrative skill and creativity. Third, the National Jazz Hall of Fame should communicate frequently with Founding Sponsors to keep their interest and excitement alive. Finally, to ensure the enthusiastic co-operation of city officials, local merchants and the Charlottesville community, he thought that more local prominence for the National Jazz Hall of Fame would prove indispensable.

THE NATIONAL JAZZ HALL OF FAME—DREAM OR REALITY?

As he leafed through the consultant's report, Mr. Rutland wondered what to make of the recommendations. While he was encouraged by a national base of support for his idea, he was unsure how the Board of Directors would react to the consultant's proposals. With less than $2,500 in the bank, how would they get the necessary funds to implement the plan? Yet he knew he had to make some tough decisions, and quickly, if he wanted to make his dream a reality.

APPENDIX 37.A   National Jazz Hall of Fame Survey

1. How would you classify your interest in jazz? (Please circle)

	NOT INTERESTED		MODERATE INTEREST		VERY ENTHUSIASTIC	
	1	2	3	4	5	1. _____

2. Rate your interest in the following categories of jazz. (Circle your answer)

	NO INTEREST		SOME INTEREST		VERY INTERESTED	
Dixieland/New Orleans (K. Oliver, P. Fountain)	1	2	3	4	5	2. _____
Big Band/Swing (B. Goodman, G. Miller)	1	2	3	4	5	3. _____
Traditional (A. Tatum, E. Garner)	1	2	3	4	5	4. _____
Improvisational (C. Parker, D. Gillespie)	1	2	3	4	5	5. _____
Jazz/Rock (M. Ferguson, P. Metheny)	1	2	3	4	5	6. _____
Fusion (M. Davis, S. Clarke)	1	2	3	4	5	7. _____
Pop Jazz (B. James, G. Benson)	1	2	3	4	5	8. _____

3. Besides Jazz, what other types of music do you usually like to listen to? (Circle your answer)

	NEVER				OFTEN	
Popular/Top 40	1	2	3	4	5	9. _____
Classical	1	2	3	4	5	10. _____

	NEVER				OFTEN	
Easy Listening	1	2	3	4	5	11. _____
Rock and Roll	1	2	3	4	5	12. _____
Country	1	2	3	4	5	13. _____
Soul/Disco	1	2	3	4	5	14. _____
Nostalgia	1	2	3	4	5	15. _____

4. How many jazz albums have you bought in the last 3 months? _____   16. _____

    in the past year? _____   17. _____

5. Do you play a musical instrument?   18. _____

    Yes _____   How many? _____   Hours per week _____   No _____   19. _____

    20. _____

    Do you sing?   Yes _____   Hours per week _____   No _____   21. _____

    22. _____

    23. _____

    Do you compose music?   Yes _____   Hours per week _____   No _____   24. _____

6. Are there any Jazz nightclubs/concert halls in your area?   Yes _____ No _____   25. _____

    If yes, how many times have you been there in the last 3 months?

    0-1 _____   2-4 _____   5-9 _____   10 or more _____   26. _____

7. How many hours per week do you listen to the radio?

    0-5 _____   5-10 _____   10-15 _____   15-20 _____   More than 20 _____   27. _____

    What format(s) do you listen to most often?

    Popular/Top 40 _____   Rock and Roll _____

    Classical _____   Jazz _____

    Easy Listening _____   Country _____

    Soul/Disco _____   Nostalgia _____

8. Have you ever visited a Hall of Fame?   Yes _____   No _____   28. _____

9. The following section is an attempt to determine the services you would expect from a National Jazz Hall of Fame. Please circle the level of your interest in each of the following services.

	LOW				HIGH	
Performance Center	1	2	3	4	5	29. _____
Concert Hall	1	2	3	4	5	30. _____
Seminars by Jazz artists	1	2	3	4	5	31. _____
Seminars by Jazz historians	1	2	3	4	5	32. _____
Student workshops	1	2	3	4	5	33. _____
Member workshops	1	2	3	4	5	34. _____
Jazz nightclub	1	2	3	4	5	35. _____
Museum with memorabilia	1	2	3	4	5	36. _____
Tourist Center	1	2	3	4	5	37. _____
Audio/Visual exhibits	1	2	3	4	5	38. _____

(Continued)

APPENDIX 37.A   (Continued)

	LOW				HIGH	
Recording studio	1	2	3	4	5	39. _____
Music chart library	1	2	3	4	5	40. _____
Shrine for Jazz greats	1	2	3	4	5	41. _____
Souvenir shop with mail order	1	2	3	4	5	42. _____
Jazz lounge	1	2	3	4	5	43. _____
School education programs	1	2	3	4	5	44. _____
Newsletter	1	2	3	4	5	45. _____
Jazz journal/Magazine	1	2	3	4	5	46. _____
Concert update	1	2	3	4	5	47. _____
Record information	1	2	3	4	5	48. _____
Musician referral center	1	2	3	4	5	49. _____
Toll free jazz "hot line"	1	2	3	4	5	50. _____
Other (Describe below)	1	2	3	4	5	51. _____

10. We would now like to ask you how much you would be willing to pay for the services you feel are essential. Please check the box below for the annual contribution you would be willing to pay for the items you circled "4" or "5" above.

$10 _____ $20 _____ $30 _____ $40 _____ $50 _____ $100 _____   52. _____

Please check here if you would <u>NOT</u> be willing to financially contribute to a National Jazz Hall of Fame.   _____

11. Would you consider donating any of your Jazz albums or memorabilia to the National Jazz Hall of Fame?

Yes _____   No _____   Do not own any _____   53. _____

12. Please circle the number indicating how often you read each of the following magazines:

	NEVER				OFTEN	
Time	1	2	3	4	5	54. _____
Barron's	1	2	3	4	5	55. _____
Esquire	1	2	3	4	5	56. _____
Harper's Bazaar	1	2	3	4	5	57. _____
Jet	1	2	3	4	5	58. _____
Inside Sports	1	2	3	4	5	59. _____
Money	1	2	3	4	5	60. _____
Omni	1	2	3	4	5	61. _____
New Republic	1	2	3	4	5	62. _____
Psychology Today	1	2	3	4	5	63. _____
Playboy	1	2	3	4	5	64. _____
Down Beat	1	2	3	4	5	65. _____
Rolling Stone	1	2	3	4	5	66. _____

	NEVER				OFTEN	
Musician	1	2	3	4	5	67. _____
The New Yorker	1	2	3	4	5	68. _____
The National Enquirer	1	2	3	4	5	69. _____

13. How many movies have you been to in the last 3 months?

0-1 _____   2-4 _____   5-9 _____   10 or more _____   70. _____

14. How many books have you read during the past year?

0-2 _____   3-6 _____   7-10 _____   More than 10 _____   71. _____

What type of books do you like to read?   (Answer below)

15. What other hobbies/activities do you regularly engage in?

16. Do you belong to any clubs or community organizations? If so, please list them in the space below.

17. Our group is considering locating the National Jazz Hall of Fame in Charlottesville, Virginia. Some other attractions in the area are the home of Thomas Jefferson, Monticello, the University of Virginia and the Blue Ridge Mountains. Would you plan a vacation to include a visit to Charlottesville and the Hall of Fame?

Yes _____   No _____   72. _____

18. What do you think about the idea of locating the Hall of Fame in Charlottesville?

19. If the Hall of Fame was located in Charlottesville, and if it offered the services you felt were essential (Question 9), would you support it?

Yes _____   No _____   73. _____

The following questions will enable us to better compare you to the nation at large. Your responses will help us very much, and will be kept STRICTLY CONFIDENTIAL.

20. In what city and state do you live? _____   74.-75. _____

21. What is your age?   76. _____

Less than 20 _____   20 to 24 _____

25 to 29 _____   30 to 34 _____

35 to 39 _____   40 to 49 _____

        50 and older _____

22. What is your sex?   Male _____   Female _____   77. _____

23. What is your race?   Caucasian _____   Black _____   Hispanic _____   Other _____   78. _____

24. What is your marital status?   Married _____   Single _____   79. _____

25. How many people are in your household?   _____   80. _____

26. What is your highest level of education?   81. _____

Have not received high school diploma _____

High school graduate _____

Some post-high school education _____

Associate's degree _____

College graduate _____   What degree? _____

University work beyond Bachelor's degree _____   What degree? _____

(Continued)

APPENDIX 37.A   (Continued)

27. What type of job do you have?   82. _____

    Student _____   Sales/Clerical _____

    Semi/Unskilled Labor _____   Professional _____

    Skilled Labor _____   Managerial _____

    Technical _____   Retired _____

28. What is your total household income?   83. _____

    Under $5,000 _____ $5,000 to $15,000 _____

    $15,000 to $25,000 _____ $25,000 to $35,000 _____

    $35,000 to $50,000 _____ $50,000 and above _____

29. How much do you contribute to non-profit organizations annually?

                                                     84. _____

    Under $25 _____ $25 to $50 _____

    $51 to $75 _____ $76 to $100 _____

    $101 to $200 _____ $200 and above _____

30. We would appreciate any other comments or suggestions.

    _____

    _____

31. Please write your name and address below if you wish to be added to our mailing list.

THANK YOU VERY MUCH!

APPENDIX 37.B   Tourist Survey

Hello, My name is _____ . I am a Graduate Student at the University of Virginia and am conducting a survey. Could I ask you a few questions?

We are conducting a survey for a group here in Charlottesville who are considering the establishment of a National Jazz Hall of Fame. We would like to get some information from you about your visit to Charlottesville and the tourist sites you plan to visit.

1. Where are you from? _____

   How far is that from Charlottesville?

   0–50 _____   50–150 _____   150–300 _____   300+ _____

2. Have you visited Charlottesville before?   yes _____   no _____

3. How long do you plan to stay here?

   one hour _____ ½ day _____ overnight _____ more _____

4. Are you stopping here on your way to another destination?

   yes _____ no _____

5. What places do you plan to visit in Charlottesville?

   Monticello _____   Ash Lawn _____   Michie Tavern _____

   U. Va. _____   Downtown _____   Castle Hill _____

   Mountains _____   Other _____

Now, I'd like to ask you some questions about the music you like to listen to.

6. What is your favorite type of music?

   Popular/Top 40 _____   Classical _____   Easy Listening _____

   Rock and Roll _____   Country _____   Soul/Disco _____

   Nostalgia _____   Jazz _____   Other _____

7. Do you have an interest in Jazz music? yes _____ no _____

8. If yes, how often do you listen to Jazz?

   SELDOM   **ALWAYS**
     1   2   3   4   5

9. If yes, what is your favorite type of Jazz?

   Dixieland _____   Big Band _____   Traditional _____

   Improvisational _____   Jazz/Rock _____   Fusion _____

   Pop/Jazz _____

10. Have you ever visited a Hall of Fame? yes _____ no _____

11. The people who are considering opening a Jazz Hall of Fame in Charlottesville plan a building which would house a collection of memorabilia, audio/visual displays, a gift shop which would sell magazines, books and records, and perhaps a performing arts center. Would you be interested in visiting such an attraction? yes _____ no _____

12. If YES, we are trying to determine what effect the location of the Hall of Fame would have on your decision to visit it. Would you visit the Hall of Fame if it was located

    More than 10 minutes from the Visitors Center? yes _____ no _____
    5 to 10 minutes away from the Visitors Center? yes _____ no _____
    Less than 5 minutes away from the Center? yes _____ no _____

13. Finally, how much do you think you would be willing to pay (per person) to visit a National Jazz Hall of Fame as described above?

    1 2 3 4 5 6 7 8 9 10

Springfield Ballet Company, Inc.

MARY K. COULTER · RONALD L. COULTER · ROBERT L. TREWATHA

The house lights dimmed. The orchestra began the familiar strains of Tchaikovsky's "Waltz of the Flowers" as the curtain rose. Another performance by the Springfield Ballet Company was underway. Joe Howard Fisk, outgoing President of the Board of Directors of the Springfield Ballet Company sat in the upper level of the partially filled theatre and said to a fellow board member, "I wonder how many more times the curtain will rise for Springfield Ballet Company performances. Our uncertain future and the survival of the troupe are the pressing problems facing our new president." Fisk realizes that a nonprofit arts organization must develop and implement strategic marketing and management skills, just as any profit-oriented enterprise must do. "Furthermore," he said, "it is our ability to formulate effective and appropriate short-run and long-run strategies that will determine if future performances by Springfield Ballet Company will continue. However, I am not sure we will ever be able to achieve efficiently our objective of building a dedicated ballet company and expanding public awareness of the arts through dance."

HISTORY OF SPRINGFIELD BALLET COMPANY

A local Springfield, Missouri, businessman and his wife created Springfield Ballet Company in August of 1976 when one of the couple's children had expressed an interest in dance. They decided to create a place for their child to receive ballet instruction and hired a married couple from a neighboring city to teach the first ballet classes in Springfield solely devoted to classical training. Later, a retired professional dancer was also employed as an instructor. The studio was developed in an old, downtown section of Springfield.

Other parents who had children interested in receiving ballet instruction were involved as officers in the original ballet organization. As a child would complete all of the instruction available, the parents of that child would leave the ballet company's Board to be replaced by a new set of interested parents. Thus, the Board was organized originally on a very personal, interest

This case was prepared by Professors Mary K. Coulter, Ronald L. Coulter, and Robert L. Trewatha of Southwest Missouri State University. It was presented at the North American Case Research Meeting, 1987. Distributed by the North American Case Research Association. All rights are reserved to the authors and the North American Case Research Association. Reprinted by permission of the authors and the North Amerian Case Research Association.

basis, and, therefore, the operations of the organization and the Board were very loosely managed.

Early Operations: 1976–1979

The early years generated enough interest in ballet that a satellite school at a small, private college approximately forty miles south of Springfield was opened. Although the satellite school did well initially, declining interest eventually forced it to close. During this period, the organization began bringing to the community guest performances by touring professional ballet companies such as the Atlanta Ballet and Chicago City Ballet, a practice that continues today. Financing for the appearances of these guest companies was obtained through the receipt of local and state grants and also by sale of public tickets for the performances.

During 1976 the Springfield Ballet Company attempted to unite the various ballet instructors from the small, local dance schools into a strong, regional ballet dance company. The rationale for this proposal was that ballet students would benefit by having the best ballet instructors in the area available to them. Instructors' expenses were to be shared through tuition payments. This effort failed because of specific fears by some dance instructors of possibly losing students permanently to other dance instructors and a general fear of competition.

Ballet Guild

A noted success of the Springfield Ballet Company during 1976 was the creation of the Springfield Ballet Guild, a fundraising unit for the Ballet that is still active today. The Guild is composed of women in the local community who are interested in the social aspects of the ballet company. Fundraising events and the sale of ballet-related items (such as leotards, sweatshirts, earrings, etc.) at performances are the main activities of the Guild. During its first year the Guild started a satellite operation in Lebanon, Missouri (a city approximately forty miles east of Springfield). Sales from tickets for garden parties held by the Guild raised approximately $3,000 during 1976. Throughout the years, however, the Guild has had a cyclical existence of formation to disbandment to reformation.

The Ballet's early development and performances were reported in the Springfield newspaper. Coverage was initially frequent and extensive, reflecting an attitude of support and a desire to have a growing and prosperous ballet in the community. Today, newspaper coverage for Springfield Ballet Company as well as other arts groups in Springfield has declined.

First Artistic Director

In 1979 the Springfield Ballet Company hired Ms. Polly Brandman as its Artistic Director. Ms. Brandman had previously been associated with the Dayton Ballet in Ohio. Her dance interests were modern and contemporary ballet styles. She was pleasant and a very competent Artistic Director for her style of ballet. To increase interest in ballet and to attract more students to the Springfield Ballet school, she conducted lecture-demonstrations in the Springfield public schools. The Board of Directors, however, felt that Springfield audiences wanted more traditional ballet performances rather than Ms. Brandman's preferred modern and contemporary ballet. Because a philosophical agreement, based on the objectives of the Springfield Ballet Company, could not be worked out between the Board and Ms. Brandman, she resigned her position as Artistic Director in 1980.

Time Period: 1980–1984

The period between 1980 and 1984 proved to be an interesting but difficult time for the Springfield Ballet Company. The Board voted to join the National Association of Regional Ballets in 1980. The association has its headquarters in New York City and its role is to promote and help regional ballet companies. To be a member of the association, a company must maintain certain standards of excellence. These standards relate to (1) having a certain number of dancers in various age categories who dance in the company, and (2) maintaining a set level of professional proficiency. Yearly dues are paid to the association by the member ballet companies. Each spring the association holds district meetings to help dancers and regional ballet organizations improve their operations and performances. Additionally, the Director of the association is available to member organizations in an advisory capacity. The Director's expertise includes fundraising, management consulting, and artistic training.

The financial picture for the Springfield Ballet Company was not strong by 1981, and financial support to help keep the organization alive was essential. Springfield Ballet Company had incurred a deficit of nearly $21,000. A grant of $4,000 funded by the Springfield Junior League and a $6,000 fundraising event helped to trim part of the deficit. In 1983, further support came from a seminar presented by the leader of the national color analysis consultant group, "Color Me Beautiful," which generated $4,000 for the ballet. This was followed in 1985 with the receipt of a $5,000 grant from the Missouri Arts Council. Unfortunately, Springfield Ballet Company's financial problems still continued because revenues were insufficient to support Springfield Ballet Company's expenses.

Time Period: 1985–Present

In 1985 the Board hired Joan Kunsch as its new Artistic Director. In addition to her regular duties as Artistic Director, she helped develop and stage a major ballet production for the community, "The Nutcracker," in December of 1985. After this production, Kunsch took a six-month study leave, which was approved by the Board. After her return, another one-month leave was requested. This leave request was unacceptable to the Board and it decided that a change in artistic director was necessary. A new Director, Kathleen Schwartz-Nolen joined the ballet in August of 1986. Her emphasis of instruction was toward the more traditional ballet form, as had been that of her predecessor.

THE COMMUNITY OF SPRINGFIELD, MISSOURI	Springfield is centrally located in the heart of the Ozark Mountain Country recreational region and is often called the Queen City of the Ozarks. For a city of approximately 150,000 residents, it has a reasonable variety of community arts organizations. In addition to the ballet, the community offers the Springfield Symphony, the Springfield Art Museum, the Springfield Regional Opera, The Chameleon Puppet Theatre, and the Springfield Little Theatre. Also, two of the five colleges located in Springfield provide various arts performances.

As a model organization to the ballet, Springfield Little Theatre has been very successful in recent years after facing several extremely tight financial years. By developing a patrons' group whereby each patron donates established levels of funding each year, the Springfield Little Theatre was able to solidify its base of operations. Patrons are given complimentary season tickets for performances. Other community arts organizations (including Springfield Ballet) have tried this format but have not had the success of Little Theatre. For one thing, the Little Theatre has received strong support from the community at large. For example, musicals have been especially popular in the community and that popularity has been translated into financial success and support for the organization. Its schedule of productions for each season includes several popular musicals that have a wide general audience appeal. In addition, many of its actors, actresses, and stage hands are involved with one of the five local colleges and university. The Springfield Little Theatre is a benchmark of success for most of the other Springfield arts organizations.

Community Support

One way the Springfield community supports the performing arts is through the annual "Salute to the Performing Arts." Now in its fifth year, this fundraising event is held at the posh University Plaza hotel in Springfield and has become one of the premiere social events of the year. Tickets to a formal dinner/dance are sold in the community. For each ticket sold at a price ranging from $125 to $150, John Q. Hammons, a successful local businessman, matches the ticket price with a personal donation. The total amount generated is then equally distributed among four performing arts groups (Symphony, Ballet, Opera and Theatre) in the city. The event has generated from $12,000 to $15,000 for each of the organizations every year of its existence. Unfortunately, 1987 will be the final year for this event.

CURRENT OPERATIONS

Springfield Ballet Company is a nonprofit organization governed by a Board of Directors and Executive Committee. The Board is very alert to the survival of the ballet and its ability to compete effectively in the local arts marketplace. The Board is currently attempting, with limited resources, to correct several areas in which the organization is weak.

Marketing

Developing a comprehensive and effective marketing program has not been a primary goal of Springfield Ballet Company in the past. As those in other types of nonprofit organizations, artistic people often feel that marketing their "product" is not necessary nor even valuable. Because competition for entertainment dollars exists in the local marketplace, Springfield Ballet Company has begun to realize that its marketing efforts have to be more sophisticated than that of the competition.

During the spring of 1985, the President of the Springfield Ballet Company Board asked a local university to conduct a marketing survey to determine the community's knowledge of and interest in the ballet. The survey's questionnaire was designed to gather information on the five major arts organizations in Springfield (Symphony, Little Theatre, Art Museum, Regional Opera and Ballet Company), so that Springfield Ballet Company's interest in the information was disguised and the community's perceptions of the other local arts organizations were also provided. Key findings from the survey were that Springfield Ballet Company was perceived to have low visibility in the community, low prestige, a limited variety of arts performances, and low performance quality. Another interesting finding was that respondents wanted to see elaborate costumes, scenery, and stage sets in Springfield Ballet Company performances.

Services Provided (Product)

Springfield Ballet Company offers dance to the community through two means: (1) dance instruction at the ballet school, and (2) dance performances by Springfield Ballet Company or by touring companies. A typical nine-month season includes two major touring performances, one to two major Springfield Ballet Company productions, and one to two smaller studio performances by Springfield Ballet Company.

During some seasons Springfield Ballet Company has presented small-scale sample performances at selected public schools throughout the area and at shopping malls. Attendance at major performances varies according to the reputation of the visiting company and the dances being performed. "The Nutcracker" (described in detail later) has been one of Springfield Ballet Company's very few successes.

The Springfield Ballet School provides instruction in classical ballet training (basic through professional), adult classes, pre-ballet, pointe, partnering, exercise (aerobics), and jazz and folk dance. Current levels of enrollment at the school are extremely disappointing.

Price

Admission prices to the performances throughout a season vary. For example, a renowned artist or dance group could possibly command higher prices for a performance. Springfield Ballet Company tries to encourage as many season ticket sales and patron contributions as possible. A 1986–1987 season ticket good for five performances (two guest ballet companies, one "Nutcracker" performance, and two studio concerts) sold for $35. A breakdown of sales is shown in Exhibit 38.1. The 1987–1988 season ticket price is the same as for the previous season. Prices are kept competitive with other local arts organizations when possible.

Promotion

Past promotional efforts have been lackluster, particularly for the dance school. The market survey reflects low visibility of Springfield Ballet Company's activities in this area.

For other activities, a mailing list of people interested in ballet is maintained, and this group receives flyers and brochures throughout the year. Other forms of promotion have been radio and TV spots, advertisements in newspapers, and posters located in various businesses throughout the area.

Place

Most of Springfield Ballet Company's performances take place at the Landers Theatre in downtown Springfield. The Landers is an old landmark theatre recently renovated to reflect its beautiful and impressive heritage. It is currently the home of Springfield Little Theatre, although other arts organizations use the stage at the Landers and work around the scheduled rehearsals and performances of the Little Theatre. Ballet and dance instruction takes place at the Springfield Ballet Company offices in the Vandivort Center, a recently renovated building housing other local arts groups next door to the Landers Theatre. A complete description of Springfield Ballet Company's facilities is included in the Operations section.

Management

The actual management of Springfield Ballet Company is a function of the working relationship between the Springfield Ballet Company employees and the Board. "Very involved" would be an accurate description of the Board's role in the operations of Springfield Ballet Company.

EXHIBIT 38.1   **Ticket Sales and Grants**

SEASON TICKETS/MEMBERSHIP DONATIONS

1986–1987 Final

33 adult × $35	=	$ 1,155
37 s/s* × 30	=	1,110
30 adult × 25	=	750
5 s/s* × 20	=	100
77 memb tickets	=	11,300
182 Total tickets	=	$14,623

1987–1988 as of July 17, 1987

338 adult × $35	=	$11,830
103 s/s* × 30	=	3,090
129 memb tickets	=	5,704
208 B. & Co. × 35	=	7,280
778 Total tickets	=	$27,904

GRANTS

1986–1987 Final

Missouri Arts Council	$ 6,000†	
Mid-America Artists Alliance	1,000	Chicago City B.
Mid-America Artists Alliance	4,650	Tulsa B. Th.
Total	$11,650	

1987–1988 as of July 17, 1987

Missouri Arts Council	$ 8,000‡	
Mid-America Artists Alliance	3,690**	B. Folklorico
Mid-America Artists Alliance	4,060	Dayton B.
Total	$15,750	

*s/s—student/senior citizen.

†Received only $5,740 because of reserved amount not released; $2000 spent on Chicago City B., $2000 spent on "Nutcracker" guest artist, $1,740 spent on management staff.

‡Following amounts must be used as a minimum: $1,800 B. Folklorico, $1,980 Dayton B.; funds used for Springfield Ballet performances can only be used for guest artists.

**This funding is for the 2-performance contract fee of $10,000.

Board of Directors

Much of the management of Springfield Ballet Company, particularly in the setting of goals, policies, and plans, has been a function of the Board of Directors. The Board of Directors is very active. Board members not only function as management of the organization but also help in soliciting funds, ushering at performances, and putting up posters in storefront windows. Board members reflect a cross-section of community individuals, who bring a particular expertise to the group. Unfortunately, many Springfield Ballet Company Board members know very little about ballet, its history, and its value as an art expression. The board currently has twenty-eight members and is authorized to increase to thirty-five members if necessary. The Executive Committee, composed of the ten Board officers, performs most of the comprehensive and detailed activities of the Board. A weekly staff meeting between the Board President, the Artistic Director, and the ballet's General Manager, if needed, is held to identify and resolve requests and problems. Several advisory committees of the Board have been formed to assist the Executive Committee in making decisions. One of the most active has been the Personnel Committee. The full Board meets monthly to (1) hear reports from the committees, the Artistic Director, and the Business Manager, and (2) vote on decisions that come before it. One step taken by the immediate past president of the Board was to conduct a training session for new Board members and interested current Board members. This training session is considered by participants as being extremely valuable in their orientation and preparation for serving on the Board.

Organizational Chart and Job Descriptions

An organizational chart does not exist for the organization, which has only two regularly paid employees—the Artistic Director and the General (Business) Manager. Other functions such as secretarial, additional dance instructors, pianists, etc. are brought in and paid as needed. The Artistic Director is a full-time position, responsible for directing Springfield Ballet Company's artistic activities including education and performances. A formal job description for this position is available but the way it is written has led to conflicts between the Board and the present Director. As noted earlier, the tenure of Artistic Directors over the last few years has been relatively short. The General Manager's position is a one-half-time position. A job description for the General Manager was recently prepared and presented to the Board during its last meeting of 1987. The Board did not accept nor implement any action relative to the document. Part-time status for this position is viewed by the Board as being appropriate at the present time.

Mission and Long-Range Plan

Besides collecting marketing information, the market survey was to help Springfield Ballet Company define what it was and how it was perceived by the public. After extensive discussion of these findings, the Board decided to develop a mission statement and long-range plan. The mission statement as presented in the long-range plan is as follows:

> Springfield Ballet, Inc. exists to EDUCATE students and the public in techniques of dance, to PERFORM at the highest level possible, and to PRESENT the finest dance available for southwest Missouri.

The long-range plan was the culmination of intense effort by the long-range planning committee over a fifteen-month period. The ad hoc, long-range planning committee was composed of five members from the Board. Included in the plan were twelve base-year goals and a series of more specific objectives for each category of goals. These are specified for five years and are intended to be updated every year so that there is an ongoing five-year plan. The introduction to the five-year plan and the list of base-year goals (note the categories) are shown in Exhibits 38.2 and 38.3.

Operations and Facility

Springfield Ballet Company brings dance to the community in two ways—education and performance.

Dance School

Springfield Ballet School has never fully realized its potential. Different types of dance instruction for various age groups are offered at the downtown studios in the Vandivort Center. During the 1986–1987 season, average enrollment at the school was 69. Predictions for 1987–1988 are for approx-

---

EXHIBIT 38.2   **Introduction**

> "And David danced before the Lord with all his might . . ."
> II Samuel 6:14
>
> This five year plan is intended as a roadmap to achievement in dance education by Springfield Ballet, Inc. Beginning with twelve base year (1986–87) goals, the plan was developed by articulating very carefully what the long range planning committee, representing a wide variety of viewpoints, wanted to see projected by the end of the fifth year (1990–91). Working backwards from those fifth year projections, each of the remaining four years was developed in logical attainable increments of growth. That articulation amounted to considerable hours of thoughtful planning and projections, shrewd calculations and a wonderful foray into dreaming. This plan can only be workable if it is monitored and refined in each of the five years of its projection. Each year another year should be added so that there is an ongoing five year plan.
>
> I should like to thank the members of my committee for their very generous gifts of spirit and of time in the development of this long range plan. As I leave the board of directors after a very happy six-year commitment, it is my sincere hope that this roadmap will augment a new plateau of achievement by an organization whose goals are worthy and laudable: To Educate, To Perform and To Present.
>
> William Brandon Bowman

imately the same number or lower. A recently conducted, very limited survey (sample size = 30) of interest in the ballet school verifies the low visibility of the school. Results of the survey are shown in Exhibit 38.4

Dance Company/Other Public Performances

One outcome of the dance school, desired by both the Board and the Artistic Director, is the opportunity it provides for the development of an ongoing, fully staffed dance company that could present dance performances throughout the year. As conditions are now, this goal remains unattainable. Low and fluctuating enrollments at the school have never afforded Springfield Ballet Company the opportunity to build a viable and ongoing dance company. Public performances by the Springfield Ballet Company currently are staffed with school enrollees and supplemented with other dancers from the community. Public performances by touring dance troupes (such as Tulsa

---

EXHIBIT 38.3   ## Mission Statement

> Springfield Ballet, Inc. exists to EDUCATE students and the public in techniques of dance, to PERFORM at the highest level possible, and to PRESENT the finest dance available for southwest Missouri.
>
> **1986–87 BASE YEAR GOALS**
>
>   I. To maintain and build Springfield Ballet School. (School)
>
>   II. To build a Springfield Ballet Company. (Company)
>
> III. To present company performances. (Company Performances)
>
> IV. To present two guest dance companies in performance. (Guest Companies)
>
>   V. To continue producing "The Nutcracker" annually. (The Nutcracker)
>
> VI. To support Springfield Ballet Guild and its projects. (Guild)
>
> VII. To maintain artistic director, general manager, school secretary and custodian. (Administration)
>
> VIII. To establish financial stability for the improvement of the administration, company, school, day-to-day operations and lease requirements. (Finances)
>
> IX. To sustain and increase community support. (Community Support)
>
>   X. To collaborate with other arts groups within this area. (Collaboration with Arts Groups)
>
> XI. To locate and establish a facility for future use of Springfield Ballet, Inc. (Facility)
>
> XII. To establish a system of orientation and guidance for members of the Board of Directors which will be monitored and updated. (Board of Directors)

EXHIBIT 38.4 **Survey Results**

CHILDREN INTERESTED IN DANCE CLASSES	
Yes	66.7%
No or No Answer	33.3%

WILLINGNESS TO SEND CHILDREN TO DANCE CLASSES	
Yes	82%
No or No Answer	18%

PREFERENCE FOR SCHOOL LOCATION	
Northwest	4.3%
Northeast	13.0%
Southwest	43.5%
Southeast	17.4%
Downtown	4.3%
Other	17.4%

TYPE OF DANCE CLASSES DESIRED	
Modern Dance	35%
Jazz	24%
Ballet	16%
Tap Dance	16%
Other	9%

Ballet, Chicago City Ballet, Alvin Alley Dance Theatre, etc.) are paid for and hosted by Springfield Ballet Company. None of the performances by visiting ballet companies has ever broken even.

Facilities

Springfield Ballet Company has been housed in its present facility in the Vandivort Center since September 1986. Exhibit 38.5 shows the layout of the facility and also compares size and cost between the previous and current locations. Equipment such as the sound system, the piano, exercise barres and mirrors are adequate, although improvements could be made if resources were available.

The Vandivort Center is also home to three other major performing arts groups and the Springfield Area Arts Council. The groups are office neighbors as well as sharing some rehearsal and performing space. All the local

EXHIBIT 38.5

Facilities

Area	CURRENT LOCATION		PREVIOUS LOCATION	
Large studio	26 × 60 ft	1560 sq ft	40 × 48 ft	1920 sq ft
Small studio	20 × 25	500	19 × 30	570
Reception area	18 × 20	360	L-shaped	210
Office #1	12 × 16	192	10 × 10	100
Office #2	12 × 26	390	12 × 15	180
W dressing rm	14 × 16	224	9 × 24	216
M dressing rm	none		9 × 16	144
Storage	9 × 16	144	basement	1000
Rent/month	$1200/$900		$650 (includes utilities), with 4.5% added 3rd, 4th, & 5th yrs of lease.	

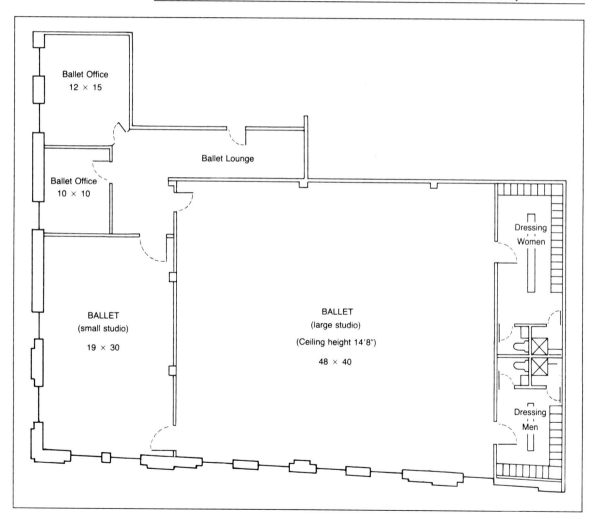

arts groups are hoping for a synergetic effect from being housed in a common location and all hope to reinforce each other's successes. Mick Dennison, Director of the Little Theatre, summed up the groups' enthusiasm when he said, "Just to have that kind of focus on these two buildings (Vandivort and Landers Theatre) as a joint center for the arts is not only good for the arts, but for the downtown area."

Financial

The financial position of Springfield Ballet Company has been improving although all is not clear sailing yet. A current balance sheet and statement of earnings are shown in Exhibits 38.6 and 38.7. In the statement of earnings, an operating surplus of $9,098 is shown. This surplus is deceiving, however, since the organization still has some outstanding liabilities including a personal loan to be repaid to one of the Directors. Exhibit 38.1 shows the breakdown of revenues from season ticket sales and membership donations for the years 1986–1987 and 1987–1988 (as of the writing of this case). One activity that has had a significant impact on changing the financial course and direction of the organization was the decision to stage and present the Nutcracker ballet.

THE NUTCRACKER

The Nutcracker ballet is a familiar, much-loved holiday tradition in many cities. Staging the Nutcracker ballet during the December holiday season has been the salvation of many struggling local ballet companies. It was with this thought in mind that Springfield Ballet Company made a commitment to preparing and presenting public performances of the Nutcracker. Cynthia Cooper, Board President during 1984–1985 and a long-time supporter of the ballet, spearheaded the drive to make this a successful and a financially sound event. She made the Nutcracker her personal cause to help change the direction and fortunes of the organization. Working closely with the Director of the National Association of Regional Ballets, she developed a fundraising campaign directed at the Nutcracker. A series of parties called "Christmas in July" were held at three exclusive homes in Springfield. Prominent (and invariably wealthy) community residents were invited and were assured that if they donated at these parties they would not be asked to donate to the Ballet for the next year. Significant cash donations as well as sponsorship of costumes and other scenery items needed for the performance were obtained. The sponsors' names appeared in program brochures and announcements. The parties were a huge success—a total of $30,000 was raised through private donations.

The first Nutcracker was presented during one weekend (3 performances) in December 1985. Although not a sellout, the presentation attracted a large crowd. Based upon the positive comments heard from the community, a commitment was made to present the Nutcracker over two December week-

EXHIBIT 38.6   **Springfield Ballet, Inc.: Balance Sheet**

	MAY 31 1987	JUNE 30 1987	MEMO: JUNE 30 1986
Assets			
Current assets:			
Cash on hand and in bank	$ 9,358	$23,460	$11,729
Cash in savings	71,252	150,005	—
Prepaid expenses	2,164	51,810	2,391
Accounts receivable	707	520	216
Deposits	25	25	25
Total current assets	83,506	225,820	14,361
Property and equipment:			
Costumes & sets	14,217	14,217	12,814
Furniture, fixtures and equipment	14,739	14,739	14,369
Leasehold improvements	354	—	354
	29,310	28,956	27,537
Less accumulated depreciation	14,583	14,811	9,357
Net property and equipment	14,727	14,145	18,180
	98,233	239,965	32,541
Liabilities and Fund Balance			
Current liabilities:			
Notes payable—current	16,000	16,000	18,306
Accounts payable	—	1,093	207
Payroll taxes payable	896	659	760
Accrued expenses	189	1,082	170
Advances for B. & Co. Concert	70,913	198,935	—
Total current liabilities	87,998	217,769	19,443
Notes payable—long-term	8,000	8,000	8,000
Fund balance—beginning of year	5,098	5,098	5,098
Current surplus (deficit)	(2,863)	9,098	
Total fund balance	2,235	14,196	5,098
	$98,233	$239,965	$32,541

ends in 1986. More funds were raised and Springfield Ballet Company was able to upgrade the scenery and costumes. The 1986 season was almost a complete sell-out. Springfield Ballet Company is hoping a community tradition is now established and is proceeding with plans to present the Nutcracker in December 1987. As each year passes, Springfield Ballet Company is able to improve the quality of the presentation (scenery, sets, costumes,

EXHIBIT 38.7   **Springfield Ballet, Inc.: Statement of Earnings**

12 Months Ended June 30, 1987	CURRENT YTD	BUDGETED YTD	PRIOR YTD
Donations	$31256	30000	56527
Grants	11073	15650	5000
Admissions	35096	44000	26985
Membership	28881	12500	5090
Tuition	13236	13070	14687
Other income	10070	5700	6915
Total revenue	129612	120920	115204
Production exp.	50197	52500	22588
Musicians	588	3490	3168
Artistic director	18678	18360	18325
General manager	9654	9192	9792
Instructors	3365	4596	2879
Receptionist	1698	0	45
Payroll taxes	2417	3587	2579
Rent	6751	10800	13200
Telephone	1951	1980	1801
Postage	3326	1290	919
Janitorial	1567	1200	978
Insurance	2014	3192	1643
Supplies	2653	1230	935
Advertising	1695	1095	943
Dues & sub.	126	258	651
Repairs & maint.	310	240	304
Miscellaneous	939	600	451
Depreciation	5808	5200	5146
Interest expense	2020	2160	2651
Art. dir. select.	136	0	522
Moving expenses	1087	0	0
Audit	960	1000	984
Bad debt	125	0	0
Newsletter	2449	0	2036
Operating expenses	$120514	121980	92540
Operating surplus (deficit)	$ 9098	(1060)	22664

paid dancers, etc.) because they are no longer starting from scratch. Although the Nutcracker Ballet has kept Springfield Ballet Company afloat financially, problems still haunt the organization.

PLANNING FOR THE FUTURE

On June 3, 1987, a telephone call was received that could be instrumental in changing the course of Springfield Ballet Company. The call, received at the Springfield Ballet Company offices, stated that Mikhail Baryshnikov and Company was going on a nationwide tour and the company's representative wanted to know if Springfield was interested in hosting a performance. The only hurdle was that a financial commitment for $92,000 was needed within a week's time or the troupe would make plans to go elsewhere. The Board immediately set about drumming up the support and, with no time to spare, accepted the Baryshnikov offer!

Currently, Springfield Ballet Company is ecstatic and the community is abuzz with excitement and anticipation. Tickets are priced at $50, $35 and $25 (in St. Louis and Tulsa—the only other two locations nearby that are hosting a performance—tickets are $100, $70 and $50). Tickets for the Springfield performance, which is to be played to a maximum of 4,000 people, are sold out. Of the 4,000 tickets, 1,000 are $50 seats; 1,000 are $35 seats; and 2,000 are $25 seats. Additional revenues can be generated from items sold at the concert, although Baryshnikov and Company receives 40% of the profits from these. Total costs for the concert (including performance fees, advertising, etc.) are projected to be approximately $100,000. The Board is already making plans to get out of debt and establish a small endowment with the profits from the concert. This may indeed be the "turning point" for Springfield Ballet Company!

BACK TO THE PRESENT

A well-deserved round of applause for the dancers arouses Joe Howard Fisk from his thoughts. To his friend and fellow Board member, he comments, "As the outgoing Board President what do I say to the new president and oncoming Board members? What help and suggestions need to be given so that Springfield Ballet Company survives and even prospers in the ever-competitive local arts marketplace? As you know, working with a small ballet company requires a lot of pieces of a complex puzzle to be put into place. What should be our strategies and plans now?"

CASE INDEX

AB Volvo (Sweden), 1004
American Greetings, 835
Anheuser-Busch Companies, Inc. . . . August A. Busch, III, 506
Apple Computer Corporation, 1987, 533
Austad's, 968
Brookstone Hospice: Heel or Heroine?, 446
Christian's, 952
Comdial Corporation, 662
Cotton Belt Exporters, 1027
Crisis in Conscience at Quasar, 420
Crisis in Geneva, 397
Dakotah, Inc., 867
Federal Express Corporation, 751
Global Marine, Inc., 671
Harley-Davidson, Inc.: The Eagle Soars Alone, 451

Hershey Foods Corporation, 774
Home Shopping Network (A), Initial Stock Offering, 882
Inner-City Paint Corporation, 907
Johnson Products Company, Inc., A Turn-around Strategy, 808
Kmart, 857
Multicon, Incorporated . . . Robotics, 610
The National Jazz Hall of Fame, 1055
Patton Septic Tank, 945
Pioneer Hi-Bred International, Inc., 690
Piper Aircraft Corporation, 627
A Problem of Silicosis, 438
The Recalcitrant Director at Byte Inc.: Corporate Legality vs. Corporate Responsibility, 432
Southern Cabinet Company, 912
Springfield Ballet Company, Inc., 1070

Springfield Remanufacturing Corporation, 648
The Standard Oil Company: British Petroleum Loses Patience, 1030
Tandy, Inc., 556
UMC, Inc., 922
Urschel Laboratories, Inc., 982
VLSI Technology, Inc., 584
The Wallace Group, 408
Walt Disney Productions—1984, 469
Xerox Corporation: Proposed Diversification, 722

NAME INDEX*

A. C. Nielsen Co., 108
A. T. Cross Co., 211
Aaker, D. A., 198
Abdelsamad, M. H., 33
Abell, D. F., 198
Abernathy, W. J., 125
Abruzzese, L., 240
Ackelsberg, R., 394
Acquisition Funding Corporation, 222
Addressograph-Multigraph Corporation, 265. *See also* AM International.
Adler, N. J., 349
Adolph Coors Company, 105, 175, 208, 209
Aerospatiale, 335
Aikman, R., 172
Airbus Industries, 225, 334
Air Canada, 170
Albertine, J., 78
Alcon Laboratories, 380
Aldridge, D., 350
Alexander, C. P., 116, 245
Alexander, L. D., 272
Alfred Dunhill PLC, 171
Allegis Corporation, 208, 210
Allied Corporation, 214, 256
Allied Signal, 61, 214
Allio, R. J., 158
Allport-Vernon-Lindzey "Study of Values", 94
Altman, E., 36, 37
American Airlines, 294
American Assembly of Collegiate Schools of Business (AACSB), 5
American Cancer Society, 355
American Can Company, 328
American Commercial Lines (ACL), 18, 159

American Cyanamid, 341
American Healthcare Systems, Inc., 365
American Hospital Supply Corporation (AHS), 8, 154, 294
American Law Institute, 61
American Management Association, 91
American Motors, 179, 208, 209
American Robot Corporation, 146
American Telephone and Telegraph, 143, 153, 181, 184, 196, 267
AM International, 264, 267
Anastassopoulos, J. P., 349
Anchor Brewing Company, 388
Anders, G., 311
Anderson, C. A., 78, 157, 235, 367
Andrews, K. R., 21, 61, 77, 78, 197, 299, 304
Anheuser-Busch, 100, 105, 109, 208, 212, 334, 365
Ansoff, H. I., 148, 157, 158, 197, 271, 274
Anthony, R. N., 78, 303, 367
A&P, 152
Apple Computer, 208, 258, 261, 381, 388
Arlow, P., 116, 394
Armco Steel, 252
Armstrong, J. S., 41
Arnwine, D., 365
Arpan, J. S., 348
Arthur D. Little, 198, 328
Ashton-Tate, Inc., 261
Associated Consultants International, 328
Atchison Topeka & Santa Fe Railway, 305
Atlas Van Lines, 222
Aupperle, K. E., 116
Avon Products, 30, 230, 322
Axtell, R. E., 349
Babian, H., 304

Bacon, J., 58, 77, 78
Badler, G., 198
Baker, H. K., 235
Baker, J. C., 77, 78
Baker, T. E., 157
Baldwin-United, 265
Baliga, B. R., 78
Ball, M., 37
Banking Act, 63
Bank of China Trust and Consultancy Company, 345
Barbato, R., 350
Barker, L., 78
Barry, T., 40
Barth, 276
Bass, B. M., 40
Bauer, R., 40
Baumback, C. M., 394
Baysinger, B. D., 77
Bazerman, M. H., 78
Beam, A., 262
Beatly, R. P., 78
Beatrice Foods, 65, 213
Beaty, D., 116
Beaunit Mills, 4
Bechtel Group, Inc., 30
Becker, G. A., 115
Beckett Aviation, 159
BeechNut, 336
Beiler, G. W., 41
Belco Petroleum Corporation, 325
Benelli, G., 78
Benjamin, R. I., 159
Bennett, A., 77
Benton, D. S., 39
Benway, S., 172
Bernstein, A., 236

*For people and companies mentioned or noted in Chapters 1–12 only. Case contributors are listed on pages xx–xxiv.

SUBJECT INDEX*